Professional VB 2005

Professional VB 2005

Bill Evjen, Billy Hollis, Rockford Lhotka,
Tim McCarthy, Rama Ramachandran,
Kent Sharkey, Bill Sheldon

Wiley Publishing, Inc.

Professional VB 2005

Published by
Wiley Publishing, Inc.
10475 Crosspoint Boulevard
Indianapolis, IN 46256
www.wiley.com

Published simultaneously in Canada

ISBN-13: 978-0-7645-7536-5
ISBN-10: 0-7645-7536-8

Manufactured in the United States of America

10 9 8 7 6 5 4 3 2 1

1B/SW/RQ/QV/IN

Library of Congress Cataloging-in-Publication Data:

Professional Visual Basic 2005 / Bill Evjen ... [et al.].
p. cm.
Includes index.
ISBN-13: 978-0-7645-7536-5 (paper/website)
ISBN-10: 0-7645-7536-8 (paper/website)
1. Microsoft Visual BASIC. 2. BASIC (Computer program language) 3. Microsoft .NET.
I. Evjen, Bill.
QA76.73.B3P7485 2005
005.2'768 — dc22

2005012585

About the Authors

Bill Evjen is an active proponent of .NET technologies and community-based learning initiatives for .NET. He has been actively involved with .NET since the first bits were released in 2000. In the same year, Bill founded the St. Louis .NET User Group (`www.stlnet.org`), one of the world's first .NET user groups. Bill is also the founder and the executive director of the International .NET Association (INETA – `www.ineta.org`), which represents more than 375,000 members worldwide.

Based in St. Louis, Missouri, Bill is an acclaimed author and speaker on ASP.NET and XML Web Services. He has written or coauthored more than 10 books, including *Professional C# 2005* and *Professional ASP.NET 2.0* (Wrox), *XML Web Services for ASP.NET*, *ASP.NET Professional Secrets* (Wiley), and more.

Bill is a technical director for Reuters, the international news and financial services company, and he travels the world speaking to major financial institutions about the future of the IT industry. He graduated from Western Washington University in Bellingham, Washington, with a Russian language degree. When he isn't tinkering on the computer, he can usually be found at his summer house in Toivakka, Finland. You can reach Bill at `evjen@yahoo.com`.

To Kalle – Welcome to the family!

Billy Hollis is coauthor of the first book ever published on Visual Basic .NET, *VB.NET Programming on the Public Beta* (Wrox Press) as well as numerous other books and articles on .NET. Billy is a Microsoft regional director and an MVP, and he was selected as one of the original .NET "Software Legends." He writes a monthly column for MSDN Online and is heavily involved in training, consultation, and software development on the Microsoft .NET platform, focusing on smart-client development and commercial packages. He frequently speaks at industry conferences such as Microsoft's Professional Developer Conference, TechEd, and COMDES. Billy is a member of the INETA speakers' bureau and speaks at user group meetings all over the United States.

Rockford Lhotka is the principal technology evangelist for Magenic Technologies (`www.magenic.com`), a company focused on delivering business value through applied technology and one of the nation's premiere Microsoft Gold Certified Partners. Rockford is the author of several books, including *Expert Visual Basic .NET* and *C# Business Objects*. He is a Microsoft Software Legend, regional director, MVP, and INETA speaker. He is a columnist for MSDN Online and contributing author for *Visual Studio Magazine*, and he regularly presents at major conferences around the world — including Microsoft PDC, Tech Ed, VS Live! and VS Connections. For more information go to `www.lhotka.net`.

For my Mom and Dad, whose love and guidance have been invaluable in my life. Thank you!

Tim McCarthy is a principal engineer at InterKnowlogy, where he architects and builds highly scalable *n*-tier web and smart-client applications utilizing the latest Microsoft platforms and technologies. Tim's expertise covers a wide range of Microsoft technologies, including, but not limited to: .NET Framework (ASP.NET/Smart Clients/Web Services), Active Directory, UDDI, SQL Server, Windows SharePoint Services/SharePoint Portal Server 2003, and Service Oriented Architecture (SOA) applications. Tim has worked as a project technical lead/member as well as in a technical consulting role for several Fortune 500 companies. He has held the Microsoft Certified Solution Developer (MCSD) and Microsoft Certified Trainer (MCT) certifications for several years and was one of the first wave of developers to earn the Microsoft Certified Application Developer (MCAD) for .NET and MCSD for .NET certifications. He also holds the Microsoft Certified Database Administrator certification for SQL Server 2000.

Tim has been an author and technical reviewer for several books from Wrox Press and most recently was a lead author on *Professional VB.NET 2003*. His other books include *Professional Commerce Server 2000*, and *Professional ADO 2.5 Programming*. Tim is currently working as a lead author on the next edition of *Professional VB.NET*. Tim has written numerous articles for the *Developer .NET Update* newsletter, developed packaged presentations for MSDN, and has written a whitepaper for Microsoft on using COM+ services in .NET. He has also written articles for *SQL Server Magazine* and *Windows & .NET Magazine*.

Tim has spoken at technical conferences around the world and several San Diego area user groups (including both .NET and SQL Server groups) and he has been a regular speaker at the Microsoft Developer Days conference in San Diego for the last several years. Tim has also delivered MSDN webcasts, many of which were repeat requests from Microsoft. Tim also teaches custom .NET classes to companies in need of expert .NET mentoring and training.

Tim holds a B.B.A. in marketing from the Illinois Institute of Technology as well as an M.B.A. in marketing from National University. Before becoming an application developer, Tim was an officer in the United States Marine Corps. Tim's passion for .NET is only surpassed by his passion for Notre Dame athletics.

I dedicate this book to everybody in my family who supports me. Jasmine, some day you will be writing books, too!

Rama Ramachandran is a software architect at DKR Capital, a major hedge fund company in Stamford, Connecticut. He is a Microsoft Certified Solutions Developer and Site-Builder and has excelled in designing and developing WinForms and Web applications using .NET, ASP.NET, Visual Basic and SQL Server. Rama has more than 15 years' experience with all facets of the software development lifecycle and has cowritten *Introducing .NET, Professional ASP Data Access, Professional Visual InterDev Programming* (all Wrox Press), and four books on classic Visual Basic.

Rama is also the "ASP Pro" at `Devx.com`, where he maintains ASP-related columns. He teaches .NET Development and Web Development for Fairfield University's master's degree in software engineering, and at the University of Connecticut. You can reach Rama at `ramabeena@hotmail.com`.

This book is dedicated to my wife, Beena, and our children, Ashish and Amit. They make my life whole. I'm great at writing about technology but get tongue-tied trying to say how much I love and care about the three of you. I am grateful to our prayer-answering God for your laughing, mischievous, adoring lives. Thanks for being there, Beens. I love you.

Kent Sharkey. Born in an igloo and raised by wolves in a strange realm called "Manitoba," Kent Sharkey wandered the wilderness until found by a group of kind technical evangelists and migrated to Redmond. He now is content strategist (yeah, he doesn't know what he's supposed to do either) for ASP.NET content on MSDN. When not answering email he dreams of sleeping, complains to everyone around (come to think of it, he does that while answering email as well), and attempts to keep his housemates (Babi, Cica, and Squirrel) happy.

As with all else, to Margaret. Thank you.

Bill Sheldon is a software architect and engineer originally from Baltimore, Maryland. Holding a degree in Computer Science from the Illinois Institute of Technology (IIT) and a Microsoft Certified Solution Developer (MCSD) qualification, Bill has been employed as an engineer since resigning his commission with the U.S. Navy following the first Gulf War. Bill is involved with the San Diego .NET User Group and writes for Windows and .NET magazines, including the twice monthly *Developer .NET Update* email newsletter. He is also a frequent online presenter for MSDN and speaks at live events such as Microsoft Developer Days. He lives with his wife, Tracie, in Southern California, where he is employed as a principal engineer with InterKnowlogy. You can reach Bill at `bills@interknowlogy.com`.

Credits

Acquisitions Editor
Katie Mohr

Development Editors
Eileen Bien Calabro
Ami Frank Sullivan

Technical Editor
Brian Patterson

Production Editor
Pamela Hanley

Copy Editor
Foxxe Editorial Services

Editorial Manager
Mary Beth Wakefield

Vice President & Executive Group Publisher
Richard Swadley

Vice President and Publisher
Joseph B. Wikert

Project Coordinator
Ryan Steffen

Graphics and Production Specialists
Carrie A. Foster
Lauren Goddard
Denny Hager
Barbara Moore
Lynsey Osborn
Alicia South

Quality Control Technicians
Laura Albert
John Greenough
Leeann Harney
Jessica Kramer
Brian H. Walls

Proofreading
TECHBOOKS Production Services

Indexing
Broccoli Information Management

Contents

Introduction

In 2002, Visual Basic took the biggest leap in innovation since it was released, with the introduction of Visual Basic .NET (as it was renamed). After more than a decade, Visual Basic was overdue for a major overhaul. But .NET goes beyond an overhaul. It changes almost every aspect of software development. From integrating Internet functionality to creating object-oriented frameworks, Visual Basic .NET challenged traditional VB developers to learn dramatic new concepts and techniques.

2005 brings us an enhanced Visual Basic language (renamed this time Visual Basic 2005). New features have been added that cement this language's position as a true object-oriented language. With Visual Basic 2005, it is still going to be a challenge for the traditional VB6 developers to learn, but it is an easy road and books like this are here to help you on your path.

First, it's necessary to learn the differences between Visual Basic 2005 and the older versions. In some cases, the same functionality is implemented in a different way. This was not done arbitrarily — there are good reasons for the changes. But you must be prepared to unlearn old habits and form new ones.

Next, you must be open to the new concepts. Full object orientation, new component techniques, new visual tools for both local and Internet interfaces — all of these and more must become part of your skill set to effectively develop applications in Visual Basic.

In this book, we cover Visual Basic virtually from start to finish. We begin by looking at the .NET Framework and end by looking at the best practices for deploying .NET applications. In between, we look at everything from database access to integration with other technologies such as XML, along with investigating the new features in detail. You will see that Visual Basic 2005 has emerged as a powerful yet easy-to-use language that will allow you to target the Internet just as easily as the desktop.

The Importance of Visual Basic

Early in the adoption cycle of .NET, Microsoft's new language, C#, got the lion's share of attention. But as .NET adoption has increased, Visual Basic's continuing importance has also been apparent. Microsoft has publicly stated that they consider Visual Basic the language of choice for applications where developer productivity is one of the highest priorities.

Future development of Visual Basic is emphasizing capabilities that enable access to the whole expanse of the .NET Framework in the most productive way, while C# development is emphasizing the experience of writing code. That fits the traditional role of Visual Basic as the language developers use in the real world to create business applications as quickly as possible.

This difference is more than academic. One of the most important advantages of the .NET Framework is that it allows applications to be written with dramatically less code. In the world of business applications, the goal is to concentrate on writing business logic and to eliminate routine coding tasks as much as possible. The value in this new world is not in churning out lots of code — it is in writing robust, useful applications with as little code as possible.

Visual Basic is an excellent fit for this type of development, which makes up the bulk of software development in today's economy. And it will grow to be an even better fit as it is refined and evolved for exactly that purpose.

Who Is This Book For?

This book is written to help experienced developers learn about Visual Basic 2005. From those who are just starting the transition from earlier versions to those who have used Visual Basic for a while and need to gain a deeper understanding, this book provides a discussion on the most common programming tasks and concepts you need.

Professional Visual Basic 2005 offers a wide-ranging presentation of Visual Basic concepts, but the .NET Framework is so large and comprehensive that no single book can cover it all. The most important area in which this book does not attempt to be complete is Web development. While chapters discussing the basics of browser-based programming in Visual Basic are included, professional Web developers should instead refer to *Professional ASP.NET 2.0* (Wrox Press).

What You Need to Use This Book

Although, it is possible to create Visual Basic applications using the command-line tools contained in the .NET Framework SDK, you will need Visual Studio 2005 (Professional or higher), which includes the .NET Framework SDK, to get the most out of this book. You may use Visual Studio .NET 2002 or Visual Studio 2003 instead, but there may be cases where much of the lessons will just not work because functionalities and capabilities will not be available in these older versions.

In addition:

- Some chapters make use of SQL Server 2005. However, you can also run the example code using Microsoft's SQL Express, which ships with Visual Studio 2005.
- Several chapters make use of Internet Information Services (IIS). IIS ships with Windows 2003 Server, Windows 2000 Server, Windows 2000 Professional, and Windows XP, although it is not installed by default.
- Chapter 21 makes use of MSMQ to work with queued transactions. MSMQ ships with Windows 2003 Server, Windows 2000 Server, Windows 2000 Professional, and Windows XP, although it is not installed by default.

What Does This Book Cover?

Chapter 1, "What Is Microsoft .NET?" — This chapter explains the importance of .NET and just how much it changes application development. You gain an understanding of why you need .NET by looking at what's wrong with the current development technologies, including COM and the DNA architectural model. Then, we look at how .NET corrects the drawbacks by using the common language runtime (CLR).

Chapter 2, "Introducing Visual Basic 2005 and Visual Studio 2005"—This chapter provides a first look at a Visual Basic application. As we develop this application, you'll take a tour of some of the new features of Visual Studio 2005.

Chapter 3, "Variables and Types"—This chapter introduces many of the types commonly used in Visual Basic. The main goal of this chapter is to familiarize you with value and reference types and to help those with a background in VB6 understand some of the key differences in how variables are defined in Visual Basic.

Chapter 4, "Object Syntax Introduction"—This is the first of three chapters that explore object-oriented programming in Visual Basic. This chapter will define objects, classes, instances, encapsulation, abstraction, polymorphism, and inheritance.

Chapter 5, "Inheritance and Interfaces"—This chapter examines inheritance and how it can be used within Visual Basic. We create simple and abstract base classes and demonstrate how to create base classes from which other classes can be derived.

Chapter 6, "The Common Language Runtime"—This chapter examines the core of the .NET platform, the common language runtime (CLR). The CLR is responsible for managing the execution of code compiled for the .NET platform. We cover versioning and deployment, memory management, cross-language integration, metadata, and the IL Disassembler.

Chapter 7, "Applying Objects and Components"—This chapter puts the theory of Chapters 4 and 5 into practice. The four defining object-oriented concepts (abstraction, encapsulation, polymorphism, inheritance) are discussed, and we explain how these concepts can be applied in design and development to create effective object-oriented applications.

Chapter 8, "Generics"—This chapter focuses on one of the biggest enhancements to Visual Basic in this version—generics. Generics enables you to make a generic collection that is still strongly typed—providing fewer chances for errors, increasing performance, and giving you Intellisense features when you are working with your collections.

Chapter 9, "Namespaces"—This chapter introduces namespaces and their hierarchical structure. An explanation of namespaces and some common ones are given. In addition, you learn how to create new namespaces, and how to import and alias existing namespaces within projects. This chapter also looks at the new `My` namespace that was made available in Visual Basic 2005.

Chapter 10, "Exception Handling and Debugging"—This chapter covers how error handling and debugging work in Visual Basic 2005 by discussing the CLR exception handler and the new `Try...Catch...Finally` structure. We also look at error and trace logging, and how you can use these methods to obtain feedback on how your program is working.

Chapter 11, "Data Access with ADO.NET 2.0"—This chapter focuses on what you will need to know about the ADO.NET object model to be able to build flexible, fast, and scalable data access objects and applications. The evolution of ADO into ADO.NET is explored, and the main objects in ADO.NET that you need to understand in order to build data access into your .NET applications are explained.

Chapter 12, "Using XML in Visual Basic 2005"—This chapter presents the features of the .NET Framework that facilitate the generation and manipulation of XML. We describe the .NET Framework's XML-related namespaces, and a subset of the classes exposed by these namespaces is examined in detail. This chapter also touches on a set of technologies that utilize XML, specifically ADO.NET and SQL Server.

Chapter 13, "Security in the .NET Framework 2.0"—This chapter examines the additional tools and functionality with regard to the security provided by .NET. `Caspol.exe` and `Permview.exe`, which assist in establishing and maintaining security policies, are discussed. The `System.Security.Permissions` namespace is looked at, and we discuss how it relates to managing permissions. Finally, we examine the `System.Security.Cryptography` namespace and run through some code to demonstrate the capabilities of this namespace.

Chapter 14, "Windows Forms"—This chapter looks at Windows Forms, concentrating primarily on forms and built-in controls. What is new and what has been changed from the previous versions of Visual Basic are discussed, along with the `System.Windows.Forms` namespace.

Chapter 15, "Windows Forms Advanced Features"—This chapter looks at some of the more advanced features that are available to you in building your Windows Forms applications.

Chapter 16, "Building Web Applications"—This chapter explores Web forms and how you can benefit from their use. Using progressively more complex examples, this chapter explains how .NET provides the power of Rapid Application Development (normally associated with Windows applications) for the development of Web applications.

Chapter 17, "ASP.NET 2.0 Advanced Features"—This chapter looks at a lot of the new and advanced features that have been made available to you with the latest release of ASP.NET 2.0. Examples of items covered include cross-page posting, master pages, site navigation, personalization, and more.

Chapter 18, "Assemblies"—This chapter examines assemblies and their use within the CLR. The structure of an assembly, what it contains, and the information it contains is examined.

Chapter 19, "Deployment"—This chapter examines the manifest of the assembly, and its role in deployment will be looked at. We also look at what Visual Studio 2005 and the CLR have to offer you when you come to deploy your applications.

Chapter 20, "Working with Classic COM and Interfaces"—This chapter discusses COM and .NET component interoperability, and what tools are provided to help link the two technologies.

Chapter 21, "Enterprise Services"—This chapter explores the .NET component services—in particular, transaction processing and queued components.

Chapter 22, "Threading"—This chapter explores threading and explains how the various objects in the .NET Framework enable any of its consumers to develop multithreaded applications. We examine how threads can be created, how they relate to processes, and the differences between multitasking and multithreading.

Chapter 23, "XML Web Services"—This chapter looks at how to create and consume Web services using Visual Basic. The abstract classes provided by the CLR to set up and work with Web services are discussed, as are some of the technologies that support Web services.

Chapter 24, "Remoting" — This chapter takes a detailed look at how to use remoting in classic three-tier application design. We look at the basic architecture of remoting and build a basic server and client that uses a singleton object for answering client requests into the business tier. We then look at how to use serialization to return more complex objects from the server to the client, and how to use the call context for passing extra data from the client to the server along with each call without having to change the object model.

Chapter 25, "Windows Services" — This chapter examines how Visual Basic is used in the production of Windows Services. The creation, installation, running, and debugging of Windows Services are covered.

Chapter 26, "Network Programming" — This chapter takes a look at working with some of the networking protocols that are available to you in your development and how to incorporate a wider network into the functionality of your applications.

Chapter 27, "Visual Basic and the Internet" — This chapter looks at how to download resources from the Web, how to design your own communication protocols, and how to reuse the Web browser control in your applications.

Appendix A, "The Visual Basic Compiler" — This appendix looks at the Visual Basic compiler `vbc.exe` and the functionality it provides.

Appendix B, "Visual Basic Resources" — This appendix provides a short list of VB resources that are out there for you.

Conventions

We have used a number of different styles of text and layout in this book to help differentiate between the different kinds of information. Here are examples of the styles we use and an explanation of what they mean:

Bullets appear indented, with each new bullet marked as follows:

- *New and important words* are in italics.
- Words that appear on the screen in menus such as File or Window are in a similar font to the one that you see on screen.
- Keyboard strokes are shown like this: Ctrl-A.
- If you see something like `Object`, you'll know that it's a filename, object name, or function name.

Code in a gray box is new, important, pertinent code:

```
Dim objMyClass as New MyClass("Hello World")
Debug.WriteLine(objMyClass.ToString)
```

Sometimes you'll see code in a mixture of styles, such as:

```
Dim objVar as Object
 objVar = Me
CType(objVar, Form).Text = "New Dialog Title Text"
```

The code with a white background is code we've already looked at and that we don't wish to examine further.

Advice, hints, and background information come in an italicized, indented paragraph like this.

Important pieces of information come in shaded boxes like this.

Customer Support

We always value hearing from our readers, and we want to know what you think about this book: what you liked, what you didn't like, and what you think we can do better next time. You can send us your comments, either by returning the reply card in the back of the book or by email to feedback@wrox.com. Please be sure to mention the book title in your message.

How to Download the Sample Code for the Book

When you visit the Wrox site, www.wrox.com, simply locate the title through our Search facility or by using one of the title lists. Click Download in the Code column or click Download Code on the book's detail page.

The files that are available for download from our site have been archived using WinZip. When you have saved the attachments to a folder on your hard drive, you need to extract the files using a decompression program such as WinZip or PKUnzip. When you extract the files, the code is usually extracted into chapter folders. When you start the extraction process, ensure that your software (WinZip, PKUnzip, and so on) is set to use folder names.

Errata

We've made every effort to make sure that there are no errors in the text or in the code. However, no one is perfect and mistakes do occur. If you find an error in one of our books, such as a spelling mistake or a faulty piece of code, we would be very grateful for feedback. By sending in errata, you may save another reader hours of frustration, and of course, you will be helping us provide even higher quality information. Simply email the information to support@wrox.com; your information will be checked and if correct, posted to the errata page for that title, or used in subsequent editions of the book.

To find errata on the Web site, go to www.wrox.com, and simply locate the title through our Advanced Search or title list. Click the Book Errata link, which is below the cover graphic on the book's detail page.

p2p.wrox.com

For author and peer discussion, join the P2P mailing lists. Our unique system provides programmer to programmer(tm) contact on mailing lists, forums, and newsgroups, all in addition to our one-to-one email support system. If you post a query to P2P, you can be confident that the many Wrox authors and other industry experts who are present on our mailing lists are examining it. At `p2p.wrox.com` you will find a number of different lists that will help you, not only while you read this book, but also as you develop your own applications.

Particularly appropriate to this book are the vb_dotnet and pro_vb_dotnet lists.

To subscribe to a mailing list just follow these steps:

1. Go to `http://p2p.wrox.com/`.
2. Choose the appropriate category from the left menu bar.
3. Click the mailing list you wish to join.
4. Follow the instructions to subscribe and fill in your email address and password.
5. Reply to the confirmation email you receive.
6. Use the subscription manager to join more lists and set your email preferences.

You can read messages in the forums without joining P2P, but in order to post your own messages, you must join.

Once you join, you can post new messages and respond to messages other users post. You can read messages at any time on the Web. If you would like to have new messages from a particular forum emailed to you, click the Subscribe to this Forum icon by the forum name in the forum listing.

For more information about how to use the Wrox P2P, be sure to read the P2P FAQs for answers to questions about how the forum software works as well as many common questions specific to P2P and Wrox books. To read the FAQs, click the FAQ link on any P2P page.

1

What Is Microsoft .NET?

New technologies force change, nowhere more so than in computers and software. Occasionally, a new technology is so innovative that it forces us to challenge our most fundamental assumptions. In the computing industry, the latest such technology is the Internet. It has forced us to rethink how software should be created, deployed, and used.

However, that process takes time. Usually, when a powerful new technology comes along, it is first simply strapped onto existing platforms. So it has been for the Internet. Before the advent of Microsoft .NET, developers used older platforms with new Internet capabilities "strapped on." The resulting systems worked, but they were expensive and difficult to produce, hard to use, and difficult to maintain.

Realizing this several years ago, Microsoft decided it was time to design a new platform from the ground up specifically for the post-Internet world. The result is called .NET. It represents a turning point in the world of Windows software for Microsoft platforms. Microsoft has staked their future on .NET and publicly stated that henceforth almost all their research and development will be done on this platform. It is expected that, eventually, almost all Microsoft products will be ported to the .NET platform. (However, the name ".NET" will evolve, as you will see at the end of the chapter.)

Microsoft is now at version 2.0 of Microsoft .NET, and the development environment associated with this version is called Visual Studio 2005. The version of Visual Basic in this version is, thus, called Visual Basic 2005, and that's what this book is all about.

What Is .NET?

Microsoft's .NET initiative is broad-based and very ambitious. It includes the .NET Framework, which encompasses the languages and execution platform, plus extensive class libraries, providing rich built-in functionality. Besides the core .NET Framework, the .NET initiative includes protocols (such as the Simple Object Access Protocol, commonly known as SOAP) to provide a new level of software integration over the Internet, via a standard known as Web Services.

Although Web Services are important (and are discussed in detail in Chapter 23), the foundation of all .NET-based systems is the .NET Framework. This chapter will look at the .NET Framework from the viewpoint of a Visual Basic developer. Unless you are quite familiar with the Framework already, you should consider this introduction an essential first step in assimilating the information about Visual Basic .NET that will be presented in the rest of this book.

The first released product based on the .NET Framework was Visual Studio .NET 2002, which was publicly launched in February 2002, and included version 1.0 of the .NET Framework. Visual Studio .NET 2003 was introduced a year later and included version 1.1 of the .NET Framework. As mentioned, the current version is Visual Studio 2005. (Note that the ".NET" part of the name has been dropped for this version.)

This book assumes that you are using VS.NET 2005. Some of the examples will work transparently with VS.NET 2002 and VS.NET 2003, but you should not count on this, because the difference between 2.0 and the earlier versions is significant.

A Broad and Deep Platform for the Future

Calling the .NET Framework a platform doesn't begin to describe how broad and deep it is. It encompasses a virtual machine that abstracts away much of the Windows API from development. It includes a class library with more functionality than any yet created. It makes available a development environment that spans multiple languages, and it exposes an architecture that makes multiple language integration simple and straightforward.

At first glance, some aspects of .NET appear similar to previous architectures, such as UCSD Pascal and Java. No doubt some of the ideas for .NET were inspired by these past efforts, but there are also many brand new architectural ideas in .NET. Overall, the result is a radically new approach to software development.

The vision of Microsoft .NET is globally distributed systems, using XML as the universal glue to allow functions running on different computers across an organization or across the world to come together in a single application. In this vision, systems from servers to wireless palmtops, with everything in between, will share the same general platform, with versions of .NET available for all of them, and with each of them able to integrate transparently with the others.

This does not leave out classic applications as you have always known them, though. Microsoft .NET also aims to make traditional business applications much easier to develop and deploy. Some of the technologies of the .NET Framework, such as Windows Forms, demonstrate that Microsoft has not forgotten the traditional business developer. In fact, such developers will find it possible to Internet- enable their applications more easily than with any previous platform.

What's Wrong with DNA and COM?

The pre-.NET technologies used for development on Microsoft platforms encompassed the COM (Component Object Model) standard for creation of components, and the DNA model for multitier software architectures. As these technologies were extended into larger, more enterprise-level settings, and as integration with the Internet began to be important, several major drawbacks became apparent. These included:

- Difficulty in integrating Internet technologies:
  - Hard to produce Internet-based user interfaces
  - No standard way for systems and processes to communicate over the Internet
  - Expensive, difficult, and undependable deployment
  - Poor cross-language integration
- Weaknesses in the most popular Microsoft tool — Visual Basic:
  - Lack of full object orientation, which made it impossible to produce frameworks in Visual Basic
  - One threading model that did not work in some contexts
  - Poor integration with the Internet
- Other weaknesses such as poor error-handling capabilities

It is important to note that all pre-.NET platforms, such as Java, also have some of these drawbacks, as well as unique ones of their own. The drawbacks related to the Internet are particularly ubiquitous.

Microsoft .NET was created with the Internet in mind. It was also designed specifically to overcome the limitations of COM and products such as Visual Basic 6 and Active Server Pages. As a result, all of the preceding limitations have been eliminated or significantly reduced in Microsoft .NET and Visual Studio 2005.

An Overview of the .NET Framework

First and foremost, .NET is a framework that covers all the layers of software development above the operating system level. It provides the richest level of integration among presentation technologies, component technologies, and data technologies ever seen on a Microsoft, or perhaps any, platform. Second, the entire architecture has been created to make it as easy to develop Internet applications as it is to develop for the desktop.

The .NET Framework actually "wraps" the operating system, insulating software developed with .NET from most operating system specifics such as file handling and memory allocation. This prepares for a possible future in which the software developed for .NET is portable to a wide variety of hardware and operating system foundations.

VS.NET supports Windows 2003, Windows XP, and all versions of Windows 2000. Programs created for .NET can also run under Windows NT, Windows 98, and Windows Me, though VS.NET does not run on these systems. Note that in some cases certain service packs are required to run .NET.

The major components of the Microsoft .NET Framework are shown in Figure 1-1.

The framework starts all the way down at the memory management and component loading level and goes all the way up to multiple ways of rendering user and program interfaces. In between, there are layers that provide just about any system-level capability that a developer would need.

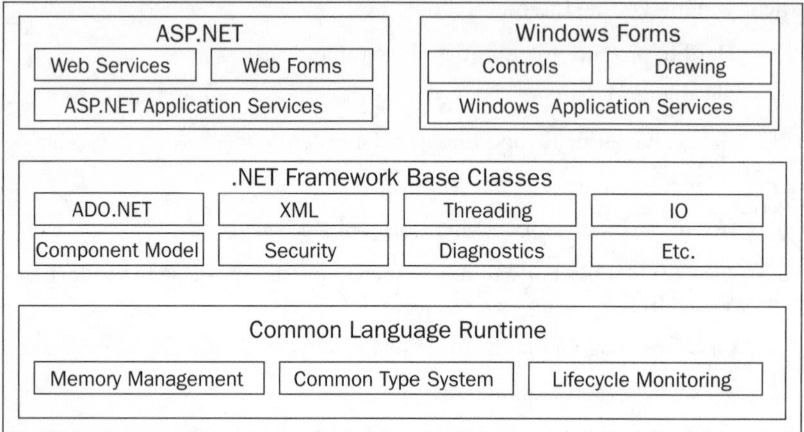

Figure 1-1

At the base is the common language runtime, often abbreviated to CLR. This is the heart of the .NET Framework — it is the engine that drives key functionality. It includes, for example, a common system of datatypes. These common types, plus a standard interface convention, make cross-language inheritance possible. In addition to allocation and management of memory, the CLR also does reference tracking for objects and handles garbage collection.

The middle layer includes the next generation of standard system Services such as classes that manage data and Extensible Markup Language (XML). These services are brought under control of the Framework, making them universally available and making their usage consistent across languages.

The top layer includes user and program interfaces. Windows Forms is a new and more advanced way to do standard Win32 screens (often referred to as "'smart clients"). Web Forms provides a new Web-based user interface. Perhaps the most revolutionary is Web Services, which provide a mechanism for programs to communicate over the Internet, using SOAP. Web Services provide an analog of COM and DCOM for object brokering and interfacing, but based on Internet technologies so that allowance is made even for integration to non-Microsoft platforms. Web Forms and Web Services, which constitute the Internet interface portion of .NET, are implemented by a part of the .NET Framework referred to as ASP.NET.

All of these capabilities are available to any language that is based on the .NET platform, including, of course, VB.NET.

The Common Language Runtime

We are all familiar with runtimes — they go back further than DOS languages. However, the common language runtime (CLR) is as advanced over traditional runtimes as a machine gun is over a musket. Figure 1-2 shows a quick diagrammatic summary of the major pieces of the CLR.

That small part in the middle of Figure 1-2 called Execution support contains most of the capabilities normally associated with a language runtime (such as the `VBRUNxxx.DLL` runtime used with Visual Basic). The rest is new, at least for Microsoft platforms.

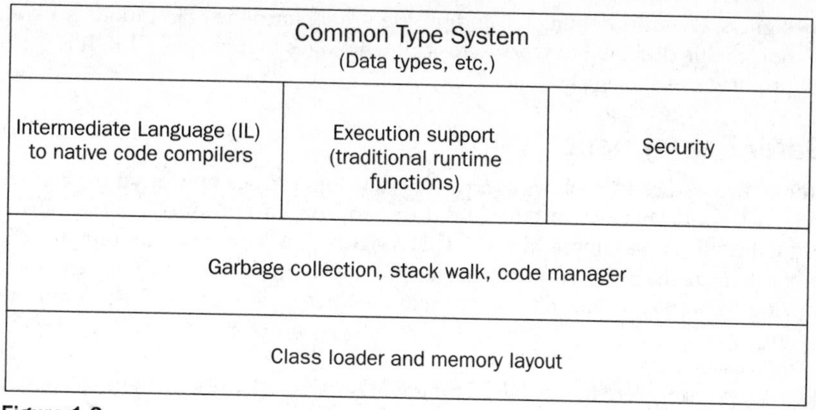

<table>
<tr><td colspan="3">Common Type System
(Data types, etc.)</td></tr>
<tr><td>Intermediate Language (IL) to native code compilers</td><td>Execution support (traditional runtime functions)</td><td>Security</td></tr>
<tr><td colspan="3">Garbage collection, stack walk, code manager</td></tr>
<tr><td colspan="3">Class loader and memory layout</td></tr>
</table>

Figure 1-2

Key Design Goals

The design of the CLR is based on the following primary goals:

- Simpler, faster development
- Automatic handling of system-level tasks such as memory management and process communication
- Excellent tool support
- Simpler, safer deployment
- Scalability

Notice that many of these design goals directly address the limitations of COM/DNA. Let's look at some of these in detail.

Simpler, Faster Development

A broad, consistent framework allows developers to write less code, and reuse code more. Using less code is possible because the system provides a rich set of underlying functionality. Programs in .NET access this functionality in a standard, consistent way, requiring less "hardwiring" and customization logic to interface with the functionality than is typically needed today.

Programming is also simpler in .NET because of the standardization of datatypes and interface conventions. As will be discussed later, .NET makes knowledge of the intricacies of COM much less important.

The net result is that programs written in VB.NET that take proper advantage of the full capabilities of the .NET Framework typically have significantly less code than equivalent programs written in earlier versions of Visual Basic. Less code means faster development, fewer bugs, and easier maintenance.

Excellent Tool Support

Although much of what the CLR does is similar to operating system functionality, it is very much designed to support development languages. It furnishes a rich set of object models that are useful to tools like designers, wizards, debuggers, and profilers, and since the object models are at the runtime level, such tools can be designed to work across all languages that use the CLR. It is expected that third parties will produce a host of such tools.

Simpler, Safer Deployment

It is hard for an experienced Windows component developer to see how anything can work without registration, GUIDs, and the like, but the CLR does. Applications produced in the .NET Framework can be designed to install with a simple XCOPY. That's right—just copy the files onto the disk and run the application (as long as the .NET Framework was previously installed, which is discussed in more detail in the following sections). This hasn't been seen in the Microsoft world since the days of DOS (and some of us really miss it).

This works because compilers in the .NET Framework embed identifiers (in the form of metadata, to be discussed later) into compiled modules, and the CLR manages those identifiers automatically. The identifiers provide all the information needed to load and run modules, and to locate related modules.

As a great by-product, the CLR can manage multiple versions of the same component (even a shared component) and have them run side by side. The identifiers tell the CLR which version is needed for a particular compiled module, because such information is captured at compile time. The runtime policy can be set in a module to use the exact version of a component that was available at compile time, to use the latest compatible version, or to specify an exact version. The bottom line is that .NET is intended to eradicate DLL hell once and for all.

This has implications that might not be apparent at first. For example, if a program needed to run directly from a CD or a shared network drive (without first running an installation program), that was not feasible in Visual Basic after version 3. That capability reappears with VB.NET. This dramatically reduces the cost of deployment in many common scenarios.

Another significant deployment benefit in .NET is that applications only need to install their own core logic. An application produced in .NET does not need to install a runtime, for example, or modules for ADO or XML. Such base functionality is part of the .NET Framework, which is installed separately and only once for each system. The .NET Framework will eventually be included with the operating system and probably with various applications. Those four-disk installs for a VB "Hello world" program are a thing of the past.

.NET programs can also be deployed across the Internet. Version 2.0 of the .NET Framework includes a new technology specifically for that purpose called ClickOnce. This is a new capability in .NET, supplementing the older "no touch deployment." You can read about ClickOnce in Chapter 19.

The .NET Framework, which includes the CLR and the Framework base classes, is required on every machine where you want to run .NET applications and code. For Windows 2003 and above, the .NET Framework is installed automatically as part of the operating system. For older operating systems, or to install a newer version of the .NET Framework, the .NET Framework is a separate installation. Deployment of .NET applications is discussed in Chapter 19.

Scalability

Since most of the system-level execution functions are concentrated in the CLR, they can be optimized and architected to allow a wide range of scalability for applications produced in the .NET Framework. As with most of the other advantages of the CLR, this one comes to all applications with little or no effort.

Memory and process management is one area where scalability can be built in. The memory management in the CLR is self-configuring and tunes itself automatically. Garbage collection (reclaiming memory that is no longer being actively used) is highly optimized, and the CLR supports many of the component management capabilities of MTS/COM+ (such as object pooling). The result is that components can run faster and, thus, support more users.

This has some interesting side effects. For example, the performance and scalability differences among languages become smaller. All languages compile to a standard bytecode called Microsoft Intermediate Language (MSIL), often referred to simply as IL, and there is a discussion later on how the CLR executes IL. With all languages compiling down to similar bytecode, it becomes unnecessary in most cases to look to other languages when performance is an issue. The difference in performance among .NET languages is minor—Visual Basic, for example, gives about the same performance as any of the other .NET languages.

Versions of the CLR are available on a wide range of devices. The vision is for .NET to be running at all levels, from smart palmtop devices all the way up to Web farms. The same development tools work across the entire range—news that will be appreciated by those who have tried to use older Windows CE development kits.

Metadata

The .NET Framework needs lots of information about an application to carry out several automatic functions. The design of .NET requires applications to carry that information within them. That is, applications are self-describing. The collected information that describes an application is called metadata.

The concept of metadata is not new. For example, COM components use a form of it called a type library, which contains metadata describing the classes exposed by the component and is used to facilitate OLE Automation. A component's type library, however, is stored in a separate file. In contrast, the metadata in .NET is stored in one place—inside the component it describes. Metadata in .NET also contains more information about the component and is better organized.

Chapter 6 on the CLR goes into more information about metadata. For now, the most important point for you to internalize is that metadata is key to the easy deployment in .NET. When a component is upgraded or moved, the necessary information about the component cannot be left behind. Metadata can never get out of sync with a .NET component, because it is not in a separate file. Everything the CLR needs to know to run a component is supplied with the component.

Multiple-Language Integration and Support

The CLR is designed to support multiple languages and allow unprecedented levels of integration among those languages. By enforcing a common type system, and by having complete control over interface calls, the CLR allows languages to work together more transparently than ever before. The cross-language integration issues of COM simply don't exist in .NET.

It is straightforward in the .NET Framework to use one language to subclass a class implemented in another. A class written in Visual Basic can inherit from a base class written in C#, or in COBOL for that matter. The VB program doesn't even need to know the language used for the base class. .NET offers full implementation inheritance with no problems that require recompilation when the base class changes.

Chapter 3 also includes more information on the multiple-language integration features of .NET.

A Common Type System

A key piece of functionality that enables multiple-language support is a common type system, in which all commonly used datatypes, even base types such as `Long` and `Boolean`, are actually implemented as objects. Coercion among types can now be done at a lower level for more consistency between languages. Also, since all languages are using the same library of types, calling one language from another doesn't require type conversion or weird calling conventions.

This results in the need for some readjustment, particularly for VB developers. For example, what was called an `Integer` in VB6 and earlier, is now known as a `Short` in VB.NET. The adjustment is worth it to bring Visual Basic in line with everything else, though, and, as a by-product, other languages get the same support for strings that Visual Basic has always had.

The CLR enforces the requirement that all datatypes satisfy the common type system. This has important implications. For example, it is not possible with the common type system to get the problem known in COM as a buffer overrun, which is the source of many security vulnerabilities. Programs written on .NET should, therefore, have fewer such vulnerabilities, because .NET is not dependent on the programmer to constantly check passed parameters for appropriate type and length. Such checking is done by default.

Chapter 3 goes into detail about the new type system in .NET.

Namespaces

One of the most important concepts in Microsoft .NET is namespaces. Namespaces help organize object libraries and hierarchies, simplify object references, prevent ambiguity when referring to objects, and control the scope of object identifiers. The namespace for a class allows the CLR to unambiguously identify that class in the available .NET libraries that it can load.

Namespaces are discussed briefly in Chapter 3 and in more detail in Chapter 9. Understanding the concept of a namespace is essential for your progress in .NET, so do not skip those sections if you are unfamiliar with namespaces.

The Next Layer — The .NET Class Framework

The next layer up in the framework provides the services and object models for data, input/output, security, and so forth. It is called the .NET Class Framework, sometimes referred to as the .NET base classes. For example, the next generation of ADO, called ADO.NET, resides here. Some of the additional functionality in the .NET Class Framework is listed below.

You might be wondering why .NET includes functionality that is, in many cases, duplication of existing class libraries. There are several good reasons:

- The .NET Class Framework libraries are implemented in the .NET Framework, making them easier to integrate with .NET-developed programs.

- The .NET Class Framework brings together most of the system class libraries needed into one location, which increases consistency and convenience.
- The class libraries in the .NET Class Framework are much easier to extend than older class libraries, using the inheritance capabilities in .NET.
- Having the libraries as part of the .NET Framework simplifies deployment of .NET applications. Once the .NET Framework is on a system, individual applications don't need to install base class libraries for functions like data access.

What Is in the .NET Class Framework?

The .NET Class Framework contains literally thousands of classes and interfaces. Here are just some of the functions of various libraries in the .NET Class Framework:

- Data access and manipulation
- Creation and management of threads of execution
- Interfaces from .NET to the outside world — Windows Forms, Web Forms, Web Services, and console applications
- Definition, management, and enforcement of application security
- Encryption, disk file I/O, network I/O, serialization of objects, and other system-level functions
- Application configuration
- Working with directory services, event logs, performance counters, message queues, and timers
- Sending and receiving data with a variety of network protocols
- Accessing metadata information stored in assemblies

Much of the functionality that a programmer might think of as being part of a language has been moved to the base classes. For example, the old VB keyword `Sqr` for extracting a square root is no longer available in .NET. It has been replaced by the `System.Math.Sqrt()` method in the framework classes.

It's important to emphasize that all languages based on the .NET Framework have these framework classes available. That means that COBOL, for example, can use the same function mentioned above for getting a square root. This makes such base functionality widely available and highly consistent across languages. All calls to `Sqrt` look essentially the same (allowing for syntactical differences among languages) and access the same underlying code. Here are examples in VB.NET and C#:

```
' Example using Sqrt in Visual Basic .NET
Dim dblNumber As Double = 200
Dim dblSquareRoot As Double
dblSquareRoot = System.Math.Sqrt(dblNumber)
Label1.Text = dblSquareRoot.ToString

' Same example in C#
Double dblNumber = 200;
Double dblSquareRoot = System.Math.Sqrt(dblNumber);
dblSquareRoot = System.Math.Sqrt(dblNumber);
label1.Text = dblSquareRoot.ToString;
```

Notice that the line using the `Sqrt()` function is exactly the same in both languages.

As a side note, a programming shop can create its own classes for core functionality, such as globally available, already compiled functions. This custom functionality can then be referenced in code the same way as built-in .NET functionality.

Much of the functionality in the base framework classes resides in a vast namespace called `System`. The `System.Math.Sqrt()` method was just mentioned. The `System` namespace contains dozens of such subcategories. The table below lists a few of the important ones, many of which you will be using in various parts of this book.

User and Program Interfaces

At the top layer, .NET provides three ways to render and manage user interfaces:

- Windows Forms
- Web Forms
- Console applications

Namespace	What It Contains	Example Classes and Subnamespaces
`System.Collections`	Creation and management of various types of collections	`Arraylist`, `Hashtable`, `SortedList`
`System.Data`	Classes and types related to basic database management (see Chapter 11 for details)	`DataSet`, `DataTable`, `DataColumn`,
`System.Diagnostics`	Classes to debug an application and to trace the execution of code	`Debug`, `Trace`
`System.IO`	Types that allow reading and writing to and from files and other data streams	`File`, `FileStream`, `Path`, `StreamReader`, `StreamWriter`
`System.Math`	Members to calculate common mathematical quantities, such as trigonometric and logarithmic functions	`Sqrt` (square root), `Cos` (cosine), `Log` (logarithm), `Min` (minimum)
`System.Reflection`	Capability to inspect metadata	`Assembly`, `Module`
`System.Security`	Types that enable security capabilities (see Chapter 24 for details)	`Cryptography`, `Permissions`, `Policy`

Windows Forms

Windows Forms is a more advanced and integrated way to do standard Win32 screens. All languages that work on the .NET Framework, including new versions of Visual Studio languages, use the Windows Forms engine, which duplicates the functionality of the old VB forms engine. It provides a rich, unified set of controls and drawing functions for all languages, as well as a standard API for underlying Windows Services for graphics and drawing. It effectively replaces the Windows graphical API, wrapping it in such a way that the developer normally has no need to go directly to the Windows API for any graphical or screen functions.

In Chapter 14, you will look at Windows Forms in more detail and note significant changes in Windows Forms versus older VB forms. Chapter 15 continues discussing advanced Windows Forms capabilities such as creation of Windows Forms visual controls.

Client Applications versus Browser-Based Applications

Before .NET, many internal corporate applications were made browser-based simply because of the cost of installing and maintaining a client application on hundreds or thousands of workstations. Windows Forms and the .NET Framework change the economics of these decisions. A Windows Forms application is much easier to install and update than an equivalent VB6 desktop application. With a simple XCOPY deployment and no registration issues, installation and updating become much easier. Internet deployment via ClickOnce also makes applications more available across a wide geographic area, with automatic updating of changed modules on the client.

That means that "smart client" applications with a rich user interface are more practical under .NET, even for a large number of users. It may not be necessary to resort to browser-based applications just to save on installation and deployment costs.

As a consequence, you should not dismiss Windows Forms applications as merely replacements for earlier VB6 desktop applications. Instead, you should examine applications in .NET and explicitly decide what kind of interface makes sense in a given case. In some cases, applications that you might have assumed should be browser-based simply because of a large number of users and wide geographic deployment instead can be smart-client-based, which can improve usability, security, and productivity.

Web Forms

The part of .NET that handles communications with the Internet is called ASP.NET. It includes a forms engine, called Web Forms, which can be used to create browser-based user interfaces.

Divorcing layout from logic, Web Forms consist of two parts:

- A template, which contains HTML-based layout information for all user interface elements
- A component, which contains all logic to be hooked to the user interface

It is as if a standard Visual Basic form was split into two parts, one containing information on controls and their properties and layout, and the other containing the code. Just as in Visual Basic, the code operates "behind" the controls, with events in the controls activating event routines in the code.

As with Windows Forms, Web Forms will be available to all languages. The component handling logic for a form can be in any language that supports .NET. This brings complete, flexible Web interface capability to a wide variety of languages. Chapters 16 and 17 go into detail on Web Forms and the controls that are used on them.

If you have used ASP.NET in previous versions of .NET, you should know that ASP.NET 2.0 has dramatic improvements. With even more built-in functionality for common browser tasks, applications can be written with far less code in ASP.NET 2.0 as compared to earlier versions. Capabilities such as user authentication can now be done with prebuilt ASP.NET components, so you no longer have to write such components yourself.

Console Applications

Although Microsoft doesn't emphasize the ability to write character-based applications, the .NET Framework does include an interface for such console applications. Batch processes, for example, can now have components integrated into them that are written to a console interface.

As with Windows Forms and Web Forms, this console interface is available for applications written in any .NET language. Writing character-based applications in previous versions of Visual Basic, for example, has always been a struggle, because it was completely oriented around a graphical user interface (GUI). VB.NET can be used for true console applications.

Web Services

Application development is moving into the next stage of decentralization. The oldest idea of an application is a piece of software that accesses basic operating system services, such as the file system and graphics system. Then we moved to applications that used lots of base functionality from other system-level applications, such as a database — this type of application added value by applying generic functionality to specific problems. The developer's job was to focus on adding business value, not on building the foundation.

Web Services represent the next step in this direction. In Web Services, software functionality becomes exposed as a service that doesn't care what the consumer of the service is (unless there are security considerations). Web Services allow developers to build applications by combining local and remote resources for an overall integrated and distributed solution.

In .NET, Web Services are implemented as part of ASP.NET (see Figure 1-1), which handles all Web interfaces. It allows programs to talk to each other directly over the Web, using the SOAP standard. This has the capacity to dramatically change the architecture of Web applications, allowing services running all over the Web to be integrated into a local application.

Chapter 23 contains a detailed discussion of Web Services.

XML as the .NET Metalanguage

Much of the underlying integration of .NET is accomplished with XML. For example, Web Services depend completely on XML for interfacing with remote objects. Looking at metadata usually means looking at an XML version of it.

ADO.NET, the successor to ADO, is heavily dependent on XML for the remote representation of data. Essentially, when ADO.NET creates what it calls a dataset (a more complex successor to a recordset), the data is converted to XML for manipulation by ADO.NET. Then, the changes to that XML are posted back to the datastore by ADO.NET when remote manipulation is finished.

Chapter 12 discusses XML in .NET in more detail, and, as previously mentioned, Chapter 11 contains a discussion of ADO.NET. With XML as an "entry point" into so many areas of .NET, integration opportunities are multiplied. Using XML to expose interfaces to .NET functions allows developers to tie components and functions together in new, unexpected ways. XML can be the glue that ties pieces together in ways that were never anticipated, both to Microsoft and non-Microsoft platforms.

The Role of COM

When the .NET Framework was introduced, some uninformed journalists interpreted it as the death of COM. That is completely incorrect. COM is not going anywhere for a while. In fact, Windows will not boot without COM.

.NET integrates very well with COM-based software. Any COM component can be treated as a .NET component by native .NET components. The .NET Framework wraps COM components and exposes an interface that .NET components can work with. This is absolutely essential to the quick acceptance of .NET because it makes .NET interoperable with a tremendous amount of older COM-based software.

Going in the other direction, the .NET Framework can expose .NET components with a COM interface. This allows older COM components to use .NET-based components as if they were developed using COM.

Chapter 20 discusses COM interoperability in more detail.

No Internal Use of COM

It is important, however, to understand that native .NET components do not interface using COM. The CLR implements a new way for components to interface, one that is not COM-based. Use of COM is only necessary when interfacing with COM components produced by non-.NET tools.

Over a long span of time, the fact that .NET does not use COM internally may lead to the decline of COM, but for any immediate purposes, COM is definitely important.

Some Things Never Change . . .

Earlier, this chapter discussed the limitations of the pre-.NET programming models. However, those models have many aspects that still apply to .NET development. Tiered layers in software architecture, for example, were specifically developed to deal with the challenges in design and development of complex applications and are still appropriate. Many persistent design issues, such as the need to encapsulate business rules, or to provide for multiple user interface access points to a system, do not go away with .NET.

Applications developed in the .NET Framework will still, in many cases, use a tiered architecture. However, the tiers will be a lot easier to produce in .NET. The presentation tier will benefit from the new interface technologies, especially Web Forms for Internet development. The middle tier will require far less COM-related headaches to develop and implement. And richer, more distributed middle tier designs will be possible by using Web Services.

The architectural skills that experienced developers have learned in earlier models are definitely still important and valuable in the .NET world.

.NET Drives Changes in Visual Basic

This chapter previously covered the limitations of Visual Basic in earlier versions. To recap, they are:

- No capability for multithreading
- Lack of implementation inheritance and other object features
- Poor error-handling ability
- Poor integration with other languages such as C++
- No effective user interface for Internet-based applications

Since VB.NET is built on top of the .NET Framework, all of these shortcomings have been eliminated. In fact, Visual Basic gets the most extensive changes of any existing language in the VS.NET suite. These changes pull Visual Basic in line with other languages in terms of datatypes, calling conventions, error handling, and, most importantly, object orientation. Chapters 4, 5, and 7 go into detail about object-oriented concepts in VB.NET, and Chapter 10 discusses error handling, which is known in .NET as "exception handling."

How .NET Affects You

One of the reasons you are probably reading this book is that you want to know how VB.NET will affect you as an existing Visual Basic developer. Here are some of the most important implications.

A Spectrum of Programming Models

In previous Microsoft-based development tools, there were a couple of quantum leaps required to move from simple to complex. A developer could start simply with ASP pages and VBScript, but when those became cumbersome, it was a big leap to learn component-based, three-tier development in Visual Basic. And it was another quantum leap to become proficient in C++, ATL, and related technologies for system-level work.

A key benefit of VB.NET and the .NET Framework is that there exists a more gradual transition in programming models from simple to full power. ASP.NET pages are far more structured than ASP pages, and code used in them is often identical to equivalent code used in a Windows Forms application. Internet development can now be done using real Visual Basic code instead of VBScript.

Visual Basic itself becomes a tool with wider applicability, as it becomes easy to do a Web interface with Web Forms, and it also becomes possible to do advanced object-oriented designs. Even system-level capabilities, such as Windows Services can be done with VB.NET (see Chapter 25). Old reasons for using another language, such as lack of performance or flexibility, are mostly gone. Visual Basic will do almost anything that other .NET languages can do.

This increases the range of applicability of Visual Basic. It can be used all the way from "scripts" (which are actually compiled on the fly) written with a text editor up through sophisticated component and Web programming in one of the most advanced development environments available.

Reducing Barriers to Internet Development

With older tools, programming for the Internet requires a completely different programming model than programming systems that will be run locally. The differences are most apparent in user interface construction, but that's not the only area of difference. Objects constructed for access by ASP pages, for example, must support `Variant` parameters, but objects constructed for access by Visual Basic forms can have parameters of any datatype. Accessing databases over the Internet requires using technologies like RDS instead of the ADO connections that local programming typically uses.

The .NET Framework erases many of these differences. Programming for the Internet and programming for local systems are much more alike in .NET than with today's systems. Differences remain — Web Forms still have significant differences from Windows Forms, for example, but many other differences, such as the way data is handled, are much more unified under .NET.

A big result of this similarity of programming models is to make Internet programming more practical and accessible. With functionality for the Internet designed in from the start, developers don't have to know as much or do as much to produce Internet systems with the .NET Framework.

Libraries of Prewritten Functionality

The evolution of Windows development languages, including Visual Basic, has been in the direction of providing more and more built-in functionality so that developers can ignore the foundations and concentrate on solving business problems. The .NET Framework continues this trend.

One particularly important implication is that the .NET Framework extends the trend of developers spending less time writing code and more time discovering how to do something with prewritten functionality. Mainframe COBOL programmers could learn everything they ever needed to know about COBOL in a year or two and very seldom need to consult reference materials after that. In contrast, today's Visual Basic developers already spend a significant portion of their time digging through reference material to figure out how to do something that they may never do again. The sheer expanse of available functionality, plus the rapidly changing pace, makes it imperative for an effective developer to be a researcher also. .NET accelerates this trend, and will probably increase the ratio of research time to coding time for a typical developer.

Easier Deployment

A major design goal in Microsoft .NET is to simplify installation and configuration of software. With DLL hell mostly gone, and with installation of compiled modules a matter of a simple file copy, developers should be able to spend less time worrying about deployment of their applications, and more time concentrating on the functionality of their systems. The budget for the deployment technology needed by a typical application will be significantly smaller.

The Future of .NET

At the Professional Developer's Conference (PDC) in Los Angeles in October of 2003, Microsoft gave the first public look at their next-generation operating system, code-named Longhorn. It was clear from even this early glimpse that .NET is at the heart of Microsoft's operating system strategy going forward.

However, the naming of what is now known as .NET is going to change. While Web Services and related technologies may still carry the .NET label going forward, the .NET Framework is called WinFX in Longhorn. This may cause some confusion in names going forward, but be assured that what you learn today about the .NET Framework and VB.NET will be important for years to come in the world of Microsoft applications.

Major Differences in .NET 2.0

If you are familiar with earlier versions of .NET, you will want to pay special attention to areas that have been significantly changed. Here is a list of some of the most important additions and changes, with the chapter you should check for more information:

Feature	Description	Chapter(s)
Edit and Continue	Allows you to make changes to code while you are running it in the integrated development environment (IDE) and have the changes take effect immediately. (This feature was available in VB6 and earlier, but was not available in Visual Basic 2002 or 2003.)	2
Partial classes	Allows code for a class to be split over multiple code modules.	4
Generics	Allows generic collections to handle specific types, declared when the collection is created.	8
Data binding	There are many new controls for data binding and new designer support such as drag-and-drop of data fields onto Windows Forms.	15
ClickOnce	New deployment technology for deploying across the Internet, with automatic updating.	19
"My" classes	Provides quick access to commonly used classes in the .NET Framework.	2
Nullable types	Allows data types that can either hold a value or be null, allowing .NET types to match up to database types more transparently.	3
Operator overloading	Allows you to define operations between arbitrary types, such as the ability to define a "+" operation for two `Account` objects.	5
IsNot keyword	Simplifies `If` statements that check if an object is `Nothing`.	2

Feature	Description	Chapter(s)
Using keyword	Automates disposing of objects created in a section of code.	4
IDE improvements	Exception manager, code snippets with automatic fill-in, improved IntelliSense, and autocorrect are a few of the new capabilities of the IDE.	2

Summary

VB.NET is not like other versions of Visual Basic. It is built with completely different assumptions, on a new platform that is central to Microsoft's entire product strategy. This chapter discussed the reasons Microsoft has created this platform and how challenges in earlier, pre-Internet technologies have been met by .NET.

This chapter has also discussed in particular how this will affect VB developers. .NET presents many new challenges for developers but simultaneously provides them with greatly enhanced functionality. In particular, Visual Basic developers now have the ability to develop object-oriented and Web-based applications far more easily and cheaply.

The next chapter takes a closer look at the VS.NET IDE, and discusses the basics of doing applications in VB.NET.

2

Introducing Visual Basic 2005 and Visual Studio 2005

Chapter 1 introduced .NET and discussed how version 2.0 of the .NET Framework is the next step in the evolution of programming on the Windows platform. This chapter takes a practical look at .NET. It starts with the creation of the standard "Hello World" Windows application using *Visual Studio 2005* (Visual Studio). After creating the initial application, you can step through simple additions to this first application. You can compare your code at each stage to understand the changes that have been made.

The chapter also covers several introductory topics associated with becoming familiar with Visual Studio and creating a simple application, including:

- Project templates
- References
- Code regions
- Forms as classes
- Class constructors
- Setting form properties
- Selecting a runtime environment
- Visual Studio environment

This chapter provides only a brief introduction to Visual Basic 2005 (VB) Windows Form applications. It will step you through creating your first .NET project and review many of the elements that are common to every .NET application. The discussion of several other project types, such as Web projects, will be covered in later chapters.

If you are familiar with Visual Studio .NET 2002 or Visual Studio 2003 and the .NET Framework version 1.x, note that while the updates to Visual Studio 2005 and the .NET Framework version 2.0 are significant, you may want to skim through this chapter, reviewing the changes.

Visual Studio .NET — Startup

Those of you making the move from COM to .NET will notice that Visual Studio 2005 has one entry for the development environment in the Start menu — there are no separate entries for Visual Basic, Visual C++, or Visual C#. All of the Visual Studio languages share the same integrated development environment (IDE). One of the changes from previous versions of Visual Studio .NET is that the environment can now be customized by project type.

When Visual Studio 2005 is started, the window shown in Figure 2-1 is displayed to permit you to configure your custom profile. Unlike previous versions of .NET, where you selected a set of preferences that you would then use for all of your development, Visual Studio 2005 allows you to select either a language-specific or task-specific profile. This book will use screen shots based on the Visual Basic Developer setting.

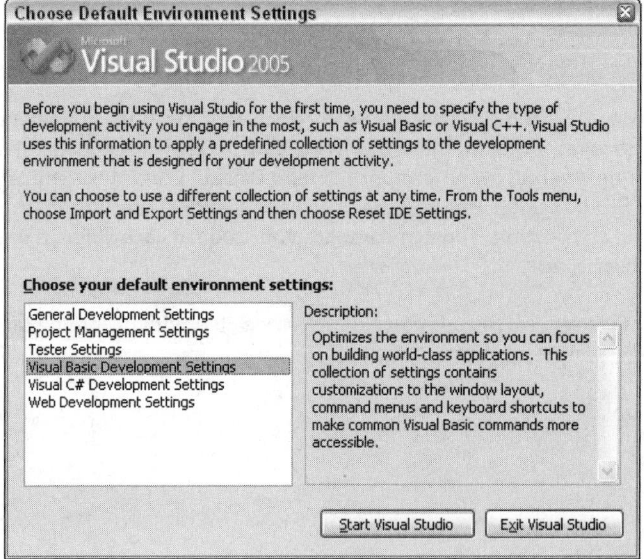

Figure 2-1

Configuration of the settings is managed through the "Import and Export Settings . . ." menu option of the Tools menu. This menu option opens a simple wizard, which first saves your current settings and then allows you to select an alternate set of settings. By default, Visual Studio ships with settings for Visual Basic, Web Development, and C# to name a few, but more importantly by exporting your settings you can create and share your own custom settings files.

The Visual Studio settings file is an XML file that allows you to capture all of your Visual Studio configuration settings. This might sound trivial, but it's not. The fact is this feature allows for standardization of

Visual Studio across different team members. The advantages of a team sharing settings go beyond just using a common look and feel. To illustrate why this can be important, let's look at a simple example of how standardizing a portion of Visual Studio can impact team development.

Tracking changes to source code can be made more difficult simply from the way that Visual Basic reformats code layout for readability. Most source control systems track code changes on a per line basis. Taking just the simple example of changing the default tab value associated with the Text Editor and reducing it from four characters to two or three characters can make code more readable and less likely to wrap. Unfortunately, if someone on the team does pick a different value, then as each engineer checks out code and makes modifications, he or she also resets the white space on every line of the source file. Thus, when the source file is checked back in, instead of having the code changes that are easily highlighted, all of the lines where the tabs were adjusted show up as changed and tracking changes becomes more difficult.

The solution is to provide a common settings file that defines settings such as the correct tab and layout for Hypertext Markup Language (HTML) elements (to name a few common settings) so that everyone starts from the same baseline. In this way developers who work together produce code that has the same layout. Engineers can then customize other settings that are specific to their view of Visual Studio.

Visual Studio .NET

Once you have set up your profile, the next step is to create your first project. Selecting File ➪ New Project opens the New Project Dialog window, shown in Figure 2-2. One of the changes in Visual Studio 2005 is that once you have selected a default environment setting, you are presented with a setting-specific project view. For Visual Basic this means that you are presented with Visual Basic project templates by default. A quick note, however: Not all project templates are listed within the New Project dialog. For example, if you want to create a Visual Basic Web site, you need to start that process by creating a new Web site instead of creating a new project. Expanding the top level of the Visual Basic tree, you may notice that this window separates project types into a series of categories. These categories include

- **Windows** — Those projects used to create code that runs as part of the standard .NET Framework. Since such projects can run on any operating system (OS) hosting the framework, the category "Windows" is something of a throwback.
- **Office** — The replacement for Visual Studio Tools for Office (VSTO). These are .NET applications that are hosted under Office 2003.
- **Smart Device** — These are projects that target the .NET Compact Framework. Such applications may run on one or more handheld devices and make use of a different runtime environment from full .NET applications.
- **Database** — This template creates a project that supports classes that will run within SQL Server 2005. All versions of SQL Server 2005 (from Express through Enterprise) support the .NET Framework as part of their runtime, and such projects have a unique set of runtime constraints. This is a very different project template from the Database project template provided under Visual Studio 2003 and still available under the Other Project Types option.

Visual Studio has other categories for projects and you have access to Other development languages and far more project types then we will cover in this one book. For now, you can select a Windows Application project template.

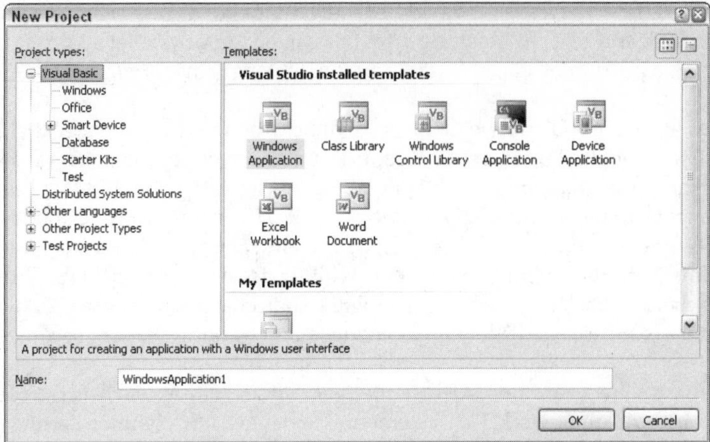

Figure 2-2

For this example, you can use `ProVB.NET` as the project name and then click the OK button. Visual Studio then takes over and uses the Windows Application template to create a new Windows Forms project. The project contains a blank form that can be customized and a variety of other elements that you can explore. Before you start customizing any code, let's first look at the elements of this new project.

The Solution Explorer

Those of you new to .NET but with previous Microsoft development tool experience will find a solution similar to a project group. However, a .NET solution can contain projects of any .NET language and also allows inclusion of the database, testing, and installation projects as part of the overall solution.

Before discussing these files in detail, let's take a look at the next step, which is to reveal a few additional details about your project. Click the second button from the left in Solution Explorer to show all of the project files, as shown in Figure 2-3. As this image shows, there are many other files that make up your project. Some of these, such as those under the My Project grouping, don't require you to edit them directly. Instead, you can double-click on the My Project entry in the Solution Explorer and open the user interface to adjust your project settings. You do not need to change any of the default settings for this project, but those of you familiar with Visual Studio 2003 should notice many of the new capabilities provided by this window. These include the ability to add and manage your project references. Similar to how a traditional Windows application allows you to reference COM components, .NET allows you to create references to other components (those implemented both with a .NET language and with COM) to extend the capabilities of your application.

The `bin` and `obj` directories that are shown in this display are used when building your project. The `obj` directory contains the first pass object files used by the compiler to create your final executable file. The "binary" or compiled version of your application is then placed in the `bin` directory by default. Of course, referring to the Microsoft Intermediate Language (MSIL) code as binary is something of a misnomer, since the actual translation to binary does not occur until runtime when your application is compiled by the Just in Time Compiler. However, Microsoft continues to use the `bin` directory as the default output directory for your project's compilation.

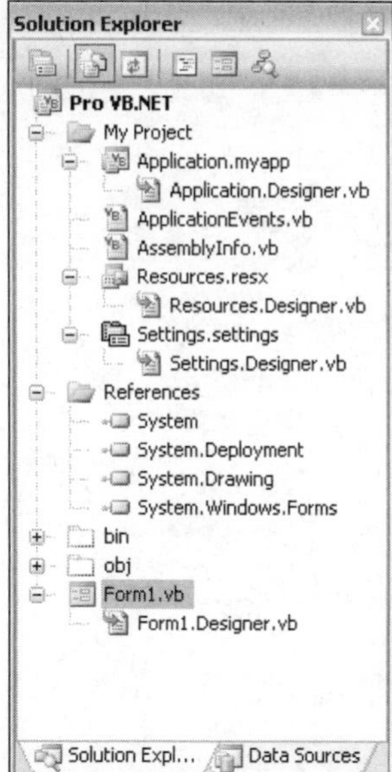

Figure 2-3

Additionally, Figure 2-3 shows that the project does not contain an `app.config` file by default. Most experienced ASP.NET developers are readily familiar with the use of `web.config` files. `App.config` files work on the same principal in that they contain XML, which is used to store project-specific settings such as database connection strings and other application-specific settings. Using a `.config` file instead of having your settings in the Windows Registry allows your applications to run side by side with another version of your application without the settings from either version impacting the other. Because each version of your application will live in its own directory, its settings will be contained in the directory with it, which enables the different versions to run with unique settings.

Finally, the Solution Explorer includes your actual source file(s). In this case, the `Form1.vb` file is the primary file associated with the default Windows form. You'll be customizing this form shortly, but before looking at that, it seems appropriate to look at some of the settings exposed by the My Project element of your new project.

My Project

Visual Studio displays a vertically tabbed display for editing your project settings. The My Project display shown in Figure 2-4 gives you access to several different aspects of your project. Most, such as Signing, Security, Publishing, and so forth, will be covered in future chapters. For this chapter, it should just be noted that this display makes it easier to carry out several tasks that once required engineers to work outside of the Visual Studio environment. For your first application, notice that you can customize your Assembly name from this screen as well as reset the type of application and object to be referenced when starting your application.

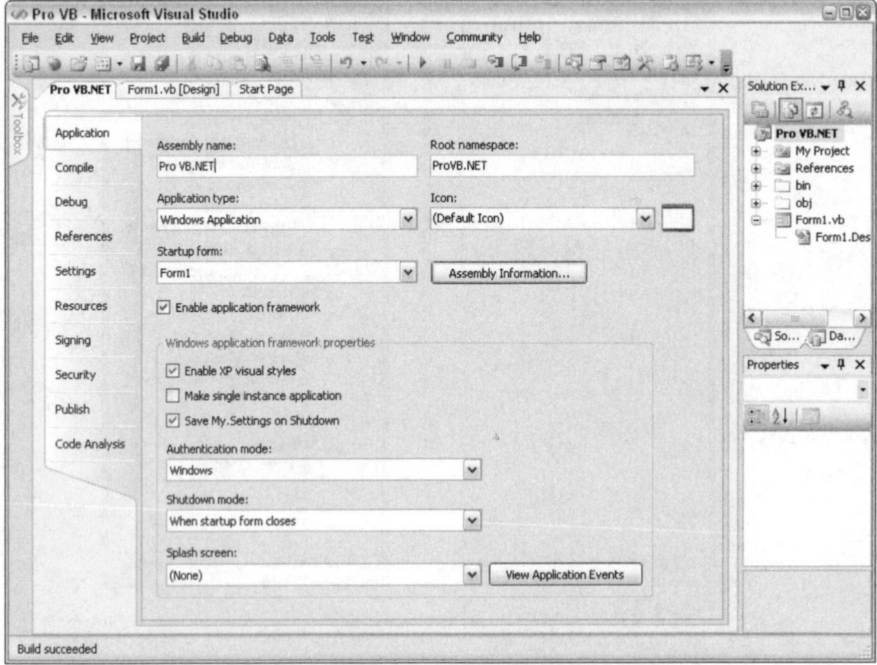

Figure 2-4

In addition, there is a button that will be discussed shortly for changing your Assembly information as well as the ability to define a root namespace for your application classes. Namespaces are covered in more detail in Chapter 9 and can be nested inside other namespaces. This nesting helps to organize classes into a logical structure, which reduces confusion and aids the developer. Just as with COM components, it's a good idea to create your own root namespace and then build your custom classes under that root. Similarly, your project already references some system namespaces.

References

It's possible to add additional references as part of your project. Select the References tab in your My Project display. From this tab, you can select other .NET class libraries and applications, as well as COM components. There is even a Shortcut tab for selecting classes defined within other projects of your current solution. Similar to the default code files that are created with a new project, each project has a default set of referenced libraries. For Windows Forms applications, the list of default namespaces is fairly short and is shown in the following table.

Reference	Description
`System`	Often referred to as the root namespace. All the base data types (`String`, `Object`, and so on) are contained within the `System` namespace. This namespace also acts as the root for all other `System` classes.
`System.Deployment`	Classes used for One Touch Deployment. This namespace is covered in more detail in Chapter 19.

Reference	Description
`System.Drawing`	Provides access to the GDI+ graphics functionality.
`System.Windows.Forms`	Classes used to create traditional Windows-based applications. This namespace is covered in more detail in Chapter 14.

Assembly Information Screen

Selecting the Assembly Information button from within your My Project window opens the Assembly Information dialog box. Within this dialog, shown in Figure 2-5 it is possible to define file properties, such as your company's name and versioning information, which will be embedded into the operating system's file attributes for your project's output. The frame of the assembly file shows that by default it contains several standard values. This dialog is new to Visual Studio 2005 and replaces the way that engineers were forced to directly edit the XML contained in the `AssemblyInfo.vb` source file associated with an application.

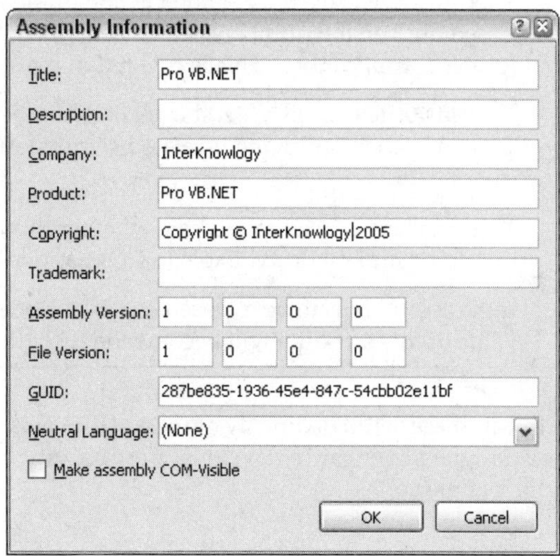

Figure 2-5

Assembly Attributes

The `AssemblyInfo.vb` file contains attribute blocks, which are used to set information about the assembly. Each attribute block has an *assembly modifier*, for example:

```
<Assembly: AssemblyTitle("")>
```

All the attributes set within this file provide information that is contained within the assembly metadata. These properties are displayed in the Assembly Information dialog. This dialog is opened from the project's properties page, on the Compile tab by selecting the Assembly Information button. The attributes contained within the file are summarized in the following table.

Attribute	Description
`Title`	Sets the name of the assembly, which appears within the file properties of the compiled file as the Description.
`Description`	This attribute is used to provide a textual description of the assembly, which is added to the `Comments` property for the file.
`Company`	Sets the name of the company that produced the assembly. The name set here appears within the Version tab of the file properties.
`Product`	Sets the product name of the resulting assembly. The product name will appear within the Version tab of the file properties.
`Copyright`	The copyright information of the assembly, this value appears on the Version tab of the file properties.
`Trademark`	Used to assign any trademark information to the assembly. This information appears within the Version tab of the file properties.
`Assembly Version`	This attribute is used to set the version number of the assembly. Assembly version numbers can be generated, which is the default setting for .NET applications. This is covered in more detail in Chapter 25.
`File Version`	This attribute is used to set the version number of the executable files. This and other deployment-related settings are covered in more detail in Chapter 25.
`COM Visible`	This attribute is used to indicate whether this assembly should be registered and made available to COM applications.
`Guid`	If the assembly is to be exposed as a traditional COM object, then the value of this attribute will become the ID of the resulting type library.

Not requiring developers to edit these settings directly at the XML level is one of the many ways that Visual Studio 2005 has been designed to enhance developer productivity. Now that you've seen some of your project settings, let's look at the code.

The New Code Window

The Form Designer opens by default when a new project is created. If you have closed it, you can easily reopen it by right-clicking `Form1.vb` in the Solution Explorer and selecting View Designer from the pop-up menu. From this window, you can also bring up the code view for this form. This can be done either by right-clicking `Form1.vb` in the Solution Explorer and selecting code view, or by right-clicking the form in the View Designer and selecting View Code from the pop-up menu.

By default you can see that the initial display of the form looks very simple. The Code Editor window should be familiar from previous development environments. There is no code in the `Form1.vb` file. This is a change from Visual Studio 2003, where you would have a generated section of code in a collapsed region in your source file. Instead, Visual Studio 2005 introduces a capability called partial classes. Partial classes will be discussed later in Chapter 4; for now you merely need to be aware that all of the generated source code for your form is located in the file `Form1.Designer.vb`. If you open this file, you'll see that there is quite a bit of custom code generated by Visual Studio already in your project. At this point, you will have a display similar to the one shown in Figure 2-6.

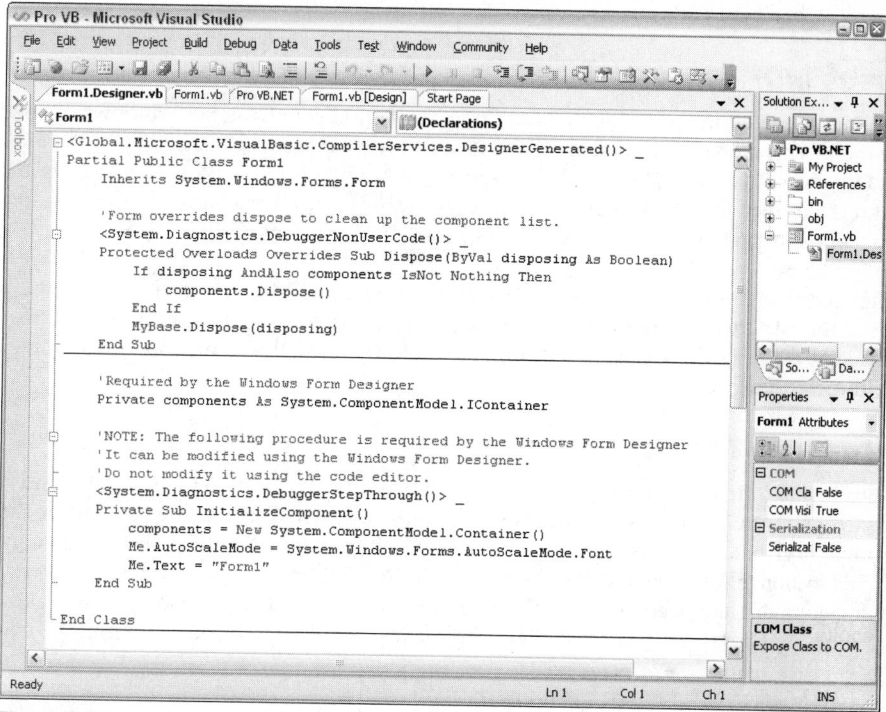

Figure 2-6

Modules inside source files in Visual Studio can be hidden on the screen — a feature known as outlining. By default there is a minus sign next to every method (sub or function). This makes it easy to hide or show code on a method-by-method basis. If the code for a method is hidden, the method declaration is still shown and has a plus sign next to it to indicate that the body code is hidden. This feature is very useful when a developer is working on a few key methods in a module and wishes to avoid scrolling through many screens of code that are not relevant to the current task.

It is also possible to hide custom regions of code. The `#Region` directive is used for this within the IDE, though it has no effect on the actual application. A region of code is demarcated by the `#Region` directive at the top and the `# End Region` directive at the end. The `#Region` directive used to begin a region should include a description. The description will appear next to the plus sign shown when the code is minimized.

The outlining enhancement was probably inspired by the fact that the Visual Studio designers generate a lot of code when a project is started. Items that were hidden in Visual Basic 6 (such as the logic that sets initial form properties) are actually inside the generated code in Visual Studio. However, seeing all of these functions in the code is an improvement because it is easier for the developer to understand what is happening, and possibly to manipulate the process in special cases.

Outlining can also be turned off by selecting Edit ➪ Outlining ➪ Stop Outlining from the Visual Studio menu. This menu also contains some other useful functions. A section of code can be temporarily hidden by highlighting it and selecting Edit ➪ Outlining ➪ Hide Selection. The selected code will be replaced with an ellipsis with a plus sign next to it, as if you had dynamically identified a region within the source code. Clicking the plus sign displays the code again.

Tabs versus MDI

You may have noticed in Figure 2-6 that the Code View and Form Designer windows opened in a tabbed environment. This tabbed environment is the default for working with the code windows inside Visual Studio. However, it is possible to toggle this setting, allowing you to work with a more traditional MDI-based interface. Such an interface opens each code window within a separate frame instead of anchoring it to the tabbed display of the integrated development environment (IDE).

To change the arrangement that is used between the tabbed and MDI interface, use the Options dialog box (accessible via Tools ➪ Options). You can also force the development environment to use the MDI as opposed to the tabbed interface (for a single session) by using the command line option `/mdi` when Visual Studio is started.

Customizing the Text Editor

Visual Studio has a rich set of customizations related to the Text Editor. Go to the Tools menu and select Options to open the Options dialog box, shown in Figure 2-7. Within the dialog box, ensure that the Show All Settings check box is selected. Next select the Text Editor folder, and then select the All Languages folder. This section allows you to make changes to the Text Editor, which are applied across every supported development language. Additionally, you can select the Basic folder. Doing so will allow you to make changes that are specific to how the Text Editor will behave when you are editing VB source code.

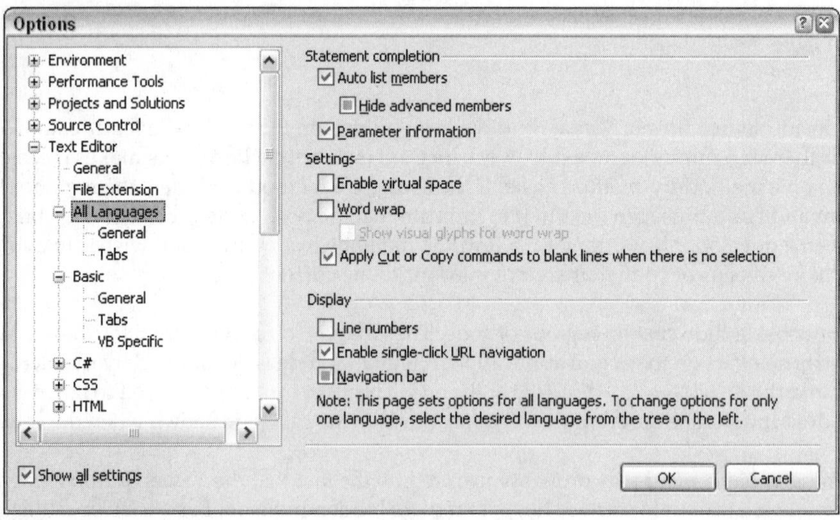

Figure 2-7

From this dialog box, it is possible to modify the number of spaces that each tab will insert into your source code and to manage several other elements of your editing environment. One little-known capability of the Text Editor that can be useful is line numbering. Checking the line numbers check box will cause the editor to number all lines, which provides an easy way to unambiguously reference lines of code.

A new feature of Visual Studio 2005 is the ability to track your changes as you edit. Enabling the Track Changes setting under the Text Editor options causes Visual Studio to provide a colored indicator of where you have modified a file. This indicator is a color bar, which resides in the left margin of your display indicating which portions of a source file have been recently edited and whether or not those changes have been saved to disk.

Extended IntelliSense

IntelliSense has always been a popular feature of Microsoft tools and applications. IntelliSense has been enhanced in Visual Studio, allowing you to not only work with the methods of a class but also to automatically display the list of possible values associated with an enumerated list of properties when one has been defined. IntelliSense also provides a tooltip-like list of parameter definitions when you are making a method call. You'll see an example of this feature later in this chapter.

Additionally, if you type `Exit` and a space, IntelliSense displays a drop-down list of keywords that could follow `Exit`. Other keywords that have drop-down lists to present available options include `Goto`, `Implements`, `Option`, and `Declare`. IntelliSense generally displays more tooltip information in the environment than before and helps the developer match up pairs of parentheses, braces, and brackets.

The Properties Window

The Properties window, shown in Figure 2-8, is, by default, placed in the lower-right corner of the Visual Studio display. Like many of the other windows in the IDE, if you close it, it can be accessed through the View menu. Alternatively, you can use the F4 key to reopen this window. The Properties window is similar to the one with which you are probably familiar from previous development environments. It is used to set the properties of the currently selected item control in the display.

For example, in the design view, select your form. You'll see the Properties window adjust to display the properties of Form1, as shown in Figure 2-8. This is the list of properties associated with your form. For example, if you want to limit how small a user can reduce the display area of your form, you can now define this as a property. For your sample, go to the `Text` property and change the default of Form1 to Professional VB.NET Intro. You'll see that once you have accepted the property change, the new value is displayed as the caption of your form. Later in the section on setting form properties in code, you'll see that unlike other environments, where properties you edit through the user interface are hidden in some binary or proprietary portion of the project, .NET properties are defined within your source file. Thus, while the Properties window may look similar to that in other environments, such as Visual Basic 6, you'll find that it is far more powerful under Visual Studio 2005.

Each control you place on your form has its own distinct set of properties. You'll notice that Visual Studio displays the Toolbox tab on the left side of your display. This tab opens a pane containing a list of the controls you can use on your form, as shown in Figure 2-9.

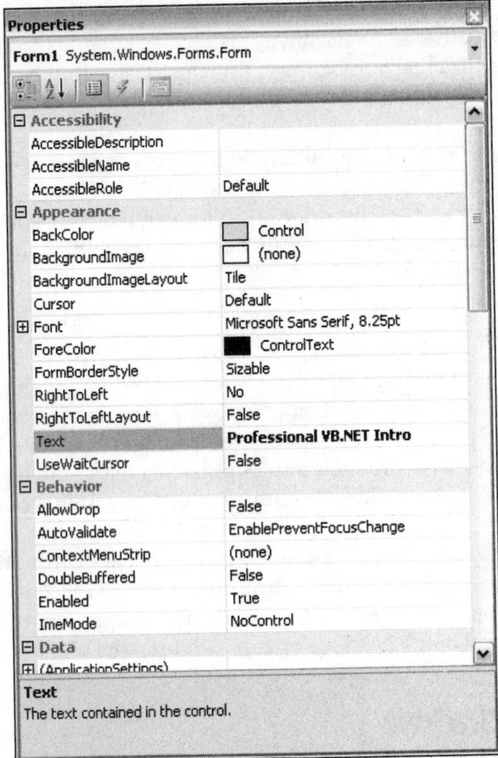

Figure 2-8

Dynamic Help

The Properties window may not have changed much from Visual Basic 6, but the Dynamic Help tab below the Properties window is new. Dynamic Help makes a guess at what you might be interested in looking at, based on what you have done recently. The options in the Dynamic Help window are categorized into three areas. The top category, entitled Help, makes a best guess on the features that the environment thinks you might be trying to use. This best guess is the same as if you pressed F1 while highlighting a keyword within your code.

Just below that is a section called Samples, and it points to a Help page that lists a variety of sample applications. The third section is a category called Getting Started, which contains a variety of help options on introductory material. One of the options in the Getting Started category is Visual Studio Walkthroughs. This contains step-by-step guides on how to perform the basic tasks for the different types of projects that can be created in Visual Studio.

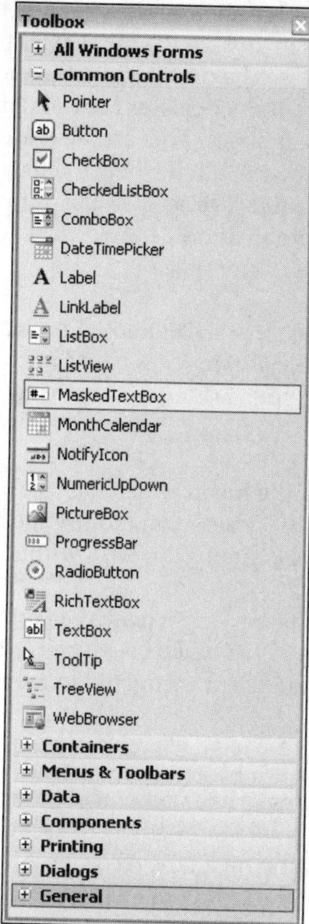

Figure 2-9

Working with Visual Basic 2005

By now, you should be reasonably familiar with some of the key windows available to you in Visual Studio. The next step is to look at the code in your sample form. Since you've already seen that the `Form1.vb` file is empty, let's open the `Form1.Designer.vb` file. To do this, go to the toolbar located in the Solution Explorer window and select the Show All Files button. This will change your project display and a small plus sign will appear next to the `Form1.vb` file. Expanding this entry displays the `Form1.Design.vb` file, and you can open this file within Visual Studio. Note that the contents of this file are generated; for now don't try to make any changes. Visual Studio will automatically regenerate the entire file when a property is changed, and as a result, any changes may be lost. The following lines start the declaration for your form in the file `Form1.Designer.vb`:

```
<Global.Microsoft.VisualBasic.CompilerServices.DesignerGenerated()> _
Partial Public Class Form1
    Inherits System.Windows.Forms.Form
```

The first line is an attribute that can be ignored. Next is the line that actually declares a new class called `Form1`. In VB, you can declare classes in any source file. This is a change from versions of Visual Basic prior to .NET, which required that classes be defined in a class module (`.cls`). You can also declare any number of classes in a single source file; since classes are not defined by their source file, however, doing so is considered a poor programming practice. This line also uses the `Partial` keyword. This keyword will be covered in more detail in Chapter 5, but in short it tells the compiler that the code for this class will exist in more than just one source file. The second line of the class declaration specifies the parent for your class. In the preceding case, your sample `Form1` class is based on the `Form` class, which is contained in the `System.Windows.Forms` namespace.

Forms are classes that derive from the `System.Windows.Forms.Form` class. This class is used to create dialog boxes and windows for traditional Windows-based applications. Chapters 4 and 5 focus on many of the new object-oriented keywords, such as `Shared` and `Inherits`, that you will use when developing more robust VB applications.

As noted, the name of your class and the file in which it exists are not tightly coupled. Thus, your form will be referenced in the code as `Form1`, unless you modify the name used in the class declaration. Similarly, you can rename the file that contains the class without changing the actual name of the class.

One of the powerful results of forms being implemented as classes is that you can now derive one form from another form. This technique is called *visual inheritance*, although the elements that are actually inherited may not be displayed. This concept is covered in much more detail in Chapters 5, 14, and 15.

Running ProVB.NET

Now that you've reviewed the elements of your generated project, let's test the code before you continue. To run an application from within Visual Studio, there are several options: The first is to click the Start button, which looks like the play button on a tape recorder. Alternatively, you can go to the Debug menu and select Start. Finally, the most common way of launching applications is to press F5.

Once the application starts, you will see an empty form display with the standard control buttons (in the upper-right corner) from which you can control the application. The form name should be Professional VB.NET Intro, which you applied earlier. At this point, the sample doesn't have any custom code to examine, so the next step is to add some simple elements to this application.

Form Properties Set in Code

As noted in the section discussing the Properties window, Visual Studio keeps every object's custom property values in the source code. To do this, Visual Studio adds a method to your form class called `InitializeComponent`. As the name suggests, this method handles the initialization of the components contained on the form. A comment before the procedure warns you that the Form Designer modifies the code contained in the procedure and that you should not modify the code directly. This module is part of the `Form1.Designer.vb` source file, and Visual Studio updates this section as changes are made through the IDE.

```
'NOTE: The following procedure is required by the Windows Form Designer
'It can be modified using the Windows Form Designer.
'Do not modify it using the code editor.
<System.Diagnostics.DebuggerStepThrough()> Private Sub _
        InitializeComponent()
```

```
    Me.SuspendLayout()
    '
    'Form1
    '
    Me.AutoScaleDimensions = New System.Drawing.SizeF(6.0!, 13.0!)
    Me.AutoScaleMode = System.Windows.Forms.AutoScaleMode.Font
    Me.ClientSize = New System.Drawing.Size(292, 266)
    Me.Name = "Form1"
    Me.Text = "Professional VB.NET Intro"
    Me.ResumeLayout(False)

End Sub
```

The seven lines of the `InitializeComponent` procedure assign values to the properties of your `Form1` class. All the properties of the form and controls are now set directly in code. When you change the value of a property of the form or a control through the Properties window, an entry will be added to `InitializeComponent` that will assign that value to the property. Previously, while examining the Properties window you set the `Text` property of the form to Professional VB.NET Intro, which caused the following line of code to be added automatically:

```
Me.Text = "Professional VB.NET Intro"
```

The code accessing the properties of the form uses the `Me` keyword. The `Me` keyword acts as a variable that refers to the instance of the current class in which it is used. When you are working within a control that is used by your form, the `Me` keyword will refer to the control if the method you are working on is part of the control class's definition, even though that method may be called by your form class. The `Me` keyword isn't necessary, but it aids in the understanding of the code, so that you immediately recognize that the property references are not simply local variables. The properties of the form class that are set in `InitializeComponent` by default are shown in the following table.

Property	Description
`Suspend Layout`	This property tells the form to not make updates to what is displayed to the user. It is called so that as each change is made the form doesn't seem to come up in pieces.
`AutoScaleDimensions`	Initializes the size of the font used to lay out the form at design time. At runtime, the font that is actually rendered is compared with this property, and the form is scaled accordingly.
`AutoScaleMode`	Indicates that the form will use fonts that are autoscaled based on the display characteristics of the runtime environment.
`ClientSize`	Sets the area in which controls can be placed (the client area). It is the size of the form minus the size of the title bar and form borders.
`Name`	This property is used to set the textual name of the form.
`ResumeLayout`	Tells the form that it should resume the normal layout and displaying of its contents.

Enhancing the Sample Application

To start enhancing the application, you are going to use the control *toolbox*. Ensure that you have closed the `Form1.designer.vb` file and switch your display to the Form1.vb [Design] tab. The Toolbox window is available whenever a form is in design mode. By default, the toolbar, shown in Figure 2-9, lives on the left-hand side of Visual Studio as a tab. When you click this tab, the control window expands and you can then drag controls onto your form. Alternatively, if you have closed the Toolbox tab, you can go to the View menu and select Toolbox.

If you haven't set up the toolbox to be permanently visible, it will slide out of the way and disappear whenever focus is moved away from it. This is a new feature of the IDE that has been added to help maximize the available screen real estate. If you don't like this feature and would like the toolbox to be permanently visible, all you need to do is click the pushpin icon on the toolbox's title bar.

Adding a Control and Event Handler

The button you've dragged onto the form is ready to go in all respects. However, Visual Studio has no way of knowing how you want to customize it. Start by going to the Properties window and changing its text property to "Hello World." You can then change the button's name property to `ButtonHelloWorld`. Having made these changes, double-click the button in the display view. Double-clicking tells Visual Studio that you want to add an event handler to this control, and by default Visual Studio adds an `On_Click` event handler for buttons. The IDE then shifts the display to the code view so that you can customize this handler (see Figure 2-10).

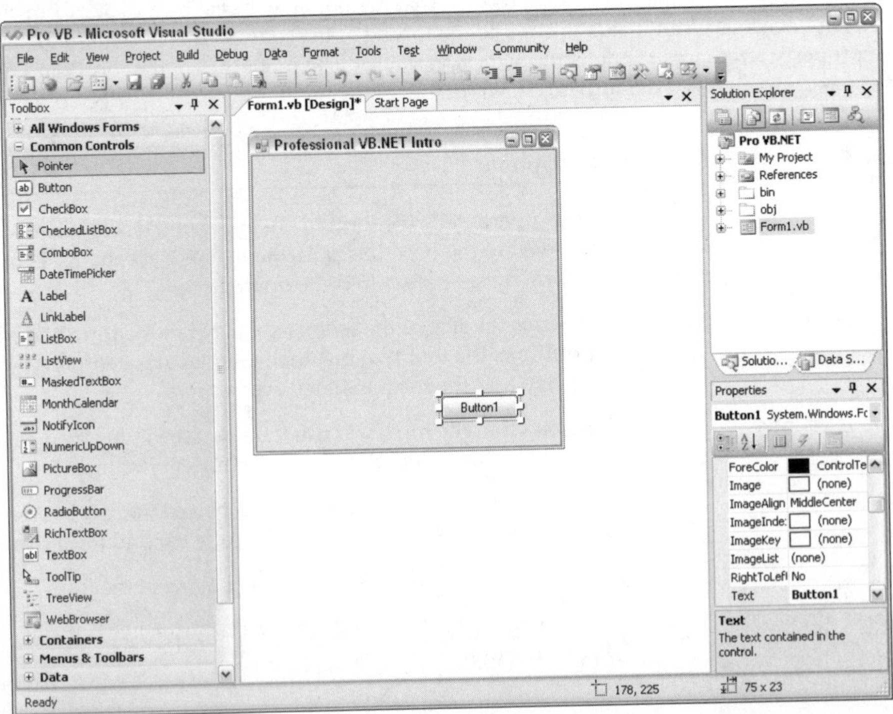

Figure 2-10

While the event handler can be added through the designer, it is also possible to add event handlers from the Code view. After you double-click the button, Visual Studio will transfer you to the Code view and display your new event handler. Notice that in the Code view there are drop-down boxes on the top of the Edit window. The boxes indicate the current object on the left, in this case your new button, and the current method on the right, in this case the Click event handler. It is possible to add new handlers for other events on your button or form using these drop-down lists.

The drop-down box on the left-hand side lists the objects for which event handlers can be added. The drop-down box on the right-hand side lists all the events for the selected object. This is similar to the previous versions of Visual Basic, apart from an enhancement that allows you to handle the events of the classes that have been overridden. For now, however, you have created a new handler for your button's click event, and it's time to look at customizing the code associated with this event.

Customizing the Code

With the Code window open to the newly added event handler for the "Hello World" button, you can start to customize this handler. Note that adding a control and event handler involves elements of generated code. Visual Studio adds code to the `Form1.Designer.vb` file By definition, the name used in the generated file for your control also links the control for which you have added this handler to the handler. These changes occur in addition to the default method implementation you see here in the editable portion of your source code.

Before you start adding new code to this method handler, however, you may want to reduce the complexity of finding some of the `Windows.Forms` enumerations that will be used in your custom code. To do this, you need to import a local reference to the `System.Windows.Forms` namespace.

Working with the Imports Statement

Go to the very first line of your code and add `Imports` statements to the generated code. The Imports statement is similar to a file-based reference for local access to the classes contained in that namespace. By default, to reference a class you need to provide its full namespace. However, when a namespace is imported into a source file, you can instead reference that class by its short name. This topic will be covered in more detail in Chapter 8. For now, you can just add the following reference to the top of `Form1.vb`:

```
Imports System.Windows.Forms
```

This line of code means that if you want the list of possible MessageBox button values all you need to reference is the enumeration `MessageBoxButtons`. Without this statement, you would need to reference `System.Windows.Forms.MessageBoxButtons` in order to use the same enumeration. An example of this is shown in the next section, where you customize the event handler. The `Imports` statement has additional capabilities to make it easy for you to work with the wide array of available namespaces in .NET. The statement is covered in more detail in Chapter 9.

Adding XML Comments

One of the new features of Visual Studio 2005 is the ability to create XML comments. XML comments are a much more powerful feature than you probably realize because they are also recognized by Visual Studio for use in IntelliSense. To add a new XML comment to your handler, go to the line before the handler and type three single quotation marks `'''`. This will trigger Visual Studio to replace your single quotation mark with the following block of comments. You can trigger these comments in front of any method, class, or property in your code.

```
''' <summary>
'''
''' </summary>
''' <param name="sender"></param>
''' <param name="e"></param>
''' <remarks></remarks>
```

Notice that Visual Studio has provided a template that offers a place to provide a summary of what this method does. It also provides placeholders to describe each parameter that is part of this method. Not only are the comments entered in these sections available within the source code, but also when it is compiled, you'll find an XML file in the project directory summarizing all of your XML comments that can be used to generate documentation and help files for said source code.

Customize the Event Handler

Now, customize the code for the button handler. This method doesn't actually do anything by default. To change this, add a command to open a message box and show the "Hello World" message. Use the `System.Windows.Forms.MessageBox` class. Fortunately, since you've imported that namespace, you can reference the `MessageBox.Show` method directly. The Show method has several different parameters, and as you see in Figure 2-11, not only does Visual Studio provide a tooltip for the list of parameters on this function, but it also provides help on the appropriate value for individual parameters.

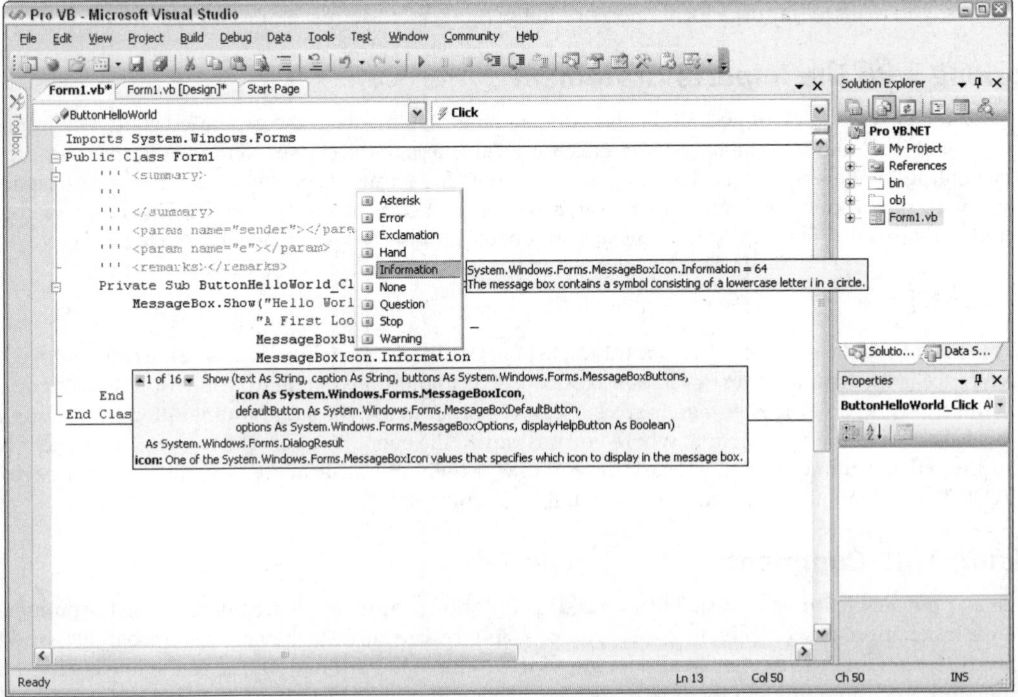

Figure 2-11

The completed call to show should look similar to the following code snippet. Note that the underscore character has been used to continue the command across multiple lines. Also note that unlike previous versions of Visual Basic, where parentheses were sometimes unnecessary, in Visual Studio 2005 the syntax now expects parentheses for every method call, but the good news is that it will automatically add them if there are no parameters required for a given call.

```
MessageBox.Show("Hello World", _
                "A First Look at VB.NET", _
                MessageBoxButtons.OK, _
                MessageBoxIcon.Information)
```

Once you have entered this line of code, you may notice a squiggly line underneath some portion of your text. This occurs if there is an error in the line you have typed. In previous versions of Visual Basic, the development environment would interrupt your progress with a dialog box, but with Visual Studio, the IDE works more like the latest version of Word. Instead of interrupting your progress, it highlights the problem and allows you to continue working on your code.

Review the Code

Now that you have created a simple Windows application, let's review the elements of the code that have been added by Visual Studio. Following is the entire `Form1.Designer.vb` source listing. Highlighted in this listing are the lines of code that have changed since the original template was used to generate this project.

```
<Global.Microsoft.VisualBasic.CompilerServices.DesignerGenerated()> _
Partial Public Class Form1
    Inherits System.Windows.Forms.Form


    'Form overrides dispose to clean up the component list.
    <System.Diagnostics.DebuggerNonUserCode()> _
    Protected Overloads Overrides Sub Dispose(ByVal disposing As Boolean)

        If disposing AndAlso components IsNot Nothing Then
               components.Dispose()
        End If
        MyBase.Dispose(disposing)
    End Sub

    'Required by the Windows Form Designer
    Private components As System.ComponentModel.Icontainer
    'NOTE: The following procedure is required by the Windows Form Designer
    'It can be modified using the Windows Form Designer.
    'Do not modify it using the code editor.
  <System.Diagnostics.DebuggerStepThrough()> _
  Private Sub InitializeComponent()
    Me. ButtonHelloWorld = New System.Windows.Forms.Button()
    Me.SuspendLayout()
    '
    'ButtonHelloWorld
    '
```

```
        Me.ButtonHelloWorld.Location = New System.Drawing.Point(112, 112)
        Me.ButtonHelloWorld.Name = "ButtonHelloWorld"
        Me.ButtonHelloWorld.Size = New System.Drawing.Size(75, 23)
        Me.ButtonHelloWorld.TabIndex = 0
        Me.ButtonHelloWorld.Text = "Hello World"
        '
        'Form1
        '
        Me.AutoScaleDimensions = New System.Drawing.SizeF(6.0!, 13.0!)
        Me.AutoScaleMode = System.Windows.Forms.AutoScaleMode.Font     Me.ClientSize =
    New System.Drawing.Size(292, 273)
        Me.Controls.Add(Me.ButtonHelloWorld)

        Me.Name = "Form1"

        Me.Text = "Professional VB.NET Intro"
        Me.ResumeLayout(False)
    End Sub
    Friend WithEvents ButtonHelloWorld As System.Windows.Forms.Button
    End Class
```

After the Class declaration in the generated file, the first change that has been made to the code is the addition of a new variable to represent the new button:

```
Friend WithEvents ButtonHelloWorld As System.Windows.Forms.Button
```

When any type of control is added to the form, a new variable will be added to the form class. Controls are represented by variables and, just as form properties are set in code, form controls are added in code. The `Button` class in the `System.Windows.Forms` namespace implements the button control on the toolbox. Each control that is added to a form has a class that implements the functionality of the control. For the standard controls, these classes are usually found in the `System.Windows.Forms` namespace. The `WithEvents` keyword has been used in the declaration of the new variable so that it can respond to events raised by the button.

The bulk of the code changes are in the `InitializeComponent` procedure. Eight lines of code have been added to help set up and display the button control. The first addition to the procedure is a line that creates a new instance of the `Button` class and assigns it to the button variable:

```
Me.ButtonHelloWorld = New System.Windows.Forms.Button()
```

Before a button is added to the form, the form's layout engine must be paused. This is done using the next line of code:

```
Me.SuspendLayout()
```

The next four lines of code set the properties of the button. The `Location` property of the `Button` class sets the location of the top-left corner of the button within the form:

```
Me.ButtonHelloWorld.Location = New System.Drawing.Point(112, 112)
```

The location of a control is expressed in terms of a `Point` structure. Next the `Name` property of the button is set:

```
Me.ButtonHelloWorld.Name = "ButtonHelloWorld"
```

The `Name` property acts in exactly the same way as it did for the form, setting the textual name of the button. The `Name` property has no effect on how the button is displayed on the form, but is used to recognize the button's context within the source code. The next two lines of code assign values to the `TabIndex` and `Text` properties of the button:

```
Me.ButtonHelloWorld.TabIndex = 0
Me.ButtonHelloWorld.Text = "Hello World"
```

The `TabIndex` property of the button is used to set the order in which the control will be selected when the user cycles through the controls on the form using the Tab key. The higher the number, the later the control will get focus. Each control should have a unique number for its `TabIndex` property. The `Text` property of a button sets the text that appears on the button.

Once the properties of the button have been set, it needs to be added to the form. This is accomplished with the next line of code:

```
    Me.Controls.Add(Me.ButtonHelloWorld)
```

This line of code adds the button to the collection of child controls for the form. The `System.Windows.Forms.Form` class (from which your `Form1` class is derived) has a property called `Controls` that keeps track of all of the child controls of the form. Whenever you add a control to a form, a line similar to the preceding one is added automatically to the form's initialization process.

Finally, near the bottom of the initialization logic is the final code change. The form is given permission to resume the layout logic:

```
Me.ResumeLayout(False)
```

In addition to the code that has been generated in the `Form1.Designer.vb` source file you have created code that lives in the `Form1.vb` source file. This code is shown here:

```
Imports System.Windows.Forms
Public Class Form1
    ''' <summary>
    '''
    ''' </summary>
    ''' <param name="sender"></param>
    ''' <param name="e"></param>
    ''' <remarks></remarks>
   Private Sub ButtonHelloWorld_Click (ByVal sender As System.Object, _
                              ByVal e As System.EventArgs) _
                              Handles ButtonHelloWorld.Click
     MessageBox.Show("Hello World", _
                                          "A First Look at VB.NET", _
```

```
                                          MessageBoxButtons.OK, _
                                          MessageBoxIcon.Information)
    End Sub
  End Class
```

This code reflects the event handler added for the button. The code contained in the handler was already covered, with the exception of the naming convention for event handlers. Event handlers have a naming convention similar to that in previous versions of Visual Basic: The control name is followed by an underscore and then the event name. The event itself may also have a standard set of parameters. At this point, you can test the application, but first perhaps a review of build options is appropriate.

Build Configurations

Prior to .NET, a Visual Basic project had only one set of properties. There was no way to have one set of properties for a debug build and a separate set for a release build. The result was that you had to manually change any properties that were environment-specific before you built the application. This has changed with the introduction of build configurations, which allow you to have different sets of project properties for debug and release builds. Visual Studio also does not limit you to only two build configurations, it is possible to create additional custom configurations. The properties that can be set for a project have been split into two groups: those that are independent of build configuration and therefore apply to all build configurations, and those that apply only to the active build configuration. For example, the Project Name and Project Location properties are the same irrespective of what build configuration is active, whereas the code optimization options differ, depending on the active build configuration. This isn't a new concept and has been available to Visual C++ developers for some time, but .NET was the first time it was available for VB developers.

Currently under Visual Studio 2005, the default settings for Visual Basic developers do not include the two build configuration settings in the project properties page. By default, Visual Basic applications are built in release mode, however if a project's build type is changed, the Visual Basic developer is by default unaware and unable to change the setting. To display these settings in Visual Studio, go to the Tools menu and select the Options menu item. On the Options dialog, select the "Projects and Solutions" tree item, and on the settings for projects and solutions, you need to select the "Show advanced build configurations" check box. This will update the user interface to properly display the build configurations.

The advantage of multiple configurations is that it is possible to turn off optimization while an application is in development and add symbolic debug information that will help locate and identify errors. When you are ready to ship the application, a single switch to the release configuration results in an executable that is optimized. The settings associated with the various build configurations are stored in the project properties. Unlike the project's display properties, which show up in the Assembly Information window discussed earlier in this chapter, project properties are accessed through the Compile tab on the project's Property pages. To access a project's Property Pages dialog box, double-click or right-click My Project in the Solution Explorer and select Open from the pop-up menu. Alternatively, it is possible to open the project's Property Pages dialog box by selecting Properties from the Project menu in Visual Studio.

At the top of this page is a drop-down list box labeled Configuration. Typically, four options are listed in this box. The currently selected configuration listed as Active, the Debug and Release options, and a final option listed as All Configurations. When changes are made on this screen, they are only applied to the selected configuration(s). Thus, on one hand, when Release is selected, any changes will be applied only to the settings for the Release build. If, on the other hand, All Configurations is selected, then any changes made will be applied to all of the configurations, Debug and Release, based on what is shown in Figure 2-12. The second drop-down box, labeled Platform, allows the selection of a target platform for the project.

The window below these two drop-downs displays the individual properties that are dependent on the active build configuration. The first such setting is the location where your project's binary files will be sent. Notice that VB now defaults to having separate bin/debug and bin/release directories, so you can keep separate copies of your executables. Below this is the Advanced button. This button opens a window that contains some low-level compiler optimizations. In most cases, you will never need to change these settings, but for those working with low-level components, they are available.

Below these settings is the label All Configurations. It should be noted that this label is somewhat misleading and would be better understood if it said: All of the available configuration settings. Of course that's a bit long, but the point is that while these settings can be different for each configuration, the grid contains all of the primary configuration settings. Visual Basic 2005 supports the default configuration elements `Option Explicit` and `Option Strict`, which will automatically reset several of the settings that you see in the grid of settings. In most cases, it is recommended that you enable both `Option Explicit` and `Option Strict`.

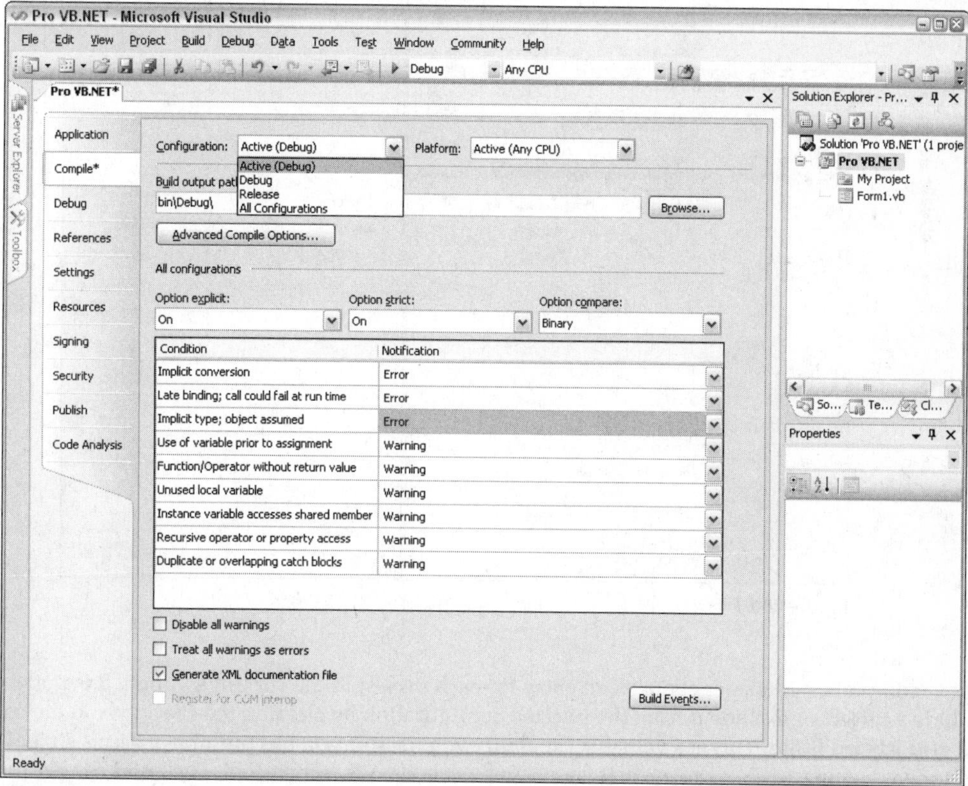

Figure 2-12

Below the grid of individual settings is a series of check boxes. The first two relate to warnings and neither is enabled. They are mutually exclusive, and the first makes warning messages disappear, which is probably a bad idea. The alternative is to treat warnings like errors, which may cause more trouble than it's worth, especially when you consider some of the items that generate warnings. Next, notice that near the bottom of Figure 2-12 is the option to generate XML comments for your assembly. These comments are generated based on the XML comments that you enter for each of the classes, methods, and properties in your source file.

Note that all of these settings are project-specific. However, when working with a solution, it is possible to have more than one project in the same solution. While you are forced to manage these settings independently for each project, there is another form of project configuration related to multiple projects. You are most likely to do this when working with integrated Setup projects, where you might only want to build the Setup project when you are working on a release build.

To customize which projects are included in each build configuration, you need the Configuration Manager for the solution. Projects are assigned to build configurations through the Configuration Manager. If, and only if, your solution has multiple projects, it is possible to open the Configuration Manager from the Build menu by selecting Configuration Manager. Alternatively, the Configuration Manager, shown in Figure 2-13, can be opened using the drop-down list box to the right of the Run button on the Visual Studio toolbar. The active configuration drop-down box contains the following options: Debug, Release, and Configuration Manager. The first two default options are the currently available configurations. However, selecting the bottom option, Configuration Manager, opens the dialog box shown in Figure 2-13.

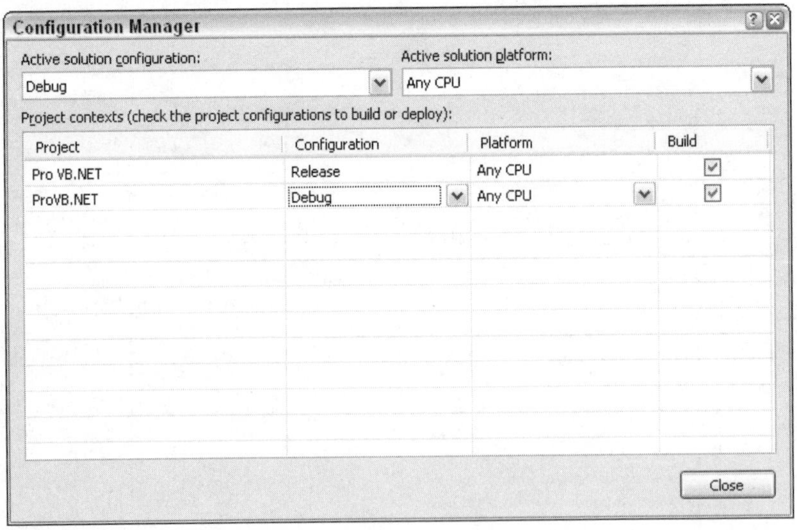

Figure 2-13

The Configuration Manager contains an entry for each project in the current solution. It is possible to include a project or exclude it from the selected configuration by clearing the check box in the column of the grid labeled Build. This is a valuable capability when a solution has multiple projects so that time isn't spent waiting while a project that isn't being worked on is recompiled. The build configuration is commonly used when a Setup project is added to a solution. The normal plan is to rebuild only the Setup package when a release version of the actual application project is created. It's important to note that regardless of the build configuration, it is possible to build any assembly by right-clicking that project and selecting the Build option from the pop-up menu.

Building Applications

For this example, it is best to just build your sample application using the Debug build configuration. The first step is to make certain that Debug is selected as the active configuration in the Configuration drop-down list box discussed in the previous section. Visual Studio provides an entire Build menu with the various options available for building an application. There are essentially two options for building applications:

- **Build** — Use the currently active build configuration to build the project.
- **Rebuild** — Clean all intermediate files (object files) and the output directory before building the project using the active build configuration.

The Build menu supports doing each of these for either the current configuration or for only the currently selected project. Thus, you can choose to only build a single project in your solution, to rebuild all of the supporting files for a single project, or to use the current configuration and build or rebuild all of the projects that have been defined as part of that configuration. Of course, anytime you choose to test run your application, the compiler will automatically attempt to perform a compilation so that you run the most recent version of your code.

You can either select Build from the menu or use the Ctrl-Shift-B keyboard combination to initiate a build. When you build your application, the Output window along the bottom edge of the development environment will open. As shown in Figure 2-14, it displays status messages associated with the build process. This window indicates your success in building your application. Once your application has been built successfully, you will find the executable file located in the targeted directory. By default, for .NET applications this is the `\ bin` subdirectory of your project files.

If there is a problem with building your application, Visual Studio provides a separate window to help coordinate any list of problems. If an error occurs, the Task List window will open as a tabbed window in the same region occupied by the Output window shown in Figure 2-14. Each error that is encountered will trigger a separate item in the Task List, and if you double-click an error, Visual Studio will automatically reposition you on the line with an error. Once your application has been built successfully, you can run it.

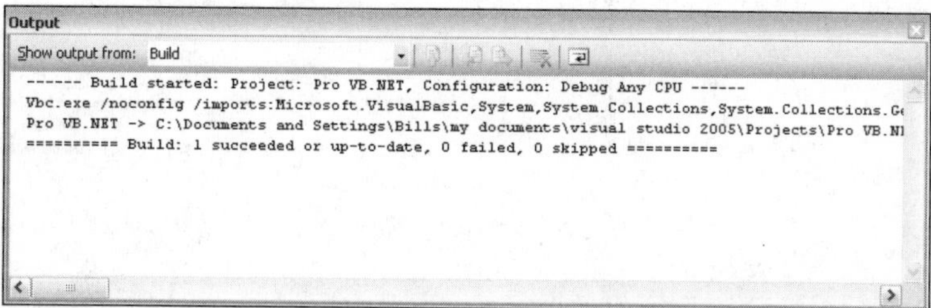

Figure 2-14

Running an Application in the Debugger

As discussed earlier, there are several ways to start your application. Starting your application launches a series of events. First, Visual Studio looks for any modified files and saves those files automatically. It then verifies the build status of your solution and rebuilds any project that does not have an updated binary, including dependencies. Finally, it initiates a separate process space and starts up your application with the Visual Studio debugger attached to that process.

Once your application is running, the look and feel of Visual Studio's IDE changes. New windows and button bars associated with debugging become visible. While your solution and code remain visible, the IDE displays additional windows such as the Autos, Locals, and Watch windows shown on the lower-right side of Figure 2-15. These windows are used by the debugger for reviewing the current value of variables within your code. On the lower-right side of Visual Studio, the Call Stack, Breakpoints, Command, and Output windows open to provide feedback on what your application is doing. These windows are discussed in more detail later in this chapter.

With your application running, select Visual Studio as the active window. Then click in the border alongside the line of code you added to open a message box when the "Hello World" button is clicked. Doing this will create a breakpoint on the selected line. If you return to your application and click the "Hello World" button, you will see that Visual Studio takes the active focus and that within your code window, the line with your breakpoint is now selected.

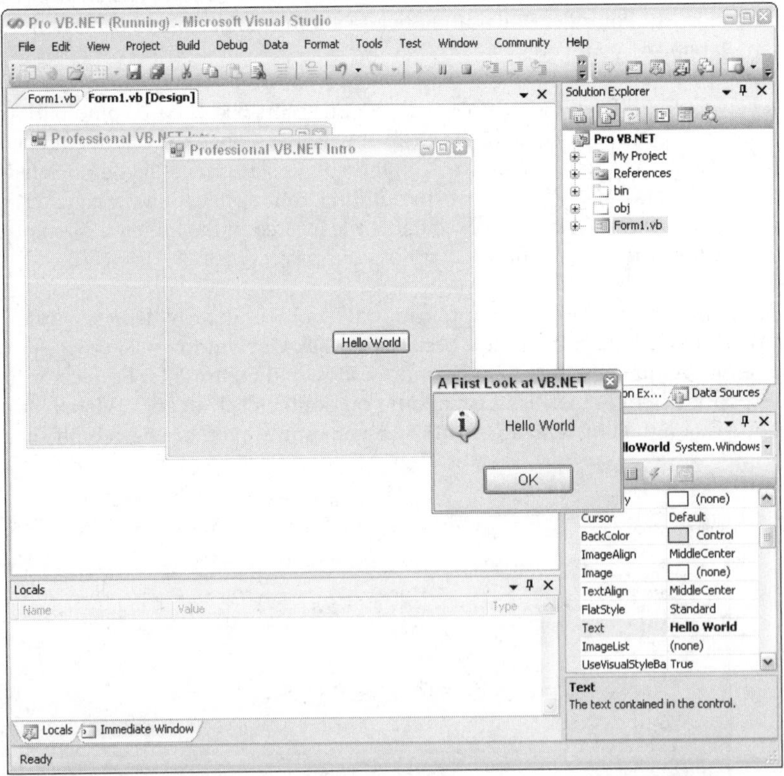

Figure 2-15

While in break mode, it is possible to update the application's running values and view the current status of your application. Chapter 10, which focuses on error handling, delves into many of the more advanced capabilities of the Visual Studio debugger. At this point, you should have a basic understanding of how to work in the Visual Studio environment. However, there are a few other elements of this environment that you will use as you develop more complex applications.

Other Debug-Related Windows

As noted earlier in this chapter, when you run an application in debug mode, Visual Studio .NET 2005 opens up a series of windows. Each of these windows provides a view of a limited set of the overall environment in which your application is running. From these windows, it is possible to find things like the list of calls used to get to the current line of code or the present value of all of the variables that are currently available. Visual Studio has a powerful debugger that is fully supported with IntelliSense, and these windows extend the debugger.

Output

As noted earlier, the build process puts progress messages in this window. Similarly, your program can also place messages in it. There are several options for accessing this window, which will be discussed in later chapters, but at the simplest level, the `Console` object will echo its output to this window during a debug session. For example, the following line of code can be added to your sample application:

```
Console.WriteLine("This is printed in the Output Window")
```

This line of code will cause the string `This is printed in the Output Window` to appear in the Output window when your application is running. You can verify this by adding this line in front of the command to open the message box and then running your application and having the debugger stop on the line where the message box is opened. Examining the contents of the Output window, you will find that your string has been displayed.

Anything written to the Output window is shown only while running a program from the environment. During execution of the compiled module, no Output window is present, so nothing can be written to it. This is the basic concept behind other objects such as the Debug and Trace objects, which are covered in more detail in Chapter 10.

Call Stack

The Call Stack window lists the procedures that are currently calling other procedures and waiting for their return. The call stack represents the path through your code that has led to the currently executing command. This can be a valuable tool when you are trying to determine what code is executing a line of code that you didn't expect to execute. This was accessed in Visual Basic 6 with a menu option on the View menu.

Breakpoints

The Breakpoints window is an enhanced breakpoint handler in which breakpoints can be defined and monitored. Earlier, you saw that you can add breakpoints directly to your code simply by selecting a line. It is also possible to add specific properties to your breakpoints, defining that a given breakpoint should only execute if a certain value is defined (or undefined) or only after it has been executed several times. This is useful for debugging problems that occur only after a certain number of iterations of a routine. (Note that breakpoints are saved when a solution is saved by the IDE.) The breakpoint handler in Visual Studio 2005 is significantly enhanced from previous versions of Visual Basic.

Locals

The Locals window is used to monitor the value of all variables that are currently in scope. This is a fairly self-explanatory window that shows a list of the current local variables and next to each item the value of the variable. As in previous versions of Visual Studio, this display supports the examination of the contents of objects and arrays via a tree-control interface.

Autos

The Autos window displays variables used in the statement currently being executed and the statement just before it. These variables are identified and listed for you automatically, hence the window's name. This window will show more than just your local variables. For example, if you are in the Debugger mode on the line to open the MessageBox in the ProVB.NET sample, you will see that the MessageBox constants that are referenced on this line are shown in this window. This window allows you to see the content of every variable involved in the currently executing command.

Watch Windows

There are four Watch windows, called Watch 1 to Watch 4. Each window can hold a set of variables or expressions for which you want to monitor the value. It is also possible to modify the value of a variable from within a Watch window. The display can be set to show variable values in decimal or hexadecimal format. To add a variable to a Watch window, right-click the variable in the Code Editor and then select Add Watch from the pop-up menu.

Useful Features of Visual Studio

The focus of most of this chapter has been on creating a simple application. When you are working with a tool such as Visual Studio .NET 2003, often your task requires some features but not others. In the preceding example, there are four in particular that are worth covering:

- The Task List
- The Command window
- The Server Explorer
- Macros in Visual Studio

The Task List

The Task List is a great productivity tool that tracks not only errors but also pending changes and additions. It's also a good way for the Visual Studio environment to communicate information that the developer needs to know, such as any current errors. The Task List is displayed by selecting the Task List from the Other Windows option of the View menu, or if there are errors found during a build of your solution, the window opens automatically.

Although it isn't immediately obvious, the Task List has several options. The quickest way to get a list of these options is to go to the View menu and select the Show Tasks option. This will provide a list of the different types of tasks that can be organized in the Task List. By default the Task List displays all tasks. However, it is possible to change this default and screen the tasks that are displayed.

The Comment option is used for tasks embedded in code comments. This is done by creating a standard comment with the apostrophe and then starting the comment with the Visual Studio keyword `TODO:`. The keyword can be followed with any text that describes what needs to be done. Once entered, the text of these comments shows up in the Task List if either the Comment option or the All option is selected. Note that a user can create his or her own comment tokens in the options for Visual Studio via the Tools ➪ Options ➪ Environment ➪ Task List menu.

Besides helping developers track these tasks, embedding the tasks in code results in another benefit. Just as with errors, clicking a task in the Task List causes the Code Editor to jump right to the location of the task without hunting through the code for it.

Finally, it is possible to enter tasks into the Task List manually. By selecting an open row of the Task List, you can add additional tasks that might be needed but that may not be associated with a particular spot in your source code. These user-entered tasks are displayed both when the View ➪ Show Tasks ➪ User option is selected, and when all tasks are displayed.

The Command Window

The Command window is one of the windows that are displayed while in debug mode. It is also possible to open this window from the Other Windows section of the View menu. When opened, the window displays a > prompt. This is a command prompt at which you can execute commands.

The Command window can be used to access Visual Studio menu options and commands by typing them instead of selecting them in the menu structure. For example, if you type `File.AddNewProject` and press Enter, the dialog box to add a new project will appear. Note that IntelliSense is available to help you enter commands in the Command window.

The Command window also has an immediate mode in which expressions can be evaluated. This mode is accessed by typing Immed at the prompt. In this mode, the window title changes to indicate that the immediate mode is active. The key difference between modes of the Command window is how the equal sign behaves. Normally, the equal sign is used as a comparison operator in the Command window. Thus the statement `a=b` is used to determine whether the value *a* is the same as *b*. In immediate mode, the statement `a=b` attempts to assign the value of *b* to *a*. This can be very useful if you are working in the debugger mode and need to modify a value that is part of a running application. To return to the command mode, type `>cmd`.

In the immediate mode, the Command window behaves very similarly to the Immediate window in Visual Basic 6.

The Server Explorer

As development has become more server-centric, developers have a greater need to discover and manipulate services on the network. The Server Explorer is a feature in Visual Studio that makes this easier. Visual Interdev started in this direction with a Server Object section in the Interdev toolbox. The Server Explorer in Visual Studio is more sophisticated in that it allows you to explore and even alter your applications database or your local registry values. With the assistance of an SQL Database project template (part of the Other Project types), it is possible to fully explore and alter an SQL Server database. You can define the tables, stored procedures, and other database objects as you might have previously done with the SQL Enterprise Manager.

However, the Server Explorer is not specific to databases. You open the Server Explorer similarly to how you open the control toolbox. When you hover over or click the Server Explorer's tab, the window will expand from the left-hand side of the IDE. Once it is open, you will see a display similar to the one shown in Figure 2-16.

It might at first seem as if this window is specific to SQL Server, but if you expand the list of available servers, as shown in Figure 2-16, you will see that you have access to several server resources. The Server Explorer even provides the ability to stop and restart services on the server. Notice the wide variety of server resources that are available for inspection or for use in the project. Having the Server Explorer available means that you don't have to go to an outside resource to find, for example, what message queues are available.

By default, you have access to the resources on your local machine. However, if you are in a domain, it is possible to add other machines, such as your Web server, to your display. The Add Server option allows a new server to be selected and inspected. To explore the event logs and registry of a server, you need to add this server to your display. Use the Add Server button shown in Figure 2-16 to open the Add Server dialog box. In this dialog box, provide the name of your server and click the OK button. This will add the new server to your display.

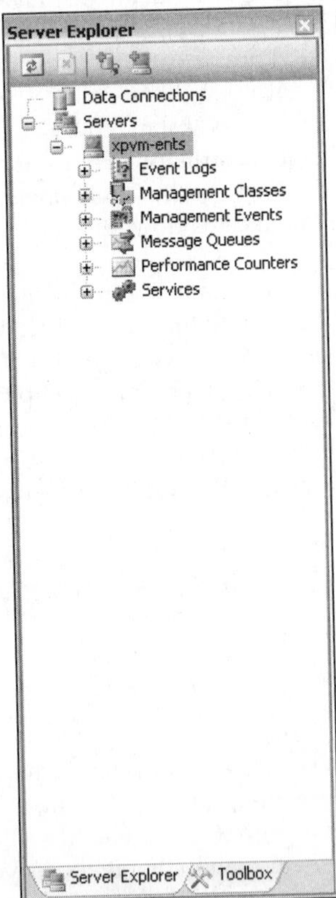

Figure 2-16

Recording and Using Macros in Visual Studio 2005

C++ developers have long had one feature that many VB developers craved—*macros*. In Visual Studio, macros become part of the environment and are available to any language. Macro options are accessible from the Tools ➪ Macros menu. The concept of macros is simple: The idea is to record a series of keystrokes and/or menu actions, and then play them back by pressing a certain keystroke combination.

For example, suppose that one particular function call with a complex set of arguments is constantly being called on in code, and the function call usually looks the same except for minor variations in the arguments. The keystrokes to code the function call could be recorded and played back as necessary, which would insert code to call the function, which could then be modified as necessary.

Macros can be far more complex than this, containing logic as well as keystrokes. The macro capabilities of Visual Studio are so comprehensive that macros have their own IDE (accessed using Tools ➪ Macros ➪ Macros IDE).

Macros can be developed from scratch in this environment, but more commonly they are recorded using the Record Temporary Macro option on the Macros menu and then renamed and modified in the above development environment. Here is an example of recording and modifying a macro:

1. Start a new window Application project.
2. In the new project, add a button to `Form1`, which was created with the project.
3. Double-click the button to get to its `Click` event routine.
4. Select Tool_Macros_Record Temporary Macro. A small toolbar will appear on top of the IDE with a button to control the recording of a macro (Pause, Stop, and Cancel).
5. Press the Enter key, and then type the following line of code:

```
Console.WriteLine("Macro test")
```

6. Press the Enter key again.
7. In the small toolbar, press the Stop button.
8. Select Tool ➪ Macros ➪ Record Temporary Macro. The Macro Explorer will appear (in the location normally occupied by the Solution Explorer) with the new macro in it. You can name the macro anything you like.
9. Right-click the macro and select Edit to get to the Macro Editor. You will see the following code in your macro:

```
DTE.ActiveDocument.Selection.NewLine()
DTE.ActiveDocument.Selection.Text = "Console.WriteLine(""A macro test"")"
DTE.ActiveDocument.Selection.NewLine()
```

The code that appears in Step 9 can vary, depending on how you typed in the line. If you made a mistake and backspaced, for example, those actions will have their own corresponding lines of code. As a result, after you record a macro, it is often worthwhile to examine the code and remove any unnecessary lines.

The code in a macro recorded this way is just standard VB code, and it can be modified as desired. However, there are some restrictions on what you can do inside the macro IDE. For example, you cannot refer to the namespace for setting up database connections because this might constitute a security violation.

To run a macro, you can just double-click it in the Macro Explorer or select Tools ➪ Macros ➪ Run Macro. You can also assign a keystroke to a macro in the Keyboard dialog box in the Tools ➪ Options ➪ Environment folder.

One final note on macros is that they essentially allow you to generate code that can then be transferred to a Visual Studio Add-In project. An Add-In project is a project designed to extend the properties of Visual Studio. To create a new Add-In project, open the New Project dialog and then go to Other Project Types – Extensibility. You can then create a Visual Studio Add-In project. Such a project allows you to essentially share your macro as a new feature of Visual Studio. For example, if Visual Studio 2005 didn't provide a standard way to get formatted comments, you might create an add-in that would allow you to automatically generate your comment template, so you wouldn't need to retype it repeatedly.

Summary

In this chapter, you have created your first sample VB application. Creating this example has helped you to explore the new Visual Studio IDE and shown how powerful the features of the IDE are. Some of the key points that were covered in this chapter include:

- How to create projects and the different project templates available
- Code regions and how you can use them to conceal code
- How to import a namespace into an application source file
- How forms are classes and how the properties of forms are set in code
- Some of the new object-oriented features of Visual Basic
- Build configurations and how to modify the build configuration of your project
- Running an application in debug mode and how to set a breakpoint

With .NET, Microsoft has brought different development languages and paradigms into a single development environment, and it is a powerful one. Users of previous versions of Visual Basic, Visual Interdev, and Visual Studio will generally find this environment familiar. The IDE offers many new features over previous development tools to help boost developer productivity.

You've also seen that Visual Studio is customizable. Various windows can be hidden, docked, or undocked; layered in tabs; and moved within the IDE. There are many tools in Visual Studio at your disposal and it's worth the effort to learn how to use them effectively.

3

Variables and Type

Experienced developers generally consider integers, characters, Booleans, and strings to be the basic building blocks of any language. In .NET, all objects share a logical inheritance from the base `Object` class. One of the advantages of this common heritage is the ability to rely on certain common methods of every variable. Another is that this allows all of .NET to build on a common type system. Having a common type system means that just as Visual Studio 2005 provides a common development environment across .NET languages (as was discussed in the last chapter), Visual Basic builds on a common type system shared across .NET languages.

Unlike the COM programming model, where different languages are needed to account for differences in how simple datatypes are stored, .NET languages can communicate without needing to abstract data. Additionally, since all datatypes are based on the core `Object` class, every variable can be ensured of having a set of common characteristics. However, this logical inheritance does not require a common physical implementation for all variables. For example, what most programmers see as some of the basic underlying types, such as `Integer`, `Long`, `Character`, and even `Byte`, are not implemented as classes. Instead .NET has a base type of object and then allows simple structures to inherit from this base class. While everything in .NET is based on the `Object` class, under the covers .NET has two major variable types: value and reference.

- Value types represent simple data storage located on the stack. They are what Visual Basic 6.0 developers would often refer to as datatypes.
- Reference types are based on complex classes with implementation inheritance from their parent classes, and custom storage on the managed heap.

Value and reference types are treated differently within assignment statements, and their memory management is handled differently. It is important to understand how theses differences affect the software you will write in Visual Basic 2005 (Visual Basic). Understanding the foundations of how data is manipulated in the .NET Framework will enable you to build more reliable and better performing applications.

The main goal of this chapter is to familiarize you with value and reference types and to allow you to understand some of the key differences in how variables are defined in Visual Basic as compared with Visual Basic 6.0. The chapter begins by looking at value types, followed by providing a clear definition of a logical grouping called primitive types. It then examines classes, how they work, and how some of the basic classes are used. Specifically, this chapter covers:

- Value versus reference types
- Value types (structures)
- Primitive types
- Reference types (classes)
- Explicit conversions
- `Option Strict` and `Option Explicit`
- Parameter passing `ByVal` and `ByRef`
- Boxing
- Retired keywords and functions

Differences of Value and Reference Types

When you start looking into the .NET Framework's underlying type systems, you often hear a conflicting set of statements. On one hand, you are told that all types inherit from the `Object` class, and on the other hand, you are told to beware when transitioning between value types and reference types. The key is that while every type, whether it is a built-in structure such as an integer or string or a custom class such as `MyEmployee`, does in fact inherit from the `Object` class. The difference between value and reference types is an underlying implementation difference.

The difference between value types and reference types is an excellent place to start, because it is a relatively simple difference. More important, as a .NET developer you generally don't need to be concerned with this difference, except in certain performance-related situations. Value and reference types behave differently when data is assigned to them:

- When data is assigned to a value type, the actual data is stored in the variable on the stack.
- When data is assigned to a reference type, only a reference is stored in the variable. The actual data is stored on the managed heap.

It is important to understand the difference between the stack and the heap. The stack is a comparatively small memory area in which processes and threads store data of fixed size. An integer or decimal value will need the same number of bytes to store their data, regardless of their actual value. This means that the location of such variables on the stack can be efficiently determined. (When a process needs to retrieve a variable, it has to search the stack. If the stack contains variables that had dynamic memory sizes, such a search could take a long time.)

Reference types do not have a fixed size. For example, a string could vary in size from 2 bytes to close to all the memory available on a system. The dynamic size of reference types means that the data they contain is stored on the heap rather than the stack. However, the address of the reference type (that is, the location of the data on the heap) does have a fixed size, and so can be stored on the stack. By only storing a reference on the stack, the program as a whole runs much more quickly, since the process can rapidly locate the data associated with a variable.

Storing the data contained in fixed and dynamically sized variables in different places results in differences in the way that variables behave. This can be illustrated by comparing the behavior of the `System.Drawing.Point` structure (a value type) and the `System.Text.StringBuilder` class (a reference type).

The `Point` structure is used as part of the .NET graphics library that is part of the `System.Drawing` namespace. The `StringBuilder` class is part of the `System.Text` namespace and is used to improve performance when you're editing strings. Namespaces are covered in detail in Chapter 8.

First, here is an example of how the `System.Drawing.Point` structure is used:

```
Dim ptX As New System.Drawing.Point(10, 20)
Dim ptY As New System.Drawing.Point

ptY = ptX
ptX.X = 200

Console.WriteLine(ptY.ToString())
```

The output from this operation will be {*X* = 10, *Y* = 20}, which seems logical. When the code copies `ptX` into `ptY`, the data contained in `ptX` is copied into the location on the stack that is associated with `ptY`. When later the value of `ptX` is changed, only the memory on the stack that is associated with `ptX` is altered. Altering the value of `ptX` had no effect on `ptY`. This is not the case with reference types. Consider the following code, which uses the `System.Text.StringBuilder` class:

```
Dim objX As New System.Text.StringBuilder("Hello World")
Dim objY As System.Text.StringBuilder

objY = objX
objX.Replace("World", "Test")

Console.WriteLine(objY.ToString())
```

The output from this operation will be "Hello Test," not "Hello World." The previous example using points demonstrated that when one value type is assigned to another, the data stored on the stack is copied. Similarly, this example demonstrates that when `objY` is assigned to `objX`, the data associated with `objX` on the stack is copied to the data associated with `objY` on the stack. However, what is copied in this case isn't the actual data, but rather the address on the managed heap where the data is actually located. This means that `objY` and `objX` now reference the same data. When the data on the heap is changed, the data associated with every variable that holds a reference to that memory is changed. This is the default behavior of reference types and is known as a shallow copy. Later in this chapter, you'll see how this behavior has been overridden for strings (which perform a deep copy).

The differences between value types and reference types go beyond how they behave when copied, and you'll encounter some of the other features provided by objects later in this chapter. First though, let's take a closer look at some of the most commonly used value types and learn how .NET works with them.

Value Types (Structures)

Value types aren't as versatile as reference types, but they can provide better performance in many circumstances. The core value types (which include the majority of primitive types) are `Boolean`, `Byte`, `Char`, `DateTime`, `Decimal`, `Double`, `Guid`, `Int16`, `Int32`, `Int64`, `SByte`, `Single`, and `TimeSpan`. These are not the only value types, but rather the subset with which most Visual Basic developers will consistently work. As you've seen, by definition value types store data on the stack.

Value types can also be referred to by their proper name: Structures. Previous versions of Visual Basic supported the user-defined type (UDT). The UDT framework has been replaced by the ability to create custom structures. The underlying principles and syntax of creating custom structures mirrors that of creating classes, which will be covered in the next chapter. This section is going to focus on some of the built-in types that are provided by the .NET Framework, and in particular, a special group of these built-in types known as primitives.

Primitive Types

Visual Basic, in common with other development languages, has a group of elements such as integers and strings that are termed *primitive types*. These primitive types are identified by keywords like `String`, `Long`, and `Integer`, which are aliases for types defined by the .NET class library. This means the line

```
Dim i As Long
```

is equivalent to the line

```
Dim i As System.Int64
```

The reason that these two different declarations are available has to do with long-term planning for your application. In most cases (as was the case when Visual Basic transitioned to .NET), you want to use the `Short`, `Integer`, and `Long` designations. When Visual Basic moved to .NET, the `Integer` type went from 16 bits to 32 bits. Code written with this `Integer` type would automatically use the larger value if you rewrote the code in .NET. Interestingly enough, however, the Visual Basic Migration Wizard actually recast Visual Basic 6 `Integer` values to Visual Basic .NET `Short` values.

This is the same reason that `Int16`, `Int32`, and `Int64` exist. These types specify a physical implementation, and therefore if your code is someday migrated to a version of .NET that maps the `Integer` value to `Int64`, those values defined as `Integer` will reflect the new larger capacity, while those declared as `Int32` will not. This could be important if your code were manipulating part of an interface where changing the physical size of the value could break the interface.

The following table lists the primitive types that Visual Basic 2005 defines and the structures or classes that they map to.

Primitive Type	.NET Class or Structure
`Byte`	`System.Byte` (structure)
`Short`	`System.Int16` (structure)
`Integer`	`System.Int32` (structure)
`Long`	`System.Int64` (structure)
`Single`	`System.Single` (structure)
`Double`	`System.Double` (structure)
`Decimal`	`System.Decimal` (structure)
`Boolean`	`System.Boolean` (structure)
`Date`	`System.DateTime` (structure)
`Char`	`System.Char` (structure)
`String`	`System.String` (class)

The `String` primitive type stands out from the other primitives. Strings are implemented as a class, not a structure. More importantly strings are the one primitive type that is a reference type.

There are certain operations you can perform on primitive types that you cannot perform on other types. For example, you can assign a value to a primitive type using a literal:

```
Dim i As Integer = 32
Dim str As String = "Hello"
```

It is also possible to declare primitive types as constant using the `Const` keyword. For example,

```
Dim Const str As String = "Hello"
```

The value of the variable `str` in the preceding line of code cannot be changed elsewhere in the application containing this code at runtime. These two simple examples illustrate the key properties of primitive types. As noted, most primitive types are, in fact, value types. So, the next step is to take a look at the specific behavior of some of the common value types in Visual Basic.

Boolean

The .NET `Boolean` type has been implemented with three values, two for `True`, and one for `False`. Two `True` values have been implemented for backward compatibility because, in contrast to most languages (in which Boolean `True` equates to `1`), Visual Basic converts a value of `True` to `-1`. This is one of the few (but not the only) legacy carryovers from Visual Basic 6.0. This was done to save developers from having to examine every Boolean expression to ensure valid return values. Of course, at the lowest level, all .NET languages operate on the basis that `0` is `False` and a nonzero value will be converted to `True`. Visual Basic works as part of a multilanguage environment, with metadata-defining interfaces, so the external value of `True` is as important as its internal value. Fortunately, Microsoft implemented Visual Basic such that, while `-1` is supported within Visual Basic, the .NET standard of `1` is exposed from Visual Basic methods to other languages.

Of course, this compromise involves making some decisions that add complexity to `True` or `False` evaluations. While a `True` value in a Boolean expression equates to `-1`, if converted to any other format, it equates to `1`. This is best illustrated by some sample Visual Basic code. Keep in mind though that this code follows poor programming practice because it references Boolean values as integers (and does so with implicit conversions):

```
Dim blnTrue As Boolean = True
Dim blnOne As Boolean = 1
Dim blnNegOne As Boolean = -1
Dim blnFalse As Boolean = False
```

The following condition, which is based on the implicit conversion of the `Boolean`, works even though the `blnOne` variable was originally assigned a value of `1`.

```
If blnOne = -1 Then
   Console.WriteLine(blnTrue)
   Console.WriteLine(blnOne.ToString)
   Console.WriteLine(Convert.ToString(Convert.ToInt32(blnNegOne)))
End If
```

The key is that implicit conversions such as the one in the preceding example work differently from explicit conversions. If you add sample code to explicitly convert the value of a `Boolean` type to an `Integer` type, and then test the result, the integer will be a positive `1`. The implicit and explicit conversion of Boolean values is not consistent in Visual Basic. Converting `blnNegOne` to an integer results in a positive value, regardless of what was originally assigned.

```
If Convert.ToInt16(blnNegOne) = 1 Then
   Console.WriteLine(blnFalse)
   Console.WriteLine(Convert.ToString(Convert.ToInt32(blnFalse)))
End If
```

This code will not compile if you are using `Option Strict` (more on this later), but it is a good illustration of what you should expect when casting implicitly rather than explicitly. The output from this code is shown in Figure 3-1.

Figure 3-1 illustrates the output when the two preceding conditionals are run as part of a test program such as the ProVisual Basic sample you created in Chapter 2. The first conditional expression demonstrates that if casting is performed between a `Boolean` and an `Integer` value then, regardless of how a `Boolean` in Visual Basic is initialized, `True` is implicitly evaluated as `–1`. The three write statements associated with this display the string representation (`True`) of a Boolean, both implicitly and explicitly, as well as the explicitly converted value.

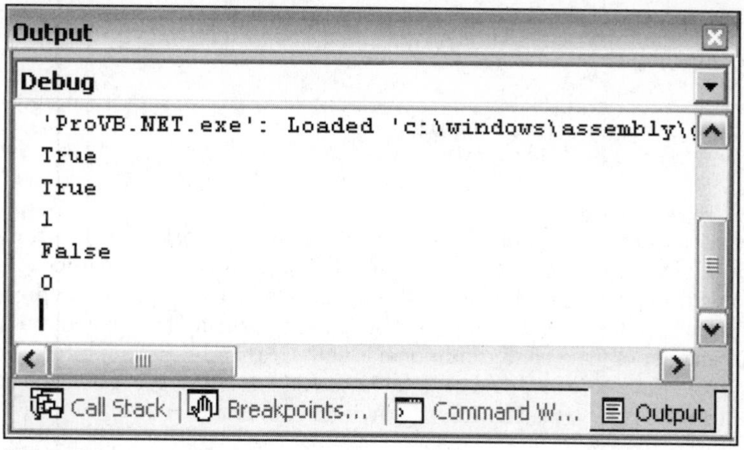

Figure 3-1

The second conditional expression performs an explicit cast from a `Boolean` to an `Integer` value. Since this condition succeeds, it demonstrates that the conversion results in a value of `1`. Behind the scenes, the reason for this is that the code used to do the explicit cast is part of the .NET Framework and, in the Framework the value of `True` is `1`. The result is that the code displays the string and converted values for a Boolean `False`.

This demonstrates the risk involved in relying on implicitly converted values. If at some point the default value associated with `True` were to change, this code would execute differently. The difference between an explicit and implicit conversion is subtle, and there are two steps to take in order to avoid difficulty:

- Always use the `True` and `False` constants in code.
- If there is any doubt as to how the return value from a method will be handled, it should be assigned to a `Boolean` variable. That `Boolean` variable can then be used in conditional expressions.

The final area where this can be an issue is across languages. Now, you need to consider the behavior of a referenced component within your Visual Basic code. You can look at a hypothetical class called `MyCSharpClass` that might have a single method `TestTrue()`. The method doesn't need any parameters, it simply returns a `Boolean`, which is always `True`.

From the Visual Basic example, you can create an instance of `MyCSharpClass` and make calls to the `TestTrue()` method:

```
Dim objMyClass as New MyCSharpClass.MyCSharpClass()

If objMyClass.TestTrue() = 1 Then
   Console.WriteLine("CSharp uses a 1 for true but does it" & _
                " implicitly convert to a 1 in VB?")
Else
```

```
        Console.WriteLine("Even classes implemented in other .NET languages" & _
                  " are evaluated implicitly as -1 in Visual Basic")
    End If

    If objMyClass.TestTrue() = True Then
        Console.WriteLine("CSharp True always converts to Visual Basic True.")
    End If
```

It's probably unclear if the first conditional in this code will ever work; after all, C# uses a value of `1` to represent `True`. However, this code is running in Visual Basic; therefore, the rules of Visual Basic apply. Even when you return a `Boolean` from a .NET language that uses `1`, not `-1`, to represent `True`, the Visual Basic compiler will ensure that the value of `True` is implicitly interpreted as – `1`. Figure 3-2 illustrates that the behavior of the second conditional is both clear and safe from future modifications of the VB language. If Visual Basic is modified at some future date to no longer use `-1` to equate to `True`, statements that instead compare to the Boolean `True` will remain unaffected.

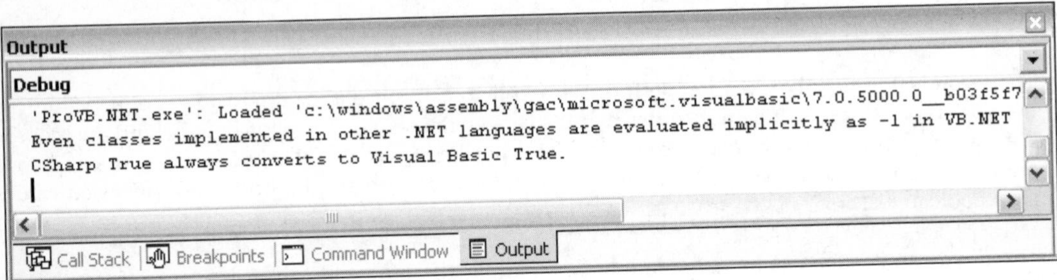

Figure 3-2

To create reusable code, it is always better to avoid implicit conversions. In the case of `Booleans`, if the code needs to check for an integer value, you should explicitly evaluate the `Boolean` and create an appropriate integer — this code will be far more maintainable and prone to fewer unexpected results. Now that `Booleans` have been covered in depth, the next step is to examine the `Integer` types that are part of Visual Basic.

The Integer Types

In Visual Basic 6.0, there were two types of integer values: the `Integer` type was limited to a maximum value of 32767 and the `Long` type supported a maximum value of 2147483647. The .NET Framework adds a new integer type, the `Short`. The `Short` is the equivalent of the `Integer` value from Visual Basic 6.0, the `Integer` has been promoted to support the range previously supported by the `Long` type, and the `Long` type is bigger than ever. In addition, each of these types also has two alternative types. In all, Visual Basic supports nine `Integer` types.

Type	Allocated Memory	Minimum Value	Maximum Value
`Short`	2 bytes	–32768	32767
`Int16`	2 bytes	–32768	32767
`UInt16`	2 bytes	0	65535

Type	Allocated Memory	Minimum Value	Maximum Value
`Integer`	4 bytes	–2147483648	2147483647
`Int32`	4 bytes	–2147483648	2147483647
`UInt32`	4 bytes	0	4294967295
`Long`	8 bytes	–9223372036854775808	9223372036854775807
`Int64`	8 bytes	–9223372036854775808	9223372036854775807
`UInt64`	8 bytes	0	18446744073709551615

Short

A `Short` value is limited to the maximum value that can be stored in 2 bytes. This means there are 16 bits and that the value can range between –32768 and 32767. This limitation may or may not be based on the amount of memory physically associated with the value; it is a definition of what must occur in the .NET Framework. This is important, because there is no guarantee that the implementation will actually use less memory than when using an `Integer` value. It is possible that, to optimize memory or processing, the operating system will allocate the same amount of physical memory used for an `Integer` type and then just limit the possible values.

The `Short` (or `Int16`) value type can be used to map SQL `smallint` values.

Integer

An `Integer` is defined as a value that can be safely stored and transported in 4 bytes (not as a 4-byte implementation). This gives the `Integer` and `Int32` value types a range from –2147483648 to 2147483647. This range is more than adequate to handle most tasks.

The main reason to use an `Int32` in place of an integer value is to ensure future portability with interfaces. For example, the `Integer` value in Visual Basic 6.0 was limited to a 2-byte value, but is now a 4-byte value. In future 64-bit platforms, the `Integer` value will be an 8-byte value. Problems could occur if an interface used a 64-bit `Integer` with an interface that expected a 32-bit `Integer` value. The solution is to use `Int32`, which would remain a 32-bit value, even on a 64-bit platform.

The new `Integer` value type matches the size of an integer value in SQL Server, which means that you can easily align the column type of a table with the variable type in your programs.

Long

The `Long` type is aligned with the `Int64` value. `Long`'s have an 8-byte range, which means that their value can range from –9223372036854775808 to 9223372036854775807.

This is a big range, but if you need to add or multiply `Integer` values, then you will often need a large value to contain the result. It's common while doing math operations on one type of integer to use a larger type to capture the result if there's a chance that the result could exceed the limit of the types being manipulated.

The `Long` value type matches the `bigint` type in SQL.

Unsigned Types

Another way to gain additional range on the positive side of an integer type is to use one of the unsigned types. The unsigned types provide a useful buffer that will hold a result that might exceed an operation by a small amount, but that isn't the main reason they exist. The `UInt16` type happens to have the same characteristics as the `Character` type, while the `UInt32` type has the same characteristics as a system memory pointer on a 32-byte system. Be forewarned that on a 64-bit system this changes to the `UInt64` type. These types are used to interface with software that expects these values and are the underlying implementation for other value types.

The Decimal Types

Just as there are a number of types to store integer values, there are three implementations of value types to store real number values. The `Single` and `Double` types work the same way in Visual Basic as they did in Visual Basic 6.0. The difference is the Visual Basic 6.0 `Currency` type (which was a specialized version of a `Double` type), which is now obsolete and a new `Decimal` value type takes its place for very large real numbers.

Type	Allocated Memory	Negative Range	Positive Range
`Single`	4 bytes	–3.402823E38 to –1.401298E-45	1.401298E-45 to 3.402823E38
`Double`	8 bytes	–1.79769313486231E308 to –4.94065645841247E-324	4.94065645841247E-324 to 1.79769313486232E308
`Currency`	Obsolete	—	—
`Decimal`	16 bytes	–79228162514264337593543950335 to 0.0000000000000000000000000001	0.0000000000000000000000000001 to 79228162514264337593543950335

Single

The `Single` type contains 4 bytes of data, and its precision can range anywhere from 1.401298E-45 to 3.402823E38 for positive values and from –3.402823E38 to –1.401298E-45 for negative values.

It can seem strange that a value that is stored using 4 bytes (the same as the `Integer` type) can store a number that is larger than even the `Long` type. This is possible because of the way that the numbers are stored—a real number can be stored with different levels of precision. Notice that there are six digits after the decimal point in the definition of the `Single` type. When a real number gets very large or very small, the stored value will contain fewer significant places.

For example, while it is possible to represent a `Long` with the value of 9223372036854775805, the `Single` type rounds this value to 9.223372E18. This seems like a reasonable action to take, but it isn't a reversible action. The following code demonstrates how this loss of data can result in errors:

```
Dim l As Long
Dim s As Single

l = Long.MaxValue
Console.WriteLine(l)

s = Convert.ToSingle(l)
s -= 1000000000000
l = Convert.ToInt64(s)

Console.WriteLine(l)
```

This code creates a `Long` that has the maximum value possible and outputs this value. Then it stores the value in a `Single`, subtracts 1000000000000, stores the value of the `Single` in the `Long`, and outputs the results, as seen in Figure 3-3, Notice that the results aren't consistent with what you might expect.

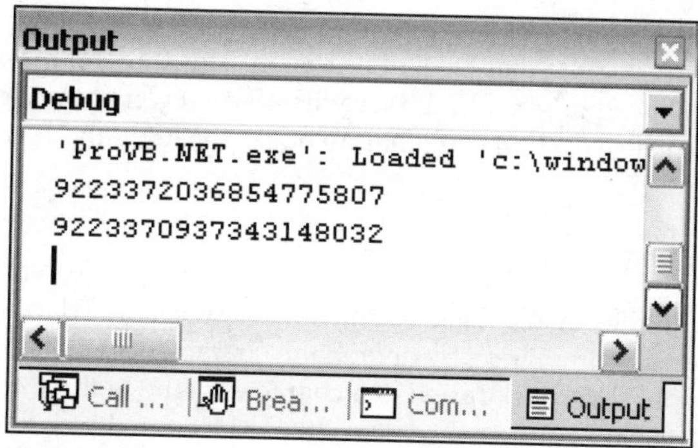

Figure 3-3

Double

The behavior of the previous example changes dramatically if you replace the value type of `Single` with `Double`. A `Double` uses 8 bytes to store values and as a result has a greater precision and range. The range for a `Double` is from 4.94065645841247E-324 to 1.79769313486232E308 for positive values and from $-$1.79769313486231E308 to – 4.94065645841247E-324 for negative values. The precision has increased so that a number can contain 15 digits before the rounding begins. This greater level of precision makes the `Double` value type a much more reliable variable for use in math operations. It's possible to represent most operations with complete accuracy with this value.

`Double` wasn't the only 8-byte decimal value in Visual Basic 6.0. One of the other variable types, `Currency`, is now obsolete. The `Currency` type was a specialized version of the `Double` type and was designed to support numbers using 19 available digits. While this was certainly better precision than the 15-digit precision available with the `Double` type, it pales in comparison to the new 28-digit `Decimal` type available in the .NET Framework.

Decimal

The `Decimal` type (new in Visual Basic) is a hybrid that consists of a 12-byte integer value combined with two additional 16-bit values that control the location of the decimal point and the sign of the overall value. A `Decimal` value will consume 16 bytes in total and can store a maximum value of 79228162514264337593543950335. This value can then be manipulated by adjusting where the decimal place is located. For example, the maximum value while accounting for four decimal places is 7922816251426433759354395.0335. This is because a `Decimal` isn't stored as a traditional number, but is rather stored as a 12-byte integer value, and the location of the decimal in relation to the available 28 digits. This means that a `Decimal` does not inherently round numbers the way a `Double` does.

As a result of the way values are stored, the closest precision to zero that a `Decimal` supports is 0.0000000000000000000000000001. And as the location of the decimal point is stored separately, it also stores a value that indicates whether its value is positive or negative. This means that the positive and negative ranges are exactly the same, regardless of the number of decimal places.

Thus, the system makes a tradeoff where the need to store a larger number of decimal places reduces the maximum value that can be kept at that level of precision. This tradeoff makes a lot of sense. After all, it's not often that you will need to store a number with 15 digits on both sides of the decimal point, and for those cases you can create a custom class that manages the logic and leverages one or more decimal values as its properties.

Char and Byte

The default character set under Visual Basic is Unicode. So, when a variable is declared as type `Char` Visual Basic creates a 2-byte value, since, by default, all characters in the Unicode character set require 2 bytes. Visual Basic supports the declaration of a character value in three ways. Placing a `$c$` following a literal string informs the compiler that the value should be treated as a character, or the `Chr` and `ChrW` methods can be used. The following code snippet shows that all three of these options work similarly, with the difference between the `Chr` and `ChrW` methods being the range of valid input values that is available. The `ChrW` method allows for a broader range of values based on wide character input.

```
Dim chrLtr_a As Char = "a"c
Dim chrAsc_a As Char = Chr(97)
Dim chrAsc_b as Char = ChrW(98)
```

To convert characters into a string that was suitable for an ASCII interface, the runtime library needed to validate each character's value to ensure it was within a valid range. This could have a performance impact for certain serial arrays. Fortunately, Visual Basic supports the `Byte` value type. This type contains a value between `0` and `255` that exactly matches the range of the ASCII character set. When interfacing with a system that uses ASCII, it is best to use a `Byte` array. The runtime knows that there is no need to perform a Unicode-to-ASCII conversion for a `Byte` array, so the interface between the systems will operate significantly faster.

In Visual Basic, the `Byte` value type expects a numeric value. Thus, to assign the letter "a" to a `Byte`, you must use the appropriate character code. One option to get the numeric value of a letter is to use the `Asc` method, as shown in the following line of code:

```
Dim bytLtrA as Byte = Asc("a")
```

DateTime

The Visual Basic `Date` keyword has always supported a structure of both date and time. Under Visual Basic, the `Date` structure has all of the same capabilities it had in Visual Basic 6.0 but is now implemented as part of the `DateTime` structure. You can, in fact, declare data values using both the `DateTime` and `Date` types. Of note, internally Visual Basic does not store date values as `Doubles`, it provides key methods for converting the new internal date representation to the Visual Basic 6.0 `Double` type. The `ToOADate` and `FromOADate` methods support backward compatibility during migration from previous versions of Visual Basic.

Visual Basic also provides a set of shared methods that provide some common dates. The concept of shared methods is covered in more detail in the next chapter, which is on object syntax, but, in short, shared methods are available even when you don't create an instance of a class. For the `DateTime` structure, the `Now()` method returns a `Date` value with the local date and time. This method has not been changed from Visual Basic 6.0, but `Today() and UtcNow()` methods have also been added. These methods can be used to initialize a `Date` object with the current local date, or the date and time based on Universal Coordinated Time (also known as Greenwich Mean Time) respectively. You can use these shared methods to initialize your classes, as shown in the following code sample:

```
Dim dteNow as Date = Now()
Dim dteToday as Date = Today()
Dim dteGMT as DateTime = DateTime.UtcNow()
```

Explicit Conversions

So far this chapter has focused primarily on implicit conversions. With implicit conversions it is safe, for example, to assign the value of a smaller type into a larger type. For example, in the following code the value of a `Short` is assigned to a `Long`.

```
Dim shtShort As Short = 32767
Dim lnhLong As Long = shtShort
```

However, the reverse of this will result in a compilation error, since the compiler doesn't have any safe way of handling the assignment when the larger value is outside the range of the smaller value. It is still possible to cast a value from a larger type to a smaller type, as shown earlier in this chapter. Using the `CType` method, it is possible to assign specific values. However, another of Visual Basic's legacy carryovers is the ability to implicitly cast across types that don't fit the traditional implicit casting boundaries.

The best way to understand how Visual Basic has maintained this capability is to understand one of the new options in Visual Basic. Under Visual Basic 6.0 it was possible to define that a module should follow the rules defined by `Option Explicit`. This capability remains under Visual Basic, but now `Option Explicit` is the default. Similarly, Visual Basic now provides a new option called `Option Strict`. It defines the support that your code should provide at compile time for implicit type conversions.

Compiler Options

Visual Studio 2005 includes a tab on the Project Settings page to edit the compiler settings for an entire project. You can access this screen by right-clicking the project in the Solution Explorer and selecting Properties from the context menu. As noted in the preceding chapter, the Project Properties dialog has a Compiler Options tab. When you select the Compiler Options tab, you should see a window similar to the one shown in Figure 3-4.

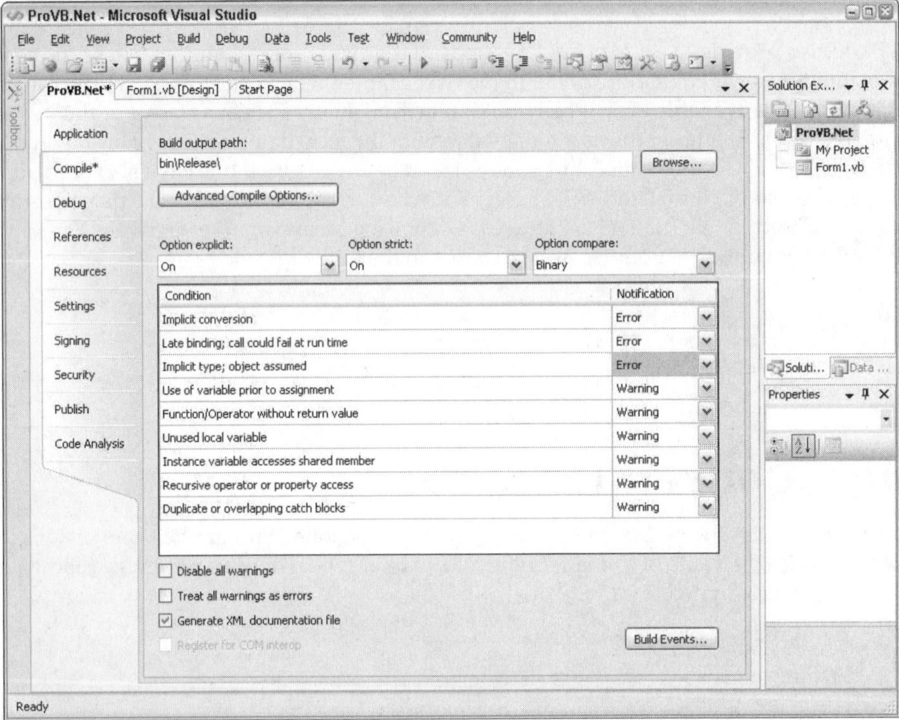

Figure 3-4

Aside from your default project file output directory, this page contains several compiler options. These options are covered here because the `Option Explicit` and `Option Strict` settings directly impact your variable usage.

- `Option Explicit` — This option has not changed from Visual Basic 6.0. When turned on it ensures that any variable name is declared. Of course, if you are using `Option Strict`, then this setting does not matter since the compiler would not recognize the type of an undeclared variable. There is, to my knowledge, no good reason to *ever* turn this option off.
- `Option Strict` — When this option is turned on, the compiler must be able to determine the type of each variable. And if an assignment between two variables requires a type conversion — for example, from `Integer` to `Boolean` — the conversion between the two types must be expressed explicitly. This setting can be edited in two ways. The first is by adding an `Option Strict` declaration to the top of your source code file. The statement within a source file will apply to all of the code entered in that source file, but only to the code in that file.

- `Option Compare`— This option determines whether strings should be compared as binary strings or if the array of characters should be compared as text. In most cases, leaving this as binary is appropriate. Doing a text comparison requires the system to convert the binary values that are stored internally prior to comparison. However, the advantage of a text-based comparison is that the character "`A`" is equal to "`a`" because the comparison is case-insensitive. This allows you to perform comparisons that don't require an explicit case conversion of the compared strings. In most cases, however, this conversion will still occur, so it's better to use binary comparison and explicitly convert the case as required.

In addition to setting `Option Explicit`, `Option Strict`, and `Option Compare` to either `On` or `Off` for your project, Visual Studio 2005 allows you to customize specific compiler conditions that may occur in your source file. Thus, unlike Visual Studio 2003, where you either turned options `On` or `Off`, with Visual Studio 2005, it is possible to choose to leverage individual settings, such as requiring early binding as opposed to runtime binding without limiting implicit conversions. These individual settings are part of the table of individual compiler settings listed below the `Option Strict` setting.

Notice that as you change your `Option Strict` setting that the notifications with the top few conditions is automatically updated to reflect the specific requirements of this new setting. In general, this table lists a set of conditions that relate to programming practices that you might want to avoid or prevent and should definitely be aware of. The use of warnings for the majority of these conditions is appropriate, since there are valid reasons why you might want to use or avoid each.

The basic idea is that these conditions represent possible runtime error conditions that the compiler can't truly detect, except to identify that an increased possibility for error exists. When you select `Warning` for a setting this is a way to avoid that practice since the compiler will warn you but allow the code to remain. On the other hand setting a practice to error prevents compilation.

An example of why these conditions are noteworthy is the warning on accessing shared member variables, if you are unfamiliar with shared member values you will find them discussed as part of the discussion of classes in Chapter 4. At this point it's just necessary to know that these values are shared across all instances of a class. Thus, if a specific instance of a class is updating a shared member value, it is appropriate to get a warning about this. Since new developers sometimes fail to realize that a shared member value is common across all instances of a class and thus if one instance updates the value, the new value is seen by all other instances, this action is one that can lead to errors.

While many of these conditions are only addressed as individual settings Visual Studio 2005 carries forward the `Option Strict` setting. Most experienced developers agree that using `Option Strict` and being forced to recognize when type conversions are occurring is a good thing. Certainly, when developing software that will be deployed in a production environment, anything that can be done that will help prevent runtime errors is a good thing. However, `Option Strict` can slow the development of a program because you are forced to explicitly define each conversion that needs to occur. If you are developing a prototype or demo component that has a limited life, you might find this option limiting.

If that were the end of the argument, then many developers would simply turn the option off— the current default— and forget about it. However, `Option Strict` has a runtime benefit. When type conversions are explicitly identified, the system does them faster. Implicit conversions require the runtime system to first identify the types involved in a conversion and then obtain the correct handler.

Another advantage of `Option Strict` is that during implementation developers are forced to consider everywhere a conversion might occur. Perhaps the development team didn't realize that some of the assignment operations resulted in a type conversion. Setting up projects that require explicit conversions means that the resulting code tends to have type consistency to avoid conversions and, thus, reduce the number of conversions in the final code. The result is not only conversions that run faster but, hopefully, a smaller number of conversions as well.

Performing Explicit Conversions

The following code is an example of how to convert between different `Integer` types when `Option Strict` is enabled.

```
Dim shrShort As Short
Dim shrUInt16 As UInt16
Dim shrInt16 As Int16
Dim intInteger As Integer
Dim intUInt32 As UInt32
Dim intInt32 As Int32
Dim lngLong As Long
Dim lngInt64 As Int64

shrShort = 0
shrUInt16 = Convert.ToUInt16(shrShort)
shrInt16 = shrShort
intInteger = shrShort
intUInt32 = Convert.ToUInt32(shrShort)

intInt32 = shrShort
lngInt64 = shrShort

lngLong = lngLong.MaxValue
If lngLong < Short.MaxValue Then
  shrShort = Convert.ToInt16(lngLong)
End If
intInteger = CInt(lngLong)
```

The preceding snippet provides some excellent examples of what might not be intuitive behavior. The first thing to note is that you can't implicitly cast from `Short` to `UInt16`, or any of the other unsigned types for that matter. That is because with `Option Strict` the compiler will not allow an implicit conversion that might result in a value out of range or in loss of data. Your first thought is that an unsigned `Short` has a maximum that is twice the maximum of a signed `Short`, but in this case, if the variable `shrShort` contained a `-1`, then the value wouldn't be in the allowable range for an unsigned type.

The second item illustrated in this code is the shared method `MaxValue`. All of the integer and decimal types have this method. As the name indicates, it returns the maximum value for the specified type. There is a matching `MinValue` method for getting the minimum value. As shared methods, the methods can be called on either an instance of the class (`LngLong.MaxValue`) or by referencing the class (`Short.MaxValue`).

One fact that isn't apparent in the code above is that, whenever possible, conversions should be avoided. Each of the `Convert.MethodName` methods has been overloaded to accept various types. However, the

CInt method (which most Visual Basic 6.0 programmers are familiar with) is defined to accept a parameter of type Object. This is important because it involves boxing the value type. As is noted later in this chapter, repeated boxing of value types has performance implications.

Finally, although this code will compile, it will not always execute correctly. It illustrates a classic intermittent error in that the final conversion statement does not check to ensure that the value being assigned to intInteger is within the maximum range for an integer type. On those occasions when LngLong is larger than the maximum allowed, this code will throw an exception.

Visual Basic has many ways to convert values. Some of them are updated versions of techniques that are familiar from Visual Basic 6.0. Others, such as the ToString method, are an inherent part of every class (although the .NET specification does not guarantee how a ToString class is implemented for each type).

The following set of conversion methods are based on the conversions supported by Visual Basic 6.0. They coincide with the primitive datatypes described earlier.

CBool()	CByte()	CChar()	CDate()
CDbl()	CDec()	CInt()	CLng()
CObj()	CShort()	CSng()	CStr()

Each of these methods has been designed to accept the input of the other primitive datatypes (as appropriate) and to convert that item to the type indicated by the method name. Thus, the CStr class is used to convert a primitive type to a String. The disadvantage of these methods is that they have been designed to support any object. This means that if a primitive type is used, the method automatically boxes the parameter prior to getting the new value. This results in a loss of performance. Finally, although these are available as methods within the VB language, they are actually implemented in a class (as with everything in the .NET Framework). Because the class uses a series of type-specific overloaded methods, the conversions run faster when the members of the Convert class are called explicitly.

```
Dim intMyShort As Integer = 200
Convert.ToInt32(intMyShort)
Convert.ToDateTime("9/9/2001")
```

The classes that are part of System.Convert implement not only the conversion methods listed earlier but also other common conversions as well. These additional methods include standard conversions for things like unsigned integers and pointers.

All of the preceding type conversions are great for value types and the limited number of classes to which they apply. However, these implementations are oriented around a limited set of known types. It is not possible to convert a custom class to an Integer using these classes. More importantly, there should be no reason to have such a conversion. Instead, a particular class should provide a method that returns the appropriate type—no type conversion will be required. However, when Option Strict is enabled, the compiler will require you to cast an object to an appropriate type before triggering an implicit conversion. But the Convert method isn't the only way to indicate that a given variable can be treated as another type.

The CType Method

The `CType` method accepts two parameters. The first parameter is the object that is having its type cast, and the second parameter is the name of the object to which it is being cast. This system allows us to cast objects from parent to child or from child to parent types. There is a limitation in the second parameter in that it can't be a variable containing the name of the casting target. Casting occurs at compile time, and any form of dynamic name selection must occur at runtime. An example of casting is shown as part of the discussion of working with the `Object` class later in this chapter.

Support for a runtime determination of object types is based on treating variables as objects and using the object metadata and the `TypeOf` operator to verify that an object supports various method and property calls. Alternatively, in Visual Basic it is possible to turn off `Option Strict` and as noted later in this chapter, your application will automatically treat objects as objects allowing for a great deal of runtime casting.

Reference Types (Classes)

A lot of the power of Visual Basic is harnessed in objects. An object is defined by its class, which describes what data, methods, and other attributes that an instance of that class will support. There are thousands of classes provided in the .NET Framework class library.

When code instantiates an object from a class, the object created is a reference type. You may recall earlier how the data contained in value and reference types is stored in different locations, but this is not the only difference between them. A class (which is the typical way to refer to a reference type) has additional capabilities, such as support for protected methods and properties, enhanced event-handling capabilities, constructors, and finalizers, and can be extended with a custom base class via inheritance. Classes can also be used to define how operators such as " =" and " +" work on an instance of the class.

The intention of this chapter is to introduce you to some commonly used classes, to complement your knowledge of the common value types already covered. Chapters 4, 5, and 7 contain a detailed look at object orientation in Visual Basic. In this chapter, you'll take a look at the features of the `Object`, `String`, `DBNull`, and `Array` classes, as well as the `Collection` classes found in the `System.Collections` namespace.

The Object Class

The `Object` class is the base class for every type in .NET—both value and reference types. At their core, every variable is an object and can be treated as such. The Visual Basic 6.0 runtime environment managed the interpretation of `Variant` objects for VB programmers. This is good in some ways because it supported a situation in which the contents of the variant could be assumed and the developer just worked as if they would be present. So long as the content of the memory area was an object of the appropriate type, the call to a method on that object would succeed. While this was simple to do, it left Visual Basic 6.0 programs open to some unusual runtime errors that are generally harder to diagnose and debug. At the same time, in ASP pages and other scripted code, `Variants` were a requirement because of the way these loosely typed languages worked. Of course, this runtime type evaluation came with its own performance implications, but this was secondary to the ease of development.

You can think of the `Object` class (in some ways) as the replacement for the `Variant` type from Visual Basic 6.0, but take care. In Visual Basic 6.0, a `Variant` type represents a variant memory location; in Visual Basic, an `Object` type represents a reference to an instance of the `Object` class. In Visual Basic 6.0, a `Variant` was implemented to provide a reference to a memory area on the heap, but its definition didn't define any specific ways of accessing this data area.

The following lines can work equally well in Visual Basic 6.0 and Visual Basic (so long as `Option Strict` is not enabled in your Visual Basic project):

```
Dim varObj
Dim objVar
```

Interestingly enough, when not using `Option Strict`, the behavior of a Visual Basic 6.0 `Variant` and a Visual Basic Object is almost identical. Since the `Object` class is the basis of all types, you can assign any variable to an object. Reference types will maintain their current reference and implementation but will be generically handled, while value types will be packaged into a box and placed into the memory location associated with the `Object`. The new `Object` supports all of the capabilities that were available from the `Variant` type but it goes beyond the Visual Basic 6.0 variant type in its support for methods. For example, there are instance methods that are available on `Object`, such as `ToString`. This method will, if implemented, return a string representation of an instance value. Since the `Object` class defines it, it can be called on any object.

```
Dim objMyClass as New MyClass("Hello World")

Console.WriteLine(objMyClass.ToString)
```

Which brings up the question of how does the `Object` class know how to convert custom classes to `String` objects? The answer to this question is that it doesn't. For this method to actually return the data in an instance of a `String`, a class must override this method. Otherwise, when this code is run, the default version of this method defined at the `Object` level will return the name of the current class (`MyClass`) as its string representation.

The `Object` class continues to fill the role of the `Variant` class even when `Object Strict` is enabled. The declaration is more explicit; anything that can be done with `Object Strict` disabled can be done with it enabled. The difference is that with `Option Strict` code must explicitly define the type of object whose property or method it plans to access. Thus, if you don't want to access only those methods available from the base `Object` class, you need to specify the actual type of the object to be used. An example of this using the `CType` variable to explicitly cast an object and call a method is as follows:

```
Dim objVar as Object

objVar = Me

CType(objVar, Form).Text = "New Dialog Title Text"
```

This snippet shows how to create a generic object under the `Option Strict` syntax. It is then assigns a copy of the current instance of a Visual Basic form. The name `Me` is reserved in Visual Basic, and its use will be described further in Chapter 6. Once it has been assigned, in order to access the `Text` property of this class, it must be cast from its base `Object` definition to a type that supports a `Text` property. The

CType command (covered earlier) accepts the object as its first parameter and the class name (without quotes) as its second parameter. In this case, the current instance variable is of type Form, and by casting this variable, the code can reference the Text property of the current form.

The String Class

Another class that will play a large role in most development projects is the String class. Having Strings defined as a class is more powerful than the Visual Basic 6.0 datatype of String with which you may be familiar. The String class is special class within .NET, because it is the one primitive type that is not a value type. To make String objects compatible with some of the underlying behavior in .NET, they have some interesting characteristics.

The following table lists a subset of the shared methods that are available from the String class.

These methods are shared, which means that the methods are not specific to any instance of a String. The String class also contains several other methods that are called based on an instance of a specific String object. The methods on the String class replace the functions that Visual Basic 6.0 had as part of the language for string manipulation and perform operations such as inserting strings, splitting strings, and searching strings.

The String() Method

The Visual Basic 6 String() method provided a single method for the creation of a String with a set length and populated with a specific character. This method no longer exists in .NET, although the same capability does exist. With the transition to classes, this capability has been added to the constructor to the String class. In fact, the String class has several different constructors for those situations in which you aren't simply assigning an existing value to a new string. Below you first see the most common default, which uses the default constructor (without any argument) to create a String, which is then assigned the constant value 'ABC'. The second declaration uses one of the parameterized versions of the String constructor. This constructor accepts two parameters, the first being a character and the second being the number of times that character should be repeated in the string.

```
Dim strConstant as String = "ABC"
Dim strRepeat as New String("A"c, 20)
```

Shared Methods	Description
Empty	This is actually a property. It can be used when an empty String is required. It can be used for comparison or initialization of a String.
Compare	Compares two objects of type String.
CompareOrdinal	Compares two Strings, without considering the local national language or culture.
Concat	Concatenates one or more Strings.
Copy	Creates a new String with the same value as an instance provided.
Equals	Determines whether two Strings have the same value.

Shared Methods	Description
Equality operator (=)	An overloaded version of the equality operator that compares two `String` objects.
Inequality operator (`op_Inequality`)	A method that accepts two `String` objects for comparison. The method returns `True` if the objects are not equal.

The second example of constructing a new string imitates the Visual Basic 6.0 `String()` method. Not only have creation methods been encapsulated, but other string-specific methods, such as character and substring searching, and case changes are now available from `String` objects.

The SubString Method

Although not removed, the `Left`, `Right`, and `Mid` methods are deprecated in Visual Basic. This is largely due to the fact that the .NET `String` class has a method called `SubString`. This single method replaces the three methods that Visual Basic 6.0 programmers are accustomed to using to create substrings. Thanks to overloading, which is covered in Chapter 5, there are two versions of this method: the first accepts a starting position and the number of characters to retrieve, while the second accepts simply the starting location. The following code shows examples of using both of these methods on an instance of a `String`.

```
Dim strMyString as String = "Hello World"

Console.WriteLine(strMystring.SubString(0,5))
Console.WriteLine(strMyString.SubString(6))
```

The PadLeft and PadRight Methods

The `LSet` and `RSet` statements from previous versions of Visual Basic have been removed. These functions have been replaced by the `PadLeft` and `PadRight` methods. These methods allow you to justify a `String` so that it is left- or right-justified. As with `SubString`, the `PadLeft`, and `PadRight` methods are overloaded. The first version of these methods requires only a maximum length of the `String` and then uses spaces to pad the `String`. The other version requires two parameters, the length of the returned `String` and the character that should be used to pad the original `String`. An example of working with the `PadLeft` method is as follows:

```
Dim strMyString as String = "Hello World"

Console.WriteLine(strMyString.PadLeft(30))
Console.WriteLine(strMyString.PadLeft(20,"."c))
```

The String Class Is Immutable

The Visual Basic `String` class isn't entirely different from the `String` type that VB programmers have used for years. The majority of `String` behaviors remain unchanged, and the majority of methods are now available as methods. However, to support the default behavior that people associate with the `String` primitive type, the `String` class isn't declared the same way that several other classes are. Strings in .NET do not allow editing of their data. When a portion of a String is changed or copied, the operating system allocates a new memory location and copies the resulting `String` to this new location. This ensures that when a `String` is copied to a second variable, the new variable references its own copy.

To support this behavior in .NET, the `String` class is defined as an immutable class. This means that each time a change is made to the data associated with a String, a new instance is created, and the original referenced memory is released for garbage collection. This is an expensive operation, but the result is that the `String` class behaves as people expect a primitive type to behave. Additionally, when a copy of a String is made, the `String` class forces a new version of the data into the referenced memory. This ensures that each instance of a `String` will reference only its own memory. Consider the following code:

```
Dim strMyString as String
Dim intLoop as Integer

For intLoop = 1 to 1000
   strMyString = strMyString & "A very long string "
Next
Console.WriteLine(strMyString)
```

This code does not perform well. For each assignment operation on the `strMyString` variable, the system allocates a new memory buffer based on the size of the new string and copies both the current value of `strMyString` and the new text that is to be appended. The system then frees the previous memory that must be reclaimed by the Garbage Collector. As this loop continues, the new memory allocation requires a larger chunk of memory. The result is that operations such as this can take a long time. However, .NET offers an alternative in the `System.Text.StringBuilder` object shown in the following sample code.

```
Dim objMyStrBldr as New System.Text.StringBuilder()
Dim intLoop as Integer

For intLoop = 1 to 1000
   ObjMyStrBldr.Append("A very long string ")
Next
Console.WriteLine(objMyStrBldr.ToString())
```

The preceding code works with strings but does not use the `String` class. The .NET class library contains a class called `System.Text.StringBuilder`, which performs better when strings will be edited repeatedly. This class does not store a string in the conventional manner — editing or appending more characters does not involve allocating new memory for the entire string. Since the preceding code snippet does not need to reallocate the memory used for the entire string, each time another set of characters is appended it performs significantly faster. In the end, an instance of the `String` class is never explicitly needed because the `StringBuilder` class implements the `ToString` method to roll up all of the characters into a string. While the concept of the `StringBuilder` class isn't new, the fact that it is now available as part of the Visual Basic implementation means developers no longer need to create their own string memory managers.

The DBNull Class and IsDBNull() Function

The `IsNull` and `IsEmpty` functions from Visual Basic 6.0 are now obsolete. Visual Basic provides alternative ways of determining if a variable has not been initialized. The first is the function `IsDBNull()`. The `IsDBNull` method accepts an object as its parameter and returns a `Boolean` that indicates if the variable has been initialized. In addition to this method, Visual Basic has access to the `DBNull` class. The class is part of the `System` namespace, and to use it you declare a local variable with the `DBNull` type. This variable is then used with an `is` comparison operator to determine if a given variable has been initialized.

```
Dim sysNull As System.DBNull
Dim strMyString As String

If strMyString Is sysNull Then
  strMyString = "Initialize my String"
End If
If Not IsDBNull(strMyString) Then
  Console.WriteLine(strMyString)
End If
```

In this code the `strMyString` variable is declared but not yet initialized, making its value null (or nothing). The first conditional is evaluated to `True` and as a result the string is initialized. The second conditional then ensures that the declared variable has been initialized. Since this was accomplished in the preceding code, this condition is also `True`. In both cases, the `sysNull` value is used not to verify the type of the object, but to verify that it has not yet been instantiated with a value.

Arrays

When Visual Basic was first announced, a lot of significant changes were planned to the way that arrays worked. A major reason for these changes involved getting rid of the `Variant_Array` structure. This structure, introduced with COM, was hidden from most VB programmers, but was nevertheless ever present. It was necessary because Visual Basic defined arrays in a unique way. The variant array has been removed not only from Visual Basic but also from every .NET language. The reason it was removed is that under .NET, arrays are handled in a consistent way. All .NET arrays at an index of zero have a defined number of elements. However, the way that an array is declared in Visual Basic varies slightly from other .NET languages such as C#.

When Visual Basic was announced, it was said that arrays would always begin at `0` and that they would be defined based on the number of elements in the array. However, in Visual Basic 6.0 the `Option Base` statement allowed arrays to be declared as starting at `1` or any other specified value. This meant that arrays were defined based on their upper limit. The Visual Basic 6.0 Option Base `This` = statement resulted in a problem when converting existing code to Visual Basic. To resolve this issue the engineers at Microsoft decided on a compromise. All arrays in .NET begin at `0`, but when an array is declared in Visual Basic the definition is based on the upper limit of the array, not the number of elements. The main result of this upper limit declaration is that arrays defined in Visual Basic have one more entry by definition than those defined with other .NET languages.

Overall, the result in the change in how arrays work means that some of the more esoteric declarations that were available in Visual Basic 6.0, such as `Dim intMyArr(15 to 30)`, are no longer supported. Still, the majority of capabilities for arrays remain unchanged. It is still possible to declare an array with multiple indices. It is also possible to declare any type as an array of that type. Since an array is a modifier of another type, the basic `Array` class is never explicitly declared for a variable's type. The `System.Array` class that serves as the base for all arrays is defined such that it cannot be created, but must be inherited. As a result, to create an `Integer` array a set of parentheses is added to the declaration of the variable. These parentheses indicate that the system should create an array of the type specified. The parentheses used in the declaration may be empty or may contain the size of the array. An array can be defined as having a single dimension using a single number, or as having multiple dimensions.

The following code illustrates some simple examples to demonstrate five different ways of creating arrays, using a simple integer array as the basis for the comparison.

```
Dim arrMyIntArray1(20) as Integer
Dim arrMyIntArray2() as Integer = {1, 2, 3, 4}
Dim arrMyIntArray3(4,2) as Integer
Dim arrMyIntArray4( , ) as Integer = _
    { {1, 2, 3, 4},{5, 6, 7, 8},{9, 10, 11, 12},{13, 14 , 15 , 16} }
Dim arrMyIntArray5() as Integer
```

In the first case, the code defines an array of integers that spans from `arrMyIntArray1(0)` to `arrMyIntArray1(20)`. This is a 21-element array, because all arrays start at `0` and end with the value defined in the declaration as the upper bound. The second statement creates an array with four elements numbered `0` through `3`, containing the values `1` to `4`. The third statement creates a multidimensional array containing five elements at the first level with each of those elements containing three child elements. The challenge, of course, is that you have to remember that all subscripts go from `0` to the upper bound, meaning that each array contains one more element than its upper bound. The result is an array with 15 elements. The next line of code, the fourth, shows an alternative way of creating the same array, but in this case there are four elements, each containing four elements, with subscripts from `0` to `3` at each level. Finally, the last line demonstrates that it is possible to simply declare a variable and indicate that the variable will be an array without specifying the number of elements in that array.

The UBound Function

Continuing to reference the arrays defined earlier, the declaration of `arrMyIntArray2` actually defined an array that spans from `arrMyIntArray2(0)` to `arrMyIntArray1(3)`. This is the case because when you declare an array by specifying the set of values it still starts at `0`. However, in this case you are not specifying the upper bound, but rather initializing the array with a set of values. If this set of values came from a database or other source it might not be clear what the upper limit on the array was. To verify the upper bound of an array, a call can be made to the `UBound` function:

```
Console.Writeline CStr(UBound(ArrMyIntArray2))
```

and

```
ArrMyIntArray2.GetUpperBound(0)
```

since it is preferable when using multi-dimension arrays.

The `UBound` function has a companion called `LBound`. The `LBound` function computes the lower bound for a given array. However, since all arrays in Visual Basic are `0`-based, it doesn't have much value anymore.

Multidimensional Arrays

As shown earlier in the sample array declarations, the definition of `arrMyIntArray3` is a multidimensional array. This declaration creates an array with 15 elements (five in the first range, each containing three elements) ranging from `arrMyIntArray3(0,0)` through `arrMyIntArray3(2,1)` to `arrMyIntArray3(4,2)`. As with all elements of an array, when it is created without specific values, the values of each of these elements is created with the default value for that type. This case also demonstrates that the size of the different dimensions can vary. It is also possible to nest deeper than two levels, but this should be done with care because such code is difficult to maintain.

The fourth declaration shown previously creates `arrMyIntArray4(, )` with predefined values. The values are mapped based on the outer set being the first dimension and the inner values being associated with the next inner dimension. For example, the value of `arrMyIntArray4(0,1)` is `2`, while the value of `arrMyIntArray4(2,3)` is `12`. The following code snippet illustrates this using a set of nested loops to traverse the array. Additionally, it provides an example of calling the `UBound` method with a second parameter to specify that you are interested in the upper bound for the second dimension of the array:

```
Dim intLoop1 as Integer
Dim intLoop2 as Integer
For intLoop1 = 0 to UBound(arrMyIntArray4)
  For intLoop2 = 0 to UBound(arrMyIntArray4, 2)
    Console.WriteLine arrMyIntArray4(intLoop1, intLoop2).ToString
  Next
Next
```

The ReDim Statement

The final declaration demonstrated previously is for `arrMyIntArray5()`. This is an example of an array that has not yet been instantiated. If an attempt were made to assign a value into this array, it would trigger an exception. The solution to this is to use the `ReDim` keyword. Although `ReDim` was part of Visual Basic 6.0, it has changed slightly in Visual Basic. The first change is that code must first `Dim` an instance of the variable; it is not acceptable to declare an array using the `ReDim` statement. The second change is that code cannot change the number of dimensions in an array. For example, an array with three dimensions cannot grow to an array of four dimensions nor can it be reduced to only two dimensions. To further extend the example, code associated with arrays, consider the following code, which manipulates some of the arrays previously declared.

```
Dim arrMyIntArray5() as Integer
```

```
 ' The statement below would compile but would cause a runtime exception.
'arrMyIntArray5(0) = 1

ReDim arrMyIntArray5(2)
ReDim arrMyIntArray3(5,4)
ReDim Preserve arrMyIntArray4(UBound(arrMyIntArray4),2)
```

The `ReDim` of `arrMyIntArray5` instantiates the elements of the array so that values can be assigned to each element. The second statement redimensions the `arrMyIntArray3` variable defined earlier. Note that it is changing the size of both the first and the second dimension. While it is not possible to change the number of dimensions in an array, it is possible to resize any of an array's dimensions. This capability is required if declarations such as `Dim arrMyIntArray6( , , ,) As Integer` are to be legal.

By the way, while it is possible to repeatedly `ReDim` a variable, this is the type of action that should ideally be done only rarely and never within a loop. If you intend to loop through a set of entries and add entries to an array, attempt to determine the number of entries you'll need before entering the loop or at a minimum `ReDim` the size of your array in chunks to improve performance.

The Preserve Keyword

The last item in the code snippet in the preceding section illustrates an additional keyword associated with redimensioning. The `Preserve` keyword indicates that the data that is stored in the array prior to redimensioning should be transferred to the newly created array. If this keyword is not used, then the data that was stored in an array is lost. Additionally, in the preceding example, the `ReDim` statement actually reduces the second dimension of the array. While this is a perfectly legal statement, it should be noted that this means that even though you have asked to preserve the data, the data values `4`, `8`, `12`, and `16` that were assigned in the original definition of this array will be discarded. These are lost because they were assigned in the highest index of the second array. Since `arrMyIntArray4(1,3)` is no longer valid, the value that resided at this location has been lost.

Arrays continue to be very powerful in Visual Basic. However, the basic array class is just that, basic. While it provides a powerful framework it does not provide a lot of other features that would allow for more robust logic to be built into the array. To achieve more advanced features, such as sorting and dynamic allocation, the base `Array` class has been inherited by the classes that make up the `Collections` namespace.

Collections

The `Collections` namespace is part of the `System` namespace and provides a series of classes that implement advanced array features. While being able to make an array of existing types is powerful, sometimes more power is needed in the array itself. The ability to inherently sort or dynamically add dissimilar objects in an array is provided by the classes of the `Collections` namespace. This namespace contains a specialized set of objects that can be instantiated for additional features when working with a collection of similar objects. The following table defines several of the objects that are available as part of the `System.Collections` namespace.

Class	Description
`ArrayList`	Implements an array whose size increases automatically as elements are added.
`BitArray`	Manages an array of `Booleans` that are stored as bit values.
`Hashtable`	Implements a collection of values organized by key. Sorting is done based on a hash of the key.
`Queue`	Implements a first in, first out collection.
`SortedList`	Implements a collection of values with associated keys. The values are sorted by key and are accessible by key or index.
`Stack`	Implements a last in, first out collection.

Each of the objects listed is focused on storing a collection of objects. This means that in addition to the special capabilities each provides it also provides one additional capability not available to objects created based on the `Array` class. In short, since every variable in .NET is based on the `Object` class, it is possible to have a collection defined, because one of these objects contains elements that are defined with different types. This is the case because each stores an array of objects, and since all classes are of type `Object`, a string could be stored alongside an integer value. The result is that it's possible within the `Collection` classes for the actual objects being stored to be different. Consider the following example code:

```
Dim objMyArrList As New System.Collections.ArrayList()
Dim objItem As Object
Dim intLine As Integer = 1
Dim strHello As String = "Hello"
Dim objWorld As New System.Text.StringBuilder("World")

' Add an integer value to the array list.
objMyArrList.Add(intLine)

' Add an instance of a string object
objMyArrList.Add(strHello)

' Add a single character cast as a character.
objMyArrList.Add(" "c)

' Add an object that isn't a primitive type.
objMyArrList.Add(objWorld)

' To balance the string, insert a break between the line
' and the string "Hello", by inserting a string constant.
objMyArrList.Insert(1, ". ")

For Each objItem In objMyArrList
  ' Output the values...
  Console.Write(objItem.ToString())
Next
```

The preceding code is an example of implementing the new `ArrayList` collection class. The collection classes, as this example shows, are more versatile than any similar structures in Visual Basic 6.0. The preceding code creates a new instance of an `ArrayList`, along with some related variables to support the demonstration. The code then shows four different types of variable being inserted into the same `ArrayList`. The code then inserts another value into the middle of the list. At no time has the size of the array been declared nor has a redefinition of the array size been required.

Part of the reason for this is that the `Add` and `Insert` methods on the `ArrayList` class are defined to accept a parameter of type `Object`. This means that the `ArrayList` object can literally accept any value in .NET. This comes at a slight performance cost for those variables that are value types because of boxing.

The System.Collections.Specialized Namespace and Generics

Visual Basic has additional classes available as part of the `System.Collections.Specialized` namespace. These classes tend to be oriented around a specific problem. For example, the `ListDictionary` class is designed to take advantage of the fact that while a hash table is very good at storing and retrieving a large number of items, it can be costly when there are only a few items. Similarly, the `StringCollection` and `StringDictionary` classes are defined so that when working with strings the time spent interpreting the type of object is reduced and overall performance is improved. The idea is that each of the classes defined in this namespace represents a specialized implementation that has been optimized for handling specific datatypes.

This specialization is different from the specialization provided by one of Visual Studio 2005's new features, Generics. The basic idea of generics is that since there is a performance cost and reliability concerns when casting to and from the object type, collections should allow you to specify what specific type they will contain. Generics not only prevent you from paying the cost of boxing for value types, but add to the ability to create type-safe code at compile time. Generics are a powerful extension to the .NET environment and are covered in detail in Chapter 8.

Parameter Passing

When an object's methods or an assembly's procedures and methods are called, it's often appropriate to provide input for the data to be operated on by the code. Visual Basic has changed the way that functions, procedures, and methods are called and how those parameters are passed. The first change actually makes writing such calls more consistent. Under Visual Basic 6.0, the parameter list for a procedure call didn't require parentheses. On the other hand, a call to a `method` did require parentheses around the parameter list. In Visual Basic, the parentheses are always required and the `Call` keyword is obsolete.

Another change in Visual Basic is the way parameters with default values are handled. As with Visual Basic 6.0, it is possible to define a function, procedure, or method that provides default values for the last parameter(s). This way it is possible to call a method such as `PadRight`, passing either with a single parameter defining the length of the string and using a default of space for the padding character, or with two parameters, the first still defining the length of the string but the second now replacing the default of space with a dash.

```
Public Function PadRight(ByVal intSize as Integer, _
                         Optional ByVal chrPad as Char = " "c)
End Function
```

To use default parameters, it is necessary to make them the last parameters in the function declaration. Visual Basic also requires that every optional parameter have a default value. It is not acceptable to just declare a parameter and assign it the `Optional` keyword. In Visual Basic, the `Optional` keyword must be accompanied by a value that will be assigned if the parameter is not passed in.

How the system handles parameters is the most important change related to them in Visual Basic. In Visual Basic 6.0, the default was that parameters were passed by reference. Passing a parameter by reference means that if changes are made to the value of a variable passed to a method, function, or procedure call, these changes were to the actual variable and, therefore, are available to the calling routine.

Passing a parameter by reference sometimes results in unexpected changes being made to a parameter's value. It is partly because of this that parameters default to passing by value in Visual Basic. The advantage of passing by value is that regardless of what a function might do to a variable while it is running, when the function is completed, the calling code still has the original value.

However, under .NET passing a parameter by value only indicates how the top-level reference for that object is passed. Sometimes referred to as a 'shallow' copy operation, the system only copies the top-level reference value for an object passed by value. This is important to remember because it means that referenced memory is not protected. Thus, while the reference passed as part of the parameter will remain unchanged for the calling method, the actual values stored in referenced objects can be updated even when an object is passed by reference.

Boxing

Normally, when a conversion (implicit or explicit) occurs, the original value is read from its current memory location and then the new value is assigned. For example, to convert a `Short` to a `Long`, the system reads the 2 bytes of `Short` data and writes them to the appropriate bytes for the `Long` variable. However, under Visual Basic if a value type needs to be managed as an object, then the system will perform an intermediate step. This intermediate step involves taking the value that is on the stack and copying it to the heap, a process referred to as boxing. As noted earlier, the `Object` class is implemented as a reference type. Therefore, the system needs to convert value types into reference types for them to be objects. This doesn't cause any problems or require any special programming, because boxing isn't something you declare or directly control. However, it does have an impact on performance.

In a situation where you are copying the data for a single value type, this is not a significant cost. However, if you are processing an array that contains thousands of values, the time spent moving between a value type and a temporary reference type can be significant.

There are ways to limit the amount of boxing that occurs. One method that has been shown to work well is to create a class based on the value type you need to work with. On first thought, this seems counterintuitive because it costs more to create a class. The key is how often you reuse the data that is contained in the class. By repeatedly using this object to interact with other objects, you will save on the creation of a temporary boxed object.

There are two important areas to examine with examples to better understand boxing. The first involves the use of arrays. When an array is created, the portion of the class that tracks the element of the array is created as a reference object, but each of the elements of the array is created directly. Thus, an array of integers consists of the array object and a set of `Integer` value types. When you update one of these values with another `Integer` value there is no boxing involved:

```
Dim arrInt(20) as Integer
Dim intMyValue as Integer = 1

arrInt(0) = 0
arrInt(1) = intMyValue
```

Neither of these assignments of an `Integer` value into the integer array that was defined previously requires boxing. In each case, the array object identifies which value on the stack needs to be referenced, and the value is assigned to that value type. The point here is that just because you have referenced an object doesn't mean you are going to box a value. The boxing only occurs when the values being assigned are being transitioned from value to reference types:

```
Dim objStrBldr as New System.Text.StringBuilder()
Dim objSortedList as New System.Collections.SortedList()
Dim intCount as Integer
For intCount = 1 to 100
  objStrBldr.Append(intCount)
  objSortedList.Add(intCount, intCount)
Next
```

The preceding snippet illustrates two separate calls to object interfaces. One of these calls requires boxing of the value `intCount`, while the other does not. There is nothing in the code to indicate which call is which. The answer is that the `Append` method of `StringBuilder` has been overridden to include a version that accepts an `Integer`, while the `Add` method of `SortedList` collection expects two objects. While the `Integer` values can be recognized by the system as objects, doing so requires the runtime library to box up these values so that they can be added to the sorted list.

The key to boxing isn't that you are working with objects as part of an action, but that you are passing a value to a parameter that expects an object or are taking an object and converting it to a value type. However, one time that boxing does not occur is when you call a method on a value type. There is no conversion to an object, so if you need to assign an `Integer` to a `String` using the `ToString` method, there is no boxing of the integer value as part of the creation of the string. On the other hand, you are explicitly creating a new `String` object, so the cost is similar.

Retired Keywords and Methods

This chapter has covered several changes from Visual Basic 6.0 that are part of Visual Basic under .NET. They include the removal of the `Currency` type, `String` function, `Rset`, and `Lset` functions. Other functions such as `Left`, `Right`, and `Mid` have been discussed as becoming obsolete, although they may still be supported. Functions such as `IsEmpty` and `IsNull` have been replaced with new versions. Additionally, this chapter has looked at some of the differences in how Visual Basic now works with arrays.

Visual Basic has removed many keywords that won't be missed. For example, the `DefType` statement has been removed. This statement was a throwback to Fortran, allowing a developer to indicate, for example, that all variables starting with the letters I, J, K, L, M, N would be integers. Most programmers have probably never used this function, and it doesn't have a logical replacement in Visual Basic under .NET.

One of the real advantages of Visual Basic under .NET is the way that it removed some of the more esoteric and obsolete functions from Visual Basic. The following list contains the majority of such functions. As with others that have already been discussed, some have been replaced; for example, the math functions are now part of the `System.Math` library, while others such as `IsObject` really don't have much more meaning than `LBound` in the context of .NET, where everything is an object and the lower bound of all arrays is `0`.

Elements of Visual Basic 6.0 Removed in .NET

Also as previously noted, the UDT has also been removed from the Visual Basic vocabulary. Instead, the ability to create a user-defined set of variables as a type has been replaced with the ability to create custom structures and classes in Visual Basic.

Remember that Visual Basic wasn't revised to work with .NET. Instead Visual Basic was rebuilt from the ground up as an entirely new language based on the .NET Framework and the syntax of Visual Basic.

`As Any`	`Now` function
`Atn` function	`Null` keyword
`Calendar` property	`On . . . GoSub`
`Circle` statement	`On . . . GoTo`
`Currency`	`Option Base`
`Date` function and statement	Option Private Module
`Date$` function	`Property Get`, `Property Let`, and `Property Set`
`Debug.Assert` method	`PSet` method
`Debug.Print` method	`Rnd` function
`DefType`	`Round` function
`DoEvents` function	`Rset`
`Empty`	`Scale` method
`Eqv` operator	`Set` statement
`GoSub` statement	`Sgn` function
`Imp` operator	`Sqr` function
`Initialize` event	`String` function
`Instancing` property	`Terminate` event
`IsEmpty` function	`Time` function and statement
`IsMissing` function	`Time$` function
`IsNull` function	`Timer` function
`IsObject` function	`Type` statement
`Let` statement	`Variant` datatype
`Line` statement	`VarType` function
`Lset`	`Wend` keyword

Summary

This chapter looked at many of the basic building blocks of Visual Basic that are used throughout project development. Understanding how they work will help you to write more stable and better performing software. There are five specific points to take note of:

- Beware of array sizes; all arrays start at `0` and are defined not by size but by the highest index.
- Remember to use the `StringBuilder` class for string manipulation.

- Use `Option Strict`; it's not just about style, it's about performance.
- Beware of parameters that are passed `ByValue` so changes are not returned.
- Take advantage of the new collection classes.

While this chapter covered many other items such as how the new `Decimal` type works and how boxing works, these five items are really the most important. Whether you are creating a new library of methods or a new user interface, these five items will consistently turn up in some form. While .NET provides a tremendous amount of power, this chapter has hopefully provided information on places where that power comes at a significant performance cost.

4

Object Syntax Introduction

Visual Basic supports the four major defining concepts required for a language to be fully object-oriented:

- **Abstraction** — Abstraction is merely the ability of a language to create "black box" code, to take a concept and create an abstract representation of that concept within a program. A `Customer` object, for instance, is an abstract representation of a real-world customer. A `DataTable` object is an abstract representation of a set of data.
- **Encapsulation** — This is the concept of a separation between interface and implementation. The idea is that you can create an interface (`Public` methods, properties, fields, and events in a class), and, as long as that interface remains consistent, the application can interact with your objects. This remains true even if you entirely rewrite the code within a given method — thus, the interface is independent of the implementation.

  Encapsulation allows you to hide the internal implementation details of a class. For example, the algorithm you use to compute pi might be proprietary. You can expose a simple API to the end user, but you hide all of the logic used by the algorithm by encapsulating it within your class.
- **Polymorphism** — Polymorphism is reflected in the ability to write one routine that can operate on objects from more than one class — treating different objects from different classes in exactly the same way. For instance, if both `Customer` and `Vendor` objects have a `Name` property, and you can write a routine that calls the `Name` property regardless of whether you're using a `Customer` or `Vendor` object, then you have polymorphism.

  Visual Basic, in fact, supports polymorphism in two ways — through late binding (much like Smalltalk, a classic example of a true object-orientated language) and through the implementation of multiple interfaces. This flexibility is very powerful and is preserved within Visual Basic.
- **Inheritance** — Inheritance is the idea that a class can gain the preexisting interface and behaviors of an existing class. This is done by inheriting these behaviors from the existing class through a process known as subclassing.

We'll discuss these four concepts in detail in Chapter 7, using this chapter and Chapter 6 to focus on the syntax that enables us to utilize these concepts.

Visual Basic is also a component-based language. Component-based design is often viewed as a successor to object-oriented design. Due to this, component-based languages have some other capabilities. These are closely related to the traditional concepts of object orientation.

- **Multiple interfaces** — Each class in Visual Basic defines a primary interface (also called the default or native interface) through its `Public` methods, properties, and events. Classes can also implement other, secondary interfaces in addition to this primary interface. An object based on this class then has multiple interfaces, and a client application can choose by which interface it will interact with the object.
- **Assembly (component) level scoping** — Not only can you define your classes and methods as `Public` (available to anyone), `Protected` (available through inheritance), and `Private` (available locally only), but you can also define them as `Friend` — meaning that they are available only within the current assembly or component. This is not a traditional object-oriented concept, but is very powerful when designing component-based applications.

In this chapter, you'll explore the creation and use of classes and objects in Visual Basic. You won't get too deeply into code. However, it is important that you spend a little time familiarizing yourself with basic object-oriented terms and concepts.

Object-Oriented Terminology

To start with, let's take a look at the word *object* itself, along with the related class and instance terms. Then we'll move on to discuss the four terms that define the major functionality in the object-oriented world — encapsulation, abstraction, polymorphism, and inheritance.

Objects, Classes, and Instances

An object is a code-based abstraction of a real-world entity or relationship. For instance, you might have a `Customer` object that represents a real-world customer, such as customer number 123, or you might have a `File` object that represents `C:\ config.sys` on your computer's hard drive.

A closely related term is class. A class is the code that defines an object, and all objects are created based on a class. A class is an abstraction of a real-world concept, and it provides the basis from which you create instances of specific objects. For example, in order to have a `Customer` object representing customer number 123, you must first have a `Customer` class that contains all of the code (methods, properties, events, variables, and so on) necessary to create `Customer` objects. Based on that class, you can create any number of objects, each one an instance of the class. Each object is identical to the others, except that it may contain different data.

You can create many instances of `Customer` objects based on the same `Customer` class. All of the `Customer` objects are identical in terms of what they can do and the code they contain, but each one contains its own unique data. This means that each object represents a different physical customer.

Composition of an Object

You use an interface to get access to an object's data and behavior. The object's data and behaviors are contained within the object, so a client application can treat the object like a black box accessible only through its interface. This is a key object-oriented concept called encapsulation. The idea is that any program that makes use of this object won't have direct access to the behaviors or data; rather, those programs must make use of our object's interface.

Let's walk through each of the three elements in detail.

Interface

The interface is defined as a set of methods (`Sub` and `Function` routines), properties (`Property` routines), events, and fields (variables) that are declared `Public` in scope.

You can also have `Private` methods and properties in your code. While these methods can be called by code within your object, they are not part of the interface and cannot be called by programs written to use our object. Another option is to use the `Friend` keyword, which defines the scope to be your current project, meaning that any code within our project can call the method, but no code outside your project (that is, from a different .NET assembly) can call the method. To complicate things a bit, you can also declare methods and properties as `Protected`, which are available to classes that inherit from your class. We'll discuss `Protected` in Chapter 6 along with inheritance.

For example, you might have the following code in a class:

```
Public Function CalculateValue() As Integer

End Function
```

Since this method is declared with the `Public` keyword, it is part of the interface and can be called by client applications that are using the object. You might also have a method such as this:

```
Private Sub DoSomething()

End Sub
```

This method is declared as being `Private`, and so it is not part of the interface. This method can only be called by code within the class — not by any code outside the class, such as the code in a program that is using one of the objects.

On the other hand, you can do something like this:

```
Public Sub CalculateValue()
  DoSomething()
End Sub
```

In this case, you're calling the `Private` method from within a `Public` method. While code using your objects can't directly call a `Private` method, you will frequently use `Private` methods to help structure the code in a class to make it more maintainable and easier to read.

Finally, you can use the Friend keyword:

```
Friend Sub DoSomething()

End Sub
```

In this case, the DoSomething method can be called by code within the class, or from other classes or modules within the current Visual Basic project. Code from outside the project will not have access to the method.

The Friend scope is very similar to the Public scope in that it makes methods available for use by code outside the object itself. However, unlike Public, the Friend keyword restricts access to code within the current Visual Basic project, preventing code in other .NET assemblies from calling the method.

Implementation or Behavior

The code inside of a method is called the implementation. Sometimes it is also called behavior, since it is this code that actually makes the object do useful work.

For instance, you might have an Age property as part of the object's interface. Within that method, you might have some code:

```
Private mAge As Integer

Public ReadOnly Property Age() As Integer
  Get
    Return mAge
  End Get
End Sub
```

In this case, the code is returning a value directly out of a variable, rather than doing something better like calculating the value based on a birth date. However, this kind of code is often written in applications, and it seems to work fine for a while.

The key concept here is to understand that client applications can use the object even if you change the implementation, as long as you don't change the interface. As long as the method name and its parameter list and return datatype remain unchanged, you can change the implementation any way you want.

The code necessary to call our Age property would look something like this:

```
theAge = myObject.Age
```

The result of running this code is that you get the Age value returned for your use. While the client application will work fine, you'll soon discover that hard-coding the age into the application is a problem and so, at some point, you'll want to improve this code. Fortunately, you can change the implementation without changing the client code:

```
Private mBirthDate As Date

Public ReadOnly Property Age() As Integer
  Get
```

```
      Return CInt(DateDiff(DateInterval.Year, mBirthDate, Now))
    End Get
  End Sub
```

You've changed the implementation behind the interface, effectively changing how it behaves, without changing the interface itself. Now, when you run the client application, you'll find that the `Age` value returned is accurate over time, whereas in the previous implementation it was not.

It is important to keep in mind that encapsulation is a syntactic tool — it allows the code to continue to run without change. However, it is not semantic, meaning that just because the code continues to run, that doesn't mean it continues to do what you actually want it to do.

In this example, the client code may have been written to overcome the initial limitations of the implementation in some way, and, thus, the client code might not only rely on being able to retrieve the `Age` value but also be counting on the result of that call being a fixed value over time.

While the update to the implementation won't stop the client program from running, it may very well prevent the client program from running correctly.

Fields or Instance Variables

The third key part of an object is its data, or state. In fact, it might be argued that the only important part of an object is its data. After all, every instance of a class is absolutely identical in terms of its interface and its implementation; the only thing that can vary at all is the data contained within that particular object.

Fields are variables that are declared so that they are available to all code within the class. Typically, fields are `Private` in scope, available only to the code in the class itself. They are also sometimes referred to as instance variables or as member variables.

You shouldn't confuse fields with properties. In Visual Basic, a `Property` is a type of method that is geared to retrieving and setting values, while a field is a variable within the class that may hold the value exposed by a `Property`.

For instance, you might have a class that has fields:

```
Public Class TheClass

  Private mName As String
  Private mBirthDate As Date

End Class
```

Each instance of the class — each object — will have its own set of these fields in which to store data. Because these fields are declared with the `Private` keyword, they are only available to code within each specific object.

While fields can be declared as `Public` in scope, this makes them available to any code using the objects in a manner you can't control. Such a choice directly breaks the concept of encapsulation, since code outside our object can directly change data values without following any rules that might otherwise be set in the object's code.

If you want to make the value of a field available to code outside of the object, you should use a property:

```
Public Class TheClass
  Private mName As String
  Private mBirthDate As Date

  Public ReadOnly Property Name() As String
    Get
      Return mName
    End Get
  End Property

End Class
```

Since the `Name` property is a method, you are not directly exposing the internal variables to client code, so you preserve encapsulation of the data. At the same time, through this mechanism, you are able to safely provide access to your data as needed.

Fields can also be declared with the `Friend` scope, which means that they are available to all code in your project. Like declaring them as `Public`, this breaks encapsulation and is strongly discouraged.

Now that you have a grasp of some of the basic object-oriented terminology, you're ready to explore the creation of classes and objects. First, you'll see how Visual Basic allows you to interact with objects, and then you'll dive into the actual process of authoring those objects.

Working with Objects

In the .NET environment, and within Visual Basic in particular, you use objects all the time without even thinking about it. Every control on a form — in fact, every form — is an object. When you open a file or interact with a database, you are using objects to do that work.

Object Declaration and Instantiation

Objects are created using the `New` keyword, indicating that you want a new instance of a particular class. There are a number of variations on how or where you can use the `New` keyword in your code. Each one provides different advantages in terms of code readability or flexibility.

The most obvious way to create an object is to declare an object variable and then create an instance of the object:

```
Dim obj As TheClass
obj = New TheClass()
```

The result of this code is that you have a new instance of `TheClass` ready for use. To interact with this new object, you will use the `obj` variable that you declared. The `obj` variable contains a reference to the object, a concept you'll explore later.

You can shorten this by combining the declaration of the variable with the creation of the instance:

```
Dim obj As New TheClass()
```

In previous versions of Visual Basic, this was a very poor thing to do because it had both negative performance and maintainability effects. However, in Visual Basic, there is no difference between the first example and this one, other than that the code is shorter.

This code both declares the variable `obj` as datatype `TheClass` and creates an instance of the class, immediately creating an object that you can use.

Another variation on this theme is:

```
Dim obj As TheClass = New TheClass()
```

Again, this both declares a variable of datatype `TheClass` and creates an instance of the class.

This third syntax example provides a great deal of flexibility while remaining compact. Though it is a single line of code, it separates the declaration of the variable's datatype from the creation of the object.

Such flexibility is very useful when working with inheritance or with multiple interfaces. You might declare the variable to be of one type—say, an interface—and instantiate the object based on a class that implements that interface. You'll revisit this syntax when interfaces are covered in detail in Chapter 6.

So far you've been declaring a variable for new objects. However, sometimes you may simply need to pass an object as a parameter to a method, in which case you can create an instance of the object right in the call to that method:

```
DoSomething(New TheClass())
```

This calls the `DoSomething` method, passing a new instance of `TheClass` as a parameter.

This can be even more complex. Perhaps, instead of needing an object reference, your method needs an `Integer`. You can provide that `Integer` value from a method on the object:

```
Public Class TheClass
  Public Function GetValue() As Integer
    Return 42
  End Function
End Class
```

You can then instantiate the object and call the method all in one shot, thus passing the value returned from the method as a parameter:

```
DoSomething(New TheClass().GetValue())
```

Obviously, you need to carefully weigh the readability of such code against its compactness. At some point, having more compact code can detract from readability rather than enhancing it.

Object References

Typically, when you work with an object, you are using a reference to that object. On the other hand, when you are working with simple datatypes, such as `Integer`, you are working with the actual value rather than with a reference. Let's explore these concepts and see how they work and interact.

When you create a new object using the `New` keyword, you store a reference to that object in a variable. For instance:

```
Dim obj As New TheClass()
```

This code creates a new instance of `TheClass`. You gain access to this new object via the `obj` variable. This variable holds a reference to the object. You might then do something like this:

```
Dim another As TheClass
another = obj
```

Now, you have a second variable, `another`, which also has a reference to the same object. You can use either variable interchangeably, since they both reference the exact same object. You need to remember that the variable you have is not the object itself but is just a reference or pointer to the object.

Dereferencing Objects

When you are done working with an object, you can indicate that you're through with it by dereferencing the object.

To dereference an object, you need to simply set the object reference to `Nothing`:

```
Dim obj As TheClass

obj = New TheClass()
obj = Nothing
```

Once any or all variables that reference an object are set to `Nothing`, the .NET runtime can tell that you no longer need that object. At some point, the runtime will destroy the object and reclaim the memory and resources consumed by the object.

Between the time that you dereference the object and the time that the .NET Framework gets around to actually destroying it, the object simply sits in the memory, unaware that it has been dereferenced. Right before .NET destroys the object, the Framework will call the `Finalize` method on the object (if it has one). The `Finalize` method will be discussed in Chapter 6.

Early versus Late Binding

One of the strengths of Visual Basic has long been that it provided access to both early and late binding when interacting with objects.

Early binding means that code directly interacts with an object by directly calling its methods. Since the Visual Basic compiler knows the object's datatype ahead of time, it can directly compile code to invoke the methods on the object. Early binding also allows the IDE to use IntelliSense to aid development efforts; it allows the compiler to ensure that you are referencing methods that exist and you are providing the proper parameter values.

Late binding means that your code interacts with an object dynamically at runtime. This provides a great deal of flexibility since the code doesn't care what type of object it is interacting with as long as the object supports the methods you want to call. Because the type of the object isn't known by the IDE or compiler, neither IntelliSense nor compile-time syntax checking is possible, but in exchange you get unprecedented flexibility.

If you enable strict type checking by using `Option Strict On` in the project properties dialog or at the top of the code modules, then the IDE and compiler will enforce early binding behavior. By default, `Option Strict` is turned off, so you have easy access to the use of late binding within the code. Chapter 4 discussed `Option Strict`.

Implementing Late Binding

Late binding occurs when the compiler can't determine the type of object that you'll be calling. This level of ambiguity is achieved through the use of the `Object` datatype. A variable of datatype `Object` can hold virtually any value, including a reference to any type of object. Thus, code such as the following could be run against any object that implements a `DoSomething` method that accepts no parameters:

```
Option Strict Off

Module LateBind
  Public Sub DoWork(ByVal obj As Object)
   obj.DoSomething()
  End Sub
End Module
```

If the object passed into this routine does not have a `DoSomething` method that accepts no parameters, then an exception will be thrown. Thus, it is recommended that any code that uses late binding always provide exception handling:

```
Option Strict Off

Module LateBind
  Public Sub DoWork(ByVal obj As Object)
     Try
       obj.DoSomething()
    Catch ex As MissingMemberException
       ' do something appropriate given failure
       ' to call this method
    End Try
  End Sub
End Module
```

Here, the call to the `DoSomething` method has been put in a `Try` block. If it works, then the code in the `Catch` block is ignored, but in the case of a failure, the code in the `Catch` block is run. You need to write code in the `Catch` block to handle the case in which the object does not support the `DoSomething` method call. This `Catch` block only catches the `MissingMemberException`, which indicates that the method doesn't exist on the object.

While late binding is flexible, it can be error prone and is slower than early bound code. To make a late bound method call, the .NET runtime must dynamically determine if the target object actually has a method that matches the one you're calling. It must then invoke that method on your behalf. This takes more time and effort than an early bound call where the compiler knows ahead of time that the method exists and can compile the code to make the call directly. With a late bound call, the compiler has to generate code to make the call dynamically at runtime.

Use of the CType Function

Whether you are using late binding or not, it can be useful to pass object references around using the `Object` datatype, converting them to an appropriate type when you need to interact with them. This is particularly useful when working with objects that use inheritance or implement multiple interfaces, concepts that will be discussed in Chapter 6.

If `Option Strict` is turned off, which is the default, you can write code that allows you to use a variable of type `Object` to make an early bound method call:

```
Module LateBind
  Public Sub DoWork(obj As Object)

    Dim local As TheClass
    local = obj
    local.DoSomething()
  End Sub
End Module
```

This code uses a strongly typed variable, `local`, to reference what was a generic object value. Behind the scenes, Visual Basic converts the generic type to a specific type so that it can be assigned to the strongly typed variable. If the conversion can't be done, you'll get a trappable runtime error.

The same thing can be done using the `CType` function. If `Option Strict` is enabled, then the previous approach will not compile, and the `CType` function must be used. Here is the same code making use of `CType`:

```
Module LateBind
  Public Sub DoWork(obj As Object)

    Dim local As TheClass
    local = CType(obj, TheClass)
    local.DoSomething()
  End Sub
End Module
```

This code declares a variable of type `TheClass`, which is an early bound datatype that you want to use. The parameter you're accepting, though, is of the generic `Object` datatype, and so you use the `CType()` method to gain an early bound reference to the object. If the object isn't of type `TheClass`, the call to `CType()` will fail with a trappable error.

Once you have a reference to the object, you can call methods by using the early bound variable, `local`.

This code can be shortened to avoid the use of the intermediate variable. Instead, you can simply call methods directly from the datatype:

```
Module LateBind
  Public Sub DoWork(obj As Object)
     CType(obj, TheClass).DoSomething()
  End Sub
End Module
```

Even though the variable you're working with is of type `Object` and, thus, any calls to it will be late bound, you use the `CType` method to temporarily convert the variable into a specific type—in this case, the type `TheClass`.

If the object passed as a parameter is not of type `TheClass`*, you will get a trappable error, so it is always wise to wrap this code in a* `Try . . . Catch` *block.*

As Chapter 6 discusses, the `CType` function can also be very useful when working with objects that implement multiple interfaces. When an object has multiple interfaces, you can reference a single object variable through the appropriate interface as needed.

Use of the DirectCast Function

Another function that is very similar to `CType` is `DirectCast`. `DirectCast` also converts values of one type into another type. It is more restrictive in its working than `CType`, but the tradeoff is that it can be somewhat faster than `CType`. `DirectCast` is used as shown in the following code:

```
Dim obj As TheClass

obj = New TheClass
DirectCast(obj, ITheInterface).DoSomething()
```

This is similar to the last example with `CType`, illustrating the parity between the two functions. There are differences, however. First, `DirectCast` works only with reference types, while `CType` accepts both reference and value types. For instance, `CType` can be used in the following code:

```
Dim int As Integer = CType(123.45, Integer)
```

Trying to do the same thing with `DirectCast` would result in a compiler error, since the value `123.45` is a value type, not a reference type.

The other difference is that `DirectCast` is not as aggressive about converting types as `CType`. `CType` can be viewed as an intelligent combination of all the other conversion functions (such as `CInt`, `CStr`, and so on). `DirectCast`, on the other hand, assumes that the source data is directly convertible and it won't take extra steps to convert the data.

As an example, consider the following code:

```
Dim obj As Object = 123.45

Dim int As Integer = DirectCast(obj, Integer)
```

If you were using `CType` this would work, since `CType` would use `CInt`-like behavior to convert the value to an `Integer`. `DirectCast`, however, will throw an exception because the value is not directly convertible to `Integer`.

Use of the TryCast Function

A function that is similar to `DirectCast` is `TryCast`. `TryCast` converts values of one type into another type, but unlike `DirectCast`, if it can't do the conversion, `TryCast` doesn't throw an exception. Instead, `TryCast` simply returns `Nothing` if the cast can't be performed. `TryCast` only works with reference values, it cannot be used with value types such as `Integer` or `Boolean`.

Using `TryCast`, you can write code like this:

```
Module LateBind
  Public Sub DoWork(obj As Object)
    Dim temp As TheClass = TryCast(obj)
    If temp Is Nothing Then
      ' the cast couldn't be accomplished
      ' so do no work
    Else
      temp.DoSomething()
    End If
  End Sub
End Module
```

If you aren't sure if a type conversion is possible, it is often best to use `TryCast`. This function avoids the overhead and complexity of catching possible exceptions from `CType` or `DirectCast` and still provides you with an easy way to convert an object to another type.

Creating Classes

Using objects is fairly straightforward and intuitive. It is the kind of thing that even the most novice programmers pick up and accept rapidly. Creating classes and objects is a bit more complex and interesting, and that is covered throughout the rest of the chapter.

Creating Basic Classes

As discussed earlier, objects are merely instances of a specific template (a class). The class contains the code that defines the behavior of its objects, as well as defining the instance variables that will contain the object's individual data.

Classes are created using the `Class` keyword and include definitions (declaration) and implementations (code) for the variables, methods, properties, and events that make up the class. Each object created based on this class will have the same methods, properties, and events, and will have its own set of data defined by the fields in the class.

The Class Keyword

If you want to create a class that represents a person — a `Person` class — you could use the `Class` keyword like this:

```
Public Class Person
    ' implementation code goes here
End Class
```

As you know, Visual Basic projects are composed of a set of files with the .vb extension. Each file can contain multiple classes. This means that, within a single file, you could have something like this:

```
Public Class Adult
  ' Implementation code goes here.
End Class

Public Class Senior
  ' Implementation code goes here.
End Class

Public Class Child
  ' Implementation code goes here.
End Class
```

The most common approach is to have a single class per file. This is because the Visual Studio .NET (VS.NET) Solution Explorer and the code-editing environment are tailored to make it easy to navigate from file to file to find code. For instance, if you create a single class file with all these classes, the Solution Explorer simply displays a single entry, as shown in Figure 4-1.

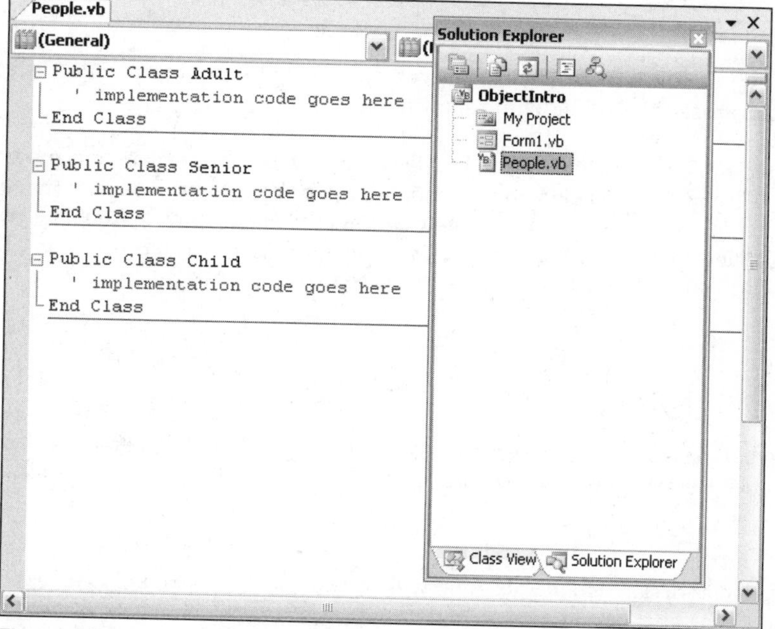

Figure 4-1

However, the VS.NET IDE does provide the Class View window. If you do decide to put multiple classes in each physical .vb file, you can make use of the Class View window to quickly and efficiently navigate through the code, jumping from class to class without having to manually locate those classes in specific code files, as shown in Figure 4-2.

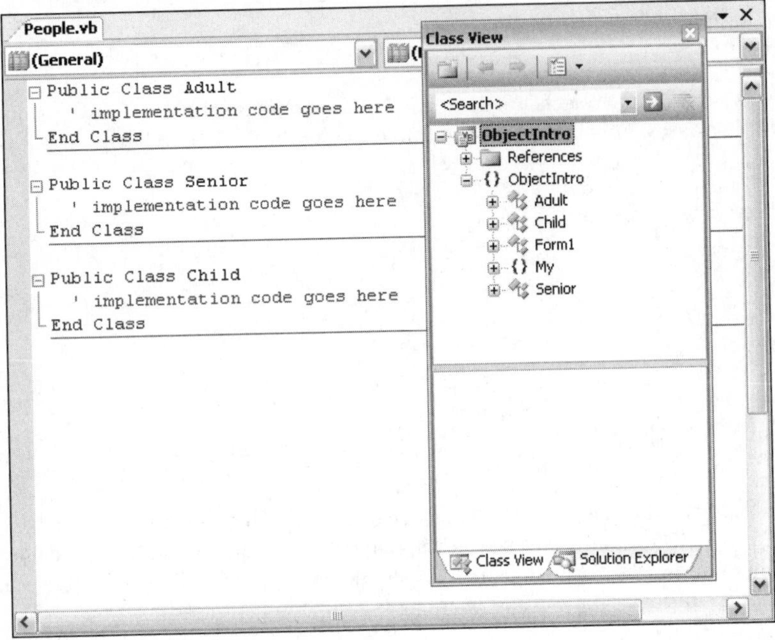

Figure 4-2

The Class View window is incredibly useful even if you keep to one class per file, since it still provides you with a class-based view of the entire application.

In this chapter, you'll stick with one class per file, because it is the most common approach. Open the VS.NET IDE and create a new Windows Application project. Name it `ObjectIntro`. Choose the Project ⇨ Add Class menu option to add a new class module to the project. You'll be presented with the standard Add New Item dialog box. Change the name to `Person.vb` and click Open. The result will be the following code, which defines the `Person` class:

```
Public Class Person

End Class
```

With the `Person` class created, you're ready to start adding code to declare the interface, implement the behaviors, and declare the instance variables.

Fields

Fields are variables declared in the class that will be available to each individual object when the application is run. Each object gets its own set of data—basically, each object gets its own copy of the fields.

Earlier, this chapter discussed how a class is simply a template from which you create specific objects. Variables that you define within the class are also simply templates — and each object gets its own copy of those variables in which to store its data.

Declaring member variables is as easy as declaring variables within the `Class` block structure. Add the following code to our `Person` class:

```
Public Class Person

  Private mName As String
  Private mBirthDate As Date

End Class
```

You can control the scope of the fields by using the following keywords:

- `Private` — Available only to code within the class
- `Friend` — Available only to code within the project/component
- `Protected` — Available only to classes that inherit from the class (discussed in detail in Chapter 6)
- `Protected Friend` — Available to code within our project/component and classes that inherit from the class whether in the project or not (discussed in detail in Chapter 6)
- `Public` — Available to code outside the class and to any projects that reference the assembly

Typically, fields are declared using the `Private` keyword, making them available only to code within each instance of the class. Choosing any other option should be done with great care, because all the other options allow code outside the class to directly interact with the variable, meaning that the value could be changed and your code would never know that a change took place.

One common exception to making fields `Private` *is the use of the* `Protected` *keyword, as discussed in Chapter 6.*

Methods

Objects typically need to provide services (or functions) that can be called when working with the object. Using their own data or data passed as parameters to the method, they manipulate information to yield a result or to perform an action.

Methods declared as `Public`, `Friend`, or `Protected` in scope define the interface of the class. Methods that are `Private` in scope are available to the code only within the class itself and can be used to provide structure and organization to code. As discussed earlier, the actual code within each method is called implementation, while the declaration of the method itself is what defines the interface.

Methods are simply routines that are coded within the class to implement the services that you want to provide to the users of an object. Some methods return values or provide information to the calling code. These are called interrogative methods. Others, called imperative methods, just perform an action and return nothing to the calling code.

In Visual Basic, methods are implemented using Sub (for imperative methods) or Function (for interrogative methods) routines within the class module that defines the object. Sub routines may accept parameters, but they don't return any result value when they are complete. Function routines can also accept parameters, and they always generate a result value that can be used by the calling code.

A method declared with the Sub keyword is merely one that returns no value. Add the following code to the Person class:

```
Public Sub Walk()
  ' implementation code goes here
End Sub
```

The Walk method presumably contains some code that performs some useful work when called but has no result value to return when it is complete.

To use this method, you might write code such as:

```
Dim myPerson As New Person()
myPerson.Walk()
```

Once you've created an instance of the Person class, you can simply invoke the Walk method.

Methods That Return Values

If you have a method that does generate some value that should be returned, you need to use the Function keyword:

```
Public Function Age() As Integer
  Return CInt(DateDiff(DateInterval.Year, mBirthDate, Now()))
End Function
```

Notice that you need to indicate the datatype of the return value when you declare a Function. In this example, you are returning the calculated age as a result of the method. You can return any value of the appropriate datatype by using the Return keyword.

You can also return the value without using the Return keyword, by setting the value of the function name itself:

```
Public Function Age() As Integer
    Age = CInt(DateDiff(DateInterval.Year, mBirthDate, Now()))
End Function
```

This is functionally equivalent to the previous code. Either way, you can use this method with code similar to the following:

```
Dim myPerson As New Person()
Dim age As Integer

age = myPerson.Age()
```

The Age method returns an Integer data value that you can use in the program as required; in this case, you're just storing it in a variable.

Indicating Method Scope

Adding the appropriate keyword in front of the method declaration indicates the scope:

```
Public Sub Walk()
```

This indicates that Walk is a Public method and is, thus, available to code outside the class and even outside the current project. Any application that references the assembly can use this method. Being Public, this method becomes part of the object's interface.

Alternately, you might choose to restrict the method somewhat:

```
Friend Sub Walk()
```

By declaring the method with the Friend keyword, you are indicating that it should be part of the object's interface only for code inside the project; any other applications or projects that make use of the assembly will not be able to call the Walk method.

```
Private Function Age() As Integer
```

The Private keyword indicates that a method is only available to the code within our particular class. Private methods are very useful to help organize complex code within each class. Sometimes the methods will contain very lengthy and complex code. In order to make this code more understandable, you may choose to break it up into several smaller routines, having the main method call these routines in the proper order. Moreover, you can use these routines from several places within the class, so, by making them separate methods, you enable reuse of the code. These subroutines should never be called by code outside the object, so you make them Private.

Method Parameters

You will often want to pass information into a method as you call it. This information is provided via parameters to the method. For instance, in the Person class, perhaps you want the Walk method to track the distance the person walks over time. In such a case, the Walk method would need to know how far the person is to walk each time the method is called. Add the following code to the Person class:

```
Public Class Person
  Private mName As String
  Private mBirthDate As Date
  Private mTotalDistance As Integer

  Public Sub Walk(ByVal distance As Integer)
     mTotalDistance += distance
  End Sub

  Public Function Age() As Integer
    Return CInt(DateDiff(DateInterval.Year, mBirthDate, Now()))
  End Function
End Class
```

With this implementation, a Person object will sum up all of the distances walked over time. Each time the Walk method is called, the calling code must pass an Integer value, indicating the distance to be walked. Our code to call this method would be similar to the following code:

```
Dim myPerson As New Person()
myPerson.Walk(12)
```

The parameter is accepted using the ByVal keyword. This indicates that the parameter value is a copy of the original value. This is the default way by which Visual Basic accepts all parameters. Typically, this is desirable because it means that you can work with the parameter inside the code, changing its value with no risk of accidentally changing the original value back in the calling code.

If you do want to be able to change the value in the calling code, you can change the declaration to pass the parameter by reference by using the ByRef qualifier:

```
Public Sub Walk(ByRef distance As Integer)
```

In this case, you'll get a reference (or pointer) back to the original value rather than receiving a copy. This means that any change you make to the Distance parameter will be reflected back in the calling code, very similar to the way object references work, as discussed earlier in this chapter.

Using this technique can be dangerous, since it is not explicitly clear to the caller of the method that the value will change. Such unintended side effects can be hard to debug and should be avoided.

Properties

The .NET environment provides for a specialized type of method called a property. A property is a method specifically designed for setting and retrieving data values. For instance, you declared a variable in the Person class to contain a name, so the Person class may include code to allow that name to be set and retrieved. This can be done using regular methods:

```
Public Sub SetName(ByVal name As String)
  mName = name
End Sub

Public Function GetName() As String
  Return mName
End Function
```

Using methods like these, you write code to interact with the object, such as:

```
Dim myPerson As New Person()

myPerson.SetName("Jones")
MsgBox(myPerson.GetName())
```

While this is perfectly acceptable, it is not as nice as it could be with the use of a property. A Property style method consolidates the setting and retrieving of a value into a single structure, and also makes the code within the class smoother overall. You can rewrite these two methods into a single property. Add the following code to the Person class:

```
Public Property Name() As String
  Get
     Return mName
  End Get
  Set(ByVal Value As String)
    mName = Value
  End Set
End Property
```

By using a property method instead, you can make the client code much more readable:

```
Dim myPerson As New Person()

myPerson.Name = "Jones"
MsgBox(myPerson.Name)
```

The `Property` method is declared with both a scope and a datatype:

```
Public Property Name() As String
```

In this example, you've declared the property as `Public` in scope, but it can be declared using the same scope options as any other method — `Public`, `Friend`, `Private`, or `Protected`.

The return datatype of this property is `String`. A property can return virtually any datatype appropriate for the nature of the value. In this regard, a property is very similar to a method declared using the `Function` keyword.

Though a `Property` method is a single structure, it is divided into two parts: a getter and a setter. The getter is contained within a `Get . . . End Get` block and is responsible for returning the value of the property on demand:

```
Get
  Return mName
End Get
```

Though the code in this example is very simple, it could be more complex, perhaps calculating the value to be returned or applying other business logic to change the value as it is returned.

Likewise, the code to change the value is contained within a `Set . . . End Set` block:

```
Set(ByVal Value As String)
   mName = Value
End Set
```

The `Set` statement accepts a single parameter value that stores the new value. The code in the block can then use this value to set the property's value as appropriate. The datatype of this parameter must match the datatype of the property itself. Having the parameter declared in this manner allows you to change the name of the variable used for the parameter value if needed.

By default, the parameter is named `Value`. However, if you dislike the name `Value`, you can change the parameter name to something else, for example:

```
Set(ByVal NewName As String)
  mName = NewName

End Set
```

In many cases, you can apply business rules or other logic within this routine to ensure that the new value is appropriate before you actually update the data within the object.

It is also possible to restrict the scope of either the `Get` or `Set` block to be more narrow than the scope of the property itself. For instance, you may want to allow any code to retrieve the property value, but only allow other code in your project to alter the value. In this case, you can restrict the scope of the `Set` block to `Friend`, while the `Property` itself is scoped as `Public`:

```
Public Property Name() As String
  Get
    Return mName
  End Get
  Friend Set(ByVal Value As String)
    mName = Value
  End Set
End Property
```

The new scope must be more restrictive than the scope of the `Property` itself. Also, either the `Get` or `Set` block can be restricted, not both. The one you don't restrict uses the scope of the `Property` method.

Parameterized Properties

The `Name` property you created is an example of a single-value property. You can also create property arrays or parameterized properties. These properties reflect a range, or array, of values. As an example, a person will often have several phone numbers. You might implement a `PhoneNumber` property as a parameterized property, storing not only phone numbers, but also a description of each number. To retrieve a specific phone number you'd write code such as:

```
Dim myPerson As New Person()
Dim homePhone As String

homePhone = myPerson.Phone("home")
```

Or, to add or change a specific phone number, you'd write the following code:

```
myPerson.Phone("work") = "555-9876"
```

Not only are you retrieving and updating a phone number property, but you're also updating a specific phone number. This implies a couple of things. First, you're no longer able to use a simple variable to hold the phone number, since you are now storing a list of numbers and their associated names. Second, you've effectively added a parameter to your property. You're actually passing the name of the phone number as a parameter on each property call.

To store the list of phone numbers, you can use the Hashtable class. The Hashtable is very similar to the standard VB Collection object, but it is more powerful — allowing you to test for the existence of a specific element. Add the following declaration to the Person class:

```
Public Class Person
  Private mName As String
  Private mBirthDate As Date
  Private mTotalDistance As Integer

  Private mPhones As New Hashtable
```

You can implement the Phone property by adding the following code to the Person class:

```
Public Property Phone(ByVal location As String) As String
  Get
    Return CStr(mPhones.Item(Location))
  End Get
  Set(ByVal Value As String)
    If mPhones.ContainsKey(location) Then
      mPhones.Item(location) = Value
    Else
      mPhones.Add(location, Value)
    End If
  End Set
End Property
```

The declaration of the Property method itself is a bit different from what you've seen:

```
Public Property Phone(ByVal location As String) As String
```

In particular, you've added a parameter, location, to the property itself. This parameter will act as the index into the list of phone numbers and must be provided both when setting or retrieving phone number values.

Since the location parameter is declared at the Property level, it is available to all code within the property, including both the Get and Set blocks.

Within your Get block, you use the location parameter to select the appropriate phone number to return from the Hashtable:

```
Get
  Return mPhones.Item(location)
End Get
```

With this code, if there is no value stored matching the location, you'll get a trappable runtime error.

Similarly, in the Set block, you use the location to update or add the appropriate element in the Hashtable. In this case, you're using the ContainsKey method of Hashtable to determine whether the phone number already exists in the list. If it does, you'll simply update the value in the list; otherwise, you'll add a new element to the list for the value:

```
Set(ByVal Value As String)
  If mPhones.ContainsKey(location) Then
    mPhones.Item(location) = Value
  Else
    mPhones.Add(location, Value)
  End If
End Set
```

In this way, you're able to add or update a specific phone number entry based on the parameter passed by the calling code.

Read-Only Properties

There are times when you may want a property to be read-only, so that it can't be changed. In the `Person` class, for instance, you may have a read-write property for `BirthDate`, but just a read-only property for `Age`. In such a case, the `BirthDate` property is a normal property, as follows:

```
Public Property BirthDate() As Date
  Get
    Return mBirthDate
  End Get
  Set(ByVal Value As Date)
   mBirthDate = Value
  End Set
End Property
```

The `Age` value, on the other hand, is a derived value based on `BirthDate`. This is not a value that should ever be directly altered and, thus, is a perfect candidate for read-only status.

You already have an `Age` method implemented as a `Function`. Remove that code from the `Person` class, because you'll be replacing it with a `Property` routine instead.

The difference between a `Function` routine and a `ReadOnly Property` is quite subtle. Both return a value to the calling code and, either way, the object is running a subroutine defined by the class module to return the value.

The difference is less a programmatic one than a design choice. You could create all your objects without any `Property` routines at all, just using methods for all interactions with the objects. However, `Property` routines are obviously attributes of an object, while a `Function` might be an attribute or a method. By carefully implementing all attributes as `ReadOnly Property` routines, and any interrogative methods as `Function` routines, you will create more readable and understandable code.

To make a property read-only, use the `ReadOnly` keyword and only implement the `Get` block:

```
Public ReadOnly Property Age() As Integer
  Get
    Return CInt(DateDiff(DateInterval.Year, mdtBirthDate, Now()))
  End Get
End Property
```

Since the property is read-only, you'll get a syntax error if you attempt to implement a `Set` block.

Write-Only Properties

As with read-only properties, there are times when a property should be write-only, where the value can be changed, but not retrieved.

Many people have allergies, so perhaps the `Person` object should have some understanding of the ambient allergens in the area. This is not a property that should be read from the `Person` object, since allergens come from the environment rather than from the person, but it is data that the `Person` object needs in order to function properly. Add the following variable declaration to the class:

```
Public Class Person
  Private mstrName As String
  Private mdtBirthDate As Date
  Private mintTotalDistance As Integer
  Private colPhones As New Hashtable()
  Private mAllergens As Integer
```

you can implement an `AmbientAllergens` property as follows:

```
Public WriteOnly Property AmbientAllergens() As Integer
  Set(ByVal Value As Integer)
    mAllergens = Value
  End Set
End Property
```

To create a write-only property, use the `WriteOnly` keyword and only implement a `Set` block in the code. Since the property is write-only, you'll get a syntax error if you attempt to implement a `Get` block.

The Default Property

Objects can implement a default property if desired. A default property can be used to simplify the use of an object at times, by making it appear as if the object has a native value. A good example of this behavior is the `Collection` object, which has a default property called `Item` that returns the value of a specific item, allowing you to write code similar to:

```
Dim mData As New HashTable()

Return mData(index)
```

Default properties must be parameterized properties. A property without a parameter cannot be marked as the default. This is a change from previous versions of Visual Basic, where any property could be marked as the default.

Our `Person` class has a parameterized property — the `Phone` property you built earlier. You can make this the default property by using the `Default` keyword:

```
Default Public Property Phone(ByVal location As String) As String
  Get
    Return CStr(mPhones.Item(location))
  End Get
  Set(ByVal Value As String)
```

```
      If mPhones.ContainsKey(location) Then
        mPhones.Item(location) = Value
      Else
        mPhones.Add(location, Value)
      End If
    End Set
  End Property
```

Prior to this change, you would have needed code such as the following to use the `Phone` property:

```
Dim myPerson As New Person()

MyPerson.Phone("home") = "555-1234"
```

But now, with the property marked as `Default`, you can simplify the code:

```
myPerson("home") = "555-1234"
```

By picking appropriate default properties, you can potentially make the use of objects more intuitive.

Events

Both methods and properties allow you to write code that interacts with your objects by invoking specific functionality as needed. It is often useful for objects to provide notification as certain activities occur during processing. You see examples of this all the time with controls, where a button indicates that it was clicked via a `Click` event, or a text box indicates that its contents have been changed via the `TextChanged` event.

Objects can raise events of their own, providing a powerful and easily implemented mechanism by which objects can notify client code of important activities or events. In Visual Basic, events are provided using the standard .NET mechanism of delegates. Before discussing delegates, let's explore how to work with events in Visual Basic.

Handling Events

We are all used to seeing code in a form to handle the `Click` event of a button, such as the following code:

```
Private Sub Button1_Click(ByVal sender As System.Object, _
  ByVal e As System.EventArgs) Handles Button1.Click

End Sub
```

Typically, we write our code in this type of routine without paying a lot of attention to the code created by the VS.NET IDE. However, let's take a second look at that code, since there are a couple of important things to note here.

First, notice the use of the `Handles` keyword. This keyword specifically indicates that this method will be handling the `Click` event from the `Button1` control. Of course, a control is just an object, so what is indicated here is that this method will be handling the `Click` event from the `Button1` object.

Also notice that the method accepts two parameters. The `Button` control class defines these parameters. It turns out that any method that accepts two parameters with these datatypes can be used to handle the `Click` event. For instance, you could create a new method to handle the event:

```
Private Sub MyClickMethod(ByVal s As System.Object, _
    ByVal args As System.EventArgs) Handles Button1.Click

End Sub
```

Even though you've changed the method name, and the names of the parameters, you are still accepting parameters of the same datatypes, and you still have the `Handles` clause to indicate that this method will handle the event.

Handling Multiple Events

The `Handles` keyword offers even more flexibility. Not only can the method name be anything you choose, but also a single method can handle multiple events if you desire. Again, the only requirement is that the method and all the events being raised must have the same parameter list.

This explains why all the standard events raised by the .NET system class library have exactly two parameters — the sender and an `EventArgs` *object. Being so generic makes it possible to write very generic and powerful event handlers than can accept virtually any event raised by the class library.*

One common scenario where this is useful is when you have multiple instances of an object that raises events, such as two buttons on a form:

```
Private Sub MyClickMethod(ByVal sender As System.Object, _
    ByVal e As System.EventArgs) _
    Handles Button1.Click, Button2.Click

End Sub
```

Notice that the `Handles` clause has been modified so that it has a comma-separated list of events to handle. Either event will cause the method to run, providing a central location in which to handle these events.

The WithEvents Keyword

The `WithEvents` keyword tells Visual Basic that you want to handle any events raised by the object within the code. For example:

```
Friend WithEvents Button1 As System.Windows.Forms.Button
```

The `WithEvents` keyword makes any events from an object available for use, while the `Handles` keyword is used to link specific events to the methods so that you can receive and handle them. This is true not only for controls on forms but also for any objects that you create.

The `WithEvents` keyword cannot be used to declare a variable of a type that doesn't raise events. In other words, if the `Button` class didn't contain code to raise events, you'd get a syntax error when you attempted to declare the variable using the `WithEvents` keyword.

The compiler can tell which classes will and won't raise events by examining their interface. Any class that will be raising an event will have that event declared as part of its interface. In Visual Basic, this means that you will have used the Event keyword to declare at least one event as part of the interface for the class.

Raising Events

Our objects can raise events just like a control, and the code using the object can receive these events by using the WithEvents and Handles keywords. Before you can raise an event from your object, however, you need to declare the event within the class by using the Event keyword.

In the Person class, for instance, you may want to raise an event any time the Walk method is called. If you call this event Walked, you can add the following declaration to the Person class:

```
Public Class Person
  Private mstrName As String
  Private mdtBirthDate As Date
  Private mintTotalDistance As Integer
  Private colPhones As New Hashtable()
  Private mintAllergens As Integer

  Public Event Walked()
```

Events can also have parameters, values that are provided to the code receiving the event. A typical button's Click event receives two parameters, for instance. In the Walked method, perhaps you want to also indicate the distance that was walked. You can do this by changing the event declaration:

```
  Public Event Walked(ByVal distance As Integer)
```

Now that the event is declared, you can raise that event within the code where appropriate. In this case, you'll raise it within the Walk method. So, anytime that a Person object is instructed to walk, it will fire an event indicating the distance walked. Make the following change to the Walk method:

```
Public Sub Walk(ByVal distance As Integer)
  mTotalDistance += distance
  RaiseEvent Walked(distance)
End Sub
```

The RaiseEvent keyword is used to raise the actual event. Since the event requires a parameter, that value is passed within parentheses and will be delivered to any recipient that handles the event.

In fact, the RaiseEvent statement will cause the event to be delivered to all code that has the object declared using the WithEvents keyword with a Handles clause for this event, or any code that has used the AddHandler method.

If more than one method will be receiving the event, the event will be delivered to each recipient one at a time. By default, the order of delivery is not defined—meaning that you can't predict the order in which the recipients will receive the event—but the event will be delivered to all handlers. Note that this is a serial, synchronous process. The event is delivered to one handler at a time, and it is not delivered to the next handler until the current handler is complete. Once you call the RaiseEvent method, the event will be delivered to all listeners one after another until it is complete; there is no way for you to intervene and stop the process in the middle.

Declaring and Raising Custom Events

As just noted, by default, you have no control over how events are raised. You can overcome this limitation by using a more explicit form of declaration for the event itself. Rather than using the simple Event keyword, you can declare a custom event. This is for more advanced scenarios, since it requires that you provide the implementation for the event itself.

Later, this chapter will discuss the concept of delegates in detail, but it is necessary to cover them briefly here in order to declare a custom event. A delegate is a definition of a method signature. When you declare an event, Visual Basic defines a delegate for the event behind the scenes based on the signature of the event. The `Walked` event, for instance, has a delegate like this:

```
Public Delegate Sub WalkedEventHandler(ByVal distance As Integer)
```

Notice how this code declares a "method" that accepts an `Integer` and has no return value. This is exactly what you defined for the event. Normally, you don't write this bit of code, because Visual Basic does it automatically. However, if you are to declare a custom event, you need to manually declare the event delegate.

You also need to declare a variable within the class where you can keep track of any code that is listening for, or handling, the event. It turns out that you can tap into the prebuilt functionality of delegates for this purpose. By declaring the `WalkedEventHandler` delegate, you have defined a datatype that automatically tracks event handlers, so you can declare the variable like this:

```
Private mWalkedHandlers As WalkedEventHandler
```

Then you can use this variable to store and raise the event within the custom event declaration:

```
Public Custom Event Walked As WalkedEventHandler
  AddHandler(ByVal value As WalkedEventHandler)
    mWalkedHandlers = _
      CType([Delegate].Combine(mWalkedHandlers, value), WalkedEventHandler)
  End AddHandler
  RemoveHandler(ByVal value As WalkedEventHandler)
    mWalkedHandlers = _
      CType([Delegate].Remove(mWalkedHandlers, value), WalkedEventHandler)
  End RemoveHandler
  RaiseEvent(ByVal distance As Integer)
    If mWalkedHandlers IsNot Nothing Then
      mWalkedHandlers.Invoke(distance)
    End If
  End RaiseEvent
End Event
```

In this case, you've used the `Custom Event` key phrase rather than just `Event` to declare the event. A `Custom Event` declaration is a block structure with three sub-blocks: `AddHandler`, `RemoveHandler`, and `RaiseEvent`.

The `AddHandler` block is called any time a new handler wants to receive the event. The parameter passed to this block is a reference to the method that will be handling the event. It is up to you to store the reference to that method, which you can do however you choose. In this implementation, you're storing it within the delegate variable just like the default implementation provided by Visual Basic.

The `RemoveHandler` block is called any time a handler wants to stop receiving our event. The parameter passed to this block is a reference to the method that was handling the event. It is up to you to remove the reference to the method, which you can do however you choose. In this implementation, you're replicating the default behavior by having the delegate variable remove the element.

Finally, the `RaiseEvent` block is called any time the event is raised. Typically, it is invoked when code within the class uses the `RaiseEvent` statement. The parameters passed to this block must match the parameters declared by the delegate for the event. It is up to you to go through the list of methods that are handling the event and to call each of those methods. In the example shown here, you're allowing the delegate variable to do that for you, which is the same behavior you get by default with a normal event.

The value of this syntax is that you could opt to store the list of handler methods in a different type of data structure, such as a `Hashtable` or collection. You could then invoke them asynchronously, or in a specific order or based on some other behavior required by the application.

Receiving Events with WithEvents

Now that you've implemented an event within the `Person` class, you can write client code to declare an object using the `WithEvents` keyword. For instance, in the project's `Form1` code module, you can write the following code:

```
Public Class Form1
  Inherits System.Windows.Forms.Form

  Private WithEvents mPerson As Person
```

By declaring the variable `WithEvents`, you are indicating that you want to receive any events raised by this object.

You can also choose to declare the variable without the `WithEvents` keyword, though, in that case, you would not receive events from the object as described here. Instead, you would use the `AddHandler` method, which is discussed after the use of `WithEvents`.

You can then create an instance of the object, as the form is created, by adding the following code:

```
Private Sub Form1_Load(ByVal sender As System.Object, _
    ByVal e As System.EventArgs) Handles MyBase.Load

  mPerson = New Person()

End Sub
```

At this point, you've declared the object variable using `WithEvents` and have created an instance of the `Person` class, so you actually have an object with which to work. You can now proceed to write a method to handle the `Walked` event from the object by adding the following code to the form. You can name this method anything you like; it is the `Handles` clause that is important because it links the event from the object directly to this method, so it is invoked when the event is raised:

```
Private Sub OnWalk(ByVal distance As Integer) Handles mPerson.Walked
  MsgBox("Person walked " & distance)
End Sub
```

You're using the `Handles` keyword to indicate which event should be handled by this method. You're also receiving an `Integer` parameter. If the parameter list of the method doesn't match the list for the event, you'll get a compiler error indicating the mismatch.

Finally, you need to call the `Walk` method on the `Person` object. Add a button to the form and write the following code for its `Click` event:

```
Private Sub Button1_Click(ByVal sender As System.Object, _
    ByVal e As System.EventArgs) Handles button1.Click

  mPerson.Walk(42)

End Sub
```

When the button is clicked, you'll simply call the `Walk` method, passing an `Integer` value. This will cause the code in your class to be run, including the `RaiseEvent` statement. The result will be an event firing back into the form, since you declared the `mPerson` variable using the `WithEvents` keyword. The `OnWalk` method will be run to handle the event, since it has the `Handles` clause linking it to the event.

The diagram in Figure 4-3 illustrates the flow of control.

The diagram illustrates how the code in the button's click event calls the `Walk` method, causing it to add to the total distance walked and then to raise its event. The `RaiseEvent` causes the `OnWalk` method in the form to be invoked and, once it is done, control returns to the `Walk` method in the object. Since you have no code in the `Walk` method after you call `RaiseEvent`, the control returns to the `Click` event back in the form, and then you're all done.

Many people have the misconception that events use multiple threads to do their work. This is not the case. Only one thread is involved in this process. Raising an event is much like making a method call, in that the existing thread is used to run the code in the event handler. This means that the application's processing is suspended until the event processing is complete.

Receiving Events with AddHandler

Now that you've seen how to receive and handle events using the `WithEvents` and `Handles` keywords, let's take a look at an alternative approach. You can use the `AddHandler` method to dynamically add event handlers through your code and `RemoveHandler` to dynamically remove them.

`WithEvents` and the `Handles` clause require that you declare both the object variable and event handler as you build the code, effectively creating a linkage that is compiled right into the code. `AddHandler`, on the other hand, creates this linkage at runtime, which can provide you with more flexibility. However, before getting too deeply into that, let's see how `AddHandler` works.

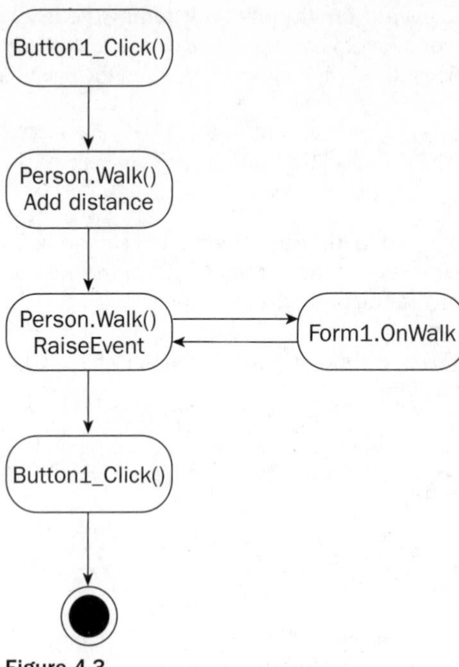

Figure 4-3

In `Form1`, you can change the way the code interacts with the `Person` object, first, by eliminating the `WithEvents` keyword:

```
Private mPerson As Person
```

and then by also eliminating the `Handles` clause:

```
Private Sub OnWalk(ByVal distance As Integer)
  MsgBox("Person walked " & distance)
End Sub
```

With these changes, you've eliminated all event handling for the object, and the form will no longer receive the event, even though the `Person` object raises it.

Now, you can change the code to dynamically add an event handler at runtime by using the `AddHandler` method. This method simply links an object's event to a method that should be called to handle that event. Any time after you've created the object, you can call `AddHandler` to set up the linkage:

```
Private Sub Form1_Load(ByVal sender As System.Object, _
    ByVal e As System.EventArgs) Handles MyBase.Load
   mPerson = New Person()
   AddHandler mPerson.Walked, AddressOf OnWalk
 End Sub
```

This single line of code does the same thing as the earlier use of `WithEvents` and the `Handles` clause, causing the `OnWalk` method to be invoked when the `Walked` event is raised from the `Person` object.

However, this linkage is done at runtime, so you have more control over the process than you would have otherwise. For instance, you could have extra code to decide which event handler to link up. Suppose that you have another possible method to handle the event in the case that a message box is not desirable. Add this code to `Form1`:

```
Private Sub LogOnWalk(ByVal distance As Integer)
  System.Diagnostics.Debug.WriteLine("Person walked " & distance)
End Sub
```

Rather than popping up a message box, this version of the handler logs the event to the Output window in the IDE.

Now, you can enhance the `AddHandler` code to decide which handler should be used dynamically at runtime:

```
Private Sub Form1_Load(ByVal sender As System.Object, _
    ByVal e As System.EventArgs) Handles MyBase.Load
  mPerson = New Person()
  If Microsoft.VisualBasic.Command = "nodisplay" Then
    AddHandler mPerson.Walked, AddressOf LogOnWalk
  Else
    AddHandler mPerson.Walked, AddressOf OnWalk
  End If
End Sub
```

If the word `nodisplay` is on the command line when the application is run, the new version of the event handler will be used; otherwise, you'll continue to use the message box handler.

The counterpart to `AddHandler` is `RemoveHandler`. `RemoveHandler` is used to detach an event handler from an event. One example of when this is useful is if you ever want to set the `mPerson` variable to `Nothing` or to a new `Person` object. The existing `Person` object has its events attached to handlers, and before you get rid of the reference to the object, you must release those references:

```
If Microsoft.VisualBasic.Command = "nodisplay" Then
  RemoveHandler mPerson.Walked, AddressOf LogOnWalk
Else
  RemoveHandler mPerson.Walked, AddressOf OnWalk
End If
mPerson = New Person
```

If you don't detach the event handlers, the old `Person` object will remain in memory because each event handler will still maintain a reference to the object even after `mPerson` no longer points to the object.

This illustrates one key reason why the `WithEvents` keyword and `Handles` clause are preferable in most cases. `AddHandler` and `RemoveHandler` must be used in pairs, and failure to do so can cause memory leaks in the application, while the `WithEvents` keyword handles these details for you automatically.

Constructor Methods

In Visual Basic, classes can implement a special method that is always invoked as an object is being created. This method is called the constructor, and it is always named New.

The constructor method is an ideal location for such initialization code, since it is always run before any other methods are ever invoked, and it is only ever run once for an object. Of course, you can create many objects based on a class, and the constructor method will be run for each object that is created.

You can implement a constructor in your classes as well, using it to initialize objects as needed. This is as easy as implementing a Public method named New. Add the following code to the Person class:

```
Public Sub New()
  Phone("home") = "555-1234"
  Phone("work") = "555-5678"
End Sub
```

In this example, you're simply using the constructor method to initialize the home and work phone numbers for any new Person object that is created.

Parameterized Constructors

You can also use constructors to allow parameters to be passed to the object as it is being created. This is done by simply adding parameters to the New method. For example, you can change the Person class as follows:

```
Public Sub New(ByVal name As String, ByVal birthDate As Date)
  mName = name
  mBirthDate = birthDate

  Phone("home") = "555-1234"
  Phone("work") = "555-5678"
End Sub
```

With this change, anytime a Person object is created, you'll be provided with values for both the name and birth date. This, however, changes how you can create a new Person object. Where you used to have code such as:

```
Dim myPerson As New Person()
```

now you will have code such as:

```
Dim myPerson As New Person("Peter", "1/1/1960")
```

In fact, since the constructor expects these values, they are mandatory — any code wishing to create an instance of the Person class must provide these values. Fortunately, there are alternatives in the form of optional parameters and method overloading (which allows you to create multiple versions of the same method, each accepting a different parameter list). These topics will be discussed later in the chapter.

Termination and Cleanup

In the .NET environment, an object is destroyed and the memory and resources it consumes are reclaimed when there are no references remaining for the object.

As discussed earlier in the chapter, when you are using objects, the variables actually hold a reference or pointer to the object itself. If you have code such as:

```
Dim myPerson As New Person()
```

you know that the `myPerson` variable is just a reference to the `Person` object you created. If you also have code like this:

```
Dim anotherPerson As Person
anotherPerson = myPerson
```

you know that the `anotherPerson` variable is also a reference to the same object. This means that this specific `Person` object is being referenced by two variables.

When there are no variables left to reference an object, it can be terminated by the .NET runtime environment. In particular, it is terminated and reclaimed by a mechanism called garbage collection, which is covered in detail in Chapter 3.

Unlike COM (and thus VB6), the .NET runtime does not use reference counting to determine when an object should be terminated. Instead, it uses a scheme known as garbage collection to terminate objects. This means that, in Visual Basic, you do not have deterministic finalization, so it is not possible to predict exactly when an object will be destroyed.

Let's review how you can eliminate references to an object. You can explicitly remove a reference by setting the variable equal to `Nothing`, with the following code:

```
myPerson = Nothing
```

You can also remove a reference to an object by changing the variable to reference a different object. Since a variable can only point to one object at a time, it follows naturally that changing a variable to point at another object must cause it to no longer point to the first one. This means that you can have code such as in the following:

```
myPerson = New Person()
```

This causes the variable to point to a brand-new object, thus releasing this reference to the prior object.

These are examples of explicit dereferencing. Visual Basic also provides facilities for implicit dereferencing of objects when a variable goes out of scope. For instance, if you have a variable declared within a method, when that method completes, the variable will be automatically destroyed, thus dereferencing any object to which it may have pointed. In fact, anytime a variable referencing an object goes out of scope, the reference to that object is automatically eliminated. This is illustrated by the following code:

```
Private Sub DoSomething()
  Dim myPerson As Person

  myPerson = New Person()
End Sub
```

Even though you didn't explicitly set the value of `myPerson` to `Nothing`, you know that the `myPerson` variable will be destroyed when the method is complete, since it will fall out of scope. This process implicitly removes the reference to the `Person` object created within the routine.

Of course, another scenario in which objects become dereferenced is when the application itself completes and is terminated. At that point, all variables are destroyed, so, by definition, all object references go away as well.

Advanced Concepts

So far, you've seen how to work with objects, how to create classes with methods, properties, and events, and how to use constructors. You've also learned how objects are destroyed within the .NET environment and how you can hook into that process to do any cleanup required by the objects.

Now let's move on to discuss some more complex topics and variations on what has been discussed so far. First, you'll cover some advanced variations of the methods you can implement in classes, including an exploration of the underlying technology behind events.

From there, you'll move on to delegates, the difference between components and classes, and .NET attributes as they pertain to classes and methods.

Overloading Methods

Methods often accept parameter values. The `Person` object's `Walk` method, for instance, accepts an `Integer` parameter:

```
Public Sub Walk(ByVal distance As Integer)
  mTotalDistance += distance
  RaiseEvent Walked(distance)
End Sub
```

Sometimes there is no need for the parameter. To address this issue, you can use the `Optional` keyword to make the parameter optional:

```
Public Sub Walk(Optional ByVal distance As Integer = 0)
  mTotalDistance += distance
  RaiseEvent Walked(distance)
End Sub
```

This doesn't provide you with a lot of flexibility, however, since the optional parameter or parameters must always be the last ones in the list. In addition, all this allows you to do is choose to pass or not to pass the parameter. Suppose that you want to do something fancier, such as allow different datatypes, or even entirely different lists of parameters.

Note that use of the `Optional` keyword makes the code harder to consume from C# or other .NET languages. If you are only working in Visual Basic, this may be a nonissue, but if you are working in a multilanguage environment, it is best to avoid use of the `Optional` keyword.

Method overloading provides exactly those capabilities. By overloading methods, you can create several methods of the same name, with each one accepting a different set of parameters or parameters of different datatypes.

As a simple example, instead of using the `Optional` keyword in the `Walk` method, you could use overloading. You'll keep the original `Walk` method, but you'll also add another `Walk` method that accepts a different parameter list. Change the code in the `Person` class back to:

```
Public Sub Walk(ByVal distance As Integer)
  mTotalDistance += distance
  RaiseEvent Walked(distance)
End Sub
```

Then you can create another method with the same name, but with a different parameter list (in this case, no parameters). Add this code to the class, without removing or changing the existing `Walk` method:

```
Public Sub Walk()
  RaiseEvent Walked(0)
End Sub
```

At this point, you have two `Walk` methods. The only way to tell them apart is by the list of parameters each accepts, the first requiring a single `Integer` parameter, the second having no parameter.

There is an `Overloads` keyword as well. This keyword is not needed for simple overloading of methods as described here, but it is required when combining overloading and inheritance. This is discussed in Chapter 6.

Now, you have the option of calling the `Walk` method in a couple of different ways. You can call it with a parameter:

```
objPerson.Walk(42)
```

or without a parameter:

```
objPerson.Walk()
```

You can have any number of `Walk` methods in the class as long as each individual `Walk` method has a different method signature.

Method Signatures

All methods have a signature, which is defined by the method name and the datatypes of its parameters.

```
Public Function CalculateValue() As Integer

End Sub
```

In this example, the signature is `i()`. The letter *i* is often used to indicate a method or function. It is appropriate here, because you don't care about the name of the function; only its parameter list is important.

If you add a parameter to the method, the signature will change. For instance, you could change the method to accept a `Double`:

```
Public Function CalculateValue(ByVal value As Double) As Integer
```

Then the signature of the method is `i(Double)`.

Notice that in Visual Basic the return value is not part of the signature. You can't overload a `Function` routine by just having its return value's datatype vary. It is the datatypes in the parameter list that must vary to utilize overloading.

Also, note that the name of the parameter is totally immaterial; only the datatype is important. This means that the following methods have identical signatures:

```
Public Sub DoWork(ByVal x As Integer, ByVal y As Integer)

Public Sub DoWork(ByVal value1 As Integer, ByVal value2 As Integer)
```

In both cases, the signature is `f(Integer, Integer)`.

The datatypes of the parameters define the method signature, but whether the parameters are passed `ByVal` or `ByRef` does not. Changing a parameter from `ByVal` to `ByRef` will not change the method signature.

Combining Overloading and Optional Parameters

Overloading is more flexible than using optional parameters, but optional parameters have the advantage that they can be used to provide default values as well as making a parameter optional.

You can combine the two concepts: overloading a method and also having one or more of those methods utilize optional parameters. Obviously, this sort of thing can get very confusing if overused, since you're employing two types of method "overloading" at the same time.

The `Optional` keyword causes a single method to effectively have two signatures. This means that a method declared as:

```
Public Sub DoWork(ByVal x As Integer, Optional ByVal y As Integer = 0)
```

has two signatures at once: `f(Integer, Integer)` and *f*`(Integer)`.

Because of this, when you use overloading along with optional parameters, the other overloaded methods cannot match either of these two signatures. However, as long as other methods don't match either signature, you can use overloading as discussed earlier. For instance, you could implement methods with the following different signatures:

```
Public Sub DoWork(ByVal x As Integer, _
      Optional ByVal y As Integer = 0)
```

and

```
Public Sub DoWork(ByVal data As String)
```

since there are no conflicting method signatures. In fact, with these two methods, you've really created three signatures:

- f(Integer, Integer)
- f(Integer)
- f(String)

The IntelliSense built into the VS.NET IDE will show that you have two overloaded methods, one of which has an optional parameter. This is different from creating three different overloaded methods to match these three signatures, in which case the IntelliSense would list three variations on the method from which you could choose.

Overloading Constructor Methods

In many cases, you may want the constructor to accept parameter values for initializing new objects, but you also want to have the ability to create objects without providing those values. This is possible through method overloading, which is discussed later, or through the use of optional parameters.

Optional parameters on a constructor method follow the same rules as optional parameters for any other `Sub` routine; they must be the last parameters in the parameter list, and you must provide default values for the optional parameters.

For instance, you can change the `Person` class as shown here:

```
Public Sub New(Optional ByVal name As String = "", _
    Optional ByVal birthDate As Date = #1/1/1900#)
  mName = name
  mBirthDate = birthDate

  Phone("home") = "555-1234"
  Phone("work") = "555-5678"
End Sub
```

Here, you've changed both the `Name` and `BirthDate` parameters to be optional, and you are providing default values for both of them. Now, you have the option of creating a new `Person` object with or without the parameter values:

```
Dim myPerson As New Person("Peter", "1/1/1960")
```

or

```
Dim myPerson As New Person()
```

If you don't provide the parameter values, then the default values of an empty `String` and `1/1/1900` will be used and the code will work just fine.

Overloading the Constructor Method

You can combine the concept of a constructor method with method overloading to allow for different ways of creating instances of the class. This can be a very powerful combination, because it allows a great deal of flexibility in object creation.

You've already explored how to use optional parameters in the constructor. Now let's change the implementation in the `Person` class to make use of overloading instead. Change the existing `New` method as follows:

```
Public Sub New(ByVal name As String, ByVal birthDate As Date)
    mName = name
    mBirthDate = birthDate
    Phone("home") = "555-1234"
    Phone("work") = "555-5678"
  End Sub
```

With this change, you require the two parameter values to be supplied.

Now add that second implementation as shown here:

```
Public Sub New()
  Phone("home") = "555-1234"
  Phone("work") = "555-5678"
End Sub
```

This second implementation accepts no parameters, meaning that you can now create `Person` objects in two different ways—either with no parameters or by passing the name and birth date:

```
Dim myPerson As New Person()
```

or

```
Dim myPerson As New Person("Fred", "1/11/60")
```

This type of capability is very powerful, because it allows you to define the various ways in which applications can create objects. In fact, the VS.NET IDE takes this into account, so, when you are typing the code to create an object, the IntelliSense tooltip will display the overloaded variations on the method, providing a level of automatic documentation for the class.

Shared Methods, Variables, and Events

So far, all of the methods you've built or used have been instance methods, methods that require us to have an actual instance of the class before they can be called. These methods have used instance variables or member variables to do their work, which means that they have been working with a set of data that is unique to each individual object.

Visual Basic allows us to create variables and methods that belong to the class rather than to any specific object. Another way to say this is that these variables and methods belong to all objects of a given class and are shared across all the instances of the class.

You can use the `Shared` keyword to indicate which variables and methods belong to the class rather than to specific objects. For instance, you may be interested in knowing the total number of `Person` objects created as the application is running—kind of a statistical counter.

Shared Variables

Since regular variables are unique to each individual `Person` object, they don't allow you to easily track the total number of `Person` objects ever created. However, if you had a variable that had a common value across all instances of the `Person` class, you could use that as a counter. Add the following variable declaration to the `Person` class:

```
Public Class Person
  Implements IDisposable

  Private Shared mCounter As Integer
```

By using the `Shared` keyword, you are indicating that this variable's value should be shared across all `Person` objects within our application. This means that if one `Person` object makes the value be `42`, all other `Person` objects will see the value as `42`: It is a shared piece of data.

You can now use this variable within the code. For instance, you can add code to the constructor method, `New`, to increment the variable so that it acts as a counter—adding 1 each time a new `Person` object is created. Change the `New` methods as shown here:

```
Public Sub New()
  Phone("home") = "555-1234"
  Phone("work") = "555-5678"
  mCounter += 1
End Sub

Public Sub New(ByVal name As String, ByVal birthDate As Date)
  mName = name
  mBirthDate = birthDate

  Phone("home") = "555-1234"
  Phone("work") = "555-5678"
  mCounter += 1
End Sub
```

The `mCounter` variable will now maintain a value indicating the total number of `Person` objects created during the life of the application. You may want to add a property routine to allow access to this value by writing the following code:

```
Public ReadOnly Property PersonCount() As Integer
  Get
    Return mCounter
  End Get
End Property
```

Notice that you're creating a regular property that returns the value of a shared variable. This is perfectly acceptable. As you'll see shortly, you could also choose to create a shared property to return the value.

Now, you could write code to use the class as follows:

```
Dim myPerson As Person

myPerson = New Person()
myPerson = New Person()
myPerson = New Person()

MsgBox(myPerson.PersonCount)
```

The resulting display would show `3`, since you've created three instances of the `Person` class.

Shared Methods

You can share not only variables across all instances of a class but also methods. Whereas a regular method or property belongs to each specific object, a shared method or property is common across all instances of the class. There are a couple of ramifications to this approach.

First, since shared methods don't belong to any specific object, they can't access any instance variables from any objects. The only variables available for use within a shared method are shared variables, parameters passed into the method, or variables declared locally within the method itself. If you attempt to access an instance variable within a shared method, you'll get a compiler error.

Also, since shared methods are actually part of the class rather than any object, you can write code to call them directly from the class without having to create an instance of the class first.

For instance, a regular instance method is invoked from an object:

```
Dim myPerson As New Person()

myPerson.Walk(42)
```

but a shared method can be invoked directly from the class itself:

```
Person.SharedMethod()
```

This saves the effort of creating an object just to invoke a method and can be very appropriate for methods that act on shared variables, or methods that act only on values passed in via parameters. You can also invoke a shared method from an object just like a regular method. Shared methods are flexible in that they can be called with or without creating an instance of the class first.

To create a shared method, you again use the `Shared` keyword. For instance, the `PersonCount` property created earlier could easily be changed to become a shared method instead:

```
Public Shared ReadOnly Property PersonCount() As Integer
  Get
    Return mCounter
  End Get
End Property
```

Since this property returns the value of a shared variable, it is perfectly acceptable for it to be implemented as a shared method. With this change, you can now find out how many `Person` objects have ever been created without having to actually create a `Person` object first:

```
MsgBox(CStr(Person.PersonCount))
```

As another example, in the `Person` class, you could create a method that compares the ages of two people. Add a shared method with the following code:

```
Public Shared Function CompareAge(ByVal person1 As Person, _
    ByVal person2 As Person) As Boolean

  Return person1.Age > person2.Age
End Function
```

This method simply accepts two parameters — each a `Person` — and returns `True` if the first is older than the second. The use of the `Shared` keyword indicates that this method doesn't require a specific instance of the `Person` class for you to use it.

Within this code, you are invoking the `Age` property on two separate objects, the objects passed as parameters to the method. It is important to recognize that you're not directly using any instance variables within the method, rather you are accepting two objects as parameters and are invoking methods on those objects. To use this method, you can call it directly from the class:

```
If Person.CompareAge(myPerson1, myPerson2) Then
```

Alternately, you can also invoke it from any `Person` object:

```
Dim myPerson As New Person()

If myPerson.CompareAge(myPerson, myPerson2) Then
```

Either way, you're invoking the same shared method, and you'll get the same behavior, whether you call it from the class or a specific instance of the class.

Shared Properties

As with other types of methods, you can also have shared property methods. Properties follow the same rules as regular methods. They can interact with shared variables, but not member variables, and they can invoke other shared methods or properties, but can't invoke instance methods without first creating an instance of the class. You can add a shared property to the `Person` class with the following code:

```
Public Shared ReadOnly Property RetirementAge() As Integer
  Get
    Return 62
  End Get
End Property
```

This simply adds a property to the class that indicates the global retirement age for all people. To use this value, you can simply access it directly from the class:

```
MsgBox(Person.RetirementAge)
```

Alternately, you can also access it from any `Person` object:

```
Dim myPerson As New Person()

MsgBox(myPerson.RetirementAge)
```

Either way, you're invoking the same shared property.

Shared Events

As with other interface elements, events can also be marked as `Shared`. For instance, you could declare a shared event in the `Person` class, such as:

```
Public Shared Event NewPerson()
```

Shared events can be raised from both instance methods and shared methods. Regular events cannot be raised by shared methods. Since shared events can be raised by regular methods, you can raise this one from the constructors in the `Person` class:

```
Public Sub New()
  Phone("home") = "555-1234"
  Phone("work") = "555-5678"
  mCounter += 1
  RaiseEvent NewPerson()
End Sub

Public Sub New(ByVal name As String, ByVal birthDate As Date)
  mName = Name
  mBirthDate = BirthDate

  Phone("home") = "555-1234"
  Phone("work") = "555-5678"
  mCounter += 1
  RaiseEvent NewPerson()
End Sub
```

The interesting thing about receiving shared events is that you can get them from either an object, such as a normal event, or from the class itself. For instance, you can use the `AddHandler` method in the form's code to catch this event directly from the `Person` class.

First, let's add a method to the form to handle the event:

```
Private Sub OnNewPerson()
  MsgBox("new person " & Person.PersonCount)
End Sub
```

Then, in the form's `Load` event, add a statement to link the event to this method:

```
Private Sub Form1_Load(ByVal sender As System.Object, _
    ByVal e As System.EventArgs) Handles MyBase.Load

    AddHandler Person.NewPerson, AddressOf OnNewPerson
```

```
      mPerson = New Person()
      If Microsoft.VisualBasic.Command = "nodisplay" Then
        AddHandler mPerson.Walked, AddressOf LogOnWalk
      Else
        AddHandler mPerson.Walked, AddressOf OnWalk
      End If
    End Sub
```

Notice that you are using the class rather than any specific object in the `AddHandler` statement. You could use an object as well, treating this like a normal event, but this illustrates how a class itself can raise an event.

When you run the application now, anytime a `Person` object is created you'll see this event raised.

Shared Constructor

A class can also have a `Shared` constructor:

```
Shared Sub New()

End Sub
```

Normal constructors are called when an instance of the class is created. The `Shared` constructor is only called once during the lifetime of an application, immediately before any use of the class.

This means that the `Shared` constructor is called before any other `Shared` methods, and before any instances of the class are created. The first time any code attempts to interact with any method on the class, or attempts to create an instance of the class, the `Shared` constructor is invoked.

Because you never directly call the `Shared` constructor, it can't accept any parameters. Also, because it is a `Shared` method, it can only interact with `Shared` variables or other `Shared` methods in the class.

Typically, a `Shared` constructor is used to initialize `Shared` fields within an object. In the `Person` class for instance, you can use it to initialize the `mCount` variable:

```
Shared Sub New()
  mCount = 0
End Sub
```

Since this method is only called once during the lifetime of the application, it is safe to do one-time initializations of values in this constructor.

Operator Overloading

Many basic datatypes, such as `Integer` and `String`, support the use of operators including +, -, =, <>, and so forth. When you create a class, you are defining a new type, and sometimes it is appropriate for types to also support the use of operators.

In your class, you can write code to define how each of these operators work when applied to objects. What does it mean when two objects are added together? Or multiplied? Or compared? If you can define what these operations mean, you can write code to implement appropriate behaviors. This is called operator overloading, since you are overloading the meaning of specific operators.

Operator overloading is done by using the `Operator` keyword, much in the same way that you create a `Sub`, `Function`, or `Property` method.

Most objects will at least provide for some type of comparison and so will often overload the comparison operators (=, <>, and maybe <, >, <=, and >=). You can do this in the `Person` class for instance, by adding the following code:

```
Public Shared Operator =(ByVal person1 As Person, _
  ByVal person2 As Person) As Boolean

  Return person1.Name = person2.Name
End Operator

Public Shared Operator <>(ByVal person1 As Person, _
  ByVal person2 As Person) As Boolean

  Return person1.Name <> person2.Name
End Operator
```

Note that you overload both the = and <> operators. Many operators come in pairs, and this includes the equality operator. If you overload =, then you must overload <> or a compiler error will result. Now that you've overloaded these operators, you can write code in `Form1` such as:

```
Dim p1 As New Person("Fred", #1/1/1960#)
Dim p2 As New Person("Mary", #1/1/1980#)
Dim p3 As Person = p1

Debug.WriteLine(CStr(p1 = p2))
Debug.WriteLine(CStr(p1 = p3))
```

Normally, it would be impossible to compare two objects using a simple comparison operator, but since you've overloaded the operator, this becomes valid code. The resulting display will show `False` and `True`.

Both the = and <> operators accept two parameters, so these are called binary operators. There are also unary operators that accept a single parameter. For instance, you might define the ability to convert a `String` value into a `Person` object by overloading the `CType` operator:

```
Public Shared Narrowing Operator CType(ByVal name As String) As Person
  Dim obj As New Person
  obj.Name = name
  Return obj
End Operator
```

To convert a `String` value to a `Person`, you assume that the value should be the `Name` property. You create a new object, set the `Name` property, and return the result. Since `String` is a broader, or less-specific, type than `Person`, this is a `Narrowing` conversion. Were you to do the reverse, convert a `Person` to a `String`, that would be a `Widening` conversion:

```
Public Shared Widening Operator CType(ByVal person As Person) As String
  Return person.Name
End Operator
```

Few non-numeric objects will overload most operators. It is difficult to imagine the result of adding, subtracting, or dividing two Customer objects against each other. Likewise, it is difficult to imagine performing bitwise comparisons between two Invoice objects. The following chart lists the various operators that can be overloaded:

Operators	Meaning
=, <>	Equality and inequality. These are binary operators to support the a = b and a <> b syntax. If you implement one, you must implement both.
>, <	Greater than and less than. These are binary operators to support the a > b and a < b syntax. If you implement one, you must implement both.
>=, <=	Greater than or equal and less than or equal. These are binary operators to support the a >= b and a <= b syntax. If you implement one, you must implement both.
IsFalse, IsTrue	Boolean conversion. These are unary operators to support the AndAlso and OrElse statements. The IsFalse operator accepts a single object and returns False if the object can be resolved to a False value. The IsTrue operator accepts a single value and returns True if the object can be resolved to a True value. If you implement one, you must implement both.
Ctype	Type conversion. This is a unary operator to support the CType(a) statement. The CType operator accepts a single object of another type and converts that object to the type of our class. This operator must be marked as Narrowing to indicate that the type is more specific than the original type or Widening to indicate that the type is broader than the original type.
+, -	Addition and subtraction. These operators can be unary or binary. The unary form exists to support the a += b and a -= b syntax, while the binary form exists to support a + b and a - b.
*, /, \, ^, Mod	Multiplication, division, exponent, and Mod. These are binary operators to support the a * b, a / b, a \ b, a ^ b, and a Mod b syntax.
&	Concatenation. This binary operator supports the a & b syntax. While this operator is typically associated with String manipulation, the & operator is not required to accept or return String values and so can be used for any concatenation operation that is meaningful for your object type.
<<, >>	Bit shifting. These binary operators support the a << b and a >> b syntax. The second parameter of these operators must be a value of type Integer, which will be the integer value to be bit shifted based on our object value.
And, Or, Xor	Logical comparison or bitwise operation. These binary operators support the a And b, a Or b, and a Xor b syntax. If the operators return Boolean results, they are performing logical comparisons. If they return results of other datatypes, then they are performing bitwise operations.
Like	Pattern comparison. This binary operator supports the a Like b syntax.

If an operator is meaningful for your datatype, you are strongly encouraged to overload that operator.

Defining AndAlso and OrElse

Notice that neither the `AndAlso` nor `OrElse` operators can be directly overloaded. This is so because these operators use other operators behind the scenes to do their work. To overload `AndAlso` and `OrElse`, you need to overload a set of other operators. Specifically:

AndAlso	OrElse
Overload the `And` operator to accept two parameters of your object's type and to return a result of your object's type.	Overload the `Or` operator to accept two parameters of your object's type and to return a result of your object's type.
Overload `IsFalse` for your object's type (meaning that you can return `True` or `False` by evaluating a single instance of your object).	Overload `IsTrue` for your object's type (meaning that you can return `True` or `False` by evaluating a single instance of your object).

If these operators are overloaded in your class, then you can use `AndAlso` and `OrElse` to evaluate statements that involve instances of your class.

Delegates

There are times when it would be nice to be able to pass a procedure as a parameter to a method. The classic case is when building a generic sort routine, where you not only need to provide the data to be sorted, but you need to provide a comparison routine appropriate for the specific data.

It is easy enough to write a sort routine that sorts `Person` objects by name or to write a sort routine that sorts `SalesOrder` objects by sales date. However, if you want to write a sort routine that can sort any type of object based on arbitrary sort criteria, that gets pretty difficult. At the same time, since some sort routines can get very complex, it would be nice to reuse that code without having to copy and paste it for each different sort scenario.

By using delegates, you can create such a generic routine for sorting, and in so doing, you can see how delegates work and can be used to create many other types of generic routines.

The concept of a delegate formalizes the process of declaring a routine to be called and calling that routine.

> *The underlying mechanism used by the .NET environment for callback methods is the delegate. Visual Basic uses delegates behind the scenes as it implements the* `Event`, `RaiseEvent`, `WithEvents`, *and* `Handles` *keywords.*

Declaring a Delegate

In your code, you can declare what a delegate procedure must look like from an interface standpoint. This is done using the `Delegate` keyword. To see how this can work, let's create a routine to sort any kind of data.

To do this, you'll declare a delegate that defines a method signature for a method that compares the value of two objects and returns a Boolean indicating whether the first object has a larger value than the second object. You'll then create a sort algorithm that uses this generic comparison method to sort data. Finally, you'll create an actual method that implements the comparison, and you'll pass the address of that method to the sort routine.

Add a new module to the project by choosing the Project ➪ Add Module menu option. Name the module `Sort.vb`, and then add the following code:

```
Module Sort

  Public Delegate Function Compare(ByVal v1 As Object, ByVal v2 As Object) _
    As Boolean

End Module
```

This line of code does something interesting. It actually defines a method signature as a datatype. This new datatype is named `Compare`, and it can be used within the code to declare variables or parameters that will be accepted by your methods. A variable or parameter declared using this datatype can actually hold the address of a method that matches the defined method signature, and you can then invoke that method by using the variable.

Any method with the signature:

```
f (Object, Object)
```

can be viewed as being of type `Compare`.

Using the Delegate Datatype

You can write a routine that accepts this datatype as a parameter, meaning that anyone calling your routine must pass us the address of a method that conforms to this interface. Add the following sort routine to the code module:

```
Public Sub DoSort(ByVal theData() As Object, ByVal greaterThan As Compare)
  Dim outer As Integer
  Dim inner As Integer
  Dim temp As Object

  For outer = 0 To UBound(theData) - 1
  For inner = outer + 1 To UBound(theData)
     If greaterThan.Invoke(theData(outer), theData(inner)) Then
       temp = theData(outer)
       theData(outer) = theData(inner)
       theData(inner) = temp
     End If
   Next
  Next
End Sub
```

The GreaterThan parameter is a variable that holds the address of a method matching the method signature defined by the Compare delegate. The address of any method with a matching signature can be passed as a parameter to our Sort routine.

Note the use of the Invoke method, which is the way that a delegate is called from the code. Also note that the routine deals entirely with the generic System.Object datatype rather than with any specific type of data. The specific comparison of one object to another is left to the delegate routine that is passed in as a parameter.

Implementing a Delegate Method

All that remains is to actually create the implementation of the delegate routine and call the sort method. On a very basic level, all you need to do is create a method that has a matching method signature. For instance, you could create a method such as:

```
Public Function PersonCompare(ByVal person1 As Object, _
  ByVal person2 As Object) As Boolean

End Function
```

The method signature of this method exactly matches that which you defined by our delegate earlier:

```
Compare(Object, Object)
```

In both cases, you're defining two parameters of type Object.

Of course, there's more to it than simply creating the stub of a method. The method needs to return a value of True if its first parameter is greater than the second parameter. Otherwise, it should be written to deal with some specific type of data.

The Delegate statement defines a datatype based on a specific method interface. To call a routine that expects a parameter of this new datatype, it must pass us the address of a method that conforms to the defined interface.

To conform to the interface, a method must have the same number of parameters with the same datatypes as were defined in our Delegate statement. In addition, the method must provide the same return type as defined. The actual name of the method doesn't matter; it is the number, order, and datatype of the parameters and the return value that count.

To find the address of a specific method, you can use the AddressOf operator. This operator returns the address of any procedure or method, allowing you to pass that value as a parameter to any routine that expects a delegate as a parameter.

The Person class already has a shared method named CompareAge that generally does what you want. Unfortunately, it accepts parameters of type Person rather than of type Object as required by the Compare delegate. You can use method overloading to solve this problem.

Create a second implementation of `CompareAge` that accepts parameters of type `Object` as required by the delegate, rather than of type `Person` as you have in the existing implementation:

```
Public Shared Function CompareAge(ByVal person1 As Object, _
    ByVal person2 As Object) As Boolean

  Return CType(person1, Person).Age > CType(person2, Person).Age
End Function
```

This method simply returns `True` if the first `Person` object's age is greater than the second's. The routine accepts two `Object` parameters rather than specific `Person` type parameters, so you have to use the `CType( )` method to access those objects as type `Person`. You accept the parameters as type `Object` because that is what is defined by the `Delegate` statement. You are matching its method signature:

```
f(Object, Object)
```

Since this method's parameter datatypes and return value match the delegate, you can use it when calling the sort routine. Place a button on the form and write the following code behind that button:

```
Private Sub Button2_Click(ByVal sender As System.Object, _
    ByVal e As System.EventArgs) Handles button2.Click

  Dim myPeople(4) As Person

  myPeople(0) = New Person("Fred", #7/9/1960#)
  myPeople(1) = New Person("Mary", #1/21/1955#)
  myPeople(2) = New Person("Sarah", #2/1/1960#)
  myPeople(3) = New Person("George", #5/13/1970#)
  myPeople(4) = New Person("Andre", #10/1/1965#)

  DoSort(myPeople, AddressOf Person.CompareAge)
End Sub
```

This code creates an array of `Person` objects and populates them. It then calls the `DoSort` routine from the module, passing the array as the first parameter and the address of the shared `CompareAge` method as the second. To display the contents of the sorted array in the IDE's output window, you can add the following code:

```
Private Sub button2_Click(ByVal sender As System.Object, _
    ByVal e As System.EventArgs) Handles button2.Click

  Dim myPeople(4) As Person

  myPeople(0) = New Person("Fred", #7/9/1960#)
  myPeople(1) = New Person("Mary", #1/21/1955#)
  myPeople(2) = New Person("Sarah", #2/1/1960#)
  myPeople(3) = New Person("George", #5/13/1970#)
  myPeople(4) = New Person("Andre", #10/1/1965#)

  DoSort(myPeople, AddressOf Person.CompareAge)
```

```
    Dim myPerson As Person

    For Each myPerson In myPeople
      System.Diagnostics.Debug.WriteLine(myPerson.Name & " " & myPerson.Age)
    Next
  End Sub
```

When you run the application and click the button, the output window will display a list of the people, sorted by age as shown in Figure 4-4.

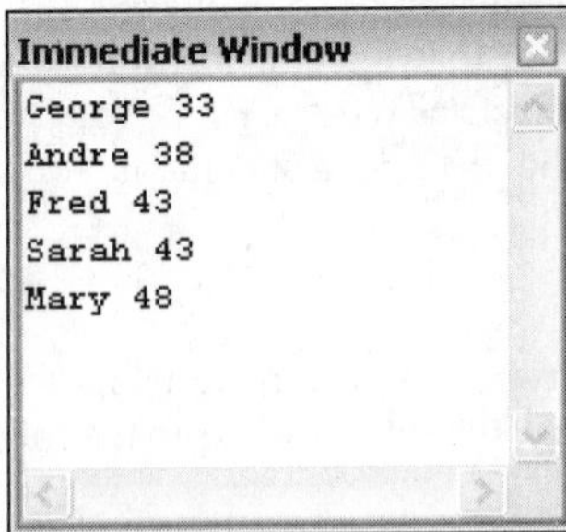

Figure 4-4

What makes this whole thing very powerful is that you can change the comparison routine without changing the sort mechanism. Simply add another comparison routine to the `Person` class:

```
  Public Shared Function CompareName(ByVal person1 As Object, _
      ByVal person2 As Object) As Boolean

    Return CType(person1, Person).Name > CType(person2, Person).Name

  End Function
```

and then change the code behind the button on the form to use that alternate comparison routine:

```
  Private Sub button2_Click(ByVal sender As System.Object, _
      ByVal e As System.EventArgs) Handles button2.Click

    Dim myPeople(4) As Person

    myPeople(0) = New Person("Fred", #7/9/1960#)
    myPeople(1) = New Person("Mary", #1/21/1955#)
    myPeople(2) = New Person("Sarah", #2/1/1960#)
    myPeople(3) = New Person("George", #5/13/1970#)
    myPeople(4) = New Person("Andre", #10/1/1965#)

    DoSort(myPeople, AddressOf Person.CompareName)

    Dim myPerson As Person

    For Each myPerson In myPeople
```

```
        System.Diagnostics.Debug.WriteLine(myPerson.Name & " " & myPerson.Age)
      Next
    End Sub
```

When you run this updated code, you'll find that the array contains a set of data sorted by name rather than by age, as shown in Figure 4-5.

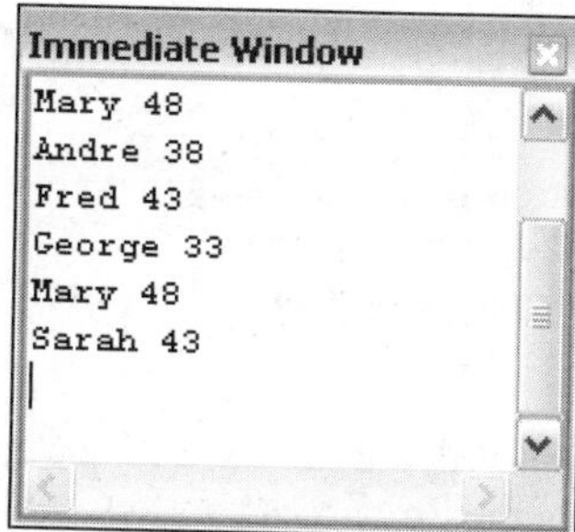

Figure 4-5

Simply by creating a new compare routine and passing it as a parameter, you can entirely change the way that the data is sorted. Better still, this sort routine can operate on any type of object, as long as you provide an appropriate delegate method that knows how to compare that type of object.

Classes versus Components

Visual Basic has another concept that is very similar to a class, the component. In fact, you can pretty much use a component and a class interchangeably, though there are some differences, which will be discussed.

A component is really little more than a regular class, but it is one that supports a graphical designer within the Visual Basic IDE. This means that you can use drag and drop to provide the code in the component with access to items from the Server Explorer or from the toolbox.

To add a component to a project, select the Project ⇨ Add Component menu option, give the component a name, and click Open in the Add New Item dialog box.

When you add a class to the project, you are presented with the Code window. When you add a component, you are presented with a graphical designer surface, much like what you'd see when adding a Web form to the project.

If you switch to the code view (by right-clicking in the Designer view and choosing View Code), you will see the code that is created automatically, just as it is with a Windows form, Web form, or regular class:

```
Public Class Component1

End Class
```

This isn't a lot more code than you'd see with a regular class, though there are differences behind the scenes. A component uses the same partial class technology as Windows Forms or Web Forms. This means that the code here is only part of the total code in the class. The rest of the code is hidden behind the designer's surface and is automatically created and managed by Visual Studio.

In the designer code is an `Inherits` statement that makes every component inherit from `System.ComponentModel.Component`. While Chapters 6 and 7 discuss the concepts of inheritance, it is important to note here that this `Inherits` line is what brings in all the support for the graphical designer in VS.NET.

The designer also manages any controls or components that are dropped on the designer. Those controls or components are automatically made available to your code. For instance, if you drag and drop a Timer control from the Windows Forms tab of the toolbox onto the component, it will be displayed in the designer.

From here, you can set its properties using the standard Properties window in the IDE, just as you would for a control on a form. Using the Properties window, set the `Name` property to `theTimer`. You now automatically have access to a `Timer` object named `theTimer`, simply by dragging and dropping and setting some properties.

This means that you can write code within the component, just as you might in a class, to use this object:

```
Public Sub Start()
  theTimer.Enabled = True
End Sub

Public Sub [Stop]()
  theTimer.Enabled = False
End Sub


Private Sub theTimer_Tick(ByVal sender As System.Object, _
  ByVal e As System.EventArgs) Handles theTimer.Tick

  ' do work
End Sub
```

For the most part, you can use a component interchangeably with a basic class, but the use of a component also provides some of the designer benefits of working with Windows Forms or Web Forms.

Summary

Visual Basic offers a fully object-oriented language with all the capabilities you would expect. In this chapter, you've explored the basic concepts around classes and objects, as well as the separation of interface from implementation and data.

You've seen how to use the `Class` keyword to create classes, and how those classes can be instantiated into specific objects, each one an instance of the class. These objects have methods and properties that can be invoked by the client code, and can act on data within the object stored in member or instance variables.

You also explored some more advanced concepts, including method overloading, shared or static variables and methods, and the use of delegates. Finally, the chapter wrapped up with a brief discussion of attributes and how they can be used to affect the interaction of classes or methods with the .NET environment.

Chapter 5 continues the discussion of object syntax as you explore the concept of inheritance and all the syntax that enables inheritance within Visual Basic. You will also walk through the creation, implementation, and use of multiple interfaces — a powerful concept that allows objects to be used in different ways, depending on the interface chosen by the client application.

Chapter 6 explores the .NET Common Language Runtime. Since the .NET platform and runtime are object-oriented at their very core, this chapter looks at how objects interact with the runtime environment. This chapter looks at topics such as using and disposing of objects and memory management.

Then Chapter 7 will wrap up the discussion of objects and object-oriented programming by applying all of this syntax. It will discuss the key object-oriented concepts of abstraction, encapsulation, polymorphism, and inheritance and show how they all tie together to provide a powerful way of designing and implementing applications.

5

Inheritance and Interfaces

Visual Basic is a fully object-oriented language. Chapter 4 covered the basics of creating classes and objects, including the creation of methods, properties, events, operators, and instance variables. You've seen the basic building blocks for abstraction, encapsulation, and polymorphism — concepts discussed in more detail in Chapter 7. The final major techniques you need to cover are inheritance and the use of multiple interfaces.

Inheritance is the idea that you can create a class that reuses methods, properties, events, and variables from another class. You can create a class with some basic functionality, then use that class as a base from which to create other, more detailed, classes. All these classes will have the same common functionality as that base class, along with new, enhanced or even completely changed functionality.

This chapter will cover the syntax that supports inheritance within Visual Basic. This includes creating the base classes from which other classes can be derived, as well as creating those derived classes.

Visual Basic also supports a related concept, multiple interfaces. You've already seen in Chapter 4 that all objects have a native or default interface, which is defined by the public methods, properties, and events declared in the class. In the .NET environment, an object can have other interfaces in addition to this native interface; in other words, .NET objects can have multiple interfaces.

These secondary interfaces define alternate ways in which your object can be accessed by providing clearly defined sets of methods, properties, and events. Like the native interface, these secondary interfaces define how the client code can interact with your object, essentially providing a "contract" that allows the client to know exactly what methods, properties, and events the object will provide. When you write code to interact with an object, you can choose which of the interfaces you want to use; basically you're choosing how you want to view or interact with that object.

You'll be using relatively basic code examples so that you can focus on the technical and syntactic issues surrounding inheritance and multiple interfaces. In Chapter 7, you'll revisit these concepts using a more sophisticated set of code as you continue to explore object-oriented programming and how to apply inheritance and multiple interfaces in a practical manner.

Inheritance

Inheritance is the concept that a new class can be based on an existing class, inheriting its interface and functionality from the original class. In Chapter 4, you explored the relationship between a class and an object, where the class is essentially a template from which objects can be created.

While this is very powerful, it doesn't provide all the capabilities you might like. In particular, there are many cases where a class only partially describes what you need for your object. You may have a class called `Person`, for instance, which has all the properties and methods that apply to all types of people, things like first name, last name, and birth date. While useful, this class probably doesn't have everything you need to describe a specific type of person, such as an employee or a customer. An employee would have a hire date and a salary, which are not included in `Person`, while a customer would have a credit rating, something neither the `Person` nor `Employee` classes would need.

Without inheritance, you'd probably end up replicating the code from the `Person` class in both the `Employee` and `Customer` classes so that they'd have that same functionality as well as the ability to add new functionality of their own.

Inheritance makes it very easy to create classes for `Employee`, `Customer`, and so forth. You don't have to recreate that code for an employee to be a person; it automatically gets any properties, methods, and events from the original `Person` class.

You can think of it this way. When you create an `Employee` class, which inherits from a `Person` class, you are effectively merging these two classes. If you then create an object based on the `Employee` class, it not only has the interface (properties, methods, and events) and implementation from the `Employee` class, but also has those from the `Person` class.

While an `Employee` object represents the merger between the `Employee` and `Person` classes, it is important to realize that the variables and code contained in each of those classes remain independent. There are two perspectives you need to understand.

From the outside, the client code that interacts with the `Employee` object will see a single, unified object that represents the merger of the `Employee` and `Person` classes.

From the inside, the code in the `Employee` class and the code in the `Person` class aren't totally intermixed. Variables and methods that are `Private` are only available within the class where they were written. Variables and methods that are `Public` in one class can be called from the other class. Variables and methods that are declared as `Friend` are only available between classes if both classes are in the same Visual Basic project. As discussed later in the chapter, there is also a `Protected` scope that is designed to work with inheritance, but again, this provides a controlled way for one class to interact with the variables and methods in the other class.

Visual Studio 2005 includes a Class Designer tool that allows you to easily create diagrams of your classes and their relationships. The Class Designer diagrams are a derivative of a standard notation called the Universal Modeling Language (UML) that is typically used to diagram the relationships between classes, objects, and other object-oriented concepts. The Class Designer diagrams more accurately and completely model .NET classes, and so this is the notation that will be used in this chapter. The relationship between the `Person`, `Employee`, and `Customer` classes is shown in Figure 5-1.

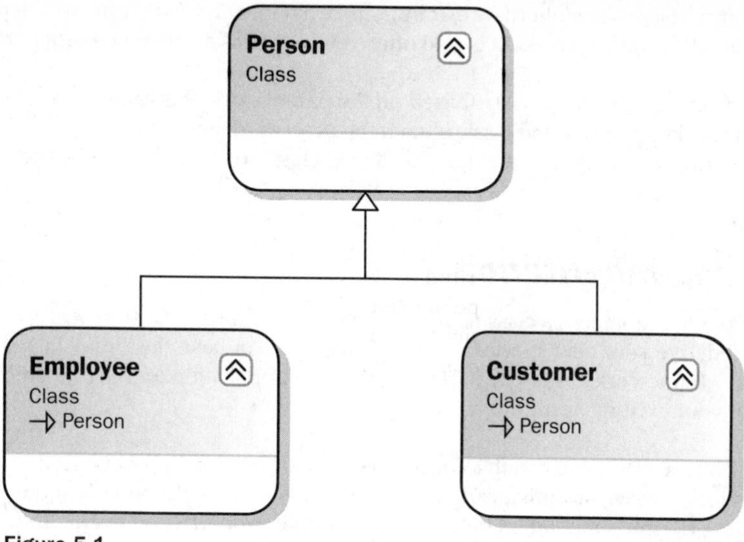

Figure 5-1

Each box in this diagram represents a class; in this case, you have `Person`, `Employee`, and `Customer` classes. The line from `Employee` back up to `Person`, terminating in a triangle, indicates that `Employee` is derived from, or inherits from, `Person`. The same is true for the `Customer` class.

Chapter 7 discusses in more detail when and how inheritance should be used in software design. This chapter covers the syntax and programming concepts necessary to implement inheritance. You'll create a base `Person` class and then use that class to create both `Employee` and `Customer` classes that inherit behavior from `Person`.

Before getting into the implementation, however, it's necessary to define some basic terms associated with inheritance. And there are a lot of terms, partly because there are often several ways to say the same thing, and the various terms are all used quite frequently and interchangeably.

Though we'll try to be consistent in the use of terminology in this book, it is important to note that in other books and articles and online all these terms are used in all their various permutations.

Inheritance, for instance, is also sometimes referred to as generalization. This is so because the class from which you are inheriting your behavior is virtually always a more general form of your new class. A person is more general than an employee, for instance.

The inheritance relationship is also referred to as an *is-a* relationship. When you create a `Customer` class that inherits from a `Person` class, that customer is a person. The employee is a person as well. Thus, you have this is-a relationship. As you'll see later in this chapter, multiple interfaces can be used to implement something similar to the is-a relationship, the *act-as* relationship.

When you create a class using inheritance, it inherits behaviors and data from an existing class. That existing class is called the base class. It is also often referred to as a superclass or a parent class.

The class you create using inheritance is based on the parent class. It is called a subclass. Sometimes, it is also called a child class or a derived class. In fact, the process of inheriting from a base class by a subclass is often referred to as deriving. You are deriving a new class from the base class. The process is also often called subclassing.

Implementing Inheritance

When you set out to implement a class using inheritance, you must first start with an existing class from which you will derive your new subclass. This existing class, or base class, may be part of the .NET system class library framework, it may be part of some other application or .NET assembly, or you may create it as part of your existing application.

Once you have a base class, you can then implement one or more subclasses based on that base class. Each of your subclasses will automatically have all of the methods, properties, and events of that base class — including the implementation behind each method, property, and event. Your subclass can add new methods, properties, and events of its own, extending the original interface with new functionality. In addition, a subclass can replace the methods and properties of the base class with its own new implementation — effectively overriding the original behavior and replacing it with new behaviors.

Essentially, inheritance is a way of merging functionality from an existing class into your new subclass. Inheritance also defines rules for how these methods, properties, and events can be merged, including control over how they can be changed or replaced, and how the subclass can add new methods, properties, and events of its own. This is what you'll explore as you go forward — what these rules are and what syntax you use in Visual Basic to make it all work.

Creating a Base Class

Virtually any class you create can act as a base class from which other classes can be derived. In fact, unless you specifically indicate in the code that your class cannot be a base class, you can derive from it (you'll come back to this later).

Create a new Windows Application project in Visual Basic. Then add a class to the project using the Project ⇨ Add Class menu option and name it `Person.vb`.

You start with the following code:

```
Public Class Person

End Class
```

At this point, you technically have a base class, since it is possible to inherit from this class even though it doesn't do or contain anything.

You can now add methods, properties, and events to this class as you normally would. All of those interface elements would be inherited by any class you might create based on `Person`. For instance, add the following code:

```
Public Class Person
  Private mName As String
  Private mBirthDate As Date

  Public Property Name() As String
    Get
      Return mName
    End Get
    Set(ByVal value As String)
      mName = value
    End Set
  End Property

  Public Property BirthDate() As Date
    Get
      Return mBirthDate
    End Get
    Set(ByVal value As Date)
      mBirthDate = value
    End Set
  End Property
End Class
```

This provides a simple method that can be used to illustrate how basic inheritance works. This class can be represented by the Class Diagram in Figure 5-2.

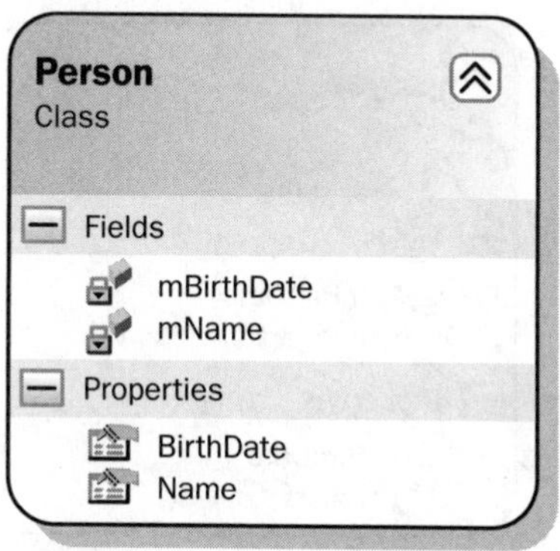

Figure 5-2

The overall box represents the `Person` class. In the top section, you have the name of the class. The next section down contains a list of the instance variables, or fields, of the class with their scope marked as `Private` (note the lock icon). The bottom section lists the properties exposed by the class, both marked as `Public`. If the class had methods or events, they would be displayed in their own sections in the diagram.

Creating a Subclass

To implement inheritance, you need to add a new class to your project. Use the Project ➪ Add Class menu option and add a new class named `Employee.vb`. You start with the following code:

```
Public Class Employee
  Private mHireDate As Date
  Private mSalary As Double

  Public Property HireDate() As Date
    Get
      Return mHireDate
    End Get
    Set(ByVal value As Date)
      mHireDate = value
    End Set
  End Property

  Public Property Salary() As Double
    Get
      Return mSalary
    End Get
    Set(ByVal value As Double)
      mSalary = value
    End Set
  End Property
End Class
```

This is a regular stand-alone class with no explicit inheritance. It can be represented by the following Class Diagram (see Figure 5-3).

Figure 5-3

Again, you can see the class name, its list of instance variables, and the properties it includes as part of its interface.

It turns out that, behind the scenes, this class inherits some capabilities from `System.Object`. In fact, every class in the entire .NET platform ultimately inherits from `System.Object` either implicitly or explicitly. This is why all .NET objects have a basic set of common functionality, including most notably the `GetType` method. This is discussed in detail later in the chapter.

While having an Employee object with a hire date and salary is useful, it should also have Name and BirthDate properties just as you implemented in the Person class. Without inheritance, you'd probably just copy and paste the code from Person directly into the new Employee class, but with inheritance you can directly reuse the code from the Person class. Let's make the new class inherit from Person.

The Inherits Keyword

To make Employee a subclass of Person, you just need to add a single line of code:

```
Public Class Employee
  Inherits Person
```

The Inherits keyword is used to indicate that a class should derive from an existing class, inheriting interface and behavior from that class. You can inherit from almost any class in your project, or from the .NET system class library or from other assemblies. It is possible to prevent inheritance, something we'll discuss later in the chapter. When using the Inherits keyword to inherit from classes outside the current project, you need to either specify the namespace that contains that class or have an Imports statement at the top of the class to import that namespace for your use.

The diagram in Figure 5-4 illustrates the fact that the Employee class is now a subclass of Person.

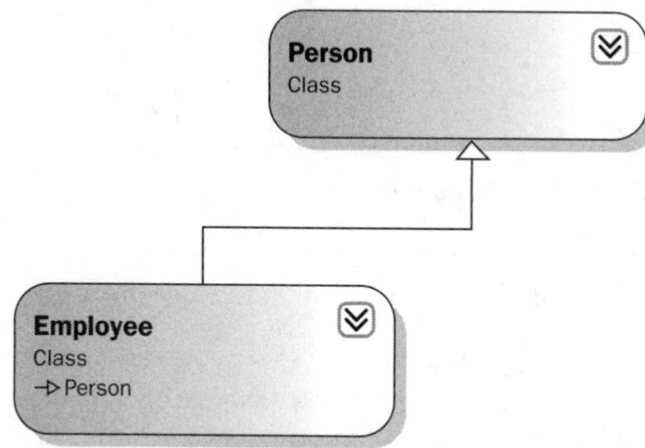

Figure 5-4

The line running from Employee back up to Person ends in an open triangle, which is the symbol for inheritance. It is this line that indicates that the Employee class also includes all the functionality and the interface from Person.

This means that an object created based on the Employee class will not only have the methods HireDate and Salary, but will also have Name and BirthDate.

To test this, bring up the designer for Form1 (which is automatically part of your project, since you created a Windows Application project) and add the following TextBox controls along with a button to the form.

Control Type	Name	Text Value
TextBox	`txtName`	<blank>
TextBox	`txtBirthDate`	<blank>
TextBox	`txtHireDate`	<blank>
TextBox	`txtSalary`	<blank>
button	`btnOK`	OK

You can also add some labels to make the form more readable. The Form Designer should now look something like Figure 5-5.

Figure 5-5

Double-click the button to bring up the code window, and enter the following code:

```
Private Sub btnOK_Click(ByVal sender As System.Object, _
                        ByVal e As System.EventArgs) Handles btnOK.Click
  Dim emp As New Employee()

  With emp
    .Name = "Fred"
    .BirthDate = #1/1/1960#
    .HireDate = #1/1/1980#
    .Salary = 30000

    txtName.Text = .Name
    txtBirthDate.Text = Format(.BirthDate, "Short date")
    txtHireDate.Text = Format(.HireDate, "Short date")
    txtSalary.Text = Format(.Salary, "$0.00")
  End With
End Sub
```

The best Visual Basic practice is to use the `With` *keyword. However, be aware that this might cause issues with portability and converting code to other languages.*

Even though Employee doesn't directly implement Name or BirthDate methods, they are available for use through inheritance. If you run this application and click the button, your controls will be populated with the values from the Employee object.

When the code in Form1 invokes the Name property on the Employee object, the code from the Person class is executed, since the Employee class has no such method built in. However, when the HireDate property is invoked on the Employee object, the code from the Employee class is executed, since it does have that method as part of its code.

From the form's perspective, it doesn't matter whether a method is implemented in the Employee class or the Person class, they are all simply methods of the Employee object. Also, since the code in these classes is merged to create the Employee object, there is no performance difference between calling a method implemented by the Employee class or a method implemented by the Person class.

Overloading Methods

Although your Employee class automatically gained the Name and BirthDate methods through inheritance, it also has methods of its own — HireDate and Salary. This shows how you've extended the base Person interface by adding methods and properties to the Employee subclass.

You can add new properties, methods, and events to the Employee class, and they will be part of any object created based on Employee. This has no impact on the Person class whatsoever, only on the Employee class and Employee objects.

You can even extend the functionality of the base class by adding methods to the subclass that have the same name as methods or properties in the base class, as long as those methods or properties have different parameter lists. You are effectively overloading the existing methods from the base class. It is essentially the same thing as overloading regular methods as discussed in Chapter 4.

For example, your Person class is currently providing your implementation for the Name property. Employees may have other names you also want to store, perhaps an informal name and a very formal name in addition to their normal name. One way to accommodate this requirement is to change the Person class itself to include an overloaded Name property that supports this new functionality. However, you're really only trying to enhance the Employee class, not the more general Person class. So, what you want is a way to add an overloaded method to the Employee class itself, even though you're overloading a method from its base class.

Overloading a method from a base class is done by using the Overloads keyword. The concept is the same as we discussed in Chapter 4, but in this case an extra keyword is involved. To overload the Name property, for instance, you can add a new property to the Employee class. First though, let's define an enumerated type using the Enum keyword. This Enum will list the different types of name you want to store. Add this Enum to the Employee.vb file, before the declaration of the class itself:

```
Public Enum NameTypes
  Informal = 1
  Formal = 2
End Enum
Public Class Employee
```

You can then add an overloaded Name property to the Employee class itself:

```
Public Class Employee
  Inherits Person

  Private mHireDate As Date
  Private mSalary As Double
  Private mNames As New Generic.Dictionary(Of NameTypes, String)

  Public Overloads Property Name(ByVal type As NameTypes) As String
    Get
      Return mNames(type)
    End Get
    Set(ByVal value As String)
      If mNames.ContainsKey(type) Then
        mNames.Item(type) = value
      Else
        mNames.Add(type, value)
      End If
    End Set
  End Property
```

This Name property is actually a property array, allowing you to store multiple values via the same property. In this case, you're storing the values in a Generic.Dictionary(Of K, V) object, which is indexed by using the Enum value you just defined. Chapter 8 will discuss generics in detail. For now, you can view this generic Dictionary just like any collection object that stores key/value data.

If you omit the Overloads *keyword here, your new implementation of the* Name *method will shadow the original implementation. Shadowing is a very different thing from overloading and is a topic covered later in the chapter.*

Though this method has the same name as the method in the base class, the fact that it accepts a different parameter list allows you to use overloading to implement it here. The original Name property, as implemented in the Person class, remains intact and valid, but now you've added a new variation with this second Name property. This is shown by Figure 5-6.

The diagram clearly indicates that the Name method in the Person class and the Name method in the Employee class both exist. If you hover over each Name property you'll see a tooltip showing the method signatures, making it very clear that each one has a different signature.

You can now change Form1 to make use of this new version of the Name property. First, add a couple of new text box controls and associated labels. The text box controls should be named txtFormal and txtInformal, and the form should now look like the one shown in Figure 5-7.

Now double-click the button to bring up the code window and add code to work with the overloaded version of the Name property.

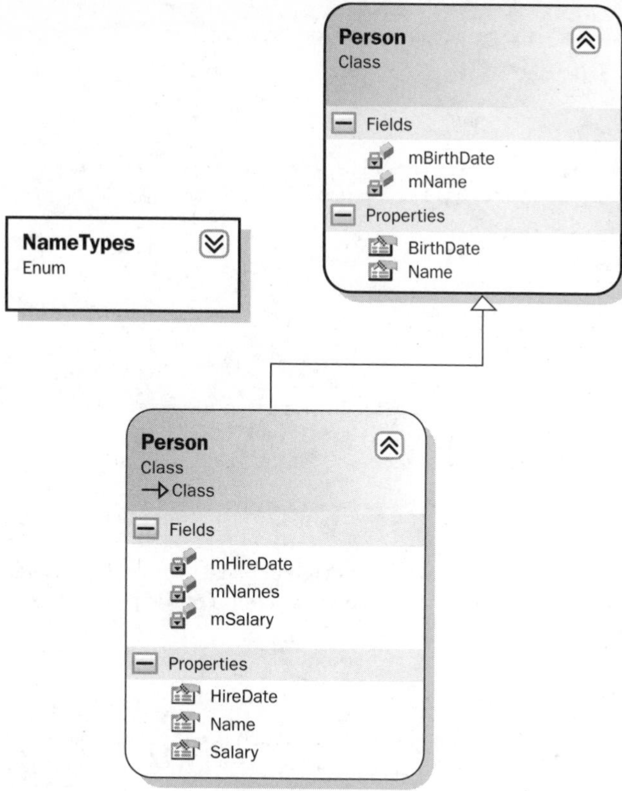

Figure 5-6

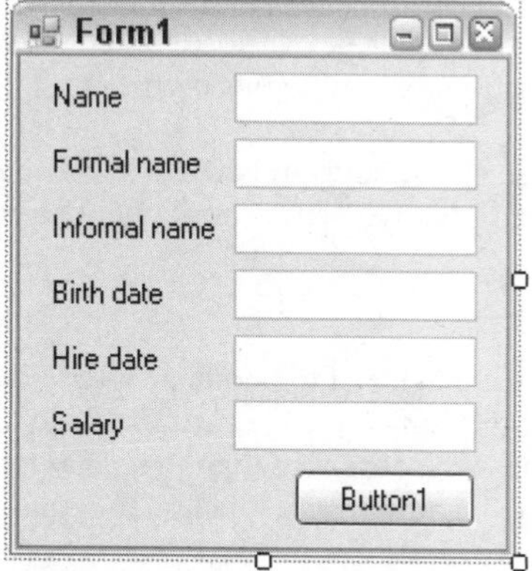

Figure 5-7

```
Private Sub btnOK_Click(ByVal sender As System.Object, _
    ByVal e As System.EventArgs) Handles btnOK.Click
  Dim emp As New Employee()

  With emp
    .Name = "Fred"
    .Name (NameTypes.Formal) = "Mr. Frederick R. Jones, Sr."
    .Name (NameTypes.Informal) = "Freddy"
    .BirthDate = #1/1/1960#
    .HireDate = #1/1/1980#
    .Salary = 30000

    txtName.Text = .Name
    txtFormal.Text = .Name (NameTypes.Formal)
    txtInformal.Text = .Name (NameTypes.Informal)
    txtBirthDate.Text = Format(.BirthDate, "Short date")
    txtHireDate.Text = Format(.HireDate, "Short date")
    txtSalary.Text = Format(.Salary, "$0.00")
  End With
End Sub
```

As you can see, the code still interacts with the original `Name` property as implemented in the `Person` class, but you are now also invoking the overloaded version of the property that is implemented in the `Employee` class.

Overriding Methods

So far, you've seen how to implement a base class and then use it to create a subclass. Finally, you extended the interface by adding methods. You've also explored how to use overloading to add methods that have the same name as methods in the base class, but with different parameters.

However, there are times when you may want not only to extend the original functionality, but also to actually change or entirely replace the functionality from the base class. Instead of leaving the existing functionality and just adding new methods or overloaded versions of those methods, you might want to entirely override the existing functionality with your own.

You can do exactly this. If the base class allows it, you can substitute your own implementation of a method in the base class—meaning that your new implementation will be used instead of the original.

The Overridable Keyword

By default, you can't override the behavior of methods on a base class. The base class must be coded specifically to allow this to occur by using the `Overridable` keyword. This is important, since you may not always want to allow a subclass to entirely change the behavior of the methods in your base class. However, if you do wish to allow the author of a subclass to replace your implementation, you can do so by adding the `Overridable` keyword to your method declaration.

Returning to your `Employee` example, you may not like the implementation of the `BirthDate` method as it stands in the `Person` class. Say, for instance, that you can't employ anyone younger than 16 years of age, so any birth date value more recent than 16 years ago is invalid for an employee.

To implement this business rule, you need to change the way the `BirthDate` property is implemented. While you could make this change directly in the `Person` class, that would not be ideal. It is perfectly acceptable to have a person under age 16, just not an employee.

Open the code window for the `Person` class and change the `BirthDate` property to include the `Overridable` keyword.

```
Public Overridable Property BirthDate() As Date
  Get
    Return mBirthDate
  End Get
  Set(ByVal value As Date)
    mBirthDate = value
  End Set
End Property
```

This change allows any class that inherits from `Person` to entirely replace the implementation of the `BirthDate` property with a new implementation.

By adding the `Overridable` keyword to your method declaration, you are indicating that you want to allow any subclass to override the behavior provided by this method. This means that you are giving permission for a subclass to totally ignore your implementation, or to extend your implementation by doing other work before or after your implementation is run.

If the subclass doesn't override this method, the method will work just like a regular method and will be automatically included as part of the subclass's interface. Putting the `Overridable` keyword on a method simply allows a subclass to override the method if you choose to have it do so.

The Overrides Keyword

In a subclass, you override a method by implementing a method of the same name, and with the same parameter list as the base class, and then using the `Overrides` keyword to indicate that you are overriding that method.

This is different from overloading, since when you overload a method you're adding a new method with the same name but a different parameter list. When you override a method, you're actually replacing the original method with a new implementation.

Without the `Overrides` keyword, you'll get a compilation error when you implement a method with the same name as one from the base class.

Open the code window for the `Employee` class and add a new `BirthDate` property:

```
Public Class Employee
  Inherits Person

  Private mHireDate As Date
  Private mSalary As Double
  Private mBirthDate As Date

  Private mNames As New Generic.Dictionary(Of NameTypes, String)
```

```
Public Overrides Property BirthDate() As Date
  Get
    Return mBirthDate
  End Get
  Set(ByVal value As Date)
    If DateDiff(DateInterval.Year, Value, Now) >= 16 Then
      mBirthDate = value
    Else
      Throw New ArgumentException( _
        "An employee must be at least 16 years old")
    End If
  End Set
End Property
```

Since you're implementing your own version of the property, you have to declare a variable to store that value within the `Employee` class. This is not ideal, and there are a couple of ways around it, including the `MyBase` keyword and the `Protected` scope.

Notice also that you've enhanced the functionality in the `Set` block, so it now raises an error if the new birth date value would make the employee be less than 16 years of age. With this code, you've now entirely replaced the original `BirthDate` implementation with a new one that enforces your business rule. This is shown in Figure 5-8.

The diagram now includes a `BirthDate` method in the `Employee` class. While perhaps not entirely intuitive, this is how the Class Diagram indicates that you've overridden the method. If you hover the mouse over the property in the `Employee` class, the tooltip will show the method signature, including the `Overrides` keyword.

If you now run your application and click the button on the form, everything should work as it did before. This is so because the birth date you're supplying conforms to your new business rule. However, you can change the code in your form to use an invalid birth date.

```
With emp
  .Name = "Fred"
  .Name(NameTypes.Formal) = "Mr. Frederick R. Jones, Sr."
  .Name(NameTypes.Informal) = "Freddy"
  .BirthDate = #1/1/2000#
```

When you run the application (from within Visual Studio .NET) and click the button, you'll get an error indicating that the birth date is invalid. This proves that you are now using the implementation of the `BirthDate` method from the `Employee` class rather than the one from the `Person` class.

Change the date value in the form back to a valid value so that your application runs properly.

The MyBase Keyword

You've just seen how you can entirely replace the functionality of a method in the base class by overriding it in your subclass. However, this can be somewhat extreme; sometimes it would be preferable to override methods so that you extend the base functionality rather than replacing the functionality.

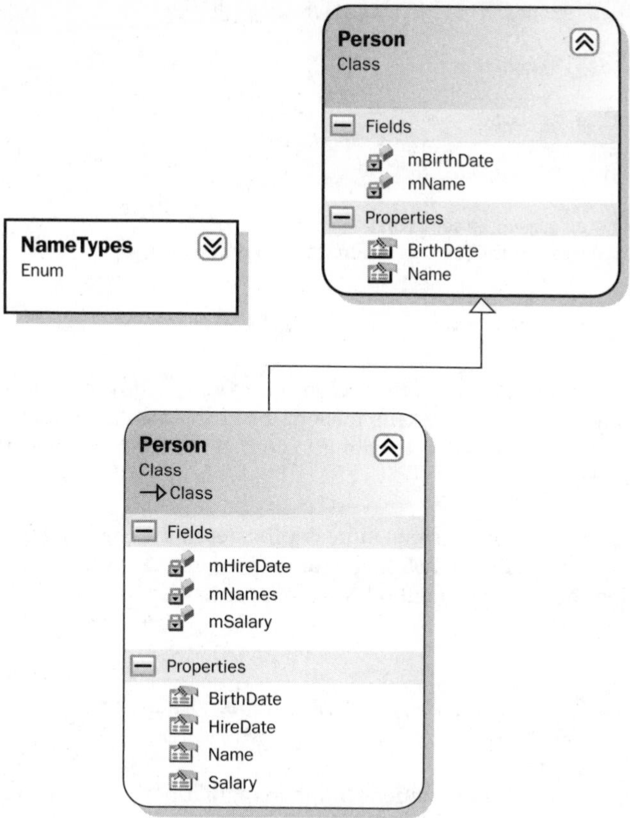

Figure 5-8

To do this, you need to override the method using the `Overrides` keyword as you just did, but within your new implementation you can still invoke the original implementation of the method. This allows you to add your own code before or after the original implementation is invoked — meaning that you can extend the behavior, while still leveraging the code in the base class.

To invoke methods directly from the base class, you can use the `MyBase` keyword. This keyword is available within any class, and it exposes all the methods of the base class for your use.

> *Even a base class like* `Person` *is an implicit subclass of* `System.Object`*, and so it can use* `MyBase` *to interact with its base class as well.*

This means that within the `BirthDate` implementation in `Employee`, you can invoke the `BirthDate` implementation in the base `Person` class. This is ideal, since it means that you can leverage any existing functionality provided by `Person`, while still enforcing your `Employee`-specific business rules.

To take advantage of this, you can enhance the code in the `Employee` implementation of `BirthDate`. First, remove the declaration of `mBirthDate` from the `Employee` class. You won't need this variable any longer, since the `Person` implementation will keep track of the value on your behalf. Then, change the `BirthDate` implementation in the `Employee` class as follows:

```
Public Overrides Property BirthDate() As Date
  Get
    Return MyBase.BirthDate
  End Get
  Set(ByVal value As Date)
    If DateDiff(DateInterval.Year, Value, Now) >= 16 Then
      MyBase.BirthDate = value
    Else
      Throw New ArgumentException( _
        "An employee must be at least 16 years old")
    End If
  End Set
End Property
```

You can now run your application and you'll see that it works just fine even though the `Employee` class no longer contains any code to actually keep track of the birth date value. You've effectively merged the `BirthDate` implementation from `Person` right into your enhanced implementation in `Employee`, creating a hybrid version of the property.

We'll discuss the `MyBase` keyword in some more depth later in the chapter. Here, you've seen how it can allow you to enhance or extend the functionality of the base class by adding your own code in the subclass but still invoking the base class method when appropriate.

Virtual Methods

The `BirthDate` method is an example of a virtual method. Virtual methods are those that can be overridden and replaced by subclasses.

Virtual methods are more complex to understand than regular nonvirtual methods. With a nonvirtual method, there is only one implementation that matches any given method signature, so there's no ambiguity about which specific method implementation will be invoked. With virtual methods, however, there may be several implementations of the same method, with the same method signature, so you need to understand the rules that govern which specific implementation of that method will be called.

When working with virtual methods, you need to keep in mind that the datatype of the object is used to determine the implementation of the method to call, rather than the type of the variable that refers to the object.

If you look at the code you've written in your form, you can see that you're declaring an object variable of type `Employee`, and you are then creating an `Employee` object that you can reference via that object.

```
Dim emp As New Employee()
```

It is not surprising, then, that you are able to invoke any of the methods that are implemented as part of the `Employee` class, and through inheritance, any of the methods implemented as part of the `Person` class:

```
With emp
  .Name = "Fred"
  .Name(NameTypes.Formal) = "Mr. Frederick R. Jones, Sr."
  .Name(NameTypes.Informal) = "Freddy"
  .BirthDate = #1/1/1960#
```

```
.HireDate = #1/1/1980#
.Salary = 30000
```

When you call the BirthDate property, you know that you're invoking the implementation contained in the Employee class, which makes sense since you know that you're using a variable of type Employee to refer to an object of type Employee.

However, because your methods are virtual methods, you can experiment with some much more interesting scenarios. For instance, suppose that you change the code in your form to interact directly with an object of type Person instead of one of type Employee:

```
Private Sub btnOK_Click(ByVal sender As System.Object, _
    ByVal e As System.EventArgs) Handles btnOK.Click
  Dim person As New Person()

  With person
    .Name = "Fred"
    .BirthDate = #1/1/1960#

    txtName.Text = .Name
    txtBirthDate.Text = Format(.BirthDate, "Short date")
  End With
End Sub
```

You can no longer call the methods implemented by the Employee class, because they don't exist as part of a Person object, but only as part of an Employee object. However, you can see that both the Name and BirthDate properties continue to function as you'd expect. When you run the application now, it will work just fine. You can even change the birth date value to something that would be invalid for Employee.

```
.BirthDate = #1/1/2000#
```

The application will now accept it and work just fine, since the BirthDate method you're invoking is the original version from the Person class.

These are the two simple scenarios, when you have a variable and object of type Employee or a variable and object of type Person. However, since Employee is derived from Person, you can do something a bit more interesting. You can use a variable of type Person to hold a reference to an Employee object.

Because of this, you can change the code in Form1 as follows:

```
Private Sub btnOK_Click(ByVal sender As System.Object, _
    ByVal e As System.EventArgs) Handles btnOK.Click

  Dim person As Person
  person = New Employee()
  With person
    .Name = "Fred"
    .BirthDate = #1/1/2000#

    txtName.Text = .Name
    txtBirthDate.Text = Format(.BirthDate, "Short date")
  End With
End Sub
```

What you're doing now is declaring your variable to be of type `Person`, but the object itself is an instance of the `Employee` class. You've done something a bit complex here, since the datatype of the variable is not the same as the datatype of the object itself. It is important to remember that a variable of a base class type can always hold a reference to an object of any subclass.

> **This is the reason that a variable of type `System.Object` can hold a reference to literally anything in .NET Framework, because all classes are ultimately derived from** `System.Object`.

This technique is very useful when creating generic routines and makes use of an object-oriented concept called polymorphism, which is discussed more thoroughly in Chapter 7. This technique allows you to create a more general routine that populates your form for any object of type `Person`. Add this code to the form:

```
Private Sub DisplayPerson(ByVal thePerson As Person)
  With thePerson
    txtName.Text = .Name
    txtBirthDate.Text = Format(.BirthDate, "Short date")
  End With
End Sub
```

Now, you can change the code behind the button to make use of this generic routine:

```
Private Sub btnOK_Click(ByVal sender As System.Object, _
    ByVal e As System.EventArgs) Handles btnOK.Click

  Dim person As Person
  person = New Employee()

  With person
    .Name = "Fred"
    .BirthDate = #1/1/2000#
  End With

  DisplayPerson(person)
End Sub
```

The benefit here is that you can pass a `Person` object or an `Employee` object to `DisplayPerson` and the routine will work the same either way.

When you run the application now, things get interesting. You'll get an error when you attempt to set the `BirthDate` property because it breaks your 16-year-old business rule, which is implemented in the `Employee` class. How can this be when your `person` variable is of type `Person`?

This clearly demonstrates the concept of a virtual method. It is the datatype of the object, in this case `Employee`, that is important. The datatype of the variable is not the deciding factor when choosing which implementation of an overridden method is invoked.

The following table shows which method is actually invoked based on the variable and object datatypes when working with virtual methods.

Variable Type	Object Type	Method Invoked
Base	Base	Base
Base	Subclass	Subclass
Subclass	Subclass	Subclass

Virtual methods are very powerful and useful when you go to implement polymorphism using inheritance. A base class datatype can hold a reference to any subclass object, but it is the type of that specific object which determines the implementation of the method. Because of this you can write generic routines that operate on many types of object as long as they derive from the same base class. We'll discuss how to make use of polymorphism and virtual methods in more detail in Chapter 7.

Overriding Overloaded Methods

Earlier, you wrote code in your `Employee` class to overload the `Name` method in the base `Person` class. This allowed you to keep the original `Name` functionality, but also extend it by adding another `Name` method that accepted a different parameter list.

You've also overridden the `BirthDate` method. The implementation in the `Employee` class replaced the implementation in the `Person` class. Overriding is a related, but different concept from overloading. It is also possible to both overload and override a method at the same time.

In the earlier overloading example, you added a new `Name` property to the `Employee` class, while retaining the functionality present in the base `Person` class. You may decide that you not only want to have your second overloaded implementation of the `Name` method, but also want to replace the existing one by overriding the existing method provided by the `Person` class.

In particular, you may want to do this so that you can store the `Name` value in the `Hashtable` object along with your `Formal` and `Informal` names.

Before you can override the `Name` method, you need to add the `Overridable` keyword to the base implementation in the `Person` class.

```
Public Overridable Property Name() As String
  Get
    Return mName
  End Get
  Set(ByVal value As String)
    mName = value
  End Set
End Property
```

With that done, the `Name` method can now be overridden by any derived classes. In the `Employee` class, you can now override the `Name` method, replacing the functionality provided by the `Person` class. First, you'll add a `Normal` option to the `Enum` that controls the types of `Name` value you can store.

```
Public Enum NameTypes
  Informal = 1
  Formal = 2
  Normal = 3
End Enum
```

Then, you can add code to the Employee class to implement a new Name property. This is in addition to the existing Name property already implemented in the Employee class:

```
Public Overloads Overrides Property Name() As String
  Get
    Return Name(NameTypes.Normal)
  End Get
  Set(ByVal value As String)
    Name(NameTypes.Normal) = value
  End Set
End Property
```

Notice that you're using both the Overrides keyword, to indicate that you're overriding the Name method from the base class, and the Overloads keyword to indicate that you're overloading this method in the subclass.

This new Name property merely delegates the call to the existing version of the Name property that handles the parameter-based names. To complete the linkage between this implementation of the Name property and the parameter-based version, you need to make one more change to that original overloaded version:

```
Public Overloads Property Name(ByVal type As NameTypes) As String
  Get
    Return mNames(Type)
  End Get
  Set(ByVal value As String)
    If mNames.ContainsKey(type) Then
      mNames.Item(type) = value
    Else
      mNames.Add(type, value)
    End If
    If type = NameTypes.Normal Then
      MyBase.Name = value
    End If
  End Set
End Property
```

This way, if the client code sets the Name property by providing the Normal index, you are still updating the name in the base class as well as in the Dictionary object maintained by the Employee class.

Shadowing

Overloading allows you to add new versions of the existing methods as long as their parameter lists are different. Overriding allows your subclass to entirely replace the implementation of a base class method with a new method that has the same method signature. As you've just seen, you can even combine these concepts not only to replace the implementation of a method from the base class but also to simultaneously overload that method with other implementations that have different method signatures.

However, any time you override a method using the `Overrides` keyword, you are subject to the rules governing virtual methods — meaning that the base class must give you permission to override the method. If the base class doesn't use the `Overridable` keyword, you can't override the method. Sometimes you may need to override a method that is not marked as `Overridable`, and shadowing allows you to do just that.

The `Shadows` keyword can also be used to entirely change the nature of a method or other interface element from the base class, although that is something which should be done with great care, since it can seriously reduce the maintainability of your code. Normally, when you create an `Employee` object, you expect that it can only act as an `Employee`, but also as a `Person` since `Employee` is a subclass of `Person`. However, with the `Shadows` keyword, you can radically alter the behavior of an `Employee` class so that it doesn't act like a `Person`. This sort of radical deviation from what is normally expected invites bugs and makes code hard to understand and maintain.

Shadowing methods is very dangerous and should be used as a last resort. It is primarily useful in cases where you have a preexisting component such as a Windows Forms control that was not designed for inheritance. If you absolutely *must* inherit from such a component, you may need to use shadowing to "override" methods or properties. There are serious limits and dangers, but it may be your only option.

You'll explore that in more detail later. First, let's see how `Shadows` can be used to override nonvirtual methods.

Overriding Nonvirtual Methods

Earlier in the chapter, we discussed virtual methods and how they are automatically created in Visual Basic when the `Overrides` keyword is employed. You can also implement nonvirtual methods in Visual Basic. Nonvirtual methods are methods that cannot be overridden and replaced by subclasses, and so most methods you implement are nonvirtual.

> **If you don't use the `Overridable` keyword when declaring a method, it is nonvirtual.**

In the typical case, nonvirtual methods are easy to understand. Since they can't be overridden and replaced, you know that there's only one method by that name, with that method signature, so when you invoke it there is no ambiguity about which specific implementation will be called. The reverse is true with virtual methods, where there may be more than one method of the same name, and with the same method signature, and you need to understand the rules governing which implementation will be invoked.

Of course, nothing is simple, and it turns out that you can override nonvirtual methods by using the `Shadows` keyword. In fact, you can use the `Shadows` keyword to override methods regardless of whether or not they have the `Overridable` keyword in the declaration.

> **The `Shadows` keyword allows you to replace methods on the base class that the Base Class Designer didn't intend to be replaced.**

Obviously, this can be very dangerous. The designer of a base class must be careful when marking a method as `Overridable`, ensuring that the base class will continue to operate properly even when that method is replaced by another code in a subclass. Designers of base classes typically just assume that if they don't mark a method as `Overridable` it will be called and not overridden. Thus, overriding a non-virtual method by using the `Shadows` keyword can have unexpected and potentially dangerous side effects, since you are doing something that the Base Class Designer assumed would never happen.

If that isn't enough complexity, it turns out that shadowed methods follow different rules from virtual methods when they are invoked. In other words, they don't act like regular overridden methods; instead, they follow a different set of rules to determine which specific implementation of the method will be invoked. In particular, when you call a nonvirtual method, it is the datatype of the variable that refers to the object that indicates which implementation of the method is called, not the datatype of the object as with virtual methods.

To override a nonvirtual method, you can use the `Shadows` keyword instead of the `Overrides` keyword. To see how this works, let's add a new property to the base `Person` class:

```
Public ReadOnly Property Age() As Integer
  Get
    Return CInt(DateDiff(DateInterval.Year, Now, BirthDate))
  End Get
End Property
```

You've added a new method, called `Age`, to the base class, and thus automatically to the subclass.

This code has a bug, introduced on purpose for illustration. The `DateDiff` parameters are in the wrong order, so you'll get negative age values from this routine. We introduced a bug because sometimes there are bugs in base classes that you didn't write and can't fix because you don't have the source code. In this case, you'll walk through the use of the `Shadows` keyword to address a bug in your base class, acting under the assumption that for some reason you can't actually fix the code in the `Person` class.

Notice that you're not using the `Overridable` keyword on this method, so any subclass is prevented from overriding the method by using the `Overrides` keyword. The obvious intent and expectation of this code is that all subclasses will use this implementation and will not override it with their own.

However, the base class cannot prevent a subclass from shadowing a method, and so it doesn't matter whether you use `Overridable` or not, either way works fine for shadowing.

Before you shadow the method, let's see how it works as a regular nonvirtual method. First, you need to change your form to use this new value. Add a text box named `txtAge` and a related label to the form. Next, change the code behind the button to use the `Age` property. You'll also include the code to display the data on the form right here to keep things simple and clear:

```
Private Sub btnOK_Click(ByVal sender As System.Object, _
    ByVal e As System.EventArgs) Handles btnOK.Click
```

```
    Dim person As Employee = New Employee()
    With person
      .Name = "Fred"
      .BirthDate = #1/1/1960#

      txtName.Text = .Name
      txtBirthDate.Text = Format(.BirthDate, "Short date")
      txtAge.Text = CStr(.Age)
    End With

  End Sub
```

Don't forget to change the birth date value to something that will be valid for an `Employee`.

At this point, you can run the application and the age field should appear in your display as expected, though with a negative value due to the bug we introduced. There's no magic or complexity here. This is basic programming with objects and basic use of inheritance as discussed at the beginning of this chapter.

Of course, you don't want a bug in your code, but if you assume you don't have access to the `Person` class, and since the `Person` class doesn't allow you to override the `Age` method, what are you to do? The answer lies in the `Shadows` keyword, which allows you to override the method anyway.

Let's shadow the `Age` method within the `Employee` class, overriding and replacing the implementation in the `Person` class even though it is not marked as `Overridable`. Add the following code to the `Employee` class:

```
  Public Shadows ReadOnly Property Age() As Integer
    Get
      Return CInt(DateDiff(DateInterval.Year, BirthDate, Now))
    End Get
  End Property
```

In many ways, this looks very similar to what you've seen with the `Overrides` keyword, in that you're implementing a method in your subclass with the same name and parameter list as a method in the base class. In this case, however, you'll find some different behavior when you interact with the object in different ways.

Technically, the `Shadows` keyword is not required here. Shadowing is the default behavior when a subclass implements a method that matches the name and method signature of a method in the base class. However, if you omit the `Shadows` keyword, the compiler will give you a warning indicating that the method is being shadowed, so it is always better to include the keyword, both to avoid the warning and to make it perfectly clear that you knew what you were doing when you chose to shadow the method.

Remember that your code in the form is currently declaring a variable of type `Employee` and is creating an instance of an `Employee` object:

```
  Dim person As Employee = New Employee()
```

This is a simple case, and, surprisingly, when you run the application now you'll see that the value of the age field is correct, indicating that you just ran the implementation of the `Age` property from the `Employee` class. At this point, you're seeing the same behavior that you got from overriding with the `Overrides` keyword.

Let's take a look at the other simple case where you're working with a variable and object that are both of datatype Person. Change the code in Form1 as follows:

```
Private Sub btnOK_Click(ByVal sender As System.Object, _
    ByVal e As System.EventArgs) Handles btnOK.Click

  Dim person As Person = New Person()

  With person
    .Name = "Fred"
    .BirthDate = #1/1/1960#

    txtName.Text = .Name
    txtBirthDate.Text = Format(.BirthDate, "Short date")
    txtAge.Text = CStr(.Age)
  End With
End Sub
```

Now, you have a variable of type Person and an object of that same type. You would expect that the implementation in the Person class would be invoked in this case, and that is exactly what happens; the age field will display the original negative value, indicating that you're invoking the buggy implementation of the method directly from the Person class. Again, this is exactly the behavior you'd expect from a method overridden via the Overrides keyword.

This next example is where things get truly interesting. Change the code in Form1 as follows:

```
Private Sub btnOK_Click(ByVal sender As System.Object, _
    ByVal e As System.EventArgs) Handles btnOK.Click

  Dim person As Person = New Employee()
  With person
    .Name = "Fred"
    .BirthDate = #1/1/1960#

    txtName.Text = .Name
    txtBirthDate.Text = Format(.BirthDate, "Short date")
    txtAge.Text = CStr(.Age)
  End With
End Sub
```

Now, you are declaring the variable to be of type Person, but you are creating an object that is of datatype Employee. You did this earlier in the chapter when exploring the Overrides keyword as well, and in that case you discovered that the version of the method that was invoked was based on the datatype of the object. The BirthDate implementation in the Employee class was invoked.

If you run the application now, you will find that the rules are different when the Shadows keyword is used. In this case, the implementation in the Person class is invoked, giving you the buggy negative value. When the implementation in the Employee class is ignored, you get the exact opposite behavior of what you got with Overrides.

The following table summarizes which method implementation is invoked based on the variable and object datatypes when using shadowing.

Variable	Object	Method Invoked
Base	Base	Base
Base	Subclass	Base
Subclass	Subclass	Subclass

In most cases, the behavior you'll want for your methods is accomplished by the `Overrides` keyword and virtual methods. However, in those cases where the Base Class Designer doesn't allow you to override a method and you want to do it anyway, the `Shadows` keyword provides you with the needed functionality.

Shadowing Arbitrary Elements

The `Shadows` keyword can be used not only to override nonvirtual methods, but it can be used to totally replace and change the nature of a base class interface element. When you override a method, you are providing a replacement implementation of that method with the same name and method signature. Using the `Shadows` keyword, you can do more extreme things, such as changing a method into an instance variable or changing a `Property` into a `Function`.

However, this can be very dangerous, since any code written to use your objects will naturally assume that you implement all the same interface elements and behaviors as your base class, because that is the nature of inheritance. Any documentation or knowledge of the original interface is effectively invalidated because the original implementation is arbitrarily replaced.

By totally changing the nature of an interface element, you can cause a great deal of confusion for programmers who will be interacting with your class in the future.

To see how you can replace an interface element from the base class, let's entirely change the nature of the `Age` property. In fact, let's change it from being a read-only property to being a read-write property. You could get even more extreme — changing it to a `Function` or `Sub`.

To do this, remove the `Age` property from the `Employee` class and add the following code:

```
Public Shadows Property Age() As Integer
  Get
    Return CInt(DateDiff(DateInterval.Year, BirthDate, Now))
  End Get
  Set(ByVal value As Integer)
    BirthDate = DateAdd(DateInterval.Year, -value, Now)
  End Set
End Property
```

With this change, the very nature of the `Age` method has changed. It is no longer a simple read-only property, now it is a read-write property that includes code to calculate an approximate birth date based on the age value supplied.

As it stands, your application will continue to run just fine. This is so because you're only using the read-only functionality of the property in your form. You can change the form to make use of the new read-write functionality:

```
Private Sub btnOK_Click(ByVal sender As System.Object, _
    ByVal e As System.EventArgs) Handles btnOK.Click

  Dim person As Person = New Employee()

  With person
    .Name = "Fred"
    .BirthDate = #1/1/1960#
    .Age = 20

    txtName.Text = .Name
    txtBirthDate.Text = Format(.BirthDate, "Short date")
    txtAge.Text = CStr(.Age)
  End With
End Sub
```

This will, however, leave you with a syntax error. The variable you're working with, `person`, is of datatype `Person`, and that datatype does not provide a writable version of the `Age` property. This means that in order to use your enhanced functionality, you must be using a variable and object of type `Employee`:

```
Dim person As Employee = New Employee()
```

If you now run the application and click the button, you'll see that the `Age` is displayed as 20, and the birth date is now a value calculated based on that age value, indicating that you are now running the shadowed version of the `Age` method as implemented in the `Employee` class.

As if that weren't odd enough, you can do some even stranger and more dangerous things. You can change `Age` into a variable, and you can even change its scope. For instance, you can comment out the `Age` property code in the `Employee` class and replace it with the following code:

```
Private Shadows Age As String
```

At this point, you've changed everything. `Age` is now a `String` instead of an `Integer`. It is a variable instead of a `Property` or `Function`. It has `Private` scope instead of `Public` scope. Your `Employee` object is now totally incompatible with the `Person` datatype, something that shouldn't occur normally when using inheritance.

This means that the code you wrote in `Form1` will no longer work. The `Age` property is no longer accessible and can no longer be used, and so your project will no longer compile. This directly illustrates the danger in shadowing a base class element such that its very nature or scope is changed by the subclass.

Since this change prevents your application from compiling, remove the line in the `Employee` class that shadows `Age` as a `String` variable, and uncomment the shadowed `Property` routine:

```
Public Shadows Property Age() As Integer
  Get
    Return CInt(DateDiff(DateInterval.Year, BirthDate, Now))
```

```
    End Get
    Set(ByVal value As Integer)
      BirthDate = DateAdd(DateInterval.Year, -value, Now)
    End Set
  End Property
```

This will restore your application to a working state, and you can move on.

Levels of Inheritance

So far, you've created a single base class and a single subclass, thus demonstrating that you can implement inheritance that is a single level deep. However, you can create inheritance relationships that are several levels deep. These are sometimes referred to as chains of inheritance.

In reality, you've been creating a two-level inheritance hierarchy so far, because you know that your base class actually derived from `System.Object`*, but for most purposes it is easiest to simply ignore that fact and treat only your classes as part of the inheritance hierarchy.*

Multiple Inheritance

Don't confuse multilevel inheritance with multiple inheritance, which is an entirely different concept that is not supported by either Visual Basic or the .NET platform itself. The idea behind multiple inheritance is that you can have a single subclass that inherits from two base classes at the same time.

For instance, you may have an application that has a class for `Customer` and another class for `Vendor`. It is quite possible that some customers are also vendors, so you might want to combine the functionality of these two classes into a `CustomerVendor` class. This new class would be a combination of both `Customer` and `Vendor`, so it would be nice to inherit from both of them at once.

While this is a useful concept, multiple inheritance is complex and somewhat dangerous. There are numerous problems with multiple inheritance, but the most obvious is that there can be collisions of properties or methods from the base classes. Suppose that both `Customer` and `Vendor` have a `Name` property. `CustomerVendor` would need two `Name` properties, one for each base class. Yet it only makes sense to have one `Name` property on `CustomerVendor`, so which base class does it link to, and how will the system operate if it doesn't link to the other one?

These are complex issues with no easy answers. Within the object-oriented community there is continual debate as to whether the advantages of code reuse outweigh the complexity that comes along for the ride.

Multiple inheritance is not supported by the .NET Framework, and so it is likewise not supported by Visual Basic. However, you can use multiple interfaces to achieve an effect similar to multiple inheritance, a topic we'll discuss later in the chapter when we talk about implementing multiple interfaces.

Multilevel Inheritance

You've seen how a subclass derives from a base class with your `Person` and `Employee` classes. However, there's nothing to stop the `Employee` subclass from being the base class for yet another class, a sub-subclass so to speak. This is not at all uncommon. In your example, you may find that you have different kinds of employees, some who work in the office and others who travel.

To accommodate this, you may want to have `OfficeEmployee` and `TravelingEmployee` classes. Of course, these are both examples of an employee and should share the functionality already present in the `Employee` class. The `Employee` class already reuses the functionality from the `Person` class. Figure 5-9 illustrates how these classes are interrelated.

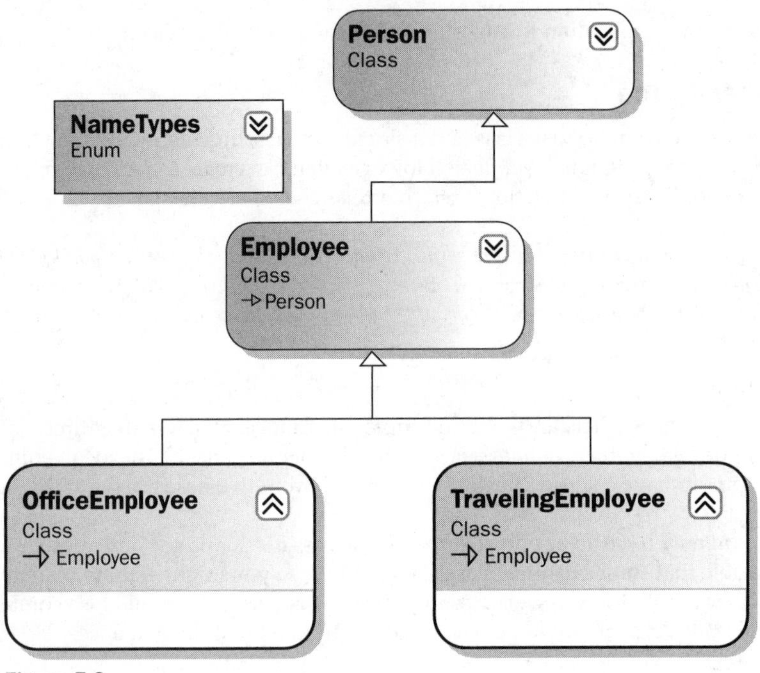

Figure 5-9

You can see that the `Employee` is a subclass of `Person`, and your two new classes are both subclasses of `Employee`. While both `OfficeEmployee` and `TravelingEmployee` are employees, and thus also people, they are each unique. An `OfficeEmployee` almost certainly has a cube or office number, while a `TravelingEmployee` will keep track of the number of miles traveled.

Add a new class to your project and name it `OfficeEmployee`. To make this class inherit from your existing `Employee` class, add the following code to the class:

```
Public Class OfficeEmployee
  Inherits Employee
End Class
```

With this change, the new class now has `Name`, `BirthDate`, `Age`, `HireDate`, and `Salary` methods. Notice that methods from both `Employee` and `Person` are inherited. A subclass always gains all the methods, properties, and events of its base class.

You can now extend the interface and behavior of `OfficeEmployee` by adding a property to indicate which cube or office number the employee occupies:

```
Public Class OfficeEmployee
  Inherits Employee

  Private mOffice As String

  Public Property OfficeNumber() As String
    Get
      Return mOffice
    End Get
    Set(ByVal value As String)
      mOffice = value
    End Set
  End Property
End Class
```

To see how this works, let's enhance your form to display this value. Add a new `TextBox` control named `txtOffice` and an associated label so that your form looks as shown in Figure 5-10.

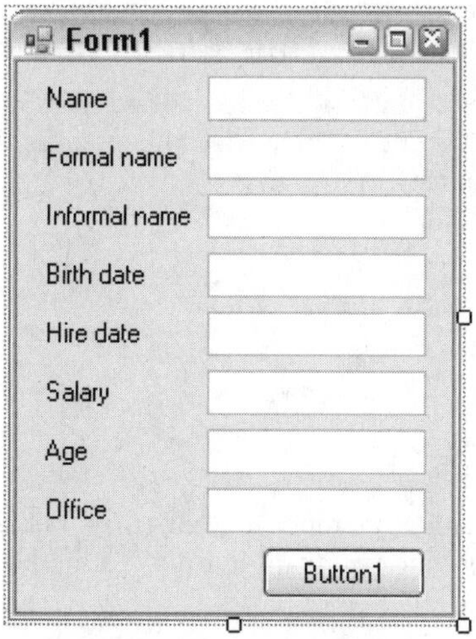

Figure 5-10

Now, change the code behind the button to make use of the new property:

```
Private Sub btnOK_Click(ByVal sender As System.Object, _
    ByVal e As System.EventArgs) Handles btnOK.Click

  Dim person As OfficeEmployee = New OfficeEmployee()

  With person
    .Name = "Fred"
    .BirthDate = #1/1/1960#
    .Age = 20
    .OfficeNumber = "A42"

    txtName.Text = .Name
```

```
        txtBirthDate.Text = Format(.BirthDate, "Short date")
        txtAge.Text = CStr(.Age)
        txtOffice.Text = .OfficeNumber
      End With
    End Sub
```

You've changed the routine to declare and create an object of type `OfficeEmployee`—thus allowing you to make use of the new property—as well as all existing properties and methods from `Employee` and `Person`, since they've been "merged" into the `OfficeEmployee` class via inheritance.

If you now run the application, you'll see that the name, birth date, age, and office values are displayed in the form.

Inheritance like this can go many levels deep, with each level extending and changing the behaviors of the previous levels. In fact, there is no specific technical limit to the number of levels of inheritance you can implement in Visual Basic. Very deep inheritance chains are typically not recommended and are often viewed as a design flaw, something discussed in more detail in Chapter 7.

Interacting with the Base Class, Your Class, and Your Object

You've already seen how you can use the `MyBase` keyword to call methods on the base class from within a subclass. The `MyBase` keyword is one of three special keywords that allow you to interact with important object and class representations:

- ❑ `Me`
- ❑ `MyBase`
- ❑ `MyClass`

The Me Keyword

The `Me` keyword provides you with a reference to your current object instance. Typically, you don't need to use the `Me` keyword, since any time you want to invoke a method within your current object you can just call that method directly.

To see clearly how this works, let's add a new method to the `Person` class that returns the data of the `Person` class in the form of a `String`. This will be a bit interesting in and of itself, since the base `System.Object` class defines the `ToString` method for this exact purpose. Remember that all classes in the .NET Framework ultimately derive from `System.Object`, even if you don't explicitly indicate it with an `Inherits` statement.

This means that you can simply override the `ToString` method from the `Object` class within your `Person` class by adding the following code:

```
Public Overrides Function ToString() As String
  Return Name
End Function
```

This implementation will return the person's `Name` property as a result when `ToString` is called.

> *By default,* `ToString` *returns the class name of the class. Up to now, if you had called the* `ToString` *method on a* `Person` *object, you would have gotten a result of* `InheritanceAndInterfaces.Person`.

Notice that the `ToString` method is calling another method within your same class, in this case the `Name` method.

You could also write this routine using the `Me` keyword:

```
Public Overrides Function ToString() As String
  Return Me.Name
End Function
```

However, this is redundant since `Me` is the default for all method calls in a class. These two implementations are identical, so typically the `Me` keyword is simply left off to avoid that extra typing.

To see how the `ToString` method now works, you can change your code in `Form1` to use this value instead of the `Name` property:

```
Private Sub btnOK_Click(ByVal sender As System.Object, _
    ByVal e As System.EventArgs) Handles btnOK.Click
  Dim objPerson As OfficeEmployee = New OfficeEmployee()

  With objPerson
    .Name = "Fred"
    .BirthDate = #1/1/1960#
    .Age = 20
    .OfficeNumber = "A42"

    txtName.Text = .ToString
    txtBirthDate.Text = Format(.BirthDate, "Short date")
    txtAge.Text = CStr(.Age)
    txtOffice.Text = .OfficeNumber
  End With
End Sub
```

When you run the application, you'll see that the person's name is displayed appropriately, which makes sense since the `ToString` method is simply returning the result from the `Name` property.

Earlier, we discussed virtual methods and how they work. Since either calling a method directly or calling it using the `Me` keyword invokes the method on the current object, this means that the method calls conform to the same rules as an external method call. In other words, your `ToString` method may not actually end up calling the `Name` method in the `Person` class if that method was overridden by a class farther down the inheritance chain such as the `Employee` or `OfficeEmployee` classes.

For example, you could override the `Name` property in your `OfficeEmployee` class such that it always returns the informal version of the person's name rather than the regular name. You can override the `Name` property by adding this method to the `OfficeEmployee` class:

```
Public Overloads Overrides Property Name() As String
  Get
    Return MyBase.Name(NameTypes.Informal)
  End Get
  Set(ByVal value As String)
    MyBase.Name = value
  End Set
End Property
```

This new version of the Name method relies on the base class to actually store the value, but instead of returning the normal name on request, now you are always returning the informal name:

```
Return MyBase.Name(NameTypes.Informal)
```

Before you can test this, you need to enhance the code in your form to actually provide a value for the informal name. Make the following change to the code:

```
Private Sub btnOK_Click(ByVal sender As System.Object,
    ByVal e As System.EventArgs) Handles btnOK.Click
  Dim objPerson As OfficeEmployee = New OfficeEmployee()

      With objPerson
   .Name = "Fred"
   .Name(NameTypes.Informal) = "Freddy"
   .BirthDate = #1/1/1960#
   .Age = 20
   .OfficeNumber = "A42"

   txtName.Text = .ToString
   txtBirthDate.Text = Format(.BirthDate, "Short date")
   txtAge.Text = CStr(.Age)
   txtOffice.Text = .OfficeNumber
  End With
End Sub
```

When you run the application, you'll find that the name field displays the informal name. Even though the ToString method is implemented in the Person class, it is invoking the implementation of Name from the OfficeEmployee class. This is because method calls within a class follow the same rules for calling virtual methods as code outside a class, such as your code in the form.

You'll see this behavior with or without the Me keyword, since the default behavior for method calls is to implicitly call them via the current object.

While methods called from within a class follow the same rules for virtual methods, this is not the case for shadowed methods. Here, you'll find that the rules for calling a shadowed method from within your class are different from those outside your class.

To see how this works, let's make the Name property in OfficeEmployee a shadowed method instead of an overridden method:

```
Public Shadows Property Name() As String
  Get
    Return MyBase.Name(NameTypes.Informal)
  End Get
  Set(ByVal value As String)
    MyBase.Name = value
  End Set
End Property
```

Before you can run your application, you'll have to adjust some code in the form. Because you've shadowed the `Name` property in `OfficeEmployee`, you'll find that the version of `Name` from `Employee` that acts as a property array is now invalid.

> **Shadowing a method replaces all implementations from higher in the inheritance chain, regardless of their method signature.**

To make your application operate, you'll need to change the variable declaration and object creation to declare a variable of type `Employee` so that you can access the property array while still creating an instance of `OfficeEmployee`:

```
Dim person As Employee = New OfficeEmployee()
```

Since your variable is now of type `Employee`, you also need to comment out the lines that refer to the `OfficeNumber` property, since it is no longer available:

```
With person
  .Name = "Fred"
  .Name(NameTypes.Informal) = "Freddy"
  .BirthDate = #1/1/1960#
  .Age = 20
  '.OfficeNumber = "A42"

  txtName.Text = .ToString
  txtBirthDate.Text = Format(.BirthDate, "Short date")
  txtAge.Text = CStr(.Age)
  'txtOffice.Text = .OfficeNumber
End With
```

When you run the application now, you'll find that it displays the name Fred rather than Freddy, meaning it is not calling the `Name` method from `OfficeEmployee`, instead it is calling the implementation provided by the `Employee` class. Remember that the code to make this call still resides in the `Person` class, but it now ignores the shadowed version of the `Name` method.

Shadowed implementations in subclasses are ignored when calling the method from within a class higher in the inheritance chain.

You'll get this same behavior with or without the `Me` keyword. So, the `Me` keyword, or calling methods directly, follows the same rules for overridden methods as any other method call. For shadowed methods, however, any shadowed implementations in subclasses are ignored and the method is called from the current level in the inheritance chain.

So, why does the `Me` keyword exist? Primarily to allow you to pass a reference to the current object as a parameter to other objects or methods. As you'll see when you look at the `MyBase` and `MyClass` keywords, things can get very confusing and there may be value in using the `Me` keyword when working with `MyBase` and `MyClass` to ensure that it is always clear which particular implementation of a method you intended to invoke.

The MyBase Keyword

While the `Me` keyword allows you to call methods on the current object instance, there are times you might want to explicitly call into methods in your parent class. Earlier, you saw an example of this when you called back into the base class from an overridden method in the subclass.

The `MyBase` keyword references only the immediate parent class, and it works like an object reference. This means that you can call methods on `MyBase`, knowing that they are being called just as if you had a reference to an object of your parent class's datatype.

> **There is no way to directly navigate up the inheritance chain beyond the immediate parent. This means that you can't direct access the implementation of a method in a base class if you are in a sub-subclass. Such a thing isn't a good idea anyway, which is why it isn't allowed.**

The `MyBase` keyword can be used to invoke or use any `Public`, `Friend`, or `Protected` element from the parent class. This includes all of those elements directly on the base class, and also any elements the base class inherited from other classes higher in the inheritance chain.

You've already used `MyBase` to call back into the base `Person` class as you implemented the overridden `Name` property in the `Employee` class.

> **Any code within a subclass can call any method on the base class by using the `MyBase` keyword.**

You can also use `MyBase` to call back into the base class implementation even if you've shadowed a method. Though we didn't remark on it at the time, you've already done this in your shadowed implementation of the `Name` property in the `OfficeEmployee` class. The highlighted lines indicate where you're calling into the base class from within a shadowed method.

```
Public Shadows Property Name() As String
  Get
    Return MyBase.Name(NameTypes.Informal)
  End Get
  Set(ByVal value As String)
    MyBase.Name = value
  End Set
End Property
```

The MyBase keyword allows you to merge the functionality of the base class into your subclass code as you deem fit.

The MyClass Keyword

As you've seen, when you use the Me keyword or call a method directly, your method call follows the rules for calling both virtual and nonvirtual methods. In other words, as you discovered earlier with the Name property, a call to Name from your code in the Person class actually invoked the overridden version of Name located in the OfficeEmployee class.

While this behavior is useful in many cases, there are also cases where you'll want to ensure that you really are running the specific implementation from your class, where even if a subclass overrode your method, you still want to ensure you're calling the version of the method that is directly in your class.

Maybe you decide that your ToString implementation in Person should always call the Name implementation that you write in the Person class, totally ignoring any overridden versions of Name in any subclasses.

This is where the MyClass keyword comes into play. This keyword is much like MyBase, in that it provides you with access to methods as though it was an object reference, in this case, a reference to an instance of the class that contains the code you're writing when using the MyClass keyword. This is true even if the instantiated object is an instance of a class derived from your class.

You've seen that a call to ToString from within Person will actually invoke the implementation in Employee or OfficeEmployee if your object is an instance of either of those types. Let's restore the Name property in OfficeEmployee so that it is an overridden method rather than a shadowed method to see how this works.

```
Public Overloads Overrides Property Name() As String
  Get
    Return MyBase.Name(NameTypes.Informal)
  End Get
  Set(ByVal value As String)
    MyBase.Name = value
  End Set
End Property
```

With this change, and based on your earlier testing, you know that the ToString implementation in Person will automatically call this overridden version of the Name property, since the call to the Name method will follow the normal rules for virtual methods. In fact, if you run the application now, you'll find that the name field on the form displays Freddy, the informal name of the person.

You can force the use of the implementation in the current class through the use of MyClass. Change the ToString method in Person as follows:

```
Public Overrides Function ToString() As String
  Return MyClass.Name
End Function
```

You are now calling the `Name` method, but you're doing it using the `MyClass` keyword. When you run the application and click the button, you'll find that the name field in the form displays Fred rather than Freddy, proving that the implementation from `Person` was invoked even though the datatype of the object itself is `OfficeEmployee`.

The `ToString` method is invoked from `Person`, since neither `Employee` nor `OfficeEmployee` provide an overridden implementation. Then, because you're using the `MyClass` keyword, the `Name` method is invoked directly from `Person`, explicitly defeating the default behavior you'd normally expect.

Constructors

As discussed in Chapter 4, you can provide a special constructor method, named `New`, on a class and it will be the first code run when an object is instantiated. You can also receive parameters via the constructor method, allowing the code that creates your object to pass data into the object during the creation process.

Constructor methods are affected by inheritance differently from regular methods. A normal `Public` method, such as `BirthDate` on your `Person` class, is automatically inherited by any subclass. From there you can overload, override, or shadow that method as we've discussed so far in this chapter.

Simple Constructors

Constructors don't quite follow the same rules. To explore the differences, let's implement a simple constructor method in your `Person` class:

```
Public Sub New()
  Debug.WriteLine("Person constructor")
End Sub
```

If you now run the application, you'll see the text displayed in the Output window in the IDE. This occurs even though the code in your form is creating an object of type `OfficeEmployee`:

```
Dim person As Employee = New OfficeEmployee()
```

As you might expect, the `New` method from your base `Person` class is invoked as part of the construction process of the `OfficeEmployee` object, simple inheritance at work. However, interesting things occur if you implement a `New` method in the `OfficeEmployee` class itself:

```
Public Sub New()
  Debug.WriteLine("OfficeEmployee constructor")
End Sub
```

Notice that you are not using the `Overrides` keyword, nor did you mark the method in `Person` as `Overridable`. These keywords have no use in this context and, in fact, will cause syntax errors if you attempt to use them on constructor methods.

When you run the application now you'd probably expect that only the implementation of `New` in `OfficeEmployee` would be invoked. Certainly, that is what would occur with a normal overridden method. But, of course, `New` isn't overridden, so when you run the application you'll find that both implementations are run. Both strings are output into the Output window in the IDE.

It is important to note that the implementation in the `Person` class ran first, followed by the implementation in the `OfficeEmployee` class. This occurs because, as an object is created, all the constructors for the classes in the inheritance chain are invoked, starting with the base class and working out through all the subclasses one by one. In fact, if you implement a `New` method in the `Employee` class you can see that it too is invoked:

```
Public Sub New()
  Debug.WriteLine("Employee constructor")
End Sub
```

When the application is run and the button clicked, you'll see all three strings in the Output window. All three constructor methods were invoked, starting with the `Person` class and working down to the `OfficeEmployee` class.

Constructors in More Depth

The rules governing constructors without parameters are pretty straightforward. However, things get a bit more interesting if you start requiring parameters on your constructors.

To understand what is going on, you need to get a slightly better understanding of how even your simple constructors are being invoked. While you see them as being invoked from the base class down through all subclasses to your final subclass, what is really happening is a bit different.

In particular, it is the subclass `New` method that is invoked first. However, Visual Basic is automatically inserting a line of code into your routine at compile time. For instance, in your `OfficeEmployee` class you have a constructor:

```
Public Sub New()
  Debug.WriteLine("OfficeEmployee constructor")
End Sub
```

Behind the scenes, Visual Basic inserts what is effectively a call to the constructor of your parent class on your behalf. You could do this manually by using the `MyBase` keyword with the following change:

```
Public Sub New()
  MyBase.New()
  Debug.WriteLine("OfficeEmployee constructor")
End Sub
```

This call must be the first line in your constructor. If you put any other code before this line, you'll get a syntax error indicating that your code is invalid. Since the call is always required, and since it always must be the first line in any constructor, Visual Basic simply inserts it for you automatically.

It is also worth noting that if you don't explicitly provide a constructor on a class by implementing a `New` method, Visual Basic creates one for you behind the scenes. The automatically created method simply has one line of code:

```
MyBase.New()
```

All classes have constructor methods, either created explicitly by you as you write a `New` method or created implicitly by Visual Basic as the class is compiled.

A constructor method is sometimes called a ctor, short for constructor. This term is often used by tools such as ILDASM or .NET Reflector.

By always calling `Mybase.New()` as the first line in every constructor, you are guaranteed that it is the implementation of `New` in your top-level base class that will actually run first. Every subclass invokes the parent class implementation all the way up the inheritance chain until only the base class remains. Then its code runs, followed by each individual subclass, as you've already seen.

Constructors with Parameters

This works great when your constructors don't require parameters. However, if your constructor does require a parameter, then it becomes impossible for Visual Basic to automatically make that call on your behalf. After all, how would Visual Basic know what values you want to pass as parameters?

To see how this works, let's change the `New` method in the `Person` class to require a `name` parameter. You can use that parameter to initialize the object's `Name` property:

```
Public Sub New(ByVal name As String)
  Me.Name = name
  Debug.WriteLine("Person constructor")
End Sub
```

Now your constructor requires a `String` parameter and uses it to initialize the `Name` property.

You are using the `Me` keyword to make your code easier to read. Interestingly enough, the compiler will actually understand and correctly compile the following code:

```
Name = name
```

But that is not at all clear to a developer reading the code. By prefixing the property name with the `Me` keyword you've made it clear that you're invoking a property on the object and providing it with the parameter value.

At this point, you'll find that your application won't compile. This is so because there is an error in the `New` method of the `Employee` class. In particular, Visual Basic's attempt to automatically invoke the constructor on the `Person` class is no longer workable, since it has no idea what data value to pass for this new `name` parameter.

There are three ways you can address this error:

- Make the `name` parameter `Optional`.
- Overload the `New` method with another implementation that requires no parameter.
- Manually provide the `Name` parameter value from within the `Employee` class.

If you make the `Name` parameter `Optional`, you're indicating that the `New` method can be called with or without a parameter. This means that one viable option is to call the method with no parameters. So, Visual Basic's default of calling it with no parameters will work just fine.

If you overload the New method, you can implement a second New method that doesn't accept any parameters, again allowing Visual Basic's default behavior to work as you've seen. Keep in mind that this solution would only invoke the overloaded version of New with no parameter; the version that requires a parameter would not be invoked.

The final way you can fix the error is by simply providing a parameter value yourself from within the New method of the Employee class. To do this, change the Employee class:

```
Public Sub New()
  MyBase.New("George")
  Debug.WriteLine("Employee constructor")
End Sub
```

By explicitly calling the New method of the parent class, you are able to provide it with the required parameter value. At this point, your application will compile, but it won't run.

Constructors, Overloading, and Variable Initialization

What isn't clear from this code is that you've now introduced a very insidious bug. The constructor in the Person class is using the Name property to set the value:

```
Public Sub New(ByVal name As String)
  Me.Name = name
  Debug.WriteLine("Person constructor")
End Sub
```

But the Name property is overridden by the Employee class, so it is that implementation that will be run. Unfortunately, that implementation makes use of a Dictionary object, which isn't available yet! It turns out that any member variables declared in a class with the New statement, such as the Dictionary object in Employee:

```
Private mNames As New Generic.Dictionary(Of NameTypes, String)
```

won't be initialized until after the constructor for that class has completed. Since you are still in the constructor for Person, there's no way the constructor for Employee can be complete. To resolve this, you need to change the Employee class a bit so that it doesn't rely on the Dictionary being created in this manner. Instead, you'll add code to create it when needed.

First, change the declaration of the variable in the Employee class:

```
Private mNames As Generic.Dictionary(Of NameTypes, String)
```

Then, update the Name property so that it creates the Hashtable object if needed:

```
Public Overloads Property Name(ByVal type As NameTypes) As String
  Get
    If mNames Is Nothing Then mNames = New Generic.Dictionary(Of NameTypes, String)
    Return mNames(type)
  End Get
  Set(ByVal value As String)
```

```
        If mNames Is Nothing Then mNames = New Generic.Dictionary(Of NameTypes, String)
        If mNames.ContainsKey(type) Then
          mNames.Item(type) = value
        Else
          mNames.Add(type, value)
        End If
        If type = NameTypes.Normal Then
          MyBase.Name = value
        End If
      End Set
    End Property
```

This will ensure that a `Dictionary` object is created in the `Employee` class code even though its constructor hasn't yet completed.

More Constructors with Parameters

Obviously, you probably don't really want to hard-code a value in a constructor as you did in the `Employee` class, so you may choose instead to change this constructor to also accept a `name` parameter. Change the `Employee` class constructor as shown:

```
    Public Sub New(ByVal name As String)
      MyBase.New(name)

      Debug.WriteLine("Employee constructor")
    End Sub
```

Of course, this just pushed the issue deeper, and now you'll find that the `OfficeEmployee` class has a compile error in its `New` method. Again, you can fix the problem by having that method accept a parameter so that it can provide it up the chain as required. Make the following change to `OfficeEmployee`:

```
    Public Sub New(ByVal name As String)
      MyBase.New(name)

      Debug.WriteLine("OfficeEmployee constructor")
    End Sub
```

Finally, the code in the form is no longer valid. You're attempting to create an instance of `OfficeEmployee` without passing a parameter value. Let's update that code and then you can run the application:

```
    Private Sub btnOK_Click(ByVal sender As System.Object, _
        ByVal e As System.EventArgs) Handles btnOK.Click

        Dim person As Employee = New OfficeEmployee("Mary")
        With person
          '.Name = "Fred"
```

You're passing a `name` value to the constructor of `OfficeEmployee`. Also, you've commented out the line of code that sets the `Name` property directly — meaning that the value passed in the constructor will be displayed in the form.

The Protected Scope

You've seen how a subclass automatically gains all the `Public` methods and properties that compose the interface of the base class. This is also true of `Friend` methods and properties; they are inherited as well and are available only to other code in the same project as the subclass.

`Private` methods and properties are not exposed as part of the interface of the subclass, meaning that the code in the subclass cannot call those methods, nor can any code using your objects. These methods are only available to the code within the base class itself. This can get confusing, since the implementations contained in the `Private` methods are inherited and are used by any code in the base class; it is just that they aren't available to be called by any other code, including code in the subclass.

There are times when you want to create methods in your base class that can be called by a subclass as well as the base class but not by code outside of those classes. Basically, you want a hybrid between `Public` and `Private`—methods that are private to the classes in the inheritance chain but are usable by any subclasses that might be created within the chain. This functionality is provided by the `Protected` scope.

`Protected` methods are very similar to `Private` methods in that they are not available to any code that calls your objects. Instead, these methods are available to code within the base class and to code within any subclass. The following table lists all the available scope options.

Scope	Description
`Private`	Available only to code within your class.
`Protected`	Available only to classes that inherit from your class.
`Friend`	Available only to code within your project/component.
`Protected Friend`	Available to classes that inherit from your class (in any project) and to code within your project/component. This is a combination of `Protected` and `Friend`.
`Public`	Available to code outside your class.

The `Protected` scope can be applied to `Sub`, `Function`, and `Property` methods. To see how the `Protected` scope works, let's add an `Identity` field to the `Person` class:

```
Public Class Person
  Private mName As String
  Private mBirthDate As String
  Private mID As String

  Protected Property Identity() As String
    Get
      Return mID
    End Get
    Set(ByVal value As String)
      mID = value
    End Set
  End Property
```

This data field represents some arbitrary identification number or value assigned to a person. This might be a Social Security number, an employee number, or whatever is appropriate.

The interesting thing about this value is that it is not currently accessible outside your inheritance chain. For instance, if you try to use it from your code in the form, you'll discover that there is no `Identity` property on your `Person`, `Employee`, or `OfficeEmployee` objects.

However, there is an `Identity` property now available inside your inheritance chain. The `Identity` property is available to the code in the `Person` class just like any other method. The interesting thing is that even though `Identity` is not available to the code in your form, it is available to the code in the `Employee` and `OfficeEmployee` classes. This is because they are both subclasses of `Person`. `Employee` is directly a subclass, and `OfficeEmployee` is indirectly a subclass of `Person` because it is a subclass of `Employee`.

Thus, you can enhance your `Employee` class to implement an `EmployeeNumber` property by using the `Identity` property. To do this, add the following code to the `Employee` class:

```
Public Property EmployeeNumber() As Integer
  Get
    Return CInt(Identity)
  End Get
  Set(ByVal value As Integer)
    Identity = CStr(value)
  End Set
End Property
```

This new property exposes a numeric identity value for the employee, but it uses the internal `Identity` property to manage that value.

You can override and shadow `Protected` elements just as you do with elements of any other scope.

Protected Variables

Up to this point, you've focused on methods and properties and how they interact through inheritance. Inheritance, and, in particular, the `Protected` scope, also has an impact on instance variables and how you work with them.

Though it is not recommended, you can declare variables in a class using `Public` scope. This makes the variable directly available to code both within and outside of your class, allowing any code that interacts with your objects to directly read or alter the value of that variable.

Variables can also have `Friend` scope, which likewise allows any code in your class or anywhere within your project to read or alter the value directly. This is also generally not recommended because it breaks encapsulation.

> **Rather than declaring variables with `Public` or `Friend` scope, it is better to expose the value using a `Property` method so that you can apply any of your business rules to control how the value is altered as appropriate.**

Of course, you know that variables can be of `Private` scope, and this is typically the case. This makes the variables accessible only to the code within your class and is the most restrictive scope.

As with methods, however, you can also use the `Protected` scope when declaring variables. This makes the variable accessible to the code in your class, and to the code in any class that derives from your class — all the way down the hierarchy chain.

There are times when this is useful, because it allows you to provide and accept data to and from subclasses, but to act on that data from code in the base class. At the same time, exposing variables to subclasses is typically not ideal, and you should use `Property` methods with `Protected` scope for this instead, since they allow your base class to enforce any business rules that are appropriate for the value, rather than just hoping that the author of the subclass only provides good values.

Events and Inheritance

So far, we've discussed methods, properties, and variables in terms of inheritance — seeing how they can be added, overridden, extended, and shadowed. In Visual Basic, events are also part of the interface of an object, and they are impacted by inheritance as well.

Inheriting Events

Chapter 4 discussed how to declare, raise and receive events from objects. You can add such an event to the `Person` class by declaring it at the top of the class:

```
Public Class Person
  Private mName As String
  Private mBirthDate As String
  Private mID As String

  Public Event NameChanged(ByVal newName As String)
```

Then, you can raise this event within the class anytime the person's name is changed:

```
Public Overridable Property Name() As String
  Get
    Return mName
  End Get
  Set(ByVal value As String)
    mName = value
    RaiseEvent NameChanged(mName)
  End Set
End Property
```

At this point, you can receive and handle this event within your form any time you're working with a `Person` object. The nice thing about this is that your events are inherited automatically by subclasses — meaning that your `Employee` and `OfficeEmployee` objects will also raise this event. Thus, you can change the code in your form to handle the event, even though you're working with an object of type `OfficeEmployee`.

First, you can add a method to handle the event to `Form1`:

```
Private Sub OnNameChanged(ByVal newName As String)
  MsgBox("New name: " & newName)
End Sub
```

Note that you're not using the `Handles` clause here. In this case, for simplicity, you'll use the `AddHandler` method to dynamically link the event to this method. However, you could have also chosen to use the `WithEvents` and `Handles` keywords, as described in Chapter 4—either way works.

With the handler built, you can use the `AddHandler` method to link this method to the event on the object:

```
Private Sub btnOK_Click(ByVal sender As System.Object, _
    ByVal e As System.EventArgs) Handles btnOK.Click

  Dim person As Employee = New OfficeEmployee("Mary")
  AddHandler person.NameChanged, AddressOf OnNameChanged

  With pPerson
    .Name = "Fred"
```

Also note that you're uncommenting the line that changes the `Name` property. With this change, you know that the event should fire when the name is changed.

When you run the application now, you'll see a message box, indicating that the name has changed and proving that the `NameChanged` event really is exposed and available even though your object is of type `OfficeEmployee` rather than of type `Person`.

Raising Events from Subclasses

One caveat you need to keep in mind is that while a subclass exposes the events of its base class, the code in the subclass cannot raise the event.

In other words, you cannot use the `RaiseEvent` method in `Employee` or `OfficeEmployee` to raise the `NameChanged` event. Only code directly in the `Person` class can raise the event.

To see this in action, let's add another event to the `Person` class, an event that can indicate the change of other arbitrary data values:

```
Public Class Person
  Private mName As String
  Private mBirthDate As String
  Private mID As String

  Public Event NameChanged(ByVal newName As String)
  Public Event DataChanged(ByVal field As String, ByVal newValue As Object)
```

You can then raise this event when the `BirthDate` is changed:

```
Public Overridable Property BirthDate() As Date
  Get
    Return mBirthDate
  End Get
```

```
    Set(ByVal value As Date)
      mBirthDate = value
      RaiseEvent DataChanged("BirthDate", value)
    End Set
  End Property
```

It would also be nice to raise this event from the `Employee` class when the `Salary` value is changed. Unfortunately, you can't use the `RaiseEvent` method to raise the event from a base class, so the following code won't work (don't enter this code):

```
  Public Property Salary() As Double
    Get
      Return mSalary
    End Get
    Set(ByVal value As Double)
      mSalary = value
      RaiseEvent DataChanged("Salary", value)
    End Set
  End Property
```

Fortunately, there is a relatively easy way to get around this limitation. You can simply implement a `Protected` method in your base class that allows any derived class to raise the method. In the `Person` class, you can add such a method:

```
  Protected Sub OnDataChanged(ByVal field As String, _
      ByVal newValue As Object)
    RaiseEvent DataChanged(field, newValue)
  End Sub
```

Then you can use this method from within the `Employee` class to indicate that `Salary` has changed:

```
  Public Property Salary() As Double
    Get
      Return mSalary
    End Get
    Set(ByVal value As Double)
      mSalary = value
      OnDataChanged("Salary", value)
    End Set
  End Property
```

Notice that the code in `Employee` is not raising the event, it is simply calling a `Protected` method in `Person`. It is the code in the `Person` class that actually raises the event, meaning that all will work as you desire.

You can enhance the code in `Form1` to receive the event. First off, you need to create a method to handle the event:

```
  Private Sub OnDataChanged(ByVal field As String, ByVal newValue As Object)
    MsgBox("New " & field & ": " & CStr(newValue))
  End Sub
```

Then, you can link this handler to the event using the `AddHandler` method:

```
Private Sub btnOK_Click(ByVal sender As System.Object, _
    ByVal e As System.EventArgs) Handles btnOK.Click

  Dim person As Employee = New OfficeEmployee("Mary")
  AddHandler person.NameChanged, AddressOf OnNameChanged
  AddHandler person.DataChanged, AddressOf OnDataChanged
```

Finally, you need to make sure that you are changing and displaying the `Salary` property:

```
With person
  .Name = "Fred"
  .Name(NameTypes.Informal) = "Freddy"
  .BirthDate = #1/1/1960#
  .Age = 20
  .Salary = 30000
  txtName.Text = .ToString
  txtBirthDate.Text = Format(.BirthDate, "Short date")
  txtAge.Text = CStr(.Age)
  txtSalary.Text = Format(.Salary, "0.00")
End With
```

When you run the application and click the button now, you'll get message boxes displaying the changes to the `Name` property, the `BirthDate` property (twice, once for the `BirthDate` property and once for the `Age` property, which changes the birth date), and the `Salary` property.

Shared Methods

In Chapter 4, you explored shared methods and how they work, providing a set of methods that can be invoked directly from the class rather than requiring that you create an actual object.

Shared methods are inherited just like instance methods and so are automatically available as methods on subclasses just as they are on the base class. If you implement a shared method in `BaseClass`, you can call that method using any class derived from `BaseClass`.

Like a regular method, shared methods can be overloaded and shadowed. They cannot, however, be overridden. If you attempt to use the `Overridable` keyword when declaring a `Shared` method, you will get a syntax error.

For instance, you can implement a method in your `Person` class to compare two `Person` objects:

```
Public Shared Function Compare(ByVal person1 As Person, _
    ByVal person2 As Person) As Boolean

  Return (person1.Name = person2.Name)

End Function
```

To test this method, let's add another button to the form, name it `btnCompare`, and set its `Text` value to `Compare`. Double-click the button to bring up the code window and enter the following code:

```
Private Sub btnCompare_Click(ByVal sender As System.Object, _
    ByVal e As System.EventArgs) Handles btnCompare.Click

  Dim emp1 As New Employee("Fred")
  Dim emp2 As New Employee("Mary")

  MsgBox(Employee.Compare(emp1, emp2))
End Sub
```

This code simply creates two `Employee` objects and compares them. Note though, that the code uses the `Employee` class to invoke the `Compare` method, displaying the result in a message box. This establishes that the `Compare` method implemented in the `Person` class is inherited by the `Employee` class as you'd expect.

Overloading Shared Methods

Shared methods can be overloaded using the `Overloads` keyword in the same manner as you overload an instance method. This means that your subclass can add new implementations of the shared method as long as the parameter list differs from the original implementation.

For example, you can add a new implementation of the `Compare` method to `Employee`:

```
Public Overloads Shared Function Compare(ByVal employee1 As Employee, _
    ByVal employee2 As Employee) As Boolean

  Return (employee1.EmployeeNumber = employee2.EmployeeNumber)

End Function
```

This new implementation compares two `Employee` objects rather than two `Person` objects, and in fact, compares them based on the employee number rather than by name.

You can enhance the code behind `btnCompare` in the form to set the `EmployeeNumber` properties:

```
Private Sub btnCompare_Click(ByVal sender As System.Object, _
    ByVal e As System.EventArgs) Handles btnCompare.Click

  Dim emp1 As New Employee("Fred")
  Dim emp2 As New Employee("Mary")

  emp1.EmployeeNumber = 1
  emp2.EmployeeNumber = 1

  MsgBox(Employee.Compare(emp1, emp2))
End Sub
```

While it might make little sense for these two objects to have the same `EmployeeNumber` value, it will prove a point. When you run the application now, even though the `Name` values of the objects are different, your `Compare` routine will return `True`, proving that you're invoking the overloaded version of the method that expects two `Employee` objects as parameters.

The overloaded implementation is available on the Employee class or any classes derived from Employee such as OfficeEmployee. The overloaded implementation is not available if called directly from Person, since that class only contains the original implementation.

Shadowing Shared Methods

Shared methods can also be shadowed by a subclass. This allows you to do some very interesting things, including converting a shared method into an instance method or vice versa. You can even leave the method as shared, but change the entire way it works and is declared. In short, just as with instance methods, you can use the Shadows keyword to entirely replace and change a shared method in a subclass.

To see how this works, you can use the Shadows keyword to change the nature of the Compare method in OfficeEmployee:

```
Public Shared Shadows Function Compare(ByVal person1 As Person, _
    ByVal person2 As Person) As Boolean

  Return (person1.Age = person2.Age)

End Function
```

Notice that this method has the same signature as the original Compare method you implemented in the Person class, but instead of comparing by name, here you're comparing by age. With a normal method you could have done this by overriding, but since Shared methods can't be overridden, the only thing you can do is shadow it.

Of course, the shadowed implementation is only available via the OfficeEmployee class. Neither the Person nor Employee classes, which are higher up the inheritance chain, are aware that this shadowed version of the method exists.

To use this from your Form1 code, you can change the code for btnCompare as follows:

```
Private Sub btnCompare_Click(ByVal sender As System.Object, _
    ByVal e As System.EventArgs) Handles btnCompare.Click

  Dim emp1 As New Employee("Fred")
  Dim emp2 As New Employee("Mary")

  emp1.Age = 20
  emp2.Age = 25
  MsgBox(OfficeEmployee.Compare(emp1, emp2))
End Sub
```

Instead of setting the EmployeeNumber values, you're now setting the Age values on your objects. More importantly, notice that you're now calling the Compare method via the OfficeEmployee class rather than via Employee or Person. This causes the invocation of the new version of the method, and the ages of the objects are compared.

Shared Events

As discussed in Chapter 4, you can create shared events, events that can be raised by shared or instance methods in a class, whereas regular events can only be raised from within instance methods.

When you inherit from a class that defines a shared event, your new subclass automatically gains that event just as it does with regular events, as discussed earlier in this chapter.

As with instance events, a shared event cannot be raised by code within the subclass, it can only be raised using the `RaiseEvent` keyword from code in the class where the event is declared. If you want to be able to raise the event from methods in your subclass, you need to implement a `Protected` method on the base class that actually makes the call to `RaiseEvent`.

This is no different from what we discussed earlier in the chapter other than to note that with a shared event you can use a method with `Protected` scope that is marked as shared to raise the event rather than using an instance method.

Creating an Abstract Base Class

So far, you've seen how to inherit from a class, how to overload and override methods, and how virtual methods work. In all of the examples so far, the parent classes have been useful in their own right and could be instantiated and do some meaningful work. Sometimes, however, you want to create a class such that it can only be used as a base class for inheritance.

MustInherit Keyword

The current `Person` class is not only being used as a base class, but can also be instantiated directly to create an object of type `Person`. Likewise, the `Employee` class is also being used as a base class for the `OfficeEmployee` class you created that derives from it.

If you want to make a class only act as a base class, you can use the `MustInherit` keyword, thereby preventing anyone from creating objects based directly on the class and requiring them instead to create a subclass and then create objects based on that subclass.

This can be very useful when you are creating object models of real-world concepts and entities. You'll discuss ways to leverage this capability in Chapter 7. You can change `Person` to use the `MustInherit` keyword:

```
Public MustInherit Class Person
```

This has no effect on the code within `Person` or any of the classes that inherit from it. However, it does mean that no code can instantiate objects directly from the `Person` class; instead you can only create objects based on `Employee` or `OfficeEmployee`.

Keep in mind that this doesn't prevent you from declaring variables of type `Person`, it merely prevents you from creating an object by using `New Person()`. You can also continue to make use of `Shared` methods from the `Person` class without any difficulty.

MustOverride Keyword

Another option you have is to create a method (`Sub`, `Function`, or `Property`) that must be overridden by a subclass. You might want to do this when you are creating a base class that provides some behaviors, but relies on subclasses to also provide some behaviors in order to function properly. This is accomplished by using the `MustOverride` keyword on a method declaration.

If a class contains any methods marked with `MustOverride`, the class itself must also be declared with the `MustInherit` keyword or you'll get a syntax error:

```
Public MustInherit Class Person
```

This makes sense. If you're requiring that a method be overridden in a subclass, it only stands to reason that your class can't be directly instantiated; it must be subclassed to be useful.

Let's see how this works by adding a `LifeExpectancy` method in `Person` that has no implementation and must be overridden by a subclass:

```
Public MustOverride Function LifeExpectancy() As Integer
```

Notice that there is no `End Function` or any other code associated with the method.

When using `MustOverride`, you cannot provide any implementation for the method in your class. Such a method is called an abstract method or pure virtual function, since it only defines the interface and no implementation.

Methods declared in this manner must be overridden in any subclass that inherits from your base class. If you don't override one of these methods, you'll generate a syntax error in the subclass, and it won't compile. This means that you need to alter the `Employee` class to provide an implementation for this method:

```
Public Overrides Function LifeExpectancy() As Integer
  Return 90
End Function
```

Your application will compile and run at this point, since you are now overriding the `LifeExpectancy` method in `Employee`, so the required condition is met.

Abstract Base Classes

You can combine these two concepts, using both `MustInherit` and `MustOverride`, to create something called an abstract base class. Sometimes, this is also referred to as a virtual class.

This is a class that provides no implementation, only the interface definitions from which a subclass can be created, for example:

```
Public MustInherit Class AbstractBaseClass
  Public MustOverride Sub DoSomething()
  Public MustOverride Sub DoOtherStuff()
End Class
```

This technique can be very useful when creating frameworks or the high-level conceptual elements of a system. Any class that inherits `AbstractBaseClass` must implement both `DoSomething` and `DoOtherStuff` or a syntax error will result.

In some ways, an abstract base class is very comparable to defining an interface using the `Interface` keyword. The `Interface` keyword will be discussed in detail later in this chapter. You could define the same interface as shown in this example with the following code:

```
Public Interface IAbstractBaseClass
  Sub DoSomething()
  Sub DoOtherStuff()
End Interface
```

Any class that implements the `IAbstractBaseClass` interface must implement both `DoSomething` and `DoOtherStuff` or a syntax error will result, and in that regard this technique is similar to an abstract base class.

Preventing Inheritance

If you want to prevent a class from being used as a base class, you can use the `NotInheritable` keyword. For instance, you can change your `OfficeEmployee` as follows:

```
Public NotInheritable Class OfficeEmployee
```

At this point, it is no longer possible to inherit from this class to create a new class. Your `OfficeEmployee` class is now sealed, meaning that it cannot be used as a base from which to create other classes.

If you attempt to inherit from `OfficeEmployee`, you'll get a compile error indicating that it cannot be used as a base class. This has no effect on `Person` or `Employee`; you can continue to derive other classes from them.

Typically, you'll want to design your classes so that they can be subclassed, because that provides the greatest long-term flexibility in the overall design. There are times, however, when you will want to make sure that your class cannot be used as a base class, and the `NotInheritable` keyword addresses that issue.

Multiple Interfaces

In Visual Basic, objects can have one or more interfaces. All objects have a primary or native interface, which is composed of any methods, properties, events, or member variables declared using the `Public` keyword. You can also have objects implement secondary interfaces in addition to their native interface by using the `Implements` keyword.

Object Interfaces

The native interface on any class is composed of all the methods, properties, events, and even variables that are declared as anything other than `Private`. Though this is nothing new, let's quickly review what is included in the native interface to set the stage for discussing secondary interfaces.

To include a method as part of your interface, you can simply declare a `Public` routine:

```
Public Sub AMethod()

End Sub
```

Notice that there is no code in this routine. Any code would be implementation and is not part of the interface. Only the declaration of the method is important when discussing interfaces. This can seem confusing at first, but it is an important distinction, since the separation of the interface from its implementation is at the very core of object-oriented programming and design.

Since this method is declared as `Public`, it is available to any code outside the class, including other applications that may make use of the assembly.

If the method has a property, you can declare it as part of the interface by using the `Property` keyword:

```
Public Property AProperty() As String

End Property
```

You can also declare events as part of the interface by using the `Event` keyword:

```
Public Event AnEvent()
```

Finally, you can include actual variables, or attributes, as part of the interface:

```
Public AnInteger As Integer
```

This is strongly discouraged, because it directly exposes the internal variables for use by code outside the class. Since the variable is directly accessible from other code, you give up any and all control over the way the value may be changed or by which code may be accessed.

Rather than making any variable `Public`, it is far preferable to make use of a `Property` method to expose the value. In that way you can implement code to ensure that your internal variable is only set to valid values and that only the appropriate code has access to the value based on your application's logic.

Using the Native Interface

In the end, the native (or primary) interface for any class is defined by looking at all the methods, properties, events, and variables that are declared as anything other than `Private` in scope. This includes any methods, properties, events, or variables that are inherited from a base class.

You're used to interacting with the default interface on most objects, so this should seem pretty straightforward. Consider a simple class:

```
Public Class TheClass
  Public Sub DoSomething()

  End Sub
```

```
    Public Sub DoSomethingElse()

    End Sub
  End Class
```

This defines a class and, by extension, also defines the native interface that is exposed by any objects you instantiate based on this class. The native interface defines two methods, `DoSomething` and `DoSomethingElse`. To make use of these methods, you simply call them:

```
Dim myObject As New TheClass()

myObject.DoSomething()

myObject.DoSomethingElse()
```

This is the same thing you've done in Chapter 4 and so far in this chapter. However, let's take a look at creating and using secondary interfaces, because they are a bit different.

Secondary Interfaces

Sometimes, it can be helpful for an object to have more than one interface, thus allowing you to interact with the object in different ways.

Inheritance allows you to create subclasses that are a specialized case of the base class. For example, your `Employee` is a `Person`.

However, there are times when you have a group of objects that are not the same thing, but you want to be able to treat them as though they were the same. You want all these objects to act as the same thing, even though they are all different.

For instance, you may have a series of different objects in an application, product, customer, invoice, and so forth. Each of these would have default interfaces appropriate to each individual object — and each of them is a different class — so there's no natural inheritance relationship implied between these classes. At the same time, you may need to be able to generate a printed document for each type of object. So, you'd like to make them all act as a printable object.

> *Chapter 7 discusses the* is-a *and* act-as *relationships in more detail.*

To accomplish this, you can define a generic interface that would enable generating such a printed document. You can call it `IPrintableObject`.

> *By convention, this type of interface is typically prefixed with a capital I to indicate that it is a formal interface.*

Each of your application objects can choose to implement the `IPrintableObject` interface. Every object that implements this interface must provide code to provide actual implementation of the interface, which is unlike inheritance, where the code from a base class is automatically reused.

By implementing this common interface, however, you are able to write a routine that accepts any object that implements the `IPrintableObject` interface and print it—while remaining totally oblivious to the "real" datatype of the object or the methods its native interface might expose.

Before you see how to use an interface in this manner, let's walk through the process of actually defining an interface.

Defining the Interface

You define a formal interface using the `Interface` keyword. This can be done in any code module in your project, but a good place to put this type of definition is in a standard module. An interface defines a set of methods (`Sub`, `Function`, or `Property`) and events that must be exposed by any class that chooses to implement the interface.

Add a module to the project using Project ➪ Add Module and name it `Interfaces.vb`. Then, add the following code to the module, outside the `Module` code block itself:

```
Public Interface IPrintableObject

End Interface
Module Interfaces

End Module
```

A code module can contain a number of interface definitions, and these definitions must exist outside any other code block. Thus, they don't go within a `Class` or `Module` block; they are at a peer level to those constructs.

Interfaces must be declared using either `Public` or `Friend` scope. Declaring a `Private` or `Protected` interface will result in a syntax error.

Within the `Interface` block of code, you can define the methods, properties, and events that will make up your particular interface. Since the scope of the interface is defined by the `Interface` declaration itself, you can't specify scopes for individual methods and events, they are all scoped the same as the interface itself.

For instance, add the following code:

```
Public Interface IPrintableObject
   Function Label(ByVal index As Integer) As String
   Function Value(ByVal index As Integer) As String
   ReadOnly Property Count() As Integer
End Interface
```

This defines a new datatype, somewhat like creating a class or structure, that you can use when declaring variables.

For instance, you can now declare a variable of type `IPrintableObject`:

```
Private printable As IPrintableObject
```

You can also have your classes implement this interface, which will require each class to provide implementation code for each of the three methods defined on the interface.

Before you implement the interface in a class, let's see how you can make use of the interface to write a generic routine that can print any object that does implement `IPrintableObject`.

Using the Interface

Interfaces define the methods and events (including parameters and datatypes) that an object is required to implement if they choose to support the interface. This means that, given just the interface definition, you can easily write code that can interact with any object that implements the interface, even though you don't know what the native datatypes of those objects will be.

To see how you can write such code, let's create a simple routine in your form that can display data to the Output window in the IDE from any object that implements `IPrintableObject`. Bring up the code window for your form and add the following routine:

```
Public Sub PrintObject(obj As IPrintableObject)
  Dim index As Integer

  For index = 0 To obj.Count
    Debug.Write(obj.Label(index) & ": ")
    Debug.WriteLine(obj.Value(index))
  Next
End Sub
```

Notice that you're accepting a parameter of type `IPrintableObject`. This is how secondary interfaces are used, by treating an object of one type as though it was actually of the interface type. As long as the object passed to this routine implements the `IPrintableObject` interface, your code will work fine.

Within the `PrintObject` routine, you're assuming that the object will implement three elements — `Count`, `Label`, and `Value` — as part of the `IPrintableObject` interface. Secondary interfaces can include methods, properties, and events, much like a default interface, but the interface itself is defined and implemented using some special syntax.

Now that you have a generic printing routine, you need a way to call it. Bring up the designer for `Form1`, add a button, and name it `btnPrint`. Double-click the button and put this code behind it:

```
Private Sub btnPrint_Click(ByVal sender As System.Object, _
    ByVal e As System.EventArgs) Handles btnPrint.Click

  Dim obj As New Employee("Andy")

  obj.EmployeeNumber = 123
  obj.BirthDate = #1/1/1980#
  obj.HireDate = #1/1/1996#

  PrintObject(obj)
End Sub
```

This code simply initializes an `Employee` object and calls the `PrintObject` routine.

Of course, this code produces compiler errors, because PrintObject is expecting a parameter that implements IPrintableObject and Employee implements no such interface.

Let's move on and implement that interface in Employee so that you can see how it works.

Implementing the Interface

Any class (other than an abstract base class) can implement an interface by using the Implements keyword. For instance, you can implement the IPrintableObject interface in Employee by adding the following line:

```
Public Class Employee
  Inherits Person
  Implements IPrintableObject
```

This will cause the interface to be exposed by any object created as an instance of Employee. Adding this line of code triggers the IDE to add skeleton methods for the interface to your class. All you need to do is provide implementations for the methods.

To implement an interface, you must implement all the methods and properties defined by that interface.

Before actually implementing the interface, however, let's create an array to contain the labels for the data fields so that you can return them via the IPrintableObject interface. Add the following code to the Employee class:

```
Public Class Employee
  Inherits Person
  Implements IPrintableObject

  Private mLabels() As String = {"ID", "Age", "HireDate"}
  Private mHireDate As Date
  Private mSalary As Double
```

To implement the interface, you need to create methods and properties with the same parameter and return datatypes as those defined in the interface. The actual name of each method or property doesn't matter because you'll be using the Implements keyword to link your internal method names to the external method names defined by the interface. As long as the method signatures match, you are all set.

This applies to scope as well. Although the interface and its methods and properties are publicly available, you don't have to declare your actual methods and properties as Public. In many cases, you can implement them as Private, so they don't become part of the native interface and are only exposed via the secondary interface.

However, if you do have a Public method with a method signature, you can use it to implement a method from the interface. This has the interesting side effect that this method provides implementation for both a method on the object's native interface and one on the secondary interface.

In this case, you'll use a Private method, so it is only providing implementation for the IPrintableObject interface. You can implement the Label method by adding the following code to Employee:

```
Private Function Label(ByVal index As Integer) As String _
      Implements IPrintableObject.Label
    Return mLabels(index)
End Function
```

This is just a regular `Private` method that returns a `String` value from the preinitialized array.

The interesting thing is the `Implements` clause on the method declaration.

```
Private Function Label(ByVal index As Integer) As String _
      Implements IPrintableObject.Label
```

By using the `Implements` keyword in this fashion, you're indicating that this particular method is the implementation for the `Label` method on the `IPrintableObject` interface. The actual name of the private method could be anything. It is the use of the `Implements` clause that makes this work. The only requirement is that the parameter datatypes and the return value datatype must match those defined by the `IPrintableObject` interface.

This is very similar to using the `Handles` clause to indicate which method should handle an event. In fact, like the `Handles` clause, the `Implements` clause allows you to have a comma-separated list of interface methods that should be implemented by this one function.

You can then move on to implement the other two elements defined by the `IPrintableObject` interface by adding this code to `Employee`:

```
Private Function Value(ByVal index As Integer) As String _
    Implements IPrintableObject.Value
  Select Case index
    Case 0
      Return CStr(EmployeeNumber)
    Case 1
      Return CStr(Age)
    Case Else
      Return Format(HireDate, "Short date")
  End Select
End Function

Private ReadOnly Property Count() As Integer _
    Implements IPrintableObject.Count
  Get
    Return UBound(mLabels)
  End Get
End Property
```

You can now run this application and click the button. The Output window in the IDE will display your results, showing the ID, age, and hire date values as appropriate.

Any object could create a similar implementation behind the `IPrintableObject` interface, and the `PrintObject` routine in your form would continue to work regardless of the native datatype of the object itself.

Reusing Common Implementation

Secondary interfaces provide a guarantee that all objects implementing a given interface will have exactly the same methods and events, including the same parameters.

The `Implements` clause links your actual implementation to a specific method on an interface. For instance, your `Value` method is linked to `IPrintableObject.Value` using the following clause:

```
Private Function Value(ByVal index As Integer) As String _
    Implements IPrintableObject.Value
```

Sometimes, your method might be able to serve as the implementation for more than one method, either on the same interface or on different interfaces.

Add the following interface definition to `Interfaces.vb`:

```
Public Interface IValues
  Function GetValue(ByVal index As Integer) As String
End Interface
```

This interface defines just one method, `GetValue`. Notice that it defines a single `Integer` parameter and a return type of `String`, the same as the `Value` method from `IPrintableObject`. Even though the method name and parameter variable name don't match, what counts here is that the parameter and return value datatypes do match.

Now bring up the code window for `Employee`. You'll have it implement this new interface in addition to the `IPrintableObject` interface:

```
Public Class Employee
  Inherits Person
  Implements IPrintableObject
  Implements IValues
```

You already have a method that returns values. Rather than reimplementing that method, it would be nice to just link this new `GetValues` method to your existing method. You can easily do this because the `Implements` clause allows you to provide a comma-separated list of method names:

```
Private Function Value(ByVal index As Integer) As String _
    Implements IPrintableObject.Value, IValues.GetValue
  Select Case Index
    Case 0
      Return CStr(EmployeeNumber)
    Case 1
      Return CStr(Age)
    Case Else
      Return Format(HireDate, "Short date")
  End Select
End Function
```

This is very similar to the use of the `Handles` keyword as discussed in Chapter 4. A single method within the class, regardless of scope or name, can be used to implement any number of methods as defined by other interfaces as long as the datatypes of the parameters and return values all match.

Combining Interfaces and Inheritance

You can combine implementation of secondary interfaces and inheritance at the same time.

When you inherit from a class that implements an interface, your new subclass automatically gains the interface and the implementation from the base class. If you specify that your base class methods are overridable, then the subclass can override those methods. This will not only override the base class implementation for your native interface, but will also override the implementation for the interface. For instance, you could declare the `Value` method as follows:

```
Public Overridable Function Value(ByVal index As Integer) As String _
    Implements IPrintableObject.Value, IValues.GetValue
```

Now it is `Public`, so it is available on your native interface, and it is part of both the `IPrintableObject` and `IValues` interfaces. This means that you can access the property three ways in client code:

```
Dim emp As New Employee()
Dim printable As IPrintableObject = emp
Dim values As IValues = emp

Debug.WriteLine(emp.Value(0))
Debug.WriteLine(printable.Value(0))
Debug.WriteLine(values.GetValue(0))
```

Note that you're also now using the `Overrides` keyword in the declaration. This means that a subclass of `Employee`, such as `OfficeEmployee`, can override the `Value` method. The overridden method will be the one invoked, regardless of whether you call the object directly or via an interface.

Combining the implementation of an interface in a base class along with overridable methods can provide a very flexible object design.

Summary

In this chapter and in Chapter 4, you've seen how Visual Basic allows you to create and work with classes and objects. Visual Basic provides the building blocks for abstraction, encapsulation, polymorphism, and inheritance.

In this chapter, you've seen how to create both simple base classes as well as abstract base classes. You've also explored how you can define formal interfaces, a concept quite similar to an abstract base class in many ways.

You've also walked through the process of subclassing, creating a new class that derives both interface and implementation from a base class. The subclass can be extended by adding new methods or altering the behavior of existing methods on the base class.

Visual Basic provides you with all the capabilities you need to build robust and sophisticated object-oriented applications. In the next chapter, we'll pull this all together by discussing abstraction, encapsulation, polymorphism, and inheritance as they pertain to building practical software.

6

The Common Language Runtime

You've seen how to create simple applications and looked at how to create classes. Now it's time not only to start tying these elements together but also to start looking at how to dispose of some of the classes that you have created. The architects of .NET realized that all procedural languages require certain base functionality. For example, many languages ship with their own runtime that provides features such as memory management. But what if instead of each language shipping with its own runtime implementation, all languages used a common runtime? This would provide languages with a standard environment and access to all of the same features. This is exactly what the common language runtime (CLR) provides.

The CLR manages the execution of code on the .NET platform. Visual Basic developers can view the CLR as a better Visual Basic runtime. However, this runtime, unlike the old stand-alone Visual Basic runtime, is common across all of .NET. The functionality exposed by the CLR is available to all .NET languages; more importantly, all of the features available to other .NET languages via the CLR are available to Visual Basic developers.

Visual Basic developers have been asking for better support for many advanced features, including operator overloading, implementation inheritance, threading, and the ability to marshal objects. Building such features into a language is not trivial. What the CLR did was allow Microsoft to concentrate on building this plumbing one time and then reuse it across multiple different programming languages. Since the CLR supports these features and because Visual Basic .NET is built on top of the CLR, Visual Basic can use these features. The result is that going forward, Visual Basic is the equal of every other .NET language, with the CLR eliminating many of the shortcomings of the previous versions of Visual Basic.

This chapter gets down into the weeds of the application runtime environment to look at:

- ❑ Elements of a .NET application
- ❑ Versioning and deployment
- ❑ Memory management and the Garbage Collector (GC)
- ❑ Microsoft Intermediate Language (MSIL)
- ❑ Integration across .NET languages

Elements of a .NET Application

A .NET application is composed of four primary entities:

- ❑ **Classes** — The basic units that encapsulate data and behavior
- ❑ **Modules** — The individual files that contain the IL for an assembly
- ❑ **Assemblies** — The primary unit of deployment of a .NET application
- ❑ **Types** — The common unit of transmitting data between modules

Classes are covered in the preceding two chapters and are defined in the source files for your application or class library. Upon compilation of your source files, you will produce a module. The code that makes up an assembly's modules may exist in a single executable (.exe) file or as a dynamic link library (.dll). A module is in fact a Microsoft Intermediate Language file, which is then used by the CLR when your application is run. However, compiling a .NET application doesn't only produce an MSIL file; it also produces a collection of files that make up a deployable application or assembly. Within an assembly, you will find several different types of files, including not only the actual executable but also configuration files, signature keys, and most importantly of all, the actual code modules.

Modules

A module contains Microsoft Intermediate Language (MSIL, often abbreviated to IL) code, associated metadata, and the assembly's manifest. By default, the Visual Basic compiler will create an assembly that is composed of a single module having both the assembly code and manifest.

IL is a platform-independent way of representing managed code within a module. Before IL can be executed, the CLR must compile it into the native machine code. The default method is for the CLR to use the JIT (Just-in-Time) compiler to compile the IL on a method-by-method basis. At runtime, as each method is called by an application for the first time, it is passed through the JIT compiler for compilation to machine code. Similarly, for an ASP.NET application, each page is passed through the JIT compiler the first time that it is requested to create an in-memory representation of the machine code that represents that page.

Additional information about the types declared in the IL is provided by the associated metadata. The metadata contained within the module is used extensively by the CLR. For example, if a client and an object reside within two different processes, the CLR will use the type's metadata to marshal data between the client and the object. MSIL is important because every .NET language compiles down to IL. The CLR doesn't care or need to know what the implementation language was, it only knows what the

IL contains. Thus, any differences in .NET languages exist at the level where the IL is generated, but once generated, all .NET languages have the same runtime characteristics. Similarly, since the CLR doesn't care which language a given module was originally written in, it can leverage modules implemented in entirely different .NET languages.

A question that constantly arises when discussing the JIT compiler and the use of a runtime environment is: "Wouldn't it be faster to compile the IL language down to native code before the user asks to run it?" Although the answer is not always "yes," Microsoft has provided a utility to handle this compilation called `Ngen.exe`. `Ngen` (short for native image generator) allows you to essentially run the JIT compiler on a specific assembly, and this assembly is then installed into the user's application cache in its native format. The obvious advantage is that now when the user asks to execute something in that assembly, the JIT compiler is not invoked, saving a small amount of time. However, unlike the JIT compiler that only compiles those portions of an assembly that are actually referenced, `Ngen.exe` needs to compile the entire codebase, so the time required for compilation is not the same as what a user will actually experience.

`Ngen.exe` is executed from the command line. The utility has been updated as part of .NET 2.0, including what is possibly the most important feature, that it now automatically detects and includes most of the dependent assemblies as part of the image generation process. To use `Ngen.exe`, you simply reference this utility followed by an action; for example, install and then your assembly reference. There are several different options available as part of the generation process, but they go beyond the scope of this chapter given that `NGen.exe` is a topic which can generate hot debate on its use and value.

So, where does the debate begin on when to use `Ngen.exe`? Keep in mind that in a server application, where the same assembly will be referenced by multiple users between machine restarts, the difference in performance on the first request is essentially lost. This means that compilation to native code is more valuable to client-side applications. Unfortunately, using `Ngen.exe` requires running it on each client machine, which can become cost-prohibitive in certain installation scenarios and in particular if you use any form of self-updating application logic. Another issue relates to using reflection, which allows you to reference other assemblies at runtime. Of course, if you don't know what assemblies you will reference until runtime, then the native image generator has a problem, since it won't know what to reference either. The key take-aways with `Ngen.exe` are that there may be occasion to use it for an application that you have created, but ensure that you fully investigate this utility and its advantages and disadvantages before doing so, and keep in mind that even native images execute within the CLR. Native image generation only changes the compilation model, not the runtime environment.

Assemblies

An assembly is the primary unit of deployment for .NET applications — it is either a dynamic link library (.dll) or an executable (.exe). An assembly is composed of a manifest, one or more modules, and (optionally) other files, such as .config, .ASPX, .ASMX, images, and so on.

The manifest of an assembly contains:

- Information about the identity of the assembly, including its textual name and version number.
- If the assembly is public, the manifest will contain the assembly's public key. The public key is used to help ensure that types exposed by the assembly reside within a unique namespace. It may also be used to uniquely identify the source of an assembly.

- A declarative security request that describes the assembly's security requirements (the assembly is responsible for declaring the security it requires). Requests for permissions fall into three categories: required, optional, and denied. The identity information may be used as evidence by the CLR in determining whether or not to approve security requests.
- A list of other assemblies that the assembly depends on. The CLR uses this information to locate an appropriate version of the required assemblies at runtime. The list of dependencies also includes the exact version number of each assembly at the time the assembly was created.
- A list of all types and resources exposed by the assembly. If any of the resources exposed by the assembly are localized, the manifest will also contain the default culture (language, currency, date/time format, and so on) that the application will target. The CLR uses this information to locate specific resources and types within the assembly.

The manifest can be stored in a separate file or in one of the modules, but by default for most applications, it will be part of the .dll or .exe file, which is compiled by Visual Studio. For Web applications, you will find that although there are a collection of .ASPX pages, the actual assembly information is located in a DLL that is referenced by those ASPX pages.

Types

The type system provides a template that is used to describe the encapsulation of data and an associated set of behaviors. It is this common template for describing data that provides the basis for the metadata that .NET uses when applications interoperate. There are two kinds of types: reference and value. The differences between these two types were discussed in Chapter 3.

Unlike COM, which is scoped at the machine level, types are scoped at either a global or the assembly level. All types are based on a common system that is used across all .NET languages. Similar to the MSIL code, which is interpreted by the CLR based upon the current runtime environment, the CLR uses a common metadata system to recognize the details of each type. The result is that unlike the different implementations of COM, which required special notation to allow translation of different datatypes between different .exe and .dll files, all .NET languages are built around a common type system.

A type has fields, properties, and methods:

- **Fields** — Variables that are scoped to the type. For example, a `Pet` class could declare a field called Name that holds the pet's name. In a well-engineered class, Fields are often kept private and exposed only as properties or methods.
- **Properties** — These look like fields to clients of the type, but can have code behind them (that usually performs some sort of data validation). For example, a `Dog` datatype could expose a property to set its gender. Code could then be placed behind the property so that it could only be set to "male" or "female," and then this property too could be saved internally to one of the fields in the `dog` class.
- **Methods** — Define behaviors exhibited by the type. For example, the `Dog` datatype could expose a method called `Sleep`, which would suspend the activity of the `Dog`.

The preceding elements make up each application. You'll note that this description mentions that some types will be defined at the application level and others globally. Under COM, all components are registered globally, and certainly if you want to expose a .NET component to COM, you must register it globally. However, with .NET it is not only possible but often encouraged that the classes and types defined in your modules are only visible at the application level. The advantage of this is that you can run several different versions of an application side by side. Of course, once you have an application that can be versioned, the next challenge is to know which version of that application you have.

Versioning and Deployment

Components and their clients are often installed at different times by different vendors. For example, a Visual Basic application might rely on a third-party grid control to display data. Runtime support for versioning is crucial in ensuring that an incompatible version of the grid control does not cause problems for the Visual Basic application.

In addition to this issue of compatibility, the deployment of applications written in previous versions of Visual Basic was problematic. Fortunately, .NET provides major improvements over the versioning and deployment offered by COM and the previous versions of Visual Basic.

Better Support for Versioning

Managing the version of components was challenging in the previous versions of Visual Basic. The version number of the component could be set, but this version number was not used by the runtime. COM components are often referenced by their ProgID, but Visual Basic does not provide any support for appending the version number on the end of the ProgID.

For those of you who are unfamiliar with the term ProgID, suffice to know that ProgIDs are developer-friendly strings used to identify a component. For example, `Word.Application` describes Microsoft Word. ProgIDs can be fully qualified with the targeted version of the component, for example, `Word.Application.10`, but this is a limited capability and relies on both the application and whether the person consuming it chooses to use this optional addendum. As you'll see in Chapter 8, Namespace is built on the basic elements of a ProgID, but provides a more robust naming system.

For many applications, .NET has removed the need to identify the version of each assembly in a central registry on a machine. However, some assemblies will be installed once and used by multiple applications. .NET provides a Global Assembly Cache (GAC), which is used to store assemblies that are intended for use by multiple applications. The CLR provides versioning support for all components that are loaded in the GAC.

The CLR provides two features for assemblies installed within the GAC:

- **Side-by-side versioning**—Multiple versions of the same component can be simultaneously stored in the GAC.
- **Automatic Quick Fix Engineering (QFE) aka hotfix support**—If a new version of a component, which is still compatible with the old version, is available in the GAC, the CLR will load the updated component. The version number, which is maintained by the developer who created the referenced assembly, drives this behavior.

The assembly's manifest contains the version numbers of referenced assemblies. The CLR uses this list at runtime to locate a compatible version of a referenced assembly. The version number of an assembly takes the following form:

```
Major.Minor.Build.Revision
```

Changes to the major and minor version numbers of the assembly indicate that the assembly is no longer compatible with the previous versions. The CLR will not use versions of the assembly that have a different major or minor number unless it is explicitly told to do so. For example, if an assembly was originally compiled against a referenced assembly with a version number of 3.4.1.9, the CLR will not load an assembly stored in the GAC unless it has a major and minor number of 3 and 4.

Incrementing the revision and build numbers indicates that the new version is still compatible with the previous version. If a new assembly that has an incremented revision or build number is loaded into the GAC, the CLR can still load this assembly for clients that were compiled against a previous version. Versioning is discussed in greater detail in Chapter 18.

Better Deployment

Applications written using the previous versions of Visual Basic and COM were often complicated to deploy. Components referenced by the application needed to be installed and registered, and for Visual Basic components, the correct version of the Visual Basic runtime needed to be available. The Component Deployment tool helped in the creation of complex installation packages, but applications could be easily broken if the dependent components were inadvertently replaced by incompatible versions on the client's computer during the installation of an unrelated product.

In .NET, most components do not need to be registered. When an external assembly is referenced, the application makes a decision on using a global copy (which must be in the GAC on the developer's system) or on copying a component locally. For most references, the external assemblies are referenced locally which means they are carried in the application's local directory structure. Using local copies of external assemblies allows the CLR to support the side-by-side execution of different versions of the same component. As noted earlier, to reference a globally registered assembly, that assembly must be located in the GAC. The GAC provides a versioning system that is robust enough to allow different versions of the same external assembly to exist side by side. For example, an application could use a newer version of ADO.NET without adversely affecting another application that relies on a previous version.

So long as the client has the .NET runtime installed (which has to be done only once), a .NET application can be distributed using a simple command like this:

```
xcopy \\server\appDirectory "C:\Program Files\appDirectory" /E /O /I
```

The preceding command would copy all of the files and subdirectories from `\\ server\appDirectory` to `C:\ Program Files\ appDirectory` and would also transfer the file's Access Control Lists (ACLs).

Besides the ability to XCopy applications, Visual Studio provides a built-in tool for constructing simple .msi installations. New with Visual Studio 2005 is the idea of a Click-Once deployment project. These deployment settings can be customized for your project solution, allowing you to integrate the deployment project with your application output.

Click-Once deployment provides an entirely new method of deployment, referred to as smart client deployment. In the smart client model, your application is placed on a central server from which the clients access the application files. Smart client deployment builds on the XML Web services architecture about which you are learning. It has the advantages of central application maintenance combined with a richer client interface and fewer server communication requirements that you have become familiar with in Windows Forms applications. Click-Once deployment is discussed in greater detail in Chapter 19.

Cross-Language Integration

Prior to .NET, interoperating with the code written in other languages was challenging. There were pretty much two options for reusing functionality developed in other languages: COM interfaces or DLLs with exported C functions. As for exposing functionality written in Visual Basic, the only option was to create COM interfaces.

Because Visual Basic is now built on top of the CLR, it's able to interoperate with the code written in other .NET languages. It's even able to derive from a class written in another language. To support this type of functionality, the CLR relies on a common way of representing types, as well as rich metadata that can describe these types.

The Common Type System

Each programming language seems to bring its own island of datatypes with it. For example, previous versions of Visual Basic represent strings using the `BSTR` structure, C++ offers `char` and `wchar` datatypes, and MFC offers the `CString` class. And the fact that the C++ `int` datatype is a 32-bit value, whereas the Visual Basic 6 `Integer` datatype is a 16-bit value, makes it difficult to pass parameters between applications written using different languages.

To help resolve this problem, C has become the lowest common denominator for interfacing between programs written in multiple languages. An exported function written in C that exposes simple C datatypes can be consumed by Visual Basic, Java, Delphi, and a variety of other programming languages. In fact, the Windows API is exposed as a set of C functions.

Unfortunately, to access a C interface, you must explicitly map C datatypes to a language's native datatypes. For example, a Visual Basic 6 developer would use the following statement to map the `GetUserNameA` Win32 function (`GetUserNameA` is the ANSI version of the `GetUserName` function):

```
' Map GetUserName to the GetUserNameA exported function
' exported by advapi32.dll.
'   BOOL GetUserName(
'       LPTSTR lpBuffer, // name buffer
'       LPDWORD nSize // size of name buffer
' );
Public Declare Function GetUserName Lib "advapi32.dll" _
Alias "GetUserNameA" (ByVal strBuffer As String, nSize As Long) As Long
```

This code explicitly mapped the `lpBuffer` C character array datatype to the Visual Basic 6 `String` parameter `strBuffer`. This is not only cumbersome, but also error prone. Accidentally mapping a variable declared as `Long` to `lpBuffer` wouldn't generate any compilation errors. However, calling the function would more than likely result in a difficult to diagnose, intermittent access violation at runtime.

COM provides a more refined method of interoperation between languages. Visual Basic 6 introduced a common type system (CTS) for all applications that supported COM, that is, variant-compatible datatypes. However, variant datatypes are as cumbersome to work with for non–Visual Basic 6 developers as the underlying C data structures that make up the variant datatypes (such as `BSTR` and `SAFEARRAY`) for Visual Basic developers. The result is that interfacing between unmanaged languages is still more complicated than it needs to be.

The CTS provides a set of common datatypes for use across all programming languages. The CTS provides every language running on top of the .NET platform with a base set of types, as well as mechanisms for extending those types. These types may be implemented as classes or as structs, but in either case they are derived from a common `System.Object` class definition.

Since every type supported by the CTS is derived from `System.Object`, every type supports a common set of methods.

Method	Description
`Boolean Equals(Object)`	Used to test equality with another object. Reference types should return `True` if the `Object` parameter references the same object. Value types should return `True` if the `Object` parameter has the same value.
`Int32 GetHashCode()`	Generates a number corresponding to the value of an object. If two objects of the same type are equal, then they must return the same hash code.
`Type GetType()`	Gets a `Type` object that can be used to access metadata associated with the type. It also serves as a starting point for navigating the object hierarchy exposed by the Reflection API (which is discussed shortly).
`String ToString()`	The default implementation returns the fully qualified name of the class of the object. This method is often overridden to output data that is more meaningful to the type. For example, all base types return their value as a string.

Metadata

Metadata is the information that enables components to be self-describing. Metadata is used to describe many aspects of a .NET component including classes, methods, and fields, and the assembly itself. Metadata is used by the CLR to facilitate all sorts of things, such as validating an assembly before it is executed or performing garbage collection while managed code is being executed.

Visual Basic developers have used metadata for years when developing and using components within their applications.

- Visual Basic developers use metadata to instruct the Visual Basic runtime on how to behave. For example, you can set the Unattended Execution property to determine whether unhandled exceptions are shown on the screen in a message box or are written to the Event Log.
- COM components referenced within Visual Basic applications have accompanying type libraries that contain metadata about the components, their methods, and their properties. You can use the Object Browser to view this information. (The information contained within the type library is what is used to drive IntelliSense.)
- Additional metadata can be associated with a component by installing it within COM+. Metadata stored in COM+ is used to declare the support a component needs at runtime, including transactional support, serialization support, and object pooling.

Better Support for Metadata

Metadata associated with a Visual Basic 6 component was scattered in multiple locations and stored using multiple formats:

- Metadata instructing the Visual Basic runtime how to behave (such as the Unattended Execution property) is compiled into the Visual Basic–generated executable.
- Basic COM attributes (such as the required threading model) are stored in the registry.
- COM+ attributes (such as the transactional support required) are stored in the COM+ catalog.

.NET refines the use of metadata within applications in three significant ways:

- .NET consolidates the metadata associated with a component.
- Since a .NET component does not have to be registered, installing and upgrading the component is easier and less problematic.
- .NET makes a much clearer distinction between attributes that should only be set at compile time and those that can be modified at runtime.

All attributes associated with Visual Basic components are represented in a common format and consolidated within the files that make up the assembly.

Since much of a COM/COM+ component's metadata is stored separately from the executable, installing and upgrading components can be problematic. COM/COM+ components must be registered to update the registry/COM+ catalog before they can be used and the COM/COM+ component executable can be upgraded without upgrading its associated metadata.

The process of installing and upgrading a .NET component is greatly simplified. Since all metadata associated with a .NET component must reside within the file that contains the component, no registration is required. Once a new component is copied into an application's directory, it can be used immediately. Since the component and its associated metadata cannot get out of sync, upgrading the component becomes much less problematic.

Another problem with COM+ is that attributes that should only be set at compile time may be reconfigured at runtime. For example, COM+ can provide serialization support for neutral components. A component that does not require serialization must be designed to accommodate multiple requests from multiple clients simultaneously. You should know at compile time whether or not a component requires support for serialization from the runtime. However, under COM+, the attribute describing whether or not client requests should be serialized can be altered at runtime.

.NET makes a much better distinction between attributes that should be set at compile time and those that should be set at runtime. For example, whether a .NET component is serializable is determined at compile time. This setting cannot be overridden at runtime.

Attributes

Attributes are used to decorate entities such as assemblies, classes, methods, and properties with additional information. Attributes can be used for a variety of purposes. They can provide information, request a certain behavior at runtime, or even invoke a particular behavior from another application. An example of this can be shown by using the `Demo` class defined in the following code block:

```
Module Module1

   <Serializable()> Public Class Demo

      <Obsolete("Use Method2 instead.")> Public Sub Method1()
         ' Old implementation ...
      End Sub

      Public Sub Method2()
         ' New implementation ...
      End Sub

   End Class

   Public Sub Main()
      Dim d As Demo = New Demo()
      d.Method1()
   End Sub
End Module
```

The sample class can be added to the `Form1` file that you created as part of your sample application in Chapter 2. Then you can add the two lines, which will create an instance of this class and call `Method1` to your event handler for your Hello World button.

The first attribute on the `Demo` class marks the class with the `Serializable` attribute. The base class library will provide serialization support for instances of the `Demo` type. For example, the `ResourceWriter` type can be used to stream an instance of the `Demo` type to disk.

The second attribute is associated with `Method1`. `Method1` has been marked as obsolete, but has not been made unavailable. When a method is marked as obsolete, there are two options, one is that Visual Studio should prevent applications from compiling. However, a better strategy for large applications is to first mark a method or class as obsolete and then prevent its use in the next release. The preceding code will cause Visual Studio to display an IntelliSense warning if `Method1` is referenced within the application, as shown in Figure 6-1. Not only does the line with `Method1` have a visual hint of the issue, but a task has also been automatically added to the Task window.

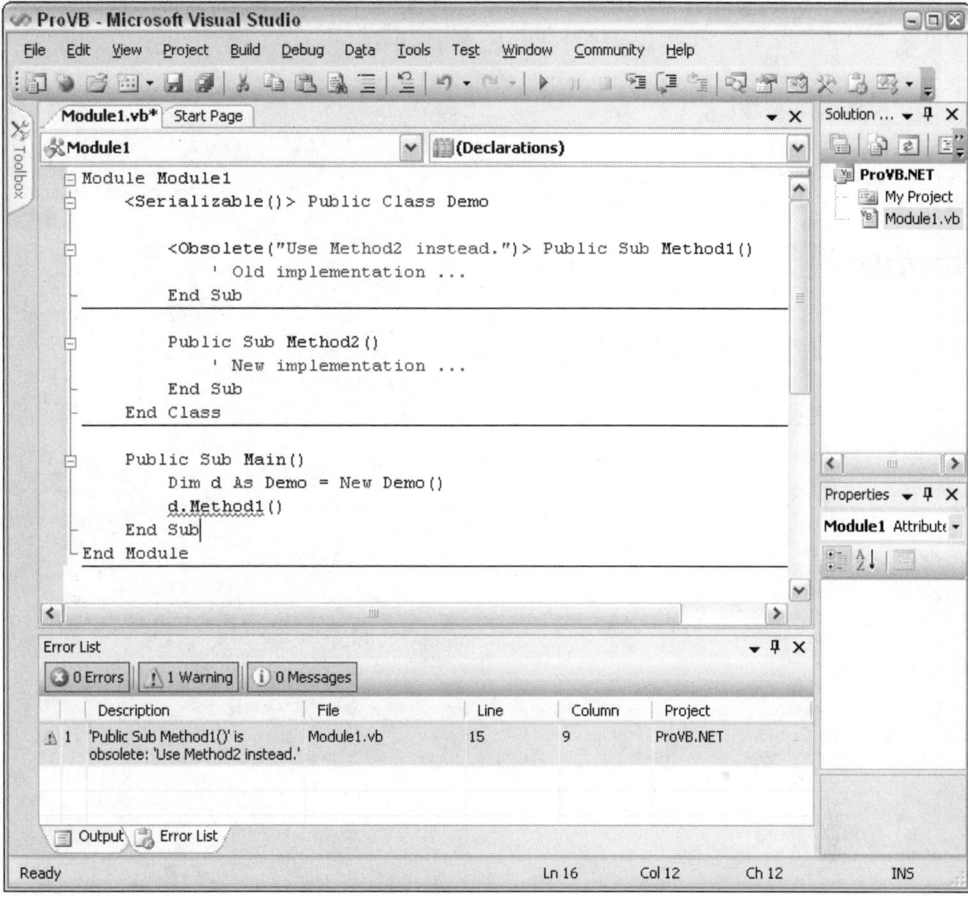

Figure 6-1

If the developer leaves this code unchanged and then compiles it, the application will compile correctly. As you see in Figure 6-2, the compilation is complete, but the developer is given a warning with a meaningful message that you would to change this code to use the correct method.

There are also times when you might need to associate multiple attributes with an entity. The following code shows an example of using both of the attributes from the previous code at the class level. Note that in this case the `Obsolete` attribute has been modified to cause a compilation error by setting its second parameter to `True`:

```
<Serializable(), Obsolete("No longer used.", True)> Public Class Demo
  ' Implementation ...
End Class
```

Attributes play an important role in the development of .NET applications, particularly XML Web services. As you'll see in Chapter 22, the declaration of a class as a Web service and of particular methods as Web methods are all handled through the use of attributes.

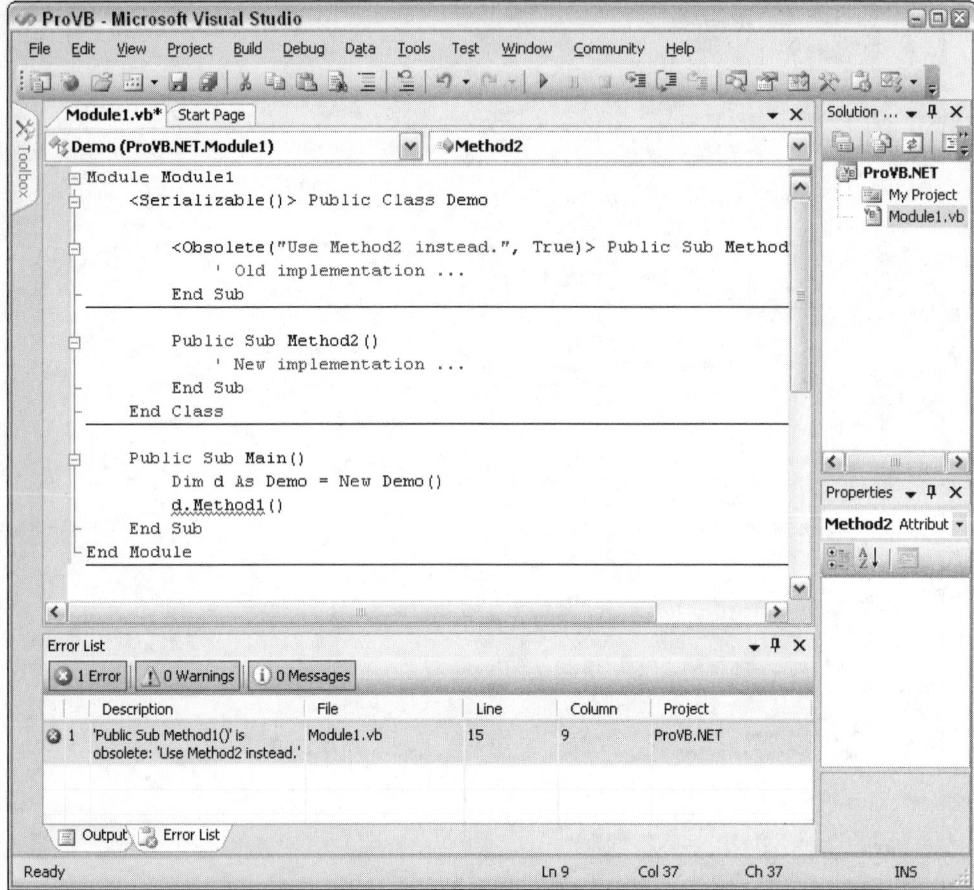

Figure 6-2

The Reflection API

The .NET Framework provides the Reflection API for accessing metadata associated with managed code. You can use the Reflection API to examine the metadata associated with an assembly and its types, and even to examine the currently executing assembly.

The `Assembly` class in the `System.Reflection` namespace can be used to access the metadata in an assembly. The `LoadFrom` method can be used to load an assembly, and the `GetExecutingAssembly` method can be used to access the currently executing assembly. The `GetTypes` method can then be used to obtain the collection of types defined in the assembly.

It's also possible to access the metadata of a type directly from an instance of that type. Since every object derives from `System.Object`, every object supports the `GetType` method, which returns a `Type` object that can be used to access the metadata associated with the type.

The `Type` object exposes many methods and properties for obtaining the metadata associated with a type. For example, you can obtain a collection of properties, methods, fields, and events exposed by the type by calling the `GetMembers` method. The `Type` object for the object's base type can also be obtained by calling the `DeclaringType` property.

A good tool that demonstrates the power of Reflection is Lutz Roeder's Reflector for .NET. Check out `www.aisto.com/roeder/dotnet`.

IL Disassembler

One of the many handy tools that ships with Visual Studio is the IL Disassembler (`ildasm.exe`). It can be used to navigate the metadata within a module, including the types the module exposes, as well as their properties and methods. The IL Disassembler can also be used to display the IL contained within a module.

The IL Disassembler can be found under your installation directory for Visual Studio 2005, with the default path being: `C:\Program Files\Microsoft Visual Studio 8\SDK\v2.0\Bin\ILDasm.exe`. Once the IL Disassembler has been started, select File and then Open. Open `mscorlib.dll`, which is located in your system directory under the default path of `C:\Windows\Microsoft.NET\Framework\V2.0.xxxx\mscorlib.dll`. Once `mscorlib.dll` has been loaded, ILDasm will display a set of folders for each namespace in this assembly. Expand the `System` namespace, then the `ValueType` namespace, and finally double-click the `Equals` method. A window similar to the one shown in Figure 6-3 will be displayed.

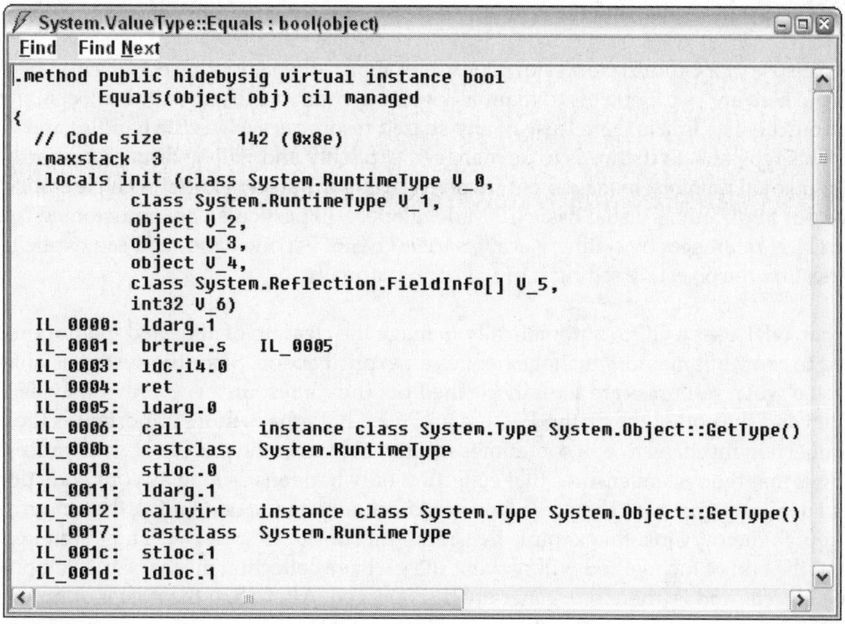

System.ValueType::Equals : bool(object)

Find Find Next

```
.method public hidebysig virtual instance bool
        Equals(object obj) cil managed
{
  // Code size       142 (0x8e)
  .maxstack  3
  .locals init (class System.RuntimeType V_0,
           class System.RuntimeType V_1,
           object V_2,
           object V_3,
           object V_4,
           class System.Reflection.FieldInfo[] V_5,
           int32 V_6)
  IL_0000:  ldarg.1
  IL_0001:  brtrue.s   IL_0005
  IL_0003:  ldc.i4.0
  IL_0004:  ret
  IL_0005:  ldarg.0
  IL_0006:  call       instance class System.Type System.Object::GetType()
  IL_000b:  castclass  System.RuntimeType
  IL_0010:  stloc.0
  IL_0011:  ldarg.1
  IL_0012:  callvirt   instance class System.Type System.Object::GetType()
  IL_0017:  castclass  System.RuntimeType
  IL_001c:  stloc.1
  IL_001d:  ldloc.1
```

Figure 6-3

Figure 6-3 shows the IL for the `Equals` method. Notice how the Reflection API is used to navigate through the instance of the value type's fields in order to determine if the values of the two objects being compared are equal.

The IL Disassembler is a very useful tool for learning how a particular module is implemented, but on the other hand, it could jeopardize your company's proprietary logic. After all, what is to prevent someone from using it to reverse engineer your code. The answer is that Visual Studio 2005, like Visual Studio 2003, ships with a third-party tool called an obfuscator. The role of the obfuscator is to make it so that the IL Disassembler cannot build a meaningful representation of your application logic.

It is beyond the scope of this chapter to completely cover the obfuscator that ships with Visual Studio 2005. However, to access this tool, you go to the Tools menu and select Dotfuscator Community Edition. The obfuscator runs against your compiled application, taking your IL file and stripping out many of the items that are embedded by default during the compilation process.

Memory Management

This section looks at one of the larger underlying elements of managed code. One of the reasons that .NET applications are referred to as "managed" is that memory deallocation is handled automatically by the system. One of the benefits of the CLR, memory management, fixes the shortcomings of the COM's memory management. Developers are accustomed to only worrying about memory management in an abstract sense. The basic rule was that every object created and every section of memory allocated needed to be released (destroyed). The CLR introduces a Garbage Collector (GC), which simplifies this paradigm. Gone are the days where a misbehaving component that failed to properly dispose of its object references or allocated and never released memory could crash a Web server.

However, the use of a GC introduces new questions about when and if objects need to be explicitly cleaned up. There are two elements to manually writing code to allocate and deallocate memory and system resources. The first is the release of any shared resources such as file handles and database connections. This type of activity needs to be managed explicitly and will be discussed shortly. The second element of manual memory management involves letting the system know when memory is no longer in use by your application. Visual Basic COM developers, in particular, are accustomed to explicitly disposing of object references by setting variables to `Nothing`. On one hand, you can explicitly show your intent to destroy the object by setting it to `Nothing` manually.

The fact that .NET uses a GC to automatically manage the cleanup of allocated memory means that you don't need to carry out memory management as an explicit action. Since the system is automatic, it's not up to you when resources are actually cleaned up; thus, a resource you previously used might sit in memory beyond the end of the method where you used it. Perhaps more important is the fact that the garbage collection mechanism will sometimes reclaim objects in the middle of your processing. The great thing is that the system ensures that collection only happens as long as your code doesn't reference the object later in the method. Therefore, you could actually end up extending the amount of time an object is kept in memory just for example by setting that object to `Nothing`. Thus, setting a variable to `Nothing` at the end of the method will prevent the garbage collection mechanism from proactively reclaiming objects, and is, therefore, generally discouraged. After all, if the goal is simply to document a developer's intention, then a comment is more appropriate.

Given this change in paradigms, the next few sections take you through a comparison of the challenges of traditional memory management and a real look under the covers of how the Garbage Collector works, the basics of some of the challenges with COM-based memory management, and then a quick look at how the GC eliminates these challenges from your list of concerns. In particular, you need to understand how you can interact with the Garbage Collector and why the `Using` command, for example, is recommended over a finalization method in .NET.

Traditional "Garbage Collection"

The Visual Basic 6 runtime environment provides limited memory management by automatically releasing objects when they are no longer referenced by any application. Once all of the references are released on an object, the runtime will automatically release the object from memory. For example, consider the following Visual Basic 6 code that uses the `Scripting.FileSystem` object to write an entry to a log file:

```
' Requires a reference to Microsoft Scripting Runtime (scrrun.dll)
Sub WriteToLog(strLogEntry As String)
 Dim objFSO As Scripting.FileSystemObject
 Dim objTS As Scripting.TextStream

 objTS = objFSO.OpenTextFile("C:\temp\AppLog.log", ForAppending)
 Call objTS.WriteLine(Date & vbTab & strLogEntry)
End Sub
```

`WriteToLog` creates two objects, a `FileSystemObject` and a `TextStream`, which are used to create an entry in the log file. Because these are COM objects, they may live either within the current application process or in their own process. Once the routine exits, the Visual Basic runtime will recognize that they are no longer referenced by an active application and dereference the objects. This results in both objects being deactivated. However, there are situations in which objects that are no longer referenced by an application will not be properly cleaned up by the Visual Basic 6 runtime. One cause of this is the circular reference.

Circular References

One of the most common situations in which the Visual Basic runtime is unable to ensure that objects are no longer referenced by the application is when objects contain a circular reference. An example of a circular reference is when object *A* holds a reference to object *B* and object *B* holds a reference to object *A*.

Circular references are problematic because the Visual Basic runtime relies on the reference counting mechanism of COM to determine whether an object can be deactivated. Each COM object is responsible for maintaining its own reference count and for destroying itself once the reference count reaches zero. Clients of the object are responsible for updating the reference count appropriately, by calling the `AddRef` and `Release` methods on the object's `IUnknown` interface. However, in this scenario, object *A* continues to hold a reference to object *B*, and vice versa, and thus the internal cleanup logic of these components is not triggered.

In addition, problems can occur if the clients do not properly maintain the COM object's reference count. For example, an object will never be deactivated if a client forgets to call `Release` when the object is no longer referenced (and no other clients call `Release` too many times). To avoid this, the Visual Basic 6 runtime takes care of updating the reference count for you, but the object's reference count can be an invalid indicator of whether or not the object is still being used by the application. As an example, consider the references that objects *A* and *B* hold.

The application can invalidate its references to *A* and *B* by setting the associated variables equal to `Nothing`. However, even though objects *A* and *B* are no longer referenced by the application, the Visual Basic runtime cannot ensure that the objects get deactivated because *A* and *B* still reference each other. Consider the following (Visual Basic 6) code:

```
 ' Class:  CCircularRef

' Reference to another object.
Dim m_objRef As Object

Public Sub Initialize(objRef As Object)
  Set m_objRef = objRef
End Sub

Private Sub Class_Terminate()
  Call MsgBox("Terminating.")
  Set m_objRef = Nothing
End Sub
```

The `CCircularRef` class implements an Initialize method that accepts a reference to another object and saves it as a member variable. Notice that the class does not release any existing reference in the `m_objRef` variable before assigning a new value. The following code demonstrates how to use this `CCircularRef` class to create a circular reference:

```
Dim objA As New CCircularRef
Dim objB As New CCircularRef

Call objA.Initialize(objB)
Call objB.Initialize(objA)

Set objA = Nothing
Set objB = Nothing
```

After creating two instances (`objA` and `objB`) of `CCircularRef`, both of which have a reference count of one, the code then calls the `Initialize` method on each object by passing it a reference to the other. Now each of the object's reference counts is equal to two: one held by the application and one held by the other object. Next, explicitly set `objA` and `objB` to `Nothing`, which decrements each object's reference count by one. However, since the reference count for both instances of `CCircularRef` is still greater than zero, the objects will not be released from memory until the application is terminated. The CLR Garbage Collector solves the problem of circular references because it looks for a reference from the root application or thread to every class, and all classes that do not have such a reference are marked for deletion, regardless of what other references they might still maintain.

The CLR's Garbage Collector

The .NET garbage collection mechanism is a very complex software, and the details of its inner workings are beyond the scope of this book. However, it is important to understand the principles behind its operation. The GC is responsible for collecting objects that are no longer referenced. The GC takes a completely different approach from that of the Visual Basic runtime to accomplish this. At certain times, and based on internal rules, a task will run through all the objects looking for those that no longer have any references from the root application thread or one of the worker threads. Those objects may then be terminated; thus, the garbage is collected.

As long as all references to an object are either implicitly or explicitly released by the application, the GC will take care of freeing the memory allocated to it. Unlike COM objects, managed objects in .NET are not responsible for maintaining their reference count, and they are not responsible for destroying themselves. Instead, the GC is responsible for cleaning up objects that are no longer referenced by the application. The GC will periodically determine which objects need to be cleaned up by leveraging the information the CLR maintains about the running application. The GC obtains a list of objects that are directly referenced by the application. Then, the GC discovers all the objects that are referenced (both directly and indirectly) by the application's "root" objects. Once the GC has identified all the referenced objects, it is free to clean up any remaining objects.

The GC relies on references from an application to objects, thus, when it locates an object that is unreachable from any of the root objects, it can clean up that object. Any other references to that object will be from other objects that are also unreachable. Thus, the GC will automatically clean up objects that contain circular references.

In some environments, such as COM, objects are destroyed in a deterministic fashion. Once the reference count reaches zero, the object will destroy itself, which means that you can tell exactly when the object will be terminated. However, with garbage collection, you can't tell exactly when an object will be destroyed. Just because you eliminate all references to an object doesn't mean that it will be terminated immediately. It will just remain in memory until the garbage collection process gets around to locating and destroying it. This is called nondeterministic finalization.

This nondeterministic nature of CLR garbage collection provides a performance benefit. Rather than expending the effort to destroy objects as they are dereferenced, the destruction process can occur when the application is otherwise idle — often decreasing the impact on the user. Of course, if garbage collection must occur when the application is active, the system may see a slight performance fluctuation as the collection is accomplished.

It is possible to explicitly invoke the GC by calling the `System.GC.Collect` method. However, this process takes time, so it is not the sort of thing that should be done in a typical application. For example, you could call this method each time you set an object variable to `Nothing`, so that the object would be destroyed almost immediately. However, this forces the GC to scan all the objects in your application — a very expensive operation in terms of performance.

It's far better to design applications so that it's acceptable for unused objects to sit in the memory for some time before they are terminated. That way, the Garbage Collector, too, can run based on its optimal rules — collecting many dereferenced objects at the same time. This means that you need to design objects that don't maintain expensive resources in instance variables. For example, database connections, open files on disk, and large chunks of memory (such as an image) are all examples of expensive resources. If you rely on the destruction of the object to release this type of resource, the system might be keeping the resource tied up for a lot longer than you expect; in fact, on a lightly utilized Web server, it could literally be days.

The first principle is working with object patterns that incorporate cleaning up such pending references before the object is released. Examples of this include calling the close method on an open database connection or file handle. In most cases, it is possible for applications to create classes that do not risk keeping these handles open. However, certain requirements, even with the best object design, can create a risk that a key resource will not be cleaned up correctly. In such an event, there are two occasions when the object could attempt to perform this cleanup: when the final reference to the object is released and immediately before the GC destroys the object.

One option is to implement the `IDisposable` interface. When implemented, this interface is used to ensure that persistent resources are released. This is the preferred method for releasing resources. The second option is to add a method to your class that the system will run immediately before an object is destroyed. This option is not recommended for several reasons, including the fact that many developers fail to remember that the garbage collector is nondeterministic, meaning that you can't, for example, reference an `SQLConnection` object from your custom object's finalizer.

Finally, as part of .NET 2.0, Visual Basic introduces the `Using` command. The `Using` command is designed to change the way that you think about object cleanup. Instead of encapsulating your cleanup logic within your object, the `Using` command creates a window around the code that is referencing an instance of your object. When your application's execution reaches the end of this window, the system automatically calls the `IDIsposable` interface for your object to ensure that it is cleaned up correctly.

The Finalize Method

Conceptually, the GC calls an Object's `Finalize` method immediately before it collects an object that is no longer referenced by the application. Classes can override the `Finalize` method to perform any necessary cleanup. The basic concept is to create a method that acts as what is in other object-oriented languages referred to as a destructor. Similarly, the `Class_Terminate` available in the previous versions of Visual Basic does not have a functional equivalent in .NET. Instead, it is possible to create a `Finalize` method that will be recognized by the GC and that will prevent a class from being cleaned up until after the finalization method is completed. An example of the structure of the `Finalize` method is:

```
Protected Overrides Sub Finalize()
  ' clean up code goes here
  MyBase.Finalize()
End Sub
```

This code uses both `Protected` scope and the `Overrides` keyword. Notice that not only does custom cleanup code go here (as indicated by the comment), but this method also calls `MyBase.Finalize()`, which causes any finalization logic in the base class to be executed as well. Any class implementing a custom `Finalize` method should always call the base finalization class.

Be careful, however, not to treat the `Finalize` method as if it was a destructor. A destructor is based on a deterministic system, where the method is called when the object's last reference is removed. In the GC system, there are key differences in how a finalizer works:

- Since the GC is optimized to only clean up memory when necessary, there will be a delay between the time when the object is no longer referenced by the application and when the GC collects it. Because of this, the same expensive resources that are released in the `Finalize` method may stay open longer than they need to be.

- The GC doesn't actually run `Finalize` methods. When the GC finds a `Finalize` method, it queues the object up for the finalizer to execute the object's method. This means that an object is not cleaned up during the current GC pass. Because of how the GC is optimized, this can result in the object remaining in memory for a much longer period.
- The GC will usually be triggered when the available memory is running low. As a result, execution of the object's `Finalize` method is likely to incur performance penalties. Therefore, the code in the `Finalize` method should be as short and quick as possible.
- There's no guarantee that a service you require is still available. For example, if the system is closing and you have a file open, .NET may have already unloaded the object required to close the file, thus a `Finalize` method can't reference an instance of any other .NET object.

All cleanup activities should be placed in the `Finalize` method. However, objects that require timely cleanup should implement a `Dispose` method that can then be called by the client application just before setting the reference to Nothing. For example:

```
Class DemoDispose
  Private m_disposed As Boolean = False

  Public Sub Dispose()
    If (Not m_disposed) Then
      ' Call cleanup code in Finalize.
      Finalize()

      ' Record that object has been disposed.
      m_disposed = True

      ' Finalize does not need to be called.
      GC.SuppressFinalize(Me)
    End If
  End Sub

  Protected Overrides Sub Finalize()
    ' Perform cleanup here \dots
    End Sub
End Class
```

The `DemoDispose` class overrides the `Finalize` method and implements the code to perform any necessary cleanup. This class places the actual cleanup code within the `Finalize` method. To ensure that the `Dispose` method only calls `Finalize` once, the value of the private `m_disposed` field is checked. Once `Finalize` has been run, this value is set to `True`. The class then calls `GC.SuppressFinalize` to ensure that the GC does not call the `Finalize` method on this object when the object is collected. If you need to implement a `Finalize` method, this is the preferred implementation pattern.

This example implements all of the object's cleanup code in the `Finalize` method to ensure that the object will be cleaned up properly before the GC collects it. The `Finalize` method still serves as a safety net in case the `Dispose` or `Close` methods were not called before the GC collects the object.

The IDisposable Interface

In some cases, the `Finalize` behavior is not acceptable. For an object that is using some expensive or limited resource, such as a database connection, a file handle, or a system lock, it is best to ensure that the resource is freed as soon as the object is no longer needed.

One way to accomplish this is to implement a method to be called by the client code to force the object to clean up and release its resources. This is not a perfect solution, but it is workable. This cleanup method must be called directly by the code using the object or via the use of the `Using` statement. The `Using` statement allows you to encapsulate an object's lifespan within a limited range and automate the calling of the `IDisposable` interface.

The .NET Framework provides the `IDisposable` interface to formalize the declaration of cleanup logic. The first thing to be aware of is that implementing the `IDisposable` interface also implies that the object has overridden the `Finalize` method. Since there is no guarantee that the `Dispose` method will be called, it is critical that `Finalize` trigger your cleanup code if it was not already executed.

Having a custom finalizer ensures that, once released, the garbage collection mechanism will eventually find and terminate the object by running its `Finalize` method. However, when handled correctly, the `IDisposable` interface ensures that any cleanup is executed immediately, so resources are not consumed beyond the time they are needed.

Note that any class that derives from `System.ComponentModel.Component` automatically inherits the `IDisposable` interface. This includes all of the forms and controls that are used in a Windows Forms UI, as well as various other classes within the .NET Framework. Since this interface is inherited, let's review a custom implementation of the `IDisposable` interface based on the `Person` class defined in the preceding chapters. The first step involves adding a reference to the interface to the top of the class:

```
Public Class Person
  Implements IDisposable
```

This interface defines two methods — Dispose and Finalize — that need to be implemented in the class. Visual Studio automatically inserts both of these methods into your code:

```
    Private disposed As Boolean = False

    ' IDisposable
    Private Overloads Sub Dispose(ByVal disposing As Boolean)
      If Not Me.disposed Then
        If disposing Then
          ' TODO: put code to dispose managed resources
        End If

        ' TODO: put code to free unmanaged resources here
      End If
      Me.disposed = True
    End Sub

#Region " IDisposable Support "
  ' This code added by Visual Basic to correctly implement the disposable pattern.
  Public Overloads Sub Dispose() Implements IDisposable.Dispose
    ' Do not change this code.
    ' Put cleanup code in Dispose(ByVal disposing As Boolean) above.
    Dispose(True)
    GC.SuppressFinalize(Me)
  End Sub
```

```
    Protected Overrides Sub Finalize()
      ' Do not change this code.
      ' Put cleanup code in Dispose(ByVal disposing As Boolean) above.
      Dispose(False)
      MyBase.Finalize()
    End Sub
  #End Region
```

Notice the use of the `Overloads` and `Overrides` keywords. The automatically inserted code is following a best practice design pattern for implementation of the `IDisposable` interface and the `Finalize` method. The idea is to centralize all cleanup code into a single method that is called by either the `Dispose()` method or the `Finalize()` method as appropriate.

Accordingly, you can add the cleanup code as noted by the `TODO:` comments in the inserted code. As mentioned in Chapter 2, the `TODO:` keyword is recognized by Visual Studio's text parser, which triggers an entry in the task list to remind you to complete this code before the project is complete. Since this code frees a managed object (the `Hashtable`), the code goes as shown here:

```
    Private Overloads Sub Dispose(ByVal disposing As Boolean)
      If Not Me.disposed Then
        If disposing Then
          ' TODO: put code to dispose managed resources
          mPhones = Nothing
        End If

        ' TODO: put code to free unmanaged resources here
      End If
      Me.disposed = True
    End Sub
```

In this case, we're using this method to release a reference to the object that the `mPhones` variable points to. While not strictly necessary, this illustrates how code can release other objects when the `Dispose` method is called. Generally, it is up to our client code to call this method at the appropriate time to ensure that cleanup occurs. Typically, this should be done as soon as the code is done using the object.

This is not always as easy as it might sound. In particular, an object may be referenced by more than one variable and just because code in one class is dereferencing the object from one variable doesn't mean that it has been dereferenced by all the other variables. If the `Dispose` method is called while other references remain, the object may become unusable and may cause errors when invoked via those other references. There is no easy solution to this problem, so careful design is required in the case that we choose to use the `IDisposable` interface.

Using IDisposable

One way to work with the `IDisposable` interface is to manually insert the calls to the interface implementation everywhere you reference the class. For example, in an application's `Form1` code, you can override the `OnLoad` event for the form. You can use the custom implementation of this method to create an instance of the `Person` object. Then you create a custom handler for the form's `OnClosed` event, and make sure to clean up by disposing of the `Person` object. To do this, add the following code to the form:

```
Private Sub Form1_Closed(ByVal sender As Object, _
    ByVal e As System.EventArgs) Handles MyBase.Closed

  CType(mPerson, IDisposable).Dispose()


End Sub
```

The `OnClosed` method runs as the form is being closed, and so it is an appropriate place to do cleanup work. Note that since the `Dispose` method is part of a secondary interface, the use of the `CType()` method to access that specific interface is needed in order to call the method.

This solution works fine for the pattern where the object implementing `IDisposable` is used within a form. However, it is less useful for other patterns such as when the object is used as part of a Web Service. In fact, even for forms, this pattern is somewhat limited in that it requires the form to define the object when the form is created, as opposed to either having the object created prior to the creation of the form or some other scenario that occurs only on other events within the form.

For these situations, Visual Basic 2005 introduces a new command keyword: `Using`. The `Using` keyword is a way to quickly encapsulate the lifecycle of an object that implements `IDisposable` and ensure that the `Dispose` method is called correctly.

```
Dim mPerson as New Person()
Using (mPerson)
  'insert custom method calls

End Using
```

What the preceding statements do is allocate a new instance of the `mPerson` object. The `Using` command then lets the compiler know to automatically clean up this object's instance when the `End Using` command is executed. The result is a much cleaner way to ensure that the `IDisposable` interface is called.

Faster Memory Allocation for Objects

The CLR introduces the concept of a managed heap. Objects are allocated on the managed heap, and the CLR is responsible for controlling access to these objects in a type-safe manner. One of the advantages of the managed heap is that memory allocations on it are very efficient. When unmanaged code (such as Visual Basic 6 or C++) allocates memory on the unmanaged heap, it typically scans through some sort of data structure in search of a free chunk of memory that is large enough to accommodate the allocation. The managed heap maintains a reference to the end of the most recent heap allocation. When a new object needs to be created on the heap, the CLR allocates memory on top of memory that has previously been allocated and then increments the reference to the end of heap allocations accordingly. Figure 3-1 is a simplification of what takes place in the managed heap for .NET.

- **State 1**—Shows a compressed memory heap with a reference to the end point on the heap.
- **State 2**—Object *B*, although no longer referenced, remains in its current memory location. The memory has not been freed and does not alter the allocation of memory or of other objects on the heap.

- **State 3** — Even though there is now a gap between the memory allocated for object *A* and object *C*, the memory allocation for *D* still occurs on the top of the heap. The unused fragment of memory on the managed heap is ignored at allocation time.
- **State 4** — After one or more allocations, before there is an allocation failure, the Garbage Collector runs. It reclaims the memory that was allocated to *B* and repositions the remaining valid objects. This compresses the active objects to the bottom of the heap creating more space for additional object allocations, as shown in Figure 6-4.

This is where the power of the GC really shines. Before the CLR is unable to allocate memory on the managed heap, the GC is invoked. The GC not only collects objects that are no longer referenced by the application, but it also has a second task, compacting the heap. This is important because if all the GC did was clean up objects, then the heap would become progressively more fragmented. When heap memory becomes fragmented, you can wind up with a not uncommon problem of having a memory allocation fail, not because there isn't enough free memory, but because there isn't enough free memory in a contiguous section of memory. Thus, not only does the GC reclaim the memory associated with objects that are no longer referenced, but it also compacts the remaining objects. The GC effectively squeezes out all of the spaces between the remaining objects, freeing up a section large managed heap for new object allocations.

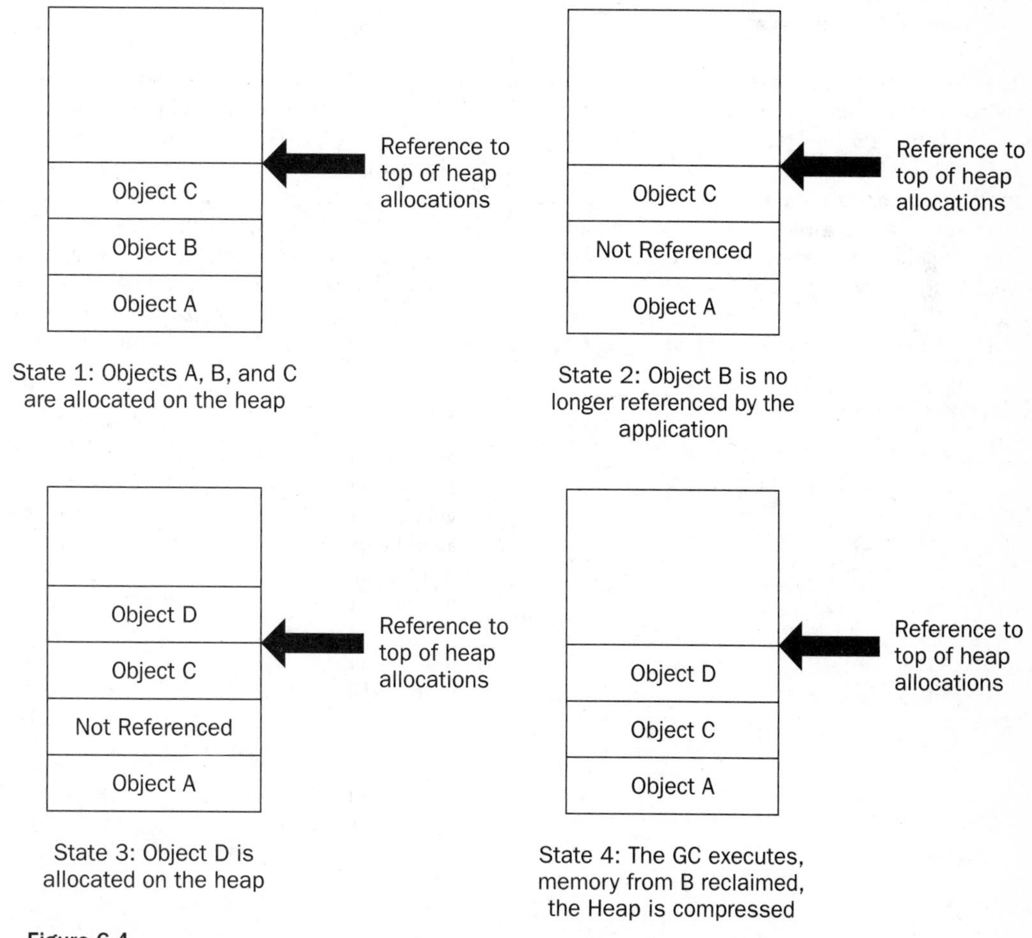

Figure 6-4

Garbage Collector Optimizations

The GC uses a concept known as generations, the primary purpose of which is to improve its performance. The theory behind generations is that objects that have been recently created tend to have a higher probability of being garbage collected than objects that have existed on the system for a longer time.

It is possible to understand generations in terms of a mall parking lot where cars represent objects created by the CLR. People have different shopping patterns when they visit the mall. Some people will spend a good portion of their day in the mall, and others will only stop long enough to pick up an item or two. Applying the theory of generations in trying to find an empty parking space for a car yields a situation in which the highest probability of finding a parking space is a place where other cars have recently parked. In other words, spaces which were occupied recently are more likely to be held by someone who just needed to quickly pick up an item or two. The longer a car has been parked in the parking lot, the higher is the probability that they are an all-day shopper and the lower the probability that their parking space will be freed up any time soon.

Generations provides a means for the GC to identify recently created objects versus long-lived objects. An object's generation is basically a counter that indicates how many times it has successfully avoided garbage collection. In versions 1.0 and 1.1 of the .NET Framework, an object's generation counter starts at zero and can have a maximum value of two.

It is possible to put this to test with a simple Visual Basic application. There are two options for this simple code, you can take the code placed within the `Sub Main` code located below and paste it into the event handler for the Hello World button that you created in Chapter 2. This will allow you to see how this code works, without creating a new project. Alternatively, you can add a new Visual Basic console application project to your solution. As you will recall from Chapter 2, when you create a new project, there are several templates to choose from, and one of them is the console application for Visual Basic. From the File menu, select Add Project ⇨ New Project. This will open the dialog box, and after you have created your new project, you will have a frame that looks similar to the code that follows. Then, within the `Main` module, add the highlighted code below. Right-click your second project, and select the Set as Startup Project option so that when you run your solution, your new project is automatically started.

```
Module Module1

  Sub Main()
    Dim myObject As Object = New Object()
    Dim i As Integer

      For i = 0 To 3
        Console.WriteLine(String.Format("Generation = {0}", _
                          GC.GetGeneration(myObject)))
        GC.Collect()
        GC.WaitForPendingFinalizers()
    Next i
  End Sub

End Module
```

Regardless of the project you use, this code sends its output to the .NET console. For a Windows application, this console defaults to the Visual Studio Output window. When you run this code, it creates an instance of an object and then iterates through a loop four times. For each loop, it displays the current generation count of `myObject` and then calls the GC. The `GC.WaitForPendingFinalizers` method blocks execution until the garbage collection has been completed.

As shown in Figure 6-5, each time the GC was run, the generation counter was incremented for `myObject`, up to a maximum of 2.

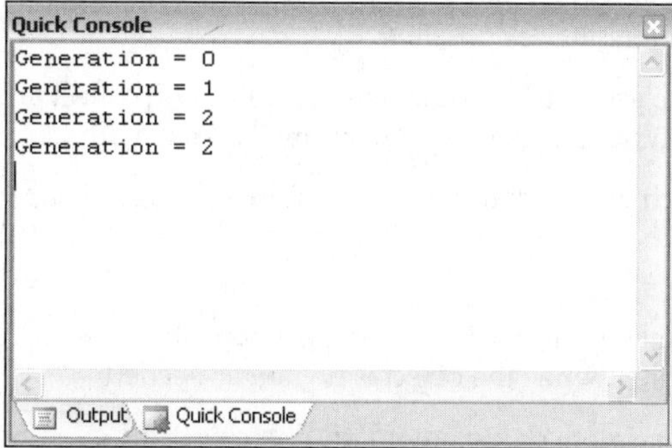

Figure 6-5

Each time the GC is run, the managed heap is compacted and the reference to the end of the most recent memory allocation is updated. After compaction, objects of the same generation will be grouped together. Generation-two objects will be grouped at the bottom of the managed heap and generation-one objects will be grouped next. Since new generation-zero objects are placed on top of the existing allocations, they will be grouped together as well.

This is significant because recently allocated objects have a higher probability of having shorter lives. Since objects on the managed heap are ordered according to generations, the GC can opt to collect newer objects. Running the GC over a limited portion of the heap will be quicker than running it over the entire managed heap.

It's also possible to invoke the GC with an overloaded version of the `Collect` method that accepts a generation number. The GC will then collect all objects no longer referenced by the application that belongs to the specified (or younger) generation. The version of the `Collect` method that accepts no parameters collects objects that belong to all generations.

Another hidden GC optimization is that a reference to an object may implicitly go out of scope and can, therefore, be collected by the GC. It is difficult to illustrate how the optimization occurs only if there are no additional references to the object, and the object does not have a finalizer. However, if an object is declared and used at the top of a module and not referenced again in a method, then in the release mode the metadata will indicate that the variable is not referenced in the later portion of the code. Once the last reference to the object is made, its logical scope ends, and if the Garbage Collector runs, the memory for that object, which will no longer be referenced, can be reclaimed before it has gone out of its physical scope.

Summary

This chapter introduced the CLR. It discussed the memory management features of the CLR, including how the CLR eliminates the circular reference problem that has plagued COM developers. Next, the chapter examined the `Finalize` method and understood why it should not be treated like the `Class_Terminate` method. Specifically, topics covered in this chapter include:

- Whenever possible, do not implement the `Finalize` method in a class.
- If the `Finalize` method is used to perform necessary cleanup, make the code for the `Finalize` method as short and quick as possible.
- There is no way to accurately predict when the GC will collect an object that is no longer referenced by the application (unless the GC is invoked explicitly).
- The order in which the GC collects objects on the managed heap is nondeterministic. This means that the `Finalize` method cannot call methods on other objects referenced by the object being collected.
- If the `Finalize` method is implemented, also implement the `IDisposable` interface that can be called by the client when the object is no longer needed.
- Leverage the `Using` keyword to automatically trigger the execution of the `IDisposable` interface.

This chapter also examined the value of a common runtime and type system that can be targeted by multiple languages. The chapter looked at how the CLR offers better support for metadata. Metadata is used to make types self-describing and is used for language elements such as attributes. Included were examples of how metadata is used by the CLR and the .NET class library and the chapter showed you how to extend metadata by creating your own attributes. Finally, there was a brief review of the Reflection API and the IL Disassembler utility (`ildasm.exe`), which can display the IL contained within a module.

7

Applying Objects and Components

Chapters 4 and 5 explored the syntax provided by Visual Basic for working with objects, creating classes, and implementing both inheritance and multiple interfaces. These are all powerful tools, providing you with the ability to create very maintainable and readable code — even for extremely complex applications.

However, just knowing the syntax and learning the tools is not enough to be successful. Successfully applying the object-oriented capabilities of Visual Basic to create applications requires an understanding of object-oriented programming. This chapter applies Visual Basic's object-oriented syntax and shows how it allows you to build object-oriented applications. It further discusses the four major object-oriented concepts — abstraction, encapsulation, polymorphism, and inheritance — which were defined in Chapter 5. You'll understand how these concepts can be applied in your design and development to create effective object-oriented applications.

Abstraction

Abstraction is the process by which you can think about specific properties or behaviors without thinking about a particular object that has those properties or behaviors. Abstraction is merely the ability of a language to create "black box" code, to take a concept and create an abstract representation of that concept within a program.

A `Customer` object, for example, is an abstract representation of a real-world customer. A `DataSet` object is an abstract representation of a set of data.

Abstraction allows you to recognize how things are similar and to ignore differences, to think in general terms and not the specifics. A `TextBox` control is an abstraction, because you can place it on a form and then tailor it to your needs by setting properties. Visual Basic allows you to define abstractions using classes.

Any language that allows a developer to create a class from which objects can be instantiated meets this criterion, and Visual Basic is no exception. You can easily create a class to represent a customer, essentially providing an abstraction. You can then create instances of that class, where each object can have its own attributes, representing a specific customer.

In Visual Basic, you implement abstraction by creating a class using the `Class` keyword. Bring up Visual Studio, and create a new Visual Basic Windows Application project named `575386ch07`. Once the project is open, add a new class to the project using the Project ➪ Add Class menu option. Name the new class `Customer`, and add some code to make this class represent a real-world customer in an abstract sense:

```
Public Class Customer
    Private mID As Guid = Guid.NewGuid
    Private mName As String
    Private mPhone As String

    Public Property ID() As Guid
      Get
        Return mID
      End Get
      Set(ByVal value As Guid)
        mID = value
      End Set
    End Property

    Public Property Name() As String
      Get
        Return mName
      End Get
      Set(ByVal value As String)
        mName = value
      End Set
    End Property

    Public Property Phone() As String
      Get
        Return mPhone
      End Get
      Set(ByVal value As String)
        mPhone = value
      End Set
    End Property
End Class
```

You know that a real customer is a lot more complex than an ID, name, and phone number. Yet at the same time, you know that in an abstract sense, your customers really do have names and phone numbers, and that you assign them unique ID numbers to keep track of them. In this case, you're using a globally unique identifier (GUID) as a unique ID. Thus, given an ID, name, and phone number, you know which customer you're dealing with, and so you have a perfectly valid abstraction of a customer within your application.

You can then use this abstract representation of a customer from within your code. To do this, you'll use data binding to link the object to a form. Before proceeding, make sure to build the project. Now click the Data | Show Data Sources menu option to open the Data Sources window. Then click the Add New Data Source link in the window to bring up the Data Source Configuration Wizard. Within the wizard, choose to add a new Object data source, and select your Customer class, as shown in Figure 7-1.

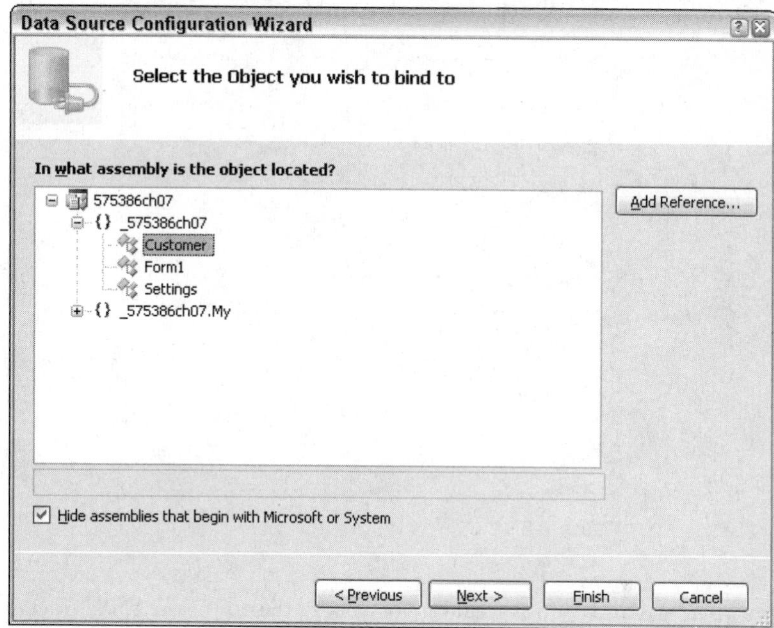

Figure 7-1

Finish the wizard and the `Customer` class should be displayed as an available data source as shown in Figure 7-2.

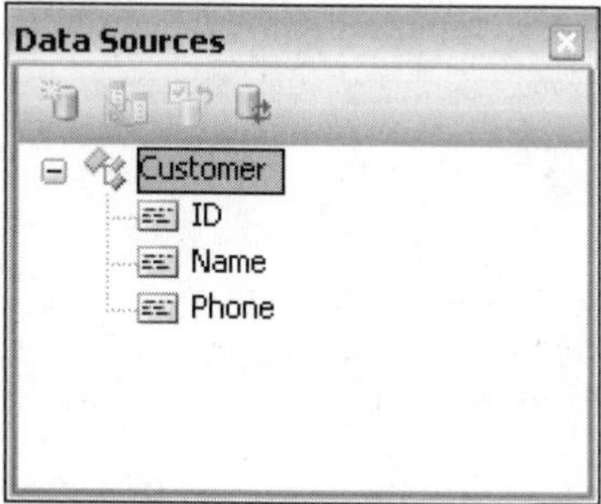

Figure 7-2

Click on `Customer` in the window. `Customer` should change its display to a combo box. Open the combo box, and change the selection from DataGridView to Details. This way you'll get a details view of the object on your form. Open the designer for `Form1` and drag the `Customer` class from the Data Sources window onto the form. The result should look something like Figure 7-3.

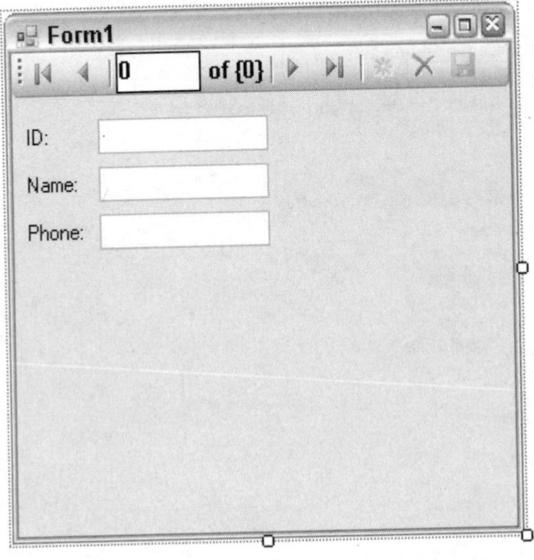

Figure 7-3

All you need to do now is add code to create an instance of the `Customer` class to act as a data source for the form. Double-click on the form to bring up its code window and add the following code:

```
Public Class Form1

  Private Sub Form1_Load(ByVal sender As System.Object, _
    ByVal e As System.EventArgs) Handles MyBase.Load

    Me.CustomerBindingSource.DataSource = New Customer

  End Sub

End Class
```

You're using the ability of Windows Forms to data bind to a property on an object. You'll learn more about data binding in Chapter 14. For now, it is enough to know that the controls on the form are automatically tied to the properties on your object.

Now, you have a simple user interface (UI) that both displays and updates the data in your `Customer` object, with that object providing the UI developer with an abstract representation of the customer. When you run the application, you'll see a display similar to that shown in Figure 7-4.

Here, you've displayed the pregenerated `ID` value, and have entered values for `Name` and `Phone` directly into the form.

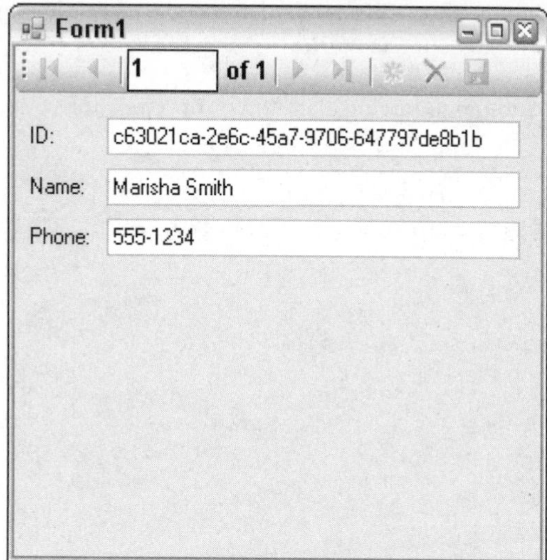

Figure 7-4

Encapsulation

Perhaps the most important of the object-oriented concepts is that of encapsulation. Encapsulation is the concept that an object should totally separate its interface from its implementation. All the data and implementation code for an object should be entirely hidden behind its interface. Another way to put this is that an object should be a black box.

The idea is that you can create an interface (by creating public methods in a class) and, as long as that interface remains consistent, the application can interact with your objects. This remains true even if you entirely rewrite the code within a given method. The interface is independent of the implementation.

Encapsulation allows you to hide the internal implementation details of a class. For example, the algorithm you use to find prime numbers might be proprietary. You can expose a simple API to the end user, but you hide all of the logic used in your algorithm by encapsulating it within your class.

This means that an object should completely contain any data it requires and that it should also contain all the code required to manipulate that data. Programs should interact with an object through an interface, using the properties and methods of the object. Client code should never work directly with the data owned by the object.

Programs interact with objects by sending messages to the object that indicate which method or property they'd like to have invoked. These messages are generated by other objects or by external sources such as the user. The object reacts to these messages through methods or properties.

Visual Basic classes entirely hide their internal data and code, providing a well-established interface of properties and methods, with the outside world.

Let's look at an example. Add the following class to your project; the code defines its native interface:

```
Public Class Encapsulation

  Public Function DistanceTo(ByVal x As Single, ByVal y As Single) As Single

  End Function

  Public Property CurrentX() As Single
    Get

    End Get
    Set(ByVal value As Single)

    End Set
  End Property

  Public Property CurrentY() As Single
    Get

    End Get
    Set(ByVal value As Single)

    End Set
  End Property

End Class
```

This creates an interface for the class. At this point, you can write client code to interact with the class, since from a client perspective all you care about is the interface. Bring up the designer for `Form1` and add a button to the form, then write the following code behind the button:

```
  Private Sub btnEncapsulation_Click(ByVal sender As System.Object, _
    ByVal e As System.EventArgs) Handles btnEncapsulation.Click

    Dim obj As New Encapsulation
    MsgBox(obj.DistanceTo(10, 10))

  End Sub
```

Even though you have no actual code in the `Encapsulation` class, you can still write code to use that class because the interface is defined.

This is a powerful idea, since it means that you can rapidly create class interfaces against which other developers can create the UI or other parts of the application, while you are still creating the implementation behind the interface.

From here, you could do virtually anything you like in terms of implementing the class. For example, you could use the values to calculate a direct distance:

```
Imports System.Math
Public Class Encapsulation
   Private mX As Single
   Private mY As Single

    Public Function DistanceTo(ByVal x As Single, ByVal y As Single) As Single
     Return CSng(Sqrt((x - mX) ^ 2 + (y - mY) ^ 2))
  End Function

    Public Property CurrentX() As Single
    Get
       Return mX
    End Get
    Set(ByVal value As Single)
       mX = value
    End Set
  End Property

  Public Property CurrentY() As Single
    Get
       Return mY
    End Get
    Set(ByVal value As Single)
       mY = value
    End Set
  End Property
End Class
```

Now, when you run the application and click the button, you'll get a meaningful value as a result.

Where encapsulation comes to the fore, however, is that you can change the implementation without changing the interface. For example, you can change the distance calculation to find the distance between the points (assuming that no diagonal travel is allowed).

```
Public Function DistanceTo(ByVal x As Single, ByVal y As Single) As Single
    Return Abs(x - mX) + Abs(y - mY)
  End Function
```

This results in a different value being displayed when the program is run.

You haven't changed the interface of the class, and so your working client program has no idea that you have switched from one implementation to the other. You have achieved a total change of behavior without any change to the client code. This is the essence of encapsulation.

Of course, the user might have a problem if you made such a change to your object. If applications were developed expecting the first set of behaviors, and then you changed to the second, there could be some interesting side effects. However, the key point is that the client programs would continue to function, even if the results were quite different from when you started.

Polymorphism

Polymorphism is often considered to be directly tied to inheritance (which is discussed next). In reality, however, it's largely independent. Polymorphism means that you can have two classes with different implementations or code, but with a common set of methods, properties, or events. You can then write a program that operates upon that interface and doesn't care about which type of object it operates at runtime.

Method Signatures

To properly understand polymorphism, you need to explore the concept of a method signature, sometimes also called a prototype. All methods have a signature, which is defined by the method's name and the datatypes of its parameters. You might have code such as this:

```
Public Function CalculateValue() As Integer

End Sub
```

In this example, the signature is:

```
f()
```

If you add a parameter to the method, the signature will change. For example, you could change the method to accept a `Double`:

```
Public Function CalculateValue(ByVal value As Double) As Integer
```

Then, the signature of the method is:

```
f(Double)
```

Polymorphism merely says that you should be able to write client code that calls methods on an object, and as long as the object provides your methods with the method signatures you expect, you don't care which class the object was created from. Let's look at some examples of polymorphism within Visual Basic.

Implementing Polymorphism

You can use several techniques to achieve polymorphic behavior:

- Late binding
- Multiple interfaces
- Reflection
- Inheritance

Late binding actually allows you to implement "pure" polymorphism, although at the cost of performance and ease of programming. Through multiple interfaces and inheritance, you can also achieve polymorphism with much better performance and ease of programming. Reflection allows you to use either late binding or multiple interfaces, but against objects created in a very dynamic way, even going so far as to dynamically load a DLL into your application at runtime so that you can use its classes.

You'll walk through each of these options to see how they are implemented and to explore their pros and cons.

Polymorphism through Late Binding

Typically, when you interact with objects in Visual Basic, you are interacting with them through strongly typed variables. For example, in `Form1` you interacted with the `Encapsulation` object with the following code:

```
Private Sub btnEncapsulation_Click(ByVal sender As System.Object, _
  ByVal e As System.EventArgs) Handles btnEncapsulation.Click

  Dim obj As New Encapsulation
  MsgBox(obj.DistanceTo(10, 10))

End Sub
```

The `obj` variable is declared using a specific type (`Encapsulation`)—meaning that it is strongly typed or early bound.

You can also interact with objects that are late bound. Late binding means that your object variable has no specific datatype, but rather is of type `Object`. To use late binding, you need to use the `Option Strict Off` directive at the top of your code file (or in the project's properties). This tells the Visual Basic compiler that you want to use late binding, so it will allow you to do this type of polymorphism. Add this to the top of the `Form1` code:

```
Option Strict Off
```

With `Option Strict` turned off, Visual Basic treats the `Object` datatype in a special way, allowing you to attempt arbitrary method calls against the object even though the `Object` datatype doesn't implement those methods.

For example, you could change the code in `Form1` to be late bound as follows:

```
Private Sub btnEncapsulation_Click(ByVal sender As System.Object, _
  ByVal e As System.EventArgs) Handles btnEncapsulation.Click

  Dim obj As Object = New Encapsulation
  MsgBox(obj.DistanceTo(10, 10))

End Sub
```

When this code is run, you'll get the same result as you did before, even though the Object datatype has no DistanceTo method as part of its interface. The late binding mechanism, behind the scenes, dynamically determines the real type of your object and invokes the appropriate method.

When you work with objects through late binding, neither the Visual Basic IDE nor the compiler can tell whether you are calling a valid method or not. In this case, there is no way for the compiler to know that the object referenced by your obj variable actually has a DistanceTo method. It just assumes that you know what you're talking about and compiles the code.

Then at runtime, when the code is actually invoked it will attempt to dynamically call the DistanceTo method. If that is a valid method, your code will work; if it is not, you'll get an error.

Obviously, there is a level of danger when using late binding, since a simple typo can introduce errors that can only be discovered when the application is actually run. However, there is also a lot of flexibility, since code that makes use of late binding can talk to any object from any class as long as those objects implement the methods you require.

There is also a substantial performance penalty for using late binding. The existence of each method is discovered dynamically at runtime, and that discovery takes time. Moreover, the mechanism used to invoke a method through late binding is not nearly as efficient as the mechanism used to call a method that is known at compile time.

To make this more obvious, you can change the code in Form1 by adding a generic routine that displays the distance:

```
Private Sub btnEncapsulation_Click(ByVal sender As System.Object, _
  ByVal e As System.EventArgs) Handles btnEncapsulation.Click

  Dim obj As New Encapsulation
  ShowDistance(obj)

End Sub
Private Sub ShowDistance(ByVal obj As Object)
   MsgBox(obj.DistanceTo(10, 10))
End Sub
```

Notice that the new ShowDistance routine accepts a parameter using the generic Object datatype—so you can pass it literally any value—String, Integer, or one of your objects. It will throw an exception at runtime, however, unless the object you pass into the routine has a DistanceTo method that matches the required method signature.

You know that your Encapsulation object has a method matching that signature, so your code works fine. However, let's add another simple class to demonstrate polymorphism. Add a new class to the project and name it Poly.vb:

```
Public Class Poly
  Public Function DistanceTo(ByVal x As Single, ByVal y As Single) As Single
    Return x + y
  End Function
End Class
```

This class is about as simple as you can get. It exposes a `DistanceTo` method as part of its interface and provides a very basic implementation of that interface.

You can use this new class in place of the `Encapsulation` class without changing the `ShowDistance` method by using polymorphism. Return to the code in `Form1` and make the following change:

```
Private Sub btnEncapsulation_Click(ByVal sender As System.Object, _
  ByVal e As System.EventArgs) Handles btnEncapsulation.Click

  Dim obj As New Poly
  ShowDistance(obj)
End Sub
```

Even though you changed the class of object you're passing to `ShowDistance` to one with a different overall interface and different implementation, the method called within `ShowDistance` remains consistent, so your code will run.

Polymorphism with Multiple Interfaces

Late binding is flexible and easy. However, it is not ideal because it defeats the IDE and compiler type checking that allow you to fix bugs due to typos during the development process, and because it has a negative impact on performance.

Another way to implement polymorphism is to use multiple interfaces. This approach avoids late binding, meaning that the IDE and compiler can check your code as you enter and compile it. Also, because the compiler has access to all the information about each method you call, your code will run much faster.

Remove the `Option Strict` directive from the code in `Form1`. This will cause some syntax errors to be highlighted in the code, but don't worry—you'll fix those soon enough.

Visual Basic not only supports polymorphism through late binding, but also implements a stricter form of polymorphism through its support of multiple interfaces. (Chapter 5 discussed multiple interfaces, including the use of the `Implements` keyword and how to define interfaces.)

With late binding you've seen how to treat all objects as equals by making them all appear using the `Object` datatype. With multiple interfaces, you can treat all objects as equals by making them all implement a common datatype or interface.

This approach has the benefit that it is strongly typed, meaning that the IDE and compiler can help you find errors due to typos, since the name and datatypes of all methods and parameters are known at design time. It is also fast in terms of performance; since the compiler knows all about the methods, it can use optimized mechanisms for calling them, especially as compared to the dynamic mechanisms used in late binding.

Let's return to the project and implement polymorphism with multiple interfaces. First, add a module to the project using the Project ➪ Add Module menu option and name it `Interfaces.vb`. Replace the `Module` code block with an `Interface` declaration:

```
Public Interface IShared
  Function CalculateDistance(ByVal x As Single, ByVal y As Single) As Single
End Interface
```

Now, you can make both the `Encapsulation` and `Poly` classes implement this interface. First, in the `Encapsulation` class add the following code:

```
Public Class Encapsulation
  Implements IShared

  Private mX As Single
  Private mY As Single

  Public Function DistanceTo(ByVal x As Single, ByVal y As Single) _
      As Single Implements IShared.CalculateDistance

    Return CSng(Sqrt((x - mX) ^ 2 + (y - mY) ^ 2))
  End Function
...
```

You can see that you're implementing the `IShared` interface, and since the `CalculateDistance` method's signature matches that of your existing `DistanceTo` method, you're simply indicating that it should act as the implementation for `CalculateDistance`.

You can make a similar change in the `Poly` class:

```
Public Class Poly
  Implements IShared
  Public Function DistanceTo(ByVal x As Single, ByVal y As Single) As Single _
      Implements IShared.CalculateDistance
        Return x + y
  End Function
End Class
```

Now, this class also implements the `IShared` interface, and you're ready to see polymorphism implemented in your code.

Bring up the code window for `Form1`, and change your `ShowDistance` method as follows:

```
Private Sub ShowDistance(ByVal obj As IShared)
  MsgBox(obj.CalculateDistance(10, 10))
End Sub
```

Note that this eliminates the compiler error you were seeing after removing the `Option Strict` directive from `Form1`.

Instead of accepting the parameter using the generic `Object` datatype, you are now accepting an `IShared` parameter—a strong datatype known by both the IDE and the compiler. Within the code itself, you are now calling the `CalculateDistance` method as defined by that interface.

This routine can now accept any object that implements `IShared`, regardless of what class that object was created from, or what other interfaces that object may implement. All you care about here is that the object implements `IShared`.

Polymorphism through Reflection

You've seen how to use late binding to invoke a method on any arbitrary object, as long as that object has a method matching the method signature you're trying to call. You've also walked through the use of multiple interfaces which allows you to achieve polymorphism through a faster, early bound technique. The challenge with these techniques is that late binding can be slow and hard to debug, and multiple interfaces can be somewhat rigid and inflexible.

You can use the concept of reflection to overcome some of these limitations. Reflection is a technology built into the .NET Framework that allows you to write code that interrogates an assembly to dynamically determine the classes and datatypes it contains. You can then use reflection to load the assembly into your process, create instances of those classes, and invoke their methods.

When you use late binding, Visual Basic makes use of the `System.Reflection` namespace behind the scenes on your behalf. You can choose to manually use reflection as well. This allows you even more flexibility in how you interact with objects.

For example, suppose that the class you want to call is located in some other assembly on disk — an assembly you didn't specifically reference from within your project when you compiled it. How can you dynamically find, load, and invoke such an assembly? Reflection allows you to do this, assuming that the assembly is polymorphic. In other words, it has either an interface you expect or a set of methods you can invoke via late binding.

To see how reflection works with late binding, let's create a new class in a separate assembly (project) and use it from within your existing application. Choose File ⇨ Add ⇨ New Project to add a new class library project to your solution. Name it `Objects`. It will start with a single class module that you can use as a starting point. Change the code in that class to the following:

```
Public Class External
  Public Function DistanceTo(ByVal x As Single, ByVal y As Single) As Single
    Return x * y
  End Function
End Class
```

Now, compile the assembly by choosing the Build ⇨ Build Objects menu option. Next, bring up the code window for `Form1`. Add an `Imports` statement at the top, and add back the `Option Strict Off` statement:

```
Option Strict Off

Imports System.Reflection
```

Remember that since you're using late binding, `Form1` also must use `Option Strict Off`. Without this, late binding is not available.

Then add a button with the following code:

```
Private Sub Button1_Click(ByVal sender As System.Object, _
     ByVal e As System.EventArgs) Handles button1.Click

  Dim obj As Object
  Dim dll As Assembly

  dll = Assembly.LoadFrom("..\..\Objects\bin\Objects.dll")

  obj = dll.CreateInstance("Objects.External")
  MsgBox(obj.DistanceTo(10, 10))
End Sub
```

There's a lot going on here, so let's walk through it a bit. First, notice that you're reverting to late binding; your `obj` variable is declared as type `Object`. You'll take a look at using reflection and multiple interfaces in a moment, but to start with you'll use late binding.

Next, you've declared a `dll` variable as type `Reflection.Assembly`. This variable will contain a reference to the `Objects` assembly that you'll be dynamically loading through your code. Note that you are not adding a reference to this assembly via Project ⇨ Add References. You'll dynamically get access to the assembly at runtime.

You then load the external assembly dynamically by using the `Assembly.LoadFrom` method:

```
dll = Assembly.LoadFrom("..\..\Objects\bin\Objects.dll")
```

This causes the reflection library to load your assembly from a file on disk at the location you specify. Once the assembly is loaded into your process, you can use the `myDll` variable to interact with it, including interrogating it to get a list of the classes it contains or to create instances of those classes.

> **You can also use the `[Assembly].Load` method, which will scan the directory where your application's .exe file is located (and the global assembly cache) for any EXE or DLL containing the Objects assembly. When it finds the assembly, it loads it into memory, making it available for your use.**

You can then use the `CreateInstance` method on the assembly itself to create objects based on any class in that assembly. In your case, you're creating an object based on the `External` class:

```
obj = dll.CreateInstance("Objects.External")
```

Now, you have an actual object to work with, so you can use late binding to invoke its `DistanceTo` method. At this point, your code is really no different from that in the earlier late binding example, except that the assembly and object were created dynamically at runtime rather than being referenced directly by your project.

At this point, you should be able to run the application and have it dynamically invoke the assembly at runtime.

Polymorphism through Reflection and Multiple Interfaces

You can also use both reflection and multiple interfaces together. You've seen how multiple interfaces allow you to have objects from different classes implement the same interface and thus be treated identically. You've also seen how reflection allows you to load an assembly and class dynamically at runtime.

You can combine these concepts by using an interface that is common between your main application and your external assembly, and also using reflection to load that external assembly dynamically at runtime.

First, you need to create the interface that will be shared across both application and assembly. To do this, add a new Class Library project to your solution named `Interfaces`. Once it is created, drag and drop the `Interfaces.vb` module from your original application into the new project. This makes the `IShared` interface part of that project and no longer part of your base application.

Of course, your base application still uses `IShared`, so you'll want to reference the `Interfaces` project from your application to gain access to the interface. Do this by right-clicking your `575386ch07` project in the Solution Explorer window and selecting the Add Reference menu option. Then add the reference, as shown in Figure 7-5.

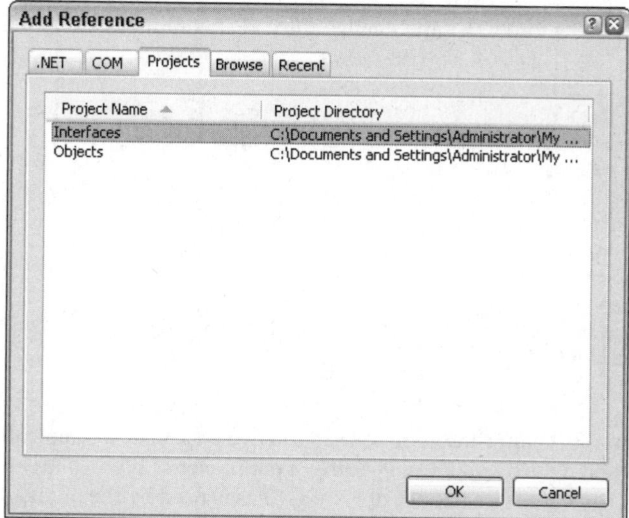

Figure 7-5

Since the `IShared` interface is now part of a separate assembly, you'll need to add an `Imports` statement to `Form1`, `Encapsulation`, and `Poly` so that they are able to locate the `IShared` interface.

```
Imports Interfaces
```

Make sure to add this to the top of all three code modules.

You also need to have the `Objects` project reference `Interfaces`, so right-click `Objects` in Solution Explorer and choose Add Reference there as well. Add the reference to `Interfaces` and click OK. At this point, both the original application and the external assembly have access to the `IShared` interface. You can now enhance the code in `Objects` by changing the `External` class:

```
Imports Interfaces
Public Class External
  Implements IShared
  Public Function DistanceTo(ByVal x As Single, ByVal y As Single) _
      As Single Implements IShared.CalculateDistance

    Return x * y
  End Function
End Class
```

With both the main application and external assembly using the same datatype, you are now ready to implement the polymorphic behavior using reflection.

First, remove the `Option Strict Off` code from `Form1`. This prohibits the use of late binding, thus ensuring that you must use a different technique for polymorphism.

Bring up the code window for `Form1` and change the code behind the button to take advantage of the `IShared` interface:

```
Private Sub btnReflection_Click(ByVal sender As System.Object, _
  ByVal e As System.EventArgs) Handles btnReflection.Click

  Dim obj As IShared
  Dim dll As Assembly

  dll = Assembly.LoadFrom("..\..\Objects\bin\Objects.dll")

  obj = CType(dll.CreateInstance("Objects.External"), IShared)
  ShowDistance(obj)
End Sub
```

All you've done here is to change the code so that you can pass your dynamically created object to the `ShowDistance` method, which you know requires a parameter of type `IShared`. Since your class implements the same `IShared` interface (from `Interfaces`) as is used by the main application, this will work perfectly. Rebuild and run the solution to see this in action.

This technique is very nice, since the code in `ShowDistance` is strongly typed, providing all the performance and coding benefits, but both the DLL and the object itself are loaded dynamically, providing a great deal of flexibility to your application.

Polymorphism with Inheritance

Inheritance, which was discussed in Chapter 5, can also be used to enable polymorphism. The idea here is very similar to that of multiple interfaces, since a subclass can always be treated as though it were the datatype of the parent class.

> **Many people consider the concepts of inheritance and polymorphism to be tightly intertwined. As you've seen, however, it is perfectly possible to use polymorphism without inheritance.**

At the moment, both your `Encapsulation` and `Poly` classes are implementing a common interface named `IShared`. You are able to use polymorphism to interact with objects of either class via that common interface. The same is true if these are child classes based on the same base class through inheritance. Let's see how this works.

In the `575386ch07` project, add a new class named `Parent`. Insert the following code into that class:

```
Public MustInherit Class Parent
  Public MustOverride Function DistanceTo(ByVal x As Single, _
      ByVal y As Single) As Single
End Class
```

As you discussed in Chapter 5, this is an abstract base class, a class with no implementation of its own. The purpose of an abstract base class is to provide a common base from which other classes can be derived.

To implement polymorphism using inheritance, you do not need to use an abstract base class. Any base class that provides overridable methods (using either `MustOverride` or `Overridable` keywords) will work fine, since all its subclasses are guaranteed to have that same set of methods as part of their interface and yet the subclasses can provide custom implementation for those methods.

In this example, you're simply defining the `DistanceTo` method as being a method that must be overridden and implemented by any subclass of `Parent`. Now, you can bring up the `Encapsulation` class and change it to be a subclass of `Parent`:

```
Public Class Encapsulation
  Inherits Parent
  Implements IShared
```

You don't need to quit implementing the `IShared` interface just because you're inheriting from `Parent`; inheritance and multiple interfaces coexist nicely. You do, however, have to override the `DistanceTo` method from the `Parent` class.

The `Encapsulation` class already has a `DistanceTo` method with the proper method signature, so you can simply add the `Overrides` keyword to indicate that this method will override the declaration in the `Parent` class:

```
Public Overrides Function DistanceTo( _
  ByVal x As Single, _ByVal y As Single) _
  As Single Implements IShared.CalculateDistance
```

At this point, the `Encapsulation` class not only implements the common `IShared` interface and its own native interface but also can be treated as though it were of type `Parent`, since it is a subclass of `Parent`. You can do the same thing to the `Poly` class:

```
Public Class Poly
  Inherits Parent
  Implements IShared
  Public Overrides Function DistanceTo( _
      ByVal x As Single, ByVal y As Single) _
      As Single Implements IShared.CalculateDistance

    Return x + y
  End Function
End Class
```

Finally, you can see how polymorphism works by altering the code in `Form1` to take advantage of the fact that both classes can be treated as though they were of type `Parent`. First, you can change the `ShowDistance` method to accept its parameter as type `Parent` and to call the `DistanceTo` method:

```
Private Sub ShowDistance(ByVal obj As Parent)
  MsgBox(obj.DistanceTo(10, 10))
End Sub
```

Then, you can add a new button to create an object of either type `Encapsulation` or `Poly` and pass it as a parameter to the method:

```
Private Sub btnInheritance_Click(ByVal sender As System.Object, _
  ByVal e As System.EventArgs) Handles btnInheritance.Click

  ShowDistance(New Poly)
  ShowDistance(New Encapsulation)


End Sub
```

Polymorphism Summary

Polymorphism is a very important concept in object-oriented design and programming, and Visual Basic provides you with ample techniques through which it can be implemented.

The following table summarizes the different techniques and their pros and cons, and provides some high-level guidelines about when to use each.

Technique	Pros	Cons	Guidelines
Late binding	Flexible, "pure" on polymorphism	Slow, hard to debug, no IntelliSense of datatype or interfaces	Use to call arbitrary methods literally any object, regardless Useful when you can't control the interfaces that will be implemented by the authors of your classes

Technique	Pros	Cons	Guidelines
Multiple interfaces	Fast, easy to debug, full IntelliSense	Not totally dynamic or flexible, requires class author to implement formal interface	Use when you are creating code that interacts with clearly defined methods that can be grouped together into a formal interface Useful when you control the interfaces that will be implemented by the classes used by your application
Reflection and late binding	Flexible, "pure" polymorphism, dynamically loads arbitrary assemblies from disk	Slow, hard to debug, no IntelliSense	Use to call arbitrary methods on objects, when you don't know at design time which assemblies you will be using
Reflection and multiple interfaces	Fast, easy to debug, full IntelliSense, dynamically loads arbitrary assemblies from disk	Not totally dynamic or flexible, requires class author to implement formal interface	Use when you are creating code that interacts with clearly defined methods that can be grouped together into a formal interface, but when you don't know at design time which assemblies you will be using
Inheritance	Fast, easy to debug, full IntelliSense, inherits behaviors from base class	Not totally dynamic or flexible, requires class author to inherit from common base class	Use when you are creating objects that have an is-a relationship, when you have subclasses that are naturally of the same datatype as a base class Polymorphism through inheritance should occur because inheritance makes sense, not because you are attempting to merely achieve polymorphism

Inheritance

Inheritance is the concept that a new class can be based on an existing class, inheriting its interface and functionality from the original class. Chapter 5 discussed the mechanics and syntax of inheritance, so we won't rehash them here. However, Chapter 5 really didn't discuss inheritance from a practical perspective, and that will be the focus of this section.

When to Use Inheritance

Inheritance is one of the most powerful object-oriented features a language can support. At the same time, inheritance is one of the most dangerous and misused object-oriented features.

Properly used, inheritance allows you to increase the maintainability, readability, and reusability of your application by offering you a clear and concise way to reuse code, via both interface and implementation. Improperly used, inheritance allows you to create applications that are very fragile, where a change to a class can cause the entire application to break or require changes.

Inheritance allows you to implement an is-a relationship. In other words, it allows you to implement a new class that is a more specific type of its base class. This means that properly used, inheritance allows you to create child classes that really are the same as the base class.

Perhaps a quick example is in order. Take a duck. You know that a duck is a bird. However, a duck can also be food, though that is not its primary identity. Proper use of inheritance would allow you to create a `Bird` base class from which you could derive your `Duck` class. You would not create a `Food` class and subclass `Duck` from `Food`, since a duck isn't really just food, it merely acts as food sometimes.

This is the challenge. Inheritance is not just a mechanism for code reuse. It is a mechanism to create classes that flow naturally from some other class. If you use it anywhere you want code reuse, you'll end up with a real mess on your hands. If you use it anywhere you just want a common interface, but where the child class is not really the same as the base class, then you should be using multiple interfaces—something we'll discuss shortly.

> **The question you must ask, when using inheritance, is whether the child class is a more specific version of the base class.**

For example, you might have different types of products in your organization. All of these products will have some common data and behaviors; they'll all have a product number, description, and price. However, if you have an agricultural application, you might have chemical products, seed products, fertilizer products, and retail products. These are all different—each having its own data and behaviors—and yet there is no doubt that each one of them really is a product. You can use inheritance to create this set of products as illustrated by the Class Diagram in Figure 7-6.

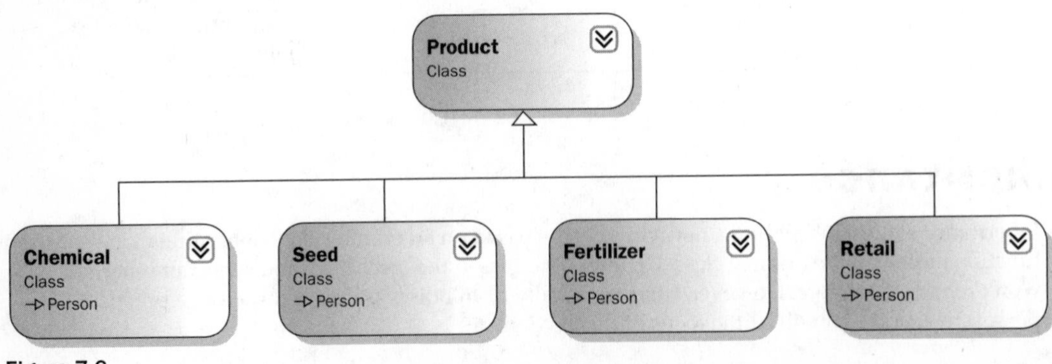

Figure 7-6

This diagram shows that you have an abstract base `Product` class, from which you derive the various types of product your system will actually use. This is an appropriate use of inheritance, because the child classes are obviously each a more specific form of the general `Product` class.

Alternately, you might try to use inheritance just as a code-sharing mechanism. For example, you may look at your application, which has `Customer`, `Product`, and `SalesOrder` classes, and decide that all of them need to be designed so that they can be printed to a printer. The code to handle the printing will all be somewhat similar, so to reuse that printing code, you create a base `PrintableObject` class. This would result in the diagram shown in Figure 7-7.

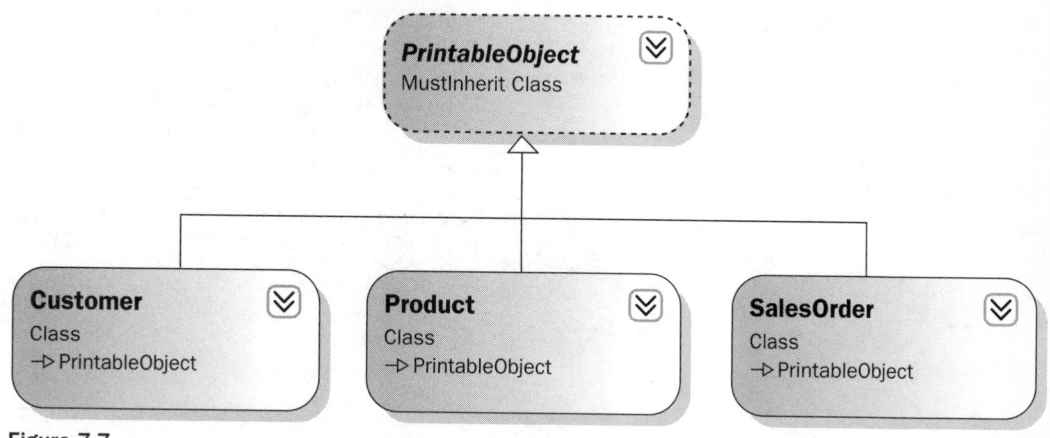

Figure 7-7

Intuitively, you know that this doesn't represent an is-a relationship. While a `Customer` can be printed, and you are getting code reuse, a customer isn't really a specific case of a printable object. Implementing a system following this design will result in a fragile design and application. This is a case where multiple interfaces are a far more appropriate technology, as you'll see later.

To illustrate this point, you might later discover that you have other entities in your organization that are similar to a customer, but are not quite the same. Upon further analysis, you may determine that `Employee` and `Customer` are related because they are specific cases of a `Contact` class. The `Contact` class provides commonality in terms of data and behavior across all these other classes (see Figure 7-8).

But now your `Customer` is in trouble, you've said it is a `PrintableObject`, and you're now saying it is a `Contact`.

You might be able to just derive `Contact` from `PrintableObject` (see Figure 7-9).

The problem with this is that now `Employee` is also of type `PrintableObject`, even if it shouldn't be. But you're stuck, since unfortunately you decided early on to go against intuition and say that a `Customer` is a `PrintableObject`.

This is a problem that could be solved by multiple inheritance, which would allow `Customer` to be a subclass of more than one base class, in this case, of both `Contact` and `PrintableObject`. However, the .NET platform and Visual Basic don't support multiple inheritance in this way. Your alternative is to use inheritance for the is-a relationship with `Contact`, and use multiple interfaces to allow the `Customer` object to act as a `PrintableObject` by implementing an `IPrintableObject` interface.

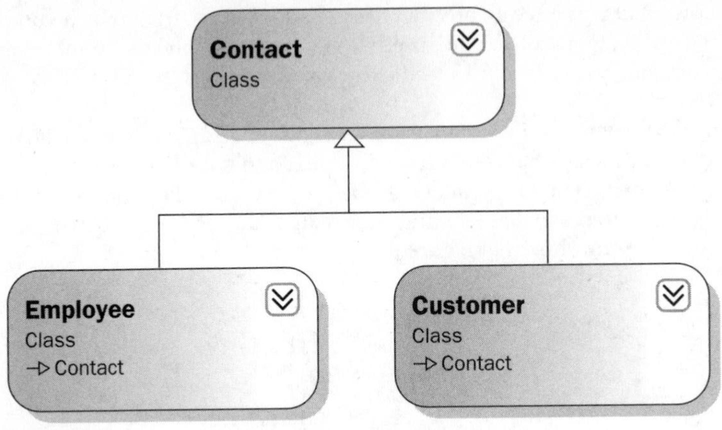

Figure 7-8

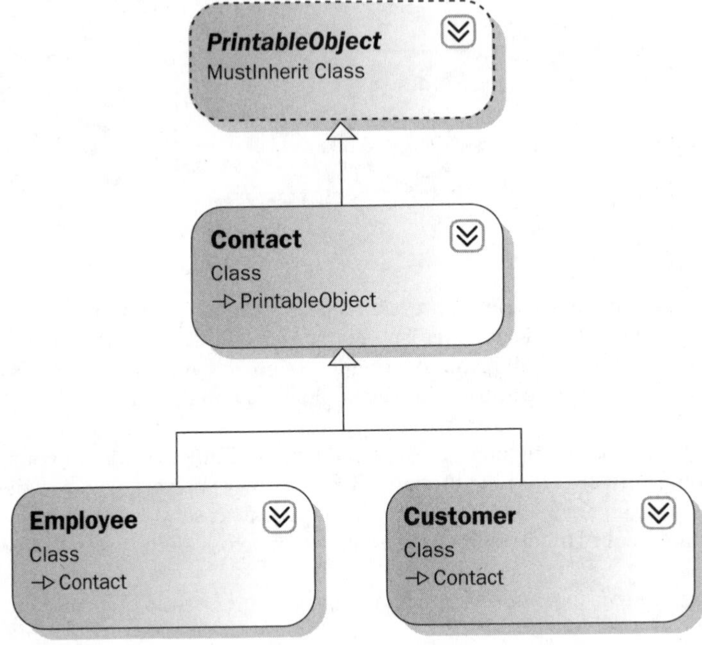

Figure 7-9

Application versus Framework Inheritance

What you've just seen is how inheritance can accidentally cause reuse of code where no reuse was desired.

However, you can take a different view of this model by separating the concept of a framework from your actual application. The way you use inheritance in the design of a framework is somewhat different from how you use inheritance in the design of an actual application.

In this context, the word framework is being used to refer to a set of classes that provide base functionality that is not specific to an application, but rather may be used across a number of applications within the organization, or perhaps even beyond the organization. The .NET Framework base class library is an example of a very broad framework you use when building your applications.

The `PrintableObject` class discussed earlier, for example, may have little to do with your specific application, but may be the type of thing that is used across many applications. If so, it is a natural candidate to be part of a framework, rather than being considered part of your actual application.

Framework classes exist at a lower level than application classes. For example, the .NET base class library is a framework on which all .NET applications are built. You can layer your own framework on top of the .NET Framework as well (see Figure 7-10).

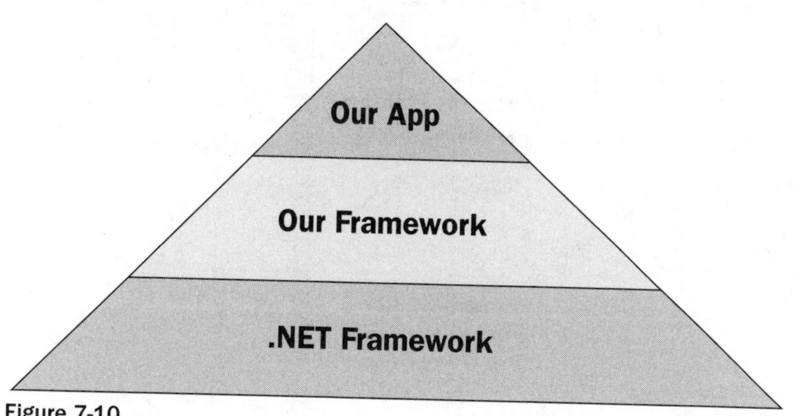

Figure 7-10

If you take this view, then the `PrintableObject` class wouldn't be part of your application at all, but rather would be part of a framework on which your application is built. In such a case, the fact that `Customer` is not a specific case of `PrintableObject` doesn't matter as much, since you're not saying that it is such a thing, but rather that it is leveraging that portion of the framework functionality.

To make all this work requires a lot of planning and forethought in the design of the framework itself. To see the dangers you face, consider that you might not only want to be able to print objects, you might also want to be able to store them in a file. So, you might not only have `PrintableObject` but also `SavableObject` as a base class.

The question then is what do you do if `Customer` should be both printable and savable? If all printable objects are savable, you might have the result shown in Figure 7-11.

Or, if all savable objects are printable, you might have the result shown in Figure 7-12.

But really neither of these provides a decent solution, since the odds are that the concept of being printable and the concept of being savable are different and not interrelated in either of these ways.

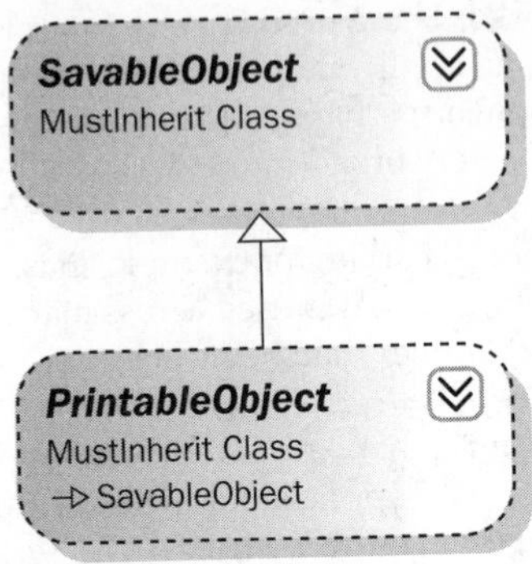

Figure 7-11

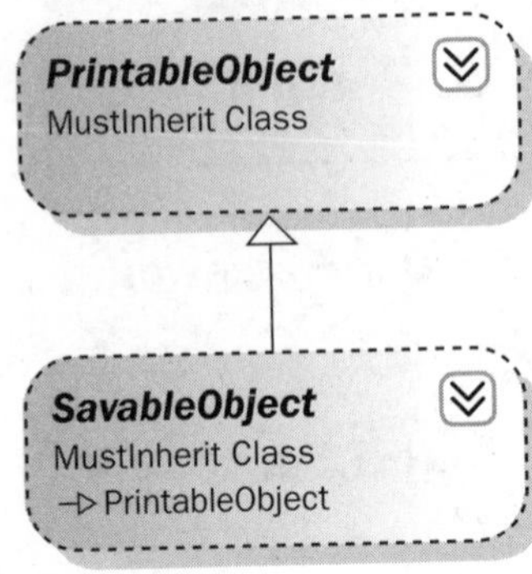

Figure 7-12

When faced with this sort of issue, it is best to avoid using inheritance and rather rely on multiple interfaces.

Inheritance and Multiple Interfaces

While inheritance is powerful, it is really geared around implementing the is-a relationship. Sometimes, you will have objects that need to have a common interface, even though they aren't really a specific case of some base class that provides that interface. We've just been exploring that issue in the discussion of the `PrintableObject`, `SavableObject`, and `Customer` classes.

Sometimes, multiple interfaces are a better alternative than inheritance. The syntax for creating and using secondary and multiple interfaces was discussed.

Multiple interfaces can be viewed as another way of implementing the is-a relationship. It is often better, however, to view inheritance as an is-a relationship and to view multiple interfaces as a way of implementing an act-as relationship.

To think about this further, we can say that the `PrintableObject` concept could perhaps be better expressed as an interface — `IPrintableObject`.

When the class implements a secondary interface such as `IPrintableObject`, you're not really saying that your class is a printable object, you're saying that it can act as a printable object. A `Customer` is a `Contact`, but at the same time it can act as a printable object. This is illustrated in Figure 7-13.

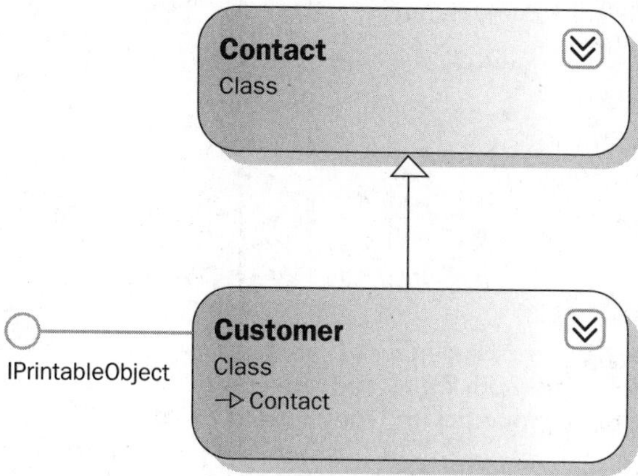

Figure 7-13

The drawback to this approach is that you get no inherited implementation when you implement `IPrintableObject`. In Chapter 5, we discussed how to reuse common code as you implement an interface across multiple classes. While not as automatic or easy as inheritance, it is possible to reuse implementation code with a bit of extra work.

Applying Inheritance and Multiple Interfaces

Perhaps the best way to see how inheritance and multiple interfaces interact is to look at an example. Returning to the original `575386ch07` project, you'll combine inheritance and multiple interfaces to create an object that has both an is-a and act-as relationship at the same time. As an additional benefit, you'll be using the .NET Framework's ability to print to a printer or Print Preview dialog.

Creating the Contact Base Class

You already have a simple `Customer` class in the project, so now let's add a `Contact` base class. Choose Project ➪ Add Class and add a class named `Contact`. Write the following code:

```
Public MustInherit Class Contact

  Private mID As Guid = Guid.NewGuid
  Private mName As String

  Public Property ID() As Guid
    Get
      Return mID
    End Get
    Set(ByVal value As Guid)
      mID = value
    End Set
```

```
    End Property

    Public Property Name() As String
      Get
        Return mName
      End Get
      Set(ByVal value As String)
        mName = value
      End Set
    End Property

  End Class
```

Subclassing Contact

Now, you can make the `Customer` class inherit from this base class, since it is a `Contact`. Also, since your base class now implements both the `ID` and `Name` properties, you can simplify the code in `Customer` by removing those properties and their related variables:

```
  Public Class Customer
    Inherits Contact

    Private mPhone As String

    Public Property Phone() As String
      Get
        Return mPhone
      End Get
      Set(ByVal value As String)
        mPhone = value
      End Set
    End Property
  End Class
```

This shows the benefit of subclassing `Customer` from `Contact`, since you're now sharing the `ID` and `Name` code across all other types of `Contact` as well.

Implementing IPrintableObject

However, you also know that a `Customer` should be able to act as a printable object. To do this in such a way that the implementation is reusable requires a bit of thought. First though, you need to define the `IPrintableObject` interface.

You'll use the standard printing mechanism provided by .NET from the `System.Drawing` namespace. As shown in Figure 7-14, add a reference to `System.Drawing.dll` to the `Interfaces` project.

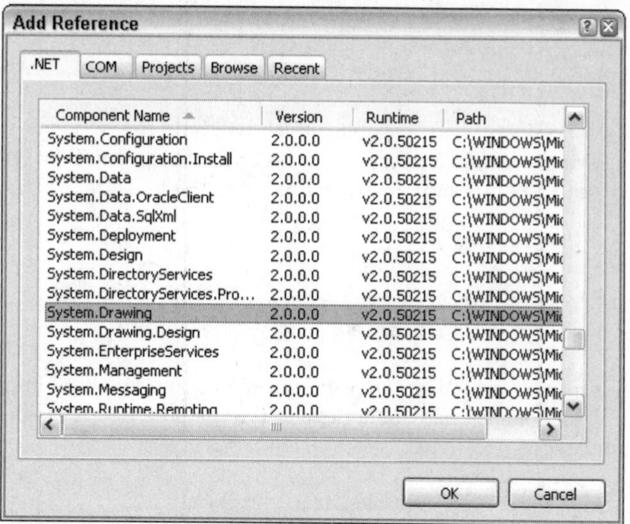

Figure 7-14

With that done, bring up the code window for `Interfaces.vb` in the `Interfaces` project and add the following code:

```
Imports System.Drawing

Public Interface IPrintableObject
  Sub Print()
  Sub PrintPreview()
  Sub RenderPage(ByVal sender As Object, _
      ByVal ev As System.Drawing.Printing.PrintPageEventArgs)
End Interface
```

This interface ensures that any object implementing `IPrintableObject` will have `Print` and `PrintPreview` methods, so you can invoke the appropriate type of printing. It also ensures the object will have a `RenderPage` method, which can be implemented by that object to render the object's data on the printed page.

At this point, you could simply implement all the code needed to handle printing directly within the `Customer` object. This isn't ideal, however, since some of the code will be common across any objects that want to implement `IPrintableObject`, and it would be nice to find a way to share that code.

To do this, let's create a new class, `ObjectPrinter`. This is a framework-style class, in that it has nothing to do with any particular application, but can be used across any application where `IPrintableObject` will be used.

Add a new class named `ObjectPrinter` to the `575386ch07` project. This class will contain all the code common to printing any object. It makes use of the built-in printing support provided by the .NET Framework class library. To use this, you need to import a couple of namespaces, so add this code to the new class:

```
Imports System.Drawing
Imports System.Drawing.Printing
Imports Interfaces
```

You can then define a `PrintDocument` variable, which will hold the reference to your printer output. You'll also declare a variable to hold a reference to the actual object you'll be printing. Notice that you're using the `IPrintableObject` interface datatype for this variable:

```
Public Class ObjectPrinter

  Private WithEvents document As PrintDocument
  Private printObject As IPrintableObject
```

Now, you can create a routine to kick off the printing process for any object implementing `IPrintableObject`. This code is totally generic; you'll write it here so it can be reused across any number of other classes:

```
  Public Sub Print(ByVal obj As IPrintableObject)
    printObject = obj

    document = New PrintDocument()
    document.Print()
  End Sub
```

Likewise, you can implement a method to show a print preview display of your object. Again, this code is totally generic, so you'll put it here for reuse:

```
  Public Sub PrintPreview(ByVal obj As IPrintableObject)
    Dim PPdlg As PrintPreviewDialog = New PrintPreviewDialog()

    printObject = obj

    document = New PrintDocument()
    PPdlg.Document = document
    PPdlg.ShowDialog()
  End Sub
```

Finally, you need to catch the `PrintPage` event that is automatically raised by the .NET printing mechanism. This event is raised by the `PrintDocument` object whenever the document determines that it needs data rendered onto a page. Typically, it is in this routine that you'd put the code to draw text or graphics onto the page surface. However, since this is a generic framework class, you won't do that here; instead, you'll delegate the call back into the actual application object that you want to print.

```
  Private Sub PrintPage(ByVal sender As Object, _
      ByVal ev As System.Drawing.Printing.PrintPageEventArgs) _
      Handles document.PrintPage

    printObject.RenderPage(sender, ev)
  End Sub

End Class
```

This allows the application object itself to determine how its data should be rendered onto the output page. Let's see how you can do that by implementing the `IPrintableObject` interface on the `Customer` class:

```
Imports Interfaces
Public Class Customer
  Inherits Contact
  Implements IPrintableObject
```

By adding this code, you require that your `Customer` class implement the `Print`, `PrintPreview`, and `RenderPage` methods. To avoid wasting paper as you test the code, let's make both the `Print` and `PrintPreview` methods the same and have them just do a print preview display:

```
  Public Sub Print() _
    Implements Interfaces.IPrintableObject.Print

    Dim printer As New ObjectPrinter()
    printer.PrintPreview(Me)

  End Sub
```

Notice that you're using an `ObjectPrinter` object to handle the common details of doing a print preview. In fact, any class you ever create that implements `IPrintableObject` will have this exact same code to implement a print preview function, relying on your common `ObjectPrinter` to take care of the details.

You also need to implement the `RenderPage` method, which is where you actually put your object's data onto the printed page:

```
Private Sub RenderPage(ByVal sender As Object, _
    ByVal ev As System.Drawing.Printing.PrintPageEventArgs) _
    Implements IPrintableObject.RenderPage

    Dim printFont As New Font("Arial", 10)
    Dim lineHeight As Single = printFont.GetHeight(ev.Graphics)
    Dim leftMargin As Single = ev.MarginBounds.Left
    Dim yPos As Single = ev.MarginBounds.Top

    ev.Graphics.DrawString("ID: " & ID.ToString, printFont, Brushes.Black, _
      leftMargin, yPos, New StringFormat())

    yPos += lineHeight
    ev.Graphics.DrawString("Name: " & Name, printFont, Brushes.Black, _
      leftMargin, yPos, New StringFormat())

    ev.HasMorePages = False

End Sub
```

All of this code is unique to your object, which makes sense since you're rendering your specific data to be printed. However, you don't need to worry about the details of whether you're printing to paper or print preview; that is handled by your `ObjectPrinter` class, which in turn uses the .NET Framework. This allows you to focus just on generating the output to the page within your application class.

By generalizing the printing code in `ObjectPrinter`, you've achieved a level of reuse that you can tap into via the `IPrintableObject` interface. Anytime you want to print a `Customer` object's data, you can have it act as an `IPrintableObject` and call its `Print` or `PrintPreview` method. To see this work, let's add a new button control to `Form1` with the following code:

```
Private Sub btnPrint_Click(ByVal sender As System.Object, _
  ByVal e As System.EventArgs) Handles btnPrint.Click

  Dim obj As New Customer
  obj.Name = "Douglas Adams"
  CType(obj, IPrintableObject).PrintPreview()

End Sub
```

This code creates a new `Customer` object and sets its `Name` property. You then use the `CType()` method to access the object via its `IPrintableObject` interface to invoke the `PrintPreview` method.

When you run the application and click the button, you'll get a print preview display showing the object's data (see Figure 7-15).

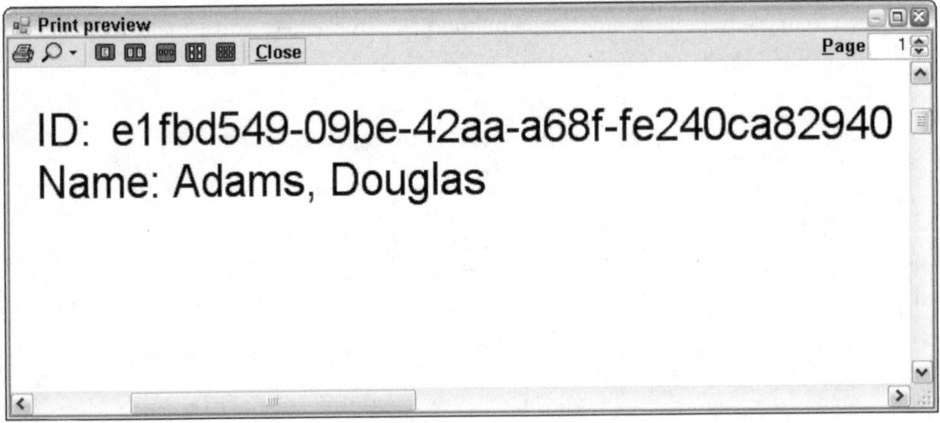

Figure 7-15

How Deep to Go?

Most of the examples discussed so far have illustrated how you can create a child class based on a single parent class. That is called single-level inheritance. However, inheritance can be many levels deep. For example, you might have a deep hierarchy, as shown in Figure 7-16.

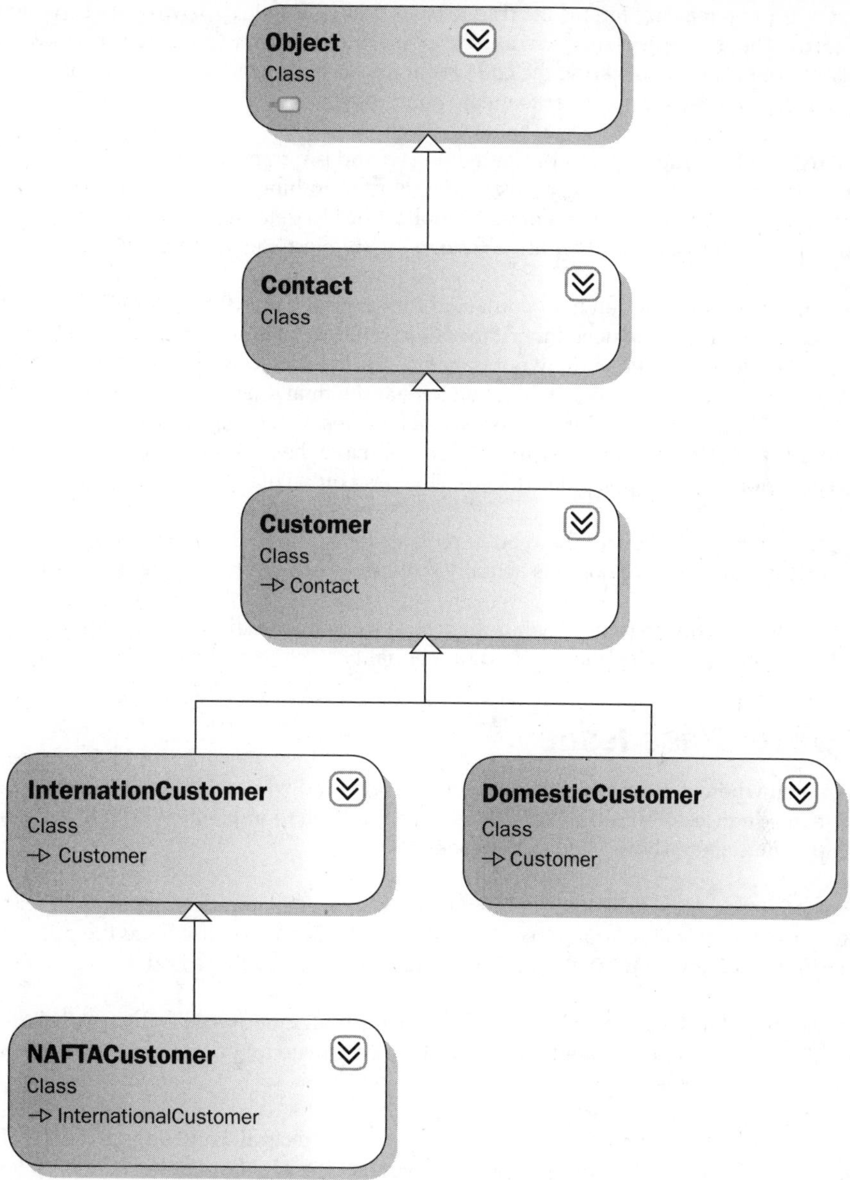

Figure 7-16

From the root of `System.Object` down to `NAFTACustomer` you have four levels of inheritance. This can be described as a four-level inheritance chain.

There is no hard and fast rule about how deep inheritance chains should go, but conventional wisdom and general experience with inheritance in other languages such as Smalltalk and C++ indicate that the deeper an inheritance chain becomes, the harder it is to maintain an application.

This happens for two reasons. First is the fragile base class or fragile superclass issue, which you'll discuss shortly. The second reason is that a deep inheritance hierarchy tends to seriously reduce readability of your code by scattering the code for an object across many different classes, all of which are combined together by the compiler to create your object.

One of the reasons for adopting object-oriented design and programming is to avoid so-called spaghetti code, where any bit of code you might look at does almost nothing useful but instead calls various other procedures and routines in other parts of your application. To determine what is going on with spaghetti code, you must trace through many routines and mentally piece together what it all means.

Object-oriented programming can help you avoid this problem, but it is most definitely not a magic bullet. In fact, when you create deep inheritance hierarchies, you are often creating spaghetti code. This is so because each level in the hierarchy not only extends the previous level's interface, but almost always also adds functionality. Thus, when you look at the final `NAFTACustomer` class it may have very little code. To figure out what it does or how it behaves, you have to trace through the code in the previous four levels of classes, and you might not even have the code for some of those classes, since they may come from other applications or class libraries you've purchased.

On one hand, you have the benefit that you're reusing code, but on the other hand, you have the drawback that the code for one object is actually scattered through five different classes.

It is important to keep this in mind when designing systems with inheritance — use as few levels in the hierarchy as possible to provide the required functionality.

Fragile Base Class Issue

You've explored where it is appropriate to use inheritance and where it is not. You've also explored how you can use inheritance and multiple interfaces in conjunction to implement both is-a and act-as relationships simultaneously within your classes.

Earlier, we noted that while inheritance is an incredibly powerful and useful concept, it can also be very dangerous if used improperly. You've seen some of this danger as we discussed the misapplication of the is-a relationship, and how you can use multiple interfaces to avoid those issues.

However, one of the most classic and common problems with inheritance is the fragile base class problem. This problem is exacerbated when you have very deep inheritance hierarchies but exists even in a single-level inheritance chain.

The issue you face is that a change in the base class always affects all child classes derived from that base class. This is a double-edged sword. On one hand, you get the benefit of being able to change code in one location and have that change automatically cascade out through all derived classes. On the other hand, a change in behavior can have unintended or unexpected consequences farther down the inheritance chain, and that can make your application very fragile and hard to change or maintain.

Interface Changes

There are obvious changes you might make, which require immediate attention. For example, you might change your `Contact` class to have `FirstName` and `LastName` instead of simply `Name` as a property. In the `Contact` class, replace the `mName` variable declaration with the following code:

```
    Private mFirstName As String
    Private mLastName As String
```

Now replace the Name property with the following code:

```
  Public Property FirstName() As String
    Get
      Return mFirstName
    End Get
    Set(ByVal value As String)
      mFirstName = value
    End Set
  End Property

  Public Property LastName() As String
    Get
      Return mLastName
    End Get
    Set(ByVal value As String)
      mLastName = value
    End Set
  End Property
```

At this point, the Task List window in the IDE will show a list of locations where you need to alter your code to compensate for the change. This is a graphic illustration of a base class change that causes cascading changes throughout your application. In this case, you've changed the base class interface, thus changing the interface of all subclasses in the inheritance chain.

To avoid having to fix code throughout your application, you should always strive to keep as much consistency in your base class interface as possible. In this case, you can implement a read-only Name property that returns the full name of the Contact:

```
  Public ReadOnly Property Name() As String
    Get
      Return mFirstName & " " & mLastName
    End Get
  End Property
```

This resolves most of the items in the Task List window. You can fix any remaining issues by using the FirstName and LastName properties. For example, in Form1 you can change the code behind your button to the following:

```
  Private Sub Button1_Click(ByVal sender As System.Object, _
       ByVal e As System.EventArgs) Handles button1.Click

    Dim obj As New Customer
    obj.FirstName = "Douglas"
    obj.LastName = "Adams"
    CType(obj, Interfaces.IPrintableObject).Print()
  End Sub
```

Any change to a base class interface is likely to cause problems, so you must think carefully before making such a change.

Implementation Changes

Unfortunately, there's another, more subtle type of change that can wreak more havoc on your application, and that is an implementation change. This is the core of the fragile base class problem.

Encapsulation provides you with separation of interface from implementation. However, keeping your interface consistent is merely a syntactic concept. If you change the implementation, you are making a semantic change, a change that doesn't alter any of your syntax but can have serious ramifications on the real behavior of the application.

In theory, you can change the implementation of a class, and as long as you don't change its interface, any client applications using objects based on that class will continue to operate without change. Of course, reality is never as nice as theory, and more often than not a change to implementation will have some consequences in the behavior of a client application.

For example, you might use a `SortedList` to sort and display some `Customer` objects. To do this, add a new button to `Form1` with code as follows:

```
Private Sub btnSort_Click(ByVal sender As System.Object, _
  ByVal e As System.EventArgs) Handles btnSort.Click

  Dim col As New Generic.SortedDictionary(Of String, Customer)
  Dim obj As Customer

  obj = New Customer()
  obj.FirstName = "Douglas"
  obj.LastName = "Adams"
  col.Add(obj.Name, obj)

  obj = New Customer()
  obj.FirstName = "Andre"
  obj.LastName = "Norton"
  col.Add(obj.Name, obj)

  Dim item As Generic.KeyValuePair(Of String, Customer)
  Dim sb As New System.Text.StringBuilder
  For Each item In col
    sb.AppendLine(item.Value.Name)
  Next
  MsgBox(sb.ToString)
End Sub
```

This code simply creates a couple of `Customer` objects, sets their `FirstName` and `LastName` properties, and inserts them into a generic `SortedDictionary` object from the `System.Collections.Generic` namespace.

Items in a `SortedDictionary` are sorted based on their key value, and you are using the `Name` property to provide that key, meaning that your entries will be sorted by name. Since your `Name` property is implemented to return first name first and last name second, your entries will be sorted by first name.

If you run the application, the dialog will display the following:

```
Andre Norton
Douglas Adams
```

However, you can change the implementation of your `Contact` class — not directly changing or impacting either the `Customer` class or your code in `Form1` — to return last name first and first name second, as shown here:

```
Public ReadOnly Property Name() As String
  Get
    Return mLastName & ", " & mFirstName
  End Get
End Property
```

While no other code requires changing, and no syntax errors are flagged, the behavior of the application is changed. When you run it, the output will now be:

```
Adams, Douglas
Norton, Andre
```

Maybe this change is inconsequential. Maybe it totally breaks the required behavior of your form. The developer making the change in the `Contact` class might not even know that someone was using that property for sort criteria.

This illustrates how dangerous inheritance can be. Changes to implementation in a base class can cascade to countless other classes in countless applications, having unforeseen side effects and consequences of which the base class developer is totally unaware.

Summary

Over the past three chapters, you've seen how object-oriented programming flows from the four basic concepts of abstraction, encapsulation, polymorphism, and inheritance. This chapter has provided some basic discussion of each concept and demonstrated how to implement them using Visual Basic.

You now understand how (when properly applied) object-oriented design and programming can allow you to create very large and complex applications that remain maintainable and readable over time. However, this is no magic bullet and these technologies and concepts can, if improperly applied, create the same hard-to-maintain code that you might create using procedural or modular design techniques.

It is not possible to fully cover all aspects of object-oriented programming in a single chapter. Before launching into a full-blown object-oriented project, we highly recommend going through other books specifically geared toward object-oriented design and programming.

8

Generics

One of the things developers often need to do is create new types to use in their programs. Early attempts at type creation led to user-defined types, or the VB `Structure` statement. Another approach is to use classes and objects to create new types. Yet another approach is to use generics.

Generics refers to the technology built into .NET 2.0 that allows you to define a code template and then to declare variables using that template. The template defines the operations that the new type can perform, and when you declare a variable based on the template, you are creating a new type. The benefit of generics over structures or objects is that a generic template makes it easier for your new types to be strongly typed. Generics also make it easier to reuse the template code in different scenarios.

The primary motivation for adding generics to .NET was to allow the creation of strongly typed collection types. Because generic collection types are strongly typed, they are significantly faster than the previous inheritance-based collection model. Any place you use collection classes in your code, you should consider revising that code to use generic collection types instead.

Visual Basic 2005 not only allows the use of preexisting generics but also the creation of your own generic templates. Because the technology to support generics was created primarily to build collection classes, it naturally follows that you might create a generic anytime you would otherwise build a normal collection class. In general, anytime you use the `Object` datatype, consider using generics instead.

In this chapter, you'll start out with a brief discussion of the use of generics, followed by a walkthrough of the syntax for defining your own generic templates.

Using Generics

There are many examples of generic templates in the .NET 2.0 BCL (Base Class Library). Many of them can be found in the `System.Collections.Generic` namespace, but others are scattered through the BCL as appropriate. Much focus is placed on the generic collection types, however, because it is here that the performance gains due to generics are most notable. In other cases, generics are used less for performance gains than for strong typing benefits.

As noted earlier, any time you use a collection datatype, you should consider using the generic equivalent instead.

A generic is often written something like `List(Of T)`. The type (or class) name is `List`. The letter `T` is a placeholder, much like a parameter. It indicates where you must provide a specific type value to customize the generic. For instance, you might declare a variable using the `List(Of T)` generic:

```
Dim data As New List(Of Date)
```

In this case, you're specifying that the type parameter, `T`, is a `Date`. By providing this type, you are specifying that the list will only contain values of type `Date`.

To make this clearer, let's contrast the new `List(Of T)` collection with the older `ArrayList` type.

When you work with an `ArrayList`, you are working with a type of collection that can store many types of values all at the same time.

```
Dim data As New ArrayList()
data.Add("Hello")
data.Add(5)
data.Add(New Customer())
```

It is loosely typed, internally always storing the values as type `Object`. This is very flexible, but is relatively slow since it is late bound. There's the advantage of being able to store any datatype, with the disadvantage that you have no control over what's in the collection.

The `List(Of T)` generic collection is quite different. It isn't a type at all, it is just a template. A type isn't created until you declare a variable using the template.

```
Dim data As New Generic.List(Of Integer)
data.Add(5)
data.Add(New Customer())' throws an exception
data.Add("Hello") ' throws an exception
```

When you declare a variable using the generic, you must provide the type of value that the new collection will hold. The end result is that a new type is created — in this case, a collection that can only hold `Integer` values.

The important thing here is that this new collection type is strongly typed for `Integer` values. Not only does its external interface (its `Item` and `Add` methods, for instance) require `Integer` values, but its internal storage mechanism only works with type `Integer`. This means that it is not late bound like `ArrayList` but rather is early bound. The end result is much higher performance, along with all the type safety benefits of being strongly typed.

Generics are useful because they typically offer a higher-performance option as compared to traditional classes. In some cases, they can also save you from writing code, since generic templates can provide code reuse where traditional classes cannot. Finally, generics can sometimes provide better type safety as compared to traditional classes, since a generic adapts to the specific type you require, while classes often must resort to working with a more general type such as `Object`.

It is important to note that generics come in two forms: generic types and generic methods. For instance, `List(Of T)` is a generic type in that it is a template that defines a complete type or class. In contrast, some otherwise normal classes have single methods that are just method templates and that assume a specific type when they are called. We'll discuss both scenarios.

Generic Types

Now that you have a basic understanding of generics and how they compare to regular types, let's get into some more detail. To do this, you'll make use of some other generic types provided in the .NET Framework. A generic type is a template that defines a complete class, structure, or interface. When you want to use such a generic, you declare a variable using the generic type, providing the real type (or types) to be used in creating the actual type of your variable.

Basic Usage

Before proceeding, create a new Windows Application project named `Generics`. On `Form1` add a `Button` (named `btnDictionary`) and a `TextBox` control (named `txtDisplay`). Set the `TextBox` control's `Multiline` property to `True` and anchor it to take up most of the form. The result should look something like Figure 8-1.

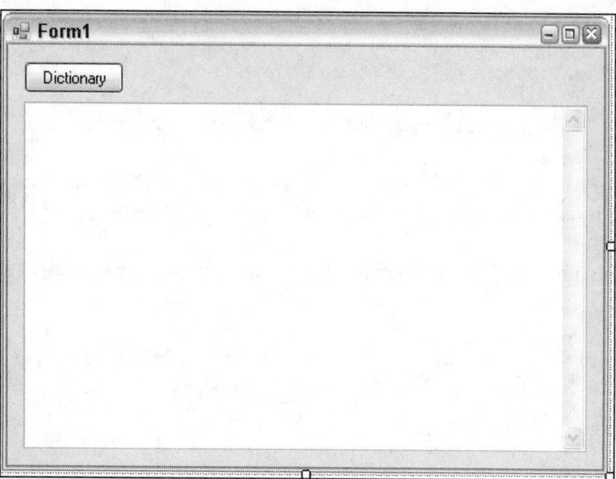

Figure 8-1

To begin, consider the `Dictionary(Of K, T)` generic. This is much like the `List(Of T)` discussed earlier, but this generic requires that you define the types of both the key data and the values to be stored. When you declare a variable as `Dictionary(Of K, T)`, the new `Dictionary` type that is created will only accept keys of the one type and values of the other.

Add the following code in the click event handler for `btnDictionary`:

```
txtDisplay.Clear()

Dim data As New Generic.Dictionary(Of Integer, String)
data.Add(5, "Rocky")
data.Add(15, "Mary")
For Each item As KeyValuePair(Of Integer, String) In data
  txtDisplay.AppendText("Data: " & item.Key & ", " & item.Value)
  txtDisplay.AppendText(Environment.NewLine)
Next
txtDisplay.AppendText(Environment.NewLine)
```

As you type, watch the IntelliSense information on the `Add` method. Notice how the key and value parameters are strongly typed based on the specific types provided in the declaration of the `data` variable. In the same code, you can create another type of `Dictionary`:

```
Dim data As New Generic.Dictionary(Of Integer, String)

Dim info As New Generic.Dictionary(Of Guid, Date)
data.Add(5, "Rocky")
data.Add(15, "Mary")
For Each item As KeyValuePair(Of Integer, String) In data
  txtDisplay.AppendText("Data: " & item.Key & ", " & item.Value)
  txtDisplay.AppendText(Environment.NewLine)
Next
info.Add(Guid.NewGuid, Now)
For Each item As KeyValuePair(Of Guid, Date) In info
  txtDisplay.AppendText("Data: " & item.Key.ToString & ", " & item.Value)
  txtDisplay.AppendText(Environment.NewLine)
Next
txtDisplay.AppendText(Environment.NewLine)
```

In this code, there are two completely different types. Both have the behaviors of a `Dictionary`, but they are not interchangeable because they have been created as different types.

Generic types may also be used as parameters and return types. For instance, add the following method to `Form1`:

```
Private Function LoadData() As Generic.Dictionary(Of Integer, String)
  Dim data As New Generic.Dictionary(Of Integer, String)
  data.Add(5, "Rocky")
  data.Add(15, "Mary")
  Return data
End Function
```

To call this method from the btnDictionary_Click method, add this code:

```
Dim results As Generic.Dictionary(Of Integer, String)
results = LoadData()
For Each item As KeyValuePair(Of Integer, String) In results
  txtDisplay.AppendText("Results: " & item.Key & ", " & item.Value)
  txtDisplay.AppendText(Environment.NewLine)
Next
txtDisplay.AppendText(Environment.NewLine)
```

The results of running this code are shown in Figure 8-2.

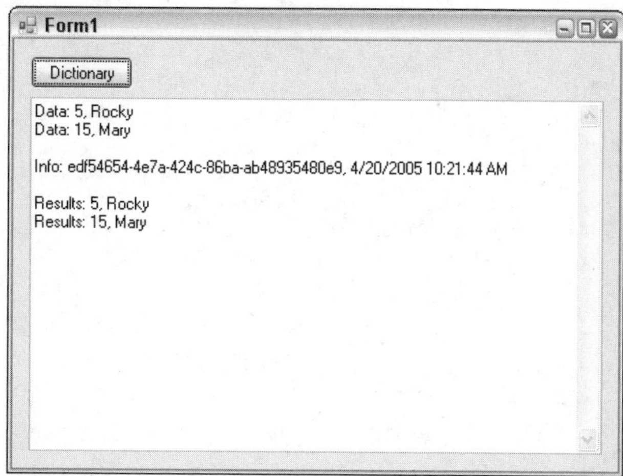

Figure 8-2

The reason this works is that both the return type of the function and the type of the data variable are exactly the same. Not only are they both Generic.Dictionary derivatives, but they have exactly the same types in the declaration.

The same is true for parameters:

```
Private Sub DoWork(ByVal values As Generic.Dictionary(Of Integer, String))
  ' do work here
End Sub
```

Again, the parameter type is not only defined by the generic type but also by the specific type values used to initialize the generic template.

Inheritance

It is possible to inherit from a generic type as you define a new class. For instance, the .NET BCL defines the System.ComponentModel.BindingList(Of T) generic type. This type is used to create collections that can support data binding. You can use this as a base class to create your own strongly typed, data-bindable collection. Add new classes named `Customer` and `CustomerList` to the project with the following code:

```
Public Class Customer
  Private mName As String

  Public Property Name() As String
    Get
      Return mName
    End Get
    Set(ByVal value As String)
      mName = value
    End Set
  End Property

End Class

Public Class CustomerList
  Inherits System.ComponentModel.BindingList(Of Customer)

  Private Sub CustomerList_AddingNew(ByVal sender As Object, _
    ByVal e As System.ComponentModel.AddingNewEventArgs) Handles Me.AddingNew

    Dim cust As New Customer
    cust.Name = "<new>"
    e.NewObject = cust

  End Sub

End Class
```

When you inherit from `BindingList(Of T)`, you must provide a specific type—in this case `Customer`. This means that your new `CustomerList` class extends and can customize `BindingList (Of Customer)`. In this case, you're providing a default value for the `Name` property of any new `Customer` object added to the collection.

When you inherit from a generic type, you can employ all the normal concepts of inheritance, including overloading and overriding methods, extending the class by adding new methods, handling events, and so forth.

To see this in action, add a new `Button` named `btnCustomer` to `Form1` and add a new form named `CustomerForm` to the project. Add a `DataGridView` control to `CustomerForm` and dock it full.

Behind `btnCustomer`, add the following code:

```
CustomerForm.ShowDialog()
```

Then add the following code behind `CustomerForm`:

```
Dim list As New CustomerList

Private Sub CustomerForm_Load(ByVal sender As System.Object, _
  ByVal e As System.EventArgs) Handles MyBase.Load

  DataGridView1.DataSource = list

End Sub
```

This code creates an instance of `CustomerList` and makes it the `DataSource` for the grid control. When you run the program and click the button to open the `CustomerForm`, notice that the grid contains a newly added `Customer` object. As you interact with the grid, new `Customer` objects are automatically added, with a default name of `<New>`. An example is shown in Figure 8-3.

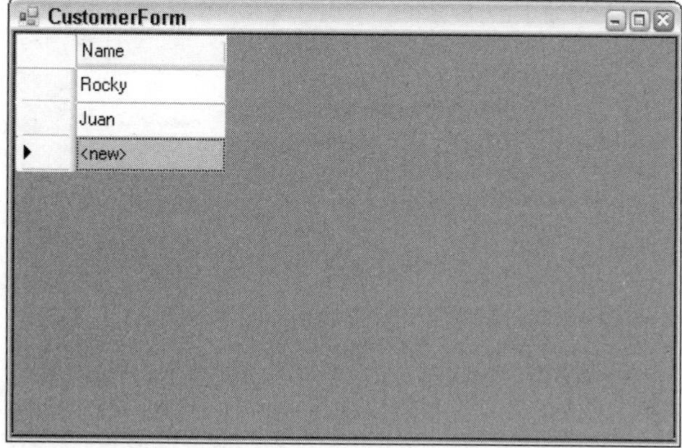

Figure 8-3

All this functionality of adding new objects and setting the default `Name` value occurs because `CustomerList` inherits from `BindingList(Of Customer)`.

Generic Methods

A generic method is a single method that is called not only with conventional parameters, but also with type information that defines the method. Generic methods are far less common than generic types. Due to the extra syntax required to call a generic method, they are also less readable than a normal method.

A generic method may exist in any class or module; it doesn't need to be contained within a generic type. The primary benefit of a generic method is avoiding the use of `CType` or `DirectCast` to convert parameters or return values between different types.

It is important to realize that the type conversion still occurs; generics merely provide an alternative mechanism to use instead of `CType` or `DirectCast`.

Without generics, code often uses the `Object` type. Add the following method to `Form1`:

```
Private Function AreEqual(ByVal a As Object, ByVal b As Object) As Boolean
  Return a.Equals(b)
End Function
```

The problem with this code is that `a` and `b` could be anything. There's no restriction here, nothing to ensure that they are even the same type. An alternative is to use generics. Add the following method to `Form1`:

```
Public Function AreEqual(Of T)(ByVal a As T, ByVal b As T) As Boolean
  Return a.Equals(b)
End Function
```

Now `a` and `b` are forced to be the same type, and that type is specified when the method is invoked.

Add a new `Button` named `btnEqual` to `Form1` with the following code in its click event:

```
Dim result As Boolean

' use normal method
result = AreEqual(1, 2)
result = AreEqual("one", "two")
result = AreEqual(1, "two")

' use generic method
result = AreEqual(Of Integer)(1, 2)
result = AreEqual(Of String)("one", "two")
'result = AreEqual(Of Integer)(1, "two")
```

But why not just declare the method as a Boolean? This code will probably cause some confusion.

The first three method calls are invoking the normal `AreEqual` method. Notice that there's no problem asking the method to compare an `Integer` and a `String`.

The second set of calls looks very odd. At first glance, they look like nonsense to many people. This is because invoking a generic method means providing two sets of parameters to the method, rather than the normal one set of parameters.

The first set of parameters defines the type or types required to define the method. This is much like the list of types you must provide when declaring a variable using a generic class. In this case, you're specifying that the `AreEqual` method will be operating on parameters of type `Integer`.

The second set of parameters is the conventional parameters that you'd normally supply to a method. What is special in this case is that the types of the parameters are being defined by the first set of parameters. In other words, in the first call, the type is specified to be `Integer`, so `1` and `2` are valid parameters. In the second call, the type is `String`, so `"one"` and `"two"` are valid. Notice that the third line is commented out. This is because `1` and `"two"` aren't the same type, so the compiler won't compile that line of code.

Creating Generics

Now that you have a good idea how to use preexisting generics in your code, let's take a look at how you can create generic templates. The primary reason to create a generic template instead of a class is to gain strong typing of your variables. Anytime you find yourself using the `Object` datatype, or a base class from which multiple types inherit, you may want to consider using generics. By using generics you can avoid the use of `CType` or `DirectCast`, which simplifies your code. If you are able to avoid the use of the `Object` datatype, you'll typically improve the performance of your code.

As discussed earlier, there are generic types and generic methods. A generic type is basically a class or structure that assumes specific type characteristics when a variable is declared using the generic. A generic method is a single method that assumes specific type characteristics, even though the method might be in an otherwise totally conventional class, structure, or module.

Generic Types

As discussed earlier, a generic type is a class, structure, or interface template. You can create such templates yourself to provide better performance, strong typing, and code reuse to the consumers of your types.

Classes

A generic class template is created in the same way that you create a normal class, with the exception that you'll require the consumer of your class to provide you with one or more types for use in your code. In other words, as the author of a generic template, you have access to the type parameters provided by the user of your generic.

For example, add a new class to the project named `SingleLinkedList`:

```
Public Class SingleLinkedList(Of T)

End Class
```

In the declaration of the type, you specify the type parameters that will be required:

```
Public Class SingleLinkedList(Of T)
```

In this case, you're requiring just one type parameter. The name, `T`, can be any valid variable name. In other words, you could declare the type like this:

```
Public Class SingleLinkedList(Of ValueType)
```

Make this change to the code in your project.

By convention (carried over from C++ templates), the variable names for type parameters are single uppercase letters. This is somewhat cryptic, and you may want to use a more descriptive convention for variable naming.

Whether you use the cryptic standard convention or more readable parameter names, the parameter is defined on the class definition. Within the class itself, you then use the type parameter anywhere that you would normally use a type (such as `String` or `Integer`).

To create a linked list, you need to define Node class. This will be a nested class (as discussed in Chapter 4):

```
Public Class SingleLinkedList(Of ValueType)
#Region " Node class "

  Private Class Node
    Private mValue As ValueType
    Private mNext As Node

    Public ReadOnly Property Value() As ValueType
      Get
        Return mValue
      End Get
    End Property

    Public Property NextNode() As Node
      Get
        Return mNext
      End Get
      Set(ByVal value As Node)
        mNext = value
      End Set
    End Property

    Public Sub New(ByVal value As ValueType, ByVal nextNode As Node)
      mValue = value
      mNext = nextNode
    End Sub
  End Class

#End Region
End Class
```

Notice how the `mValue` variable is declared as `ValueType`. This means that the actual type of `mValue` will depend on the type supplied when an instance of `SingleLinkedList` is created.

Because `ValueType` is a type parameter on the class, you can use `ValueType` as a type anywhere in the code. As you write the class, you can't tell what type `ValueType` will be. That information will be provided by the user of your generic class. Later, when someone declares a variable using your generic type, that person will specify the type—like this:

```
Dim list As New SingleLinkedList(Of Double)
```

At this point, a specific instance of your generic class is created, and all cases of `ValueType` within your code are replaced by the VB compiler with `Double`. Essentially, this means that for this specific instance of `SingleLinkedList`, the `mValue` declaration ends up as:

```
Private mValue As Double
```

Of course, you never get to see this code, since it is dynamically generated by the .NET JIT compiler at runtime based on your generic template code.

The same is true for methods within the template. In your example, there's a constructor method, which accepts a parameter of type `ValueType`. It is important to remember that `ValueType` will be replaced by a specific type when a variable is declared using your generic.

So, what type is `ValueType` when you're writing the template itself? Since it can conceivably be any type when the template is used, `ValueType` is treated like the `Object` type as you create the generic template. This severely restricts what you can do with variables or parameters of `ValueType` within your generic code.

The `mValue` variable is of `ValueType`, which means it is basically of type `Object` for the purposes of your template code. This means you can do assignments (like you do in the constructor code), and you can call any methods that are on the `System.Object` type:

- `Equals`
- `GetHashValue`
- `GetType`
- `ToString`

No operations beyond these basics are available by default. Later in the chapter, you'll discuss the concept of constraints, which allow you to restrict the types that can be specified for a type parameter. Constraints have the side benefit that they expand the operations you can perform on variables or parameters defined based on the type parameter.

However, this capability is enough to complete the `SingleLinkedList` class. Add the following code to the class after the `End Class` from the `Node` class:

```
  Private mHead As Node

  Default Public ReadOnly Property Item(ByVal index As Integer) As ValueType
    Get
      Dim current As Node = mHead
      For index = 1 To index
        current = current.NextNode
        If current Is Nothing Then
          Throw New Exception("Item not found in list")
        End If
      Next
      Return current.Value
    End Get
  End Property

  Public Sub Add(ByVal value As ValueType)
    mHead = New Node(value, mHead)
```

```
End Sub

Public Sub Remove(ByVal value As ValueType)
  Dim current As Node = mHead
  Dim previous As Node = Nothing
  While current IsNot Nothing
    If current.Value.Equals(value) Then
      If previous Is Nothing Then
        ' this was the head of the list
        mHead = current.NextNode
      Else
        previous.NextNode = current.NextNode
      End If
      Exit Sub
    End If
    previous = current
    current = current.NextNode
  End While

  ' You got to the end without finding the item.
  Throw New Exception("Item not found in list")

End Sub

Public ReadOnly Property Count() As Integer
  Get
    Dim result As Integer = 0
    Dim current As Node = mHead
    While current IsNot Nothing
      result += 1
      current = current.NextNode
    End While
    Return result
  End Get
End Property
```

Notice that the `Item` property and the `Add` and `Remove` methods all use `ValueType` either as return types or parameter types. More importantly, note the use of the `Equals` method in the `Remove` method:

```
If current.Value.Equals(value) Then
```

The reason this compiles is that `Equals` is defined on `System.Object` and, thus, is universally available. This code could not use the = operator, because that isn't universally available.

To try out the `SingleLinkedList` class, add a button to `Form1` named `btnList` and add the following code to `Form1`:

```
Private Sub btnList_Click(ByVal sender As System.Object, _
  ByVal e As System.EventArgs) Handles btnList.Click

  Dim list As New SingleLinkedList(Of String)
  list.Add("Rocky")
  list.Add("Mary")
```

```
    list.Add("Erin")
    list.Add("Edward")
    list.Add("Juan")
    list.Remove("Erin")

    txtDisplay.Clear()
    txtDisplay.AppendText("Count: " & list.Count)
    txtDisplay.AppendText(Environment.NewLine)
    For index As Integer = 0 To list.Count - 1
      txtDisplay.AppendText("Item: " & list.Item(index))
      txtDisplay.AppendText(Environment.NewLine)
    Next

  End Sub
```

When you run the code, you'll see a display similar to Figure 8-4.

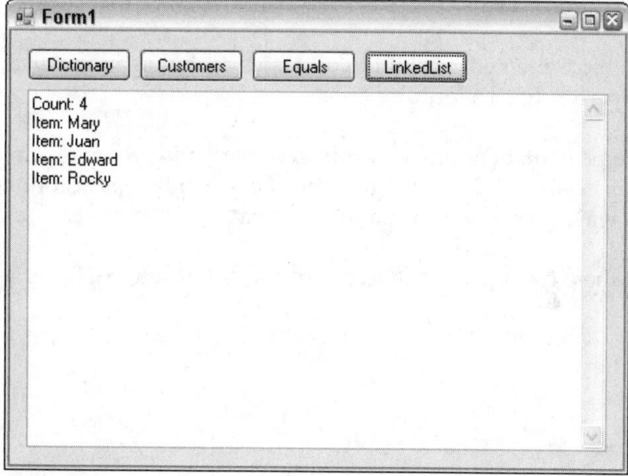

Figure 8-4

Other Generic Class Features

Earlier in the chapter, you used the `Dictionary` generic, which specifies multiple type parameters. To declare a class with multiple type parameters, you use syntax like this:

```
Public Class MyCoolType(Of T, V)
  Private mValue As T
  Private mData As V

  Public Sub New(ByVal value As T, ByVal data As V)
    mValue = value
    mData = data
  End Sub

End Class
```

Also, it is possible to use regular types in combination with type parameters, like this:

```
Public Class MyCoolType(Of T, V)
  Private mValue As T
  Private mData As V
  Private mActual As Double

  Public Sub New(ByVal value As T, ByVal data As V, ByVal actual As Double)
    mValue = value
    mData = data
    mActual = actual
  End Sub

End Class
```

Other than the fact that variables or parameters of types `T` or `V` must be treated as type `System.Object`, you can write virtually any code you choose. The code in a generic class is really no different from the code you'd write in a normal class.

This includes all the object-oriented capabilities of classes, including inheritance, overloading, overriding, events, methods, properties, and so forth.

However, there are some limitations on overloading. In particular, when overloading methods with a type parameter, the compiler doesn't know what that specific type might be at runtime. Thus, you can only overload methods in ways where the type parameter (that could be any type) doesn't lead to ambiguity.

For instance, adding these two methods to `MyCoolType` will result in a compiler error:

```
Public Sub DoWork(ByVal data As Integer)
  ' do work here
End Sub

Public Sub DoWork(ByVal data As V)
  ' do work here
End Sub
```

This isn't legal because the compiler can't know whether `V` will be `Integer` at runtime. If `V` was to end up defined as `Integer`, then you'd have two identical method signatures in the same class. Likewise, the following is not legal:

```
Public Sub DoWork(ByVal value As T)
  ' do work here
End Sub

Public Sub DoWork(ByVal data As V)
  ' do work here
End Sub
```

Again, there's no way for the compiler to be sure that `T` and `V` will represent different types at runtime.

However, you can declare overloaded methods like this:

```
Public Sub DoWork(ByVal data As Integer)
  ' do work here
```

```
    End Sub

    Public Sub DoWork(ByVal value As T, ByVal data As V)
      ' do work here
    End Sub
```

This works because there's no possible ambiguity between the two method signatures. Regardless of what types `T` and `V` end up being, there's no way the two `DoWork` methods can have the same signature.

Classes and Inheritance

Not only can you create basic generic class templates, but you can also combine the concept with inheritance.

This can be as basic as having a generic template inherit from an existing class:

```
Public Class MyControls(Of T)
  Inherits Control

End Class
```

In this case, the `MyControls` generic class inherits from the Windows Forms `Control` class, thus gaining all the behaviors and interface elements of a `Control`.

Alternately, a conventional class can inherit from a generic template. Suppose that you have a simple generic template:

```
Public Class GenericBase(Of T)

End Class
```

It is quite practical to inherit from this generic class as you create other classes:

```
Public Class Subclass
  Inherits GenericBase(Of Integer)

End Class
```

Notice how the Inherits statement not only references `GenericBase` but also provides a specific type for the type parameter of the generic type. Anytime you use a generic type, you must provide values for the type parameters, and this is no exception. This means that your new `Subclass` actually inherits from a specific instance of `GenericBase` where `T` is of type `Integer`.

Finally, you can also have generic classes inherit from other generic classes. For instance, you can create a generic class that inherits from the `GenericBase` class:

```
Public Class GenericSubclass(Of T)
  Inherits GenericBase(Of Integer)

End Class
```

As with the previous example, this new class inherits from an instance of `GenericBase` where `T` is of type `Integer`.

But things can get far more interesting. It turns out that you can use type parameters to specify the types for other type parameters. For instance, you could alter `GenericSubclass` like this:

```
Public Class GenericSubclass(Of V)
  Inherits GenericBase(Of V)

End Class
```

Notice that you're specifying that the type parameter for `GenericBase` is `V`—which is the type provided by the caller when it declares a variable using `GenericSubclass`. So, if a caller does this:

```
Dim obj As GenericSubclass(Of String)
```

then `V` is of type `String`, meaning that `GenericSubclass` is inheriting from an instance of `GenericBase` where its `T` parameter is also of type `String`. The type flows through from the subclass into the base class.

If that's not complex enough, consider the following class definition:

```
Public Class GenericSubclass(Of V)
  Inherits GenericBase(GenericSubclass(Of V))

End Class
```

In this case, the `GenericSubclass` is inheriting from `GenericBase`, where the `T` type in `GenericBase` is actually a specific instance of the `GenericSubclass` type. A caller can create such an instance like this:

```
Dim obj As GenericSubclass(Of Date)
```

In this case, the `GenericSubclass` type has a `V` of type `Date`. It also inherits from `GenericBase`, which has a `T` of type `GenericSubclass(Of Date)`.

Such complex relationships are typically not useful, but it is important to recognize how types flow through generic templates, especially when inheritance is involved.

Structures

You can also define generic `Structure` types. Structures were discussed in Chapter 3. The basic rules and concepts are the same as for defining generic classes. For instance:

```
Public Structure MyCoolStructure(Of T)
  Public Value As T
End Structure
```

As with generic classes, the type parameter or parameters represent real types that will be provided by the user of the structure in actual code. Thus, anywhere you see a `T` in the structure, it will be replaced by a real type such as `String` or `Integer`.

Code can use the structure in a manner similar to how a generic class is used:

```
Dim data As MyCoolStructure(Of Guid)
```

When the variable is declared, an instance of the `Structure` is created based on the type parameter provided. In this example, an instance of `MyCoolStructure` that holds `Guid` objects has been created.

Interfaces

Finally, you can define generic Interface types. Generic interfaces are a bit different from generic classes or structures, because they are implemented by other types when they are used. You can create a generic interface using the same syntax used for classes and structures:

```
Public Interface ICoolInterface(Of T)
  Public Sub DoWork(ByVal data As T)
  Public Function GetAnswer() As T
End Interface
```

Then the interface can be used within another type. For instance, you might implement the interface in a class:

```
Public Class ARegularClass
  Implements ICoolInterface(Of String)

  Public Sub DoWork(ByVal data As String) _
   Implements ICoolInterface(Of String).DoWork

  End Sub

  Public Function GetAnswer() As String _
    Implements ICoolInterface(Of String).GetAnswer

  End Function

End Class
```

Notice that you provide a real type for the type parameter in the `Implements` statement and `Implements` clauses on each method. In each case, you're specifying a specific instance of the `ICoolInterface` interface — one that deals with the `String` datatype.

As with classes and structures, an interface can be declared with multiple type parameters. Those type parameter values can be used in place of any normal type (such as `String` or `Date`) in any `Sub`, `Function`, `Property`, or `Event` declaration.

Generic Methods

You've already seen examples of methods declared using type parameters such as `T` or `V`. While these are examples of generic methods, they've been contained within a broader generic type such as a class, structure, or interface.

It is also possible to create generic methods within otherwise normal classes, structures, interfaces, or modules. In this case, the type parameter isn't specified on the class, structure, or interface but rather is specified directly on the method itself.

For instance, you can declare a generic method to compare equality like this:

```
Public Module Comparisons

  Public Function AreEqual(Of T)(ByVal a As T, ByVal b As T) As Boolean
    Return a.Equals(b)
  End Function

End Module
```

In this case, the `AreEqual` method is contained within a module, though it could as easily be contained in a class or structure.

Notice that the method accepts two sets of parameters. The first set of parameters are the type parameters, in this example just `T`. The second set of parameters are the normal parameters that a method would accept. In this example, the normal parameters have their types defined by the type parameter, `T`.

As with generic classes, it is important to remember that the type parameter is treated as a `System.Object` type as you write the code in your generic method. This severely restricts what you can do with parameters or variables declared using the type parameters. Specifically, you can do assignment and call the four methods common to all `System.Object` variables.

Later in the chapter, we'll discuss constraints, which allow you to restrict the types that can be assigned to the type parameters and also expand the operations that can be performed on parameters and variables of those types.

As with generic types, a generic method can accept multiple type parameters:

```
Public Class Comparisons

  Public Function AreEqual(Of T, R)(ByVal a As Integer, ByVal b As T) As R
    ' implement code here
  End Function

End Class
```

In this example, the method is contained within a class rather than a module. Notice that it accepts two type parameters, `T` and `R`. The return type is set to type `R`, while the second parameter is of type `T`. Also look at the first parameter, which is a conventional type. This illustrates how you can mix conventional types and generic type parameters in the method parameter list and return types, and by extension within the body of the method code.

Constraints

At this point, you've seen how to create and use generic types and methods. However, there have been serious limits on what you can do when creating generic type or method templates thus far. This is because the compiler treats any type parameters as the type `System.Object` within your template code. The end result is that you can assign the values and call the four methods common to all `System.Object` instances but can do nothing else. In many cases, this is too restrictive to be useful.

Constraints offer a solution and at the same time provide a control mechanism.

Constraints allow you to specify rules about the types that can be used at runtime to replace a type parameter. Using constraints, you can ensure that a type parameter is a `Class` or a `Structure`, or that it implements a certain interface or inherits from a certain base class.

Not only do constraints let you restrict the types available for use, but they also give the VB compiler valuable information. For example, if the compiler knows that a type parameter must always implement a given interface, then the compiler will allow you to call the methods on that interface within your template code.

Type Constraints

The most common type of constraint is a type constraint. A type constraint restricts a type parameter to be a subclass of a specific class or to implement a specific interface. This idea can be used to enhance the `SingleLinkedList` to sort items as they are added. First, change the declaration of the class itself to add the `IComparable` constraint:

```
Public Class SingleLinkedList(Of ValueType As IComparable)
```

With this change, `ValueType` is not only guaranteed to be equivalent to `System.Object`, but it is also guaranteed to have all the methods defined on the `IComparable` interface.

This means that within the Add method you can make use of any methods in the `IComparable` interface (as well as those from `System.Object`). The end result is that you can safely call the `CompareTo` method defined on the `IComparable` interface, because the compiler knows that any variable of type `ValueType` will implement `IComparable`:

```
Public Sub Add(ByVal value As ValueType)
  If mHead Is Nothing Then
    ' List was empty, just store the value.
    mHead = New Node(value, mHead)

  Else
    Dim current As Node = mHead
    Dim previous As Node = Nothing
    While current IsNot Nothing
      If current.Value.CompareTo(value) > 0 Then
        If previous Is Nothing Then
          ' this was the head of the list
          mHead = New Node(value, mHead)
        Else
          ' insert the node between previous and current
          previous.NextNode = New Node(value, current)
        End If
        Exit Sub
      End If
      previous = current
      current = current.NextNode
    End While
    ' you're at the end of the list, so add to end
    previous.NextNode = New Node(value, Nothing)
  End If
End Sub
```

Note the call to the `CompareTo` method:

```
If current.Value.CompareTo(value) > 0 Then
```

This is possible because of the `IComparable` constraint on `ValueType`. If you run the code now, the items should be displayed in sorted order, as shown in Figure 8-5.

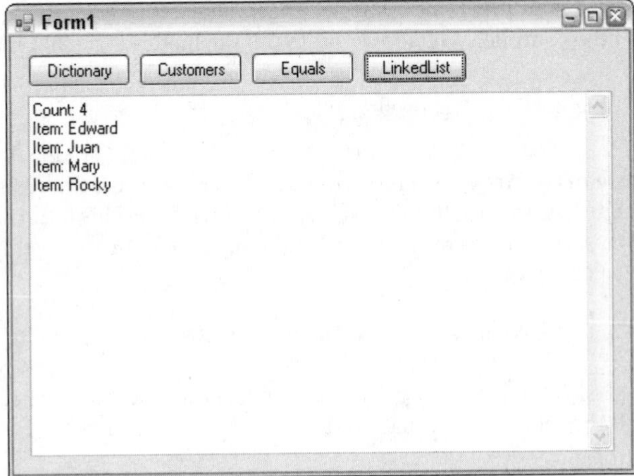

Figure 8-5

Not only can you constrain a type parameter to implement an interface, but you can also constrain it to be a specific type (class) or subclass of that type. For example, you could implement a generic method that works on any Windows Forms control:

```
Public Shared Sub ChangeControl(Of C As Control)(ByVal control As C)

  control.Anchor = AnchorStyles.Top Or AnchorStyles.Left

End Sub
```

The type parameter, `C`, is constrained to be of type `Control`. This restricts calling code to only specify this parameter as `Control` or a subclass of `Control` such as `TextBox`.

Then the parameter to the method is specified to be of type `C`, which means that this method will work against any `Control` or subclass of `Control`. Because of the constraint, the compiler now knows that the variable will always be some type of `Control` object and so it allows you to use any methods, properties, or events exposed by the `Control` class as you write your code.

Finally, it is possible to constrain a type parameter to be of a specific generic type. For instance:

```
Public Class ListClass(Of T, V As Generic.List(Of T))

End Class
```

In this case, you're specifying that the V type must be a List(Of T), whatever type T might be. A caller can use your class like this:

```
Dim list As ListClass(Of Integer, Generic.List(Of Integer))
```

Earlier in the chapter, we discussed how inheritance and generics interact. If you recall, things can get quite complex. The same is true when you constrain type parameters based on generic types.

Class and Structure Constraints

Another form of constraint allows you to be more general. Rather than enforcing the requirement for a specific interface or class, you can specify that a type parameter must be either a reference type or value type.

To specify that the type parameter must be a reference type, you use the Class constraint:

```
Public Class ReferenceOnly(Of T As Class)

End Class
```

This ensures that the type specified for T must be the type of an object. Any attempt to use a value type, such as Integer or a Structure, would result in a compiler error.

Likewise, you can specify that the type parameter must be a value type such as Integer or a Structure by using the Structure constraint:

```
Public Class ValueOnly(Of T As Structure)

End Class
```

In this case, the type specified for T must be a value type. Any attempt to use a reference type such as String, an interface, or a class would result in a compiler error.

New Constraints

Sometimes, you'll want to write generic code that creates instances of the type specified by a type parameter. In order to know that you can actually create instances of a type, you need to know that the type has a default public constructor. You can do this using the New constraint:

```
Public Class Factories(Of T As New)

  Public Function CreateT() As T
    Return New T
  End Function


End Class
```

The type parameter, T, is constrained so that it must have a public default constructor. Any attempt to specify a type for T that doesn't have such a constructor will result in a compile error.

Because you know that `T` will have a default constructor, you are able to create instances of the type as shown in the `CreateT` method.

Multiple Constraints

In many cases, you'll need to specify multiple constraints on the same type parameter. For instance, you might want to require that a type be both a reference type and have a public default constructor.

Essentially, you're providing an array of constraints, so you use the same syntax you use to initialize elements of an array:

```
Public Class Factories(Of T As {New, Class})

  Public Function CreateT() As T
    Return New T
  End Function


End Class
```

The constraint list can include two or more constraints, letting you specify a great deal of information about the types allowed for this type parameter.

Within your generic template code, the compiler is aware of all the constraints applied to your type parameters, so it allows you to use any methods, properties, and events specified by any of the constraints applied to the type.

Generics and Late Binding

One of the primary limitations of generics is that variables and parameters declared based on a type parameter are treated as type `System.Object` inside your generic template code. While constraints offer a partial solution, expanding the type of those variables based on the constraints, you are still very restricted in what you can do with the variables.

One key example is the use of common operators. There's no constraint you can apply that tells the compiler that a type supports the + or – operators. This means that you can't write generic code like this:

```
Public Function Add(Of T)(ByVal val1 As T, ByVal val2 As T) As T
  Return val1 + val2
End Function
```

This will generate a compiler error, because there's no way for the compiler to verify that variables of type `T` (whatever that is at runtime) will support the + operator. Since there's no constraint that you can apply to `T` to ensure that the + operator will be valid, there's no direct way to use operators on variables of a generic type.

One alternative is to use Visual Basic's native support for late binding to overcome the limitations you're seeing here. It is important to remember that late binding incurs substantial performance penalties, because a lot of work is done dynamically at runtime rather than by the compiler when you build your project. It is also important to remember the risks that come with late binding. Specifically the fact that the code can fail at runtime in ways that early bound code can't fail. But given those caveats, late binding can be used to solve your immediate problem.

To enable late binding, make sure to put `Option Strict Off` at the top of the code file containing your generic template (or set the project property to change `Option Strict` project-wide). Then you can rewrite the `Add` function as follows:

```
Public Function Add(Of T)(ByVal val1 As T, ByVal val2 As T) As T
  Return CObj(value1) + CObj(value2)
End Function
```

By forcing the `value1` and `value2` variables to be explicitly treated as type `Object`, you're telling the compiler that it should use late binding semantics. Combined with the `Option Strict Off` setting, the compiler assumes that you know what you're doing and it allows the use of the + operator even though its validity can't be confirmed.

The compiled code uses dynamic late binding to invoke the + operator at runtime. If that operator does turn out to be valid for whatever type `T` is at runtime, then this code will work great. In contrast, if the operator is not valid, a runtime exception will be thrown.

Summary

Generics allow you to create class, structure, interface, and method templates. These templates gain specific types based on how they are declared or called at runtime.

Generics provide you with another code reuse mechanism along with procedural and object-oriented concepts.

They also allow you to change code that uses parameters or variables of type `Object` (or other general types) to use specific datatypes. This often leads to much better performance and increases the readability of your code.

9

Namespaces

Even if you didn't realize it, you've been using namespaces since Chapter 2. For example, `System`, `System.Diagnostics`, and `System.Windows.Forms` are all namespaces contained within the .NET Framework. Namespaces are an easy concept to understand, but in this chapter, we'll put the ideas behind them on a firm footing — and clear up any misconceptions you might have about how they are used and organized.

If you're familiar with COM, you'll find that the concept of namespaces is the logical extension of programmatic identifier (`ProgID`) values. For example, the functionality of Visual Basic 6's `FileSystemObject` is now mostly encompassed in the .NET's `System.IO` namespace, though this is not a one-to-one mapping. However, namespaces are about more than a change in name; they represent the logical extension of the COM naming structure, expanding its ease of use and extensibility.

In addition to the traditional `System` and `Microsoft` namespaces (for example, used in the things such as Microsoft's Web Services Enhancements), .NET Framework 2.0 introduces a new way to get at some tough-to-find namespaces using the new `My` namespace. The `My` namespace is a powerful way of "speed-dialing-specific" functionalities in the base.

This chapter covers:

- What namespaces are
- Which namespaces are used in Visual Studio (Visual Studio 2005) projects by default
- Referencing namespaces and using the `Imports` statement
- How the compiler searches for class references
- How to alias namespaces
- Creating our own namespaces
- Using the new `My` namespace

Let's begin this chapter by defining what a namespace is (and isn't).

What Is a Namespace?

Namespaces are a way of organizing the vast number of classes, structures, enumerations, delegates, and interfaces that the .NET Framework class library provides. Namespaces are a hierarchically structured index into a class library, which is available to all of the .NET languages, not only Visual Basic 2005 (with the exception of the new `My` namespace). The namespaces, or object references, are typically organized by function. For example, the `System.IO` namespace contains classes, structures, and interfaces for working with input/output streams and files. These classes in this namespace do not necessarily inherit from the same base classes (apart from `Object`, of course).

A namespace is a combination of a naming convention and an assembly, which organizes collections of objects and prevents ambiguity in object references. A namespace can be, and often is, implemented across several physical assemblies, but, from the reference side, it is the namespace that ties these assemblies together. A namespace consists of not only classes but also other (child) namespaces. For example, `IO` is a child namespace of the `System` namespace.

Namespaces provide identification beyond the component name. With a namespace, it is possible to put a more meaningful title (for example, `System`) followed by a grouping (for example, `Text`) to group together a collection of classes that contain similar functions. For example, the `System.Text` namespace contains a powerful class called `StringBuilder`. To reference this class, you can use the fully qualified namespace reference of `System.Text.StringBuilder`, as shown here:

```
Dim sb As New System.Text.StringBuilder
```

The structure of a namespace is not a reflection of the physical inheritance of classes that make up a namespace. For example, the `System.Text` namespace contains another child namespace called `RegularExpressions`. This namespace contains several classes, but they do not inherit or otherwise reference the classes that make up the `System.Text` namespace.

Figure 9-1 shows how the `System` namespace contains the `Text` child namespace, which also has a child namespace, called `RegularExpressions`.

Both of these child namespaces, `Text` and `RegularExpressions`, contain a number of objects in the inheritance model for these classes, as shown in Figure 9-1.

As you can see in the figure, while some of the classes in each namespace do inherit from each other, and while all of the classes eventually inherit from the generic `Object`, the classes in `System.Text.RegularExpressions` do not inherit from the classes in `System.Text`.

You might be wondering at this point what all the fuss is about. To emphasize the usefulness of namespaces, we can draw another good example from this figure. If you make a reference to `System.Drawing.Imaging.Encoder` in your application, you are making a reference to a completely different `Encoder` class than the namespace that is shown in Figure 9-1 — `System.Text.Encoder`. Being able to clearly identify classes that have the same name though very different functions and disambiguate them is yet another advantage of namespaces.

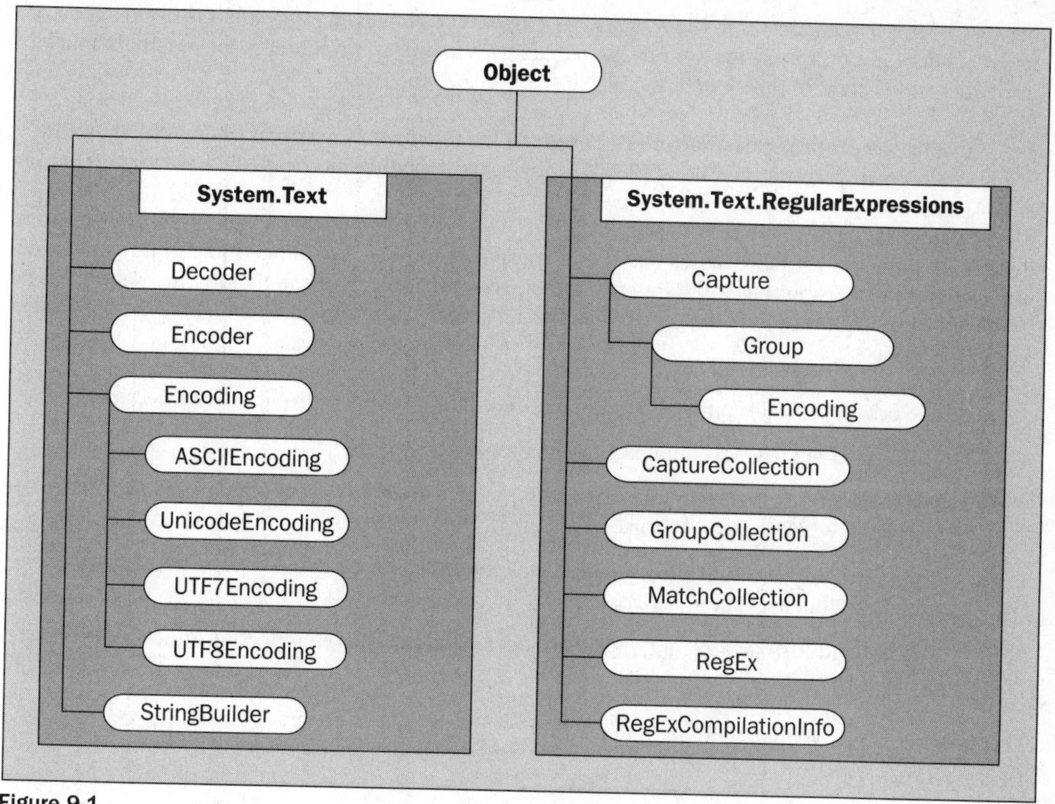

Figure 9-1

If you are an experienced COM developer, you may note that unlike a `ProgID`, which is a one-level relationship between the project assembly and class, a single namespace can use child namespaces to extend the meaningful description of a class. The `System` namespace, imported by default as part of every project created with Visual Studio, contains not only the default `Object` class, but also many other classes that are used as the basis for every .NET language.

However, what if a class you need isn't available in your project? The problem may be with the references in your project. For example, by default, the `System.DirectoryServices` namespace, used for getting programmatic access to the Active Directory objects, isn't part of your project's assembly. Using it requires adding a reference to the project assembly. The concept of referencing a namespace is very similar to the ability to reference a COM object in VB6.

In fact, with all this talk about referencing, it's probably a good idea to look at an example of adding an additional namespace to a project. Before doing that, you need to know a little bit about how a namespace is implemented.

Namespaces are implemented in .NET assemblies. The `System` namespace is implemented in an assembly called `System.dll` provided with Visual Studio. By referencing this assembly, the project gains the ability to reference all of the child namespaces of `System` that happen to be implemented in this assembly. Using the preceding table, the project can import and use the `System.Text` namespace because its implementation is in the `System.dll` assembly. However, although it is listed above, the project cannot import or use the `System.Data` namespace unless it references the assembly that implements this child of the `System` namespace, `System.Data.dll`.

Let's create a sample project so that you can examine the role that namespaces play within it. Using Visual Studio 2005, create a new Visual Basic 2005 Windows Application project called `Namespace_Sampler`.

The `Microsoft.VisualBasic.Compatibility.VB6` library isn't part of Visual Basic 2005 projects by default. To gain access to the classes that this namespace provides, you'll need to add it to your project. You can do this by using the Add Reference dialog box (available by right-clicking the References node in the Solution Explorer). This dialog box has five tabs, each containing elements that can be referenced from your project:

- The first tab (.NET) contains .NET assemblies that have been provided by Microsoft.
- The second tab (COM) contains COM components.
- The third tab (Projects) contains any custom .NET assemblies from any of the various projects contained within your solution.
- The fourth tab (Browse) allows you to look for any component files (.dll, .tlb, .olb, .ocx, .exe, or .manifest) that are on the network.
- The last and fifth tab (Recent) lists the most recently made references for quick-referencing capabilities.

The Add Reference dialog is shown in Figure 9-2.

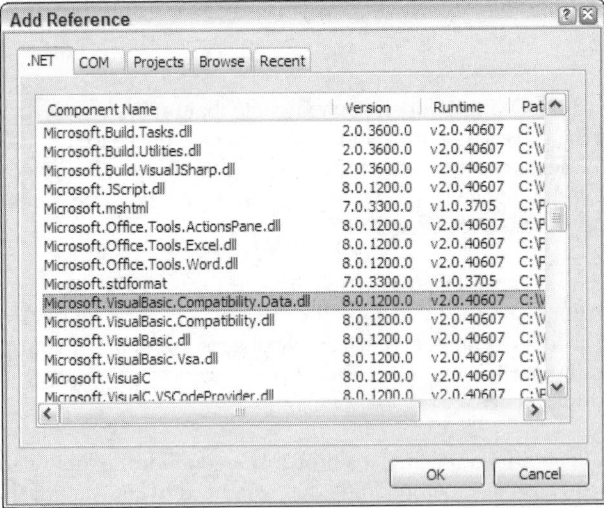

Figure 9-2

The available .NET namespaces are listed by a component name. This is the same as the namespace name. From the dialog, you will see a few columns that supply the namespace of the component, the version number of the component, the version of the .NET Framework that the particular component is targeted for, and the path location of the file. You can select a single namespace to make a reference to by clicking your mouse on the component that you are interested in. Holding down the Ctrl key and pressing the mouse button will allow you to select multiple namespaces to reference. To select a range of namespaces, first click on either the first or last component in the dialog that is contained in the range choice, then complete the range selection by holding down the Shift key and using the mouse to select the other component in the range. Once you have selected all the components that you are interested in referencing, press the OK button.

The example in Figure 9-2 is importing some namespaces from the `Microsoft.VisualBasic` namespace, even though only one selection has been made. This implementation, while a bit surprising at first, is very powerful. First, it shows the extensibility of namespaces — the single `Microsoft.VisualBasic.Compatibility.VB6` namespace is implemented in two separate assemblies. Second, it allows you to include only the classes that you need — in this case, those that are related to the VB6 (Visual Basic 6) environment or to database tools, or both types. There are some interesting points about the `Microsoft.VisualBasic` namespace that you should be aware of. First, this namespace gives you access to all those functions that VB6 developers have had for years. Microsoft has implemented these in the .NET Framework and has made them available for your use within your .NET projects. Since these functions have been implemented in the .NET Framework, there is absolutely no performance hit for using them, but you will most likely find the functionality that they provide available to you in newer .NET namespaces. One big point is that contrary to what the name of the namespace suggests, this namespace is available for use by all of the .NET languages. So, this means that even a C# developer could also use the `Microsoft.VisualBasic` namespace if he or she so desired.

Namespaces and References

Highlighting their importance to every project, references (including namespaces) are no longer hidden from view — available only after opening a dialog box as they were in VB6. As shown in the Solution Explorer window in Figure 9-3, every new project comes with a set of referenced namespaces. (If you don't see the references listed in Solution Explorer, press the Show All Files button from the Solution Explorer menu.)

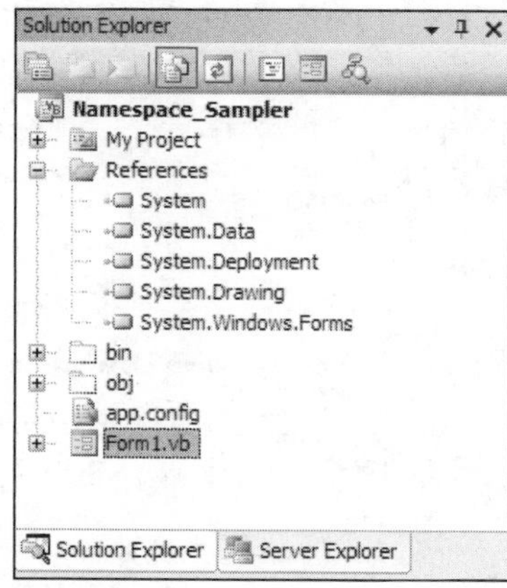

Figure 9-3

The list of default references changes based on the type of project. The example in Figure 9-3 shows the default references for a Windows Forms project in Visual Studio 2005. If the project type is an ASP.NET Web Application, the list of references changes appropriately — the reference to the `System.Windows.Forms` namespace assembly changes and is replaced by a reference to `System.Web`. If the project type is an ASP.NET Web Service (not shown), then the `System.Windows.Forms` namespace is replaced by references to the `System.Web` and `System.Web.Services` namespaces.

In addition to making the namespaces available, references play a second important role in your project. One of the advantages of .NET is using services and components built on the common language runtime (CLR), which allow you to avoid DLL conflicts. The various problems that can occur related to DLL versioning, commonly referred to as DLL hell, involve two types of conflict.

The first situation occurs when you have a component that requires a minimum DLL version, and an older version of the same DLL causes your product to break. The alternative situation is when you require an older version of a DLL, and a new version is incompatible. In either case, the result is that a shared file, outside of your control, creates a systemwide dependency that impacts your software. As part of .NET, it is possible, but not required, to indicate that a DLL should be shipped as part of your project to avoid an external dependency.

To indicate that a referenced component should be included locally, you can select the reference in Solution Explorer and then examine the properties associated with that reference. One editable property is called `Copy Local`. You will see this property and its value in the Properties window within Visual Studio 2005. For those assemblies that are part of a Visual Studio 2005 installation, this value defaults to `False`. However, for custom references, this property will default to `True` to indicate that the referenced DLL should be included as part of the assembly. Changing this property to `True` changes the path associated with the assembly. Instead of using the path to the referenced file's location on the system, the project creates a subdirectory based on the reference name and places the files required for the implementation of the reference in this subdirectory, as shown in Figure 9-4.

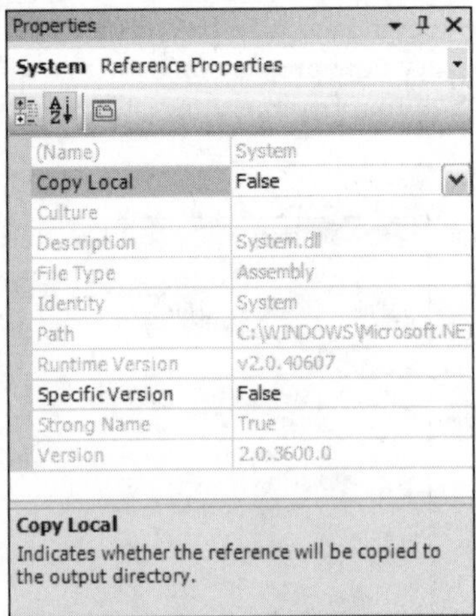

Figure 9-4

The benefit of this is that even if another version of the DLL is later placed on the system, your project's assembly will continue to function. However, this protection from a conflicting version comes at a price. Future updates to the namespace assembly to fix flaws will be in the system version but not in the private version that is part of your project's assembly. To resolve this, Microsoft's solution is to place new versions in directories based on their version information. If you examine the path information for all of the Visual Studio 2005 references, you will see that it includes a version number. As new versions of these DLLs are released, they will be installed in a separate directory. This method allows for an escape from DLL hell, by keeping new versions from stomping on old versions, and also allows for old versions to be easily located for maintenance updates. For this reason, in many cases, it is better to leave alone the default behavior of Visual Studio 2005, which is set to only copy locally custom components, until your organization implements a directory structure with version information similar to that of Microsoft.

The Visual Basic 2005 compiler will not allow you to add a reference to your assembly if the targeted implementation includes a reference that isn't also referenced in your assembly. The good news is that the compiler will help. If, after adding a reference, that reference doesn't appear in the IntelliSense list generated by Visual Studio 2005, go ahead and type the reference to a class from that reference. The compiler will flag it with one of its Microsoft Word–like spelling or grammar error underlines. Then when you click the underlined text, the compiler will tell you which other assemblies need to be referenced in the project in order to use the class in question.

Common Namespaces

The generated list of references shown in Solution Explorer for the newly created `Namespace_Sampler` project includes most, but not all, of the namespaces that are part of your Windows Application project. For example, one namespace not displayed as a reference is `Microsoft.VisualBasic` and the accompanying `Microsoft.VisualBasic.dll`. Every Visual Basic 2005 project includes the namespace `Microsoft.VisualBasic`. This namespace is part of the Visual Studio project templates for Visual Basic 2005 and is, in short, what makes Visual Basic 2005 different from C# or any other .NET language. The implicit inclusion of this namespace is the reason that you can call `IsDBNull` and other methods of Visual Basic 2005 directly. The only difference in the default namespaces that are included with Visual Basic 2005 and C# Windows Application projects is that the former use `Microsoft.VisualBasic` and the latter use `Microsoft.CSharp`.

To see all of the namespaces that are imported automatically, such as the `Microsoft.VisualBasic` namespace, right-click the project name in Solution Explorer and select Properties from the context menu. This will open the project properties in the Visual Studio document window. Select the References tab from the left-hand navigation, and you will see the reference `Microsoft.VisualBasic` at the top of the list. This is illustrated in Figure 9-5.

When looking at the project's global list of imports in the textarea at the bottom of the page, you can see that in addition to the `Microsoft.VisualBasic` namespace, the `System.Collections` and `System.Diagnostics` namespaces are also imported into the project. This is signified by the checkmarks next to the namespace. Unlike the other namespaces in the list, these namespaces are not listed as references in the textarea directly above this. That is because the implementation of the `System.Collections` and `System.Diagnostics` namespaces is part of the referenced `System.dll`. Similarly to `Microsoft.VisualBasic`, importing these namespaces allows references to the associated classes, such that a fully qualified path is not required. Since these namespaces contain commonly used classes, it is worthwhile to always include them at the project level.

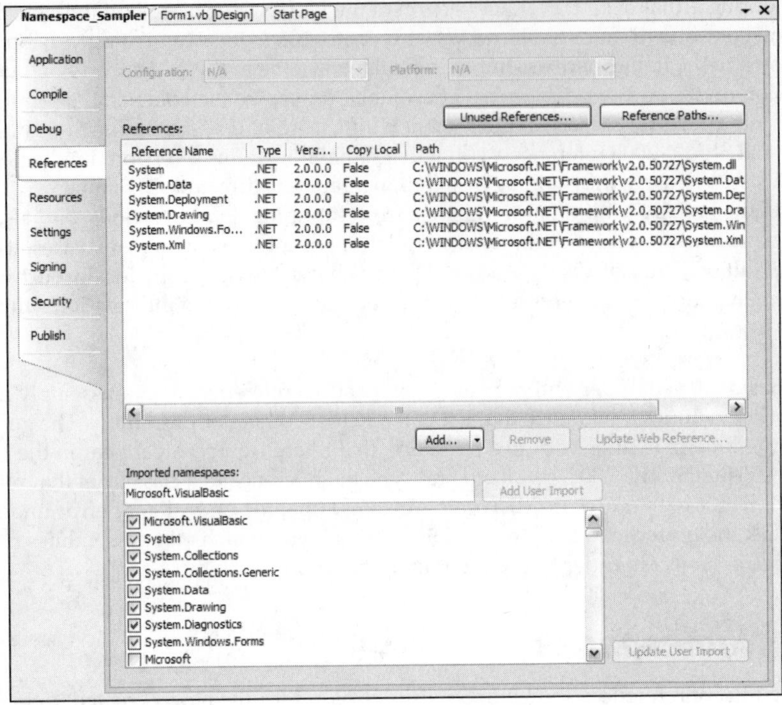

Figure 9-5

The following listing brings together brief descriptions of some of the namespaces commonly used in Visual Basic 2005 projects:

- `System.Collections` — Contains the classes that support various feature-rich object collections. Included automatically, it has classes for arrays, lists, dictionaries, queues, hash tables, and so on. As of .NET 2.0, this namespace also includes the ability to work with the new generics — a way to build type-safe collections.
- `System.Data` — Contains the classes to support the core features of ADO.NET.
- `System.Diagnostics` — Included in all Visual Basic 2005 projects, this namespace includes the debugging classes. The `Trace` and `Debug` classes provide the primary capabilities, but the namespace contains dozens of classes to support debugging.
- `System.Drawing` — Simple drawing classes to support Windows Application projects.
- `System.EnterpriseServices` — Not included automatically, the `System.EnterpriseServices` implementation must be referenced to make it available. This namespace contains the classes that interface .NET assemblies with COM+.
- `System.IO` — This namespace contains important classes that allow you to read and write to files as well as data streams.

- `System.Text` — This commonly used namespace allows you to work with text in a number of different ways, usually in regard to string manipulation. One of the more popular objects that this namespace offers is the `StringBuilder` object.
- `System.Threading` — This namespace contains the objects to work with and manipulate threads within your application.
- `System.Web` — This is the namespace that deals with one of the more exciting features of the .NET Framework — ASP.NET. This namespace provides the objects that deal with browser-server communications. Two of the main objects include the `HttpRequest` object, which deals with the request from the client to the server, and the `HttpResponse` object, which deals with the response from the server to the client.
- `System.Web.Services` — This is the main namespace you use when you are creating XML Web Services, one of the more powerful capabilities that is provided with the .NET Framework. This namespace provides you with the classes that deal with SOAP messages and the manipulation of these messages.
- `System.Windows.Forms` — The classes to create Windows Forms in Windows Application projects. This namespace contains the form elements.

Of course, to really make use of the classes and other objects in the above listing, you really need more detailed information. In addition to resources such as Visual Studio 2005's help files, the best source of information is the Object Browser. It is available directly in the Visual Studio 2005 IDE. You will find it by selecting View ➪ Object Browser if you are using Visual Studio 2005 or 2003 or View ➪ Other Windows ➪ Object Browser if you are using Visual Studio 2002. The Visual Studio 2005 Object Browser is shown in Figure 9-6.

The Object Browser displays each of the referenced assemblies and allows you to drill down into the various namespaces. The previous screen shot illustrates how the `System.dll` implements a number of namespaces, including some that are part of the `System` namespace. By drilling down into a namespace, it is possible to see some of the classes available. By further selecting a class, the browser shows not only the methods and properties associated with the selected class but also a brief outline of what that class does.

Using the Object Browser is an excellent way to gain insight not only into which classes and interfaces are available via the different assemblies included in your project but also into how they work. As you can guess, the ability to actually see not only which classes are available but what and how to use them is important in being able to work efficiently. To work effectively in the .NET CLR environment requires finding the right class for the task.

Importing and Aliasing Namespaces

Not all namespaces should be imported at the global level. Although you have looked at the namespaces that are included at this level, it is much better to import namespaces only in the module where they will be used. Importing a namespace at the module level does not change setting the reference, but does mean that you don't add it into the list of imports on the project's property page. Similarly to variables used in a project, it is possible to define a namespace at the module level. The advantage of this is similar to the use of local variables in that it helps to prevent different namespaces from interfering with each other. As this section will show, it is possible for two different namespaces to contain classes or even child namespaces with the same name.

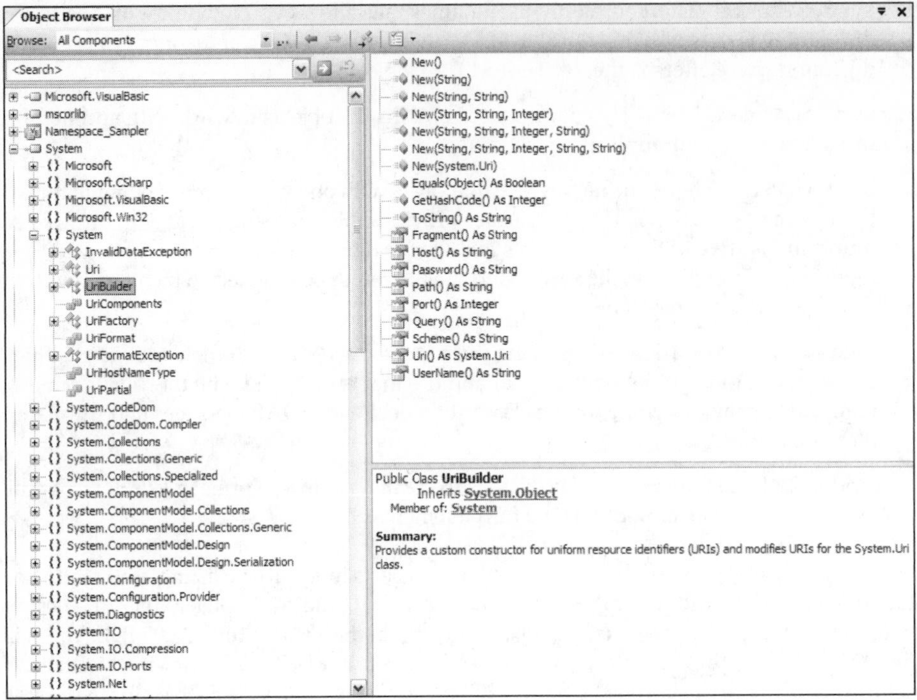

Figure 9-6

Importing Namespaces

The development environment and compiler need a way to prioritize the order in which namespaces should be checked when a class is referenced. It is always possible to unequivocally specify a class by stating its complete namespace path. This is referred to as fully qualifying your declaration. Here is an example of fully qualifying a `StringBuilder` object:

```
Dim sb As New System.Text.StringBuilder
```

However, if every reference to every class needed its full namespace declaration, that would make Visual Basic 2005 and every other .NET language very difficult to program in. After all, who would want to type `System.Collections.ArrayList` each time they wanted an instance of the `ArrayList` class. If you review the global references, you'll see the `System.Collections` namespace. Thus, you can just type `ArrayList` whenever you need an instance of this class as the reference to the larger `System.Collections` namespace has already been made by the application.

In theory, another way to reference the `StringBuilder` class is to use `Text.StringBuilder`, but with all namespaces imported globally, there is a problem with this. The problem is caused by what is known as namespace crowding. Because there is a second namespace, `System.Drawing`, which has a child called `Text`, the compiler doesn't have a clear location for the `Text` namespace and, therefore, cannot resolve the `StringBuilder` class. The solution to this problem is to make it so that only a single version of the `Text` child namespace is found locally. Then the compiler will use this namespace regardless of the global availability of the `System.Drawing.Text` namespace.

`Imports` statements specify to the compiler those namespaces that the code will use.

```
Imports Microsoft.Win32
Imports System
Imports SysDraw = System.Drawing
```

Once they are imported into the file, you are not required to fully qualify your object declarations in your code. For instance, if you imported the `System.Data.SqlClient` namespace into your file, you would then be able to create a `SqlConnection` object in the following manner:

```
Dim conn As New SqlConnection
```

Each of the `Imports` statements from above illustrates a different facet of importing namespaces. The first, `Imports Microsoft.Win32`, is a namespace that is not imported at the global level. Looking at the reference list, you may not see the Microsoft assembly referenced directly. However, opening the Object Browser reveals that this namespace is actually included as part of the `System.dll`.

As noted earlier, the `StringBuilder` references become ambiguous because both `System.Text` and `System.Drawing.Text` are valid namespaces at the global level. As a result, the compiler has no way to distinguish which `Text` child namespace is being referenced. Without any clear indication, the compiler flags `Text.StringBuilder` declarations in the command handler. However, using the `Imports System` declaration in the module tells the compiler that, before checking namespaces imported at the global level, it should attempt to match incomplete references at the module level. Since the `System` namespace is declared at this level, while `System.Drawing` (for the moment) is not, there is no ambiguity as to which child namespace `Text.StringBuilder` belongs to.

This demonstrates how the compiler looks at each possible declaration:

- First, see if the item is a complete reference such as `System.Text.StringBuilder`.
- If the declaration does not match a complete reference, then the compiler tries to see if the declaration is from a child namespace of one of the module-level imports.
- Finally, if a match has not been found, the compiler looks at the global-level imports to see if the declaration can be associated with a namespace imported for the entire assembly.

While the preceding logical progression of moving from a full declaration through module- to global-level imports does resolve the majority of issues, it does not handle all possibilities. Specifically, if we imported `System.Drawing` at the module level, the namespace collision would return. This is where the third import statement becomes important — this import statement uses an alias.

Referencing Namespaces in ASP.NET

Making a reference to a namespaces in ASP.NET is quite similar to working with Windows Forms, but you have to take some simple, additional steps. From your ASP.NET solution, first make a reference to the assemblies from the References folder just as you do with Windows Forms. Once there, import these namespaces at the top of the page file in order to avoid having to fully qualify the reference each and every time on that particular page.

For example, instead of using System.Collections.Generic for each instance of use, use the <%# Import %> page directive at the top of the ASP.NET page (if the page is constructed using the inline coding style) or use the Imports keyword at the top of the ASP.NET page's code-behind file (just as is done with Windows Forms applications). This is how to perform this task when using inline coding for ASP.NET pages:

```
<%# Import Namespace="System.Collections.Generic" %>
```

Now that this reference is in place on the page, you can gain access to everything this namespace contains without the need to fully qualify the object you are accessing. It is important to note that the Import keyword in the inline example is not missing an "s" at the end. When importing in this manner, it is Import (without the "s") instead of Imports — as it is in the ASP.NET code-behind model and in Windows Forms.

In ASP.NET 1.0/1.1, if you used a particular namespace on each page of your application, you would have to have the Import statement on each and every page where it was needed. ASP.NET 2.0 introduces the ability to use the web.config file to make a global reference so that you don't need to make further references on the pages themselves. This is done as illustrated here in the following example.

```
<pages>
   <namespaces>
      <add namespace="System.Drawing" />
      <add namespace="Wrox.Books" />
   </namespaces>
</pages>
```

In this example, using the <namespaces> element in the web.config file, references are made to the System.Drawing namespace and the Wrox.Books namespace. Because these references are now contained within the web.config file, there is no need to again reference them on any of the ASP.NET pages that are contained within this solution.

Aliasing Namespaces

Aliasing has two benefits in .NET. The first is that aliasing allows a long namespace such as System.EnterpriseServices to be replaced with a shorthand name such as COMPlus. The second is that it adds a way to prevent ambiguity among child namespaces at the module level.

As noted earlier, the System and System.Drawing namespaces both contain a child namespace of Text. Since you will be using a number of classes from the System.Drawing namespace, it follows that this namespace should be imported into the form's module. However, were this namespace imported along with the System namespace, the compiler would once again find references to the Text child namespace ambiguous. However, by aliasing the System.Drawing namespace to SysDraw, the compiler knows that it should only check the System.Drawing namespace when a declaration begins with that alias. The result is that although multiple namespaces with the same child namespace are now available at the module level, the compiler knows that one (or more) of them should only be checked at this level when they are explicitly referenced.

Aliasing as defined above is done in the following fashion:

```
Imports SysDraw = System.Drawing
```

Creating Your Own Namespaces

Every assembly created in .NET is part of some root namespace. By default, this logic actually mirrors COM in that assemblies are assigned a namespace that matches the project name. However, unlike COM, in .NET it is possible to change this default behavior. In this way, just as Microsoft has packaged the system-level and CLR classes using well-defined names, it is possible for you to create your own namespaces. Of course, it's also possible to create projects that match existing namespaces and extend those namespaces, but that is very poor programming practice.

Creating an assembly in a custom namespace can be done at one of two levels. However, unless you want the same name for each assembly that will be used in a large namespace, you will normally reset the root namespace for the assembly. This is done through the assembly's project pages, reached by right-clicking the solution name in the Solution Explorer window and working off of the first tab (Application) within the Properties page that opens up in the Document window, as shown in Figure 9-7.

The next step is optional, but, depending on whether you want to create a class at the top level or at a child level, you can add a `Namespace` command to your code. There is a trick to being able to create top-level namespaces, or multiple namespaces within the modules that make up an assembly. Instead of replacing the default namespace with another name, you can delete the default namespace and define the namespaces only in the modules, using the `Namespace` command.

The `Namespace` command is accompanied by an `End Namespace` command. This `End Namespace` command must be placed after the `End Class` tag for any classes that will be part of the namespace. The following code demonstrates the structure used to create a `MyMetaNamespace` namespace, which contains a single class:

```
Namespace MyMetaNamespace
    Class MyClass1
        'Code
    End Class
End Namespace
```

You can then utilize the `MyClass1` object simply by referencing its namespace, `MyMetaNamespace.MyClass1`. It is also possible to have multiple namespaces in a single file, as shown here:

```
Namespace MyMetaNamespace1
    Class MyClass1
        'Code
    End Class
 End Namespace

Namespace MyMetaNamespace2
   Class MyClass2
      'Code
    End Class
 End Namespace
```

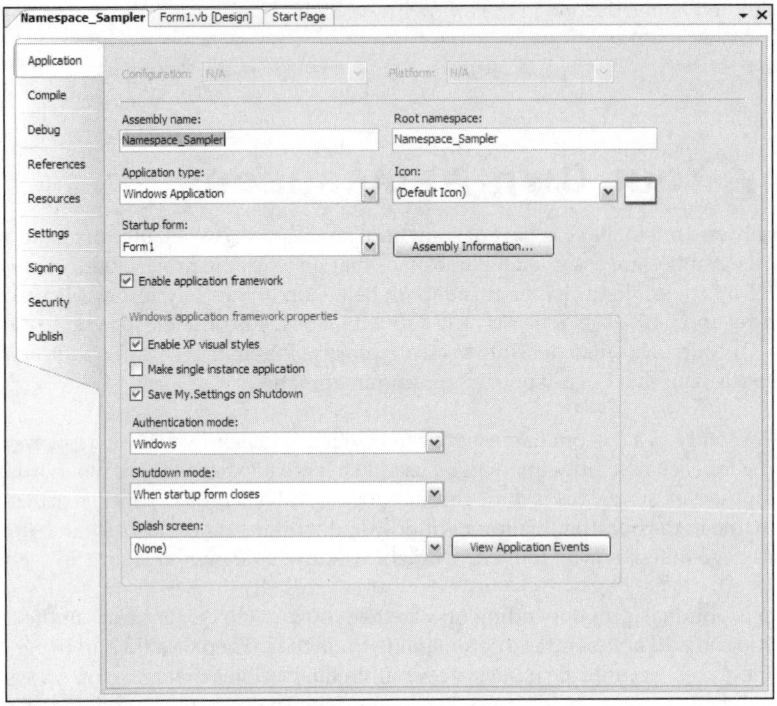

Figure 9-7

Using this kind of structure, if you want to utilize `MyClass1`, you get at it through the namespace `MyMetaNamespace.MyClass1`. This does not give you access to `MyMetaNamespace2` and the objects that it offers; instead, you have to make a separate reference to `MyMetaNamespace2.MyClass2`.

The `Namespace` command can also be nested. Using nested `Namespace` commands is how child namespaces are defined. The same rules apply — each `Namespace` must be paired with an `End Namespace` and must fully encompass all of the classes that are part of that namespace. In this example, the `MyMetaNamespace` has a child namespace called `MyMetaNamespace.MyChildNamespace`.

```
Namespace MyMetaNamespace
    Class MyClass1
       'Code
    End Class

    Namespace MyChildNamespace
       Class MyClass2
          'Code
       End Class
    End Namespace
End Namespace
```

This is another point to be aware of when you make references to other namespaces within your own custom namespaces. Let's look at an example of this.

```
Imports System
Imports System.Data
Imports System.Data.SqlClient

Namespace MyMetaNamespace1
    Class MyClass1
        'Code
    End Class
End Namespace

Namespace MyMetaNamespace2
   Imports System.IO

   Class MyClass2
      'Code
   End Class
End Namespace
```

In this example, there are a number of different namespaces referenced in the file. The three namespaces referenced at the top of the code listing — the `System`, `System.Data`, and `System.Data.SqlClient` namespace references, are available to each and every namespace that is developed in the file. This is so because these three references are sitting outside of any particular namespace declarations. However, this is quite different for the `System.IO` namespace reference. Because this reference is made within the `MyMetaNamespace2` namespace, it is unavailable to any other namespace in the file.

> **When you create your own namespaces, Microsoft recommends that you use a convention of `CompanyName.TechnologyName`, for example, `Wrox.Books`. This helps to ensure that all libraries are organized in a consistent way.**

Sometimes when you are working with custom namespaces, you might find that you have locked yourself out of accessing a particular branch of a namespace, purely due to naming conflicts. For this reason, Visual Basic has introduced the new `Global` keyword in this latest version, which can be used as the outermost root class available in the .NET Framework class library. Figure 9-8 shows a diagram of how the class structure looks with the new `Global` keyword.

This means that you can make specifications such as:

```
Global.System.String
```

or

```
Global.Wrox.System.Titles
```

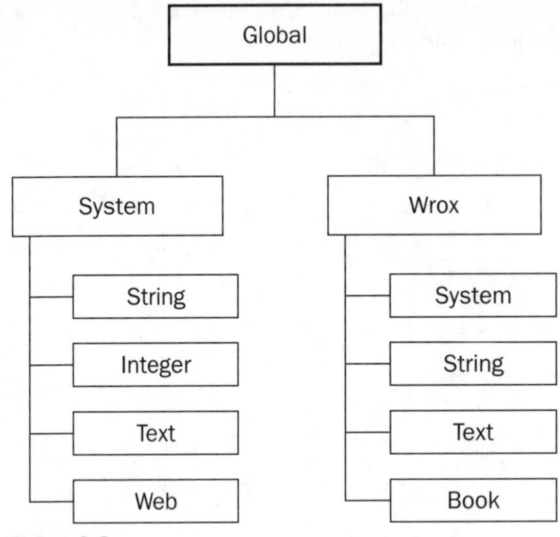

Figure 9-8

My

The `My` keyword is a novel concept to quickly give you access to your application, your users, your resources, the computer, or the network on which the application resides. The `My` keyword has been referred to as a way of speed-dialing common but complicated resources that you need access to. Using the `My` keyword, you can quickly get access to a wide variety of items such as user details or specific settings of the requestor's browser.

Though not really considered a true namespace, the `My` object declarations that you make work the same as the .NET namespace structure you are used to working with. To give you an example, let's first look at how you get at the user's machine name using the traditional namespace structure:

```
Environment.MachineName.ToString()
```

For this example, you simply need to use the `Environment` class and use this namespace to get at the `MachineName` property. Now let's look at how you would accomplish this same task using the new `My` keyword:

```
My.Computer.Info.MachineName.ToString()
```

As you are looking at this example, you might be wondering what the point is if the example, which is using `My`, is lengthier than the first example that just works off of the `Environment` namespace. Just remember that it really isn't about the length of what you type to get access to specific classes, but instead is about a logical way to find often accessed resources without the need to spend too much time hunting them down. Would you have known to look in the `Environment` class to get the machine name of the user's computer? Maybe, but maybe not. Using `My.Computer.Info.MachineName.ToString()` is a tremendously more logical approach, and once compiled, this namespace declaration will be set to work with the same class as previously without a performance hit.

If you type the `My` keyword in your Windows Forms application, you will notice that IntelliSense provides you with six items to work with — `Application`, `Computer`, `Forms`, `Resources`, `User`, and `WebServices`. Though this new keyword works best in the Windows Forms environment, there are still things that you can use in the Web Forms world. If you are working for a Web application, then you will have three items off of the `My` keyword — `Application`, `Computer`, and `User`. Each of these is broken down in the following sections.

My.Application

The `My.Application` namespace gives you quick access to specific settings and points that deal with your overall application. The following table details the properties and methods of the `My.Application` namespace.

Property/Method	Description
`ApplicationContext`	Returns the contextual information about the thread of the Windows Forms application.
`AssemblyInfo`	Provides quick access to the assembly of the Windows Forms. You can get at assembly information such as version number, name, title, copyright information, and more.
`ChangeCurrentCulture`	A method that allows you to change the culture of the current application thread.
`ChangeCurrentUICulture`	A method that allows you to change the culture that is being used by the Resource Manager.
`CurrentCulture`	Returns the current culture which is being used by the current thread.
`CurrentDirectory`	Returns the current directory for the application.
`CurrentUICulture`	Returns the current culture that is being used by the Resource Manager.
`Deployment`	Returns an instance of the `ApplicationDeployment` object, which allows for programmatic access to the application's ClickOnce features.
`IsNetworkDeployed`	Returns a `Boolean` value which indicates whether the application was distributed via the network using the ClickOnce feature. If `True`, then the application was deployed using ClickOnce — otherwise `False`.
`Log`	This property allows you to write to your application's event log listeners.
`MainForm`	Allows access to properties of the main form (initial form) for the application.

Table continued on following page

Property/Method	Description
`OpenForms`	Returns a `FormCollection` object, which allows access to the properties of the forms which are currently open.
`SplashScreen`	Allows you to programmatically assign the splash screen for the application.

While there is much that can be accomplished using the `My.Application` namespace, for an example of its use, let's focus on the use of the `AssemblyInfo` property. This property provides access to the information that is stored in the application's `AssemblyInfo.vb` file as well as other details about the class file. In one of your applications, you can create a message box that is displayed using the following code:

```
MessageBox.Show("Company Name: " & My.Application.AssemblyInfo.CompanyName & _
      vbCrLf & _
   "Description: " & My.Application.AssemblyInfo.Description & vbCrLf & _
   "Directory Path: " & My.Application.AssemblyInfo.DirectoryPath & vbCrLf & _
   "Copyright: " & My.Application.AssemblyInfo.LegalCopyright & vbCrLf & _
   "Trademark: " & My.Application.AssemblyInfo.LegalTrademark & vbCrLf & _
   "Name: " & My.Application.AssemblyInfo.Name & vbCrLf & _
   "Product Name: " & My.Application.AssemblyInfo.ProductName & vbCrLf & _
   "Title: " & My.Application.AssemblyInfo.Title & vbCrLf & _
   "Version: " & My.Application.AssemblyInfo.Version.ToString())
```

From this example, you can see that we can get at quite a bit of information concerning the assembly of the application that is running. Running this code will produce a message box similar to the one shown in Figure 9-9.

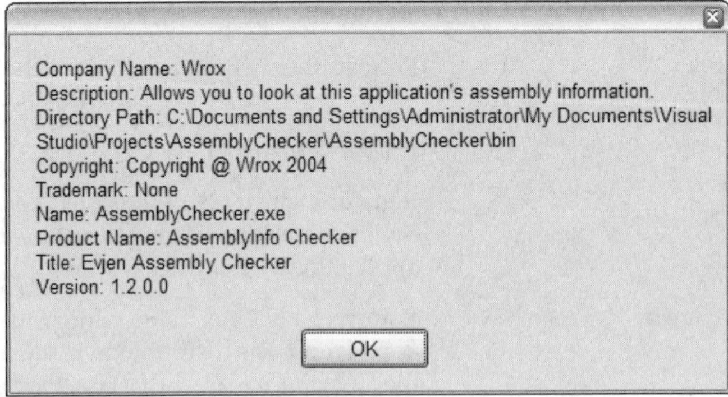

Figure 9-9

Another interesting property to look at from the `My.Application` namespace is the `Log` property. This property allows you to work with the log files for your application. For instance, you can easily write to the system's Application Event Log by first changing the application's `app.config` file to include the following:

```
<?xml version="1.0" encoding="utf-8" ?>
<configuration>
    <system.diagnostics>
        <sources>
            <source name="Microsoft.VisualBasic.MyServices.Log.WindowsFormsSource"
             switchName="DefaultSwitch">
                <listeners>
                    <add name="EventLog"/>
                </listeners>
            </source>
        </sources>
        <switches>
            <add name="DefaultSwitch" value="Information" />
        </switches>
        <sharedListeners>
            <add name="EventLog" type="System.Diagnostics.EventLogTraceListener"
             initializeData="EvjenEventWriter"/>
        </sharedListeners>
    </system.diagnostics>
</configuration>
```

Once the configuration file is in place, you can then record entries to the Application Event Log as illustrated here in the following simple example:

```
Private Sub Form1_Load(ByVal sender As System.Object, _
   ByVal e As System.EventArgs) Handles MyBase.Load

    My.Application.Log.WriteEntry("Entered Form1_Load", _
       TraceEventType.Information, 1)

End Sub
```

You could also just as easily use the `WriteExceptionEntry` method in addition to the `WriteEntry` method. After running this application and looking in the Event Viewer, you will see the event shown in Figure 9-10.

The previous example showed how to write to the Application Event Log when working with the objects that write to the event logs. In addition to the Application Event Log, there is also a Security Event Log and a System Event Log. It is important to note that when using these objects, it is impossible to write to the Security Event Log, and it is only possible to write to the System Event Log if the application does it under either the Local System or Administrator accounts.

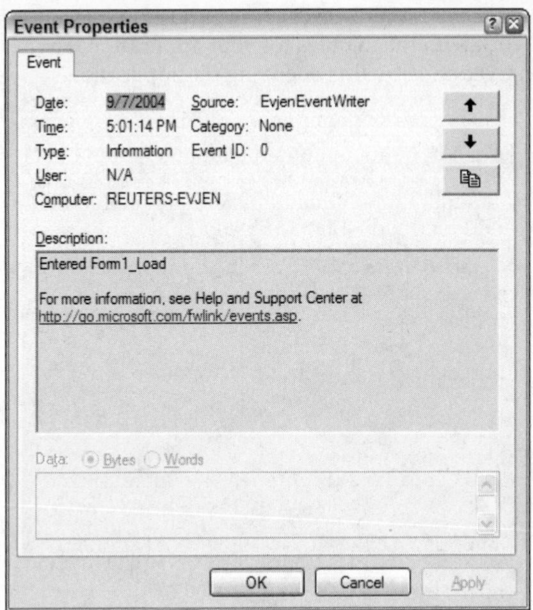

Figure 9-10

In addition to writing to the Application Event Log, you can also just as easily write to a text file. Just as with writing to the Application Event Log, writing to a text file also means that you are going to need to make changes to the `app.config` file.

```
<?xml version="1.0" encoding="utf-8" ?>
<configuration>
    <system.diagnostics>
        <sources>
            <source name="Microsoft.VisualBasic.MyServices.Log.WindowsFormsSource"
             switchName="DefaultSwitch">
                <listeners>
                    <add name="EventLog"/>

                    <add name="FileLog" />
                </listeners>
            </source>
        </sources>
        <switches>
            <add name="DefaultSwitch" value="Information" />
        </switches>
        <sharedListeners>
            <add name="EventLog" type="System.Diagnostics.EventLogTraceListener"
             initializeData="EvjenEventWriter"/>

            <add name="FileLog"
             type="System.Diagnostics.FileLogTraceListener, Microsoft.VisualBasic,
```

```
            Version=8.0.1200.0, Culture=neutral, PublicKeyToken=b03f5f7f11d50a3a"
            initializeData="FileLogWriter" />

        </sharedListeners>
    </system.diagnostics>
</configuration>
```

Now with this `app.config` file in place, you simply need to run the same `WriteEntry` method as before. Though this time, in addition to writing the Application Event Log, the information will also be written to a new text file. You will find the text file at `C:\Documents and Settings\[ username ]\Application Data\[ AssemblyCompany ]\[ AssemblyProduct ]\[ Version ]`. For instance, in my example, the log file was found at `C:\Documents and Settings\Administrator\Application Data\Wrox\Log Writer\1.2.0.0\`. In the .log file found, you will see a line such as:

```
Microsoft.VisualBasic.MyServices.Log.WindowsFormsSource
     Information      1      Entered Form1_Load
```

Though split here on two lines (due to the width of the paper for this book), you will find this information in a single line within the .log file. By default it is separated by tabs, but you can also change the delimiter yourself by adding a delimiter attribute to the FileLog section in the `app.config` file. This is:

```
<add name="FileLog"
 type="System.Diagnostics.FileLogTraceListener, Microsoft.VisualBasic,
 Version=8.0.1200.0, Culture=neutral, PublicKeyToken=b03f5f7f11d50a3a"

 initializeData="FileLogWriter" delimiter=";" />
```

In addition to writing to event logs and text files, you can also write to XML files, console applications, and more.

My.Computer

The `My.Computer` namespace can be used to work with the parameters and details of the computer in which the application is running. The following table details the objects contained in this namespace.

Property	Description
`Audio`	This object allows you to work with audio files from your application. This includes starting, stopping, and looping audio files.
`Clipboard`	This object allows you to read and write to the clipboard.
`Clock`	This allows for access to the system clock to get at GMT and the local time of the computer that is running the application. You can also get at the tick count, which is the number of milliseconds that has elapsed since the computer was started.

Table continued on following page

Property	Description
`FileSystem`	This object provides a large collection of properties and methods that allow for programmatic access to drives, folders, and files. This includes the ability to read, write, and delete items in the file system.
`Info`	This provides access to the computer's details such as amount of memory, the operating system type, which assemblies are loaded, and the name of the computer itself.
`Keyboard`	This object provides access to knowledge of which keyboard keys are pressed by the end user. Also included is a single method, `SendKeys`, which allows you to send the pressed keys to the active form.
`Mouse`	This provides a handful of properties that allow for detection of the type of mouse installed, and provides such details as whether the left and right mouse buttons have been swapped, whether a mouse wheel exists, and details on how much to scroll when the user uses the wheel.
`Name`	This is a read-only property that provides access to the name of the computer.
`Network`	This object provides a single property and some methods to enable you to interact with the network to which the computer where the application is running is connected. With this object, you can use the `IsAvailable` property to first check that the computer is connected to a network. If this is positive, the `Network` object allows you to upload or download files, and ping the network.
`Ports`	This object can provide notify one if there are available ports as well as allowing for access to the ports.
`Printers`	This object allows determination of which printers are available to the application as well as provides the ability to define default printers and print items to any of the printers available.
`Registry`	This object provides programmatic access to the registry and the registry settings. Using the `Registry` object, you can determine if keys exist, determine values, change values, and delete keys.
`Screen`	Provides the ability to work with one or more screens which may be attached to the computer.

There is a lot to the My.Computer namespace, so it is impossible to touch upon most of it. For an example of using this namespace, let's take a look at the FileSystem property. The FileSystem property allows for you to easily and logically access drives, directories, and files on the computer.

To illustrate the use of this property, first start off by creating a Windows Form with a DataGridView and a Button control. It should appear as shown in Figure 9-11.

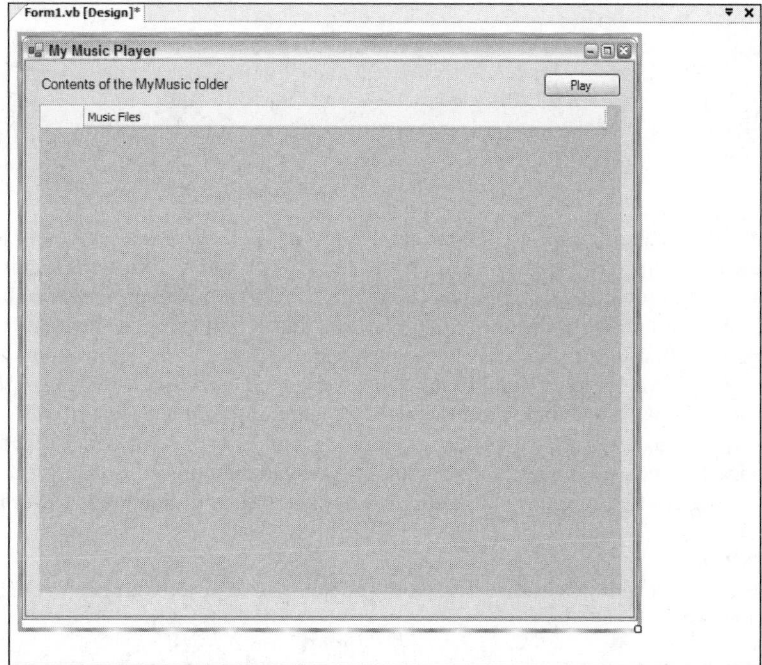

Figure 9-11

This little application will look in the user's My Music folder and list all of the .wma files found therein. Once listed, the user of the application will be able to select one of the listed files, and after pressing the Play button, the file will be launched and played inside Microsoft's Windows Media Player.

The first step after getting the controls on the form in place is to make a reference to the Windows Media Player DLL. You will find this on the COM tab, and the location of the DLL is C:\WINDOWS\System32\wmp.dll. This will give you an object called WMPLib in the References folder of your solution.

You might be wondering why you would make a reference to a COM object in order to play a .wma file from your application instead of using the My.Computer.Audio namespace that is provided to you. The Audio property only allows for the playing of .wav files, because to play .wma, .mp3, and similar files, the user must have the proper codecs on his or her machine. These codecs are not part of the Windows OS, but are part of Windows Media Player.

Now that the reference to the `wmp.dll` is in place, let's put some code in the `Form1_Load` event.

```
Private Sub Form1_Load(ByVal sender As System.Object, _
    ByVal e As System.EventArgs) Handles MyBase.Load

        For Each MusicFile As String _
          In My.Computer.FileSystem.GetFiles _
          (My.Computer.FileSystem.SpecialDirectories.MyMusic, True, "*.wma")
             Dim MusicFileInfo As System.IO.FileInfo = _
                My.Computer.FileSystem.GetFileInfo(MusicFile.ToString())
             Me.DataGridView1.Rows.Add(MusicFileInfo.Directory.Parent.Name & _
                "\" & MusicFileInfo.Directory.Name & "\" & MusicFileInfo.Name)
        Next

End Sub
```

In this example, the `My.Computer.FileSystem.GetFiles` method points to the My Music folder through the use of the `SpecialDirectories` property. This property allows for logical and easy access to folders such as Desktop, My Documents, My Pictures, Programs, and more. Though it is possible to use just this first parameter with the `GetFiles` method, this example makes further definitions. The second parameter defines the `recurse` value—which states whether the subfolders should be perused as well. By default, this is set to `False`, but it has been changed to `True` for this example. The last parameter defines the wildcard that should be used in searching for elements. In this case, the value of the `wildcard` is `*.wma`, which instructs the `GetFile` method to get only the files that are of type `.wma`. Once retrieved with the `GetFile` method, the retrieved file is then placed inside the `DataGridView` control, again using the `My.Computer.FileSystem` namespace to define the value of the item placed within the row.

Once the `Form1_Load` event is in place, the last event to construct is the `Button1_Click` event. This is illustrated here:

```
Private Sub Button1_Click(ByVal sender As System.Object, _
   ByVal e As System.EventArgs) Handles Button1.Click
      Dim MediaPlayer As New WMPLib.WindowsMediaPlayer
      MediaPlayer.openPlayer(My.Computer.FileSystem.SpecialDirectories.MyMusic & _
         "\" & DataGridView1.SelectedCells.Item(0).Value)
End Sub
```

From this example, you can see that it is pretty simple to play one of the provided .wma files. It is as simple as creating an instance of the `WMPLib.WindowsMediaPlayer` object and using the `openPlayer` method, which takes as a parameter the location of the file to play. In this case, you are again using the `SpecialDirectories` property. The nice thing about using this property is that it could be more difficult to find the user's My Music folder due to the username changing the actual location of the files that the application is looking for, but using the `My` namespace allows it to figure out the exact location of the items. When built and run, the application provides a list of available music files and allows you to easily select one for playing in the Media Player. This is illustrated in Figure 9-12.

Figure 9-12

Though it would have been really cool if it were possible to play these types of files using the `Audio` property from the `My.Computer` namespace, it is still possible to use the `My.Computer.Audio` namespace for playing .wav files and system sounds.

To play a system sound, you use the following construct:

```
My.Computer.Audio.PlaySystemSound(SystemSounds.Beep)
```

The system sounds in the `SystemSounds` enumeration include: `Asterisk`, `Beep`, `Exclamation`, `Hand`, and `Question`.

My.Forms

The `My.Forms` namespace is just a quick and logical way of getting at the properties and methods of the forms that are contained within your solution. For instance, to get at the first form in your solution (assuming that it's named `Form1`), you use the following namespace construct:

```
My.Form.Form1
```

To get at other forms, you simply change the namespace so that the name of the form that you are trying to access follows the `Form` keyword in the namespace construction.

My.Resources

The `My.Resources` namespace is a tremendously easy way of getting at the resources stored in your application. If you open up the `MyResources.resx` file from the My Projects folder in your solution, you can easily create as many resources as you wish. As an example, I created a single `String` resource titled `MyResourceString` and gave it a value of `St. Louis Rams`.

To access the resources that you create, you use the simple reference as shown here:

```
My.Resources.MyResourceString.ToString()
```

Using IntelliSense, you will find all of your created resources listed after you type the period after the `My.Resources` string.

My.User

The `My.User` namespace allows you to work with the `IPrincipal` interface. You can use the `My.User` namespace to figure out if the user is authenticated or not, what the user's name is, and more. For instance, if you have a login form in your application, you could allow access to a particular form with code similar to the following:

```
If (Not My.User.IsInRole("Administrators")) Then
   ' Code here
End If
```

You can also just as easily get at the user's name with the following:

```
My.User.Identity.Name
```

As well, you can check if the user is authenticated by using:

```
If My.User.Identity.IsAuthenticated Then
   ' Code here
End If
```

My.WebServices

When not using the `My.WebServices` namespace, you access your Web Services references in a lengthier manner. The first step in either case is to make a Web reference to some remote XML Web service in your solution. These references will then appear in the Web References folder in Solution Explorer in Visual Studio 2005. Before the introduction of the `My` namespace, you would have accessed the values that the Web reference exposed in the following manner:

```
Dim ws As New ReutersStocks.GetStockDetails
Label1.Text = ws.GetLatestPrice.ToString()
```

This works, but now with the `My` namespace, you can use the following construct:

```
Label1.Text = My.WebServices.GetStockDetails.GetLatestPrice.ToString()
```

Summary

The introduction of namespaces with the .NET Framework provides a powerful tool that helps to abstract the logical capabilities from their physical implementation. While there are differences in the syntax of referencing objects from a namespace and referencing the same object from a COM-style component implementation, there are several similarities. This chapter introduced namespaces and their hierarchical structure, and demonstrated

- That namespace hierarchies are not related to class hierarchies
- How to review and add references to a project
- How to import and alias namespaces at the module level
- How to create custom namespaces
- How to use the new `My` namespace

Namespaces play an important role in enterprise software development. The fact that namespaces allow you to separate the implementation of related functional objects, while retaining the ability to group these objects, improves the overall maintainability of your code. Everyone who has ever worked on a large project has been put in the situation where a fix to a component has been delayed because of the potential impact on other components in the same project. Regardless of the logical separation of components in the same project, developers who took part in the development process worried about testing. With totally separate implementations for related components, it is not only possible to alleviate this concern but also easier than ever before for a team of developers to work on different parts of the same project.

10

Exception Handling and Debugging

All professional-grade programs need to handle unexpected conditions. In programming languages before Microsoft .NET, this was often called error handling. Unexpected conditions generated error codes, which were trapped by programming logic that took appropriate action.

The common language runtime in .NET does not generate error codes. When an unexpected condition occurs, the CLR creates a special object called an exception. This object contains properties and methods that describe the unexpected condition in detail and communicate various items of useful information about what went wrong.

Because .NET deals with exceptions instead of errors, the term "error handling" is seldom used in the .NET world. Instead, now refer to exception handling. This term refers to the techniques used in .NET to detect exceptions and take appropriate action.

In this chapter, we will cover how exception handling works in Visual Basic .NET (VB.NET). There are many improvements over pre-.NET versions of Visual Basic. This chapter will discuss the common language runtime (CLR) exception handler in detail and the programming methods that are most efficient in catching errors. Specifically, it will discuss:

- A brief review of error handling in Visual Basic 6 (VB6)
- The general principles behind exception handling
- The `Try . . . Catch . . . Finally` structure, the `Exit Try` statement, and nested `Try` structures
- The exception object's methods and properties

- Exception handling between managed and unmanaged code, and how VB.NET assists you in that area
- Capabilities in Visual Studio .NET to work with exceptions
- Error and trace logging and how you can use these methods to obtain feedback on how your program is working

You'll begin with a quick review of error handling in previous versions of Visual Basic to use as a reference point. Then you will look at the new ways of handling exceptions in .NET.

A Brief Review of Error Handling in VB6

For compatibility, Visual Basic .NET still supports the old-style syntax for error handling that was used in Visual Basic 6 and earlier versions. That means you can still use the syntax presented in this review. However, it is strongly recommended that you avoid using this old-style syntax in favor of the exception handling features that are native to .NET.

The old-style syntax in VB6 was handed down from DOS versions of BASIC. The `On Error` construct was created in an era when line labels and `GoTo` statements were commonly used. Such error handling is difficult to use and has limited functionality compared to more modern alternatives.

In VB6, a typical routine with error handling code looks like this:

```
Private Function OpenFile(sFileName As String) As Boolean

On Error GoTo ErrHandler:
Open sFileName For Random As #1
OpenFile = True
Exit Sub

ErrHandler:
Select Case Err.Number
    Case 53 ' File not found
        MessageBox.Show "File not found"
    Case Else
        MessageBox.Show "Other error"
End Select
OpenFile = False

End Function
```

The top of the routine points to a section of code called an error handler, which is usually placed at the bottom of the routine. The error handler gets control as soon as an error is detected in the routine, and it looks at the error number to see what to do. The error number is available as a property of the `Err` object, which is a globally available object that holds error information in VB6.

If the error handler can take care of the error without breaking execution, it can resume execution with the line of code that generated the error (`Resume`) or the one after that (`Resume Next`) or at a particular location (`Resume {LineLabel}`).

This structure becomes more complex if the error handling needs to vary in the routine. Multiple `On Error GoTo` statements must be used to send errors to various error handlers, like this:

```
Private Function OpenFile(sFileName As String) As Boolean

On Error GoTo ErrHandler1
' Do calculations here
Dim i As Integer
i = Len(sFileName)
Dim j As Integer
j = 100 \ i

On Error GoTo ErrHandler2
Open sFileName For Random As #1
OpenFile = True
Exit Function

ErrHandler1:
Select Case Err.Number
    Case 6 ' Overflow
        MessageBox.Show "Overflow"
    Case Else
        MessageBox.Show "Other error"
End Select

OpenFile = False
Exit Function

ErrHandler2:
Select Case Err.Number
    Case 53 ' File not found
        MessageBox.Show "File not found"
    Case Else
        MessageBox.Show "Other error"
End Select
OpenFile = False

End Function
```

With this type of error handling, it is easy to get confused about what should happen under various conditions. You must change the error handling pointer as necessary or errors will be incorrectly processed. There is very little information available about the error during the process, except for the error number. You can't tell, for example, the line number on which the error was generated without single-stepping through the code.

Such logic can rapidly become convoluted and unmanageable. There's a much better way to manage errors in VB.NET, called *structured exception handling*. The rest of this chapter will discuss this new way to work with code errors, and you will use the term structured exception handling throughout, except for the small sections that discuss compatibility with older error-handling techniques.

Exceptions in .NET

.NET implements a systemwide, comprehensive approach to exception handling. As noted in the chapter introduction, the concept of an error is expanded to exceptions, which are objects that contain a set of information relevant to the error. Such an object is an instance of a class that derives from a class named `System.Exception`.

Important Properties and Methods of an Exception

The `Exception` class has properties that contain useful information about the exception.

Property	Description
`HelpLink`	A string indicating the link to help for this exception.
`InnerException`	Returns the `exception` object reference to an inner (nested) exception.
`Message`	A string that contains a description of the error, suitable for displaying to users.
`Source`	A string containing the name of an object that generated the error.
`StackTrace`	A read-only property that holds the stack trace as a text string. The stack trace is a list of the pending method calls at the point that the exception was detected. That is, if `MethodA` called `MethodB`, and an exception occurred in `MethodB`, the stack trace would contain both `MethodA` and `MethodB`.
`TargetSite`	A read-only string property that holds the method that threw the exception.

The two most important methods of the `Exception` class are:

Method	Description
`GetBaseException`	Returns the first exception in the chain
`ToString`	Returns the error string, which might include as much information as the error message, the inner exceptions, and the stack trace, depending on the error

You will see these properties and methods used in the code examples given later, once you have covered the syntax for detecting and handling exceptions.

How Exceptions Differ from the Err Object in VB6

Because an exception contains all of the information needed about an error, structured exception handling does not use error numbers and the `Err` object. The exception object contains all the relevant information about the error.

However, where there is only one global `Err` object in VB6, there are many types of exception objects in VB.NET. For example, if a divide by zero is done in code, then an `OverflowException` is generated. There are several dozen types of exception classes in VB.NET, and in addition to using the ones that are available in the .NET Framework, you can inherit from a class called `ApplicationException` and then create your own exception classes (see Chapter 6 for a discussion of inheritance).

In .NET, all exceptions inherit from `System.Exception`. Special-purpose exception classes can be found in many namespaces. The following table lists four representative examples of the classes that extend `Exception`:

Namespace	Class	Description
`System`	`InvalidOperationException`	Generated when a call to an object method is inappropriate because of the object's state
`System`	`OutOfMemoryException`	Results when there is not enough memory to carry out an operation
`System.XML`	`XmlException`	Often caused by an attempt to read invalid XML
`System.Data`	`DataException`	Represents errors in ADO.NET components

There are literally dozens of exception classes scattered throughout the .NET Framework namespaces. It is common for an exception class to reside in a namespace with the classes that commonly generate the exception. For example, the `DataException` class is in `System.Data`, with the ADO.NET components that often generate a `DataException` instance.

Having many types of exceptions in VB.NET enables different types of conditions to be trapped with different exception handlers. This is a major advance over VB6. The syntax to do that is discussed next.

Structured-Exception-Handling Keywords in VB.NET

Structured exception handling depends on several new keywords in VB.NET. They are:

- `Try`—Begin a section of code in which an exception might be generated from a code error. This section of code is often called a `Try` block. In some respects, this would be the equivalent of an `On Error` statement in VB6. However, unlike an `On Error` statement, a `Try` statement does not indicate where a trapped exception should be routed. Instead, the exception is automatically routed to a `Catch` statement (discussed next).

- `Catch`—Begin an exception handler for a type of exception. One or more `Catch` code blocks come after a `Try` block, with each `Catch` block catching a different type of exception. When an exception is encountered in the `Try` block, the first Catch block that matches that type of exception will receive control.

  A `Catch` statement is analogous to the line label used in a VB6 `On Error` statement, but the ability to route different types of exceptions to different `Catch` statements is a radical improvement over VB6.
- `Finally`—Contains code that runs when the `Try` block finishes normally, or if a `Catch` block receives control and then finishes. That is, the code in the `Finally` block always runs, regardless of whether an exception was detected. Typically, the `Finally` block is used to close or dispose of any resources, such as database connections, that might have been left unresolved by the code that had a problem. There is no equivalent of a `Finally` in VB6.
- `Throw`—Generate an exception. This is similar to `Err.Raise` in VB6. It's usually done in a `Catch` block when the exception should be kicked back to a calling routine or in a routine that has itself detected an error such as a bad argument passed in.

The Try, Catch, and Finally Keywords

Here is an example showing some typical simple structured exception handling code in VB.NET. In this case, the most likely source of an error is the `iItems` argument. If it has a value of zero, this would lead to dividing by zero, which would generate an exception.

First, create a Windows Application in Visual Basic 2005, and place a button on the default `Form1` created in the project. In the button's click event, place the following two lines of code:

```
Dim sngAvg As Single
sngAvg = GetAverage(0, 100)
```

Then put the following function in the form's code:

```
Private Function GetAverage(iItems As Integer, iTotal As Integer) as Single
    ' Code that might throw an exception is wrapped in a Try block
    Try
        Dim sngAverage As Single

        ' This will cause an exception to be thrown if iItems = 0
        sngAverage = CSng(iTotal \ iItems)

        ' This only executes if the line above generated no error
        MessageBox.Show("Calculation successful")
        Return sngAverage

    Catch excGeneric As Exception
        ' If the calculation failed, you get here
        MessageBox.Show("Calculation unsuccessful - exception caught")
        Return 0
     End Try

End Function
```

In this code, you are trapping all the exceptions with a single generic exception type, and you don't have any `Finally` logic. Run the program, and press the button. You will be able to follow the sequence better if you place a breakpoint at the top of the `GetAverage` function and step through the lines.

Here is a more complex example that traps the divide-by-zero exception explicitly. This second version of the `GetAverage` function (notice that the name is `GetAverage2`) also includes a `Finally` block:

```
Private Function GetAverage2(iItems As Integer, iTotal As Integer) as Single
     ' Code that might throw an exception is wrapped in a Try block
    Try
        Dim sngAverage As Single

        ' This will cause an exception to be thrown.
        sngAverage = CSng(iTotal \ iItems)

        ' This only executes if the line above generated no error.
        MessageBox.Show("Calculation successful")
        Return sngAverage

     Catch excDivideByZero As DivideByZeroException
        ' You'll get here with an DivideByZeroException in the Try block
        MessageBox.Show("Calculation generated DivideByZero Exception")
        Return 0

    Catch excGeneric As Exception
        ' You'll get here when any exception is thrown and not caught in
        ' a previous Catch block.
        MessageBox.Show("Calculation failed - generic exception caught")
        Return 0

    Finally
        ' Code in the Finally block will always run.
         MessageBox.Show("You always get here, with or without an error")
    End Try

End Function
```

In this code, there are two `Catch` blocks for different types of exceptions. If an exception is generated, .NET will go down the `Catch` blocks looking for a matching exception type. That means the `Catch` blocks should be arranged with specific types first and more generic types later.

Place the code for `GetAverage2` in the form, and place another button on `Form1`. In the `Click` event for the second button, place the code:

```
Dim sngAvg As Single
sngAvg = GetAverage2(0, 100)
```

Run the program again and press the second button. As before, it's easier to follow if you set a breakpoint early in the code and then step through the code line by line.

The Throw Keyword

Sometimes a `Catch` block is unable to handle an error. Some exceptions are so unexpected that they should be "sent back up the line" to the calling code, so that the problem can be promoted to code that can decide what to do with it. A `Throw` statement is used for that purpose.

A `Throw` statement, like an `Err.Raise`, ends execution of the exception handler — that is, no more code in the `Catch` block after the `Throw` statement is executed. However, `Throw` does not prevent code in the `Finally` block from running. That code still runs before the exception is kicked back to the calling routine.

You can see the `Throw` statement in action by changing the earlier code for `GetAverage2` to look like this:

```
Private Function GetAverage3(iItems As Integer, iTotal as Integer) as Single
    ' Code that might throw an exception is wrapped in a Try block
    Try
        Dim sngAverage As Single

        ' This will cause an exception to be thrown.
        sngAverage = CSng(iTotal \ iItems)

        ' This only executes if the line above generated no error.
        MessageBox.Show("Calculation successful")
        Return sngAverage

    Catch excDivideByZero As DivideByZeroException
        ' You'll get here with an DivideByZeroException in the Try block.
        MessageBox.Show("Calculation generated DivideByZero Exception")

        Throw excDivideByZero
        MessageBox.Show("More logic after the throw - never executed")

    Catch excGeneric As Exception
        ' You'll get here when any exception is thrown and not caught in
        ' a previous Catch block.
        MessageBox.Show("Calculation failed - generic exception caught")

        Throw excGeneric
    Finally
        ' Code in the Finally block will always run, even if
        ' an exception was thrown in a Catch block.
        MessageBox.Show("You always get here, with or without an error")
    End Try
End Function
```

Here is some code to call `GetAverage3`. You can place this code in another button's click event to test it out.

```
Try
    Dim sngAvg As Single
    sngAvg = GetAverage3(0, 100)
Catch exc As Exception
    MessageBox.Show("Back in the click event after an error")
Finally
    MessageBox.Show("Finally block in click event")
End Try
```

Throwing a New Exception

`Throw` can also be used with exceptions that are created on the fly. For example, you might like your earlier function to generate an `ArgumentException`, since you can consider a value of `iItems` of zero to be an invalid value for that argument.

In such a case, a new exception must be instantiated. The constructor allows you to place your own custom message into the exception. To show how this is done, let's change the aforementioned example to throw your own exception instead of the one caught in the `Catch` block.

```
Private Function GetAverage4(iItems As Integer, iTotal as Integer) as Single

    If iItems = 0 Then
        Dim excOurOwnException As New _
             ArgumentException("Number of items cannot be zero")

         Throw excOurOwnException
    End If


  ' Code that might throw an exception is wrapped in a Try block.
    Try
        Dim sngAverage As Single

        ' This will cause an exception to be thrown.
        sngAverage = CSng(iTotal \ iItems)

        ' This only executes if the line above generated no error.
        MessageBox.Show("Calculation successful")
        Return sngAverage

    Catch excDivideByZero As DivideByZeroException
        ' You'll get here with an DivideByZeroException in the Try block.
        MessageBox.Show("Calculation generated DivideByZero Exception")
        Throw excDivideByZero
        MessageBox.Show("More logic after the thrown - never executed")
    Catch excGeneric As Exception
        ' You'll get here when any exception is thrown and not caught in
        ' a previous Catch block.
        MessageBox.Show("Calculation failed - generic exception caught")
         Throw excGeneric
    Finally
        ' Code in the Finally block will always run, even if
        ' an exception was thrown in a Catch block.
        MessageBox.Show("You always get here, with or without an error")
    End Try
End Function
```

This code can be called from a button with similar code for calling `GetAverage3`. Just change the name of the function called to `GetAverage4`.

This technique is particularly well suited to dealing with problems detected in property procedures. Property `Set` procedures often do checking to make sure the property is about to be assigned a valid value. If not, throwing a new `ArgumentException` (instead of assigning the property value) is a good way to inform the calling code about the problem.

The Exit Try Statement

The `Exit Try` statement will, under a given circumstance, break out of the `Try` or `Catch` block and continue at the `Finally` block. In the following example, you are going to exit a `Catch` block if the value of `iItems` is `0`, because you know that your error was caused by that problem.

```
Private Function GetAverage5(iItems As Integer, iTotal as Integer) As Single
    ' Code that might throw an exception is wrapped in a Try block.
  Try
      Dim sngAverage As Single

      ' This will cause an exception to be thrown.
      sngAverage = CSng(iTotal \ iItems)

      ' This only executes if the line above generated no error.
      MessageBox.Show("Calculation successful")
      Return sngAverage

  Catch excDivideByZero As DivideByZeroException
      ' You'll get here with an DivideByZeroException in the Try block.

      If iItems = 0 Then
          Return 0
          Exit Try
      Else
          MessageBox.Show("Error not caused by iItems")
      End If

      Throw excDivideByZero
      MessageBox.Show("More logic after the thrown - never executed")

  Catch excGeneric As Exception
      ' You'll get here when any exception is thrown and not caught in
      ' a previous Catch block.
      MessageBox.Show("Calculation failed - generic exception caught")
      Throw excGeneric
  Finally
      ' Code in the Finally block will always run, even if
      ' an exception was thrown in a Catch block.
      MessageBox.Show("You always get here, with or without an error")
  End Try
End Sub
```

In your first `Catch` block, you have inserted an `If` block so that you can exit the block given a certain condition (in this case if the overflow exception was caused by the value of `intY` being `0`). The `Exit Try` goes immediately to the `Finally` block and completes the processing there:

```
If iItems = 0 Then
  Return 0
  Exit Try
Else
  MessageBox.Show("Error not caused by iItems")
End If
```

Now, if the overflow exception is caused by something other than division by zero, you'll get a message box displaying `Error not caused by iItems`.

Nested Try Structures

In some cases, particular lines in a `Try` block may need special exception processing. Also, errors can occur within the `Catch` portion of the `Try` structures and can cause further exceptions to be thrown. For both of these scenarios, nested `Try` structures are available. You can alter the example under the section "The Throw Keyword" to demonstrate the following code:

```
Private Function GetAverage6(iItems As Integer, iTotal as Integer) As Single
    ' Code that might throw an exception is wrapped in a Try block.
    Try
        Dim sngAverage As Single


        ' Do something for performance testing....
        Try
            LogEvent("GetAverage")
        Catch exc As Exception
            MessageBox.Show("Logging function unavailable")
        End Try


        ' This will cause an exception to be thrown.
        sngAverage = CSng(iTotal \ iItems)

        ' This only executes if the line above generated no error.
        MessageBox.Show("Calculation successful")
        Return sngAverage

    Catch excDivideByZero As DivideByZeroException
        ' You'll get here with an DivideByZeroException in the Try block.
        MessageBox.Show("Error not divide by 0")
        Throw excDivideByZero
        MessageBox.Show("More logic after the thrown - never executed")
    Catch excGeneric As Exception
        ' You'll get here when any exception is thrown and not caught in
        ' a previous Catch block.
        MessageBox.Show("Calculation failed - generic exception caught")
        Throw excGeneric
    Finally
        ' Code in the Finally block will always run, even if
        ' an exception was thrown in a Catch block.
        MessageBox.Show("You always get here, with or without an error")
    End Try
End Function
```

In this example, you are assuming that a function exists to log an event. This function would typically be in a common library, and might log the event in various ways. We will actually discuss logging of exceptions in detail later in the chapter, but a simple LogEvent function might look like this:

```
Public Function LogEvent(ByVal sEvent As String)
    FileOpen(1, "logfile.txt", OpenMode.Append)
    Print(1, DateTime.Now & "-" & sEvent & vbCrLf)
    FileClose(1)

End Function
```

In this case, you don't want a problem logging an event, such as a "disk full" error, to crash the routine. The code for the GetAverage function puts up a message box to indicate trouble with the logging function.

A Catch block can be empty. In that case, it has a similar effect as On Error Resume Next in VB6. The exception is ignored. However, execution does not pick up with the line after the line that generated the error, but instead picks up with either the Finally block or the line after the End Try if no Finally block exists.

Using Exception Properties

The earlier examples have displayed hard-coded messages into message boxes, and this is obviously not a good technique for production applications. Instead, a message box describing an exception should give as much information as possible concerning the problem. To do this, various properties of the exception can be used.

The most brutal way to get information about an exception is to use the ToString method of the exception. Suppose that you modify the earlier example of GetAverage2 to change the displayed information about the exception like this:

```
Private Function GetAverage2(ByVal iItems As Integer, ByVal iTotal As Integer) _
        As Single
    ' Code that might throw an exception is wrapped in a Try block.
    Try
        Dim sngAverage As Single

        ' This will cause an exception to be thrown.
        sngAverage = CSng(iTotal \ iItems)
        ' This only executes if the line above generated no error.
         MessageBox.Show("Calculation successful")
        Return sngAverage

    Catch excDivideByZero As DivideByZeroException
        ' You'll get here with an DivideByZeroException in the Try block.

         MessageBox.Show(excDivideByZero.ToString)
        Throw excDivideByZero
        MessageBox.Show("More logic after the thrown - never executed")

    Catch excGeneric As Exception
        ' You'll get here when any exception is thrown and not caught in
        ' a previous Catch block.
```

```
            MessageBox.Show("Calculation failed - generic exception caught")
            Throw excGeneric
        Finally
            ' Code in the Finally block will always run, even if
            ' an exception was thrown in a Catch block.
            MessageBox.Show("You always get here, with or without an error")
        End Try
    End Function
```

When the function is accessed with `iItems = 0`, a message box similar to the one in Figure 10-1 will be displayed.

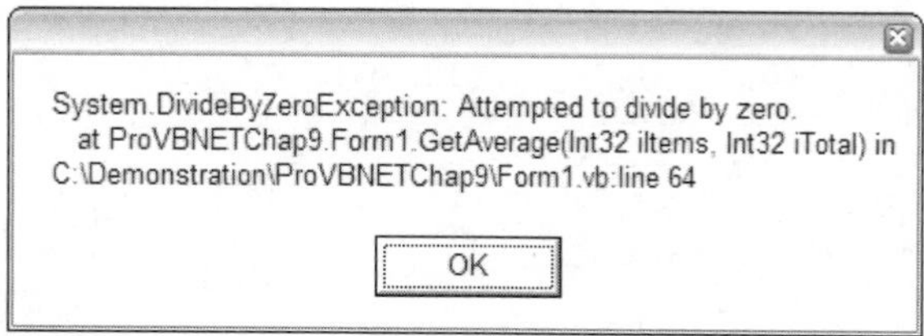

Figure 10-1

The Message Property

The message in the aforementioned box is helpful to a developer, because it contains a lot of information. But it's not something you would typically want a user to see. Instead, the user normally needs to see a short description of the problem, and that is supplied by the `Message` property.

If the previous code is changed so that the `Message` property is used instead of `ToString`, then the message box will change to look something like Figure 10-2.

The InnerException and TargetSite Properties

The `InnerException` property is used to store an exception trail. This comes in handy when multiple exceptions occur. It's quite common for an exception to occur that sets up circumstances whereby further exceptions are raised. As exceptions occur in a sequence, you can choose to stack your exceptions for later reference by use of the `InnerException` property of your `Exception` object. As each exception joins the stack, the previous `Exception` object becomes the inner exception in the stack.

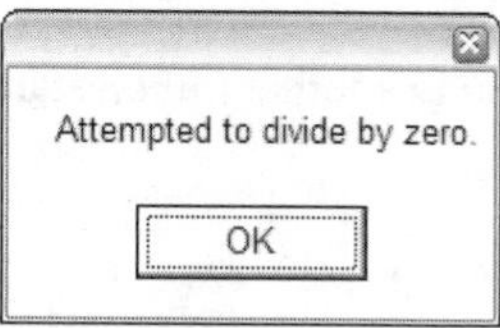

Figure 10-2

For simplicity, you'll start a new code sample, with just a subroutine that generates its own exception. You'll include code to add a reference to an `InnerException` object to the exception you are generating with the `Throw` method.

Your example will also include a message box to show what's stored in the exception's `TargetSite` property. As you'll see in the results, `TargetSite` will contain the name of the routine generating the exception, in this case `HandlerExample`. Here's the code:

```
Sub HandlerExample()
  Dim intX As Integer
  Dim intY As Integer
  Dim intZ As Integer
  intY = 0
  intX = 5
  ' First Required Error Statement.
  Try
    ' Cause a "Divide by Zero"
    intZ = CType((intX \ intY), Integer)
  ' Catch the error.
  Catch objA As System.DivideByZeroException
    Try
      Throw (New Exception("0 as divisor", objA))
    Catch objB As Exception
      Messagebox.Show(objB.Message)
      Messagebox.Show(objB.InnerException.Message)
      Messagebox.Show(objB.TargetSite.Name)
    End Try
  Catch
    Messagebox.Show("Caught any other errors")
  Finally
    Messagebox.Show(Str(intZ))
  End Try
End Sub
```

As before, you catch the divide-by-zero error in the first `Catch` block, and the exception is stored in `objA` so that you can reference its properties later.

You throw a new exception with a more general message (`"0 as divisor"`) that is easier to interpret, and you build up your stack by appending `objA` as the `InnerException` object using an overloaded constructor for the Exception object:

```
Throw (New Exception("0 as divisor", objA))
```

You catch your newly thrown exception in another `Catch` statement. Note how it does not catch a specific type of error:

```
Catch objB As Exception
```

Then you display three message boxes:

```
Messagebox.Show(objB.Message)
Messagebox.Show(objB.InnerException.Message)
Messagebox.Show(objB.TargetSite.Name)
```

The message box that is produced by your custom error, which is held in the `objB` variable, is shown in Figure 10-3.

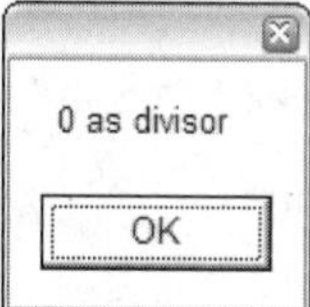

Figure 10-3

The `InnerException` property holds the exception object that was generated first. The `Message` property of the `InnerException` is shown in Figure 10-4.

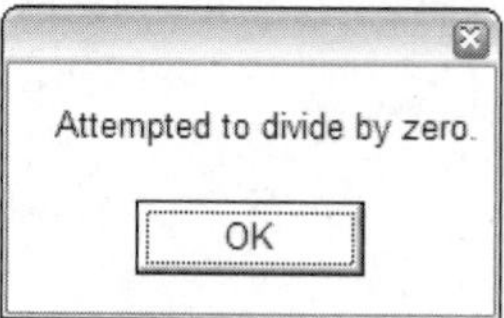

Figure 10-4

As mentioned earlier, the `TargetSite` property gives you the name of the method that threw your exception. This information comes in handy when troubleshooting and could be integrated into the error message so that the end user could report the method name back to you. Figure 10-5 shows a message box displaying the `TargetSite` from the previous example.

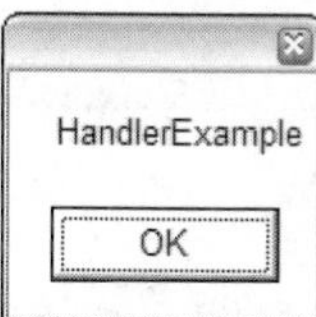

Figure 10-5

Source and StackTrace

The `Source` and `StackTrace` properties provide the user with information regarding where the error occurred. This supplemental information can be invaluable for the user to pass on to the troubleshooter in order to help get errors resolved more quickly. The following example uses these two properties and shows the feedback when the error occurs:

```
Sub HandlerExample2()
  Dim intX As Integer
  Dim intY As Integer
  Dim intZ As Integer
  intY = 0
  intX = 5
  ' First Required Error Statement.
  Try
    ' Cause a "Divide by Zero"
    intZ = CType((intX \ intY), Integer)
  ' Catch the error.
  Catch objA As System.DivideByZeroException

    objA.Source = "HandlerExample2"
    Messagebox.Show("Error Occurred at :" & _
        objA.Source & objA.StackTrace)

  Finally
    Messagebox.Show(Str(intZ))
  End Try
End Sub
```

The output from your `Messagebox` statement is very detailed and gives the entire path and line number where your error occurred, as shown in Figure 10-6.

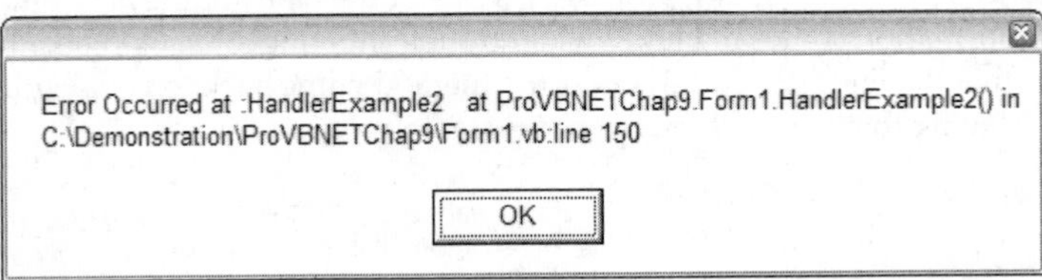
Error Occurred at :HandlerExample2   at ProVBNETChap9.Form1.HandlerExample2() in C:\Demonstration\ProVBNETChap9\Form1.vb:line 150
OK

Figure 10-6

Notice that this information was also included in the `ToString` method that was examined earlier (refer back to Figure 10-1).

GetBaseException

The `GetBaseException` method comes in very handy when you are deep in a set of thrown exceptions. This method returns the originating exception, which makes debugging easier and helps keep the troubleshooting process on track by sorting through information that can be misleading.

```
Sub HandlerExample3()
  Dim intX As Integer
  Dim intY As Integer
  Dim intZ As Integer
  intY = 0
  intX = 5
  ' First Required Error Statement.
  Try
    ' Cause a "Divide by Zero"
    intZ = CType((intX \ intY), Integer)
  ' Catch the error.
  Catch objA As System.DivideByZeroException

    Try
      Throw (New Exception("0 as divisor", objA))
    Catch objB As Exception
      Try
        Throw (New Exception("New error", objB))
      Catch objC As Exception
        Messagebox.Show(objC.GetBaseException.Message)
      End Try
    End Try

  Finally
    Messagebox.Show(Str(intZ))
  End Try
End Sub
```

The `InnerException` property provides the information that the `GetBaseException` method needs, so as your example executes the `Throw` statements, it sets up the `InnerException` property. The purpose of the `GetBaseException` method is to provide the properties of the initial exception in the chain that was produced. Hence, `objC.GetBaseException.Message` returns the `Message` property of the original `OverflowException` message even though you've thrown multiple errors since the original error occurred:

```
Messagebox.Show(objC.GetBaseException.Message)
```

To put it another way, the code traverses back to the exception caught as `objA` and displays the same message as the `objA.Message` property would, as shown in Figure 10-7.

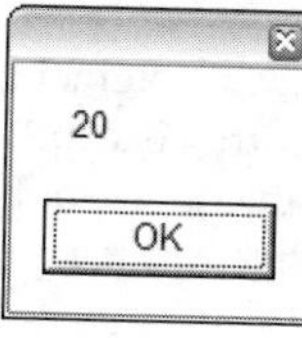

Figure 10-7

HelpLink

The HelpLink property gets or sets the help link for a specific Exception object. It can be set to any string value, but is typically set to a URL. If you create your own exception in code, you might want to set HelpLink to some URL describing the error in more detail. Then the code that catches the exception can go to that link. You could create and throw your own custom application exception with code like the following:

```
Dim exc As New ApplicationException("A short description of the problem")
exc.HelpLink = "http://mysite.com/somehtmlfile.htm"
Throw exc
```

When trapping an exception, the HelpLink can be used to launch a viewer so that the user can see the details about the problem. The following example shows this in action, using the built-in Explorer in Windows:

```
Sub HandlerExample4()
Try
    Dim exc As New ApplicationException("A short description of the problem")
    exc.HelpLink = "http:// mysite.com/somehtmlfile.htm "
    Throw exc

    ' Catch the error.
Catch objA As System.Exception
    Shell("explorer.exe " & objA.HelpLink)

End Try
End Sub
```

This results in launching Internet Explorer to show the page specified by the URL.

Most exceptions thrown by the CLR or the .NET Framework's classes have a blank HelpLink property. You should only count on using HelpLink if you have previously set it to a URL (or some other type of link information) yourself.

Interoperability with VB6-Style Error Handling

Since VB.NET still supports the older On Error statement, it is possible that you will be using code that handles errors that way instead of the structured exception handling. It is possible to use both techniques in a single program. However, it is not possible to use both forms in a single routine. If you attempt to use both On Error and Try . . . Catch in a single routine, you will get a syntax error.

However, the VB compiler allows the two techniques for handling errors to communicate with one another. For example, suppose that you have a routine that uses On Error and then uses Err.Raise to promote the error to the calling code. Also suppose that the calling code makes the call in a Try . . . Catch block. In that case, the error created by Err.Raise becomes an exception in the calling code and is trapped by a Catch block just as a normal exception would be. Here's a code example to illustrate.

First, create a subroutine that creates an error with `Err.Raise`, like this:

```
Private Sub RaiseErrorWithErrRaise()
    Err.Raise(53)    ' indicates File Not Found
End Sub
```

Then call this routine from a button's click event, with the call inside a `Try . . . Catch` block, like this:

```
Private Sub Button2_Click(ByVal sender As System.Object, _
    ByVal e As System.EventArgs) Handles Button2.Click
    Trºy
        RaiseErrorWithErrRaise()
    Catch ex As Exception
        MessageBox.Show(ex.Message)
    End Try
End Sub
```

When the button is clicked, it will display a message box with `File Not Found`. Even though the `File Not Found` error was raised by `Err.Raise`, it was translated to a .NET exception automatically.

Similarly, exceptions that are generated by a `Throw` statement in a called routine can be trapped by `On Error` in a calling routine. The exception is then translated into an `Err` object that works like the VB6 `Err` object.

Error Logging

Error logging is important in many applications for thorough troubleshooting. It is common for end users of the applications to not remember what the error said exactly. Recording specific errors in a log allows you to get the specific error message without recreating the error.

While error logging is very important, you only want to use it to trap specific levels of errors because it carries overhead and can reduce the performance of your application. You want to only log errors that will be critical to your application integrity — for instance, an error that would cause the data that the application is working with to become invalid.

There are three main approaches to error logging:

- ❑ Write error information in a text file or flat file located in a strategic location.
- ❑ Write error information to a central database.
- ❑ Write error information to the Event Log that is available on the Windows OS (NT, 2000, XP, and 2003). The .NET Framework includes a component that can be used to write and read from the System, Application, and Security Logs on any given machine.

The type of logging you choose depends on the categories of errors you wish to trap and the types of machines you will run your application on. If you choose to write to the event log, you need to categorize the errors and write them in the appropriate log file. Resource-, hardware-, and system-level errors fit best into the System Event Log. Data access errors fit best into the Application Event Log. Permission errors fit best into the Security Event Log.

Event logs are not available on Windows 98 or Windows ME, even though .NET supports these systems. If you expect to support these operating systems on client machines, you will not be able to use the built-in Event Log classes shown here. Logging on these systems will require building your own custom log. You may want your logging component to check the OS version and decide whether to log to an Event Log or a custom log.

The Event Log

There are three Event Logs available: the System, Application, and Security Logs. Events in these logs can be viewed using the Event Viewer, which is accessed from the Control Panel. Access Administrative Tools and then select the Event Viewer subsection to view events. Typically, your applications would use the Application event log.

Event logging is available in your program through an Event Log component. It can both read and write to all of the available logs on a machine. The `EventLog` component is part of the `System.Diagnostics` namespace. The component allows adding and removing custom Event Logs, reading and writing to and from the standard Windows Event Logs, and creating customized Event Log entries.

Event Logs can get full, as they have a limited amount of space, so you only want to write critical information to your Event Logs. You can customize each of your system Event Log's properties by changing the log size and determining how the system will handle events that occur when the log is full. You can configure the log to overwrite data when it is full or overwrite all events older than a given number of days. It is important to remember that the Event Log that is written to is based on where the code is running from, so that if there are many tiers, you can locate the proper Event Log information to research the error further.

There are five types of Event Log entries you can make. These five types are divided into event type entries and audit type entries.

Event type entries are:

- **Information** — Added when events such as a service starting or stopping occurs
- **Warning** — Occurs when a noncritical event occurs that might cause future problems, such as disk space getting low
- **Error** — Should be logged when something occurs that will prevent normal processing, such as a startup service not being able to start

Audit type entries will usually go into the Security Log and can be either:

- **Success audit** — For example, a success audit might be a successful login through an application to an SQL Server
- **Failure audit** — A failure audit might come in handy if a user doesn't have access to create an output file on a certain file system

If you don't specify the type of Event Log entry, an information type entry is generated.

Each entry in an Event Log has a `Source` property. The `Source` property is required and is a programmer-defined string that is assigned to an event that helps categorize the events in a log. A new `Source` must be defined prior to being used in an entry in an Event Log. The `SourceExists` method is used to determine if a particular source already exists on the given computer. We recommend that you use a string that is relevant to where the error originated, such as the component name. Packaged software often uses the software name as the Source in the Application Log. This helps group errors that occur by specific software package.

The `EventLog` component is in the `System.Diagnostics` namespace. To use it conveniently, you need to include an `Imports System.Diagnostics` statement in the declarations section of your code.

> **Certain security rights must be obtained in order to manipulate Event Logs. Ordinary programs can read all of the Event Logs and write to the Application Event Log. Special privileges, on the administrator level, are required to perform tasks such as clearing and deleting Event Logs. Your application should not normally need to do these tasks, or to write to any log besides the Application Event Log.**

The most common events, methods, and properties for the `EventLog` component are listed and described in the following tables.

Events, Methods, and Properties

The following table describes the relevant event.

Event	Description
`EntryWritten`	Generated when an event is written to a log

The following table describes the relevant methods.

Methods	Description
`CreateEventSource`	Creates an event source in the specified log
`DeleteEventSource`	Deletes an event source and associated entries
`WriteEntry`	Writes a string to a specified log
`Exists`	Can be used to determine if a specific event log exists
`SourceExists`	Used to determine if a specific source exists in a log
`GetEventLogs`	Retrieves a list of all event logs on a particular computer
`Delete`	Deletes an entire Event Log — use this method with care

The following table describes the relevant properties.

Properties	Description
`Source`	Specifies the source of the entry to be written.
`Log`	Used to specify a log to write to. The three logs are System, Application, and Security. The System Log is the default if not specified.

Here is an example that illustrates some of these methods and properties:

```
Sub LoggingExample1()
  Dim objLog As New EventLog()
  Dim objLogEntryType As EventLogEntryType
  Try
    Throw (New EntryPointNotFoundException())
  Catch objA As System.EntryPointNotFoundException
    If Not objLog.SourceExists("Example") Then
      objLog.CreateEventSource("Example", "System")
    End If
    objLog.Source = "Example"
    objLog.Log = "System"
    objLogEntryType = EventLogEntryType.Information
    objLog.WriteEntry("Error: " & objA.Message, objLogEntryType)
  End Try
End Sub
```

You have declared two variables — one to instantiate your log and one to hold your entry's type information. Note that you need to check for the existence of a source prior to creating it. These two lines of code accomplish this:

```
If Not objLog.SourceExists("Example") Then
  objLog.CreateEventSource("Example", "System")
```

Once you have verified or created your source, you can set the `Source` property of the `EventLog` object, set the `Log` property to specify which log you want to write to, and `EventLogEntryType` to `Information` (other choices are `Warning`, `Error`, `SuccessAudit`, and `FailureAudit`). If you attempt to write to a source that does not exist in a specific log, you will get an error. After you have set these three properties of the `EventLog` object, you can then write your entry. In this example, you concatenated the word `Error` with the actual exception's `Message` property to form the string to write to the log:

```
objLog.Source = "Example"
objLog.Log = "System"
objLogEntryType = EventLogEntryType.Information
objLog.WriteEntry("Error: " & objA.Message, objLogEntryType)
```

Writing to Trace Files

As an alternative for platforms that don't support event logging, or if you can't get direct access to the Event Log, you can write your debugging and error information to trace files. A trace file is a text-based file that you generate in your program to track detailed information about an error condition. Trace files are also a good way to supplement your event logging if you wish to track detailed information that would potentially fill the Event Log.

A more detailed explanation of the variety of trace tools and uses in debugging follows in "Analyzing Problems and Measuring Performance via the Trace Class," but you will cover some of the techniques for using the `StreamWriter` interface in your development of a trace file in this section.

The concepts involved in writing to text files include setting up streamwriters and debug listeners. The `StreamWriter` interface is handled through the `System.IO` namespace and allows you to interface with the files in the file system on a given machine. The `Debug` class interfaces with these output objects through listener objects. The job of any listener object is to collect, store up, and send the stored output to text files, logs, and the Output window. In your example, you will use the `TextWriterTraceListener` interface.

As you will see, the `StreamWriter` object opens an output path to a text file, and by binding the `StreamWriter` object to a listener object you can direct debug output to a text file.

Trace listeners are output targets and can be a `TextWriter` or an `EventLog`, or can send output to the default Output window (which is `DefaultTraceListener`). The `TextWriterTraceListener` accommodates the `WriteLine` method of a `Debug` interface by providing an output object that stores up information to be flushed to the output stream, which you set up by the `StreamWriter` interface.

The following table lists some of the commonly used methods from the `StreamWriter` object.

Method	Description
`Close`	Closes the `StreamWriter`.
`Flush`	Flushes all content of the `StreamWriter` to the output file designated upon creation of the `StreamWriter`.
`Write`	Writes byte output to the stream. Optional parameters allow designation of where in the stream (offset).
`WriteLine`	Writes characters followed by a line terminator to the current stream object.

The following table lists some of the methods associated with the `Debug` object, which provides the output mechanism for your text file example to follow.

The following example shows how you can open an existing file (called `mytext.txt`) for output and assign it to the `Listeners` object of the `Debug` object so that it can catch your `Debug.WriteLine` statements.

Method	Description
`Assert`	Checks a condition and displays a message if `False`
`Close`	Executes a flush on the output buffer and closes all listeners
`Fail`	Emits an error message in the form of an Abort/Retry/Ignore message box
`Flush`	Flushes the output buffer and writes it to the listeners
`Write`	Writes bytes to the output buffer
`WriteLine`	Writes characters followed by a line terminator to the output buffer
`WriteIf`	Writes bytes to the output buffer if a specific condition is `True`
`WriteLineIF`	Writes characters followed by a line terminator to the output buffer if a specific condition is `True`

```
Sub LoggingExample2()
  Dim objWriter As New _
      IO.StreamWriter("C:\mytext.txt", True)
   Debug.Listeners.Add(New TextWriterTraceListener(objWriter))
  Try
    Throw (New EntryPointNotFoundException())
  Catch objA As System.EntryPointNotFoundException
    Debug.WriteLine(objA.Message)
    objWriter.Flush()
    objWriter.Close()
    objWriter = Nothing
  End Try
End Sub
```

Looking in detail at this code, you first create a `StreamWriter` that is assigned to a file in your local file system:

```
Dim objWriter As New _
    IO.StreamWriter("C:\mytext.txt", True)
```

You then assign your `StreamWriter` to a debug listener by using the `Add` method:

```
Debug.Listeners.Add(New TextWriterTraceListener (objWriter))
```

In this example, you force an exception and catch it, writing the `Message` property of the `Exception` object (which is `Entry point was not found.`) to the debug buffer through the `WriteLine` method:

```
Debug.WriteLine(objA.Message)
```

You finally flush the listener buffer to the output file and free your resources.

```
objWriter.Flush()
objWriter.Close()
objWriter = Nothing
```

Analyzing Problems and Measuring Performance via the Trace Class

The trace tools in the .NET Framework revolve around the `Trace` class, which provides properties and methods that help you trace the execution of your code. By default, tracing is enabled in VB.NET, so not unlike your previous debug discussion, all you have to do is set up the output and utilize its capabilities.

You can specify the detail level you want to perform for your tracing output by configuring trace switches. You will show an example of setting a trace switch shortly, but first you need to cover what a trace switch can do and what the settings for trace switches mean.

Trace switches can be either `BooleanSwitch` or `TraceSwitch`. `BooleanSwitch` has a value of either `0` or `1` and is used to determine if tracing is off or on, respectively, while `TraceSwitch` allows you to specify a level of tracing based on five enumerated values. You can manage a `BooleanSwitch` or `TraceSwitch` as an environment variable. Once a switch is established, you can create and initialize it in code and use it with either trace or debug.

A `TraceSwitch` can have five enumerated levels that can be read as `0–4` or checked with four properties provided in the switch class interface. The four properties return a Boolean value based on whether the switch is set to a certain level or higher. The five enumerated levels for `TraceSwitch` are as follows.

Level	Description
0	None
1	Only error messages
2	Warning and error messages
3	Information, warning, and error messages
4	Verbose, information, warning, and error messages

The four properties are `TraceError`, `TraceWarning`, `TraceInfo`, and `TraceVerbose`. For example, if your switch was set at number `2` and you asked for the `TraceError` or `TraceWarning` properties, they would return `True`, while the `TraceInformation` and `TraceVerbose` properties would return `False`.

An environment variable is either managed via the command line or under My computer ➪ Properties ➪ Advanced within the Environment Variables button.

Within the Environment Variables button, you add a new `User` variable, giving it the `SwitchName` and `Value` for that switch.

From the command line, type

```
Set _Switch_MySwitch   = 0
```

The value on the left of the = symbol is the name of the switch, and the value on its right is either `0` or `1` for a `BooleanSwitch` or `0–4` for a `TraceSwitch`. Note that there is a space between the word `Set` and the leading underscore of `_Switch`. Once you have typed this line, if you follow that by the plain `SET` command at the command line, it will show your new switch as an environment variable, as shown in Figure 10-8.

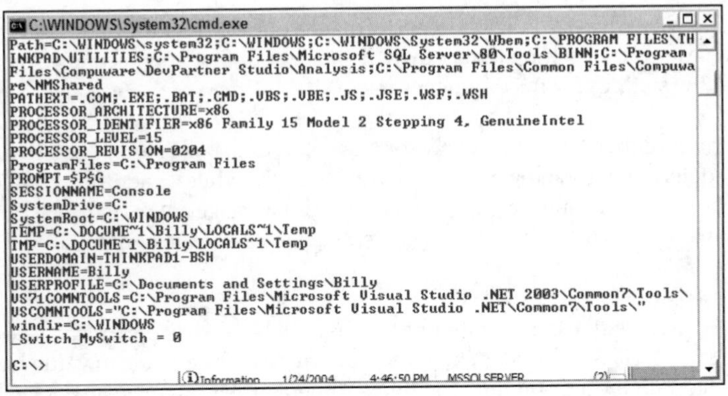

```
C:\WINDOWS\System32\cmd.exe
Path=C:\WINDOWS\system32;C:\WINDOWS;C:\WINDOWS\System32\Wbem;C:\PROGRAM FILES\TH
INKPAD\UTILITIES;C:\Program Files\Microsoft SQL Server\80\Tools\BINN;C:\Program
Files\Compuware\DevPartner Studio\Analysis;C:\Program Files\Common Files\Compuwa
re\NMShared
PATHEXT=.COM;.EXE;.BAT;.CMD;.VBS;.VBE;.JS;.JSE;.WSF;.WSH
PROCESSOR_ARCHITECTURE=x86
PROCESSOR_IDENTIFIER=x86 Family 15 Model 2 Stepping 4, GenuineIntel
PROCESSOR_LEVEL=15
PROCESSOR_REVISION=0204
ProgramFiles=C:\Program Files
PROMPT=$P$G
SESSIONNAME=Console
SystemDrive=C:
SystemRoot=C:\WINDOWS
TEMP=C:\DOCUME~1\Billy\LOCALS~1\Temp
TMP=C:\DOCUME~1\Billy\LOCALS~1\Temp
USERDOMAIN=THINKPAD1-BSH
USERNAME=Billy
USERPROFILE=C:\Documents and Settings\Billy
VS71COMNTOOLS=C:\Program Files\Microsoft Visual Studio .NET 2003\Common7\Tools\
VSCOMNTOOLS="C:\Program Files\Microsoft Visual Studio .NET\Common7\Tools\"
windir=C:\WINDOWS
_Switch_MySwitch = 0

C:\>
```

Figure 10-8

For the example that follows, you have the output directed to the default Output window:

```
Sub TraceExample1()
  Dim objTraceSwitch As TraceSwitch
  objTraceSwitch = New TraceSwitch("ExampleSwitch", "Test Trace Switch")
  objTraceSwitch.Level = TraceLevel.Error
  Try
    Throw (New EntryPointNotFoundException())
  Catch objA As System.EntryPointNotFoundException
    Trace.WriteLineIf(objTraceSwitch.TraceVerbose, _
        "First Trace " & objA.Source)
    Trace.WriteLineIf(objTraceSwitch.TraceError, _
        "Second Trace " & objA.Message)
  End Try
End Sub
```

You begin by assigning your switch to an existing registry entry and setting its level:

```
objTraceSwitch = New TraceSwitch("ExampleSwitch", "Test Trace Switch")
objTraceSwitch.Level = TraceLevel.Error
```

After you throw your exception, you first cause your trace output listener to catch the `Source` property of your `Exception` object based on whether the value of your switch is `TraceVerbose` or better:

```
Trace.WriteLineIf(objTraceSwitch.TraceVerbose, _
    "First Trace " & objA.Source)
```

Since the tracing level is set to `Error`, this line is skipped and you continue by writing a trace to the Output window to include the message information if the level is set to `Error`:

```
Trace.WriteLineIf(objTraceSwitch.TraceError, _
    "Second Trace " & objA.Message)
```

As you can see in your Output window shown, you successfully wrote only the second trace line based on the level being `Error` on your trace switch, as can be seen in Figure 10-9.

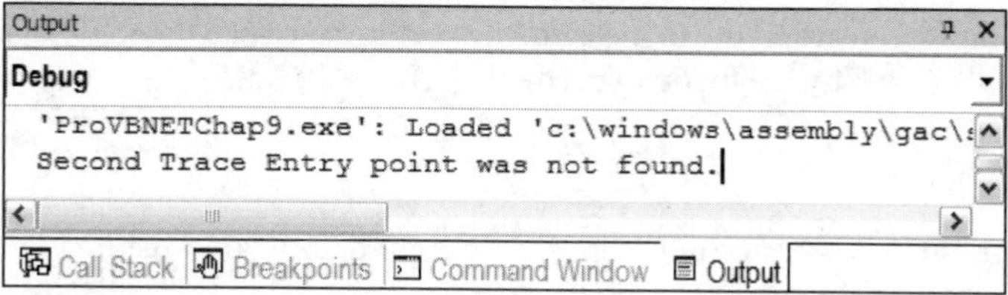

Figure 10-9

The other thing you want the ability to do is to determine the performance of your application. Overall, your application might appear to be working fine, but it is always a good thing to be able to measure the performance of your application so that environment changes or degradation over time can be counteracted. The basic concept here is to use conditional compilation so that you can turn on and off your performance-measuring code:

```
Sub TraceExample2()
  Dim connInfo As New Connection()
  Dim rstInfo As New Recordset()
  #Const bTrace = 1
  Dim objWriter As New _
    IO.StreamWriter(IO.File.Open("c:\mytext.txt", IO.FileMode.OpenOrCreate))
  connInfo.ConnectionString = "Provider = sqloledb.1" & _
    ";Persist Security Info = False;" & "Initial Catalog = Northwind;" & _
    "DataSource = LocalServer"
  connInfo.Open(connInfo.ConnectionString, "sa")
  Trace.Listeners.Add(New TextWriterTraceListener(objWriter))
  #If bTrace Then
    Trace.WriteLine("Begun db query at " & now())
  #End If
  rstInfo.Open("SELECT CompanyName, OrderID, " & _
```

```
      "OrderDate FROM Orders AS a LEFT JOIN Customers" & _
      " AS b ON a.CustomerID = b.CustomerID WHERE " & _
      "a.CustomerID = 'Chops'", connInfo, _
      CursorTypeEnum.adOpenForwardOnly, _
      LockTypeEnum.adLockBatchOptimistic)
    #If bTrace Then
```

```
      Trace.WriteLine("Ended db query at " & now())
    #End If
    Trace.Listeners.Clear()
    objWriter.Close()
    rstInfo.Close()
    connInfo.Close()
    rstInfo = Nothing
    connInfo = Nothing
```

End SubThis subroutine uses ADO, so be sure to add a reference to an ADO library and an `Imports ADODB` statement in the declarations section of the module.

In this simple example, you are trying to measure the performance of a database query using a conditional constant defined as `bTrace` by the following code:

```
#Const bTrace = 1
```

You establish your database connection strings, then right before you execute your query you write to a log file based on whether you are in tracing mode or not:

```
#If bTrace Then
  Trace.WriteLine("Begun db query at " & now())
#End If
```

Again, after your query returns you'll write to your log only if you are in tracing mode:

```
#If bTrace Then
  Trace.WriteLine("Ended db query at" & now())
#End If
```

It is always important to remember that tracing will potentially slow the application down, so you want to use this functionality only when troubleshooting and not let it run all the time.

Summary

As mentioned in Chapter 1, a major weakness of pre-.NET versions of Visual Basic was limited error-handling capabilities. As you've seen in this chapter, this problem has been thoroughly addressed. Errors and unexpected conditions are now packaged as exceptions, and these exception objects have special syntax to detect and manage them. The `Try . . . Catch . . . Finally . . . End Try` construct brings VB.NET's error-handling capabilities on par with other advanced languages.

In this chapter, we reviewed the exception object and all the syntax that is available to work with exceptions. We've looked at the various properties of exceptions and discussed how to use the exposed information. We've also covered how to promote exceptions to consuming code using the `Throw` statement, and how structured exception handling interoperates with old-style `On Error`.

As discussed, any new code you write should use the new exception-handling capabilities of .NET. Avoid using the old-style `On Error` except for maintenance tasks in old code.

We also covered some other topics related to error handling, such as:

- Error logging to Event Logs and trace files
- Instrumentation and measuring performance
- Tracing techniques

Using the full capabilities for error handling that are now available in VB.NET can make the applications more reliable and help diagnose problems faster when they do occur. Proper use of tracing and instrumentation can also help you tune your application for better performance.

11

Data Access with ADO.NET 2.0

ADO.NET 1.*x* was the successor to ActiveX Data Objects 2.6 (ADO). The main goal of ADO.NET 1.*x* was to allow developers to easily create distributed, data sharing applications in the .NET Framework. The main goals of ADO.NET 2.0 are to improve the performance of existing features in ADO.NET 1.*x*, to be easier to use, and to add new features with out breaking backward compatibility.

Throughout this chapter, when ADO.NET is mentioned without a version number after it (that is, 1.x or 2.0), this means that the statement applies to all versions of ADO.NET.

ADO.NET 1.*x* was built upon industry standards such as XML, and it provided a data access interface to communicate with data sources such as SQL Server and Oracle. ADO.NET 2.0 builds upon these concepts, while increasing performance. Applications can use ADO.NET to connect to these data sources and retrieve, manipulate, and update data. ADO.NET 2.0 does not break any compatibility with ADO.NET 1.*x*, it only adds to the stack of functionality.

In solutions that require disconnected or remote access to data, ADO.NET 2.0 uses XML to exchange data between programs or with Web pages. Any component that can read XML can make use of ADO.NET components. A receiving component does not even have to be an ADO.NET component if a transmitting ADO.NET component packages and delivers a data set in an XML format. Transmitting information in XML-formatted data sets enables programmers to easily separate the data-processing and user interface components of a data-sharing application onto separate servers. This can greatly improve both the performance and maintainability of systems that support many users.

For distributed applications, ADO.NET 1.*x* proved that the use of XML data sets provided performance advantages relative to the COM marshaling used to transmit disconnected data sets in ADO. Since transmission of data sets occurred through XML streams in a simple text-based standard accepted throughout the industry, receiving components did not have to have any of the architectural restrictions required by COM. XML data sets used in ADO.NET 1.*x* also avoided the processing cost of converting values in the Fields collection of a `Recordset` to data types recognized by COM. Virtually, any two components from different systems can share XML data sets provided that they both use the same XML schema for formatting the data set. This continues to be true in ADO.NET 2.0, but the story gets better. The XML integration in ADO.NET 2.0 is even stronger now, and extensive work was done to improve the performance of the `DataSet` object, particularly in the areas of serialization and memory usage.

ADO.NET also supports the scalability required by Web-based data-sharing applications. Web applications must often serve hundreds, or even thousands, of users. By default, ADO.NET does not retain lengthy database locks or active connections that monopolize limited resources. This allows the number of users to grow with only a small increase in the demands made on the resources of a system.

In this chapter, we will see that ADO.NET 2.0 is a very extensive and flexible API for accessing many types of data. And since ADO.NET 2.0 is an incremental change to ADO.NET 1.*x*, all previous ADO.NET knowledge that was learned can be leveraged. In fact, to get the most out of this chapter you should be fairly familiar with ADO.NET 1.*x* and also the entire .NET Framework 1.*x*.

In this chapter, we will understand how to use the ADO.NET 2.0 object model in order to build flexible, fast, scalable data access objects and applications. Specifically, we will focus on:

- The ADO.NET 2.0 architecture
- Some of the new features offered in ADO.NET 2.0, specifically batch updates, `DataSet` performance improvements, and asynchronous processing
- Working with the Common Provider Model
- Building a data access component

ADO.NET 2.0 Architecture Enhancements

The main design goals of ADO.NET 2.0 are the following:

- To add many new customer-driven features yet still remain backward compatible with ADO.NET 1.*x*
- Improve upon performance of ADO.NET 1.*x*
- Provide more power for power users
- Take advantage of new SQL Server 2005 features

In distributed applications, the concept of working with disconnected data is very common. A disconnected model means that once you have retrieved the data that you need, the connection to the data source is dropped—you work with the data locally. The reason why this model is so popular is that it frees up precious database server resources, which leads to highly scalable applications. The ADO.NET solution for disconnected data is the `DataSet` object.

ADO.NET Components

To better support the disconnected model, the ADO.NET components separate data access from data manipulation. This is accomplished via two main components, the `DataSet` and the .NET Data Provider. Figure 11-1 illustrates the concept of separating data access from data manipulation.

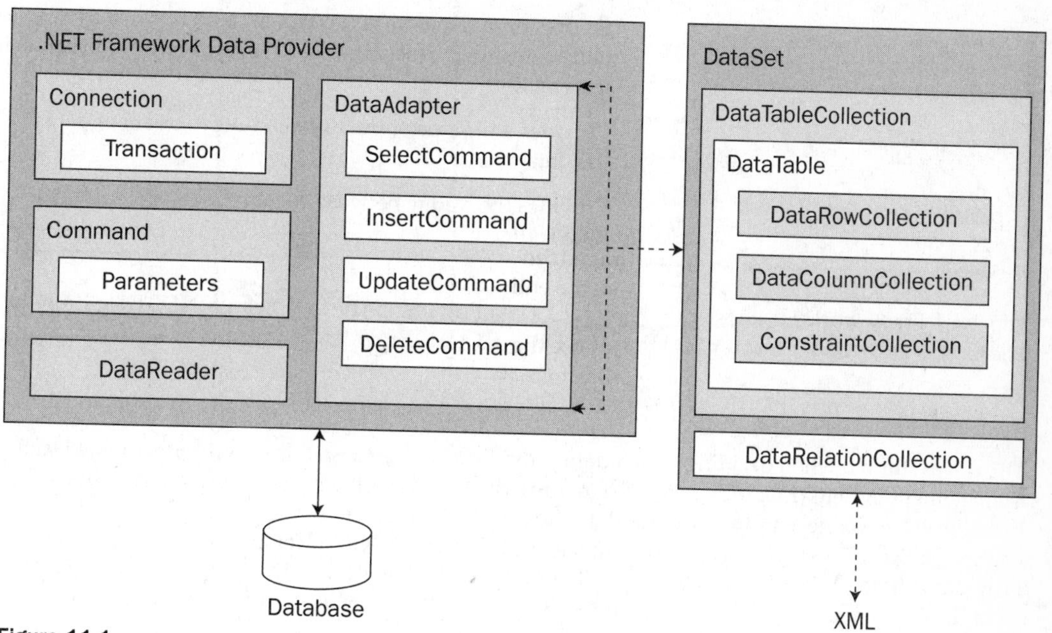

Figure 11-1

The `DataSet` is the core component of the disconnected architecture of ADO.NET. The `DataSet` is explicitly designed for data access independent of any data source. As a result, it can be used with multiple and differing data sources, with XML data, or even to manage data local to an application such as an in-memory data cache. The `DataSet` contains a collection of one or more `DataTable` objects made up of rows and columns of data, as well as primary key, foreign key, constraint, and relation information about the data in the `DataTable` objects. It is basically an in-memory database, but the cool thing is that it does not care whether its data is obtained from a database, an XML file, a combination of the two, or somewhere else. You can apply inserts, updates, and deletes to the `DataSet` and then push the changes back to the data source, no matter where the data source lives! We will take a more in-depth look at the `DataSet` object family and its ADO.NET 2.0 enhancements later in this chapter.

The other core element of the ADO.NET architecture is the .NET Data Provider, whose components are designed for data manipulation (as opposed to data access with the `DataSet`). These components are listed in the following table.

The `DataAdapter` uses `Command` objects to execute SQL commands at the data source to both load the `DataSet` with data, and also to reconcile changes made to the data in the `DataSet` with the data source. We will take a closer look at this later when we cover the `DataAdapter` object in more detail.

.NET Data Providers can be written for any data source, though this is beyond the scope of this chapter.

Object	Activity
`Connection`	Provides connectivity to a data source
`Command`	Enables access to database commands to return and modify data, run stored procedures, and send or retrieve parameter information
`DataReader`	Provides a high-performance, read-only stream of data from the data source
`DataAdapter`	Provides the bridge between the `DataSet` object and the data source

The .NET Framework 2.0 ships with three .NET Data Providers: The SQL Server .NET Data Provider, The Oracle .NET Data Provider, and the OLE DB .NET Data Provider.

Do not confuse the OLE DB .NET Data Provider with generic OLE DB providers.

The rule of thumb when deciding which data provider to use is to first use a .NET Relational Database Management System (RDBMS)–specific data provider if it is available, and to use the .NET OLE DB Provider when connecting to any other data source. So, if you were writing an application that was using SQL Server, then you would want to use the SQL Server .NET Data Provider. The .NET OLE DB Provider is used to access any data source that is exposed through OLE DB, such as Microsoft Access, Open DataBase Connectivity (ODBC), and so on. We will be taking a closer look at these later on.

.NET Data Providers

.NET Data Providers are used for connecting to a RDBMS-specific database (such as SQL Server or Oracle), executing commands, and retrieving results. Those results are either processed directly (via a `DataReader`), or placed in an ADO.NET `DataSet` (via a `DataAdapter`) in order to be exposed to the user in an ad hoc manner, combined with data from multiple sources, or passed around between tiers. .NET Data Providers are designed to be lightweight, to create a minimal layer between the data source and the .NET programmer's code, and to increase performance while not sacrificing any functionality. Currently, the .NET Framework supports three data providers: the SQL Server .NET Data Provider (for Microsoft SQL Server 7.0 or later), the Oracle .NET Data Provider, and the OLE DB .NET Data Provider. Most RDBMS vendors are now producing their own .NET Data Providers in order to encourage .NET developers to use their databases.

Connection Object

To connect to a specific data source, we use a data `Connection` object. To connect to Microsoft SQL Server 7.0 or later, we need to use the `SqlConnection` object of the SQL Server .NET Data Provider. We need to use the `OleDbConnection` object of the OLE DB .NET Data Provider to connect to an OLE DB data source, or the OLE DB Provider for SQL Server (SQLOLEDB) to connect to versions of Microsoft SQL Server earlier than 7.0.

Connection String Format — OleDbConnection

For the OLE DB .NET Data Provider, the connection string format is identical to the connection string format used in ADO with the following exceptions:

- The `Provider` keyword is required.
- The URL, `Remote Provider`, and `Remote Server` keywords are not supported.

Here is an example `OleDbConnection` connection string connecting to an Oracle database (note this is all one line):

```
Provider=msdaora;Data Source=MyOracleDB;User Id=myUsername;Password=myPassword;
```

Connection String Format — SqlConnection

The SQL Server .NET Data Provider supports a connection string format that is similar to the OLE DB (ADO) connection string format. The only thing that you need to leave off, obviously, is the provider name-value pair, since we know we are using the SQL Server .NET Data Provider. Here is an example of a `SqlConnection` connection string:

```
data source=(local);initial catalog=pubs;Integrated Security=SSPI;
```

Command Object

After establishing a connection, you can execute commands and return results from a data source (such as SQL Server) using a `Command` object. A `Command` object can be created using the `Command` constructor, or by calling the `CreateCommand` method of the `Connection` object. When creating a `Command` object using the `Command` constructor, you need to specify a SQL statement to execute at the data source, and a `Connection` object. The `Command` object's SQL statement can be queried and modified using the `CommandText` property. The following code is an example of executing a `SELECT` command and returning a `DataReader` object:

```
' Build the SQL and Connection strings.
Dim sql As String = "SELECT * FROM authors"
Dim connectionString As String = "Initial Catalog=pubs;" _
 & "Data Source=(local);Integrated Security=SSPI;"
' Initialize the SqlCommand with the SQL
' and Connection strings.
Dim command As SqlCommand = New SqlCommand(sql, _
    New SqlConnection(connectionString))
' Open the connection.
command.Connection.Open()
' Execute the query, return a SqlDataReader object.
' CommandBehavior.CloseConnection flags the
' DataReader to automatically close the DB connection
' when it is closed.
Dim dataReader As SqlDataReader = _
    command.ExecuteReader(CommandBehavior.CloseConnection)
```

The `CommandText` property of the `Command` object will execute all SQL statements in addition to the standard `SELECT`, `UPDATE`, `INSERT`, and `DELETE` statements. For example, you could create tables, foreign keys, primary keys, and so on, by executing the applicable SQL from the `Command` object.

The Command object exposes several Execute methods to perform the intended action. When returning results as a stream of data, ExecuteReader is used to return a DataReader object. ExecuteScalar is used to return a singleton value. In ADO.NET 2.0, the ExecuteRow method has been added which returns a single row of data in the form of a SqlRecord object. ExecuteNonQuery is used to execute commands that do not return rows, which usually includes stored procedures that have output parameters and/or return values. (We'll talk about stored procedures in a later section.)

When using a DataAdapter with a DataSet, Command objects are used to return and modify data at the data source through the DataAdapter object's SelectCommand, InsertCommand, UpdateCommand, and DeleteCommand properties.

> **Note that the DataAdapter object's SelectCommand property must be set before the Fill method is called.**

The InsertCommand, UpdateCommand, and DeleteCommand properties must be set before the Update method is called. We will take a closer look at this when we look at the DataAdapter object.

Using Stored Procedures with Command Objects

In this section, we'll take a quick look at how to use stored procedures, before delving into a more complex illustration of how we can build a reusable data access component that also uses stored procedures later in the chapter. The motivation for using stored procedures is simple. Imagine you have this code

```
SELECT au_lname FROM authors WHERE au_id='172-32-1176'
```

If you pass that to SQL Server using ExecuteReader on SqlCommand (or any execute method, for that matter), what happens is that SQL Server has to compile the code before it can run it, in much the same way that VB .NET applications have to be compiled before they can be executed. This compilation takes up SQL Server's time, so it's a pretty obvious leap to deduce that if you can reduce the amount of compilation that SQL Server has to do, database performance should be increased. (Compare the speed of execution of a compiled application against interpreted code.)

That's what stored procedures are all about: we create a procedure, store it in the database, and because the procedure is known of and understood ahead of time, it can be compiled ahead of time ready for use in our application.

Stored procedures are very easy to use, but the code to access them is sometimes (in my opinion) a little verbose. In the next section, we'll see some code that can make accessing stored procedures a little more straightforward, but to make things a little clearer we'll start by building a simple application that demonstrates how to create and call a stored procedure.

Creating a Stored Procedure

To create a stored procedure, you can either use the tools in Visual Studio .NET, or you can use the tools in SQL Server's Enterprise Manager if you are using SQL Server 2000 or in SQL Server Management Studio if you are using SQL Server 2005. (Although technically you can use a third-party tool or just create the stored procedure in a good old-fashioned SQL script.)

For our example, we'll build a stored procedure that returns all of the columns for a given author ID. The SQL to do this will look like this:

```
SELECT
    au_id, au_lname, au_fname, phone,
   address, city, state, zip, contract
FROM
    authors
WHERE
    au_id = whatever author ID we want
```

The whatever author ID we want part is important. When using stored procedures, we typically have to be able to provide parameters into the stored procedure and use them from within code. This isn't a book about SQL Server, so I'm only going to show you in principle how to do this. There are many resources on the Web about building stored procedures (they've been around a very long time, and they're most definitely not a .NET-specific feature).

Variables in SQL Server are prefixed by the `@` symbol. So, if we have a variable called `au_id`, our SQL will look like this:

```
SELECT
    au_id, au_lname, au_fname, phone,
    address, city, state, zip, contract
FROM
    authors
WHERE
    au_id = @au_id
```

In Visual Studio 2005, stored procedures can be accessed using the Server Explorer. Simply add a new data connection (or use an existing data connection), and then drill down into the Stored Procedures folder in the management tree. In this screenshot, you'll see a number of stored procedures already loaded. The `byroyalty` procedure is a stored procedure provided by the pubs database developers. Figure 11-2 illustrates the stored procedures of the pubs database in Visual Studio 2005.

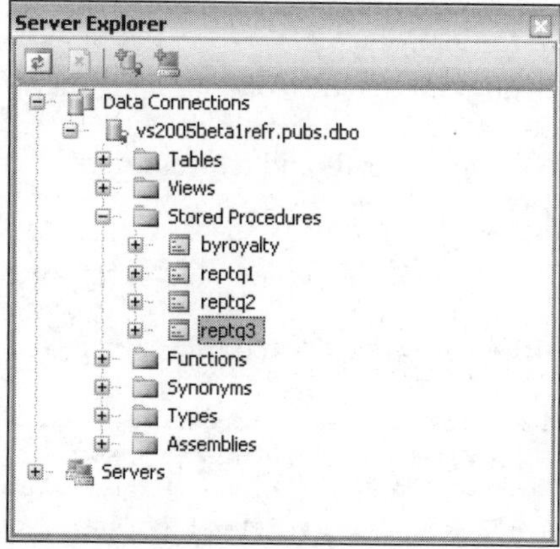

Figure 11-2

To create a new stored procedure, just right-click the Stored Procedures folder in the Server Explorer and select Add New Stored Procedure. This will then display the Editor window.

A stored procedure can be either a single SQL statement, or a complex set of statements. T-SQL supports branches, loops, and other variable declarations, which can make for some pretty complex stored procedure code. However, our stored procedure is just a single line of SQL. We need to declare the parameter that we want to pass in (`@au_id`), and the name of the procedure: `usp_authors_Get_By_ID`. Here's code for the stored procedure:

```
CREATE PROCEDURE usp_authors_Get_By_ID
    @au_id varchar(11)
AS
SELECT
    au_id, au_lname, au_fname, phone,
    address, city, state, zip, contract
FROM
    authors
WHERE
    au_id = @au_id
```

Click OK to save the stored procedure in the database. We're now able to access this stored procedure from code.

Calling the Stored Procedure

Calling the stored procedure is just an issue of creating a `SqlConnection` object to connect to the database and a `SqlCommand` object to run the stored procedure.

In the sample code for this chapter, you will see a solution called `Examples.sln`, and in it there will be a project called AdoNetFeaturesTest.

For all of the data access examples in this chapter, you will need the pubs database, which can be downloaded from MSDN. Also, make sure to run the `examples.sql` *file — available with the code download for this chapter — in SQL Server 2005 Management Studio before running the code examples. This will create the necessary stored procedures and function in the pubs database.*

Now you have to decide what you want to return out of calling the stored procedure. In this case you will return an instance of the SqlDataReader object. In the `TestForm.vb` file, there is a method called `GetAuthorSqlReader` that takes an author ID and returns an instance of a `SqlDataReader`. Here is the code for this method:

```
Private Function GetAuthorSqlReader(ByVal authorId As String) As SqlDataReader
    ' Build a SqlCommand
    Dim command As SqlCommand = New SqlCommand("usp_authors_Get_By_ID", _
        GetPubsConnection())
    ' Tell the command we are calling a stored procedure
    command.CommandType = CommandType.StoredProcedure
    ' Add the @au_id parameter information to the command
    command.Parameters.Add(New SqlParameter("@au_id", authorId))
    ' The reader requires an open connection
    command.Connection.Open()
    ' Execute the sql and return the reader
    Return command.ExecuteReader(CommandBehavior.CloseConnection)
End Function
```

Notice that in the SqlCommand's constructor call we have factored out creating a connection to the pubs database into a separate helper method. This will be used later in other code examples in your form.

Here is the code for the GetPubsConnection helper method:

```
Private Function GetPubsConnection() As SqlConnection
    ' Build a SqlConnection based on the config value.
    Return New _
        SqlConnection(ConfigurationSettings.AppSettings("dbConnectionString"))
End Function
```

The most significant thing this code does is to grab a connection string to the database from the application's configuration file, the app.config file. Here is what the entry in the app.config file looks like:

```
<appSettings>
    <add key="dbConnectionString" value="data source=(local);initial
        catalog=pubs;Integrated Security=SSPI;" />
</appSettings>
```

Although the helper method does not do much, it is nice to place this code in a separate method. This way, if the code to get a connection to the databases needs to be changed, the code will only have to be changed in one place.

Accessing a stored procedure is more verbose (but not more difficult) than accessing a normal SQL statement through the methods discussed thus far. The approach is:

- Create a SqlCommand object
- Configure it to access a stored procedure by setting the CommandType property
- Add parameters that exactly match those in the stored procedure itself
- Execute the stored procedure using one of the SqlCommand's Execute*** methods

There's no real need to build an impressive UI for this application, since we're about to move on to a far more interesting discussion. I have simply added a Button named getAuthorByIdButton that calls the GetAuthorSqlRecord helper method and display's the selected author's name. Here is the Button's Click event handler:

```
Private Sub _getAuthorByIdButton_Click(ByVal sender As System.Object, _
    ByVal e As System.EventArgs) Handles _getAuthorByIdButton.Click
    Dim reader As SqlDataReader = Me. GetAuthorSqlReader ("409-56-7008")
    If reader.Read()
        MsgBox(reader("au_fname").ToString() & "  " _
            & reader("au_lname").ToString())
    End If

    reader.Close()
End Sub
```

Here I've hard-coded an author ID of 409-56-7008. Run the code now and you should see the result shown in Figure 11-3.

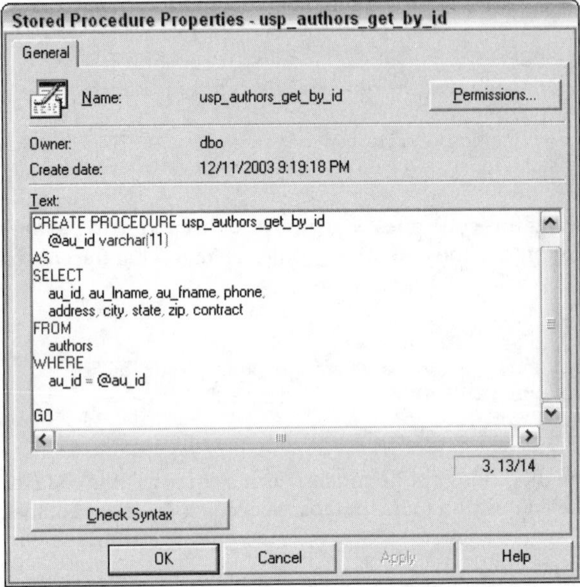

Figure 11-3

DataReader Object

You can use the `DataReader` to retrieve a read-only, forward-only stream of data from the database. Using the `DataReader` can increase application performance and reduce system overhead because only one buffered row at a time is ever in memory. With the `DataReader` object, you are getting as close to the raw data as possible in ADO.NET; you do not have to go through the overhead of populating a `DataSet` object, which sometimes may be expensive if the `DataSet` contains a lot of data. The disadvantage of using a `DataReader` object is that it requires an open database connection and increases network activity.

After creating an instance of the `Command` object, a `DataReader` is created by calling the `ExecuteReader` method of the `Command` object. Here is an example of creating a `DataReader` and iterating through it to print out its values to the screen:

```
Private Sub TraverseDataReader()

    ' Build the SQL and Connection strings.
    Dim sql As String = "SELECT * FROM authors"
    Dim connectionString As String = "Initial Catalog=pubs;" _
        & "Data Source=(local);Integrated Security=SSPI;"

    ' Initialize the SqlCommand with the SQL query and connection strings.
    Dim command As SqlCommand = New SqlCommand(sql, _
        New SqlConnection(connectionString))
    ' Open the connection.
```

```
        command.Connection.Open()
        ' Execute the query, return a SqlDataReader object.
        ' CommandBehavior.CloseConnection flags the
        ' DataReader to automatically close the DB connection
        ' when it is closed.
        Dim reader As SqlDataReader = _
            command.ExecuteReader(CommandBehavior.CloseConnection)
        ' Loop through the records and print the values.
        Do While reader.Read
            Console.WriteLine(reader.GetString(1) & " " & reader.GetString(2))
        Loop
        ' Close the DataReader (and its connection).
        reader.Close()

    End Sub
```

In this code snippet, we use the `SqlCommand` object to execute the query via the `ExecuteReader` method. This method returns a populated `SqlDataReader` object to us, and then we loop hrough it and print out the author names. The main difference with this code compared to looping through the rows of a `DataTable` is that we have to stay connected while we loop through the data in the `DataReader` object; this is so because the `DataReader` reads in only a small stream of data at a time to conserve memory space.

At this point an obvious design question is whether to use the `DataReader` *or the* `DataSet`*. The answer to this question really depends upon performance. If you want high performance, and you are only going to access the data that you are retrieving once, then the* `DataReader` *is the way to go. If you need access to the same data multiple times, or if you need to model a complex relationship in memory, then the* `DataSet` *is the way to go. As always, you will need to test each option thoroughly before deciding which one is the best.*

The `Read` method of the `DataReader` object is used to obtain a row from the results of the query. Each column of the returned row may be accessed by passing the name or ordinal reference of the column to the `DataReader`, or, for best performance, the `DataReader` provides a series of methods that allow you to access column values in their native data types (`GetDateTime`, `GetDouble`, `GetGuid`, `GetInt32`, and so on). Using the typed accessor methods when the underlying data type is known will reduce the amount of type conversion required (converting from type `Object`) when retrieving the column value.

The `DataReader` provides a nonbuffered stream of data that allows procedural logic to efficiently process results from a data source sequentially. The `DataReader` is a good choice when retrieving large amounts of data; only one row of data will be cached in memory at a time. You should always call the `Close` method when you are through using the `DataReader` object, as well as closing the `DataReader` object's database connection; otherwise, the connection won't be closed until the Garbage Collector gets around to collecting the object. Note how we used the `CommandBehavior.CloseConnection` enumeration value on the `SqlDataReader.ExecuteReader` method. This tells the `SqlCommand` object to automatically close the database connection when the `SqlDataReader.Close` method is called.

If your command contains output parameters or return values, they will not be available until the `DataReader` *is closed.*

Executing Commands Asynchronously

In ADO.NET 2.0, additional support has been to allow Command objects to execute their commands asynchronously. This can be a huge perceived performance gain in many applications, especially in Windows Forms applications. This can come in really handy, especially if you ever have to execute a long-running SQL statement. We will look at how this new functionality lets us add asynchronous processing to enhance the responsiveness of an application.

The SqlCommand object provides three different asynchronous call options, BeginExecuteReader, BeginExecuteNonQuery, and BeginExecuteXmlReader. Each of these methods has a corresponding "end" method, that is, EndExecuteReader, EndExecutreNonQuery, and EndExecuteXmlReader. Since we have just finished covering the DataReader object, let's look at an example using the BeginExecuteReader method to execute a long-running query.

In the AdoNetFeaturesTest project, I have added a Button and an associated Click event handler to the form that will initiate the asynchronous call to get a DataReader instance:

```
Private Sub _testAsyncCallButton_Click(ByVal sender As System.Object, _
        ByVal e As System.EventArgs) Handles _testAsyncCallButton.Click

        ' Build a connection for the async call to the database.
        Dim connection As SqlConnection = GetPubsConnection()
        connection.ConnectionString &= "Asynchronous Processing=true;"

        ' Build a command to call the stored procedure.
        Dim command As New SqlCommand("usp_Long_Running_Procedure", connection)

        ' Set the command type to stored procedure.
        command.CommandType = CommandType.StoredProcedure

        ' The reader requires an open connection.
        connection.Open()

        ' Make the asynchronous call to the database.
        command.BeginExecuteReader(AddressOf Me.AsyncCallback, _
        command, CommandBehavior.CloseConnection)
    End Sub
```

The first thing we do is to reuse our helper method GetPubsConnection to get a connection to the pubs database. The next step that we do, which is very important, is to append the statement Asynchronous Processing=true to our Connection object's connection string. This must be set in order for ADO.NET 2.0 to make asynchronous calls to SQL Server.

After getting the connection set, we then build a SqlCommand object and initialize it to be able to execute the usp_Long_Running_Procedure stored procedure. This procedure uses the SQL Server 2005 WAITFOR DELAY statement to create a 20 second delay before it executes the usp_Authors_Get_All stored procedure. As you can probably guess, the usp_authors_Get_All stored procedure simply selects all of the authors from the authors table. The delay is put in simply to demonstrate the fact that while this stored procedure is executing, we can performs other tasks in our Windows Forms application. Here is the SQL code for the usp_Long_Running_Procedure stored procedure:

```
CREATE PROCEDURE usp_Long_Running_Procedure
AS
SET NOCOUNT ON

WAITFOR DELAY '00:00:20'
EXEC usp_authors_Get_All
```

The last line of code in the Button's Click event handler is the call to BeginExecuteReader. In this call, the first thing we are passing in is a delegate method (Me.AsyncCallback) for the System.AsyncCallback delegate type. This is how the .NET Framework will call us back once the method is finished running asynchronously. We then pass in our initialized SqlCommand object so that it can be executed for us, as well as the CommandBehavior value for the DataReader. In this case, we passed in the CommandBehavior.CloseConnection value so that the connection to the database will be closed once the DataReader has been closed. We will cover the DataReader in more detail in the next section.

Now that we have initiated the asynchronous call, and have defined a callback for our asynchronous call, let's look at the actual method that is getting called back, the AsyncCallback method:

```
Private Sub AsyncCallback(ByVal ar As IAsyncResult)
    ' Get the command that was passed from the AsyncState of the IAsyncResult.
    Dim command As SqlCommand = CType(ar.AsyncState, SqlCommand)
    ' Get the reader from the IAsyncResult.
    Dim reader As SqlDataReader = command.EndExecuteReader(ar)
    ' Get a table from the reader.
    Dim table As DataTable = Me.GetTableFromReader(reader, "Authors")
    ' Call the BindGrid method on the Windows main thread, passing in the table.
    Me.Invoke(New BindGridDelegate(AddressOf Me.BindGrid), _
        New Object() {table})
End Sub
```

The first line of the code is simply getting the SqlCommand object back from the AsyncState property of the IAsyncResult that was passed in to you. Remember, when we called BeginExecuteReader earlier we passed in our SqlCommand object. We need it so that we can call the EndExecuteReader method on the next line. This method gives us our SqlDataReader. On the next line, we then transform the SqlDataReader into a DataTable (we will cover that transformation later when we talk about the DataSet is disussed). The last line of this method is probably the most important. If we tried to just take our DataTable and bind it to the grid, it would not work, because right now we are executing on a thread other than the main Windows thread. There is a helper method named BindGrid to do the data binding, but it must be called only in the context of the Windows main thread. To bring the data back to the main Windows thread, it has to be marshaled via the Invoke method of the Form object. Invoke takes two arguments, the delegate of the method you want to call, and optionally any parameters for that method. In this case I have define a delegate for the BindGrid method, called BindGridDelegate. Here is the delegate declaration:

```
Private Delegate Sub BindGridDelegate(ByVal table As DataTable)
```

Notice how the signature is exactly the same as the BindGrid method shown here:

```
Private Sub BindGrid(ByVal table As DataTable)
    ' Clear the grid.
    Me._authorsGridView.DataSource = Nothing
    ' Bind the grid to the DataTable.
    Me._authorsGridView.DataSource = table
End Sub
```

Here is another look at the call to the form's Invoke method:

```
        Me.Invoke(New BindGridDelegate(AddressOf Me.BindGrid), _

            New Object() {table})
```

In the line of code, we pass in a new instance of the BindGridDelegate delegate and initialize it with a pointer to the BindGrid method. As a result, the .NET worker thread that was executing our query can now safely join up with the main Windows thread.

DataAdapter Objects

Each .NET Data Provider included with the .NET Framework has a DataAdapter object. The OLE DB .NET Data Provider includes an OleDbDataAdapter object, and the SQL Server .NET Data Provider includes a SqlDataAdapter object. A DataAdapter is used to retrieve data from a data source and populate DataTable objects and constraints within a DataSet. The DataAdapter also resolves changes made to the DataSet back to the data source. The DataAdapter uses the Connection object of the .NET Data Provider to connect to a data source, and Command objects to retrieve data from, and resolve changes to, the data source from a DataSet object. This differs from the DataReader, in that the DataReader uses the Connection to access the data directly, without having to use a DataAdapter. The DataAdapter essentially decouples the DataSet object from the actual source of the data, whereas the DataReader is tightly bound to the data in a read-only fashion.

The SelectCommand property of the DataAdapter is a Command object that retrieves data from the data source. A nice, convenient way to set the DataAdapter's SelectCommand property is to pass in a Command object in the DataAdapter's constructor. The InsertCommand, UpdateCommand, and DeleteCommand properties of the DataAdapter are Command objects that manage updates to the data in the data source according to the modifications made to the data in the DataSet. The Fill method of the DataAdapter is used to populate a DataSet with the results of the SelectCommand of the DataAdapter. It also adds or refreshes rows in the DataSet to match those in the data source. In this example, the code shows how to fill a DataSet object with information from the authors table in the pubs database:

```
Private Sub TraverseDataSet()
    ' Build the SQL and Connection strings.
    Dim sql As String = "SELECT * FROM authors"
    Dim connectionString As String = "Initial Catalog=pubs;" _
        & "Data Source=(local);Integrated Security=SSPI;"

    ' Initialize the SqlDataAdapter with the SQL
    ' and Connection strings, and then use the
    ' SqlDataAdapter to fill the DataSet with data.
    Dim adapter As New SqlDataAdapter(sql, connectionString)
```

```
        Dim authors As New DataSet
        adapter.Fill(authors)

        ' Iterate through the DataSet's table.
        For Each row As DataRow In authors.Tables(0).Rows
            Console.WriteLine(row("au_fname").ToString _
                & " " & row("au_lname").ToString)
        Next

        ' Print the DataSet's XML.
        Console.WriteLine(authors.GetXml())
        Console.ReadLine()

    End Sub
```

Note how we use the `SqlDataAdapter`'s constructor to pass in and set the `SelectCommand`, as well as passing in the connection string in lieu of a `SqlCommand` object that already has an initialized `Connection` property. We then just call the `SqlDataAdapter` object's `Fill` method and pass in an initialized `DataSet` object. If the `DataSet` object is not initialized, the `Fill` method will raise an exception (`System.ArgumentNullException`).

In ADO.NET 2.0, a significant performance improvement was made in the way that the `DataAdapter` updates the database. In ADO.NET 1.*x*, the `DataAdapter`'s `Update` method would loop through each row of every `DataTable` object in the `DataSet` and then subsequently make a trip to the database for each row that was being updated. In ADO.NET 2.0, batch update support was added to the `DataAdapter`. This means that when the `Update` method is called, the `DataAdapter` batches all of the updates from the `DataSet` in one trip to the database.

Now, let's take a look at a more advanced example in which we use a `DataAdapter` to insert, update, and delete data from a `DataTable` back to the pubs database:

```
    Private Sub _batchUpdateButton_Click(ByVal sender As System.Object, _
            ByVal e As System.EventArgs) Handles _batchUpdateButton.Click

            ' Build insert, update, and delete commands.

            ' Build the parameter values.
            Dim insertUpdateParams() As String = {"@au_id", "@au_lname", "@au_fname", _
                "@phone", "@address", "@city", "@state", "@zip", "@contract"}
```

This code starts out by initializing a string array of parameter names to pass into the `BuildSqlCommand` helper method.

```
            ' Insert command.
            Dim insertCommand As SqlCommand = BuildSqlCommand("usp_authors_Insert", _
                insertUpdateParams)
```

Next,we pass the name of the stored procedure to execute and the parameters for the stored procedure to the BuildSqlCommand helper method. This method returns an initialized instance of the SqlCommand class. Here is the BuildSqlCommand helper method:

```
Private Function BuildSqlCommand(ByVal storedProcedureName As String, _
        ByVal parameterNames() As String) As SqlCommand
    ' Build a SqlCommand.
    Dim command As New SqlCommand(storedProcedureName, GetPubsConnection())
    ' Set the command type to stored procedure.
    command.CommandType = CommandType.StoredProcedure
    ' Build the parameters for the command.
    ' See if any parameter names were passed in.
    If Not parameterNames Is Nothing Then
        ' Iterate through the parameters.
        Dim parameter As SqlParameter = Nothing
        For Each parameterName As String In parameterNames
            ' Create a new SqlParameter.
            parameter = New SqlParameter()
            parameter.ParameterName = parameterName
            ' Map the parameter to a column name in the DataTable/DataSet.
            parameter.SourceColumn = parameterName.Substring(1)
            ' Add the parameter to the command.
            command.Parameters.Add(parameter)
        Next
    End If
    Return command
End Function
```

This method first initializes a SqlCommand class and passes in the name of a stored procedure, and it then uses the GetPubsConnection helper method to pass in a SqlConnection object to the SqlCommand. The next step is to set the command type of the SqlCommand to a stored procedure. This is important to do because ADO.NET uses this to optimize how the stored procedure is called on the database server. We then check to see if any parameter names have been passed (via the parameterNames string array), and if there were any, We then iterate through them. While iterating through the parameter names, We build up SqlParameter objects and add them to the SqlCommand's collection of parameters. The most important step in building up the SqlParameter object is to set its SourceColumn property. This is what the DataAdapter later uses to map the name of the parameter to the name of the column in the DataTable when its Update method is called. An example of such a mapping is associating the @au_id parameter name with the au_id column name. As you can see in the code, the mapping is assuming that the stored procedure parameters all have exactly the same names as the columns, except for the mandatory @ character in front of the parameter. That is why when assigning the SqlParameter's SourceColumn property value, we use the Substring method to strip off the @ character to make sure that it will map correctly.

We then call the BuildSqlCommand method two more times to build your update and delete SqlCommand objects.

```
        ' Update command.
        Dim updateCommand As SqlCommand = BuildSqlCommand("usp_authors_Update", _
```

```
        insertUpdateParams)

    ' Delete command.
    Dim deleteCommand As SqlCommand = BuildSqlCommand("usp_authors_Delete", _
        New String() {"@au_id"})
```

Now that the SqlCommand objects have been created, the next step is to create a SqlDataAdapter object. Once the SqlDataAdapter is created, we set its InsertCommand, UpdateCommand, and DeleteCommand properties with the respective SqlCommand objects that we just built.

```
    ' Create an adapter.
    Dim adapter As New SqlDataAdapter()

    ' Associate the commands with the adapter.
    adapter.InsertCommand = insertCommand
    adapter.UpdateCommand = updateCommand
    adapter.DeleteCommand = deleteCommand
```

The next step is to get a DataTable instance of the authors table from the pubs database. You do this by calling the GetAuthorsSqlReader helper method to first get a DataReader and then the GetTableFromReader helper method to load a DataTable from a DataReader.

```
    ' Get the authors reader.
    Dim reader As SqlDataReader = GetAuthorsSqlReader()
    ' Load a DataTable from the reader.
    Dim table As DataTable = GetTableFromReader(reader, "Authors")
```

Once we have our DataTable filled with data, the next step is to begin modifying it so we can test the new batch update capability of the DataAdapter. The first change we will make is an insert in the DataTable. In order to add a row, we first call the DataTable's NewRow method to give us a DataRow initialized with the same columns as our DataTable.

```
    ' Add a new author to the DataTable.
    Dim row As DataRow = table.NewRow
```

Once that is done, we then go ahead and set the values of the columns of the DataRow:

```
    row("au_id") = "335-22-0707"
    row("au_fname") = "Tim"
    row("au_lname") = "McCarthy"
    row("phone") = "760-930-0075"
    row("contract") = 0
```

Finally, we call the Add method of the DataTable's DataRowCollection property and pass in the newly populated DataRow object:

```
    table.Rows.Add(row)
```

Now that there is a new row in the DataTable, the next test is to update one of the rows in the DataTable:

```
    ' Change an author in the DataTable.
    table.Rows(0)("au_fname") = "Updated Name!"
```

And finally, we will delete a row from the DataTable. In this case, it will be the second to last row in the DataTable:

```
        ' Delete the second to last author from the table
        table.Rows(table.Rows.Count - 2).Delete()
```

Now that we have performed an insert, update, and delete action on our DataTable it is time to send the changes back to the database. We do this by calling the DataAdapter's Update method, and passing in either a DataSet or a DataTable. Note how we are calling the GetChanges method of the DataTable; this is important, because we only want to send the changes to the DataAdapter:

```
        ' Send only the changes in the DataTable to the database for updating.
        adapter.Update(table.GetChanges())
```

To prove that the update worked, we get back a new DataTable from the server using the same technique as before, and then bind it to the grid with our helper method to see the changes that were made:

```
        ' Get the new changes back from the server to show that the update worked.
        reader = GetAuthorsSqlReader()
        table = GetTableFromReader(reader, "Authors")
        ' Bind the grid to the new table data.
        BindGrid(table)
    End Sub
```

SQL Server .NET Data Provider

The SQL Server .NET Data Provider uses Tabular Data Stream (TDS), to communicate with the SQL Server. This offers a great performance increase, since TDS is SQL Server's native communication protocol. As an example of how much of an increase you can expect, when I ran some simple tests accessing the authors table of the pubs database we saw the SQL Server .NET Data Provider perform about 70 percent faster than the OLE DB .NET Data Provider.

The SQL Server .NET Data Provider is lightweight and performs very well, thanks to not having to go through the OLE DB or ODBC layer. What it actually does is that it establishes a networking connection (usually sockets based) and drags data from this directly into managed code and vice versa.

This is very important, since going through the OLE DB or ODBC layers means that the CLR has to marshal (convert) all of the COM data types to .NET CLR data types each time data is accessed from a data source. When using the SQL Server .NET Data Provider, everything runs within the .NET CLR, and the TDS protocol is faster than the other network protocols previously used for SQL Server.

To use this provider, you need to include the System.Data.SqlClient namespace in your application. Also, it will only work for SQL Server 7.0 and above. I highly recommend using SQL Server .NET Data Provider any time you are connecting to a SQL Server 7.0 and above database server. The SQL Server .NET Data Provider requires the installation of MDAC 2.6 or later.

OLE DB .NET Data Provider

The OLE DB .NET Data Provider uses native OLE DB through COM Interop (see Chapter 17 for more details) to enable data access. The OLE DB .NET Data Provider supports both manual and automatic transactions. For automatic transactions, the OLE DB .NET Data Provider automatically enlists in a transaction and obtains transaction details from Windows 2000 Component Services. The OLE DB .NET Data Provider does not support OLE DB 2.5 interfaces. OLE DB Providers that require support for OLE DB 2.5 interfaces will not function properly with the OLE DB .NET Data Provider. This includes the Microsoft OLE DB Provider for Exchange and the Microsoft OLE DB Provider for Internet Publishing. The OLE DB .NET Data Provider requires the installation of MDAC 2.6 or later. To use this provider, you need to include the `System.Data.OleDb` namespace in your application.

The DataSet Component

The `DataSet` object is central to supporting disconnected, distributed data scenarios with ADO.NET. The `DataSet` is a memory-resident representation of data that provides a consistent relational programming model regardless of the data source. The `DataSet` represents a complete set of data including related tables, constraints, and relationships among the tables; basically, like having a small relational database residing in memory.

> *Since the* `DataSet` *contains a lot of metadata in it, you need to be careful about how much data you try to stuff into it, since it will be consuming memory.*

The methods and objects in a `DataSet` are consistent with those in the relational database model. The `DataSet` can also persist and reload its contents as XML and its schema as XSD. It is completely disconnected from any database connections; therefore, it is totally up to you to fill it with whatever data you need in memory.

ADO.NET 2.0 has added several new features to `DataSet` and `DataTable` classes as well as adding enhancements to existing features. The new features we will talk about in this section are the following:

- The binary serialization format option.
- Additions to make the `DataTable` more of a stand-alone object.
- The ability to expose `DataSet` and `DataTable` data as a stream (`DataReader`) and also loading stream data into a `DataSet` or `DataTable`.

DataTableCollection

An ADO.NET `DataSet` contains a collection of zero or more tables represented by `DataTable` objects. The `DataTableCollection` contains all of the `DataTable` objects in a `DataSet`.

A `DataTable` is defined in the `System.Data` namespace and represents a single table of memory-resident data. It contains a collection of columns represented by the `DataColumnCollection`, which defines the schema and rows of the table. It also contains a collection of rows represented by the `DataRowCollection`, which contains the data in the table. Along with the current state, a `DataRow` retains its original state and tracks changes that occur to the data.

DataRelationCollection

A DataSet contains relationships in its DataRelationCollection object. A relationship (represented by the DataRelation object) associates rows in one DataTable with rows in another DataTable. The relationships in the DataSet can have constraints, which are represented by UniqueConstraint and ForeignKeyConstraint objects. It is analogous to a JOIN path that might exist between the primary and foreign key columns in a relational database. A DataRelation identifies matching columns in two tables of a DataSet.

Relationships enable you to see what links information within one table to another. The essential elements of a DataRelation are the name of the relationship, the two tables being related, and the related columns in each table. Relationships can be built with more than one column per table, with an array of DataColumn objects for the key columns. When a relationship is added to the DataRelationCollection, it may optionally add ForeignKeyConstraints that disallow any changes that would invalidate the relationship.

ExtendedProperties

DataSet (as well as DataTable and DataColumn) has an ExtendedProperties property. ExtendedProperties is a PropertyCollection where a user can place customized information, such as the SELECT statement that was used to generate the resultset, or a date/time stamp of when the data was generated. Since the ExtendedProperties contains customized information, this is a good place to store extra user-defined data about the DataSet (or DataTable or DataColumn), such as a time when the data should be refreshed. The ExtendedProperties collection is persisted with the schema information for the DataSet (as well as DataTable and DataColumn). The following code is an example of adding an expiration property to a DataSet:

```
Private Shared Sub DataSetExtended()

    ' Build the SQL and Connection strings.
    Dim sql As String = "SELECT * FROM authors"
    Dim connectionString As String = "Initial Catalog=pubs;" _
        & "Data Source=(local);Integrated Security=SSPI;"

    ' Initialize the SqlDataAdapter with the SQL
    ' and Connection strings, and then use the
    ' SqlDataAdapter to fill the DataSet with data.
    Dim adapter As SqlDataAdapter = _
        New SqlDataAdapter(sql, connectionString)
    Dim authors As New DataSet
    adapter.Fill(authors)

    ' Add an extended property called "expiration."
    ' Set its value to the current date/time + 1 hour.
    authors.ExtendedProperties.Add("expiration", _
        DateAdd(DateInterval.Hour, 1, Now))

    Console.Write(authors.ExtendedProperties("expiration").ToString)
    Console.ReadLine()

End Sub
```

This code starts out by filling a `DataSet` with the authors table from the pubs database. We then add a new extended property, called expiration, and set its value to the current date and time plus one hour. We then simply read it back. As you can see, it is very easy to add extended properties to `DataSet` objects. The same pattern also applies to `DataTable` and `DataColumn` objects.

Creating and Using DataSet Objects

The ADO.NET `DataSet` is a memory-resident representation of the data that provides a consistent relational programming model, regardless of the source of the data it contains. A `DataSet` represents a complete set of data including the tables that contain, order, and constrain the data, as well as the relationships between the tables. The advantage to using a `DataSet` is that the data in a `DataSet` can come from multiple sources, and it is fairly easy to get the data from multiple sources into the `DataSet`. Also, you can define your own constraints between the data tables in a `DataSet`.

There are several methods of working with a `DataSet`, which can be applied independently or in combination. You can:

- Programmatically create `DataTables`, `DataRelations`, and `Constraints` within the `DataSet` and populate them with data
- Populate the `DataSet` or a `DataTable` from an existing RDBMS using a `DataAdapter`
- Load and persist a `DataSet` or `DataTable` using XML
- Load a `DataSet` from an XSD schema file
- Load a `DataSet` or a `DataTable` from a `DataReader`

Here is a typical usage scenario for a `DataSet` object:

1. A client makes a request to a Web service.
2. Based on this request, the Web service populates a `DataSet` from a database using a `DataAdapter` and returns the `DataSet` to the client.
3. The client then views the data and makes modifications.
4. When finished viewing and modifying the data, the client passes the modified `DataSet` back to the Web service, which again uses a `DataAdapter` to reconcile the changes in the returned `DataSet` with the original data in the database.
5. The Web service may then return a `DataSet` that reflects the current values in the database.
6. (Optional) The client can then use the `DataSet` class's `Merge` method to merge the returned `DataSet` with the client's existing copy of the `DataSet`; the `Merge` method will accept successful changes and mark with an error any changes that failed.

The design of the ADO.NET `DataSet` makes this scenario fairly easy to implement. Since the `DataSet` is stateless, it can be safely passed between the server and the client without tying up server resources such as database connections. Although the `DataSet` is transmitted as XML, Web services and ADO.NET automatically transform the XML representation of the data to and from a `DataSet`, creating a rich, yet simplified, programming model. In addition, because the `DataSet` is transmitted as an XML stream, non-ADO.NET clients can consume the same Web service as that consumed by ADO.NET clients.

Similarly, ADO.NET clients can interact easily with non-ADO.NET Web services by sending any client DataSet to a Web service as XML and by consuming any XML returned as a DataSet from the Web service. One thing to be careful of is the size of the data; if there are a large number of rows in the tables of your DataSet, then it will eat up a lot of bandwidth.

Programmatically Creating DataSet Objects

You can programmatically create a DataSet object to use as a data structure in your programs. This could be quite useful if you have complex data that needs to be passed around to another object's method. For example, when creating a new customer, instead of passing 20arguments about the new customer to a method, you could just pass the programmatically created DataSet object with all of the customer information to the object's method.

Here is the code for building an ADO.NET DataSet object that is comprised of related tables:

```
Private Sub BuildDataSet()

    Dim customerOrders As New Data.DataSet("CustomerOrders")
    Dim customers As Data.DataTable = customerOrders.Tables.Add("Customers")
    Dim orders As Data.DataTable = customerOrders.Tables.Add("Orders")
    Dim row As Data.DataRow

    With customers
        .Columns.Add("CustomerID", Type.GetType("System.Int32"))
        .Columns.Add("FirstName", Type.GetType("System.String"))
        .Columns.Add("LastName", Type.GetType("System.String"))
        .Columns.Add("Phone", Type.GetType("System.String"))
        .Columns.Add("Email", Type.GetType("System.String"))
    End With

    With orders
        .Columns.Add("CustomerID", Type.GetType("System.Int32"))
        .Columns.Add("OrderID", Type.GetType("System.Int32"))
        .Columns.Add("OrderAmount", Type.GetType("System.Double"))
        .Columns.Add("OrderDate", Type.GetType("System.DateTime"))
    End With

    customerOrders.Relations.Add("Customers_Orders", _
    customerOrders.Tables("Customers").Columns("CustomerID"), _
    customerOrders.Tables("Orders").Columns("CustomerID"))

    row = customers.NewRow()
    row("CustomerID") = 1
    row("FirstName") = "Miriam"
    row("LastName") = "McCarthy"
    row("Phone") = "555-1212"
    row("Email") = "tweety@hotmail.com"
    customers.Rows.Add(row)

    row = orders.NewRow()
    row("CustomerID") = 1
    row("OrderID") = 22
    row("OrderAmount") = 0
    row("OrderDate") = #11/10/1997#
```

```
        orders.Rows.Add(row)

        Console.WriteLine(customerOrders.GetXml())
        Console.ReadLine()

    End Sub
```

Here is what the resulting XML of the DataSet looks like:

```
<CustomerOrders>
  <Customers>
    <CustomerID>1</CustomerID>
    <FirstName>Miriam</FirstName>
    <LastName>McCarthy</LastName>
    <Phone>555-1212</Phone>
    <Email>tweety@hotmail.com</Email>
</Customers>
<Orders>
  <CustomerID>1</CustomerID>
  <OrderID>22</OrderID>
  <OrderAmount>0</OrderAmount>
  <OrderDate>1997-11-10T00:00:00.0000</OrderDate>
</Orders>
</CustomerOrders>
```

We start out by first defining a DataSet object (customerOrders) named CustomerOrders. We then create two tables, one for customers (customers), and one for orders (orders), we then define the columns of the tables. Notice how we call the Add method of the DataSet's Tables collection. We then define the columns of each of the tables and create a relation in the DataSet between the Customers table and the Orders table on the CustomerID column. Finally, we create instances of Rows for the tables, add the data, and then append the Rows to the Rows collection of the DataTable objects. If you create a DataSet object with no name, it will be given the default name of NewDataSet.

ADO.NET DataTable Objects

A DataSet is made up of a collection of tables, relationships, and constraints. In ADO.NET, DataTable objects are used to represent the tables in a DataSet. A DataTable represents one table of in-memory relational data. The data is local to the .NET application in which it resides, but can be populated from a data source such as SQL Server using a DataAdapter.

The DataTable class is a member of the System.Data namespace within the .NET Framework class library. You can create and use a DataTable independently or as a member of a DataSet, and DataTable objects can also be used by other the .NET Framework objects, including the DataView. You access the collection of tables in a DataSet through the DataSet object's Tables property.

The schema, or structure, of a table is represented by columns and constraints. You define the schema of a DataTable using DataColumn objects as well as ForeignKeyConstraint and UniqueConstraint objects. The columns in a table can map to columns in a data source, contain calculated values from expressions, automatically increment their values, or contain primary key values.

If you populate a DataTable from a database, it will inherit the constraints from the database, so you do not have to do all of that work manually. A DataTable must also have rows in which to contain and order the data. The DataRow class represents the actual data contained in the table. You use the DataRow and its properties and methods to retrieve, evaluate, and manipulate the data in a table. As you access and change the data within a row, the DataRow object maintains both its current and original state.

You can create parent/child relationships between tables within a database, like SQL Server, using one or more related columns in the tables. You create a relationship between DataTable objects using a DataRelation, which can then be used to return a row's related child or parent rows.

ADO.NET 2.0 Enhancements to the DataSet and DataTable

One of the main complaints developers had in ADO.NET 1.*x* was with the performance of the DataSet and its DataTable children, in particular when there is a large amount of data in them. The performance hit comes in two different ways; the first way is the time it takes to actually load a DataSet with a lot of data. As the number of rows in a DataTable increases, the time to load a new row increases almost proportionally to the number of rows in the DataTable. The second way is when the large DataSet is serialized and remoted. A key feature of the DataSet is the fact that it automatically knows how to serialize itself, especially when we want to pass it between application tiers. The only problem is that the serialization is quite verbose and takes up a lot of memory and network bandwidth. Both of these performance problems are addressed in ADO.NET 2.0.

Indexing

The first improvement to the DataSet family was that the indexing engine for the DataTable has been completely rewritten and it now scales much better for large datasets. The addition of the new indexing engine results in faster basic inserts, updates, and deletes, which also means faster Fill and Merge operations. Just as in relational database design, if you are dealing with large DataSets it really pays big dividends now if you add unique keys and foreign keys to your DataTable. The nice part, though, is that you do not have to change any of your code at all to take advantage of this new feature.

Serialization

The second improvement made to the DataSet family was adding new options to the way that the DataSet and DataTable are serialized. The main complaint about retrieving DataSet objects from Web services and remoting calls was that they were way too verbose and took up too much network bandwidth. In ADO.NET 1.*x*, the DataSet serializes as XML, even when using the binary formatter. In ADO.NET 2.0, in addition to this behavior, we can also specify true binary serialization, by setting the newly added RemotingFormat property to SerializationFormat.Binary rather than (the default) SerializationFormat.XML. In the AdoNetFeaturesTest project of the Examples solution I have added a Button (_serializationButton) to the form and its associated Click event handler that demonstrates how to serialize a DataTable in binary format:

```
Private Sub _serializationButton_Click(ByVal sender As System.Object, _
    ByVal e As System.EventArgs) Handles _serializationButton.Click

        ' Get the authors reader.
        Dim reader As SqlDataReader = GetAuthorsSqlReader()
        ' Load a DataTable from the reader
        Dim table As DataTable = GetTableFromReader(reader, "Authors")
```

This code starts out by calling the helper methods GetAuthorsSqlReader and GetTableFromReader to get a DataTable of the authors from the pubs database. The next code block, shown below, is where we are actually serializing the DataTable out to a binary format:

```
        Using fs As New FileStream("c:\authors.dat", FileMode.Create)
            table.RemotingFormat = SerializationFormat.Binary
            Dim format As New BinaryFormatter
            format.Serialize(fs, table)
        End Using

        ' Tell the user what happened.
        MsgBox("Successfully serialized the DataTable!")
    End Sub
```

This code takes advantage of the newly added Using statement for VB.NET to wrap up creating and disposing of a FileStream instance that will hold a serialized DataTable data. The next step is to set the DataTable's RemotingFormat property to the SerializationFormat.Binary enumeration value. Once that is done, simply create a new BinaryFormatter instance, and then call its Serialize method to serialize the DataTable into the FileStream instance. Then finish by showing a message box to the user that the data has been serialized.

DataReader Integration

Another nice feature of the DataSet and DataTable classes is the ability to both read from and write out to a stream of data in the form of a DataReader. We'll first take a look at how you can load a DataTable from a DataReader. To demonstrate this, I have added a Button (_loadFromReaderButton) and its associated Click event handler to TestForm.vb of the AdoNetFeaturesTest project in the Examples solution:

```
    Private Sub _loadFromReaderButton_Click(ByVal sender As System.Object, _
        ByVal e As System.EventArgs) Handles _loadFromReaderButton.Click

        ' Get the authors reader.
        Dim reader As SqlDataReader = GetAuthorsSqlReader()

        ' Load a DataTable from the reader.
        Dim table As DataTable = GetTableFromReader(reader, "Authors")

        ' Bind the grid to the table.
        BindGrid(table)
        End Sub
```

This method is a controller method, meaning that it only calls helper methods. It starts out by first obtaining a SqlDataReader from the GetAuthorsReader helper method. It then calls the GetTableFromReader helper method to transform the DataReader into a DataTable. The GetTableFromReader method is where we actually get to see the DatatTable's new load functionality:

```
    Private Function GetTableFromReader(ByVal reader As SqlDataReader, _
        ByVal tableName As String) As DataTable
        ' Create a new DataTable using the name passed in.
        Dim table As New DataTable(tableName)
```

```
        ' Load the DataTable from the reader.
        table.Load(reader)
        ' Close the reader.
        reader.Close()
        Return table
    End Function
```

This method starts out by first creating an instance of a DataTable and initializing it with the name passed in from the tableName argument. Once the new DataTable has been initialized, we call the new Load method and pass in the SqlDataReader that was passed into the method via the reader argument. This is where the DataTable takes the DataReader and populates the DataTable instance with the column names and data from the DataReader. The next step is to close the DataReader, since we have finished our use of it, and finally, return the newly populated DataTable.

DataTable Independence

One of the most convenient enhancements to ADO.NET 2.0 has been the addition of several methods from the DataSet class to the DataTable class. The DataTable is now much more versatile and useful than it was in ADO.NET 1.*x*. The DataTable now supports all of the same read and write methods for XML as the DataSet, specifically the ReadXml, ReadXmlSchema, WriteXml, and WriteXmlSchema methods.

Also, the Merge method of the DataSet has now been added to the DataTable as well. In addition to the existing functionality of the DataSet class, some of the new features of the DataSet class have also been added to the DataTable class, namely the RemotingFormat property, the Load method, and the GetDataReader method.

Working with the Common Provider Model

In ADO.NET 1.*x*, you could either code to the provider-specific classes, such as SqlConnection, or the generic interfaces, such as IDbConnection. If there was the possibility that the database you were programming against would change during your project, or if you were creating a commercial package intended to support customers with different databases, then you had to use the generic interfaces. You can't call a constructor on an interface, so most generic programs included code that accomplished the task of obtaining the original IDbConnection by means of their own factory method, such as a GetConnection method that would return a provider-specific instance of the IDbConnection interface.

ADO.NET 2.0 has a more elegant solution for getting the provider-specific connection. Each data provider registers a ProviderFactory class and a provider string in the .NET machine.config. There is a base ProviderFactory class (DbProviderFactory) and a System.Data.Common.ProviderFactories class that can return a DataTable of information about different data providers registered in machine.config, and it can also return the correct ProviderFactory given the provider string (called ProviderInvariantName) or a DataRow from the DataTable. Instead of writing your own framework to build connections based on the name of the provider, ADO.NET 2.0 makes it much more straightforward, flexible, and easier to solve this problem.

Let's look at an example of using the common provider model to connect to the pubs database and display some rows from the authors table. In the `AdoNetFeaturesTest` project, on the `TestForm.vb` Form, the `_providerButton Button`'s `Click` event handler shows this functionality. I have broken down this code into six steps, and we will look at each step.

The first step is get the provider factory object based on a configuration value of the provider's invariant name:

```
Private Sub _providerButton_Click(ByVal sender As System.Object, _
 ByVal e As System.EventArgs) Handles _providerButton.Click
        ' 1. Factory
        ' Create the provider factory from config value.
        Dim factory As DbProviderFactory =
DbProviderFactories.GetFactory(ConfigurationSettings.AppSettings("providerInvariant
Name"))
```

We are able to get the factory via the `DbProviderFactories` object's `GetFactory` method and passing in the string name of the provider invariant that we are storing in the project's `app.config` file. Here is the entry in the `app.config` file:

```
<add key="providerInvariantName" value="System.Data.SqlClient" />
```

In this case, we are using the SQL Server data provider. Once we have the factory object, the next step is to use it to create a connection:

```
        ' 2. Connection
        ' Create the connection from the factory.
        Dim connection As DbConnection = factory.CreateConnection()
        ' Get the connection string from config.
        connection.ConnectionString =
ConfigurationSettings.AppSettings("dbConnectionString")
```

The connection is created by calling the `DbProviderFactory`'s `CreateConnection` method. In this case, the factory will be giving back a `SqlConnection`, because we chose to use the `System.Data.SqlClient` provider invariant. To keep our code generic, we will not be directly programming against any of the classes in the `System.Data.SqlClient` namespace. Note how the connection class we declared was a `DbConnection` class, which is part of the `System.Data` namespace.

The next step is to create a `Command` object, so we can retrieve the data from the authors table:

```
        ' 3. Command
        ' Create the command from the connection.
        Dim command As DbCommand = connection.CreateCommand()
        ' Set the type of the command to stored procedure.
        command.CommandType = CommandType.StoredProcedure
        ' Set the name of the stored procedure to execute.
        command.CommandText = "usp_authors_Get_All"
```

Begin by declaring a generic `DbCommand` class variable and then using the `DbConnection`'s `CreateCommand` method to create the `DbCommand` instance. Once we have done that, we set the command type to stored procedure and then set the stored procedure name.

In this example, we will be using a DbDataAdapter to fill a DataTable with the author's data. Here is how we create and initialize the DbDataAdapter:

```
        ' 4. Adapter
        ' Create the adapter from the factory.
        Dim adapter As DbDataAdapter = factory.CreateDataAdapter()
        ' Set the adapter's select command.
        adapter.SelectCommand = command
```

Just as you did when we created DbConnection instance, agai use the factory to create DbDataAdapter. After creating it, then set the SelectCommand property's value to the instance of the previously initialized DbCommand instance.

After finishing these steps, the next step is to create a DataTable and fill it using the DataAdapter:

```
        ' 5. DataTable
        ' Create a new DataTable.
        Dim authors As New DataTable("Authors")
        ' Use the adapter to fill the DataTable.
        adapter.Fill(authors)
```

The final step is to bind the table to the form's grid:

```
        ' 6.  Grid
        ' Populate the grid with the data.
        BindGrid(authors)
```

We already looked at the BindGrid helper method in the asynchronous example earlier. In this example, we are simply reusing this generic method again.

```
    Private Sub BindGrid(ByVal table As DataTable)

        ' Clear the grid.

        Me._authorsGridView.DataSource = Nothing

        ' Bind the grid to the DataTable.

        Me._authorsGridView.DataSource = table

    End Sub
```

The main point to take away from this example is that we were able to easily write database-agnostic code in just a few short lines of code. Although this was possible to do in ADO.NET 1.*x*, it required a lot of lines of code to create this functionality; you had to write your own abstract factory classes and factory methods in order to create instances of the generic database interfaces, such as IDbConnection, IDbCommand, and so on.

Connection Pooling Enhancements in ADO.NET 2.0

Pooling connections can significantly enhance the performance and scalability of your application. Both the SQL Client .NET Data Provider and the OLE DB .NET Data Provider automatically pool connections using Windows Component Services and OLE DB Session Pooling, respectively. The only requirement is that you must use the exact same connection string each time if you want to get a pooled connection.

ADO.NET 2.0 enhances the connection pooling functionality offered in ADO.NET 1.*x* by allowing you to close all of the connections currently kept alive by the particular managed provider that you are using. You can clear a specific connection pool by using the shared `SqlConnection.ClearPool` method or clear all of the connection pools in an application domain by using the shared `SqlConnection.ClearPools` method. Both the SQL Server and Oracle managed providers implement this functionality.

Building a Data Access Component

To better demonstrate what we have learned so far about ADO.NET, we are going to build a data access component. This component is designed to abstract the processing of stored procedures. The component we are building will be targeted at SQL Server, and it is assumed that all data access to the database will be through stored procedures. The idea of only using stored procedures to access data in a database has a number of advantages, such as scalability, performance, flexibility, security, and so on. The only disadvantage is that you have to use stored procedures, and not SQL strings. Through the process of building this component we will see how stored procedures are implemented in ADO.NET. We will also be building on the knowledge that we have gained from the previous chapters.

This component's main job is to abstract stored procedure calls to SQL Server, and one of the ways we do this is by passing in all of the stored procedure parameter metadata as XML. We will look at this XML later in this section. The other job of the component is to demonstrate the use of some of the new objects in ADO.NET.The code for this project is quite extensive and you will only examine the key parts of it in this chapter. The full source is available in the code download.Let's start with the beginning of the component. The first thing we do is declare the class and the private members of the class:

```
Option Explicit On
Option Strict On

Imports System
Imports System.Data
Imports System.Data.SqlClient
Imports System.Xml
Imports System.Collections
Imports System.Diagnostics

''' <summary>
''' This class wraps stored procedure calls to SQL Server. It requires that all
''' stored procedures and their parameters be defined in an XML document before
''' calling any of its methods. The XML can be passed in as an XmlDocument
''' instance or as a string of XML.  The only exceptions to this rule are
''' stored procedures that do not have parameters. This class also caches
```

```
''' SqlCommand objects. Each time a stored procedure is executed, a SqlCommand
''' object is built and cached into memory so that the next time the stored
''' procedure is called the SqlCommand object can be retrieved from memory.
''' </summary>
Public NotInheritable Class StoredProcedureHelper

    Private _connectionString As String = ""
    Private _spParamXml As String = ""
    Private _spParamXmlDoc As XmlDocument = Nothing
    Private _spParamXmlNode As XmlNode = Nothing
    Private _commandParametersHashTable As New Hashtable()

    Private Const ExceptionMsg As String = "There was an error in the method.  " _
        & "Please see the Windows Event Viewer Application log for details"
```

Start out with the `Option` statements. Note that when using the `Option Strict` statement. This helps prevent logic errors and data loss that can occur when you work between variables of different types. Next, import the namespaces that we need for the component. In this case, most of your dependencies are on `System.Data.SqlClient`. We'll call the class `StoredProcedureHelper`, to indicate that it wraps calling stored procedures to SQL Server. Next, declare the private data members. Then use the `ExceptionMsg` constant to indicate a generic error message for any exceptions that we throw.

Constructors

Now, we get to declare our constructors for the `StoredProcedureHelper` class. This is where we can really take advantage of method overloading, and it gives you a way to pass data to your class upon instantiation. First,declare a default constructor:

```
''' <summary>
''' Default constructor.
''' </summary>
Public Sub New()
End Sub
```

The default constructor is provided in case people want to pass data to your class through public properties instead of through constructor arguments.

The next constructor we create allows for a database connection string to be passed in. By abstracting the database connection string out of this component, we give users of our component more flexibility in how they decide to store and retrieve their database connection strings. Here is the code for the constructor:

```
''' <summary>
''' Overloaded constructor.
''' </summary>
''' <param name="connectionString">The connection string to the
''' SQL Server database.</param>
Public Sub New(ByVal connectionString As String)
    Me._connectionString = connectionString
End Sub
```

The only difference between this constructor and the default constructor is that we are passing in a database connection string.

In the next constructor, we pass in both a database connection string and a string of XML representing the stored procedure parameters for the stored procedures we want to call. Here is the code for the constructor:

```
''' <summary>
''' Overloaded constructor.
''' </summary>
''' <param name="connectionString">The connection string to the
''' SQL Server database.</param>
''' <param name="spParamXml">A valid XML string which conforms to
''' the correct schema for stored procedure(s) and their
''' associated parameter(s).</param>
Public Sub New(ByVal connectionString As String, ByVal spParamXml As String)
    Me.New(connectionString)
    Me._spParamXml = spParamXml
    Me._spParamXmlDoc = New XmlDocument
    Try
        Me._spParamXmlDoc.LoadXml(spParamXml)
        Me._spParamXmlNode = Me._spParamXmlDoc.DocumentElement
    Catch e As XmlException
        LogError(e)
        Throw New Exception(ExceptionMsg, e)
    End Try
End Sub
```

This constructor sets the database connection string by calling the first overloaded constructor. This is a handy technique that will keep you from having to write duplicate code in your constructors. The constructor then loads the stored procedure parameter configuration into a private `XmlDocument` instance variable as well as a private `XmlNode` instance variable.

The remaining constructors allow you to pass in combinations of database connection strings as well as either a valid `XmlDocument` instance representing the stored procedure parameters or a valid `XmlNode` instance that represents the stored procedure parameters.

Properties

Now, let's look at the properties of our class. The object contains the following properties: `ConnectionString`, `SpParamXml`, and `SpParamXmlDoc`. All of the properties are provided as a courtesy in case the user of the object did not want to supply them via a constructor call. The `ConnectionString` property performs the same functionality as the first overloaded constructor we looked at. The `SpParamXml` property allows the user of the object to pass in a valid XML string representing the stored procedures parameter metadata. All of the properties are read-write. The `SpParamXmlDoc` property allows the user to pass in an `XmlDocument` instance representing the stored procedures' parameter metadata.

Here is the code for the `SpParamXml` property:

```
''' <summary>
''' A valid XML string which conforms to the correct schema for
''' stored procedure(s) and their associated parameter(s).
''' </summary>
```

```
Public Property SpParamXml() As String
    Get
        Return Me._spParamXml
    End Get
    Set(ByVal Value As String)
        Me._spParamXml = Value
        ' Set the XmlDocument instance to null, since
        ' an XML string is being passed in.
        Me._spParamXmlDoc = Nothing
        Try
            Me._spParamXmlDoc.LoadXml(Me._spParamXml)
            Me._spParamXmlNode = Me._spParamXmlDoc.DocumentElement
        Catch e As XmlException
            LogError(e)
            Throw New Exception(ExceptionMsg)
        End Try
    End Set
End Property
```

The interesting thing to note about this property is that it makes sure to reset the `XmlDocument` instance to `Nothing` before trying to load the document. This is in case it was already set in one of the overloaded constructors, or from a previous call to this property. It also sets the `XmlNode` instance to the `DocumentElement` property of the `XmlDocument` instance, thus keeping them both in sync.

Stored Procedure XML Structure

In this case, rather than having the user of this class be responsible for populating the `Parameters` collection of a `Command` object, we will abstract it out into an XML structure. The structure is very simple; it basically allows you to store the metadata for one or more stored procedures at a time. This has a huge advantage in the fact that you can change all of the parameters on a stored procedure without having to recompile this project. The following is what the XML structure for the metadata looks like:

```
<StoredProcedures>
 <StoredProcedure name>
  <Parameters>
   <Parameter name size datatype direction isNullable sourceColumn />
  </Parameters>
 </StoredProcedure>
</StoredProcedures>
```

Here is what some sample data for the XML structure looks like:

```
<?xml version="1.0"?>
<StoredProcedures>
 <StoredProcedure name="usp_Get_Authors_By_States">
  <Parameters>
   <Parameter name="@states" size="100" datatype="VarChar"
    direction="Input" isNullable="True" />
   <Parameter name="@state_delimiter" size="1" datatype="Char"
    direction="Input" isNullable="True" />
  </Parameters>
 </StoredProcedure>
</StoredProcedures>
```

The valid values for the direction attribute are `Input`, `Output`, `ReturnValue`, and `InputOutput`. These values map directly to the `System.Data.Parameter` enumeration values. The valid values for the datatype attribute are `BigInt`, `Binary`, `Bit`, `Char`, `DateTime`, `Decimal`, `Float`, `Image`, `Int`, `Money`, `NChar`, `NText`, `NVarChar`, `Real`, `SmallDateTime`, `SmallInt`, `SmallMoney`, `Text`, `Timestamp`, `TinyInt`, `UniqueIdentifier`, `VarBinary`, `VarChar`, and `Variant`. These values map directly to the `System.Data.SqlDbType` enumeration values.

Methods

We have just finished looking at the stored procedure XML structure the class expects, as well as the public properties and public constructors for the class. Now, let's turn our attention to the public methods of our class.

ExecSpReturnDataSet

This public function executes a stored procedure and returns a `DataSet` object. It takes a stored procedure name (`String`), an optional `DataSet` name (`String`), and an optional list of parameter names and values (`IDictionary`). Here is the code for `ExecSpReturnDataSet`:

```
''' <summary>
''' Executes a stored procedure with or without parameters and returns a
''' populated DataSet object.
''' </summary>
''' <param name="spName">The name of the stored procedure to execute.</param>
''' <param name="dataSetName">An optional name for the DataSet instance.</param>
''' <param name="paramValues">A name-value pair of stored procedure parameter
''' name(s) and value(s).</param>
''' <returns>A populated DataSet object.</returns>
Public Function ExecSpReturnDataSet(ByVal spName As String, _
                ByVal dataSetName As String, _
                ByVal paramValues As IDictionary) As DataSet
    Dim command As SqlCommand = Nothing
    Try
        ' Get the initialized SqlCommand instance.
        command = GetSqlCommand(spName)
        ' Set the parameter values for the SqlCommand.
        SetParameterValues(command, paramValues)
        ' Initialize the SqlDataAdapter with the SqlCommand object.
        Dim sqlDA As New SqlDataAdapter(command)

        ' Initialize the DataSet.
        Dim ds As New DataSet()

        If Not (dataSetName Is Nothing) Then
            If dataSetName.Length > 0 Then
                ds.DataSetName = dataSetName
            End If
        End If

        ' Fill the DataSet.
        sqlDA.Fill(ds)

        ' Return the DataSet.
```

```
            Return ds
        Catch e As Exception
            LogError(e)
            Throw New Exception(ExceptionMsg, e)
        Finally
            ' Close and release resources.
            DisposeCommand(command)
        End Try
    End Function
```

This function uses three main objects to accomplish its mission: the `SqlCommand`, `SqlDataAdapter`, and the `DataSet` objects. We first wrap everything in a `Try-Catch-Finally` block to make sure that we trap any exceptions that are thrown and to properly close and release the `SqlCommand` and `SqlConnection` resources. The first thing we do is to call a helper method, `GetSqlCommand`, in order to get a fully initialized `SqlCommand` instance, to include any `SqlParameter` objects the `SqlCommand` may have based on our object's internal `XmlDocument`. Here is the code for `GetSqlCommand` and its overload:

```
''' <summary>
''' Initializes a SqlCommand object based on a stored procedure name
''' and a SqlTransaction instance. Verifies that the stored procedure
''' name is valid, and then tries to get the SqlCommand object from
''' cache. If it is not already in cache, then the SqlCommand object
''' is initialized and placed into cache.
''' </summary>
''' <param name="transaction">The transaction that the stored
''' procedure will be executed under.</param>
''' <param name="spName">The name of the stored procedure to execute.</param>
''' <returns>An initialized SqlCommand object.</returns>
Public Function GetSqlCommand(ByVal transaction As SqlTransaction, _
    ByVal spName As String) As SqlCommand

    Dim command As SqlCommand = Nothing

    ' Get the name of the stored procedure.
    If spName.Length < 1 Or spName.Length > 127 Then
        Throw New ArgumentOutOfRangeException("spName", _
            "Stored procedure name must be from 1 - 128 characters.")
    End If

    ' See if the command object is already in memory.
    Dim hashKey As String = Me._connectionString & ":" & spName
    command = CType(_commandParametersHashTable(hashKey), SqlCommand)
    If command Is Nothing Then
        ' It was not in memory.
        ' Initialize the SqlCommand.
        command = New SqlCommand(spName, GetSqlConnection(transaction))

        ' Tell the SqlCommand that we are using a stored procedure.
        command.CommandType = CommandType.StoredProcedure

        ' Build the parameters, if there are any.
        BuildParameters(command)

        ' Put the SqlCommand instance into memory.
```

```
            Me._commandParametersHashTable(hashKey) = command
        Else
            ' It was in memory, but we still need to set the
            ' connection property.
            command.Connection = GetSqlConnection(transaction)
        End If

        ' Return the initialized SqlCommand instance.
        Return command
    End Function

    ''' <summary>
    ''' Overload. Initializes a SqlCommand object based on a stored
    ''' procedure name, with no SqlTransaction instance.
    ''' Verifies that the stored procedure name is valid, and then tries
    ''' to get the SqlCommand object from cache. If it is not already in
    ''' cache, then the SqlCommand object is initialized and placed into cache.
    ''' </summary>
    ''' <param name="spName">The name of the stored procedure to execute.</param>
    ''' <returns>An initialized SqlCommand object.</returns>
    Public Function GetSqlCommand(ByVal spName As String) As SqlCommand
        ' Return the initialized SqlCommand instance.
        Return GetSqlCommand(Nothing, spName)
    End Function
```

The difference between this method and its overload is that the first method takes in a `SqlTransaction` instance argument, and the overload does not require the `SqlTransaction` instance to be passed in. The overload simply calls the first method and passes in a value of `Nothing` for the `SqlTransaction` argument.

This method first performs a check to make sure that the stored procedure name is between 1 and 128 characters long, in accordance with the SQL Server object naming conventions. If it is not, then we throw an exception. The next step this method performs is to try to get an already initialized `SqlCommand` object from the object's private `Hashtable` variable, `_commandParametersHashTable`, using the object's database connection string and the name of the stored procedure as the key. If the `SqlCommand` was not found, then go ahead and build the `SqlCommand` object by calling its constructor and passing in the stored procedure name and a `SqlConnection` instance returned from the `GetSqlConnection` helper method. The code then sets the `SqlCommand`'s `CommandType` property. We make sure that we pass in the `CommandType.StoredProcedure` enumeration value, since we are executing a stored procedure.

Once the `SqlCommand` object is properly initialized, we pass it to the `BuildParameters` method. We will take a look at this method in more detail later. After this step, the `SqlCommand` is fully initialized, and then place it into the object's internal cache (the `_commandParametersHashTable Hashtable` variable). Finally, the `SqlCommand` is returned to the calling code.

Getting back to the `ExecSpReturnDataSet` method, now that the `SqlCommand` object has been properly initialized, we need to set the values of the parameters. This will be done via another helper method called `SetParameterValues`. `SetParameterValues` take two arguments, a reference to a `SqlCommand` object, and an `IDictionary` interface. We are using an `IDictionary` interface instead of a class such as a `Hashtable` (which implements the `IDictionary` interface) in order to make the code more flexible. This is a good design practice and works quite well, for example, in the case where the user of the class has built his or her own custom dictionary object that implements the `IDictionary` interface. It then loops through the SqlCommand's Parameters collection and sets each SqlParameter's value based on the corresponding name-value pair in the IDictionary object as long as the parameter's direction is not Output. Following is the code for the SetParameterValues method:

```
''' <summary>
''' Traverses the SqlCommand's SqlParameters collection and sets the values
''' for all of the SqlParameter(s) objects whose direction is not Output and
''' whose name matches the name in the dictValues IDictionary that was
''' passed in.
''' </summary>
''' <param name="command">An initialized SqlCommand object.</param>
''' <param name="dictValues">A name-value pair of stored procedure parameter
''' name(s) and value(s).</param>
Public Sub SetParameterValues(ByVal command As SqlCommand, _
    ByVal dictValues As IDictionary)
    If command Is Nothing Then
        Throw New ArgumentNullException("command", _
            "The command argument cannot be null.")
    End If
    ' Traverse the SqlCommand's SqlParameters collection.
    Dim parameter As SqlParameter
    For Each parameter In command.Parameters
        ' Do not set Output parameters.
        If parameter.Direction <> ParameterDirection.Output Then
            ' Set the initial value to DBNull.
            parameter.Value = TypeCode.DBNull
            ' If there is a match, then update the parameter value.
            If dictValues.Contains(parameter.ParameterName) Then
                parameter.Value = dictValues(parameter.ParameterName)
            Else
                ' There was not a match.
                ' If the parameter value cannot be null, throw an exception.
                If Not parameter.IsNullable Then
                    Throw New ArgumentNullException(parameter.ParameterName, _
                        "Error getting the value for the " _
                        & parameter.ParameterName & " parameter.")
                End If
            End If
        End If
    Next parameter
End Sub
```

When traversing the SqlCommand's Parameters collection, if a SqlParameter's value cannot be found in the IDictionary instance, then a check is made to see whether the SqlParameter's value is allowed to be null or not. If it is allowed, then the value is set to DBNull; otherwise, an exception is thrown.

After setting the values of the parameters, the next step is to pass the SqlCommand object to the SqlDataAdapter's constructor:

```
' Initialize the SqlDataAdapter with the SqlCommand object.
Dim sqlDA As New SqlDataAdapter(command)
```

The next step is to try to set the name of the DataSet using the dataSetName method argument:

```
' Try to set the name of the DataSet.
If Not (dataSetName Is Nothing) Then
    If dataSetName.Length > 0 Then
        ds.DataSetName = dataSetName
    End If
End If
```

After doing this, we then call the Fill method of the SqlDataAdapter to fill the DataSet object:

```
' Fill the DataSet.
sqlDA.Fill(ds)
```

Then return the DataSet object back to the caller:

```
' Return the DataSet.
Return ds
```

If an exception was caught, then log the exception data to the Windows Application Log via the LogError private method, and then throw a new exception with the generic exception message. We nest the original exception inside of the new exception via the innerException constructor parameter:

```
Catch e As Exception
    LogError(e)
    Throw New Exception(ExceptionMsg, e)
```

In the Finally block, close and release the SqlCommand object's resources via the DisposeCommand helper method:

```
Finally
    ' Close and release resources
    DisposeCommand(command)
```

The DisposeCommand helper function closes the SqlCommand's SqlConnection property and disposes of the SqlCommand object:

```
''' <summary>
''' Disposes a SqlCommand and its underlying SqlConnection.
''' </summary>
''' <param name="command"></param>
Private Sub DisposeCommand(ByVal command As SqlCommand)
    If Not (command Is Nothing) Then
        If Not (command.Connection Is Nothing) Then
            command.Connection.Close()
            command.Connection.Dispose()
        End If
        command.Dispose()
    End If
End Sub
```

BuildParameters

This private method is the heart of this object and does the most work. It is responsible for parsing the stored procedure parameter XML and mapping all of the `SqlParameter` objects into the `Parameters` property of the `SqlCommand` object. Here is the signature of the method:

```
''' <summary>
''' Finds the parameter information for the stored procedure from the
''' stored procedures XML document and then uses that information to
''' build and append the parameter(s) for the SqlCommand's
''' SqlParameters collection.
''' </summary>
''' <param name="command">An initialized SqlCommand object.</param>
Private Sub BuildParameters(ByVal command As SqlCommand)
```

The first thing we do in this method is to see if in fact there is any XML being passed in or not. Here is the code that checks for the XML:

```
' See if there is an XmlNode of parameter(s) for the stored procedure.
If Me._spParamXmlNode Is Nothing Then
    ' No parameters to add, so exit.
    Return
End If
```

The last code simply checks if there is an `XmlNode` instance of parameter information. If the `XmlNode` has not been initialized, then we exit the method. It is entirely possible that users of this object may have stored procedures with no parameters at all. We have chosen an `XmlNode` object to parse the XML, as loading all of the stored procedure XML into memory will not hurt performance; it is a small amount of data. As an alternative, we could have used an `XmlReader` object to load in only what we needed into memory at runtime.

The next step is to clear the `SqlCommand` object's `Parameters` collection:

```
' Clear the parameters collection for the SqlCommand
command.Parameters.Clear()
```

We then use the name of the stored procedure as the key in the XPath query of the XML, and then execute the following XPath query to get the list of parameters for the stored procedure:

```
' Get the node list of <Parameter>'s for the stored procedure.
Dim xpathQuery As String = "//StoredProcedures/StoredProcedure[@name='" _
    & command.CommandText & "']/Parameters/Parameter"
Dim parameterNodes As XmlNodeList = Me._spParamXmlNode.SelectNodes(xpathQuery)
```

This query is executed off the `XmlDocument` object and returns an `XmlNodeList` object. We then start the loop through the `Parameter` elements in the XML and retrieve all of the mandatory `Parameter` attributes:

```
Dim parameterNode As XmlElement
For Each parameterNode In parameterNodes
    ' Get the attribute values for the <Parameter> element.

    ' Get the attribute values for the <Parameter> element.
```

```
        ' name
        Dim parameterName As String = parameterNode.GetAttribute("name")
        If parameterName.Length = 0 Then
            Throw New ArgumentNullException("name", "Error getting the 'name' " _
                & "attribute for the <Parameter> element.")
        End If

        ' size
        Dim parameterSize As Integer = 0
        If parameterNode.GetAttribute("size").Length = 0 Then
            Throw New ArgumentNullException("size", "Error getting the 'size' " _
                & "attribute for the <Parameter> element.")
        Else
            parameterSize = Convert.ToInt32(parameterNode.GetAttribute("size"))
        End If

        ' datatype
        Dim sqlDataType As SqlDbType
        If parameterNode.GetAttribute("datatype").Length = 0 Then
            Throw New ArgumentNullException("datatype", "Error getting the " _
                & "'datatype' attribute for the <Parameter> element.")
        Else
            sqlDataType = CType([Enum].Parse(GetType(SqlDbType), _
                parameterNode.GetAttribute("datatype"), True), SqlDbType)
        End If

        ' direction
        Dim parameterDirection As ParameterDirection = parameterDirection.Input
        If parameterNode.GetAttribute("direction").Length > 0 Then
            parameterDirection = CType([Enum].Parse(GetType(ParameterDirection), _
                parameterNode.GetAttribute("direction"), True), ParameterDirection)
        End If
    End If
```

Since these attributes are mandatory, if any of them are missing, we throw an exception. The interesting part of this code is that we are using the `Enum.Parse` static method to convert the string value from the XML into the correct .NET enumeration data type for the `sqlDataType` and `parameterDirection` variables. This is possible because the probable values in the XML for these attributes map directly to the names of their respective enumeration data types in .NET. Next, get the optional attributes:

```
' Get the optional attribute values for the <Parameter> element.

' isNullable
Dim isNullable As Boolean = False
Try
    If parameterNode.GetAttribute("isNullable").Length > 0 Then
        isNullable = Boolean.Parse(parameterNode.GetAttribute("isNullable"))
    End If
Catch
End Try

' sourceColumn -- This must map to the name of a column in a DataSet.
```

```
Dim sourceColumn As String = ""
Try
    If parameterNode.GetAttribute("sourceColumn").Length > 0 Then
        sourceColumn = parameterNode.GetAttribute("sourceColumn")
    End If
Catch
End Try
```

These attributes are optional mainly because of their data types. Since `isNullable` is Boolean, just go ahead and convert it to `False` if it is missing, and if `sourceColumn` is missing, just ignore it entirely.

Now, we are ready to create the `SqlParameter` object and set its `Direction` property. We do so with the following code:

```
' Create the parameter object.  Pass in the name, datatype,
' and size to the constructor.
Dim sqlParameter As SqlParameter = New SqlParameter(parameterName, _
    sqlDataType, parameterSize)

'Set the direction of the parameter.
sqlParameter.Direction = parameterDirection
```

We then set the optional property values of the `SqlParameter` object:

```
' If the optional attributes have values, then set them.
' IsNullable
If isNullable Then
    sqlParameter.IsNullable = isNullable
End If
' SourceColumn
sqlParameter.SourceColumn = sourceColumn
```

Finally, add the `SqlParameter` object to the `SqlCommand` object's `Parameters` collection, complete the loop, and finish the method:

```
' Add the parameter to the SqlCommand's parameter collection.
        command.Parameters.Add(sqlParameter)
    Next parameterNode
End Sub
```

Next, we are going to look at `ExecSpReturnDataReader`. This function is almost identical to `ExecSpReturnDataSet`, except that it returns a `SqlDataReader` object instead of a `DataSet` object.

ExecSpReturnDataReader

This public function executes a stored procedure and returns a `SqlDataReader` object. Similar to the `ExecSpReturnDataSet` method, it takes a stored procedure name (`String`) and an optional list of parameter names and values (`IDictionary`). Here is the code for `ExecSpReturnDataReader`:

```
''' <summary>
''' Executes a stored procedure with or without parameters and returns a
''' SqlDataReader instance with a live connection to the database. It is
```

```
''' very important to call the Close method of the SqlDataReader as soon
''' as possible after using it.
''' </summary>
''' <param name="spName">The name of the stored procedure to execute.</param>
''' <param name="paramValues">A name-value pair of stored procedure parameter
''' name(s) and value(s).</param>
''' <returns>A SqlDataReader object.</returns>
Public Function ExecSpReturnDataReader(ByVal spName As String, _
    ByVal paramValues As IDictionary) As SqlDataReader

    Dim command As SqlCommand = Nothing
    Try
        ' Get the initialized SqlCommand instance.
        command = GetSqlCommand(spName)

        ' Set the parameter values for the SqlCommand.
        SetParameterValues(command, paramValues)

        ' Open the connection.
        command.Connection.Open()

        ' Execute the sp and return the SqlDataReader.
        Return command.ExecuteReader(CommandBehavior.CloseConnection)
    Catch e As Exception
        LogError(e)
        Throw New Exception(ExceptionMsg, e)

    End Try

End Function
```

This function uses two objects to accomplish its mission: the `SqlCommand` and `SqlDataReader` objects. The only part where this function differs from `ExecSpReturnDataSet` is right after we call the `SetParameterValues` private method. In this case, we have to make sure that the `SqlCommand` object's `SqlConnection` is opened. This is because the `SqlDataReader` requires an open connection. Then call the `ExecuteReader` method of the `SqlCommand` object to get the `SqlDataReader` object, passing in the `CommandBehavior.CloseConnection` value for the method's behavior argument.

Since this method returns a `SqlDataReader` object, which requires an open database connection, do not close the connection in this method. It is up to the caller to close the `SqlDataReader` and the connection when finished. Since we used the `CommandBehavior.CloseConnection` value for the behavior argument, the user of the method only has to remember to call the `SqlDataReader`'s `Close` method in order to close the underlying `SqlConnection` object.

The next function we are going to look at, `ExecSpReturnXmlReader`, is almost identical to the last two functions, except that it returns an `XmlReader` instead of a `DataSet` or a `SqlDataReader`.

ExecSpReturnXmlReader

This public function executes a stored procedure and returns an `XmlReader` instance. The function requires that the stored procedure contains a `FOR XML` clause in its SQL statement. Once again, it takes a stored procedure name (`String`) and an optional list of parameter names and values (`IDictionary`). Here is the code for `ExecSpReturnXmlReader`:

```
''' <summary>
''' Executes a stored procedure with or without parameters and returns an
''' XmlReader instance with a live connection to the database. It is
''' very important to call the Close method of the XmlReader as soon
''' as possible after using it. Only use this method when calling stored
''' procedures that return XML results (FOR XML ...).
''' </summary>
''' <param name="spName">The name of the stored procedure to execute.</param>
''' <param name="paramValues">A name-value pair of stored procedure parameter
''' name(s) and value(s).</param>
''' <returns>An XmlReader object.</returns>
Public Function ExecSpReturnXmlReader(ByVal spName As String, _
    ByVal paramValues As IDictionary) As XmlReader

    Dim command As SqlCommand = Nothing
    Try
        ' Get the initialized SqlCommand instance.
        command = GetSqlCommand(spName)
        ' Set the parameter values for the SqlCommand.
        SetParameterValues(command, paramValues)

        ' Open the connection.
        command.Connection.Open()

        ' Execute the sp and return the XmlReader.
        Return command.ExecuteXmlReader()
    Catch e As Exception
        LogError(e)
        Throw New Exception(ExceptionMsg, e)
    End Try
End Function
```

The only difference between this method and `ExecSpReturnDataReader` is that you call the `ExecuteXmlReader` method of the `SqlCommand` object instead of the `ExecuteReader` method. Similarly to the `ExecSpReturnDataReader` method, users of this method need to close the returned `XmlReader` when finished using it in order to properly release resources.*This method will only work with SQL Server 2000 and above*Next, you look at the `ExecSp` method which only needs the `SqlCommand` object to get its work done. Its job is to execute stored procedures that do not return result sets.

ExecSp

This public method executes a stored procedure and does not return a value. It takes a stored procedure name (`String`) and an optional list of parameter names and values (`IDictionary`) for its arguments. Here is the code for `ExecSp`:

```
''' <summary>
''' Executes a stored procedure with or without parameters that
''' does not return output values or a resultset.
''' </summary>
```

```
''' <param name="transaction">The transaction that the stored procedure
''' will be executed under.</param>
''' <param name="spName">The name of the stored procedure to execute.</param>
''' <param name="paramValues">A name-value pair of stored procedure parameter
''' name(s) and value(s).</param>
Public Sub ExecSp(ByVal spName As String, ByVal paramValues As IDictionary)

    Dim command As SqlCommand = Nothing
    Try
        ' Get the initialized SqlCommand instance.
        command = GetSqlCommand(transaction, spName)
        ' Set the parameter values for the SqlCommand.
        SetParameterValues(command, paramValues)

        ' Run the stored procedure.
        RunSp(command)

    Catch e As Exception
        LogError(e)
        Throw New Exception(ExceptionMsg, e)
    Finally
        ' Close and release resources.
        DisposeCommand(command)
    End Try
End Sub
```

It is almost identical to the other `Exec*` functions, except when it executes the stored procedure. The code inside of the private `RunSp` method opens up the `SqlCommand`'s `SqlConnection` object and then it calls the `SqlCommand` object's `ExecuteNonQuery` method. This ensures that the `SqlCommand` does not return any type of `DataReader` object to read the results. This method will be mostly used to execute `INSERT`, `UPDATE`, and `DELETE` stored procedures that do not return any results. This method also has an overload that does not include the `SqlTransaction` argument.

Following is the code for `RunSp`:

```
''' <summary>
''' Opens the SqlCommand object's underlying SqlConnection and calls
''' the SqlCommand's ExecuteNonQuery method.
''' </summary>
''' <param name="command">An initialized SqlCommand object.</param>
Private Sub RunSp(ByRef command As SqlCommand)
    ' Open the connection.
    command.Connection.Open()

    ' Execute the stored procedure.
    command.ExecuteNonQuery()
End Sub
```

Finally, the last public function you are going to create is `ExecSpOutputValues`.

ExecSpOutputValues

This last public function in the component executes a stored procedure and returns an `IDictionary` object that contains output parameter name-value pairs. It is not meant for stored procedures that return result sets. As with the previous examples, this function takes a stored procedure name (`String`) and an optional list of parameter names and values (`IDictionary`) for its arguments. Here is the code for `ExecSpOutputValues`:

```
''' <summary>
''' Executes a stored procedure with or without parameters and returns an
''' IDictionary instance with the stored procedure's output parameter
''' name(s) and value(s).
''' </summary>
''' <param name="transaction">The transaction that the stored procedure
''' will be executed under.</param>
''' <param name="spName">The name of the stored procedure to execute.</param>
''' <param name="paramValues">A name-value pair of stored procedure parameter
''' name(s) and value(s).</param>
''' <returns>An IDictionary object.</returns>
Public Function ExecSpOutputValues(ByVal transaction As SqlTransaction, _
                                   ByVal spName As String, _
                                   ByVal paramValues As IDictionary) As IDictionary

    Dim command As SqlCommand = Nothing
    Try
        ' Get the initialized SqlCommand instance.
        command = GetSqlCommand(transaction, spName)
        ' Set the parameter values for the SqlCommand.
        SetParameterValues(command, paramValues)

        ' Run the stored procedure.
        RunSp(command)

        ' Get the output values.
        Dim outputParams As New Hashtable()
        Dim param As SqlParameter
        For Each param In command.Parameters
            If param.Direction = ParameterDirection.Output _
                Or param.Direction = ParameterDirection.InputOutput Then
                outputParams.Add(param.ParameterName, param.Value)
            End If
        Next param
        Return outputParams

    Catch e As Exception
        LogError(e)
        Throw New Exception(ExceptionMsg, e)
    Finally
        ' Close and release resources.
        DisposeCommand(command)
    End Try
End Function
```

This function is almost identical to ExecSp, except that after the SqlCommand.ExecuteNonQuery method is called we iterate through the SqlCommand object's Parameters collection and look for all of the parameters that are output parameters. Next, take the values of the output parameters and add the name-value pair to the IDictionary instance that we return. This method also has an overload that does not include the SqlTransaction argument.

Using DataSet Objects to Bind to DataGrids

Now that we have built the data access component, it is time to test it. A nice way to test it is to call the ExecSpReturnDataSet method, take the DataSet object that was created, and then bind the DataSet to a DataGrid. (You can find more about data binding in Chapter 14.) We also get to see how easily the DataSet and the DataGrid control integrate together. I have created a Windows Application project called SqlServerWrapperTestHarness and have added it to the Examples solution. It contains references to System, System.Data, System.Drawing, System.Windows.Forms, and System.Xml, as well as a project reference to the SqlServerWrapper project. I have added a form to the project named TestForm.vb, with two buttons, one for testing the ExecSpReturnDataSet method and one for testing the ExecSpReturnSqlRecord method. In this example, we will only be looking at the code for testing the ExecSpReturnDataSet method. Figure 11-4 shows what the test form looks like.

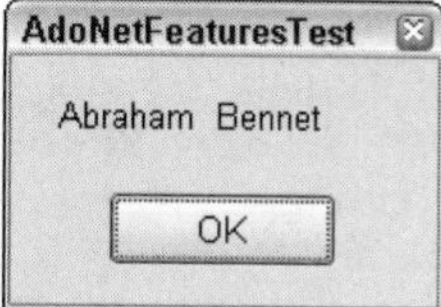

Figure 11-4

Figure 11-5 shows what your references should look like.

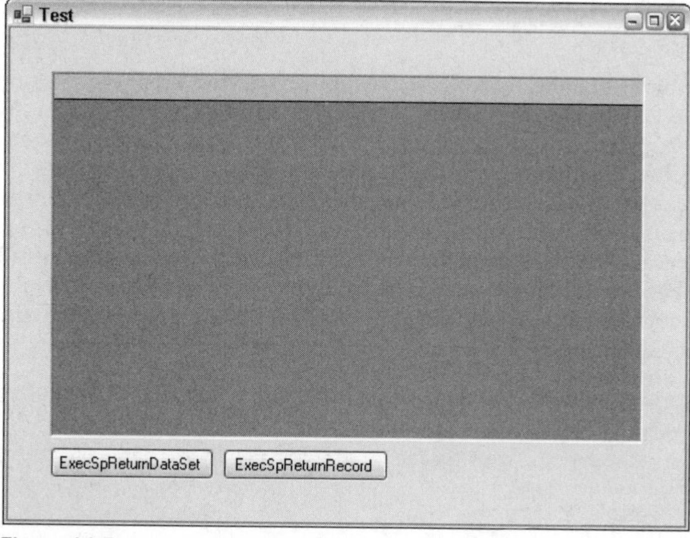

Figure 11-5

Here is the code dare the declarations and private members of the form:

```
Option Explicit On
Option Strict On
```

```
Imports SqlServerWrapper
Imports System.Data.SqlClient
Imports System.Xml
Imports System.Configuration

Public Class TestForm
    Inherits System.Windows.Forms.Form

    Private _helper As StoredProcedureHelper = Nothing
```

These declarations should look pretty familiar by now. Note that we are declaring a private variable (`_helper`) for the `StoredProcedureHelper` class that we are using so we can get to the class from other parts of the Form instead of just a `Button Click` event handler.

Next, we initialize the `_helper` variable in the form's `Load` event handler:

```
Private Sub TestForm_Load(ByVal sender As System.Object, _
    ByVal e As System.EventArgs) Handles MyBase.Load
    ' Set the SQL connection string
    Dim connectionString As String =
ConfigurationSettings.AppSettings("dbConnectionString")

    ' Call the SqlServer wrapper constructor and
    ' pass the DB connection string and the stored procedures config.
    helper = New StoredProcedureHelper(connectionString, _
        CType(ConfigurationSettings.GetConfig("StoredProcedureSettings"), _
        XmlNode))
    End Sub
```

As in the other examples before, this code starts out by retrieving a connection string to the pubs database from the `app.config` file. We then create a new instance of the `StoredProcedureHelper` and assign it to the `_helper` class variable. During the constructor call to the `StoredProcedureHelper` class, first pass in the connection string, and then pass in an `XmlNode` of the stored procedure metadata for the `StoredProcedureHelper` class to consume. This is interesting in the fact that we are passing the stored procedure metadata in to our class via the `GetConfig` method of the `ConfigurationSettings` class. This is so because we have created a section inside of our `app.config` file called `StoredProcedureSettings`, and we have configured a `SectionHandler` to let the .NET Framework application configuration functionality consume our XML and give it back to us as an `XmlNode`. Here is what this section looks like inside of the `app.config` file:

```
<configSections>
    <section name="StoredProcedureSettings"
type="SqlServerWrapper.StoredProcedureSectionHandler, SqlServerWrapper" />
  </configSections>
  <StoredProcedureSettings>
```

```
    <StoredProcedures>
      <StoredProcedure name="usp_Get_Authors_By_States">
        <Parameters>
          <Parameter name="@states" datatype="VarChar" direction="Input"
isNullable="false" size="100" />
          <Parameter name="@state_delimiter" datatype="Char" direction="Input"
isNullable="false" size="1" />
        </Parameters>
      </StoredProcedure>
      <StoredProcedure name="usp_Get_Author_By_ID">
        <Parameters>
          <Parameter name="@au_id" datatype="VarChar" direction="Input"
isNullable="false" size="11" />
        </Parameters>
      </StoredProcedure>
    </StoredProcedures>
  </StoredProcedureSettings>
```

This is nice because we do not need to include a separate XML file for the project; we just integrate seamlessly into the `app.config` file. Note how we are defining what class in what assembly will handle consuming the `<StoredProcedureSettings>` section in the `<section>` element. The requirement for this to work is that the class defined must implement the `System.Configuration.IConfigurationSectionHandler` interface. Here is the code for the section handler:

```
Option Explicit On
Option Strict On
```

```
Imports System
Imports System.Configuration
Imports System.Xml
Imports System.Xml.Serialization
Imports System.Xml.XPath

Public Class StoredProcedureSectionHandler
    Implements IConfigurationSectionHandler

    Public Function Create(ByVal parent As Object, _
        ByVal configContext As Object, _
        ByVal section As System.Xml.XmlNode) As Object _
            Implements IConfigurationSectionHandler.Create
        Return section("StoredProcedures")
    End Function
End Class
```

This code is pretty simple; just return the XML node named `StoredProcedures` to the caller of the handler.

Back to our `Button`'s `Click` event handler, once we have the `StoredProcedureHelper` class instance fully initialized, we then create the parameter values for the stored procedure we want to execute and pass these arguments to the `ExecSpReturnDataSet` method:

```
' Add the two parameter name-values.
Dim params As New Hashtable
params.Add("@states", "CA")
params.Add("@state_delimiter", "^")

' Execute the sp, and get the DataSet object back.
Dim ds As DataSet = _helper.ExecSpReturnDataSet("usp_Get_Authors_By_States", _
    "", params)
```

The last step is to actually bind the data to the form's grid:

```
' Bind the DataGrid to the DataSet object.
dgdAuthors.SetDataBinding(ds.Tables(0), Nothing)
```

Finally, the results should look like Figure 11-6.

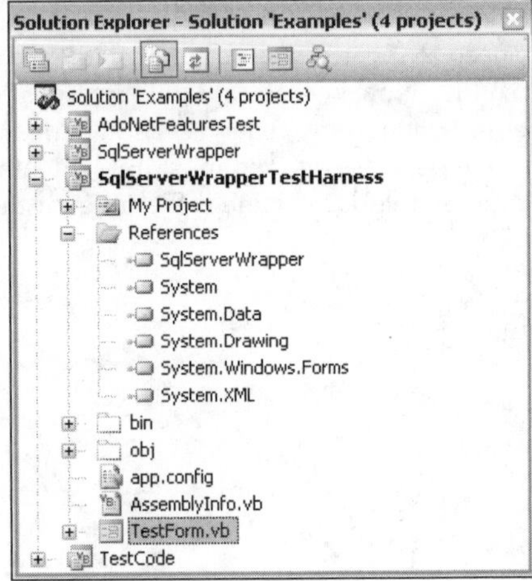

Figure 11-6

Summary

This chapter took a look at ADO.NET and the new features of ADO.NET 2.0. We have seen and used the main objects in ADO.NET that you need to quickly get up and running in order to build data access into your .NET applications. We took a fairly in-depth look at the `DataSet` and `DataTable` classes, since these are the core classes of ADO.NET.

We looked at stored procedures; first by showing how to create them in SQL Server and then how to access them from our code. Finally, we built our own custom data access component, which made it easy to call stored procedures and separate data access code from the rest of business logic code in a .NET application.

12

Using XML in Visual Basic 2005

In this chapter, we'll look at how you can generate and manipulate Extensible Markup Language (XML) using Visual Basic 2005. However, using XML in Visual Basic is a vast area to cover (more than possibly could be covered in this chapter). The .NET Framework exposes five XML-specific namespaces that contain over a hundred different classes. In addition, there are dozens of other classes that support and implement XML-related technologies, such as ADO.NET, SQL Server, and BizTalk. Consequently, we'll concentrate on the general concepts and the most important classes.

Visual Basic relies on the classes exposed in the following XML-related namespaces to transform, manipulate, and stream XML documents:

- `System.Xml` provides core support for a variety of XML standards (including DTD, namespace, DOM, XDR, XPath, XSLT, and SOAP).
- `System.Xml.Serialization` provides the objects used to transform objects to and from XML documents or streams using serialization.
- `System.Xml.Schema` provides a set of objects that allow schemas to be loaded, created, and streamed. This support is achieved using a suite of objects that support the in-memory manipulation of the entities that compose an XML schema.
- `System.Xml.XPath` provides a parser and evaluation engine for the XML Path Language (XPath).
- `System.Xml.Xsl` provides the objects necessary when working with Extensible Stylesheet Language (XSL) and XSL Transformations (XSLT).

The XML-related technologies utilized by Visual Basic include other technologies that generate XML documents and allow XML documents to be managed as a data source:

- **ADO** — The legacy COM objects provided by ADO have the ability to generate XML documents in stream or file form. ADO can also retrieve a previously persisted XML document and manipulate it. (Although ADO will not be used in this chapter, ADO and other legacy COM APIs can be accessed seamlessly from Visual Basic.)
- **ADO.NET** — This uses XML as its underlying data representation: the in-memory data representation of the ADO.NET `DataSet` object is XML; the results of data queries are represented as XML documents; XML can be imported into a `DataSet` and exported from a `DataSet`. (ADO.NET is covered in Chapter 11.)
- **SQL Server 2000** — XML-specific features were added to SQL Server 2000 (`FOR XML` queries to retrieve XML documents and `OPENXML` to represent an XML document as a rowset). Visual Basic can use ADO.NET to access SQL Server's XML-specific features (the documents generated and consumed by SQL Server can then be manipulated programmatically). Recently, Microsoft also released SQLXML, which provides an SQL Server 2000 database with some excellent XML capabilities, such as the ability to query a database using XQuery, get back XML result sets from a database, work with data just as if it was XML, take huge XML files and have SQLXML convert them to relational data, and much more. SQLXML allows you to perform these functions and more via a set of managed .NET classes. You can download SQLXML for free from the Microsoft SQLXML Web site at `http://msdn.microsoft.com/sqlxml`.
- **SQL Server 2005** — SQL Server has now been modified with XML in mind. SQL Server 2005 can natively understand XML because it is now built into the underlying foundation of the database. The ability to query and understand XML documents is a valuable addition to this database server. SQL Server 2005 also comes in a lightweight (and free) version called SQL Server Express Edition.

In this chapter, we'll make sense of this range of technologies by introducing some basic XML concepts and demonstrating how Visual Basic, in conjunction with the .NET Framework, can make use of XML. Specifically, you will:

- Learn the rationale behind XML.
- Look at the namespaces within the .NET Framework class library that deal with XML and XML-related technologies.
- Take a closer look at some of the classes contained within these namespaces.
- Gain an overview of some of the other Microsoft technologies that utilize XML, particularly SQL Server and ADO.NET.

At the end of this chapter, you will be able to generate, manipulate, and transform XML using Visual Basic.

An Introduction to XML

XML is a tagged markup language similar to HTML. In fact, XML and HTML are distant cousins and have their roots in the Standard Generalized Markup Language (SGML). This means that XML leverages one of the most useful features of HTML — readability. However, XML differs from HTML in that XML represents data, while HTML is a mechanism for displaying data. The tags in XML describe the data, for example:

```
<?xml version="1.0" encoding="utf-8"?>
<Movies>
  <FilmOrder name="Grease" filmId="1" quantity="21"></FilmOrder>
  <FilmOrder name="Lawrence of Arabia" filmId="2" quantity="10"></FilmOrder>
  <FilmOrder name="Star Wars" filmId="3" quantity="12"></FilmOrder>
  <FilmOrder name="Shrek" filmId="4" quantity="14"></FilmOrder>
</Movies>
```

This XML document is used to represent a store order for a collection of movies. The standard used to represent an order of films would be useful to movie rental firms, collectors, and others. This information can be shared using XML because:

- The data tags in XML are self-describing.
- XML is an open standard and supported on most platforms today.

XML supports the parsing of data by applications not familiar with the contents of the XML document. XML documents can also be associated with a description (a schema) that informs an application as to the structure of the data within the XML document.

At this stage, XML looks simple — it's just a human-readable way to exchange data in a universally accepted way. The essential points that you should understand about XML are

- XML data can be stored in a plain text file.
- A document is said to be well formed if it adheres to the XML standard.
- Tags are used to specify the contents of a document, for example, `<FilmOrder>`.
- XML elements (also called nodes) can be thought of as the objects within a document.
- Elements are the basic building blocks of the document. Each element contains a start tag and end tag. A tag can be both a start and an end tag, for example, `<FilmOrder/>`. Such a tag is said to be empty.
- Data can be contained in the element (the element content) or within attributes contained in the element.
- XML is hierarchical. One document can contain multiple elements, which can themselves contain child elements, and so on. However, an XML document can only have one root element.

This last point means that the XML document hierarchy can be thought of as a tree containing nodes:

- The example document has a root node, `<Movies>`.
- The branches of the root node are elements of type `<FilmOrder>`.
- The leaves of the XML element, `<FilmOrder>`, are its attributes: `name`, `quantity`, and `filmId`.

Of course, we're interested in the practical use of XML by Visual Basic. A practical manipulation of the example XML is to display for the staff of the movie supplier firm a particular movie order in some application so that this supplier could fill the order, and then save the information to a database. In this chapter, you'll look at how you can perform such tasks using the functionality provided by the .NET Framework class library.

XML Serialization

The simplest way to demonstrate Visual Basic's support for XML is not with a complicated technology, such as SQL Server or ADO.NET. Instead, we will demonstrate a practical use of XML by serializing a class.

The serialization of an object means that it is written out to a stream, such as a file or a socket (this is also known as dehydrating an object). The reverse process can also be performed: An object can be deserialized (or rehydrated) by reading it from a stream.

> *The type of serialization you are discussing in this chapter is XML serialization, where XML is used to represent a class in serialized form.*

To help you understand XML serialization, let's examine a class named `FilmOrder` (which can be found in the code download from `www.wrox.com`). This class is implemented in Visual Basic and is used by the company for processing an order for movies. This class could be instantiated on a firm's PDA, laptop, or even mobile phone (so long as the .NET Framework was installed).

An instance of `FilmOrder` corresponding to each order could be serialized to XML and sent over a socket using the PDA's cellular modem. (If the person making the order had a PDA which did not have a cellular modem, the instance of `FilmOrder` could be serialized to a file.) The order could then be processed when the PDA was dropped into a docking cradle and synced. What we are talking about here is data in a propriety form, an instance of `FilmOrder` being converted into a generic form — XML — that can be universally understood.

The `System.Xml.Serialization` namespace contains classes and interfaces that support the serialization of objects to XML and the deserialization of objects from XML. Objects are serialized to documents or streams using the `XmlSerializer` class. Let's look at how you can use `XmlSerializer`. First, you need to define an object that implements a default constructor, such as `FilmOrder`:

```
Public Class FilmOrder

   ' These are Public because we have yet to implement
   ' properties to provide program access.

   Public name As String
   Public filmId As Integer
   Public quantity As Integer

   Public Sub New()
   End Sub

   Public Sub New(ByVal name As String, _
                  ByVal filmId As Integer, _
```

```
                    ByVal quantity As Integer)
        Me.name = name
        Me.filmId = filmId
        Me.quantity = quantity
    End Sub
End Class
```

This class should be created in a console application. From there, let's move onto the module. Within the module's `Sub Main`, create an instance of `XmlSerializer`, specifying the object to serialize and its type in the constructor:

```
Dim serialize As XmlSerializer = _
  New XmlSerializer(GetType(FilmOrder))
```

Create an instance of the same type as was passed as parameter to the constructor of `XmlSerializer`:

```
Dim MyFilmOrder As FilmOrder = _
  New FilmOrder("Grease", 101, 10)
```

Call the `Serialize` method of the `XmlSerializer` instance, and specify the stream to which the serialized object is written (parameter one, `Console.Out`) and the object to be serialized (parameter two, `prescription`):

```
serialize.Serialize(Console.Out, MyFilmOrder)
Console. WriteLine()
```

To make reference to the `XmlSerializer` object, you are going to have to make reference to the `System.Xml.Serialization` namespace:

```
Imports System.Xml
Imports System.Xml.Serialization
```

Running the module, the following output is generated by the preceding code:

```
<?xml version="1.0" encoding="IBM437"?>
<FilmOrder xmlns:xsd="http://www.w3.org/2001/XMLSchema"
                     xmlns:xsi="http://www.w3.org/2001/XMLSchema-instance">
  <name>Grease</name>
  <filmId>101</filmId>
  <quantity>10</quantity>
</FilmOrder>
```

This output demonstrates the default way that the `Serialize` method serializes an object:

- Each object serialized is represented as an element with the same name as the class, in this case `FilmOrder`.
- The individual data members of the class serialized are contained in elements named for each data member, in this case `name`, `filmId`, and `quantity`.

Also generated are

- The specific version of XML generated, in this case `1.0`
- The encoding used, in this case `IBM437`
- The schemas used to describe the serialized object, in this case `www.w3.org/2001/XMLSchema-instance` and `www.w3.org/2001/XMLSchema`

A schema can be associated with an XML document and describe the data it contains (name, type, scale, precision, length, and so on). Either the actual schema or a reference to where the schema resides can be contained in the XML document. In either case, an XML schema is a standard representation that can be used by all applications that consume XML. This means that applications can use the supplied schema to validate the contents of an XML document generated by the `Serialize` method of `XmlSerializer`.

The code snippet that demonstrated the `Serialize` method of `XmlSerializer` displayed the XML generated to `Console.Out`. Clearly, we do not expect an application to use `Console.Out` when it would like to access a `FilmOrder` object in XML form. The basic idea shown was how serialization can be performed in just two lines of code (one call to a constructor and one call to method). The entire section of code responsible for serializing the instance of `FilmOrder` is

```
Try
    Dim serialize As XmlSerializer = _
                New XmlSerializer(GetType(FilmOrder))
    Dim MyMovieOrder As FilmOrder = _
            New FilmOrder("Grease", 101, 10)
    serialize.Serialize(Console.Out, MyMovieOrder)
    Console.Out.WriteLine()
    Console.Readline()
Catch ex As Exception
    Console.Error.WriteLine(ex.ToString())
End Try
```

The `Serialize` method's first parameter is overridden so that it can serialize XML to a file (the file name is given as type `String`), a `Stream`, a `TextWriter`, or an `XmlWriter`. When serializing to `Stream`, `TextWriter`, or `XmlWriter`, adding a third parameter to the `Serialize` method is permissible. This third parameter is of type `XmlSerializerNamespaces` and is used to specify a list of namespaces that qualify the names in the XML-generated document. The permissible overrides of the `Serialize` method are:

```
Public Sub Serialize(Stream, Object)
Public Sub Serialize(TextWriter, Object)
Public Sub Serialize(XmlWriter, Object)
Public Sub Serialize(Stream, Object, XmlSerializerNamespaces)
Public Sub Serialize(TextWriter, Object, XmlSerializerNamespaces)
Public Sub Serialize(XmlWriter, Object, XmlSerializerNamespaces)
```

An object is reconstituted using the `Deserialize` method of `XmlSerializer`. This method is overridden and can deserialize XML presented as a `Stream`, a `TextReader`, or an `XmlReader`. The overloads for `Deserialize` are:

```
Public Function Deserialize(Stream) As Object
Public Function Deserialize(TextReader) As Object
Public Function Deserialize(XmlReader) As Object
```

Before demonstrating the `Deserialize` method, we will introduce a new class, `WXClientMultiPrescription`. This class contains an array of prescriptions (an array of `WXClientPrescription` objects). `WXClientMultiPrescription` is defined as follows:

```
Public Class FilmOrder_Multiple

    Public multiFilmOrders() As FilmOrder

    Public Sub New()
    End Sub

    Public Sub New(ByVal multiFilmOrders() As FilmOrder)
        Me.multiFilmOrders = multiFilmOrders
    End Sub
End Class
```

The `FilmOrder_Multiple` class contains a fairly complicated object, an array of `FilmOrder` objects. The underlying serialization and deserialization of this class is more complicated than that of a single instance of a class that contains several simple types. However, the programming effort involved on your part is just as simple as before. This is one of the great ways in which the .NET Framework makes it easy for you to work with XML data, no matter how it is formed.

To work through an example of the deserialization process, let's start by first creating a sample order stored as an XML file called `Filmorama.xml`.

```
<?xml version="1.0" encoding="utf-8" ?>
<FilmOrder_Multiple xmlns:xsi="http://www.w3.org/2001/XMLSchema-instance"
 xmlns:xsd="http://www.w3.org/2001/XMLSchema">
   <multiFilmOrders>
         <FilmOrder>
            <name>Grease</name>
            <filmId>101</filmId>
            <quantity>10</quantity>
         </FilmOrder>
         <FilmOrder>
            <name>Lawrence of Arabia</name>
            <filmId>102</filmId>
            <quantity>10</quantity>
         </FilmOrder>
         <FilmOrder>
            <name>Star Wars</name>
            <filmId>103</filmId>
            <quantity>10</quantity>
         </FilmOrder>
   </multiFilmOrders>
</FilmOrder_Multiple>
```

Once the XML file is in place, the next step is to change your console application so it will take this XML file and deserialize its contents.

From there, it is important to make sure that your console application has made the proper namespace references:

```
Imports System.Xml
Imports System.Xml.Serialization
Imports System.IO
```

Then, the following code demonstrates an object of type `FilmOrder_Multiple` being deserialized (or rehydrated) from a file, `Filmorama.xml`. This object is deserialized using this file in conjunction with the `Deserialize` method of `XmlSerializer`:

```
' Open file, ..\Filmorama.xml
Dim dehydrated As FileStream = _
   New FileStream("..\Filmorama.xml", FileMode.Open)

' Create an XmlSerializer instance to handle deserializing, ' FilmOrder_Multiple
Dim serialize As XmlSerializer = _
   New XmlSerializer(GetType(FilmOrder_Multiple))

' Create an object to contain the deserialized instance of the object.
Dim myFilmOrder As FilmOrder_Multiple = _
   New FilmOrder_Multiple

' Deserialize object
myFilmOrder = serialize.Deserialize(dehydrated)
```

Once deserialized, the array of prescriptions can be displayed:

```
Dim SingleFilmOrder As FilmOrder

For Each SingleFilmOrder In myFilmOrder.multiFilmOrders
   Console.Out.WriteLine("{0}, {1}, {2}", _
      SingleFilmOrder.name, _
      SingleFilmOrder.filmId, _
      SingleFilmOrder.quantity)
Next

Console.ReadLine()
```

This example is just code that serializes an instance of type, `FilmOrder_Multiple`. The output generated by displaying the deserialized object containing an array of film orders is:

```
Grease, 101, 10
Lawrence of Arabia, 102, 10
Star Wars, 103, 10
```

`XmlSerializer` also implements a `CanDeserialize` method. The prototype for this method is:

```
Public Overridable Function CanDeserialize(ByVal xmlReader As XmlReader) _
   As Boolean
```

If CanDeserialize returns True, then the XML document specified by the xmlReader parameter can be deserialized. If the return value of this method is False, then the specified XML document cannot be deserialized.

The FromTypes method of XmlSerializer facilitates the creation of arrays that contain XmlSerializer objects. This array of XmlSerializer objects can be used in turn to process arrays of the type to be serialized. The prototype for FromTypes is:

```
Public Shared Function FromTypes(ByVal types() As Type) As XmlSerializer()
```

Before we further explore the System.Xml.Serialization namespace, we need to take a moment to consider the various uses of the term "attribute."

Source Code Style Attributes

Thus far you have seen attributes applied to a specific portion of an XML document. Visual Basic has its own flavor of attributes, as do C# and each of the other .NET languages. These attributes refer to annotations to the source code that specify information (or metadata) that can be used by other applications without the need for the original source code. We will call such attributes Source Code Style attributes.

In the context of the System.Xml.Serialization namespace, Source Code Style attributes can be used to change the names of the elements generated for the data members of a class or to generate XML attributes instead of XML elements for the data members of a class. To demonstrate this, we will use a class called ElokuvaTilaus, which contains data members named name, filmId, and quantity. It just so happens that the default XML generated when serializing this class is not in a form that can be readily consumed by an external application. As an example of this, assume that a Finnish development team has written this external application, and hence the XML element and attribute names are in Finnish (minus the umlauts) rather than in English.

To rename the XML generated for a data member, name, a Source Code Style attribute will be used. This Source Code Style attribute would specify that when ElokuvaTilaus is serialized, the name data member would be represented as an XML element, <Nimi>. The actual Source Code Style attribute that specifies this is:

```
<XmlElementAttribute("Nimi")> Public name As String
```

ElokuvaTilaus also contains other Source Code Style attributes:

- <XmlAttributeAttribute("ElokuvaId")> — Specifies that filmId is to be serialized as an XML attribute named ElokuvaId
- <XmlAttributeAttribute("Maara")> — Specifies that quantity is to be serialized as an XML attribute named Maara

`ElokuvaTilaus` is defined as follows:

```
Imports System.Xml.Serialization

Public Class ElokuvaTilaus

  ' These are Public because we have yet to implement
  ' properties to provide program access.

  <XmlElementAttribute("Nimi")> Public name As String
  <XmlAttributeAttribute("ElokuvaId")> Public filmId As Integer
  <XmlAttributeAttribute("Maara")> Public quantity As Integer

  Public Sub New()
  End Sub

  Public Sub New(ByVal name As String, _
                 ByVal filmId As Integer, _
                 ByVal quantity As Integer)
    Me.name = name
    Me.filmId = filmId
    Me.quantity = quantity
  End Sub

End Class
```

`ElokuvaTilaus` can be serialized as follows:

```
Dim serialize As XmlSerializer = _
    New XmlSerializer(GetType(ElokuvaTilaus))
Dim MyMovieOrder As ElokuvaTilaus = _
    New ElokuvaTilaus("Grease", 101, 10)

serialize.Serialize(Console.Out, MyMovieOrder)
```

The output generated by this code reflects the Source Code Style attributes associated with class `ElokuvaTilaus`:

```
<?xml version="1.0" encoding="IBM437"?>
<ElokuvaTilaus xmlns:xsi="http://www.w3.org/2001/XMLSchema-instance"
 xmlns:xsd="http://www.w3.org/2001/XMLSchema"
 ElokuvaId="101" Maara="10">
    <Nimi>Grease</Nimi>
</ElokuvaTilaus>
```

The value of `filmId` is contained in an XML attribute, `ElokuvaId`, and the value of `quantity` is contained in an XML attribute, `Maara`. The value of `name` is contained in an XML element, `Nimi`.

The example has only demonstrated the Source Code Style attributes exposed by the `XmlAttributeAttribute` and `XmlElementAttribute` classes in the `System.Xml .Serialization` namespace. A variety of other Source Code Style attributes exist in this namespace that also control the form of XML generated by serialization. The classes associated with such Source Code Style attributes include `XmlTypeAttribute`, `XmlTextAttribute`, `XmlRootAttribute`, `XmlIncludeAttribute`, `XmlIgnoreAttribute`, and `XmlEnumAttribute`.

System.Xml Document Support

The `System.Xml` namespace implements a variety of objects that support standards-based XML processing. The XML-specific standards facilitated by this namespace include XML 1.0, Document Type Definition (DTD) support, XML namespaces, XML schemas, XPath, XQuery, XSLT, DOM Level 1 and DOM Level 2 (Core implementations), as well as SOAP 1.1, SOAP 1.2, SOAP Contract Language, and SOAP Discovery. The `System.Xml` namespace exposes over 30 separate classes in order to facilitate this level of XML standard's compliance.

With respect to generating and navigating XML documents, there are two styles of access:

- **Stream-based** — `System.Xml` exposes a variety of classes that read XML from and write XML to a stream. This approach tends to be a fast way to consume or generate an XML document because it represents a set of serial reads or writes. The limitation of this approach is that it does not view the XML data as a document composed of tangible entities, such as nodes, elements, and attributes. An example of where a stream could be used is when receiving XML documents from a socket or a file.
- **Document Object Model (DOM)–based** — `System.Xml` exposes a set of objects that access XML documents as data. The data is accessed using entities from the XML document tree (nodes, elements, and attributes). This style of XML generation and navigation is flexible but may not yield the same performance as stream-based XML generation and navigation. DOM is an excellent technology for editing and manipulating documents. For example, the functionality exposed by DOM might make merging your checking, savings, and brokerage accounts simpler.

XML Stream-Style Parsers

When demonstrating XML serialization, you alluded to XML stream-style parsers. After all, when an instance of an object was serialized to XML, it had to be written to a stream, and when it was deserialized, it was read from a stream. When an XML document is parsed using a stream parser, the parser always points to the current node in the document. The basic architecture of stream parsers is shown in Figure 12-1.

The classes that access a stream of XML (read XML) and generate a stream of XML (write XML) are contained in the `System.Xml` namespace and are

- `XmlWriter` — This abstract class specifies a noncached, forward-only stream that writes an XML document (data and schema).
- `XmlReader` — This abstract class specifies a noncached, forward-only stream that reads an XML document (data and schema).

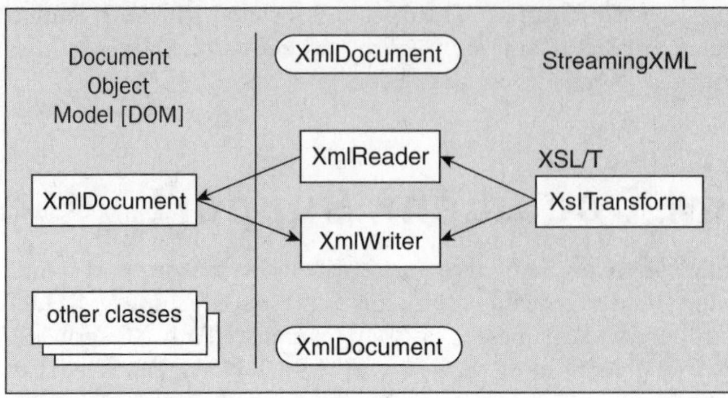

Figure 12-1

Your diagram of the classes associated with the XML stream-style parser referred to one other class, `XslTransform`. This class is found in the `System.Xml.Xsl` namespace and is not an XML stream-style parser. Rather, it is used in conjunction with `XmlWriter` and `XmlReader`. This class will be reviewed in detail later.

The `System.Xml` namespace exposes a plethora of additional XML manipulation classes in addition to those shown in the architecture diagram. The classes shown in the diagram include

- `XmlResolver` — This abstract class resolves an external XML resource using a Uniform Resource Identifier (URI). `XmlUrlResolver` is an implementation of an `XmlResolver`.
- `XmlNameTable` — This abstract class provides a fast means by which an XML parser can access element or attribute names.

Writing an XML Stream

An XML document can be created programmatically in .NET. One way to perform this task is by writing the individual components of an XML document (schema, attributes, elements, and so on) to an XML stream. Using a unidirectional write-stream means that each element and its attributes must be written in order — the idea is that data is always written at the head of the stream. To accomplish this, you use a writable XML stream class (a class derived from `XmlWriter`). Such a class ensures that the XML document you generate correctly implements the W3C Extensible Markup Language (XML) 1.0 specification and the Namespaces in XML specification.

But why would this be necessary since you have XML serialization? You need to be very careful here to separate interface from implementation. XML serialization worked for a specific class, `ElokuvaTilaus`. The class is a proprietary implementation and not the format in which data is exchanged. For this one specific case, the XML document generated when `ElokuvaTilaus` is serialized just so happens to be the XML format used when placing an order for some movies. `ElokuvaTilaus` was given a little help from Source Code Style attributes so that it would conform to a standard XML representation of a film order summary.

In a different application, if the software used to manage an entire movie distribution business wants to generate movie orders, it will have to generate a document of the appropriate form. The movie distribution management software will achieve this by using the `XmlWriter` object.

Before reviewing the subtleties of `XmlWriter`, it is important to note that this class exposes over 40 methods and properties. The example presented in this section will provide an overview that touches on a subset of these methods and properties. This subset will allow an XML document that corresponds to a movie order to be generated.

For this example, let's build a module that generates an XML document corresponding to a movie order. You will use an instance of `XmlWriter`, `FilmOrdersWriter`, which will actually be a file on disk. This means that the XML document generated is streamed to this file. Since the `FilmOrdersWriter` variable represents a file, it must be

- **Created** — The instance of `XmlWriter` `FilmOrdersWriter` is created using the `Create` method as well as by assigning all the properties of this object with the `XmlWriterSettings` object.
- **Opened** — The file the XML is streamed to, `FilmOrdersProgrammatic.xml`, is opened by passing the file name to the constructor associated with `XmlWriter`.
- **Generated** — The process of generating the XML document is described in detail at the end of this section.
- **Closed** — The file (the XML stream) is closed using the `Close` method of `XmlWriter` or by simply using the `Using` keyword.

Before you go about creating the `XmlWriter` object, you will first need to customize how the object will operate by using the `XmlWriterSettings` object. This object, which is new to .NET 2.0, allows you to configure the behavior of the `XmlWriter` object before you instantiate it.

```
Dim myXmlSettings As New XmlWriterSettings
myXmlSettings.Indent = True
myXmlSettings.NewLineOnAttributes = True
```

The `XmlWriterSettings` object allows for a few settings on how the XML creation will be handled by the `XmlWriter` object. The following table details the properties of the `XmlWriterSettings` class.

Property	Initial Value	Description
`CheckCharacters`	`True`	This property, if set to `True`, will perform a character check upon the contents of the `XmlWriter` object. Legal characters can be found at `www.w3.org/TR/REC-xml#charsets`.
`CloseOutput`	`False`	This property will get or set a value indicating whether the `XmlWriter` should also close the underlying stream or `System.IO.TextWriter` when the `XmlWriter.Close` method is called.

Table continued on following page

Property	Initial Value	Description
ConformanceLevel	ConformanceLevel Document	Allows the XML to be checked to make sure that it follows certain specified rules. Possible conformance level settings include Document, Fragment, and Default.
Encoding	Encoding.UTF8	Defines the encoding of the XML generated.
Indent	False	Defines whether the XML generated should be indented or not. Setting this value to True will properly indent child nodes from parent nodes.
IndentChars	Two spaces	Specifies the number of spaces by which child nodes will be indented from parent nodes. This setting only works when the Indent property is set to True.
NewLineChars	\r\n	Assigns the characters that are used to define line breaks.
NewLineHandling	System.Xml .NewLineHandling .Replace	This property gets or sets a value indicating whether to normalize line breaks in the output.
NewLineOnAttributes	False	Defines whether a node's attributes should be written to a new line in the construction. This will occur if set to True.
OmitXmlDeclaration	False	Defines whether an XML declaration should be generated in the output. This omission only occurs if set to True.
OutputMethod	System.Xml .XmlOutputMethod .Xml	This property gets the method used to serialize the System.Xml.XmlWriter output.

Once the XmlWriterSettings object has been instantiated and assigned the values you deem necessary, the next steps are to invoke the XmlWriter object as well as make the association between the XmlWriterSettings object and the XmlWriter object.

The basic infrastructure for managing the file (the XML text stream) and applying the settings class is:

```
Dim FilmOrdersWriter As XmlWriter = _
   XmlWriter.Create("..\FilmOrdersProgrammatic.xml", myXmlSettings)

FilmOrdersWriter.Close()
```

or the following, if you are utilizing the `Using` keyword, which is new to the .NET Framework 2.0 and highly recommended:

```
Using FilmOrdersWriter As XmlTextWriter = _
   XmlWriter.Create("..\FilmOrdersProgrammatic.xml", myXmlSettings)

End Using
```

With the preliminaries completed (file created and formatting configured), the process of writing the actual attributes and elements of your XML document can begin. The sequence of steps used to generate your XML document is:

- Write an XML comment using the `WriteComment` method. This comment describes from whence the concept for this XML document originated and generates the following code:

```
<!-- Same as generated by serializing, ElokuvaTilaus -->
```

- Begin writing the XML element, `<ElokuvaTilaus>`, by calling the `WriteStartElement` method. You can only begin writing this element because its attributes and child elements must be written before the element can be ended with a corresponding `</ElokuvaTilaus>`. The XML generated by the `WriteStartElement` method is:

```
<ElokuvaTilaus>
```

- Write the attributes associated with `<ElokuvaTilaus>` by calling the `WriteAttributeString` method twice. The XML generated by calling the `WriteAttributeString` method twice adds to the `ElokuvaTilaus`XML element that is currently being written to:

```
<ElokuvaTilaus ElokuvaId="101" Maara="10">
```

- Using the `WriteElementString` method, write the child XML element `<Nimi>` contained in the XML element, `<ElokuvaTilaus>`. The XML generated by calling this method is:

```
<Nimi>Grease</Nimi>
```

- Complete writing the `<ElokuvaTilaus>` parent XML element by calling the `WriteEndElement` method. The XML generated by calling this method is:

```
</ElokuvaTilaus>
```

Let's now put all this together in the `Module1.vb` file shown here:

```
Imports System.Xml
Imports System.Xml.Serialization
Imports System.IO

Module Module1

    Sub Main()

        Dim myXmlSettings As New XmlWriterSettings
```

```
        myXmlSettings.Indent = True
        myXmlSettings.NewLineOnAttributes = True

        Using FilmOrdersWriter As XmlWriter = _
            XmlWriter.Create("..\FilmOrdersProgrammatic.xml", myXmlSettings)

            FilmOrdersWriter.WriteComment(" Same as generated " & _
               "by serializing, ElokuvaTilaus ")
            FilmOrdersWriter.WriteStartElement("ElokuvaTilaus")
            FilmOrdersWriter.WriteAttributeString("ElokuvaId", "101")
            FilmOrdersWriter.WriteAttributeString("Maara", "10")
            FilmOrdersWriter.WriteElementString("Nimi", "Grease")
            FilmOrdersWriter.WriteEndElement() ' End ElokuvaTilaus

        End Using

    End Sub

End Module
```

Once this is run, you will then find the XML file `FilmOrdersProgrammatic.xml` created in the same folder as the `Module1.vb` file. The content of this file is:

```
<?xml version="1.0" encoding="utf-8"?>
<!-- Same as generated by serializing, ElokuvaTilaus -->
<ElokuvaTilaus
  ElokuvaId="101"
  Maara="10">
  <Nimi>Grease</Nimi>
</ElokuvaTilaus>
```

The previous XML document is the same in form as the XML document generated by serializing the `ElokuvaTilaus` class. Notice how in the previous XML document the `<Nimi>` element is indented two characters and that each attribute is on a different line in the document? This was achieved using the `XmlWriterSettings` class.

The sample application covered only a small portion of the methods and properties exposed by the XML stream-writing class, `XmlWriter`. Other methods implemented by this class include methods that manipulate the underlying file, such as the `Flush` method, and methods that allow XML text to be written directly to the stream, such as the `WriteRaw` method.

The `XmlWriter` class also exposes a variety of methods that write a specific type of XML data to the stream. These methods include `WriteBinHex`, `WriteCData`, `WriteString`, and `WriteWhiteSpace`.

You can now generate the same XML document in two different ways. You have used two different applications that took two different approaches to generating a document that represents a standardized movie order. However, there are even more ways to generate XML, depending on the circumstances. For example, you could receive a movie order from a store, and this order would have to be transformed from the XML format used by the supplier to your own order format.

Reading an XML Stream

In .NET, XML documents can be read from a stream as well. The way a readable stream works is that data is traversed in the stream in order (first XML element, second XML element, and so on). This traversal is very quick because the data is processed in one direction, and features, such as write and move backward in the traversal, are not supported. At any given instance, only data at the current position in the stream can be accessed.

Before exploring how an XML stream can be read, you need to understand why it should be read in the first place. To answer this question, let's return to your movie supplier example. Imagine that the application that manages the movie orders can generate a variety of XML documents corresponding to current orders, preorders, and returns. All the documents (current orders, preorders, and returns) can be extracted in stream form and processed by a report-generating application. This application prints up the orders for a given day, the preorders that are going to be due, and the returns that are coming down back to the supplier. The report-generating application processes the data by reading in and parsing a stream of XML.

One class that can be used to read and parse such an XML stream is `XmlReader`. Other classes in the .NET Framework are derived from `XmlReader`, such as `XmlTextReader`, which can read XML from a file (specified by a string corresponding to the file's name), a `Stream`, or an `XmlReader`. For demonstration purposes, you will use an `XmlReader` to read an XML document contained in a file. Reading XML from a file and writing it to a file is not the norm when it comes to XML processing, but a file is the simplest way to access XML data. This simplified access allows you to focus more on XML-specific issues.

In creating a sample, the fist step is to make the proper imports into the `Module1.vb` file:

```
Imports System.Xml
Imports System.Xml.Serialization
Imports System.IO
```

From there, the next step in accessing a stream of XML data is to create an instance of the object that will open the stream (the `readMovieInfo` variable of type `XmlReader`) and then to open the stream itself. Your application performs this as follows (where `MovieManage.xml` will be the name of the file containing the XML document):

```
Dim myXmlSettings As New XmlReaderSettings()
Using readMovieInfo As XmlReader = XmlReader.Create(fileName, myXmlSettings)
```

You will notice that like the `XmlWriter` has a settings class, the `XmlReader` also has a settings class. Though you can make assignments to the `XmlReaderSettings` object, in this case you do not. Later, this chapter will detail the `XmlReaderSettings` object.

The basic mechanism for traversing each stream is to traverse from node to node using the `Read` method. Node types in XML include element and white space. Numerous other node types are defined, but for the sake of this example you will focus on traversing XML elements and the white space that is used to make the elements more readable (carriage returns, linefeeds, and indentation spaces). Once the stream is positioned at a node, the `MoveToNextAttribute` method can be called to read each attribute contained in an element. The `MoveToNextAttribute` method will only traverse attributes for nodes that contain attributes (nodes of type element). An example of an `XmlReader` traversing each node and then traversing the attributes of each node follows:

```
    While readMovieInfo.Read()
        ' Process node here.
        While readMovieInfo.MoveToNextAttribute()
            ' Process attribute here.
        End While
    End While
```

This code, which reads the contents of the XML stream, does not utilize any knowledge of the stream's contents. However, a great many applications know exactly how the stream they are going to traverse is structured. Such applications can use `XmlReader` in a more deliberate manner and not simply traverse the stream without foreknowledge.

Once the example stream has been read, it can be cleaned up using the `End Using` call:

```
End Using
```

This `ReadMovieXml` subroutine takes the file name containing the XML to read as a parameter. The code for the subroutine is as follows and is basically the code just outlined:

```
Private Sub ReadMovieXml(ByVal fileName As String)
    Dim myXmlSettings As New XmlReaderSettings()
    Using readMovieInfo As XmlReader = XmlReader.Create(fileName, myXmlSettings)
        While readMovieInfo.Read()
            ShowXmlNode(readMovieInfo)
            While readMovieInfo.MoveToNextAttribute()
                ShowXmlNode(readMovieInfo)
            End While
        End While
    End Using

    Console.ReadLine()
End Sub
```

For each node encountered after a call to the `Read` method, `ReadMovieXml` calls the `ShowXmlNode` subroutine. Similarly, for each attribute traversed, the `ShowXmlNode` subroutine is called. This subroutine breaks down each node into its subentities.

- **Depth** — The `Depth` property of `XmlReader` determines the level at which a node resides in the XML document tree. To understand depth, consider the following XML document composed solely of elements: `<A><B></B><C><D></D></C></A>`. Element `<A>` is the root element and when parsed would return a `Depth` of `0`. Elements `<B>` and `<C>` are contained in `<A>` and are hence a `Depth` value of `1`. Element `<D>` is contained in `<C>`. The `Depth` property value associated with `<D>` (depth of `2`) should, therefore, be one more than the `Depth` property associated with `<C>` (depth of `1`).
- **Type** — The type of each node is determined using the `NodeType` property of `XmlReader`. The node returned is of enumeration type, `XmlNodeType`. Permissible node types include `Attribute`, `Element`, and `Whitespace`. (Numerous other node types can also be returned including `CDATA`, `Comment`, `Document`, `Entity`, and `DocumentType`.)
- **Name** — The type of each node is retrieved using the `Name` property of `XmlReader`. The name of the node could be an element name, such as `<ElokuvaTilaus>`, or an attribute name, such as `ElokuvaId`.

- **Attribute Count** — The number of attributes associated with a node is retrieved using the `AttributeCount` property of `XmlReader's NodeType`.
- **Value** — The value of a node is retrieved using the `Value` property of `XmlReader`. For example, the element node `<Nimi>` contains a value of `Grease`.

Subroutine `ShowXmlNode` is implemented as follows:

```
Private Sub ShowXmlNode(ByVal reader As XmlReader)

    If reader.Depth > 0 Then
        For depthCount As Integer = 1 To reader.Depth
            Console.Write("  ")
        Next
    End If

    If reader.NodeType = XmlNodeType.Whitespace Then

        Console.Out.WriteLine("Type: {0} ", reader.NodeType)

    ElseIf reader.NodeType = XmlNodeType.Text Then

        Console.Out.WriteLine("Type: {0}, Value: {1} ", _
                              reader.NodeType, _
                              reader.Value)

    Else

        Console.Out.WriteLine("Name: {0}, Type: {1}, " & _
                              "AttributeCount: {2}, Value: {3} ", _
                              reader.Name, _
                              reader.NodeType, _
                              reader.AttributeCount, _
                              reader.Value)
    End If

End Sub
```

Within the `ShowXmlNode` subroutine, each level of node depth adds two spaces to the output generated:

```
If reader.Depth > 0 Then
  For depthCount As Integer = 1 To reader.Depth
    Console.Write("  ")
  Next
End If
```

You add these spaces in order to make the output generated human-readable (so you can easily determine the depth of each node displayed). For each type of node, `ShowXmlNode` displays the value of the `NodeType` property. The `ShowXmlNode` subroutine makes a distinction between nodes of type `Whitespace` and other types of nodes. The reason for this is simple: A node of type `Whitespace` does not contain a name or attribute count. The value of such a node is any combination of white-space characters (space, tab, carriage return, and so on). Therefore, it does not make sense to display the properties if the `NodeType` is `XmlNodeType.WhiteSpace`. Nodes of type `Text` have no name associated with them and so for this type, subroutine `ShowXmlNode` only displays the properties `NodeType` and `Value`. For all other node types, the `Name`, `AttributeCount`, `Value`, and `NodeType` properties are displayed.

For the finalization of this module, add a `Sub Main` as follows:

```
Sub Main(ByVal args() As String)
   ReadMovieXml("..\MovieManage.xml")
End Sub
```

An example construction of the `MovieManage.xml` file is:

```
<?xml version="1.0" encoding="utf-8" ?>
<MovieOrderDump>

 <FilmOrder_Multiple>
    <multiFilmOrders>
       <FilmOrder>
          <name>Grease</name>
          <filmId>101</filmId>
          <quantity>10</quantity>
       </FilmOrder>
       <FilmOrder>
          <name>Lawrence of Arabia</name>
          <filmId>102</filmId>
          <quantity>10</quantity>
       </FilmOrder>
       <FilmOrder>
          <name>Star Wars</name>
          <filmId>103</filmId>
          <quantity>10</quantity>
       </FilmOrder>
    </multiFilmOrders>
 </FilmOrder_Multiple>

 <PreOrder>
    <FilmOrder>
       <name>Shrek III - Shrek Becomes a Programmer</name>
       <filmId>104</filmId>
       <quantity>10</quantity>
    </FilmOrder>
 </PreOrder>

 <Returns>
    <FilmOrder>
       <name>Star Wars</name>
       <filmId>103</filmId>
       <quantity>2</quantity>
    </FilmOrder>
 </Returns>

</MovieOrderDump>
```

Running this module produces the following output (a partial display since it would be rather lengthy):

```
Name: xml, Type: XmlDeclaration, AttributeCount: 2, Value: version="1.0"
encoding="utf-8"
Name: version, Type: Attribute, AttributeCount: 2, Value: 1.0
Name: encoding, Type: Attribute, AttributeCount: 2, Value: utf-8
Type: Whitespace
Name: MovieOrderDump, Type: Element, AttributeCount: 0, Value:
 Type: Whitespace
 Name: FilmOrder_Multiple, Type: Element, AttributeCount: 0, Value:
  Type: Whitespace
  Name: multiFilmOrders, Type: Element, AttributeCount: 0, Value:
   Type: Whitespace
   Name: FilmOrder, Type: Element, AttributeCount: 0, Value:
    Type: Whitespace
    Name: name, Type: Element, AttributeCount: 0, Value:
     Type: Text, Value: Grease
```

This example managed to use three methods and five properties of `XmlReader`. The output generated was informative but far from practical. `XmlReader` exposes over 50 methods and properties, which means that you have only scratched the surface of this highly versatile class. The remainder of this section will look at the `XmlReaderSettings` class, introduce a more realistic use of `XmlReader`, and demonstrate how the classes of `System.Xml` handle errors.

The XmlReaderSettings Class

Just like the `XmlWriter` object, the `XmlReader` object requires settings to be applied for instantiation of the object. This means that you can apply settings for how the `XmlReader` object behaves for when it is reading whatever XML that you might have for it. This includes settings for how to deal with white space, schemas, and more. The following table details these settings.

Property	Initial Value	Description
`CheckCharacters`	`True`	This property, if set to `True`, will perform a character check upon the contents of the retrieved object. Legal characters can be found at `www.w3.org/TR/REC-xml#charsets`.
`CloseInput`	`False`	This property gets or sets a value indicating whether the underlying stream or `System.IO.TextReader` should be closed when the reader is closed.
`ConformanceLevel`	`ConformanceLevel.Document`	Allows for the XML to be checked to make sure that it follows certain specified rules. Possible conformance level settings include `Document`, `Fragment`, and `Default`.
`DtdValidate`	`False`	Defines whether the `XmlReader` should perform a DTD validation.

Table continued on following page

Property	Initial Value	Description
IgnoreComments	False	Defines whether comments should be ignored or not.
IgnoreInlineSchema	True	Defines whether any inline schemas should be ignored or not.
IgnoreProcessing Instructions	False	Defines whether processing instructions contained within the XML should be ignored.
IgnoreSchema Location	True	Defines whether the xsi: schemaLocation or xsi: noNamespaceSchemaLocation attributes should be ignored or not.
IgnoreValidation Warnings	True	Defines whether the XmlReader object should ignore all validation warnings.
IgnoreWhitespace	False	Defines whether the XmlReader object should ignore all insignificant white space.
LineNumberOffset	0	Defines the line number which the LineNumber property starts counting within the XML file.
LinePositionOffset	0	Defines the line number which the LineNumber property starts counting with the XML file.
NameTable	An empty XmlNameTable object	Allows the XmlReader to work with a specific XmlNameTable object that is used for atomized string comparisons.
ProhibitDtd	True	This property gets or sets a value indicating whether to prohibit document type definition (DTD) processing.
Schemas	An empty XmlSchemaSet object	Allows the XmlReader to work with an instance of the XmlSchemaSet class.
ValidationFlags		This property gets or sets a value indicating the schema validation settings.
ValidationType	ValidationType .None	This property gets or sets a value indicating whether the System.Xml .XmlReader will perform validation or type assignment when reading.
XmlResolver	A new XmlResolver with no credentials	This property sets the XmlResolver to access external documents.

An example of using this setting class to modify the behavior of the XmlReader class is:

```
Dim myXmlSettings As New XmlReaderSettings()
myXmlSettings.IgnoreWhitespace = True
myXmlSettings.IgnoreComments = True

Using readMovieInfo As XmlReader = XmlReader.Create(fileName, myXmlSettings)
   ' Use XmlReader object here.
End Using
```

In this case, the `XmlReader` object that is created will behave in that it will ignore the white space that it encounters as well as ignoring any of the XML comments. These settings, once established with the `XmlReaderSettings` object are then associated to the `XmlReader` object through its `Create` method.

Traversing XML Using XmlTextReader

An application can easily use `XmlReader` to traverse a document that is received in a known format. The document can thus be traversed in a deliberate manner. You implemented a class that serialized arrays of movie orders. The next example will take an XML document containing multiple XML documents of that type and traverse them. Each movie order will be forwarded to the movie supplier by sending a fax. The document will be traversed as follows:

```
Read root element: <MovieOrderDump>
    Process each <FilmOrder_Multiple> element
        Read <multiFilmOrders> element
            Process each <FilmOrder>
                Send fax for each movie order here
```

The basic outline for the program's implementation is to open a file containing the XML document to parse and to traverse it from element to element.

```
Dim myXmlSettings As New XmlReaderSettings()

Using readMovieInfo As XmlReader = XmlReader.Create(fileName, myXmlSettings)
      readMovieInfo.Read()
      readMovieInfo.ReadStartElement("MovieOrderDump")

      Do While (True)

         '****************************************************
         '* Process FilmOrder elements here                  *
         '****************************************************

      Loop

      readMovieInfo.ReadEndElement()  '  </MovieOrderDump>

End Using
```

The previous code opened the file using the constructor of `XmlReader`, and the `End Using` statement takes care of shutting everything down for you. The previous code also introduced two methods of the `XmlReader` class:

- `ReadStartElement(String)` — This verifies that the current in the stream is an element and that the element's name matches the string passed to method `ReadStartElement`. If the verification is successful, the stream is advanced to the next element.
- `ReadEndElement()` — This verifies that the current element is an end tab, and if the verification is successful the stream is advanced to the next element.

The application knows that an element, `<MovieOrderDump>`, will be found at a specific point in the document. The `ReadStartElement` method verifies this foreknowledge of the document format. Once all the elements contained in element `<MovieOrderDump>` have been traversed, the stream should point to the end tag `</MovieOrderDump>`. The `ReadEndElement` method verifies this.

The code that traverses each element of type `<FilmOrder>` similarly uses the `ReadStartElement` and `ReadEndElement` methods to indicate the start and end of the `<FilmOrder>` and `<multiFilmOrders>` elements. The code that ultimately parses the list of prescription and faxes the movie supplier (using the `FranticallyFaxTheMovieSupplier` subroutine) is:

```
Dim myXmlSettings As New XmlReaderSettings()

Using readMovieInfo As XmlReader = XmlReader.Create(fileName, myXmlSettings)
      readMovieInfo.Read()
      readMovieInfo.ReadStartElement("MovieOrderDump")

      Do While (True)
         readMovieInfo.ReadStartElement("FilmOrder_Multiple")
         readMovieInfo.ReadStartElement("multiFilmOrders")

         Do While (True)
            readMovieInfo.ReadStartElement("FilmOrder")
            movieName = readMovieInfo.ReadElementString()
            movieId = readMovieInfo.ReadElementString()
            quantity = readMovieInfo.ReadElementString()
            readMovieInfo.ReadEndElement() ' clear </FilmOrder>

            FranticallyFaxTheMovieSupplier(movieName, movieId, quantity)

            ' Should read next FilmOrder node
            ' else quits
            readMovieInfo.Read()

            If ("FilmOrder" <> readMovieInfo.Name) Then
               Exit Do
            End If
         Loop

         readMovieInfo.ReadEndElement() ' clear </multiFilmOrders>
         readMovieInfo.ReadEndElement() ' clear </FilmOrder_Multiple>

         ' Should read next FilmOrder_Multiple node
         ' else you quit
         readMovieInfo.Read() ' clear </MovieOrderDump>

         If ("FilmOrder_Multiple" <> readMovieInfo.Name) Then
            Exit Do
         End If
```

```
        Loop

        readMovieInfo.ReadEndElement()   '  </MovieOrderDump>

    End Using
```

Three lines within the previous code contain a call to the `ReadElementString` method:

```
movieName = readMovieInfo.ReadElementString()
movieId = readMovieInfo.ReadElementString()
quantity = readMovieInfo.ReadElementString()
```

While parsing the stream, it was known that an element named `<name>` existed and that this element contained the name of the movie. Rather than parsing the start tag, getting the value, and parsing the end tag, it was easier just to get the data using the `ReadElementString` method. This method retrieves the data string associated with an element and advances the stream to the next element. The `ReadElementString` method was also used to retrieve the data associated with the XML elements `<filmId>` and `<quantity>`.

The output of this example was a fax, which we won't show because the emphasis of this example is on showing that it is simpler to traverse a document when its form is known. The format of the document is still verified by `XmlReader` as it is parsed.

The `XmlReader` class also exposes properties that give more insight into the data contained in the XML document and the state of parsing: `IsEmptyElement`, `EOF`, and `IsStartElement`. This class also allows data in a variety of forms to be retrieved using methods such as `ReadBase64`, `ReadHex`, and `ReadChars`. The raw XML associated with the document can also be retrieved, using `ReadInnerXml` and `ReadOuterXml`. Once again, you have only scratched the surface of the `XmlReader` class. You will find this class to be quite rich in functionality.

Handling Exceptions

XML is text and could easily be read using mundane methods such as `Read` and `ReadLine`. A key feature of each class that reads and traverses XML is inherent support for error detection and handling. To demonstrate this, consider the following malformed XML document found in the file named `malformed.XML`:

```
<?xml version="1.0" encoding="IBM437" ?>
<ElokuvaTilaus ElokuvaId="101", Maara="10">
   <Nimi>Grease</Nimi>
<ElokuvaTilaus>
```

This document may not immediately appear to be malformed. By wrapping a call to the method you developed (`movieReadXML`), you can see what type of exception is raised when `XmlReader` detects the malformed XML within this document:

```
Try
    movieReadXML("..\Malformed.xml")
Catch xmlEx As XmlException
    Console.Error.WriteLine("XML Error: " + xmlEx.ToString())
Catch ex As Exception
    Console.Error.WriteLine("Some other error: " + ex.ToString())
End Try
```

The methods and properties exposed by the `XmlReader` class raise exceptions of type `System.Xml.XmlException`. In fact, every class in the `System.Xml` namespace raises exceptions of type `XmlException`. Although this is a discussion of errors using an instance of type `XmlReader`, the concepts reviewed apply to all errors generated by classes found in the `System.Xml` namespace.

The properties exposed by `XmlException` include

- `LineNumber` — The number of the line within an XML document where the error occurred.
- `LinePosition` — The position within the line specified by `LineNumber` where the error occurred.
- `Message` — The error message that corresponds to the error that occurred. This error took place at the line in the XML document specified by `LineNumber` and within the line at the position specified by `LinePostion`.
- `SourceUri` — Provides the URI of the element or document in which the error occurred.

The error displayed when subroutine `movieReadXML` processes `malformed.xml` is:

```
XML Error: System.Xml.XmlException: The ',' character, hexadecimal value 0x2C,
 cannot begin a name. Line 2, position 49.
```

Looking closely at the document, there is a comma separating the attributes in element, `<FilmOrder>` `(ElokuvaTilaus="101", Maara="10")`. This comma is invalid. Removing the comma and running the code again gives the following output:

```
XML Error: System.Xml.XmlException: This is an unexpected token. Expected
'EndElement'. Line 5, position 27.
```

Once again, you can recognize the precise error. In this case, you do not have an end element, `</ElokuvaTilaus>`, but you do have an opening element, `<ElokuvaTilaus>`.

The properties provided by the `XmlException` class (`LineNumber`, `LinePosition`, and `Message`) provide a useful level of precision when tracking down errors. The `XmlReader` class also exposes a level of precision with respect to the parsing of the XML document. This precision is exposed by the `XmlReader` through properties such as `LineNumber` and `LinePosition`.

Using the MemoryStream Object

A very useful class that can greatly help you when working with XML is `System.IO.MemoryStream`. Rather than needing a network or disk resource backing the stream (as in `System.Net.Sockets.NetworkStream` and `System.IO.FileStream`), `MemoryStream` backs itself onto a block of memory. Imagine that you want to generate an XML document and email it. The built-in classes for sending email rely on having a `System.String` containing a block of text for the message body. But, if you want to generate an XML document, you need a stream.

If the document is reasonably sized, you should write the document directly to memory and copy that block of memory to the email. This is good from a performance and reliability perspective because you don't have to open a file, write it, rewind it, and read the data back in again. However, you must consider scalability in this situation because if the file is very large, or you have a great number of smaller files, you could run out of memory (in which case you'll have to go the "file" route).

In this section, you'll see how to generate an XML document to a `MemoryStream` object. You'll read the document back out again as a `System.String` value and email it. What you'll do is create a new class called `EmailStream` that extends `MemoryStream`. This new class will contain an extra method called `CloseAndSend` that, as its name implies, will close the stream and send the email message.

First, you'll create a new console application project called `EmailStream`. The first job is to create a basic `Customer` object that contains a few basic members and that can be automatically serialized by .NET through use of the `SerializableAttribute` attribute:

```
<Serializable()> Public Class Customer

    ' members...
    Public Id As Integer
    Public FirstName As String
    Public LastName As String
    Public Email As String

End Class
```

The fun part now is the `EmailStream` class itself. This needs access to the `System.Web.Mail` namespace, so you'll need to add a reference to the `System.Web` assembly. The new class should also extend `System.IO.MemoryStream`, as shown here:

```
Imports System.IO
Imports System.Web.Mail

Public Class EmailStream
    Inherits MemoryStream
```

The first job of `CloseAndSend` is to start putting together the mail message. This is done by creating a new `System.Web.Mail.MailMessage` object and configuring the sender, recipient, and subject.

```
  ' CloseAndSend - close the stream and send the email...
Public Sub CloseAndSend(ByVal fromAddress As String, _
                        ByVal toAddress As String, _
                        ByVal subject As String)

    ' Create the new message...
    Dim message As New MailMessage
    message.From = fromAddress
    message.To = toAddress
    message.Subject = subject
```

This method will be called once the XML document has been written to the stream, so you can assume at this point that the stream contains a block of data. To read the data back out again, you have to rewind the stream and use a `System.IO.StreamReader`. Before you do this, the first thing you should do is call `Flush`. Traditionally, streams have always been buffered, that is, the data is not sent to the final destination (the memory block in this case, but a file in the case of a `FileStream` and so on) each and every time the stream is written. Instead, the data is written in (pretty much) a nondeterministic way. Because you need all the data to be written, you call `Flush` to ensure that all the data has been sent to the destination and that the buffer is empty.

In a way, EmailStream is a great example of buffering. All of the data is held in a memory "buffer" until you finally send the data on to its destination in a response to an explicit call to this method:

```
      ' Flush and rewind the stream...

      Flush()
      Seek(0, SeekOrigin.Begin)
```

Once you've flushed and rewound the stream, you can create a StreamReader and dredge all the data out into the Body property of the MailMessage object:

```
      ' Read out the data...

      Dim reader As New StreamReader(Me)
      message.Body = reader.ReadToEnd()
```

After you've done that, you close the stream by calling the base class method:

```
      ' Close the stream...

      Close()
```

Finally, you send the message:

```
      ' Send the message...

      SmtpMail.Send(message)

   End Sub
```

To call this method, you need to add some code to the Main method. First, you create a new Customer object and populate it with some test data:

```
Imports System.Xml.Serialization

Module Module1

  Sub Main()

    ' Create a new customer...
    Dim customer As New Customer
    customer.Id = 27
    customer.FirstName = "Bill"
    customer.LastName = "Gates"
    customer.Email = "bill.gates@microsoft.com"
```

After you've done that, you can create a new EmailStream object. You then use XmlSerializer to write an XML document representing the newly created Customer instance to the block of memory that EmailStream is backing to:

```
        ' Create a new email stream...
        Dim stream As New EmailStream

        ' Serialize...
        Dim serializer As New XmlSerializer(customer.GetType())
        serializer.Serialize(stream, customer)
```

At this point, the stream will be filled with data, and after all the data has been flushed, the block of memory that `EmailStream` backs on to will contain the complete document. Now, you can call `CloseAndSend` to email the document.

```
        ' Send the email...
        stream.CloseAndSend("evjen@yahoo.com", _
           "evjen@yahoo.com", "XML Customer Document")

    End Sub

End Module
```

You probably already have Microsoft SMTP Service properly configured — this service is necessary to send email. You also need to make sure that the email addresses used in your code goes to your email address! Run the project, check your email, and you should see something, as shown in Figure 12-2.

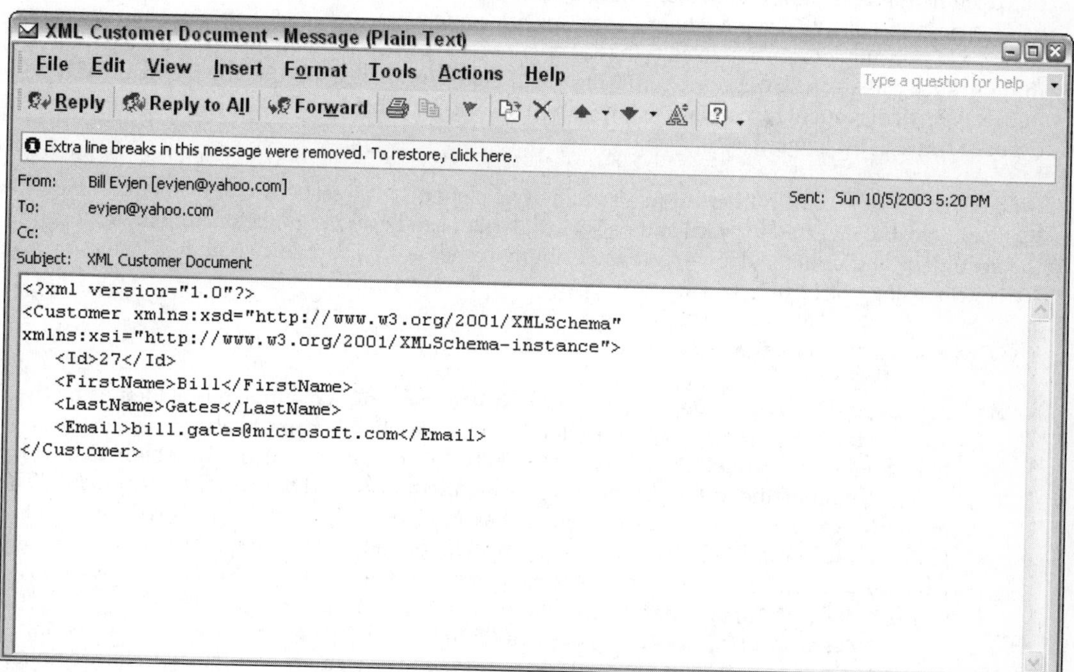

Figure 12-2

Document Object Model (DOM)

The classes of the `System.Xml` namespace that support the Document Object Model (DOM) interact as illustrated in Figure 12-3.

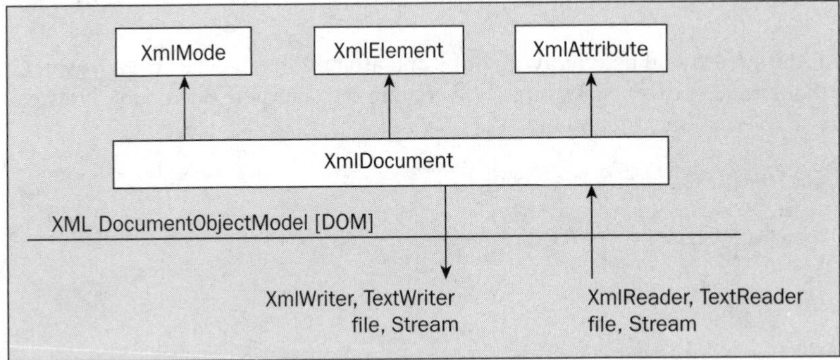

Figure 12-3

Within this diagram, an XML document is contained in a class named `XmlDocument`. Each node within this document is accessible and managed using `XmlNode`. Nodes can also be accessed and managed using a class specifically designed to process a specific node's type (`XmlElement`, `XmlAttribute`, and so on). XML documents are extracted from `XmlDocument` using a variety of mechanisms exposed through such classes as `XmlWriter`, `TextWriter`, `Stream`, and a file (specified by file name of type `String`). XML documents are consumed by an `XmlDocument` using a variety of load mechanisms exposed through the same classes.

Where a DOM-style parser differs from a stream-style parser is with respect to movement. Using DOM, the nodes can be traversed forward and backward. Nodes can be added to the document, removed from the document, and updated. However, this flexibility comes at a performance cost. It is faster to read or write XML using a stream-style parser.

The DOM-specific classes exposed by `System.Xml` include

- `XmlDocument` — Corresponds to an entire XML document. A document is loaded using the `Load` method. XML documents are loaded from a file (the file name specified as type `String`), `TextReader`, or `XmlReader`. A document can be loaded using `LoadXml` in conjunction with a string containing the XML document. The `Save` method is used to save XML documents. The methods exposed by `XmlDocument` reflect the intricate manipulation of an XML document. For example, the following self-documenting creation methods are implemented by this class: `CreateAttribute`, `CreateDataSection`, `CreateComment`, `CreateDocumentFragment`, `CreateDocumentType`, `CreateElement`, `CreateEntityReference`, `CreateNode`, `CreateProcessingInstruction`, `CreateSignificantWhitespace`, `CreateTextNode`, `CreateWhitespace`, and `CreateXmlDeclaration`. The elements contained in the document can be retrieved. Other methods support the retrieving, importing, cloning, loading, and writing of nodes.
- `XmlNode` — Corresponds to a node within the DOM tree. This class supports datatypes, namespaces, and DTDs. A robust set of methods and properties are provided to create, delete, and replace nodes: `AppendChild`, `CloneNode`, `InsertAfter`, `InsertBefore`, `PrependChild`,

RemoveAll, RemoveChild, and ReplaceChild. The contents of a node can similarly be traversed in a variety of ways: FirstChild, LastChild, NextSibling, ParentNode, and PreviousSibling.

- XmlElement — Corresponds to an element within the DOM tree. The functionality exposed by this class contains a variety of methods used to manipulate an element's attributes: GetAttribute, GetAttributeNode, RemoveAllAttributes, RemoveAttributeAt, RemoveAttributeNode, SetAttribute, and SetAttributeNode.
- XmlAttribute—Corresponds to an attribute of an element (XmlElement) within the DOM tree. An attribute contains data and lists of subordinate data. For this reason, it is a less complicated object than an XmlNode or an XmlElement. An XmlAttribute can retrieve its owner document (property, OwnerDocument), retrieve its owner element (property, OwnerElement), retrieve its parent node (property, ParentNode), and retrieve its name (property, Name). The value of an XmlAttribute is available via a read-write property named Value.

Given the diverse number of methods and properties (and there are many more than those listed here) exposed by XmlDocument, XmlNode, XmlElement, and XmlAttribute, it should be clear that any XML 1.0–compliant document can be generated and manipulated using these classes. In comparison to their XML stream counterparts, these classes afford more flexible movement within and editing of XML documents.

A similar comparison could be made between DOM and data serialized and deserialized using XML. Using serialization, the type of node (for example, attribute or element) and the node name are specified at compile time. There is no on-the-fly modification of the XML generated by the serialization process.

Other technologies that generate and consume XML are not as flexible as DOM. This includes ADO.NET and ADO, which generate XML of a particular form. Out of the box, SQL Server 2000 does expose a certain amount of flexibility when it comes to the generation (FOR XML queries) and consumption of XML (OPENXML) . SQL Server 2005 has more support from XML and even supports an XML datatype. SQL Server 2005 also expands upon the FOR XML query with FOR XML TYPE. The choice between using classes within DOM and a version of SQL Server is a choice between using a language, such as Visual Basic, to manipulate objects or installing SQL Server and performing most of the XML manipulation in SQL.

DOM Traversing Raw XML Elements

The first DOM example will load an XML document into an XmlDocument object using a string that contains the actual XML document. This scenario is typical of an application that uses ADO.NET to generate XML but then uses the objects of DOM to traverse and manipulate this XML. ADO.NET's DataSet object contains the results of ADO.NET data access operations. The DataSet class exposes a GetXml method. This method retrieves the underlying XML associated with the DataSet. The following code demonstrates how the contents of the DataSet are loaded into the XmlDocument:

```
Dim xmlDoc As New XmlDocument
Dim ds As New DataSet

' Set up ADO.NET DataSet() here
xmlDoc.LoadXml(ds.GetXml())
```

This example will simply traverse each XML element (XmlNode) in the document (XmlDocument) and display the data accordingly. The data associated with this example will not be retrieved from a DataSet but will instead be contained in a string, rawData. This string is initialized as follows:

```
Dim rawData As String = _
    "<multiFilmOrders>" & _
    "  <FilmOrder>" & _
    "    <name>Grease</name>" & _
    "    <filmId>101</filmId>" & _
    "    <quantity>10</quantity>" & _
    "  </FilmOrder>" & _
    "  <FilmOrder>" & _
    "    <name>Lawrence of Arabia</name>" & _
    "    <filmId>102</filmId>" & _
    "    <quantity>10</quantity>" & _
    "  </FilmOrder>" & _
    "</multiFilmOrders>"
```

The XML document in rawData is a portion of the XML hierarchy associated with a prescription written at your dental office. The basic idea in processing this data is to traverse each <FilmOrder> element in order to display the data it contains. Each node corresponding to a <FilmOrder> element can be retrieved from your XmlDocument using the GetElementsByTagName method (specifying a tag name of FilmOrder). The GetElementsByTagName method returns a list of XmlNode objects in the form of a collection of type XmlNodeList. Using the For Each statement to construct this list, the XmlNodeList (movieOrderNodes) can be traversed as individual XmlNode elements (movieOrderNode). The code for handling this is as follows:

```
Dim xmlDoc As New XmlDocument
Dim movieOrderNodes As XmlNodeList
Dim movieOrderNode As XmlNode

xmlDoc.LoadXml(rawData)

' Traverse each <FilmOrder>
movieOrderNodes = xmlDoc.GetElementsByTagName("FilmOrder")

For Each movieOrderNode In movieOrderNodes

    '**********************************************************
    ' Process <name>, <filmId> and <quantity> here
    '**********************************************************

Next
```

Each XmlNode can then have its contents displayed by traversing the children of this node using the ChildNodes method. This method returns an XmlNodeList (baseDataNodes) that can be traversed one XmlNode list element at a time:

```
Dim baseDataNodes As XmlNodeList
Dim bFirstInRow As Boolean

baseDataNodes = movieOrderNode.ChildNodes
bFirstInRow = True
For Each baseDataNode As XmlNode In baseDataNodes
```

```
    If (bFirstInRow) Then
      bFirstInRow = False
    Else
      Console.Out.Write(", ")
    End If
    Console.Out.Write(baseDataNode.Name & ": " & baseDataNode.InnerText)
  Next
  Console.Out.WriteLine()
```

The bulk of the previous code retrieves the name of the node using the `Name` property and the `InnerText` property of the node. The `InnerText` property of each `XmlNode` retrieved contains the data associated with the XML elements (nodes) `<name>`, `<filmId>`, and `<quantity>`. The example displays the contents of the XML elements using `Console.Out`. The XML document is displayed as follows:

```
name: Grease, filmId: 101, quantity: 10
name: Lawrence of Arabia, filmId: 102, quantity: 10
```

Other, more practical, methods for using this data could have been implemented, including:

- The contents could have been directed to an ASP.NET `Response` object. The data retrieved could have been used to create an HTML table (`<table>` table, `<tr>` row, and `<td>` data) that would be written to the `Response` object.
- The data traversed could have been directed to a `ListBox` or `ComboBox` Windows Forms control. This would allow the data returned to be selected as part of a GUI application.
- The data could have been edited as part of your application's business rules. For example, you could have used the traversal to verify that the `<filmId>` matched the `<name>`. For example, if you really wanted to validate the data entered into the XML document in any manner.

The example in its entirety is:

```
Dim rawData As String = _
    "<multiFilmOrders>" & _
    "  <FilmOrder>" & _
    "    <name>Grease</name>" & _
    "    <filmId>101</filmId>" & _
    "    <quantity>10</quantity>" & _
    "  </FilmOrder>" & _
    "  <FilmOrder>" & _
    "    <name>Lawrence of Arabia</name>" & _
    "    <filmId>102</filmId>" & _
    "    <quantity>10</quantity>" & _
    "  </FilmOrder>" & _
    "</multiFilmOrders>"

Dim xmlDoc As New XmlDocument
Dim movieOrderNodes As XmlNodeList
Dim movieOrderNode As XmlNode
Dim baseDataNodes As XmlNodeList
Dim bFirstInRow As Boolean

xmlDoc.LoadXml(rawData)
' Traverse each <FilmOrder>
movieOrderNodes = xmlDoc.GetElementsByTagName("FilmOrder")
```

```
For Each movieOrderNode In movieOrderNodes
  baseDataNodes = movieOrderNode.ChildNodes
  bFirstInRow = True
  For Each baseDataNode As XmlNode In baseDataNodes
    If (bFirstInRow) Then
      bFirstInRow = False
    Else
      Console.Out.Write(", ")
    End If
    Console.Out.Write(baseDataNode.Name & ": " & baseDataNode.InnerText)
  Next
  Console.Out.WriteLine()
Next
```

DOM Traversing XML Attributes

This next example will demonstrate how to traverse data contained in attributes and how to update the attributes based on a set of business rules. In this example, the `XmlDocument` object is populated by retrieving an XML document from a file. After the business rules edit the object, the data will be persisted back to the file.

```
Dim xmlDoc As New XmlDocument

xmlDoc.Load("..\MovieSupplierShippingListV2.xml")

'*******************************************
' Business rules process document here

'*******************************************
xmlDoc.Save("..\MovieSupplierShippingListV2.xml")
```

The data contained in the file, `MovieSupplierShippingListV2.xml`, is a variation of the dental prescription. You have altered your rigid standard (for the sake of example) so that the data associated with individual movie orders is contained in XML attributes instead of XML elements. An example of this movie order data is:

```
<FilmOrder name="Grease" filmId="101" quantity="10" />
```

You have already seen how to traverse the XML elements associated with a document, so let's assume that you have successfully retrieved the `XmlNode` associated with the `<FilmOrder>` element.

```
Dim attributes As XmlAttributeCollection
Dim filmId As Integer
Dim quantity As Integer

attributes = node.Attributes()
For Each attribute As XmlAttribute In attributes
  If 0 = String.Compare(attribute.Name, "filmId") Then
    filmId = attribute.InnerXml
  ElseIf 0 = String.Compare(attribute.Name, "quantity") Then
    quantity = attribute.InnerXml
  End If
Next
```

The previous code traverses the attributes of an XmlNode by retrieving a list of attributes using the Attributes method. The value of this method is used to set the attributes object (datatype, XmlAttributeCollection). The individual XmlAttribute objects (variable, attribute) contained in attributes are traversed using a For Each loop. Within the loop, the contents of the filmId and the quantity attribute are saved for processing by your business rules.

Your business rules execute an algorithm that ensures that the movies in the company's order are provided in the correct quantity. This rule is that the movie associated with filmId=101 must be sent to the customer in batches of six at a time due to packaging. In the event of an invalid quantity, the code for enforcing this business rule keeps removing a single order from the quantity value until the number is divisible by six. Then this number is assigned to the quantity attribute. The Value property of the XmlAttribute object is used to set the correct value of the order's quantity. The code performing this business rule is:

```
If filmId = 101 Then
  ' This film comes packaged in batches of six.
  Do Until (quantity / 6) = True
    quantity -= 1
  Loop

  Attributes.ItemOf("quantity").Value = quantity
End If
```

What is elegant about this example is that the list of attributes was traversed using For Each. Then ItemOf was used to look up a specific attribute that had already been traversed. This would not have been possible by reading an XML stream with an object derived from the XML stream reader class, XmlReader.

You can use this code as follows:

```
Sub TraverseAttributes(ByRef node As XmlNode)
    Dim attributes As XmlAttributeCollection
    Dim filmId As Integer
    Dim quantity As Integer
        attributes = node.Attributes()
    For Each attribute As XmlAttribute In attributes
        If 0 = String.Compare(attribute.Name, "filmId") Then
            filmId = attribute.InnerXml
        ElseIf 0 = String.Compare(attribute.Name, "quantity") Then
            quantity = attribute.InnerXml
        End If
    Next

    If filmId = 101 Then
       ' This film comes packaged in batches of six
       Do Until (quantity / 6) = True
          quantity -= 1
       Loop

       Attributes.ItemOf("quantity").Value = quantity
```

```
        End If

    End Sub

    Sub WXReadMovieDOM()

        Dim xmlDoc As New XmlDocument
        Dim movieOrderNodes As XmlNodeList
        xmlDoc.Load("..\MovieSupplierShippingListV2.xml")

        ' Traverse each <FilmOrder>
        movieOrderNodes = xmlDoc.GetElementsByTagName("FilmOrder")

        For Each movieOrderNode As XmlNode In movieOrderNodes
            TraverseAttributes(movieOrderNode)
        Next

        xmlDoc.Save("..\MovieSupplierShippingListV2.xml")

    End Sub
```

XSLT Transforms

XSLT is a language that is used to transform XML documents so that they can be presented visually. You have performed a similar task before. When working with XML serialization, you rewrote the `FilmOrder` class. This class was used to serialize a movie order object to XML using nodes that contained English-language names. The rewritten version of this class, `ElokuvaTilaus`, serialized XML nodes containing Finnish names. Source Code Style attributes were used in conjunction with the `XmlSerializer` class to accomplish this transformation. Two words in this paragraph send chills down the spine of any experienced developer: rewrote and rewritten. The point of an XSL Transform is to use an alternate language (XSLT) to transform the XML rather than rewriting the source code, SQL commands, or some other mechanism used to generate XML.

Conceptually, XSLT is straightforward. A file with an .xslt extension describes the changes (transformations) that will be applied to a particular XML file. Once this is completed, an XSLT processor is provided with the source XML file and the XSLT file, and performs the transformation. The `System.Xml.Xsl.XslTransform` class is such an XSLT processor. A new processor in .NET 2.0 is the `XslCompiledTransform` object found at `System.Xml.XslCompiledTransform`. You will take a look at using both of these processors.

The XSLT file is itself an XML document, although certain elements within this document are XSLT-specific commands. There are dozens of XSLT commands that can be used in writing an XSLT file. In the first example, you will explore the following XSLT elements (commands):

- `stylesheet` — This element indicates the start of the style sheet (XSL) in the XSLT file.
- `template` — This element denotes a reusable template for producing specific output. This output is generated using a specific node type within the source document under a specific context. For example, the text `<xsl: template match="/">` selects all root notes (`"/"`) for the specific transform template.

- ❑ `for-each` — This element applies the same template to each node in the specified set. Recall that you demonstrated a class (`FilmOrder_Multiple`) that could be serialized. This class contained an array of prescriptions. Given the XML document generated when a `FilmOrder_Multiple` is serialized, each prescription serialized could be processed using `<xsl:for-each select = "FilmOrder_Multiple/multiFilmOrders/FilmOrder">`.
- ❑ `value-of` — This element retrieves the value of the specified node and inserts it into the document in text form. For example, `<xsl:value-of select="name" />` would take the value of XML element, `<name>`, and insert it into the transformed document.

The `FilmOrder_Multiple` class when serialized generates XML such as the following (where . . . indicates where additional `<FilmOrder>` elements may reside):

```
<?xml version="1.0" encoding="you-ascii" ?>
<FilmOrder_Multiple>
    <multiFilmOrders>
        <FilmOrder>
            <name>Grease</name>
            <filmId>101</filmId>
            <quantity>10</quantity>
        </FilmOrder>
        ...
    </multiFilmOrders>
</FilmOrder_Multiple>
```

The previous XML document is used to generate a report that is viewed by the manager of the movie supplier. This report is in HTML form, so that it can be viewed via the Web. The XSLT elements you previously reviewed (`stylesheet`, `template`, and `for-each`) are all the XSLT elements required to transform the XML document (in which data is stored) into an HTML file (show that the data can be displayed). An XSLT file `DisplayThatPuppy.xslt` contains the following text that is used to transform a serialized version, `FilmOrder_Multiple`:

```
<?xml version="1.0" encoding="UTF-8" ?>
<xsl:stylesheet xmlns:xsl="http://www.w3.org/1999/XSL/Transform" version="1.0">
 <xsl:template match="/">
     <HTML>
     <TITLE>What people are ordering</TITLE>
     <BODY>
         <TABLE BORDER="1">
           <TR>
             <TD><B>Film Name</B></TD>
             <TD><B>Film ID</B></TD>
             <TD><B>Quantity</B></TD>
           </TR>
           <xsl:for-each select=
            "FilmOrder_Multiple/multiFilmOrders/FilmOrder">
           <TR>
              <TD><xsl:value-of select="name" /></TD>
              <TD><xsl:value-of select="filmId" /></TD>
              <TD><xsl:value-of select="quantity" /></TD>
           </TR>
           </xsl:for-each>
```

```
            </TABLE>
          </BODY>
        </HTML>
    </xsl:template>
  </xsl:stylesheet>
```

In the previous XSLT file, the XSLT elements are marked in boldface. These elements perform operations on the source XML file containing a serialized `FilmOrder_Multiple` object and generate the appropriate HTML file. Your file contains a table (marked by the table tag, `<TABLE>`) that contains a set of rows (each row marked by a table row tag, `<TR>`). The columns of the table are contained in table data tags, `<TD>`. The previous XSLT file contains the header row for the table:

```
<TR>
    <TD><B>Film Name</B></TD>
    <TD><B>Film ID</B></TD>
    <TD><B>Quantity</B></TD>
</TR>
```

Each row containing data (an individual prescription from the serialized object, `FilmOrder_Multiple`) is generated using the XSLT element, `for-each`, to traverse each `<FilmOrder>` element within the source XML document:

```
<xsl:for-each select=
    "FilmOrder_Multiple/multiFilmOrders/FilmOrder">
```

The individual columns of data are generated using the `value-of` XSLT element, in order to query the elements contained within each `<FilmOrder>` element (`<name>`, `<filmId>`, and `<quantity>`):

```
<TR>
    <TD><xsl:value-of select="name" /></TD>
    <TD><xsl:value-of select="filmId" /></TD>
    <TD><xsl:value-of select="quantity" /></TD>
</TR>
```

The code to create a displayable XML file using the `XslTransform` object is:

```
Dim myXslTransform As XslTransform = New XslTransform

Dim destFileName As String = "..\ShowIt.html"

myXslTransform.Load("..\DisplayThatPuppy.xslt")
myXslTransform.Transform("..\FilmOrders.xml", destFileName)

System.Diagnostics.Process.Start(destFileName)
```

This consists of only seven lines of code with the bulk of the coding taking place in the XSLT file. Your previous code snippet created an instance of a `System.Xml.Xsl.XslTransform` object named `myXslTransform`. The `Load` method of this class is used to load the XSLT file you previously reviewed, `DisplayThatPuppy.xslt`. The `Transform` method takes a source XML file as the first parameter, which in this case was a file containing a serialized `FilmOrder_Multiple` object. The second parameter is the destination file that will be created by the transform (file name `ShowIt.html`). The `Start` method of the `Process` class is used to display the HTML file. The `Start` method launches a process that is most suitable for displaying the file provided. Basically, the extension of the file dictates which application will be used to display the file. On a typical Windows machine, the program used to display this file is Internet Explorer, as shown in Figure 12-4.

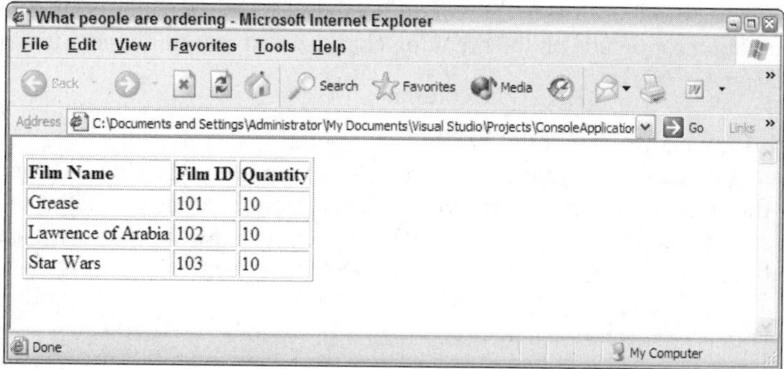

Figure 12-4

Do not confuse displaying this HTML file with ASP.NET. Displaying an HTML file in this manner takes place on a single machine without the involvement of a Web server. Using ASP.NET is more complex than displaying an HTML page in the default browser.

As was demonstrated, the backbone of the `System.Xml.Xsl` namespace is the `XslTransform` class. This class uses XSLT files to transform XML documents. `XslTransform` exposes the following methods and properties:

- `XmlResolver`—This get/set property is used to specify a class (abstract base class, `XmlResolver`) that is used to handle external references (import and include elements within the style sheet). These external references are encountered when a document is transformed (method, `Transform`, is executed). The `System.Xml` namespace contains a class, `XmlUrlResolver`, which is derived from `XmlResolver`. The `XmlUrlResolver` class resolves the external resource based on a URI.
- `Load`—This overloaded method loads an XSLT style sheet to be used in transforming XML documents. It is permissible to specify the XSLT style sheet as a parameter of type `XPathNavigator`, file name of XSLT file (specified as parameter type, `String`), `XmlReader`, or `IXPathNavigable`. For each of type of XSLT supported, an overloaded member is provided that allows an `XmlResolver` to also be specified. For example, it is possible to call `Load(String, XmlResolver)` where `String` corresponds to a file name and `XmlResolver` is an object that handles references in the style sheet of type `xsl:import` and `xsl:include`. It would also be permissible to pass in a value of `Nothing` for the second parameter of the `Load` method (so that no `XmlResolver` would be specified). Note that there have been considerable changes to the parameters that the `Load` method takes between versions 1.0 and 1.1 of the .NET Framework. Look at the SDK documentation for details on the breaking changes that you might encounter when working with the `XslTransform` class.

- `Transform`—This overloaded method transforms a specified XML document using the previously specified XSLT style sheet and an `XmlResolver`. The location where the transformed XML is to be output is specified as a parameter to this method. The first parameter of each overloaded method is the XML document to be transformed. This parameter can be represented as an `IXPathNavigable`, XML file name (specified as parameter type, `String`), or `XPathNavigator`. Note that there have been considerable changes to the parameters that the `Transform` method takes between versions 1.0 and 1.1 of the .NET Framework. Look at the SDK documentation for details on the breaking changes that you might encounter when working with the `XslTransform` class.

The most straightforward variant of the `Transform` method is `Transform(String, String, XmlResolver)`. In this case, a file containing an XML document is specified as the first parameter, and a file name that receives the transformed XML document is specified as the second parameter, and the `XmlResolver` used as the third parameter. This is exactly how the first XSLT example utilized the `Transform` method:

```
myXslTransform.Transform("..\FilmOrders.xml", destFileName)
```

The first parameter to the `Transform` method can also be specified as `IXPathNavigable` or `XPathNavigator`. Either of these parameter types allows the XML output to be sent to an object of type `Stream`, `TextWriter`, or `XmlWriter`. When these two flavors of input are specified, a parameter containing an object of type `XsltArgumentList` can be specified. An `XsltArgumentList` object contains a list of arguments that are used as input to the transform.

When working with a .NET 2.0 project, it is preferable to use the `XslCompiledTransform` object instead of the `XslTransform` object, because the `XslTransform` object is considered obsolete. When using the new `XslCompiledTransform` object, you construct the file using the following code:

```
Dim myXsltCommand As New XslCompiledTransform()
Dim destFileName As String = "..\ShowIt.html"
myXsltCommand.Load("..\DisplayThatPuppy.xslt")
myXsltCommand.Transform("..\FilmOrders.xml", destFileName)
System.Diagnostics.Process.Start(destFileName)
```

Just like the `XslTransform` object, the `XslCompiledTransform` object uses the `Load` and `Transform` methods. The `Load` method provides the following signatures:

```
XslCompiledTransform.Load (IXPathNavigable)
XslCompiledTransform.Load (String)
XslCompiledTransform.Load (XmlReader)
XslCompiledTransform.Load (IXPathNavigable, XsltSettings, XmlResolver)
XslCompiledTransform.Load (String, XsltSettings, XmlResolver)
XslCompiledTransform.Load (XmlReader, XsltSettings, XmlResolver)
```

In this case, `String` is a representation of the .xslt file that should be used in the transformation. `XmlResolver` has already been explained and `XsltSettings` is an object that allows you to define which XSLT additional options to permit. The previous example used a single parameter, `String`, which showed the location of the style sheet:

```
myXsltCommand.Load("..\DisplayThatPuppy.xslt")
```

The `XslCompiledTransform` object's `Transform` method provides the following signatures:

```
XslCompiledTransform.Transform (IXPathNavigable, XmlWriter)
XslCompiledTransform.Transform (String, String)
XslCompiledTransform.Transform (String, XmlWriter)
XslCompiledTransform.Transform (XmlReader, XmlWriter)
XslCompiledTransform.Transform (IXPathNavigable, XsltArgumentList, Stream)
XslCompiledTransform.Transform (IXPathNavigable, XsltArgumentList, TextWriter)
XslCompiledTransform.Transform (IXPathNavigable, XsltArgumentList, XmlWriter)
XslCompiledTransform.Transform (String, XsltArgumentList, Stream)
XslCompiledTransform.Transform (String, XsltArgumentList, TextWriter)
XslCompiledTransform.Transform (String, XsltArgumentList, XmlWriter)
XslCompiledTransform.Transform (XmlReader, XsltArgumentList, Stream)
XslCompiledTransform.Transform (XmlReader, XsltArgumentList, TextWriter)
XslCompiledTransform.Transform (XmlReader, XsltArgumentList, XmlWriter)
XslCompiledTransform.Transform (XmlReader, XsltArgumentList, XmlWriter, XmlResolver)
```

In this case, `String` represents the location of specific files (whether it is source files or output files). Some of the signatures also allow for output to `XmlWriter` objects, streams, and `TextWriter` objects. These can be done by also providing additional arguments using the `XsltArgumentList` object. In the previous example, you used the second signature `XslCompiledTransform.Transform(String, String)`, which asked for the source file and the destination file (both string representations of the location of said files).

```
myXsltCommand.Transform("..\FilmOrders.xml", destFileName)
```

The `XslCompiledTransform` object example will produce the same table as was generated using the `XslTransform` object.

XSLT Transforming between XML Standards

The first example used four XSLT elements to transform an XML file into an HTML file. Such an example has merit, but it does not demonstrate an important use of XSLT. Another major application of XSLT is to transform XML from one standard into another standard. This may involve renaming elements/attributes, excluding elements/attributes, changing datatypes, altering the node hierarchy, and representing elements as attributes and vice versa.

A case of differing XML standards could easily happen to your software that automates movie orders coming into a supplier. Imagine that the software, including its XML representation of a movie order, is so successful that you sell 100,000 copies. However, just as you're celebrating, a consortium of the largest movie supplier chains announces that they will no longer be accepting faxed orders and that they are introducing their own standard for the exchange of movie orders between movie sellers and buyers.

Rather than panic, you simply ship an upgrade that comes complete with an XSLT file. This upgrade (a bit of extra code plus the XSLT file) transforms your XML representation of a movie order into the XML representation dictated by the consortium of movie suppliers. Using an XSLT file allows you to ship the upgrade immediately. If the consortium of movie suppliers revises their XML representation, you are not obliged to change your source code. Instead, you can simply ship the upgraded XSLT file that will ensure that each movie order document is compliant.

The specific source code that executes the transform is:

```
Dim myXsltCommand As New XslCompiledTransform()
myXsltCommand.Load("..\ConvertLegacyToNewStandard.xslt")
myXsltCommand.Transform("..\MovieOrdersOriginal.xml", "..\MovieOrdersModified.xml")
```

The three lines of code are

1. Create an `XslCompiledTransform` object.
2. Use the `Load` method to load an XSLT file (`ConvertLegacyToNewStandard.xslt`).
3. Use the `Transform` method to transform a source XML file (`MovieOrdersOriginal.xml`) into a destination XML file (`MovieOrdersModified.xml`).

Recall that the input XML document (`MovieOrdersOriginal.xml`) does not match the format required by your consortium of movie supplier chains. The content of this source XML file is:

```
<?xml version="1.0" encoding="you-ascii" ?>
<FilmOrder_Multiple>
    <multiFilmOrders>
        <FilmOrder>
            <name>Grease</name>
            <filmId>101</filmId>
            <quantity>10</quantity>
        </FilmOrder>
        ...
    </multiFilmOrders>
</FilmOrder_Multiple>
```

The format exhibited in the previous XML document does not match the format of the consortium of movie supplier chains. To be accepted by the collective of suppliers, you must transform the document as follows:

- Rename element `<FilmOrder_Multiple>` to `<Root>`.
- Remove element `<multiFilmOrders>`.
- Rename element `<FilmOrder>` to `<DvdOrder>`.
- Remove element `<name>` (the film's name is not to be contained in the document).
- Rename element `<quantity>` to `HowMuch` and make `HowMuch` an attribute of `<DvdOrder>`.
- Rename element `<filmId>` to `FilmOrderNumber` and make `FilmOrderNumber` an attribute of `<DvdOrder>`.
- Display attribute `HowMuch` before attribute `FilmOrderNumber`.

A great many of the steps performed by the transform could have been achieved using an alternative technology. For example, you could have used Source Code Style attributes with your serialization to generate the correct XML attribute and XML element name. If you had known in advance that a consortium of suppliers was going to develop a standard, you could have written your classes to be serialized based on the standard. The point was that you didn't know and now one standard (your legacy standard) has to be converted into a newly adopted standard of the movie suppliers' consortium. The worst thing you could do would be to change your working code and then force all users working with the application to upgrade. It is vastly simpler to add an extra transformation step to address the new standard.

The XSLT file that facilitates the transform is named `ConvertLegacyToNewStandard.xslt`. A portion of this file is implemented as follows:

```
<xsl:template match="FilmOrder">
    <!-- rename <FilmOrder> to <DvdOrder> -->
    <xsl:element name="DvdOrder">
       <!-- Make element 'quantity' attribute HowMuch
            Notice attribute HowMuch comes before attribute FilmOrderNumber -->
        <xsl:attribute name="HowMuch">
            <xsl:value-of select='quantity'></xsl:value-of>
        </xsl:attribute>
        <!-- Make element filmId attribute FilmOrderNumber -->
        <xsl:attribute name="FilmOrderNumber">
            <xsl:value-of select='filmId'></xsl:value-of>
        </xsl:attribute>
    </xsl:element>
    <!-- end of DvdOrder element -->
</xsl:template>
```

In the previous snippet of XSLT, the following XSLT elements are used to facilitate the transformation:

- `<xsl:template match="FilmOrder">` — All operations in this `template` XSLT element will take place on the original document's `FilmOrder` node.
- `<xsl:element name="DvdOrder">` — The element corresponding to the source document's `FilmOrder` element will be called `DvdOrder` in the destination document.
- `<xsl:attribute name="HowMuch">` — An attribute named `HowMuch` will be contained in the previously specified element. The previously specified element is `<DvdOrder>`. This `attribute` XSLT element for `HowMuch` comes before the `attribute` XSLT element for `FilmOrderNumber`. This order was specified as part of your transform to adhere to the new standard.
- `<xsl:value-of select='quantity'>` — Retrieve the value of the source document's `<quantity>` element and place it in the destination document. This instance of XSLT element, `value-of`, provides the value associated with attribute `HowMuch`.

Two new XSLT elements have crept into your vocabulary: `element` and `attribute`. Both of these XSLT elements live up to their names. Specifying the XSLT element named `element` places an element in the destination XML document. Specifying the XSLT element named `attribute` places an attribute in the destination XML document. The XSLT transform found in `ConvertLegacyToNewStandard.xslt` is too long to review completely. When reading this file in its entirety, you should remember that this XSLT file contains inline documentation to specify precisely what aspect of the transformation is being performed at which location in the XSLT document. For example, the following XML code comments inform you about what the XSLT element `attribute` is about to do:

```
<!-- Make element 'quantity' attribute HowMuch
      Notice attribute HowMuch comes before attribute FilmOrderNumber -->
<xsl:attribute name="HowMuch">
```

```
        <xsl:value-of select='quantity'></xsl:value-of>
    </xsl:attribute>
```

The previous example spanned several pages but contained just three lines of code. This demonstrates that there is more to XML than learning how to use it in Visual Basic and the .NET Framework. Among other things, you also need a good understanding of XSLT, XPath, and XQuery.

Other Classes and Interfaces in System.Xml.Xsl

We just took a good look at XSLT and the `System.Xml.Xsl` namespace, but there is a lot more to it than that. The other classes and interfaces exposed by `System.Xml.Xsl` namespace include

- `IXsltContextFunction` — This interface accesses at runtime a given function defined in the XSLT style sheet.
- `IXsltContextVariable` — This interface accesses at runtime a given variable defined in the XSLT style sheet.
- `XsltArgumentList` — This class contains a list of arguments. These arguments are XSLT parameters or XSLT extension objects. The `XsltArgumentList` object is used in conjunction with the `Transform` method of `XslTransform` and `XslCompiledTransform`.
- `XsltContext` — This class contains the state of the XSLT processor. This context information allows XPath expressions to have their various components resolved (functions, parameters, and namespaces).
- `XsltException`, `XsltCompileException` — These classes contain the information pertaining to an exception raised while transforming data. `XsltCompileException` is derived from `XsltException`.

ADO.NET

ADO.NET allows Visual Basic applications to generate XML documents and to use such documents to update persisted data. ADO.NET natively represents its `DataSet`'s underlying datastore in XML. ADO.NET also allows SQL Server — specific XML support to be accessed. In this chapter, your focus is on those features of ADO.NET that allow the XML generated and consumed to be customized. ADO.NET is covered in detail in Chapter 11.

The `DataSet` properties and methods that are pertinent to XML include `Namespace`, `Prefix`, `GetXml`, `GetXmlSchema`, `InferXmlSchema`, `ReadXml`, `ReadXmlSchema`, `WriteXml`, and `WriteXmlSchema`. An example of code that uses the `GetXml` method is:

```
Dim adapter As New _
    SqlDataAdapter("SELECT ShipperID, CompanyName, Phone " & _
                   "FROM Shippers", _
                   "SERVER=localhost;UID=sa;PWD=sa;Database=Northwind;")
Dim ds As New DataSet

adapter.Fill(ds)
Console.Out.WriteLine(ds.GetXml())
```

The previous code uses the sample Northwind database (which comes with SQL Server and MSDE) and retrieves all rows from the Shippers table. This table was selected because it contains only three rows of data. The XML returned by GetXml is as follows (where . . . signifies that <Table> elements were removed for the sake of brevity):

```
<NewDataSet>
  <Table>
    <ShipperID>1</ShipperID>
    <CompanyName>Speedy Express</CompanyName>
    <Phone>(503) 555-9831</Phone>
  </Table>
  ...
</NewDataSet>
```

What you are trying to determine from the previous XML document is how to customize the XML generated. The more customization you can perform at the ADO.NET level, the less need there will be later. With this in mind, you notice that the root element is <NewDataSet> and that each row of the DataSet is returned as an XML element, <Table>. The data returned is contained in an XML element named for the column in which the data resides (<ShipperID>, <CompanyName>, and <Phone>, respectively).

The root element, <NewDataSet>, is just the default name of the DataSet. This name could have been changed when the DataSet was constructed by specifying the name as a parameter to the constructor:

```
Dim ds As New DataSet("WeNameTheDataSet")
```

If the previous version of the constructor was executed, then the <NewDataSet> element would be renamed <WeNameTheDataSet>. After the DataSet has been constructed, you can still set the property DataSetName, thus changing <NewDataSet> to a name such as <WeNameTheDataSetAgain>:

```
ds.DataSetName = "WeNameTheDataSetAgain"
```

The <Table> element is actually the name of a table in the DataSet's Tables property. Programmatically, you can change <Table> to <WeNameTheTable>.

```
ds.Tables("Table").TableName = "WeNameTheTable"
```

You can customize the names of the data columns returned by modifying the SQL to use alias names. For example, you could retrieve the same data but generate different elements using the following SQL code:

```
SELECT ShipperID As TheID, CompanyName As CName, Phone As TelephoneNumber FROM
Shippers
```

Using the previous SQL statement, the <ShipperID> element would become the <TheID> element. The <CompanyName> element would become <CName> and <Phone> would become <TelephoneNumber>. The column names can also be changed programmatically by using the Columns property associated with the table in which the column resides. An example of this follows, where the XML element <TheID> is changed to <AnotherNewName>.

```
ds.Tables("WeNameTheTable").Columns("TheID").ColumnName = "AnotherNewName"
```

This XML could be transformed using System.Xml.Xsl. This XML could be read as a stream (XmlTextReader) or written as a stream (XmlTextWriter). The XML returned by ADO.NET could even be deserialized and used to create an object or objects using XmlSerializer. What is important is to recognize what ADO.NET-generated XML looks like. If you know its format, then you can transform it into whatever you like.

ADO.NET and SQL Server 2000's Built-In XML Features

Those interested in fully exploring the XML-specific features of SQL Server should take a look at *Professional SQL Server 2000 Programming* (Wrox Press, ISBN 0764543792). However, since the content of that book is not .NET-specific, the next example will form a bridge between *Professional SQL Server 2000 Programming* and the .NET Framework.

Two of the major XML-related features exposed by SQL Server are

- FOR XML — The FOR XML clause of an SQL SELECT statement allows a rowset to be returned as an XML document. The XML document generated by a FOR XML clause is highly customizable with respect to the document hierarchy generated, per-column data transforms, representation of binary data, XML schema generated, and a variety of other XML nuances.
- OPENXML — The OPENXML extension to Transact-SQL allows a stored procedure call to manipulate an XML document as a rowset. Subsequently, this rowset can be used to perform a variety of tasks, such as SELECT, INSERT INTO, DELETE, and UPDATE.

SQL Server's support for OPENXML is a matter of calling a stored procedure call. A developer who can execute a stored procedure call using Visual Basic in conjunction with ADO.NET can take full advantage of SQL Server's support for OPENXML. FOR XML queries have a certain caveat when it comes to ADO.NET. To understand this caveat, consider the following FOR XML query:

```
SELECT ShipperID, CompanyName, Phone FROM Shippers FOR XML RAW
```

Using SQL Server's Query Analyzer, this FOR XML RAW query generated the following XML:

```
<row ShipperID="1" CompanyName="Speedy Express" Phone="(503) 555-9831"/>
<row ShipperID="2" CompanyName="United Package" Phone="(503) 555-3199"/>
<row ShipperID="3" CompanyName="Federal Shipping" Phone="(503) 555-9931"/>
```

The same FOR XML RAW query can be executed from ADO.NET as follows:

```
Dim adapter As New _
    SqlDataAdapter("SELECT ShipperID, CompanyName, Phone " & _
                   "FROM Shippers FOR XML RAW", _
                   "SERVER=localhost;UID=sa;PWD=sa;Database=Northwind;")
Dim ds As New DataSet

adapter.Fill(ds)
Console.Out.WriteLine(ds.GetXml())
```

The caveat with respect to a FOR XML query is that all data (the XML text) must be returned via a result set containing a single row and a single column named XML_F52E2B61-18A1-11d1-B105- 00805F49916B.

The output from the previous code snippet demonstrates this caveat (where . . . represents similar data not shown for reasons of brevity):

```
<NewDataSet>
  <Table>
    <XML_F52E2B61-18A1-11d1-B105-00805F49916B>
      &lt;row ShipperID="1" CompanyName= "Speedy Express" Phone="(503)
       555-9831"/&gt;
      ...
    </XML_F52E2B61-18A1-11d1-B105-00805F49916B>
  </Table>
</NewDataSet>
```

The value of the single row and single column returned contains what looks like XML, but it contains `/<` instead of the less-than character, and `/>` instead of the greater-than character. The symbols < and > cannot appear inside XML data. For this reason, they must be entity-encoded (that is, represented as `/>` and `/<`). The data returned in element `<XML_F52E2B61-18A1-11d1-B105- 00805F49916B>` is not XML but is data contained in an XML document.

To fully utilize `FOR XML` queries, the data must be accessible as XML. The solution to this quandary is the `ExecuteXmlReader` method of the `SQLCommand` class. When this method is called, an `SQLCommand` object assumes that it is executed as a `FOR XML` query and returns the results of this query as an `XmlReader` object. An example of this follows (again found in `VBNetXML05`):

```
Dim connection As New _
    SqlConnection("SERVER=localhost;UID=sa;PWD=sa;Database=Northwind;")
Dim command As New _
    SqlCommand("SELECT ShipperID, CompanyName, Phone " & _
               "FROM Shippers FOR XML RAW")
Dim memStream As MemoryStream = New MemoryStream
Dim xmlReader As New XmlTextReader(memStream)

connection.Open()
command.Connection = connection
xmlReader = command.ExecuteXmlReader()
' Extract results from XMLReader
```

The `XmlReader` created in this code is of type `XmlTextReader`, which derives from `XmlReader`. The `XmlTextReader` is backed by a `MemoryStream`, hence it is an in-memory stream of XML that can be traversed using the methods and properties exposed by `XmlTextReader`. Streaming XML generation and retrieval has been discussed earlier.

Using the `ExecuteXmlReader` method of the `SQLCommand` class, it is possible to retrieve the result of `FOR XML` queries. What makes `FOR XML` style of queries so powerful is that it can configure the data retrieved. The three types of `FOR XML` queries support the following forms of XML customization:

- `FOR XML RAW` — This type of query returns each row of a result set inside an XML element named `<row>`. The data retrieved is contained as attributes of the `<row>` element. The attributes are named for the column name or column alias in the `FOR XML RAW` query.
- `FOR XML AUTO` — By default, this type of query returns each row of a result set inside an XML element named for the table or table alias contained in the `FOR XML AUTO` query. The data

retrieved is contained as attributes of this element. The attributes are named for the column name or column alias in the FOR XML AUTO query. By specifying FOR XML AUTO, ELEMENTS it is possible to retrieve all data inside elements rather than inside attributes. All data retrieved must be in attribute or element form. There is no mix-and-match capability.

- FOR XML EXPLICIT — This form of the FOR XML query allows the precise XML type of each column returned to be specified. The data associated with a column can be returned as an attribute or an element. Specific XML types, such as CDATA and ID, can be associated with a column returned. Even the level in the XML hierarchy in which data resides can be specified using a FOR XML EXPLICIT query. This style of query is fairly complicated to implement.

FOR XML queries are flexible. Using FOR XML EXPLICIT and the dental database, it would be possible to generate any form of XML medical prescription standard. The decision that needs to be made is where XML configuration takes place. Using Visual Basic, a developer could use XmlTextReader and XmlTextWriter to create any style of XML document. Using the XSLT language and an XSLT file, the same level of configuration can be achieved. SQL Server and, in particular, FOR XML EXPLICIT allow the same level of XML customization, but this customization takes place at the SQL level and may even be configured to stored procedure calls.

XML and SQL Server 2005

As a representation for data, XML is ideal in that it is a self-describing data format that allows you to provide your datasets as complex datatypes as well as providing order to your data. SQL Server 2005 embraces this direction.

More and more developers are turning to XML as a means of data storage. For instance, Microsoft Office allows documents to be saved and stored as XML documents. As more and more products and solutions are turning toward XML as a means of storage, this allows for a separation between the underlying data and the presentation aspect of what is being viewed. XML is also being used as a means of communicating datasets across platforms and across the enterprise. The entire XML Web services story is a result of this new capability. Simply said, XML is a powerful alternative to your data storage solutions.

Just remember that the power of using XML isn't only about storing data as XML somewhere (whether that is XML files or not), but is also about the ability to quickly get at this XML data and to be able to query the data that is retrieved.

SQL Server 2005 makes a big leap toward XML in adding an XML datatype. This allows you to unify the relational data aspects of the database and the new desires to work with XML data.

FOR XML has also been expanded from within this latest edition of SQL Server. This includes a new TYPE directive which returns an XML datatype instance. Also, from the Framework, .NET 2.0 adds a new namespace — System.Data.SqlXml — which allows you to easily work with the XML data that comes from SQL Server 2005. The SqlXml object is an XmlReader-derived type. Another addition is the use of the SqlDataReader object's GetXml method.

Summary

Ultimately, XML could be the underpinnings of electronic commerce, banking transactions, and data exchange of almost every conceivable kind. The beauty of XML is that it isolates data representation from data display. Technologies, such as HTML, contain data that is tightly bound to its display format. XML does not suffer this limitation, yet at the same time has the readability of HTML. Accordingly, the XML facilities available to a Visual Basic application are vast, and there are a large number of XML-related features, classes, and interfaces exposed by the .NET Framework.

In this chapter, you saw how to use `System.Xml.Serialization.XmlSerializer` to serialize classes. Source Code Style attributes were introduced in conjunction with serialization. This style of attributes allows the customization of the XML serialized to be extended to the source code associated with a class. What is important to remember about the direct of serialization classes is that a required change in the XML format becomes a change in the underlying source code. Developers should resist the temptation to rewrite the serialized classes in order to conform to some new XML data standard (such as the prescription format endorsed by your consortium of pharmacies). Technologies, such as XSLT, exposed via the `System.Xml.Query` namespace should be examined first as alternatives. You saw how to use XSLT style sheets to transform XML data using the classes found in the `System.Xml.Xsl` namespace.

The most useful classes and interfaces in the `System.Xml` namespace were reviewed, including those that support document-style XML access: `XmlDocument`, `XmlNode`, `XmlElement`, and `XmlAttribute`. The `System.Xml` namespace also contains classes and interfaces that support stream-style XML access: `XmlReader` and `XmlWriter`.

Finally, you looked at using XML with Microsoft's SQL Server.

13

Security in the .NET Framework 2.0

This chapter will cover the basics of security and cryptography. We'll begin with a brief discussion of the .NET Framework's security architecture, because this will have an impact on the solutions that we may choose to implement.

The .NET Framework provides us with additional tools and functionality with regard to security. We now have the `System.Security.Permissions` namespace, which allows us to control code access permissions along with role-based and identity permissions. Through our code, we can control access to objects programmatically, as well as receive information on the current permissions of objects. This security framework will assist us in finding out if we have permissions to run our code, instead of getting halfway through execution and having to deal with permission-based exceptions. In this chapter we will cover:

- Concepts and definitions
- Permissions
- Roles
- Principals
- Code access permissions
- Role based permissions
- Identity permissions
- Managing permissions
- Managing policies
- Cryptography

Cryptography is the cornerstone of the .NET Web Services security model, so in the second half of this chapter we discuss the basis of cryptography and how to implement it. Specifically, we will cover:

- Hash algorithms
- SHA
- MD5
- Secret key encryption
- Public key cryptography standard
- Digital signatures
- Certification
- Secure Sockets Layer communications

Let's begin the chapter by taking a look at some security concepts and definitions.

As always, the code for this chapter is available for download from www.wrox.com, which you'll need in order to follow along.

Security Concepts and Definitions

Before going on, let's detail the different types of security that we will be illustrating in this chapter and how they can relate to real scenarios.

Security Type	Related Concept in Security.Permissions Namespace or Utility	Purpose
NTFS	None	Allows for detailing of object rights (e.g. locking down of specific files)
Security Policies	`Caspol.exe` utility, `PermView.exe` utility	Set up overall security policy for a machine or user from an operating system level.
Cryptographic	Strong name and assembly, generation, `SignCode.exe` utility	Use of Public key infrastructure and Certificates
Programmatic	Groups and permission sets	For use in pieces of code that are being called into. Provides extra security to prevent users of calling code from violating security measures implemented by the program that are not provided for on a machine level

There are many approaches to providing security on our machines where our shared code is hosted. If multiple shared code applications are on one machine, each piece of shared code can get called from many front-end applications. Each piece of shared code will have its own security requirements for accessing environment variables — such as the registry, the file system, and other items — on the machine that it is running on. From an NTFS perspective, the administrator of our server can only lock down those items on the machine that are not required to be accessed from any piece of shared code running on it. Therefore, some applications will want to have additional security built in to prevent any calling code from doing things it is not supposed to do. The machine administrator can further assist the programmers by using the utilities provided with .NET to establish additional machine and/or user policies that programs can implement. As a further step along this line, the .NET environment has given us programmatic security through Code Access security, Role Based security, and Identity security. As a final security measure, we can use the cryptographic methods provided to require the use of certificates in order to execute our code.

Security in the .NET infrastructure has some basic concepts that we will discuss here. Code security is managed and accessed in the .NET environment through the use of security policies. Security policies have a relationship that is fundamentally tied to either the machine that code is running on, or to particular users under whose context the code is running. To this end, any modifications to the policy are done either at the machine or user level.

We establish the security policy on a given set of code by associating it with an entity called a group. A group is created and managed within each of the machine- and user-based policies. These group classifications are set up so that we can place code into categories. We would want to establish new code groups when we are ready to categorize the pieces of code that would run on a machine, and assign the permissions that users will have to access the code. For instance, if we wanted to group all Internet applications and then group all non-Internet applications together, we would establish two groups and associate each of our applications with its respective group. Now that we've got the code separated into groups, we can define different permission sets for each group. If we wanted to limit our Internet applications' access to the local file system, we could create a permission set that limits that access and associates the Internet application group with the new permission set. By default, the .NET environment gives us one code group named `All Code` that is associated with the `FullTrust` permission set.

Permission sets are unique combinations of security configurations that determine what each user with access to a machine can do on that machine. Each set determines what a user has access to, for instance, whether they can read environment variables, the file system, or execute other portions of code. Permission sets are maintained at the machine and user levels through the utility `Caspol.exe`. Through this utility, we can create our own permission sets, though there are seven permission sets that ship with the .NET infrastructure that are also useful, as shown in the following table.

Permission Set	Explanation
`FullTrust`	Allows full access to all resources — adds assembly to a special list that has `FullTrust` access
`Everything`	Allows full access to everything covered by default named permission sets, only differs from `Full-Trust` in that the group does not get added to the `FullTrust` Assembly List

Table continued on following page

Permission Set	Explanation
`Nothing`	Denies all access including `Execution`
`Execution`	Allows execution-only access
`SkipVerification`	Allows objects to bypass all security verification
`Internet`	Grants default rights that are normal for Internet applications
`LocalInternet`	Grants rights that are not as restricted as Internet, but not full trust

Security that is used within the programming environment also makes use of permission sets. Through code we can control access to files in a file system, environment variables, file dialogs, isolated storage, reflections, registry, sockets, and UI. Isolated storage and virtual file systems are new operating system level storage locations that can be used by programs and are governed by the machine security policies. These file systems keep a machine safe from file system intrusion by designating a regulated area for file storage. The main access to these items is controlled through code access permissions.

Although many methods that we use in Visual Basic 2005 give an identifiable return value, the only return value that we will get from security methods is if the method fails. If a security method succeeds, it will not give a return value. If it fails, it will return an exception object reflecting the specific error that occurred.

Permissions in the System.Security.Permissions Namespace

The `System.Security.Permissions` namespace is the namespace that we will use in our code to establish and use permissions to access many things such as the file system, environment variables, and the registry within our programs. The namespace controls access to both operating system level objects as well as code objects. In order to use the namespace in our project, we need to include the `Imports System.Security.Permissions` line with any of our other `Imports` statements in our project. Using this namespace gives us access to using the `CodeAccessPermission` and `PrincipalPermission` classes for using role-based permissions and also utilizing information supplied by `Identity` permissions. `CodeAccessPermission` is the main class that we will use as it controls access to the operating system level objects our code needs in order to function. Role-based permissions and `Identity` permissions grant access to objects based on the identity that the user of the program that is running carries with them.

In the following table, those classes that end with `Attribute`, such as `EnvironmentPermissionAttribute`, are the classes that allow us to modify the security level at which our code is allowed to interact with each respective object. The attributes that we can specify reflect either `Assert`, `Deny`, or `PermitOnly` permissions.

If permissions are asserted, we have full access to the object, while if we have specified `Deny` permissions we are not allowed to access the object through our code. If we have `PermitOnly` access, only objects within our program's already determined scope can be accessed, and we cannot add any more resources beyond that scope. In our table, we also deal with security in regard to Software Publishers. A Software Publisher is a specific entity that is using a digital signature to identify itself in a Web-based application. The following is a table of the namespace members that apply to Windows Forms programming with an explanation of each.

Class	Description
`CodeAccessSecurityAttribute`	Specifies security access to objects such as the registry and file system
`DataProtectionPermission`	Controls ability to access data and memory. This is a new class in the .NET Framework 2.0.
`DataProtectionPermissionAttribute`	Allows security actions to be added for data protections via code
`EnvironmentPermission`	Controls ability to see and modify system and user environment variables
`EnvironmentPermissionAttribute`	Allows security actions for environment variables to be added via code
`FileDialogPermission`	Controls ability to open files via a file dialog
`FileDialogPermissionAttribute`	Allows security actions to be added for File Dialogs via code
`FileIOPermission`	Controls ability to read and write files in the file system
`FileIOPermissionAttribute`	Allows security actions to be added for file access attempts via code
`GacIdentityPermission`	Defines the identity permissions for files which come from the Global Assembly Cache (GAC). This is a new class in the .NET Framework 2.0.
`GacIdentityPermissionAttribute`	Allows security actions to be added for files which originate from the GAC
`IsolatedStorageFilePermission`	Controls ability to access a private virtual file system within the isolated storage area of an application
`IsolatedStorageFilePermission Attribute`	Allows security actions to be added for private virtual file systems via code
`IsolatedStoragePermission`	Controls ability to access the isolated storage area of an application
`IsolatedStoragePermission Attribute`	Allows security actions to be added for the isolated storage area of an application
`KeyContainerPermission`	Controls ability to access key containers. This is a new class in the .NET Framework 2.0.

Table continued on following page

Class	Description
KeyContainerPermissionAccess Entry	Defines the access rights for particular key containers
KeyContainerPermissionAccess EntryCollection	Represents a collection of KeyContainer-PermissionAccessEntry objects
KeyContainerPermissionAccess EntryEnumerator	Represents the enumerators for the objects contained in the KeyContainerPermissionAccess EntryCollection object
KeyContainerPermissionAttribute	Allows security actions to be added for key containers
PermissionSetAttribute	Allows security actions to be added for a permission set
PrincipalPermission	Controls the ability to make checks against an active principal
PrincipalPermissionAttribute	Allows for checking against a specific user. Security principals are a user and role combination used to establish security identity
PublisherIdentityPermission	Allows for ability to access based on the identity of a software publisher
PublisherIdentityPermission Attribute	Allows security actions to be added for a software publisher
ReflectionPermission	This controls the ability to access nonpublic members of a given type
ReflectionPermissionAttribute	Allows for security actions to be added for public and nonpublic members of a given type
RegistryPermission	Controls the ability to access registry keys and values
RegistryPermissionAttribute	Allows security actions to be added for registry keys and values
ResourcePermissionBase	Controls the ability to work with the code access security permissions
ResourcePermissionBaseEntry	Allows you to define the smallest part of a code access security permission set
SecurityAttribute	Controls which security attributes are representing code, used to control the security when creating an assembly
SecurityPermission	The set of security permission flags for use by .NET; this collection is used when we want to specify a permission flag in our code

Class	Description
`SecurityPermissionAttribute`	Allows security actions for the security permission flags
`StorePermission`	Controls ability to access stores which contain X509 certificates. This is a new class in the .NET Framework 2.0.
`StorePermissionAttribute`	Allows security actions to be added for access stores which contain X509 certificates
`UIPermission`	Controls ability to access user interfaces and use the windows clipboard
`UIPermissionAttribute`	Allows security actions to be added for UI Interfaces and the use of the clipboard

Code Access Permissions

Code access permissions are controlled through the `CodeAccessPermission` class within the `System.Security` namespace, and its members make up the majority of the permissions we'll use in our attempt to secure our code and operating environment. The following is a table of the class methods and an explanation of their use.

Method	Description
`RevertAll`	Reverses all previous `assert`, `deny` or `permit-only` methods
`RevertAssert`	Reverses all previous assert methods
`RevertDeny`	Reverses all previous deny methods
`RevertPermitOnly`	Reverses all previous permit-only methods
`Assert`	Sets the permission to full access so that the specific resource can be accessed even if the caller hasn't been granted permission to access the resource
`CheckAsset`	Checks the validity of accessing the asserted resource through a permission object. This method can be overridden.
`CheckDemand`	Checks the validity of accessing the demanded resource through a permission object. This method can be overridden.
`CheckDeny`	Checks the validity of accessing the denied resource through a permission object. This method can be overridden.

Table continued on following page

Method	Description
`CheckPermitOnly`	Checks the validity of accessing permitted resources through a permission object. This method can be overridden.
`Copy`	Copies a permission object
`Demand`	Returns whether or not all callers in the call chain have been granted the permission to access the resource in a given manner
`Deny`	Denies all callers access to the resource
`Equals`	Determines if a given object is the same instance of the current object
`FromXml`	Establishes a permission set given a specific XML encoding. This parameter is an XML encoding
`GetHashCode`	Returns a hash code associated with a given object
`GetType`	Returns the type of a given object
`Intersect`	Returns the permissions two permission objects have in common
`IsSubsetOf`	Returns result of whether the current permission object is a subset of a specified permission
`PermitOnly`	Determines that only those resources within this permission object can be accessed even if code has been granted permission to other objects
`ToString`	Returns a string representation of the current permission object
`ToXml`	Creates an XML representation of the current permission object
`Union`	Creates a permission that is the union of two permission objects

Role-Based Permissions

Role-based permissions are permissions granted based on the user and the role that code is being called with. Users are generally authenticated within the operating system platform and hold a Security Identifier (SID) that is associated within a security context. The SID can further be associated with a role, or a group membership that is established within a security context. The .NET role functionality supports those users and roles associated within a security context and also has support for generic and custom users and roles through the concept of principals. A principal is an object that holds the current caller credentials, which is termed the identity of the user. Principals come in two types: Windows principals and non-Windows principals. Windows-based Principal objects are objects that store the Windows SID information regarding the current user context associated with the code that is calling into the module where we are using role-based permissions. NonWindows Principals are principal objects that are created programmatically via a custom login methodology which are made available to the current thread.

Role-based permissions are not set against objects within our environment like code access permissions. They are instead a permission that is checked within the context of the current user and role that a user is part of. Within the `System.Security.Permissions` namespace, the concept of the principals and the `PrincipalPermission` class of objects are used to establish and check permissions. If a programmer passes the user and role information during a call as captured from a custom login, the `PrincipalPermission` class can be used to verify this information as well. During the verification, if the user and role information is `Null`, then permission is granted, regardless of the user and role. The `PrincipalPermission` class does not grant access to objects, but has methods that determine if a caller has been given permissions according to the current permission object through the `Demand` method. If a security exception is generated then the user does not have sufficient permission.

The following table lists the methods in the `PrincipalPermission` class and a description of each.

Method	Description
`Copy`	Copies a permission object
`Demand`	Returns whether or not all callers in the call chain have been granted the permission to access the resource in a given manner
`Equals`	Determines if a given object is the same instance of the current object
`FromXml`	Establishes a permission set given a specific XML encoding
`GetHashCode`	Returns a hash code associated with a given object
`GetType`	Returns the type of a given object
`Intersect`	Returns the permissions two permission objects have in common specified in the parameter
`IsSubsetOf`	Returns the result of whether the current permission object is a subset of a specified permission
`IsUnrestricted`	Returns the result of whether the current permission object is unrestricted
`ToString`	Returns a string representation of the current permission object
`ToXml`	Creates an XML representation of the current permission object
`Union`	Creates a permission that is the union of two permission objects

As an example of how we might use these methods, here is a code snippet which captures the current Windows principal information and displays it on the screen in the form of a message box output. Each element of the principal information could be used in a program to validate against, and thus, restrict code execution based on the values in the principal information. In our example, we have inserted an `Imports System.Security.Principal` line at the top of our module so we could use the identity and principal objects:

```
Imports System.Security.Principal
Imports System.Security.Permissions

Private Sub btnRoleBasedPermissions_Click(ByVal sender As System.Object, _
   ByVal e As System.EventArgs) Handles btnRoleBasedPermissions.Click

   Dim objIdentity As WindowsIdentity = WindowsIdentity.GetCurrent
   Dim objPrincipal As New WindowsPrincipal(objIdentity)
   MessageBox.Show(objPrincipal.Identity.IsAuthenticated.ToString())
   MessageBox.Show(objIdentity.IsGuest.ToString())
   MessageBox.Show(objIdentity.ToString())
   objIdentity = Nothing
   objPrincipal = Nothing

End Sub
```

In this code we have illustrated a few of the properties that could be used to validate against when a caller wants to run our code. Sometimes we want to make sure that the caller is an authenticated user, and not someone who bypassed the security of our machine with custom login information. This is achieved through the following line of code:

```
MessageBox.Show(objPrincipal.Identity.IsAuthenticated.ToString())
```

and will output in the `MessageBox` as either `True` or `False` depending on whether the user is authenticated or not.

Another piece of information to ensure that our caller is not bypassing system security would be to check and see if the account is operating as a guest. We do this by the following line of code:

```
MessageBox.Show(objIdentity.IsGuest.ToString())
```

Once again, the `IsGuest` returns either `True` or `False`, based on whether the caller is authenticated as a guest.

The final `MessageBox` in our example displays the `ToString` value for the identity object. This is a value that tells us what type of identity it is, either a Windows Identity or non-Windows Identity. The line of code that executes it is:

```
MessageBox.Show(objIdentity.ToString())
```

The output from the `IsString()` method is shown in the screen shot in Figure 13-1.

Again, the principal and identity objects are used in verifying the identity or aspects of the identity of the caller that is attempting to execute our code. Based on this information, we can lock down or release certain system resources. We will show how to lock down and release system resources through our code access permissions examples coming up.

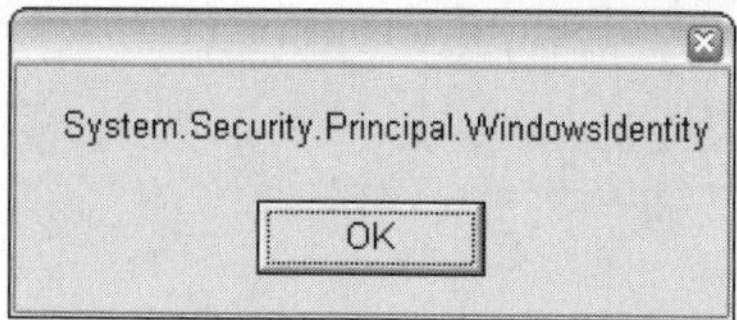

Figure 13-1

Identity Permissions

Identity permissions are pieces of information, also called evidence, by which a piece of code can be identified. Examples of the evidence would be the strong name of the assembly or the digital signature associated with the assembly.

A strong name is a combination of the name of a program, its version number, and its associated cryptographic key and digital signature files.

Identity permissions are granted by the runtime based on information received from the trusted host, or someone who has permission to provide the information. Therefore, they are permissions that we don't specifically request. Identity permissions provide additional information to be used by the runtime when we configure items in the `Caspol.exe` utility. The additional information that the trusted host can supply includes the digital signature, the application directory, or the strong name of the assembly.

Managing Code Access Permissions

In this section, we'll be looking at the most common type of permissions — that of programmatic access — and how they are used. As our example, we created a Windows Form and placed four buttons on it. This Windows Form will be used to illustrate the concept we previously mentioned, namely that, if a method fails, an exception object is generated which contains our feedback. Note at this point, that in the case of a real-world example we would be setting up permissions for a calling application. In many instances we don't want a calling application to be able to access the registry, or we want a calling application to be able to read memory variables, but not change them. However, in order to demonstrate the syntax of our commands, in our examples that follow, we have placed the attempts against the objects we have secured in the same module. In our examples, we first set up the permission that we want and grant the code the appropriate access level we wish it to be able to utilize. Then we use code that accesses our security object to illustrate the effect our permissions have on the code that accesses the objects. We'll also be tying together many of the concepts discussed so far by way of these examples.

To begin with, let's look at an example of trying to access a file in the file system, which will illustrate the use of the `FileIOPermission` class in our `Permissions` namespace. In the first example, the file `C:\testsecurity\testing.txt` has been secured at the operating system level so that no one can access it. In order to do this, the system administrator would set the operating system security on the file to no access:

```
Imports System.Security.Principal
Imports System.Security.Permissions
Imports System.IO

Private Sub btnFileIO_Click(ByVal sender As System.Object, _
```

```
    ByVal e As System.EventArgs) Handles btnFileIO.Click

    Dim oFp As FileIOPermission = New _
      FileIOPermission(FileIOPermissionAccess.Write, "C:\testsecurity\testing.txt")

    oFp.Assert()

    Try
      Dim objWriter As New IO.StreamWriter _
        (File.Open("C:\testsecurity\testing.txt", IO.FileMode.Open))
      objWriter.WriteLine("Hi there!")
      objWriter.Flush()
      objWriter.Close()
      objWriter = Nothing
    Catch objA As System.Exception
      MessageBox.Show(objA.Message)
    End Try

End Sub
```

Let's walk through the code. In this example, we are going to attempt to open a file in the `C:\testsecurity` directory called `testing.txt`. We set the file access permissions within our code so that the method, irrespective of who called it, should be able to get to it with the following lines:

```
Dim oFp As FileIOPermission = New _
  FileIOPermission(FileIOPermissionAccess.Write, "C:\testsecurity\testing.txt")

oFp.Assert()
```

We used the `Assert` method, which declares that the resource should be accessible even if the caller has not been granted permission to access the resource. However, in this case, since the file is secured at the operating system level (by the system administrator), we get the following error, as illustrated in Figure 13-2, that was caught in our exception handling.

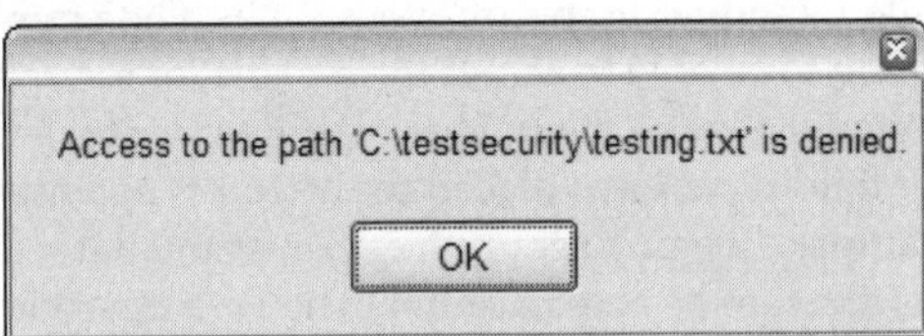

Figure 13-2

Now, let's look at that example again with full operating system rights, but the code permissions set to `Deny`:

```
Protected Sub btnFileIO_Click(ByVal sender As Object, ByVal e As System.EventArgs)

    Dim oFp As FileIOPermission = New _
      FileIOPermission(FileIOPermissionAccess.Write, _
```

```
            "C:\testsecurity\testing.txt")

      oFp.Deny()

      Try
        Dim objWriter As New IO.StreamWriter _
           (File.Open("C:\testsecurity\testing.txt", _
           IO.FileMode.Open))
        objwriter.WriteLine("Hi There")
        objWriter.Flush()
        objWriter.Close()
        objWriter = Nothing

      Catch objA As System.Exception
        messagebox.Show(objA.Message)

      End Try

   End Sub
```

The Deny method denies all callers access to the object, regardless of whether the operating system granted them permission. This is usually a good thing to put into place as not every method you implement needs full and unfettered access to system resources. This helps prevent accidental security vulnerabilities which your method may expose. With the Deny method, we catch the following error in our exception handler as shown in Figure 13-3.

Figure 13-3

As you can see, this error differs from the first by reflecting a `System.Security.Permissions.FileIOPermission` failure as opposed to an operating system level exception.

Now, let's look at an example of how we would use the `EnvironmentPermission` class of the namespace to look at `EnvironmentVariables`.

```
Protected Sub btnTestEnvironmentPermissions_Click _
   (ByVal sender As Object, ByVal e As System.EventArgs) _
    Handles btnTestEnvironmentPermissions.Click

   Dim oEp As EnvironmentPermission = New EnvironmentPermission _
      (EnvironmentPermissionAccess.Read, "Temp")

   Dim sEv As String
```

```
    oEp.Assert()

    Try
        sEv = Environment.GetEnvironmentVariable("Temp")
        MessageBox.Show("Assert was a success")
    Catch objA As System.Exception
        MessageBox.Show("Assert failed")
    End Try

    System.Security.CodeAccessPermission.RevertAssert()
    oEp.Deny()

    Try
       sEv = Environment.GetEnvironmentVariable("Temp")
       MessageBox.Show("Deny was a success")
    Catch objA As System.Exception
        MessageBox.Show("Deny failed")
    End Try

    MessageBox.Show(oEp.ToString)

End Sub
```

There is a lot going on in this example, so let's look at it carefully. We first establish an environment variable permission and use the `Assert` method to ensure access to the code that follows:

```
Dim oEp As EnvironmentPermission = New EnvironmentPermission _
   (EnvironmentPermissionAccess.Read, "Temp")

Dim sEv As String
oEp.Assert()
```

We then try to read the environment variable into a string. If the string read succeeds, we then pop up a message box to reflect the success. If the read fails, a message box is shown reflecting the failure:

```
Try
    sEv = Environment.GetEnvironmentVariable("Temp")
    MessageBox.Show("Assert was a success")
Catch objA As System.Exception
    MessageBox.Show("Assert failed")
End Try
```

Next, we revoke the assert we previously issued by using the `RevertAssert` method and establish `Deny` permissions:

```
System.Security.CodeAccessPermission.RevertAssert()
oEp.Deny()
```

We then try again to read the variable, and write the appropriate result to a message box:

```
Try
    sEv = Environment.GetEnvironmentVariable("Temp")
    MessageBox.Show("Deny failed")
```

```
    Catch objA As System.Exception
        MessageBox.Show("Deny was a success")
    End Try
```

We finally write the ToString of the method to another message box. Following is the output of all three message boxes as a result of running our subroutine. The first two message box messages give us the feedback from our Assert and Deny code, followed by the output of our ToString method:

```
Assert was a success

Deny failed

<IPermission class="System.Security.Permissions.EnvironmentPermission, mscorlib,
 Version=2.0.3600.0, Culture=neutral, PublicKeyToken=b77a5c561934e089"
 version="1" Read="Temp" />
```

As you can see, the ToString method is an XML representation of the permission object that is currently in effect. The first and second message boxes that are output are the system information of the version of the Visual Basic security environment that was running at the time the button was clicked. The third message box is the environment variable name surrounded by the Read tags, which was the permission in effect at the time the ToString method was executed.

Let's look at one more example of where the permissions would affect us in our program functionality, that of accessing the registry. We would generally access the registry on the computer that was the central server for a component in our Windows Forms application.

When we use the EventLog methods to create entries in the machine Event Logs, we access the registry. To illustrate this concept, in the following code example we'll deny permissions to the registry and see the result:

```
Protected Sub btnTestRegistryPermissions_Click(ByVal sender As Object, _
                                        ByVal e As System.EventArgs) _
                                        Handles btnTestRegistryPermissions.Click

    Dim oRp As New _
        RegistryPermission(Security.Permissions.PermissionState.Unrestricted)
    oRp.Deny()

    Dim objLog As New EventLog
    Dim objLogEntryType As EventLogEntryType

    Try
        Throw (New EntryPointNotFoundException)
    Catch objA As System.EntryPointNotFoundException
        Try
            If Not System.Diagnostics.EventLog.SourceExists("Example") Then
                System.Diagnostics.EventLog.CreateEventSource("Example", "System")
            End If

            objLog.Source = "Example"
            objLog.Log = "System"
```

```
            objLogEntryType = EventLogEntryType.Information
            objLog.WriteEntry("Error: " & objA.message, objLogEntryType)
        Catch objB As System.Exception
            MessageBox.Show(objB.Message)
        End Try
    End Try

End Sub
```

As we walk through our code, we start with setting up the registry permission and setting it to `Deny` access:

```
Dim oRp As New _
    RegistryPermission(Security.Permissions.PermissionState.Unrestricted)
oRp.Deny()
```

Next, we set up to `Throw` an exception on purpose in order to set up writing to an Event Log:

```
Throw (New EntryPointNotFoundException)
```

When the exception is caught, it checks the registry to make sure a specific type of registry entry source is already in existence:

```
If Not System.Diagnostics.EventLog.SourceExists("Example") Then
   System.Diagnostics.EventLog.CreateEventSource("Example", "System")
End If
```

And at this point our code fails with the following error message as shown in Figure 13-4.

Figure 13-4

These examples can serve as a good basis for use in developing classes that access the other objects within the scope of the `Permissions` namespace, such as reflections and UI permissions.

Managing Security Policy

As we stated in the introduction to the chapter, we have two new command-line utilities (`Caspol.exe` and `Permview.exe`) that help us configure and view security policy at both machine and user levels. When we manage security policy at this level we are doing so as an administrator of a machine or user policy for a machine that is hosting code that will be called from other front-end applications. `Caspol.exe` is a command-line utility that has many options to give us the ability to configure our security policies (`Caspol` stands for Code Access Security Policy). User and machine policy are associated with groups and permission sets. There is one group that is provided for us, the `AllCode` Group.

The Caspol utility has two categories of commands for us to review. The first category listed in the following table is the set of commands that give us feedback on the current security policy.

Command	Short Command	Parameters	Effect
`-List`	`-l`	None	This lists the combination of the following three options
`-ListGroups`	`-lg`	None	This will list only groups
`-ListPset`	`-lp`	None	This will list only permission sets
`-ListFulltrust`	`-lf`	None	This will list only assemblies which have full trust privileges
`-Reset`	`-rs`	None	This will reset the machine and user policies to the default for .NET. This is handy if a policy creates a condition that is not recoverable. Use this command carefully as you will lose all changes made to the current policies
`--ResolveGroup`	`-rsg`	Assembly File	This will list what groups are associated with a given assembly file
`--ResolvePerm`	`-rsp`	Assembly File	This will list what permission sets are associated with a given assembly file

This is not the list in its entirety, but a listing of some of the more important commands. Now let's look at some examples of output from our previous listed commands.

If we wanted to list the groups active on our local machine at the Visual Studio Command Prompt, we would type the following:

```
Caspol -Machine -ListGroups
```

The output will look similar to the following, as illustrated in Figure 13-5 (though it will differ slightly depending upon the machine you are working on).

Let's talk about the previous screen, so that we know some of the other things that are listed besides what we specifically requested. On the third line, we see that code access security checking is `ON`. On the following line we see that the machine is checking for the user's right to execute the `Caspol` utility, since Execution checking is `ON`. The Policy change prompt is `ON`, so if the user executes a `Caspol` command that will change system policy, there will be an "Are You Sure?" style prompt which appears to confirm that this is really intentional.

```
Visual Studio Command Prompt

C:\Documents and Settings\Administrator>Caspol -Machine -ListGroups
Microsoft (R) .NET Framework CasPol 2.0.40607.16
Copyright (C) Microsoft Corporation. All rights reserved.

Security is ON
Execution checking is ON
Policy change prompt is ON

Level = Machine

Code Groups:

1.  All code: Nothing
   1.1.  Zone - MyComputer: FullTrust
      1.1.1.  StrongName - 002400000480000094000000060200000024000052534131000400
0001000100007D1FA57C4AED9F0A32E84AA0FAEFD0DE9E8FD6AEC8F87FB03766C834C99921EB23BE
79AD9D5DCC1DD9AD236132102900B723CF980957FC4E177108FC607774F29E8320E92EA05ECE4E82
1C0A5EFE8F1645C4C0C93C1AB99285D622CAA652C1DFAD63D745D6F2DE5F17E5EAF0FC4963D261C8
A12436518206DC093344D5AD293: FullTrust
      1.1.2.  StrongName - 00000000000000000400000000000000: FullTrust
   1.2.  Zone - Intranet: LocalIntranet
      1.2.1.  All code: Same site Web
      1.2.2.  All code: Same directory FileIO - 'Read, PathDiscovery'
   1.3.  Zone - Internet: Internet
      1.3.1.  All code: Same site Web
   1.4.  Zone - Untrusted: Nothing
   1.5.  Zone - Trusted: Internet
      1.5.1.  All code: Same site Web
   1.6.  Application: Nothing
      1.6.1.  All code: Same site Web
      1.6.2.  All code: Same directory FileIO - 'Read'
Success

C:\Documents and Settings\Administrator>_
```

Figure 13-5

The level is also listed on our screen prior to our requested output, which is detailed at the bottom listing the groups present on the machine. There are two levels that the policies pertain to, those being the machine and the user. When changing policy, if the user is not an administrator, the user policy is affected unless the user specifically applies the policy to the machine through use of the `-machine` switch, as illustrated in our screenshot. If the user is an administrator, the machine policy is affected unless the user specifically applies the policy to the user level through the use of the `-user` switch.

Let's now look at another request result example. This time we will ask for a listing of all of the permission sets on our machine. At the Command Prompt we would type the following:

```
Caspol -machine -listpset
```

And we would see the output similar to the following screen shot. The following output has been shortened for space considerations, but the output would contain a listing of all of the code explicitly set to execute against the seven permission sets that we mentioned in our definitions section. Also, note that the output is an XML representation of a permission object. The listing details the named permission sets and what each one has as active rights. For instance, the fifth permission set is named `LocalIntranet`, while the next lines detail the `Permission` class, being an environment permission with read access to the environment variable - `USERNAME`. The next class detail is regarding `FileDialogpermissions`, and it lists those as being unrestricted. The screen shot shown in Figure 13-6 then goes on to detail the effective settings for `IsolatedStorage` and others.

```
Visual Studio Command Prompt

C:\Documents and Settings\Administrator>Caspol -Machine -Listpset
Microsoft (R) .NET Framework CasPol 2.0.40607.16
Copyright (C) Microsoft Corporation. All rights reserved.

Security is ON
Execution checking is ON
Policy change prompt is ON

Level = Machine

Named Permission Sets:

1. FullTrust (Allows full access to all resources) =
<PermissionSet class="System.Security.NamedPermissionSet" version="1" Unrestrict
ed="true" Name="FullTrust" Description="Allows full access to all resources" />

2. SkipVerification (Grants right to bypass the verification) =
<PermissionSet class="System.Security.NamedPermissionSet" version="1" Name="Skip
Verification" Description="Grants right to bypass the verification">
   <IPermission class="System.Security.Permissions.SecurityPermission, mscorlib
, Version=2.0.3600.0, Culture=neutral, PublicKeyToken=b77a5c561934e089" version=
"1" Flags="SkipVerification" />
</PermissionSet>

3. Execution (Permits execution) =
<PermissionSet class="System.Security.NamedPermissionSet" version="1" Name="Exec
ution" Description="Permits execution">
   <IPermission class="System.Security.Permissions.SecurityPermission, mscorlib
, Version=2.0.3600.0, Culture=neutral, PublicKeyToken=b77a5c561934e089" version=
"1" Flags="Execution" />
</PermissionSet>

4. Nothing (Denies all resources, including the right to execute) =
<PermissionSet class="System.Security.NamedPermissionSet" version="1" Name="Noth
ing" Description="Denies all resources, including the right to execute" />

5. LocalIntranet (Default rights given to applications on the local intranet) =
<PermissionSet class="System.Security.NamedPermissionSet" version="1" Name="Loca
lIntranet" Description="Default rights given to applications on the local intran
et">
   <IPermission class="System.Security.Permissions.EnvironmentPermission, mscor
lib, Version=2.0.3600.0, Culture=neutral, PublicKeyToken=b77a5c561934e089" versi
on="1" Read="USERNAME" />
   <IPermission class="System.Security.Permissions.FileDialogPermission, mscorl
ib, Version=2.0.3600.0, Culture=neutral, PublicKeyToken=b77a5c561934e089" versio
n="1" Unrestricted="true" />
   <IPermission class="System.Security.Permissions.IsolatedStorageFilePermissio
n, mscorlib, Version=2.0.3600.0, Culture=neutral, PublicKeyToken=b77a5c561934e08
9" version="1" Allowed="AssemblyIsolationByUser" UserQuota="9223372036854775807"
 Expiry="9223372036854775807" Permanent="True" />
   <IPermission class="System.Security.Permissions.ReflectionPermission, mscorl
ib, Version=2.0.3600.0, Culture=neutral, PublicKeyToken=b77a5c561934e089" versio
n="1" Flags="ReflectionEmit" />
   <IPermission class="System.Security.Permissions.SecurityPermission, mscorlib
, Version=2.0.3600.0, Culture=neutral, PublicKeyToken=b77a5c561934e089" version=
"1" Flags="Assertion, Execution, BindingRedirects" />
```

Figure 13-6

Let's now look at the second category of commands that go with the `Caspol` utility as shown in the following table. These commands are those that we will use to actually modify policy.

Command	Short Command	Parameters	Effect
`-AddFullTrust`	`-af`	`Assembly File Name`	Adds a given `Assembly` file to the full trust permission set
`-AddGroup`	`-ag`	`Parent Label, Membership, Permission Set Name`	Adds a code group to the code group hierarchy
`-AddPSet`	`-ap`	`Permission Set Path, Permission Set Name`	Adds a new named permission set to the policy; the permission set should be an XML file
`-ChgGroup`	`-cg`	`Membership, Permission Set Name`	Changes a code group's information
`-ChgPset&`	`-cp`	`File Name, Permission Set Name`	Changes a named permission set's information
`-Force&`	`-f&`		This option is not recommended. It forces `Caspol` to accept policy changes even if the change could cause `Caspol` itself not to be able to be executed
`-Recover`	`-r&`		Recovers policy information from a backup file that is controlled by the utility
`-RemFullTrust`	`-rf`	`Assembly File Name`	Removes a given `Assembly` file from the full trust permission set
`-RemGroup`	`-rg`	`Label`	Removes a code group
`-RemPSet`	`-rp`	`Permission Set Name`	Removes a permission set. The seven default sets cannot be removed

Again, this is not a comprehensive list of all the available commands, therefore you should consult the MSDN documentation for the complete listing, if needed. Let's begin our discussion of these commands with a few more definitions that will help us understand the parameters that go with our commands. An assembly file is created within Visual Basic each time we do a build where our version is a release version. An assembly needs to have a strong name associated with it in order to be used in our permissions groupings. An assembly gets a strong name from being associated with a digital signature uniquely identifying the assembly. We carry out this association in addition to providing other pieces of evidence to be used with the strong name within the `AssemblyInfo.vb` file of our project. To do this, open up the `AssemblyInfo.vb` file within Visual Studio 2005. This file is automatically created for you by Visual Studio when you create a project. Simply add a new assembly attribute to the list as shown here:

```
<Assembly: AssemblyKeyFileAttribute("myKey.snk")>
```

This associates our assembly with an existing originating key file in order for Visual Studio to generate a strong name during the build process. Be sure that you place the key file in the project directory as this is where Visual Studio will be looking for it during the build process.

During the build, Visual Studio has generated the strong name, and then we can add our assembly to our security configuration. Place the executable, `SecurityApp.exe` (your executable will be the name of your project), which was created from our build, into the `C:\testsecurity` directory on the local machine for use with our policy method illustrations.

If we wanted to add our assembly to the `fulltrust` permission set, we would type

```
Caspol -addfulltrust C:\testsecurity\SecurityApp.exe
```

The following is a screen shot of the outcome of our command (Figure 13-7).

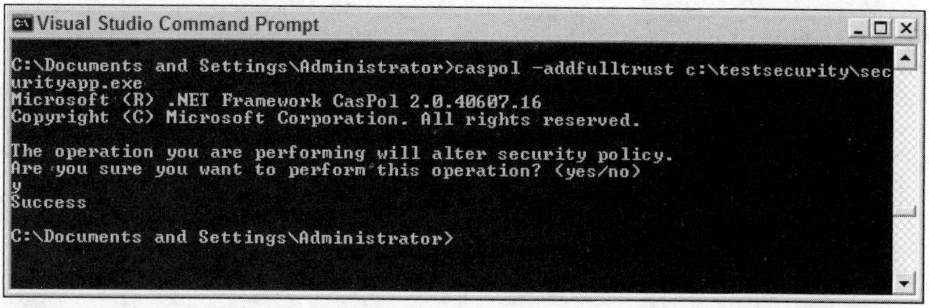

```
Visual Studio Command Prompt

C:\Documents and Settings\Administrator>caspol -addfulltrust c:\testsecurity\sec
urityapp.exe
Microsoft (R) .NET Framework CasPol 2.0.40607.16
Copyright (C) Microsoft Corporation. All rights reserved.

The operation you are performing will alter security policy.
Are you sure you want to perform this operation? (yes/no)
y
Success

C:\Documents and Settings\Administrator>
```

Figure 13-7

As we can see, we were prompted before our command altered our security policy, and then our new application was added to the `fulltrust` assembly list. We can confirm it was added by issuing the following command:

```
Caspol -listfulltrust
```

The excerpt of output from our command that includes our new assembly would look like what is shown in Figure 13-8.

In the screen shot, we can see our application name, version, and key information that was associated with our .exe file when we did our build.

Now, let's look at the creation and addition of a permission set to our permission sets in our security policy. Permission sets can be created by hand, in any text editor, in an XML format and saved as an .xml file (for this example we have saved it as `securityexample.xml`). Following is a listing from one such file that was created for this example:

```
<PermissionSet class="System.Security.NamedPermissionSet" version="1">
   <Permission class="System.Security.Permissions.FileIOPermission, mscorlib,
         SN=03689116d3a4ae33" version="1">
      <Read> C:\TestSecurity </Read>
   </Permission>
```

```
    <Permission class="System.Security.Permissions.EnvironmentPermission,
             mscorlib, SN=03689116d3a4ae33" version="1">
       <Read> [TEMP] </Read>
     </Permission>
     <Name>SecurityExample</Name>
     <Description>Gives Full File Access</Description>
</PermissionSet>
```

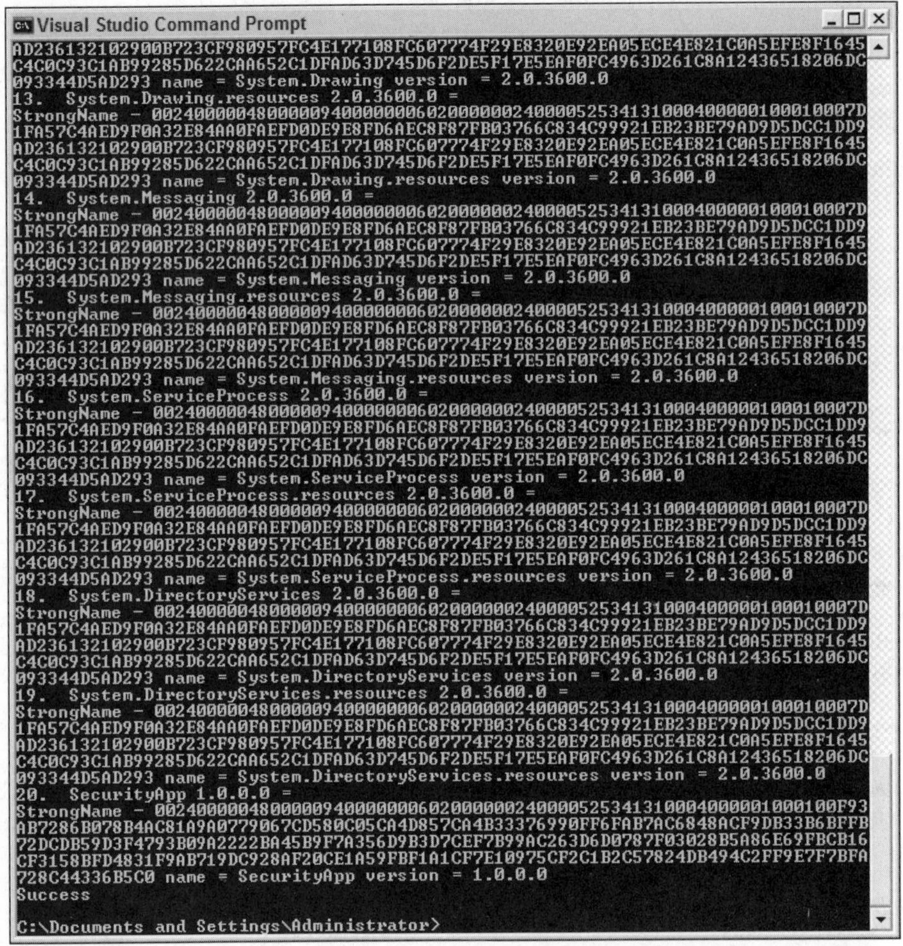

Figure 13-8

The listing has multiple permissions within the permission set. The listing sets up read file permissions within one set of tags as shown:

```
<Permission class="System.Security.Permissions.FileIOPermission, mscorlib,
           SN=03689116d3a4ae33" version="1">
   <Read> C:\TestSecurity </Read>
</Permission>
```

We then set up read access to our `Temp` environment variable in the second set of permission tags:

```
<Permission class="System.Security.Permissions.EnvironmentPermission,
          mscorlib, SN=03689116d3a4ae33" version="1">
   <Read> [TEMP] </Read>
</Permission>
```

The listing also gives our custom permission set the name of `SecurityExample` with a description:

```
<Name>SecurityExample</Name>
<Description>Gives Full File Access</Description>
```

When we want to add our permission set to our policy, we would type the following command:

```
Caspol -addpset C:\testsecurity\securityexample.xml securityexample
```

In the last command, we are issuing the `-addpset` flag to indicate that we want to add a permission set, followed by the XML file containing our permission set, followed finally by the name of our permission set. The outcome of our command looks like the following screen shot (Figure 13-9).

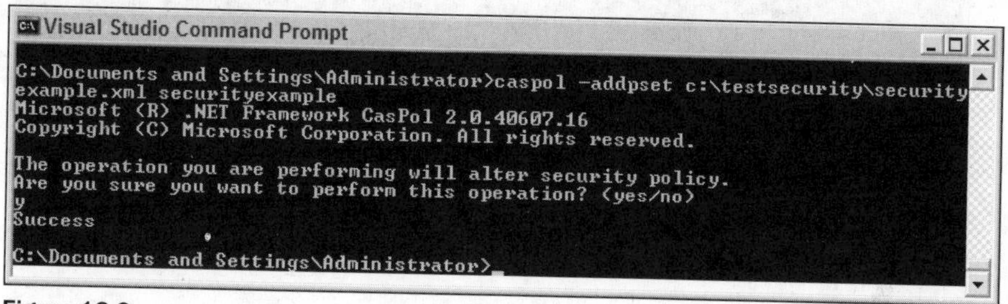

```
Visual Studio Command Prompt
C:\Documents and Settings\Administrator>caspol -addpset c:\testsecurity\security
example.xml securityexample
Microsoft (R) .NET Framework CasPol 2.0.40607.16
Copyright (C) Microsoft Corporation. All rights reserved.

The operation you are performing will alter security policy.
Are you sure you want to perform this operation? (yes/no)
y
Success

C:\Documents and Settings\Administrator>_
```

Figure 13-9

We can then list our security permission sets by typing `Caspol -listpset`. Here is the excerpt (Figure 13-10) that shows our new security permission set.

As you can see, typing `Caspol -listpset` gives a listing of just the permission sets within our policy. Our named permission set `SecurityExample` shows up under the `Named Permission Sets` heading, and its description is listed just after its name.

Now that we have a permission set, we can add a group that our assembly object fits into and which enforces our new permission set. We add this group by using the `AddGroup` switch in `Caspol`. The `AddGroup` switch has a couple of parameters that need more explanation. The first parameter is `parent_label`. When we look at the group screen shot that follows, we can see our `All code` group has a `1.` before it. The labels within code groups have a hierarchy that gets established when we add groups, and so we need to specify what our parent label would be. In our case, since the only one that exists is `1.`, that is what we'll be designating.

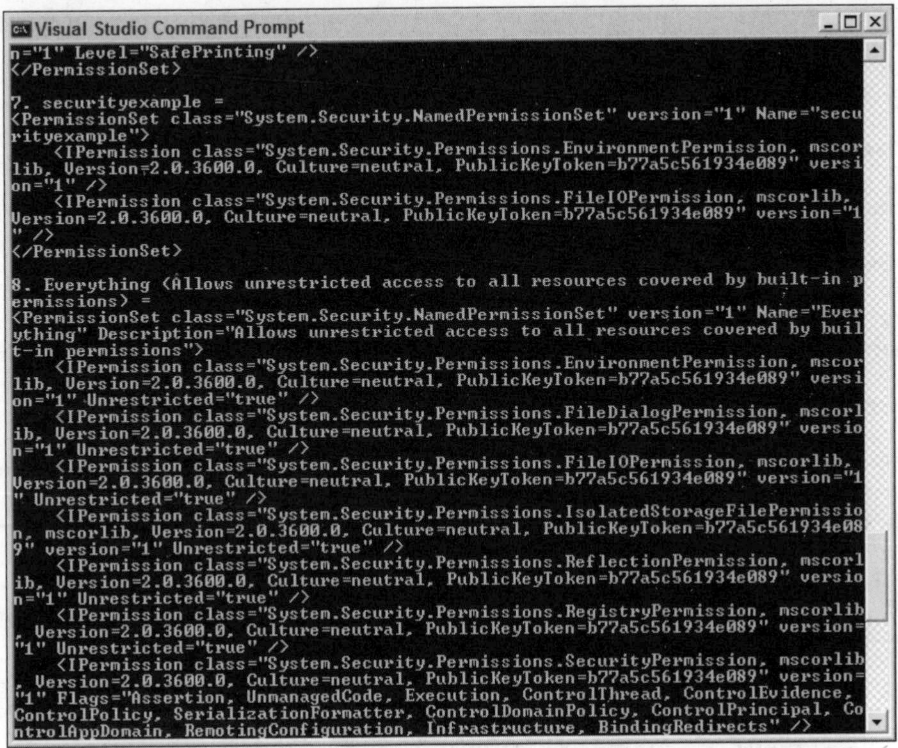

Visual Studio Command Prompt
n="1" Level="SafePrinting" />
</PermissionSet>
7. securityexample =
<PermissionSet class="System.Security.NamedPermissionSet" version="1" Name="secu
rityexample">
<IPermission class="System.Security.Permissions.EnvironmentPermission, mscor
lib, Version=2.0.3600.0, Culture=neutral, PublicKeyToken=b77a5c561934e089" versi
on="1" />
<IPermission class="System.Security.Permissions.FileIOPermission, mscorlib,
Version=2.0.3600.0, Culture=neutral, PublicKeyToken=b77a5c561934e089" version="1
" />
</PermissionSet>
8. Everything (Allows unrestricted access to all resources covered by built-in p
ermissions) =
<PermissionSet class="System.Security.NamedPermissionSet" version="1" Name="Ever
ything" Description="Allows unrestricted access to all resources covered by buil
t-in permissions">
<IPermission class="System.Security.Permissions.EnvironmentPermission, mscor
lib, Version=2.0.3600.0, Culture=neutral, PublicKeyToken=b77a5c561934e089" versi
on="1" Unrestricted="true" />
<IPermission class="System.Security.Permissions.FileDialogPermission, mscorl
ib, Version=2.0.3600.0, Culture=neutral, PublicKeyToken=b77a5c561934e089" versio
n="1" Unrestricted="true" />
<IPermission class="System.Security.Permissions.FileIOPermission, mscorlib,
Version=2.0.3600.0, Culture=neutral, PublicKeyToken=b77a5c561934e089" version="1
" Unrestricted="true" />
<IPermission class="System.Security.Permissions.IsolatedStorageFilePermissio
n, mscorlib, Version=2.0.3600.0, Culture=neutral, PublicKeyToken=b77a5c561934e08
9" version="1" Unrestricted="true" />
<IPermission class="System.Security.Permissions.ReflectionPermission, mscorl
ib, Version=2.0.3600.0, Culture=neutral, PublicKeyToken=b77a5c561934e089" versio
n="1" Unrestricted="true" />
<IPermission class="System.Security.Permissions.RegistryPermission, mscorlib
, Version=2.0.3600.0, Culture=neutral, PublicKeyToken=b77a5c561934e089" version=
"1" Unrestricted="true" />
<IPermission class="System.Security.Permissions.SecurityPermission, mscorlib
, Version=2.0.3600.0, Culture=neutral, PublicKeyToken=b77a5c561934e089" version=
"1" Flags="Assertion, UnmanagedCode, Execution, ControlThread, ControlEvidence,
ControlPolicy, SerializationFormatter, ControlDomainPolicy, ControlPrincipal, Co
ntrolAppDomain, RemotingConfiguration, Infrastructure, BindingRedirects" />

Figure 13-10

Since we designate `1`, the new group will become a child of 1. The second parameter is `membership`. The `membership` parameter has a certain list of options that we can put in based on the following table. Each option designates a piece of information we are providing about the pieces of code that we will add to our group. For instance, we would state that we will only be adding code that had a specific signature with the `-Pub` option, or add only code in a certain application directory with the `-AppDir` option.

Option	Description
`-All`	All code
`-Pub`	Code that has a specific signature on a certificate file
`-Strong`	Code that has a specific strong name, as designated by a file name, code name, and version
`-Zone`	Code that fits into the following zones: MyComputer, Intranet, Trusted, Internet, or Untrusted
`-Site`	Originating on a Web site

Option	Description
`-Hash`	Code that has a specific assembly hash
`-AppDir`	A specific application directory
`-SkipVerif`	Code that requests the `skipverification` permission
`-URL`	Originating at a specific URL
`-Custom`	Code that requires a custom membership condition.

The third parameter to the `AddGroup` command is the permission set name that we want to be associated with our group. The group that we will create will be under parent label 1, and we will designate the `-Zone` parameter as being `MyComputer` since our code lives on a local drive. We will also associate the new group with our `SecurityExample` permission set by typing the following command:

```
Caspol -addgroup 1. -Zone MyComputer SecurityExample
```

We can see that our output from the command was successful in the screen shot shown in Figure 13-11.

In our screen shot (Figure 13-12), we use the `-listgroups` command to list our new group.

In the screen shot, we can see that a 1.6 level was added with our `SecurityExample` permission set attached to all code that fits into the MyComputer Zone. Now, let's verify that our assembly object fits into the MyComputer Zone by using our `resolveperm` command. This is illustrated in Figure 13-13.

As we can see at the bottom of the screen shot, it lists which `ZoneIdentityPermission` the assembly object has been associated with — MyComputer. In addition, each assembly will get a `URLIdentityPermission` specifying the location of the executable.

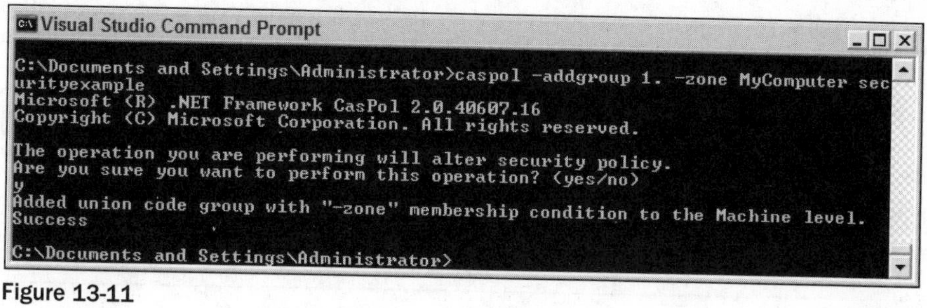

```
Visual Studio Command Prompt
C:\Documents and Settings\Administrator>caspol -addgroup 1. -zone MyComputer sec
urityexample
Microsoft (R) .NET Framework CasPol 2.0.40607.16
Copyright (C) Microsoft Corporation. All rights reserved.

The operation you are performing will alter security policy.
Are you sure you want to perform this operation? (yes/no)
y
Added union code group with "-zone" membership condition to the Machine level.
Success

C:\Documents and Settings\Administrator>
```

Figure 13-11

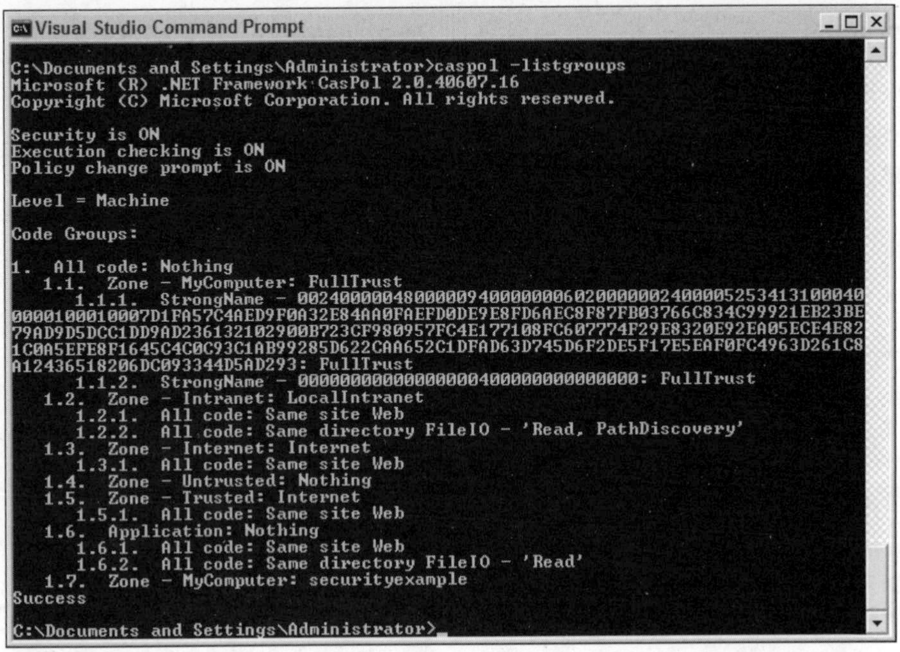

```
Visual Studio Command Prompt

C:\Documents and Settings\Administrator>caspol -listgroups
Microsoft (R) .NET Framework CasPol 2.0.40607.16
Copyright (C) Microsoft Corporation. All rights reserved.

Security is ON
Execution checking is ON
Policy change prompt is ON

Level = Machine

Code Groups:

1.  All code: Nothing
   1.1.  Zone - MyComputer: FullTrust
      1.1.1.  StrongName - 002400000480000094000000060200000024000052534131000400
00010001007D1FA57C4AED9F0A32E84AA0FAEFD0DE9E8FD6AEC8F87FB03766C834C99921EB23BE
79AD9D5DCC1DD9AD236132102900B723CF980957FC4E177108FC607774F29E8320E92EA05ECE4E82
1C0A5EFE8F1645C4C0C93C1AB99285D622CAA652C1DFAD63D745D6F2DE5F17E5EAF0FC4963D261C8
A12436518206DC093344D5AD293: FullTrust
      1.1.2.  StrongName - 00000000000000000400000000000000: FullTrust
   1.2.  Zone - Intranet: LocalIntranet
      1.2.1.  All code: Same site Web
      1.2.2.  All code: Same directory FileIO - 'Read, PathDiscovery'
   1.3.  Zone - Internet: Internet
      1.3.1.  All code: Same site Web
   1.4.  Zone - Untrusted: Nothing
   1.5.  Zone - Trusted: Internet
      1.5.1.  All code: Same site Web
   1.6.  Application: Nothing
      1.6.1.  All code: Same site Web
      1.6.2.  All code: Same directory FileIO - 'Read'
   1.7.  Zone - MyComputer: securityexample
Success

C:\Documents and Settings\Administrator>_
```

Figure 13-12

Not only do we have the utility that helps us with managing security permission sets and groups, but we also have a utility that views the security information regarding an assembly called `Permview.exe`. (`Permview` stands for Permissions Viewer.)

`Permview` is not as complex as `Caspol` because its main purpose is to give a certain type of feedback regarding the security requests of assemblies. In fact, the `Permview` utility only has two switches, one for the output location, and one for declarative security to be included in the output. In order to specify an output location the switch is `/Output` and then a file path is appended to the command line after the switch. The `Permview` utility brings up another concept we have yet to cover, that of declarative security.

Declarative security is displayed in the `Permview` utility with the `/Decl` switch, and is security that a piece of code requests at an assembly level. Since it is at the assembly level, the line which requests the security is at the top of the Visual Basic module, even before our `Imports` statements. We can request one of three levels of security, as shown in the following table.

Level	Description
`RequestMinimum`	Permissions the code must have in order to run
`RequestOptional`	Permissions that code may use, but could run without
`RequestRefused`	Permissions that you want to ensure are never granted to the code

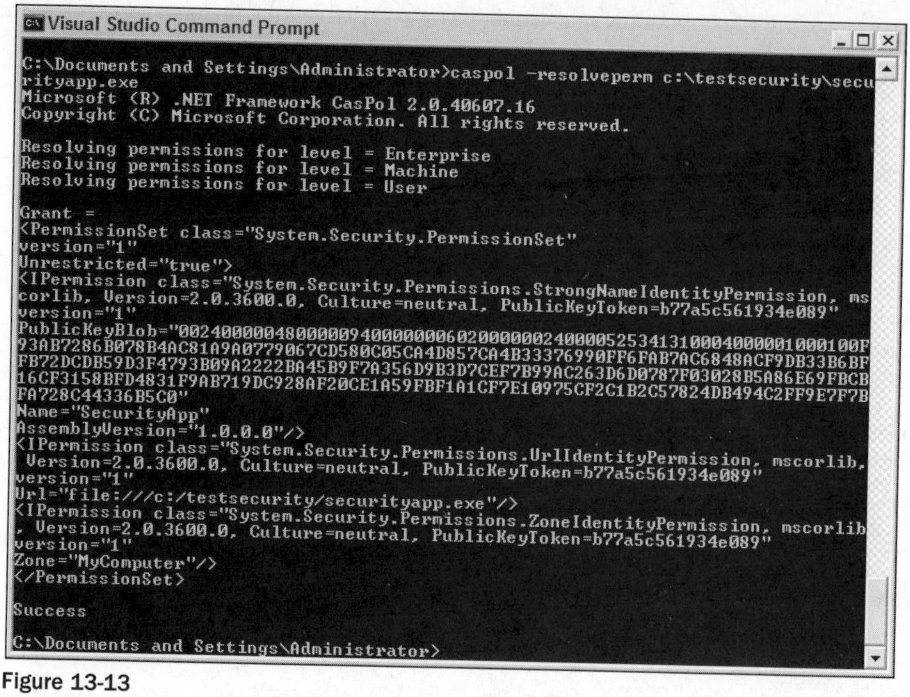

```
Visual Studio Command Prompt
C:\Documents and Settings\Administrator>caspol -resolveperm c:\testsecurity\secu
rityapp.exe
Microsoft (R) .NET Framework CasPol 2.0.40607.16
Copyright (C) Microsoft Corporation. All rights reserved.

Resolving permissions for level = Enterprise
Resolving permissions for level = Machine
Resolving permissions for level = User

Grant =
<PermissionSet class="System.Security.PermissionSet"
version="1"
Unrestricted="true">
<IPermission class="System.Security.Permissions.StrongNameIdentityPermission, ms
corlib, Version=2.0.3600.0, Culture=neutral, PublicKeyToken=b77a5c561934e089"
version="1"
PublicKeyBlob="0024000004800000940000000602000000240000525341310004000001000100F
93AB7286B078B4AC81A9A0779067CD580C05CA4D857CA4B3337699 0FF6FAB7AC6848ACF9DB33B6BF
FB72DCDB59D3F4793B09A2222BA45B9F7A356D9B3D7CEF7B99AC263D6D0787F03028B5A86E69FBCB
16CF3158BFD4831F9AB719DC928AF20CE1A59FBF1A1CF7E10975CF2C1B2C57824DB494C2FF9E7F7B
FA728C44336B5C0"
Name="SecurityApp"
AssemblyVersion="1.0.0.0"/>
<IPermission class="System.Security.Permissions.UrlIdentityPermission, mscorlib,
 Version=2.0.3600.0, Culture=neutral, PublicKeyToken=b77a5c561934e089"
version="1"
Url="file:///c:/testsecurity/securityapp.exe"/>
<IPermission class="System.Security.Permissions.ZoneIdentityPermission, mscorlib
, Version=2.0.3600.0, Culture=neutral, PublicKeyToken=b77a5c561934e089"
version="1"
Zone="MyComputer"/>
</PermissionSet>

Success

C:\Documents and Settings\Administrator>
```

Figure 13-13

Requesting permissions at the assembly level will help ensure that the code will be able to run, and not get permission-based security exceptions. Since we have users calling our code, the declarative security ensures the callers have proper security to do all that our code requires, otherwise a security exception will be thrown. The following is an example of the syntax of how we would request minimum permissions, and the code would be placed at the top of our procedure. This example also illustrates syntax as described in the table at the beginning of our chapter regarding permissions in the `Security.Permissions` namespace. It also illustrates the use of a security constant, `SecurityAction.RequestMinimum` for the type of security we are requesting:

```
<Assembly: SecurityPermissionAttribute(SecurityAction.RequestMinimum)>
```

Once this line is added to our assembly by means of the `AssemblyInfo.vb` file, `Permview` will report on what the assembly requested by listing minimal, optional, and refused permission sets, including our security permission set under the minimal set listing.

Figuring the Minimum Permissions Required for Your Application

Before the .NET Framework 2.0, one of the big requests from developers who were building and deploying applications was the need for understanding which permissions were required for the application to run. This was sometimes a difficult task as developers would build their applications under Full Trust and then the applications would be deployed to a machine where it wouldn't have those kinds of privileges.

The .NET Framework 2.0 introduces a new tool that can be used to fully understand which permissions your application is going to need in order to run on another machine. This command-line tool, `PermCalc.exe`, does this by emulating the complete path of your assembly and all the permissions that it would require.

To use `PermCalc.exe`, open up the Visual Studio Command Prompt and navigate to the location of the assembly you want to check. `PermCalc.exe` takes the following command structure:

```
PermCalc.exe [Options] <assembly>
```

Or you can also have `PermCalc.exe` evaluate more than a single assembly.

```
PermCalc.exe [Options] <assembly> <assembly>
```

As an example of this, we ran the `PermCalc.exe` tool on the `SecurityApp.exe` and were given the following results:

```
Microsoft (R) .NET Framework Permissions Calculator.
Copyright (C) Microsoft Corporation 2003. All rights reserved.

<Assembly Name="C:\Documents and Settings\Administrator\My Documents\Visual
 Studio\Projects\SecurityApp\SecurityApp\obj\Debug\securityapp.exe">
<PermissionSet class="System.Security.PermissionSet"
 version="1">
<IPermission class="System.Security.Permissions.EnvironmentPermission, mscorlib,
 Version=2.0.3600.0, Culture=neutral, PublicKeyToken=b77a5c561934e089"
 version="1"
 Unrestricted="true"/>
<IPermission class="System.Security.Permissions.FileIOPermission, mscorlib,
 Version=2.0.3600.0, Culture=neutral, PublicKeyToken=b77a5c561934e089"
 version="1"
 Unrestricted="true"/>
<IPermission class="System.Security.Permissions.RegistryPermission, mscorlib,
 Version=2.0.3600.0, Culture=neutral, PublicKeyToken=b77a5c561934e089"
 version="1"
 Unrestricted="true"/>
<IPermission class="System.Security.Permissions.SecurityPermission, mscorlib,
 Version=2.0.3600.0, Culture=neutral, PublicKeyToken=b77a5c561934e089"
 version="1"
 Flags="UnmanagedCode, Execution, ControlEvidence, ControlPrincipal,
 RemotingConfiguration"/>
<IPermission class="System.Net.SocketPermission, System, Version=2.0.3600.0,
 Culture=neutral, PublicKeyToken=b77a5c561934e089"
 version="1"
 Unrestricted="true"/>
<IPermission class="System.Diagnostics.PerformanceCounterPermission, System,
 Version=2.0.3600.0, Culture=neutral, PublicKeyToken=b77a5c561934e089"
 version="1"
```

```
 Unrestricted="true"/>
<IPermission class="System.Net.NetworkInformation.NetworkInformationPermission,
 System, Version=2.0.3600.0, Culture=neutral, PublicKeyToken=b77a5c561934e089"
 version="1"
 Access="Read"/>
</PermissionSet>

</Assembly>
```

From this output, you can see the permissions that would be required for the application to run on someone's machine. These results were generated using the command:

```
PermCalc.exe -under SecurityApp.exe
```

The option `-Under` should be used when you are unsure of the exact permissions as `PermCalc.exe` actually always overestimates the permissions by default. Using `-Under` forces `PermCalc.exe` to underestimate the permissions instead.

Using Visual Studio to Figure Minimum Permissions

Looking at the properties of your solution in Visual Studio, you will notice that there is a new Security tab. One of the problems in testing your application's security and permissioning situations in the past was that as a developer, you were always forced to develop your programs under Full Trust. This means that you have access to the system's resources in a very open and free manner. This was an issue because the programs that you build typically cannot run under Full Trust and you still have to test the application's abilities to tap into the system's resources in which the program is being run.

The new Security tab is a new GUI face to the `PermCalc.exe` tool and allows you to run your applications under different types of zones. Figure 13-14 shows a screen shot of this new page from the solution property page.

After checking the Enable ClickOnce Security Settings check box, you will be able to select whether the application will be running on the client machine under full trust or whether the application will only have a partial trust status. You will also be able to select the zone in which your application will run. The options include

- Local Intranet
- Internet
- Custom

After selecting the zone type you are wishing to test the application in, you can then examine all of the various permissions that are required by the application in order to run.

Pressing the Calculate Permissions button on the form will do just that (shown in Figure 13-15). Visual Studio will examine the assembly and provide you with information on what permissions for which assemblies would be required to run the application in the zone specified.

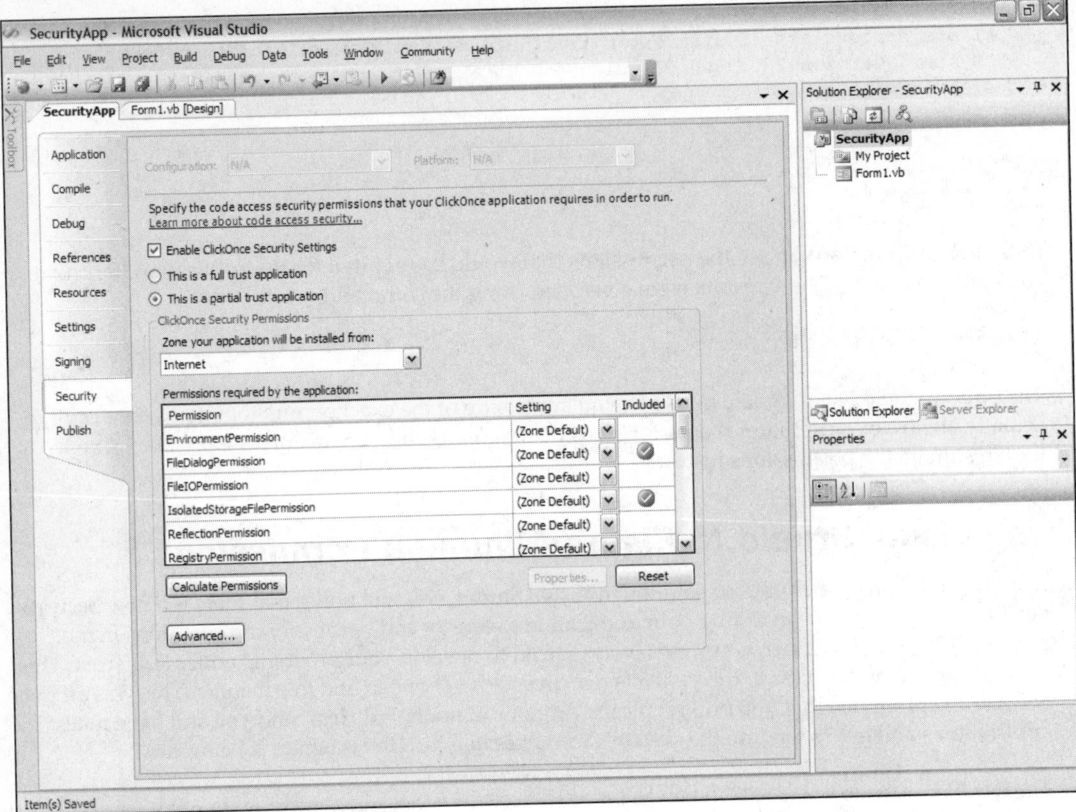

Figure 13-14

Figure 13-15

Once analyzed, Visual Studio will present information on what is needed from each of the assemblies in order for the application to function. This is illustrated in Figure 13-16.

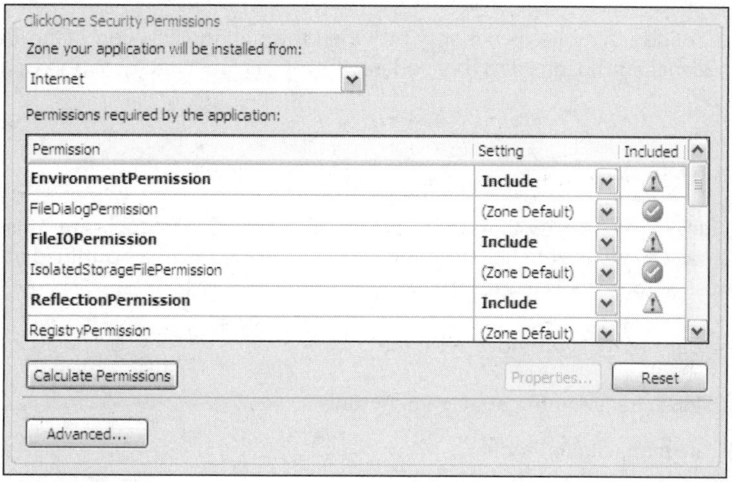

Figure 13-16

What makes this section of the application's property pages even better is that from the textbox of assemblies listed, you can highlight selected assemblies and fine-tune their permissions even further—granulizing the permissions the assemblies are allowed to work with. For instance, highlighting the `FileIOPermission` line in the textbox and pressing the Properties button allows you to fine-tune how the permissioning around this assembly will function. The dialog that appears in this situation is shown in Figure 13-17.

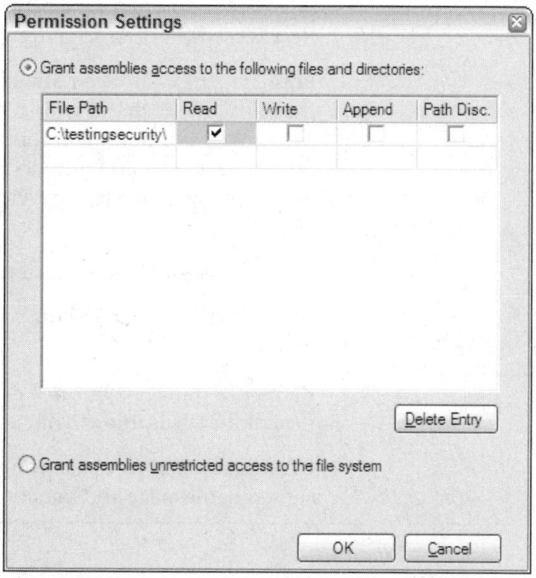

Figure 13-17

From this screen shot, you can see that the `FileIOPermission` part of the permission settings allows you to specify the file path that the assembly is allowed to access as well as the actions that the assembly is allowed to take in the path defined.

The ability to examine assemblies is not only provided through the new command-line tool, `PermCalc.exe`, but even Visual Studio joins the fray and allows for easy management and understanding of your applications.

Security Tools

Microsoft provides many security tools in its .NET SDK. Most of these tools are console-based utility applications. These can be used to help implement the security processes outlined above. We won't be discussing the use of these tools in great detail.

There are two groups of tools provided with the SDK:

- Permissions and assembly management tools
- Certificate management tools

Permissions and Assembly Management Tools

Program Name	Function
`Caspol.exe`	Stands for Code Access Security Policy tool. Lets you view and modify security settings
`Signcode.exe`	File signing tool; lets you digitally sign your executable files
`Storeadm.exe`	Administration tool for isolated storage management. Restricts code access to filing system
`Permcalc.exe`	Emulates the complete path of your assembly and all of the permissions that it would require. It can also evaluate assemblies and provide information on the permissions an end user would require to run the program. This is a new command-line tool provided by the .NET Framework 2.0.
`Permview.exe`	Displays assembly's requested access permissions
`Peverify.exe`	Checks if the executable file will pass the runtime test for type-safe coding
`Secutil.exe`	Extracts a public key from a certificate and puts it in a format that is usable in your source code
`Sn.exe`	Creates assemblies with strong names; that is, digitally signed namespace and version info

Certificate Management Tools

Program Name	Function
`Makecert.exe`	Creates an X.509 certificate for testing purposes
`Certmgr.exe`	Assembles certificates into a CTL (Certificate Trust List). Can also be used for revoking
`Chktrust.exe`	Validates a signed file containing data, its PKCS#7 hash, and a X.509 certificate
`Cert2spc.exe`	Creates an SPC (Software Publisher Certificate) from an X.509 certificate

Dealing with Exceptions Using the SecurityException Class

In this latest release of the .NET Framework , the `SecurityException` class has been greatly expanded in order to provide considerably more detailed information on the types of exceptions that are encountered in a security context.

In the past, using .NET Framework versions 1.0/1.1, the `SecurityException` class provided very little information in the way of actually telling you what was wrong and why the exception was thrown. Due to this limitation, the .NET Framework 2.0 has added a number of new properties to the `SecurityException` class. The following table details the properties of the `SecurityException` class.

Properties	Description
`Action`	Retrieves the security action which caused the exception to occur
`Demanded`	Returns the permissions, permission sets, or permission set collections which caused the error to occur
`DenySetInstance`	Returns the denied permissions, permissions sets, or permission set collections which caused the security actions to fail
`FailedAssemblyInfo`	Returns information about the failed assembly
`FirstPermissionThatFailed`	Returns the first permission contained in the permission set or permission set collection which failed
`GrantedSet`	Returns the set of permissions that caused the security actions to fail
`Method`	Returns information about the method that is connected to the exception

Table continued on following page

Properties	Description
`PermissionState`	Returns the state of the permission that threw the exception
`PermissionType`	Returns the type of the permission that threw the exception
`PermitOnlySetInstance`	Returns a permission set or permission set collection which is part of the permit-only stack frame if a security action has failed
`RefusedSet`	Returns the permissions that were refused by the assembly
`Url`	Returns the URL of the assembly which caused the exception
`Zone`	Returns the zone of the assembly which caused the exception

As you can see, there is a lot of information that you can get your hands on if there is a security exception that is thrown in your application. For instance, you can use something similar to the following `Catch` section of code to check for security errors:

```
Dim myFile as FileStream

Try
   myFile = My.Computer.FileSystem.GetFileInfo("C:\testingsecurity\testing.txt")
Catch ex As Security.SecurityException
   MessageBox.Show(ex.Method.Name.ToString())
End Try
```

One nice addition to the `SecurityException` class is in how Visual Studio so easily works with it. If you encounter a `SecurityException` error while working in the debug mode of your solution, you will see something similar to the following warning directly in the IDE as shown in Figure 13-18.

The nice thing is the detailed error notification that is shown in Figure 13-14. Also, it is possible to get Visual Studio to provide a detailed view of the error by breaking down the `SecurityException` object in the Locals window of Visual Studio when you catch the error using a `Try-Catch` statement.

Now that we've covered the permissions side of .NET security, let's take a look at cryptography.

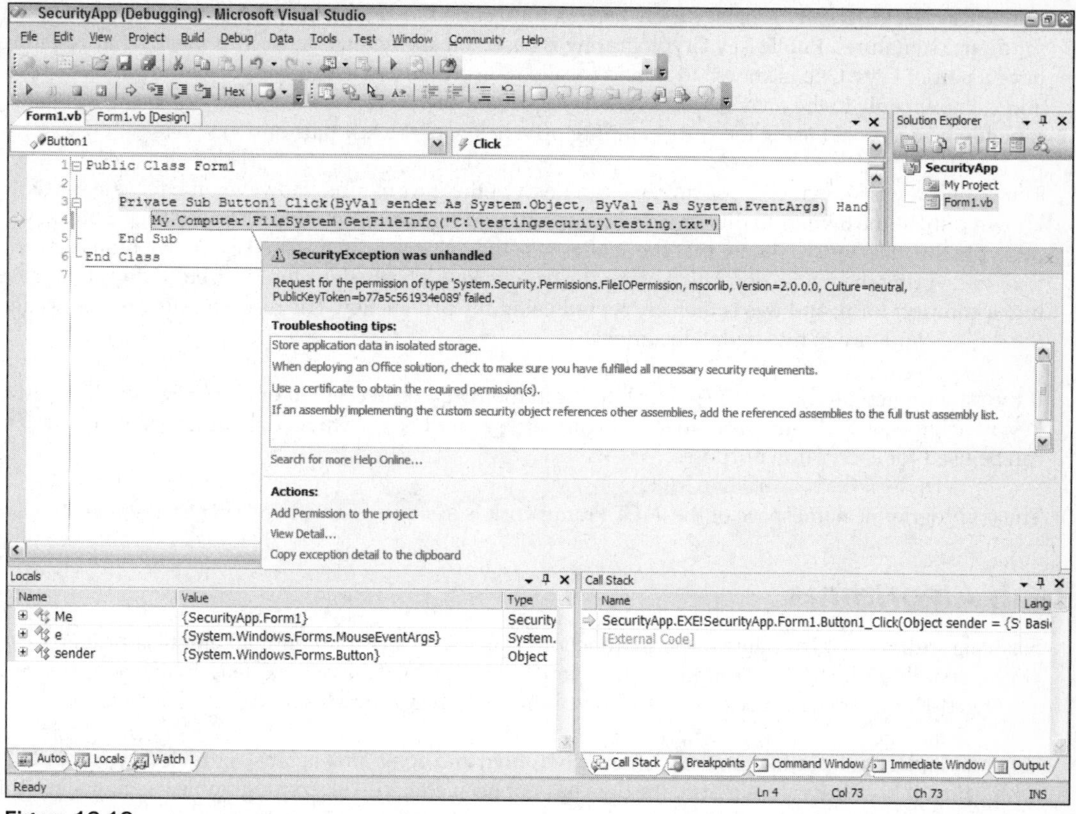

Figure 13-18

Cryptography Basics

Rather than being a general exposition of cryptography, this section is meant to familiarize you with basic techniques required to deal with .NET security and protecting your Web Services through encryption. The three building blocks we need are hashing algorithms, secret key encryption, and an understanding of the Public Key Cryptographic System (PKCS).

Hashing algorithms digest long sequences of data into short footprints, the most popular being 64-bit hash keys. The two most popular hashing algorithms are SHA (Secured Hash Algorithm) and MD5 (Message Digest version 5). These hash keys are used for signing digital documents; in other words, the hash is generated and encrypted using a private key.

Secret key encryption is commonly used to protect data through passwords and pass phrases (long phrases that would be difficult to guess). Secret key encryption is suitable for situations where the encrypted data needs to be accessed by the same person who protected it.

Public Key Cryptography is most widely used in protecting the data through encryption. It is also used for digital signatures. Public Key Cryptography is based on asymmetric keys. This means that you always have a pair of keys. One is known to all and is called the public key. The other key of the pair is kept secret and is known only to the owner. This is called the private key. If we use the public key to encrypt data, it can only be decrypted using the corresponding private key of the key pair, and vice versa.

The public key is known to all, so any one can decrypt the information. However, the private key is known only to the owner, so this process acts as a digital signature. In other words, if the public key decrypts the message, we know that the sender was the owner of the private key. As we hinted, rather than encrypting the whole document using the private key, a hash algorithm is used to digest the data into a compact form, and this is then encrypted using the private key. The result of this process is called the digital signature of the digital document.

If the data is encrypted using the public key, it can then only be decrypted by the corresponding private key, which means that only the owner of the private key will be able to read the unencrypted data. This can be used for encryption purposes.

The cryptographic namespace of the .NET Framework is `System.Security.Cryptography`.

Hash Algorithms

Hash algorithms are also called one-way functions. This is because of their mathematical property of nonreversibility. The hash algorithms reduce large binary strings into a fixed-length binary byte array. This fixed-length binary array is used for computing digital signatures, as explained earlier.

To verify a piece of information, the hash is recomputed and compared against a previously computed hash value. If both the values match, the data has not been altered. The cryptographic hashing algorithms map a large stream of binary data to a much shorter fixed length, so it is theoretically possible to have two different documents having the same hash key.

Although, in theory, it is possible that two documents may have the same MD5 hash key and a different check sum, it is computationally impossible to create a forged document having the same hash key as the original hash value. Take the case of a virus attack on an executable code. In the late eighties, the state-of-art was to create a check sum or a CRC (Cyclic Redundancy Check) as a protection measure against accidental or malicious damage to the code integrity.

Virus makers drew cunning designs to create viruses that added padding code to the victim's files so that the check sum and CRC remained unchanged in spite of the infection. However, using MD5 hash values, this kind of stealth attack is rendered unfeasible.

Windows Meta Files (WMF) still use check sums in the file header. For example, the .NET Framework class `System.Drawing.Imaging.WmfPlaceableFileHeader` has a read/write property of type `short` called `Checksum`. However, due to ease of computation, this check sum is used as a cheap mode of protection against accidental damage rather than against malicious attacks.

Here is a simple program to calculate a check sum:

```
' Cryptography/Checksum.vb

Imports System
Imports System.IO

Module Module1
```

This is the entry point for the program. Here, we check to see if we've received the correct argument from the command line to run the program, and stop the program if we haven't:

```
Public Sub Main(ByVal CmdArgs() As String)
    If (CmdArgs.Length <> 1) Then
        Console.WriteLine("usage: Checksum <filename>")
        End
    End If
```

First, we open the file for which the check sum is to be computed:

```
Dim fs As FileStream = File.OpenRead(CmdArgs(0))
```

We then compute the check sum and close the file, and then output the result to the screen:

```
    Dim sum As Short = compute(fs)
    fs.Close()
    Console.WriteLine(sum)
End Sub
```

The following method computes the check sum:

```
Function compute(ByVal strm As Stream)
        Dim sum As Long = 0
        Dim by As Integer
        strm.Position = 0
        by = strm.ReadByte
        While (by <> -1)
            sum = (((by Mod &HFF) + sum) Mod &HFFFF)
            by = strm.ReadByte
        End While
        Return CType((sum Mod &HFFFF), Short)
    End Function
End Module
```

Compile this program with:

```
vbc Checksum.vb
```

and run it with:

```
Checksum <filename>
```

Due to their unsafe nature, check sum and CRC are sometimes termed as poor cousins of cryptographic hash algorithms. We will now look into classes provided by the .NET Framework to cater for cryptographic grade algorithms.

Cryptographic Hash Algorithms

The abstract class `System.Security.Cryptography.HashAlgorithm` represents the concept of cryptographic hash algorithms within the .NET Framework. The framework provides eight classes which extend the `HashAlgorithm` abstract class. These are

- `MD5CryptoServiceProvider` (extends abstract class `MD5`)
- `RIPEMD160Managed` (extends abstract class `RIPEMD160`)
- `SHA1CryptoServiceProvider` (extends abstract class `SHA1`)
- `SHA256Managed` (extends abstract class `SHA256`)
- `SHA384Managed` (extends abstract class `SHA384`)
- `SHA512Managed` (extends abstract class `SHA512`)
- `HMACSHA1` (extends abstract class `KeyedHashAlgorithm`)
- `MACTripleDES` (extends abstract class `KeyedHashAlgorithm`)

The last two classes belong to a class of algorithm called keyed hash algorithms. The keyed hashes extend the concept of cryptographic hash with the use of a shared secret key. This is used for computing the hash of data transported over an unsecured channel.

The following is an example of computing a hash value of a file:

```
' Cryptography/TestKeyHash.vb

Imports System
Imports System.IO
Imports System.Security.Cryptography
Imports System.Text
Imports System.Runtime.Serialization.Formatters

Module Module1
    Public Sub Main(ByVal CmdArgs() As String)
        If (CmdArgs.Length <> 1) Then
            Console.WriteLine("usage: TestKeyHash <filename>")
            End
        End If
```

Here, we create the object instance of the .NET SDK Framework class with a salt (a random secret to confuse a potential snooper):

```
Dim key() As Byte = Encoding.ASCII.GetBytes( _
"My Secret Key".ToCharArray())
Dim hmac As HMACSHA1 = New HMACSHA1(key)
Dim fs As FileStream = File.OpenRead(CmdArgs(0))
```

The next four lines compute the hash, convert the binary hash into a printable base 64 format, close the file, and then print the base 64 encoded string as the result of hashing to the screen:

```
        Dim hash() As Byte = hmac.ComputeHash(fs)
        Dim b64 As String = Convert.ToBase64String(hash)
        fs.Close()
        Console.WriteLine(b64)
    End Sub
End Module
```

The code can be compiled at the command line using the following:

```
vbc TestKeyHash.vb
```

To execute the code, give the following command at the console prompt:

```
TestKeyHash TestKeyHash.vb
```

This should produce a hashed output:

```
IOEj/D0rOxjEqCD8qHoYm+yWw6I=
```

The previous example uses an instance of the `HMACSHA1` class. The output displayed is a `Base64` encoding of the binary hash result value. `Base64` encoding is widely used in MIME and XML file formats to represent binary data. To recover the binary data from a `Base64` encoded string, we could use the following code fragment:

```
Dim orig() As Byte = Convert.FromBase64String(b64)
```

The XML parser, however, does this automatically. We will come across this in later examples.

SHA

SHA (Secured Hashing Algorithm) is a block cipher and operates on a block size of 64 bits. However, the subsequent enhancements of this algorithm have bigger key values, thus increasing the value range and therefore enhancing the cryptographic utility. We must note that the bigger the key value sizes, the longer it takes to compute the hash. Moreover, for relatively smaller data files, smaller hash values are more secure. To put it another way, the hash algorithm's block size should be less than or equal to the size of the data itself.

The hash size for the `SHA1` algorithm is 160 bits. Here is how to use it, which is similar to the HMACSHA1 code discussed previously:

```
 ' Cryptography/TestSHA1.vb

Imports System
Imports System.IO
Imports System.Security.Cryptography
Imports System.Text
Imports System.Runtime.Serialization.Formatters

Module Module1
    Public Sub Main(ByVal CmdArgs() As String)
        If (CmdArgs.Length <> 1) Then
```

```
                Console.WriteLine("usage: TestSHA1 <filename>")
            End
        End If
        Dim fs As FileStream = File.OpenRead(CmdArgs(0))


        Dim sha As SHA1 = New SHA1CryptoServiceProvider
        Dim hash() As Byte = sha.ComputeHash(fs)

        Dim b64 As String = Convert.ToBase64String(hash)
        fs.Close()
        Console.WriteLine(b64)
    End Sub
End Module
```

The .NET Framework provides bigger key size algorithms as well, namely SHA256, SHA384, and SHA512. The numbers at the end of the name indicate their block size.

The class `SHA256Managed` extends the abstract class `SHA256`, which in turn extends the abstract class `HashAlgorithm`. The Forms Authentication module of ASP.NET security (`System.Web.Security.FormsAuthenticationModule`) uses SHA1 as one of its valid formats to store and compare user passwords.

MD5

MD5 stands for Message Digest version 5. It is a cryptographic, one-way hash algorithm. The MD5 algorithm competes well with SHA. MD5 is an improved version of MD4, devised by Ron Rivest of RSA fame. In fact, FIPS PUB 180-1 states that SHA-1 is based on similar principles to MD4. The salient features of this class of algorithms are

- It is computationally unfeasible to forge an MD5 hash digest.
- MD5 is not based on any mathematical assumption such as the difficulty of factoring large binary integers.
- MD5 is computationally cheap, and therefore suitable for low latency requirements.
- It is relatively simple to implement.

The MD5 is the de facto standard for hash digest computation, due to the popularity of RSA.

The .NET Framework provides an implementation of this algorithm through the class `MD5CryptoServiceProvider` in the `System.Security.Cryptography` namespace. This class extends the `MD5` abstract class, which in turn extends the abstract class `HashAlgorithm`. This class shares a common base class with SHA1, so the examples previously discussed can be modified easily to accommodate this:

```
Dim fs As FileStream = File.OpenRead(CmdArgs(0))


Dim md5 As MD5 = New MD5CryptoServiceProvider
Dim hash() As Byte = md5.ComputeHash(fs)
```

```
Dim b64 As String = Convert.ToBase64String(hash)
fs.Close()
Console.WriteLine(b64)
```

RIPEMD-160

Based on MD5, RIPEMD-160 started as a project in Europe called RIPE (RACE Integrity Primitives Evaluation) in 1996. By 1997, the design of RIPEMD-160 was finalized. RIPEMD-160 is a 160-bit hash algorithm and is meant to be a replacement for MD4 and MD5.

The .NET Framework 2.0 introduces the `RIPEMD160` class to work with this latest iteration of encryption techniques. The following code demonstrates the use of this class:

```
Dim fs As FileStream = File.OpenRead(CmdArgs(0))

Dim myRIPEMD As New RIPEMD160Managed
Dim hash() As Byte = myRIPEMD.ComputeHash(fs)

Dim b64 As String = Convert.ToBase64String(hash)
fs.Close()
Console.WriteLine(b64)
```

Secret Key Encryption

Secret key encryption is widely used to encrypt data files using passwords. The simplest technique is to seed a random number using a password, and then encrypt the files with an XOR operation using this random number generator.

The .NET Framework represents the secret key by an abstract base class `SymmetricAlgorithm`. Four concrete implementations of different secret key algorithms are provided by default:

- `DESCryptoServiceProvider` (extends abstract class `DES`)
- `RC2CryptoServiceProvider` (extends abstract class `RC2`)
- `RijndaelManaged` (extends abstract class `Rijndael`)
- `TripleDESCryptoServiceProvider` (extends abstract class `TripleDES`)

Let's explore the `SymmetricAlgorithm` design. As will be clear from the following example code, two separate methods are provided to access encryption and decryption. Here is a console application program that encrypts and decrypts a file given a secret key:

```
' Cryptography/SymEnc.vb

Imports System.Security.Cryptography
Imports System.IO
Imports System.Text
Imports System

Module Module1
   Public Sub Main(ByVal CmdArgs() As String)
```

```
        If (CmdArgs.Length <> 4) Then
            UsageAndExit()
        End If
```

Here, we compute the index of the algorithm that we'll use:

```
Dim algoIndex As Integer = CmdArgs(0)
If (algoIndex < 0 Or algoIndex >= algo.Length) Then
   UsageAndExit()
End If
```

We open the input and output files (the file name represented by `CmdArgs(3)` is the output file, and `CmdArgs(2)` is the input file):

```
Dim fin As FileStream = File.OpenRead(CmdArgs(2))
Dim fout As FileStream = File.OpenWrite(CmdArgs(3))
```

We create the symmetric algorithm instance using the .NET Framework class `SymmetricAlgorithm`. This will use the algorithm name indexed by the `CmdArgs(0)` parameter. After this, we'll set the key parameters, and display them on-screen for information:

```
Dim sa As SymmetricAlgorithm = _
    SymmetricAlgorithm.Create(algo(algoIndex))
sa.IV = Convert.FromBase64String(b64IVs(algoIndex))
sa.Key = Convert.FromBase64String(b64Keys(algoIndex))
Console.WriteLine("Key " + CType(sa.Key.Length, String))
Console.WriteLine("IV " + CType(sa.IV.Length, String))
Console.WriteLine("KeySize: " + CType(sa.KeySize, String))
Console.WriteLine("BlockSize: " + CType(sa.BlockSize, String))
Console.WriteLine("Padding: " + CType(sa.Padding, String))
```

At this point, we check to see which operation is required, and execute the appropriate static method:

```
    If (CmdArgs(1).ToUpper().StartsWith("E")) Then
        Encrypt(sa, fin, fout)
    Else
        Decrypt(sa, fin, fout)
    End If
End Sub
```

Here is where the encryption itself takes place:

```
Public Sub Encrypt(ByVal sa As SymmetricAlgorithm, _
                   ByVal fin As Stream, _
                   ByVal fout As Stream)
    Dim trans As ICryptoTransform = sa.CreateEncryptor()
    Dim buf() As Byte = New Byte(2048) {}
    Dim cs As CryptoStream = _
        New CryptoStream(fout, trans, CryptoStreamMode.Write)
    Dim Len As Integer
    fin.Position = 0
Len = fin.Read(buf, 0, buf.Length)
```

```
        While (Len > 0)
            cs.Write(buf, 0, Len)
            Len = fin.Read(buf, 0, buf.Length)
        End While
        cs.Close()
        fin.Close()
    End Sub
```

Here's the decryption method:

```
    Public Sub Decrypt(ByVal sa As SymmetricAlgorithm, _
                       ByVal fin As Stream, _
                       ByVal fout As Stream)
        Dim trans As ICryptoTransform = sa.CreateDecryptor()
        Dim buf() As Byte = New Byte(2048) {}
        Dim cs As CryptoStream = _
            New CryptoStream(fin, trans, CryptoStreamMode.Read)
        Dim Len As Integer
        Len = cs.Read(buf, 0, buf.Length)
        While (Len > 0)
            fout.Write(buf, 0, Len)
            Len = cs.Read(buf, 0, buf.Length)
        End While
        fin.Close()
        fout.Close()
    End Sub
```

This next method prints usage information:

```
    Public Sub UsageAndExit()
        Console.Write("usage SymEnc <algo index> <D|E> <in> <out> ")
        Console.WriteLine("D =decrypt, E=Encrypt")
        For i As Integer = 0 To (algo.Length - 1)
            Console.WriteLine("Algo index: {0} {1}", i, algo(i))
        Next i
        End
    End Sub
```

The static parameters used for object creation are indexed by `CmdArgs(0)`. How we arrive at these magic numbers will be discussed shortly:

```
        Dim algo() As String = {"DES", "RC2", "Rijndael", "TripleDES"}
        Dim b64Keys() As String = {_
            "YE32PGCJ/g0=", _
            "vct+rJ09WuUcR61yfxniTQ==", _
            "PHDPqfwE3z25f2UYjwwfwg4XSqxvl8WYmy+2h8t6AUg=", _
            "Q1/lWoraddTH3IXAQUJGDSYDQcYYuOpm"}
        Dim b64IVs() As String = {_
            "onQX8hdHeWQ=", _
            "jgetiyz+pIc=", _
            "pd5mgMMfDI2Gxm/SKl5I8A==", _
            "6jpFrUh8FF4="}
    End Module
```

After compilation, this program can encrypt and decrypt using all four of the symmetric key implementations provided by the .NET Framework. The secret keys and their initialization vectors (IV) have been generated by a simple source code generator, which we will examine shortly.

The following commands encrypt and decrypt files using the DES algorithm. With the first command, we take a text file, `1.txt`, and use the DES algorithm to create an encrypted file called `2.bin`. The next command decrypts this file back and stores it into `3.bin`:

```
SymEnc 0 E 1.txt 2.bin
SymEnc 0 D 2.bin 3.bin
```

The first parameter of the `SymEnc` program is an index to the string array, which determines the algorithm to be used:

```
Dim algo() As String = {"DES", "RC2", "Rijndael", "TripleDES"}
```

The string defining the algorithm is passed as a parameter to the static `Create` method of the abstract class `SymmetricAlgorithm`. This class has an abstract factory design pattern:

```
Dim sa As SymmetricAlgorithm = _
    SymmetricAlgorithm.Create(algo(algoIndex))
```

To encrypt, we get an instance of the `ICryptoTransform` interface by calling the `CreateEncryptor` method of the `SymmetricAlgorithm` class extender:

```
Dim trans As ICryptoTransform = sa.CreateEncryptor()
```

Similarly, for decryption, we get an instance of the `ICryptoTransform` interface by calling the `CreateDecryptor` method of the `SymmetricAlgorithm` class instance:

```
Dim trans As ICryptoTransform = sa.CreateDecryptor()
```

We use the class `CryptoStream` for both encryption and decryption. However, the parameters to the constructor differ. For encryption we use the following code:

```
Dim cs As CryptoStream = _
    New CryptoStream(fout, trans, CryptoStreamMode.Write)
```

Similarly, for decryption we use the following code:

```
Dim cs As CryptoStream = _
    New CryptoStream(fin, trans, CryptoStreamMode.Read)
```

We call the `Read` and `Write` methods of the `CryptoStream` for decryption and encryption, respectively. For generating the keys, we use a simple code generator listed as follows:

```
' Cryptography/SymKey.vb

Imports System.Security.Cryptography
Imports System.Text
Imports System.IO
```

```
Imports System
Imports Microsoft.VisualBasic.ControlChars

Module Module1
    Public Sub Main(ByVal CmdArgs() As String)
        Dim keyz As StringBuilder = New StringBuilder
        Dim ivz As StringBuilder = New StringBuilder
        keyz.Append("Dim b64Keys() As String = { _" + VbCrLf)
        ivz.Append(VbCrLf + "Dim b64IVs() As String = { _" + VbCrLf )
```

The algorithm names for symmetric keys used by .NET SDK are given the correct index values here:

```
Dim algo() As String = {"DES", "RC2", "Rijndael", "TripleDES"}
```

For each of the algorithms, we generate the keys and IV:

```
        Dim comma As String = ", _" + VbCrLf

        For i As Integer = 0 To 3
           Dim sa As SymmetricAlgorithm = SymmetricAlgorithm.Create(algo(i))

           sa.GenerateIV()
           sa.GenerateKey()

           Dim Key As String
           Dim IV As String

           Key = Convert.ToBase64String(sa.Key)
           IV = Convert.ToBase64String(sa.IV)
           keyz.AppendFormat(tab + """" + Key + """" + comma)
           ivz.AppendFormat(tab + """" + IV + """" + comma)
           If i = 2 Then comma = " "
        Next i
```

Here, we print or emit the source code:

```
        keyz.Append("}"})
        ivz.Append("}"})
        Console.WriteLine(keyz.ToString())
        Console.WriteLine(ivz.ToString())
    End Sub
End Module
```

The preceding program creates a random key and an initializing vector for each algorithm. This output can be inserted directly into the `SymEnc.vb` program. The simplest way to do this is to type

```
SymKey > keys.txt
```

This will redirect the information into a file called `keys.txt`, which you can then use to cut and paste the values into your program. We use the `StringBuilder` class along with the control character `crlf` (carriage return and line feed) to format the text so that it can be inserted directly into your program. We then convert the binary data into Base64 encoding using the public instance method `ToBase64String` of the class Convert. Kerberos, the popular network authentication protocol supported by Windows Server 2003, Windows 2000, and all of the UNIX flavors, uses secret key encryption for implementing security.

In this next section, we will look into public key encryption.

PKCS

The Public Key Cryptographic System is a type of asymmetric key encryption. This system uses two keys, one private and the other public. The public key is widely distributed whereas the private key is kept secret. One cannot derive or deduce the private key by knowing the public key, so the public key can be safely distributed.

The keys are different, yet complementary. That is, if you encrypt data using the public key, only the owner of the private key can decipher it, and vice versa. This forms the basis of PKCS encryption.

If the private key holder encrypts a piece of data using their private key, any person having access to the public key can decrypt it. The public key, as the name suggests, is available publicly. This property of the PKCS is exploited along with a hashing algorithm, such as SHA or MD5, to provide a verifiable digital signature process.

The abstract class `System.Security.Cryptography.AsymmetricAlgorithm` represents this concept in the .NET Framework. Two concrete implementations of this class are provided by default, and they are

- `DSACryptoServiceProvider`, which extends the abstract class `DSA`
- `RSACryptoServiceProvider`, which extends the abstract class `RSA`

DSA (Digital Signature Algorithm) was specified by NIST (National Institute of Standards and Technology) in January 2000. The original DSA standard was, however, issued by NIST, way back in August 1991. DSA cannot be used for encryption and is good for only digital signature. We will discuss digital signature in more detail in the next subsection.

RSA algorithms can also be used for encryption as well as digital signatures. RSA is the de facto standard and has much wider acceptance than DSA. RSA is a tiny bit faster than DSA as well.

RSA algorithm is named after its three inventors: Rivest, Shamir, and Adleman. It was patented in the USA, but the patent expired on September 20, 2000. RSA can be used for both digital signature and data encryption. It is based on the assumption that large numbers are extremely difficult to factor. The use of RSA for digital signatures is approved within the FIPS PUB 186-2 and defined in the ANSI X9.31 standard document.

To gain some practical insights into RSA implementation of the .NET Framework, consider the following code:

```
' Cryptography/TestRSAKey.vb

Imports System.Security.Cryptography.Xml

Module Module1
```

```
    Sub Main()
        Dim RSA As RSAKeyValue = New RSAKeyValue
        Dim str As String = RSA.Key.ToXmlString(True)
        System.Console.WriteLine(str)
    End Sub
End Module
```

This code creates a pair of private and public keys and prints it out at the command line in XML format. To compile the preceding code, simply open a console session, run `corvar.bat` (if necessary), set the .NET SDK paths, and compile the program by typing the following command:

```
TestRSAKey.vb
```

This should produce a file called `TestRSAKey.exe`. Execute this program and redirect the output to a file such as `key.xml`:

```
TestRSAKey > key.xml
```

The file `key.xml` contains all the private and public members of the generated RSA key object. You can open this XML file in Internet Explorer 5.5 or above. If you do so, you will notice that the private member variables are also stored in this file. The binary data representing the large integers is encoded in `Base64` format.

The program listed above uses an `RSAKeyValue` instance to generate a new key pair. The class `RSAKeyValue` is contained in the `System.Security.Cryptography.Xml` namespace. This namespace can be thought of as the XML face of the .NET cryptographic framework. It contains a specialized, lightweight implementation of XML for the purpose of cryptography, and the model allows XML objects to be signed with a digital signature.

The `System.Security.Cryptography.Xml` namespace classes depend upon the classes contained in the `System.Security.Cryptography` namespace for the actual implementation of cryptographic algorithms.

The `key.xml` file, generated by redirecting the output of the Visual Basic test program `TestRSAKey`, contains both private and public keys. However, we need to keep the private key secret while making the public key widely available. Therefore, we need to separate out the public key from the key pair. Here is the program to do it:

```
' Cryptography/TestGetPubKey.vb

Imports System.Text
Imports System.Security.Cryptography
Imports System.IO
Imports System.Security.Cryptography.Xml
Imports System

Module Module1
    Public Sub Main(ByVal CmdArgs() As String)
        If (CmdArgs.Length <> 1) Then
            Console.WriteLine("usage: TestGetPubKey <key pair xml>")
            End
        End If
        Dim xstr As String = File2String(CmdArgs(0))
```

The following code creates an instance of the RSA implementation and reinitializes the internal variables through the XML formatted string:

```
        Dim rsa As RSACryptoServiceProvider = New RSACryptoServiceProvider
        rsa.FromXmlString(xstr)
        Dim x As String = rsa.ToXmlString(False)
        Console.WriteLine(x)
    End Sub

    Public Function File2String(ByVal fname As String)
        Dim finfo As FileInfo = New FileInfo(fname)
        Dim buf() As Byte = New Byte(finfo.Length) {}
        Dim fs As FileStream = File.OpenRead(fname)
        fs.Read(buf, 0, buf.Length)
        Return (New ASCIIEncoding).GetString(buf)
    End Function
End Module
```

This program is logically similar to `TestRSAKey.vb`, except that it has to read the key file and pass a different parameter in the `ToXmlString` method.

The cryptography classes use a lightweight XML implementation, thus avoiding the elaborate ritual of parsing the fully-formed generic XML data containing serialized objects. This has another advantage of speed because it bypasses the DOM parsers. To compile the previous code, type:

```
vbc /r:System.Security.dll TestGetPubKey.vb
```

This should produce the file `TestGetPubKey.exe`. Run this file, giving `key.xml` as the name of the input file, and redirect the program's output to `pub.xml`. This file will contain an XML formatted public key. The binary data, basically binary large integers, are `Base64` encoded. You may recall that `key.xml` contains both the public and private key pairs, and was generated by redirecting the output of `TestRSAKey.exe`. The following line will redirect `key.xml`'s public key to `pub.xml`:

```
TestGetPubKey key.xml > pub.xml
```

Now, let's write a program to test the encrypt and decrypt feature of the RSA algorithm:

```
' Cryptography/TestCrypt.vb

Imports System
Imports System.IO
Imports System.Security.Cryptography.Xml
Imports System.Security.Cryptography
Imports System.Text

Module Module1
    Public Sub Main(ByVal CmdArgs() As String)
        If (CmdArgs.Length <> 4) Then
            Console.WriteLine("usage: TestCrypt <key xml> <E|D> <in> <out>")
            Console.WriteLine(" E= Encrypt, D= Decrypt (needs private key)")
            End
        End If
```

Here, we read the public or private key into memory:

```
Dim xstr As String = File2String(CmdArgs(0))
```

We create an instance of an RSA cryptography service provider and initialize the parameters based on the XML lightweight file name passed in `CmdArgs(0)`:

```
Dim RSA As New RSACryptoServiceProvider
RSA.FromXmlString(xstr)
```

We display the key file name:

```
Console.WriteLine("Key File: " + CmdArgs(0))
Dim op As String= "Encrypted"
```

We read the input file and store it into a byte array:

```
Dim info As FileInfo = New FileInfo(CmdArgs(2))
Dim inbuflen As Integer = CType(info.Length, Integer)
Dim inbuf() As Byte = New Byte(inbuflen-1) {}
Dim outbuf() As Byte
Dim fs As FileStream = File.OpenRead(CmdArgs(2))
fs.Read(inbuf, 0, inbuf.Length)
fs.Close()
```

We either encrypt or decrypt depending on `CmdArgs(1)` option:

```
If (CmdArgs(1).ToUpper().StartsWith("D")) Then
    op = "Decrypted"
    outbuf = rsa.Decrypt(inbuf, False)
Else
    outbuf = rsa.Encrypt(inbuf, False)
End If
```

We'll write back the result in the output buffer into the file and display the result:

```
    fs = File.OpenWrite(CmdArgs(3))
    fs.Write(outbuf, 0, outbuf.Length)
    fs.Close()
    Console.WriteLine(op + " input [" + CmdArgs(2) + "] to output [" _
                  + CmdArgs(3) + "]")
End Sub
```

Here's a helper method to read the file name passed as an argument and convert the content to string:

```
    Public Function File2String(ByVal fname As String)
        Dim finfo As FileInfo = New FileInfo(fname)
        Dim buf() As Byte = New Byte(finfo.Length) {}
        Dim fs As FileStream = File.OpenRead(fname)
        fs.Read(buf, 0, buf.Length)
        fs.Close()
        Return (New ASCIIEncoding).GetString(buf)
    End Function
End Module
```

This test program encrypts or decrypts a short file depending on the parameters supplied to it. It takes four parameters, the XML formatted private or public key file, option `E` or `D` standing for encrypt or decrypt options, respectively, and input and output file names.

This program can be compiled with the following command:

```
vbc /r:System.Security.dll TestCrypt.vb
```

The previous command will produce a PE file `TestCrypt.exe`. To test the encrypt and decrypt functions, we'll create a small plain-text file called `1.txt`. Recall that we had also created two other files, `key.xml` and `pub.xml`. The file `key.xml` contains a key pair and `pub.xml` contains the public key extracted from the file `key.xml`.

Let's encrypt the plain-text file `plain.txt`. To do so, use the following command:

```
TestCrypt pub.xml E 1.txt rsa.bin
```

Note that we have used the public key file to encrypt it. You can type the output on the console, but this won't make any sense to us because it contains binary data. You could use a binary dump utility to dump out the file's content. If you do this, you will notice that the total number of bytes is 128 compared to the input of 13 bytes. This is because the RSA is a block cipher algorithm and the block size equals the key size, so the output will always be in multiples of the block size. You may wish to rerun the preceding examples with larger files to see the resulting encrypted file length.

Let us now decrypt the file to get back the original text. Use the following command to decrypt:

```
TestCrypt key.xml D rsa.bin decr.txt
```

Note that we used the `key.xml` file, which also contains the private key, to decrypt. That's because we use the public key to encrypt and private key to decrypt. In other words, anyone may send encrypted documents to you if they know your public key, but only you can decrypt the message. The reverse is true for digital signatures, which we will cover in the next section.

Digital Signature Basics

Digital signature is the encryption of a hash digest (for example, MD5 or SHA-1) of data using a public key. The digital signature can be verified by decrypting the hash digest and comparing it against a hash digest computed from the data by the verifier.

As noted earlier, the private key is known only to the owner, so the owner can sign a digital document by encrypting the hash computed from the document. The public key is known to all, so anyone can verify the signature by recomputing the hash and comparing it against the decrypted value, using the public key of the signer.

The .NET Framework provides DSA and RSA digital signature implementations by default. We will consider only DSA, as RSA was covered in the previous section. Both of the implementations extend the same base class, so all programs for DSA discussed below will work for RSA as well.

We will go through the same motions of producing a key pair and a public key file and then sign and verify the signature:

```
' Cryptography/GenDSAKeys.vb

Imports System
Imports System.Security.Cryptography
Imports FileUtil

Module Module1
    Public Sub Main(ByVal CmdArgs() As String)
        Dim dsa As DSACryptoServiceProvider = New DSACryptoServiceProvider
        Dim prv As String = dsa.ToXmlString(True)
        Dim pub As String = dsa.ToXmlString(False)
        Dim fileutil As FileUtil = New FileUtil
        fileutil.SaveString("dsa-key.xml", prv)
        fileutil.SaveString("dsa-pub.xml", pub)
        Console.WriteLine("Created dsa-key.xml and dsa-pub.xml")
    End Sub
End Module
```

This code generates two XML formatted files `dsa-key.xml` and `dsa-pub.xml`, containing private and public keys, respectively. Before we can run this, however, we need to create the `FileUtil` class used to output our two files:

```
' Cryptography/FileUtil.vb

Imports System.IO
Imports System.Text

Public Class FileUtil
    Public Sub SaveString(ByVal fname As String, ByVal data As String)
        SaveBytes(fname, (New ASCIIEncoding).GetBytes(data))
    End Sub

    Public Function LoadString(ByVal fname As String)
        Dim buf() As Byte = LoadBytes(fname)
        Return (New ASCIIEncoding).GetString(buf)
    End Function

    Public Function LoadBytes(ByVal fname As String)
        Dim finfo As FileInfo = New FileInfo(fname)
        Dim length As String = CType(finfo.Length, String)
        Dim buf() As Byte = New Byte(length) {}
        Dim fs As FileStream = File.OpenRead(fname)
        fs.Read(buf, 0, buf.Length)
        fs.Close()
        Return buf
    End Function

    Public Sub SaveBytes(ByVal fname As String, ByVal data() As Byte)
        Dim fs As FileStream = File.OpenWrite(fname)
        fs.SetLength(0)
        fs.Write(data, 0, data.Length)
        fs.Close()
    End Sub
End Class
```

The following code signs the data:

```
' Cryptography/DSASign.vb

Imports System
Imports System.IO
Imports System.Security.Cryptography
Imports System.Text
Imports FileUtil

Module Module1
    Public Sub Main(ByVal CmdArgs() As String)
        If CmdArgs.Length <> 3 Then
            Console.WriteLine("usage: DSASign <key xml> <data> <sign>")
            End
        End If
        Dim fileutil As FileUtil = New FileUtil
        Dim xkey As String = fileutil.LoadString(CmdArgs(0))
        Dim fs As FileStream = File.OpenRead(CmdArgs(1))
```

The DSA provider instance is created and the private key is reconstructed from the XML format using the following two lines of code:

```
Dim dsa As DSACryptoServiceProvider = New DSACryptoServiceProvider
dsa.FromXmlString(xkey)
```

The next line signs the file:

```
        Dim sig() As Byte = dsa.SignData(fs)
        fs.Close()
        fileutil.SaveString(CmdArgs(2), Convert.ToString(sig))
        Console.WriteLine("Signature in {0}} file", CmdArgs(2))
    End Sub
End Module
```

To verify the signature, we'll use the following sample code:

```
' Cryptography/DSAVerify.vb

Imports System
Imports System.IO
Imports System.Security.Cryptography
Imports System.Text
Imports FileUtil

Module Module1
    Public Sub Main(ByVal CmdArgs() As String)
        If CmdArgs.Length <> 3 Then
            Console.WriteLine("usage: DSAVerify <key xml> <data> <sign>")
            End
        End If
        Dim fileutil As FileUtil = New FileUtil
        Dim xkey As String = fileutil.LoadString(CmdArgs(0))
```

```
        Dim data() As Byte = fileutil.LoadBytes(CmdArgs(1))
        Dim xsig As String = fileutil.LoadString(CmdArgs(2))
        Dim dsa As DSACryptoServiceProvider = New DSACryptoServiceProvider
        dsa.FromXmlString(xkey)
        Dim xsigAsByte() As Byte = New Byte(xsig) {}
        Dim verify As Boolean
        verify = dsa.VerifyData(data, xsigAsByte)
        Console.WriteLine("Signature Verification is {0}", verify)
    End Sub
End Module
```

The actual verification is done using the highlighted code fragment.

The next four commands listed compile the source files:

```
vbc /target:library FileUtil.vb
vbc /r:FileUtil.dll GenDSAKeys.vb
vbc /r:FileUtil.dll DSASign.vb
vbc /r:FileUtil.dll DSAVerify.vb
```

There are many helper classes within the `System.Security.Cryptography` and the `System.Security.Cryptography.Xml` namespaces, which provide many features to help deal with digital signatures and encryption, and, at times, provide overlapping functionality. Therefore, there is more than one way of doing the same thing.

X509 Certificates

X509 is a public key certificate exchange framework. A public key certificate is a digitally signed statement by the owner of a private key, trusted by the verifier (usually a certifying authority) that certifies the validity of the public key of another entity. This creates a trust relationship between two unknown entities. This is an ISO standard specified by the document ISO/IEC 9594-8. X.509 certificates are also used in SSL (Secure Sockets Layer), which is covered in the next section.

There are many certifying authority services available over the Internet. VeriSign (`www.verisign.com`) is the most popular one. This company was also founded by the RSA trio themselves. You can also run your own Certificate Authority (CA) service over an Intranet using Microsoft Certificate Server.

The Microsoft .NET Framework SDK also provides tools for generating certificates for testing purposes.

```
makecert -n CN=Test test.cer
```

This command generates a test certificate. You can view it by double-clicking the `test.cer` file from Windows Explorer. The certificate is shown in Figure 13-19.

From the same dialog box, you could also install this certificate on your computer by clicking the Install Certificate button at the bottom of the dialog box.

Three classes dealing with X509 certificates are provided in the .NET Framework in the namespace `System.Security.Cryptography.X509Certificates`. Here is a program that loads and manipulates the certificate created earlier:

Figure 13-19

```
' Cryptography/LoadCert.vb

Imports System
Imports System.Security.Cryptography.X509Certificates

Module Module1
    Public Sub Main(ByVal CmdArgs() As String)
        If CmdArgs.Length <> 1 Then
            Console.Write("usage loadCert <cert file> ")
            End
        End If
        Dim cert As X509Certificate = _
            X509Certificate.CreateFromCertFile(CmdArgs(0))
        Console.WriteLine("hash= {0}", cert.GetCertHashString())
        Console.WriteLine("effective Date= {0}", _
                          cert.GetEffectiveDateString())
        Console.WriteLine("expire Date= {0}", _
                          cert.GetExpirationDateString())
        Console.WriteLine("Issued By= {0}", cert.GetIssuerName())
        Console.WriteLine("Issued To= {0}", cert.GetName())
        Console.WriteLine("algo= {0}", cert.GetKeyAlgorithm())
        Console.WriteLine("Pub Key= {0}", cert.GetPublicKeyString())
    End Sub
End Module
```

The static method loads `CreateFromCertFile` (the certificate file) and creates a new instance of the class `X509Certificate`.

The next section deals with SSL, which uses X509 certificates for establishing the trust relationship.

Secure Sockets Layer

SSL (Secure Sockets Layer) protocol provides privacy and reliability between two communicating applications over the Internet. SSL is built over the TCP layer. In January 1999, IETF (Internet Engineering Task Force) adopted an enhanced version of SSL 3.0 and called it TLS, which stands for Transport Layer Security. TLS is backwardly compatible with SSL, and is defined in RFC 2246. However, the name SSL stayed due to wide acceptance of this Netscape protocol name.

SSL provides connection-oriented security and has the following four properties:

- Connection is private and encryption is valid for that session only.
- Symmetric key cryptography, like DES, is used for encryption. However, the session secret key is exchanged using public key encryption.
- Digital certificates are used to verify the identities of the communicating entities.
- Secure hash functions, like SHA and MD5, are used for message authentication code (MAC).

The SSL protocol sets the following goals for itself:

- **Cryptographic security** — Uses symmetric key for session and public key for authentication
- **Interoperability** — Interpolates OS and programming languages
- **Extensibility** — Adds new protocols for encrypting data which are allowed within the SSL framework
- **Relative efficiency** — Reduces computation and network activity by using caching techniques

The following is a simplified discussion of the SSL algorithm sequence.

Two entities communicating using SSL protocols must have a public-private key pair, optionally with digital certificates validating their respective public keys.

At the beginning of a session, the client and server exchange information to authenticate each other. This ritual of authentication is called the Handshake Protocol. During this, a session ID, the compression method, and the cipher suite to be used are negotiated. If the certificates exist, they are then exchanged. Although certificates are optional, either the client or the server may refuse to continue with the connection and end the session in the absence of a certificate.

After receiving each other's public keys, a set of secret keys based on a randomly generated number is exchanged by encrypting it with each other's public keys. After this, the application data exchange can commence. The application data will be encrypted using a secret key, and a signed hash of the data is sent to verify the data integrity.

Microsoft implements the SSL client in the .NET Framework classes. However, the server-side SSL can be used by deploying your service through the IIS Web server.

The following code fragment can be used to access SSL protected Web servers from the .NET platform:

```
Dim req As WebRequest = WebRequest.Create("https://www.reuters.com")
Dim result As WebResponse = req.GetResponse()
```

Note that the preceding URL starts with `https`, which signals the `WebRequest` class (part of `System.Net`) to use SSL protocol. Interestingly, the same code is useful for accessing unsecured URLs as well.

The following is a program for accessing a secured URL. It takes care of the minor details, such as encoding, for us:

```
' Cryptography/GetWeb.vb

Imports System
Imports System.IO
Imports System.Net
Imports System.Text

Module Module1
    Public Sub Main(ByVal CmdArgs() As String)
        If CmdArgs.Length <> 1 Then
            Console.WriteLine("usage: GetWeb url")
            Console.WriteLine("example: GetWeb https://www.reuters.com")
            End
        End If
        Dim ms As String
```

We call the `Create()` method (which we'll see in a moment) with a URL and an encoding format:

```
    Try
        ms = Create(CmdArgs(0), "utf-8")
    Catch x As Exception
        Console.WriteLine(x.StackTrace)
        Console.WriteLine("Bad URL: {0}", CmdArgs(0))
    End Try
    Console.WriteLine(ms)
End Sub
```

Now, we come to the `Create()` method. Using the .NET Framework `WebRequest` object, we create an HTTP secured request object and get its response stream:

```
Function Create(ByVal url As String, ByVal encod As String) As String
    Dim req As WebRequest = WebRequest.Create(url)
    Dim result As WebResponse = req.GetResponse()
    Dim ReceiveStream As Stream = result.GetResponseStream()
```

We create an encoding instance from the .NET Framework object, `Encoding`:

```
Dim enc As Encoding = System.Text.Encoding.GetEncoding(encod)
```

Here, we'll create the stream reader:

```
Dim sr As StreamReader = New StreamReader(ReceiveStream, enc)
```

We read the stream fully — the entire Web page or serialized object is read into the `responseString`:

```
            Dim response As String = sr.ReadToEnd()
            Return response
        End Function
        Dim MaxContentLength As Integer = 16384 ' 16k
    End Module
```

The preceding console application gets a secured (SSL) protected URL and displays the content on the console. To compile the code, give the following command:

```
vbc /r:System.dll GetWeb.vb
```

Summary

In this chapter, we covered the basics of security and cryptography. We started with an overview of the security architecture of the .NET Framework, and looked at four types of security: NTFS, security policies, cryptographic, and programmatic.

We went on to examine the security tools and functionality that the .NET Framework provides. We examined the `System.Security.Permissions` namespace, and learned how we can control code access permissions, role-based permissions, and identity permissions. We looked at how we can manage code access permissions and manage security policies for our code. We used two tools — `Caspol.exe` and `Permview.exe` — that help us to configure and view security at both the machine and user levels.

In the second half of the chapter, we turned our attention to cryptography, both the underlying theory and how it can be applied within our applications. We looked at the different types of cryptographic hash algorithms, including SHA, MD5, Secret Key Encryption, and PKCS. We also understood how we can use digital certificates (specifically, X509 certificates) and Secure Socket Layers.

14

Windows Forms

Windows Forms is the part of the .NET Framework base classes used to create user interfaces for local applications, often called Win32 clients. It is dramatically improved over the forms and controls available in pre-.NET versions of Visual Basic. Although some familiar controls have been retired, no significant functionality has been lost, and lots of new capabilities have been added.

Windows Forms uses the version number of the related .NET Framework. Thus, the version in Visual Basic 2005 is Windows Forms 2.0. This chapter will sometimes refer to the version number to emphasize differences from the versions included in Visual Basic 2002 and 2003. Those versions are Windows Forms 1.0 and 1.1, respectively.

After explaining why Windows Forms is an important user interface option for .NET applications, this chapter will start its technical content by summarizing the changes in Windows Forms 2.0. This will allow those with some experience in previous versions of Windows Forms to quickly identify key changes.

Then the chapter will look at forms, controls, and their behaviors, with emphasis on those elements that are most important for routine application development. Windows Forms is one of the larger namespaces in .NET, and there is too much there to discuss everything. Instead, this chapter highlights those things developers need to know first.

The next chapter (Chapter 15) includes more advanced treatment of certain aspects of Windows Forms. After gaining a basic understanding of the key capabilities in this chapter, you'll be ready to go on to the more advanced concepts in that chapter.

The Importance of Windows Forms

The first versions of .NET emphasized ASP.NET and Web Forms because of the popularity of browser-based development. However, as discussed in Chapter 1, "smart client" applications are becoming more prevalent under .NET because it offers cheaper and more flexible deployment than older COM-based client software. (Deployment is discussed in detail in Chapter 19.)

This transition to "smart client" applications results in Windows Forms gaining greater importance. Windows Forms applications can even be "Internet-enabled" by using Web services to access and manage data on remote Internet servers.

It's also more practical in .NET-based systems to support both browser-based and smart-client user interfaces in the same system. Middle-tier components can easily be designed to work with both. So it's not an "either or" choice — Windows Forms interfaces may be mixed with browser-based Web Forms interfaces.

Summary of Changes in Windows Forms version 2.0

If you have already used Windows Forms 1.0 or 1.1, much of the material in this chapter will be familiar to you. To help you zero in on the new capabilities in Windows Forms 2.0, here is a summary of changes and additions.

Default Instances of Forms

In VB6 and earlier, a form named `Form1` could be shown by merely including the line:

```
Form1.Show
```

The capability was not available in Visual Basic 2002 and 2003. Instead, a form was treated the same as any other class, and had to be instantiated before use. Typical code to show a form in Windows Forms 1.0 and 1.1 looked like this:

```
Dim f As New Form1
f.Show
```

The second form is still recommended because it fits object-oriented conventions. However, the first form is again available in Visual Basic. It is slightly changed, because method calls in .NET normally have parentheses at the end, so the new form looks like this:

```
Form1.Show()
```

However, the editor inserts those parentheses automatically.

Showing a form without instancing it, as in the first form above, is referred to as using the default instance of the form. That default instance is available from anywhere in a project containing a form. There is only one default instance, and any reference to it will bring up the same underlying instance of the form.

Another way to get to the default instance of a form is through the new `My` namespace. The following line has exactly the same effect of showing the default instance of a form:

```
My.Forms.Form1.Show()
```

Changes in Existing Controls

The base `Control` class, which is a base class for all Windows Forms controls, has some new properties in Windows Forms 2.0. Since all controls inherit from this class, all Windows Forms controls gain these new properties and the new functionality that goes along with them.

Two of the new properties, `Padding` and `Margin`, are most useful when used in conjunction with some new controls, `TableLayoutPanel` and `FlowLayoutPanel`. Those two properties are discussed later, in the section discussing these new controls. The other new properties are discussed here.

MaximumSize and MinimumSize Properties

The `MaximumSize` and `MinimumSize` properties specify the maximum and minimum height and width of a control. Forms had these properties in Windows Forms 1.0 and 1.1, but now all controls have them.

If the maximum height and width are both set to the default value of 0, then there is no maximum. Similarly, if the minimum height and width are set to zero, there is no minimum. The form or control can be any size.

If these properties are set to anything else, the settings become limits on the size of the control. For example, if the `MaximumSize` height and width are both set to 100, then the control cannot be bigger than 100 × 100 pixels. The visual designer will not make the control any larger on the form design surface. Attempting to set the height or width of the control in code at runtime to a value greater than 100 will cause it to be set to 100 instead.

The `MaximumSize` and `MinimumSize` properties can be reset at runtime to enable sizing of the controls outside the limits imposed at design time. However, the properties have a return type of `Point`, so resetting either property requires creating a `Point` structure. For example, you can reset the `MinimumSize` property for a button named `Button1` with the following line of code:

```
Button1.MinimumSize = New Point(20, 20)
```

This sets the new minimum width and height to 20 pixels.

UseWaitCursor Property

Windows Forms interfaces can make use of threading or asynchronous requests to allow tasks to happen in the background. If a control is waiting for some asynchronous request to finish, it is helpful to indicate that to the user by changing the mouse cursor when the mouse is inside the control. Normally, the cursor used is the familiar hourglass, which is called the `WaitCursor` in Windows Forms.

For any control, setting the `UseWaitCursor` property to True causes the cursor to change to the hourglass (or whatever is being used for the `WaitCursor`) while the mouse is positioned inside the control. This allows a control to visually indicate that it is waiting for something. The typical usage is to set `UseWaitCursor` to `True` when an asynchronous process is begun and then set it back to false when the process is finished and the control is ready for normal operation again.

AutoCompletion in Text Boxes and Combo Boxes

Text boxes and combo boxes get new properties for autocompletion of text entries. This capability was often added manually or with third-party controls in previous versions, but is now built in. The `AutoCompleteMode` controls how autocompletion works in the control, while the `AutoCompleteSource` and `AutoCompleteCustomSource` properties tell the control where to get entries for autocompletion.

An example of autocompletion in action is shown later, in the section entitled "Advanced Capabilities for Data Entry."

New Controls

Windows Forms 2.0 includes a number of new controls. Some are brand new and offer completely new functionality. Others are replacements for existing controls, offering additional functionality.

WebBrowser Control

Even smart client applications often need to display HTML or browse Web sites. Windows Forms 1.0 or 1.1 did not include a true Windows Forms control for browsing. The legacy ActiveX browsing control built into Windows could be used via interoperability, but this had drawbacks for deployment and versioning.

The legacy ActiveX control is still the ultimate foundation for browsing capability, but Windows Forms 2.0 includes an intelligent Windows Forms wrapper that makes it much easier to use and deploy the control.

MaskedTextbox control

Windows Forms 1.0 offered replacements for almost all of the controls available in Visual Basic 6, but one notable exception was the `MaskedEdit` control. In Windows Forms 1.0 and 1.1, masked edit capabilities were available only through third-party controls or by doing your own custom development.

That omission has now been rectified. The `MaskedTextbox` control resembles the old `MaskedEdit` control in functionality. It allows a mask for input and a variety of useful properties to control user interaction with the control. More information on this control is available in the section entitled "Advanced Capabilities for Data Entry."

TableLayoutPanel and FlowLayoutPanel Controls

Browser-based user interfaces are good at dynamically arranging controls at runtime, because browser windows can be different sizes for different users. Forms-based interfaces have traditionally lacked such capabilities. Dynamic positioning can be done in forms, but it requires writing a lot of sizing and positioning logic.

Two new controls in Windows Forms 2.0 mimic layout capabilities in a browser, giving better options for dynamic positioning of controls.

- The `TableLayoutPanel` creates a virtual table, with cells for each control. The position of controls in the panel is thereby determined by the position of the enclosing cell.
- The `FlowLayoutPanel` allows the position of each control to be relative to the position of the previous control in the panel. This allows a set of controls to be added to a panel without worrying about detailed positioning, while still assuring that the controls will be accessible to the user and not hidden by other controls.

Just about any control can be placed in these containers. To gain control over how controls are arranged in a `TableLayoutPanel` or a `FlowLayoutPanel`, all Windows Forms controls now include a `Margin` property. This property allows extra space to be included around a control when the automatic layout is done.

The containers themselves have a `Padding` property that specifies the amount of extra space to leave around the inside edge of the control. This also affects dynamic layout of contained controls.

An example illustrating usage of both controls, plus the `Padding` and `Margin` properties, is included in the section entitled "Dynamic Sizing and Positioning of Controls."

Replacements for Older Windows Forms Controls

The `Toolbar`, `MainMenu`, `ContextMenu`, and `StatusBar` controls in Windows Forms 1.0 and 1.1 offered basic functionality, and these controls are still available in Windows Forms 2.0. But in most cases, you will not want to use these controls because there are new replacements with significantly enhanced capabilities. Since the old versions are still available, the new versions have different names. The table that follows summarizes these replacements.

Old Control	New Control	Most Important New Capabilities
`Toolbar`	`ToolStrip`	Allows many new types of controls on the toolbar. Supports "rafting," which allows the toolbar to be detached by the user and float over the application. Allows user to add or remove buttons or other toolbar elements. Includes new cosmetics, allowing toolbars to look like those in Office 2003.
`MainMenu`	`MenuStrip`	The new menu controls both inherit from `ToolStrip`, which allows new cosmetics and more flexible placement.
`ContextMenu`	`ContextMenuStrip`	
`StatusBar`	`StatusStrip`	Inherits from `ToolStrip`, which allows new cosmetics and makes it easier to embed other controls in a status bar.

The old versions no longer show up by default in the toolbox. If you want to use them in new projects, you must add them to the toolbox by right-clicking on the Windows Forms Toolbox tab and selecting Choose Items. Then place a checkmark on the older control that you want added to the toolbox. However, you'll probably only want to use the older controls for compatibility with older projects and use the improved versions for new development.

These controls are covered in more detail, including examples, in the sections entitled "Toolbars and the New ToolStrip Control" and "Menus."

The System.Windows.Forms Namespace

You've already seen how namespaces are used to organize related classes in the .NET Framework. The main namespace used for Windows Forms classes is `System.Windows.Forms`. The classes in this namespace are contained in the `System.Windows.Forms.dll` assembly.

If your application needs to have user interface support, it must contain a reference to the `System.Windows.Forms.dll` assembly. If you choose a Windows Application project or Windows Control Library project in VS.NET, that reference is added by default. In some other cases, such as creating a library that will work with controls, you will need to add that reference manually. (You can see more about creating controls in Windows Forms in Chapter 15.)

Using Forms

Before .NET, forms in Visual Basic were special types of modules, with a special section containing layout information. That changed with the advent of VB.NET and Windows Forms. A form is just another class in VB.NET. There is a special section of code maintained by the Visual Forms Designer, but the code in that section is the same as any other VB.NET code.

A class becomes a form based on inheritance. A form must have the `System.Windows.Forms` class in its inheritance tree. That causes the form to have the behavior and object interface a form requires.

In the previous section on changes in Windows Forms 2.0, we discussed that forms can be used by referring to a default instance. However, the preferred technique is to treat a form the same as any other class, which means creating an instance of the form and using the instance. Typical code would look like this:

```
Dim f As New Form1
f.Show()
```

There is one circumstance in which loading a form the same way as a class instance yields undesirable results. Let's cover that next.

Showing Forms via Sub Main

When a form is instanced via the technique above, it is referenced by an object variable, which establishes an object reference to the instance. References are covered in detail in Chapter 3.

References can go away as object variables go out of scope or are set to other references or to `Nothing`. When all object references to a form are gone, the form is disposed of, and therefore, vanishes. This is particularly apparent if you want to start your application with a `Sub Main`, and then show your first form inside `Sub Main`. You might think this code would work:

```
' This code will not work in VB.NET!!
Sub Main()

    ' Do start up work here
    ' After start up work finished, show the main form...
    Dim f As New Form1
    f.Show()

End Sub
```

What happens if you try this, however, is that `Form1` briefly appears and then immediately vanishes, and the application quits. That's because the object variable f went out of scope, and it was the only reference to the form that was shown. So, the form was destroyed because it had no references pointing to it.

To get around this behavior, you could use the default instance as the startup form. However, there's a better way that stays within good object-oriented conventions. Replace the line that shows the form, as shown in the following code:

```
' This code will not work in VB.NET!!
Sub Main()

    ' Do start up work here
    Dim f As New Form1

    Application.Run(f)

End Sub
```

Now `Sub Main` will transfer control to the form, and the form will not vanish when `Sub Main` ends.

Setting the Startup Form

Instead of using `Sub Main` as your application entry point, you can also define a startup form, which is the form that will be loaded first when your application begins. To define the startup form, you need to open the Properties dialog box for the project and set the Startup object setting. Do this using the Project ➪ Properties menu. You can also invoke the window by right-clicking the project name in Solution Explorer, and selecting Properties from the context menu. The Properties dialog box for a Windows Application is shown in Figure 14-1.

If the Properties menu item doesn't appear under your Project menu, open the Solution Explorer (Ctrl-Alt-L), highlight the project name (it will be in bold font), then try again.

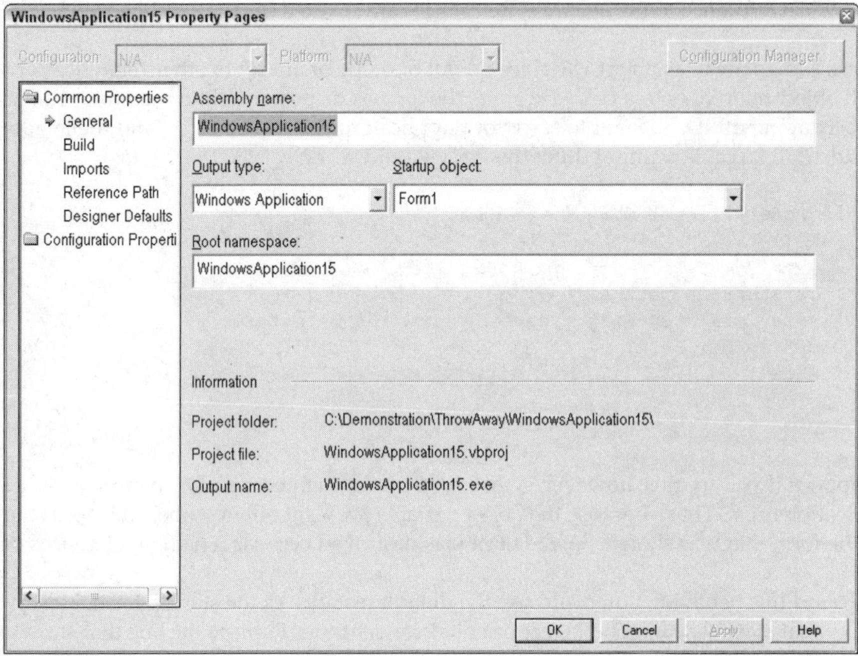

Figure 14-1

Startup Location

Often, you'll want a form to be centered on the screen when it first appears. VB.NET does this automatically for you when you set the `StartPosition` property. The following table shows the settings and their meanings.

StartPosition Value	Effect
`Manual`	Show the form positioned at the values defined by the form's `Location` property
`CenterScreen`	Show the form centered on the screen
`WindowsDefaultLocation`	Show the form at the windows default location
`WindowsDefaultBounds`	Show the form at the windows default location, with the windows default bounding size
`CenterParent`	Show the form centered in its owner

Form Borders

Forms have a number of border options in Windows Forms. The `FormBorderStyle` property is used to set the border option, and the options can affect the way a form can be manipulated by the user. The options available for `FormBorderStyle` include:

- `None`—No border, and the user cannot resize the form
- `FixedSingle`—Single 3-D border, and the user cannot resize the form
- `Fixed3D`—3-D border, and the user cannot resize the form
- `FixedDialog`—Dialog box style border, and the user cannot resize the form
- `Sizeable`—Same as FixedSingle, except that the user can resize the form
- `FixedToolWindow`—Single border, and the user cannot resize the form
- `SizeableToolWindow`—Single border, and the user can resize the form

Each of these has a different effect on the buttons that appear in the title bar of the form. For details, check the help topic for the `FormBorderStyle` property.

Always on Top—The TopMost Property

Some forms need to remain visible at all times, even when they do not have the focus. Examples are floating toolbars and tutorial windows. In VB.NET, forms have a property called `TopMost`. Set it to `True` to have a form overlay others even when it does not have the focus.

Note that a form with `TopMost` set to `True` will be on top of all applications, not just the hosting application. If you need a form to only be on top of other forms in the application, this capability is provided by an owned form.

Owned Forms

As with the `TopMost` property, an owned form floats above the application, but does not interfere with using the application. An example is a search-and-replace box. However, an owned form is not on top of all forms, just the form that is its owner.

When a form is owned by another form, it is minimized and closed with the owner form. Owned forms are never displayed behind their owner form, but they do not prevent their owner form from gaining the focus and being used. However, if you want to click on the area covered by an owned form, the owned form has to be moved out of the way first.

A form can only have one "owner" at a time. If a form that is already owned by `Form1` is added to the owned forms collection for `Form2`, then the form is no longer owned by `Form1`.

There are two ways to make a form owned by another form. It can be done in the owner form or in the owned form.

AddOwnedForm() Method

In the owner form, another form can be made owned with the `AddOwnedForm()` method. Here is code to make an instance of `Form2` become owned by `Form1`. This code would reside somewhere in `Form1` and would typically be placed just before the line that shows the instance of `Form2` to the screen.

```
Dim frm As New Form2
Me.AddOwnedForm(frm)
```

Owner Property

The relationship can also be set up in the owned form. This is done with the `Owner` property of the form. Here is a method that would work inside `Form2` to make it owned by a form that is passed in as an argument to the function:

```
Public Sub MakeMeOwned(frmOwner As Form)
    Me.Owner = frmOwner
End Sub
```

Since this technique requires a reference to the owner inside the owned form, it is not used as often as using the `AddOwnedForm()` method in the `Owner` form.

OwnedForms Collection

The owner form can access its collection of owned forms with the `OwnedForms` property. Here is code to loop through the forms owned by a form:

```
Dim frmOwnedForm As Form
For Each frmOwnedForm In Me.OwnedForms
  Console.WriteLine(frmOwnedForm.Text)
Next
```

The owner form can remove an owned form with the `RemoveOwnedForm` property. This could be done in a loop like the previous one, with code like the following:

```
Dim frmOwnedForm As Form
For Each frmOwnedForm In Me.OwnedForms
  Console.WriteLine(frmOwnedForm.Text)

  Me.RemoveOwnedForm(frmOwnedForm)
Next
```

This loop would cause an owner form to stop owning all of its slaved forms. Note that those deslaved forms would not be unloaded, they would simply no longer be owned.

Notice that no matter how a form becomes an owned form, a reference to it is placed in the `OwnedForms` collection. This can have an undesirable side effect. If you close a form and remove all other references to it from your application, you might expect it to disappear entirely from your application. But the extra reference in the `OwnedForms` collection can cause the form to hang around, taking up resources. To prevent that, it's a good idea to remove an owned form from the `OwnedForms` collection before closing it.

Making Forms Transparent and Translucent

Windows Forms offers advanced capabilities to make forms translucent or parts of a form transparent. You can even change the entire shape of a form.

The Opacity Property

The `Opacity` property measures how opaque or transparent a form is. A value of 0 percent makes the form fully transparent. A value of 100 percent makes the form fully visible. Any value greater than 0 and less than 100 makes the form partially visible, as if it was a ghost. Note that an opacity value of 0 percent disables the ability to click the form.

Very low levels of opacity, in the range of 1 or 2 percent, make the form effectively invisible, but still allow the form to be clickable. This means that the `Opacity` property has the potential to create mischievous applications that sit in front of other applications and "steal" their mouse clicks and other events.

Percentage values are used to set the Opacity in the Property Window. However, if you want to set the `Opacity` *property in code, you must use values between 0 and 1 instead, with 0 being equivalent to 0 percent and 1 being equivalent to 100 percent.*

Tool and dialog windows that should not completely obscure their background are one example of a usage for `Opacity`. Setting expiration for a "free trial" by gradually fading out the application's user interface is another.

The following block of code shows how to fade a form out and back in when the user clicks a button named `Button1`. You may have to adjust the `Step` value of the array, depending on the performance of your computer:

```
Private Sub Button1_Click(ByVal sender As System.Object, _
                          ByVal e As System.EventArgs) _
                          Handles Button1.Click
    Dim i As Double
    For i = -1 To 1 Step 0.005
      ' Note - opacity is a value from 0.0 to 1.0 in code
      Me.Opacity = System.Math.Abs(i)
    Next i
End Sub
```

The TransparencyKey Property

Instead of making an entire form translucent or transparent, the `TransparencyKey` property allows you to specify a color that will become transparent on the form. This allows you to make some sections of a form transparent, while other sections are unchanged.

For example, if `TransparencyKey` is set to a red color, and some areas of the form are that exact shade of red, they will be transparent. Whatever is behind the form will show through in those areas, and if you click in one of those areas, you will actually be clicking the object behind the form.

`TransparencyKey` can be used to create irregularly shaped "skin" forms. A form can have its `BackgroundImage` property set with an image, and by just painting a part of the image with the `TransparencyKey` color, you can make parts of the form disappear.

The Region Property

Another way to gain the capability of "skins" is by using the `Region` property of a form. The `Region` property allows a shape for a form to be encoded as a "graphics path," thereby changing the shape from the default rectangle to another shape. A path can contain line segments between points, curves and arcs, and outlines of letters, in any combination.

Let's do an example that will change the shape of a form to an arrow. Create a new Windows application. Set the `FormBorderStyle` property of `Form1` to None. Then place the following code in the `Load` event for `Form1`:

```
Dim PointArray(6) As Point
PointArray(0) = New Point(0, 40)
PointArray(1) = New Point(200, 40)
PointArray(2) = New Point(200, 0)
PointArray(3) = New Point(250, 100)
PointArray(4) = New Point(200, 200)
PointArray(5) = New Point(200, 160)
PointArray(6) = New Point(0, 160)
Dim myGraphicsPath As _
System.Drawing.Drawing2D.GraphicsPath = _
        New System.Drawing.Drawing2D.GraphicsPath

myGraphicsPath.AddPolygon(PointArray)
Me.Region = New Region(myGraphicsPath)
```

When the program is run, `Form1` will appear in the shape of a right-pointing arrow. If you lay out the points in the array, you will see that they have become the vertices of the arrow.

Visual Inheritance

By inheriting from `System.Windows.Forms.Form`, any class automatically gets all the properties, methods, and events that a form based on Windows Forms is supposed to have. However, a class does not have to inherit directly from the `System.Windows.Forms.Form` class to become a Windows form. It can become a form by inheriting from another form, which itself inherits from `System.Windows.Forms.Form`. In this way, controls originally placed on one form can be directly inherited by a second form. Not only is the design of the original form inherited, but also any code associated with these controls (the processing logic behind an Add New button, for example). This means that it is possible to create a base form with processing logic required in a number of forms, and then create other forms which inherit the base controls and functionality.

VB.NET provides an Inheritance Picker tool to aid in this process. It should be noted at this point, however, that a form must be compiled into either an `.exe` or `.dll` file before it can be used by the

Inheritance Picker. Once that is done, the addition of a form that inherits from another form in the project can be performed via the Project ➪ Add Inherited Form.

Scrollable Forms

Some applications need countless (or so it seems) fields on a single screen. Try as you may, no amount of reorganizing and reducing spaces between the fields helps the situation. While you could split the data entry into multiple screens, it is often done with regret. (Imagine what the Web surfing would be like if scrolling a Web page was impossible.)

Forms in VB.NET are based on a class called `ScrollableControl`. This base class will give you, free of charge, scrollbars to pull controls into view that are off the edge of your forms.

The scrollable control class on which a form is based automatically gives a form scrollbars when it is sized smaller than the child controls sited on it. To enable this feature, set the `AutoScroll` property of your form to `True`. When you run your program, resize the form to make it smaller than the controls require and presto — instant scrolling.

> **You cannot have both `Autoscroll` and `IsMdiContainer` set to `True` at the same time.**

Forms at Runtime

The lifecycle of a form is like that of all objects. It is created, and later destroyed. Forms have a visual component, so they use system resources, such as handles. These are created and destroyed at interim stages within the lifetime of the form. Forms can be created and will hold state as a class, but will not appear until they are activated. Likewise, closing a form doesn't destroy its state.

The following table summarizes the states of a form's existence, how you get the form to that state, the events that occur when the form enters a state, and a brief description of each.

Code	Events Fired	Description
`MyForm = New Form1`	`Load`	The form's `New()` method will be called (as will `InitializeComponent`).
`MyForm.Show()` or	`HandleCreated`	Use `Show()` for modeless display.
`MyForm.ShowDialog()`	`Load`	Use `ShowDialog()` for modal display.
	`VisibleChanged`	The `HandleCreated` event only fires the first time the form is shown or after it has previously been closed.
	`Activated`	

Table continued on following page

Code	Events Fired	Description
`MyForm.Activate()`	`Activated`	A form can be activated when it is visible but does not have the focus.
`MyForm.Hide()`	`Deactivate`	Hides the form (sets the `Visible` property to `False`).
	`VisibleChanged`	
`MyForm.Close()`	`Deactivate`	Closes the form and calls `Dispose` to release the window's resources.
	`Closing`	During the `Closing` event, you can set the `CancelEventArgs.Cancel` property to `True` to abort the close.
	`Closed`	
	`VisibleChanged`	
	`HandleDestroyed`	Also called when the user closes the form using the control box or X button.
	`Disposed`	The `Deactivate` event will only fire if the form is currently active.
		Note: There is no longer an `Unload` event. Use the `Closing` or `Closed` event instead.
`MyForm.Dispose()`	None	Use the `Close()` method to finish using your form.
`MyForm = Nothing`	None	Releasing the reference to the form flags it for garbage collection. The Garbage Collector will call the form's `Finalize()` method.

Controls

The controls included in Windows Forms provide basic functionality for a wide range of applications. The controls in Windows Forms 2.0 are very similar to those previous versions of Windows Forms, but there are some significant differences to the controls in VB6. This section will cover the features that all controls use (such as docking) and then address each of the standard controls available to you. Important changes from older versions of Visual Basic (VB6 and earlier) will be briefly mentioned.

Control Tab Order

The VS2005 design environment allows you to set the tab order of the controls on a form simply by clicking them in sequence. To activate the feature, open a form in the designer and select the View ➪ Tab Order menu item. This will show a small number in the upper-left corner of each control on your form representing the tab index of that control.

To set the values, simply click on each control in the sequence you want the tab flow to operate. The screen shot in Figure 14-2 shows a simple form with the tab order feature enabled.

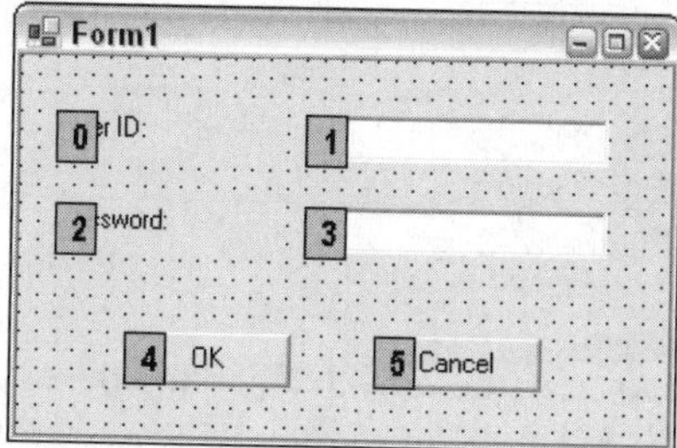

Figure 14-2

In VB.NET, it is possible to have two or more controls with the same tab index value. At runtime, Visual Basic will break the tie by using the z-order of the controls. The control that is highest in the z-order will receive the focus first. The z-order is a ranking number that determines which controls are in front of or behind other controls. (The term comes from the z-axis, which is an axis that is perpendicular to the traditional x- and y-axes.) The z-order can be changed by right-clicking the control and selecting Bring to Front.

Control Arrays

Control arrays, which were a feature of VB6 and earlier versions, are not present in VB.NET. There were two capabilities for which they were needed:

- To have a single method handle the events of multiple controls
- To dynamically add new controls to your form at runtime

Both of these capabilities can also be accomplished in VB.NET, but the techniques used are different. The .NET Framework allows for any type of control to be created on the fly and for events to be attached dynamically to controls at runtime.

Since control arrays don't exist in VB.NET, you can no longer assign the same name to multiple controls on your form. Furthermore, the `Index` property is gone from the standard set of control properties.

To get the control array effect, you need to connect a single method to multiple control events. Then, since you are without the `Index` property, your handler will need a way to determine what control fired the event. To do this, simply use the `Sender` parameter of the event.

A simple example is helpful to see how to set this up. First, create a new Windows application, and set the `Text` property of the blank `Form1` to `Add Dynamic Control Demo`. Then add two buttons to the form, as shown in Figure 14-3.

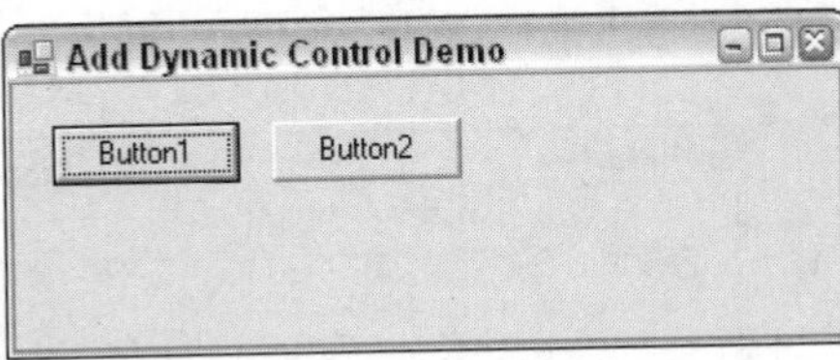

Figure 14-3

Double-click `Button1` to switch over to the code that handles the `Button1.Click` event. To make this method respond to the `Button2.Click` event as well, simply add the `Button2.Click` event handler to the end of the `Handles` list, and then add some simple code to display a message box indicating what button triggered the event:

```
' Note the change in the method name from Button1_Click. Since
' two objects are hooked up, it's a good idea to avoid having the
' method specifically named to a single object.
Private Sub Button_Click(ByVal sender As System.Object, _
                ByVal e As System.EventArgs) _
        Handles Button1.Click, Button2.Click
    Dim buttonClicked As Button
    buttonClicked = CType(sender, Button)
    ' Tell the world what button was clicked
    MessageBox.Show("You clicked " & buttonClicked.Text)
End Sub
```

Run the program and click the two buttons. Each one will trigger the event and display a message box with the appropriate text from the button that was clicked.

Next, you'll enhance the program to add a third button dynamically at runtime. First, add another button to your form that will trigger the addition of `Button3`, as shown in Figure 14-4.

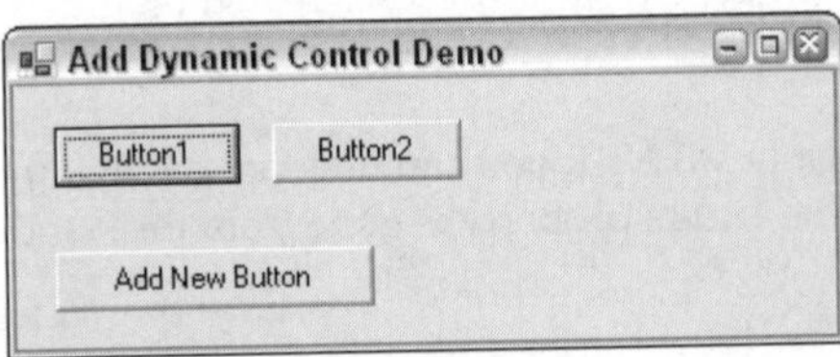

Figure 14-4

Name the new button `AddNewButton` and add the following code to handle its `Click` event:

```
Private Sub AddNewButton_Click(ByVal sender As System.Object, _
                    ByVal e As System.EventArgs) _
                    Handles addNewButton.Click

    Dim newButton As Button

    ' Create the new control
    newButton = New Button()

    ' Set it up on the form
    newButton.Location = New System.Drawing.Point(184, 16)
    newButton.Size = New System.Drawing.Size(75, 23)
    newButton.Text = "Button3"

    ' Add it to the form's controls collection
    Me.Controls.Add(newButton)

    ' Hook up the event handler.
    AddHandler newButton.Click, AddressOf Me.Button_Click
End  Sub
```

When the `AddNewButton` button is clicked, the code creates a new button, sets its size and position, and then does two essential things. First, it adds the button to the form's controls collection, and second, it connects the `Click` event of the button to the method that will handle it.

With this done, run the program and click the `addNewButton` button. `Button3` will appear. Then, simply click `Button3` to prove that the click event is being handled. You should get the result, as shown in Figure 14-5.

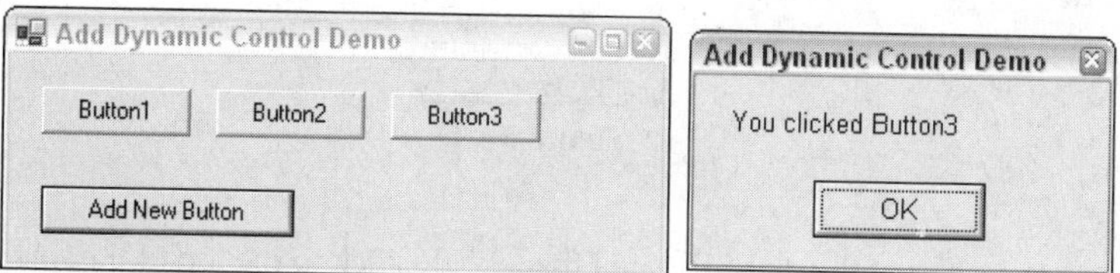

Figure 14-5

Automatic Resizing and Positioning of Controls

Windows Forms 2.0 includes a variety of ways to allow user interfaces to be dynamic. Controls can be set to automatically stretch and reposition themselves as a form is resized. Controls can also be dynamically arranged inside some special container controls intended for that purpose. This section covers all these ways of allowing dynamic sizing and positioning of controls.

Docking

Docking refers to gluing a control to the edge of a parent control. If the parent control moves or is stretched, the docked control will do the same. Good examples of docked controls are menu bars and status bars, which are typically docked to the top and bottom of a form, respectively. Docking is similar to the `Align` property of controls such as the VB6 status bar, but in VB.NET, all visual controls have a `Dock` property.

To work through an example, create a new Windows application and place a label on a form. Then set the background color of the label to white, make its font bold, place a solid border around it, and set its `TextAlign` to `MiddleCenter`. If you also set the `Text` property of the form to `AutoResize_Demo` and the `Text` property of the label to `Automatic Resizing Rocks!`, then the result when you show the form should look something like Figure 14-6.

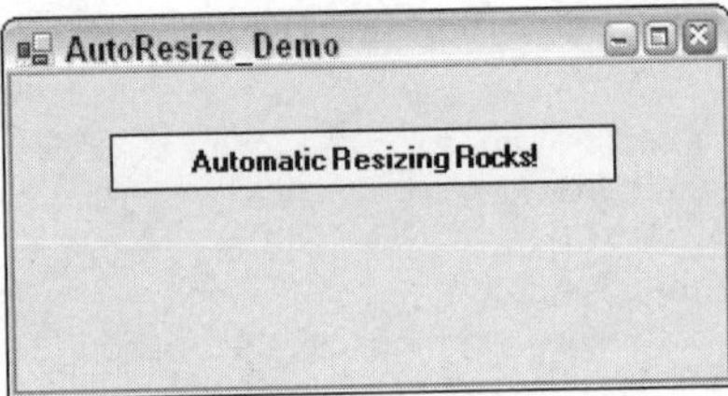

Figure 14-6

Suppose that you need to glue this label to the top of the form. To do this, view the `Dock` property of the label. If you pull it down you'll see a small graphic like that in Figure 14-7.

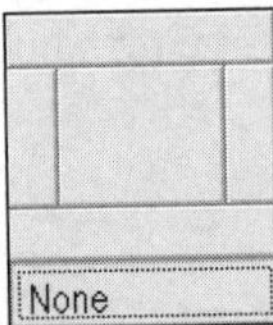

Figure 14-7

Simply click the top section of the graphic to tell the label to stick to the top of the form. The other sections give you other effects. (A status bar would use the bottom section, for example. Clicking the box in the middle causes the control to fill the form.) The label control will immediately "stick" to the top of your form. When you run your program and stretch the window sideways, you'll get the effect, as shown in Figure 14-8.

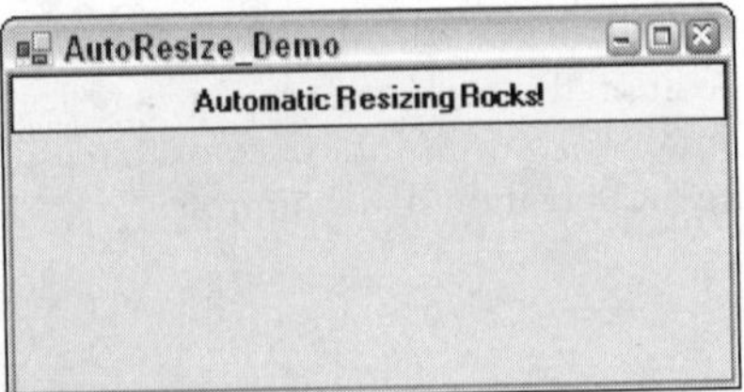

Figure 14-8

If you attempt to dock multiple controls to the same edge, VB.NET must decide how to break the tie. Precedence is given to controls in reverse z-order. In other words, the control that is furthest back in the z-order will be the first control that is next to the edge. If you dock two controls to the same edge and want to switch them, right-click the control you want docked first and select Send to Back.

If you want a gap between the edge of your form and the docked controls, set the `DockPadding` property of the parent control. You can set a different value for each of the four directions (`Left`, `Right`, `Top`, `Bottom`). You can also set all four properties to the same value using the `All` setting.

Anchoring

Anchoring is similar to docking, except that you can specifically define the distance each edge of your control will maintain from the edges of a parent. To see it in action, add a button to the form in the docking example. The result should look like Figure 14-9.

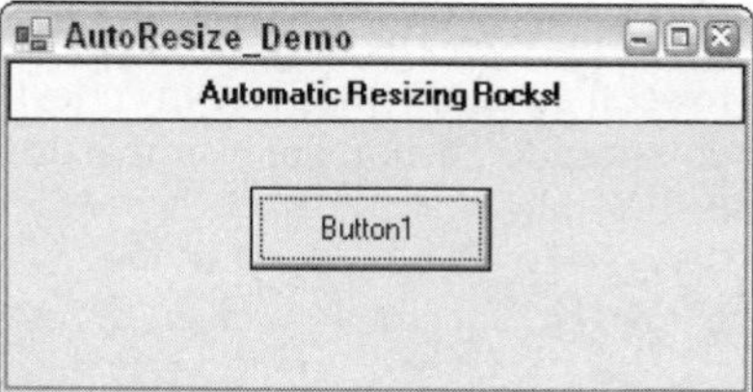

Figure 14-9

Dropping down the `Anchor` property of the button gives you the graphic in Figure 14-10.

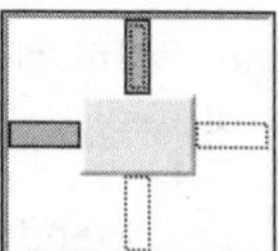

Figure 14-10

The four rectangles surrounding the center box allow you to toggle the anchor settings of the control. The graphic shows the default anchor setting of `Top, Left` for all controls.

When the setting is on (dark gray), the edge of your control will maintain its starting distance from the edge of the parent as the parent is resized. If you set the anchor to two opposing edges (such as the left and right edges), the control will stretch to accommodate this, as shown in Figure 14-11.

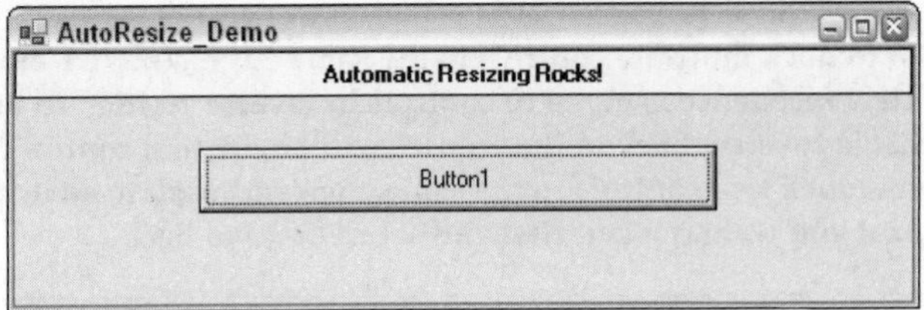

Figure 14-11

One of the most common uses of anchoring is to set the `Anchor` property for buttons in the lower-right portion of a form. Setting the `Anchor` property of a button to `Bottom, Right` will cause the button to maintain a constant distance to the bottom-right corner of the form.

Note that you should set the Anchor properties of your controls after you have designed the entire form since the anchoring effect occurs at design time as well. It can be very frustrating at design time when you need to adjust the size of your form but don't want the controls to move around.

You can also set the `Anchor` property in code. The most common time this would be needed would be for a control created on the fly. To set the Anchor property in code, you must add together the anchor styles for all the sides to which you need to anchor. For example, to set the Anchor property to `Bottom, Left` would require a line of code like this:

```
MyControl.Anchor = AnchorStyles.Bottom + AnchorStyles.Right
```

The Splitter Control

The splitter control is a great new tool that helps with resizing as well. A splitter lets a user decide the width (or height) of sections that make up a form. Windows Explorer uses a splitter to divide the folder tree view and folder content windows.

Placing a splitter on your form at design time is a bit tricky if you're new to the feature. To save yourself some frustration, follow this basic sequence of steps:

- Place one panel on the form that will act as the left half of the form, and set its `Dock` property to `Left`.
- Place the splitter control on the form; it will automatically dock. Be sure the splitter is sited on the form itself, and not within the panel. Place a button in the panel, and set the button's `Anchor` property to `Top, Left, Right`.
- Your form should now look something like Figure 14-12 (you've made the splitter extra fat and turned on their borders so you can see them).

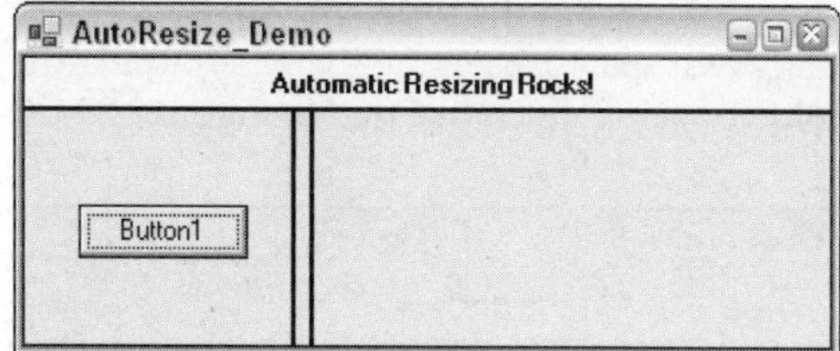

Figure 14-12

- Next, add another panel that will act as the right panel, and set its dock property to `Fill`. This tells it to take up the remaining space on the form
- Add a button to the right panel, and as with the first, set its `Anchor` property to `Top, Left, Right`.

When you run the form, the splitter will automatically operate and adjust sizes of the two panels, and in turn, the size of the two buttons, as shown in Figure 14-13.

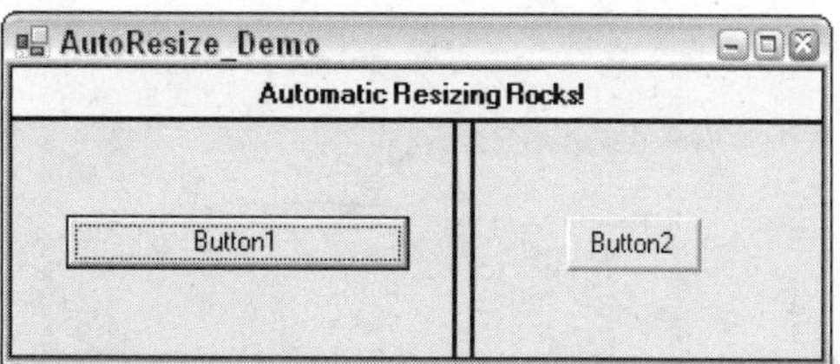

Figure 14-13

It's a good idea to change the back color of the splitter to a bright color like red at design time. This will make it easier to see and select. At runtime, change the color to something less vibrant.

FlowLayoutPanel Control

The summary of new features mentioned a new control for Windows Forms 2.0 called the `FlowLayoutPanel` control. This control allows dynamic layout of controls contained within the FlowLayoutPanel, based on the size of the `FlowLayoutPanel`. The following walkthrough will demonstrate this control in action.

Start a new Windows application project. On the blank `Form1` included in the new project, place a `FlowLayoutPanel` control toward the top of the form, and make it a bit less than the width of the form. Set the `Anchor` property for the `FlowLayoutPanel` to `Top`, `Left`, and `Right`.

Place a button in the bottom-right corner of the form, and set the `Anchor` property for the button to `Bottom` and `Right`. Then place two text boxes in the `FlowLayoutPanel`, keeping their default sizes. The form you have created should now look much like that in Figure 14-14.

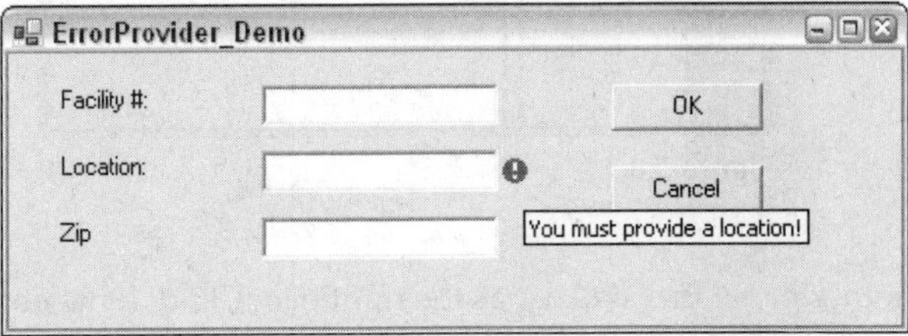

Figure 14-14

Now run the application. The initial layout will be similar to the design-time layout. However, if you resize the form to about half of its original width, the layout of the text boxes will change. Since there is no longer enough room for them to be arranged side by side, the arrangement will automatically switch, and the form will look more like that in Figure 14-15.

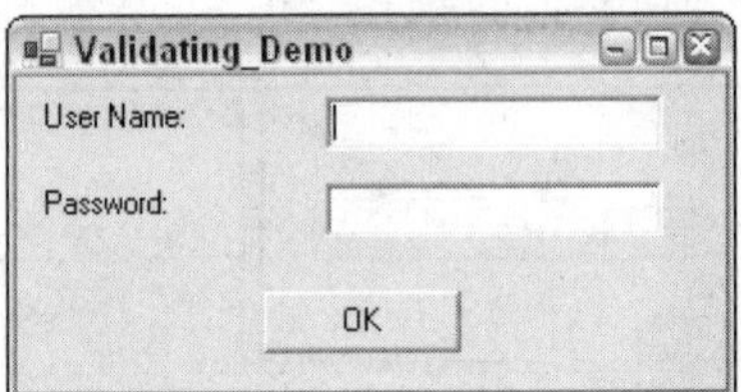

Figure 14-15

Padding and Margin properties

To assist in positioning controls in the `FlowLayoutPanel`, all controls have a new property called `Margin`. There are settings for `Margin.Left`, `Margin.Right`, `Margin.Top`, and `Margin.Bottom`. These settings determine how much space is reserved around a control when calculating its automatic position in a `FlowLayoutPanel`.

You can see the `Margin` property in action by changing the `Margin` property for one or more of the text boxes in the previous example. If you change all the `Margin` settings for the first `Textbox` to 20 pixels, for example, and run the application, the form will look like Figure 14-16.

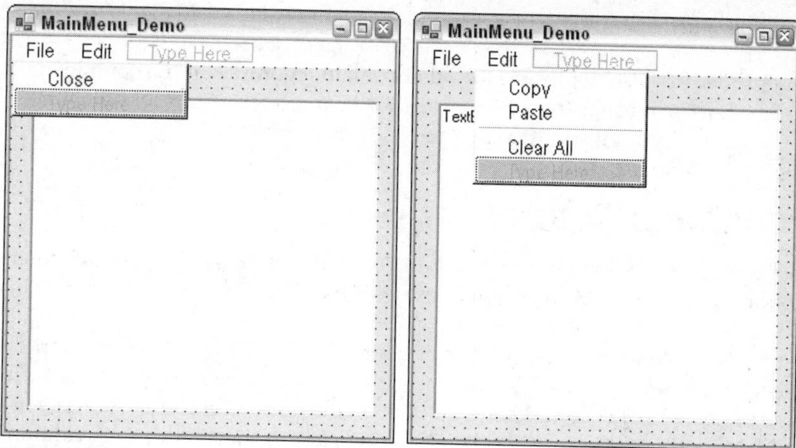

Figure 14-16

The first text box now has a 20 pixel separation from all the other controls in the `FlowLayoutPanel`, as well as a 20 pixel separation from the edges of the `FlowLayoutPanel` itself.

The `Padding` property is for the `FlowLayoutPanel` or other container control. When a control is embedded into a `FlowLayoutPanel`, the `Padding.Left`, `Padding.Right`, `Padding.Top`, and `Padding.Bottom` properties of the `FlowLayoutPanel` determine how far away from the inside edge of the container to position the control.

You can see the `Padding` property in action by changing the `Padding` property for the `FlowLayoutPanel` in the previous example. If you set all `Padding` settings to 20 pixels, and reset the `Margin` property for the first `Textbox` back to the default, then the form will look like Figure 14-17 in the visual designer.

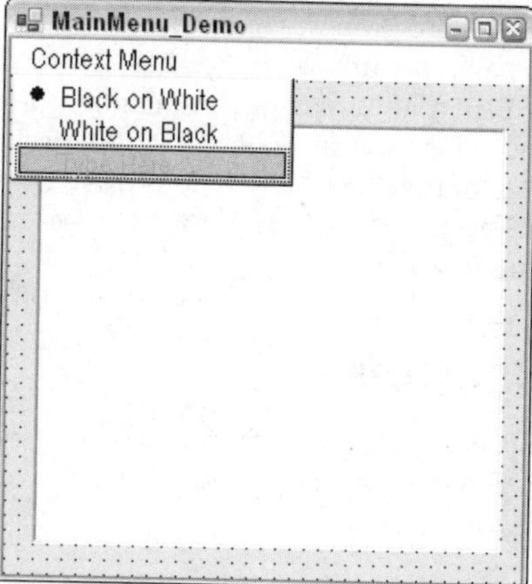

Figure 14-17

Notice that all the controls in the FlowLayoutPanel are now at least 20 pixels from the edges.

The Padding property is also applicable for other container controls, if the contained controls have their Dock property set. If the settings for Padding are not zero, a docked control will be offset from the edge of the container by the amount specified by the Padding property.

TableLayoutPanel Control

The other new control for dynamic layout is the TableLayoutPanel. This control consists of a table of rows and columns, resulting in a rectangular array of cells. You can place one control in each cell.

The dimensions of the columns and rows can be controlled by setting some key properties. For columns, set the number of columns with the ColumnCount property, and then control each individual column with the ColumnStyles collection. When you click on the button for the ColumnStyles collection, you'll get a designer window that allows you to set two key properties for each column — the SizeType and Width properties.

SizeType can be set to one of the following enumerations:

- Absolute — Sets the column width to a fixed size in pixels
- AutoSize — Indicates that the size of the column should be managed by the TableLayoutPanel, which will allocate width to the column depending on the widest control contained in the column
- Percent — Sets the percentage of the TableLayoutPanel to use for the width of the column

The Width property is only applicable if you do not choose a SizeType of AutoSize. It sets either the number of pixels for the width of the column (if the SizeType is Absolute) or the percentage width for the column (if the SizeType is set to Percent).

Similarly, for rows, there is a RowCount property to set the number of rows, and a RowStyles collection to manage the size of the rows. Each row in RowStyles has a SizeType, which works the same way as SizeType does for Columns, except that it manages the height of the row instead of the width of a column. The Height property is used for rows instead of a Width property, but it works in a corresponding way. Height is either the number of pixels (if SizeType is Absolute) or a percentage of the height of the TableLayoutPanel (if SizeType is Percent). If SizeType is AutoSize, then a row is sized to the height of the tallest control in the row.

Extender Provider Controls

There is a new family of controls in Windows Forms that can only be used in association with other controls. Each of these controls, called extender provider controls, causes new properties to appear for every other control on the form.

Extender provider controls have no visible manifestation, so they appear in the component tray. The three extender provider controls currently available are the HelpProvider, the ToolTip, and the ErrorProvider. All three controls work in basically the same way. Each extender provider control implements the properties that are "attached" to other controls. The best way to see how this works is to go through an example, so let's do that with a `ToolTip` control.

ToolTip

The `ToolTip` control is the simplest of the extender providers. It adds just one property to each control, named `ToolTip on ToolTip1` (assuming the `ToolTip` control has the default name of `ToolTip1`). This property works exactly the same way the `ToolTipText` property works in VB6, and in fact, replaces it.

To see this in action, create a Windows Forms application. On the blank `Form1` that is created for the project, place a couple of buttons. Take a look at the properties window for `Button1`. Notice that it does not have a `ToolTip` property of any kind.

Drag over the `ToolTip` control, which will be placed in the component tray. Go back to the properties window for `Button1`. A property named `ToolTip on ToolTip1` is now present. Set any string value you like for this property.

Now run the project, and hover the mouse pointer over `Button1`. You will see a tooltip containing the string value you entered for the `ToolTip on ToolTip1` property.

HelpProvider

The `HelpProvider` control allows controls to have associated context-sensitive help available by pressing F1. When a `HelpProvider` control (named `HelpProvider1` by default) is added to a form, all controls on the form get these new properties, which show up in the controls' Properties window.

Property	Usage
`HelpString on HelpProvider1`	Provides a pop-up tooltip for the control when shape F1 is pressed while the control has the focus. If the `HelpKeyword` and `HelpNavigator` properties (see later) are set to provide a valid reference to a help file, then the `HelpString` value is ignored in favor of the information in the help file.
`HelpKeyword on HelpProvider1`	Provides a keyword or other index to use in a help file for context-sensitive help for this control. The `HelpProvider1` control has a property that indicates the help file to use. This replaces the `HelpContextID` property in VB6.
`HelpNavigator on HelpProvider1`	Contains an enumerated value that determines how the value in `HelpKeyword` is used to refer to the help file. There are several possible values for displaying such elements as a topic, an index, or a table of contents in the help file.
`ShowHelp on HelpProvider1`	Determines whether the `HelpProvider` control is active for this control.

Filling in the HelpString property immediately causes the control to provide tooltip help when F1 is pressed while the control has the focus. The HelpProvider control has a property to point to a help file (either an HTML help file or a Win32 help file), and the help topic in the HelpTopic property points to a topic in this file.

ErrorProvider

The ErrorProvider control presents a simple, visual way to indicate to a user that a control on a form has an error associated with it. The added property for controls on the form when an ErrorProvider control is used is called Error on ErrorProvider1 (assuming the ErrorProvider has the default name of ErrorProvider1). Setting this property to a string value causes the error icon to appear next to a control, and for the text to appear in a tooltip if the mouse hovers over the error icon.

Here is a screen with several text boxes, and an error icon next to one (with a tooltip). The error icon and tooltip are displayed and managed by the ErrorProvider control, as shown in Figure 14-18.

The ErrorProvider control's default icon is the red circle with an exclamation point. When the Error property for the text box is set, the icon will blink for a few moments, and hovering over the icon will cause the tooltip to appear. The code for this behavior in the example screen is explained in the next topic.

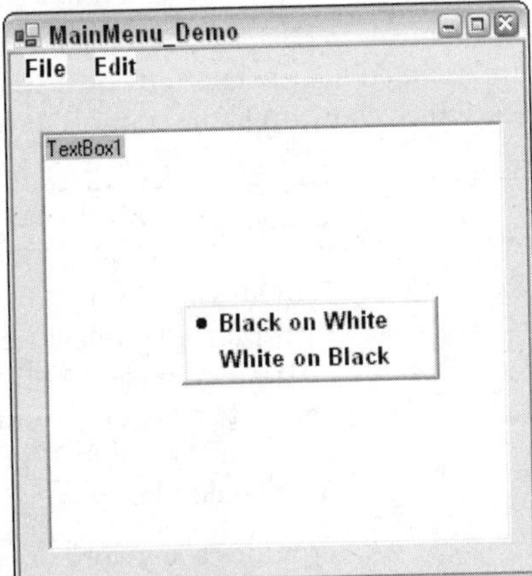

Figure 14-18

Properties of Extender Providers

In addition to providing other controls with properties, extender provider controls also have properties of their own. For example, the ErrorProvider control has a property named BlinkStyle. When it is set to NeverBlink, the blinking of the icon is stopped for all controls that are affected by the ErrorProvider.

Other properties of the ErrorProvider allow you to change things such as the icon used, and where the icon will appear in relation to the field that has the error. For instance, you might want the icon to show up beneath a field, instead. You can also have multiple error providers on your form. For example, you may wish to give the user a warning rather than an error. A second error provider with a yellow icon could be used to provide this feature.

Working with Extender Provider Controls in Code

Setting the Error property in the previous example can be done with the Property window, but this is not very useful for on-the-fly error management. However, setting the Error property in code is not done with typical property syntax. By convention, extender provider controls have a method for each property they need to set, and the arguments for the method include the associated control and the property setting. To set the Error property in the previous example, the following code was used:

```
ErrorProvider1.SetError(txtName, "You must provide a location!")
```

The name of the method to set a property is the word Set prefixed to the name of the property. This line of code shows that the Error property is set with the SetError (), method of the ErrorProvider.

There is a corresponding method to get the value of the property, and it is named with Get prefixed to the name of the property. To find out what the current Error property setting for txtName is, you would use the following line:

```
sError = ErrorProvider1.GetError(txtName)
```

Similar syntax is used to manipulate any of the properties managed by an extender provider control. The discussion of the tooltip provider earlier talked about setting the tooltip property in the Properties window. To set that same property in code, the syntax would be

```
ToolTip1.SetToolTip(Button1, "New tooltip for Button1")
```

Advanced Capabilities for Data Entry

New for Windows Forms 2.0 are a couple of advanced capabilities for data entry. Textbox and Combobox controls now have autocompletion capabilities, and a new MaskedTextbox allows entry of formatted input such as phone numbers.

Autocompletion

Responsive user interfaces help users accomplish their purposes, thereby making them more productive. One classic way to do this is with autocompletion.

An example of autocompletion is IntelliSense in Visual Studio. Using IntelliSense, the user only has to type in a few letters, and Visual Studio presents a list of probable entries matching those letters. If what the user wants is in the list, the user need only indicate that, rather than typing the entire entry.

Autocompletion is available in Windows Forms 2.0 with text boxes and combo boxes. Both use a set of properties to control how autocompletion works and where the list of entries available to the user comes from.

To see autocompletion in action, create a Windows Application project. Drag a text box from the toolbox onto the blank `Form1` created for the project.

Set the `AutocompleteMode` for the text box to `Suggest` in the Property window. Then set the `AutocompleteSource` to `CustomSource`. Finally, click the button in the setting window for `AutoCompleteCustomSource`. You'll see a window for entering entries that is very similar to the window for entering items for a list box or combo box.

Enter the following items into the dialog:

```
Holder
Holland
Hollis
Holloway
Holly
Holstein
Holt
```

Now, start the project, and type "Hol" into the text box. As soon as you start typing, a drop-down will appear that contains entries matching what you've typed, which includes all seven elements in the list. If you then type another `l`, the list will decrease to four elements that begin with `Holl`. (See Figure 14-19.) If you then type an `o`, the list will contain only the entry `Holloway`.

The `AutoCompleteMode` has two other modes. The `Append` mode does not automatically present a drop-down, but instead appends the rest of the closest matching entry to the text in the `Textbox` or `ComboBox`, and highlights the untyped characters. This allows the closest matching entry to be placed in the textarea without the user explicitly selecting an entry.

The `SuggestAppend` mode combines `Suggest` and `Append`. The current best match is displayed in the textarea, and the drop-down with other possibilities is automatically displayed. This mode is the one most like IntelliSense.

You can also set the list of items to be included in the autocompletion list at runtime, and this would be the most common usage scenario. A list of items from a database table would typically be loaded for autocompletion.

MaskedTextbox Control

The new features summary discussed the addition of a `MaskedTextbox` control, which fills in for the old VB6 `MaskedEdit` control. If you have used `MaskedEdit` in VB6, the `MaskedTextbox` will feel quite familiar.

After dragging a `MaskedTextbox` control to a form, you will typically want to first set the mask associated with the control. You can do this in the property window by selecting the `Mask` property, but you can also click the right-pointing arrow on the right side of the `MaskedTextbox`. In either case, you can either construct a mask manually or select one of the commonly used masks from a list.

If you need to create your own mask, you will need to design it based on a set of formatting characters:

Mask Character	Description
`#`	Digit placeholder.
`.`	Decimal placeholder. The actual character used is the one specified as the decimal placeholder in your international settings. This character is treated as a literal for masking purposes.
`,`	Thousands separator. The actual character used is the one specified as the thousands separator in your international settings. This character is treated as a literal for masking purposes.
`:`	Time separator. The actual character used is the one specified as the time separator in your international settings. This character is treated as a literal for masking purposes.
`/`	Date separator. The actual character used is the one specified as the date separator in your international settings. This character is treated as a literal for masking purposes.
`\`	Treat the next character in the mask string as a literal. This allows you to include the `#`, `&`, `A`, and `?` characters in the mask. This character is treated as a literal for masking purposes.
`&`	Character placeholder. Valid values for this placeholder are ANSI characters in the following ranges: 32–126 and 128–255.
`>`	Convert all the characters that follow to uppercase.
`<`	Convert all the characters that follow to lowercase.
`A`	Alphanumeric character placeholder (entry required). For example: a–z, A–Z, or 0–9.
`a`	Alphanumeric character placeholder (entry optional).
`9`	Digit placeholder (entry optional). For example: 0–9.
`C`	Character or space placeholder (entry optional). This operates exactly like the `&` placeholder, and ensures compatibility with Microsoft Access.
`?`	Letter placeholder. For example: a–z or A–Z.
Literal	All other symbols are displayed as literals; that is, as themselves.

Literal characters are simply inserted automatically by the `MaskedTextbox` control. If you have literal characters for the parentheses in a phone number, for example, the user need not type these for them to show up in the textarea of the control.

As an example of a mask, suppose that you have an account number that must consist of exactly two uppercase letters and five digits. You could construct a mask of `>??00000`. The first character forces all letters to uppercase. The two question marks specify two required alphabetic characters, and the five zeros specify five required digits.

Once you have set the `Mask` for the `MaskedTextbox`, all entries into the control will be coerced to the `Mask` pattern. Keystrokes that don't fit will be thrown away.

You have two options for fetching the text information entered by the user in a `MaskedTextbox`. The `InputText` property will get the entry without any of the literal placeholder characters. For example, if you are using a mask for phone number, `InputText` will just return the ten digits in the phone number. If you want the text exactly as it appears in the control, then you should use the normal `Text` property.

Validating Data Entry

Most controls that you place on a form require that their content be validated in some way. A text box might require a numeric value only or simply require that the user provide any value and not leave it blank.

The `ErrorProvider` control just covered makes this task significantly easier than it was in previous versions. To illustrate the use of this control in data validation, create a new Windows application project and change the `Text` property for the blank `Form1` to `Validating Demo`. Then place two text boxes on the form that will hold a username and password, as shown in Figure 14-19.

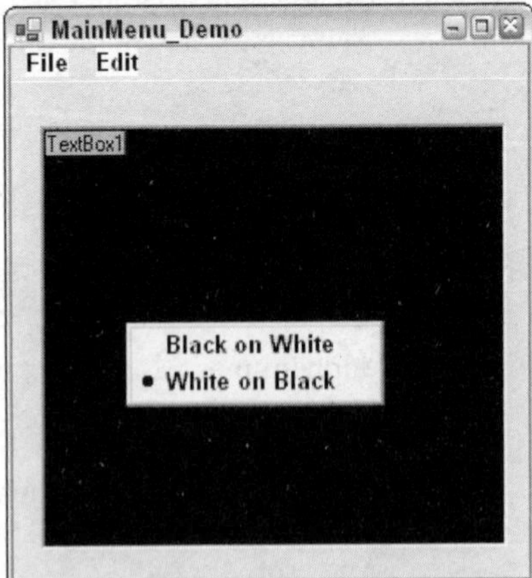

Figure 14-19

Name the first text box `UserNameTextBox` and the second text box `PasswordTextBox`. You also need to drag an `ErrorProvider` control onto the form, which will cause it to appear in the Component Tray. In the next section, you'll add the code that will simply verify that the user has filled in both text boxes and given a visual indication, via the `ErrorProvider`, if either of the fields has been left blank.

The Validating Event

The `Validating` event fires when your control begins its validation. It is here that you need to place your code that will validate your control, and set a visual indication for the error. Insert the following code to see this in action:

```
Private Sub UserNameTextBox_Validating(ByVal sender As Object, _
                              ByVal e As System.ComponentModel.CancelEventArgs) _
                              Handles UserNameTextBox.Validating
    If userNameTextbox.Text = "" Then
        ErrorProvider1.SetError(UserNameTextBox, "User Name cannot be blank")
    Else
        ErrorProvider1.SetError(UserNameTextBox, "")
    End If
End Sub
Private Sub PasswordTextBox_Validating(ByVal sender As Object, _
                              ByVal e As System.ComponentModel.CancelEventArgs) _
                              Handles PasswordTextBox.Validating
    If passwordTextbox.Text = "" Then
        ErrorProvider1.SetError(PasswordTextBox, "Password cannot be blank")
    Else
        ErrorProvider1.SetError(PasswordTextBox, "")
    End If
End Sub
```

Run the program and the tab between the controls without entering any text to get the error message. You'll see an icon blink next to each of the text box controls, and if you hover over an error icon, you'll see the appropriate error message.

There is also a `Validated` event that fires after a control's `Validating` event. It can be used, for example, to do a final check after other events have manipulated the contents of the control.

The CausesValidation Property

The `CausesValidation` property determines if the control will participate in the validation events on the form. A control with a `CausesValidation` setting of `True` (it is `True` by default) will have two effects:

- The control's `Validating/Validated` events will fire when appropriate.
- The control will trigger the `Validating/Validated` events for other controls.

It is important to understand that the validation events fire for a control not when the focus is lost but when the focus shifts to a control that has a `CausesValidation` value of `True`.

To see this effect, set the CausesValidation property of the password text box in your application to False (be sure to leave it True for the username and OK button). When you run the program, tab off the username text box and again to the OK button. Notice that it isn't until the focus reaches the OK button that the validating event of the username text box fires. Also, notice that the validating event of the password field never fires.

Ultimately, if you determine that the control is not valid, you need to decide how to act. That may include setting the focus to the control that needs attention (as well as indicating the error with an ErrorProvider).

Toolbars and the New ToolStrip Control

As mentioned in the summary of new features in Windows Forms 2.0, the ToolStrip control replaces the Toolbar control from Windows Forms 1.0 and 1.1. ToolStrip has many improvements. It supports movement to other sides of a form than the place it was laid out, and you have much more flexibility in placing items on the toolbar. It also integrates better with the IDE to assist in creating toolbars and manipulating the many settings available.

The ToolStrip does not sit alone on a form. When a ToolStrip is dragged onto a form, the container that actually sits on the form is called a RaftingContainer. This container handles the positioning, so that the toolbar created by a ToolStrip can be dragged to other parts of the form.

The ToolStrip sits inside the RaftingContainer and is the container for toolbar elements. It handles the sizing of the toolbar, movement of toolbar elements, and other general toolbar functions.

The items on the toolbar must be from a set of controls specially designed to serve as toolbar items. All of these items inherit from the ToolStripItem base class. The controls available for toolbar items are:

Control	Description
ToolStripButton	Replicates the functionality of a regular Button for a toolbar
ToolStripLabel	Replicates the functionality of a regular Label for a toolbar
ToolStripSeparator	A visual toolbar element that displays a vertical bar to separate other groups of elements (no user interaction)
ToolStripComboBox	Replicates the functionality of a regular ComboBox for a toolbar. This item must be contained within a ToolStrip-ControlHost (see below).
ToolStripTextBox	Replicates the functionality of a regular TextBox for a toolbar. This item must be contained within a ToolStrip-ControlHost (see below)
ToolStripControlHost	A hosting container for other controls that reside on a ToolStrip. It can host any of the following controls: ToolStripComboBox, ToolStripTextBox, other Windows Forms controls, or user controls.

Control	Description
ToolStripDropDownItem	A hosting container for toolbar elements that feature drop-down functionality. Can host a ToolStripMenuItem, a ToolStripSplitButton, or a ToolStripDropDownButton.
ToolStripDropDownButton	A button that supports drop-down functionality. Clicking the button shows a list of options, and the user must then click the one desired. This item is used when the user needs to select from a group of options, no one of which is used a large majority of the time.
ToolStripSplitButton	A combination of a regular button and a drop-down button. This item is often used when there is a frequently used option to click, but you also need to offer the user other options that are less frequently used.
ToolStripMenuItem	A selectable option displayed on a menu or context menu. This item is typically used with the menu controls that inherit from the ToolStrip, and which are discussed in the section later in this chapter entitled "Menus."

Notice that almost any control can be hosted on a toolbar using the ToolStripControlHost. However, for buttons, text boxes, labels, and combo boxes, it is much easier to use the ToolStrip version instead of the standard version.

Creating a ToolStrip and Adding Toolbar Elements

Let's do an example to see how to build a toolbar using the ToolStrip control. Create a new Windows application. Add a ToolStrip control to the blank Form1 that is included with the new project. Make the form about twice its default width, so that you have plenty of room to see the ToolStrip as you work on it.

The ToolStrip will be positioned at the top of the form by default. It will not contain any elements, though if you highlight the ToolStrip control in the component tray, a "menu designer" will appear in the ToolStrip.

The easiest way to add multiple elements to the ToolStrip is to use the designer dialog for the ToolStrip. Highlight the ToolStrip in the component tray and click the button in the properties window for the Items property. You'll see a designer dialog that looks like Figure 14-20.

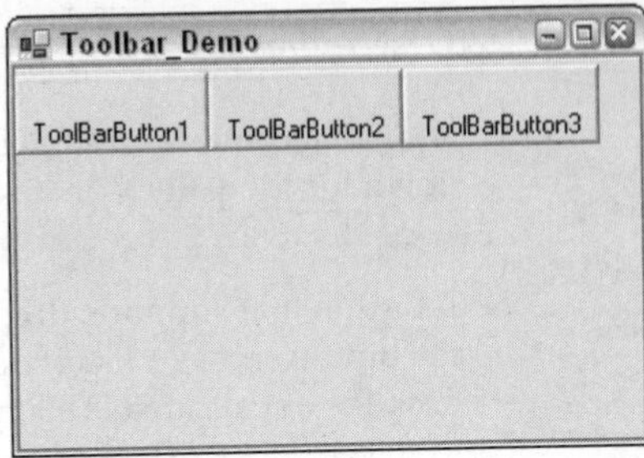

Figure 14-20

The drop-down in the upper left contains the different types of items that can be placed on the toolbar. Add one each of the following types, with the setting specified:

`ToolStripButton`	Set the `Text` property to `Go`.
`ToolStripComboBox`	Set the `Text` property to blank. Set `DropDownStyle` to `DropDownList`. Open the Items dialog and add the names of some colors.
`ToolStripSplitButton`	Set the `Text` property to `Options`.
`ToolStripTextBox`	Set the `Text` property to blank.

Then click OK in the dialog, and the `ToolStrip` will look like the one in Figure 14-21.

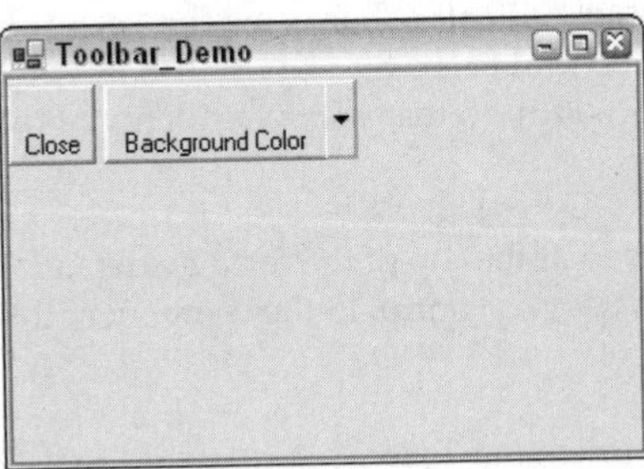

Figure 14-21

You can now handle events on any of these toolbar elements the same way you would any other controls. You can double-click to get a `Click` event routine or access the event routines through the drop-downs in the Code Editor.

Run your program and, using the mouse, grab the dotted handle on the far-left edge of the toolbar. If you drag this to the right, the toolbar will be repositioned. If you drag it to other positions on the form, the entire toolbar will dock to different edges of the form.

Allowing the User to Move Toolbar Elements

By default, the `AllowReorder` property of the `ToolStrip` is set to `False`. If you change that to `True`, then the elements on the toolbar can be moved around in relation to one another at runtime (reordered).

Change the `AllowReorder` property to `True` for the `ToolStrip`, and run your program again. Hold down the Alt key, and drag elements on the toolbar around. They will assume new positions on the toolbar when you drop them.

Creating a Standard Set of Toolbar Elements

If you need a toolbar that has the typical visual elements for cut, copy, paste, and so on, it is not necessary for you to create the elements. The designer will do it for you.

Create a new form in your project, and drag a `ToolStrip` onto the form. As before, it will be positioned at the top and will not contain any elements.

With the `ToolStrip` highlighted in the component tray, click the `Item` property. Below the properties in the Property window, a link named Insert Standard Items will appear. Click that link, and elements will be inserted into the `ToolStrip` to make it look like the one in Figure 14-22.

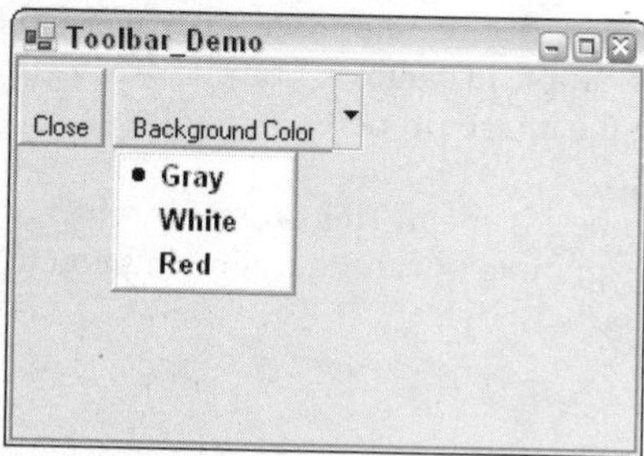

Figure 14-22

Altering Toolbar Elements in the Designer

When a `ToolStrip` or element with a `ToolStrip` is highlighted in the Visual Designer, a small right-pointing arrow is displayed on the right-hand side of the element. If you click this arrow, you will see a dialog that allows you to change the most commonly used properties of the element. This is just a convenience feature — the properties window can also be used to change these properties, along with any other properties of the element.

Menus

Menus are added to a form in VB.NET 2005 by dragging controls called `MenuStrip` or `ContextMenuStrip` onto your form. `MenuStrip` implements a standard Windows-style menu at the top of the form. `ContextMenuStrip` allows a pop-up menu with a right mouse button click.

These controls are actually subclasses of the `ToolStrip`, so much of the information you learned earlier in this chapter for working with the `ToolStrip` also applies to the `MenuStrip` and `ContextMenuStrip`.

When dragged onto the form, these controls appear in the component tray just as the `ToolStrip` does, and you access the designer for these controls the same way as you do for the `ToolStrip`. However, because these are menus, the most common way of adding items is to type items directly into the menu designer that appears when the control is highlighted.

The menu designer is extremely intuitive — the menu appears on your form just as it would at runtime, and you simply fill in the menu items you need. Each item can be renamed, and each can have a `Click` event associated with it.

Adding Standard Items to a Menu

If your form's menu needs to have the standard top-level options (File, Edit, and so on) and the typical options under these items, then you can have all these typical options inserted for you automatically.

To see this capability in action, drag a `MenuStrip` to a form, and then click the right arrow at the right edge of the `MenuStrip` to bring up the designer dialog. Click the link at the bottom of the dialog that says Insert Standard Items.

Icons and Checkmarks for Menu Items

Each item on a menu has an `Image` property. Setting this property to an image causes the image to appear on the left side of the text for the menu option. You can see this property in use by looking at the standard items inserted in the example just above. The File ➪ Save option has an icon of a diskette, which was produced by setting the image property of that item.

Items can also have checkmarks beside them. This is done by changing the `Checked` property of the item to `True`. This can be done at design time or runtime, allowing you to manipulate the checkmarks on menus as necessary.

Context Menus

To implement a context menu for a form or any control on a form, drag a `ContextMenuStrip` to the form, and add the menu items. Items are added and changed the same way as with the `MenuStrip`.

To hook a context menu to a control, set the control's `ContextMenuStrip` property to the `ContextMenuStrip` menu control you want to use. Then, when your program runs and you right-click in the control, the context menu will pop up.

Dynamically Manipulating Menus at Runtime

Menus can be adjusted at runtime using code. Context menus, for instance, may need to change depending on the state of your form. The following walkthrough shows how to add a new menu item to a context menu and also how to clear the menu items.

First, create a new Windows application. On the blank `Form1` for the project, drag over a `MenuStrip` control. Using the menu designer, type in a top-level menu option of `File`. Under that option, type in options for `Open` and `Save`.

Now place a button on the form. Double-click the button to get its `Click` event, and place the following code into the event:

```
Dim NewItem As New ToolStripMenuItem
NewItem.Text = "Save As"
' Set any other properties of the menu item you like.

FileToolStripMenuItem.DropDownItems.Add(NewItem)
AddHandler NewItem.Click, _
     AddressOf Me.NewMenuItem_Click
```

Then add the event handler referenced in this code at the bottom of the form's code:

```
Private Sub NewMenuItem_Click(ByVal sender As System.Object, _
                              ByVal e As System.EventArgs)
   MessageBox.Show("New menu item clicked!")
End Sub
```

If you now run the program and look at the menu, it will only have File and Save options. Clicking the button will cause a new Save As item to be added to the menu, and it will be hooked to the event routine called `NewMenuItem_Click`.

Common Dialogs

VB.NET provides you with seven common dialog controls. Each is a control that will open a predefined form that is identical to the one used by the operating system. The next sections outline the use and basic properties of each control that customizes their use.

OpenFileDialog and SaveFileDialog

These two controls will open the standard dialog control that allows a user to select files on the system. They are virtually identical, except for the buttons and labels that appear on the actual dialog box when it is shown to the user. Each prompts the user for a file on the system, by allowing the user to browse the files and folders available.

Use the following properties to set up the dialog boxes.

Property	Comments
`InitialDirectory`	Defines the initial location that will be displayed when the dialog box opens. For example: `OpenFileDialog1.InitialDirectory = "C:\Program Files"`
`Filter`	String that defines the Files of type list. Separate items using the pipe character. Items are entered in pairs with the first of each pair being the description of the file type, and the second half as the file wildcard. For example: `OpenFileDialog1.Filter = "All Files$|*.* |Text Files|*.txt|Rich Text Files|*.rtf"`

Table continued on following page

Property	Comments
`FilterIndex`	Integer that specifies the default filter item to use when the dialog box opens. For example, with the above filter used, default to text files as follows: `OpenFileDialog1.FilterIndex = 2`
`RestoreDirectory`	Boolean value that, if `True`, will force the system's default directory to be restored to the location it was in when the dialog box was first opened. This is `False` by default.
`Filename`	Holds the full name of the file that the user selected, including the path.
`ShowDialog()`	Displays the dialog.

The following code will open the standard dialog box asking the user to select a file that currently exists on the system, and will simply display the choice in a message box upon return:

```
OpenFileDialog1.InitialDirectory = "C:\"
OpenFileDialog1.Filter = "Text files|*.txt|All files|*.*"
OpenFileDialog1.FilterIndex = 1
OpenFileDialog1.RestoreDirectory = True
OpenFileDialog1.ShowDialog()
MessageBox.Show("You selected """ & OpenFileDialog1.FileName & """")
```

ColorDialog Control

As the name implies, this control gives the user a dialog box from which to select a color. Use the following properties to set up the dialogs boxes.

Using these properties looks something like this:

```
ColorDialog1.Color = TextBox1.BackColor
ColorDialog1.AllowFullOpen = True
ColorDialog1.ShowDialog()
TextBox1.BackColor = ColorDialog1.Color
```

Property	Comments
`Color`	The `System.Drawing.Color` that the user selected. You can also use this to set the initial color selected when the user opens the dialog.
`AllowFullOpen`	Boolean value that, if `True`, will allow the user to select any color. If `False`, the user is restricted to the set of default colors.
`ShowDialog()`	Displays the dialog.

FontDialog Control

This control will display the standard dialog box, allowing a user to select a font. Use the following properties to set up the dialog boxes.

Property	Comments
`Font`	The `System.Drawing.Font` that the user selected. Also used to set the initial font.
`ShowEffects`	Boolean value that, if `True`, will make the dialog box display the text effects options of underline and strikeout.
`ShowColor`	Boolean value that, if `True`, will make the dialog box display the combo box of the font colors. The `ShowEffects` property must be `True` for this to have an effect.
`FixedPitchOnly`	Boolean value that, if `True`, will limit the list of font choices to only those that have a fixed pitch (such as Courier, or Lucida console).
`ShowDialog()`	Displays the dialog.

Using these properties looks like this:

```
FontDialog1.Font = TextBox1.Font
FontDialog1.ShowColor = True
FontDialog1.ShowEffects = True
FontDialog1.FixedPitchOnly = False
FontDialog1.ShowDialog()
TextBox1.Font = FontDialog1.Font
```

Printer Dialog Controls

There are three more common dialog controls: `PrintDialog`, `PrintPreviewDialog`, and `PageSetupDialog`. They can all be used to control the output of a file to the printer. You can use these in conjunction with the `PrintDocument` component to run and control print jobs.

Drag and Drop

Implementing a drag-and-drop operation in the .NET Framework is accomplished by a short sequence of events. Typically, it begins in a `MouseDown` event of one control, and always ends with the `DragDrop` event of another.

To demonstrate the process, you'll begin with a new Windows Application. Add two list boxes to your form, and add three items to the first using the `Items` Property Designer. This application will allow you to drag the items from one list box into the other.

The first step in making drag and drop work is specifying whether or not a control will accept a drop. By default, all controls will reject such an act and not respond to any attempt by the user to drop something onto them. In your case, set the `AllowDrop` property of the second list box (the one without the items added) to `True`.

The next item of business is to invoke the drag-and-drop operation. This is typically done in the `MouseDown` event of the control containing the data you want to drag (although you're not restricted to it). The `DoDragDrop` method is used to start the operation. This method defines the data that will be dragged, and the type of dragging that will be allowed. In the present situation, you'll drag the text of the selected list box item, and you'll permit both a move and a copy of the data to occur.

Switch over to the code window of your form and add the following code to the `MouseDown` event of `ListBox1`:

```
Private Sub ListBox1_MouseDown(ByVal sender As Object, _
                               ByVal e As System.Windows.Forms.MouseEventArgs) _}
                               Handles ListBox1.MouseDown
   Dim DragDropResult As DragDropEffects
   If e.Button = MouseButtons.Left Then
      DragDropResult = ListBox1.DoDragDrop( _
                 ListBox1.Items(ListBox1.SelectedIndex), _
                 DragDropEffects.Move Or DragDropEffects.Copy)
      ' Leave some room here to check the result of the operation
      ' (You'll fill it in next).
   End If
End Sub
```

You'll notice the comment here about leaving room to check the result of the operation. You'll fill that in shortly. For now, calling the `DoDragDrop` method has got you started.

The next step involves the recipient of the data, in your case, `ListBox2`. There are two events here that will be important to monitor — the `DragEnter` and `DragDrop` events.

As can be predicted by the name, the `DragEnter` event will occur when the user first moves over the recipient control. The `DragEnter` event has a parameter of type `DragEventArgs` that contains an `Effect` property and a `KeyState` property.

The `Effect` property allows you to set the display of the drop icon for the user to indicate if a move or a copy will occur when the mouse button is released. The `KeyState` property allows you to determine the state of the Ctrl, Alt, and Shift keys. It is a Windows standard that when both a move or a copy can occur, a user is to indicate the copy action by holding down the Ctrl key. Therefore, in this event, you will check the `KeyState` property and use it to determine how to set the `Effect` property.

Add the following code to the `DragEnter` event of `ListBox2`:

```
Private Sub ListBox2_DragEnter(ByVal sender As Object, _
                               ByVal e As DragEventArgs) _
                               Handles ListBox2.DragOver
   If e.KeyState = 9 Then ' Control key
      e.Effect = DragDropEffects.Copy
   Else
      e.Effect = DragDropEffects.Move
   End If
End Sub
```

Note that you can also use the DragOver event if you want, but it will fire continuously as the mouse moves over the target control. In this situation, you only need to trap the initial entry of the mouse into the control.

The final step in the operation occurs when the user lets go of the mouse button to drop the data at its destination. This is captured by the DragDrop event. The parameter contains a property holding the data that is being dragged. It's now a simple process of placing it into the recipient control as follows:

```
Private Sub ListBox2_DragDrop(ByVal sender As Object, _
                              ByVal e As System.Windows.Forms.DragEventArgs) _
                              Handles ListBox2.DragDrop
   ListBox2.Items.Add(e.Data.GetData(DataFormats.Text))
End Sub
```

One last step — you can't forget to manipulate ListBox1 if the drag and drop was a move. Here's where you'll fill in the hole you left in the MouseDown event of ListBox1. Once the DragDrop has occurred, the initial call that invoked the procedure will return a result indicating what ultimately happened. Go back to the ListBox1_MouseDown event and enhance it to remove the item from Listbox1 if it was moved (and not simply copied):

```
Private Sub ListBox1_MouseDown(ByVal sender As Object, _
           ByVal e As System.Windows.Forms.MouseEventArgs) _
           Handles ListBox1.MouseDown
   Dim DragDropResult As DragDropEffects

   If e.Button = MouseButtons.Left Then
      DragDropResult = ListBox1.DoDragDrop( _
                  ListBox1.Items(ListBox1.SelectedIndex), _
                  DragDropEffects.Move Or DragDropEffects.Copy)

      ' If operation is a move (and not a copy), then remove then
      ' remove the item from the first list box.
      If DragDropResult = DragDropEffects.Move Then
        ListBox1.Items.RemoveAt(ListBox1.SelectedIndex)
      End If

   End If
End Sub
```

When you're done, run your application and drag the items from `Listbox1` into `Listbox2`. Try a copy by holding down the control key when you do it. The screen shot in Figure 14-23 shows the result after `Item1` has been moved and `Item3` has been copied a few times.

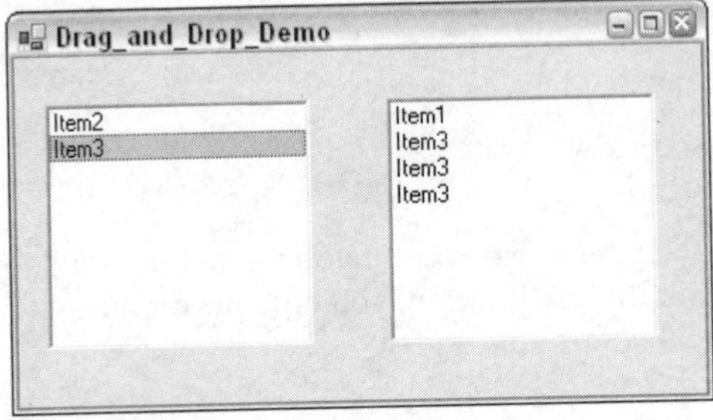

Figure 14-23

Panel and GroupBox Container Controls

In VB6, a `Frame` control can be used as a container to group controls. A set of option buttons (the VB6 version of radio buttons) placed in a frame control automatically becomes related as one option group. Frames are also often used in VB6 to separate areas of a form into functional areas, or to group controls for showing and hiding. If a frame is hidden, all the controls in it are hidden. Sometimes, frames in VB6 are used with a border (with or without a title for the frame) and other times without a border.

The functionality in the frame control for VB6 is divided into two controls in VB.NET. They are called the `GroupBox` control and the `Panel` control.

Each is like the VB6 frame control in the following ways:

- They can serve as a container for other controls.
- If they are hidden or moved, the action affects all the controls in the container.

The `GroupBox` control is the one that most closely resembles a frame control visually. It acts just like a VB6 frame control, with one significant exception. There is no way to remove its border. It always has a border, and it can have a title, if needed. The border is always set the same way. Figure 14-24 shows a form with a `GroupBox` control containing three `RadioButtons`.

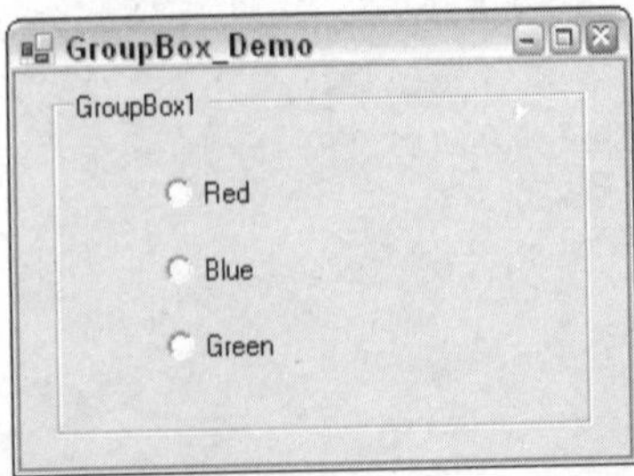

Figure 14-24

The Panel control has three major differences from GroupBox:

- It has options for displaying its border in the BorderStyle property, with a default of no border.
- It has the capability to scroll if its AutoScroll property is set to True.
- It has no ability to set a title or caption.

Figure 14-25 shows a form containing a Panel control with its border set to FixedSingle, with scrolling turned on, and with a CheckedListBox that is too big to display all at once (which forces the Panel to show a scrollbar).

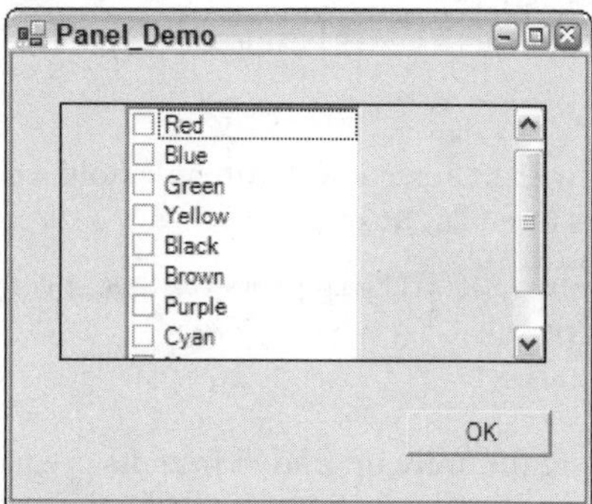

Figure 14-25

Summary of Standard Windows.Forms Controls

VB.NET of course contains most of the controls that you are accustomed to using in pre-.NET versions. The following few pages list the basic controls that are generally quite intuitive and don't warrant a full example to explain. Where appropriate, the important differences from pre-.NET versions of Visual Basic are stated.

- Button
    - Known as CommandButton in VB6 and earlier.
    - Now uses the Text property instead of Caption.
    - Can now display both an icon and text simultaneously. The image is set using the Image property (instead of Picture). The image position can be set using the ImageAlign property (left, right, center, and so on).
    - Text on the button can be aligned using the TextAlign property.
    - Can now have different appearances using the FlatStyle property.
    - No longer has the Default and Cancel properties. These are now managed by the form itself using the AcceptButton and CancelButton properties.

- `CheckBox`
  - Now uses the `Text` property instead of `Caption`.
  - Can now appear as a toggle button using the `Appearance` property.
  - Check box and text can now be positioned within the defined area using the `CheckAlign` and `TextAlign` properties.
  - Uses the `CheckState` property instead of `Value`.
  - Has a `FlatStyle` property controlling the appearance of the check box.
- `CheckedListBox`
  - A list box that has check boxes beside each item (see `Listbox`).
- `ComboBox`
  - As with the new `ListBox` control, can now hold a collection of objects instead of an array of strings (see `ListBox`).
  - Now has a `MaxDropDownItems` property that specifies how many items to display when the list opens.
- `DataGrid`
  - This has been significantly upgraded from its predecessor in VB6. In essence, the `DataGrid` is a front-end user interface to the data objects in the .NET Framework.
  - You can find more information on this control in Chapter 16.
- `DateTimePicker`
  - Formerly known as a `DTPicker`.
- `DomainUpDown` — New!
  - A simple one-line version of a list box.
  - Can hold a collection of objects and will display the `ToString()` result of an item in the collection.
  - Can wrap around the list to give a continuous scrolling effect using the `Wrap` property.
- `HScrollBar`
  - Unchanged.
- `ImageList`
  - Same as previous versions, but with an improved window for managing the images within the list. The `MaskColor` property is now `TransparentColor`.
- `Label`
  - Essentially the same as previous versions.
  - `Caption` is now `Text`.
  - Can now display an image and text.

- The TextAlign property is especially useful. The text of a label beside a text box in VB6 would always be a few pixels higher than the text in the text box. Now by setting the label's TextAlign property so that the vertical alignment is Middle, this problem is solved.
- Can now specify if a mnemonic should be interpreted (if UseMnemonic is True, the first ampersand (&) in the Text property will indicate to underline the following character and have it react to the Alt key shortcut, placing the focus on the next control in the tab order that can hold focus, such as a text box).

- LinkLabel—New!
    - Identical to a label, but behaves like a hyperlink with extra properties such as LinkBehavior (for example, HoverUnderline), LinkColor, and ActiveLinkColor.
- ListBox
    - A list box can now hold a collection of objects, instead of an array of strings. Use the DisplayMember property to specify what property of the objects to display in the list, and the ValueMember property to specify what property of the objects to use as the values of the list items. (This is similar to the ItemData array from previous versions.) For example, the combo box can store a collection of, say, employee objects, and display to the user the Name property of each, as well as retrieve the EmployeeId as the value of the item currently selected.
    - Can no longer be set to display check boxes using a Style property. Use the CheckedListBox control instead.
- ListView
    - Same functionality as the VB6 version but with an improved Property Editor that allows you to define the list view item collection and its subitems at design time.
    - Subitems can have their own font display properties.
    - New HeaderStyle property instead of HideColumnHeaders.
- MonthCalendar
    - Formerly known as MonthView.
- NotifyIcon—New!
    - Great new control that gives you an icon in the system tray.
    - Tooltip of the icon is set by the Text property of the control.
    - Pop-up menus are set using a ContextMenu control (see the "Menus" section earlier in chapter).
- NumericUpDown—New!
    - A single-line text box that displays a number and up/down buttons that increment/decrement the number when clicked.
- PictureBox
    - Image property defines the graphic to display instead of Picture.
    - Use the SizeMode property to autostretch or center the picture.

- `ProgressBar`
  - Now has a `Step()` method that automatically increments the value of the progress bar by the amount defined in the `Step` property.
- `RadioButton`
  - Formerly known as `OptionButton`.
  - Use `Checked` property to specify value (formerly `Value`).
  - Use `CheckAlign` and `TextAlign` to specify where the radio button and text appear in relation to the area of the control.
- `RichTextBox`
  - Essentially the same control as before with a few new properties such as `ZoomFactor`, `WordWrap`, `DetectURLs`, and `AutoWordSelection`.
  - Use the `Lines()` array to get or set specific individual lines of text of the control.
- `StatusBar`
  - Has a `Panels` collection and a `ShowPanels` property. If `False`, the status bar will display only the `Text` property. This would be equivalent to setting the VB6 status bar control `Style` property to `sbrSimple`.
  - The `StatusBar` control docks to the bottom of the parent control by default. (See the section on docking.) You could change this if you wanted to (although it's not apparent how intuitive a floating status bar would be).
- `TabControl`
  - Formerly known as the `TabStrip` control.
  - Now has a `TabPages` collection of `TabPage` objects. A `TabPage` object is a subclass of the `Panel` control specialized for use in the `TabControl`.
  - Uses the `Appearance` property to display the tabs as buttons, if desired (formerly the `Style` property of the `TabStrip` control).
- `TextBox`
  - Now has a `CharacterCasing` property that can automatically adjust the text entered into upper- or lowercase.
  - `ReadOnly` property now used to prevent the text from being edited. This used to be the `Locked` property. (The `Locked` property now determines if the control can be moved or resized.)
  - Now has `Cut`, `Copy`, `Paste`, `Undo`, and `ClearUndo` methods.
- `Timer`
  - Essentially unchanged from previous versions.
  - The timer is now disabled by default.
  - You cannot set the interval to zero to disable it.

- `TrackBar`
    - Formerly known as the `Slider` control, it is essentially unchanged.
- `TreeView`
    - Has the same functionality as in VB6 but with a new Node Tree Editor that allows you to visually design the tree.
- `VScrollBar`
    - Unchanged.

Retired Controls

The following list outlines the controls from VB6 that you won't find in VB.Net and how to reproduce their functionality:

- `Spinner`
    - Use the `DomainUpDown` or `NumericUpDown` control.
- `Line` and `Shape`
    - VB.NET has no `Line` or `Shape` control, nor any immediate equivalent. A "cheap" way of reproducing a horizontal or vertical line is to use a label control. Set its background color to that of the line you want, and then either the `Size.Height` or `Size.Width` value to 1.
    - Diagonal lines and shapes must be drawn using GDI+ graphics methods.
- `DirListBox`, `FileListBox`, `DriveListBox`
    - You would typically use these controls to create a file system browser similar to Windows Explorer. VB.NET has no equivalent controls. You can use the `OpenFileDialog` and `SaveFileDialog` (see previous section) to accomplish your needs in most circumstances.
- `Image`
    - Use the `PictureBox` control.

Using ActiveX Controls

While VB.NET is optimized to use Windows Forms controls, you can certainly place an ActiveX control on your form and use it as well. You'll see how to do this in Chapter 20.

Other Handy Programming Tips

Here are some other handy programming tips for using Windows Forms:

- **Switch the focus to a control** — Use the `.Focus()` method. To set the focus to `TextBox1`, for example, use the following code:

```
TextBox1.Focus()
```

- **Change the cursor** — To switch the cursor to an hourglass, for example, use the `Cursor` object as follows:

```
Cursor.Current = Cursors.WaitCursor ' hourglass
Cursor.Current = Cursors.Default ' pointer
```

- **Quickly determine the container control or parent form** — With the use of group boxes and panels, controls are often contained many times removed from the ultimate form. You can now use the `FindForm` method to immediately get a reference to the form. Use the `GetContainerControl` method to access the immediate parent of a control.
- **Traversing the tab order** — Use the `GetNextControl` method of any control to get a reference to the next control on the form in the tab order.
- **Convert client coordinates to screen coordinates (and back)** — Want to know where a control is in screen coordinates? Use the `PointToScreen` method. Convert back using the `PointToClient` method.
- **Change the z-order of controls at runtime** — Controls now have both `BringToFront` and `SendToBack` methods.
- **Locate the mouse pointer** — The control class now exposes a `MousePosition` property that returns the location of the mouse in screen coordinates.
- **Managing child control** — Container controls, such as a group box or panel, can use the `HasChildren` property and `Controls` property to determine the existence of, and direct references to, child controls, respectively.
- **Maximize, minimize, restore a form** — Use the form's `WindowState` property.

MDI Forms

MDI (Multiple Document Interface) forms are forms that are created to hold other forms. The MDI form is often referred to as the parent, and the forms displayed within the MDI parent are often called children. Figure 14-26 shows a typical MDI parent with several children displayed within it.

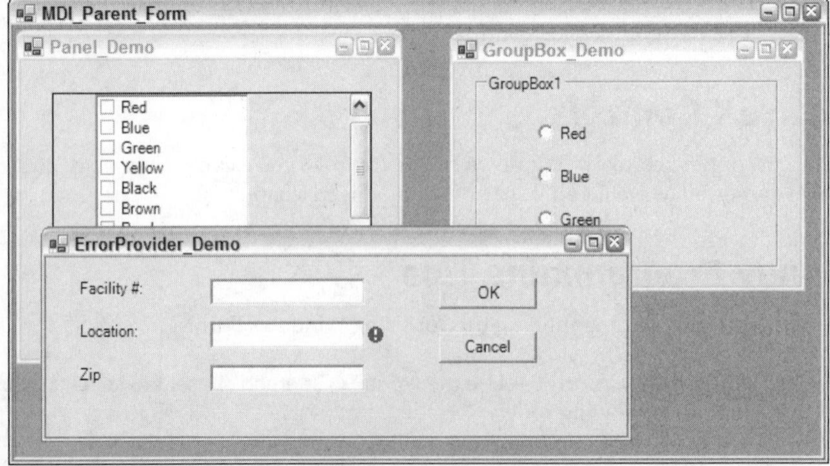

Figure 14-26

Creating an MDI Parent Form

In VB.NET, a regular form is converted to an MDI parent form by setting the `IsMDIContainer` property of the form to `True`. This is normally done in the Properties window at design time.

A form can also be made into an MDI parent at runtime by setting the `IsMDIContainer` property to `True` in code. However, the design of an MDI form is usually rather different from that of a normal form, so this approach is not often needed.

Differences in MDI Parent Forms between VB6 and VB.NET

In VB6, an MDI parent form can only contain controls that have a property called `Align`. This property determines to which side of the MDI parent form the control is supposed to be docked. Typical controls like buttons and text boxes cannot be added directly to an MDI parent form. They must be added to a container control, such as a `PictureBox`, which has an `Align` property.

In VB.NET, an MDI parent can contain any control that a regular form can contain. Buttons, labels, and the like can be placed directly on the MDI surface. Such controls will appear in front of any MDI child forms that are displayed in the MDI client area.

It is still possible to use controls like `PictureBoxes` to hold other controls on a VB.NET MDI parent, and these controls can be docked to the side of the MDI form. In fact, every control in VB.NET has the equivalent of the `Align` property, called `Dock`. The `Dock` property was previously discussed in the section on changes to controls in VB.NET.

MDI Child Forms

In VB.NET, a form becomes an MDI child at runtime by setting the form's `MDIParent` property to point to an MDI parent form. This makes it possible to use a form as either a stand-alone form or an MDI child in different circumstances. In fact, the `MDIParent` property cannot be set at design time—it must be set at runtime to make a form an MDI child. (Note that this is completely different from VB6, where it was necessary to make a form an MDI child at design time.)

It is possible to have any number of MDI child forms displayed in the MDI parent client area. The currently active child form can be determined with the `ActiveForm` property of the MDI parent form.

An MDI Example in VB.NET

To see these changes to MDI forms in action, you can do the following step-by-step exercise. It shows the basics of creating an MDI parent and making it display an MDI child form.

1. Create a new Windows Application. It will have an empty form named `Form1`. Change both the name of the form and the form's `Text` property to `MDIParentForm`.
2. In the Properties window, set the `IsMDIContainer` property for `MDIParentForm` to `True`. This designates the form as an MDI container for child windows. (Setting this property also causes the form to have a different default background color.)
3. From the toolbox, drag a `MainMenu` control to the form. Create a top-level menu item called File with submenu items called New MDI Child and Quit. Also create a top-level menu item called Window. The File ⇨ New MDI Child menu option will create and show new MDI child forms

at runtime, and the Window menu will keep track of the open MDI child windows. (For more information on working with `MainMenu` controls, see the section on menu controls earlier in the chapter.)

4. In the Menu Option Editor at the top of the form, right-click the Window menu item and select Properties. In the Properties window, set the `MDIList` property to `True`. This will enable the Window menu to maintain a list of open MDI child windows with a checkmark next to the active child window.

5. Now, you need to create an MDI child form to use as a template for multiple instances. To do this, select Project ⇨ Add Windows Form and then Open in the Add New Item dialog box. That will result in a new blank form named `Form2`. Place any controls you like on the form. As an alternative, you can reuse any of the forms created in previous exercises in this chapter.

6. Now go back to `MDIParentForm`. In the menu editing bar, double-click the New MDI Child option under File. The Code Editor will appear, with the cursor in the event routine for that menu option. Place the following code in the event:

```
Protected Sub MenuItem2_Click(ByVal sender As Object,
                              ByVal e As System.EventArgs)

    ' This line may change if you are using a form with a different name.
    Dim NewMDIChild As New Form2()
    'Set the Parent Form of the Child window.
    NewMDIChild.MDIParent = Me
    'Display the new form.
    NewMDIChild.Show()

End Sub
```

7. In the menu editing bar for `MDIParentForm`, double-click the Quit option under File. The Code Editor will appear, with the cursor in the event routine for that menu option. Place the following code in the event:

```
Protected Sub MenuItem3_Click(ByVal sender As Object, _
                              ByVal e As System.EventArgs)

    End
End Sub
```

8. Now run and test the program. Use the File ⇨ New MDI Child option to create several child forms. Note how the Window menu option automatically lists them with the active one checked and allows you to activate a different one.

Arranging Child Windows

MDI parent forms have a method called `LayoutMDI` that will automatically arrange child forms in the familiar cascade or tile layout. For the example above, add a menu item to your Windows menu called Tile Vertical and insert the following code into the menu item's `Click` event to handle it:

```
Me.LayoutMdi(MDILayout.TileVertical)
```

To see an example of the rearrangement, suppose that the MDI form in Figure 14-26 is rearranged with the `MDILayout.TileVertical` option. It would then look similar to the image in Figure 14-27.

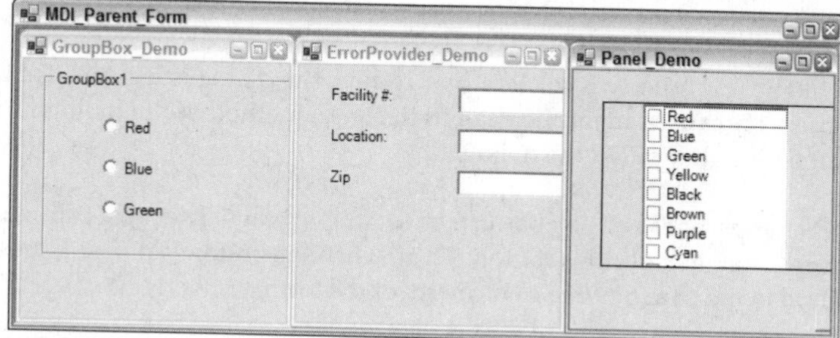

Figure 14-27

Dialog Forms

In VB6 and earlier, forms were shown with the `Show` method, and this technique is still used in VB.NET. In both VB6 and VB.NET, the `Show` method by default displays modeless forms, which are forms that allow the user to click off them onto another form in the application.

In VB6, dialog boxes were displayed with the `vbModal` parameter (or a hard-coded value of `1`) after the form's `Show` method. This caused the form to be a modal form, which meant that it was the only active form in the application until it was exited.

Showing a form modally is done differently in VB.NET. A Windows Form has a `ShowDialog()` method that takes the place of the `Show` method with the `vbModal` parameter. Here is code for showing a modal dialog in VB.NET:

```
Dim frmDialogForm As New DialogForm
frmDialogForm.ShowDialog()
```

DialogResult

It is common when showing a dialog form to need to get information about what action the user selected. This was often done with a custom property in VB6, but VB.NET has a built-in property for that purpose. When a form is shown with the `ShowDialog()` method, the form has a property called `DialogResult` to indicate its state.

The `DialogResult` property can take the following enumerated results:

- `DialogResult.Abort`
- `DialogResult.Cancel`
- `DialogResult.Ignore`
- `DialogResult.No`
- `DialogResult.None`

- `DialogResult.OK`
- `DialogResult.Retry`
- `DialogResult.Yes`

When the `DialogResult` property is set, as a by-product, the dialog is hidden. That is, setting the `DialogResult` property causes an implicit call to the `Hide` method of the dialog form, so that control is released back to the form that called the dialog.

The `DialogResult` property of a dialog box can be set in two ways. The most common way is to associate a `DialogResult` value with a button. Then, when the button is pressed, the associated value is automatically placed in the `DialogResult` property of the form.

To set the `DialogResult` value associated with a button, the `DialogResult` property of the button is used. If this property is set for the button, it is unnecessary to set the `DialogResult` in code when the button is pressed. Here is an example that uses this technique.

In VS.NET, start a new VB.NET Windows Application. On the automatic blank form that comes up (named `Form1`), place a single button and set its `Text` property to `Dialog`.

Property	Value for First Button	Value for Second Button
`Name`	`BtnOK`	`btnCancel`
`Text`	`OK`	`Cancel`
`DialogResult`	`OK`	`Cancel`

Now, add a new Windows Form using the Project ➪ Add Windows Form... menu, and name it `DialogForm.vb`. Place two buttons on `DialogForm` and set the following properties for the buttons:

Do not put any code in `DialogForm` at all. The form should look like the one shown in Figure 14-28.

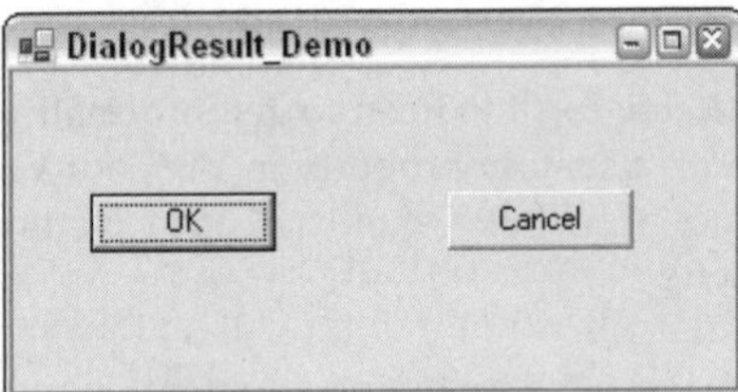

Figure 14-28

On the first form, `Form1`, place the following code in the `Click` event for `Button1`:

```
Private Sub Button1_Click(ByVal sender As System.Object, _
  ByVal e As System.EventArgs) Handles Button1.Click
```

```
    Dim frmDialogForm As New DialogForm()
    frmDialogForm.ShowDialog()

    ' You're back from the dialog - check user action.
    Select Case frmDialogForm.DialogResult
      Case DialogResult.OK
        MsgBox("The user pressed OK")
      Case DialogResult.Cancel
        MsgBox("The user pressed cancel")
  End Select

    frmDialogForm = Nothing

  End Sub
```

Now, run and test the code. When a button is pressed on the dialog form, a message box should be displayed (by the calling form) indicating the button that was pressed.

The second way to set the `DialogResult` property of the form is in code. In a `Button_Click` event, or anywhere else in the dialog form, a line like this can be used to set the `DialogResult` property for the form, and simultaneously hide the dialog form, giving control back to the calling form.

```
  Me.DialogResult = DialogResult.Ignore
```

This particular line sets the dialog result to `DialogResult.Ignore`, but setting the dialog result to any of the permitted values will also hide the dialog form.

Summary

The new features and improvements to Windows Forms in VS.NET simplify development of rich client and smart client interfaces, and allow new capabilities that user interface designers did not have in earlier versions of Visual Basic. Coupled with the easy deployment of .NET applications, you can expect a resurgence in forms-based programs.

Becoming a capable Windows Forms developer requires becoming familiar with the controls that are available, and their properties, events, and methods. This takes time. If you are coming from the VB6 world, much of your expertise will continue to be useful with Windows Forms, and this chapter has highlighted the most important differences you need to know about. If you are less familiar with form-based interfaces, you can expend a fair amount of time using the reference documentation to find the control capabilities you need.

However, many professional Windows Forms developers need to go beyond just creating forms and laying out controls. Complex applications often also require creation of new controls or enhancement of built-in controls. The capabilities for doing this were limited in the earlier versions of Visual Basic, but are much more impressive in VB.NET. Accordingly, the next chapter will discuss how to create and modify Windows Forms controls.

15

Windows Forms Advanced Features

The previous chapter discussed the basics of Windows Forms 2.0. Using the capabilities presented in that chapter, you can create straightforward user interfaces for systems written in VB.NET along with the built-in capabilities of forms and controls available in Windows Forms 2.0.

However, as applications become larger, and require more and more forms to present information to the user, it becomes more important to use the advanced capabilities of the .NET environment to better structure the application. The main defect of large systems that you should strive to avoid is redundant code. Repeated code patterns end up being used (in slightly different variations) in many, many places in an application.

Examples of functions that often result in repeated code include making sure that fields are entered by the user, that the fields are formatted correctly, and that `null` fields in the database are handled correctly (and don't cause runtime errors). Writing similar code many times for such functions has a number of drawbacks:

- It takes longer to write the application because there is more code to be handled.
- It is more difficult to debug, again because of having more code.
- The application is less reliable, because when a bug is found, it is difficult to find all the places to fix it.
- The application is more difficult to enhance, again because it is necessary to go to many places in the code to enhance the same basic functionality.

In VB6 and earlier systems, the techniques available to reduce redundant code were limited. You could write functions to be accessed from various places, for example, and you could write `UserControls` to encapsulate some functionality.

Your options in Visual Basic .NET are much broader. Using the full object-oriented capabilities of the .NET environment, plus additional capabilities specific to Windows Forms programming, you can componentize your logic, allowing the same code to be used in lots of places in your application.

This chapter discusses techniques for componentizing code in Windows Forms applications. It is assumed that you have already read Chapters 5 and 7 on inheritance and other object-oriented techniques available in .NET before working with this chapter.

Packaging Logic in Visual Controls

As we saw in the last chapter, Windows Forms user interfaces are based on using controls. A control is simply a special type of .NET class (just as forms are). As a fully object-oriented programming environment, VB.NET gives us the capability to inherit and extend classes, and controls are no exception. It is, therefore, possible to create new controls that go beyond what the built-in controls can do.

There are four primary sources of controls for use on Windows Forms interfaces:

- Controls packaged with the .NET Framework (referred to in this chapter as built-in controls)
- Existing ActiveX controls that are imported into Windows Forms (these were mentioned in Chapter 14, and are also discussed in Chapter 20)
- Third-party .NET-based controls from a software vendor
- Custom controls that are created for a specific purpose in a particular project or organization

If you are able to build your application with controls from the first three categories, so much the better. Using prewritten functionality that serves the purpose is generally a good idea. However, this chapter assumes you need to go beyond such prepackaged functionality.

If you are primarily familiar with versions of Visual Basic before the .NET era (VB6 and earlier), then the only technique available for such packaging was `UserControls`. While `UserControls` are also available in Visual Basic .NET (and are much improved), they are only one of several techniques available for writing visual controls.

Developing Custom Controls in .NET

There are three basic techniques for the creation of custom Windows Forms controls in .NET, corresponding to three different starting points. This range of options gives the flexibility to choose a technique that allows an appropriate balance between simplicity and flexibility. You can:

- Inherit from an existing control
- Build a composite control (using the `UserControl` class as your starting point)
- Write a control from scratch (using the very simple `Control` class as your starting point)

These are in rough order of complexity, from simplest to most complex. Let's look at each of these with a view to understanding the scenarios in which each one is useful.

Inherit from an Existing Control

The simplest technique starts with a complete Windows Forms control that is already developed. A new class is created that inherits the existing control. (See Chapter 5 for a complete discussion of inheritance in .NET.) This new class has all the functionality of the base class from which it inherits and the new logic can be added to create additional functionality in this new class or, indeed, to override functionality from the parent (when permitted).

Most of the built-in Windows Forms controls can be used as the base class for such an inherited control. There are a few exceptions, such as the `NotifyIcon` control, and the `ProgressBar`. If you are in doubt about any particular control, you can check the Visual Studio Help. The declaration for a class that cannot be inherited will have the `NotInheritable` keyword included at the beginning.

Third-party controls may also be candidates for extension into new custom controls through inheritance. As with Windows Forms controls, some third-party controls can be inherited and others cannot.

Here are some typical examples where it might make sense to extend an existing Windows Forms control:

- A text box with built-in validation for specific types of information
- A self-loading list box, combo box, or data grid
- A menu control that varies its options based on the current user
- A `NumericUpDown` control that generates a special event when it reaches 80 percent of its maximum allowed value

Each of these scenarios starts with an existing control that simply needs some additional functionality. The more often such functionality is needed in your project, the more sense it makes to package it in a custom control. If a text box that needs special validation or editing will be used in only one place, it probably doesn't make sense to create an inherited control. In that case, simply adding some logic in the form where the control is used to handle the control's events and manipulating the control's properties and methods is probably sufficient. But where such functionality is needed in many locations in an application, packaging the functionality in an inherited control can centralize the logic and facilitate reuse, thereby removing maintenance headaches.

Build a Composite Control

In some cases, a single existing control does not furnish the needed functionality, but a combination of two or more existing controls does. Here are some typical examples:

- A set of buttons with related logic that are always used together (such as "Save," "Delete," and "Cancel" buttons on a file maintenance form)
- A set of text boxes to hold a name, address, and phone number, with the combined information formatted and validated in a particular way
- A set of option buttons with a single property exposed as the chosen option
- A data grid together with buttons that alter its appearance or behavior in specific ways

As with inherited controls, composite controls are only appropriate for situations that require the same functionality in multiple places. If the functionality is only needed once, then simply placing the relevant controls on the form and including appropriate logic right in the form is usually better.

Composite controls are the closest relative to VB6 `UserControls`, and because of that, they are sometimes referred to as `UserControls`. In fact, the base class used to create composite controls is the `UserControl` class in .NET.

Write a Control from Scratch

If a control needs to have special functionality not related to any existing control, then it can be written from scratch to draw its own visual interface and implement its own logic. This option requires more work, but allows us to do just about anything that is possible within .NET and Windows Forms, including very sophisticated drawing of a user interface.

To write a control from scratch, it is necessary to inherit from the `Control` class, which gives basic functionality such as properties for colors and size. With this basic functionality already built in, the main tasks to be performed to get a custom control working are to add on any specific properties and methods needed for this control, to write the rendering logic that will paint the control to the screen, and to handle mouse and keyboard input to the control.

Inheriting from an Existing Control

With this background on the options for creating custom controls, the next step is to look in depth at the procedures used for their development. First up is creating a custom control by inheriting from an existing control and extending it with new functionality. This is the simplest method for the creation of new controls, and the best way to introduce generic techniques that apply to all new controls.

After describing the general steps needed to create a custom control via inheritance, two examples will illustrate the details. It is important to understand that many of the techniques described for working with a control created through inheritance also apply to the other ways that a control can be created. Whether inheriting from the `Control` class, the `UserControl` class, or from an existing control, a control is a .NET class. Creating properties, methods, and events, and coordinating these members with the VS.NET designers, is done in a similar fashion, regardless of the starting point.

Overview of the Process

Here are the general stages involved in the creation of a custom control via inheritance from an existing control. This is not a step-by-step recipe, but just an overview. An example follows that goes into more detail on specific steps, but those steps will carry out the following stages:

1. For the first stage, it is necessary to create or open a Windows Control Library project, and add a new `UserControl` to the project using the option on the Project menu. The class that is created will inherit from the `System.Windows.Forms.UserControl` namespace. The line that specifies the inherited class must be changed to inherit from the control that is being used as the starting point.

2. The class file then gets new logic added as necessary to add new functionality, before the project is compiled with a `Build` operation in order to create a DLL containing the new control's code.
3. The control is now ready to be used. It can be placed in the Windows Forms toolbox with the Add/Remove Items option in Visual Studio 2003 (or the Customize Toolbox option in Visual Studio 2002). From that point forward, it can be dragged onto forms like any other control.

Step 2, of course, is where the effort lies. New logic for the custom control may include new properties, methods, and events. It may also include intercepting events for the base control and taking special actions as necessary. All of this logic relies on basic object-oriented capabilities of the .NET Framework.

However, there are several coding techniques that are specific to developing Windows Forms controls. While our example will include adding routine properties and events, we will focus on these special techniques for programming controls.

Adding Additional Logic to a Custom Control

This section discusses how to place new logic in an inherited control, with special emphasis on techniques that go beyond basic object orientation. A detailed example using the techniques follows this section.

Creating a Property for a Custom Control

Creating a property for a custom control is just like creating a property for any other class. It is necessary to write a property procedure, and to store the value for the property somewhere, most often in a module-level variable.

Properties typically need a default value, that is, a value the property will take on automatically when a control is instantiated. As you might expect, you can use your own internal logic in a control to set a default value for a property. Typically, this means setting the module-level variable that holds the property value to some initial value. That can be done when the module-level variable is declared, or it can be done in the constructor for the control.

Using the constructor to initialize the value is especially useful if the default value is different for different instantiations of the control, as in the case where the default `Text` property for a button is the name of the button.

Here's the code for a typical simple property for a custom control:

```
Dim mnMaxItemsSelected As Integer = 10
Public Property MaxItemsSelected() As Integer
  Get
    Return mnMaxItemsSelected
  End Get
  Set(ByVal Value As Integer)
    If Value < 0 Then
      Throw New ArgumentException("Property value cannot be negative")
    Else
      mnMaxItemsSelected = Value
    End If
  End Set
End Property
```

Once a property is created for a control, it automatically shows up in the Properties window for the control. However, there are some additional capabilities that you can use to make the property work better with the designers and the Property window in VS.NET.

Coordinating a Property with the Visual Studio IDE

The Visual Studio IDE needs to work with the default value of a property in two important ways:

- To reset the value of the property (done when a user right-clicks the property in the Property Window and selects Reset)
- To decide whether to set the property in code. A property that is at its default value normally does not need to be explicitly set in the designer-generated code.

There are two ways to accomplish these tasks. For properties that take simple values, such as integers, Booleans, floating point numbers, or strings, .NET provides an attribute. For properties that take complex types, such as structures, enumerated types, or object references, there are two methods that need to be implemented.

Attributes

You can learn more about attributes in Chapter 6. However, let's go over a couple of important notes since this may be the first time you have needed to use them.

Attributes reside in namespaces, just as components do. The attributes used in this chapter are in the `System.ComponentModel` namespace. To use attributes, the project must have a reference to the assembly containing the namespace for the attributes. For `System.ComponentModel`, that's no problem — the project will automatically have the reference.

However, the project will not automatically have an "Imports" for that namespace. This could be done without this by using a full namespace path for each attribute. That would mean referring to a `DefaultValue` attribute in code like this:

```
<System.ComponentModel.DefaultValue(4)> Public Property
MyProperty() As Integer
```

This is a bit clumsy. To make it easy to refer to the attributes in code, you should put this line at the beginning of all the modules that will need to use the attributes discussed in this chapter:

```
Imports System.ComponentModel
```

Then, the preceding line can be written more simply as

```
< DefaultValue(4)> Public Property MyProperty() As Integer
```

All of the examples in this chapter will assume that the Imports statement has been placed at the top of the class, so all attributes will be referenced by their short name. If you get a compile error on an attribute, it's likely that you've left off that line.

Finally, note that an attribute for a property must be on the same line of code as the property declaration. Of course, line continuation characters can be used so that an attribute is on a separate physical line but still on the same logical line in the program. For example, the last example could also be written as

```
< DefaultValue(4)> _
Public Property MyProperty() As Integer
```

Setting a Default Value with an Attribute

There are various attributes of the .NET Framework that can be assigned in metadata to classes, properties, and methods. The one for creating a default value is called, appropriately enough, `DefaultValue`. Let's change the last code for a simple property to include a `DefaultValue` attribute:

```
Dim mnMaxItemsSelected As Integer = 10
  <DefaultValue(10)> Public Property MaxItemsSelected() As Integer
    Get
      Return mnMaxItemsSelected
    End Get
    Set(ByVal Value As Integer)
      If Value < 0 Then
        Throw New ArgumentException("Property value cannot be negative")
      Else
        mnMaxItemsSelected = Value
      End If
    End Set
End Property
```

Including the `DefaultValue` attribute allows the Property window to reset the value of the property back to the default value. That is, if you right-click the property in the Property window, and select Reset off of the pop-up context menu, the value of the property will return to 10 from any other value to which it happens to be set.

Another effect of the attribute can be seen in the code generated by the visual designer. If the property above is set to any value that is not the default, a line of code appears in the designer-generated code to set the property value. This is called serializing the property.

That is, if the value of `MaxItemsSelected` is set to 5, then a line of code something like this appears in the designer-generated code:

```
MyControl.MaxItemsSelected = 5
```

If the property has the default value of 10 (because it was never changed, or because it was reset to 10), the line to set the property value is not present in the designer-generated code. That is, the property does not need to be serialized in code if the value is at the default.

To see serialized code, you need to look in the partial class that holds the Windows Forms Designer generated code. This partial class will not be visible in the Solution Explorer by default. To see it, you'll need to press the Show All Files button in the Solution Explorer.

Alternate Techniques for Working with the IDE

The last sample property returned an `Integer`. Some custom properties return more complex types, such as structures, enumerated types, or object references. These properties cannot use a simple `DefaultValue` attribute to take care of resetting and serializing the property. An alternate technique is needed.

For complex types, designers check to see if a property needs to be serialized by using a method on the control containing the property. The method returns a Boolean value that indicates whether a property needs to be serialized (`True` if it does, `False` if it does not)

If a property is named `MyProperty`, then the method to check serialization is called `ShouldSerializeMyProperty`. It would typically look something like the following code:

```
Public Function ShouldSerializeMyProperty() As Boolean
  If mnMyProperty = mnMyPropertysDefaultValue Then
    Return False
  Else
    Return True
  End If
End Function
```

If a property in a custom control does not have a related `ShouldSerializeXXX` method or a `DefaultValue` attribute, then the property is always serialized. Code for setting the property's value will always be included by the designer in the generated code for a form. For that reason, it's a good idea to always include either a `ShouldSerializeXXX` method or a `DefaultValue` attribute for every new property created for a control.

If you include both a `DefaultValue` attribute and a `ShouldSerializeXXX` method, the `DefaultValue` attribute takes precedence and the `ShouldSerializeXXX` method is ignored.

Providing a Reset Method for a Control Property

The alternate way to reset a property's value to the default is a special reset method. As an example of this, in the case of a property named `MyProperty`, the reset method is named `ResetMyProperty`. It typically looks something like the following code:

```
Public Sub ResetMyProperty()
  mnMyProperty = mnMyPropertysDefaultValue
End Sub
```

To allow the Property window to reset the value of a property, either a `DefaultValue` attribute or a reset method must be present. If you include both a `DefaultValue` attribute and a reset method, the `DefaultValue` attribute takes precedence and the reset method is ignored.

As with the `ShouldSerializeXXX` method, the default property value can be called from an attribute if one has been included with the property declaration.

Other Useful Attributes

`DefaultValue` is not the only attribute that is useful for properties. The `Description` attribute is also one that should be used with most properties. It contains a text description of the property that shows up in the Properties windows when a property is selected. To include a `Description` attribute, the declaration of the preceding property would look like the following code:

```
<DefaultValue(100), _
Description("This is a description for my property")> _
Public Property MyProperty() As Integer
```

Such a property will look like Figure 15-1 when highlighted in the Property window.

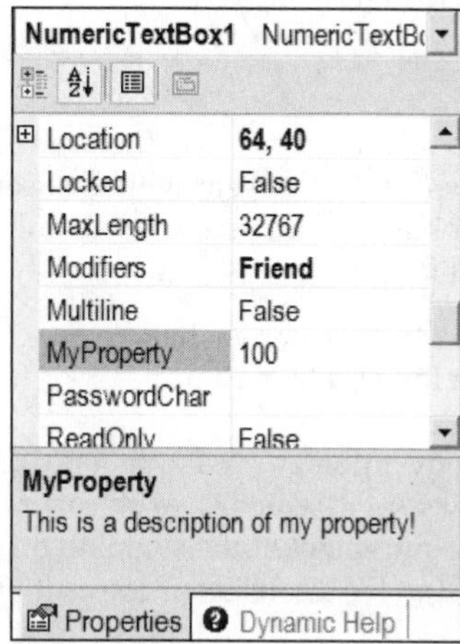

Figure 15-1

Another attribute you will sometimes need is the `Browsable` attribute. As mentioned earlier, a new property appears in the Properties window automatically. In some cases, you may need to create a property for a control that you do not want to show up in the Properties window. In that case, you use a `Browsable` attribute set to `False`. Here is code similar to the last one, making a property nonbrowsable in the Properties window:

```
<Browsable(False)> _
Public Property MyProperty() As Integer
```

A final attribute you may want to use is the `Category` attribute. Properties can be grouped by category in the Properties window by pressing a button at the top of the window. Standard categories include Behavior, Appearance, etc. You can have your property appear in any of those categories, or you can make up a new category of your own. To assign a category to a property, use code like this:

```
<Category("Appearance")> _
Public Property MyProperty() As Integer
```

Defining a Custom Event for the Inherited Control

Adding events to classes was covered in Chapter 4. In summary, the process is as follows:

- Declare the event in the control. The event can have any arguments that are appropriate, but they cannot have named arguments, optional arguments, or arguments that are `ParamArrays`. Here is code for declaring a generic event:

```
Public Event MyEvent(ByVal MyFirstArgument As Integer, _
                     ByVal MySecondArgument As String)
```

- Elsewhere in the control's code, implement code to raise the event. The location and circumstances of this code vary depending on the nature of the event, but a typical line that raises the preceding event looks like the following code:

```
RaiseEvent MyEvent(nValueForMyFirstArgument, sValueForMySecondArgument)
```

- Often this code will be in a method that raises the event. This allows the raising of the event to be done in a uniform fashion. If the event will be raised from several places in your control, doing it with a method is preferred. If the event will only be raised in one place, the code to do it can just be placed in that location.
- The form that contains the control can now handle the event. The process for doing that is the same as handling an event for a built-in control.

You may recall that the standard convention in .NET is to use two arguments for an event — `Sender`, which is the object raising the event, and `e`, which is an object of type `EventArgs` or of a type that inherits from `EventArgs`. This is not a requirement of the syntax (you can actually use any arguments you like when you declare your event), but it's a consistent convention throughout the .NET Framework, so it will be followed in this chapter.

Now, it's time to illustrate the concepts on creating properties and events for a control. The following example creates a new control that contains a custom property and a custom event. The property uses several of the attributes discussed above.

Creating a CheckedListBox that Limits the Number of Selected Items

This example inherits the built-in `CheckedListBox` control, and extends its functionality. If you are not familiar with this control, it works just like a normal `ListBox` control, except that selected items are indicated with a check in a check box at the front of the item rather than highlighting the item.

To extend the functionality of this control, the example will include the creation of a property called `MaxItemsSelected`. This property will hold a maximum value for the number of items that a user can select. The event that fires when a user checks on an item is then monitored to see if the maximum has already been reached.

If selection of another item would exceed the maximum number, the selection is prevented, and an event is fired to let the consumer form know that the user has tried to exceed the maximum limit. The code that handles the event in the form can then do whatever is appropriate. In our case, a message box is used to tell the user that no more items can be selected.

The DefaultValue, Description, and Category attributes are placed on the MaxItemsSelected property to assist in the designer.

Here is the step-by-step construction of our example:

1. Start a new Windows Control Library project in Visual Studio .NET (VS.NET). Give it the name LimitedCheckedListBox. In the Solution Explorer, select the UserControl1.vb file, right-click it, and select Rename. Name the module LimitedCheckedListBox.vb, before bringing up the code window for this class. Then bring up the code window and place the following line in the declarations at the top of the class (before the line declaring the class):

```
Imports System.ComponentModel
```

   This allows us to utilize the attributes required from the System.ComponentModel namespace.

2. Next we need to specify the actual class we want to inherit from. The designer will have inserted the UserControl class as the base class, but we need to change that to the CheckedListBox class.

   The line inserted by the designer is in the file LimitedCheckedListBox.Designer.vb. This is a partial class to hold the designer code. The partial class code file LimitedCheckedListBox.Designer.vb will not be shown by default.

   To see this code file, click the button in the Solution Explorer to show All Files (it's the middle button at the top of the Solution Explorer. Double click the LimitedCheckedListBox.Designer.vb to open it in the code window. Then alter the class declaration so that it reads as follows:

```
Partial Public Class LimitedCheckedListBox
    Inherits System.Windows.Forms.CheckedListBox
```

3. Now, go back to the LimitedCheckedListBox.vb module and begin adding code specifically for this control. First, we need to implement the MaxSelectedItems property. A module level variable is needed to hold the property's value, so insert this line just under the class declaration line:

```
Private mnMaxSelectedItems As Integer = 4
```

4. Now create the code for the property itself. Insert the following code into the class just above the line that says End Class:

```
<DefaultValue(4), Category("Behavior"), _
Description("The maximum number of items allowed to be checked")> _
Public Property MaxSelectedItems() As Integer
  Get
    Return mnMaxSelectedItems
  End Get
  Set(ByVal Value As Integer)
    If Value < 0 Then
      Throw New ArgumentException("Property value cannot be negative")
    Else
      mnMaxSelectedItems = Value
    End If
  End Set
End Property
```

This code sets the default value of the `MaxSelectedItems` property to 4, and sets a description for the property to be shown in the Properties window when the property is selected there. It also specifies that the property should appear in the Behavior category when properties in the Properties window are sorted by category.

5. Next, declare the event that will be fired when a user selects too many items. The event will be named `MaxItemsExceeded`. Just under the code for Step 3, insert the following line:

```
Public Event MaxItemsExceeded(Sender As Object, e As EventArgs)
```

6. Next, insert code into the event routine that fires when the user clicks on an item. For the `CheckedListBox` base class, this is called the `ItemCheck` property. Open the left-hand drop-down box in the code window and select the option `LimitedCheckedListBox` Events. Then, select the `ItemCheck` event in the right-hand drop-down box of the code window. The following code will be inserted to handle the `ItemCheck` event:

```
Private Sub LimitedCheckedListBox_ItemCheck(ByVal sender As Object, _
            ByVal e As System.Windows.Forms.ItemCheckEventArgs) _
             Handles MyBase.ItemCheck

End Sub
```

7. The following code should be added to the `ItemCheck` event to monitor it for too many items:

```
Private Sub LimitedCheckedListBox_ItemCheck(ByVal sender As Object, _
            ByVal e As System.Windows.Forms.ItemCheckEventArgs) _
             Handles MyBase.ItemCheck
If (Me.CheckedItems.Count >= mnMaxSelectedItems) _
   And (e.NewValue = CheckState.Checked) Then
   RaiseEvent MaxItemsExceeded(Me, New EventArgs)
   e.NewValue = CheckState.Unchecked
End If
End Sub
```

8. Build the project to create a DLL containing the `LimitedCheckedListBox` control.

9. Add a new Windows Application project to the solution (using the File ➪ Add Project ➪ New Project menu) to test the control. Name the new project anything you like. Right-click the project in the Solution Explorer, and select Set as Startup Project in the pop-up menu. This will cause your Windows application to run when you press F5 in Visual Studio.

10. In the new Windows Forms project, right-click the Windows Forms tab in the toolbox, and select Choose Items. In the dialog box that appears, click the tab for .NET Framework Components, and browse to select the `LimitedCheckedListBox.dll` file. Return to the Choose Items dialog, and click the OK button.

11. Scroll to the bottom of the controls on the Windows Forms tab. The `LimitedCheckedListBox` control should be there.

12. The Windows Application will have a `Form1` that was created automatically. Drag a `LimitedCheckedListBox` control onto `Form1`, just as you would a normal list box. Change the `CheckOnClick` event for the `LimitedCheckedListBox` to `True` (to make testing easier). This property was inherited from the base `CheckedListBox` control.

13. In the Items property of the LimitedCheckedListBox, click the button to add some items. Insert the following list of colors: Red, Yellow, Green, Brown, Blue, Pink, and Black. At this point, your Windows Application Project should have a Form1 that looks something like Figure 15-2.

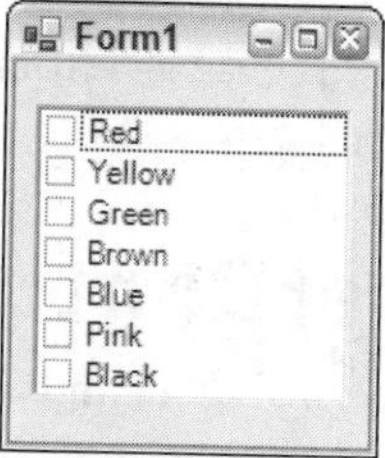

Figure 15-2

14. Bring up the code window for Form1. In the left-hand drop-down box above the code window, select LimitedCheckedListBox1 to get to its events. Then, in the right-hand drop-down box, select the MaxItemsExceeded event. The empty event will look like the following code:

```
Private Sub LimitedCheckedListBox1_MaxItemsExceeded( _
            ByVal sender As System.Object, e As System.EventArgs) _
            Handles LimitedCheckedListBox1.MaxItemsExceeded

  End Sub
```

15. Now insert the following code to handle the event:

```
MsgBox("You are attempting to select more than " & _
       LimitedCheckedListBox1.MaxSelectedItems & _
       " items. You must uncheck some other item " & _
        " before checking this one.")
```

16. Now start the Windows Application project. Check and uncheck various items in the list box to see that the control works as it is supposed to. You should get a message box whenever you attempt to check more than four items. (Four items is the default maximum, and it was not changed.) If you uncheck some items, then you can check items again until the maximum is once again exceeded. When finished, close the form to stop execution.

17. If you want to check the serialization of the code, look at the designer-generated code in the partial class for Form1 (named LimitedCheckedListBox.Designer.vb), and examine the properties for LimitedCheckedListBox1. Note how there is no line of code that sets MaxSelectedItems. Remember, if you don't see the partial class in the Solution Explorer, you'll need to press the Show All button at the top of the Solution Explorer.

18. Go back to the design mode for Form1 and select LimitedCheckedListBox1. In the Properties window, change the MaxSelectedItems property to 3.

19. Now, return to the partial class and look again at the code that declares the properties for LimitedCheckedListBox1. Note that there is now a line of code that sets MaxSelectedItems to the value of 3.

20. Go back to the design mode for `Form1` and select `LimitedCheckedListBox1`. In the Properties window, right-click the `MaxSelectedItems` property. In the pop-up menu, select Reset. The property will change back to a value of `4`, and the line of code that sets the property that you looked at in the last step will be gone.

These last few steps showed that the `DefaultValue` attribute is working as it should.

The Control and UserControl Base Classes

In the earlier example, a new control was created by inheriting from an existing control. As is standard with inheritance, this means the new control began with all the functionality of the control from which it inherited. Then new functionality was added.

This chapter didn't discuss the base class for this new control (`CheckedListBox`), because you probably already understand a lot about the properties, methods, events, and behavior of that class. However, you are not likely to be as familiar with the base classes used for the other techniques for control creation, so it's appropriate to discuss them now.

There are two generic base classes that are used as a starting point to create a control. It is helpful to understand something about the structure of these classes to see when the use of each is appropriate.

The classes discussed in this chapter are all in the System.Windows.Forms namespace. There are similarly named classes for some of these in the System.Web.UI namespace (which is used for Web forms), but these classes should not be confused with anything discussed in this chapter. Chapter 17 will cover the creation of Web controls.

The Control Class

The `Control` class is contained within the `System.Windows.Forms` namespace and contains base functionality to define a rectangle on the screen, provide a handle for it, and process routine operating system messages. This gives the class the ability to perform such functions as handling user input through the keyboard and mouse. The `Control` class serves as the base class for any component that needs a visual representation on a Win32-type graphical interface. Besides built-in controls and custom controls that inherit from the `Control` class, the `Form` class also ultimately derives from the `Control` class.

In addition to these low-level windowing capabilities, the `Control` class also includes such visually related properties as `Font`, `ForeColor`, `BackColor`, and `BackGroundImage`. The `Control` class also has properties that are used to manage layout of the control on a form, such as docking and anchoring.

The Control class does not contain any logic to paint to the screen except to paint a background color or show a background image. While it does offer access to the keyboard and mouse, it does not contain any actual input processing logic except for the ability to generate standard control events such as Click and KeyPress. The developer of a custom control based on the Control class must provide all of the functions for the control beyond the basic capabilities provided by the Control class.

Here are some of the most important members of the `Control` class (from the perspective of a VB developer).

Property	Description
AllowDrop	If set to True then this control will allow drag-and-drop operations and events to be used
Anchor	Determines which edges of the control are anchored to the container's edges
BackColor Font ForeColor	Visual properties which are the same as corresponding properties in Visual Basic 6 and earlier
CanFocus	A read-only property that indicates whether the control can receive focus
Causes	Indicates whether entering the control causes validation on the control
Validation	itself or on controls contained by this control that require validation
Controls	A collection of child controls which this control contains
Dock	Controls to which edge of the container this control is docked to
Enabled	Property indicating whether the control is currently enabled
Location Size	Properties that relate to the size and position of the control
Visible	Property that indicates whether the control is currently visible on the screen
BringToFront	Brings this control to the front of the z-order
DoDragDrop	Begins a drag-and-drop operation
Focus	Attempts to set focus to this control
Hide	Hides the control by setting the visible property to False
Refresh	Forces the control to repaint itself, and to force a repaint on any of its child controls
Show	Makes the control display by setting the visible property to True
Update	Forces the control to paint any currently invalid areas

A standard set of events is also furnished by the Control class, including events for clicking the control (Click, DoubleClick), events for keystroke handling (KeyUp, KeyPress, KeyDown), events for mouse handling (MouseUp, MouseHover, MouseDown, etc.), and events for handling drag-and-drop operations (DragEnter, DragOver, DragLeave, DragDrop). Also included are standard events for managing focus and validation in the control (GotFocus, Validating, Validated). See the help files on the Control class for details on these events and a comprehensive list.

The UserControl Class

The built-in functionality of the Control class is a great starting point for controls that will be built from scratch, with their own display and keyboard handling logic. However, there is limited capability in the Control class to use it as a container for other controls.

That means that composite controls do not typically use the Control class as a starting point. Composite controls combine two or more existing controls, so the starting point must be able to manage contained controls. The class that meets this requirement is the UserControl class. Since it ultimately derives from the Control class, it has all of the properties, methods, and events listed earlier.

However, the UserControl class does not derive directly from the Control class. It derives from the ContainerControl class, which, in turn, derives from the ScrollableControl class.

As the name suggests, the ScrollableControl class adds support for scrolling the client area of the control's window. Almost all the members implemented by this class relate to scrolling. They include AutoScroll, which turns scrolling on or off, and controlling properties such as AutoScrollPosition, which gets or sets the position within the scrollable area.

The ContainerControl class derives from ScrollableControl and adds the ability to support and manage child controls. It manages the focus and the ability to tab from control to control. It includes properties such as ActiveControl to point to the control with the focus, and Validate, which validates the most recently changed control that has not had its validation event fired.

Neither ScrollableControl nor ContainerControl are usually inherited from directly; they add functionality that is needed by their more commonly used child classes: Form and UserControl.

The UserControl class can contain other child controls, but the interface of UserControl does not automatically expose these child controls in any way. Instead, the interface of UserControl is designed to present a single, unified interface to outside clients such as forms or container controls. Any object interface that is needed to access the child controls must be specifically implemented in your custom control. The following example demonstrates this.

The external interface of the UserControl class consists exclusively of members inherited from other classes, though it does overload many of these members to gain functionality suitable for its role as a base class for composite controls.

A Composite UserControl

Our earlier examples showed inheriting an existing control, which was the first of the three techniques for created custom controls. The next step up in complexity and flexibility is to combine more than one existing control to become a new control. This is similar to the process of creating a UserControl in VB6, but it is easier to do in VB.NET.

The main steps in the process of creating a UserControl are:

- Start a new Windows Control Library project, and assign names to the project and the class representing the control.
- The project will contain a design surface that looks a lot like a form. You can drag controls onto this surface just as you would a form. Write logic loading and manipulating the controls as necessary, very much like you would with a form. It is usually particularly important to handle resizing when the UserControl is resized. This can be done by using the Anchor and Dock properties of the constituent controls, or you can create resize logic that will reposition and resize the controls on your UserControl when it is resized on the form containing it.

- ❑ Create properties of the `UserControl` to expose functionality to a form that will use it. This typically means creating a property to load information into and get information out of the control. Sometimes properties to handle cosmetic elements are also necessary.
- ❑ Build the control and refer to it in a Windows Application exactly as was done for the inherited controls discussed earlier.

There is a key difference between this type of development and inheriting a control, as we did in the preceding examples. A UserControl will not by default expose the properties of the controls it contains. It will expose the properties of the UserControl class plus any custom properties that we give it. If you want properties for contained controls to be exposed, you must explicitly create logic to expose them.

Creating a Composite UserControl

To demonstrate the process of creating a composite `UserControl`, the next exercise will build one that is similar to what is shown in Figure 15-3.

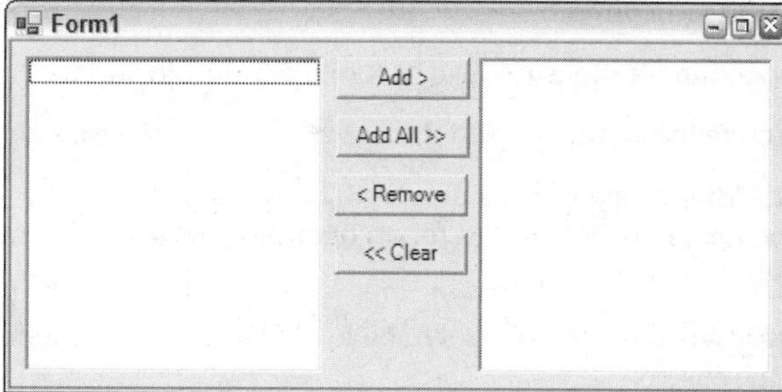

Figure 15-3

This type of layout is common in wizards and in other user interfaces that require selection from a long list of items. The control has one list box holding a list of items that can be chosen (on the left), and another list box containing the items chosen so far (on the right). Buttons allow items to be moved back and forth.

Loading this control means loading items into the left list box, which we call `lstSource` and refer to as the source list box. Getting selected items back out will involve exposing the items that are selected in the right list box, named `lstTarget` and referred to in our discussion as the target list box.

The buttons in the middle that transfer elements back and forth will be called `btnAdd`, `btnAddAll`, `btnRemove`, and `btnClear`, from top to bottom, respectively.

There are lots of ways to handle this kind of interface element in detail. A production-level version would have the following characteristics:

- ❑ Buttons would gray out (disable) when they are not appropriate. For example, `btnAdd` would not be enabled unless an item was selected in `lstSource`.
- ❑ Items that have been transferred from `lstSource` to `lstTarget` would not be shown in `lstSource`. If they are removed from `lstTarget`, they should show in `lstSource` again.

- Items could be dragged and dropped between the two list boxes.
- Items could be selected and moved with a single double-click.

Such a production-type version contains too much code to discuss in this chapter. For simplicity, the exercise will have the following limitations:

- Buttons do not gray out when they should be unavailable.
- Items transferred from `lstSource` will not disappear from the list. This means that it will be possible to add duplicate items to `lstTarget`.
- Drag-and-drop is not supported. (Implementation of drag-and-drop was discussed in Chapter 14, if you are interested in adding it to the example.)
- No double-clicking is supported.

This leaves the following general tasks to make the control work:

- Create a `UserControl` project.
- Add the list boxes and buttons to the `UserControl` design surface.
- Add logic to resize the controls when the `UserControl` changes size.
- Add logic to transfer elements back and forth between the list boxes when buttons are pressed. (More than one item may be selected for an operation, so several items may need to be transferred when a button is pressed.)
- Expose properties to allow the control to be loaded and selected items to be fetched by the form that contains the control.

How Does Resize Work?

The steps outlined above are fairly straightforward. Even the resize logic is made easy by using the built-in capabilities of Windows Forms controls. The list boxes can be docked to the sides to help manage their resizing, then only their width needs to be managed. The buttons need to have an area set aside for them and then be properly positioned within the area.

Setting a Minimum Size

Since we need the buttons to always be visible, our `UserControl` needs to have a minimum size. To take care of that, we will need to set the `MinimumSize` property for the `UserControl` in the designer. The `MinimumSize` property is inherited from the `Control` class, and was discussed in the previous chapter.

Exposing Properties of Subcontrols

Most of the controls contained in the composite control in this exercise do not need to expose their interfaces to the form that will be using the composite control. The buttons, for example, are completely private to the `UserControl`—none of their properties or methods need to be exposed.

The easiest way to load up the control is to expose the appropriate properties of the source list box. Similarly, the easiest way to allow access to the selected items is to expose the appropriate properties of the target list box. In this way, the `UserControl` will expose a limited number of their properties.

As an example, the exercise also includes a `Clear` method that clears both list boxes simultaneously. This allows the control to be flushed and reused by a form that consumes it.

Stepping Through the Example

Here is the step-by-step procedure to build our composite `UserControl`:

1. Start a new Windows Control Library project. Name it `SelectComboControl`.
2. Right-click on the `UserControl1.vb` module that is generated for the project, and select Rename. Change the name of the module to `SelectCombo.vb`. This will automatically also change the name of your class to `SelectCombo`.
3. Go to the design surface for the control. Drag two list boxes and four buttons onto the control and arrange them so that they look something like Figure 15-4.

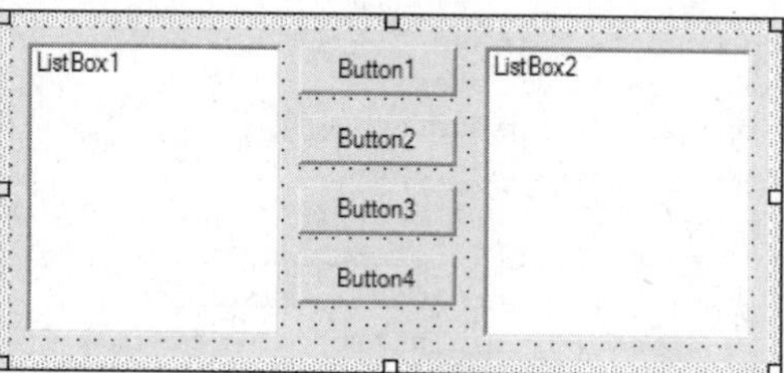

Figure 15-4

4. Change the names and properties of these controls as shown in the following table.

Original Name	New Name	Properties to Set for Control
`Listbox1`	`lstSource`	`Dock` = Left
`Listbox2`	`lstTarget`	`Dock` = Right
`Button1`	`btnAdd`	`Text` = "Add >"
`Button2`	`btnAddAll`	`Text` = "Add All >>"
`Button3`	`btnRemove`	`Text` = "< Remove"
`Button4`	`btnClear`	`Text` = "<< Clear"

5. Click on an unoccupied area of the `UserControl` so that the properties for the `UserControl` itself appear in the Properties window. Set the `MinimumSize` height and width to 200 twips each. We will also need to know how wide the area for the buttons should be. Set up a variable

to hold the size of the area for the buttons. That code should go just under the class declaration lines, and should look like the following code:

```
' Make the width of the area for the buttons 100 twips
Dim mnButtonAreaWidth As Integer = 100
```

6. Set up resize logic to arrange these controls when the composite control is resized. Go to the code window for the class. Get an empty `Resize` event by selecting SelectCombo Events in the left-hand drop-down box, and then Resize in the right-hand box. Place this code in the `Resize` event:

```
Private Sub SelectCombo_Resize(ByVal sender As Object, _
                               ByVal e As System.EventArgs) _
                               Handles MyBase.Resize

    'Set source and target list boxes to appropriate width. Note that
    'docking the list boxes makes their height the right size automatically.
    Dim nListboxWidth As Integer
    nListboxWidth = CInt(0.5 * (Me.Size.Width - mnButtonAreaWidth))
    lstSource.Size = New Size(nListboxWidth, lstSource.Size.Height)
    lstTarget.Size = New Size(nListboxWidth, lstSource.Size.Height)

    'Now position the buttons between the list boxes.
    Dim nLeftButtonPosition As Integer
    nLeftButtonPosition = nListboxWidth + _
        ((mnButtonAreaWidth - btnAdd.Size.Width) \2)
    btnAdd.Location = New Point(nLeftButtonPosition, btnAdd.Location.Y)
    btnAddAll.Location = New Point(nLeftButtonPosition, _
                                   btnAddAll.Location.Y)
    btnRemove.Location = New Point(nLeftButtonPosition, _
                                   btnRemove.Location.Y)
    btnClear.Location = New Point(nLeftButtonPosition, btnClear.Location.Y)
End sub
```

7. Put logic in the class to transfer items back and forth between the list boxes and clear the target list box when `btnClear` is pressed. This logic is surprisingly short because it involves manipulating the collections of items in the list boxes. Here are the `click` events for each of the buttons:

```
Private Sub btnAdd_Click(ByVal sender As Object, _
                         ByVal e As System.EventArgs) _
                         Handles btnAdd.Click
    Dim objItem As Object
    For Each objItem In lstSource.SelectedItems
      lstTarget.Items.Add(objItem)
    Next objItem
End Sub

Private Sub btnAddAll_Click(ByVal sender As Object, _
                            ByVal e As System.EventArgs) _
                            Handles btnAddAll.Click
    Dim objItem As Object
    For Each objItem In lstSource.Items
      lstTarget.Items.Add(objItem)
    Next objItem
End Sub
```

```
Private Sub btnClear_Click(ByVal sender As Object, _
                           ByVal e As System.EventArgs) _
                           Handles btnClear.Click
    lstTarget.Items.Clear()
End Sub

Private Sub btnRemove_Click(ByVal sender As Object, _
                            ByVal e As System.EventArgs) _
                            Handles btnRemove.Click
    ' Have to go through the collection in reverse
    ' because we are removing items.
    Dim nIndex As Integer
    For nIndex = lstTarget.SelectedItems.Count - 1 To 0 Step -1
      lstTarget.Items.Remove(lstTarget.SelectedItems(nIndex))
    Next nIndex
End Sub
```

The logic in the `Click` event for `btnRemove` has one oddity to take into account, which concerns items being removed from the collection. It is necessary to go through the collection in reverse. Otherwise the removal of items will cause the looping enumeration to be messed up and a runtime error will be generated.

8. Create the public properties and methods of the composite control. In our case, we need the following members.

Member	Purpose
`Clear` method	Clears both list boxes of their items
`Add` method	Adds an item to the source list box
`AvailableItem` property	An indexed property to read the items in the source list box
`AvailableCount` property	Exposes the number of items in the source list box
`SelectedItem` property	An indexed property to read the items in the target list box
`SelectedCount` property	Exposes the number of items available in the target list box

The code for these properties and methods is as follows:

```
Public ReadOnly Property SelectedItem(ByVal iIndex As Integer) As Object
  Get
    Return lstTarget.Items(iIndex)
  End Get
End Property

Public ReadOnly Property SelectedCount() As Integer
  Get
    Return lstTarget.Items.Count
  End Get
End Property

Public ReadOnly Property AvailableCount() As Integer
  Get
```

```
      Return lstSource.Items.Count
    End Get
  End Property

  Public Sub Add(ByVal objItem As Object)
    lstSource.Items.Add(objItem)
  End Sub

  Public ReadOnly Property AvailableItem(ByVal iIndex As Integer) As Object
    Get
      Return lstSource.Items(iIndex)
    End Get
  End Property

  Public Sub Clear()
    lstSource.Items.Clear()
    lstTarget.Items.Clear()
  End Sub
```

9. Build the control. Then create a Windows Application project to test it in. As in previous examples, it will be necessary to refer to the control using Choose Items. Then it can be dragged from the toolbox, have items added in code (via the `Add` method), be resized, and so on. When the project is run, the buttons can be used to transfer items back and forth between the list boxes, and the items in the target list box can be read with the `SelectedItem` property.

Keep in mind that you can also use the techniques for inherited controls in composite controls too. You can create custom events, apply attributes to properties, and create `ShouldSerialize` and `Reset` methods to make properties work better with the designer. (That wasn't necessary here because most of our properties were `ReadOnly`.)

Building a Control from Scratch

If your custom control needs to draw its own interface, you should use the `Control` class as your starting point. Such a control gets a fair amount of base functionality from the `Control` class. A partial list of properties and methods of the `Control` class was included earlier in the chapter. These properties arrange for the control to automatically have visual elements such as background and foreground colors, fonts, window size, and so on.

However, such a control does not automatically use any of that information to actually display anything (except for a `BackgroundImage`, if that property is set). A control derived from the `Control` class must implement its own logic for painting the control's visual representation. In all but the most trivial examples, such a control also needs to implement its own properties and methods to gain the functionality it needs.

The techniques used in the earlier example for default values and the `ShouldSerialize` and `Reset` methods all work fine with the controls created from the `Control` class, so that capability will not be discussed again. Instead, this section will focus on the capability that is very different in the `Control` class — the logic to paint the control to the screen.

Painting a Custom Control with GDI+

The base functionality used to paint visual elements for a custom control is in the part of .NET called GDI+. A complete explanation of GDI+ is too complex for this chapter, but here is an overview of some of the main concepts needed.

GDI+

GDI+ is an updated version of the old GDI (Graphics Device Interface) functions provided by the Windows API. GDI+ provides a new API for graphics functions, which then takes advantage of the Windows graphics library.

The GDI+ functions can be found in the `System.Drawing` namespace. Some of the classes and members in this namespace will look familiar if you have used the Win32 GDI functions. Classes are available for such items as pens, brushes, and rectangles. Naturally, the `System.Drawing` namespace makes these capabilities much easier to use than the equivalent API functions.

The `System.Drawing` namespace enables you to manipulate bitmaps and indeed utilize various structures for dealing with graphics such as `Point`, `Size`, `Color`, and `Rectangle`. In addition to this, there are a number of classes available to developers, including:

- `Cursors`—Contains the various cursors that you would need to set in your application, such as an hourglass or an insertion `I-beam` cursor
- `Font`—Includes capabilities like font rotation
- `Graphics`—Contains methods to perform routine drawing constructs, including lines, curves, ellipses, and so on.
- `Icon`, `Pen`, and `Brush`
- The `Pen` and `Brush` classes

The System.Drawing Namespace

The `System.Drawing` namespace includes many classes and it also includes some subsidiary namespaces. We will be using one of those in our example: `System.Drawing.Text`. First, let's look at important classes in `System.Drawing`.

The System.Drawing.Graphics Class

Many of the important drawing functions are members of the `System.Drawing.Graphics` class. Methods like `DrawArc`, `DrawEllipse`, and `DrawIcon` have self-evident actions. There are over 40 methods that provide drawing-related functions in the class.

Many drawing members require one or more points as arguments. A point is a structure in the `System.Drawing` namespace. It has X and Y values for horizontal and vertical positions, respectively. When a variable number of points are needed, an array of points may be used as an argument. The next example uses points.

The `System.Drawing.Graphics` class cannot be directly instantiated. That is, you can't just enter code like this to get an instance of the `Graphics` class:

```
Dim grfGraphics As New System.Drawing.Graphics() ' This does not work!!
```

That's because the constructor for the class is private. It is only supposed to be manipulated by objects that can set the `Graphics` class up for themselves. There are several ways to get a reference to a `Graphics` class, but the one most commonly used in the creation of Windows controls is to get one out of the arguments in a `Paint` event. That technique is used in our example further down. For now, to understand the capabilities of GDI+ a little better, let's do a quick example on a standard Windows Form.

Using GDI+ Capabilities in a Windows Form

Here is an example of a form that uses the `System.Drawing.Graphics` class to draw some graphic elements on the form surface. The example code runs in the `Paint` event for the form, and draws an ellipse, an icon (which it gets from the form itself), and two triangles, one in outline and one filled.

Start a Windows Application project in VB.NET. On the `Form1` that is automatically created for the project, place the following code in the `Paint` event for the form:

```
Dim grfGraphics As System.Drawing.Graphics
grfGraphics = e.Graphics

' Need a pen for the drawing. We'll make it violet.
Dim penDrawingPen As New _
      System.Drawing.Pen(System.Drawing.Color.BlueViolet)

' Draw an ellipse and an icon on the form
grfGraphics.DrawEllipse(penDrawingPen, 30, 150, 30, 60)
grfGraphics.DrawIcon(Me.Icon, 90, 20)

' Draw a triangle on the form.
' First have to define an array of points.
Dim pntPoint(2) As System.Drawing.Point

pntPoint(0).X = 150
pntPoint(0).Y = 150

pntPoint(1).X = 150
pntPoint(1).Y = 200

pntPoint(2).X = 50
pntPoint(2).Y = 120

grfGraphics.DrawPolygon(penDrawingPen, pntPoint)

' Do a filled triangle.
' First need a brush to specify how it is filled.
Dim bshBrush As System.Drawing.Brush
bshBrush = New SolidBrush(Color.Blue)
```

```
    ' Now relocate the points for the triangle.
    ' We'll just move it 100 twips to the right.
    pntPoint(0).X += 100
    pntPoint(1).X += 100
    pntPoint(2).X += 100
    grfGraphics.FillPolygon(bshBrush, pntPoint)
```

Then, start the program and, when it comes up, the form will look something like Figure 15-5.

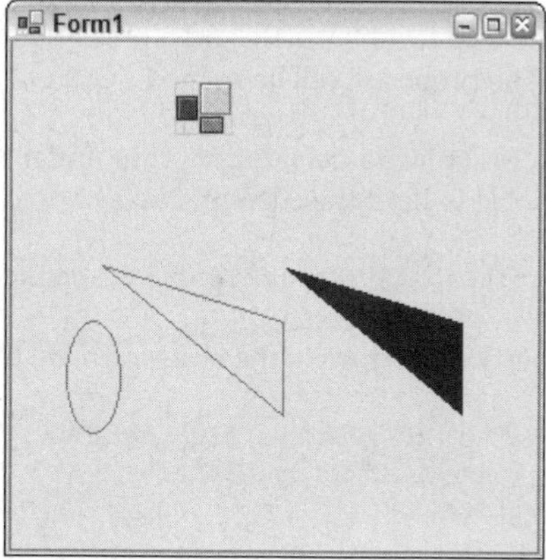

Figure 15-5

As you can see, the graphics functions are not difficult to use. The hardest part is figuring out how to initialize the objects needed, such as the graphics object itself, and the necessary brushes and pens.

For an example, you will create a custom control that displays a "traffic light," with red, yellow, and green signals that can be displayed via a property of the control. GDI+ classes will be used to draw the traffic light graphics in the control.

First, start a new project in VB.NET of the Windows Control Library type, and name it `"TrafficLight"`. The created module will have a class in it named `UserControl1`. We want a different type of control class, so you need to get rid of this one. Right-click on this module in the Solution Explorer and select Delete.

Now right-click on the project, and select Add New Item. Select the item type of Custom Control, and name it `TrafficLight.vb`.

As with the other examples in this chapter, it is necessary to include the `Imports` statement for the namespace containing the attribute we will use. This line should go at the very top of the code module for `TrafficLight.vb`:

```
    Imports System.ComponentModel
```

The TrafficLight control needs to know which "light" to display. There are three states the control can be in: red, yellow, and green. An enumerated type will be used for these states. Add the following code just below the last code:

```
Public Enum TrafficLightStatus
    statusRed = 1
    statusYellow = 2
    statusGreen = 3
End Enum
```

The example will also need a module-level variable and a property procedure to support changing and retaining the state of the light. The property will be named Status.

To handle the Status property, first place a declaration right under the last enumeration declaration that creates a module level variable to hold the current status:

```
Private mStatus As TrafficLightStatus = TrafficLightStatus.statusGreen
```

Then, insert the following property procedure in the class to create the Status property:

```
<Description("Status (color) of the traffic light")> _
Public Property Status() As TrafficLightStatus
    Get
        Status = mStatus
    End Get
    Set(ByVal Value As TrafficLightStatus)
        If mStatus <> Value Then
            mStatus = Value
            Me.Invalidate()
        End If
    End Set
End Property
```

The Invalidate method of the control is used when the Status property changes, and it forces a complete redraw of the control. Ideally, this type of logic should be placed in all of the events that affect the rendering of the control.

Now, add procedures to make the property serialize and reset properly. These routines look like this:

```
Public Function ShouldSerializeStatus() As Boolean
    If mStatus = TrafficLightStatus.statusGreen Then
        Return False
    Else
        Return True
    End If
End Function

Public Sub ResetStatus()
    Me.Status = TrafficLightStatus.statusGreen
End Sub
```

Now, place code to handle the `Paint` event, that is, to draw the "traffic light" when the control repaints. We will use some code similar to that in the section on drawing with the GDI+ (above). The code generated for the new custom control will already have a blank `Paint` event inserted. You just need to insert the highlighted code below into that event, below the comment line that says "Add your custom paint code here":

```
Protected Overrides Sub OnPaint(ByVal pe As _
                        System.Windows.Forms.PaintEventArgs)
    MyBase.OnPaint(pe)

    'Add your custom paint code here
    Dim grfGraphics As System.Drawing.Graphics
    grfGraphics = pe.Graphics

    ' Need a pen for the drawing the outline. We'll make it black.
    Dim penDrawingPen As New _
        System.Drawing.Pen(System.Drawing.Color.Black)

    ' Draw the outline of the traffic light on the control.
     ' First have to define an array of points.
     Dim pntPoint(3) As System.Drawing.Point

    pntPoint(0).X = 0
    pntPoint(0).Y = 0

    pntPoint(1).X = Me.Size.Width - 2
    pntPoint(1).Y = 0

    pntPoint(2).X = Me.Size.Width - 2
    pntPoint(2).Y = Me.Size.Height - 2

    pntPoint(3).X = 0
    pntPoint(3).Y = Me.Size.Height - 2

    grfGraphics.DrawPolygon(penDrawingPen, pntPoint)

    ' Now ready to draw the circle for the "light"
    Dim nCirclePositionX As Integer
    Dim nCirclePositionY As Integer
    Dim nCircleDiameter As Integer
    Dim nCircleColor As Color

    nCirclePositionX = Me.Size.Width * 0.02
    nCircleDiameter = Me.Size.Height * 0.3
    Select Case Me.Status
        Case TrafficLightStatus.statusRed
            nCircleColor = Color.OrangeRed
            nCirclePositionY = Me.Size.Height * 0.01
        Case TrafficLightStatus.statusYellow
            nCircleColor = Color.Yellow
            nCirclePositionY = Me.Size.Height * 0.34
        Case TrafficLightStatus.statusGreen
            nCircleColor = Color.LightGreen
            nCirclePositionY = Me.Size.Height * 0.67
    End Select
```

```
    Dim bshBrush As System.Drawing.Brush
    bshBrush = New SolidBrush(nCircleColor)
    ' Draw the circle for the signal light
     grfGraphics.FillEllipse(bshBrush, nCirclePositionX, _
                nCirclePositionY, nCircleDiameter, nCircleDiameter)
End Sub
```

Now, build the control library by selecting Build from the Build menu. This will create a `DLL` in the `/bin` directory where the control library solution is saved.

Then, start a new Windows Application project and right-click the Windows Forms tab in the toolbox. In the Add/Remove Items dialog box, first make sure that the .NET Components tab is selected, and then use the Browse button to point to the deployed `DLL` for the control library. The toolbox should now contain the `TrafficLight` control.

Drag a `TrafficLight` control onto the form in the Windows Application project. Notice that its property window includes a `Status` property. Set that to `statusYellow`. Note that the rendering on the control on the form's design surface changes to reflect this new status. Also, change the background color of the `TrafficLight` control to a darker gray to improve its cosmetics. (The `BackColor` property for `TrafficLight` was inherited from the `Control` class.)

At the top of the code for the form, place the following line to make the enumerated value for the traffic light's status available.

```
Imports TrafficLight.TrafficLight
```

Add three buttons (named `btnRed`, `btnYellow`, and `btnGreen`) to the form to make the traffic light control display as red, yellow, and green. The logic for the buttons will look something like the following code:

```
Private Sub btnRed_Click(ByVal sender As System.Object, _
               ByVal e As System.EventArgs) Handles btnRed.Click
    TrafficLight1.Status = TrafficLightStatus.statusRed
End Sub

Private Sub btnYellow_Click(ByVal sender As System.Object, _
              ByVal e As System.EventArgs) Handles btnYellow.Click
    TrafficLight1.Status = TrafficLightStatus.statusYellow
End Sub

Private Sub btnGreen_Click(ByVal sender As System.Object, _
              ByVal e As System.EventArgs) Handles btnGreen.Click
    TrafficLight1.Status = TrafficLightStatus.statusGreen
End Sub
```

In the Solution Explorer, right-click your test Windows Application, and select "Set as Startup Project." Then press F5 to run.

When your test form comes up, you can change the "signal" on the traffic light by pressing the buttons. Figure 15-6 shows a sample screen.

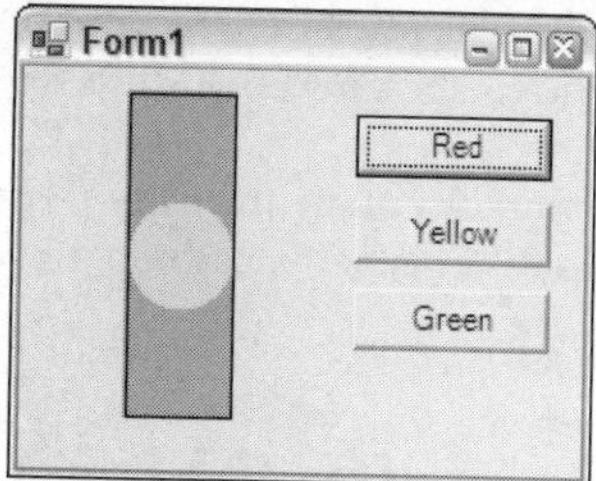

Figure 15-6

Of course, you can't see the color in a black-and-white screen shot, but as you might expect from its position, the circle above is yellow. The "red light" displays at the top of the control, and the "green light" displays at the bottom. These positions are all calculated in the `Paint` event logic, depending on the value of the `Status` property.

Attaching an Icon for the Toolbox

By default, the icon that appears in the toolbox next to your control's name is a gear-shaped icon. However, you can use an attribute on the class declaration that defines your control to specify a different icon to place in the toolbox.

The attribute needed is the `ToolboxBitmap` attribute. It can be used in several ways.

If the icon you want to use is already defined for another control, you can have your control get the icon out of the existing control. Suppose, for example, you want to use the icon for a `Textbox` as the icon for our `TrafficLight` control. In that case, the line that declares the class

```
Public Class TrafficLight
```

should be changed to add the attribute as follows:

```
<ToolboxBitmap(GetType(System.Windows.Forms.TextBox))> _
Public Class TrafficLight
```

You can also use an icon that resides in a graphic file. There are a lot of these included with VS.NET in the "`Common7\backslash Graphics\backslash Icons`" subdirectory of the VS.NET directory (which is usually under "Program Files" on your main system drive). Or, you can define your own icons in the Paint accessory of Windows by defining an image size of 16 x 16 pixels, and then painting the icon.

In either case, the `ToolboxBitmap` attribute is used to refer to the file containing the icon you want, as shown below.

```
<ToolboxBitmap("C:\TestData\RedLightIcon.bmp")> _
Public Class TrafficLight
```

After adding the attribute, just rebuild the control to incorporate the icon in the control's DLL. Note that you must remove the control from the toolbox and read it to see the changed icon.

It's also possible to get a toolbox bitmap out of an arbitrary resource compiled into an assembly, but discussing all the concepts required to do that is beyond the scope of this chapter.

Embedding Controls in Other Controls

Another technique that is valuable for creating custom controls is to use embedding of other controls. In a sense, the `UserControl` does this. However, when a `UserControl` is used as the base class, it only exposes by default the properties of the `UserControl` class. Instead, you may want to use a control such as a `Textbox` or `Grid` as the starting point, but embed a `Button` in the `Textbox` or `Grid` to get some new functionality.

The embedding technique relies on the fact that in Windows Forms, all controls can be containers for other controls. Visual Basic developers are familiar with the idea that `Panels` and `GroupBoxes` can be containers, but in fact a `TextBox` or `Grid` can also be a container of other controls.

This technique is best presented with an example. The standard `ComboBox` control does not have a way for the user to reset to a "no selection" state. Once an item is selected, setting to that state requires code that sets the `SelectedIndex` to `-1`.

We will create a `ComboBox` that has a button to reset the selection state back to "no selection." That allows the user to access that capability directly.

Now that we have done several controls in examples, rather than proceed step-by-step, we'll just show the code for such a `ComboBox`, and discuss how the code works.

```
Public Class SpecialComboBox
    Inherits ComboBox

    Dim WithEvents btnEmbeddedButton As Button

    Public Sub New()

        Me.DropDownStyle = ComboBoxStyle.DropDownList

        ' Fix up the embedded button.
        btnEmbeddedButton = New Button
        btnEmbeddedButton.Width = SystemInformation.VerticalScrollBarWidth
        btnEmbeddedButton.Top = 2
        btnEmbeddedButton.Height = Me.Height - 8
        btnEmbeddedButton.BackColor = SystemColors.Control
        btnEmbeddedButton.FlatStyle = FlatStyle.System
        btnEmbeddedButton.Text = "t"
        Dim fSpecial As New Font("Wingdings 3", Me.Font.Size - 1)
        btnEmbeddedButton.Font = fSpecial

        btnEmbeddedButton.Left = Me.Width - btnEmbeddedButton.Width - _
            SystemInformation.VerticalScrollBarWidth - 5
```

```
        Me.Controls.Add(btnEmbeddedButton)
        btnEmbeddedButton.Anchor = CType(AnchorStyles.Right _
            Or AnchorStyles.Top Or AnchorStyles.Bottom, AnchorStyles)
        btnEmbeddedButton.BringToFront()

    End Sub

    Private Sub btnEmbeddedButton_Click(ByVal sender As Object, _
            ByVal e As System.EventArgs) Handles btnEmbeddedButton.Click
        Me.SelectedIndex = -1
        Me.Focus
    End Sub

    Private Sub BillysComboBox_DropDownStyleChanged(ByVal sender As Object, _
            ByVal e As System.EventArgs) Handles MyBase.DropDownStyleChanged
        If Me.DropDownStyle <> ComboBoxStyle.DropDownList Then
            Me.DropDownStyle = ComboBoxStyle.DropDownList
            Throw New _
              InvalidOperationException("DropDownStyle must be DropDownList")
        End If
    End Sub
End Class
```

As in our first example in the chapter, this example inherits from a built-in control. Thus it immediately gets all of the capabilities of the standard `ComboBox`. All we need to add is the ability to reset the selected state.

To do that, we need a button for the user to press. The class declares the button as a private object named `btnEmbeddedButton`. Then, in the constructor for the class, the button is instantiated, and its properties are set as necessary. The size and position of the button need to be calculated. This is done using the size of the `ComboBox` and a special system parameter called `SystemInformation.VerticalScrollBarWidth`. This parameter is chosen because it is also used to calculate the size of the button used to drop down a combo box. Thus our new embedded button will be exactly the same width as the button that the regular `ComboBox` displays for dropping down the list.

Of course, we need to display something in the new button to indicate its purpose. For simplicity, the code above displays a lower case "t" using the WingDings 3 font (which all Windows systems should have installed). This will cause a left-pointing triangle to appear, as seen in Figure 15-6, which is a screen shot of the control in use.

The button is then added to the `Controls` collection of the `ComboBox`. You may be surprised to find out that a `ComboBox` even has a `Controls` collection for embedded controls, but all controls in Windows Forms have one.

Finally, the `Anchor` property of the new button is set to maintain the position if the `SpecialComboBox` is resized by its consumer.

Besides the constructor, only a couple of small routines are needed. The `click` event for the button must be handled, and in it the `SelectedIndex` must be set to `-1`. And, since this functionality is only for combo boxes with a style of `DropDownList`, the `DropDownStyleChanged` event of the `ComboBox` must be trapped, and the style prevented from being set to anything else.

Summary

This chapter discussed the creation of custom controls in VB.NET, and illustrated how much easier it is to do this in comparison with the previous versions of Visual Basic. The advent of full inheritance capabilities in VB.NET means that it is a lot easier for developers to utilize functionality simply by inheriting from the namespaces built into the .NET Framework. It is probably best to start by overriding these existing controls in order to learn the basics of creating properties and coordinating them with the designer, building controls and testing them, and so on. These techniques can then be extended by the creation of composite controls, as we have illustrated with worked examples within this chapter.

You have seen how to create controls by:

- Inheriting from another control
- Building a composite control
- Writing a control from scratch, based on the `Control` class, although this took more work than the other two methods

In the course of writing a control from scratch, it was necessary to discuss the basics of GDI+. However, if you are going to do extensive work with GDI+, you will need to seek out additional resources to aid in that effort.

The key concept that you should take away from this chapter is that Windows Forms controls are a great way to package functionality that will be reused across many forms, and to create more dynamic, responsive user interfaces much more quickly with much less code.

16

Building Web Applications

Shipping as part of Visual Studio 2005 (VS.Net 2005), Microsoft introduced ASP.Net version 2.0, an enhanced version of its Web Application development technology. Almost every aspect of Web development with ASP.Net has undergone improvements asked for by end users. ASP.Net 2.0 introduces a new feature, a host of new controls, and an improved code-behind model. In this chapter you will take a quick look at building Web applications with Visual Studio 2005, using ASP.Net version 2.0. In the next chapter, you will find information about some advanced features of ASP.Net version 2.0

ASP.Net first provided a visual metaphor for creating Web forms with code behind controls in a manner very similar to windows-based forms. In addition, ASP.Net introduced a number of server controls that enabled a programmer to drag and drop onto a design surface and obtain complex HTML-based UI elements such as grids and calendars without having to write complex code. ASP.Net also provided automatic state management and saving of control properties across round trips from the browser to the Web server. Now, ASP.Net version 2 goes beyond to provide additional productivity, performance, and feature enhancements.

> **This chapter explores Web forms and how you can benefit from their use, but it is only meant to whet your appetite. If you want to learn more, read *Beginning ASP.NET 2.0 and Databases* (Wiley, 2006).**

A Web Site in Action

In VS.Net 2005, a Web application is called a Web Site. This is to distinguish it from the previous version where a Web application was bound to Internet Information Server (IIS) and to physical folders in the IIS root. Web sites in Visual Studio 2005 can exist within a file system, within a local IIS Web site, or on a remote Web site. The easiest way to learn about Web sites is to see them in action, and then take them apart to see how they are constructed. Let's look at a very simple Web form — the quintessential "Hello World" example.

Setting Up the Environment

To be able to create ASP.NET applications with VS.Net 2005, you do not need to be running Internet Information Server (IIS). Visual Studio 2005 ships with its own lightweight Web server application that can be used as a temporary Web server while developing ASP.Net Web applications. Once you finish development, you can deploy an ASP.Net application to a production server. On the production server, you will need to be running IIS.

The HelloWorld Web Form

Create a new ASP.NET Web site in VS.NET by selecting File ➪ New ➪ Web Site. Click "Visual Basic," and then click the "ASP.Net Web site" template. You may choose a location for your Web site or accept the default `C:\WebSites\` as your location. Name the Web site HelloWorld, thereby making your location `C:\WebSites\HelloWorld`, as shown in Figure 16-1.

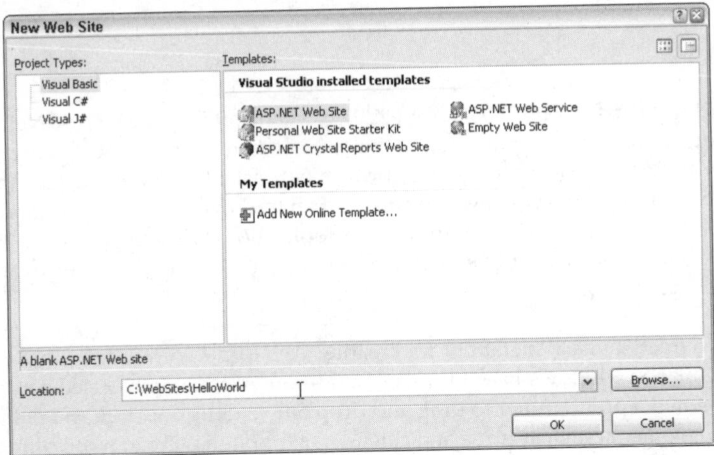

Figure 16-1

Click OK and you will be presented with a new solution. VS.NET has created a new Web form for you, called `default.aspx` (`aspx` is the extension for ASP.NET Web pages).

By default, this version of Visual Studio .Net opens up a Web form in source view — you get to see the HTML that makes up the Web page. You can also set it to open up in design view by setting an option under Tools ➪ Options. In design view, you work with a WYSIWYG (What You See Is What You Get) Web page editor.

Switch to design view by clicking the Design tab at the bottom of the page. You can treat the Web form in front of you as a normal VB form, dropping controls onto it by dragging them from the toolbox. For now, drag a `Label` control from the toolbox and drop it onto the top left of the form. Use the Properties window to set its caption (its `Text` property) to "Hello World." Your screen will look like Figure 16-2.

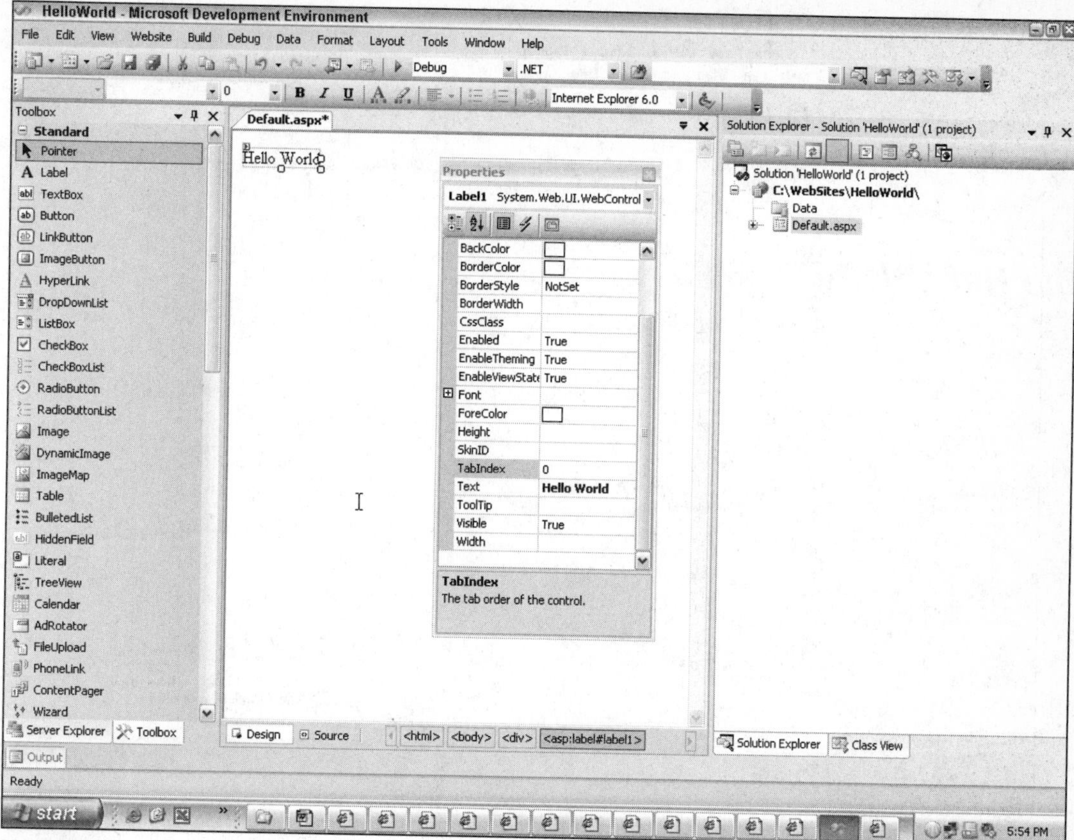

Figure 16-2

For this example, that's all you need to do. You can now execute your application. Remember, you have created your Web page within a folder called `C:\WebSites`. It is not linked to your local Internet Information Server (even if you have one). In previous versions of ASP.Net, when you created a new ASP.Net project, VS.Net automatically linked it to your local Web server, and created an application within the IIS root enabling it to be executed.

In ASP.Net 2.0, VS.Net 2005 executes your ASP.Net Web site by using a special lightweight Web server that ships with VS.Net 2005. This lightweight Web server — the Visual Web Developer Web Server — enables you to execute ASP.Net applications on your development machine even if you do not have IIS installed. It also enables you to develop file system-based Web sites as opposed to developing Web sites that are within the IIS root alone.

Normally, VS.NET executes applications in a special debug mode that allows you to monitor the progress of your application. For now, you simply want to execute your application in the release mode or the production mode, so select Debug ➪ Start Without Debugging from the menu, or press Control + F5. If all goes well, your browser will open the `default.aspx` file and you will see an image similar to Figure 16-3.

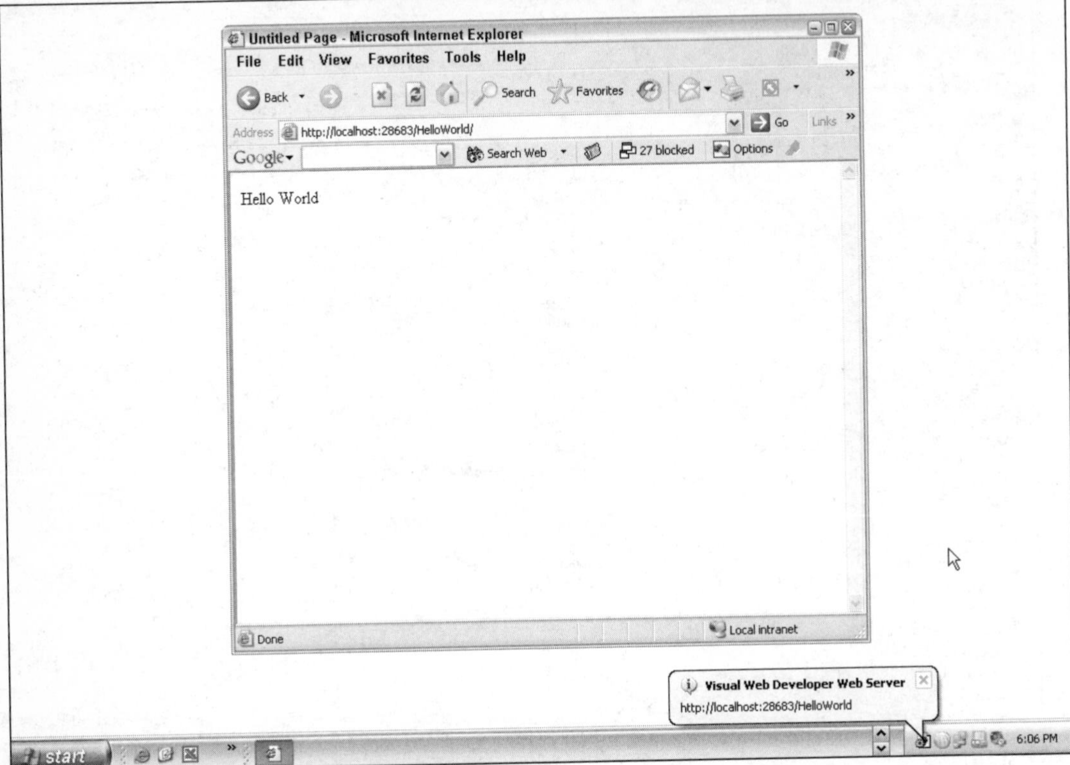

Figure 16-3

If you are running Windows XP with Service Pack 2, chances are, you will not see the page displayed in Figure 16-3. Instead, you will probably see an error image similar to Figure 16-4.

The error message you see appears because Windows XP's firewall blocks the Visual Web Developer Web Server that VS.Net uses to launch your Web application. To fix this, click the Unblock button to allow Windows XP's firewall to consider the Visual Web Developer WebServer to be a "friendly" application, and then refresh your browser to view your page. You will need to do this only once since XP remembers your settings.

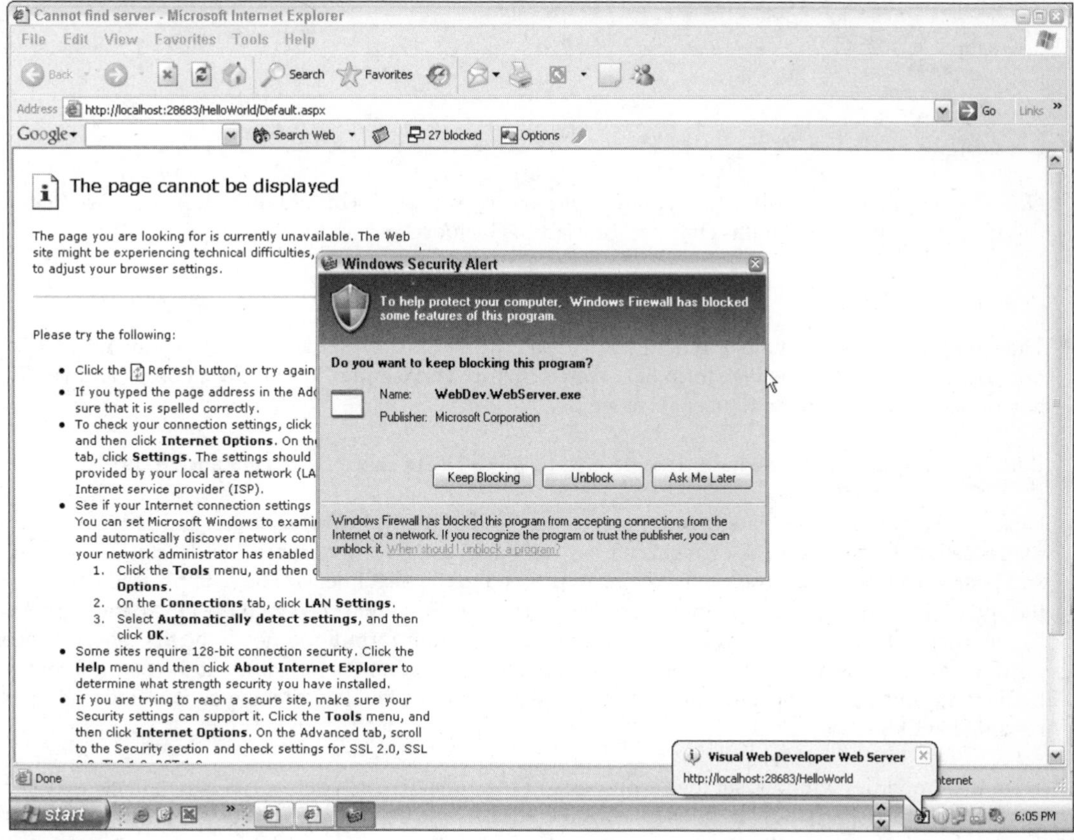

Figure 16-4

Right-click the browser and select View Source to see what the output produced by your solution looks like. You will see that it is pure HTML, generated at runtime by your aspx file (tidied up a bit here):

```
<!DOCTYPE html PUBLIC "-//W3C//DTD XHTML 1.1//EN"
"http://www.w3.org/TR/xhtml11/DTD/xhtml11.dtd">

<html xmlns="http://www.w3.org/1999/xhtml" >
<head><title>
 Untitled Page
</title></head>
<body>
    <form method="post" action="default.aspx" id="form1">
<div>
<input type="hidden" name="__VIEWSTATE"
value="/wEPDwUJODExMDE5NzY5ZGTQYknpxOG8TrYU95K/Cp6yZZc6Lg==" />
</div>

    <div>
```

```
        <span id="Label1">Hello World</span>

    </div>
    </form>
</body>
</html>
```

Notice that there is an HTML `form` within your page, even though you did not ask for one. You'll look at this more closely later on in this chapter. Your label is included within the `span` tag:

```
        <span id="Label1">Hello World</span>
```

The `span` tag acts as a container to hold your `Label`. Close the browser and return to your VS.NET solution to see what makes this Web form tick. Web forms are very similar to Windows Forms, and you'll see how much alike they are with this next example.

Within your application, you have a single Web form, `default.aspx`. Let's enhance it further.

Back in VS.Net designer, position your mouse at the end of the HelloWorld `Label` and press Shift+Enter to proceed to the next line. (In VS.Net 2005, asp.net pages use flow-layout by default. You cannot drag and position a label to an absolute position. To proceed to the next line, you have to press Shift+Enter at the end of the line. If you press Enter at the end of the line, you will proceed to the next paragraph, just like in Microsoft Word.). Drag and drop another `Label` to your form underneath the first one, and again, position your mouse at its end and press Shift+Enter to proceed to the next line. Add a `Button` control to the form underneath the new `Label`. Widen the width of the label by clicking on it and dragging its resizing handles.

From the Properties window, set the `ID` property of the `Label` (which defines its name) to be `lblText`. Leave its `Text` property as `Label`. Then, click the `Button` and set its `ID` property to `btnSubmit` and its `Text` property to `Submit`. By this time, your screen looks similar to Figure 16-5.

Now, double-click the button and watch what happens. You will be taken to the code behind the form, and your cursor will blink within the `btnSubmit_Click` event code, just like in Visual Basic 6! Wait a minute, though. This isn't a Windows Form, so how can buttons have code behind them?

In ASP.NET, controls do have code behind them. As you can see, you have a subroutine called `btnSubmit_Click` that will be executed when the button is clicked. This code is executed — on the server, not the client browser — whenever the form is submitted to the server. You'll see more details later on. For now, enter the following as the code for the click event:

```
Sub btnSubmit_Click(ByVal sender As System.Object, _
                            ByVal e As System.EventArgs) _


   lblText.Text = "Hello World from Button Submit Code."
End Sub
```

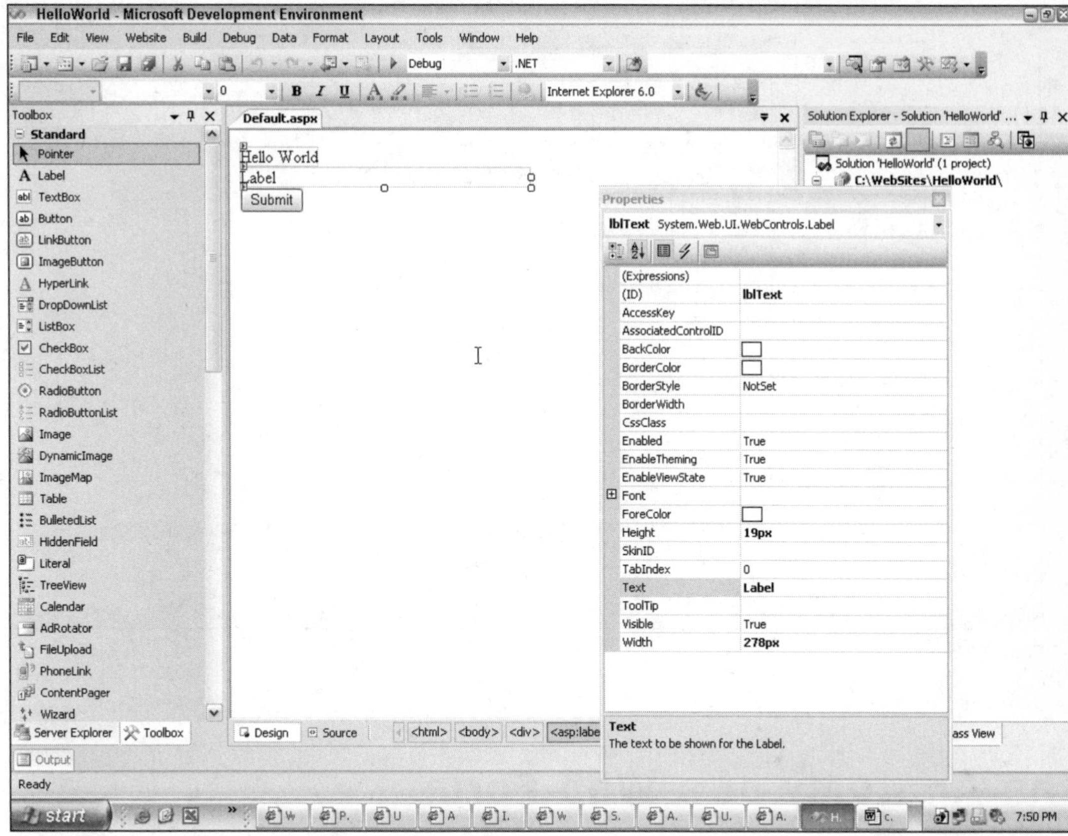

Figure 16-5

Notice how IntelliSense works when you type this line. Although ASP programmers had this functionality with InterDev, VS.NET's IntelliSense provides more HTML elements for use in your code.

Close the code window (saving any changes you have made), and return to the design mode for the form. Then execute the ASP.Net Web application by pressing Ctrl-F5 again. The Web form — `default.aspx` — opens up in the browser, displaying two labels and a button. The second label has the default caption of Label. Click the Submit button and the text "Hello World from Button Submit Code" will appear within the second label as shown in Figure 16-6.

When you click the Submit button, the code behind the button is executed, just like a Windows Form.

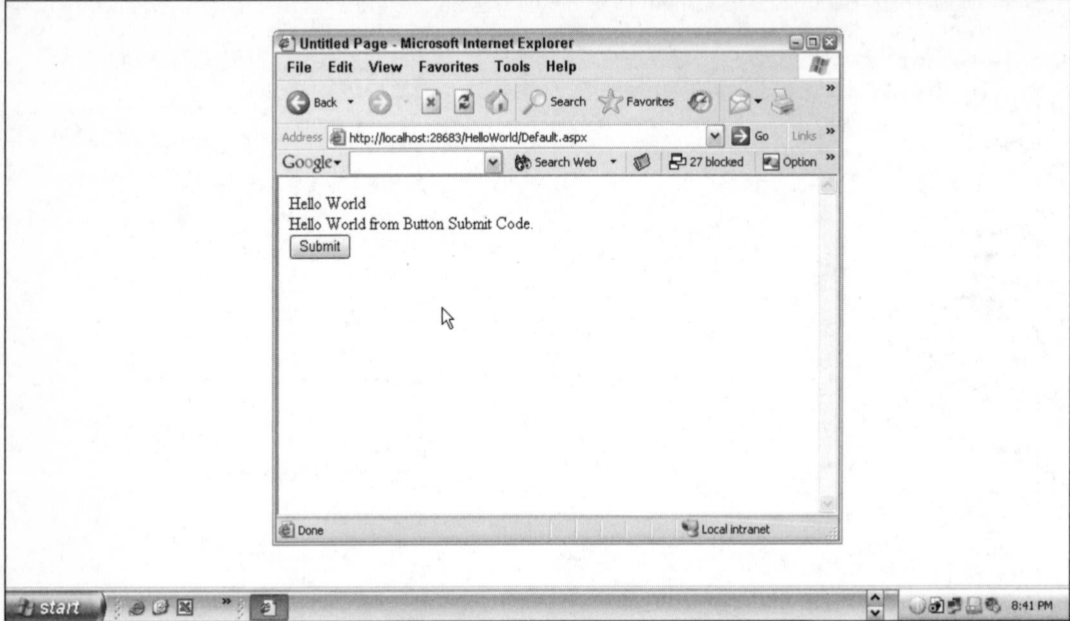

Figure 16-6

The Anatomy of a Web Form

Web forms bridge the gap between VB programming and traditional ASP programming. By offering a visual technique to drag and drop controls onto a page, and code for events behind the controls, Web forms bring a very familiar metaphor to Web development.

A Web form is made up of two components: the visual elements that you can see in the design view and the code behind the controls and the page. The visual elements form the template for the presentation of the Web page in the end user's browser. The code is executed on the server when the page loads and in response to other events that you have coded for.

ASP.Net provides two models for managing these two separate components:

- Single-file page model
- Code-behind page model

Single-File Page Model

In the single-file page model, both components reside within the same physical .aspx file. The code components are enclosed within a `<script> </script>` block that contains an attribute `runat="server"`. This attribute separates script blocks that execute within a browser (client-side code) from script blocks that execute on the server (server-side code). You can use any text editor to create a single-file page model .aspx page. In fact, if your default.aspx page was built using a single-file page model, it would look like this:

```
<%@ Page Language="VB" %>

<script runat=server>
    Sub btnSubmit_Click(ByVal sender As Object, ByVal e As System.EventArgs)
        lblText.Text = "Hello World from Button Submit Code."
    End Sub
</script>

<!DOCTYPE html PUBLIC "-//W3C//DTD XHTML 1.1//EN"
"http://www.w3.org/TR/xhtml11/DTD/xhtml11.dtd">

<html xmlns="http://www.w3.org/1999/xhtml" >
<head runat="server">
    <title>Untitled Page</title>
</head>
<body>
    <form id="form1" runat="server">
    <div>
        <asp:Label ID="Label1" Runat="server" Text="Hello World"></asp:Label>
        <br />
        <asp:Label ID="lblText" Runat="server" Text="Label" Width="278px"
Height="19px"></asp:Label>
        <br />
        <asp:Button ID="btnSubmit" Runat="server" Text="Submit"
OnClick="btnSubmit_Click" />

    </div>
    </form>
</body>
</html>
```

Notice that the page does not contain an explicit class declaration. However, at runtime, the single-file page is treated as a class that derives from the `System.Web.UI.Page` class and includes all controls on the page as members of the derived class. The server-side script code within the page becomes part of this derived class.

Code-Behind Page Model

When you create a Web form in VS.Net 2003, by default it separates the code component from the markup responsible for the visual elements into two separate physical files. In the case of your `default.aspx` page, the HTML responsible for the visual elements was within the aspx page, while the code for the controls was placed in a separate `default.aspx.vb` page. This is what the `default.aspx` page is comprised of:

```
<%@ Page Language="VB" AutoEventWireup="false" CompileWith="Default.aspx.vb"
ClassName="Default_aspx" %>

<!DOCTYPE html PUBLIC "-//W3C//DTD XHTML 1.1//EN"
"http://www.w3.org/TR/xhtml11/DTD/xhtml11.dtd">
```

```
<html xmlns="http://www.w3.org/1999/xhtml" >
<head runat="server">
    <title>Untitled Page</title>
</head>
<body>
    <form id="form1" runat="server">
    <div>
        <asp:Label ID="Label1" Runat="server" Text="Hello World"></asp:Label>
        <br />
        <asp:Label ID="lblText" Runat="server" Text="Label" Width="278px"
Height="19px"></asp:Label>
        <br />
        <asp:Button ID="btnSubmit" Runat="server" Text="Submit"
OnClick="btnSubmit_Click" />

    </div>
    </form>
</body>
</html>
```

And the `default.aspx.vb` page consists of the following:

```
Partial Class Default_aspx

    Sub btnSubmit_Click(ByVal sender As Object, ByVal e As System.EventArgs)
        lblText.Text = "Hello World from Button Submit Code."
    End Sub
End Class
```

Notice that there is no server-side `<script></script>` block with a `runat=server` attribute in the aspx page. Also notice that the .aspx page has a `@ Page` directive that indicates the location of the separate code-behind page.

```
<%@ Page Language="VB" AutoEventWireup="false" CompileWith="Default.aspx.vb"
ClassName="Default_aspx" %>
```

The code-behind .vb page contains all the code for the page. However, notice that the code is declared within a class declared with the `Partial` keyword indicating that it is part of a class and not the complete class definition.

```
Partial Class Default_aspx
```

At runtime, the compiler reads in the .aspx page and the file it references within the `@Page` directive, combines the two into a single class, and compiles them as a unit into a single class.

Single-file page models and code-behind page models are functionally identical. There is no benefit or performance difference between the two models. Which one you choose will depend solely upon your style. For pages that do not contain much code, a single-file page model will be more efficient in managing code pieces. For a cleaner separation of code and markup, a code-behind page model is more efficient. Besides, the code behind an aspx page can be used in more than one aspx page in the code-behind page model.

Figure 16-7 shows the two components that make up your `default.aspx` Web form within your example Web application.

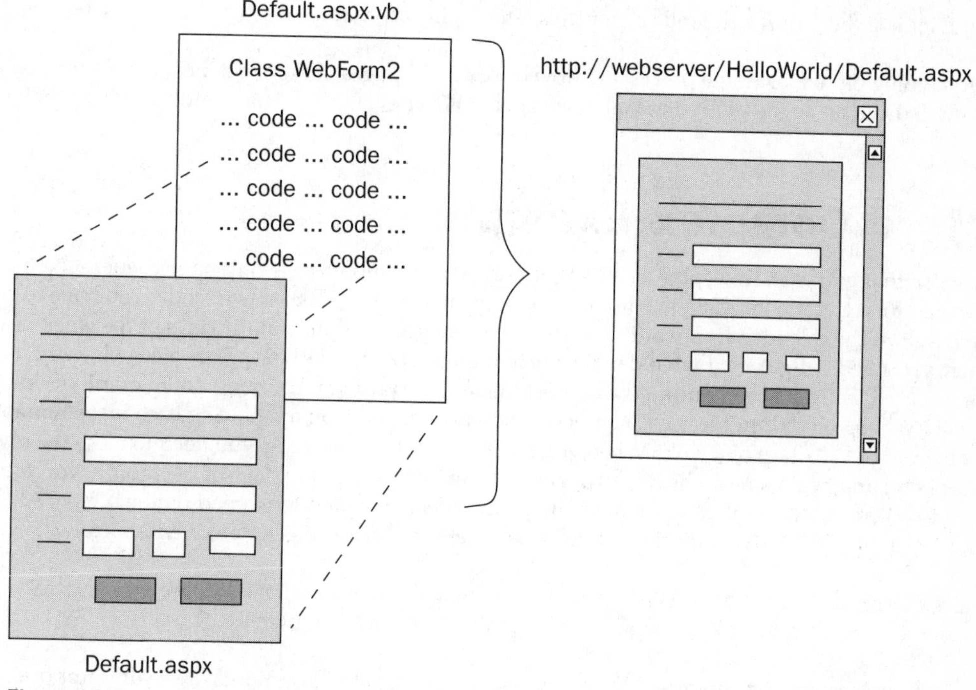

Figure 16-7

By dividing the components into separate files and, therefore, within the VS.NET environment, into separate views, Web forms provide a very familiar environment for the VB programmer. With traditional Visual Basic, you first paint the form by dragging and dropping controls, and then write the code for the events that the controls expose. When developing Web forms, you first create the look of your Web page by dragging and dropping controls onto the page, and then you write code for the events exposed by the controls.

The Template for Presentation

The .aspx file forms the user interface component of the Web form and serves as a template for its presentation in the browser. This .aspx file is the `Page` and it contains HTML markup and Web forms specific elements. You can drag and drop several types of controls onto a Web form, including:

- HTML controls
- Web form controls
- Validation controls
- Data related controls

- COM and .NET components registered on your machine
- Items from your clipboard

You'll look at these different kinds of controls later on in this chapter.

Before going on to look at the processing flow of ASP.NET pages, let's take a look at another example that will drive home the point that Web forms make Web development uncannily like VB development.

A More Complex Example

Suppose that you wish to display a calendar for the current month in a Web page. Generating a dynamic calendar for a traditional ASP page involves writing at least 50 to 100 lines of code. You have to create a table to host the calendar, figure out the month and the year, and output the days of the week header. Then, you need to figure out what day the current month begins with and how many days there are in the month. Finally, you can output the days of the month starting with 1 and going on till the end of the month. When you output the days, you need to make sure that you are placing each week horizontally in one row (a `<TR>` tag) of a table. When you reach the end of one week, you need to close the row (a `</TR>` tag) and begin a new one. Finally, when you are done with the days of the month, you probably need to output a few blank days to make the table appear even and look good on the screen. All this takes up a lot of ASP code, especially if you want the calendar to be generated dynamically.

There was an alternative before Web forms. You could simply use a client-side ActiveX control — a `Calendar` control in your Web page. However, this had its own problems.

ActiveX controls are not supported by all browsers; in fact, only IE on Windows really supports them. The `Calendar` control may not exist on your users' computers, so you have to worry about distributing it. Also, an ActiveX control will only work on the Windows platform, so your Web site users on Macs, for example, will not be able to view the page properly.

> **Web forms bring the ease of development with an ActiveX control to the world of ASP and Web development, but they output standard HTML on demand.**

In your HelloWorld Web site, add a new Web form. From the menu, select Website ⇨ Add New Item. In the dialog box that pops up, select Web Form, and name it `Calendar.aspx`. Remember to open up the Web form in the design view. From your toolbox, look for the `Calendar` control under the Web forms group. Double-click or drag it onto the form. That's it, you now have a fully functional calendar in your Web page, albeit a very plain looking one, as shown in Figure 16-8.

Before you run this Web form, let's make it look a little better. Click on the `Calendar` control on the page. On the top-right corner of the control you should see a little right-pointing arrow. Click it to open up the "`Common Calendar Tasks`" menu. Select the `Auto Format` menu option. You can now use the Auto Format dialog box to select from a number of predefined visual formats for your calendar. Click on each format to view a preview. Finally, select the `Colorful 2` option and click OK. Your `Calendar` control is instantly transformed visually using the styles defined in the Auto Format option.

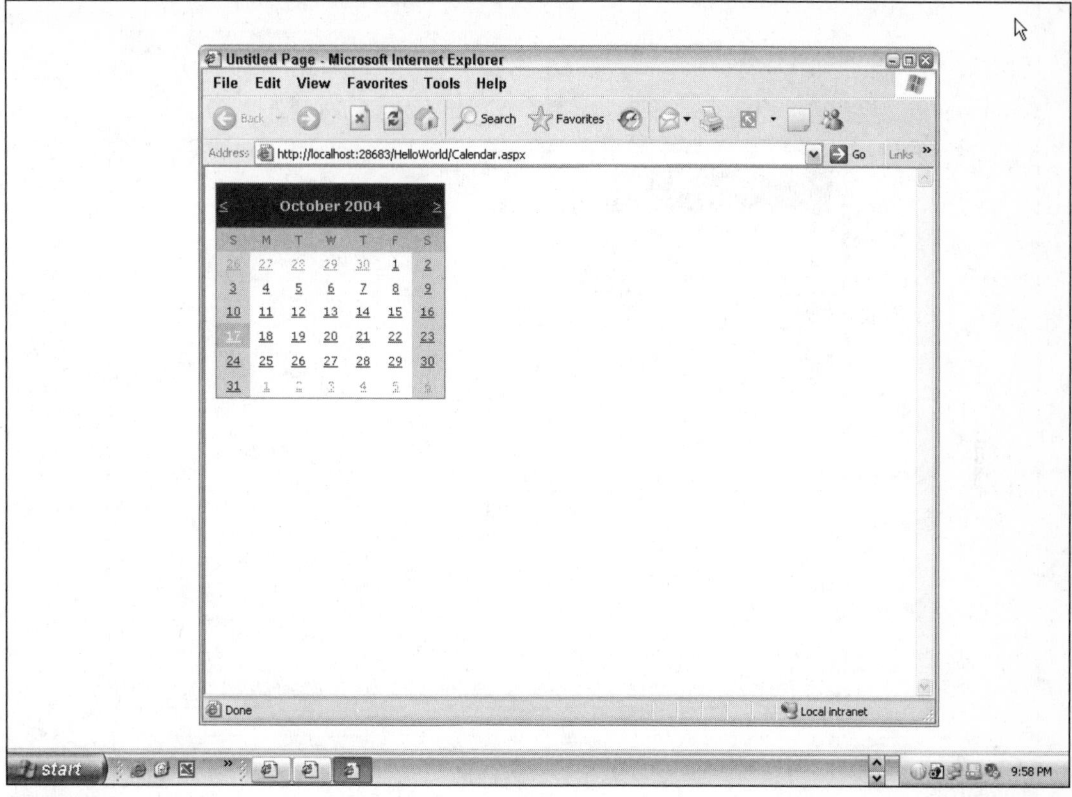

Figure 16-8

We now need to make sure that the `Calendar.aspx` page opens up when we run the application. To ensure this, right click on the `Calendar.aspx` page in the Solution Explorer and select `Set as Start Page` from the context menu. Run the Web site by pressing Ctrl-F5.

All you did was drag and drop a calendar control onto a Web page in your design environment and set a few properties to make it look different. In your browser, you should have a Web page that looks like Figure 16-9.

This is not a static calendar painted on the browser. It is fully interactive. Click any day and it becomes highlighted in green. Click another day and the selection changes. Click the other months listed at the top of the calendar and the month view automatically changes. Your Web form contains the `Calendar` control that is being executed at runtime.

The `Calendar` control is a Web form server control that is outputting plain HTML to be viewed in the browser (IE and Netscape version 4.0 or above). And you developed it using Visual Basic .NET (VB.NET), just like developing and deploying a VB.NET Windows Form.

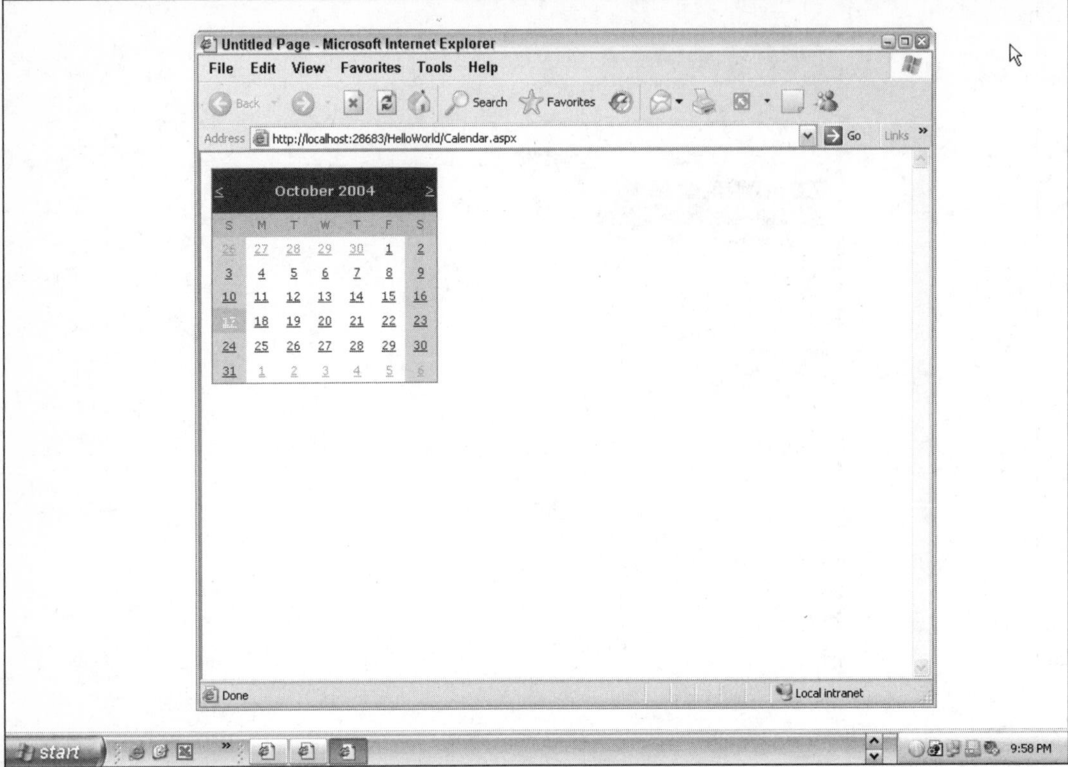

Figure 16-9

The Processing Flow of ASP.NET Web Forms

Traditional Web development, especially ASP development, has always involved generating an HTML page and adding script code to it. An ASP page in traditional ASP (ASP versions prior to ASP.NET) was therefore a plain text file separated into blocks of ASP code and HTML code. When a browser requested an ASP page from the Web server, the ASP engine kicked in and parsed the page, before its output was sent back to the browser. At runtime, the ASP engine would interpret the ASP code one line at a time. It would execute each line that contained ASP script code, and would output unchanged every line that contained plain HTML text. The traditional ASP Web development model was therefore one of HTML pages with code added to them.

Figure 16-10 shows a simplistic view of how the processing flow takes place in traditional ASP.

Web forms turn this paradigm of Web development upside down. With Web forms, every page is actually an executable program. The page's execution results in HTML text being outputted. You can therefore focus on developing with controls and code elements that output HTML, instead of worrying about interspersing code around HTML text.

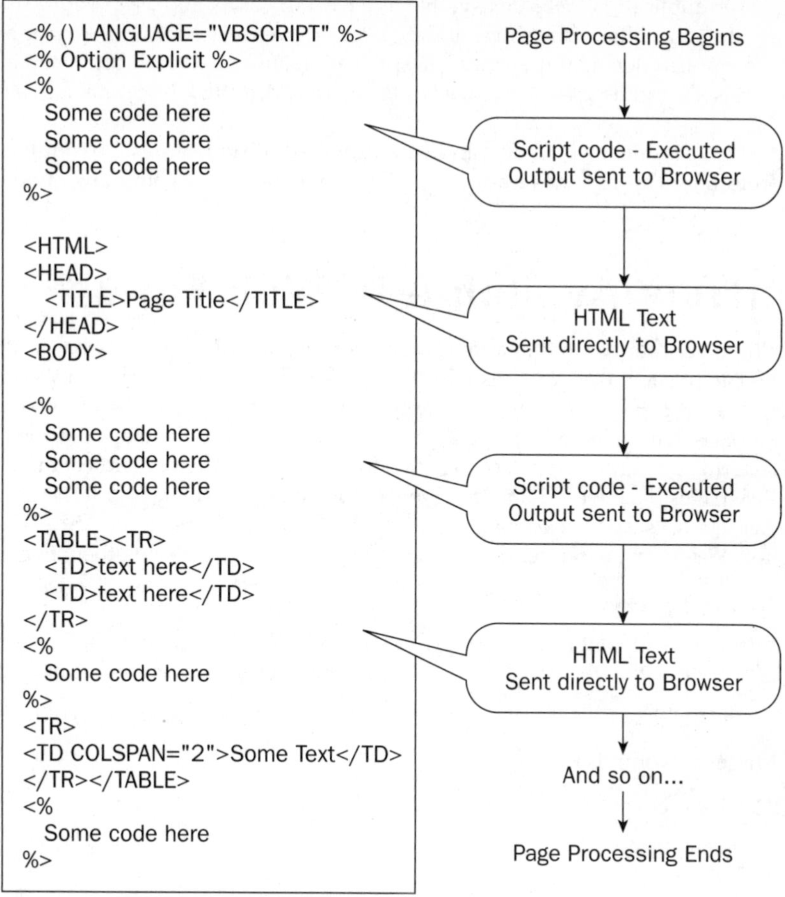

Figure 16-10

So, what exactly is a Web form? Well, a VB.NET Web form is an ASP.NET page. As you've already seen, Web forms (or ASP.NET pages) are text files with an .aspx extension. On a .NET server (or indeed any IIS server where the .NET Framework has been installed), when a browser requests an .aspx file, the ASP.NET runtime parses and compiles the page. This process is similar to the way that the ASP engine in ASP 3.0 and below parsed the page. The main difference is that the ASP.NET runtime compiles the page into a .NET class file. The code is compiled and not interpreted line by line each time the page is executed using a script engine. This results in improved runtime performance since the Web page code is compiled and stored in cache for reuse.

A typical Web application Web site (that is, a Web site that contains Web forms) developed in VB.NET will have at least one .aspx file. If you incorporate controls and code on the form, the code itself is placed in the .vb file. That is, if your Web form is called `Default`, you will end up with `Default.aspx` and `Default.aspx.vb`. The .aspx file corresponds to the traditional ASP .asp file and contains primarily HTML code that defines your Web page. The .aspx.vb file contains the code-behind-the-Web-page VB code.

In addition, a Web application Web site usually has a `Global.asax` and a `Web.config` file. The `Global.asax` file is the .NET counterpart of the `Global.asa` file used in ASP Web applications. It contains code for event handlers that fire when the application and the session begin and end. A complete description of this file and its uses is available in *Professional ASP.NET 1.0 Special Edition* (Wiley, 2002).

The `Web.config` file is new to .NET. It is an XML-formatted file that stores the configuration settings for your Web application. This includes features such as debug mode and compiling options.

The Controls Available in Web Forms

Using a paradigm very similar to the earlier versions of Visual Basic, Microsoft has introduced the concept of adding controls to a Web form visually. Every control you need to use in a Web form, whether it is a `text box` or a `button` control, you can simply drag and drop from a controls toolbox. Remember, however, that this is not the same as dragging and dropping controls in an application like FrontPage. The controls are dragged and dropped onto a Web form, but they do not manifest themselves as ActiveX Controls in Web pages. That would limit the Web applications you create to Internet Explorer alone, since a browser like Netscape does not support ActiveX Controls. Instead, the ASP.Net controls you drag and drop onto a Web form are rendered at runtime as pure HTML, allowing them to be used within all browsers.

Web form controls are different from controls used in VB.NET Windows Forms. This is because Web form controls operate within the ASP.NET page framework. There are four kinds of controls for use in Web forms:

- HTML server controls
- ASP.NET server controls
- Validation controls
- User controls

Before you take a look at these types, let's examine the idea behind server-side controls.

The Concept of Server-Side Controls

Like in traditional ASP, you can use the `<%and the %>` tags to separate ASP code from plain HTML code. However, if you rely on these tags to delimit ASP code, you will be responsible for the maintaining state when the page is submitted back to the server.

This means that, if you want to create an interactive Web application, you will be responsible for obtaining the data from the `Request` object, passing it back to the browser when the page returns, and keeping track of it. This task — maintaining state — has been a big worry for ASP programmers up till now.

For example, consider the case where you have a form with a single text box and a button that submits the form, as shown in Figure 16-11.

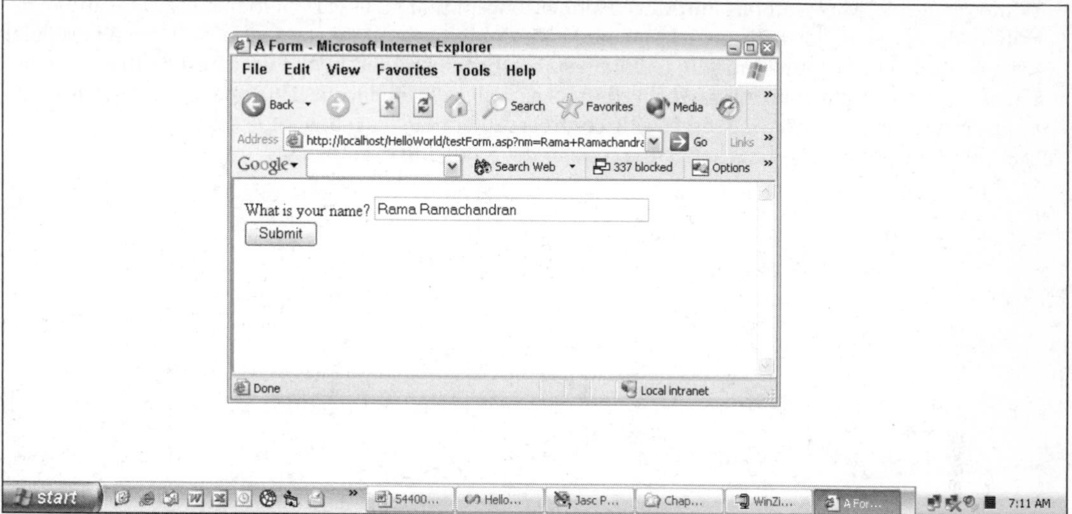

Figure 16-11

When the form is submitted, assume that it returns with the value of the text box intact. To be able to do this, you will need to code a form in this manner:

```
<html>
<head>
   <title>A Form</title>
</head>

<body>
   <form action="testForm.asp">
     What is your name?
      <input type="text" name="nm" value="<%= Request("nm") %>" size="40"
             maxlength="40"><br>
     <input type="submit" name="cmd" value=" Submit ">
   </form>
</body>
</html>
```

The programmer is responsible for maintaining the value of the text entered in the text box and returning it back to the browser.

```
value="<%= Request("nm") %>"
```

You do this by obtaining the value of the text box (named `"nm"`) from the `Request` object, and using that value as the `value` attribute of the text box. The first time around, since the `Request` object does not have a value named `nm`, it will be blank and so the user will see a blank text box. When the user enters a value and presses the Submit button, the same form is returned, but this time, with the value of the text box filled in.

With Web forms, Microsoft has introduced a new concept that takes care of managing state automatically without having to write any incremental code. Web forms allow you to indicate that a particular form control needs to automatically maintain state when submitted by the user. You do this by using the `runat="server"` attribute for the form controls as well as for the form. This one line change makes your form controls behave like server-side controls rather than just client-side controls. To take your example from above, you can change the code to the following example:

```
<html>
<head>
   <title>A Form</title>
</head>

<body>

   <form action="testForm.aspx" runat="server">
     What is your name?
     <asp:textbox runat="server" name="nm"
                  size="40" maxlength="40" /><br>
     <input type="submit" name="cmd" value=" Submit ">
   </form>
</body>
</html>
```

Save the file with an .aspx extension (to make sure that the ASP.NET runtime handles its processing correctly) and you will get automatic state maintenance without writing any further code. Notice the differences. First, it is an .aspx file. Second, the `FORM` tag itself has an indication `runat="server"`:

```
   <form action="testForm.aspx" runat="server">
```

This causes the ASP.NET runtime to create additional code to handle the state. This is done via a hidden form field that is appended to your form. If you chose to view the source of your file in the browser, this is what you would see in place of the `form` tag code:

```
<form name="_ctl0" method="post" action="testForm.aspx" id="_ctl0">
<input type="hidden" name="__VIEWSTATE"
value="dDwyMTA1NTI4MTE3Ozs++XTC7CS2N3CQ7xiWjEu4Q5P+URk=" />
```

The ASP.NET runtime has added additional code, including a form `NAME` and an `ID`, as well as a hidden field called_`VIEWSTATE`. ASP.NET uses this hidden field to transfer state information between the browser and the Web server. It compresses the information needed into a cryptic field value. All controls on the Web page that need their state information maintained are automatically tagged within this single hidden field value.

Notice too that, instead of using a simple `INPUT` tag for your text box, you used the special `asp:textbox` tag. This is required to make sure that the text box behaves like a server-side control.

HTML Server Controls

HTML Server Controls are HTML elements exposed to the server by using the `runat="server"` attribute. In VS.NET, HTML Server Controls are included within the Web forms group of the toolbox. The regular HTML Form Controls (`TextBox`, `CheckBox`, `Listbox`, and so on) are available within the HTML group.

HTML Server Controls are identical to regular HTML Form controls in look, feel, and behavior, except that the presence of the `runat="server"` enables you to program them within the Web forms page framework.

HTML Server Controls are available for the HTML elements most commonly used on a Web page to make it interactive, such as the `FORM` tag, the HTML `<input>` elements (`TextBox`, `CheckBox`, and `Submit` button), `ListBox` (`select`), `Table`, and `Image`. These predefined HTML Server Controls share the basic properties of the generic controls, and, each control typically provides its own set of properties and its own event.

In the VS.NET environment, you can create a regular HTML control by clicking the HTML group within your toolbox and then dragging a `Text Field` control onto the Web form. Then give it the name `txt First_Name` by changing its `ID` property. This will result in a regular HTML control with something like the following code:

```
<input style="Z-INDEX: 102; LEFT: 221px; POSITION: absolute; TOP: 249px"
       type="text">
```

To convert a regular HTML control to an HTML Server Control (and vice versa), simply right-click the control in the design mode and select (or uncheck) the menu option Run As Server Control. If you select it, you will see the following code:

```
<input style="Z-INDEX: 102; LEFT: 221px; POSITION: absolute; TOP: 249px"
       type="text"

       id="Text1" name="Text1" runat="server">
```

Notice the difference between the above two sections of code, the final attribute that denotes that this is a server control.

HTML controls are created from classes in the .NET Framework class library's `System.Web.UI.HtmlControls` namespace. Regular HTML controls are parsed and rendered simply as HTML elements. For example, a regular `Text Field` HTML control will be parsed and rendered as an HTML text box.

By converting HTML controls to HTML Server Controls, you gain the ability to:

- Write code for events generated on the control that are executed on the server side, rather than on the client side. For example, you can respond with server-side code to the `Click` event of a `Button`.
- Write code for events in client script. Since they are displayed as standard HTML form controls, they retain the ability to handle client-side script as always.
- Automatically maintain the values of the control on a round-trip when the browser submits the page to the server.
- Bind the value of the control to a field, property, method, or expression in your server-side code.

HTML Server Controls are included for backward compatibility with existing ASP applications. They make it easier to convert traditional ASP applications to ASP.NET (Web forms) applications. However, everything that can be done with HTML Server Controls can be done — with more programmatic control — by using the new ASP.NET Server Controls.

ASP.NET Server Controls

HTML controls are just wrappers around regular HTML tags and do not offer any programmatic advantage in terms of controlling their look and feel. ASP.NET Server Controls, on the other hand, do not necessarily map to a single HTML element and provide a much richer UI output. You have already seen this with your `Calendar` ASP.NET Server Control.

VB.NET ships with over 20 ASP.NET Server Controls, ranging from simple controls like `TextBox`, `Button`, and `Label`, to more complex Server Controls such as `AdRotator`, `Calendar`, and `DataGrid`. These controls can all be found in the `System.Web.UI.WebControls` namespace.

When you drag and drop each of these controls onto your Web form, they display their own distinctive UI. For example, a `TextBox` may simply be visible as a text box, but the `Calendar` control or the `DataGrid` control will appear as a tabular construct.

Behind the scenes, these controls are prefixed with the `asp:` tag. For example, in `Default.aspx`, when you placed a `Label` on the page and set its `Text` property to `"Hello World"`, your `Label` uses the following code to define it:

```
<asp:label id="Label1" runat="server">Hello World</asp:label>
```

You can view the HTML source of any control by right-clicking anywhere on the page and selecting View HTML Source from the context menu. Similarly, when you drag a `Button` onto the form, instead of obtaining the normal HTML `INPUT TYPE="SUBMIT"` text, you get the following code:

```
<asp:button id="btnSubmit"
runat="server"
text="Submit"></asp:button>
```

Notice that the code does not represent a regular HTML control, but rather, an ASP.NET control. The attributes refer to the ASP.NET control's properties. At runtime, the ASP.NET control is rendered on the Web page by using plain HTML, which depends on the browser type as well as the settings on the control. For example, the button above may be rendered on the target browser either as an `INPUT TYPE="SUBMIT"` HTML element, or as a `<BUTTON>` tag, depending on the browser type.

The following ASP Server Controls ship with VB.NET and are available for use in a Web form, and are found in the `Standard` section of the toolbox.

Control	Purpose
`Label`	Displays noneditable text
`TextBox`	Displays editable text in a box
`Button`	Displays a button, usually used to carry out an action
`LinkButton`	Behaves like a button, but appears like a hyperlink
`ImageButton`	Displays a button with an image rather than with text

Control	Purpose
`HyperLink`	Creates a hyperlink for navigation
`DropDownList`	Presents a list in a drop-down combo box
`ListBox`	Presents a list of items in a scrollable box
`CheckBox`	Displays a single check box allowing users to check on or off
`CheckBoxList`	Displays a set of check boxes as a group; useful when you want to bind it to data from a database
`RadioButton`	Displays a single radio button
`RadioButtonList`	Displays a group of radio buttons where only one radio button from the group can be selected
`Image`	Displays an image
`DynamicImage` (New in Ver 2)	Displays an image generated by a .Net component or .aspx page
`ImageMap` (New in Ver 2)	Displays an image with hot spots that can be used as an image map for navigation in a page
`Table`	Creates a table
`BulletedList` (New in Ver 2)	Data aware list generated in the form of an bulleted list
`TreeView` (New in Ver 2)	Displays information in a treeview format
`Panel`	Creates a bounding box on the Web form that acts as a container for other controls
`Calendar`	Displays an interactive calendar
`AdRotator`	Displays a sequence of images, either in predetermined or random order
`FileUpload` (New in Ver 2)	Creates a control capable of allowing a user to select a file and have it uploaded to the server
`ContentPage` (New in Ver 2)	Provides Previous, Next page links
`Wizard` (New in Ver 2)	Creates a wizard interface
`MultiView` and `View` (New in Ver 2)	Displays information within a container control allowing the developer to programmatically present different views of a page
`GridView` (New in Ver 2)	Displays information (usually from a database) in a tabular format with rows and columns
`DataList`	Displays information from a database, very similar to the `Repeater` control
`Repeater`	Displays information from a database using HTML elements that you specify, repeating the display once for each record
`DetailsView` (New in Ver 2)	Displays detail information in tabular format
`FormsView` (New in Ver 2)	Displays single record view of data

Validation Controls

Validation Controls are different from HTML or ASP.NET Server Controls in that they do not possess a visual identity. Their purpose is to provide easy client-side or server-side validation for other controls. For example, you may have a text box that you need the user to fill in, and you may need to only accept certain entries. For example, it could be a text box that requires a date in a certain format, like DD/MM/YY. Validation Controls allow you to generate validation scripts (client- or server-side) with a few clicks.

To use Validation Controls, you first attach the Validation Control to an input control and then set its parameters, so as to test for things like:

- Data entry in a required field
- Specific values or patterns of characters
- Entries between ranges

VB.NET ships with the following Validation Controls, also in the Web forms section of the toolbox.

Control	Purpose
`RequiredFieldValidator`	Ensures that the user does not leave a field blank
`CompareValidator`	Compares the user's entry against another value—a constant, the property of another control, or even a database value
`RangeValidator`	Makes sure that the user's entry is between the lower and upper boundary values specified
`RegularExpressionValidator`	Checks to make sure that the entry matches a pattern defined by the developer
`CustomValidator`	Checks the user's entry against validation logic that you code

The easiest way to understand the power and capability of Validation Controls is to see them in action.

Add a new Web form to your HelloWorld solution (call it `Validation.aspx`). Switch to design view and drag a `TextBox` control onto the Web form and change its `ID` property to `txtName`. Then drag a `RequiredFieldValidator` control from your toolbox onto the Web form, right next to the `TextBox`. Proceed to the next line and add a `Button` control onto the form, below the `TextBox`, and set its `Text` property to `Submit`.

Now, let's set the properties for the Validation Control. Change its `ID` to `rfvTxtName`, to signify to ourselves that it is going to be bound to the `TextBox` you just created. Then, click the `ControlToValidate` property and select the `txtName` `TextBox` from the drop-down list that appears. By doing so, you have bound the Validation Control to the `txtName` `TextBox` ASP.NET Server Control. Finally, change the `ErrorMessage` property to the text that you want to display if the user is in error: "`Required Field. Please enter your name.`"

When you are done, your screen should look like Figure 16-12.

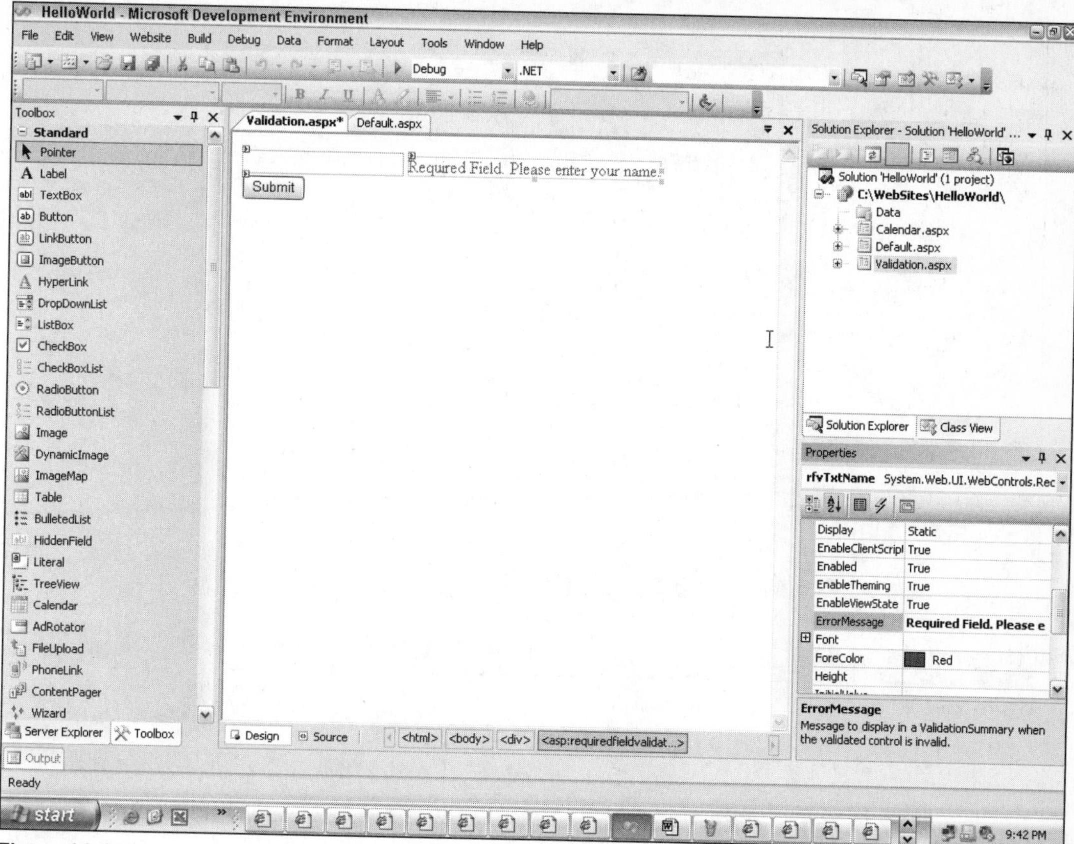

Figure 16-12

Set `Validation.aspx` as the startup page and press Ctrl-F5 to run your Web site. You should see the page in the browser with just a text box and a button visible. Do not type anything into the text box. Just click the button to simulate a user submitting the form without entering a required field: Your form submission is not accepted and you get a red error message reminding you that the field is required, as shown in Figure 16-12.

If you check the code behind this page, you will find that the Validation Controls write a lot of client-side JavaScript code to handle the data validation. However, you did not have to worry about it, you just dragged and dropped the Validation Control. The other Validation Controls also work in the same way: drop a Validation Control, attach it to a Server Control, and set the validation parameters.

User Controls

The final set of controls available are the User Controls. Similar to traditional VB User Controls, these are Web forms that you create and then use within other Web forms (see Figure 16-13). This allows you to build visual components for your Web forms — useful when creating toolbars, template UI elements, and so on. (User Controls are covered in the next chapter.)

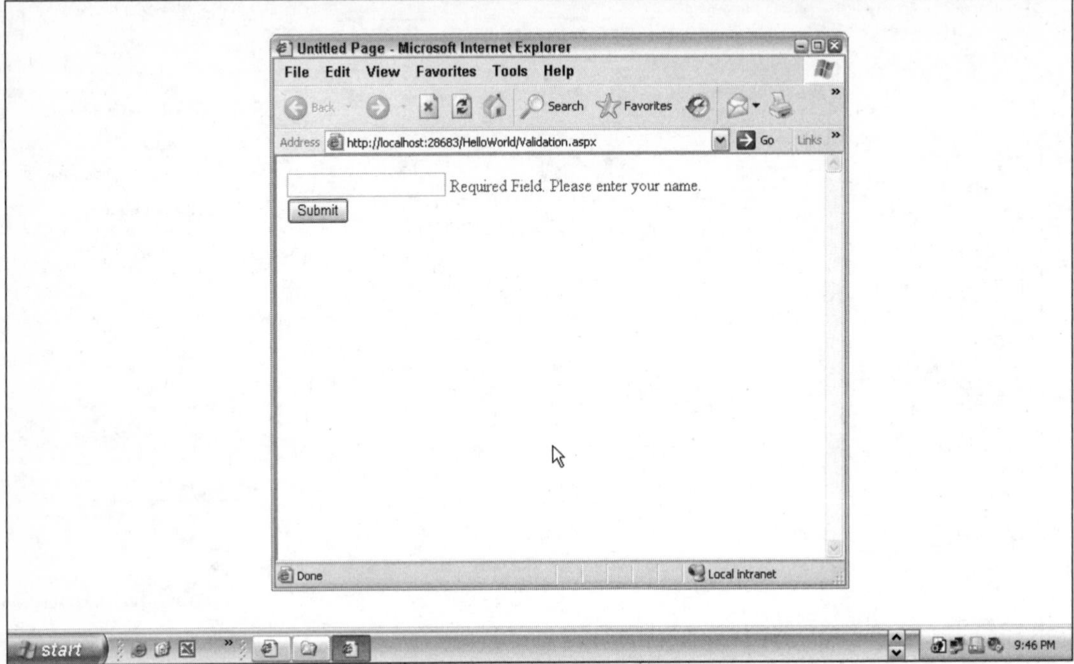

Figure 16-13

Events in Web Forms

Events in the world of Windows Forms are triggered by one of three different circumstances. An event can occur when the user makes an action: moves the mouse, uses the keyboard, and so on. An event can occur when the system makes an action: loads a page, reacts to another process or application, and so on. Finally, an event can occur without the engagement of either users or system, simply being caused by the passage of time.

In the world of the Web, however, the very stateless nature of the HTTP protocol forces Web pages to have different event handling strategies. Consider the following:

- A browser requests a Web page.
- The Web server serves the page by processing its code in a linear fashion.
- The output of the server processing is sent back to the browser as HTML.
- The browser renders the page on the screen based on the HTML output.
- At this point, the page no longer exists on the server.
- The user takes some action on the Web page.

- ❑ If the server has to react to this action, the page has to be posted back to the Web server before the Web server can react to the action.
- ❑ This process continues over and over.

Web forms expose events to the Web developer, allowing you to write code for the events. This code is different from client-side script. The code for the event is evaluated and executed on the server.

If a Web form can trigger an event for the mouse activity on a button, for instance, in such a way that the server can take action on the event, then the form will need to be posted every time the user moves the mouse. This is not practical, and because of this, Web forms expose very limited events for different controls (usually only the `Click` event).

The Web Form's Lifecycle

VB developers trying to create Web forms face a few shocks, the first of which is the concept of a Web form's lifecycle. Imagine developing a traditional VB form that goes through the following event code each time you display it on-screen:

1. `Form_Initialize:` No problem.
2. `Form_Load:` No problem.
3. `Form_QueryUnload:` Huh?
4. `Form_Unload:` What?
5. `Form_Terminate:` No kidding?

This is the VB6 form's equivalent of the ASP.NET Web form's cycle. This would be nonsensical for a VB6 form because it would load itself and then unload immediately afterwards.

In the case of Web forms, when a browser requests a page, the Web form is first loaded, then its events are handled, and finally it is discarded or unloaded from memory before the HTML output is sent to the browser. So, a Web form goes through the cycle of load and unload each time that a browser makes a request for it.

Let's take a look at the stages in the life of a Web form on the Web server before its output is sent to the browser:

- ❑ **Configuration** — This is very similar to the `Form_Initalize` and the `Form_Load` stages of a VB6 form. This is the first stage of a Web form's lifecycle on the Web server. During this stage, the page and control states are restored and then the page's `Page_Load` event is raised.

  The `Page_Load` event is built into every page. Since it occurs in the first stage of a Web form's processing, this event is a useful tool for the Web developer. The `Page_Load` event can be used to modify control properties, set up data binding or database access, and restore information from previously saved values before the page is visible on the browser.
- ❑ **Event handling** — If this is the first time that the browser has requested the page, no further events need to be handled. However, if this page is called in response to a form event, then the corresponding event handler in the page is called during this stage. Code within the event handler is then executed.

- **Cleanup** — This is the final stage in the page's lifecycle. It is the equivalent of the `Form_Unload` and `Form_Terminate` events of traditional Visual Basic. Remember, in the case of a Web form, at the end of its processing, the page is discarded. The cleanup stage handles the destruction by closing files and database connections by invoking the `Page_Unload` event. Like the `Page_Load` event, the `Page_Unload` event is built into every page. It can be used to clean up — delete variables and arrays from memory, remove objects from memory, close database connections, and so on.

Event Categories

If you have written HTML code, you know that controls on a Web page can have events associated with them. These are client-side events raised within a browser. The controls on ASP.NET Web forms also support the HTML client-side events, but in addition expose more events that you as a developer can utilize in your code. In fact, the controls in ASP.NET Web forms expose events in a manner very similar to standard Visual Basic controls on a windows form.

Events in Web forms can be classified into different categories:

- Intrinsic events
- Client-side events versus server-side events
- Postback versus non-postback events
- Bubbled events
- Application and session events

Intrinsic Events

Most Web form controls support a click-type event. This is necessitated by the fact that, in order for an event to be processed, the Web form needs to be posted back to the server. Some Web form controls also support an `OnChange` event that is raised when the control's value changes.

Client-Side versus Server-Side Events

ASP.NET Server Controls only support server-side events. However, the HTML elements that are outputted by these Server Controls support client-side events themselves. For example, the `MouseOver` event is used to change the source of an `Image` control and display a different image when the user rolls the mouse over the control. If you decide to use the ASP.NET `ImageButton` Server Control, you will be able to write code for the `ImageButton`'s `Click` event, which will be processed on the server. However, you can also write client-side code for the `MouseOver` event of the `ImageButton` to handle the rollover. If you write code for both the client- and server-side events, only the server-side event will be processed.

Postback versus Non-Postback Events

Server-side event processing happens when the form is posted back to the server. By default, these click-type events are postback events. The `OnChange` event is raised when a control's value changes. For example, if you write code for the `OnChange` event of a `TextBox`, when the user changes its value, the event is not fired immediately. Instead, these changes are cached by the control until the next time that a post occurs. When the Web form is posted back to the server, all the pending events are raised and processed.

On the server side, all of the `OnChange` events that were cached and raised before the `Click` event that posted the form are processed before the posting `Click` event.

Client-side events are automatically processed in the client browser without making a round trip to the browser. So, for example, validation client-side scripts do not need a postback to the server.

Bubbled Events

ASP.NET server controls such as the `Repeater`, `DataList`, and `DataGrid` controls can contain child controls that themselves raise events. For example, each row in a `DataGrid` control can contain one or more buttons. Events from the nested controls are bubbled; that is, they're sent to the container. The container in turn raises a generic event called `ItemCommand` with parameters that allow you to discover which individual control raised the original event. By responding to this single event, you can avoid having to write individual event handlers for child controls.

Application and Session Events

Continuing the tradition of ASP application and session events, VB.NET Web forms support the same high-level events. These events are not specific to a single page, but, rather, work at the user and/or Web application level. These events include the `ApplicationStart` and `ApplicationEnd` events for the application-level scope, and the `SessionStart` and `SessionEnd` events for the session-level (individual user) scope. You can write code for these special events within the `Global.asax` file.

Web Forms versus ASP

It is very easy to think of Web forms (ASP.NET) as the next version of ASP, that Microsoft has released a new version of ASP and is just calling it ASP.NET to equate it to the other .NET initiatives. ASP 3.0, for instance, was basically the previous version (ASP 2.0) but with new functionality, performance improvements, and one new object. This is most definitely not the case with ASP.NET and ASP 3.0.

While Web forms are the next version of ASP (ASP ceases to exist as a separate offering from Microsoft with the introduction of ASP.NET, though it will continue to be supported), it is not just an update. It is vastly different.

Let's consider the differences between ASP.NET and ASP 3.0:

- ASP was an interpreted application. This leads to poor performance, as compared to executable Windows desktop applications.

  Web forms are compiled into class `.dll` files and are invoked as "applications" on the Web server. This leads to vastly improved performance. The performance drop you see when you test your application for the very first time is, in fact, indicative of this change. ASP.NET checks to see if the source code for the page has changed in any way. If it has (like in your testing mode), it recompiles the page and saves the compiled output for all subsequent requests.

- In ASP, you are entirely responsible for managing view state and control state via code. If you want a form control to display the value entered by the user before the form is posted, you have to obtain the value from the `Request` object and use it as part of the `VALUE` attribute of the control. The onus is entirely on the Web developer.

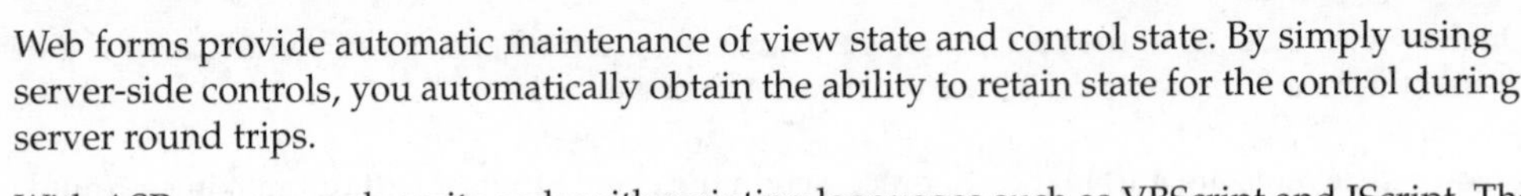

Web forms provide automatic maintenance of view state and control state. By simply using server-side controls, you automatically obtain the ability to retain state for the control during server round trips.

- With ASP, you can only write code with scripting languages such as VBScript and JScript. These languages do not support typed variables or early binding on objects.

  Web forms support VB.NET code as well as C# code. You can use a coding language that supports typed variables (`Dim x As Integer`) as well as early binding on objects (`Dim objRS As ADODB.Recordset`). This results in additional benefits, like IntelliSense making it easier to assign property values and invoke methods on objects.

- With ASP, you are responsible for generating client-side validation code. When you have forms with large numbers of controls that need validation, this can be a cumbersome task, even if you have created custom routines that can simply be copied and pasted. You still need to write the code yourself to invoke these routines.

  Web forms provide a very robust, drag-and-drop, validation control feature. Not only can you drag and drop your way to setting up validation parameters—required fields, types of accepted input, range of accepted input, and so on—Web forms also write the client-side validation routines for you.

- If you have used COM components with ASP applications, you know that every time you need to change and update the COM component on the Web server, you need to release the component from the Web server (or COM+) before you can overwrite it with the new component. ASP programmers are used to bringing down the Web server or stopping and starting the COM+ services to allow such changes.

  With Web forms, because of just-in-time compiling to native code, components can be updated without having to stop and start the Web services.

- ASP configuration settings are stored in the metabase (meta information database) of the IIS Web server. This makes it difficult to port the ASP application from one server to another. The metabase configuration settings have to be set up individually on the new Web server each time you move the ASP application.

  With Web forms, all configuration settings are stored in an XML-formatted text file that can be easily moved from one Web application directory to another. The XML-formatted `Config.web` file allows you to create portable configuration settings.

- Debugging of ASP applications has always been a daunting task. The only surefire way to debug ASP applications running on a Web server is to pepper the ASP page with `response.write` statements, to output the values of variables in your code. This is similar to peppering a VB form with `Debug.Print` statements.

  Web forms provide an automatic tracing capability. When you set the `Trace` and the `TraceMode` properties of a Web form, ASP.NET automatically maintains a log of actions performed, and their timestamp. When the page is rendered on the browser, ASP.NET automatically appends an HTML table listing all of the trace activity. You can also write your own tracing code to be appended to this log.

Transferring Control among Web Forms

Earlier in this chapter, it was mentioned that VB developers would get a shock when they try to create Web forms, because the familiar metaphor of VB development is turned upside down in the world of Web form development. Well, get ready for shock number two!

In a traditional VB application, suppose you have two forms, `Form1` and `Form2`. If you want the application to transfer control from `Form1` (which is currently open on the screen) to `Form2`, all it takes is the following code:

```
Load Form2
Form2.show
```

Of the two lines above, the first line is optional. You can use the first line if you plan to set some properties for `Form2`'s controls, or invoke a subroutine within `Form2` before showing it.

How do you do the same with a Web form? Can you "show" `WebForm2` from `WebForm1`? The answer will surprise you. No, you can't. Not in the way that you can with traditional Visual Basic.

There are two ways to transfer control from one Web form to another:

- **Hyperlink** — In `WebForm1`, you can create a hyperlink to allow the user to navigate to `WebForm2` by using a `Hyperlink` HTML tag (`<A>`). If you wish, you can pass additional arguments to the second form when navigating to it, by using the Query String (the portion of the URL that appears after the question mark in a browser's address bar). This technique of transferring control is very fast, since it transfers control to the second page directly without having to post the first page and process its events/contents.
- **Redirecting** — The second technique is to use the server-side `Response.Redirect` method to transfer control to a second page. The `Response.Redirect` issues an `Object Moved` command to the browser, forcing the browser to request the second page via a client-side request. Another similar technique is to use the `Server.Transfer` method to transfer control to a second page. The `Server.Transfer` method directly transfers control and session state to the second page without making a client round trip.

A Final Example

You'll wrap up this chapter by building a small Web Forms application. Your application is a Loan Slicer application. Consider the scenario — you have a current home mortgage loan and you pay a certain sum of money as your monthly payment towards the loan. However, by simply making one additional payment per year towards the principal repayment, you can drastically reduce the life of the loan and pay it off faster. This is loan slicing. You want to build a Web form application that will allow an end user to figure out not only what the monthly payment for a mortgage loan will be (that would be a wimpy little application), but also to see how the loan gets sliced off if the user wishes to pay an additional sum each month towards the principal.

You begin by asking the user to enter the principal loan amount, the interest rate per annum, and the number of years for which the loan will be taken.

You then calculate the monthly payment due for the loan, and display a table of how the payments slowly eat their way through the loan till the loan is fully paid off. If the user wishes to view the "loan slicing" effect, he can specify a new monthly payment value higher than the original amount, and see how quickly the loan gets paid off.

You'll build this loan slicer using the US mortgage loan formula.

So, let's begin. Start VS.NET and select New website. Select the template type to be ASP.NET Web site and give it the name LoanSlicer.

VS.NET creates a default Web form, `Default.aspx`.

Drag a `Label` control onto this form and position it at the top left (you can move it around by inserting or deleting paragraph marks, just as you would move an inserted object in a Microsoft Word file). Set its:

- `ID` property to be `lblTitle`
- `Text` property to be "`Acme Loan Slicer`"
- `Font, Size` property to `Large`
- `Font, Bold` property to `True`
- `Font, Name` property to `Verdana`

Press Enter to the right of the `Label` to create a new paragraph. Then, in sequence, insert a `Label` control, a `TextBox` control, and a `RequiredFieldValidator` control. Your Web form should look like Figure 16-14.

Set the properties for these controls as shown in the following table.

Control	Property	Value
`Label`	`ID`	`Leave this unchanged.`
	`Text`	`Principal amount ($)`
	`Font, Bold`	`True`
	`Font, Name`	`Verdana`
`TextBox`	`ID`	`TxtPrincipal`
`RequiredFieldValidator`	`ID`	`RfvPrincipal`
	`ControlToValidate`	`TxtPrincipal`
	`ErrorMessage`	`(Required. Please try again.)`

Insert two more rows of `Label`, `TextBox`, and `RequiredFieldValidator` controls, placing each set underneath the one above. To move to the next line without creating a new paragraph, use Shift+Enter to create a soft return (`<BR>` tag).

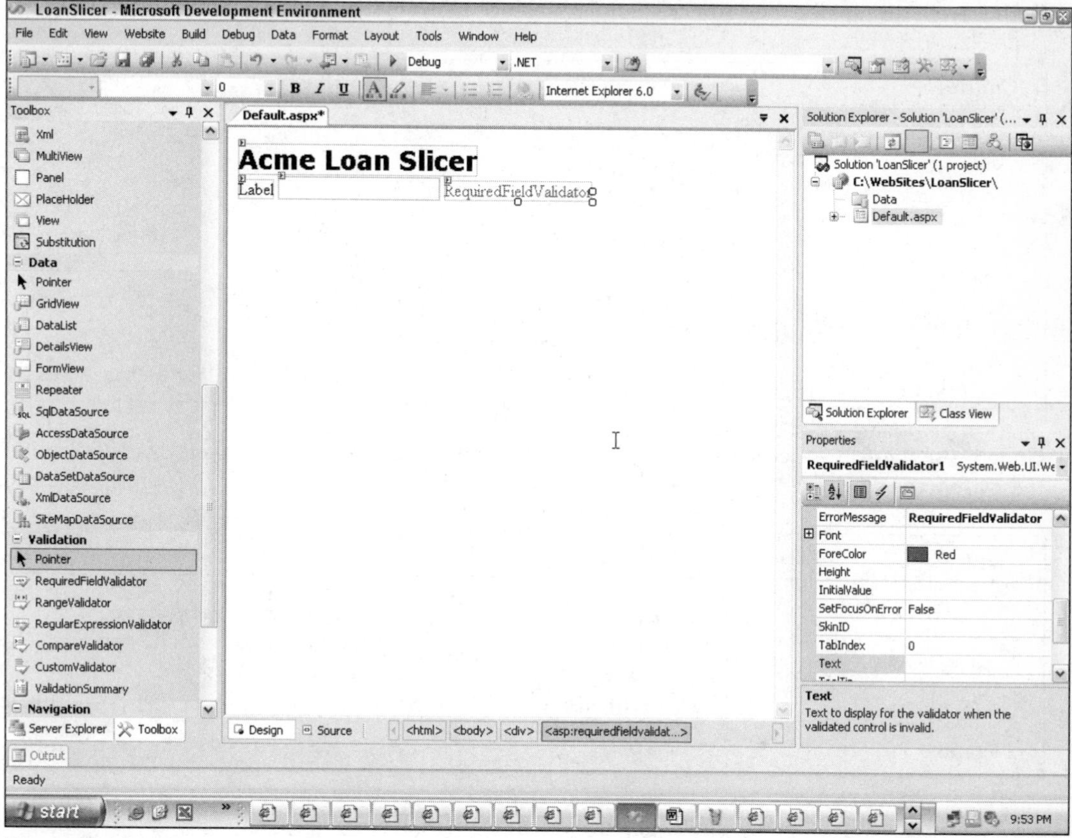

Figure 16-14

Set the properties for the second row of controls as shown in the following table.

Control	Property	Value
`Label`	`ID`	`Leave this unchanged`
	`Text`	`Interest rate (%)`
	`Font, Bold`	`True`
	`Font, Name`	`Verdana`
`TextBox`	`ID`	`TxtInterest`
`RequiredFieldValidator`	`ID`	`RfvInterest`
	`ControlToValidate`	`TxtInterest`
	`ErrorMessage`	`(Required. Please try again.)`

Set the properties for the third row of controls as shown in the following table.

Control	Property	Value
Label	ID	Leave this unchanged
	Text	Period (years)
	Font, Bold	True
	Font, Name	Verdana
TextBox	ID	TxtYears
RequiredFieldValidator	ID	RfvYears
	ControlToValidate	TxtYears
	ErrorMessage	(Required. Please try again.)

Underneath these three sets of controls, place another row with a Label and a TextBox control, with these properties.

Control	Property	Value
Label	ID	Leave this unchanged.
	Text	Loan slicer monthly amount ($)
	Font, Bold	True
	Font, Name	Verdana
TextBox	ID	TxtSlicerAmount

Underneath these four rows of controls, place a Button with these properties.

Control	Property	Value
Button	ID	BtnCalculate
	Text	Calculate

Next, place a Label control beneath the Button and set its properties.

Control	Property	Value
Label	ID	LblMonthlyPayment
	Text	Monthly payment
	Font, Bold	True
Control	Property	Value
	Font, Name	Verdana
	BackColor	Light blue (#C0FFFF)

And, finally, underneath the label, place a `GridView` control. For the `GridView` control, first set the following minimal but very important properties.

Control	Property	Value
`DataGrid`	`ID` `Visible`	`grdValues` `False`

To set the appearance of the `DataGrid` control, instead of setting individual properties, click the AutoFormat link at the bottom of the Properties window. From the list, experiment with the look you want. Figure 16-15 shows Mocha.

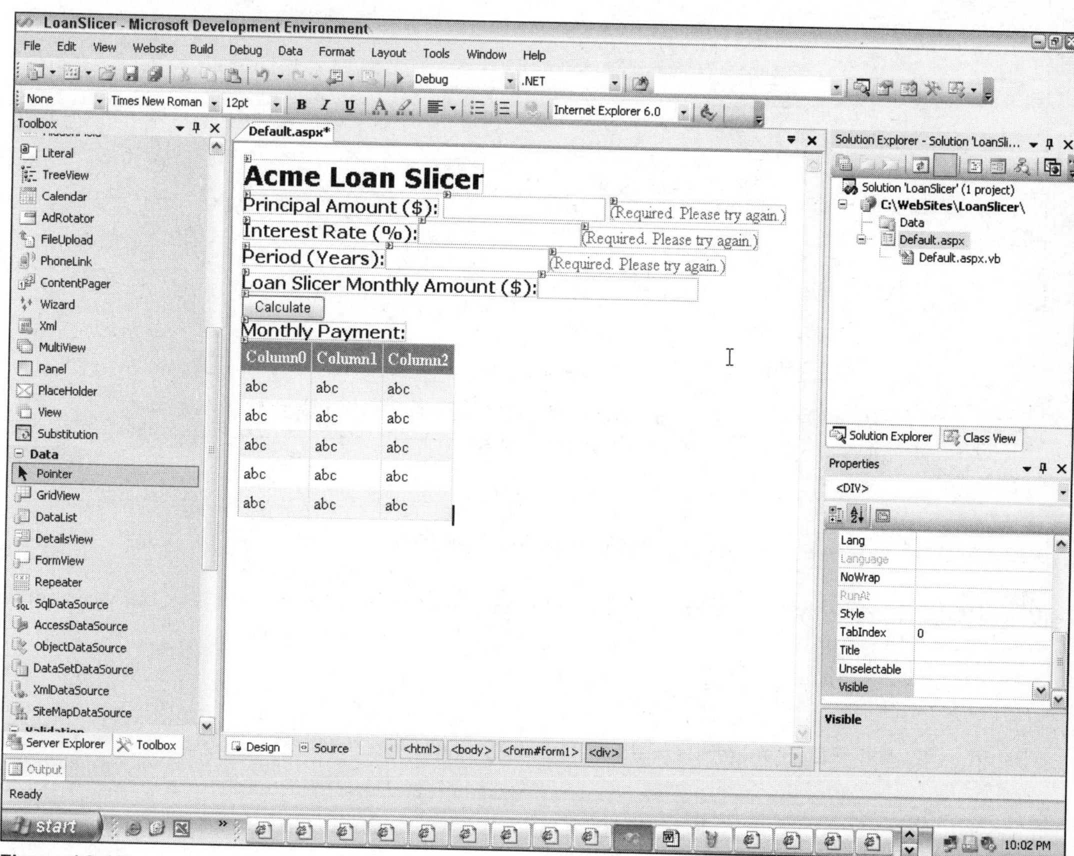

Figure 16-15

Before you go any further, let's test out this Web form. You have not placed any code in it and so it shouldn't do much, but at least you can make sure that it looks fine.

Press Ctrl-F5 to run the Web site. You should get the Web form displayed in a browser. The `GridView` and the `RequiredFieldValidator` controls should be invisible. Go ahead and click the `Calculate` button without entering any values in any of the text boxes. You should get the red error messages next to each text box as shown in Figure 16-16.

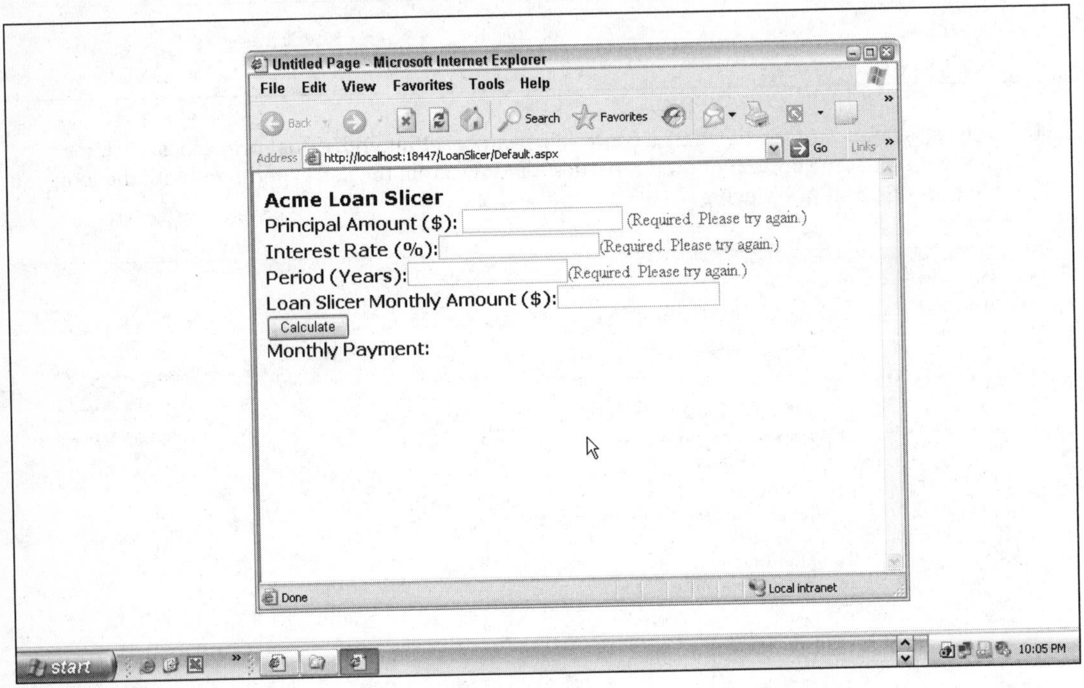

Figure 16-16

You are all set. Now let's proceed to write code for the form.

Calculating the monthly payment for a mortgage loan is a little convoluted to explain, but very simple to code. Here is the formula:

```
MP = P * ( MI / 1 -- ( 1 + MI )\ ( --N ) )
```

Assuming the following (where * is multiply, / is divide, and ^, is "raise to the power of").

Variable Name	Represents
`MP`	Monthly payment
`P`	Principal loan amount (the amount borrowed)
`MI`	Monthly interest rate in decimals (that is, the annual interest rate divided by 1,200)
`N`	Number of months in the loan

This is the formula that you will be using for calculating your monthly payment. Once you calculate the monthly payment, it is simple to construct a grid containing the following information.

A	B	C	D	E	F	G	H	I
Month/ year	Loan amount	Original Payment	Interest paid	Principal paid	Balance loan	New payment	New principal paid	New balance loan

Let's begin by adding code to your `Calculate` button. Double-click the button to add a call to a subroutine you will be building as part of the next step:

```
Sub btnCalculate_Click(ByVal sender As Object, ByVal e As System.EventArgs)
   CalculateValues()
End Sub
```

At the bottom of the `Default.aspx.vb` class, before the `End Class` statement, add this `CalculateValues` subroutine:

```
Private Sub CalculateValues()
  Dim dblPrincipal As Double
  Dim dblInterest As Double
  Dim lngYears As Long
  Dim dblMonthlyPayment As Double
  Dim dblMonthlyInterest As Double
  Dim lngN As Long

  ' -- Get values from the text boxes
  dblPrincipal = CDbl(Me.txtPrincipal.Text)
  dblInterest = CDbl(Me.txtInterest.Text)
  lngYears = CLng(Me.txtYears.Text)
  ' -- Calculated intermediary values
  dblMonthlyInterest = (dblInterest / (12 * 100))
  lngN = lngYears * 12
  ' -- Monthly Payment calculation:
  dblMonthlyPayment = (dblPrincipal * (dblMonthlyInterest / (1 - (1 + _
      dblMonthlyInterest) _  (-lngN))))

  ' -- Assign the value to the Blue label
  Me.lblMonthlyPayment.Text = "Monthly Payment: " & _
      format(dblMonthlyPayment, "$#,##0.00")

End Sub
```

After declaring all the variables you will be using, you first obtain your values from the text boxes on the form, converting them to appropriate data types along the way:

```
dblPrincipal = CDbl(Me.txtPrincipal.Text)
dblInterest = CDbl(Me.txtInterest.Text)
lngyears = CLng(Me.txtYears.Text)
```

You then calculate the intermediary variable values:

```
dblMonthlyInterest = (dblInterest / (12 * 100))
lngN = lngYears * 12
```

Finally, you are ready to calculate the monthly payment:

```
dblMonthlyPayment = (dblPrincipal * (dblMonthlyInterest / (1 - (1 + _
    dblMonthlyInterest) ^ (-lngN))))
```

You store this in the variable `dblMonthlyPayment`. You output this value as the `Text` property of the blue label on the screen, performing some formatting so that it is presented as a dollar amount:

```
Me.lblMonthlyPayment.Text = "Monthly Payment: " & _
    format(dblMonthlyPayment, "$#,##0.00")
```

That was the easy part. Let's test it again by running your application. Enter the following values: Principal = 100,000; Interest Rate = 6.75; Years = 10. You should get the output shown in Figure 16-17.

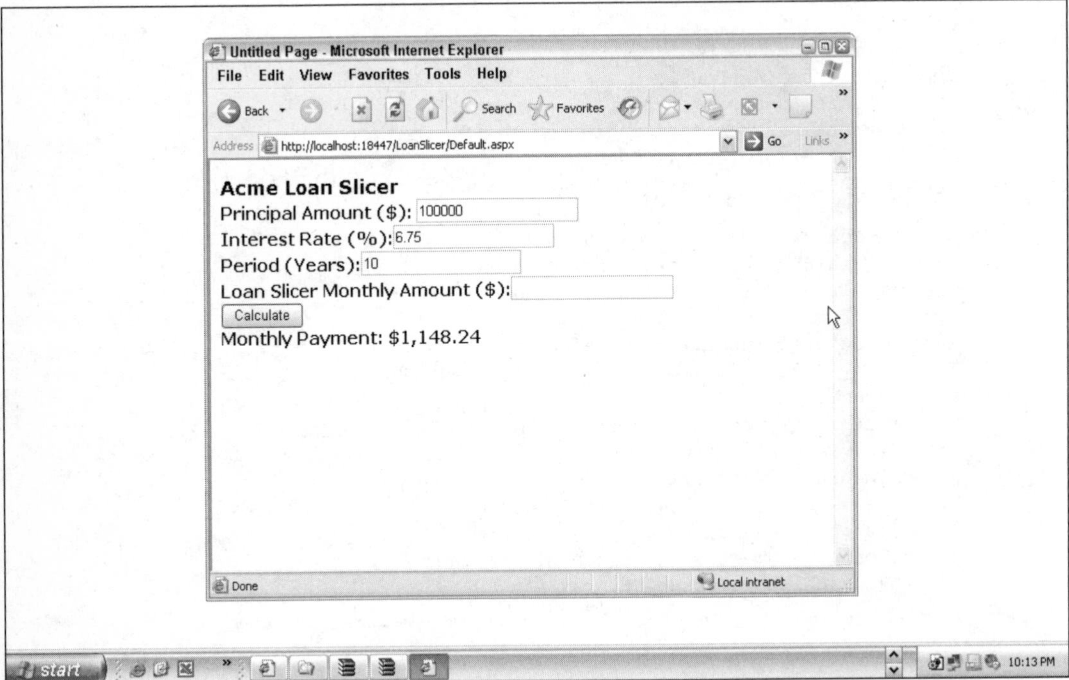

Figure 16-17

Now comes the more difficult part—populating the `GridView` with your values.

Before you look at the code, let's understand what you are trying to do. You need to display a `GridView` full of rows and columns that represent your loan payouts. You want to display the current loan amount, the monthly payment, the interest paid, the principal paid, and the balance loan amount for every month of every year in the loan period.

In addition, if the user has entered a Loan Slicer Monthly Amount—an amount that he/she is willing to pay that is larger than the monthly payment due—you need to also figure out how the new monthly payment will pay off the loan faster, and therefore "slice" it.

Normally, a `GridView` is bound to a database. You don't have a database in this scenario. You could dump the values into a database and have the `GridView` then read the database. But that would be very inefficient. A better way would be to create your own "database" on the fly. You can do that by creating a `DataTable` object and populating it with values. Your `GridView` can be bound to a `DataView` object at runtime. To do so, you need to write code as follows:

```
OurGridViewObject.DataSource = OurDataViewObject
```

A `DataView` object can be created and initialized by an existing `DataTable` object. Therefore, you can create a `DataView` object by using a `DataTable` object, as follows:

```
OurDataViewObject = New DataView(OurDataTableObject)
```

A `DataTable` object in turn consists of rows and columns, or rather `DataRow` objects and `DataColumn` objects. To create a row for a table, you use a `DataRow` object as follows:

```
OurDataTable.Rows.Add OurDataRow
```

The `DataColumn` objects can also be created at runtime by using the following code:

```
OurDataTable.Columns.Add OurDataColumn
```

And finally, you can create a `DataColumn` object by passing the `Column` definition as follows:

```
OurDataColumn = New DataColumn(strColumnName, ColumnDataType)
```

You can put all of this code together in the following `BuildPayoutGrid` subroutine. Add the following code to the bottom of the `CalculateValues` subroutine, immediately before the `End Sub`:

```
BuildPayoutGrid(dblPrincipal, dblMonthlyInterest, dblMonthlyPayment)
```

Since we will be referencing data objects from the `System.Data` namespace, add the following line at the very top of your `Default.aspx.vb` page above the `Partial Class Default_aspx` declaration:

```
Imports System.Data
Partial Class Default_aspx
```

Then, add the code for the `BuildPayOutGrid` subroutine itself to the bottom of the page:

```
Private Sub BuildPayoutGrid(ByVal dblP As Double, ByVal dblMI As Double, _
                            ByVal dblM As Double)
  ' -- Variables to hold our output data
  Dim dtPayout As DataTable
  Dim drPayout As DataRow
  Dim datMonthYear As Date
  Dim dblSlicerAmount As Double
  Dim dblNewBalance As Double
  Dim dblMonthlyInterestPaid As Double

  ' -- Make sure we have the new "Loan Slicer" monthly amount
  dblSlicerAmount = CDbl(Me.txtSlicerAmount.Text)
  ' -- if the user has not entered one, add one additional payment
  ' -- per year as the new slicer amount
  If dblSlicerAmount = 0 Then
    dblSlicerAmount = dblM + (dblM / 12)
  End If
  Me.txtSlicerAmount.Text = CStr(dblSlicerAmount)
  ' -- Create a new DataTable
  dtPayout = New DataTable()
  ' -- Create nine string columns
  dtPayout.Columns.Add(New DataColumn("Month/Year", GetType(String)))
  dtPayout.Columns.Add(New DataColumn("Loan Amount", GetType(String)))
  dtPayout.Columns.Add(New DataColumn("Original Payment", _
      GetType(String)))
  dtPayout.Columns.Add(New DataColumn("Interest Paid", GetType(String)))
  dtPayout.Columns.Add(New DataColumn("Principal Paid", GetType(String)))
   dtPayout.Columns.Add(New DataColumn("Balance Amount", GetType(String)))
   dtPayout.Columns.Add(New DataColumn("New Payment", GetType(String)))
  dtPayout.Columns.Add(New DataColumn("New Principal Paid", _
      GetType(String)))
  dtPayout.Columns.Add(New DataColumn("New Balance Amount", _
      GetType(String)))   dblNewBalance = dblP
  ' -- Populate it with values
  ' -- Start with current Month/Year
  datMonthYear = Now()
  Do While dblP > 0
    ' -- Create a new row for our table
    drPayout = dtPayout.NewRow()         drPayout(0) =
MonthName(Month(datMonthYear)) & ", " & _
        Year(datMonthYear)
    drPayout(1) = Format(dblP, "$ #,##0.00")
    drPayout(2) = Format(dblM, "$ #,##0.00")
    dblMonthlyInterestPaid = (dblP * dblMI)
    drPayout(3) = Format(dblMonthlyInterestPaid, "$ #,##0.00")
    drPayout(4) = Format(dblM - dblMonthlyInterestPaid, "$ #,##0.00")
    drPayout(5) = Format(dblP - (dblM - dblMonthlyInterestPaid), _
        "$ #,##0.00")
    ' -- new values
    If dblNewBalance >= 0 Then
      drPayout(6) = Format(dblSlicerAmount, "$ #,##0.00")
```

```
        drPayout(7) = Format(dblSlicerAmount - dblMonthlyInterestPaid, _
            "$ #,##0.00")
        drPayout(8) = Format(dblNewBalance - (dblSlicerAmount - _
            dblMonthlyInterestPaid), "$ #,##0.00")
      Else
        drPayout(6) = "PAID"
        drPayout(7) = "IN"
        drPayout(8) = "FULL"
      End If
      ' -- Add the row to the table
      dtPayout.Rows.Add(drPayout)
      ' -- Next month
      datMonthYear = DateAdd(DateInterval.Month, 1, datMonthYear)
      ' -- Starting Loan Amount is previous month's Ending balance
      dblP = (dblP - (dblM - dblMonthlyInterestPaid))
      dblNewBalance = (dblNewBalance - (dblSlicerAmount - _
          dblMonthlyInterestPaid))
    Loop
    ' -- Create a new DataView and bind it to the GridView
    With me.grdValues
      .Visible = True
      .DataSource = New DataView(dtPayout)
      .DataBind()
    End With

  End Sub
```

Let's examine this code piece by piece. You begin by declaring the variables you will need:

```
Dim dtPayout As DataTable
Dim drPayout As DataRow
Dim datMonthYear As Date
Dim dblSlicerAmount As Double
Dim dblNewBalance As Double
Dim dblMonthlyInterestPaid As Double
```

The code first makes sure that there is a valid "Loan Slicer" amount in the text box on the screen. If not, it simply adds one additional monthly payment per year to calculate a new, larger monthly payment. Finally, the text box is updated with the new "slicer" amount:

```
dblSlicerAmount = CDbl(Me.txtSlicerAmount.Text)
' -- if the user has not entered one, add one additional payment
' -- per year as the new slicer amount
If dblSlicerAmount = 0 Then
    dblSlicerAmount = dblM + (dblM / 12)
End If
Me.txtSlicerAmount.Text = CStr(dblSlicerAmount)
```

You then create a blank `DataTable`:

```
dtPayout = New DataTable()
```

You make sure that the DataTable has the columns you will need. You do this by adding DataColumns to the DataTable. These DataColumns are created on the fly by passing column definition arguments to the DataColumn that is being created:

```
dtPayout.Columns.Add(New DataColumn("Month/Year", GetType(String)))
dtPayout.Columns.Add(New DataColumn("Loan Amount", GetType(String)))
dtPayout.Columns.Add(New DataColumn("Original Payment", _
    GetType(String)))
dtPayout.Columns.Add(New DataColumn("Interest Paid", GetType(String)))
dtPayout.Columns.Add(New DataColumn("Principal Paid", GetType(String)))
dtPayout.Columns.Add(New DataColumn("Balance Amount", GetType(String)))

dtPayout.Columns.Add(New DataColumn("New Payment", GetType(String)))
dtPayout.Columns.Add(New DataColumn("New Principal Paid", _
    GetType(String)))
dtPayout.Columns.Add(New DataColumn("New Balance Amount", _
    GetType(String)))
```

The code then stores the loan amount in a new variable to calculate the effect of the new "slicer" amount also:

```
dbNewBalance = dbIp
```

You are now ready to populate the DataTable columns with values, and the DataTable with rows. To do so, you begin with the current month:

```
datMonthYear = Now()
```

You need to dump the output as long as there is an outstanding balance on the loan. Therefore, you use a Do...While...Loop till the loan amount reduces to zero:

```
Do While dblP > 0
```

The code then begins the process of creating a "database on the fly" by creating a new row for the DataTable. This new row will automatically have nine columns addressed by the column numbers 0 to 8:

```
drPayout = dtPayout.NewRow()
```

You set the values for each column in the current row. This is relatively simple. You know the initial loan amount and the monthly payment. You can then calculate the monthly interest on the outstanding loan amount and, from that, figure out how much of the monthly payment is interest and how much is the payoff of the principal itself. The balance is the amount of the loan left:

```
drPayout(0) = MonthName(Month(datMonthYear)) & ", " & _
    Year(datMonthYear)
drPayout(1) = Format(dblP, "$ #,##0.00")
drPayout(2) = Format(dblM, "$ #,##0.00")

dblMonthlyInterestPaid = (dblP * dblMI)
```

```
drPayout(3) = Format(dblMonthlyInterestPaid, "$ #,##0.00")
drPayout(4) = Format(dblM - dblMonthlyInterestPaid, "$ #,##0.00")
drPayout(5) = Format(dblP - (dblM - dblMonthlyInterestPaid), _
    "$ #,##0.00")
```

The last three columns of figures are calculated based on the new "slicer" amount using the same logic as the original amount. What this means is that the first six columns will show the loan being paid out month after month, based on the bank's monthly payment figure, while the last three columns will show the loan getting sliced and paid off much faster because of the larger monthly payment. Since you know that the loan will get sliced, you also add logic to display a text "PAID IN FULL", instead of negative numbers when the loan balance reaches zero:

```
If dblNewBalance >= 0 Then
    drPayout(6) = Format(dblSlicerAmount, "$ #,##0.00")
    drPayout(7) = Format(dblSlicerAmount - dblMonthlyInterestPaid, _
        "$ #,##0.00")
    drPayout(8) = Format(dblNewBalance - (dblSlicerAmount - _
        dblMonthlyInterestPaid), "$ #,##0.00")
Else
    drPayout(6) = "PAID"
    drPayout(7) = "IN"
    drPayout(8) = "FULL"
End If
```

Once you have filled nine columns with figures, you are ready to add the row to the `DataTable`:

```
dtPayout.Rows.Add(drPayout)
```

Since you are in a loop, you need to get your data ready for the next pass. The code increments the date by one month and updates the value of the loan amount to the balance amount remaining. You do the same for the new sliced loan balance and then complete the loop:

```
datMonthYear = DateAdd(DateInterval.Month, 1, datMonthYear)
' -- Starting Loan Amount is previous month's Ending balance
    dblP = (dblP - (dblM - dblMonthlyInterestPaid))
    dblNewBalance = (dblNewBalance - (dblSlicerAmount - _
        dblMonthlyInterestPaid))

Loop
```

When you finish processing the loop, you will have a `DataTable` filled with values. The code then creates a `DataView` based on the `DataTable` and assigns it to the `DataSource` property of the `GridView`, all in one swoop. You also make sure that the `GridView` is visible (remember, in design mode, you had set it to be invisible). Finally, invoke the `Bind` method to actually bind the `GridView` to the `DataView` created on the fly:

```
With dgValues
    .Visible = True
    .DataSource = New DataView(dtPayout)
    .DataBind()
End With
```

That's it, you will get a neat HTML table filled with rows and columns of output from the `GridView`. Run the application and enter a Principal Amount of 100,000, an Interest Rate of 6.75, a Period value of 10, and a Loan Slicer Amount value of 1,500. (See Figure 16-18.)

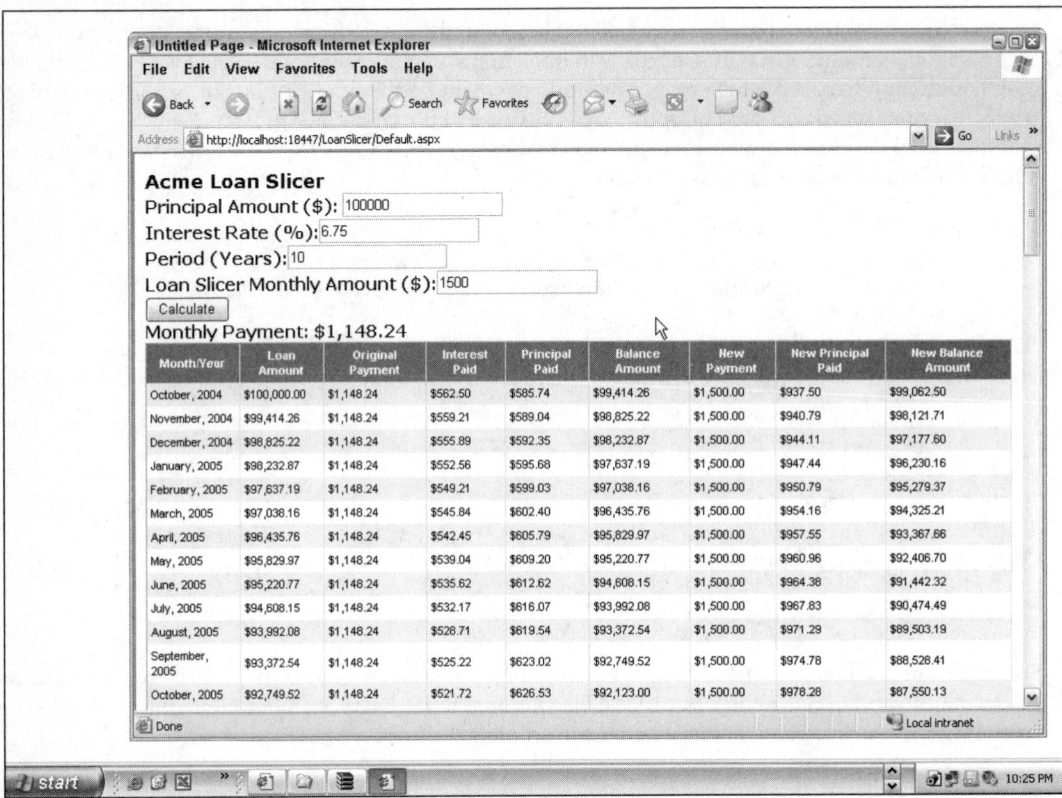

Month/Year	Loan Amount	Original Payment	Interest Paid	Principal Paid	Balance Amount	New Payment	New Principal Paid	New Balance Amount
October, 2004	$100,000.00	$1,148.24	$562.50	$585.74	$99,414.26	$1,500.00	$937.50	$99,062.50
November, 2004	$99,414.26	$1,148.24	$559.21	$589.04	$98,825.22	$1,500.00	$940.79	$98,121.71
December, 2004	$98,825.22	$1,148.24	$555.89	$592.35	$98,232.87	$1,500.00	$944.11	$97,177.60
January, 2005	$98,232.87	$1,148.24	$552.56	$595.68	$97,637.19	$1,500.00	$947.44	$96,230.16
February, 2005	$97,637.19	$1,148.24	$549.21	$599.03	$97,038.16	$1,500.00	$950.79	$95,279.37
March, 2005	$97,038.16	$1,148.24	$545.84	$602.40	$96,435.76	$1,500.00	$954.16	$94,325.21
April, 2005	$96,435.76	$1,148.24	$542.45	$605.79	$95,829.97	$1,500.00	$957.55	$93,367.66
May, 2005	$95,829.97	$1,148.24	$539.04	$609.20	$95,220.77	$1,500.00	$960.96	$92,406.70
June, 2005	$95,220.77	$1,148.24	$535.62	$612.62	$94,608.15	$1,500.00	$964.38	$91,442.32
July, 2005	$94,608.15	$1,148.24	$532.17	$616.07	$93,992.08	$1,500.00	$967.83	$90,474.49
August, 2005	$93,992.08	$1,148.24	$528.71	$619.54	$93,372.54	$1,500.00	$971.29	$89,503.19
September, 2005	$93,372.54	$1,148.24	$525.22	$623.02	$92,749.52	$1,500.00	$974.78	$88,528.41
October, 2005	$92,749.52	$1,148.24	$521.72	$626.53	$92,123.00	$1,500.00	$978.28	$87,550.13

Figure 16-18

If you scroll down the page, you can see that your calculations are on the mark. At the end of 10 years, you have completely paid off your loan amount. However, because of your Loan Slicing feature, you see that, by simply paying (about) an additional $350 per month, one can cut down the loan from 10 years to around 7.5 years. The `GridView` ends when the principal loan amount reduces to zero. Long before that, the Loan Slicer indicates that you have PAID IN FULL your loan (see Figure 16-19).

And there you have it. A simple Web Forms application with a slight twist. You also saw how to bind a `GridView` to a non-database source that you are calculating on the fly.

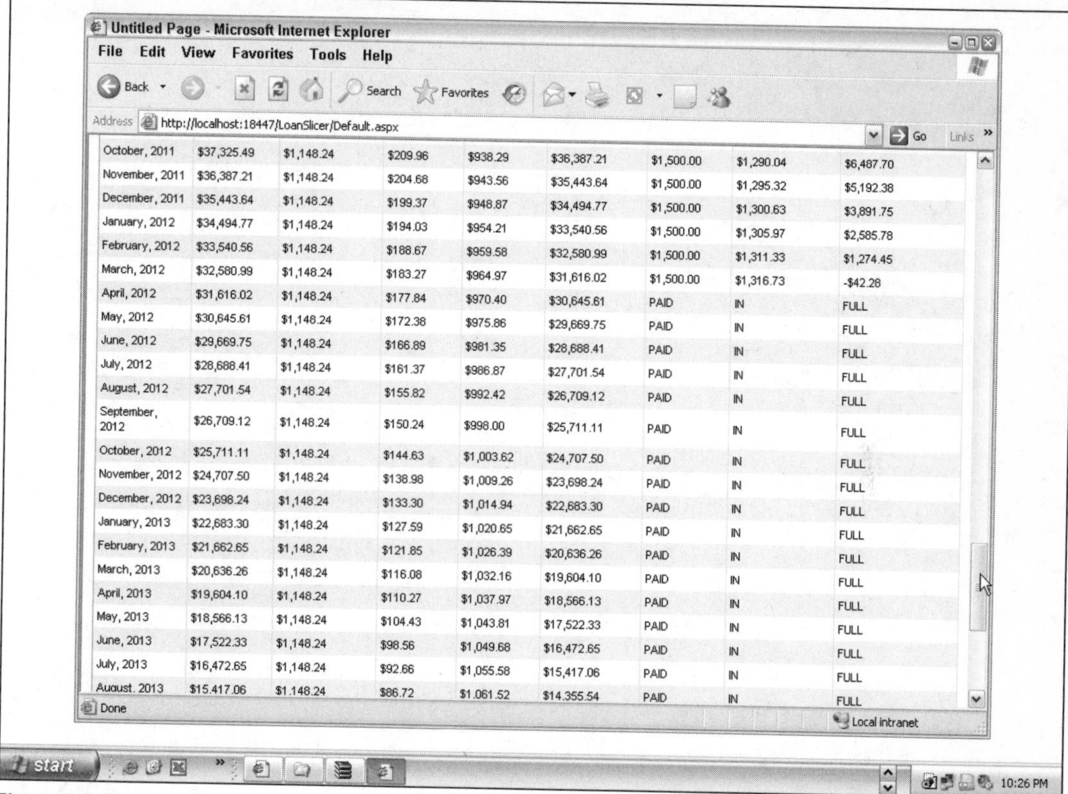

October, 2011	$37,325.49	$1,148.24	$209.96	$938.29	$36,387.21	$1,500.00	$1,290.04	$6,487.70
November, 2011	$36,387.21	$1,148.24	$204.68	$943.56	$35,443.64	$1,500.00	$1,295.32	$5,192.38
December, 2011	$35,443.64	$1,148.24	$199.37	$948.87	$34,494.77	$1,500.00	$1,300.63	$3,891.75
January, 2012	$34,494.77	$1,148.24	$194.03	$954.21	$33,540.56	$1,500.00	$1,305.97	$2,585.78
February, 2012	$33,540.56	$1,148.24	$188.67	$959.58	$32,580.99	$1,500.00	$1,311.33	$1,274.45
March, 2012	$32,580.99	$1,148.24	$183.27	$964.97	$31,616.02	$1,500.00	$1,316.73	-$42.28
April, 2012	$31,616.02	$1,148.24	$177.84	$970.40	$30,645.61	PAID	IN	FULL
May, 2012	$30,645.61	$1,148.24	$172.38	$975.86	$29,669.75	PAID	IN	FULL
June, 2012	$29,669.75	$1,148.24	$166.89	$981.35	$28,688.41	PAID	IN	FULL
July, 2012	$28,688.41	$1,148.24	$161.37	$986.87	$27,701.54	PAID	IN	FULL
August, 2012	$27,701.54	$1,148.24	$155.82	$992.42	$26,709.12	PAID	IN	FULL
September, 2012	$26,709.12	$1,148.24	$150.24	$998.00	$25,711.11	PAID	IN	FULL
October, 2012	$25,711.11	$1,148.24	$144.63	$1,003.62	$24,707.50	PAID	IN	FULL
November, 2012	$24,707.50	$1,148.24	$138.98	$1,009.26	$23,698.24	PAID	IN	FULL
December, 2012	$23,698.24	$1,148.24	$133.30	$1,014.94	$22,683.30	PAID	IN	FULL
January, 2013	$22,683.30	$1,148.24	$127.59	$1,020.65	$21,662.65	PAID	IN	FULL
February, 2013	$21,662.65	$1,148.24	$121.85	$1,026.39	$20,636.26	PAID	IN	FULL
March, 2013	$20,636.26	$1,148.24	$116.08	$1,032.16	$19,604.10	PAID	IN	FULL
April, 2013	$19,604.10	$1,148.24	$110.27	$1,037.97	$18,566.13	PAID	IN	FULL
May, 2013	$18,566.13	$1,148.24	$104.43	$1,043.81	$17,522.33	PAID	IN	FULL
June, 2013	$17,522.33	$1,148.24	$98.56	$1,049.68	$16,472.65	PAID	IN	FULL
July, 2013	$16,472.65	$1,148.24	$92.66	$1,055.58	$15,417.06	PAID	IN	FULL
August, 2013	$15,417.06	$1,148.24	$86.72	$1,061.52	$14,355.54	PAID	IN	FULL

Figure 16-19

Summary

Web forms are the future for Web development in the Microsoft .NET Framework and this chapter gave you an overview of what you can accomplish with them in VB.NET. Web forms provide you with the power of Rapid Application Development for developing Web applications. They are to Web applications what Visual Basic was to Windows applications when it was first released.

Web forms are built on the common language runtime and provide all the benefits of those technologies, including a managed execution environment, type safety, inheritance, and dynamic compilation for improved performance. Web forms provide a familiar "code behind forms" design metaphor for Visual Basic programmers. They automatically manage state and values for controls when a Web page is posted back to the server. Additionally, Web forms can generate an enormous amount of HTML code and client-side JavaScript code for data validation with a few clicks of your mouse.

17

ASP.NET 2.0 Advanced Features

ASP.NET is an exciting technology. It allows for the creation and delivery of remotely generated applications (Web applications) accessible via a simple browser — a container that many are rather familiar with. The idea of Web-based applications (in our case, ASP.NET applications) is that there is only a single instance of the application that is delivered out to the end user over HTTP. This means that the end users viewing your application will always have the latest and greatest version at their disposal. Because of this, many companies today are looking at ASP.NET to not only deliver the company's Web site, but to deliver some of their latest applications for their employees, partners, and customers.

The last chapter took a look at some of the basics of ASP.NET 2.0. This chapter will continue on the path and show you some additional and exciting technologies that you will find in ASP.NET 2.0 including master pages, configuration, data access, and more.

This will be a chapter where we will attempt to touch upon many topics as ASP.NET has become a rather large offering with many possibilities and capabilities. Sit back, pull up that keyboard, and enjoy!

Applications and Pages

The previous chapter took a look at the structure of ASP.NET pages and their lifecycle. There is quite a bit you can do with the applications and pages in ASP.NET to change how they behave or to change how you compile and deliver them. This section will look at some of these possibilities.

Cross-Page Posting

The way in which Active Server Pages 2.0/3.0 (also called *classic ASP*) worked was that values from forms were usually posted to other pages. These pages were usually steps in a process that the end user worked through. With the introduction of ASP.NET on the other hand, pages in this environment posted back results to themselves in a step called a *postback*. One of the biggest requests of Web developers in the ASP.NET world has been the ability to do postbacks not only to the page from whence the values originated, but also the ability to do postbacks to other pages within the application. This new feature is something that has been provided with the release of ASP.NET 2.0.

Cross-page posting (as it is referred) is an easy functionality to achieve now. It gives you the ability to post page values from one page (`Page1.aspx`) to an entirely different page (`Page2.aspx`). Normally, when posting to the same page (as with ASP.NET 1.0/1.1), you could capture the postback in a postback event as shown here:

```
If Page.IsPostBack Then
   ' do work here
End If
```

Now, let's take a look at `Page1.aspx` and see how you accomplish cross-page posting with ASP.NET 2.0.

```
<%@ Page Language="VB" %>

<script runat="server">
    Protected Sub Button1_Click(ByVal sender As Object, _
       ByVal e As System.EventArgs)

        Label1.Text = "Your name is: " & TextBox1.Text & "<br>" & _
            "Your appointment is on: " & Calendar1.SelectedDate.ToLongDateString()
    End Sub
</script>

<html xmlns="http://www.w3.org/1999/xhtml" >
<head runat="server">
    <title>Cross-Page Posting</title>
</head>
<body>
    <form id="form1" runat="server">
    <div>
        What is your name?<br />
        <asp:TextBox ID="TextBox1" Runat="server"></asp:TextBox>
        <br />
        <br />
        When is your appointment?<br />
        <asp:Calendar ID="Calendar1" Runat="server">
        </asp:Calendar><br />
        <asp:Button ID="Button1" OnClick="Button1_Click" Runat="server"
         Text="Do a PostBack to this Page" />
        <br />
        <br />
        <asp:Button ID="Button2" Runat="server"
         Text="Do a PostBack to Another Page" PostBackUrl="~/page2.aspx" />
        <br />
```

```
            <br />
            <asp:Label ID="Label1" Runat="server"></asp:Label>
        </div>
        </form>
    </body>
    </html>
```

With `Page1.aspx`, you can see that there is nothing really different about this page — except for the `Button2` server control. This page contains a new attribute which you will find with the `Button`, `ImageButton`, and `LinkButton` controls — the `PostBackUrl` attribute. The value of this attribute points to the location of the file that this page should post to. In this case, the `PostBackUrl` attribute states that this page should post to `Page2.aspx`. You can see that this is the only thing needed on the `Page1.aspx` to cause it to post back to another page. As for `Button1`, you can see that this is a simple button which will cause the page to post back to itself. This is nothing new as this has been the case even in ASP.NET 1.*x*. You can see the event handler for this postback in the `OnClick` attribute within the `Button1` control. Pressing this button will cause the page to post back to itself and to populate the `Label1` control that is at the bottom of the page.

Clicking on the second button, though, will post to the second page, which is shown here:

```
<%@ Page Language="VB" %>

<script runat="server">
    Protected Sub Page_Load(ByVal sender As Object, ByVal e As System.EventArgs)
        Dim pp_TextBox1 As TextBox
        Dim pp_Calendar1 As Calendar

        pp_TextBox1 = CType(PreviousPage.FindControl("TextBox1"), TextBox)
        pp_Calendar1 = CType(PreviousPage.FindControl("Calendar1"), Calendar)

        Label1.Text = "Your name is: " & pp_TextBox1.Text & "<br>" & _
            "Your appointment is on: " & _
            pp_Calendar1.SelectedDate.ToLongDateString()
    End Sub
</script>

<html xmlns="http://www.w3.org/1999/xhtml" >
<head runat="server">
    <title>Second Page</title>
</head>
<body>
    <form id="form1" runat="server">
    <div>
        <asp:Label ID="Label1" Runat="server"></asp:Label>
    </div>
    </form>
</body>
</html>
```

In this page, the first step is that in the `Page_Load` event, instances of both the `TextBox` and `Calendar` controls are created. From here, these instances are populated with the values of these controls on the previous page (`Page1.aspx`) by using the `PreviousPage.FindControl()` method. The `String` value assigned to the `FindControl` method is the `Id` value of the ASP.NET server control from the originating page (in our case, `TextBox1` and `Calendar1`). Once you have assigned the values to these control instances, you can then start working with the new controls and their values as if they were posted from the same page.

You can also expose the server controls and other items as properties from `Page1.aspx`. This is illustrated here in this partial code sample:

```
<%@ Page Language="VB" %>

<script runat="server">
    Public ReadOnly Property pp_TextBox1() As TextBox
        Get
            Return TextBox1
        End Get
    End Property

    Public ReadOnly Property pp_Calendar1() As Calendar
        Get
            Return Calendar1
        End Get
    End Property

    Protected Sub Button1_Click(ByVal sender As Object, _
       ByVal e As System.EventArgs)

        Label1.Text = "Your name is: " & TextBox1.Text & "<br>" & _
            "Your appointment is on: " & Calendar1.SelectedDate.ToLongDateString()
    End Sub
</script>
```

Once you have exposed the properties you want from `Page1.aspx`, then you can easily get at these properties in the cross-page postback by then using the new `PreviousPageType` page directive. This is illustrated here in the following example:

```
<%@ Page Language="VB" %>
<%@ PreviousPageType VirtualPath="~/Page1.aspx" %>

<script runat="server">
    Protected Sub Page_Load(ByVal sender As Object, ByVal e As System.EventArgs)
        Label1.Text = "Your name is: " & PreviousPage.pp_TextBox1.Text & "<br>" & _
            "Your appointment is on: " & _
            PreviousPage.pp_Calendar1.SelectedDate.ToLongDateString()
    End Sub
</script>
```

After your properties on `Page1.aspx`, you can access them easily by strongly typing the `PreviousPage` property on `Page2.aspx` by the use of the `PreviousPageType` directive. The `PreviousPageType` directive specifies the page the post will come from. Using this directive allows you to specifically point at `Page1.aspx`. This is done using the `VirtualPath` attribute of the `PreviousPageType` directive. The `VirtualPath` attribute takes a `String` value whose value is the location of the directing page.

Once this association has been made, you can then use the `PreviousPage` property and you will see that the `pp_TextBox1` and `pp_Calendar1` properties that were created on `Page1.aspx` are now present in Visual Studio 2005's IntelliSense. You will find that working with the `PreviousPage` property is a bit easier and is less error prone than using weak-typing. This is shown here in Figure 17-1.

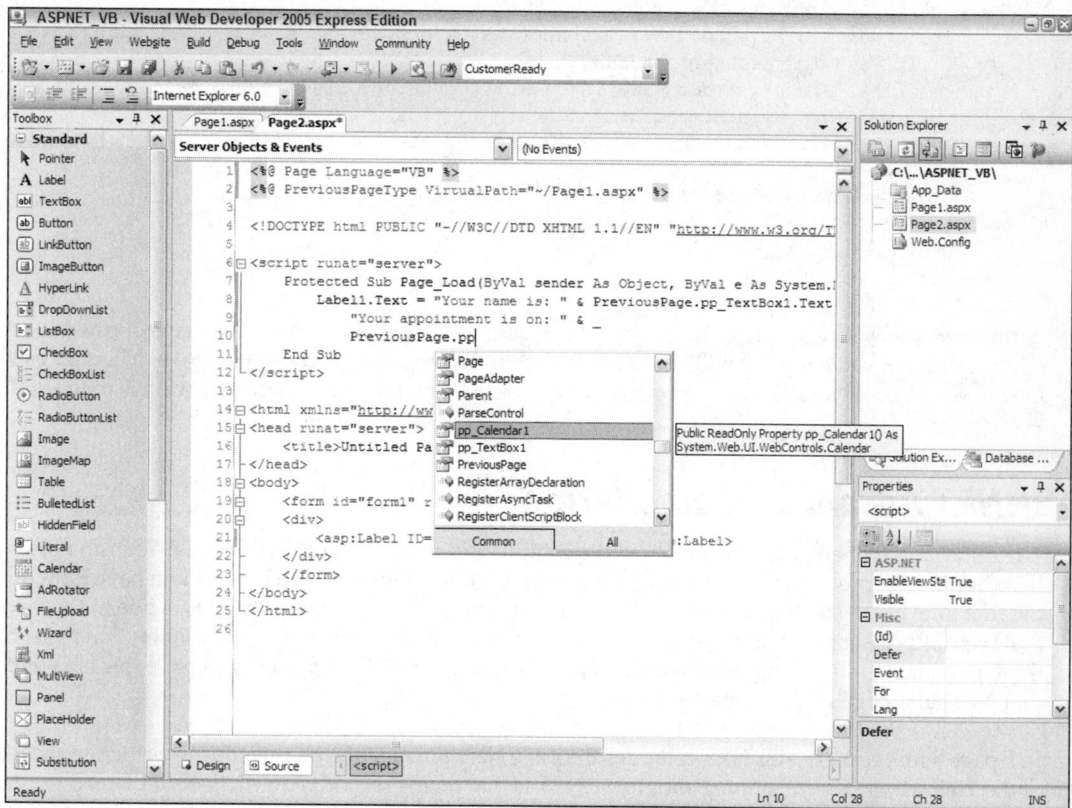

Figure 17-1

One thing to be careful of is to guard against browsers hitting a page that is expecting information from a cross-page post and this action causing errors if the information the second page is expecting isn't there. Pages that were looking for postback information was something you always had to guard against before — even when dealing with ASP.NET pages (1.0/1.1) that performed postbacks to themselves. With standard pages that aren't cross-page posting, you would protect your code from this postback behavior through the use of the `Page.IsPostBack` property as shown here:

```
If Page.IsPostBack Then
    ' code here
End If
```

When cross-page posting, you will want to use the `Page.IsCrossPagePostBack` property.

```
<%@ Page Language="VB" %>
<%@ PreviousPageType VirtualPath="~/Page1.aspx" %>

<script runat="server">
    Protected Sub Page_Load(ByVal sender As Object, ByVal e As System.EventArgs)
        If Page.IsCrossPagePostBack Then
         Label1.Text = "Your name is: " & PreviousPage.pp_TextBox1.Text & "<br>" & _
              "Your appointment is on: " & _
              PreviousPage.pp_Calendar1.SelectedDate.ToLongDateString()
        Else
          Server.Transfer("Page1.aspx")
        End If
    End Sub
</script>
```

In this example, if someone hits this page without going to `Page1.aspx` first to get cross-posted to `Page2.aspx`, then the request will be checked to see if the request is a cross-post. If it is (checked using the `Page.IsCrossPagePostBack` property), then the code is run, otherwise the request is redirected to `Page1.aspx`.

ASP.NET Advanced Compilation

The last chapter, Chapter 16, covered how the compilation process works in ASP.NET. You can notice this compilation process and how it works when you hit one of the ASP.NET pages you have built for the first time in the fact that it takes a few seconds for the page to be generated. This is due to the fact that the ASP.NET application is being compiled into intermediate code when you first hit that page. One thing that makes this situation even less enjoyable is that each and every page will have this lag when that particular page is first requested.

In a page's first request, ASP.NET compiles the page class into a DLL and then this is written to the disk of the Web server. The great thing about ASP.NET is that on the second request, instead of need to compile the page again, the DLL is accessed instead — making the request for the page far quicker than otherwise. You will notice this yourself if you hit the refresh button on your browser to re-request the same page. You will notice a new snappiness to the page.

Due to how the pages are compiled in ASP.NET, whenever you make changes to your pages within your application, the application is recompiled again and each and every page will again have this initial drag as it is compiled. This can be quite a pain if you are working with larger sites and you really can't afford this kind of pause to page generation (even if it is only one time).

ASP.NET 2.0 includes a couple of precompilation tools so that you don't have to experience this cost of page-by-page compilation. Both of these processes precompile your entire application at once. The first precompilation option is to invoke `precompile.axd` directly in the browser as if it was a page of your application. If you are using the Web server that is built into Visual Studio 2005, your request would be structured in the following format:

```
http://[host]:[port]/[application name]/precompile.axd
```

Though if you are using Microsoft's Internet Information Server, your request would be structured in the following format:

```
http://[host]/[application name]/precompile.axd
```

Once run, and if successful, you will be notified in large bold text:

```
The application was successfully precompiled.
```

If there is an error on any of the pages of your application, you will be notified of this through this compilation process which will make note of the page and line of the error. If successful, this precompilation process will have gone through each element of your application and will have successfully compiled it all into a DLL, thereby removing the churn you would normally experience hitting each of your pages for the first time.

The other method of precompilation is for when you are going to need to precompile your applications that are meant to be deployed. Contained within the .NET Framework 2.0, you will find a tool—`aspnet_compiler`. You will find this tool at `C:\Windows\Microsoft.NET\Framework\v2.0.[xxxxx]\`.

This is a command-line tool and you will simply need to navigate the aforementioned location to use it. In the simplest case, you would use the following structure to precompile your ASP.NET application.

```
aspnet_compiler -v [Application Name] -p[Physical Location] [Target]
```

For an example of using this compiler, let's suppose that you are compiling an application called `Wrox` which is located at `C:\Websites\Wrox`. For this, you would use the following construction:

```
aspnet_compiler -v /Wrox -p C:\Websites\Wrox c:\Wrox
```

If successful, the application will be compiled. The output of a successful compilation is shown here in Figure 17-2.

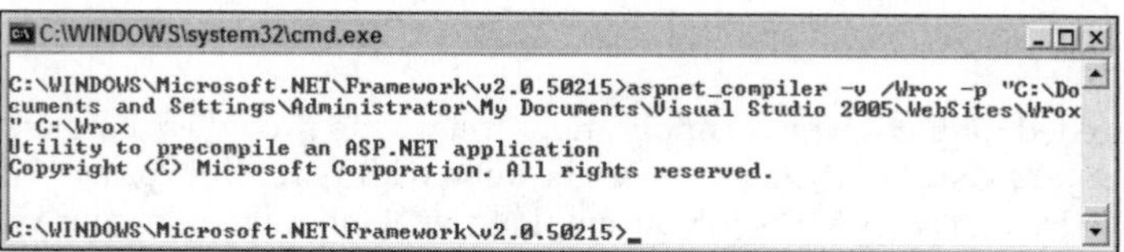

Figure 17-2

The nice thing about this compilation process is that it hides your code for you by packaging it into a DLL where it will be quite hidden for casually prying eyes. If you look at the target location of the compilation process, you will still see the same structure and files as you had before, but if you look at the contents of the .aspx files, you will see the following:

```
This is a marker file generated by the precompilation tool,
And should not be deleted!
```

If you look at what was compiled by the `aspnet_compiler` tool, you will find a `Code.dll` in the `bin` folder. This is where all the code from the pages is located. To deploy this precompiled application, you will not only need to move the `Code.dll` file, but each folder and placer file which was generated by the compiler. Move everything that was generated by the compiler to the target server and the ASP.NET application will be able to run without any concerns.

One important point about this second precompilation process is that it doesn't precompile each and every file that is contained within your application. The files that are excluded from the precompilation process include:

- HTML files
- XML files
- XSD files
- Web.config files
- Text files

If you want these types of files also precompiled along with the rest of your files, one trick is to change the file extensions of the files that allow for it to be an .aspx extension. Doing this will cause these files' contents to also be batched in with the content from the other pages in the compilation process, thereby obfuscating their contents.

Master Pages

Many Web applications are built so that each of the pages of the application has some similarities. For instance, there might be a common header that is used on each and every page of your applications There also may be other common page elements including navigation sections, advertisements, footers, and more. It really isn't so common to have your Web pages each have their own unique look and feel to them. What people are looking for in their applications is some kind of commonality to give the end user what works through a multipaged application.

What is really needed for these types of applications is a way to provide a template that can be used by your pages—a sort of visual inheritance (as can be done with Windows Forms). With a new feature in ASP.NET 2.0 called *master pages*, you can now employ visual inheritance in your Web applications.

The use of master pages means that you are working with a template file (the master page) which has a .master extension. Once a .master page is created, you can then take a *content page*, with an .aspx extension, and make an association between the two files. Doing this will allow ASP.NET to take these two files and combine them into a single Web page to display in a browser. Figure 17-3 shows a diagram of how this works.

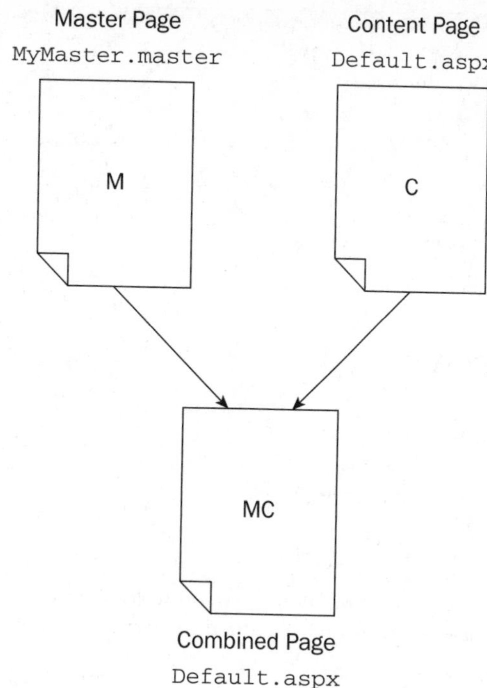

Figure 17-3

Let's now take a look at how we would make this work by first creating the master page.

Creating a Master Page

The first step is to create a template that will end up being our master page. You can build a master page using any text editor (such as Notepad), but you will find it far easier to use Visual Studio 2005 or Visual Web Developer, as I will show you here.

Start within the Solution Explorer. Right-click on the solution and select Add New Item. In the Add New Item dialog, you will find the option to add a master page to the solution. This is illustrated here in Figure 17-4.

Your master page options are quite similar to that of working with a standard .aspx page. You can either create master pages to be inline or you can have master pages which utilize the code-behind model. If you wish to use the code-behind model, make sure that you have the 'Place code in separate file' check box checked in the dialog — otherwise leave it blank. Creating an inline master page will produce a single .master file. Using the code-behind model produces a `.master` file in addition to a `.master.vb` or `.master.cs` file.

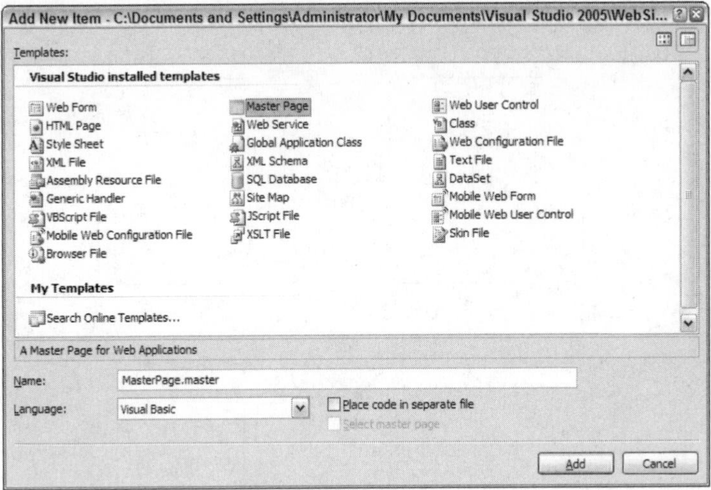

Figure 17-4

A master page should be built so that it contains one or more content regions that are utilized by the content pages. The following master page example (named `Wrox.master`) contains two of these content areas:

```
<%@ Master Language="VB" %>

<!DOCTYPE html PUBLIC "-//W3C//DTD XHTML 1.1//EN"
 "http://www.w3.org/TR/xhtml11/DTD/xhtml11.dtd">

<script runat="server">

</script>

<html xmlns="http://www.w3.org/1999/xhtml" >
<head runat="server">
    <title>Wrox</title>
</head>
<body>
    <form id="form1" runat="server">
    <div>
        <table cellpadding="3" border="1">
            <tr bgcolor="silver">
                <td colspan="2"><h1>The Wrox Company Homepage</h1></td>
            </tr>
            <tr>
                <td>
                    <asp:ContentPlaceHolder ID="ContentPlaceHolder1"
                     Runat="server">
                    </asp:ContentPlaceHolder>
                </td>
```

```
                    <td>
                        <asp:ContentPlaceHolder ID="ContentPlaceHolder2"
                         Runat="server">
                        </asp:ContentPlaceHolder>
                    </td>
                </tr>
                <tr>
                    <td colspan="2">Copyright 2006 - Wrox</td>
                </tr>
            </table>
        </div>
        </form>
</body>
</html>
```

The first thing to notice is the `<% Master %>` directive at the top of the page instead of the standard `<% Page %>` directive. This specifies that this is a master page and cannot be generated without a content page associated with it. It isn't a page that you can pull up in the browser. In this case, the `Master` directive simply uses the `Language` attribute and nothing more, but you will find that it has a number of other attributes at its disposal to fine-tune the behavior of the page.

The idea is to code the master page as you would any other `.aspx` page. This master page contains a simple table and two areas that are meant for the content pages. These areas are defined with the use of the `ContentPlaceHolder` server control. This page contains two `ContentPlaceHolder` controls. It will be *only* in these two specified areas where content pages will be allowed to interject content into the dynamically created page (as you will shortly see).

The nice thing about working with master pages is that you don't only have to work with them in the code view of the IDE, but Visual Studio 2005 also allows for you to work with them in the design view as well. This is illustrated here in Figure 17-5.

You can see that in this view, you can work with the master page by simply dragging and dropping controls onto the design surface just as you would with any typical .aspx page.

Creating the Content Page

Now that there is a master page in your project that you can utilize, the next step is to create a content page which will do just that. To do this, again right-click on the solution from within the Solution Explorer of Visual Studio 2005 and select Add New Item. This time though, we are going to add a typical Web Form to the project. Though, before you hit the Add button, be sure that you check the Select a Master Page check box in the dialog. This informs VS2005 that we are going to be building a content page that will be associated with a master page. Doing this will then pull up a new dialog, which will allow you to select a master page to associate this new file with. This is shown here in Figure 17-6.

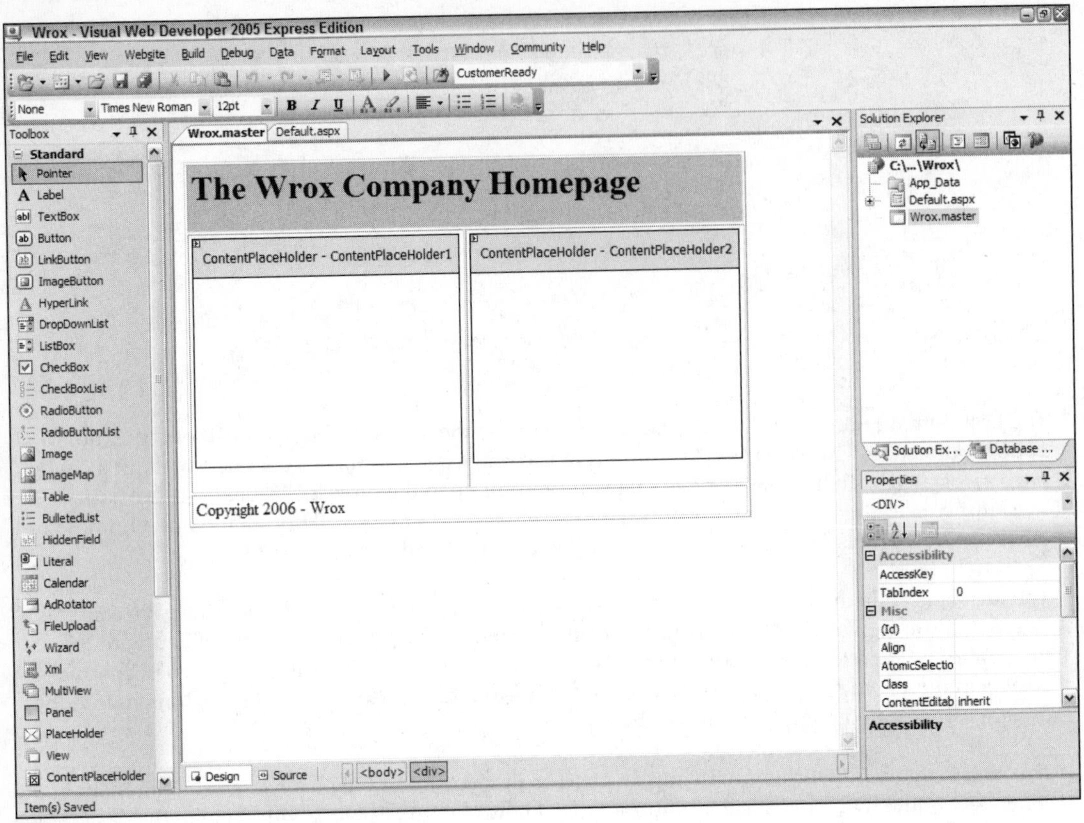

Figure 17-5

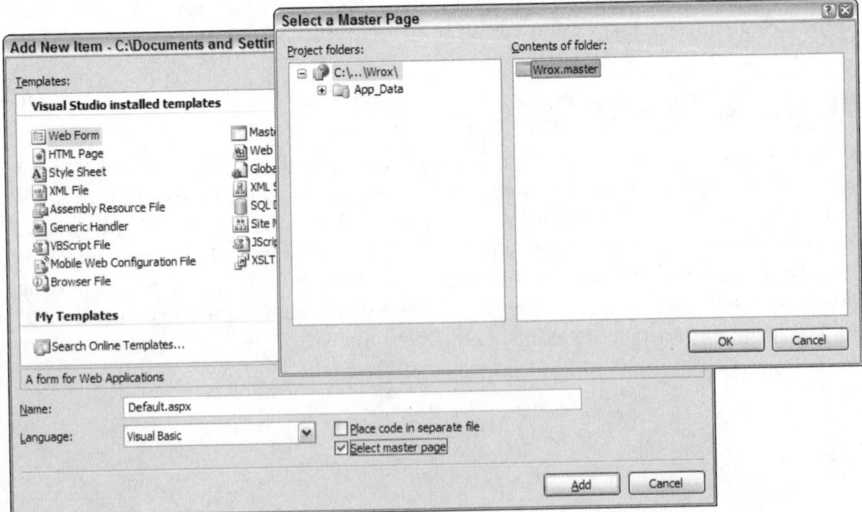

Figure 17-6

In this case, if you have been following along with the example, you should only have a single master page available in the dialog, though it is possible to have as many different master pages as you wish in a single project. Select the `Wrox.master` page and press the OK button.

The page created will have only a single line of code to it:

```
<%@ Page Language="VB" MasterPageFile="~/Wrox.master" Title="Untitled Page" %>
```

There is quite a bit that is different with this file than a typical .aspx page. First off, there is none of the default HTML code, script tags, and DOCTYPE declarations that are the norm. The other change is the addition of the `MasterPageFile` attribute in the `Page` directive. This new attribute makes the association to the master page which will be used for this content page. In this case, it is the `Wrox.master` file that we created earlier.

Though there isn't much to show while in the Source view of Visual Studio when looking at a content page, the real power of master pages can be seen when you switch to the Design view of the same page. This is shown here in Figure 17-7.

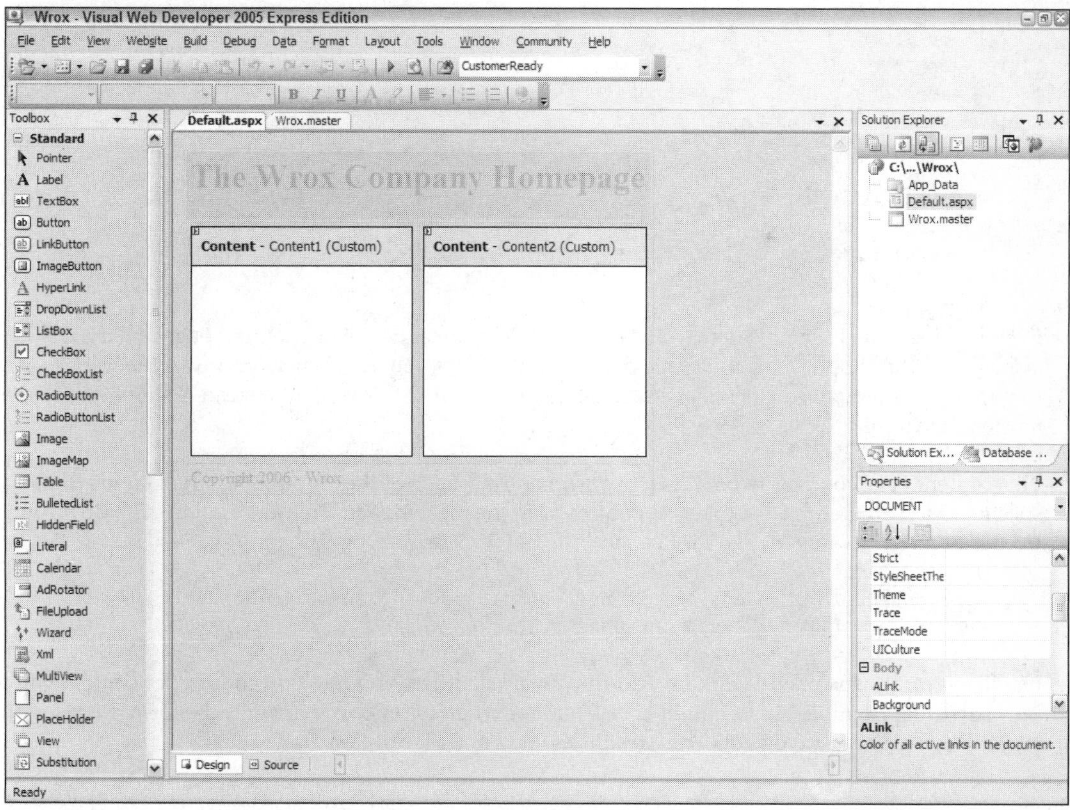

Figure 17-7

This view shows you the entire template and the two content areas that this content page is allowed to deal with. All the grayed-out areas are off limits and do not allow for any changes from the content page — while the lighted areas allow for you to deal with any type of content you wish. For instance, not only can you place raw text in these content areas, but anything that you would normally place into a typical .aspx page can also be placed in these content areas as well. For an example of this, let's create a simple form in one of the content areas and place an image in the other. This code is shown here:

```
<%@ Page Language="VB" MasterPageFile="~/Wrox.master" Title="My Content Page" %>

<script runat="server">
 Protected Sub Button1_Click(ByVal sender As Object, ByVal e As System.EventArgs)
    Label1.Text = "Hello " & Textbox1.Text
 End Sub
</script>

<asp:Content ID="Content1" ContentPlaceHolderID="ContentPlaceHolder1"
 Runat="server">
   <b>Enter in your name:<br />
   <asp:TextBox ID="TextBox1" Runat="server"></asp:TextBox>
   <asp:Button ID="Button1" Runat="server" Text="Submit" OnClick="Button1_Click" />
   <br />
   <br />
   <asp:Label ID="Label1" Runat="server"></asp:Label>
   </b>
</asp:Content>

<asp:Content ID="Content2" ContentPlaceHolderID="ContentPlaceHolder2"
 Runat="server">
    <asp:Image ID="Image1" Runat="server" ImageUrl="wrox_logo.gif" />
</asp:Content>
```

Even looking at this example here, you can see the differences between a content page and a regular .aspx page. Most importantly, this page doesn't contain any `<form>` element or any of the `<html>` structure that you would normally see in a typical Web form. All of this content instead is stored inside the master page itself.

This content page contains two `Content` server controls. Each of these `Content` server controls map to a specific `<asp:ContentPlaceHolder>` control from the master page. This association is made through the use of the `ContentPlaceHolderID` attribute of the `Content` control.

```
<asp:Content ID="Content1" ContentPlaceHolderID="ContentPlaceHolder1"
 Runat="Server"> ... </asp:Content>
```

Just like typical .aspx pages, you can create any event handlers you might need for your content page. This particular example uses a button-click event for when the end user submits the form. Running this example would produce the following results as shown in Figure 17-8.

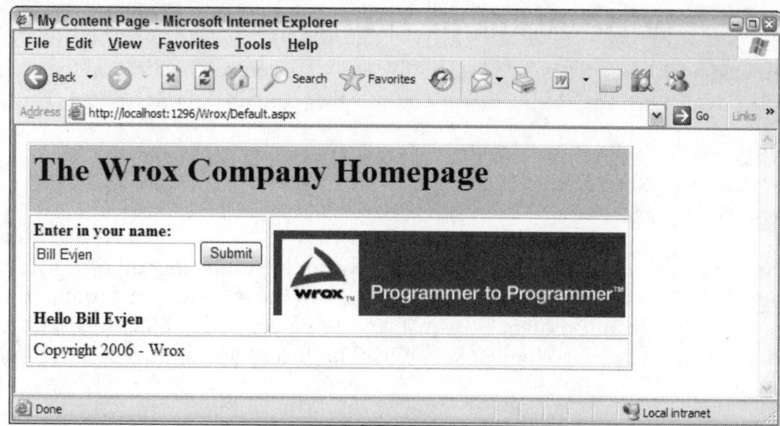

Figure 17-8

Declaring the Master Page Application-Wide

As shown in our examples thus far, we have been declaring the master page from the content page through the use of the `MasterPageFile` attribute of the `Page` directive.

```
<%@ Page Language="VB" MasterPageFile="~/Wrox.master" Title="My Content Page" %>
```

You can apply this attribute to each and every one of your content pages or you can make this declaration in the `web.config` file of your application as shown here:

```
<configuration>
   <system.web>
      <pages masterPageFile="~/Wrox.master"></pages>
   </system.web>
</configuration>
```

From the `<pages>` node in the `web.config` file, you make the declaration that all your content pages will use a specific master page through the use of the `masterPageFile` attribute. Doing this means that your content pages can simply use the following `Page` directive construction:

```
<%@ Page Language="VB" Title="My Content Page" %>
```

The nice thing with making the master page declaration in the `web.config` file is you don't have to make this declaration on any of your solution's content pages, and if you decide to change the template and associate all the content pages to a brand new master page, it is a simple change in one spot to change each and every content page instantaneously.

Doing this will have no effect on the regular .aspx pages in your solution. They will still function as normal. Also, if you have a content page that you wish to associate to a different master page than the one that is specified in the `web.config` file, then you simply need to use the `MasterPageFile` attribute in the `Page` directive of the page. This will override any declaration that you might have in the `web.config` file.

Providing Default Content in Your Master Page

Earlier, we showed how to use a basic `ContentPlaceHolder` control. In addition to using it as it was shown, you also create `ContentPlaceHolder` controls that contain default content. This is illustrated here:

```
<asp:ContentPlaceHolder ID="ContentPlaceHolder1" Runat="server">
   Here is some default content!
</asp:ContentPlaceHolder>
```

For default content, you can again use whatever you want, including any other ASP.NET server controls. A content page that uses a master page that contains one of these `ContentPlaceHolder` controls can then either override the default content—by just specifying content (which overrides the original content declared in the master page)—or just keep the default content contained in the control.

Data-Driven Applications

ASP.NET 2.0 provides some unique data access server controls that make it easy for you to get at the data you need. As data for your applications finds itself in more and more types of data stores, it can sometimes be a nightmare to figure out how to get at and aggregate these information sets onto a Web page in a simple and logical manner. ASP.NET data source controls are meant to work with a specific type of data store by connecting to the data store and performing operations such as Inserts, Updates, and Deletes—all on your behalf. The following table details the new data source controls at your disposal.

Data Source Control	Description
`SqlDataSource`	Enables you to work with any SQL-based database, such as Microsoft SQL Server or even Oracle
`AccessDataSource`	Enables you to work with a Microsoft Access file (.mbd)
`ObjectDataSource`	Enables you to work with a business object or a Visual Studio 2005 data component
`XmlDataSource`	Enables you to work with the information from an XML file or even a dynamic XML source (for example, an RSS feed)
`SiteMapDataSource`	Enables you to work with the hierarchical data represented in the site map file (.sitemap)

ASP.NET itself provides a number of server controls that you can use for data-binding purposes. That means that you can use these data source controls as the underlying data systems for a series of controls with very little work on your part. These data-bound controls in ASP.NET include:

- <asp:GridView>
- <asp:DataGrid>
- <asp:DetailsView>
- <asp:TreeView>
- <asp:Menu>
- <asp:DataList>
- <asp:Repeater>
- <asp:DropDownList>
- <asp:BulletedList>
- <asp:CheckBoxList>
- <asp:RadioButtonList>
- <asp:ListBox>
- <asp:AdRotator>

The newest and most thought of control in the bunch is the `GridView` control. This control was introduced in ASP.NET 2.0 and makes the `DataGrid` control more or less obsolete. The `GridView` control allows paging, sorting, and editing with very little work on your part. This next section takes a look at using the `GridView` control with SQL Server and allowing for these advanced features.

Using the GridView and SqlDataSource Controls

For an example of using these two controls together to display some information, let's turn to Visual Studio 2005. Start a new page and drag and drop a `GridView` control onto the design surface of the page. Pulling up the smart tag for the control on the design surface, you can click the Auto Format link to give your `GridView` control a better look and feel rather than the default look of the control.

Next, drag and drop an `SqlDataSource` control onto the design surface. This control is a middle-tier component, and therefore, it will appear as a gray box on the design surface. The first step is to configure the `SqlDataSource` control to work with the data we want from our Microsoft SQL Server instance. This is shown in Figure 17-9.

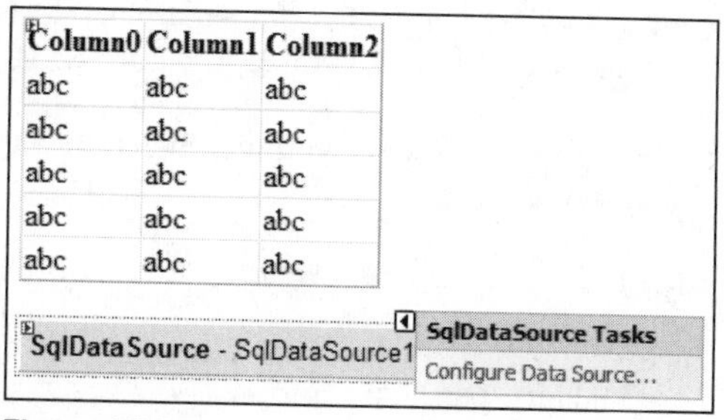

Figure 17-9

Working through the configuration process for the `SqlDataSource` control, you must choose your data connection and then whether you want to store this connection in the `web.config` file (shown in Figure 17-10). This is highly advisable.

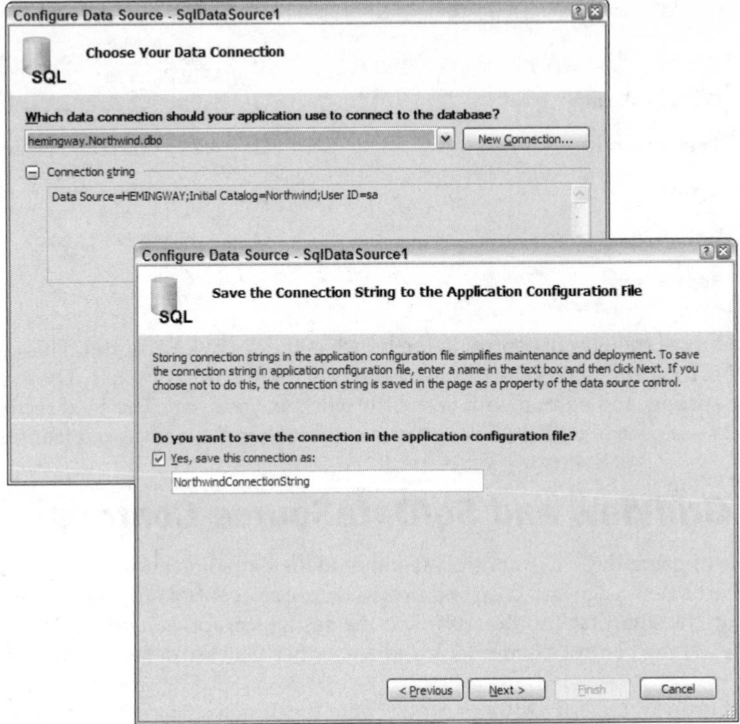

Figure 17-10

From this configuration process, you also get to choose the table that you are going to work with, and test out the queries that the wizard will generate. For our example, select the Customers table and select every row by checking the * check box. This is illustrated in Figure 17-11.

Once you work through the configuration process, you will then notice that your web.config file has changed to now include the connection string.

```
<configuration xmlns="http://schemas.microsoft.com/.NetConfiguration/v2.0">

   <connectionStrings>
      <add name="NorthwindConnectionString"
       connectionString="Server=.;Integrated Security=True;Database=Northwind"
       providerName="System.Data.SqlClient" />
   </connectionStrings>

   <system.web>
      ...
   </system.web>
</configuration>
```

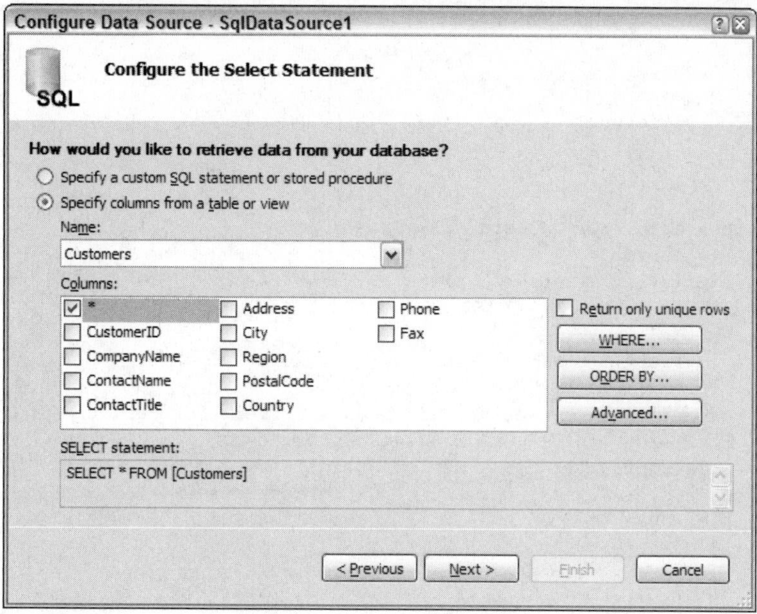

Figure 17-11

Once you have configured the `SqlDataSource` control, the next step is to tie the `GridView` control to this `SqlDataSource` control instance. This can be done through the `GridView` control's smart tag as shown here in Figure 17-12. You can also enable paging and sorting for the control in the same form.

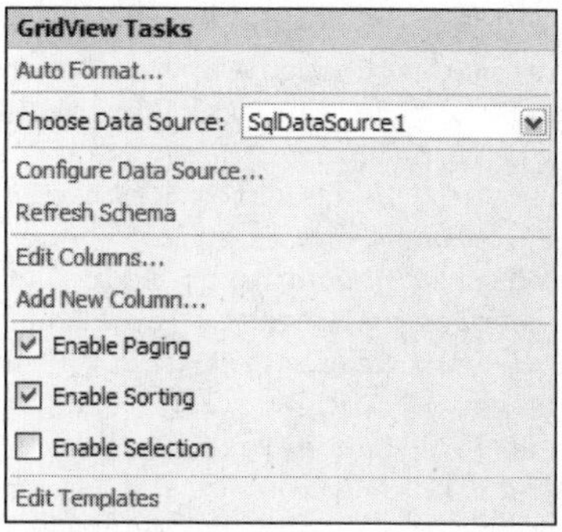

GridView Tasks
Auto Format...
Choose Data Source: SqlDataSource1
Configure Data Source...
Refresh Schema
Edit Columns...
Add New Column...
Enable Paging
Enable Sorting
Enable Selection
Edit Templates

Figure 17-12

The code generated by the wizard (it would also be how you would code it yourself) is shown here:

```
<%@ Page Language="VB" %>

<script runat="server">

</script>

<html xmlns="http://www.w3.org/1999/xhtml" >
<head runat="server">
    <title>GridView Example</title>
</head>
<body>
    <form id="form1" runat="server">
    <div>
        <asp:GridView ID="GridView1" Runat="server" BorderWidth="1px"
         BackColor="White" GridLines="Vertical"
         CellPadding="3" BorderStyle="Solid" BorderColor="#999999"
         ForeColor="Black" DataSourceID="SqlDataSource1"
         DataKeyNames="CustomerID" AutoGenerateColumns="False" AllowPaging="True"
         AllowSorting="True">
            <FooterStyle BackColor="#CCCCCC"></FooterStyle>
            <PagerStyle ForeColor="Black" HorizontalAlign="Center"
             BackColor="#999999"></PagerStyle>
            <HeaderStyle ForeColor="White" Font-Bold="True"
             BackColor="Black"></HeaderStyle>
            <AlternatingRowStyle BackColor="#CCCCCC"></AlternatingRowStyle>
            <Columns>
                <asp:BoundField ReadOnly="True" HeaderText="CustomerID"
                 DataField="CustomerID"
                 SortExpression="CustomerID"></asp:BoundField>
                <asp:BoundField HeaderText="CompanyName" DataField="CompanyName"
                 SortExpression="CompanyName"></asp:BoundField>
                <asp:BoundField HeaderText="ContactName" DataField="ContactName"
                 SortExpression="ContactName"></asp:BoundField>
                <asp:BoundField HeaderText="ContactTitle" DataField="ContactTitle"
                 SortExpression="ContactTitle"></asp:BoundField>
                <asp:BoundField HeaderText="Address" DataField="Address"
                 SortExpression="Address"></asp:BoundField>
                <asp:BoundField HeaderText="City" DataField="City"
                 SortExpression="City"></asp:BoundField>
                <asp:BoundField HeaderText="Region" DataField="Region"
                 SortExpression="Region"></asp:BoundField>
                <asp:BoundField HeaderText="PostalCode" DataField="PostalCode"
                 SortExpression="PostalCode"></asp:BoundField>
                <asp:BoundField HeaderText="Country" DataField="Country"
                 SortExpression="Country"></asp:BoundField>
                <asp:BoundField HeaderText="Phone" DataField="Phone"
                 SortExpression="Phone"></asp:BoundField>
                <asp:BoundField HeaderText="Fax" DataField="Fax"
                 SortExpression="Fax"></asp:BoundField>
            </Columns>
```

```
            <SelectedRowStyle ForeColor="White" Font-Bold="True"
             BackColor="#000099"></SelectedRowStyle>
        </asp:GridView>
        <asp:SqlDataSource ID="SqlDataSource1" Runat="server"
         SelectCommand="SELECT * FROM [Customers]"
         ConnectionString="<%$ ConnectionStrings:NorthwindConnectionString %>">
        </asp:SqlDataSource>
    </div>
    </form>
</body>
</html>
```

Let's first examine this code by looking at the `SqlDataSource` control. This control has some important attributes to pay attention to. The first is the `SelectCommand` attribute. This is the SQL query that you will be using. In our case, it is a `Select * From [Customers]` query (meaning that we are grabbing everything from the Customers table of the Northwind database). The second attribute to pay attention to is the `ConnectionString` attribute. The interesting thing with this attribute is the use of `<%$ ConnectionStrings:NorthwindConnectionString %>` to get at the connection string. This value points at the settings that are placed inside the `web.config` file for those that don't want to hard-code their connection strings directly in the code of their pages. If you did want to do this, you would use something similar to the following construction:

```
ConnectionString="Server=(local);Trusted_Connection=True;Integrated Security=SSPI;
   Persist Security Info=True;Database=Northwind"
```

Now looking to the GridView control, you can see how simple it was to add the ability to perform paging and sorting capabilities to the control. It was simply a matter of adding the attributes `AllowPaging` and `AllowSorting` to the control and setting their values to `True` (they are set to `False` by default).

```
<asp:GridView ID="GridView1" Runat="server" BorderWidth="1px"
 BackColor="White" GridLines="Vertical"
 CellPadding="3" BorderStyle="Solid" BorderColor="#999999"
 ForeColor="Black" DataSourceID="SqlDataSource1"
 DataKeyNames="CustomerID" AutoGenerateColumns="False" AllowPaging="True"
 AllowSorting="True">
   <!-- Inner content removed for clarity -->
</asp:GridView>
```

Each of the columns from the Customers table of the Northwind database are defined in the control through the use of the `<asp:BoundField>` control, a subcontrol of the `GridView` control. The `BoundField` control allows you to specify the header text of the column through the use of the `HeaderText` attribute. The `DataField` attribute actually ties the values that are displayed in this column to a particular value coming from the Customers table, and the `SortExpression` attribute should use the same values for sorting—unless you are sorting on a different value than what is being displayed.

In the end, your page should look something similar to the following as shown here in Figure 17-13.

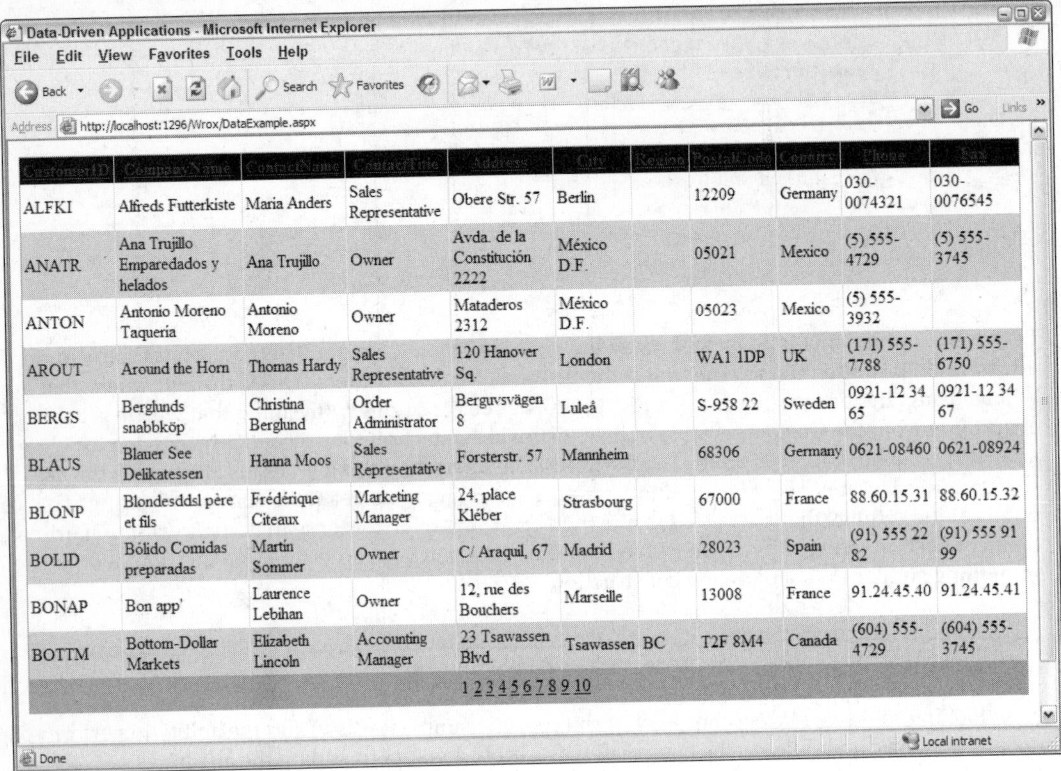

CustomerID	CompanyName	ContactName	ContactTitle	Address	City	Region	PostalCode	Country	Phone	Fax
ALFKI	Alfreds Futterkiste	Maria Anders	Sales Representative	Obere Str. 57	Berlin		12209	Germany	030-0074321	030-0076545
ANATR	Ana Trujillo Emparedados y helados	Ana Trujillo	Owner	Avda. de la Constitución 2222	México D.F.		05021	Mexico	(5) 555-4729	(5) 555-3745
ANTON	Antonio Moreno Taquería	Antonio Moreno	Owner	Mataderos 2312	México D.F.		05023	Mexico	(5) 555-3932	
AROUT	Around the Horn	Thomas Hardy	Sales Representative	120 Hanover Sq.	London		WA1 1DP	UK	(171) 555-7788	(171) 555-6750
BERGS	Berglunds snabbköp	Christina Berglund	Order Administrator	Berguvsvägen 8	Luleå		S-958 22	Sweden	0921-12 34 65	0921-12 34 67
BLAUS	Blauer See Delikatessen	Hanna Moos	Sales Representative	Forsterstr. 57	Mannheim		68306	Germany	0621-08460	0621-08924
BLONP	Blondesddsl père et fils	Frédérique Citeaux	Marketing Manager	24, place Kléber	Strasbourg		67000	France	88.60.15.31	88.60.15.32
BOLID	Bólido Comidas preparadas	Martín Sommer	Owner	C/ Araquil, 67	Madrid		28023	Spain	(91) 555 22 82	(91) 555 91 99
BONAP	Bon app'	Laurence Lebihan	Owner	12, rue des Bouchers	Marseille		13008	France	91.24.45.40	91.24.45.41
BOTTM	Bottom-Dollar Markets	Elizabeth Lincoln	Accounting Manager	23 Tsawassen Blvd.	Tsawassen	BC	T2F 8M4	Canada	(604) 555-4729	(604) 555-3745

1 2 3 4 5 6 7 8 9 10

Figure 17-13

Allowing for Editing and Deleting of Records with the GridView

Now let's expand upon the previous example by allowing for the editing and deleting of records that are displayed in the `GridView`. If you are using the Visual Studio 2005 `SqlDataSource` configuration wizard to accomplish these tasks, then you are going to have to take some extra steps beyond what was previously shown in the preceding `GridView` example.

Go back to the `SqlDataSource` control on the design surface of your Web page and pull up the control's smart tag. You will find the option to Configure Data Source. Select this option to reconfigure the `SqlDataSource` control to allow for the editing and deletion of the data from the Customers table of the Northwind database.

When you come to the screen in the Configure Select Statement dialog (see Figure 17-14), click the Advanced Options button.

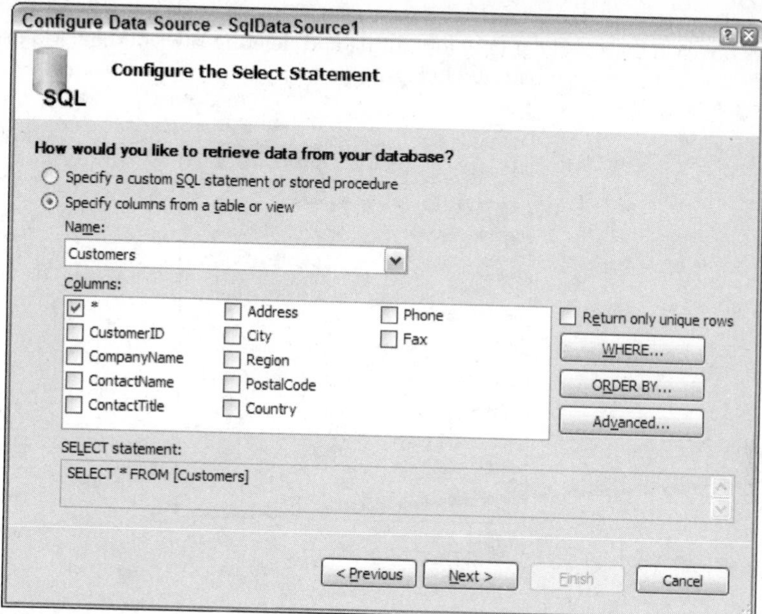

Figure 17-14

This will pull up a new dialog titled Advanced SQL Generation Options as shown here in Figure 17-15.

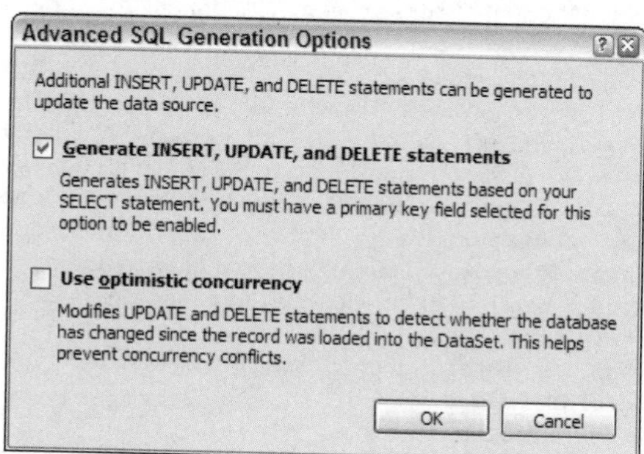

Figure 17-15

As shown in this dialog, make sure you select the Generate Insert, Update, and Delete statements check box. This will construct the `SqlDataSource` control to be able to not only handle the simple Select query, but will also add the Update and Delete queries to the control as well. After this, press OK and then work through the rest of the wizard until you are finished.

The next step is to go back to the `GridView` control's smart tag and select the Refresh Schema. You will also find check boxes in the smart tag now for editing and deleting rows of data. Make sure both of these check boxes are checked. This is illustrated in Figure 17-16.

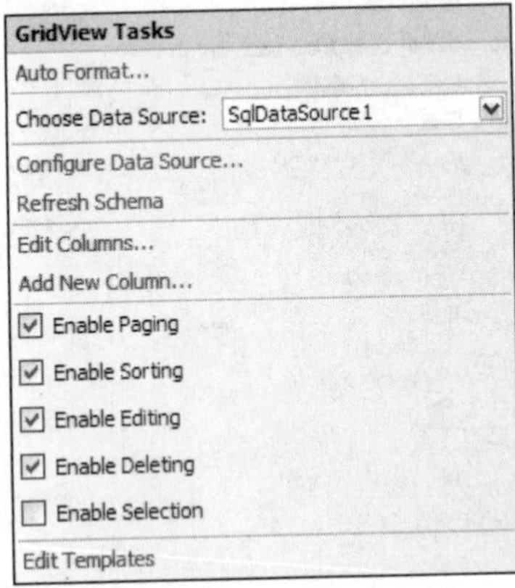

Figure 17-16

Now let's look at what changed in the code. First off, the `SqlDataSource` control has now changed to allow for the updating and deletion of data.

```
<asp:SqlDataSource ID="SqlDataSource1" Runat="server"
 SelectCommand="SELECT * FROM [Customers]"
 ConnectionString="<%$ ConnectionStrings:AppConnectionString1 %>"
 DeleteCommand="DELETE FROM [Customers] WHERE [CustomerID] = @original_CustomerID"
 InsertCommand="INSERT INTO [Customers] ([CustomerID], [CompanyName],
    [ContactName], [ContactTitle], [Address], [City], [Region], [PostalCode],
    [Country], [Phone], [Fax]) VALUES (@CustomerID, @CompanyName, @ContactName,
    @ContactTitle, @Address, @City, @Region, @PostalCode, @Country, @Phone, @Fax)"
 UpdateCommand="UPDATE [Customers] SET [CompanyName] = @CompanyName, [ContactName]
    = @ContactName, [ContactTitle] = @ContactTitle, [Address] = @Address, [City] =
    @City, [Region] = @Region, [PostalCode] = @PostalCode, [Country] = @Country,
    [Phone] = @Phone, [Fax] = @Fax WHERE [CustomerID] = @original_CustomerID">
          <DeleteParameters>
              <asp:Parameter Type="String" Name="CustomerID"></asp:Parameter>
          </DeleteParameters>
          <UpdateParameters>
              <asp:Parameter Type="String" Name="CompanyName"></asp:Parameter>
              <asp:Parameter Type="String" Name="ContactName"></asp:Parameter>
              <asp:Parameter Type="String" Name="ContactTitle"></asp:Parameter>
              <asp:Parameter Type="String" Name="Address"></asp:Parameter>
              <asp:Parameter Type="String" Name="City"></asp:Parameter>
              <asp:Parameter Type="String" Name="Region"></asp:Parameter>
              <asp:Parameter Type="String" Name="PostalCode"></asp:Parameter>
              <asp:Parameter Type="String" Name="Country"></asp:Parameter>
              <asp:Parameter Type="String" Name="Phone"></asp:Parameter>
              <asp:Parameter Type="String" Name="Fax"></asp:Parameter>
              <asp:Parameter Type="String" Name="CustomerID"></asp:Parameter>
          </UpdateParameters>
```

```
            <InsertParameters>
                <asp:Parameter Type="String" Name="CustomerID"></asp:Parameter>
                <asp:Parameter Type="String" Name="CompanyName"></asp:Parameter>
                <asp:Parameter Type="String" Name="ContactName"></asp:Parameter>
                <asp:Parameter Type="String" Name="ContactTitle"></asp:Parameter>
                <asp:Parameter Type="String" Name="Address"></asp:Parameter>
                <asp:Parameter Type="String" Name="City"></asp:Parameter>
                <asp:Parameter Type="String" Name="Region"></asp:Parameter>
                <asp:Parameter Type="String" Name="PostalCode"></asp:Parameter>
                <asp:Parameter Type="String" Name="Country"></asp:Parameter>
                <asp:Parameter Type="String" Name="Phone"></asp:Parameter>
                <asp:Parameter Type="String" Name="Fax"></asp:Parameter>
            </InsertParameters>
</asp:SqlDataSource>
```

From this code, you can see that there are now other queries that have been added to the control. Using the `DeleteCommand`, `InsertCommand`, and `UpdateCommand` attributes of the `SqlDataSource` control, these functions can now be performed just as `Select` queries were enabled through the use of the `SelectCommand` attribute. As you can see in the queries, there are a lot of parameters defined within them. These parameters are then assigned through the `<DeleteParameters>`, `<UpdateParameters>`, and `<InsertParameters>` elements. Within each of these subsections, the actual parameters are defined through the use of the `<asp:Parameter>` control where you also assign the datatype of the parameter (through the use of the `Type` attribute) and the name of the parameter.

Besides these changes to the `SqlDataSource` control, there is only one small change that has been made to the `GridView` control as shown here:

```
<Columns>
    <asp:CommandField ShowDeleteButton="True"
     ShowEditButton="True"></asp:CommandField>
    <asp:BoundField ReadOnly="True" HeaderText="CustomerID" DataField="CustomerID"
     SortExpression="CustomerID"></asp:BoundField>
    <asp:BoundField HeaderText="CompanyName" DataField="CompanyName"
     SortExpression="CompanyName"></asp:BoundField>
    <asp:BoundField HeaderText="ContactName" DataField="ContactName"
     SortExpression="ContactName"></asp:BoundField>
    <asp:BoundField HeaderText="ContactTitle" DataField="ContactTitle"
     SortExpression="ContactTitle"></asp:BoundField>
    <asp:BoundField HeaderText="Address" DataField="Address"
     SortExpression="Address"></asp:BoundField>
    <asp:BoundField HeaderText="City" DataField="City"
     SortExpression="City"></asp:BoundField>
    <asp:BoundField HeaderText="Region" DataField="Region"
     SortExpression="Region"></asp:BoundField>
    <asp:BoundField HeaderText="PostalCode" DataField="PostalCode"
     SortExpression="PostalCode"></asp:BoundField>
    <asp:BoundField HeaderText="Country" DataField="Country"
     SortExpression="Country"></asp:BoundField>
    <asp:BoundField HeaderText="Phone" DataField="Phone"
     SortExpression="Phone"></asp:BoundField>
    <asp:BoundField HeaderText="Fax" DataField="Fax"
     SortExpression="Fax"></asp:BoundField>
</Columns>
```

The only change that is needed for the `GridView` control is the addition of a new column that will allow for editing and deleting commands to be initiated from. This is done through the use of the `<asp:CommandField>` control. From this control, you can see that we also enabled the Edit and Delete buttons through a `Boolean` value.

Once built and run, your new page will look like the following as shown here in Figure 17-17.

Data-Driven Applications - Microsoft Internet Explorer

File Edit View Favorites Tools Help

Address http://localhost:1296/Wrox/DataExample.aspx

	CustomerID	CompanyName	ContactName	ContactTitle	Address	City	Region	PostalCode	Country	Phone	Fax
Edit Delete	ALFKI	Alfreds Futterkiste	Maria Anders	Sales Representative	Obere Str. 57	Berlin		12209	Germany	030-0074321	030-0076545
Edit Delete	ANATR	Ana Trujillo Emparedados y helados	Ana Trujillo	Owner	Avda. de la Constitución 2222	México D.F.		05021	Mexico	(5) 555-4729	(5) 555-3745
Edit Delete	ANTON	Antonio Moreno Taquería	Antonio Moreno	Owner	Mataderos 2312	México D.F.		05023	Mexico	(5) 555-3932	
Edit Delete	AROUT	Around the Horn	Thomas Hardy	Sales Representative	120 Hanover Sq.	London		WA1 1DP	UK	(171) 555-7788	(171) 555-6750
Edit Delete	BERGS	Berglunds snabbköp	Christina Berglund	Order Administrator	Berguvsvägen 8	Luleå		S-958 22	Sweden	0921-12 34 65	0921-12 34 67
Edit Delete	BLAUS	Blauer See Delikatessen	Hanna Moos	Sales Representative	Forsterstr. 57	Mannheim		68306	Germany	0621-08460	0621-08924
Edit Delete	BLONP	Blondesddsl père et fils	Frédérique Citeaux	Marketing Manager	24, place Kléber	Strasbourg		67000	France	88.60.15.31	88.60.15.32
Edit Delete	BOLID	Bólido Comidas preparadas	Martín Sommer	Owner	C/ Araquil, 67	Madrid		28023	Spain	(91) 555 22 82	(91) 555 91 99
Edit Delete	BONAP	Bon app'	Laurence Lebihan	Owner	12, rue des Bouchers	Marseille		13008	France	91.24.45.40	91.24.45.41
Edit Delete	BOTTM	Bottom-Dollar Markets	Elizabeth Lincoln	Accounting Manager	23 Tsawassen Blvd.	Tsawassen	BC	T2F 8M4	Canada	(604) 555-4729	(604) 555-3745

1 2 3 4 5 6 7 8 9 10

Local intranet

Figure 17-17

Don't Stop There!

This chapter has limited space, so there is only room to go through this one example, but it is important to realize that there are so many other `DataSource` controls at your disposal. The `ObjectDataSource` control is rather powerful for those that wish to enforce a strict *n*-tier model and separate the data retrieval logic into an object that the `GridView` and other data-bound controls can work with. The `XmlDataSource` control is one control that you will most likely find yourself using a lot as more and more data is getting stored as XML—including dynamic data (such as Web logs via RSS). These `DataSource` controls are fine-tuned for the type of data stores for which they are targeted and you will find a lot of benefit in exploring their capabilities in detail.

Navigation

People rarely build Web applications that are made up of just a single page instance. Instead, applications are usually made up of multiple pages that are all related to each other in some fashion. Some applications have a workflow on how end users can work from page to page, while other applications have a navigation structure that allows for free roaming throughout. Sometimes a navigation structure of a site can get rather complex, and managing this complexity is something that can get rather cumbersome.

ASP.NET 2.0 includes a way of managing the navigational structure of your Web applications. This new system, which allows you to completely manage your application's navigation, allows for you to first define your navigational structure through an XML file and can then be bound to a couple of different server controls which are focused on navigation.

This makes it rather easy when you have to introduce changes either to the structure of your navigation or even name changes to pages which are contained within this structure. Instead of going from page to page throughout your entire application, changing titles or page destinations, you can now make these changes in one place — an XML file — and the changes will be instantaneously reflected throughout your entire application.

The first step in working with the ASP.NET navigation system is to first reflect your navigational structure in the `web.sitemap` file — which is basically the XML file that will contain the complete site structure.

For instance, let's suppose that you want to have the following site structure:

```
Home
      Books
      Magazines
            U.S. Magazines
            European Magazines
```

This site structure has three levels to it and multiple items in the lowest level. With this structure, you can then reflect this in the `web.sitemap` file as follows:

```
<?xml version="1.0" encoding="utf-8" ?>
<siteMap xmlns="http://schemas.microsoft.com/AspNet/SiteMap-File-1.0" >
   <siteMapNode url="default.aspx" title="Home" description="The site homepage">
      <siteMapNode url="books.aspx" title="Books"
       description="Books from our catalog" />
      <siteMapNode url="magazines.aspx" title="Magazines"
       description="Magazines from our catalog">
         <siteMapNode url="magazines_us.aspx" title="U.S. Magazines"
          description="Magazines from the U.S." />
         <siteMapNode url="magazines_eur.aspx" title="European Magazines"
          description="Magazines from Europe" />
      </siteMapNode>
   </siteMapNode>
</siteMap>
```

To create a `web.sitemap` file in Visual Studio 2005, get to the Add New Items dialog and you will see the option of adding a Site Map. In this file, you can place the above content. To move a level down in the hierarchy, you would nest `<siteMapNode>` elements within other `<siteMapNode>` elements. A `<siteMapNode>` element can contain a couple of different attributes. These attributes are defined in the following table.

Attribute	Description
`Title`	The `title` attribute provides a textual description of the link. The `String` value used here is the text used for the link.
`Description`	The `description` attribute not only reminds you what the link is for, but is also used for the `ToolTip` attribute on the link. The `ToolTip` attribute is the yellow box that shows up next to the link when the end user hovers the cursor over the link for a couple of seconds.
`Url`	The `url` attribute describes where the file is located in the solution. If the file is in the root directory, simply use the file name, such as `default.aspx`. If the file is located in a subfolder, be sure to include the folders in the `String` value used for this attribute. For example, `MySubFolder/MyFile.aspx`.
`Roles`	If ASP.NET security trimming is enabled, you can use the `roles` attribute to define which roles are allowed to view and click the provided link in the navigation.

Using the SiteMapPath Server Control

One of the available server controls that work with a `web.sitemap` file is the `SiteMapPath` control. This control provides a popular structure which you will find on many Web sites on the Internet. Some folks call this feature *breadcrumb navigation*, but whatever you call it, you will find it very easy to implement in ASP.NET.

To see an example of this control at work, let's create a page that would be at the bottom of the site map structure. So, within the project that contains your `web.sitemap` file, create an ASP.NET page named `magazines_us.aspx`. On this page, simply drag and drop a `SiteMapPath` control onto the page. You will find this control under the Navigation section in the Visual Studio Toolbox. This control's code looks as follows:

```
<asp:SiteMapPath ID="SiteMapPath1" Runat="server"></asp:SiteMapPath>
```

What else do you need to do to get this control to work? Well, nothing! Simply build and run the page and you will then see the following results as shown here in Figure 17-18.

From this example, you can see that the `SiteMapPath` control defines the end user's place in the application's site structure. It shows the current page the user is on (U.S. Magazines) as well as the two pages that are above it in the hierarchy.

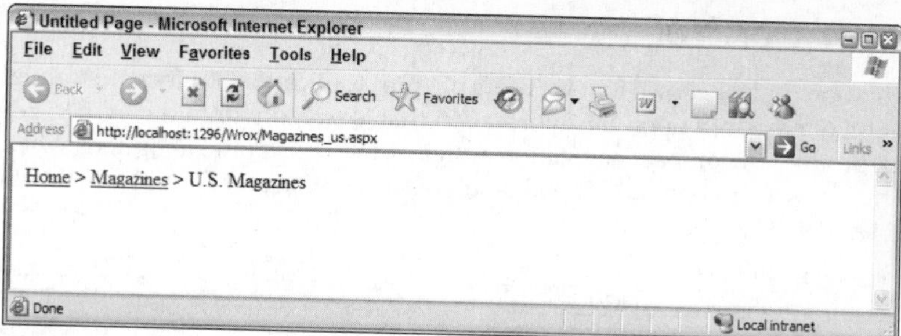

Figure 17-18

The SiteMapPath control requires no DataSource control, as it will automatically bind itself to any .sitemap file that it finds in the project, and nothing is required on your part to make this happen. The SiteMapPath's smart tag allows you to customize the look and feel of the control as well so you can produce other results in how it displays as illustrated in Figure 17-19.

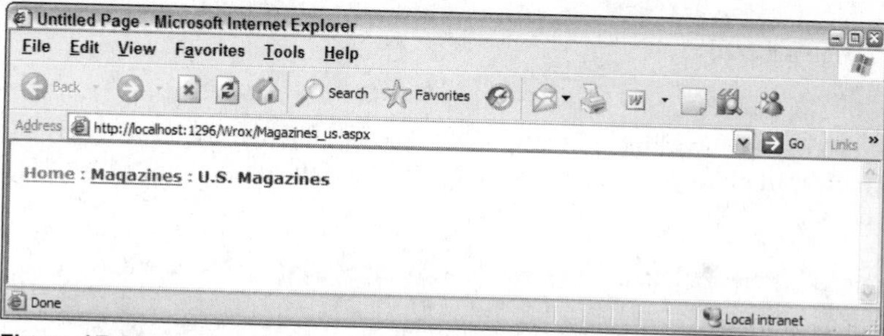

Figure 17-19

The code for this version of the SiteMapPath control is as follows:

```
<asp:SiteMapPath ID="SiteMapPath1" Runat="server" PathSeparator=" : "
 Font-Names="Verdana" Font-Size="0.8em">
   <PathSeparatorStyle Font-Bold="True" ForeColor="#507CD1"></PathSeparatorStyle>
   <CurrentNodeStyle ForeColor="#333333"></CurrentNodeStyle>
   <NodeStyle Font-Bold="True" ForeColor="#284E98"></NodeStyle>
   <RootNodeStyle Font-Bold="True" ForeColor="#507CD1"></RootNodeStyle>
</asp:SiteMapPath>
```

From this example, you can see a lot of style elements and attributes that can be used with the SiteMapPath control. There are many options at your disposal in order to give you the ability to create breadcrumb navigation that is unique.

Menu Server Control

Another navigation control allows for end users of your application to navigate throughout the pages your application offers based upon the information that is stored within the `web.sitemap` file. The `Menu` server control produces a compact navigation system which pops out suboptions when the end user hovers their mouse over an option. The end result of the `Menu` server control when bound to the site map is as shown here in Figure 17-20.

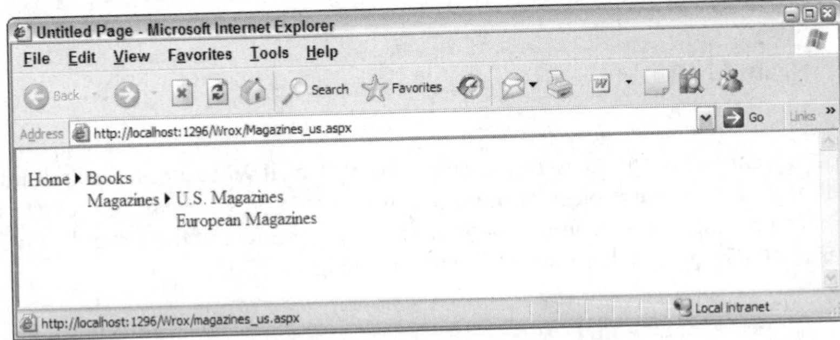

Figure 17-20

To build this, you must be working off of the `web.sitemap` file that we created earlier. After the `web.sitemap` file is in place, place a `Menu` server control on the page along with a `SiteMapDataSource` control.

```
<asp:Menu ID="Menu1" Runat="server" DataSourceID="SiteMapDataSource1">
</asp:Menu>
<asp:SiteMapDataSource ID="SiteMapDataSource1" Runat="server" />
```

The `SiteMapDataSource` control will automatically work with the application's `web.sitemap` file. In addition to the `SiteMapDataSource` control, the other item included is the `Menu` server control, which uses the typical `ID` and `Runat` attributes in addition to the `DataSourceID` attribute to connect this control with what is retrieved from the `SiteMapDataSource` control.

Like the other controls provided by ASP.NET, you can easily modify the look and feel of this control. Clicking on the Auto Format link in the control's smart tag, you can give the control the 'Classic' look and feel. This setting would produce the following result as shown here in Figure 17-21.

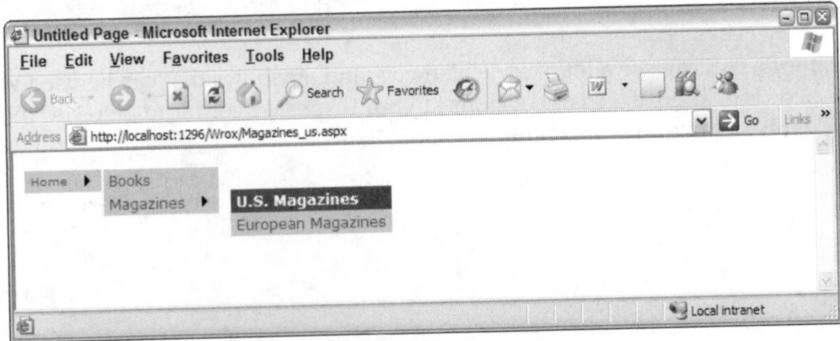

Figure 17-21

Like the other controls, you can see that there are a lot of subelements that contribute to the changing of the control's style. This is illustrated here in the following code example:

```
<asp:Menu ID="Menu1" Runat="server" DataSourceID="SiteMapDataSource1"
 Font-Names="Verdana" Font-Size="0.8em" BackColor="#B5C7DE" ForeColor="#284E98"
 StaticSubMenuIndent="10px" DynamicHorizontalOffset="2">
   <StaticSelectedStyle BackColor="#507CD1"></StaticSelectedStyle>
   <StaticMenuItemStyle HorizontalPadding="5"
    VerticalPadding="2"></StaticMenuItemStyle>
   <DynamicMenuStyle BackColor="#B5C7DE"></DynamicMenuStyle>
   <DynamicSelectedStyle BackColor="#507CD1"></DynamicSelectedStyle>
   <DynamicMenuItemStyle HorizontalPadding="5"
    VerticalPadding="2"></DynamicMenuItemStyle>
   <DynamicHoverStyle ForeColor="White" Font-Bold="True"
    BackColor="#284E98"></DynamicHoverStyle>
   <StaticHoverStyle ForeColor="White" Font-Bold="True"
    BackColor="#284E98"></StaticHoverStyle>
</asp:Menu>
```

The TreeView Server Control

The last navigation server control that we will look at is the `TreeView` server control. This control allows you to render a hierarchy of data. The `TreeView` control is not only meant for displaying what is contained within the `.sitemap` file, but you can also use this control to represent other forms of hierarchal data — such as data that you might store in a standard XML file.

You may have encountered a similar `TreeView` control in .NET when using the IE Web Controls, which also contained a `TreeView` control. That `previous TreeView` control was limited to working only in Microsoft's Internet Explorer, while this new `TreeView` control will work in a wide variety of browsers.

The `TreeView` control is similar to that of the `Menu` control in that it won't bind automatically to the `web.sitemap` file, but instead requires an underlying `DataSource` control. The code for displaying the contents of the `.sitemap` file is shown here in the following example:

```
<asp:TreeView ID="TreeView1" Runat="server" DataSourceID="SiteMapDataSource1">
</asp:TreeView>
<asp:SiteMapDataSource ID="SiteMapDataSource1" Runat="server" />
```

As with the `Menu` control example, a `SiteMapDataSource` is needed. After a basic `SiteMapDataSource` control is in place, position a `TreeView` control on the page and set the `DataSourceId` property to `SiteMapDataSource1`. This simple construction produces the result as shown here in Figure 17-22.

Remember that by using the Auto Format link from the control's smart tag, you can format the `TreeView` control with a wide variety of looks and feels.

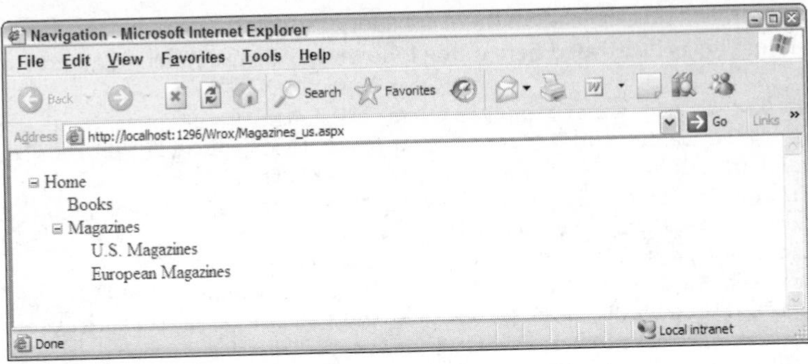

Figure 17-22

The `TreeView` is not only meant for site maps, but instead (as stated) it can build upon any underlying hierarchal data set. For instance, you can display a hierarchal data structure from a standard XML file just as easily. Let's suppose you have an XML file as follows:

```
<?xml version="1.0" encoding="utf-8" ?>
<Hardware>
   <Item Category="Motherboards">
      <Option Choice="Asus" />
      <Option Choice="Abit" />
   </Item>
   <Item Category="Memory">
      <Option Choice="128mb" />
      <Option Choice="256mb" />
      <Option Choice="512mb" />
   </Item>
   <Item Category="Hard Drives">
      <Option Choice="40GB" />
      <Option Choice="80GB" />
      <Option Choice="100GB" />
   </Item>
   <Item Category="Drives">
      <Option Choice="CD" />
      <Option Choice="DVD" />
      <Option Choice="DVD Burner" />
   </Item>
</Hardware>
```

It's quite obvious that this XML file is not meant for site navigation purposes, but instead it is meant for an end user to make selections from. As stated, the `TreeView` control is quite extensible. For an example of this, let's create a page that uses the above XML file. The code for the page is shown here:

```
<%@ Page Language="VB" %>

<script runat="server">
    Protected Sub Button1_Click(ByVal sender As Object, _
       ByVal e As System.EventArgs)

        If TreeView1.CheckedNodes.Count > 0 Then
            Label1.Text = "We are sending you information on:<p>"
```

```
            For Each node As TreeNode In TreeView1.CheckedNodes
                Label1.Text += node.Text & " " & node.Parent.Text & "<br>"
            Next
        Else
            label1.Text = "You didn't select anything. Sorry!"
        End If
    End Sub
</script>

<html xmlns="http://www.w3.org/1999/xhtml" >
<head runat="server">
    <title>The TreeView Control</title>
</head>
<body>
    <form id="form1" runat="server">
    <div>
        Please select the following items that you are interesting in:
        <br />
        <br />
        <asp:TreeView ID="TreeView1" Runat="server"
         DataSourceID="XmlDataSource1" ShowLines="True">
            <DataBindings>
                <asp:TreeNodeBinding TextField="Category"
                 DataMember="Item"></asp:TreeNodeBinding>
                <asp:TreeNodeBinding ShowCheckBox="True" TextField="Choice"
                 DataMember="Option"></asp:TreeNodeBinding>
            </DataBindings>
        </asp:TreeView> <br />
        <br />
        <asp:Button ID="Button1" Runat="server"
         Text="Submit Choices" OnClick="Button1_Click" />
        <br />
        <br />
        <asp:Label ID="Label1" Runat="server"></asp:Label>
        <asp:XmlDataSource ID="XmlDataSource1" Runat="server"
         DataFile="~/Hardware.xml">
        </asp:XmlDataSource>
    </div>
    </form>
</body>
</html>
```

In this example, we are using an `XmlDataSource` control instead of the `SiteMapDataSource` control. The `XmlDataSource` control associates itself with the XML file from earlier (`Hardware.xml`) through the use of the `DataFile` attribute.

The `TreeView` control then binds itself to the `XmlDataSource` control through the use of the `DataSourceID` attribute which here is pointed to `XmlDataSource1`. Another interesting addition in the root `TreeView` node is the addition of the `ShowLines` attribute being set to `True`. This feature of the `TreeView` will cause each of the nodes in the hierarchy to show their connection to their parent node through a visual line.

When working with XML files, which can basically be of any construction, you are actually going to have to bind the nodes of the `TreeView` control to specific values that come from the XML file. This is done through the use of the `<DataBindings>` element. The `<DataBindings>` element encapsulates one or more `TreeNodeBinding` objects. Two of the more important available properties of a `TreeNodeBinding` object are the `DataMember` and `TextField` properties. The `DataMember` property points to the name of the XML element that the `TreeView` control should look for. The `TextField` property specifies the XML attribute of that particular XML element. If you do this correctly with the use of the `<DataBindings>` construct, you get the result shown here in Figure 17-23.

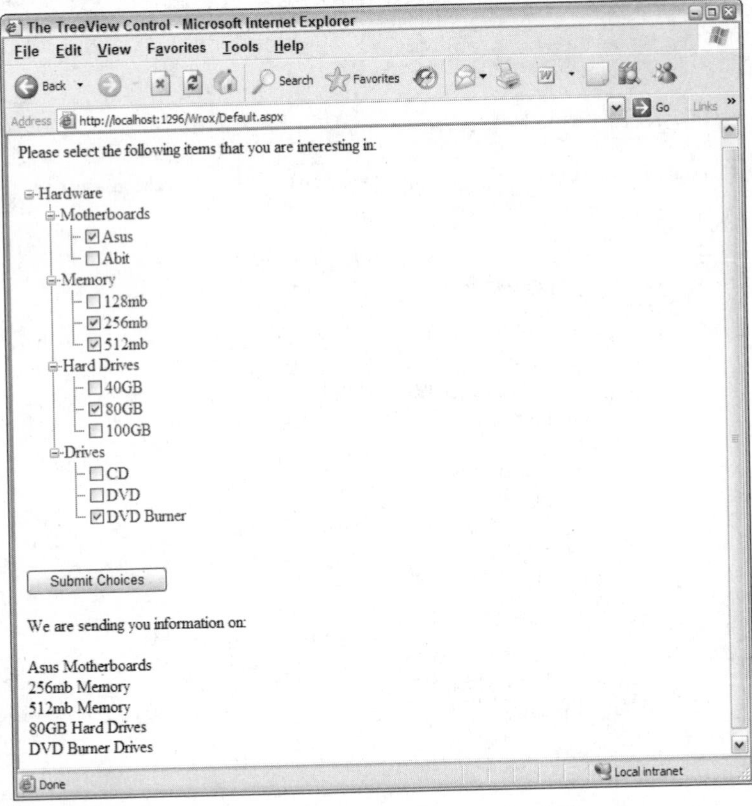

Figure 17-23

In the button `click` event from our example, you can see how easy it is to iterate through each of the checked nodes from the `TreeView` selection by creating instances of `TreeNode` objects. These selections are made from one of the `TreeNodeBinding` objects which sets the `ShowCheckBox` property to `True`.

Membership and Role Management

ASP.NET contains a built-in membership and role management system that can be initiated through either code or through the ASP.NET Web Site Administration Tool. This is an ideal system to use to authenticate users to access a page or even your entire site. This management system not only provides a new API suite for managing users, but it also gives you some server controls that interact with this API.

The first set in setting up your site's security and the user roles, open up the ASP.NET Web Site Administration Tool. You will be able to launch this tool through a button in the Visual Studio 2005 Solution Explorer or by clicking Build ➪ Configuration Manager in the Visual Studio menu. From the tool, which will open up in the Document window, click on the Security tab. Figure 17-24 shows what this tab of the tool looks like.

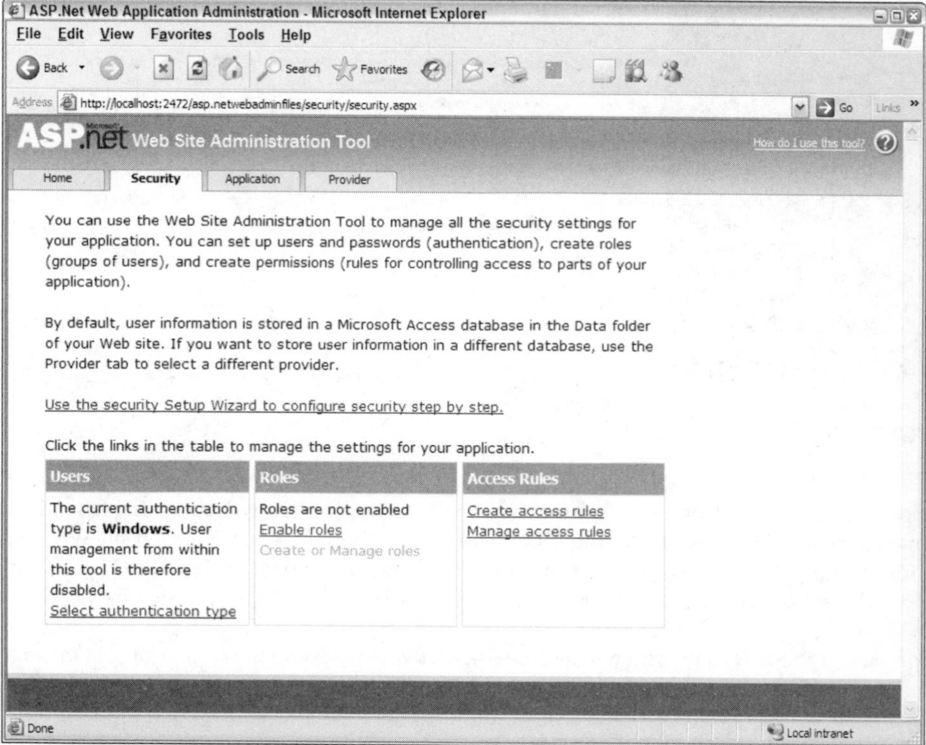

Figure 17-24

The first step is to click the link to start up the Security Setup Wizard. This launched wizard is shown here in Figure 17-25.

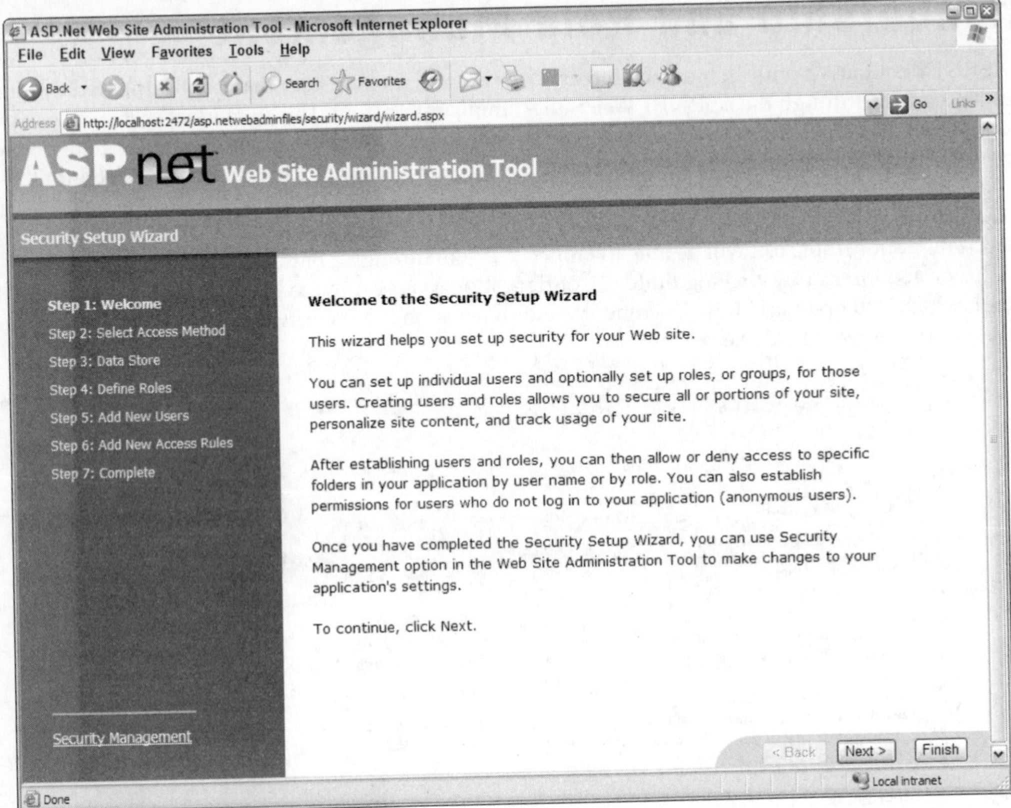

Figure 17-25

The first question asked from the wizard is whether your application will be available on the public Internet or if it will be hosted on an intranet. If you select Internet, then your Web site will be enabled with forms authentication. If you select Intranet, then your site will be configured to work with Windows Integrated Authentication. For our demonstration purposes, select the Internet option.

Working through the wizard, you will also be asked if you are going to work with role management. Enable role management by checking the appropriate check box and add a role titled `Manager`. After this step, you will actually be able to enter users into the system. Fill out information for each user you want in the system. This is shown in Figure 17-26.

The next step is to then create the access rules for your site. You can pick specific folders and apply the rules for the folder. For this example, I made it so that anyone in the `Manager` role would have access to the site, while anonymous users would be denied access. This is shown here in Figure 17-27.

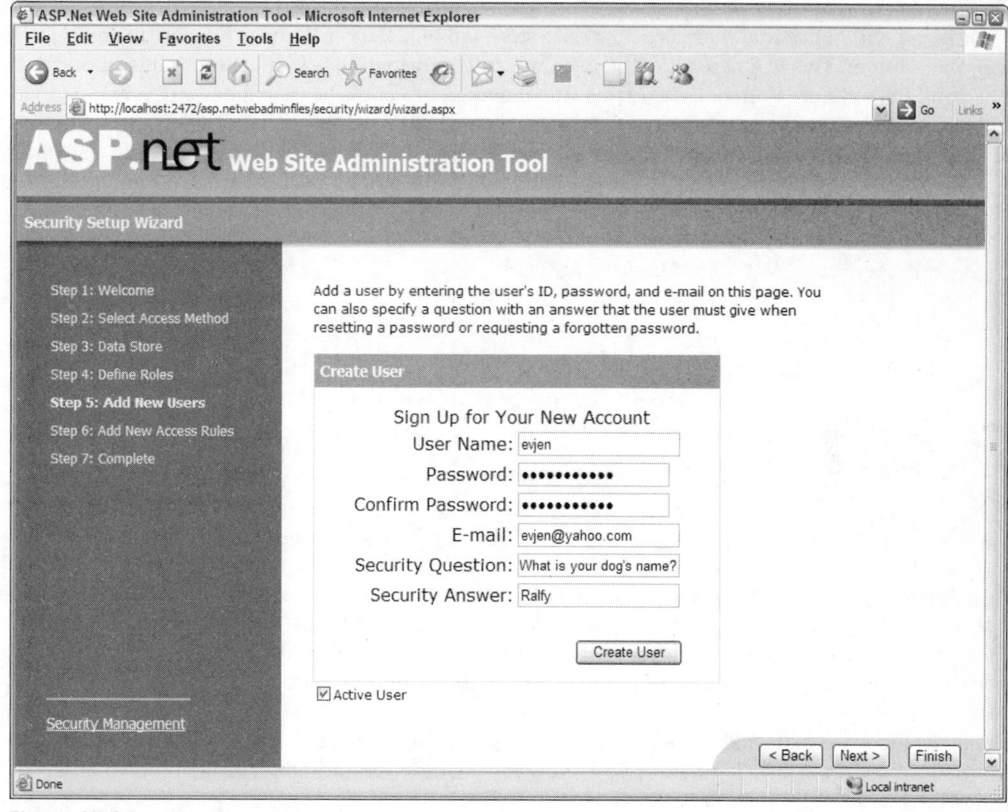

Figure 17-26

Add New Access Rule

Select a directory for this rule:

Wrox

Rule applies to:

Role Manager

User

All Users

Anonymous Users

Search for users

Permission:

Allow

Deny

Add This Rule

Rules that appear dimmed are inherited from the parent and cannot be changed at this level.

Permission	Users And Roles	Delete
Allow	Manager	Delete
Deny	[anonymous]	Delete
Allow	[all]	Delete

< Back Next > Finish

Figure 17-27

Clicking the Finish button will of course finish the wizard. If you refresh the Solution Explorer in Visual Studio, you will notice that there is a new data store (an SQL Server Express Edition .mdb file) in the App_Data folder. This is where all of the user and role information is being stored. It is important to note that you can configure both of the systems (the membership and role management systems) to work with other data stores besides these SQL Express data files. For example, you can configure these systems to work with a full-blown version of Microsoft's SQL Server. You will also notice in the Solution Explorer, that if you didn't already have a web.config file, you have one now. The contents added to the web.config file include:

```
<?xml version="1.0" encoding="utf-8"?>
<configuration>
    <system.web>
        <authorization>
            <allow roles="Manager" />
            <deny users="?" />
        </authorization>
        <roleManager enabled="true" />
        <authentication mode="Forms" />
    </system.web>
</configuration>
```

From this you can see all the settings that we enabled. In the <authorization> section, we allow for users that are in the role of Manager, while we also deny all anonymous users (defined with a question mark). The <roleManager> element turns on the role management system, while the <authentication> element turns on forms authentication. Now, let's utilize these configurations.

The next step is to create a login page as everyone will be hitting any page in this application as an anonymous user first. The login page will allow for people to enter in their credentials in order to be authorized in the Manager role that we created earlier.

ASP.NET includes a slew of controls that make working with the membership and role management systems easier. On the login page (Login.aspx), let's place a simple Login server control on the page.

```
<asp:Login ID="Login1" Runat="server"></asp:Login>
```

The nice thing here is that you have to do absolutely nothing to tie this Login control to the .mdf database that was created earlier through the wizard. Now go back to another page in the application (besides the Login.aspx page) and start up that page. In my case, I started up Default.aspx (which only contains a simple text statement), but from Figure 17-28 you can see (by looking at the URL specified in the browser) that I was redirected to Login.aspx instead as I wasn't yet authenticated.

The Login.aspx page allows me to enter my credentials, which then authorize me in the Manager role. Hitting the Login button causes the browser to redirect me to the appropriate page. I am now authenticated and authorized for the site!

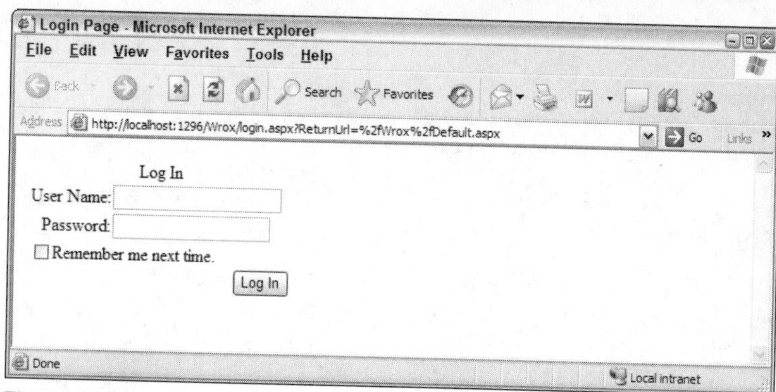

Figure 17-28

Personalization

Many Web applications have features that allow for personalization of some kind. This might be as simple as greeting the users by name or it might deal with more advanced issues such as content placement. Whatever the case, personalization techniques have always had a tricky approach. Developers used anything from cookies, sessions, or database entries to control the personalization that users placed on their pages.

ASP.NET 2.0 includes a simple to use and configure personalization system. It is as simple as making entries in the `web.config` file to get the personalization system started. Like the membership and role management systems, the personalization system also uses an underlying data store. In our example, we will continue to work with the SQL Server Express Edition .mdb file.

For our example, we are going to create two properties — `FirstName` and `LastName`, both of type `String`. For this, we will need to alter the `web.config` file. The changed `web.config` file is shown here:

```
<?xml version="1.0"?>
<configuration>
   <system.web>
      <profile>
         <properties>
            <add name="FirstName" type="System.String" />
            <add name="LastName" type="System.String" />
         </properties>
      </profile>
   </system.web>
</configuration>
```

Now that the profile properties we are going to store for each user are configured in the `web.config` file, the next step is to build a simple ASP.NET page that utilizes these property settings. Create a simple page that contains two `TextBox` controls that ask the end user for their first and last name. We will then input the values collected into the personalization engine via a button `click` event. The code for this page is as follows:

```
<%@ Page Language="VB" %>

<script runat="server">
    Protected Sub Button1_Click(ByVal sender As Object, _
       ByVal e As System.EventArgs)

        Profile.FirstName = TextBox1.Text
        Profile.LastName = TextBox1.Text

        Label1.Text = "First name: " & Profile.FirstName & _
            "<br>Last name: " & Profile.LastName
    End Sub
</script>

<html xmlns="http://www.w3.org/1999/xhtml" >
<head runat="server">
    <title>Welcome Page</title>
</head>
<body>
    <form id="form1" runat="server">
    <div>
        First name:<br />
        <asp:TextBox ID="TextBox1" Runat="server"></asp:TextBox>
        <br />
        Last name:<br />
        <asp:TextBox ID="TextBox2" Runat="server"></asp:TextBox>
        <br />
        <asp:Button ID="Button1" Runat="server" Text="Submit Information"
         OnClick="Button1_Click" />
        <br />
        <br />
        <asp:Label ID="Label1" Runat="server"></asp:Label>
    </div>
    </form>
</body>
</html>
```

With this page, when the page is posted back to itself, the values placed into the two text boxes are placed into the personalization engine and associated with this particular user through the use of the `Profile` object. When working with the `Profile` object in Visual Studio, you will notice that the custom properties you created are provided to you through IntelliSense. Once stored in the personalization engine, they are then available to you on any page within the application through the use of the same `Profile` object.

Configuring ASP.NET

Configuring ASP.NET is something that has been greatly enhanced in this release of ASP.NET. Instead of purely working with various XML configuration files to manage how ASP.NET works and performs, you can now use an MMC ASP.NET Snap-In. To get at this new ASP.NET configuration tool, open up IIS

(5.0 or 6.0) and expand the Web Sites folder. This folder shows a list of all the Web sites configured to work with IIS. Remember that not all of your Web sites are configured to work in this manner. It is also possible that you have built your Web application so that it is making use of the new ASP.NET built-in Web server.

After you find the application you are looking for in the Web Sites folder, right-click that application and select Properties from the list

Selecting the Properties option brings up the MMC console. The far-right tab is the ASP.NET tab. Click this tab to get the results shown here in Figure 17-29.

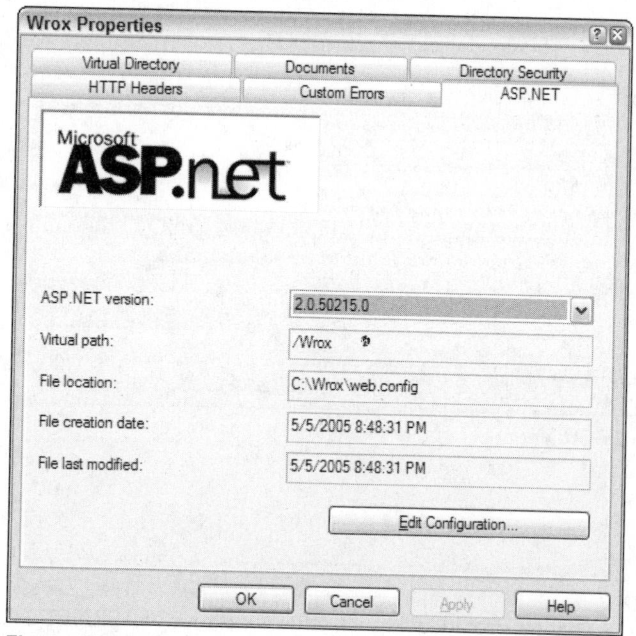

Figure 17-29

You should also note that selecting one of the application folders lets you edit the `web.config` file from the MMC snap-in; selecting Properties for the default Web site (the root node) lets you edit the `machine.config` file as well.

In addition to being able to edit the ASP.NET features that are shown in Figure 17-29, the ASP.NET tab also includes an Edit Configuration button that provides a tremendous amount of modification capabilities to use in the `web.config` file. When you click this button, you will then be provided with a multi-tabbed GUI titled ASP.NET Configuration Settings (shown here in Figure 17-30).

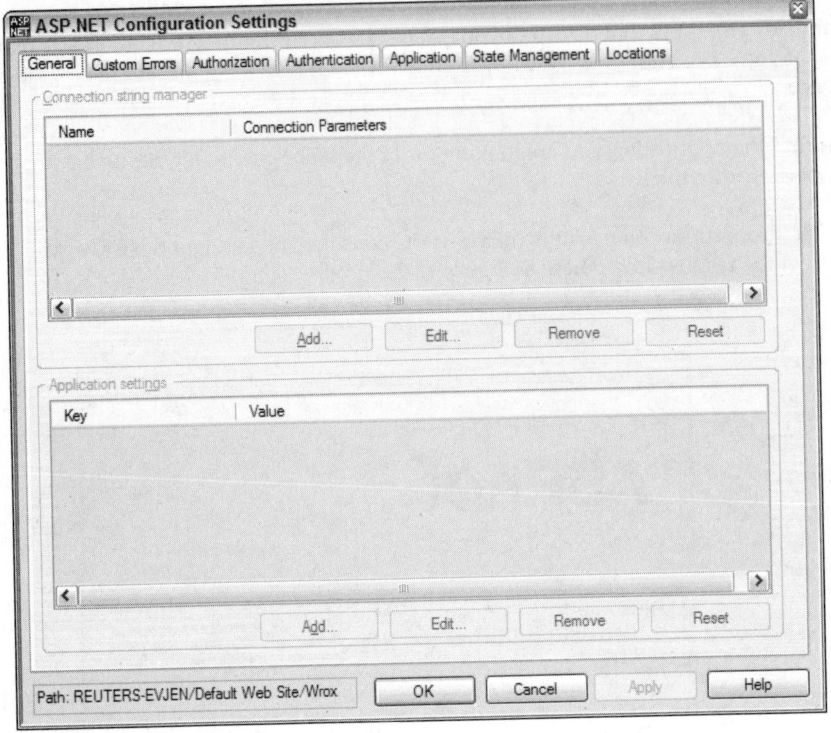

Figure 17-30

Summary

This and the previous chapter provided a quick whirlwind tour of ASP.NET 2.0 and some of the application features that you can give to the projects you develop. ASP.NET is really focused around the area of developer productivity and works very hard at providing you access to features and functions that most Web sites need to employ today. This chapter took a look at the following ASP.NET technologies:

- Cross-page posting
- ASP.NET compilation techniques
- Master page
- The datasource controls
- The new navigation system and some of the navigation server controls
- Membership and role management

The nice thing with the features presented is that you can utilize the wizards that are built into the underlying technology, or you can simply avoid these wizards and employ the technologies yourself. Either way is fine. The other nice feature about the technologies introduced is that they all allow for a huge amount of customization. You can alter the behavior and output of these technologies so that in the end, you get exactly what you are looking for. If you want to dig deeper into ASP.NET, be sure to take a look at Wrox's *Professional ASP.NET 2.0*.

18

Assemblies

By now, you've probably developed some programs in .NET, so you've seen the modules produced by the .NET compilers, which have file extensions of .dll or .exe. Most .NET modules are DLLs, including class libraries and those that serve as code-behind for ASP.NET. Windows applications, console applications, and Windows Services are examples of .NET modules that are executables and thus have an extension of .exe.

These .NET compiled modules, both DLLs and EXEs, are referred to as assemblies. Assemblies are the unit of deployment in .NET, containing both compiled code and metadata that is needed by the .NET Common Language Runtime (CLR) to run the code. Metadata includes information such as the code's identity and version, dependencies on other assemblies, and a list of types and resources exposed by the assembly.

Basic development in .NET doesn't require you to know any more than that. However, as your applications become more complex, and as you begin considering such issues as deployment and maintenance of your code, you need to understand more about assemblies. This chapter addresses that need. This chapter looks at:

- What assemblies are and how they are used
- The general structure of an assembly
- How assemblies can be versioned
- The Global Application Cache (GAC), including how and when to use it
- How assemblies are located and loaded by the CLR

Once this chapter has covered these essentials, Chapter 19 will use this information to discuss deployment in depth.

Assemblies

The assembly is used by the CLR as the smallest unit for:

- Deployment
- Version control
- Security
- Type grouping
- Code reuse

An assembly must contain a manifest, which tells the CLR what else is in the assembly. The other elements can be any of the following three categories:

- Type metadata
- Microsoft Intermediate Language (MSIL) code
- Resources

An assembly can be just one file. Figure 18-1 details the contents of a single-file assembly.

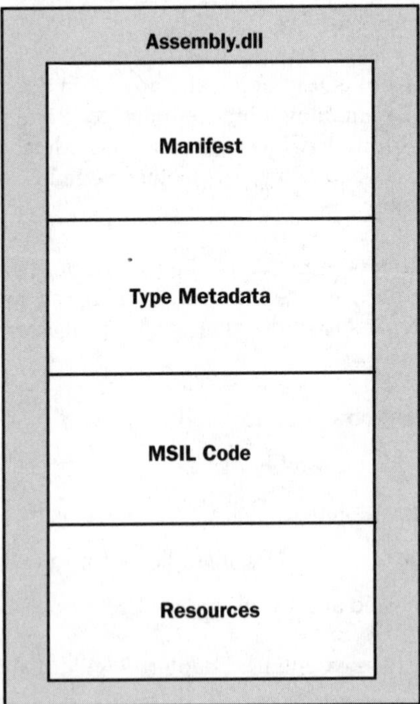

Figure 18-1

Alternatively, the structure can be split across multiple files, as shown in Figure 18-2. This is just one example of a multiple-file assembly configuration.

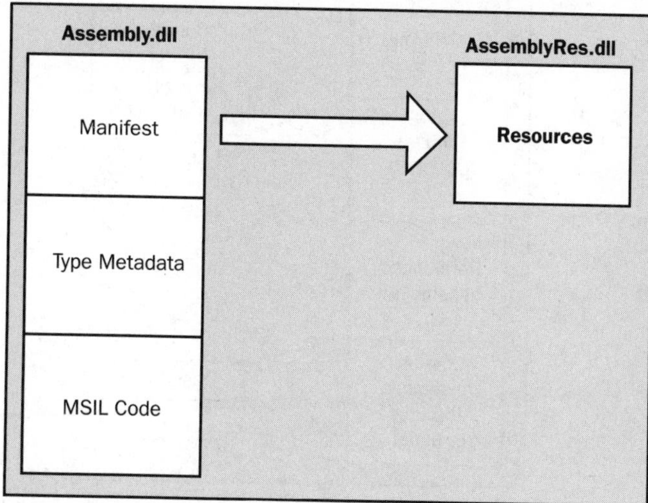

Figure 18-2

An assembly can only have one manifest section across all the files that make up the assembly. There is nothing stopping you, however, from having a resource section (or any of the other sections of type `Metadata` and MSIL code) in each of the files that make up an assembly. The ability to split an assembly across multiple files can help with deployment and specifically on-demand downloading.

The Manifest

The manifest is the part of the assembly that contains a list of the other elements contained in the assembly and basic identification information for the assembly. The manifest contains the largest part of the information that allows the assembly to be self-describing. Elements listed in the manifest are placed in appropriate sections. The manifest includes the sections displayed in Figure 18-3. We'll cover these sections later in the chapter.

To look at the manifest for a particular assembly, you can use the IL Disassembler (`Ildasm.exe`), which is part of the .NET Framework SDK. When `Ildasm.exe` loads up, you can browse for an assembly to view by selecting Open from the File menu. Once an assembly has been loaded into `Ildasm.exe`, it will disassemble the metadata contained within the assembly and present you with a tree view layout of the data. Initially, the tree view shows only top-level elements, as illustrated in Figure 18-4.

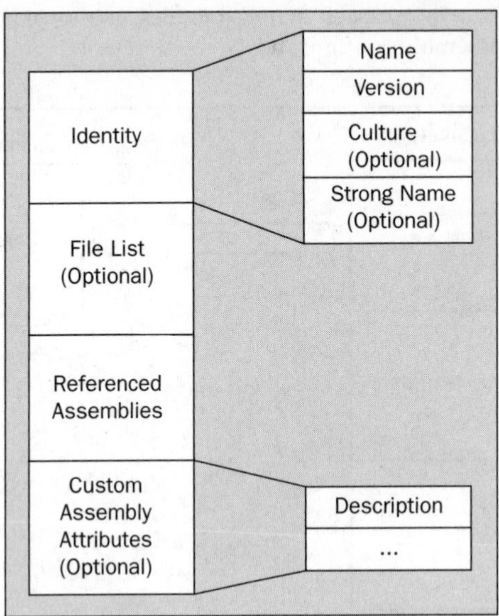

Figure 18-3

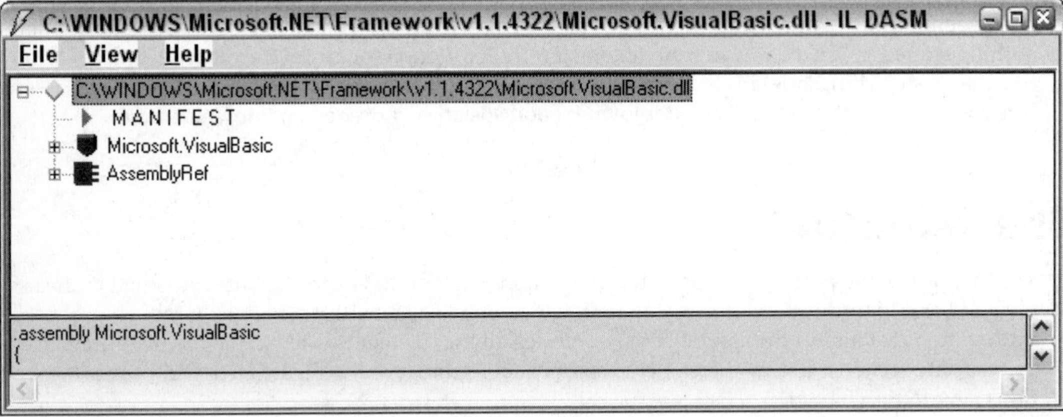

Figure 18-4

The full path of the assembly you are viewing will represent the root node. You will notice that the first node below the root is called MANIFEST and, as you've probably have guessed, it contains all the information about the assembly's manifest. If you double-click this node, a new window will be displayed, containing the information contained within the manifest, as shown in Figure 18-5.

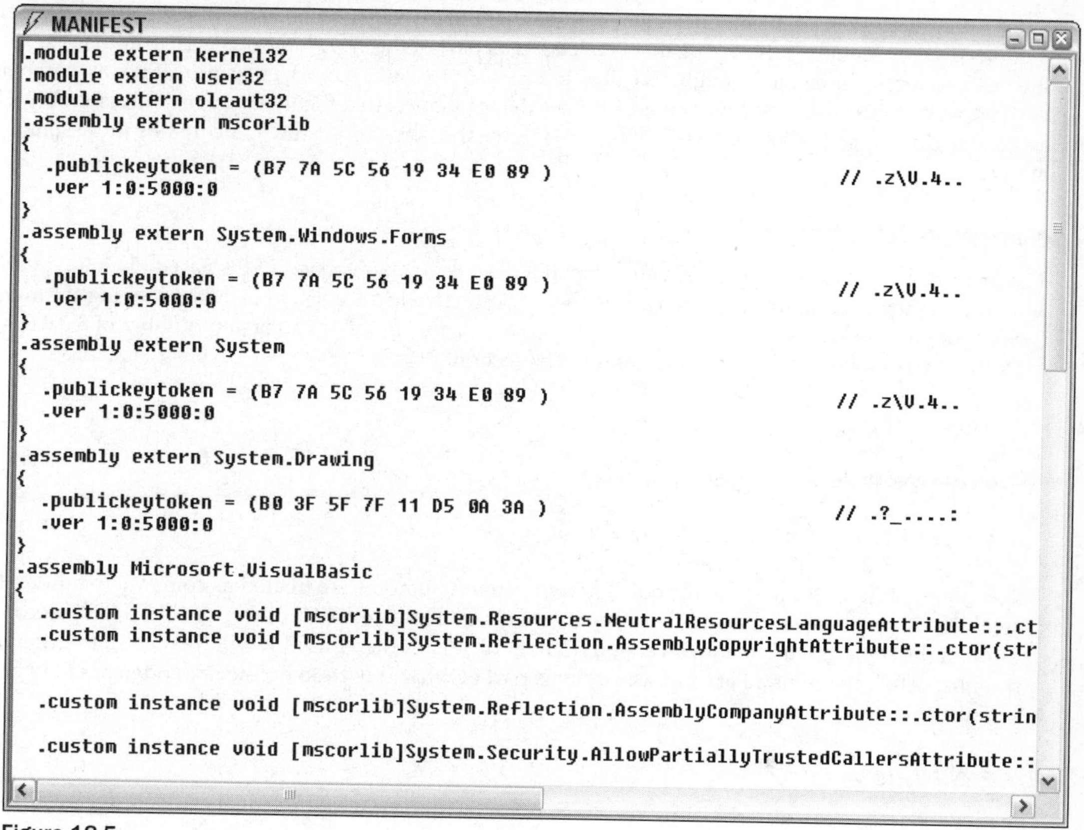

```
MANIFEST
.module extern kernel32
.module extern user32
.module extern oleaut32
.assembly extern mscorlib
{
  .publickeytoken = (B7 7A 5C 56 19 34 E0 89 )                         // .z\V.4..
  .ver 1:0:5000:0
}
.assembly extern System.Windows.Forms
{
  .publickeytoken = (B7 7A 5C 56 19 34 E0 89 )                         // .z\V.4..
  .ver 1:0:5000:0
}
.assembly extern System
{
  .publickeytoken = (B7 7A 5C 56 19 34 E0 89 )                         // .z\V.4..
  .ver 1:0:5000:0
}
.assembly extern System.Drawing
{
  .publickeytoken = (B0 3F 5F 7F 11 D5 0A 3A )                         // .?_....:
  .ver 1:0:5000:0
}
.assembly Microsoft.VisualBasic
{
  .custom instance void [mscorlib]System.Resources.NeutralResourcesLanguageAttribute::.ct
  .custom instance void [mscorlib]System.Reflection.AssemblyCopyrightAttribute::.ctor(str

  .custom instance void [mscorlib]System.Reflection.AssemblyCompanyAttribute::.ctor(strin

  .custom instance void [mscorlib]System.Security.AllowPartiallyTrustedCallersAttribute::
```

Figure 18-5

The Identity Section

The identity section of the manifest is what is used to uniquely identify this particular assembly. This section contains some standard information, such as the version number, and may also contain some optional elements, such as a strong name for the assembly (which we'll discuss below). There are certain restrictions on the information that must appear in the identity section, depending on the type of assembly. Assemblies come in two types: application-private and shared. (We will cover the differences between the two types shortly.)

The identity section of an assembly can be found by looking for the `.assembly` (without a following `extern`) directive in the Manifest window of `Ildasm.exe`. In Figure 18-5, the line that denotes the beginning of the identity section is:

```
.assembly Microsoft.VisualBasic
```

From the earlier figure of the manifest, you can see that the identity section can contain a number of subsections. Every assembly has a name that is declared as part of the `.assembly` directive; in the case of the last line, you can see the assembly is called `Microsoft.VisualBasic`. The name of the assembly is very important, because this is what the CLR uses to locate the actual file that contains the assembly. The extension .dll is appended to the assembly name to give the name of the file that contains the assembly manifest.

The Version Number

The identity section must also contain an entry that describes what version of the assembly it is. A version number for an assembly is presented by the .ver directive in `Ildasm.exe` and by looking through the output you can see that the `Microsoft.VisualBasic` assembly has a version number of 8:0:0:0, as indicated by the following entry in the `.assembly` section:

```
.ver 8:0:0:0
```

As you can see, there are four parts to a version number:

```
Major : Minor : Build : Revision
```

Assemblies that have the same name but different version numbers are treated as completely different assemblies. If you have an assembly on your machine that has a version number of 1.5.2.3 and another version of the same assembly with a version number of 1.6.0.1, then the CLR will treat them as different assemblies. The version number of an assembly is part of what is used to define dependencies between assemblies.

Strong Names

The identity section can also contain an optional strong name. The strong name is not a name as such but is, in fact, a public key that has been generated by the author of the assembly to uniquely identify the assembly. A strong name is used to ensure that your assembly has a unique signature compared to other assemblies that may have the same name. Strong names were introduced to combat DLL hell by providing an unambiguous way to differentiate among assemblies.

A strong name is based on public-private key encryption and creates a unique identity for your assembly. You can create a key pair that is used to create a strong name by using the SN tool included in the .NET Framework SDK (there is an example of how to do this in Chapter 21). The public key is stored in the identity section of the manifest. A signature of the file containing the assembly's manifest is created and stored in the resulting PE file. The .NET Framework uses these two signatures when resolving type references to ensure that the correct assembly is loaded at runtime. A strong name is indicated in the manifest by the `.publickey` directive in the `.assembly` section.

The Culture

The final part of an assembly's identity is its culture, which is optional. Cultures are used to define what country/language the assembly is targeted for.

The combination of name, strong name, version number, and culture is used by the CLR to enforce version dependencies. So, you could create one version of your assembly targeted at English users another for German users, another for Finnish users, and so on.

Cultures can be general as in the case of English or more specific as in the case of US-English. Cultures are represented by a string that can have two parts to it: primary and secondary (optional). The culture for English is `en`, and the culture for US-English is `en-us`.

If a culture is not indicated in the assembly, it is then assumed that the assembly can be used for any culture. Such an assembly is said to be culture-neutral.

A culture can be assigned to an assembly by including the attribute `AssemblyCulture` from the `System.Reflection` namespace in your assembly's code (usually within the `AssemblyInfo.vb` file):

```
<Assembly: AssemblyCulture("en")>
```

The culture of an assembly is represented in the manifest by the `.locale` directive in the `.assembly` section:

```
.locale = (65 00 6E 00 00 00)                                    // e.n...
```

Referenced Assemblies

The next section of the manifest that you are going to look at is the referenced assemblies section. As the name suggests, this section is where information is recorded about all the assemblies that you reference. An assembly reference is indicated in the manifest by the use of the `.assembly extern` directive, as shown in Figure 18-6.

```
MANIFEST
.assembly extern mscorlib
{
  .publickeytoken = (B7 7A 5C 56 19 34 E0 89 )                    // .z\V.4..
  .ver 1:0:5000:0
}
```

Figure 18-6

You can see in Figure 18-6 that various pieces of information are stored about an assembly when it is referenced. The first piece of information stored is the name of the assembly. This is included as part of the `.assembly extern` directive. The screenshot shows a reference to the `mscorlib` assembly. This name of the reference is used to determine the name of the file that contains the implementation of the assembly. The CLR takes the name of the assembly reference and appends `.dll`. So, in the last example, the CLR will look for a file called `mscorlib.dll` when it resolves the type references. The assembly `mscorlib` is a special assembly in .NET that contains all the definitions of the base types used in .NET and is referenced by all assemblies. The process that the CLR goes through to resolve a type reference is discussed later in this chapter.

The .publickeytoken Directive

If the assembly being referenced contains a strong name, then a hash of the public key of the referenced assembly is stored as part of the record to the external reference. This hash is stored in the manifest using the `.publickeytoken` directive as part of the `.assembly extern` section. The assembly reference shown in Figure 18-6 contains a hash of the strong name of the `mscorlib` assembly. The stored hash of the strong name is compared at runtime to a hash of the strong name (`.publickey`) contained within the referenced assembly to help ensure that the correct assembly is loaded. The value of the `.publickeytoken` is computed by taking the lower 8 bytes of a hash (SHA1) of the strong name of the referenced assemblies.

The .Ver Directive

The version of the assembly being referenced is also stored in the manifest. This version information is used with the rest of the information stored about a reference to ensure that the correct assembly is loaded; this will be discussed later. If an application references version 1.1.0.0 of an assembly, it will not load version 2.1.0.0 of the assembly unless a version policy (discussed later) exists to say otherwise. The version of the referenced assembly is stored in the manifest using the `.ver` directive as part of a `.assembly extern` section.

The .Locale Directive

If an assembly that is being referenced has a culture, then the culture information will also be stored in the external assembly reference section using the `.locale` directive. The combination of name, strong name (if it exists), version number, and culture are what make up a unique version of an assembly.

Assemblies and Deployment

The information in the manifest allows reliable determination of the identity and version of an assembly. This is the basis for the deployment options available in .NET, and for the side-by-side execution of assemblies that helps .NET overcome DLL hell. This section looks at these issues in detail.

Application-Private Assemblies

We mentioned earlier that assemblies can be of two types. The first is an application-private assembly. As the name implies, this type of assembly is used by one application only and is not shared. This is the default style of assembly in .NET and is the main mechanism by which an application can be independent of changes to the system.

Application-private assemblies are deployed into the application's own directory. Because application-private assemblies are not shared, they do not need a strong name. This means that, at a minimum, they only need to have a name and version number in the identity section of the manifest. Because the assemblies are private to the application, the application does not perform version checks on the assemblies, since the application developer has control over the assemblies that are deployed to the application directory. If strong names exist, however, the CLR will check that they match.

If all the assemblies that an application uses are application-private and the CLR is already installed on the target machine, then deployment is quite simple. Chapter 19 discusses this implication in more detail.

We'll discuss shared assemblies and the global application cache next.

Shared Assemblies

The second type of assembly is the shared assembly and, as the name suggests, this type of assembly can be shared among several different applications that reside on the same server. This type of assembly should only be used when it is important to share assemblies among many applications. For example, a Windows Forms control purchased as part of a package may be used in many of your applications, and thus it is better to install a shared version of the assembly rather than copies of it for each application. The .NET Framework assemblies themselves are also examples of shared assemblies.

There are certain requirements that are placed upon shared assemblies. The assembly needs to have a globally unique name, which is not a requirement of application-private assemblies. As mentioned earlier, strong names are used to create a globally unique name for an assembly. As the assembly is shared, all references to the shared assembly are checked to ensure the correct version is being used by an application.

Shared assemblies are stored in the (GAC), which is usually located in the `assembly` folder in the `Windows` directory (for example in Windows XP, `C:\Windows\Assembly`). However, it's not enough to just copy an assembly into that directory. The process for placing an assembly in the GAC is similar in concept to registering a COM DLL. That process is discussed in detail later.

No other changes to the code of the assembly are necessary to differentiate it from that of an application-private assembly. In fact, just because an assembly has a strong name does not mean that it has to be deployed as a shared assembly; it could just as easily be deployed in the application directory as an application-private assembly.

Installing a shared assembly into the GAC requires administrator rights on the machine. This is another factor complicating deployment of shared assemblies. Because of the extra effort involved in the creation and deployment of shared assemblies, you should avoid this type of assembly unless you really need it.

The Global Assembly Cache (GAC)

Each computer that has the .NET runtime installed has a GAC. However, assemblies in the GAC are always stored in the same folder, no matter which version of .NET you have. The folder is a subfolder of your main Windows folder, and it is named Assembly. If you have multiple versions of the .NET Framework, assemblies in the GAC for all of them are stored in this directory.

As previously noted, a strong name is required for an assembly placed in that GAC. That strong name is used to identify a particular assembly in the GAC. However, another piece of metadata is also used for verification of an assembly. When an assembly is created, a hash of the assembly is placed in the metadata. If an assembly is changed (with a binary editor, for example), the hash of the assembly will no longer match the hash in the metadata. The metadata hash is checked against the actual hash when an assembly is placed in the GAC with the `gacutil.exe` utility described later. If the two hash codes do not match, the installation cannot be completed.

The strong name is also used when an application resolves a reference to an external assembly. It checks that the public key stored in the assembly is equal to the hash of the public key stored as part of the reference in the application. If the two do not match, then the application knows that the external assembly has not been created by the original author of the assembly.

You can view the assemblies that are contained within the GAC by navigating to the directory using the Windows Explorer. This is shown in Figure 18-7.

assembly

File Edit View Favorites Tools Help

Back Search Folders

Address C:\WINDOWS\assembly Go

Global Assembly Name	Type	Version	Culture	Public Key Token
Microsoft.Matrix.Framework		0.6.0.0		6f763c9966660626
Microsoft.Matrix.Framework.Mobile		0.6.0.0		6f763c9966660626
Microsoft.Matrix.WebHost		0.6.0.0		6f763c9966660626
Microsoft.mshtml		7.0.3300.0		b03f5f7f11d50a3a
Microsoft.StdFormat		7.0.3300.0		b03f5f7f11d50a3a
Microsoft.Vbe.Interop		11.0.0.0		71e9bce111e9429c
Microsoft.VisualBasic		7.0.5000.0		b03f5f7f11d50a3a
Microsoft.VisualBasic.Compatibility		7.0.5000.0		b03f5f7f11d50a3a
Microsoft.VisualBasic.Compatibility.Data		7.0.5000.0		b03f5f7f11d50a3a
Microsoft.VisualBasic.Vsa		7.0.5000.0		b03f5f7f11d50a3a
Microsoft.VisualC		7.0.5000.0		b03f5f7f11d50a3a
Microsoft.VisualStudio	Native Images	1.0.5000.0		b03f5f7f11d50a3a
Microsoft.VisualStudio.VCCodeModel		7.0.5000.0		b03f5f7f11d50a3a
Microsoft.VisualStudio.VCProject		7.0.5000.0		b03f5f7f11d50a3a
Microsoft.VisualStudio.VCProjectEngine		7.0.5000.0		b03f5f7f11d50a3a
Microsoft.VisualStudio.VSHelp		7.0.3300.0		b03f5f7f11d50a3a
Microsoft.Vsa		7.0.5000.0		b03f5f7f11d50a3a
Microsoft.Vsa.Vb.CodeDOMProcessor		7.0.5000.0		b03f5f7f11d50a3a
Microsoft.VSDesigner	Native Images	7.0.5000.0		b03f5f7f11d50a3a
Microsoft.VSDesigner.Mobile	Native Images	7.0.5000.0		b03f5f7f11d50a3a
Microsoft_VsaVb		7.0.5000.0		b03f5f7f11d50a3a
mscomctl		10.0.4504.0		31bf3856ad364e35
mscorcfg		1.0.5000.0		b03f5f7f11d50a3a

Figure 18-7

The `gacutil.exe` utility that ships with .NET is used to add and remove assemblies from the GAC. To add an assembly into the GAC using the `gacutil.exe` tool, use the following command line:

```
gacutil.exe /i myassembly.dll
```

Recall that the assembly being loaded must have a strong name.

To remove an assembly, use the `/u` option like this:

```
gacutil.exe /u myassembly.dll
```

`gacutil.exe` has a number of other options. You can examine them and see examples of their usage by typing in the command:

```
gacutil.exe /?
```

Versioning Issues

Although COM was a landmark achievement in Windows programming history, it left much to be desired when it came to maintaining backward compatibility. COM used type libraries to describe its interfaces and each interface was represented by a GUID. Each interface ID was stored in the registry along with other related entries which made for a complex set of interrelated registry entries. The separation between the registry entries and the actual DLL on disk made it extremely easy for things to go wrong. A wrong registry entry or simply a mismatched GUID rendered the DLL useless.

The problem is that COM DLLs are not self-describing. They rely heavily on the registry having the correct entries. Another problem lies with the operating system not being able to best resolve differences between different DLL versions. Prior versions of Visual Basic relied on the `Server.coClass` and not the actual version of the DLL. This means it's not possible to require a certain version of a COM DLL as a dependency. A different DLL with the same nominal version number may be indistinguishable from the one desired.

.NET's versioning scheme was specifically designed to alleviate the problems of COM. The major capabilities of .NET that solve versioning issues are:

- Application isolation
- Side-by-side execution
- Self-describing components

Application Isolation

For an application to be isolated it should be self-contained and independent. This means that the application should rely on its own dependencies for ActiveX controls, components, or files, and not have those files shared with other applications. The option of having application isolation is essential for a good solution to versioning problems.

If an application is isolated, components are owned, managed by, and used by the parent application alone. If a component is used by another application, even if it is the same version, the other application must have its very own copy. This ensures that each application can install and uninstall dependencies and not interfere with other applications.

> **Does this sound familiar? This is what most early Windows and DOS applications did until COM required registration of DLLs in the registry and placement of shared DLLs in the system directory. The wheel surely does turn!**

The .NET Framework caters to application isolation by allowing us to create application-private assemblies that are for individual applications and are repeated physically on disk for each client. This means that each client is independent from the other. This isolation works best for many scenarios. It is sometimes referred to as a "zero-impact" deployment because there is no chance of causing problems for any other application by either installing or uninstalling such an application.

Side-by-Side Execution

Side-by-side execution occurs when multiple versions of the same assembly can run at the same time. Side-by-side execution is performed by the CLR. Components that are to execute side-by-side must be installed within the application directory or a subdirectory of it. This ensures application isolation (as discussed earlier).

With application assemblies, versioning is not much of an issue. The interfaces are dynamically resolved by the CLR. You can replace an application assembly with a different version, and the CLR will load it and make it work with the other assemblies in the application, as long as the new version does not have any interface incompatibilities. The new version may even have elements of the interface that are new and that don't exist in the old version (new properties or methods). As long as the existing class interface elements used by the other application assemblies are unchanged, the new version will work fine. When we discuss exactly how the CLR locates a referenced assembly below, you'll see more about how this works.

Self-Describing

In the earlier section on the manifest, the self-describing nature of .NET assemblies was mentioned. The term self-describing means that all the information the CLR needs to know to load and execute an assembly is inside the assembly itself.

Self-describing components are essential to .NET's side-by-side execution. Once the extra version is known by the CLR to be needed, everything else about the assembly needed to run side-by-side is in the assembly itself. Each application can get its own version of an assembly, and all the work to coordinate the versions in memory is performed transparently by the CLR.

Versioning becomes more important with shared assemblies. Without good coordination of versions, .NET applications with shared assemblies are subject to some of the same problems as COM applications. In particular, if a new version of a shared assembly is placed in the GAC, there must be a means to control which applications get which version of a shared assembly. This is accomplished with versioning policy.

Version Policies

As discussed earlier, a version number comprises four parts: major, minor, build, and revision. The version number is used as part of the identity of the assembly. When a new version of a shared assembly is created and placed in the GAC, any of these parts can change. Which ones change affects how the CLR views compatibility for the new assembly.

When the version number of a component only changes by its build and revision parts, it is compatible. This is often referred to as Quick Fix Engineering (QFE). It's only necessary to place the new assembly in the GAC, and it will automatically be considered compatible with applications that were created to use the older version that had different numbers for the build and revision.

If either the major or minor build number changes, however, compatibility is not assumed by the CLR. In that case, there are manual ways to indicate compatibility if necessary, and these are covered later in this section.

When an application comes across a type that is implemented in an external reference, the CLR has to determine what version of the referenced assembly to load. What steps does the CLR go through to ensure the correct version of an assembly is loaded? To answer this question, you need to look at version policies and how they affect what version of an assembly is loaded.

The Default Versioning Policy

Let's start by looking at the default versioning policy. This policy is what is followed in the absence of any configuration files on the machine that modify the versioning policy. The default behavior of the runtime is to consult the manifest for the name of the referenced assembly and the version of the assembly to use.

If the referenced assembly does not contain a strong name, it is assumed that the referenced assembly is application-private and is located in the application directory. The CLR takes the name of the referenced assembly and appends .dll to create the file name that contains the referenced assembly's manifest. The CLR then searches in the application's directory for the file name and, if it's found, it will use the version that was found even if the version number is different from the one specified in the manifest. Therefore, the version numbers of application-private assemblies are not checked, because the application developer, in theory, has control over which assemblies are deployed to the application's directory. If the file cannot be found, the CLR will raise a `System.IO.FileNotFoundException`.

Automatic Quick Fix Engineering Policy

If the referenced assembly contains a strong name, the process by which an assembly is loaded is different:

1. The three different types of assembly configuration files (discussed later) are consulted, if they exist, to see if they contain any settings that will modify which version of the assembly the CLR should load.
2. The CLR will then check to see if the assembly has been requested and loaded in a previous call. If it has, it will use the loaded assembly.
3. If the assembly is not already loaded, the GAC is then queried for a match. If a match is found, then this assembly will be used by the application.
4. If any of the configuration files contains a `codebase` (discussed later) entry for the assembly, the assembly is looked for in the location specified. If the assembly cannot be found in the location specified in the `codebase`, a `TypeLoadException` is raised to the application.
5. If there are no configuration files or if there are no `codebase` entries for the assembly, the CLR then moves on to probe for the assembly starting in the application's base directory.
6. If the assembly still hasn't been found, the CLR will ask the Windows Installer service if it has the assembly in question. If it does, then the assembly is installed and the application uses this newly installed assembly. This is a feature called on-demand installation.

If the assembly hasn't been found by the end of this entire process, a `TypeLoadException` will be raised.

Although a referenced assembly contains a strong name, this does not mean that it has to be deployed into the GAC. This allows application developers to install a version with the application that is known to work. The GAC is consulted to see if it contains a version of an assembly with a higher `build.revision` number to enable administrators to deploy an updated assembly without having to reinstall or rebuild the application. This is known as the Automatic Quick Fix Engineering Policy.

Configuration Files

The default versioning policy described earlier may not be the most appropriate policy for your requirements. Fortunately, you can modify this policy through the use of XML configuration files to meet your specific needs. There are three types of configuration files that can be created:

- The first is an application configuration file, and it is created in the application directory. As the name implies, this configuration file applies to a single application only. To do this, you need to create the application configuration file in the application directory with the same name as the application file name and appending `.config`. For example, suppose that you have a Windows Forms application called `HelloWorld.exe` installed in the `C:\ HelloWorld` directory. The application configuration file would be: `C:\HelloWorld\HelloWorld.exe.config`.
- The second type of configuration file is called the machine configuration file. It is named `machine.config` and can be found in the `C:\Windows\ Microsoft.NET\ Framework \v2.0.xxxx\ CONFIG` directory. The `machine.config` file overrides any other configuration files on a machine and can be thought of as containing glo.bal settings.
- The third type of configuration file is the security configuration file, and it contains information regarding the code access security system. The code access security system allows you to grant/deny access to resources by an assembly. This configuration file must be located within the `Windows` directory.

The main purpose of the configuration file is to provide binding-related information to the developer or administrator who wishes to override the default policy handling of the CLR.

Specifically, the configuration file, as it's written in XML, has a root node named `<configuration>` and must have the end node of `</configuration>` present to be syntactically correct.

The configuration file is divided into specific types of nodes that represent different areas of control. These areas are:

- Startup
- Runtime
- Remoting
- Crypto
- Class API
- Security

Although all of these areas are important, in this chapter you will look only at the first two.

All of the settings that are going to be discussed can be added to the application configuration file. Some of the settings (these will be pointed out) can also be added to the machine configuration file. If a setting in the application configuration file conflicts with that of one in the machine configuration file, then the setting in the machine configuration is used. When we talk about assembly references in the following discussion of configuration settings, we are talking exclusively about shared assemblies (which implies that the assemblies have a strong name, since assemblies in the GAC are required to have one).

Startup Settings

The <startup> node of the application and machine configuration files has a <requiredRuntime> node that specifies the runtime version required by the application. This is so because different versions of the CLR can run on a machine side by side. The following example shows how you would specify the version of the .NET runtime inside the configuration file:

```
<configuration>
  <startup>

    <requiredRuntime version ="2.0.xxxx" safemode ="true"/>
  </startup>
</configuration>
```

Runtime Settings

The runtime node, which is written as <runtime> (not to be confused with <requiredRuntime>), specifies the settings that manage how the CLR handles garbage collection and versions of assemblies. With these settings, you can specify which version of an assembly the application requires or redirect it to another version entirely.

Loading a Particular Version of an Assembly

The application and machine configuration files can be used to ensure that a particular version of an assembly is loaded. You can indicate whether this version should be loaded all the time or only to replace a specific version of the assembly. This functionality is supported through the use of the <assemblyIdentity> and <bindingRedirect> elements in the configuration file. For example:

```
<configuration>
  <runtime>
    <assemblyBinding xmlns="urn:schemas-microsoft-com:asm.v1">
      <dependentAssembly>
        <assemblyIdentity name="AssemblyName"
                          publickeytoken="b77a5c561934e089"
                          culture="en-us"/>
          <bindingRedirect oldVersion="*"
                           newVersion="2.0.50.0"/>
      </dependentAssembly>
    </assemblyBindings>
  </runtime>
</configuration>
```

The <assemblyBinding> node is used to declare settings for the locations of assemblies and redirections via the <dependentAssembly> node and also the <probing> node (which you will look at shortly).

In the last example, when the CLR resolves the reference to the assembly named AssemblyName, it will load version 2.0.50.0 instead of the version that appears in the manifest. If you would like to only load version 2.0.50.0 of the assembly when a specific version is referenced, then you can replace the value of the oldVersion attribute with the version number that you would like to replace (for example, 1.5.0.0). The publickeytoken attribute is used to store the hash of the strong name of the assembly to replace. This is used to ensure that the correct assembly is identified. The same is true of the culture attribute.

Defining the Location of an Assembly

The location of an assembly can also be defined in both the application and machine configuration files. You can use the <codeBase> element to inform the CLR of the location of an assembly. This enables you to distribute an application and have the externally referenced assemblies downloaded the first time they are used. This is called on-demand downloading. For example:

```
<configuration>
  <runtime>
    <assemblyBinding xmlns="urn:schemas-microsoft-com:asm.v1">
      <dependentAssembly>
        <assemblyIdentity name="AssemblyName"
                          publickeytoken="b77a5c561934e089"
                          culture="en-us"/>
        <codeBase version="2.0.50.0"
                  href="http://www.wrox.com/AssemblyName.dll/>
      </dependentAssembly>
    </assemblyBindings>
  </runtime>
</configuration>
```

From the previous example, you can see that whenever a reference to version 2.0.50.0 of the assembly AssemblyName is resolved (and the assembly isn't already on the users computer), the CLR will try to load the assembly from the location defined in the href attribute. The location defined in the href attribute is a standard URL and can be used to locate a file across the Internet or locally.

If the assembly cannot be found or the details in the manifest of the assembly defined in the href attribute do not match those defined in the configuration file, the loading of the assembly will fail and you will receive a TypeLoadException. If the version of the assembly in the preceding example is actually 2.0.60.0, then the assembly will load, because the version number is only different by build and revision number.

Providing the Search Path

The final use of configuration files that you will look at is that of providing the search path for use when locating assemblies in the application's directory. This setting only applies to the application configuration file. By default, the CLR will only search for an assembly in the application's base directory—it will not look in any subdirectories. You can modify this behavior by using the <probing> element in an application configuration file. For example:

```
<configuration>
  <runtime>
    <assemblyBinding xmlns="urn:schemas-microsoft-com:asm.v1">
      <probing privatePath="regional"/>
    </assemblyBinding>
  </runtime>
</configuration>
```

The privatePath attribute can contain a list of directories relative to the application's directory (separated by a semicolon) that you would like the CLR to search in when trying to locate an assembly. The privatePath attribute cannot contain an absolute pathname.

As part of an assembly reference being resolved, the CLR will check in the application's base directory for it. If it cannot find it, it will look through in order all the subdirectories specified in the `privatePath` variable, as well as looking for a subdirectory with the same name as the assembly. If the assembly being resolved is called `AssemblyName`, the CLR will also check for the assembly in a subdirectory called `AssemblyName`, if it exists.

This isn't the end of the story, though. If the referenced assembly being resolved contains a culture setting, the CLR will also check for culture-specific subdirectories in each of the directories it searches in. For example, if the CLR is trying to resolve a reference to an assembly named `AssemblyName` with a culture of `en` and a `privatePath` equal to that in the last example, and the application being run has a home directory of `C:\ExampleApp`, the CLR will look in the following directories (in the order they are shown):

- `C:\ExampleApp`
- `C:\ExampleApp\en`
- `C:\ExampleApp\en\AssemblyName`
- `C:\ExampleApp\regional\en`
- `C:\ExampleApp\regional\en\AssemblyName`

As you can see, the CLR can probe quite a number of directories to locate an assembly.

When an external assembly is resolved by the CLR, it consults the configuration files first to see if it needs to modify the process by which it resolves an assembly. As discussed, the resolution process can be modified to suit your needs.

Dynamic Loading of Assemblies

The discussion above about locating and loading assemblies refers to assemblies that are known at compile time through the application's references. There is an alternative method of locating and loading an assembly that is useful for certain scenarios.

In this technique, the location of the assembly is supplied by the application, using a URL or file name. The normal rules for locating the assembly do not apply—only the location specified by the application is used.

The location is just a string variable, and so it may come from a configuration file or database. In fact, the assembly to be loaded may be newly created, and perhaps did not even exist when the original application was compiled. Because the information to load the assembly can be passed into the application on the fly at runtime, this type of assembly loading is called dynamic loading.

The Assembly Class

References to assemblies, and operations to be performed on assemblies in code are mostly contained in a .NET Framework class called the `Assembly` class. It is part of the `System.Reflection` namespace. In the code examples that follow, assume that the following `Imports` statement is at the top of the code module:

```
Imports System.Reflection
```

The `Assembly` class has a shared method called `LoadFrom`, which takes a URL or file name, and returns a reference to the assembly at that location. Here's a code example of `LoadFrom` in action:

```
Dim asmDynamic As [Assembly]
asmDynamic = [Assembly].LoadFrom("http://www.dotnetmasters.com/loancalc2.dll")
```

The brackets around `Assembly` are needed because it is a reserved keyword in Visual Basic. The brackets indicate that the word applies to the `Assembly` class, and the keyword is not being used.

After these lines are executed, the code contains a reference to the assembly at the given location. That allows other operations on the assembly to take place. One such operation is to get a reference to a particular type (which could be a class, structure, or enumeration) in the assembly. The reference to a type is needed to instantiate the type when an assembly is loaded dynamically. The `GetType` method of the `Assembly` class is used to get the reference, using a string that represents the identification of the type. The identification consists of the full namespace path that uniquely identifies the type within the current application.

For example, suppose that you wanted to get an instance of a certain form that was in the assembly, with a namespace path of `MyProject.Form1`. The following line of code would get a reference to the type for that form:

```
Dim typMyForm As Type = formAsm.GetType("MyProject.Form1")
```

The type reference can then be used to generate an instance of the type. To do this you need another class in `System.Reflection` called the `Activator` class. This class has a shared method called `CreateInstance`, which takes a type reference, and returns an instance of that type. (If you are familiar with Active Server Pages and older versions of Visual Basic, `CreateInstance` is functionally similar to the `CreateObject` function in those environments.) You could, thus, get an instance of the form with these lines:

```
Dim objForm As Object
objForm = Activator.CreateInstance(typeMyForm)
```

`CreateInstance` always returns a generic object. That means it may be necessary to coerce the returned reference to a particular type to gain access to the type's interface. For example, assuming that you knew the object was actually a Windows Form, you could coerce the instance above into the type of `System.Windows.Forms.Form` and then do normal operations that are available on a form:

```
Dim FormToShow As Form = CType(objForm, System.Windows.Forms.Form)
FormToShow.MdiParent = Me
FormToShow.Show()
```

At this point, the form will operate normally. It will behave no differently from a form that was in a referenced assembly.

If the newly loaded form needs to load other classes that are in the dynamic assembly, nothing special needs to be done. For example, suppose that the form just shown needs to load an instance of another form, named `Form2`, that resides in the same dynamically loaded assembly. The standard code to instantiate a form will work fine. The CLR will automatically load the `Form2` type because it already has a reference to the assembly containing `Form2`.

Furthermore, suppose that the dynamically loaded form needs to instantiate a class from another DLL that is not referenced by the application. For example, suppose that the form needs to create an instance of a `Customer` object, and the `Customer` class is in a different DLL. As long as that DLL is in the same folder as the dynamically loaded DLL, the CLR will automatically locate and load the second DLL.

Putting Assemblies to Work

The previous code examples include hard-coded strings for the location of the assembly and the identification of the type. There are uses for such a technique, such as certain types of Internet deployment of an application. However, when using dynamic loading, it is common for these values to be obtained from outside the code. For example, a database table or an XML-based configuration file can be used to store the information.

This enables you to add new capabilities to an application on the fly. A new assembly with new functionality can be written, and then the location of the assembly and the identity of the type to load from the assembly can be added to the configuration file or database table.

Unlike application assemblies automatically located by the CLR, which must be in the application's directory or a subdirectory of it, dynamically loaded assemblies can be anywhere the application knows how to get to. Possibilities include:

- A Web site (as in the example above)
- A directory on the local machine
- A directory on a shared network machine

However, the security privileges available to code do vary, depending on where the assembly was loaded from. Code loaded from a URL via HTTP, as shown earlier, has a very restricted set of privileges by default compared to code loaded from a local directory. Chapter 13 has details on code access security, default security policies, and how default policies can be changed.

Summary

Assemblies are the basic unit of deployment and versioning in .NET. Simple applications can be written and installed without knowing much about assemblies. More complex applications require an in-depth understanding of the structure of assemblies, the metadata they contain, and how assemblies are located and loaded by the CLR.

You have looked at how the identity of an assembly is used to allow multiple versions of an assembly to be installed on a machine and run side by side. This chapter covered how an assembly is versioned, and the process by which the CLR resolves an external assembly reference and how you can modify this process through the use of configuration files.

You also looked at how an assembly stores information such as version number, strong name, and culture about any external assemblies that it references. You also saw how this information is checked at runtime to ensure that the correct version of the assembly is referenced and how you can use versioning policies to override this in the case of a buggy assembly. The assembly is the single biggest aid in reducing the errors that can occur due to DLL hell and in helping with deployment.

The chapter also discussed the capability to load an assembly dynamically, based on a location that is derived at runtime. This capability is useful for some special deployment scenarios, such as simple Internet deployment.

Understanding all these elements helps you understand how to structure an application, when and how to use shared assemblies, and the deployment implications of your choices for assemblies.

Simple applications are usually done with no strong names or shared assemblies, and all assemblies for the application are deployed to the application directory. Versioning issues are rare as long as class interfaces are consistent.

Complex applications may require shared assemblies to be placed in the GAC, which means that those assemblies must have strong names, and you must control your version numbers. You also need to understand your options for allowing an application to load a different version of an assembly than the one it would load by default, or to load assemblies dynamically using an application-specific technique to determine the assembly's location. This chapter has covered the basics for all of these needs.

19

Deployment

.NET has many effects on how we create and use software. Some of the most dramatic changes are in the area of deployment. .NET offers a host of deployment options that were not available for older, COM-based software. These options completely change the economics of deployment. The changes are so important that they can even alter the preferred architecture for a system written in .NET.

As experienced developers know, deployment is the process of taking an application that has been developed and placing it in the production environment in which it will be used. This can include many steps. Setting up databases, placing software in appropriate directories on servers, and configuring options for a particular installation are some of the actions that fall under the deployment category.

But deployment is not just concerned with the initial process of getting an application up and running. Deployment also includes handling of changes and upgrades to the application. Depending on the application and the number of users, dealing with these maintenance tasks can be far more complex than the initial installation of the application.

This chapter is going to look at what VS.NET and the CLR have to offer to help in deployment of applications. Now that you understand assemblies (covered in the previous chapter), we are going to start discussing the problems that occur when you deploy applications, along with a number of terms that are used when talking about application deployment. You will then move to look at what the CLR contains that helps alleviate some of the deployment issues discussed previously. The remainder of the chapter covers:

- Creating deployment projects in VS.NET, which allow initial installation of applications
- Deployment of the .NET Framework itself on systems where it does not already reside
- Updating applications on servers, including components and ASP.NET applications
- Installing and updating Windows Forms applications on client machines

This last subject covers the most common options for client deployment, including a new deployment technology in Visual Studio 2005 and .NET Framework 2.0 called ClickOnce.

Deployment in .NET is a huge topic and we can't hope to cover every aspect in the pages that we have for this chapter. What this chapter should give you is an understanding of, a basic knowledge of, and the desire to learn more about the options available to you.

Application Deployment

This section begins by discussing the main issues associated with application deployment and defining a few common terms that are used. It then moves on to discuss the deployment options available prior to .NET. Hopefully, this will give you an understanding of the issues to be overcome when considering deployment in .NET.

In the context of this chapter, *application deployment* includes two principle functions:

- The process of taking an application, packaging it up, and installing it on another machine
- The process of updating an application that has already been installed with new or changed functionality

Deployment can, in some cases, also include placing the .NET Framework itself on a particular machine. This task will be broken out as a separate task for this chapter. We will assume for most of the chapter that the .NET Framework is installed on any machines in question. During the discussion of creating deployment projects, we will discuss what to do if the .NET Framework is not available on a system.

Why Is Deployment Easier in .NET?

Pre-.NET applications for Microsoft Windows were typically based on a technology called COM. While COM had many interesting benefits as a development platform, its most significant weak point was deployment. All components in a COM environment had to be *registered*, which means that they had a record embedded in the local machine's registry to assist in identifying and locating the component.

COM components also had inflexible versioning capabilities, which resulting in the possibility that two versions that were both needed by applications could not simultaneously be available on the same machine. As mentioned previously, the versioning requirements of COM led to a condition colloquially referred to as DLL hell.

DLL Hell

What does DLL hell mean? The term is actually used to describe a number of problems that can arise when multiple applications share a common component. The common component is usually a .dll or a COM component. The problems usually arise for one of three following reasons:

- The first common cause of DLL hell is installing a new application that overwrites a shared component with a version that is not compatible with the version that already resides on the computer. Any applications that relied on the previous version of the component could well be rendered unusable. This often occurrs when installing an application that overwrites a system file (for example, `MFC42.dll`) with an older version. Any application that relied on the functionality of the newer version will stop working. When installing an application on the computer, the installer should check that it is not overwriting a newer version of the component. However, not all installations do this check.

- The second cause is installing a new version of a shared component that is binarily compatible (the public interface matches exactly) with the previous version, but in which, when updating the functionality, a new bug has been introduced into the component that could cause any application that depends on the component to misbehave or stop working. This type of error can be very hard to diagnose.
- The third common cause is an application that uses a feature of a common component that is actually an undocumented and unexpected behavior in the component: a side effect. When this shared component is updated with a newer version, the side effect may well have disappeared, breaking any applications that depended on it. There are many undocumented API calls available in DLLs; the problem is that, because they are undocumented, they may well disappear in a subsequent version without warning.

As the discussion indicates, DLL hell can be caused by a variety of reasons and the effects can be wide ranging. Applications may stop working, but worse still, it could introduce subtle bugs that may lie undetected for some time. It may be some time before you realize an application has stopped working, which can make it significantly harder to detect the cause of the problem.

Microsoft has tried to address some of these issues with the latest versions of Windows by introducing Windows File Protection and private DLLs:

- As the name suggests Windows File Protection is a mechanism by which the OS protects a list of system DLLs from being overwritten with a different version. Normally, only service packs and other OS updates can update the DLLs that are protected, although this can be overridden by changing some registry keys. This should reduce some of the causes of DLL hell that are caused by the overwriting of system DLLs.
- The second feature introduced is that of private DLLs. Private DLLs are used by one particular application only and are not shared among different applications. If an application relies on a specific version of a .dll file or COM component, then it can be installed in the application directory and a .local file created in the directory to inform that OS to look for private DLLs first and then move on to look for shared DLLs.

However, while these capabilities have helped, DLL hell and the need for component registration still cause COM applications to be difficult and expensive to deploy and maintain. One of the primary goals in designing .NET was to overcome these COM deployment drawbacks. All versions of .NET include features to simplify deployment, including two key ones — eliminating registration and side-by-side execution of DLLs.

No Registration in .NET

As covered in the previous chapter, assemblies in .NET are self-describing. All the information needed to execute an assembly is normally contained in the assembly itself. Thus, there is no need to place any information in the Windows registry. As long as the CLR can locate an assembly needed by an application (the process of location was discussed in the previous chapter), then the assembly can be run.

Side-by-Side Execution

Multiple versions of an assembly can be executed by .NET, even if they have exactly the same interface and nominal version number. The previous chapter explained why this is true. The implication for deployment is that each application can deploy the assemblies it needs and be assured that there will be no conflict with the assemblies needed by other applications.

These .NET capabilities, thus, allow many deployment possibilities, from simple to complex. Let's start by looking at the simplest method of deployment, which harkens back to the days of DOS—XCOPY deployment.

XCOPY Deployment

The term *XCOPY deployment* was coined to describe an ideal deployment scenario. Its name derives from the DOS `xcopy` command that is used to copy an entire directory structure from one location to another. XCOPY deployment relates to a scenario where all you have to do to deploy an application is to copy the directory (including all child directories) to the computer that you would like to run the program.

Why can't you use XCOPY deployment at present for older Windows applications? The main reason is that installing an application currently is a multistep process. First, the component needs to be copied to the machine, and then the component must be registered on the machine, creating a dependency between the component and the registry. The application requires the entry in the registry to activate the component. Because of this coupling between the component and the registry, it is not possible to install the component simply by copying it from one machine to another.

All but the simplest of applications also require other dependencies (such as databases, message queues, document extensions) to be created on the new computer. The CLR tries to overcome the problem of the coupling between the registry and components, but at present it cannot help with the dependencies that are required by more advanced applications. You are closer to XCOPY deployment with .NET, and in some cases you may actually be able to achieve a form of it.

Using the Windows Installer

Microsoft introduced the *Windows Installer* service as part of Windows 2000 as a way to simplify installation of applications. Although the Windows Installer service was released as part of Windows 2000, it can also be installed on previous versions of Windows and is automatically installed with several Microsoft applications (such as Microsoft Office). The Windows Installer service is what Microsoft calls an *operating system component*. The service implements all the required rules that a setup needs (for instance, *do not overwrite a system file with an older version*).

Instead of creating an executable that contains all the rules to install the application, you create a file, called a *Windows Installer package file*, which describes what needs to be done to install your application. Such files have an extension of .msi, which is an acronym derived from "Microsoft Installer."

An application is described in the resulting Windows Installer package as being made up of three parts: components, features, and products. Each part is made up of any number of the previous parts. For example, a product is made up of several features, and a feature may contain one or more components. The component is the smallest part of the installation and contains a group of files and other resources that need to be installed together. You will not be going into the underlying details of the Windows Installer architecture. If you are interested then you should take a look at the Windows Installer SDK documentation on MSDN.

The files that make up a product can be packaged externally in a number of cabinet files or the files can be packaged up into the resultant .msi file. As you will see later, there are a number of options within the deployment project templates that allow you to specify how the product's files are packaged. When the user requests that a particular application be installed he or she can just double-click the .msi file (assuming the Windows Installer service is installed). If the Windows Installer service is not installed there is usually a `Setup.exe` file that will install the Windows Installer service first. The service will read the file and determine what needs to be done (such as which files need to be copied and where they need to be copied to) to install the application. All the installation rules are implemented centrally by the service and do not need to be distributed as part of a setup executable. The Windows Installer package file contains a list of actions (such as *copy file mfc40.dll to the windows system folder*) and what rules need to be applied to these actions. It does not contain the implementation of the rules.

The Windows Installer service also provides a rich API that developers can use to include features, such as on-demand installing, into their applications. One of the biggest complaints about previous installers is that if the installation fails, the user's computer is often left in an unstable state. The Windows Installer service overcomes this by providing a rollback method. If the installation fails for some reason, the Windows Installer service will rollback the computer to its original state, so you could say that the installation is transactional.

You can manually create a Windows Installer package file using the Windows Installer SDK tools. However, this is not very user-friendly, so Microsoft integrated creation of MSI files into the development environment. Three out of the four actual deployment/setup templates in VS.NET use Windows Installer technology. You will look at these in more detail later in the chapter.

Once an MSI file has been created for an application, the application can be installed by merely double-clicking on the MSI file in Windows Explorer. The Windows Installer will take over and use the MSI file to determine what steps are needed for application installation.

Since projects installed with the Windows Installer may have registry entries, file extension associations, and other changes to a user's configuration, the actions of the Windows Installer may be monitored by programs such anti-spyware. It is often helpful to inform the user performing the install that such installation actions may be questioned by other programs, and that they should allow the installation to proceed or the resulting installation may not be complete.

Let's take a look at the deployment project templates that are available within VS.NET and see how they can create MSI files for easy installation of an application.

Visual Studio .NET Deployment Projects

VS.NET provides a set of project templates that can be used to help package your application and deploy it. Most of these templates use Windows Installer technology. We will start by taking a look at the different templates and what they should be used for, after which we will take a practical look at their creation.

Project Templates

Visual Studio .NET includes five project templates that can be used for setup and deployment in .NET. Before we discuss the project templates, we need to define the difference between setup and deployment. A *setup* is an application/process that you use to package your application and that provides an easy mechanism by which it can be installed on another machine. *Deployment* is the process of installing an application on another machine, usually through a setup application/process.

The five project templates available within VS.NET can be created by the same means as any other project in VS.NET, by using the New Project dialog box, as shown in Figure 19-1.

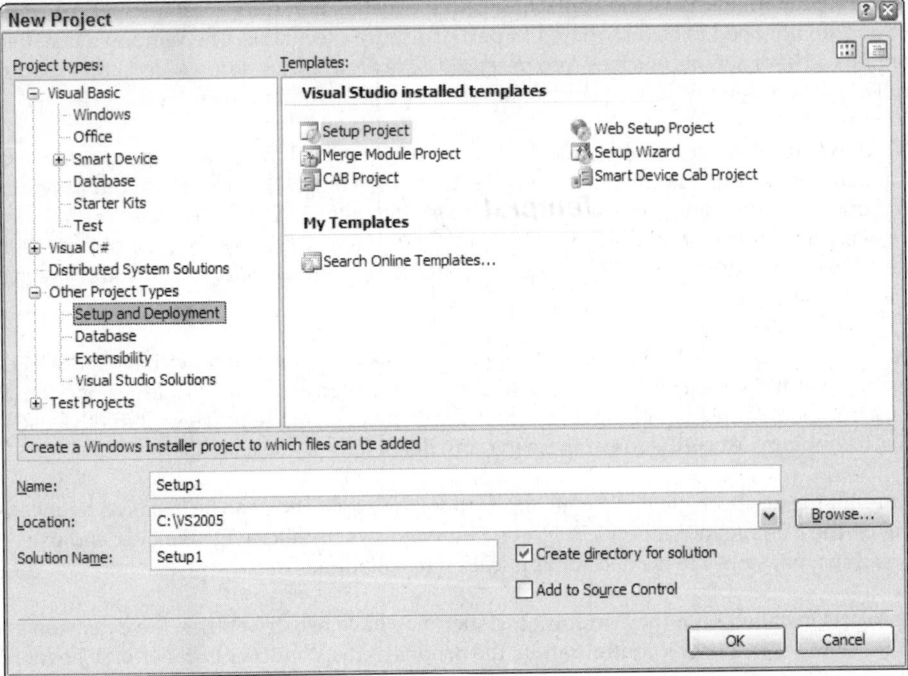

Figure 19-1

As you can see from the Figure 19-1, you need to select the Other Project Types node and then the Setup and Deployment Projects node from the tree view of project types on the left of the dialog box. Of the six available project templates there are four actual project templates:

- CAB Project
- Merge Module Project
- Setup Project
- Web Setup Project
- Smart Device CAB Project

and one wizard (called the Setup Wizard) that can be used to help create any of the project templates listed except the Smart Device CAB Project.

Let's now consider each of the project types in turn.

The Cab Project Template

As its name implies, the Cab Project template is used to create a *cabinet file*. A cabinet file (.cab) can contain any number of files. It is usually used to package components into a single file that can then be placed on a Web server so that the cab file can be downloaded by a Web browser.

Controls hosted within Internet Explorer are often packaged into a cabinet file and a reference added to the file in the Web page that uses the control. When Internet Explorer encounters this reference, it will check that the control isn't already installed on the user's computer, at which point it will download the cabinet file, extract the control, and install it to a protected part of the user's computer.

You can compress cabinet files to reduce their size and consequently the time it takes to download them.

The Merge Module Project Template

The Merge Module Project template is used to create a *merge module*, which is similar to a cabinet file in that it can be used to package a group of files. The difference is that a merge module file (.msm) cannot be used by itself to install the files that it contains. The merge module file created by this project template can be used within another setup project.

Merge modules were introduced as part of the Microsoft Windows Installer technology to enable a set of files to be packaged up into an easy to use file that could be reused and shared between Windows Installer–based setup programs. The idea is to package up all the files and any other resources (for example, registry entries, bitmaps, and so on) that are dependent on each other into the merge module.

This type of project can be very useful for packaging a component and all its dependencies. The resulting merge file can then be used in the setup program of each application that uses the component. This allows applications such as Crystal Reports to have a prepackaged deployment set that can be integrated into the deployment of other applications.

Microsoft suggests that a merge module should not be modified once it has been distributed, which means a new one should be created. The notion of packaging everything up into a single redistributable file can help alleviate the issues of DLL hell, because the package contains all dependencies.

The Setup Project Template

The Setup Project template is used to create a standard Windows Installer setup for an application. This type of project will probably be familiar to you if you have used the Visual Studio Installer add-on for Visual Studio 6. The Setup Project template can be used to create a setup package for a standard Windows application, which is normally installed in the `Program Files` directory of a user's computer.

The Web Setup Project Template

The Web Setup Project template is used to create a Windows Installer setup program that can be used to install a project into a virtual directory of a Web server. It is intended to be used to create a setup program for a Web application, which may contain ASP.NET Web Forms or Web Services that must be exposed to the Web.

The Smart Device CAB Project Template

The Smart Device CAB Project template is used to create a CAB file for an application that runs on a device containing the .NET Compact Framework, such as a PocketPC device. Such applications are often referred to a "mobile applications", and have many capabilities and limitations that do not apply to other .NET-based applications. This book does not discuss mobile applications, so we will not discuss this template type any further.

The Setup Wizard

The Setup Wizard can be used to help guide you through the creation of any of the previous setup and deployment project templates except the Smart Device CAB template. The steps that the wizard displays to you depend on whether the wizard was started to add a project to an existing solution or started to create a totally new project.

Creating a Deployment Project

A deployment project can be created in exactly the same way as any other project in Visual Studio 2005 by using the New ➪ Project option from the File menu or by using the New Project button on the Visual Studio start page.

You can also add a deployment project to an existing solution by using the Add Project item from the File menu. You will then be presented with the Add New Project dialog box, where you can select a deployment template.

Walkthroughs

Now that you have looked at how you can create a deployment project, the next two sections are going to contain practical walkthroughs of the creation of two deployment projects. The two walkthroughs are going to cover:

- A Windows application
- An ASP.NET Web application

Each these scenarios details a different deployment project template. They have been chosen because they are the most common deployment scenarios. You can use the walkthroughs and apply or modify them to your own needs. You will not use the wizard to create the deployment projects in the walkthroughs, so that you will be able to understand what is required to create a deployment project. The wizard can be used to help guide you through the creation of a deployment project and, therefore, hides from you some of the necessary background steps. However, the wizard can be very useful in providing the base for a deployment project.

A Windows Application

The first deployment scenario that you are going to look at is that of a Windows application where a user installs and runs an application on his local machine. In deploying this application, you will need to ensure that everything the application needs is distributed with the application's executable. This type of deployment scenario is one of the most typical that you will come across.

In this deployment scenario, the package needs to be created in such a way that it will guide the user through the process of installing the application on his or her machine. The best deployment template for this scenario is the Setup Project, and this is what you will be using throughout this section.

Before getting into the specifics of this project type, you need to create an application that will serve as the desktop application you want to deploy. For this example, you are going to use the Windows application project type. Create a new project, and choose Windows Application from the list of available Visual Basic project templates. Name the project "SampleForDeployment".You will not add any code to the project and will use it just as the new project wizard originally created it. Following this, you should have a solution with just one project.

After this, add a new project to the solution and choose Setup Project from the list of available Setup and Deployment Project templates. You will now have a Visual Studio solution containing two projects, as shown in Figure 19-2.

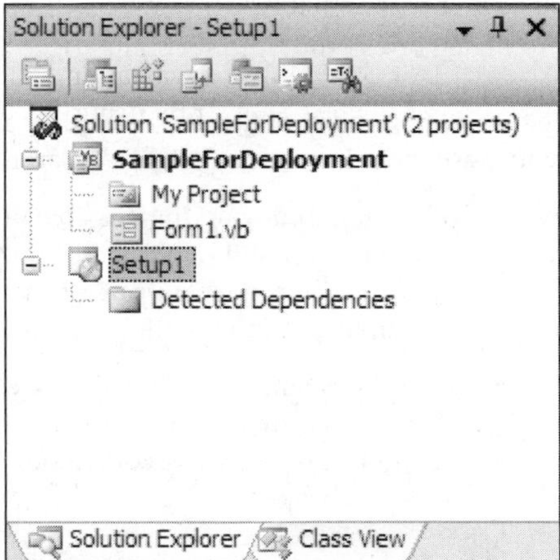

Figure 19-2

The deployment project does not contain any files at present, just a folder called Detected Dependencies, which is discussed later. Notice also the buttons that appear along the top of Solution Explorer. These are used to access the editors of this deployment project template and will be discussed later in this chapter.

Next, you need to add files to the setup project, and in particular you need to add the file created by the Windows application project. You can add files to the setup deployment project in two ways. The first is to make sure the setup project is the active project and then choose the Add Item from the Project menu. The second method is to right-click the setup project file in Solution Explorer and choose Add from the pop-up menu. Both these methods enable you to choose from one of four options:

- If you select File from the submenu, you will be presented with a dialog box that will allow you to browse for and select a particular file to add to the setup project. This method is sufficient if the file you are adding is not the output from another project within the solution. This option is very useful in Web setup projects, because it allows you include external business components (if they are used) and so on.

- The Merge Module option allows you to include a merge module in the deployment project. If you select this option, you will be presented with a dialog box that you can use to browse for and select a merge module to include in your project. Third-party vendors can supply merge modules or you can create your own with Visual Studio.
- The Assembly option can be used to select a .NET component (assembly) to be included in the deployment project. If you select this option, you will be presented with a window that you can use to select an assembly to include from those that are installed on your machine.
- If the deployment project is part of a solution (as in this walkthrough), you can use the Project ⇨ Add ⇨ Project Output submenu item. As the name implies, this allows you to add the output from any of the projects in the solution to the setup project.

You want to add the output of the Windows application project to the setup project. Select the Project Output menu item to bring up the dialog box (shown in Figure 19-3) that will enable you to accomplish this task.

The Add Project Output Group dialog box is split into several parts:

- The combo box at the top contains a list of the names of all the nondeployment projects in the current solution. In your case there is only one project—SampleForDeployment.
- Below the combo box is a list box containing all the possible outputs from the selected project. If you click a possible output, a description of the selected output appears in the Description box at the bottom. You are interested in the Primary output, so make sure that this is selected. The different types of output are summarized in the following table.
- Below the list of possible outputs is a combo box that allows you to select the configuration to use for the selected project. You will use the (Active) option, because this will use whatever configuration is in effect when the project is built. The combo box will also contain all the possible build configurations for the selected project.

Click OK to return to the solution.

Project Output	Description
Primary output	The primary output of a project is the resulting DLL or EXE that is produced by building the particular project.
Localized resources	The localized resource of a project is a DLL that contains only resources. The resources within the DLL are specific to a culture or locale. This is often called a satellite DLL.
Debug Symbols	When the particular project in question is compiled a special file is created that contains special debugging information about the project. These are called *debug symbols*. The debug symbols for a project have the same name as the primary output but with an extension of .pdb. The debug symbols provide information to a debugger when an application is being run through it.
Content Files	ASP.NET Web applications have content files that are part of the Web site, such as HTLM files, images files, and so forth. This option allows inclusion of such content as part of a deployment.

Project Output	Description
Source Files	This will include all the source files for the selected project including the project file. The solution file is *not* included.
Documentation Files	Source code for a project may contain comments that are formatted so that documentation in an XML format can automatically be produces. This option accesses those XML documentation files.
XML Serialization Assemblies	A project may contain XML schemas. If so, assemblies can be generated that contain classes based on those schemas. This option includes those assemblies.

Now, not only has the output from the Windows application been added to the Setup project, but the Detected Dependencies folder also contains an entry.

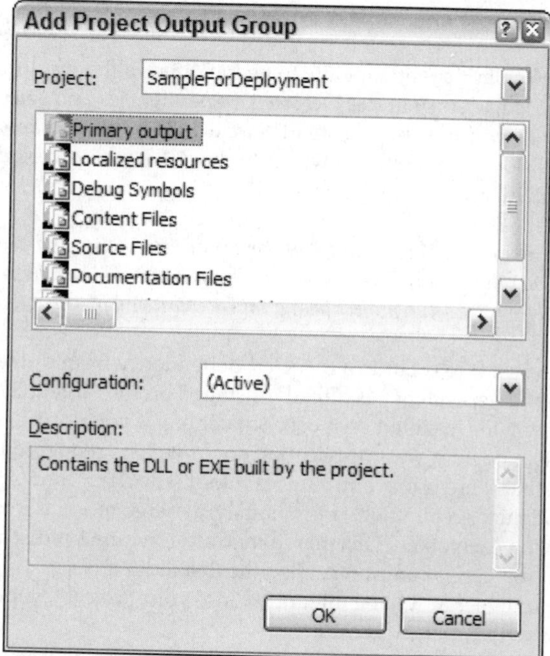

Figure 19-3

Whenever you add a .NET component to this deployment project, its dependencies are added to this folder. The dependencies of the dependencies will also be added and so on until all the required files have been added. This functionality has been included to help ensure that all the dependencies of an application are deployed along with the application. The files listed in the Detected Dependencies folder will be included in the resulting setup and, by default, will be installed into the application's directory as application-private assemblies. This is shown in Figure 19-4. This default behavior helps reduce the possible effects of DLL hell by making the application use its own copies of dependent files.

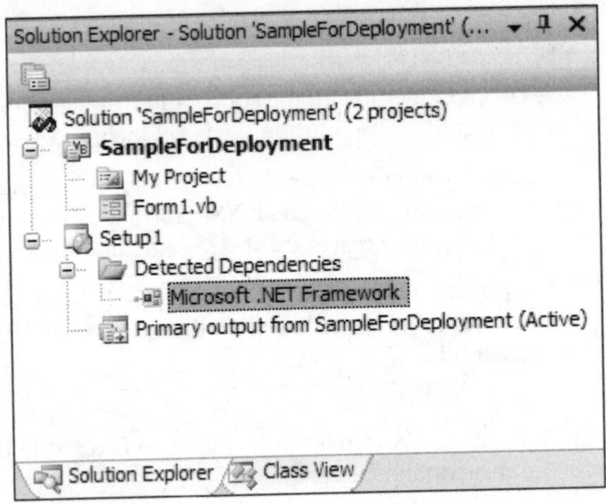

Figure 19-4

If you do not want a particular dependency file to be included in the resulting setup, you can exclude it by right-clicking the particular entry under Detected Dependencies and selecting Exclude from the pop-up menu. The dependency will then have a small "circle and slash" icon before its name to indicate that it has been excluded. This does not apply, however to the .NET Framework dependency. Ith is handled in a special way,, as you will see later in the chapter.)

> *Dependencies can also be excluded by selecting the particular dependency and using the Properties window to set the* `Exclude` *property to* `True`*. The listed dependencies will be refreshed whenever a .NET file is added to or removed from the setup project taking into account any files that have already been excluded.*

You may decide that you want to exclude a detected dependency from the setup of an application because you know that the dependency is already installed on the target computer. This is fine if you have tight control over what is installed on a user's machine. If you don't and you deploy the application with the missing dependency, your application could well be rendered unusable. In the previous screenshot you can see that there is one entry in the folder. The `Microsoft .NET Framework entry` is a merge module dependency. As mentioned previously, a merge module is used to package a group of files that are dependent on each other. This merge module contains a redistributable version of the CLR and will be installed on the user's computer when the installation is run. All dependencies must have a complete installation package that will be integrated into your project's deployment package, and that is normally accomplished with a merge module.

You can select an item in the setup project in Solution Explorer and that particular item's properties will be displayed in the Properties window. For example, if you select the root node of the setup project (Setup), the Properties window will change to show you the details of the setup project.

> *As with any other project in VS.NET, there are a set of project properties that can also be modified. The project properties are accessed by right-clicking the project file and choosing Properties from the pop-up menu. These properties will be covered later.*

We are not going to include a discussion of every single property of all the different project items, because this would probably fill a whole book. Instead, we will take a look at the properties from the root setup node and each of the two different project items. We are going to start with the root setup node (Setup). Before we start the discussion, make sure that the node is selected and take some time to browse the list of available properties. The root setup node represents the resulting output from this deployment project type: Windows Installer package (.msi). Therefore, the Properties window contains properties that will affect the resulting .msi that is produced.

Properties of the Root Setup Node

The first property you are going to look at is `ProductName`. This property, as the name tells you, is used to set the textual name of the product that this Windows Installer package is installing. By default, it is set to the name of the setup project (in this case `Setup1`). The value of this property is used throughout the steps of the resulting setup. For instance, it is used for the text of the title bar when the resulting .msi file is run. The property is used along with the `Manufacturer` property to construct the default installation directory:

```
C:\ProgramFiles\<Manufacturer>\<ProductName>
```

The `ProductName` property is also used by the Add/Remove Programs control panel applet (see Figure 19-5) to show that the application is installed.

Figure 19-5

From the screenshot in Figure 19-5, you can see there is a link that you can click to get support information about the selected application. That link yields a dialog similar to the one in Figure 19-6.

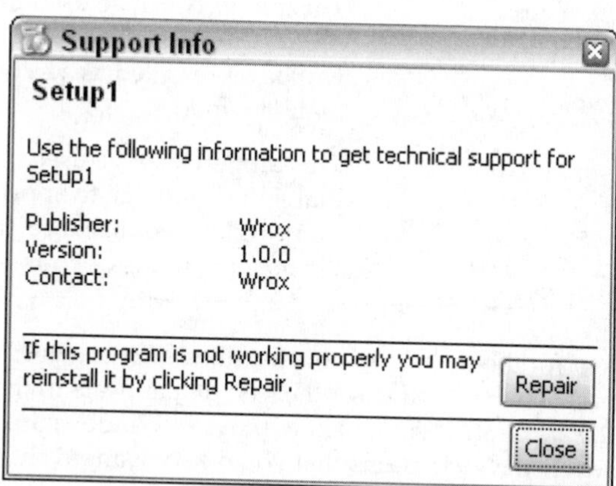

Figure 19-6

A number of the properties of the setup project can be used to customize the support information that is shown. The following table contains details of how the properties relate to the support information that is shown.

Support Information	Related Properties	Description
Publisher	`Manufacturer`	The `Manufacturer` property is used to help create the default installation directory for the project and provide a textual display of the manufacturer of the application contained within the Windows Installer package.
Version	`ManufacturerUrl`	This property is used in conjunction with the `Manufacturer` property to make a hyperlink for the Publisher part of the support information. If a value is entered, the name of the Publisher will be underlined, which can then be clicked to allow you to visit the publisher's Web site. If a value is not included the publisher's name does not act as a hyperlink.
	`Version`	This is the version number of the Windows Installer package. It can be changed to match the version number of the application that the package installs. But this has to be done manually.
Contact	`Author`	This property is used to hold the name of the company/person that created the Windows Installer package. By default this has the same value as the `Manufacturer` property.
Support Information	`SupportPhone`	This property can be used to provide a support telephone number for the application.
	`SupportUrl`	This property can be used to provide a URL for the product's support Web site. The value of this property will be represented as a hyperlink in the support information window.
Comments	`Description`	This property can be used to include any information that you would like to appear in the support information window. For instance, it could be used to detail the opening hours of your support department.

The next property to look at for the root setup node is called `AddRemoveProgramsIcon`. As you can probably guess, this property enables you to set the icon that appears in the Add/Remove Programs control panel applet for the application contained within this Windows Installer package. You can select (None) from the drop-down list, which means that you do not want to change the icon, and the default icon will be used. Alternatively, you have the option to (Browse) for an icon, which brings up a window that allows you to find and select the particular icon you would like to use. You do not have to use a stand-alone icon file; you can use an icon from an executable or DLL that is contained within the project. The last option, the Icon option is used when an icon has been selected and will then be used in the Add/Remove Programs list.

The remainder of the properties for the root setup node are summarized in the following table.

Property	Description
`DetectNewer InstalledVersion`	If this property is set to `True` and a newer version of the application is found on the machine, then the installation will not continue. If the property is set to `False`, then this check will not occur, and the application will install even if there is a newer version on the computer already.
`Keywords`	This property enables you to set a number of keywords that can be used to locate this installer.
`Localization`	This property is used to set which locale this installer has been designed to run in. The values of this property will affect what string resources are used within the installation.
`ProductCode`	This property is a GUID that is used to uniquely identify the particular version of the application contained within it.
`RemovePrevious Version`	If this property is set to `True` and an older version of the application is found on the machine, then the installation will remove the old version and continue on with the installation. If the property is set to `False` then this check is not done.
`SearchPath`	This property is used to specify a search path that VS.NET uses when it builds the setup project and needs to find the detected dependencies.
`Subject`	This property is used to provide an additional text string of what the installation is used for.
`Title`	This property is used to set the textual title of the application that is installed. By default, this property will have the same name as the setup project.
`Upgrade Code`	This property is a GUID and is used to uniquely identify a product. This property should stay the same for all versions of the same application. The `ProductCode` and `PackageCode` properties change, depending on the specific version of the product.

Properties of the Primary Output Project Item

You are now going to move on and take a quick look at the properties of the primary output project item in the following table.

Property	Description
`Condition`	This enables you to enter a condition that will be evaluated when the installation is run. If the condition evaluates to `True`, then the file will be installed; if the condition evaluates to `False`, then the file won't be installed. If you only wanted a particular file to be installed and the installation was being run on Microsoft Windows 2000 or better, you could enter the following for the condition: `VersionNT >= 5`.
`Dependencies`	Selecting this property will display a window that shows all the dependencies of the selected project output.
`Exclude`	You can use this property to indicate whether you want the project output to be excluded from the resulting Windows Installer package.
`ExcludeFilter`	This property enables you to exclude files from the project output using wildcards. For example, if you enter a wildcard `*.txt`, then all files that are part of the project output that have an extension of .txt will be excluded from the resulting Windows Installer package. Selecting this property will display a window that will allow you to enter any number of wildcards.
`Folder`	As mentioned previously, this property allows you to select the target folder for the project outputs.
`Hidden`	This property allows you to install the files that make up the project output as hidden files. This property basically toggles on/off option of the hidden attribute of the files.
`KeyOutput`	This property expands to provide information about the main file that makes up the project output. In your case, it will show information of the `Windows Application.exe` file.
`Outputs`	Selecting this property will display a window that lists all the files that are part of the project output and where these files are located on the development machine.
`PackageAs`	This property can be used to indicate whether the project output should be packaged according to what is defined in the project properties (`vsdpa Default`) or externally (`vsdpaLoose`) to the resulting Windows Installer package. The default is to use the project properties setting.
`Permanent`	This property is used to indicate whether the files that make up the project output should be removed when the application is uninstalled (`False`) or left behind (`True`). It is advisable that all the files that are installed by an application be removed when the application is uninstalled. Therefore, this property should be set to `False`, which it is the default.
`ReadOnly`	This property is used to set the read-only file attribute of all the files that make up the project output. As the name suggests, this makes the file read-only on the target machine.
`Register`	This property allows you to instruct the Windows Installer to register the files contained within the project output as COM objects. This only really applies to projects (for example, the Class Library project template) that have been compiled with the `Register for COM Interop` project property set.

Property	Description
`SharedLegacy`	This property indicates whether the files that make up the project output are to be reference counted, once installed. This really only applies to files that are going to be shared across multiple applications. When the installation is removed, the files will only be uninstalled if their reference count is equal to zero.
`System`	This property indicates that the files contained within the project output are to be treated as system files and protected by Windows file protection.
`Transitive`	This property indicates whether the condition specified in the condition property is reevaluated when the installation is rerun on the computer at a later date. If the value is `True`, then the condition is checked on each additional run of the installation. A value of `False` will cause the condition only to be run the first time the installation is run on the computer. The default value is `False`.
`Vital`	This property is used to indicate that the files contained within the project output are vital to the installation—if the installation of these files fails then the installation as a whole should fail. The default value is `True`.

Properties of the Detected Dependency Items

Here is a brief look at the properties of files that reside in the `DetectedDependencies` folder. You will only cover the properties that are different to those of the project output item (discussed earlier). Most of the additional properties are read-only and cannot be changed. They are used purely to provide information to the developer.

Property	Description
`MergeModuleProperties`	A merge module can contain a number of custom configurable properties. If the selected merge module contains any, they will appear here. In the case of the example, there are no custom properties.
`Author`	This property stores the name of the author of the merge module. `[Read-only]`
`Description`	This property is used to store a textual description of the merge module. `[Read-only]`
`LanguageIds`	This property is used to indicate what language the selected merge module is targeted at. `[Read-only]`
`ModuleDependencies`	Selecting this property will show a window that lists all the dependencies of the selected merge module. `[Read-only]`
`ModuleSignature`	This property will display the unique signature of the merge module. `[Read-only]`
`Subject`	This property is used to display additional information about the merge module. `[Read-only]`
`Title`	This property is used simply to state the title of the merge module. `[Read-only]`

Table continued on following page

Property	Description
`Version`	This property is used to store the version number of the selected merge module. The version number of the merge module usually changes, because the version number of the files it contains changes. `[Read-only]`

Of course, some projects will also contain other .dll files in this folder. Some of the additional properties that may be encountered for these files are listed in the following table.

Property	Description
`DisplayName`	This contains the file name of the selected assembly. `[Read-only]`
`Files`	Selecting this property will display a window that will list all the files that make up the selected assembly. `[Read-only]`
`HashAlgorithm`	This property shows what hash algorithm was used by the manifest in hashing the files contents (to stop tampering). `[Read-only]`
`Language`	This property will show what language this assembly is targeted at. This property relates to the culture of an assembly. If the property is empty, then the assembly is culture (language)–independent. `[Read only]`
`PublicKey` `PublicKeyToken`	These two properties are used to show information about the strong name of the selected assembly. If an assembly has a strong name, then either of these two properties will contain a value (other than all 0s). One or the other of these properties is used normally, not both. `[Read only]`
`SourcePath`	This property contains the location of where the selected assembly can be found on the development computer. `[Read only]`
`TargetName`	This property contains the file name of the assembly, as it will appear on the target machine. `[Read only]`
`Version`	This property shows you the version number of the selected assembly. `[Read only]`

This has been a brief look at the Setup Project template. It uses all the project defaults and provides a standard set of steps to the users when they run the Windows Installer package. More often than not, this simple approach of including a single application file and its dependencies is not good enough. Fortunately, the setup project can be customized extensively to meet your needs. You can create shortcuts, directories, registry entries, and so on. These customizations and more can be accomplished using the set of built-in editors, which will be covered after the next walkthrough.

An ASP.NET Web Application

The other deployment scenario you are going to look at is that of a Web application that has been created using the ASP.NET Web application project template. It is assumed that the Web application is being developed on a development Web server and that you will need to create a deployment project to transfer the finished application to the production Web server. Although the previous deployment scenario is one of the most typical, this scenario has to come a very close second.

From the simple requirements defined earlier, you can see that the best deployment template to use is the Web Setup Project template. There is one major difference between this template and the previous Setup Project template: the Web Setup Project will, by default, deploy the application to a virtual directory of the Web server on which the setup is run, whereas a setup project will deploy the application to the `Program Files` folder on the target machine by default. There are, obviously, some properties that differ between the two project templates, but other than that they are pretty similar. They both produce a Windows Installer package and have the same set of project properties discussed later in the chapter.

As with the other walkthroughs, you need to create an application that you can use for deployment. However, an ASP.NET Web Application is not one of the project templates available with the New Project dialog as seen in Figure 19-1. As discussed in Chapters 2 and 16, such applications are created with the File | New | Web Site option.

Using that option, create a new ASP.NET Web Application by selecting File | New | Web Site, and then selecting the ASP.NET Web Site template. You are not going to add any code to this web site, since it is being used purely as a base for the deployment project.

Now, add a Web Setup Project template using the normal File | New Project dialog. Your solution should now contain two projects.

As with the previous walkthrough, the deployment project does not contain any files at present. There is also a folder called `Detected Dependencies` in Solution Explorer (shown in Figure 19-7) that acts in exactly the same way as in the previous walkthrough.

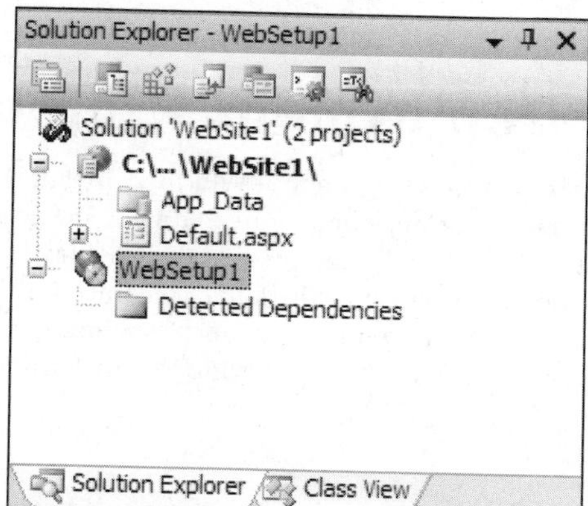

Figure 19-7

The next step that you need to look at is adding the output of the Web application to the deployment project. This is accomplished in pretty much the same way as the previous walkthrough, by right-clicking on the WebSetup1 project and selecting Add | Project Output. Note that when you add the project representing the web site, the only option you have for the type of files to add is "Content Files", which encompasses the files that make up the web site.

The resulting project should look like Figure 19-8.

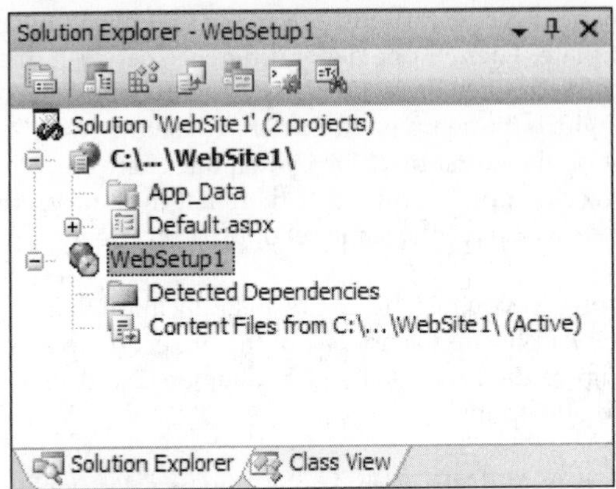

Figure 19-8

Now if you build the solution, the resulting Windows Installer package will include the compiled code of the Web application along with its dependencies, as well as the other files that make up a Web application, ASP.NET files, stylesheets, and so on.

Most of the topics discussed in the last walkthrough apply to this walkthrough. As mentioned earlier, the setup project and Web setup project are very similar and only really differ in where they install the application by default.

Modifying the Deployment Project

In the last two walkthroughs, you created the default Windows Installer package for the particular project template. You didn't customize the steps or actions that were performed when the package was run. What if you want to add a step to the installation process that displays a `ReadMe` file to the user? Or what if you need to create registry entries on the installation computer? The walkthroughs did not cover how to customize the installation to suit your needs, which is what this section is going to focus on. There are six editors that you can use to customize a Windows Installer–based deployment project:

- File System Editor
- Registry Editor
- File Types Editor
- User Interface Editor
- Custom Actions Editor
- Launch Conditions Editor

The editors are accessible through the View ➪ Editor menu option or by using the corresponding buttons at the top of Solution Explorer.

You can also modify the resulting Windows Installer package through the project's Properties window. In this section, you are going to take a brief look at each of the six editors and the project properties, and see how they can be used to modify the resulting Windows Installer package. We will only be able to cover the basics of each of the editors, which is enough to get you going. You will use the project created in the Windows application walkthrough in this section.

Project Properties

The first step you take in customizing the Windows Installer package is to use the project properties. The project properties dialog box is accessed by right-clicking the root of the setup project and selecting Properties from the pop-up menu. You can also select the Properties item from the Project menu when the setup project is the active project. Both of these methods will bring up the project properties dialog box as illustrated in Figure 19-9.

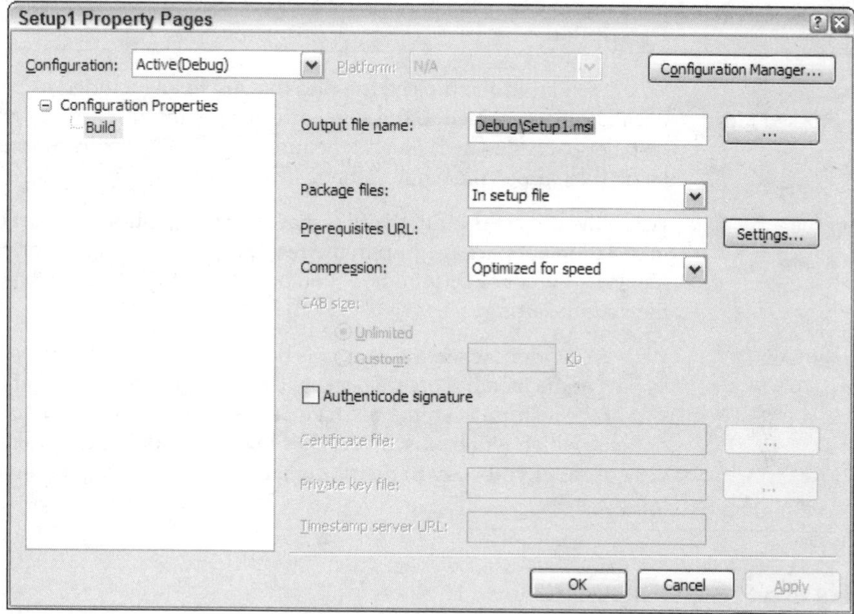

Figure 19-9

As you can see from Figure 19-9, there is only one page that you can use to set the properties of the project: Build.

The Build Page

Now it's time to take a look at the Build page and how the options can be used to affect the way that the resulting Windows Installer package is built.

Build Configurations

The first thing to notice is that, as with most other projects in VS.NET, you can create different build configurations. You can modify the properties of a project for the currently active build configuration or you can modify the properties for all the build configurations. You use the Configuration combo box to change what build configuration you want to alter the properties for. In Figure 19-9, notice that you are modifying the properties for the currently active build configuration: Debug. The button labeled Configuration Manager allows you to add, remove, and edit the build configurations for this project.

Moving on, you can see an option called Output file name, which can be used to modify where the resulting Windows Installer package (.msi) file will be created. You can modify the file name and path directly or you can press the Browse button.

Package Files

By using the next setting, Package files, you can specify how the files that make up the installation are packaged up. The following table describes the possible settings.

Package	Description
As loose uncompressed files	When you build the project, the files that are to be included as part of the installation are copied to the same directory as the resulting Windows Installer package (.msi) file. As mentioned earlier, this directory can be set using the Output file name setting.
In setup file	When the project is built, the files that are to be included as part of the installation are packaged up in the resulting Windows Installer package file. When you use this method, you only have one file to distribute. This is the default setting.
In cabinet file(s)	With this option, when the project is built, the files that are to be included as part of the installation are packaged into a number of cabinet files. The size of the resulting cabinet files can be restricted by the use of a number of options, which will be discussed later in this section. This option can be very useful if you want to distribute the installation program on a set of floppy disks.

Prerequisites and Prerequisites URL

Prerequisites, in the context of the setup project properties, are standard components that may be needed to install or run the application, but that are not a part of the application. There are several of these, as can be seen in the dialog shown in Figure 19-10, which is displayed when the Settings button next to Prerequisites URL is pressed.

The .NET Framework 2.0 will be checked by default. You should only uncheck it if you are sure that all the machines upon which your application will be installed already have the Framework installed.

If the box for any of these prerequisites is checked, the resulting installation package will automatically check for the presence of that prerequisite and install it if required. If you are installing from a CD or network share, it is common for the packages that install these prerequisites to be placed in the same place as your installation package. The default settings assume that this is true and will install the prerequisites from that location.

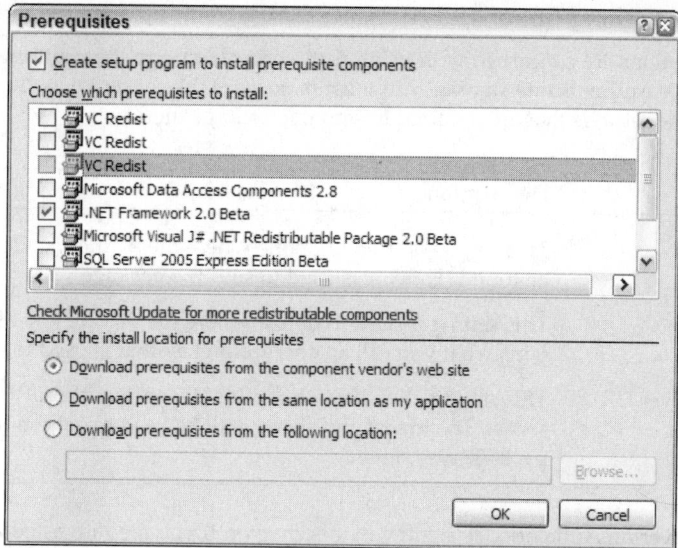

Figure 19-10

However, you can specify a different location for packages that install prerequisites by selecting the Download prerequisites from the following location: option at the bottom of the dialog and then specifying the URL at which the packages will be located.

If your application will only be installed on Windows XP or later, it is unnecessary to have the Windows Installer 2.0 prerequisite.

Compression

You also have the option to modify the compression used when packaging the files that are to be contained within the installation program. The three options (`Optimized for speed`, `Optimized for size`, and `None`) are pretty self-explanatory and will not be covered in this book. The default, however, is `Optimized for speed`.

Setting the Cabinet File Size

If you want to package the files in cabinet files, then you have the option to specify the size of those resulting cabinet file(s):

- The first option you have is to let the resulting cabinet file be of an unlimited size. What this effectively means is that all the files will be packaged into one big cabinet file. The resulting size of the cabinet file will also be dependent on the compression method selected.
- If you are installing from floppy disks or CDs, creating one large cabinet file is not practical. In this case, you can use the second option to specify the maximum size of the resulting cabinet file(s). If you select this option, you need to fill in the maximum size that a cabinet file can be (this figure is in KB). If all the files that need to be contained within this installation exceed this size, then multiple cabinet files will be created.

Using the Solution Signing Options

The final set of options are concerned with using Authenticode to sign the resulting Windows Installer package. To enable Authenticode signing, you must make sure the check box is checked. This will enable you to set the three settings that are required to sign the package file.

Setting	Description
Certificate file	This setting is used to define where the Authenticode certificate file can be found. This file is used to sign the package.
Private key file	This setting is used to define where the private key file is. This file contains what you call an encryption key that is used to sign the package.
Timestamp server URL	This setting allows you to optionally specify the URL of a timestamp server. The timestamp server will be used to get the time of when the package was signed.

We will not be covering Authenticode signing in this chapter. If you are interested in this option, you should consult the MSDN documentation for Authenticode.

The File System Editor

Now that we have taken a look at the project properties, we are going to move on to look at the editors that are available for to customize the resulting Windows Installer package. You will need to make sure that the current active project is the setup project.

Start by taking a look at the File System Editor. This editor is automatically displayed for you in VS.NET's Document Window when you first create the Setup project. You can also get at this editor and the other editors that are available to you via the View ➪ Editor menu option in the VS.NET IDE. The first editor you will look at, the File System Editor, is used to manage all the file system aspects of the installation including:

- Creating folders on the user's machine
- Adding files to the folders defined
- Creating shortcuts

Basically, this is the editor that you use to define what files need to be installed and where they are installed on the user's machine.

The File System Editor is split into two panes in the Document Window, as shown in Figure 19-11.

The left pane shows a list of the folders that have been created automatically for the project (discussed earlier in the chapter). When you select a folder in the left pane, two things happen: first, the right pane of the editor displays a list of the files that are to be installed into the selected folder, and second, the Properties window will change to show you the properties of the currently selected folder.

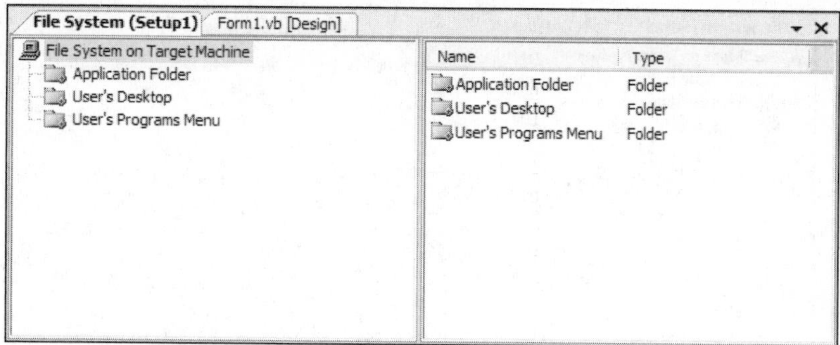

Figure 19-11

Adding Items to a Folder

To add an item that needs to be installed to a folder, you can either right-click the folder in the left pane and choose Add from the pop-up menu or you can select the required folder and right-click in the right pane and again choose Add from the pop-up menu. You will be presented with four options, three of which were discussed earlier in the walkthroughs:

- Project output
- File
- Assembly

The fourth option (Folder) allows you to add a subfolder to the currently selected folder. This subfolder then becomes a standard folder that can be used to add files. If you add any .NET components or executables, the dependencies of these components will also be added to the installation automatically.

Adding Special Folders

When you create a new deployment project, a set of standard folders will be created for you (listed in the desktop application section). What if the folders created do not match your requirements? Well, you can also use the File System editor to add special folders. To add a special folder, right-click anywhere in the left pane (other than on a folder), and you will be presented with a pop-up menu that has one item: Add SpecialFolder. Alternatively, it's available through the Action ➪ Add Special Folder menu option. This menu item (shown in Figure 19-12) expands to show you a list of folders that you can add to the installation (folders already added to the project will be grayed out).

As you can see from Figure 19-12, there are a number of system folders that you can choose from. They are summarized in the following table.

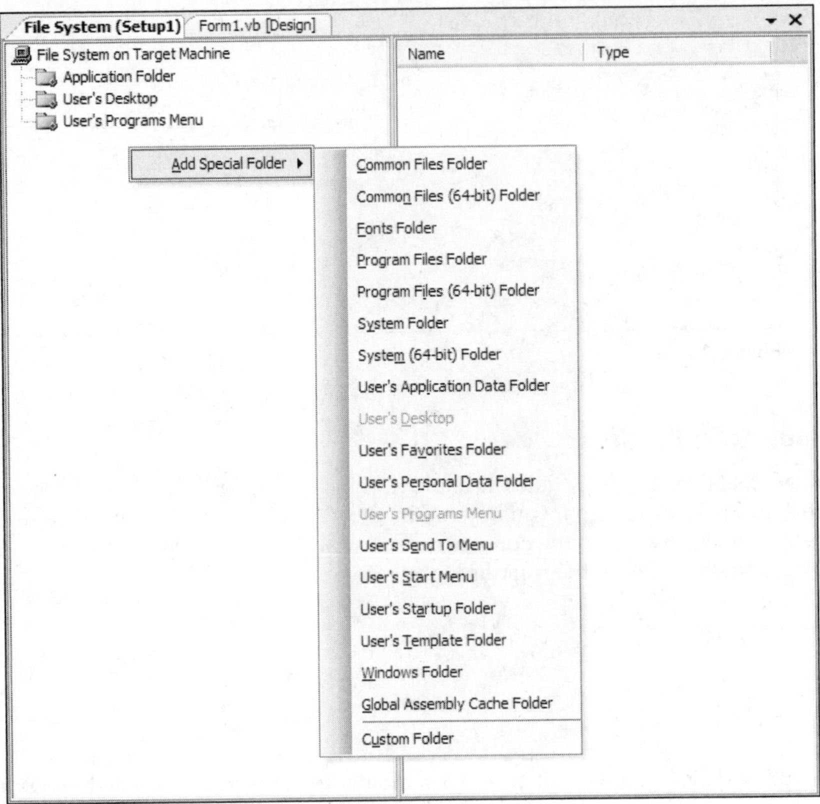

Figure 19-12

Name	Description	Windows Installer Property
Common Files Folder	Files (nonsystem) that are shared by multiple applications are usually installed to this folder.	`[CommonFilesFolder]`
Common Files Folder (64-bit)	Same as Common Files Folder, except that it's for 64-bit systems.	`[CommonFiles64Folder]`
Fonts Folder	This folder is used to contain all the fonts that are installed on the computer. If your application used a specific font you want to install it into this folder.	`[FontsFolder]`
Program Files Folder	Most applications are installed in a directory below the program files folder. This acts as root directory for installed applications.	`[ProgramFilesFolder]`
Program Files Folder (64-bit)	Same as Program Files Folder, except that it's for 64-bit systems.	`[ProgramFiles 64Folder]`

Name	Description	Windows Installer Property
System Folder	This folder is used to store shared system files. The folder typically holds files that are part of the OS.	`[SystemFolder]`
System Folder (64-bit)	Same as System Folder, except that it's for 64-bit systems.	`[System64Folder]`
User's Application Data Folder	This folder is used to store data on a per-application basis that is specific to a user.	`[CommonAppDataFolder]`
User's Desktop	This folder represents the user's desktop. This folder can be used to create and display a shortcut to your application that a user can use to start your application.	`[DesktopFolder]`
User's Favorite Folder	This folder is used as a central place to store links to the user's favorite Web sites, documents, folders, and so on.	`[FavoritesFolder]`
User's Personal Data Folder	This folder is where a user will store important files. It is normally referred to as My Documents.	`[PersonalFolder]`
User's Programs Menu	This folder is where shortcuts are created to applications that appear on the user's Program menu. This is an ideal place to create a shortcut to your application.	`[ProgramMenuFolder]`
User's Send To Menu	This folder stores all the user's send to shortcuts. A send to shortcut is displayed when you right-click a file in the Windows Explorer and choose Send To. The send to shortcut usually invokes an application passing in the pathname of the files it was invoked from.	`[SendToFolder]`
User's Start Menu	This folder can be used to add items to the user's Start menu. This is not often used.	`[StartMenuFolder]`
User's Startup Folder	This folder is used to start applications whenever the user logs in to the computer. If you would like your application to start every time the user logs in, then you can add a shortcut to your application in this folder.	`[StartupFolder]`
User's Template Folder	This folder contains templates specific to the logged-in user. Templates are usually used by applications like Microsoft Office 2000.	`[TemplateFolder]`
Windows Folder	This folder is the windows root folder. This is where the OS is installed.	`[WindowsFolder]`
Global Assembly Cache Folder	This folder is used to store all the shared assemblies on the user's computer.	

If none of the built-in folders match your requirements, you can even use the item at the bottom of the list to create your own custom folder. This is where the Windows Installer property column of the preceding table comes. Suppose that you wanted to create a new directory in the user's favorites folder called Wrox Press, you could accomplish this by adding the correct special folder and then adding a subfolder to it. Another way to accomplish this is to create a custom folder, the process of which we will discuss now.

Right-click in the left pane of the File Editor, and choose Custom Folder from the pop-up menu.

The new folder will be created in the left pane of the editor. The name of the folder will be edit mode, so enter the text Wrox Press and press Enter.

The folder will now be selected, and the Properties window will have changed to show the properties of the new folder. The properties of a folder are summarized in the following table.

Property	Description
`(Name)`	This is the name of the selected folder. The name property is used within the setup project as the means by which you select a folder.
`AlwaysCreate`	This property is used to indicate whether this folder should be created on installation even if it's empty (`True`). If the value is `False` and there are no files to be installed into the folder, then the folder will not be created. The default is `False`.
`Condition`	This enables you to enter a condition that will be evaluated when the installation is run. If the condition evaluates to `True` then the folder will be created; if the condition evaluates to `False` then the folder won't be created.
`DefaultLocation`	This is where you define where the folder is going to be created on the target machine. You can enter a literal folder name (such as `C:\Temp`), or you can use a Windows Installer property, or a combination of the two. A Windows Installer property contains information that is filled in when the installer is run. In the last table of special folders, there was a column called Windows Installer property. The property defined in this table would be filled in with the actual location of the special folder at runtime. Therefore, if you enter `[WindowsFolder]` as the text for this property, the folder created represents the Windows special folder.
`Property`	This property is used to define a Windows Installer property that can be used to override the `DefaultLocation` property of the folder when the installation is run.
`Transitive`	This property indicates whether the condition specified in the condition property is reevaluated on subsequent (re)installs. If the value is `True`, then the condition is checked on each additional run of the installation. A value of `False` causes the condition only to be run the first time the installation is run on the computer. The default value is `False`.

Set the `DefaultLocation` property to `[FavoritesFolder]\Wrox Press`.

You could now add some shortcuts to this folder using the technique described in the following section. When the installation is run, a new folder will be added to the user's favorite folder called Wrox Press.

Creating Shortcuts

The final aspect of the File System Editor that you are going to look at is that of creating shortcuts. The first step in creating a shortcut is to locate the file that is to be the target of the shortcut. Select the target file and right-click it. The pop-up menu that appears will include an option to create a shortcut to the selected file, which will be created in the same folder. Select this option.

To add the shortcut to the user's desktop, you need to move this shortcut to the folder that represents the user's desktop. Likewise, you could move this shortcut to the folder that represents the user's programs menu. Cut and paste the new shortcut to the User's Desktop folder in the left pane of the editor. The shortcut will now be added to the user's desktop when the installation is run. You will probably want to rename the shortcut, which can be accomplished easily via the Rename option of the pop-up menu.

You have only taken a brief look at the File System Editor. I would encourage you to explore what can be accomplished by using the editor.

The Registry Editor

The next editor that you are going to look at is the Registry Editor, which is used to:

- Create registry keys
- Create values for registry keys
- Import a registry file

Like the File System Editor, the Registry Editor is split into two panes, as illustrated in Figure 19-13.

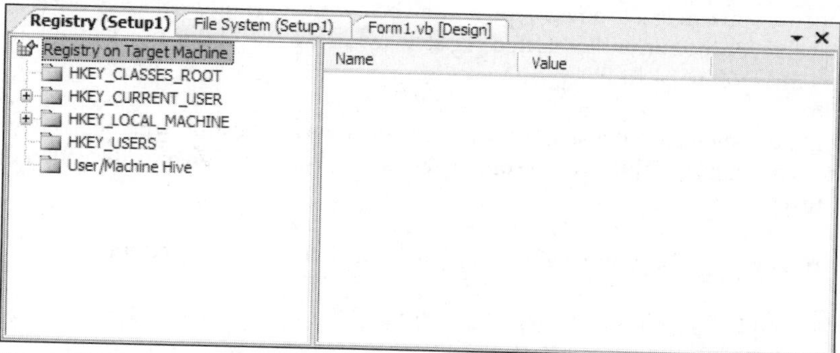

Figure 19-13

The left pane of the editor represents the registry keys on the target computer. When you select a registry key, two things happen: the right pane of the editor will be updated to show the values that are to be created under the selected registry key, and if the registry key selected is not a root key in the left pane, the Properties window will be updated with a set of properties for this registry key.

When you create a new deployment project, a set of registry keys will be created for you that correspond to the standard base registry keys of Windows. Notice in Figure 19-13 that there is a key defined with a name of `[Manufacturer]`. When the installation is run, this will be replaced with the value of the `Manufacturer` property that you discussed earlier in the chapter. `[Manufacturer]` is a property of the installation and can be used elsewhere within the installation. There are a number of these properties defined that can be used in much the same way (you should consult the "Property Reference" topic in the MSDN documentation for a full list).

Adding a Value to a Registry Key

So, how do you add a value to a registry key? First, select the required registry key (or create it) that is going to hold the registry values, and then there are a number of ways to add the registry value:

- Right-click the registry key and use the resulting pop-up menu
- Right-click in the right-hand pane and use the resulting pop-up menu
- Use the Action menu

The menu items contained within the Action menu will depend on where the current focus is. For illustrational purposes here, select one of the Software registry keys. The Action menu will contain one item, New, which contains a number of menu items:

- Key
- String value
- Environment string value
- Binary value
- DWORD value

Using this menu, you can create a new registry key below the currently selected key (via Key), or you can create a value for the currently selected registry key using one of the four Value types: String, Environment String, Binary, and DWORD.

Take a look at how to create a registry entry that informs the application whether or not to run in the debug mode. The registry value must be applicable to a particular user, must be called `Debug`, and must contain the text `True` or `False`.

The first step is to select the following registry key in the left pane of the editor:

```
HKEY_CURRENT_USER\Software [Manufacturer].
```

The registry key `HKEY>\_CURRENT>\_USER` is used to store registry settings that apply to the currently logged-in user.

Now, you want to create a value so that it is applicable to only this application and not all applications created by you. What you need to do is create a new registry key below the `HKEY>\_CURRENT>\_USER\Software\[Manufacturer]` key that is specific to this product, so select the Action ⇨ New ⇨ Key menu item.

When the key is created, the key name will be editable, so give it a name of `[ProductName]` and press Enter. This creates a key that is given the name of the product contained within this Windows Installer package. The `ProductName` property of the setup was discussed earlier in this chapter.

Now that you have created the correct registry key, the next step is to create the actual registry value. Make sure that your new registry key is selected, and choose String Value from the Action ➪ New menu and give the new value a name of Debug.

Once the value has been created, you can set a default value for it, in this case `False`. Make sure that the new value is selected; the Properties window will have changed to show you the details for this value. Notice that there is a property called `Value`, which is used to set the initial value. Enter `False` as the value for the `Value` property, and that's it. The end result is displayed in Figure 19-14.

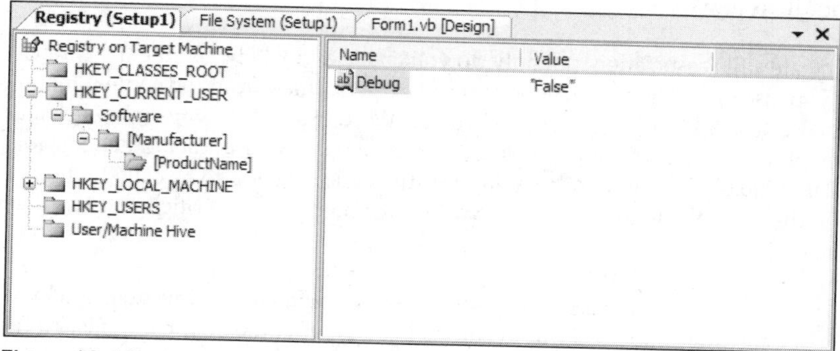

Figure 19-14

When the Windows Installer package is run the Debug registry, value will be created. As you can see, manipulating the Windows Registry is straightforward.

You can move most keys and values in the Registry Editor around by using cut and paste or simply by dragging and dropping the required item.

If a value already exists in the registry, the Windows Installer package will overwrite the existing value with that defined in the Registry Editor.

The alternative to creating registry entries during installation is to have your application create registry entries the first time they are needed. However, this has one significant difference from registry keys created with a Windows Installer package. The uninstall corresponding to a Windows Installer installation will automatically remove any registry keys created during the install. If the registry entries are created by the application instead, the uninstall has no way to know that these registry entries should be removed.

Importing Registry Files

If you already have a registry file that contains the registry settings that you would like to be created, you can import the file into the Registry Editor, which saves you from having to manually enter the information. To import a registry file, you need to make sure the root node (Registry onTarget Machine) is selected in the left pane of the editor. You can then use the Import item of the Action menu to select the registry file to import.

Registry manipulation should be used with extreme caution. Windows relies heavily on the registry and as a result of this you can cause yourself a great number of problems if you delete/overwrite/change registry values and keys without knowing the full consequences of the action.

If you want to create the registry entries that are required to create file associations, you can use the editor covered next.

The File Types Editor

The File Types Editor can be used to create the required registry entries to establish a *file association* for the application being installed. A file association is simply a link between a particular file extension and a particular application. For example, the file extension .doc is normally associated with Microsoft WordPad or Microsoft Word.

When you create a file association, not only do you create a link between the file extension and the application, but you also define a set of actions that can be performed from the context menu of the file with the associated extension. Looking at your Microsoft Word example, if you right-click a document with an extension of .doc, you get a context menu that can contain any number of actions, for example, Open and Print. The action in bold (Open, by default) is the default action to be called when you double-click the file, so in the example double-clicking a Word document will start Microsoft Word and load the selected document.

So, how do you create a file extension using the editor? We will answer this question by walking through the creation of a file extension for the application. Let's say that the application uses a file extension of .set and that the file is to be opened in the application when it is double-clicked. To accomplish this, start the File Types editor, which unlike the last two editors, has only one pane to its interface, as shown in Figure 19-15.

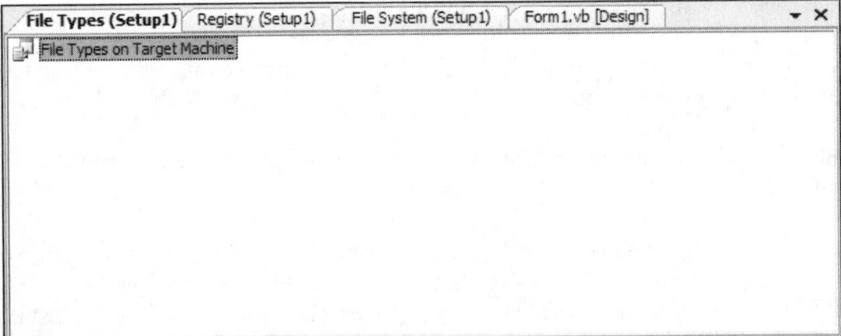

Figure 19-15

To add a new file type, you need to make sure the root element (File Types on Target Machine) is selected in the editor. You can then choose Add File Type from the Action menu. Give the new file type the name, Example File Type.

Before continuing, you must set the extension and application that this file type uses. These are both accomplished using the Properties window (shown in Figure 19-16).

Enter .set as the value for the Extensions property.

To associate an application with this file type, you need to use the `Command` property. The ellipsis button for this property presents you with a dialog box where you can select an executable file contained within any of the folders defined in the File System Editor. In this case, you'll select `Primary Output from WindowsApplication (active)` from the `Application Folder` as the value for `Command`.

When this new file type was first created, a default action was added for you called `&Open`—select it. Now take a look at the Properties window again. Notice the `Arguments` property: you can use this to add command-line arguments to the application defined in the last step. In the case of the default action that has been added for you, the arguments are `"%1"`, where the value `"%1"` will be replaced by the file name that invoked the action. You can add your own hard-coded arguments (such as `/d`). An action is set to be the default by right-clicking it and selecting Set as Default from the pop-up menu.

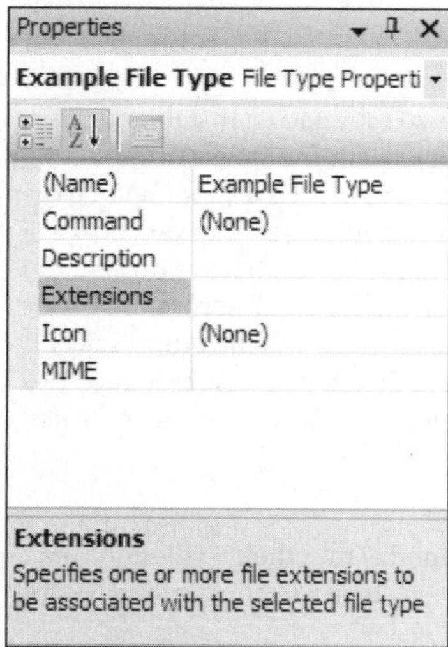

Figure 19-16

The User Interface Editor

The User Interface Editor is used to manage the interface that the user relies on to proceed through the installation of the application. The editor allows you to define the dialog boxes that are displayed to the user and in what order they are shown. The User Interface Editor looks like the example in Figure 19-17.

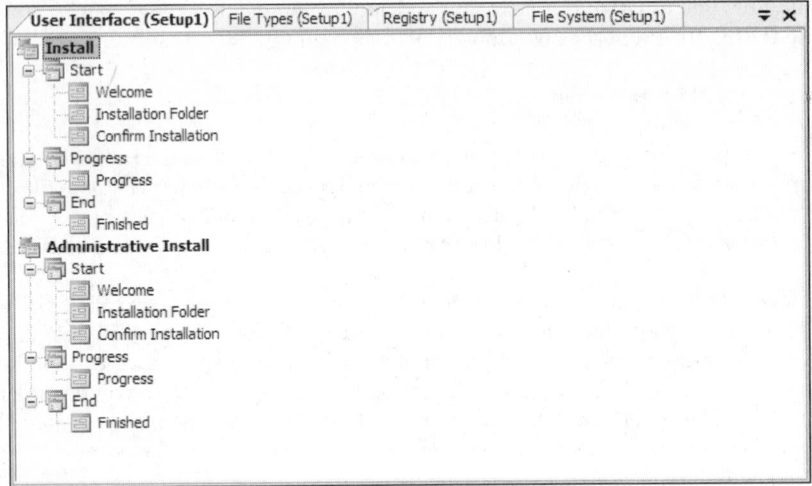

Figure 19-17

The editor uses a tree view with two root nodes: Install and Admininstrative Install. Below each of these nodes there are three nodes that represent the stages of installation: Start, Progress, and End. Each of the three stages can contain a number of dialog boxes that will be displayed to the user when the resulting Windows Installer package is run. A default set of dialog boxes is predefined when you create the deployment project. The default dialog boxes that are present depend on the type of deployment project: Setup Project or Web Setup Project. Figure 19-17 shows the dialog boxes that were added by default to a Setup Project. However, if you are creating a Web Setup Project the Installation Folder dialog box will be replaced by an Installation Address dialog box. Using Figure 19-17, the following section discusses the two modes that the installer can be run in and what the three stages of the installation are.

Installation Modes

Start by taking a look at the two modes that the installation runs: Install and Admininstrative Install. These basically distinguish between an end user installing the application and a system administrator performing a network setup.

To use the Administrative Install mode of the resulting Windows Installer package you can use `msiexec.exe` *with the/a command-line parameter:*

```
msiexec.exe /a <PACKAGE>.msi
```

The Install mode will be the one that is most used and is what you will use in this discussion. As mentioned earlier, the steps the installation goes through can be split into three stages and are represented as subnodes of the parent installation mode.

The Start Stage

The Start stage is the first stage of the installation and contains the dialog boxes that need to be displayed to the user before the actual installation of the files begins. The Start stage should be used to gather any information from the user that may affect what is installed and where it is installed. This stage is commonly used to ask the user to select the base installation folder for the application and to ask the user what parts of the system he or she would like to install. Another very common task at this stage is to ask users what their name is and what organization they work for. At the end of this stage the Windows Installer service will determine how much disk space is required on the target machine and check that this amount of space is available. If the space is not available, the user will receive an error and the installation will not continue.

The Progress Stage

The Progress stage is the second stage of the installer and is where the actual installation of the files occurs. There isn't usually any user interaction in this stage of installation. There is normally one dialog box that indicates the current progress of the installation. The current progress of the installation is calculated automatically.

The End Stage

Once the actual installation of the files has finished, the installer moves into the End stage. The most common use of this stage is to inform the user that the installation has been completed successfully. It is often used to provide the option of running the application straight away or to view any release notes.

Customizing the Order of Dialog Boxes

The order in which the dialog boxes appear within the tree view determines the order in which they are presented to the user when the resulting Windows Installer package is run. Dialog boxes cannot be moved between different stages.

The order of the dialog boxes can be changed by dragging the respective dialog boxes to the position in which you want them to appear. You can also move a particular dialog box up or down in the order in by right-clicking the dialog box and selecting either Move Up or Move Down.

Adding Dialog Boxes

A set of predefined dialog boxes has been added to the project for you, allowing for actions such as prompting a user for a registration code, but what happens if these do not match your requirements? As well as being able to modify the order in which the dialog boxes appear, you can also add or remove dialog boxes to and from any of the stages.

When adding a dialog box, you have the choice of using a built-in dialog box or importing one. To illustrate how to add a dialog box, consider an example of adding a dialog box to display a `ReadMe` file to the user of Windows Installer package. The `ReadMe` file needs to be displayed before the actual installation of the files occurs.

The first step is to determine the mode in which the dialog box is to be shown: Install or Administrative Install. In this case, you are not interested in the Admin mode, so you will use the Install mode. After this, you need to determine the stage at which the dialog box is to be shown. In the example, you want to display the `ReadMe` file to the user before the actual installation of the files occurs, which means that you will have to show the `ReadMe` file in the Start stage. Make sure the Start node is selected below the Install parent node.

You are now ready to add the dialog box. Using the Action menu again, select the Add Dialog menu item, which will display a dialog box (see Figure 19-18) where you can choose from the built-in dialog boxes.

As you can see in Figure 19-18, there are a number of built-in dialog boxes to choose from. Each dialog box has a short description that appears at the bottom of the window to inform you of its intended function. In this case, you want to use the Read Me dialog box, so select it and click on OK.

New dialog boxes are always added as the last dialog box in the stage that they are added to, so now you need to move it into the correct position. In this case, you want the Read Me dialog box to be shown immediately after the Welcome dialog box, so drag and drop it into position.

Properties of the Dialog Boxes

Like most other project items in Visual Studio, dialog boxes have a set of properties that you can change to suit your needs using the Properties window. If you make sure a dialog box is selected, you will notice that the properties window changes to show the properties of the selected dialog box. The properties that appear depend on the dialog box selected. Details of all the properties of the built-in dialog boxes can be found by looking at the "Properties of the User Interface Editor" topic in the MSDN documentation.

The Custom Actions Editor

The Custom Actions Editor is used for fairly advanced installations and allows you to define actions that are to be performed due to one of the following installation events: Install, Commit, Rollback, and Uninstall. For example, you can use this editor to define an action that creates a new database when the installation is committed.

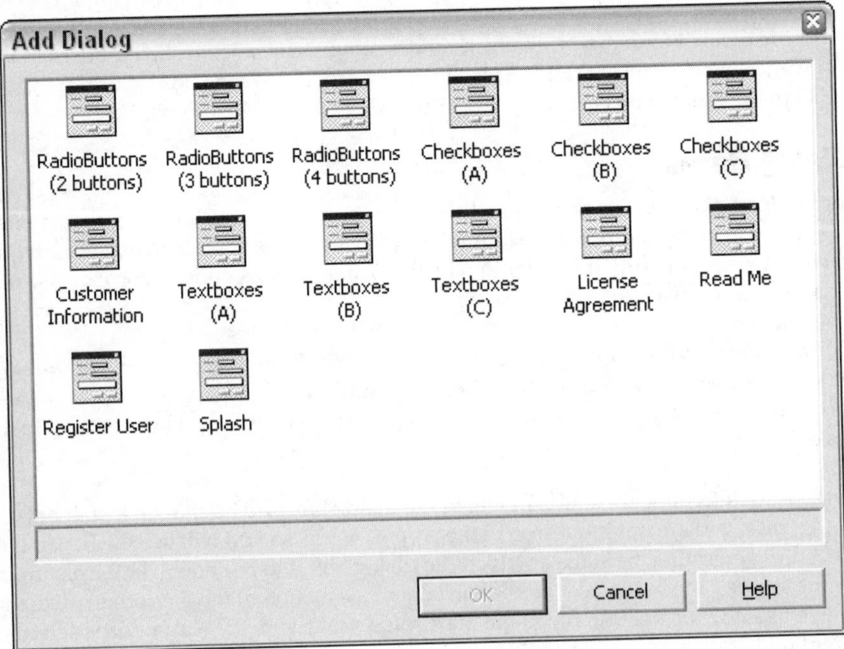

Figure 19-18

The custom actions that are added using this editor can be windows script-based, compiled executables, or DLLs.

Before we continue with the discussion of this editor, make sure that it is loaded by right-clicking on the Setup1 project and selecting View | Custom Actions. Once it is loaded, you will notice that it uses a tree view to represent the information, much like the User Interface Editor. There are four nodes that represent each of the four installation events that you can add custom actions to. This is displayed in Figure 19-19.

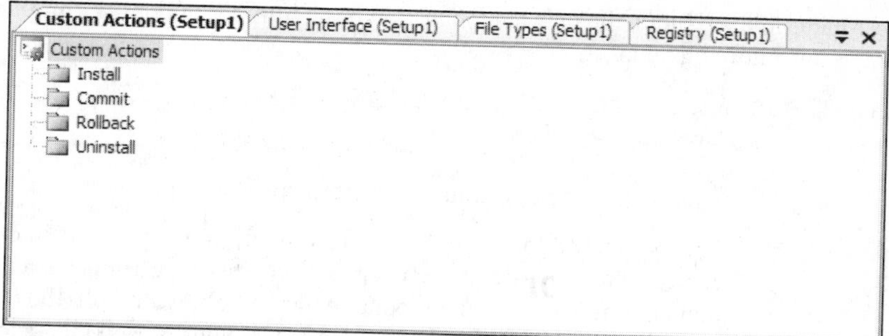

Figure 19-19

As with the User Interface Editor, the order in which the actions appear determines the order in which they are run, and this can be modified simply by dragging and dropping the actions or by using the context menus of the actions to move them up or down.

Adding a Custom Action

To add a custom action you must select the node of the event into which you want to install the action. You can then use the Action menu to select the executable, DLL, or script that implements the custom action. The four actions that are defined in the editor are defined in the following table.

Event	Description
`Install`	The actions defined for this event will be run when the installation of the files has finished, but before the installation has been committed.
`Commit`	The actions defined for this event will be run when the installation has been committed and has therefore been successful.
`Rollback`	The actions defined for this event will be run when the installation fails and rolls back the machine to the same state as before the install was started.
`Uninstall`	The actions defined for this event will be run when the application is being uninstalled from the machine.

Suppose that you want to start your application up as soon as the installation is completed successfully. Use the following process to accomplish this.

First, decide when the action must occur. Using the preceding table, you can see that the `Commit` event will be run when the installation has been successful. Make sure that this node is selected in the editor. You are now ready to add the actual action you would like to happen when the `Commit` event is called. Using the Action menu again, select the Add Custom Action menu item, which will display a dialog box that you can use to navigate for and select a file (.exe, .dll, or windows script) from any that are included in the File System Editor. In this example select `Primary output from WindowsApplication (Active)`, which is contained within the Application Folder.

As with most items in the editors, the new custom action has a number of relevant properties that are summarized in the following table.

Property	Description
`(Name)`	This is the name given to the selected custom action.
`Arguments`	This property allows you to pass command-line arguments into the executable that makes up the custom action. This only applies to custom actions that are implemented in executable files (.exe). By default, the first argument passed in can be used to distinguish what event caused the action to run. The first argument can have the following values:

`/Install`
`/Commit`
`/Rollback`
`/Uninstall`
`Condition`
	This enables you to enter a condition that will be evaluated before the custom action is run. If the condition evaluates to `True`, then the custom action will run; if the condition evaluates to `False`, then the custom action will not run.

`CustomActionData`	This property allows you to pass additional information to the custom action.
`EntryPoint`	This property is used to define the entry point in the DLL that implements the custom action. This only applies to custom actions that are implemented in dynamic linked libraries (.dll). If no value is entered, then the installer will look for an entry point in the selected DLL with the same name as the event that caused the action to run (`Install`, `Commit`, `Rollback`, `Uninstall`).
`InstallerClass`	If the custom action is implemented by an Installer class in the selected component, then this property must be set to `True`. If not, it must be set to `False`. (consult the MSDN documentation for more information on the Installer class, which is used to create special installers for such .NET applications as Windows Services. The Installer class is located in the `System.Configuration.Install` namespace)
`SourcePath`	This property will show the path to the actual file on the developer's machine that implements the custom action.

Set the `InstallClass` property to equal `False`, because your application does not contain an installer class.

That's it. When you run the Windows Installer package and the installation is successful, the application will automatically start. The custom action that you implemented earlier is very simple, but custom actions can be used to accomplish any customized installation actions that you could want. I suggest that you take some time to play around with what can be accomplished using custom actions. For instance, try creating a custom action that writes a short file into the application directory.

The Launch Conditions Editor

The Launch Conditions Editor can be used to define a number of conditions for the target machine that must be met before the installation will run. For example, if your application relies on the fact that the user must have Microsoft Word 2000 installed on his or her machine to run your application, you can define a launch condition that will check this.

You can define a number of searches that can be performed to help create launch conditions:

- ❑ File search
- ❑ Registry search
- ❑ Windows Installer search

As with the Custom Actions Editor, the Launch Conditions Editor (shown in Figure 19-20) uses a tree view to display the information contained within it.

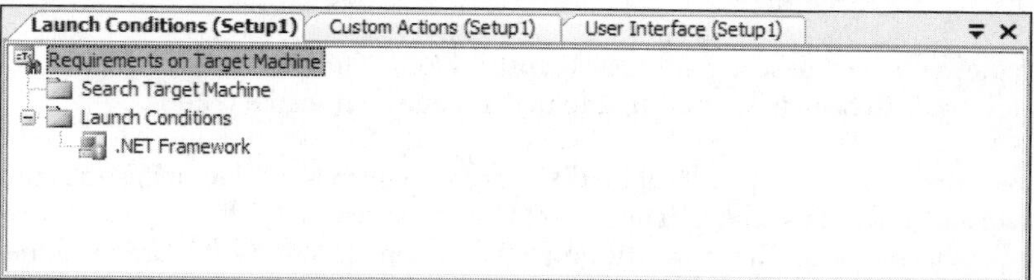

Figure 19-20

There are two root nodes: the first, (Search Target Machine) is used to display the searches that have been defined, the second (Launch Conditions) contains a list of the conditions that will be evaluated when the Windows Installer package is run on the target machine.

As with many of the other editors, the order in which the items appear below these two nodes determines the order in which the searches are run and the order in which the conditions are evaluated. If you wish, you can modify the order of the items in the same manner as previous editors.

The searches are run and then the conditions are evaluated as soon as the Windows Installer package is run, before any dialog boxes are shown to the user.

We are now going to look at an example of adding a file search and launch condition to a setup project. For argument's sake, let's say that you want to make sure that your users have Microsoft Word 2003 installed on their machine before they are allowed to run the installation for your application.

Adding a File Search

To add a file search, you begin by searching for the Microsoft Word 2003 executable.

Making sure the Search Target Machine node is currently selected in the editor, add a new file search by selecting the Add File Search item from the Action menu. The new item should be given a meaningful name, so enter `Word2003Search`. The end result is shown in Figure 19-21.

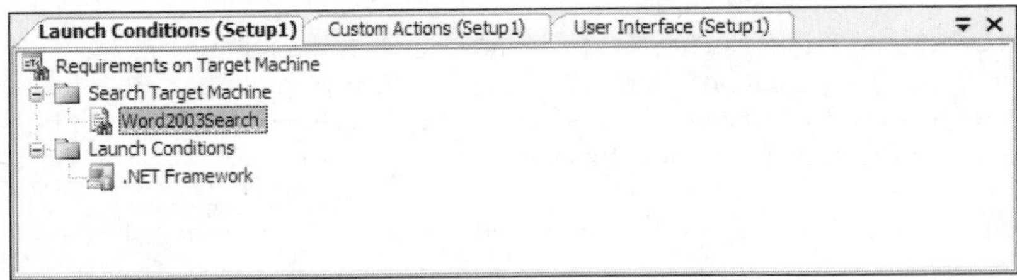

Figure 19-21

Modifying the File Search Properties

Like most items contained within the editors mentioned in this chapter, the new file search item has a set of properties that you can modify using the Properties window. The properties of the file search item determine the criteria that will be used when searching for the file. Most of the properties are self-explanatory and have been covered in previous sections, so they will not be covered in this chapter.

In this example , you need to search for the Microsoft Word 2003 executable, which means that a number of these properties will need to be modified to match your own search criteria.

The first property that requires modification is `FileName`, which is used to define the name of the file that the search will look for. In this case, you need to search for Microsoft Word 2003 executable, so enter `winword.exe` as the value for this property. Previous versions of Microsoft Word used the same file name.

There is no need to search for the file from the root of the hard drive. The `Folder` property can be used to define the starting folder for the search. By default, the value is `[SystemFolder]`, which indicates that the search will start from the Windows `system` folder. There are a number of these built-in values; if you are interested, you can look up what these folders correspond to in the "Adding Special Folders," section.

In this example, you do not want to search the Windows `system` folder because Microsoft Word is usually installed in the `Program Files` folder. Set the value of the `Folder` property to `[ProgramFilesFolder]` to indicate that this should be your starting folder.

When the search starts it will only search the folder specified in the `Folder` property, as indicated by the default value (`0`) of the `Depth` property. The `Depth` property is used to specify how many levels of sub-folders the search will look in from the starting folder specified above for the file in question. There are performance issues relating to the `Depth` property. If a search is performed for a file that is very deep in the file system hierarchy, it can take a long time to find the file. Therefore, it is advisable that, wherever possible, you should use a combination of the `Folder` and `Depth` properties to decrease the possible search range. The file that you are searching for in your example will probably be at a depth of greater than `1`, so change the value to `3`.

There may be different versions of the file that you are searching for on a user's machine. You can use the remaining properties to specify a set of requirements for the file that must be met for it to be found, for example, minimum version number, minimum file size.

You are searching for the existence of Microsoft Word 2003; this means that you will need to define the minimum version of the file that you want to find. To search for the correct version of `winword.exe`, you need to enter `11.0.0.0` as the value for the `MinVersion` property. This will ensure that the user has Microsoft Word 2003 or later installed and not an earlier version.

The result of the file search will need to be assigned to a Windows Installer property so that you can use it to create a launch condition later. This is going to be a bit of a tongue twister. You need to define the name of the Windows Installer property that is used to store the result of the file search using the `Property` property. Enter `WORDEXISTS` as the value for the `Property` property. If the file search is successful, the full path to the found file will be assigned to this Windows Installer property; otherwise, it will be left blank. At this point, the Properties window should look as shown in Figure 19-22.

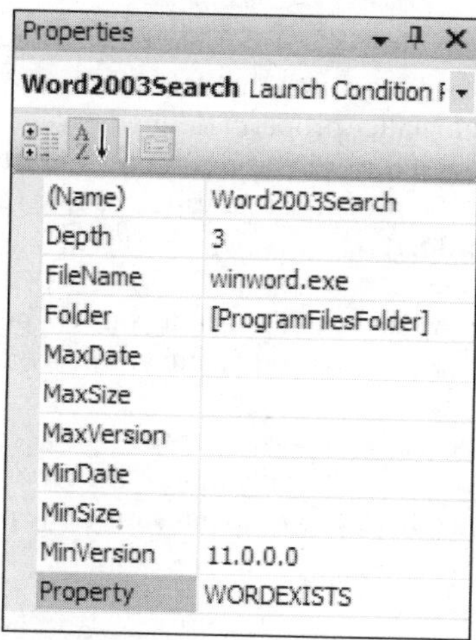

Figure 19-22

Creating a Launch Condition

A file search alone is pretty useless. Which takes you on to the second step of the process of ensuring the user has Microsoft Word 2003 installed, creating a launch condition. You can use the results of the file search described earlier to create a launch condition.

Make sure that the Launch Conditions node is selected in the editor, and add a new launch condition to the project by selecting Add Launch Condition from the Action menu. You need to give this new item a meaningful name; in this case (see Figure 19-23), you will give it a name of `Word2KExists`.

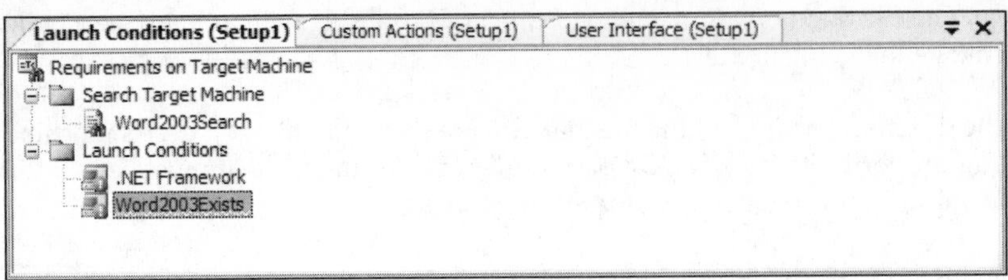

Figure 19-23

This new item has a number of properties that you will need to modify. The first property you will change is called `Message`, and it is used to set the text of the message box that will appear if this condition is not met. Enter any meaningful description that explains why the installation cannot continue.

The next property that you will need to change is called `Condition`, and it is used to define a valid deployment condition that is to be evaluated when the installation runs. The deployment condition entered must evaluate to `True` or `False`. When the installer is run, the condition will be evaluated; if the result of the condition is `False`, then the message defined will be displayed to the user and the installation will stop.

For this example, you need to enter a condition that takes into account if the `winword.exe` file was found. You can use the Windows Installer property defined earlier (`WORDEXISTS`) as part of the condition. Because the property is empty if the file was not found and nonempty if the file was found, you can perform a simple test on whether the property is empty to create the condition. Enter `WORDEXISTS <> ""` as the value for the `Condition` property.

Hopefully, from the preceding discussion of this search you will be able to apply the knowledge gained, to understand how to use the other searches and create your own launch conditions.

We have now finished the brief discussion of the editors that you can use to modify the resulting Windows Installer package to suit your needs. You have only looked briefly at the functionality of the editors, but they are extremely powerful so we advise you to spend some time playing around with them.

Building

The final step is concerned with how to build the deployment or setup project you have created. There is basically no difference between how you build a Visual Basic .NET application and a deployment/setup project. If the project is the only project contained within the solution, then you can just use the Build item from the Build menu, which will cause the project to be built. As with the other projects, you will be informed of what is happening during the build through the Output window.

The deployment/setup project can also be built as part of a multiproject solution. If the Build Solution item is chosen from the Build menu, all the projects in the solution will be built. Any deployment or setup projects will be built last. This is to ensure that if they contain the output from another project in the solution, they pick up the latest build of that project.

As with most other project templates in Visual Studio, you can set the current build configuration to be used when building the project. This will not be covered in this chapter because it is covered in Appendix A. As you can see, building a setup/deployment project is basically the same as building any other project template.

Internet Deployment of Windows Applications

The earlier discussions of creating an installation package for your application presumed that you were able to transfer the MSI file to each machine that needed installation, either electronically or via some storage medium such as a CD-ROM. This works well for installations within an organization and can work acceptably for initial installation from CD-ROMs on distributed systems.

However, the availability of the Internet has raised the bar for acceptable deployment of Windows-based client applications. Perhaps the most important advantage of browser-based applications has been their ease of deployment for the user. For Windows Forms applications to be cost-competitive with browser-based applications, low-cost deployment over the Internet is needed.

Fortunately, there are several ways to get low-cost deployment over the Internet. These include:

- "No-touch" deployment
- Deployment with ClickOnce, a new capability in Visual Studio 2005 and the .NET Framework 2.0
- Components or libraries that contain deployment capabilities, such as the Application Updater Application Block

Different deployment techniques are suitable for different applications. Let's look at each technique, and discuss how it works and what kinds of applications it is suitable for use with.

No-Touch Deployment

Built into all versions of the .NET Framework is the capability to run applications from a Web server instead of from the local machine. There are two ways to do this, depending on how the application is launched.

First, an application EXE that exists on a Web server can be launched via a standard HTML hyperlink. An application named `MyApp.exe` that is located at `www.mycompany.com/apps` can be launched with the following HTML in a Web page:

```
<a href="http://www.mycompany.com/apps/MyApp.exe">Launch MyApp</a>
```

When the hyperlink is clicked on a system with the .NET Framework installed, Internet Explorer will transfer control to the .NET Framework to launch the program. The Framework then tries to load the EXE assembly, which does not yet exist on the client. At that point, the assembly is automatically fetched from the deployment Web server and placed on the local client machine. It resides on the client machine in something called the *application download cache*, which is a special directory on the system managed by the .NET. Framework.

If the EXE tries to load a class from another application assembly (typically a DLL), then that assembly is assumed to be in the same directory on the Web server as the EXE. The application assembly will also be transferred to the application download cache and loaded for use.

This process will continue for any other application assemblies that are needed. The application is said to *trickle-feed* to the client system.

Automatic Updating

Whenever an assembly in the application download cache is needed, the .NET Framework automatically checks for a new version in the appropriate directory on the Web server. Thus, the application can be updated for all client machines by simply placing an assembly on the Web server.

Using a Launch Application

One drawback of this technique for deploying the application is that it cannot be launched except from a Web page. (The Web page can be local to the machine, however.)

To get around this limitation, you can get a similar deployment capability by using a small launching application that uses dynamic loading to start the main application. Dynamic loading was discussed in the previous chapter. In this case, the location for the assembly used in dynamic loading will be the URL of the assembly on the Web server.

An application that uses this technique still gets all the trickle feeding and auto-update features of an application launched straight from a URL.

Limitations of No-Touch Deployment

No-touch deployment is useful for simple applications, but has some serious drawbacks for more complex applications. The biggest issues are:

- An active Internet connection is required to run the application — no offline capability is available
- Only assemblies can be deployed via no-touch deployment — application files such as configuration files cannot be included
- Applications deployed via no-touch deployment are subject to code-access security limitations, as discussed in Chapter 13 on security
- No-touch deployment has no capability to deploy any prerequisites for the application or any COM components that it may need

Given the limitations of no-touch deployment, Microsoft has added an alternative to the .NET Framework 2.0 called ClickOnce. It is essentially a complete replacement for no-touch deployment. Thus, while no-touch deployment is still supported in .NET Framework 2.0, it is no longer recommended for use, and we will not discuss it further.

ClickOnce Deployment

A more advanced form of Internet and network deployment uses a new technology in .NET Framework 2.0 called ClickOnce. It is intended to overcome the limitations of no-touch deployment and to provide a robust, easy-to-implement deployment option for a wide range of applications.

ClickOnce has several advantages over alternatives such as no-touch deployment, including:

Updating from a Web server with user control — No-touch deployment only allows completely automatic updating from the Web server. ClickOnce can be configured for completely automatic updates from a Web server, but can also be set up to allow more control by the user over when the application is installed and uninstalled.

Offline Access — Applications deployed with ClickOnce can be configured to run in an offline condition also. Applications that can be run offline have a shortcut installed on the Start menu.

ClickOnce also has advantages over applications installed with Windows Installer. These include auto-updating of the application from the deployment server, and installation of the application by users who are not administrators. (Windows Installer applications require the active user to be an administrator. ClickOnce applications can be installed by users with reduced permissions.)

ClickOnce deployment can be done from a Web server, a network share, or read-only media such as a CD-ROM or DVD_ROM. The following discussion assumes you are using a Web server for deployment, but you can substitute a network share if you do not have access to a Web server.

Important Note: ClickOnce does not require the .NET Framework 2.0 to be installed on the Web server you use for ClickOnce deployment. However, it does require that the Web server understand how to handle files with extensions ".application" and ".manifest". The configuration for these extensions is done automatically if the .NET Framework 2.0 is installed on the Web server. However, on servers that do not contain the Framework, you will probably have to do the configuration manually.

Each extension that a Web server can handle must be associated with an option called a "MIME type" that tells the web server how to handle that file extensions when serving a file. The MIME type for each extension used by ClickOnce should be set to "application/x-ms-application." If you do not know how to configure MIME types for your Web server, your should ask a network administrator or other profession that is able to do so.

Configuring an Application for ClickOnce

No special work need be done to prepare a typical Windows application to be deployed via ClickOnce. Unlike the deployment options discussed earlier, it is not necessary to add additional projects to the solution. If you use standard options in ClickOnce, it is also unnecessary to add any custom logic to your application. All of the work to enable ClickOnce deployment for an application can be performed by selecting options in the IDE.

It is possible to control the ClickOnce deployment by writing your own custom logic controlling the ClickOnce deployment processes. However, that capability is beyond the scope of this book and is not discussed. Instead, the chapter will cover basic configuration of ClickOnce and common options that do not require that you write any code.

Online vs. Locally Installed Applications

Applications installed via ClickOnce are one of two types:

- **Online Applications**, which can only be accessed by the user when the system has a connection to the web site used to deploy the application
- **Offline Applications**, which can also be used when there is no connection available

Online applications must be launched with a URL (Uniform Resource Locator), a standard filename, or a UNC (Universal Naming Convention) filename. This may be done in various ways, such as clicking a link in a Web page, typing a URL into the Address textbox of a browser, typing a filename into the Address textbox of Windows Explorer, or selecting a shortcut on the local machine that contains the URL or filename. However, ClickOnce does not automatically add any such mechanisms to a user's machine to access the application. That is up to you.

Offline applications can also be launched with a URL or UNC, and are always launched that way the first time. The differences are:

- When ClickOnce does the initial installation of the application on the user's machine, by default it places a shortcut to the application on the user's Start | Programs menu.
- The application can be started from the shortcut, and will run with no connection to the original location used for installation. Of course, any functionality of the application that depends on a network or Internet connection will be affected if the system is not online. It is your responsibility to build the application in such a way that it functions properly when offline.

Deploying an Online Application

A walk-through of deployment for a simple Windows application will demonstrate the basics of ClickOnce. This first walk-through will deploy an online application to a Web server, which is one of the simpler user scenarios for ClickOnce.

First, create a simple Windows Application in Visual Studio, and name it SimpleApp. On the blank Form1 that is created as part of the application, place a single button.

To enable ClickOnce deployment, access the Build menu, and select the Publish SimpleApp option. The ClickOnce publishing wizard will appear. The first screen in the wizard is shown in Figure 19-24.

The location will default to a local web server, but as discussed earlier, deployment can be done to a network share or even a local directory. You should change the location if the default is not appropriate for your circumstances. Once you've verified the location to publish, press the Next button.

Next, you must select of the two types of ClickOnce applications discussed earlier. Since this example is for an online application, you should click the second option to make the application only available online, as shown in Figure 19-25

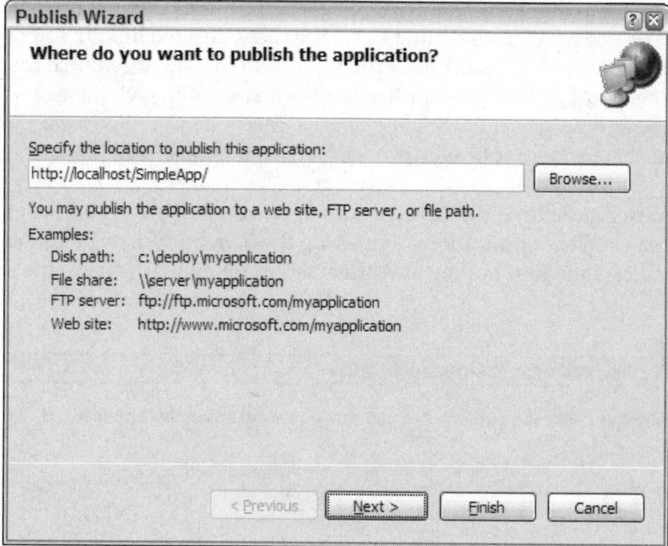

Figure 19-24

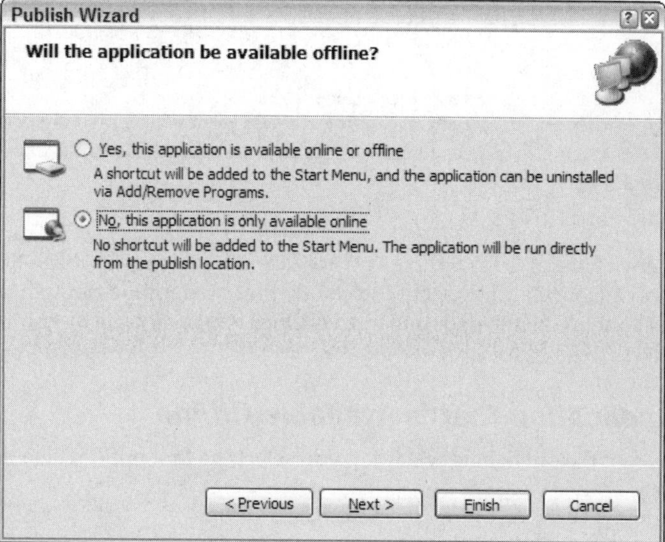

Figure 19-25

Now you can press the Next button to see a summary of your selection, and then press the Finish button. The ClickOnce deployment process will then begin. A new item will be added to your project called "SimpleApp_TemporaryKey.pfx", a complete build will be done, a new virtual directory will be created for the application on the Web server, and the files needed to deploy the application will be copied to that virtual directory. (The new item is discussed below, in the section on "Signing the Manifest".)

When the process is complete, a web page will be generated that contains the link needed to deploy the application. The Web page will have a Run button that activates the link. If you click this button, the application will be deployed by ClickOnce. (You may wish to view the source for this web page to obtain the HTML needed to launch the application from your own web pages.)

First, the pre-requisites for the application are verified. In this case, that just means the .NET Framework.

Then a Security Warning dialog is displayed asking if it is acceptable to run the application, as shown in Figure 19-26. You can run the application by pressing the Run button, or press the Cancel button, which aborts the process. Press the Run button, and after a short delay you will see the application's form appear.

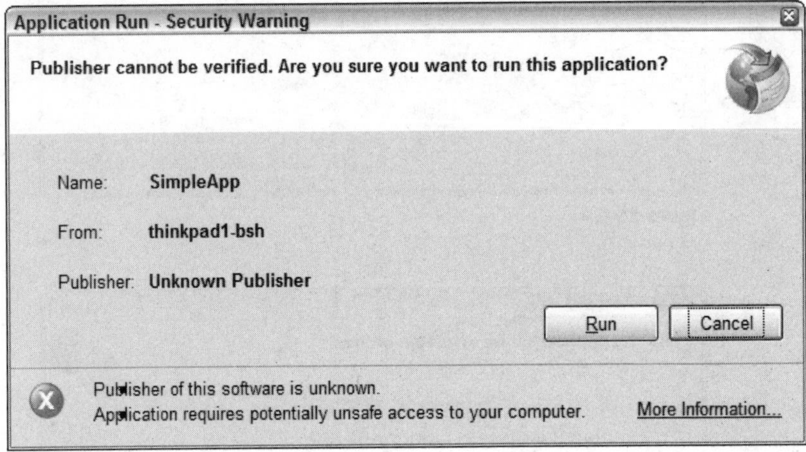

Figure 19-26

If you now make any changes to the SimpleApp application, you must publish the application again to make the changes available via ClickOnce. You can do that by stepping through the publishing wizard once again. More about automatic updating of ClickOnce applications is discussed below in the topic "The Update Process".

Deploying an Application That is Available Offline

In the second screen of the publishing wizard, if you select the first option, then the installation process has some differences.

- The web page that ClickOnce generates to test the deployment will have a button that says "Install" instead of "Run".
- When the button is pressed, a shortcut to the application is added to the user's Start | Programs menu. The shortcut will be in the program folder that is named for the company name that was entered when Visual Studio was installed.
- The application will be launched at the end of the install process, as it was with an online app. However, future launches can be accomplished with the same URL or via the shortcut in the Start menu.

Files and Directories Produced by ClickOnce

The virtual directory used by ClickOnce to deploy your application contains a number of files for different aspects of the deployment. Figure 19-27 shows what the directory for SimpleApp looks like after ClickOnce has finished copying all files needed.

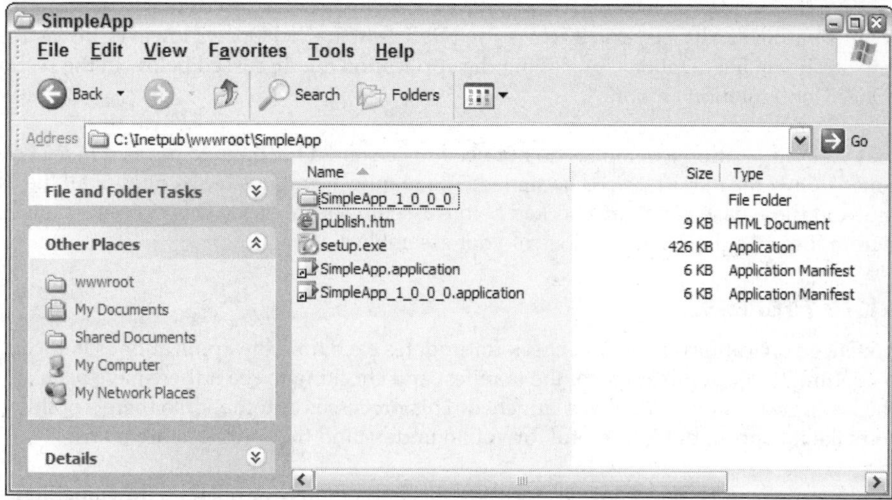

Figure 19-27

The virtual directory contains a folder for the first version of SimpleApp, which by default is version 1.0.0.0. It also contains the Web page that was displayed after ClickOnce finished, which is named publish.htm.

The next file is Setup.exe. This is an executable that does not need the .NET Framework to run. It is used during the ClickOnce process for all the activities that must take place before the application is launched. This includes activities such as checking for the presence of the .NET Framework. It is discussed further in the section below entitled "The Bootstrapper".

The next file is SimpleApp.application. The ".application" extention is specific to ClickOnce, and indicates a special file called a "manifest". This is an XML-based file that contains all the information needed to deploy the application, such as what files are needed and what options have been chosen. There is also a file named SimpleApp_1_0_0_0.application, which is the manifest specifically associated with version 1.0.0.0.

Each version of the application has it's own manifest, and the one named SimpleApp.application (with no embedded version number) it typically the currently active one. (Thus, the link to the application does not need to change when the version number changes.)

Other files associated with a version are in the folder for that version.

Signing the Manifest

Since the manifest controls the update process, it is essential that ClickOnce be assured that the manifest is valid. This is done by signing the manifest, using a public-private key pair. As long as a third party does not have the key pair, they cannot "spoof" a manifest, preventing any malicious interference in the ClickOnce deployment process.

A key pair is automatically generated when you publish with ClickOnce. However, you can supply your own key pair if you like. Options for signing the application are discussed below in the section entitled "ClickOnce Configuration Options".

Note that your application assemblies do not need to be signed for them to be used in a ClickOnce deployment. Only the manifest need be signed. The manifest contains hash codes of all the assemblies involved, and those hash codes are checked before assemblies are used. This prevents malicious third parties from inserting their own versions of your assemblies.

The Update Process

All ClickOnce applications by default check for updates each time the application is launched. This is done by getting the current version of the manifest and checking to see if there have been any changes since the last time the application was launched. This process is automatic, so there's nothing you need to do to make it happen, but it's helpful for you to understand the steps that are taken.

For an online application, if a change is detected, it is immediately applied by downloading any changed files. Then the application is launched. In spirit this is similar to a browser-based application, because the user does not have any option to use an older version.

For an application available offline, if changes are detected, the user is asked if the update should be made. The user can choose to decline the update. There is a configuration option that allows you to specify a minimum version number, and that can force a user to accept an update. We will look at ClickOnce configuration options later.

If an update is made for an offline application, the previous version is kept. The user then has the ability to roll back to that version using their Add/Remove Programs option in the Control Panel. The user can also uninstall the ClickOnce-deployed application from that same location.

Only one version back is kept. If there are older versions, they are removed when a new version is installed, so that the only versions available at any point in time are the current version and the one immediately before it. If a roll back is made to the immediately preceding version, it cannot be rolled back any further to earlier versions.

You can control the update process by including code in your application that detects when changes have been made, and applies the changes as necessary. As previously mentioned, this chapter will not cover writing such logic. There are samples available in the MSDN documentation for this capability.

ClickOnce Configuration Options

In Visual Studio 2005, the properties for a Windows Application project now include several pages that affect ClickOnce. (You can get to the properties for a project by right-clicking on it in the Solution Explorer, and selecting Properties.)

The Signing tab page includes options for signing the ClickOnce manifest. There are buttons to select a particular certificate from a store or a file, or to generate a new test certification for signing. This page also contains an option to sign the assembly that is compiled from the project, but as mentioned above, this is not necessary for ClickOnce to operate. A typical example of the Signing tab page is shown in Figure 19-28.

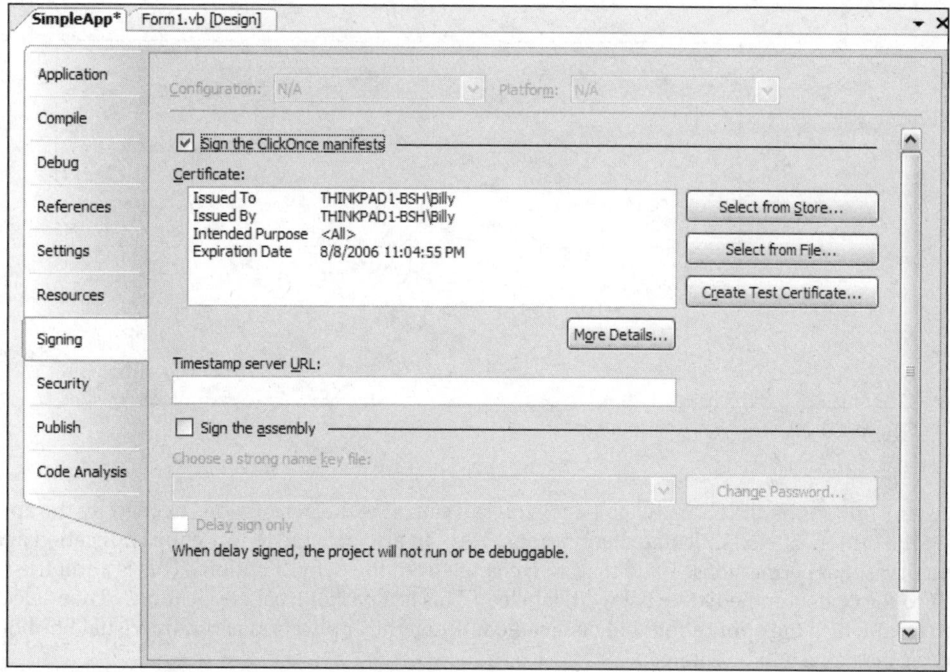

Figure 19-28

The Security tab page controls options relating to the code access security permissions needed by the application to run. Since the application is being deployed from a source off of the local machine if you use ClickOnce, code access security limitations are in effect as described in Chapter 13. A typical example of the Security tab page is shown in Figure 19-29

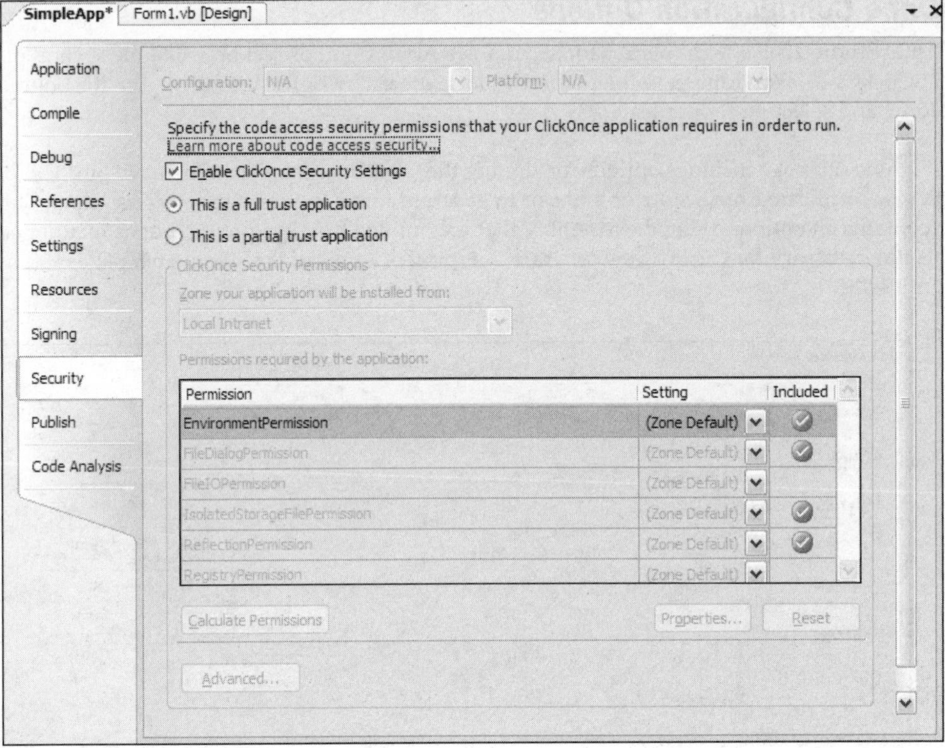

Figure 19-29

Using the options on the Security tab page, you can calculate the permissions needed by the application, using the button labeled Calculate Permissions. You can also arrange to test your application against a particular set of permissions. To do that, you change from the default option "This is a full trust application" to the option immediately below it, labeled "This is a partial trust application". Then select the zone from which the application will be installed. When the application is run by Visual Studio, permission for that zone will be enforced.

All of the other ClickOnce configuration options are on the tab page labeled Publish. Such a page is shown in Figure 19-30.

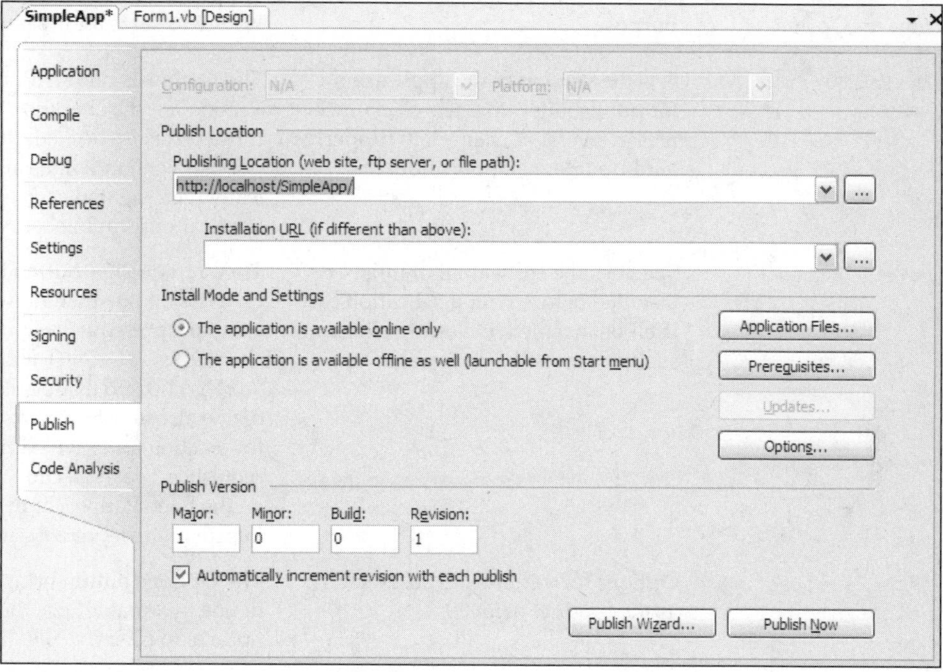

Figure 19-30

There are many options that you can set with the Publish page, but here are some of the most important:

Property/Option	Purpose	Where to set it on the page
`Publishing Location`	Specifies the virtual directory, network directory, or local directory to which the application will be published by ClickOnce.	Textbox labeled "Publishing Location". (Note that this can also be set in the first screen of the publish wizard.)
`Installation URL`	Specifies the location from which your application will be deployed by users. By default, this is the same as the Publishing Location, but may be set to be elsewhere.	Textbox labeled "Installation URL"
`Install Mode`	Selects the online only vs. offline mode for the application.	Option buttons under "Install Mode and Settings". (Note that this can also be set in the second screen of the publish wizard.)

Table continued on following page

Property/Option	Purpose	Where to set it on the page
`Publish Version`	Sets the version of the application for publishing purposes. ClickOnce requires version changes to properly auto-update the application.	The textboxes under "Publish Version". If the checkbox under those boxes is checked, the publish version will be automatically incremented each time the application is published.
`Prerequisites`	Specifies the software that must be installed before your application can itself be installed, including elements such as the .NET Framework.	The Prerequisites button brings up a dialog box that allows standard prerequisites to be checked off. The .NET Framework is checked by default. The dialog also allows you to specify the location for downloading prerequisites. See the section below on the Bootstrapper for more information on prerequisites.
`Miscellaneous options`	Options for various purposes such as the product name.	The Options button brings up a dialog box that allows these options to be set.
`Update options`	Options that control the update process, including when the application updates (before or after it starts), the minimum version number required, etc.	These options are only available for applications that can run offline. The Updates button brings up a dialog box controlling these options.

The Bootstrapper

Because applications deployed by ClickOnce is a part of the .NET Framework, the .NET Framework must be available on the user's machine before your application can be installed and run. In addition, your application may require other items such as a database or COM component to be installed.

To provide for such needs, ClickOnce includes a "bootstrapper" that runs as the first step in the ClickOnce process. The bootstrapper is not a .NET program, so it can run on systems that do not yet have the .NET Framework installed. The bootstrapper is contained in a program called Setup.exe, which is included by ClickOnce as part of the publishing process.

When setup.exe runs, it checks for the prerequisites needed by the application, as specified in the Prerequisites options discussed above. If needed, these options are then downloaded and installed. Only if the user's system contains installed prerequisites does ClickOnce attempt to install and run your Windows application.

The MSDN documentation includes more details on configuring and using the ClickOnce bootstrapper.

ClickOnce vs. Other Deployment Technologies

ClickOnce is a complete replacement for no-touch deployment. However, there are other deployment scenarios for which ClickOnce may not be the ideal solution. For example, ClickOnce can only deploy a per-user installation. ClickOnce cannot install an application once to be used by all users on the system.

ClickOnce may be used in combination with technologies such as the Windows Installer. If you create .msi files, as discussed earlier in the chapter, you may include them as part of ClickOnce's bootstrapper process. This is an advanced technique not discussed in this book, but you can learn more about this capability in the MSDN documentation.

For cases in which ClickOnce is not appropriate, you may wish to use more customized deployment technologies. These are discussed next.

Custom Deployment Options

If an application needs deployment capabilities not covered by the technologies discussed so far, it may be necessary to use alternatives technologies, or even develop them yourself. For example, you can create a deployment function that checks via a Web Service to see when updating needs to take place and that uses FTP to transfer files from a Web server to a client machine.

Updater Application Block

Rather than start from scratch on such deployment/installation technology, you can look at starting points such as the Updater Application Block. Created by Microsoft's Patterns and Practices Group, the Updater Application Block can be downloaded from Microsoft's Web site. It includes manifest-based checking of modules for updating, and background transfer of new modules using the same transfer technology as Windows Update.

You can use the Updater Application Block as is, or customize it for your own needs. For example, you could create a version that allows different classes of users to have different update strategies, so that new updates go out to a select group of users first.

Summary

An application must be deployed to be useful. How an individual application should be deployed depends heavily on circumstances. Factors such as the geographic distribution of the application, its complexity, and how often it will be updated all must be considered to choose an appropriate strategy.

The main possibilities for deployment are:

- XCOPY deployment
- Installation via the Windows Installer
- No-touch deployment
- ClickOnce deployment
- Deployment with other technologies such as the Application Updater Block

This chapter has covered each of these, with some discussion of their applicability. It will be helpful for you to understand all of these options to make appropriate decisions for the deployment of individual applications.

On one hand, simple utilities, for example, might be best installed by simply copying files. On the other hand, stand-alone applications that have many dependencies on COM-based components will more often use Windows Installer technology. Applications that depend on Web Services for data will often be best deployed with ClickOnce. Corporate applications with special needs for security during installation, or that need to install an application once for multiple users, may be better off using the Application Updater Block.

It's also helpful to understand that these options are not mutually exclusive. You may have an application with COM dependencies that needs to use an .msi file for an initial install, but then gets the rest of the application and future updates via ClickOnce or the Application Updater Block. Whatever your application, the plethora of application deployment technologies available for .NET-based applications means you should be able to find an option or combination that suits your needs.

20

Working with Classic COM and Interfaces

However much we try, we just can't ignore the vast body of technology surrounding Microsoft's Component Object Model, or COM. Over the years, this model has been the cornerstone of so much Microsoft-related development that we have to take a long, hard look at how we are going to integrate all that stuff into the new world of .NET.

This chapter starts by taking a brief backward glance at COM, then compares it with the way that components interact in .NET, and finally it takes a look at the tools Microsoft provides to help link the two together. Having looked at the theory, we then try it out by building a few example applications. First, we take a legacy basic COM object and run it from a Visual Basic 2005 program. Then we repeat the trick with a full-blown ActiveX control. Finally, we turn things around and try running some Visual Basic code in the guise of a COM object.

> **More information on how to make COM and VB6 code interoperate with the .NET platform can be found in *Professional Visual Basic Interoperability: COM and VB6 to .NET* (Wiley, 2002).**

As all that is done, try to remember one thing: COM is, to a large extent, where .NET came from. In evolutionary terms, COM's kind of like Lucy, the *Australopithecus* from ancient Ethiopia. So, if it seems a little clunky at times, let's not to be too hard on it. In fact, let's not refer to it as "Nasty, tired, clunky old COM" at all. Let's simply call it "Classic COM."

Classic COM

Before looking into COM-.NET interoperability, it's important to be aware of the main points about COM itself. This section doesn't attempt to do anything more than skim the surface, however. While the basic concepts are fundamentally simple, the underlying technology is anything but. Some of the most impenetrable books on software that have ever been written have COM as their subject, and we have no wish to add to these.

COM was Microsoft's first full-blown attempt at creating a language-independent standard for programming. The idea was that interfaces between components would be defined according to a binary standard. This would mean that you could, for the first time, invoke a VB component from a VC++ application, and vice versa. It would also be possible to invoke a component in another process or even on another machine, via Distributed COM (DCOM). You won't be looking at out-of-process servers here, however, because the vast majority of components developed to date are in-process. To a large extent, DCOM was fatally compromised by bandwidth, deployment, and firewall problems and never achieved a high level of acceptance.

A COM component implements one or more *interfaces*, some of which are standards provided by the system, and some of which are custom interfaces defined by the component developer. An interface defines the various methods that an application may invoke. Once specified, an interface definition is supposed to be inviolate so that, even if the underlying code changes, applications that use the interface don't need to be rebuilt. If the component developers find that they have left something out, they should define a new interface containing the extra functionality in addition to that in the original interface. This has, in fact, happened with a number of standard Microsoft interfaces. For example, the `IClassFactory2` interface extends the `IClassFactory` interface by adding features for managing the creation of licensed objects.

The key to getting applications and components to work together is *binding*. COM offers two forms of binding, early and late:

- In *early binding*, the application uses a *type library* at compile time to work out how to link in to the methods in the component's interfaces. A type library can either come as a separate file, with the extension .tlb, or as part of the DLL containing the component code.
- In *late binding*, no connection is made between the application and its components at compile time. Instead, the COM runtime searches through the component for the location of the required method when the application is actually run. This has two main disadvantages: It's slower and it's unreliable. If a programming error is made (for example, the wrong method is called, or the right method with the wrong number of arguments), it doesn't get caught at compile time.

If a type library is not explicitly referred to, there are two ways to identify a COM component, by *class ID*, which is actually a GUID, and by *ProgID*, which is a string and looks something like `"MyProject.MyComponent"`. These are all cross-referenced in the registry. In fact, COM makes extensive use of the registry to maintain links between applications, their components, and their interfaces. All experienced COM programmers know their way around the registry blindfolded.

VB6 has a lot of COM features embedded into it, to the extent that many VB6 programmers aren't even aware that they are developing COM components. For instance, if you create a DLL containing an instance of a VB6 class, you will in fact have created a COM object without even asking for one. The relative ease of this process is demonstrated during the course of this chapter.

There are clearly similarities between COM and .NET. So, to a large extent, all you've got to do to make them work together is put a wrapper around a COM object to turn it into an assembly, and vice versa.

COM and .NET in Practice

It's time to get serious and see if all this seamless integration really works. To do this, we're going to have to simulate a legacy situation. Let's imagine that your enterprise depends on a particular COM object that was written for you a long time ago by a wayward genius (who subsequently abandoned software development and has gone to live in a monastery in Tibet). Anyway, all you know is that the code works perfectly and you need it for your .NET application.

You have one, or possibly two, options here. If you have the source (which is not necessarily the case) and you have sufficient time (or, to put it another way, money), you can upgrade the object to .NET and continue to maintain it under Visual Studio 2005. For the purist, this is the ideal solution for going forward. However, maintaining the source as it is under Visual Studio isn't really a viable option. Visual Studio does offer an upgrade path, but it doesn't cope well with COM objects using interfaces specified as abstract classes.

If upgrading to .NET isn't an option, all you can do is simply take the DLL for the COM object, register it on the .NET machine, and use the .NET interoperability tools. This is the path that you're going to take.

So, what you need is a genuine legacy COM object, and what you're going to have to use is genuine legacy VB6. For the next section, then, you're going to be using VB6. If you've already disposed of VB6, or never had it in the first place, feel free to skip this section. The DLL is available as part of the code download, in any case.

A Legacy Component

For your legacy component, you're going to imagine that you have some kind of analytics engine that requires a number of calculations. Because of the highly complex nature of these calculations, their development has been given to specialists, while the user interface for the application has been given to UI specialists. A COM interface has been specified that all calculations must confirm to. This interface has the name `IMegaCalc` and has the following methods.

Method	Description
`Sub AddInput (InputValue as Double)`	Add input value to calculation
`Sub DoCalculation ( )`	Do calculation
`Function GetOutput ( ) as Double`	Get output from calculation
`Sub Reset ( )`	Reset calculation for next time

Step 1: Defining the Interface

The first thing you have to do is define your interface. In VB6, the way to do this is to create an abstract class, that is, one without any implementation. So, create an ActiveX DLL project called `MegaCalculator`. You do this by creating a new project and then changing its name to `MegaCalculator` by means of the Project ⇨ Project1 Properties dialog box. Having done that, create a class called `IMegaCalc`. This is what the code looks like:

```
Option Explicit

Public Sub AddInput(InputValue As Double)
End Sub

Public Sub DoCalculation()
End Sub

Public Function GetOutput() As Double
End Function

Public Sub Reset()
End Sub
```

From the main menu, select File ⇨ Make MegaCalculator.dll to define and register the interface.

Step 2: Implementing the Component

For the purposes of this demonstration, the actual calculation that you're going to perform is going to be fairly mundane: In fact, you're going to calculate the mean of a series of numbers. So, create another ActiveX DLL project, called `MeanCalculator` this time. You need to add a reference to the type library for the interface that you're going to implement, so select the MegaCalculator DLL via the References dialog box that appears when you select Project ⇨ References.

Having done that, you can go ahead and write the code for the mean calculation. You do this in a class called `MeanCalc`:

```
Option Explicit

Implements IMegaCalc

Dim mintValue As Integer
Dim mdblValues() As Double
Dim mdblMean As Double

Private Sub Class_Initialize()
  IMegaCalc_Reset
End Sub

Private Sub IMegaCalc_AddInput(InputValue As Double)
  mintValue = mintValue + 1
  ReDim Preserve mdblValues(mintValue)
  mdblValues(mintValue) = InputValue
End Sub
```

```
Private Sub IMegaCalc_DoCalculation()
  Dim iValue As Integer
  mdblMean = 0#
  If (mintValue = 0) Then Exit Sub

  For iValue = 1 To mintValue
    mdblMean = mdblMean + mdblValues(iValue)
  Next iValue

  mdblMean = mdblMean / mintValue
End Sub

Private Function IMegaCalc_GetOutput() As Double
  IMegaCalc_GetOutput = mdblMean
End Function

Private Sub IMegaCalc_Reset()
  mintValue = 0
End Sub
```

As before, you select File ➪ Make MeanCalculator.dll to build and register the component. It has a default interface called `MeanCalc` (which contains no methods, and is thus invisible to the naked eye), plus an implementation of `IMegaCalc`.

Step 3: Registering the Legacy Component

You now have your legacy component. If you're developing your new .NET application on the same machine, you don't need to do anything more because your component would already have been registered by the build process. However, if you're working on an entirely new machine, you'll need to register it there. The easiest way to do this is to open a command box, and register it with the following command using `regsvr32.exe` found in `C:\Windows\system32`:

```
regsvr32 MeanCalculator.dll
```

Then you should see the result shown in Figure 20-1.

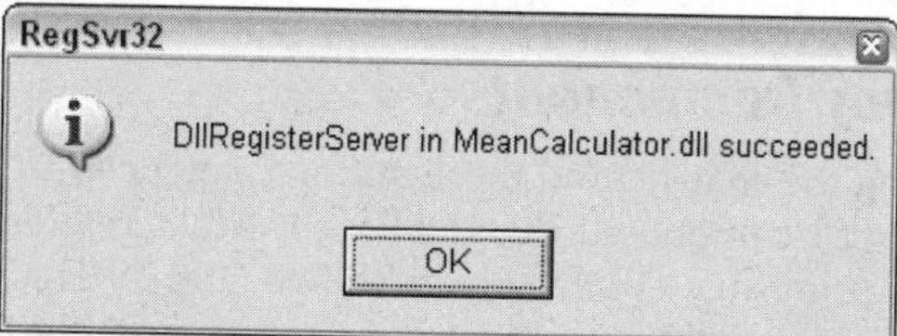

Figure 20-1

Because `MeanCalculator` implements an interface from `MegaCalculator`, you'll also have to repeat the trick with that DLL:

```
regsvr32 MegaCalculator.dll
```

and what you see is shown in Figure 20-2.

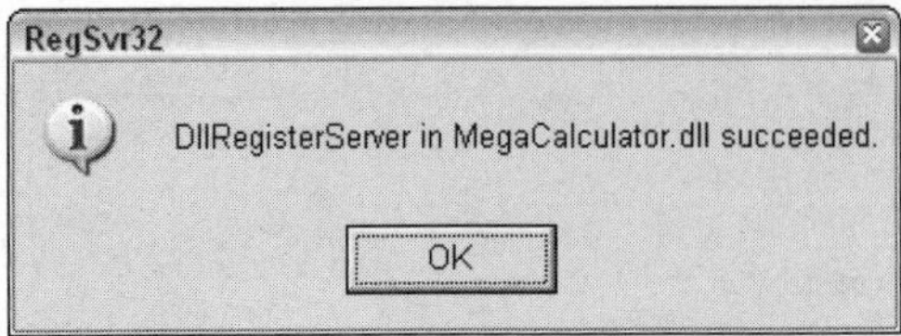

Figure 20-2

You're now ready to use your classic component from a .NET application.

The .NET Application

For your .NET application, all you're going to do is instantiate a `MeanCalc` object and get it to work out a mean for you. So, create a Windows Application project in Visual Basic called `CalcApp`. What the form looks like is shown in Figure 20-3.

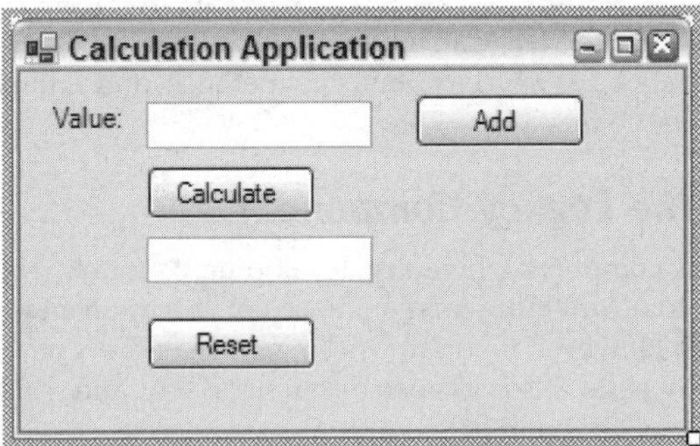

Figure 20-3

The two text boxes are called `txtInput` and `txtOutput`, respectively; the second one is not enabled for user input. The three command buttons are `btnAdd`, `btnCalculate`, and `btnReset`, respectively.

Referencing the Legacy Component

Before you dive into writing the code behind those buttons, you need to make your new application aware of the `MeanCalculator` component. So, you have to add a reference to it, via the Project ➪ Add Reference menu item. This brings up a dialog box with five tabs: .NET, COM, Projects, Browse, and Recent. Select `MeanCalculator` and `MegaCalculator` in turn from the COM tab (see Figure 20-4).

Now, press the OK button. Notice that, in the list of references in the Solution Explorer, you can now see both `MeanCalculator` and `MegaCalculator` (see Figure 20-5).

Inside the .NET Application

Now that you've successfully got your component referenced, you can go ahead and finish coding your application. First, add a global variable (`mobjMean`) to hold a reference to an instance of the mean calculation component:

```
Public Class Form1

    Dim mobjMean As MeanCalculator.MeanCalc
```

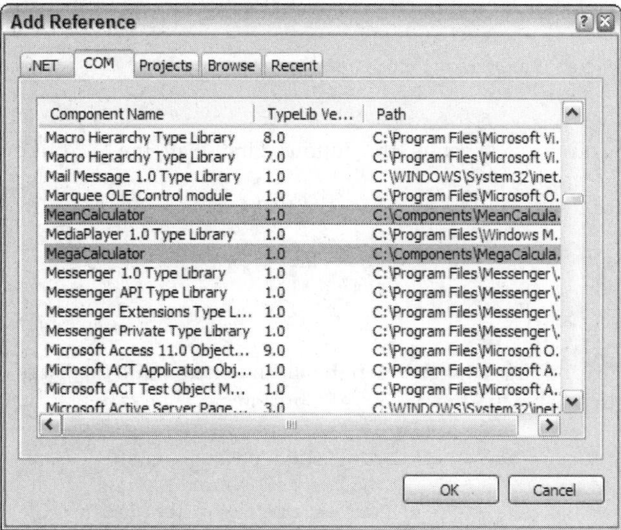

Figure 20-4

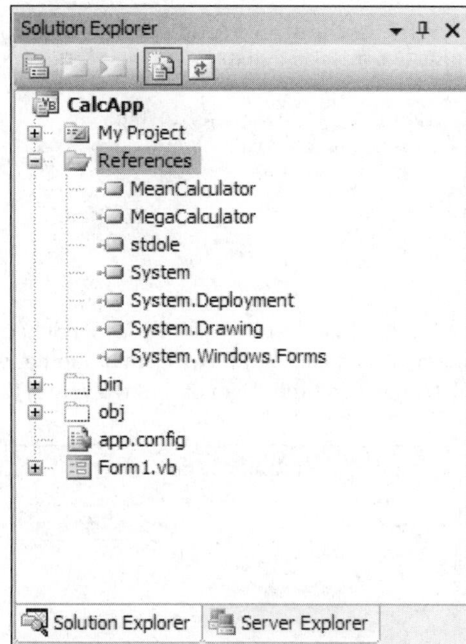

Figure 20-5

Next, you need to create a `Form1_Load` event where you will add the following instruction, which will create the component that you're going to use:

```
Private Sub Form1_Load(ByVal sender As Object, _
   ByVal e As System.EventArgs) Handles Me.Load

    mobjMean = New MeanCalculator.MeanCalc()
End Sub
```

Finally, you need to add the code behind the buttons. First of all, the `Add` button:

```
Private Sub btnAdd_Click(ByVal sender As Object, _
                         ByVal e As System.EventArgs) _
                         Handles btnAdd.Click
  mobjMean.AddInput(CDbl(txtInput.Text))
End Sub
```

All you're doing here is adding whatever's in the input text box into the list of numbers for the calculation. Next, here's the code behind the `Calculate` button:

```
Private Sub btnCalculate_Click(ByVal sender As Object, _
                               ByVal e As System.EventArgs) _
                               Handles btnCalculate.Click
  mobjMean.DoCalculation()
  txtOutput.Text = mobjMean.GetOutput()
End Sub
```

This performs the calculation, retrieves the answer, and puts it into the output text box. Finally, the code behind the `Reset` button simply resets the calculation:

```
Private Sub btnReset_Click(ByVal sender As Object, _
             ByVal e As System.EventArgs) Handles btnReset.Click
    mobjMean.Reset()
End Sub
```

Trying It All Out

Of course, the proof of the pudding is in the eating, so let's see what happens when you run your application. First, put one value in, say 2, and click Add. Now, enter another value, say 3, and click Add once more. When you click Calculate, you'll get the mean of the two values (2.5 in this case; see Figure 20-6).

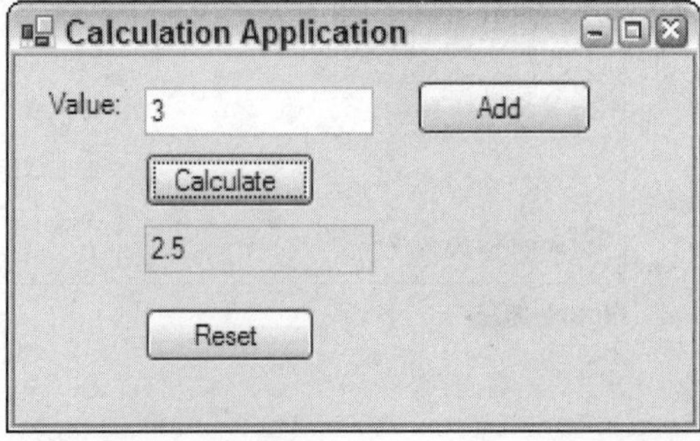

Figure 20-6

Using TlbImp Directly

In the preceding example, there's actually quite a lot going on under the covers. Every time you import a COM DLL into Visual Studio, it's creating a *default interop assembly*, which is basically a .NET assembly that acts as a wrapper for the COM object. If you're doing this a lot, it might be better to do the wrapping once and for all, and then let your application developers import the resulting .NET assembly instead. Let's see how you might do that.

The process that creates the default interop assembly on behalf of Visual Studio is called `TlbImp.exe`. The name stands for *Type Library Import*, and that's pretty much what it does. It comes as part of the .NET Framework SDK, and you might find it convenient to extend the `PATH` environment variable to include the `\bin` directory of the .NET Framework SDK.

`TlbImp` takes a COM DLL as its input and generates a .NET assembly DLL as its output. By default, the .NET assembly has the same name as the type library, which will — in the case of VB6 components — always be the same as the COM DLL. This means that you'll have to explicitly specify a different output file. You do this by using the `/out:` switch. So that you can see what's going on at each step in the process, you'll also specify `/verbose`:

```
tlbimp MegaCalculator.dll /out:MegaCalculatorNet.dll /verbose
```

For this example, start with `MegaCalculator`, because `MeanCalculator` has a reference to `MegaCalculator`. If you start with `MeanCalculator`, you will notice that you will get an error saying that there is a reference to `MegaCalculator` and that `TlbImp` will not be able to overwrite the `MegaCalculator.dll`. The way to get around this is to start with `MegaCalculator` by giving `TlbImp` the command as shown above. Once this is accomplished, `TlbImp` will inform you of the success or failure in creating a .NET assembly of the name `MegaCalculatorNet.dll`.

Now that `MegaCalculatorNet.dll` is in place, you can work with `MeanCalculator` and make sure that the reference now points to the new `MegaCalculatorNet.dll`. You accomplish this by using the following command:

```
tlbimp MeanCalculator.dll /out:MeanCalculatorNet.dll
   reference:MegaCalculatorNet.dll /verbose
```

What happens with this command is shown in Figure 20-7.

```
Visual Studio Command Prompt

C:\Components>tlbimp MeanCalculator.dll /out:MeanCalculatorNet.dll /reference:Me
gaCalculatorNet.dll /verbose
Microsoft (R) .NET Framework Type Library to Assembly Converter 2.0.40607.16
Copyright (C) Microsoft Corporation.  All rights reserved.

Resolved referenced file 'MeanCalculator.dll' to file 'C:\Components\MeanCalcula
tor.dll'.
Type '_MeanCalc' imported.
Resolving reference to type library 'MegaCalculator'.
A reference to type library 'MegaCalculator' has been resolved to user specified
 assembly 'MegaCalculatorNet'.
Type 'MeanCalc' imported.
Type library imported to C:\Components\MeanCalculatorNet.dll

C:\Components>
```

Figure 20-7

Notice that `TlbImp` has encountered a reference to another COM type library, `MegaCalculator`, and it has very kindly in turn imported `MegaCalculatorNet` instead.

Having converted your COM DLLs into .NET assemblies, you can now reference them in an application as you would any other .NET DLL.

Late Binding

We've shown that you can successfully do early binding on COM components within a .NET application. But what if you want to do late binding? What if you don't have access to a type library at application development time? Can you still make use of the COM components? Does the .NET equivalent of late binding even exist?

The answer is that, yes, it does, but, no, it's not as transparent as with VB6. Let's take a look at what one used to do in VB6. If you wanted to do early binding, you would do this:

```
Dim myObj As MyObj
Set myObj = New MyObj

MyObj.MyMethod (...)
```

For late binding, it would look like this instead:

```
Dim myObj As Object
Set myObj = CreateObject ("MyLibrary.MyObject")

MyObj.MyMethod (...)
```

There's actually an enormous amount of stuff going on under the covers here; if you're interested in looking into this further, try *VB COM: Visual Basic 6 Programmer's Introduction to COM.*

An Example for Late Binding

For your sample, let's extend the calculator to a more generic framework that can feed inputs into a number of different calculation modules rather than just the fixed one. You'll keep a table in memory of calculation ProgIDs and present the user with a combo box to select the right one.

The Sample COM Object

The first problem you encounter with late binding is that you can only late-bind to the default interface, which, in this case, is `MeanCalculator.MeanCalc`, not `MeanCalculator.IMegaCalc`. So, you're going to have to redevelop your COM object as a stand-alone library, with no references to other interfaces.

As before, you'll build a DLL under VB6, copy it over to your .NET environment, and reregister it there. You'll call this VB6 DLL `MeanCalculator2.dll`, and the code in the class (called `MeanCalc`) should look like this:

```
Option Explicit

Dim mintValue As Integer
Dim mdblValues() As Double
Dim mdblMean As Double

Private Sub Class_Initialize()
  Reset
End Sub

Public Sub AddInput(InputValue As Double)
  mintValue = mintValue + 1
  ReDim Preserve mdblValues(mintValue)
  mdblValues(mintValue) = InputValue
End Sub

Public Sub DoCalculation()
  Dim iValue As Integer
  mdblMean = 0#

  If (mintValue = 0) Then Exit Sub

  For iValue = 1 To mintVal
    mdblMean = mdblMean + mdblValues(iValue)
  Next iValue

  mdblMean = mdblMean / mintValue
End Sub

Public Function GetOutput() As Double
  GetOutput = mdblMean
End Function

Public Sub Reset()
  mintValue = 0
End Sub
```

As before, you'll need to move this across to your .NET machine and register it using `RegSvr32`.

The Calculation Framework

For your generic calculation framework, you'll create a new application in Visual Basic 2005 called `CalcFrame`. You'll basically use the same dialog box as last time, but with an extra combo box at the top (see Figure 20-8).

The new combo box is called `cmbCalculation`. You've also disabled the controls `txtInput`, `btnAdd`, `btnCalculate`, and `btnReset`, until you know if the selected calculation is valid.

Start off by importing the `Reflection` namespace; you'll need this for handing all the late binding:

```
Imports System.Reflection
```

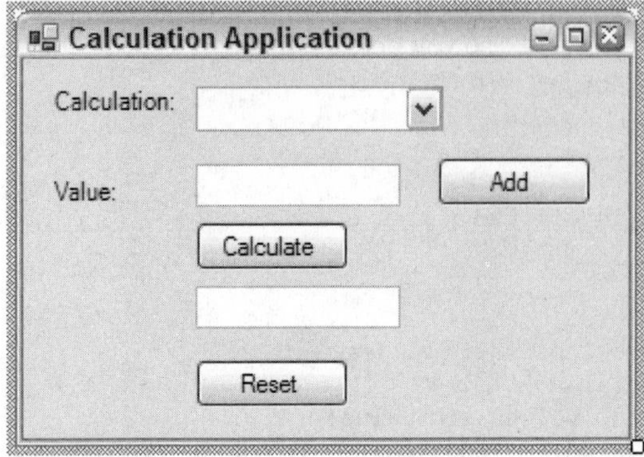

Figure 20-8

Then add a few member variables:

```
Public Class Form1
    Inherits System.Windows.Forms.Form

    Private mstrObjects() As String
    Private mnObject As Integer
    Private mtypCalc As Type
    Private mobjcalc As Object
```

Next, add a few lines to `Form1_Load`:

```
Private Sub Form1_Load(ByVal sender As Object, _
   ByVal e As System.EventArgs) Handles Me.Load

    mnObject = 0
    AddObject("Mean", "MeanCalculator2.MeanCalc")
    AddObject("StdDev", "StddevCalculator.StddevCalc")

    If (mnObject > 0) Then
        cmbCalculation.SelectedIndex = 0
    End If

End Sub
```

What you're doing here is building up a list of calculations. Once finished, you select the first one in the list. Let's just take a look at that subroutine `AddObject`:

```
Private Sub AddObject(ByVal strName As String, ByVal strObject As String)
    cmbCalculation.Items.Add(strName)
    mnObject = mnObject + 1
    ReDim Preserve mstrObjects(mnObject)
    mstrObjects(mnObject - 1) = strObject
End Sub
```

In this code segment, you're adding the calculation name to the combo box and its `ProgID` to an array of strings. Neither of these is sorted, so you get a one-to-one mapping between them. Check out what happens when you select a calculation via the combo box:

```
Private Sub cmbCalculation_SelectedIndexChanged(ByVal sender As Object, _
                                                ByVal e As System.EventArgs) _
                            Handles cmbCalculation.SelectedIndexChanged
    Dim intIndex As Integer
    Dim bEnabled As Boolean

    intIndex = cmbCalculation.SelectedIndex
    mtypCalc = Type.GetTypeFromProgID(mstrObjects(intIndex))

    If (mtypCalc Is Nothing) Then
        mobjcalc = Nothing
        bEnabled = False
    Else
        mobjcalc = Activator.CreateInstance(mtypCalc)
        bEnabled = True
    End If

    txtInput.Enabled = bEnabled
    btnAdd.Enabled = bEnabled
    btnCalculate.Enabled = bEnabled
    btnReset.Enabled = bEnabled
End Sub
```

There are two key calls here. The first is to `Type.GetTypeFromProgID`. This takes the incoming `ProgID` string and converts it to a `Type` object. This may either succeed or fail; if it fails, you disable all controls and let the user try again. If it succeeds, however, you go on to create an instance of the object described by the type. You do this in the call to the static method `Activator.CreateInstance`.

So, let's assume that your user has selected a calculation that you can successfully instantiate. What next? The next thing is that the user enters a number and clicks the Add button.

```
Private Sub btnAdd_Click(ByVal sender As Object, _
   ByVal e As System.EventArgs) Handles btnAdd.Click

   Dim objArgs() As [Object] = {CDbl(txtInput.Text)}
   mtypCalc.InvokeMember("AddInput", BindingFlags.InvokeMethod, _
      Nothing, mobjcalc, objArgs)

End Sub
```

The important call here is to `InvokeMember`. Let's take a closer look. There are five parameters here:

- The first parameter is the name of the method that you want to call: `AddInput` in this case. So, instead of going directly to the location of the routine in memory, you ask the .NET runtime to find it for you.
- The value from the `BindingFlags` enumeration tells it to invoke a method.

- The next parameter is to provide language-specific binding information, which isn't needed in this case.
- The fourth parameter is a reference to the COM object itself (the one that you instantiated using `Activator.CreateInstance`).
- Finally, the fifth parameter is an array of objects representing the arguments for the method. In this case, there's only one argument, the input value.

Something very similar to this is going on underneath VB6 late binding, except that here it's exposed in all its horror. In some ways, that's no bad thing, because it should bring it home that late binding is something to avoid, if at all possible. Anyway, let's carry on and complete the program. Here are the remaining event handlers:

```
Private Sub btnCalculate_Click(ByVal sender As Object, _
            ByVal e As System.EventArgs) Handles btnCalculate.Click

    Dim objResult As Object
    mtypCalc.InvokeMember("DoCalculation", BindingFlags.InvokeMethod, _
                          Nothing, mobjcalc, Nothing)
    objResult = mtypCalc.InvokeMember("GetOutput", _
                  BindingFlags.InvokeMethod, Nothing, mobjcalc, Nothing)
    txtOutput.Text = objResult

End Sub

Private Sub btnReset_Click(ByVal sender As Object, _
              ByVal e As System.EventArgs) Handles btnReset.Click

    mtypCalc.InvokeMember("Reset", BindingFlags.InvokeMethod, _
       Nothing, mobjcalc, Nothing)

End Sub
```

Running the Calculation Framework

Let's quickly complete the job by running the application. Here's what happens when you select the nonexistent calculation `StdDev` (see Figure 20-9).

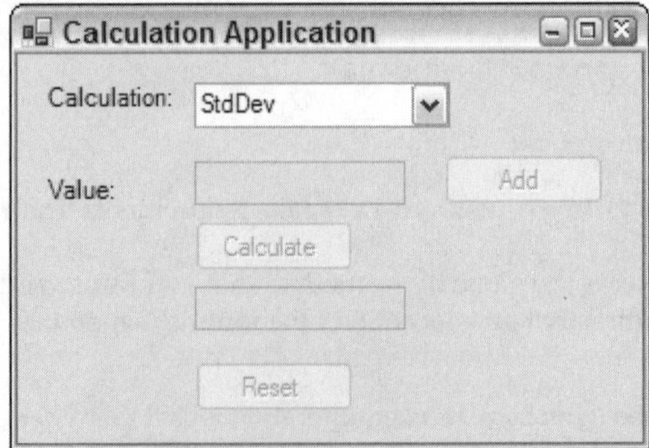

Figure 20-9

As you can see in the screen shot, the input fields have been disabled, as desired. And, here's what happens when you repeat the earlier calculation using Mean (see Figure 20-10). This time, the input fields are enabled, and you can carry out your calculation as before.

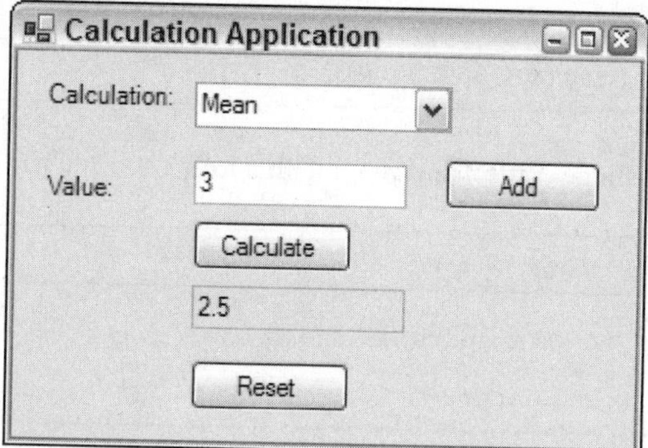

Figure 20-10

One final word about late binding. You took care to ensure that you checked to see that the object was successfully instantiated. In a real-life application, you would also need to take care that the method invocations were successful, ensuring that all exceptions were caught—you don't have the luxury of having the compiler find your bugs for you.

ActiveX Controls

Let's move on from basic COM objects to ActiveX controls You're going to do pretty much the same as you did with the basic COM component (apart from late binding, which has no relevance to ActiveX controls)—build a legacy control using VB6 and then import it into a Visual Basic project.

A Legacy ActiveX Control

For your legacy control, you're going to build a simple buttonlike object that is capable of interpreting a mouse click and can be one of two colors according to its state. You do this by taking a second foray into VB6; once again, if you don't have VB6 handy, feel free to skip the next section, download the OCX file, and pick it up when you start developing your .NET application.

Step 1: Create the Control

This time, you need to create an ActiveX Control project. You'll call the project `Magic`, and the control class `MagicButton`, so as to give a proper impression of its remarkable powers. From the toolbox, you select a `Shape` control and place it on the `UserControl` form that VB6 provides you with. Rename the shape to `shpButton`, and change its properties as follows.

Property	Value
FillStyle	0 — Solid
Shape	4 — Rounded Rectangle
FillColor	Gray (&H00808080&)

Add a label on top of the shape control and rename this to lblText. Change its properties as follows.

Property	Value
BackStyle	0 – Transparent
Alignment	2 – Center

Switch to the code view of MagicButton.

Now, add two properties called Caption and State, and an event called Click, as well as code to handle the initialization of the properties and persisting them, to ensure that the shape resizes correctly and that the label is centered. You also need to handle mouse clicks. The code in MagicButton should look like this:

```
Option Explicit

Public Event Click()

Dim mintState As Integer

Public Property Get Caption() As String
  Caption = lblText.Caption
End Property

Public Property Let Caption(ByVal vNewValue As String)
  lblText.Caption = vNewValue
  PropertyChanged ("Caption")
End Property

Public Property Get State() As Integer
  State = mintState
End Property

Public Property Let State(ByVal vNewValue As Integer)
  mintState = vNewValue
  PropertyChanged ("State")

  If (State = 0) Then
    shpButton.FillColor = &HFFFFFF&
  Else
    shpButton.FillColor = &H808080&
  End If
End Property
```

```
Private Sub UserControl_InitProperties()
  Caption = Extender.Name
  State = 1
End Sub

Private Sub UserControl_ReadProperties(PropBag As PropertyBag)
  Caption = PropBag.ReadProperty("Caption", Extender.Name)
  State = PropBag.ReadProperty("State", 1)
End Sub

Private Sub UserControl_WriteProperties(PropBag As PropertyBag)
  PropBag.WriteProperty "Caption", lblText.Caption
  PropBag.WriteProperty "State", mintState
End Sub

Private Sub UserControl_Resize()
  shpButton.Move 0, 0, ScaleWidth, ScaleHeight
  lblText.Move 0, (ScaleHeight - lblText.Height) / 2, ScaleWidth
End Sub

Private Sub lblText_Click()
  RaiseEvent Click
End Sub

Private Sub UserControl_MouseUp(Button As Integer, Shift As Integer, _
                                X As Single, Y As Single)
  RaiseEvent Click
End Sub
```

If you build this, you'll get an ActiveX control called `Magic.ocx`.

Step 2: Registering Your Legacy Control

You now have your legacy control. As before, if you're developing your new .NET application on the same machine, you don't need to do anything more, because your control will already have been registered by the build process. However, if you're working on an entirely new machine, you'll need to register it there. As before, you need to open up a command box and register it with the following command:

```
regsvr32 Magic.ocx
```

Having done that, you're ready to build your .NET application.

A .NET Application, Again

This .NET application is going to be even more straightforward than the last one. All you're going to do this time is show a button that will change color whenever the user clicks it. Let's create a Windows Application project in Visual Basic called `ButtonApp`. Before you start to develop it, however, you need to extend the toolbox to incorporate your new control. You do this via the Tools ⇨ Choose Toolbox Items menu item (see Figure 20-11).

When you click the OK button, you can see that your magic button class is now available to you in the toolbox (see Figure 20-12).

Let's add one to your form (see Figure 20-13).

Notice that references to AxMagic and Magic have just been added to the project in the Solution Explorer window (see Figure 20-14).

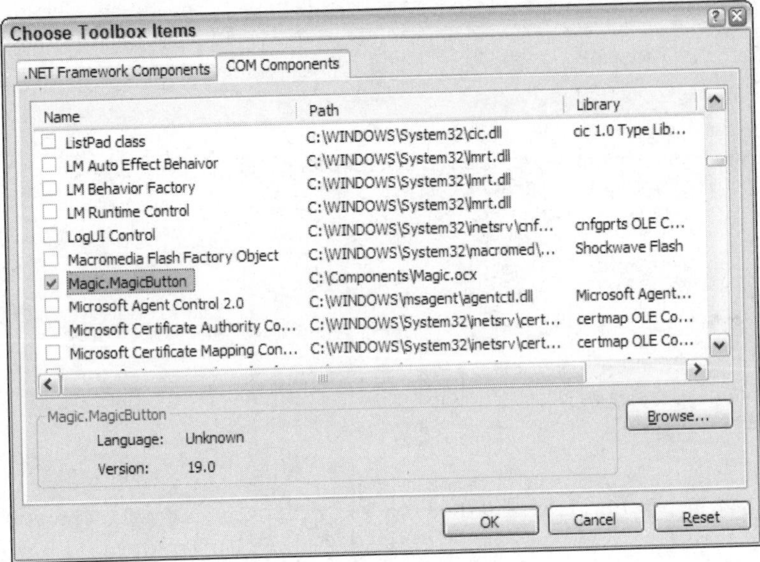

Figure 20-11

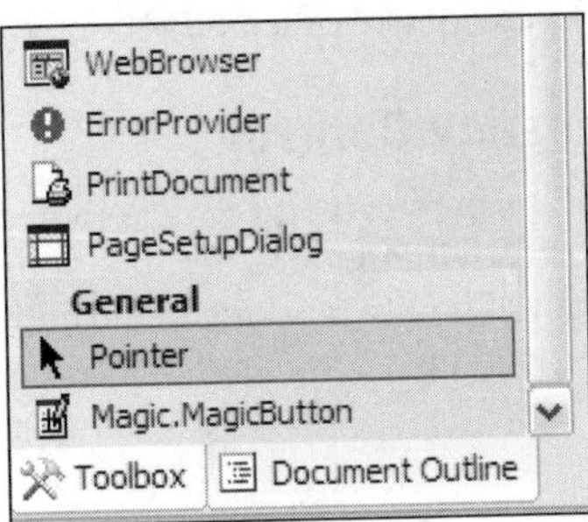

Figure 20-12

All you need to do now is initialize the Caption property to ON, change the Text of the form to Button Application, and code up a handler for the mouse Click event:

```
Private Sub AxMagicButton1_ClickEvent(ByVal sender As Object, _
        ByVal e As System.EventArgs) Handles AxMagicButton1.ClickEvent

    AxMagicButton1.CtlState = CType(1 - AxMagicButton1.CtlState, Short)
    If (AxMagicButton1.CtlState = 0) Then
        AxMagicButton1.Caption = "OFF"
    Else
```

```
        AxMagicButton1.Caption = "ON"
    End If

End Sub
```

Something slightly peculiar happened here. In the course of importing the control into .NET, the variable `State` mutated into `CtlState`. This happened because there is already a class in the `AxHost` namespace called `State`, which is used to encapsulated the persisted state of an ActiveX control. (So, maybe you should have called it something else.)

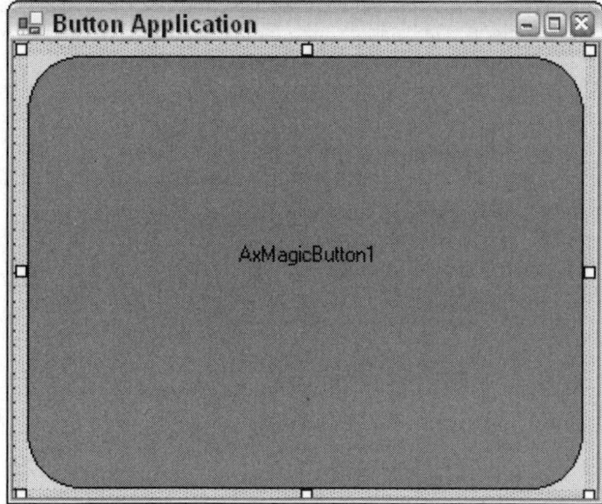

Figure 20-13

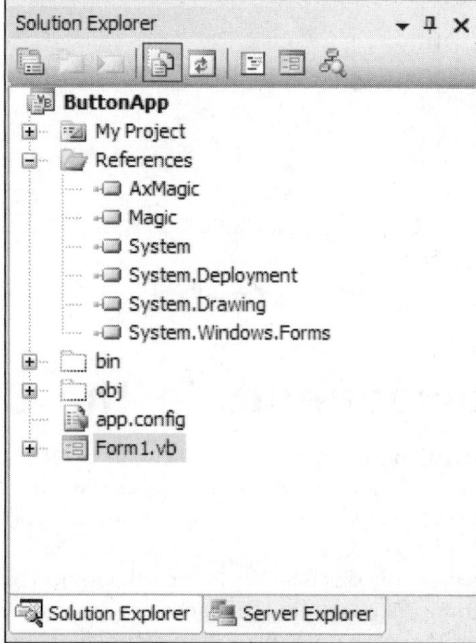

Figure 20-14

Trying It All Out, Again

So, what happens when you run this one? First of all, notice the control in the "ON" position (see Figure 20-15).

If you click the control, it changes to the "OFF" position (see Figure 20-16).

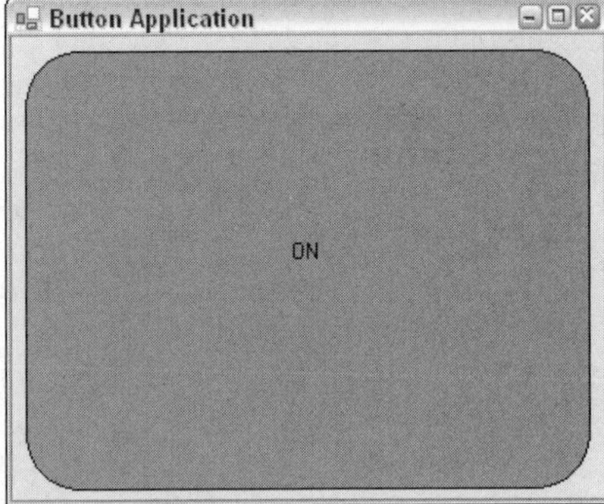

Figure 20-15

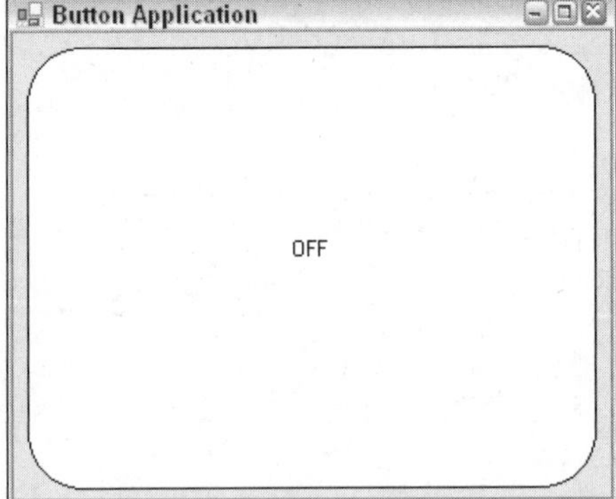

Figure 20-16

Using .NET Components in the COM World

So, you've established beyond all doubt that you can use your COM legacy components with your .NET-based applications. You don't have to throw everything out *quite* yet. It's now time to consider the opposite question: Can you run .NET components in the COM world?

Actually, the first question is probably this one: Why on earth would you want to run .NET components in the COM world? It's not immediately obvious, in fact, because migration to .NET would almost certainly be application-led in most cases, rather than component-led. However, it's possible (just) to imagine a situation in which a particularly large application remains not based on .NET, while component development moves over to .NET. Well, let's pretend that that's the case for the next section. The technology's quite cool, anyway.

A .NET Component

Let's take a look at your definitely nonlegacy component. You'll implement an exact copy of the functionality that you did earlier with `MegaCalculator` and `MeanCalculator`, except using Visual Basic rather than VB6.

Start off by creating a Class Library project called `MegaCalculator2`. This is the entire code of the class library:

```
Public Interface IMegaCalc

  Sub AddInput(ByVal InputValue As Double)

  Sub DoCalculation()
  Function GetResult() As Double
  Sub Reset()

End Interface
```

Next, you create another Class Library project, called `MeanCalculator3`. This will contain a class called `MeanCalc` that is going to implement the `IMegaCalc` interface in a precise analog of the `MeanCalc` in your original VB6 `MeanCalculator` project. As before, you'll need to add a reference to `MegaCalculator2` first, although this time it will be a true .NET Framework reference, and you'll have to browse for it (see Figure 20-17).

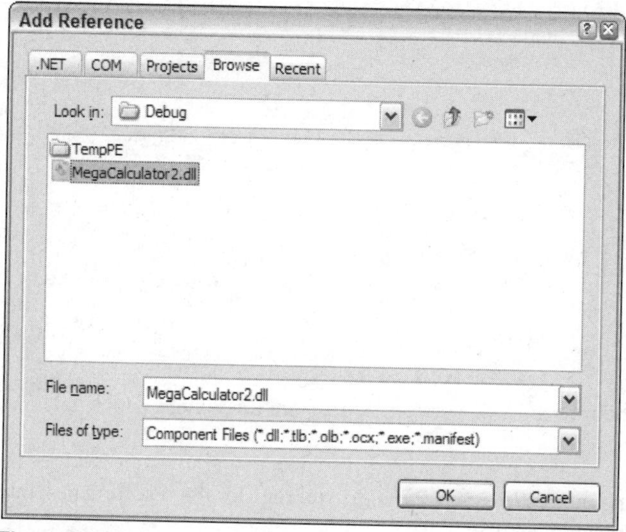

Figure 20-17

This is what the code looks like:

```
Public Class MeanCalc
  Implements MegaCalculator2.IMegaCalc

  Dim mintValue As Integer
  Dim mdblValues() As Double
  Dim mdblMean As Double

  Public Sub AddInput(ByVal InputValue As Double) _
      Implements MegaCalculator2.IMegaCalc.AddInput
    mintValue = mintValue + 1
    ReDim Preserve mdblValues(mintValue)
    mdblValues(mintValue - 1) = InputValue
  End Sub

  Public Sub DoCalculation()_
      Implements MegaCalculator2.IMegaCalc.DoCalculation
    Dim iValue As Integer

    mdblMean = 0

    If (mintValue = 0) Then Exit Sub

    For iValue = 0 To mintValue - 1 Step 1
      mdblMean = mdblMean + mdblValues(iValue)
    Next iValue

    mdblMean = mdblMean / iValue
  End Sub

  Public Function GetResult() As Double Implements _
                MegaCalculator2.IMegaCalc.GetResult
    GetResult = mdblMean
  End Function

  Public Sub Reset() Implements MegaCalculator2.IMegaCalc.Reset
    mintValue = 0
  End Sub

  Public Sub New()
    Reset()
  End Sub

End Class
```

This is all quite similar to the VB6 version, apart from the way in which `Implements` is used. Let's build the assembly.

Now we come to the interesting part: How do you register the resulting assembly so that a COM-enabled application can make use of it?

RegAsm

The tool provided with the .NET Framework SDK to register assemblies for use by COM is called `RegAsm`. `RegAsm` is very simple to use. If all you're interested in is late binding, then you simply run it like this (see Figure 20-18).

The only problem with `RegAsm`, in fact, is finding the thing. It's usually found lurking in `%SystemRoot%\Microsoft.NET\Framework\<version>`, where `<version>` is the current .NET Framework version number. You might find it useful to add this to your path in the system environment. You can also use the Visual Studio command prompt.

```
Visual Studio 2005 Command Prompt
C:\VB_Book\Code\MeanCalculator3\bin>regasm MeanCalculator3.dll
Microsoft (R) .NET Framework Assembly Registration Utility 2.0.50727.7
Copyright (C) Microsoft Corporation 1998-2004.  All rights reserved.

Types registered successfully

C:\VB_Book\Code\MeanCalculator3\bin>_
```

Figure 20-18

However, there's probably even less reason for late binding to an exported .NET component than there is for early binding, so we'll move on to look at early binding. For this, you need a type library, so you need to add another parameter, `/tlb` (see Figure 20-19).

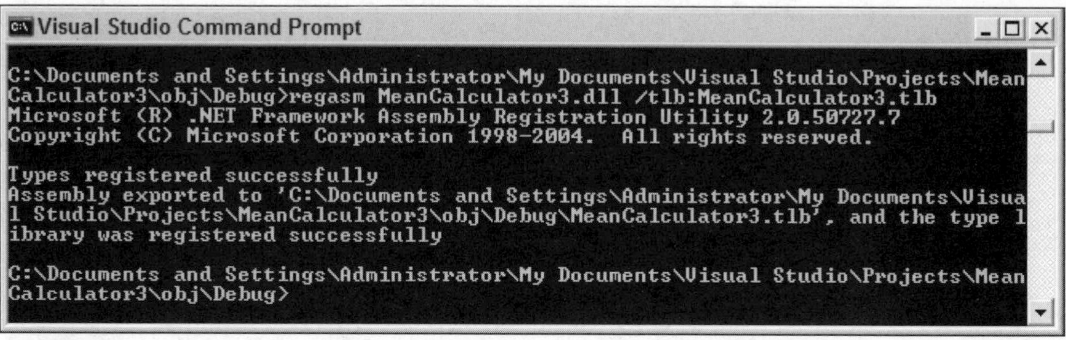

Visual Studio Command Prompt
C:\Documents and Settings\Administrator\My Documents\Visual Studio\Projects\Mean
Calculator3\obj\Debug>regasm MeanCalculator3.dll /tlb:MeanCalculator3.tlb
Microsoft (R) .NET Framework Assembly Registration Utility 2.0.50727.7
Copyright (C) Microsoft Corporation 1998-2004. All rights reserved.
Types registered successfully
Assembly exported to 'C:\Documents and Settings\Administrator\My Documents\Visua
l Studio\Projects\MeanCalculator3\obj\Debug\MeanCalculator3.tlb', and the type l
ibrary was registered successfully
C:\Documents and Settings\Administrator\My Documents\Visual Studio\Projects\Mean
Calculator3\obj\Debug>

Figure 20-19

If you now take a look in the target directory, you see that not only do you have the original `MeanCalculator3.dll`, but you've also acquired a copy of the `MegaCalculator2.dll` and two type libraries: `MeanCalculator3.tlb` and `MegaCalculator2.tlb`. You'll need both of these, so it was good of `RegAsm` to provide them for you. You need the `MegaCalculator2` type library for the same reason that .NET needed the `MegaCalculator` assembly, because it contains the definition of the `IMegaCalc` interface that `MeanCalculator` is using.

Testing with a VB6 Application

Turning the tables again, you need to build a VB6 application to see if this is really going to work. Let's copy the type libraries over to your pre-.NET machine (if that's where VB6 is running) and create a Standard EXE project in VB6. You'll call this `CalcApp2`. You'll need to create references to the two new type libraries, so go to the References dialog box, browse to find them, and select them (see Figure 20-20).

Now you've got all you need to create your application. Create it the same as you did for the Visual Basic `CalcApp` (see Figure 20-21).

As before, the text boxes are `txtInput` and `txtOutput`, respectively, and the command buttons are `btnAdd`, `btnCalculate`, and `btnReset`. Here's the code behind it:

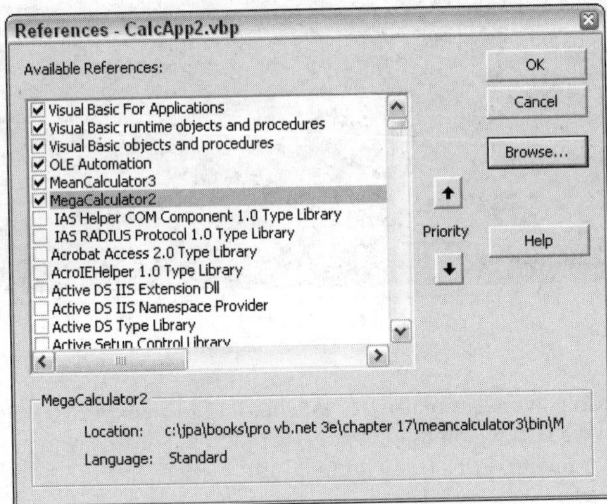

Figure 20-20

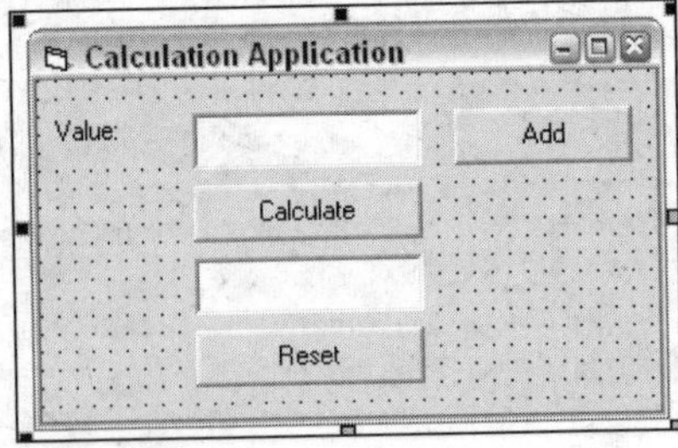

Figure 20-21

```
Option Explicit

Dim mobjCalc As MeanCalculator3.MeanCalc
Dim mobjMega As MegaCalculator2.IMegaCalc
```

```
Private Sub btnAdd_Click()
  mobjMega.AddInput (txtInput.Text)
End Sub

Private Sub btnCalculate_Click()
  mobjMega.DoCalculation
  txtOutput.Text = mobjMega.GetResult
End Sub

Private Sub btnReset_Click()
  mobjMega.Reset
End Sub

Private Sub Form_Load()
  Set mobjCalc = New MeanCalculator3.MeanCalc
  Set mobjMega = mobjCalc
End Sub
```

Notice that, this time, you have to explicitly get hold of a reference to the interface `IMegaCalc`. The default interface of the component, `MeanCalc`, is entirely empty.

You make the executable via the File ➪ Make `CalcApp2.exe` menu item, and then you can move it back to your .NET machine (unless, of course, you're already there). Let's run it up and see what happens (see Figure 20-22).

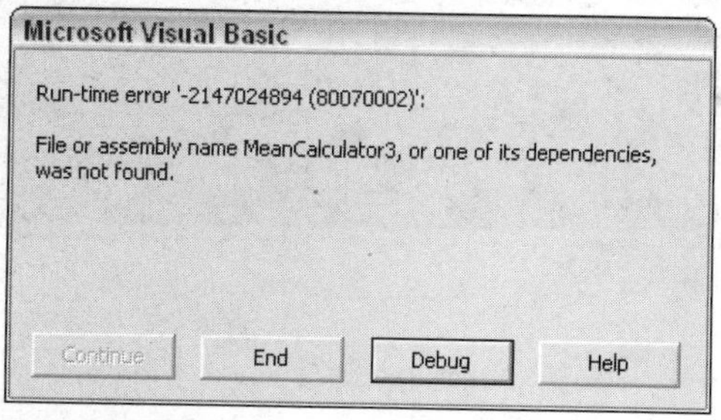

Figure 20-22

Well, that's not *quite* what you expected. What's happened here?

In COM, the location of the DLL containing the component is available via the registry. In .NET, the assembly always has to be either in the current directory or the global assembly. All the registry is doing for you here is converting a COM reference to a .NET one; it's not finding the .NET one for you.

But it's easy to sort out. All you have to do to resolve matters is move the two assemblies, for `MegaCalculator3` and `MeanCalculator2`, to your current directory, and try again (see Figure 20-23).

That's better. So you've established that in the unlikely event of having to run .NET from a COM-oriented application, Microsoft has provided you with the tools.

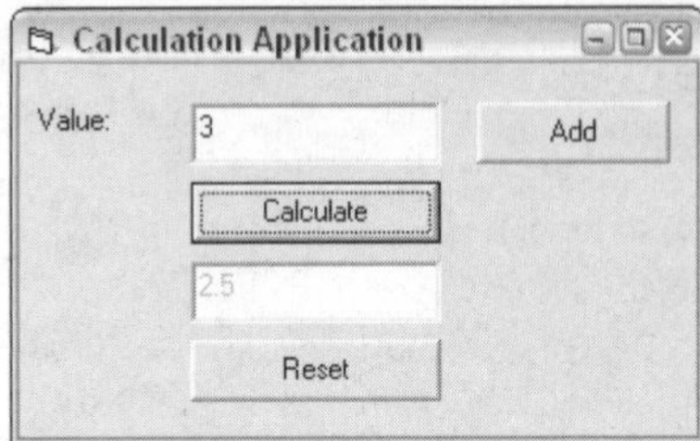

Figure 20-23

TlbExp

In fact, Microsoft has provided you with not one, but *two* alternative tools. The other one is `TlbExp`, which, as its name suggests, is the counterpart of `TlbImp`. This is how you can use `TlbExp` to achieve the same result as `RegAsm` in the previous section (see Figure 20-24).

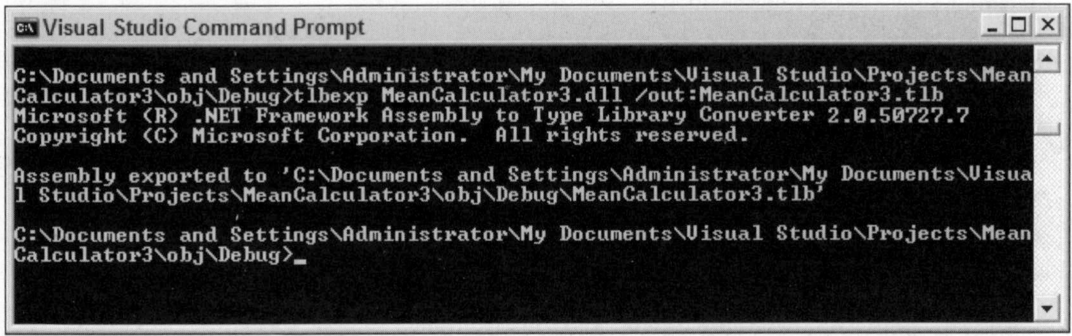

Figure 20-24

Summary

COM isn't going to go away for quite some time, so .NET applications have to interoperate with COM, and they have to do it well. This chapter looked at how all this works in practice.

- You managed to make a .NET application early bind to a COM component, using the import features available in Visual Basic.
- You looked at the underlying tool, `Tlbimp`.
- You managed to make it late bind as well, although it wasn't a pleasant experience.
- You incorporated an ActiveX control into a .NET user interface, again using the features of Visual Basic.
- You looked at using `Regasm` and `TlbExp` to export type libraries from .NET assemblies, so as to enable VB6 applications to use .NET assemblies as if they were COM components.

21

Enterprise Services

The previous chapter explored the vast hinterland of legacy software known as COM. This chapter looks at "what COM did next" and how it fits into the world of .NET, in the shape of *.NET Enterprise Services*. You would be forgiven for thinking that Enterprise Services is yet another version of legacy software, except that much of it hasn't been around for long enough to be considered as legacy. However, there is more to it than that. The features made available by Enterprise Services are still very valuable today for creating scalable, distributed applications.

To understand Enterprise Services, go back in time to around 1997. At this time, a number of technologies began to emerge from Microsoft, including *Microsoft Transaction Server* (MTS) *Microsoft Message Queuing* (MSMQ), and *Microsoft Clustering Services*. The aim of these developments was to bring something that had previously been esoteric, specialized, and generally mainframe-based within the scope of standard PC technology, and put these technologies in the hands of developers.

Handling transactions involved a considerable extension to the NT/COM runtime. It also involved the introduction of several new standard COM interfaces, some to be used or implemented by transactional components and some to be used or implemented by the underlying resource managers, such as SQL Server. These additions, along with some other innovations relating to areas like asynchronous COM, came to be known as *COM +*.

This chapter explores the .NET Enterprise Services. In particular, it looks at transaction processing and queued components. This is an enormous subject that could easily fill a whole book by itself, so this chapter only scratches the surface of it. However, by the end of the chapter, you will understand how all the various pieces fit together.

Let's start by looking at what transactions are, and how they fit into Visual Basic 2005 (VB).

You can find more information about transactions in .NET in *Professional VB.NET Transactions* (Wiley, 2002)

Transactions

A *transaction* is one or more linked units of processing placed together as a single unit of work, which either succeeds or fails. If the unit of work succeeds, the work is then committed. If the unit fails, then every item of processing is rolled back and the process is placed back to its original state.

The standard transaction example involves transferring money from account A to account B. The money must either end up in account B (and nowhere else), or — if something goes wrong — stay in account A (and go nowhere else). This avoids the very undesirable case in which we have taken money from account A but haven't put it in account B.

The ACID Test

Transaction theory starts with *ACID*. According to the ACID theory, all transactions should have the following properties:

- *Atomicity* — A transaction is *atomic*; that is, everything is treated as one unit. However many different components the transaction involves, and however many different method calls on those components there are, the system treats it as a single operation that either entirely succeeds or entirely fails. If it fails, the system is left in a state as if the transaction had never happened.
- *Consistency* — All changes are done in a consistent manner. The system goes from one valid state to another.
- *Isolation* — Transactions that are going on at the same time are isolated from each other. If transaction A changes the system from state 1 to state 2, transaction B will see the system in either state 1 or 2, but not some half-baked state in between the two.
- *Durability* — If a transaction has been committed, the effect will be permanent, even if the system fails.

Let's illustrate this with a concrete example. Imagine that, having spent a happy afternoon browsing in your favorite bookstore, you decide to shell out some of your hard-earned dollars for a copy of, yes, *Professional VB.NET*, 3rd Edition (wise choice). You take the copy to the checkout and exchange a bit of cash for the book. A transaction is going on here: You pay money and the store provides you with a book.

There are only two reasonable outcomes — either you get the book and the store gets their money or you don't get the book and the store doesn't get their money. If, for example, there is insufficient credit on your card, you'll walk out of the shop without the book In that case, the transaction doesn't happen. The only way for the transaction to complete is for you to get the book and the store to get its money. This is the principle of atomicity.

If, on the other hand, the store decides to provide you with a copy of some other book instead, you might reasonably feel that you have ended up with an outcome that wasn't originally on the agenda. This would be a violation of the principle of consistency.

Let's now imagine that there is one copy of the book in the storeroom. However, another potential buyer has gone up to the till next to you. As far as the person at the next till is concerned, your respective transactions are isolated from each other (even though you are competing for the same resource). Either your transaction succeeds or the other person's does. What very definitely *doesn't* happen is that the bookstore decides to exert the wisdom of Solomon and give you half each.

Once you have taken the book home, let's imagine that the bookstore calls you up and asks you if they could have the book back. Apparently, some important customer (well, far more important than you, anyway) needs a copy. You would feel that this was a tad unreasonable, and a violation of the principle of durability.

At this point, it's worth considering what implications all this is likely to have on the underlying components. How can you ensure that all of the changes in the system can be unwound if the transaction is aborted at some point? Perhaps you're in the middle of updating dozens of database files, and something goes wrong.

There are three aspects to rescuing this situation with transactions:

- Knowledge that something has gone wrong
- Knowledge to perform the recovery
- Coordination of the recovery process

The middle part of the process is handled by the resource managers themselves; the likes of SQL Server and Oracle are fully equipped to deal with two-phase commit and rollback (even if the resource manager in question is restarted part-way through a transaction), so you don't need to worry about any of that. The last part of the process, coordination, is handled by the .NET runtime (or at least the Enterprise Services part of it). The first part, knowing that something is wrong, is shared between the components themselves and the .NET runtime. This isn't at all unusual: Sometimes a component can detect that something has gone wrong itself and signal that recovery is necessary, whilst, on other occasions, it may not be able to do so because it has crashed.

Later you will see how all this works as you build a transactional application. However, before that, take a look at how transactions are implemented within .NET Enterprise Services.

Transactional Components

But what actually are the components that are managed by Enterprise Services? What purpose do they serve? To answer that, we need to consider what a typical real-world *n*-tier application looks like. The bottom tier is the persistent data store, typically an industry-standard database such as SQL Server or Oracle. However, there are other possible data stores, including the file system. These are termed "resource managers," as they manage . . . resources. The software here is concerned with maintaining the integrity of the application's data and providing rapid and efficient access to it. The top tier is the user interface. This is a completely different specialization, and the software here is concerned with presenting a smooth, easy to follow front end to the end user. This layer shouldn't actually do any data manipulation at all, apart from whatever formatting is necessary to meet each user's presentational needs. The interesting stuff is in the tiers in between, in particular, the business logic. In the .NET/COM+ transactional model, the software elements that implement this are components running under the control of the Enterprise Services runtime.

Typically, these components are called into being to perform some sort of transaction and then, to all intents and purposes, disappear again. For example, a component might be called into play to transfer information from one database to another in such a way that the information was either in one database or the other, but not both. This component might have a number of different methods, each of which did a different kind of transfer. However, each method call would carry out a complete transfer:

```
Public Sub TransferSomething()
  TakeSomethingFromA
  AddSomethingToB
End Sub
```

Crucially, this means that most transaction components have no concept of *state*; there are no properties that hold values between method calls. The reason for this can be seen if you imagine what would happen if you had a number of instances of the above component all vying for the attention of the database. If instance one of the control started the transfer, remembering the state or current values of A and B just after instance two had done the same, you could end up with the state being different between the two instances. This would violate the isolation of the transaction. Persistence is left to the outside tiers in this model. This takes a little bit of getting used to at first because it runs counter to everything that you learned in object-orientation 101 classes, so let's take a minute or two to consider what we're actually gaining from this.

The business logic is the area of the system that requires all the transactional management. Anything that happens here needs to be monitored and controlled to ensure that all the ACID requirements are met. The neatest way to do this in a component-oriented framework is to develop the business logic as components that are required to implement a standard interface. The transaction management framework can then use this interface to monitor and control how the logic is implemented from a transactional point of view. The transaction interface is a means for the business logic elements to talk to the transaction framework and for the transaction framework to talk back to the logic elements.

So what's all this about not having state? Well, if we maintain state inside our components, then we've immediately got ourselves a scaling problem. The middle tiers of our application are now seriously resource-hungry. If you want an analogy from another area of software, consider why the Internet scales so well. The reason that it does is because HTTP is a stateless protocol. Every HTTP request stands in isolation, so no resources are tied up in maintaining any form of session. It's the same with transactional components.

This is not to say that you can't ever maintain state inside your transactional components. You can. However, it's not recommended.

An Example of Transactions

For our transaction example, we're going to build a simple business logic component that transfers data from one bank account (Wrox's, in fact) to another one. Wrox's bank account will be represented by a row in one database, whilst the other will be represented by a row in another one.

There's one important point that we should make right from the start. You can't have transactions without any resource managers. It's very tempting to think that you can experiment with transactional component services without actually involving, say, a database, because (as we shall see) none of the methods in the transactional classes makes any explicit references to one. However, if you do try to do this, you will find that your transactions don't actually trouble the system's statistics. Fortunately, you don't need to go out and lay out your hard-earned cash for a copy of SQL Server (nice though that is), because Visual Studio .2005 (VS) comes with a lightweight (but fully functional) copy of SQL Server, which goes under the name of *SQL Express 2005*, or *SQL Express*.

Creating Our Databases

The first thing to do, then, is set up the databases. Check to see if the Database Explorer tab is visible in Visual Studio 2005 (see Figure 21-1). If not, open it using the View, Database Explorer menu item. You need to create a new database in the Data Connections tree.

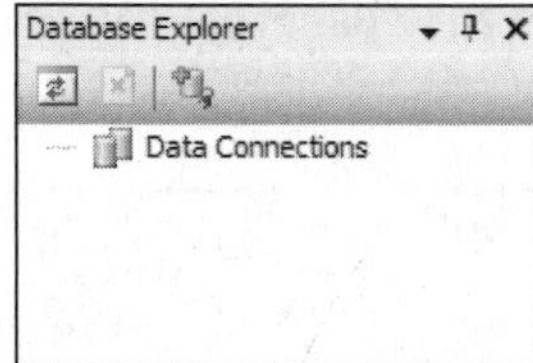

Figure 21-1

Next, right-click Data Connections, and select New Database from the menu. Alternately, you can click the icon that looks like a plus sign over a can with a plug (not quite the universal symbol for a database, but it will have to do). A further dialog box appears (see Figure 21-2).

Enter the database name (BankOfWrox) and elect to use Windows NT Integrated Security (which means that it uses the same security as Windows itself). You should now see BankOfWrox in the list of data connections (see Figure 21-3).

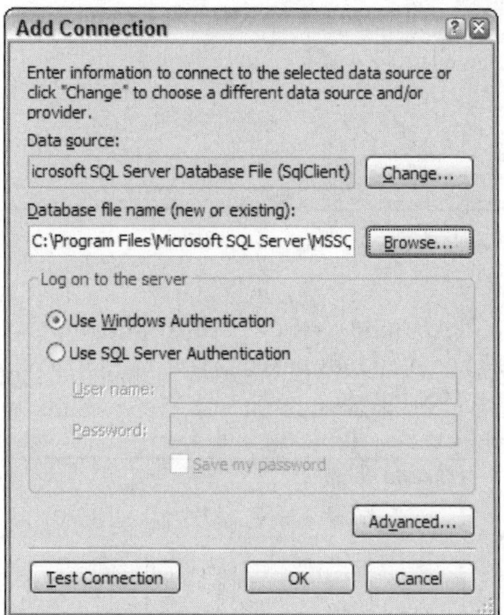

Figure 21-2

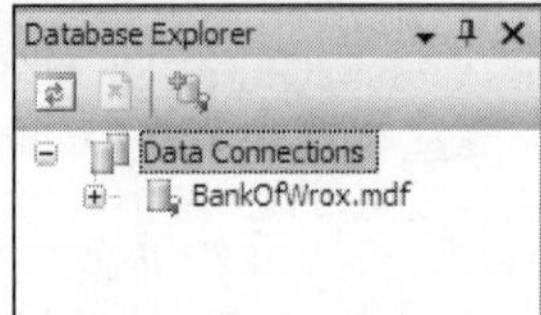

Figure 21-3

Now, set up the database. If you open up the new node, you should see a number of other nodes, including Tables. Right-click this, then select New Table from the menu. A further dialog box should appear (see Figure 21-4).

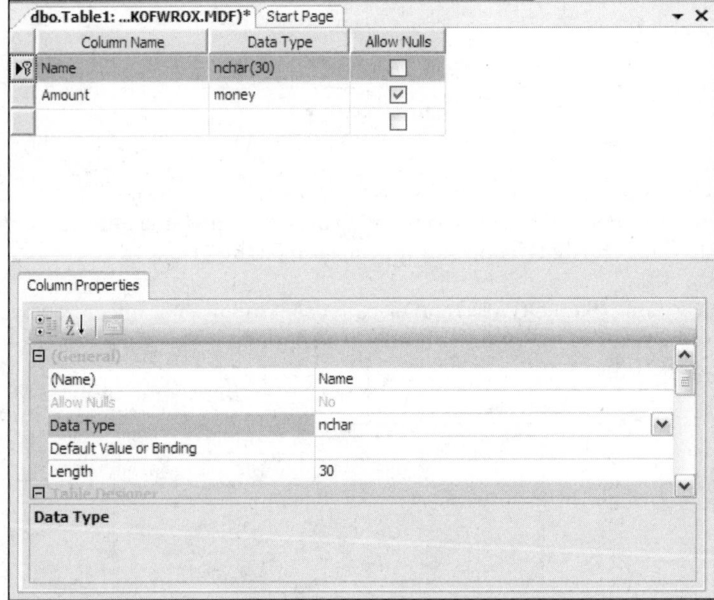

Figure 21-4

Create two columns, Name and Amount, as shown. Make sure that Name is set up to be the primary key. When you click the Close box, you'll be asked if you want to save changes to Table1. Select `Yes`, and another dialog box will appear (see Figure 21-5).

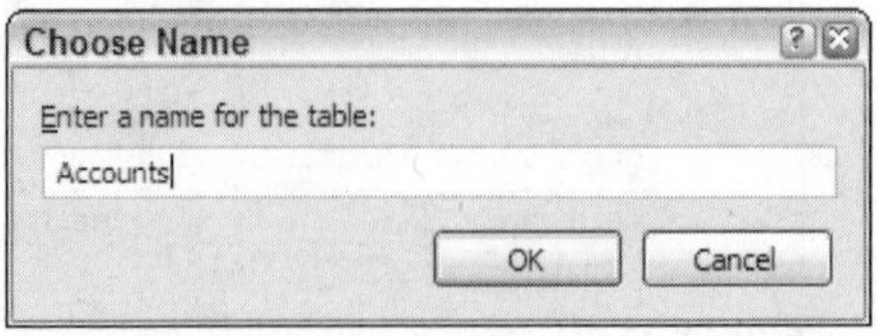

Choose Name

Enter a name for the table:

Accounts

OK Cancel

Figure 21-5

Use the name Accounts for the table. You should now see a child node called Accounts below Tables in the tree.

Okay, that's `BankOfWrox` created. Repeat the whole process for `BankOfMe`. The structure is exactly the same (although it doesn't need to be for the purposes of this example). Don't forget to set Name as the primary key. While we could have created these two as separate rows in the same database, it doesn't really simulate the scenario where Enterprise Services is intended (interapplication communication).

Populating Our Databases

The next thing to do is populate our databases. If we right-click over Accounts for either database, and select Show Table Data from Table from the menu, we will see a grid which will enable us to add rows and initialize the values of their columns (see Figure 21-6).

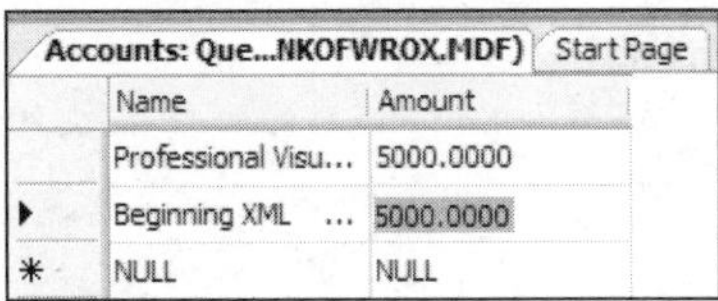

Figure 21-6

Enter two accounts in `BankOfWrox`, Professional Visual Basic 2005 and Beginning XML, and allocate $5,000 to each. Now repeat the process for `BankOfMe`, setting up one account, `Me`, with $0 in it. (So you're either (a) broke or (b) wise enough not to leave any cash lying around in this sort of account.)

The Business Logic

The next step is to create our transactional component to support our business logic. Create a new Class Library project called `Transactions`. Then, add a reference to `System.EnterpriseServices` (see Figure 21-7).

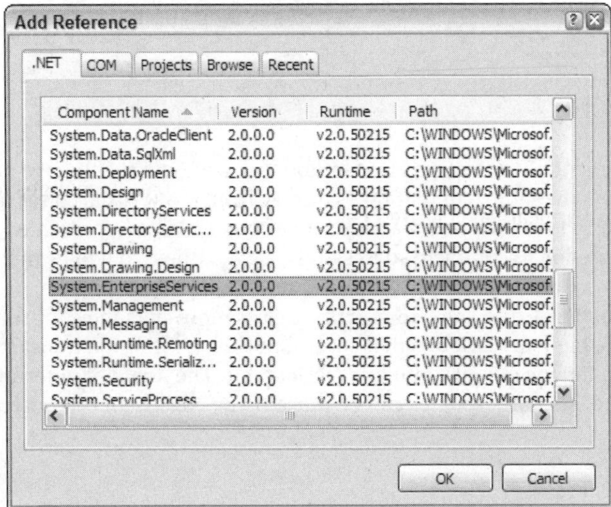

Figure 21-7

This reference is needed because, in order to come under the control of the Enterprise Services runtime, the component needs to inherit from the `System.EnterpriseServices .ServicedComponent` class:

```
Imports System.EnterpriseServices
Imports System.Configuration
Imports System.Data.SqlClient

<Assembly: ApplicationName("WroxTransactions")>
<Assembly: ApplicationAccessControl(True)>
Public Class BankTransactions
    Inherits ServicedComponent
```

Here's the main function in our component, `TransferMoney`:

```
Public Sub TransferMoney(ByVal amount As Decimal, _
  ByVal sourceBank As String, _
  ByVal sourceAccount As String, _
  ByVal destinationBank As String, _
  ByVal destinationAccount As String)

    Try
        Withdraw(sourceBank, sourceAccount, amount)
        Try
            Deposit(destinationBank, destinationAccount, amount)
        Catch ex As Exception
            'deposit failed
            Throw New _
              ApplicationException("Error transfering money, deposit failed.", _
              ex)
        End Try
        'both operations succeeded
        ContextUtil.SetComplete()
    Catch ex As Exception
        'withdraw failed
        Throw New _
          ApplicationException("Error transfering money, withdrawal failed.", _
          ex)
    End Try
End Sub
```

Ignoring, for the moment, the references to `ContextUtil`, we can see that we have effectively divided up the logic into two halves, the half that takes money from the Wrox account (represented by the private function `Withdraw`), and the half that adds it to your account (represented by the private function `Deposit`). For the function to complete successfully, each of the two halves must complete successfully.

So what does `ContextUtil` do? The `ContextUtil` class represents the context of the transaction. Within that context, there are basically two bits that control the behavior of the transaction from the point of view of each participant: the *consistent* bit and the *done* bit. The done bit determines whether or not the transaction is finished, so that resources can be reused. The consistent bit determines whether or not the transaction was successful from the point of view of the participant. This is established during the first phase of the two-phase commit process. In complex distributed transactions involving more than one participant, the overall consistency and doneness are voted on, so that a transaction is only consistent or done when everyone agrees that it is. If a transaction completes in an inconsistent state, it is not allowed to proceed to the second phase of the commit.

In this case, there is only a single participant, but the principal remains the same. We can determine the overall outcome by setting these two bits, which is done via `SetComplete` and `SetAbort`, which are static methods in the `ContextUtil` class. Both of these set the done bit to `True`. `SetComplete` also sets the consistent bit to `True`, whereas `SetAbort` sets the consistent bit to `False`. In this example, `SetComplete` is only set if both halves of the transaction are successful.

The First Half of the Transaction

Now it's time to see what's going on in the two halves of the transaction itself. Note that we're putting the SQL commands into the component to reduce the number of files you need to touch. However, in a real application, you would likely want to create stored procedures for each database call.

1. First of all, here's the function that takes the money out of the Wrox account:

```
Private Sub Withdraw(ByVal bank As String, _
  ByVal account As String, _
  ByVal amount As Decimal)
```

2. Start by establishing a connection to our database and retrieving the current account balance from it:

```
Dim ConnectionString As String
Dim SQL As String
Dim conn As SqlConnection = Nothing
Dim cmdCurrent As SqlCommand
Dim currentValue As Decimal
Dim cmdUpdate As SqlCommand
ConnectionString = My.Settings.Item(bank).ToString
SQL = String.Format("SELECT Amount FROM Accounts WHERE Name = '{0}'", _
  account)
```

3. The call to `ExecuteScalar` retrieves a single value from the database; in this case, the Amount for the requested account. Note that we have started an exception handler with the `Try` keyword. We'll finish the Try block in a moment:

```
Try
        conn = New SqlConnection(ConnectionString)
        conn.Open()

        cmdCurrent = New SqlCommand(SQL, conn)
        currentValue = CDec(cmdCurrent.ExecuteScalar())
```

4. Note the current balance, and see if we can afford to transfer the amount asked for. If not, we raise an `Exception`:

```
'check for overdrafts
        If amount > currentValue Then
            Throw New ArgumentException("Attempt to overdraft account")
        End If
```

5. Otherwise, subtract the amount and update the table accordingly:

```
'otherwise, we're good to withdraw
        SQL = _
          String.Format("UPDATE Accounts SET Amount = {0} WHERE Name = '{1}'", _
          currentValue - amount, account)
        cmdUpdate = New SqlCommand(SQL, conn)
        cmdUpdate.ExecuteNonQuery()
```

6. Finally, close the exception handler, and the database:

```
Catch ex As Exception
        Throw New DataException("Error withdrawing", ex)
    Finally
        If Not conn Is Nothing Then
            conn.Close()
        End If
    End Try
End Sub
```

The Second Half of the Transaction

The second half of the transaction is similar, except that the failure conditions are slightly different. First of all, stipulate that we don't want any transfer of less than $50. Secondly, we've inserted a bug such that an attempt to transfer a negative amount will cause a divide by zero. (You'll see why we did this rather bizarre act of sabotage in a little while.) Here's the code:

```
Private Sub Deposit(ByVal bank As String, _
  ByVal account As String, _
  ByVal amount As Decimal)
    Dim ConnectionString As String
    Dim SQL As String
    Dim conn As SqlConnection = Nothing
    Dim cmdCurrent As SqlCommand
    Dim currentValue As Decimal
    Dim cmdUpdate As SqlCommand

    ConnectionString = My.Settings.Item(bank).ToString
    SQL = String.Format("SELECT Amount FROM Accounts WHERE Name = '{0}'", _
```

```
        account)

      If amount < 0 Then
          amount = amount / 0
      ElseIf amount < 50 Then
          Throw New ArgumentException("Value of deposit must be greater than $50")
      Else
          Try
              conn = New SqlConnection(ConnectionString)
              conn.Open()

              'get the current value
              cmdCurrent = New SqlCommand(SQL, conn)
              currentValue = CDec(cmdCurrent.ExecuteScalar())

              SQL = _
               String.Format("UPDATE Accounts SET Amount = {0} WHERE Name = '{1}'", _
                currentValue + amount, account)

              cmdUpdate = New SqlCommand(SQL, conn)
              cmdUpdate.ExecuteNonQuery()
          Finally
              If Not conn Is Nothing Then
                  conn.Close()
              End If
          End Try
      End If

  End Sub
```

Our business logic component is complete. Let's see how we bring it under the control of Enterprise Services. First of all, of course, we need to build our DLL in VS.NET.

Why did we add the divide by zero error? This will give you a chance to see what happens to the transaction when an exception occurs in your code. The transaction will automatically fail and roll back. This means that your data will still be in a good state at the end.

Registering Our Component

Because the Enterprise Services infrastructure is COM-oriented, you need to expose the .NET component as a COM component and register it with Component Services. Component Services handles all transaction coordination; that is, Component Services tracks any changes and restores the data should the transaction fail. First, some changes to the component are needed to enable this COM interaction. Prepare to take a trip down memory lane.

All COM components must have a GUID (Global Unique Identifier) that uniquely identifies it to the COM infrastructure. This was done for you in Visual Basic 6.0, but with .NET it requires you to add a value. In addition, your component will need an attribute to make it visible to COM. You can set both of these in the Assembly information dialog. Double-click the My Project item in the Solution Explorer. On the Application page, click Assembly Information. There should already be a `Guid` assigned to your component. You will need to check off COM Visible. This makes all of the `Public` types accessible to COM (see Figure 21-8).

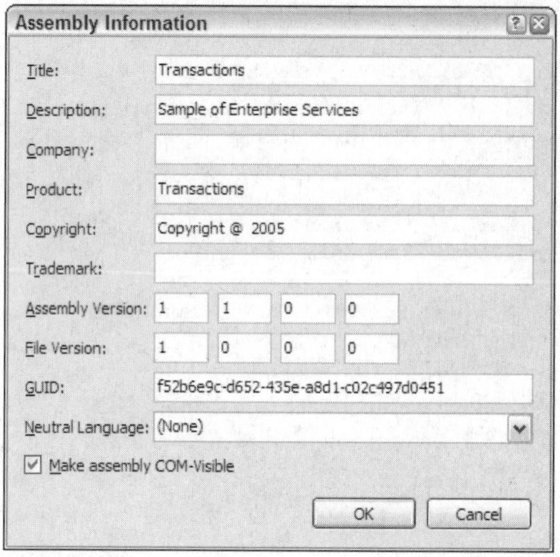

Assembly Information				
Title:	Transactions			
Description:	Sample of Enterprise Services			
Company:				
Product:	Transactions			
Copyright:	Copyright @ 2005			
Trademark:				
Assembly Version:	1	1	0	0
File Version:	1	0	0	0
GUID:	f52b6e9c-d652-435e-a8d1-c02c497d0451			
Neutral Language:	(None)			

☑ Make assembly COM-Visible

OK Cancel

Figure 21-8

You should also update the Assembly Version as you make changes to the component.

In Chapter 18, you can find more information about strong names and assemblies in general.

The problem is that the assembly is a private assembly. In order to make it available to the transaction framework, it needs to be a shared assembly. To do this, we need to give the assembly a *cryptographically strong name*, generally referred to as its *strong name*.

Cryptographically strong means that the name has been signed with the private key of a dual key pair. This isn't the place to go into a long discussion on dual key cryptography, but the essence of this is as follows: A pair of keys are generated, one public and one private. If something is encrypted using the private key, it can only be decrypted using the public key from that pair, and vice versa.

This means that it is an excellent tool for preventing tampering with information. If, for example, the name of an assembly was to be encrypted using the private key of a pair, then the recipient of a new version of that assembly could verify the origin of that new version, and be confident that it was not a rogue version from some other source. This is because only the original creator of the assembly retains access to its private key.

Giving the Assembly a Strong Name

We now have to make sure that our assembly uses the strong name. You can create a new strong name file, or assign an existing strong name file on the Signing tab of the My Project dialog (see Figure 21-9).

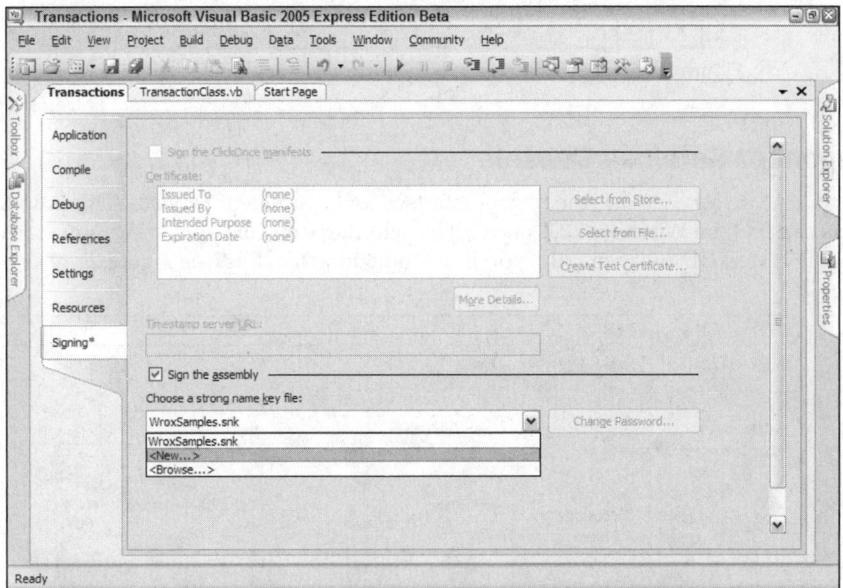

Figure 21-9

Registering with Component Services

Once we've built the DLL again, we can run `RegSvcs` once more (see Figure 21-10).

RegSvcs does a number of things at this point. First, it creates a COM Type Library for the DLL. This enables it to communicate with COM. In addition, it creates a COM+ application for the component.

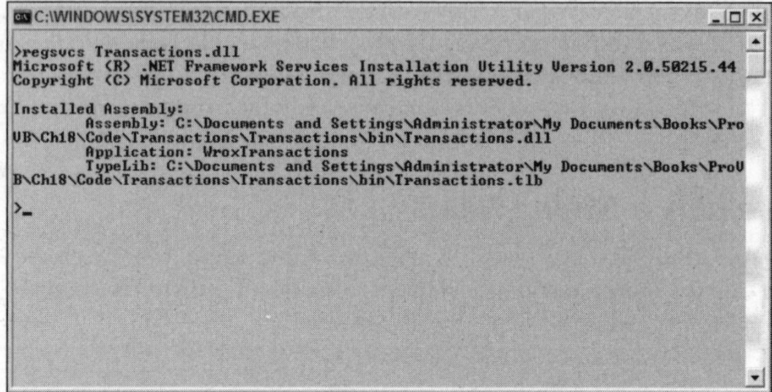

Figure 21-10

The Component Services Console

The *Component Services Console* is the control interface for Component Services. This is an MMC snap-in, which you can find (on Windows 2000 and XP) by selecting Control Panel ➪ Administrative Tools ➪ Component Services. If you open it up, you'll see something like this (see Figure 21-11).

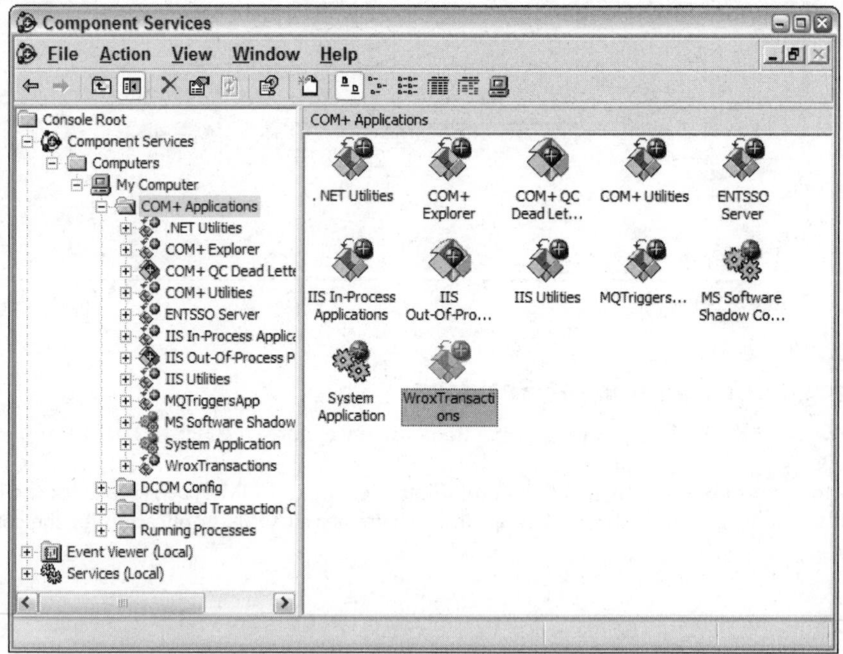

Figure 21-11

You should be able to find the sample, under COM+ Applications. A COM+ application is a set of related COM+ components that have been packaged together. `RegSvcs` creates a new application for every component that it registers. If you want to bundle together a series of components from separate DLLs, you can do this, but you can only do it by creating a new application via the Component Services Console (try right-clicking COM+ Applications and then selecting New). We'll explore the console a little more as we go on.

Now, we need a test application. Secondly, and more importantly, we need to tell Component Services that we're interested in transactions.

A Test Application

Deal with the first problem straightaway by creating a Windows Application project called `TestBankTransactions` and a very simple form (see Figure 21-12).

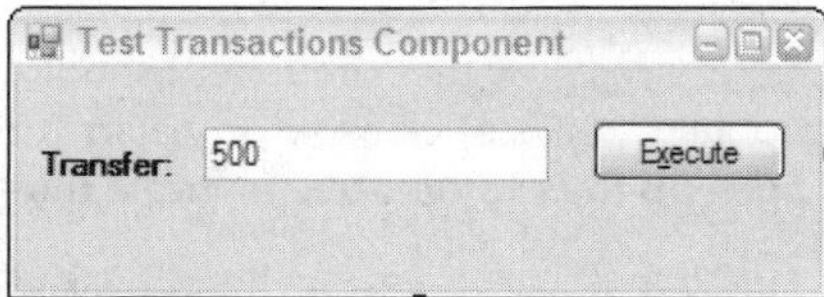

Figure 21-12

The text field is called `TransferField` and the command button is called `TransferButton`.

In order to access the transactional component, add references to a couple of DLLs. First, add a reference to the transactional component DLL itself. We'll need to browse for this, as it isn't currently in the global assembly cache.

Secondly, in order to access the objects in this DLL, we also need to make our application aware of the `System.EnterpriseServices` assembly, so add a reference to that as well.

Having done that, it's time to import `Transactions` into the application:

```
Imports Transactions
Public Class MainForm
```

Here's the code behind our `TransferButton` button:

```
Private Sub TransferButton_Click(ByVal sender As System.Object, _
  ByVal e As System.EventArgs) Handles TransferButton.Click
    Dim txn As New BankTransactions
    Try
        txn.TransferMoney(CDec(Me.TransferField.Text), _
          "BankOfWrox", "Professional Visual Basic ", _
          "BankOfMe", "Me")
```

```
        MessageBox.Show(String.Format("{0:C} transfered from {1} to {2}", _
            CDec(Me.TransferField.Text), "BankOfWrox", "BankOfMe"), _
            "Transfer Succeeded", _
            MessageBoxButtons.OK, _
            MessageBoxIcon.Information)

    Catch ex As Exception
        MessageBox.Show(ex.Message, "Transfer failed", _
          MessageBoxButtons.OK, _
          MessageBoxIcon.Error)

    End Try

End Sub
```

The Transaction Attribute

Now it's time to tell Component Services how the component should enter a transaction. There are two ways of doing this: via the Component Services Console or via an attribute in code. To do it via the Component Services Console, open up the explorer tree to locate the `Transactions` component.

Next, right-click over this, and select Properties from the menu, then select the Transactions tab (see Figure 21-13).

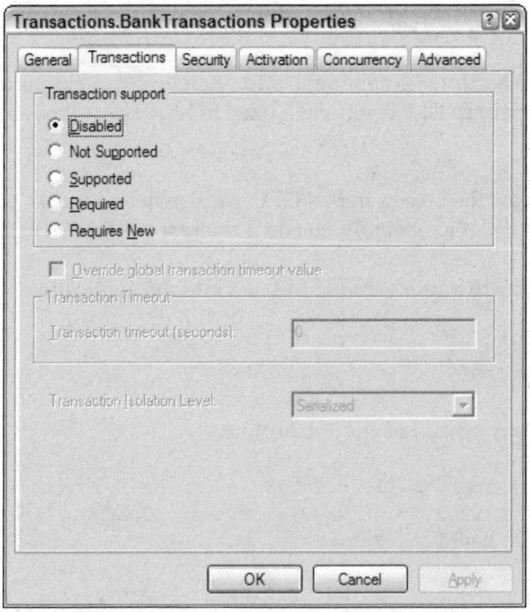

Figure 21-13

Finally, select one of the available options; we'll discuss what these all mean in a moment.

However, it's a little tiresome to require our system manager to do this every time, especially if we already know that our component is always going to have the same transaction characteristics. So there's an alternative mechanism available to us: We can explicitly set up an attribute in the code for our component.

Attributes are items of declarative information that can be attached to the elements of code, such as classes, methods, data members, and properties. Anything that uses these can query their values at runtime. One such attribute is called `TransactionAttribute`, and, unsurprisingly, this is used for specifying the transaction characteristics of a component class. The value of this attribute is taken from an enumeration called `TransactionOption`. Both `TransactionAttribute` and `TransactionOption` are found within the `System.EnterpriseServices` namespace. That enumeration can take the following values.

Value	Description
`Disabled`	Ignore any transaction in the current context; this is the default.
`NotSupported`	Create the component in a context with no governing transaction.
`Required`	Share a transaction if one exists; create a new transaction if necessary.
`RequiresNew`	Create the component with a new transaction, regardless of the state of the current context.
`Supported`	Share a transaction if one exists. If it doesn't, create the component in a transaction-free.

The available values are exactly the same as the ones shown in the `Transaction` tab. This case is a stand-alone transaction, so either `RequiresNew` or `Required` is equally valid.

Before changing the component, deregister the current version to avoid any confusion (see Figure 21-14).

Now go back to the `Transactions` project and make the change:

```
<Transaction(TransactionOption.RequiresNew)> _
Public Class BankTransactions
   Inherits ServicedComponent
```

Having made the change, rebuild `Transactions` and then reregister it as before.

Now run the test application.

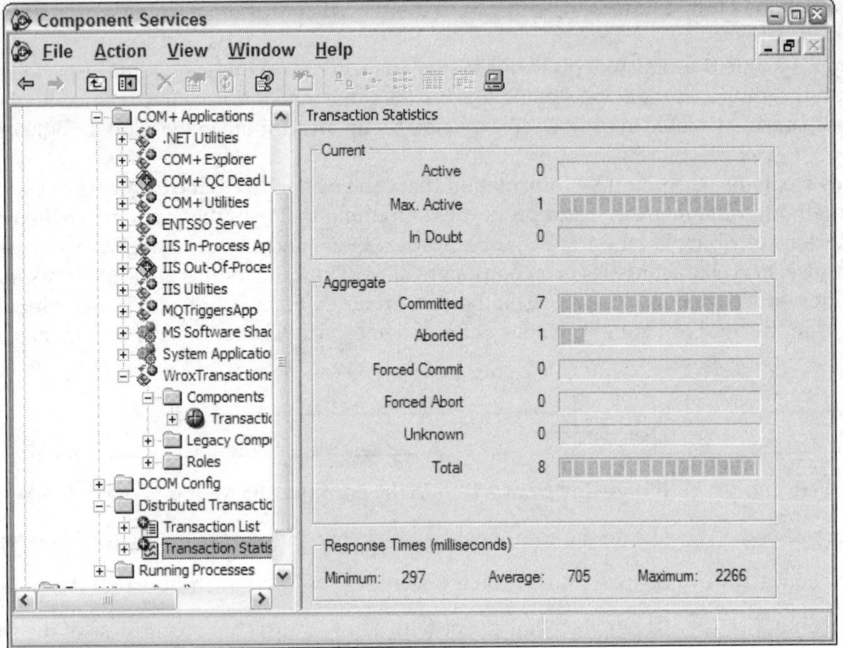

Figure 21-14

Enter 1000 and hit the Confirm button. You might be able to see the number of current active transactions briefly go from none to one (depending on your computer, this may be too fast to see), followed by the number of committed transactions and the total both going up by one. Great, we've implemented our first transaction. And if we check the two databases, we can see that the amount in `BankOfWrox's` Professional Visual Basic account has been reduced to $4,000, whereas Jon's account in `BankOfMe` has been increased by $1,000.

Invalid Data

So what happens if we enter a value that we know is invalid? There are two options here: Either try to transfer more money than there is in the Professional Visual Basic account, or try to transfer less than our "approved limit." Run the application again and try to transfer $10. As expected, the transaction will fail, and no changes will be made to the accounts. Professional Visual Basic still has $4,000, and your account still has $1,000. This isn't too much of a big deal, because the invalid condition is spotted before any database manipulation is carried out. If we look at the transaction statistics, we can see that the number of *aborted* transactions has been incremented this time.

However, try to transfer $10,000. This time around, the first part of the transaction is successful, but the *second* part fails. Again, the number of aborted transactions is incremented. But what's happened to the database? Well, fortunately for everyone concerned, we see that there is still $4,000 in the Professional Visual Basic account, and still $1,000 in your account. The *entire* transaction has failed.

Something Goes Wrong

Remember that bit of mindless vandalism that we did to the `Deposit` function so that it would divide by zero if we entered a negative value? Here's where we get to try it out. Run the application again, and try to transfer $-1. You should receive an error message. But we were halfway through a transaction! Never mind, because looking at the transaction statistics, we see that the aborted count has gone up by one. More importantly, if we check the databases, we see that Professional Visual Basic *still* has $4,000, and the other account still has $1,000. So we're protected against software failures as well.

Other Aspects of Transactions

There are a number of other topics that relate to transactions, such as Just-In-Time activation and Object Pooling.

Just-In-Time

Creating and deleting components takes time. So, instead of discarding the component when finished with it, why not keep it around in case another instance is required? The mechanism by which this is done is called *Just-In-Time* (JIT) *activation*, and it's set by default for all automatic transactional components (it's unset by default for all other COM+ components, however). This is another reason why holding state is a bad thing within components, because it limits the ability to share components.

All good transactional components are entirely stateless. However, real life dictates differently, because, for example, we might want to maintain a link to our database, one that would be expensive to set up every time. The JIT mechanism provides us with a couple of methods that we can override in the `ServicedComponent` class in this case.

The method that gets invoked when a JIT component gets activated is called `Activate`, and the component that gets invoked when it is deactivated is called, unsurprisingly, `Deactivate`. In `Activate` and `Deactivate` you should put the things that you would normally put in your constructor and deconstructor. In addition, JIT can be activated by adding the `JustInTimeActivation` attribute to any class within `ServicedComponent`.

Object Pooling

We can, if we want, take this a stage further and maintain a pool of objects already constructed and prepared to be activated whenever required. When the object is no longer required (that is, it's deactivated), it is returned to the pool until the next time it is required. By retaining objects, we do not have to continually create them from new, which in turn reduces the performance costs of our application. We can use the `ObjectPooling` attribute within our class to determine how the pool is to operate:

```
<Transaction(TransactionOption.RequiresNew), _
ObjectPooling(MinPoolSize:=5, MaxPoolSize:=20, _
                        CreationTimeOut:=30)> _
Public Class BankTransactions
```

Holding Things Up

A JIT-activated component will be deactivated whenever the current method call returns, unless we tell it otherwise. The way that we control this is by means of methods in the `ContextUtil` class. The `ContextUtil` is the favored method to obtain information about the context of the COM+ object.

If we invoke `ContextUtil.DisableCommit`, we are effectively telling Component Services that we are not finished yet; in other words, we're setting the consistency and done bits of the transaction to `False`. The transaction is in an indeterminate state for the time being. Once we are happy that everything is complete, call `ContextUtil.EnableCommit`, setting the consistency to `True` and the done bit to `False`. This says that it is okay for the component to be deactivated at the end of the current method call. However, it doesn't say whether or not the transaction is complete or not. It's up to us to invoke either `SetComplete`, setting both the consistency and done parts to true, or `SetAbort`, which sets the consistency to false and done to true, in other words, aborting the call.

As has been shown, `ContextUtil` allows us to control the activity of the object and retrieve any information about its context.

Queued Components

The traditional component programming model is very much a *synchronous* one. Put simply, you invoke a method and you get a result. However, a little thought reveals the unfortunate fact that an awful lot of real-world problems are inherently *asynchronous*. You can't always wait for a response to your request before moving on to the next task. The real-world analogy here is the difference between phoning someone, and sending them an email. Phoning someone is a synchronous process. Either they answer the phone (a successful transaction), or they don't (or you've called a wrong number, another form of unsuccessful transaction). Emailing someone is asynchronous; you have no control over how long the email takes to arrive, or when the person will actually look at the email. So, if we are to be able to tackle everything that the real world throws at us, we need to introduce an asynchronous component model for those scenarios where it is most appropriate.

Why only some scenarios? The synchronous model is quite simple to manage, because the three possible outcomes of a request are quite straightforward to handle. First of all, the request can be successful. Secondly, the software can crash. Finally, the software can simply not respond at all; in which case, it times out. However, when dealing with asynchronous requests, expect all manner of unusual conditions. For example, the target system may not currently be operational, so we will have to make a decision on how long to wait before it comes back up again. Each outstanding request takes up system resources, so they need to be managed carefully. We need to be able to know when the response comes back. We need to make certain that the recipient only receives a given message once. And so on.

We are, in fact, dealing with a different infrastructure than MTS here, an infrastructure to handle reliable messaging. Microsoft's product to tackle this type of problem is MSMQ, or Microsoft Message Queue.

The idea behind reliable messaging is that once you have asked the system to send a message to a given target, you can effectively stop worrying about it. The system will handle storing and forwarding of messages to their target, and will handle retries and timeouts for you, ensuring it is only received once, and returning messages to the dead letter queue if all else fails. MSMQ is, in fact, a whole technology in itself, and can seem quite complex. However, Enterprise Services provides a handy, simple abstraction called *queued components*.

Queued components take the sometimes gnarly aspects of working with MSMQ and make them easier to work with rather than the raw queue handling. Instead, you have the ideas of recorders, listeners, and players. Recorders create messages that are put on a queue. Eventually, a listener receives the message. This could happen immediately, or it could take weeks if the two components are disconnected. Finally, the player does whatever the message requests.

Naturally, this places some restrictions on the kind of component that can be used. For example, we can't have any output arguments, and we can't have any return value. If we have either of these, the values can't be set until the player has finally done the action, removing the benefit of the asynchronous aspects of the call. However, there are some cool things that we can do, and we're going to explore them in the next section.

> **In order to run the Queued Components examples, MSMQ is needed, which comes with Windows 2000 and XP. However, you need to install it separately using the Add Windows Components dialog.**

An Example of Queued Components

We're going to write a very simple logging component that takes a string as its input, and writes it out to a sequential file, as well as outputting it in a message box. For the purposes of a simple example, the client and the server will be on the same machine; however, in a production scenario, they would be separate. The benefit of using queued components here is that the logging doesn't slow down the main process. So let's create a Class Library project called `Reporter`. As usual with component services, add a reference to the `System.EnterpriseServices` namespace. The first thing is to define an interface:

```
Imports System.IO
Imports System.EnterpriseServices
Public Interface IReporter
  Sub Log(ByVal message As String)
End Interface
```

Notice that our Log method follows the requirements listed previously. There is no return value, and all parameters are input only. We need to separate the interface from the implementation because the implementation, residing on the server, is going to be sitting on another machine somewhere. The client isn't the slightest bit interested in the details of this; all it needs to know is how to interface to it.

Take a look at the actual implementation. As with the transactional component, we inherit from `ServicedComponent`, and we also implement the interface that we just defined. However, notice the `<InterfaceQueuing()>` attribute that indicates to the component services runtime that the interface can be queued (we did the same for the interface):

```
<InterfaceQueuing(Interface:="IReporter")> Public Class Reporter
  Inherits ServicedComponent
  Implements IReporter
```

In the logging method, all we do is output a message box, open up a `StreamWriter` component to append to our log file, and then close it again:

```
Sub Log(ByVal message As String) Implements IReporter.Log
    MsgBox(strText)
    Using writer As StreamWriter = _
          New StreamWriter("c:\account.log", True)
            writer.WriteLine(String.Format("{0}: {1}", _
              DateTime.Now, message))
            writer.Close()
        End Using
  End Sub
End Class
```

And that's it for the code for the component. Take a look at what to do to enable queuing. Click the Show All Files button on the Solution Explorer to see the hidden files for the project. Open the My Project item and then open the AssemblyInfo.vb file. Ensure that it has the attributes listed below:

```
'Enterprise Services attributes
<Assembly: EnterpriseServices.ApplicationAccessControl(False, _
    Authentication:=EnterpriseServices.AuthenticationOption.None)>
<Assembly: EnterpriseServices.ApplicationQueuing(Enabled:=True, _
    QueueListenerEnabled:=True)>
<Assembly: EnterpriseServices.ApplicationName("WroxQueue")>
<Assembly: EnterpriseServices.ApplicationActivation(EnterpriseServices
.ActivationOption.Server)>
```

Next, we ensure that queuing is correctly enabled for this component. The next line is a special line to enable message queuing to work correctly in a workgroup environment, by switching off authentication. If we didn't do this, we would need to set up an entire domain structure. (In a production scenario, that's exactly what we would use, so you would need to remove this line.) Finally, we ensure that the component runs as a server, rather than as a library. This was optional in the case of transactional components, but it's mandatory for queued components. We'll soon see why. In addition, you should add a strong name file to your project as you did with the Transactions component.

Consoles Again

It's time to build our component. Once built, register it using `RegSvcs` just like you did with the Transactions component.

Take a look at the Component Services Console to see how it's going (see Figure 21-15).That looks fine, but there's one other console to look at right now. This is the *Computer Management Console*. Get to this either from the system console, or by right-clicking the My Computer icon, and selecting Manage from the menu. Tucked away, right at the bottom, is the relevant part. You'll need to open up Services and Applications to find it. Take a closer look in Figure 21-15.

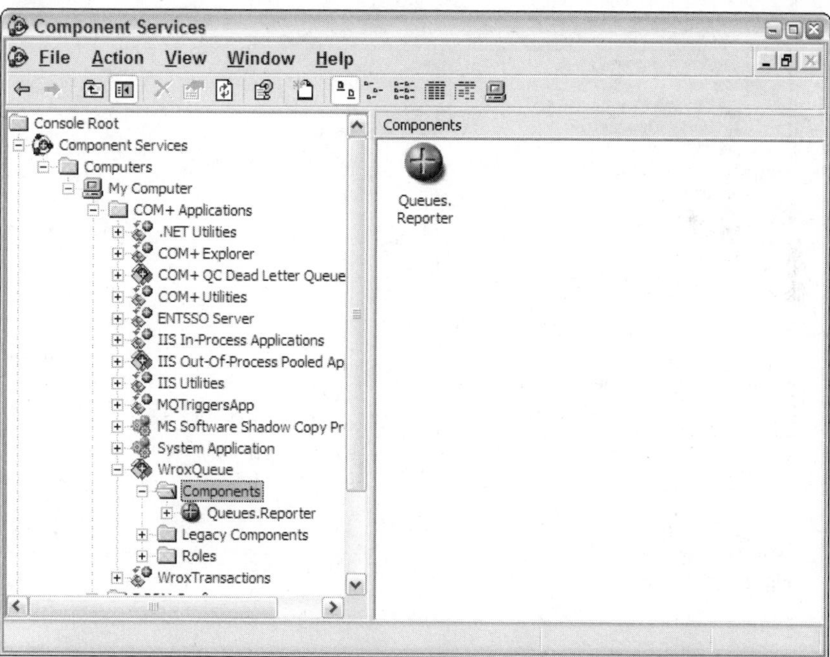

Figure 21-15

Component Services has set up some queues for us. There are five queues feeding into the main one, so the infrastructure is ready. Remember, by the way, that all this would be running on the server machine in a production scenario, not the client.

Building the Client

The problem is that all of the code you've written in this project is built on top of the MSMQ infrastructure, which is, inevitably, a COM infrastructure. Worse, the current tasks involve *marshaling* COM objects into a stream suitable for inserting into a queued message. For the purposes of this discussion, think of marshaling as basically intelligently serializing the contents of a method invocation on an interface. We do this in such a way that they can then be deserialized at the other end and turned into a successful invocation of the same method in a remote implementation of the interface. We get COM to do this for us by constructing a *moniker*, which is basically an intelligent name.

We'll start by creating a Windows Application project called `TestReporter`. We need to add a reference to our `Reporter` component, in the usual manner. Here's the form (see Figure 21-16).

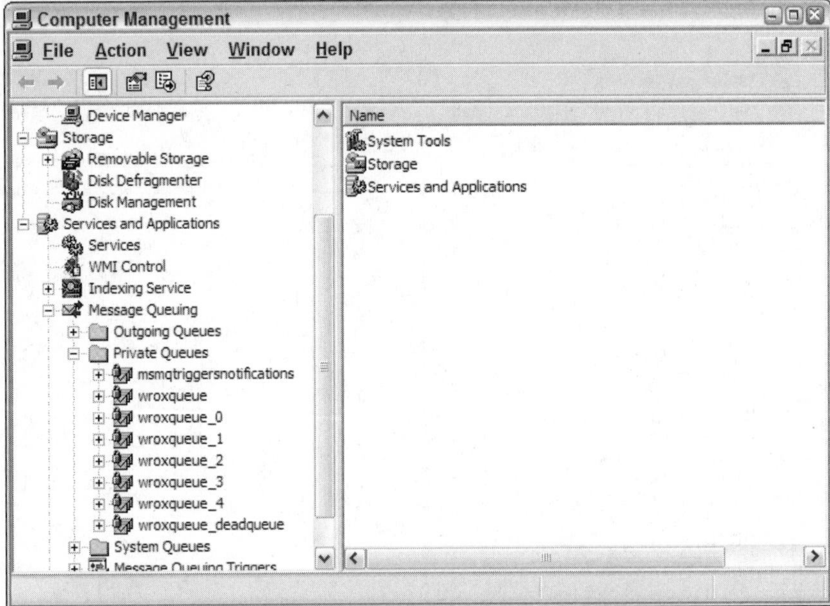

Figure 21-16

The text box is called `MessageField`, and the button is called `SendButton`. Here's the code:

```
Imports System.Runtime.InteropServices
Public Class MainForm
  Inherits System.Windows.Forms.Form
  Private Sub SendButton_Click(ByVal sender As System.Object, _
                          ByVal e As System.EventArgs) _
                          Handles SendButton.Click
```

Here's the crucial section. The important things to note are the references to our interface and how we instantiate the object:

```
        Dim logger As Queues.IReporter

        Try
            logger = CType(Marshal.BindToMoniker("queue:/new:Queues.Reporter"), _
              Queues.IReporter)
```

Here's the queued call:

```
logger.Log(Me.MessageField.Text)
```

Finally, we have to release the reference to the underlying COM object:

```
            Marshal.ReleaseComObject(logger)
            MessageBox.Show("Message sent")

        Catch ex As Exception
            MessageBox.Show(ex.Message, "Error sending message")
        End Try
```

It's not pretty, but you only have to do it once to be able to do it many times over.

Queuing Invocations

Now, try using this application to put a message onto the queue. Run it up and enter a suitable message., such as "Hello everyone".

Click the Send button and nothing happens. Time to take a look at our message queue (see Figure 21-17).

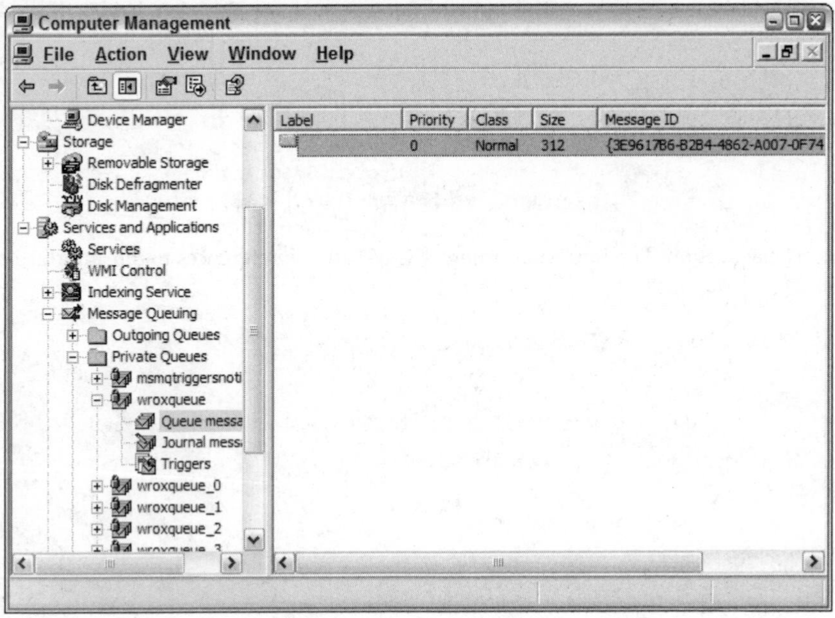

Figure 21-17

We've definitely created a message. So that represents our invocation. If we were to be able to read it, we would see the message you typed in earlier embedded somewhere in it. (Unfortunately, the console only allows us to inspect the start of the message, but if we do so, we can see the name of our component in there.)

But why hasn't anything happened? The answer is that we haven't actually started our server. Remember, we said that our component had to run as a server? This is why. The server has to sit there all the time, serving the incoming queue. So let's go to the Component Services Console, right-click Reporter, select Start from the menu, and we're off. Lo and behold, there's the message box (see Figure 21-18).

Figure 21-18

Now that the message has been delivered, go back to the Component Services Console. Right-clicking over the message queue and selecting Refresh shows that the message has indeed been removed from the queue.

Look in `account.log` and notice that it has been updated as well. Now, running the application results in the message boxes popping up straightaway.

Transactions with Queued Components

Now, why did we tell you to call that file `account.log`? The thing is that MSMQ is like SQL Server, a resource manager, and it can take part in transactions. At first, this is a little counterintuitive, because how on earth can anything so asynchronous as MSMQ have anything to do with transactions? The point is that it is *reliable*. If we take the transaction to go up to the point at which a message is securely in the queue, we have definitely got something that can participate. What happens at the other end of the queue is an entirely separate transaction. Of course, if something goes wrong there, we may need to look at setting up a compensating transaction coming back the other way to trigger some kind of rollback.

For the final example, then, we're going to take our original transactional component and add in a queued element, so that not only does the transfer of money take place, but the fact also gets logged to a remote file. Use exactly the same queued component as last time. And that's why we called the file `account.log`.

Start off by making a clone of `TestTransactions`, called `TestQueuedTransactions`. We need to add a reference to `Queues` and an import statement:

```
Imports System.Runtime.InteropServices
```

We also need a new private subroutine:

```
    Private Shared Sub LogTransaction(ByVal amount As Decimal, _
      ByVal sourceBank As String, ByVal sourceAccount As String, _
      ByVal destinationBank As String, ByVal destinationAccount As String)

        Dim logger As Queues.IReporter

        Try
            logger = CType(Marshal.BindToMoniker("queue:/new:Queues.Reporter"), _
              Queues.IReporter)

            logger.Log(String.Format("{0:c} transfered from {1}:{2} to {3}:{4}", _
                amount, _
                sourceBank, sourceAccount, _
                destinationBank, destinationAccount))

            Marshal.ReleaseComObject(logger)
            MessageBox.Show("Message sent")

        Catch ex As Exception
            MessageBox.Show(ex.Message, "Error sending message")
        End Try
    End Sub
```

This may look kind of familiar to the previous queued component example application. Finally, add a call to this subroutine in the button click event handler:

```
    Private Sub TransferButton_Click(ByVal sender As System.Object, ByVal e As
System.EventArgs) Handles TransferButton.Click
        Dim txn As New Transactions.BankTransactions
        Try
            txn.TransferMoney(CDec(Me.TransferField.Text), _
              "BankOfWrox", "Professional VB", _
              "BankOfMe", "Me")
            LogTransaction(CDec(Me.TransferField.Text), _
              "BankOfWrox", "Professional VB", _
              "BankOfMe", "Me")

            MessageBox.Show(String.Format("{0:C} transfered from {1} to {2}", _
                CDec(Me.TransferField.Text), "BankOfWrox", "BankOfMe"), _
                "Transfer Succeeded", _
                MessageBoxButtons.OK, _
                MessageBoxIcon.Information)

        Catch ex As Exception
            MessageBox.Show(ex.Message, "Transfer failed", _
              MessageBoxButtons.OK, _
              MessageBoxIcon.Error)

        End Try
    End Sub
```

So we're including a queued component into our transaction. It's been deliberately placed at the start to see if it genuinely takes part in the two-phase committal. If the transaction fails, we shouldn't see any messages come through.

We also need to make a small change to our `Reporter` component. However, we need to shut it down via the Component Services Console first. The change is very simple. To ensure that the queued component takes part in the transaction, it must be marked with the `Transaction` attribute:

```
<InterfaceQueuing(Interface:="Reporter.IReporter"), _
Transaction(TransactionOption.Required)> _
Public Class Reporter
```

If we now transfer $1,000, we see the usual "Transfer complete" message box. And if we now start up the Reporter component, we also see the message box from our queued component (see Figure 21-19).

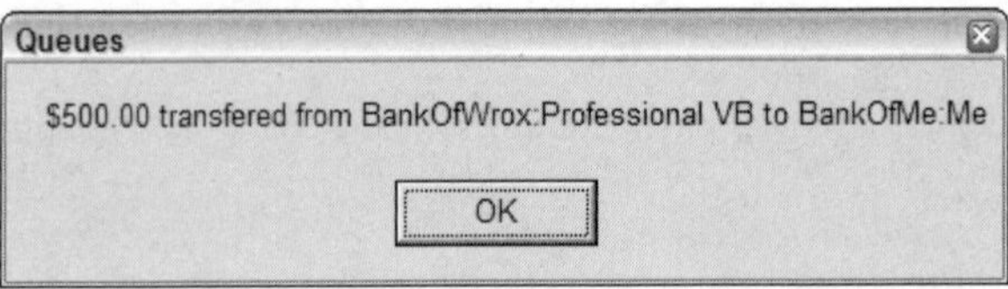

Figure 21-19

If we try it again, we see the queued message coming through first. So we know it's okay for valid transfers. What happens if we try to transfer $100? As we know from the earlier example, this will fail, and indeed, we see the "Transfer failed" message box from the main component. But not a peep out of the queued component.

Summary

This chapter looked at the .NET Component Services, those parts of .NET that address issues required for serious enterprise computing. To begin with, we looked at transactions and their importance in maintaining data correctness when multiple simultaneous changes may happen to your data. Properly applied, transactions can ensure that even with multiple users editing data, your database will always reflect the correct data. In addition, we looked at asynchronous processing using MSMQ and Queued Components. Many scenarios, such as logging or other background processes, are better handled using asynchronous code. Queued Components make building these asynchronous handlers much easier.

There are many other aspects of Enterprise Services that we haven't looked at, including *role-based security*, *object constructors*, and more. It is definitely worth investing in the many other books relating to this topic for more details on these features.

22

Threading

One of the things that the move from 16-bit to 32-bit computing gave us was the ability to write code that made use of threads, but although Visual C++ developers have been able to use threads for some time, Visual Basic developers haven't had a really reliable way to do so, until now. Previous techniques involved accessing the threading functionality available to Visual C++ developers. Although this worked, without adequate debugger support in the Visual Basic environment, actually developing multithreaded code was nothing short of a nightmare.

For most developers, the primary motivation for multithreading is the ability to perform long-running tasks in the background, while still providing the user with an interactive interface. Another common scenario is when building server-side code that can perform multiple long-running tasks at the same time. In that case, each task can be run on a separate thread, allowing all the tasks to run in parallel.

This chapter introduces you to the various objects in the .NET Framework that enable any .NET language to be used to develop multithreaded applications.

What Is a Thread?

The term *thread* is short for *thread of execution*. When your program is running, the CPU is actually running a sequence of processor instructions, one after another. You can think of these instructions, one after another, as forming a thread that is being executed by the CPU. What we call a thread is, in effect, a pointer to the currently executing instruction in the sequence of instructions that make up our application. This pointer starts at the top of the program and moves through each line, branching and looping when it comes across decisions and loops and, at a time when the program is no longer needed, the pointer steps outside of the program code and the program is effectively stopped.

Most applications have only one thread, so they are only executing one sequence of instructions. Some applications have more than one thread, so they can simultaneously execute more than one sequence of instructions.

It is important to realize that each CPU in your computer can only execute one thread at a time, with the exception of hyperthreaded processors that essentially contain multiple CPUs inside a single CPU. This means that if you only have one CPU, then your computer can only execute one thread at a time. Even if an application has several threads, only one can run at a time in this case. If your computer has two or more CPUs, then each CPU will run a different thread at the exact same time. In this case, more than one thread in your application may run at the same exact time, each on a different CPU.

Of course, when you have a computer with only one CPU that several programs can actively be running at the same time, the statements in the previous paragraph fly in the face of visual evidence. Yet it is true that only one thread can execute at a time on a single-CPU machine. What you may *perceive* to be simultaneously running applications is really an illusion created by the Windows operating system through a technique called preemptive multithreading, which is discussed later in the chapter.

All applications have at least one thread—otherwise they couldn't do any work, as there'd be no pointer to the thread of execution.

The principle of a thread is that it allows your program to perform multiple actions, potentially at the same time. Each sequence of instructions is executed independently of other threads.

The classic example of *multithreaded* functionality is Microsoft Word's spell checker. When the program starts, the execution pointer starts at the top of the program and eventually gets itself into a position where you're able to start writing code.

However, at some point Word will start another thread and create another execution pointer. As you type, this new thread examines the text and flags any spelling errors as you go, underlining them with a red wavy line (see Figure 22-1).

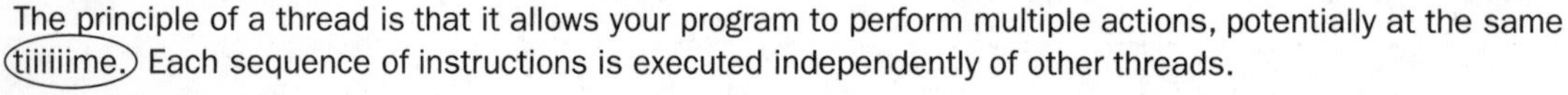

The principle of a thread is that it allows your program to perform multiple actions, potentially at the same tiiiiime. Each sequence of instructions is executed independently of other threads.

Figure 22-1

Every application has one primary thread. This thread serves as the main process thread through the application. Imagine you have an application that starts up, loads a file from disk, performs some processing on the data in the file, writes a new file, and then quits. Functionally, it might look like Figure 22-2.

In this simple application, we need to use only a single thread. When the program is told to run, Windows creates a new process and also creates the *primary thread*. To understand more about exactly what it is that a thread does, you need to understand a little more about how Windows and the computer's processor deal with different processes.

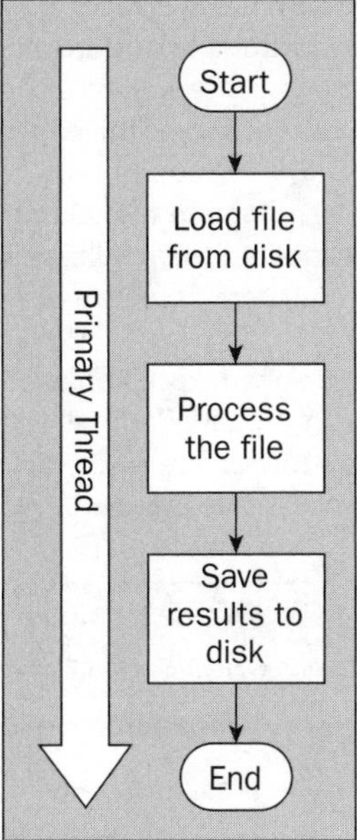

Figure 22-2

Processes, AppDomains, and Threads

Windows is capable of keeping many programs in memory at once and allowing the user to switch between them. Windows can also run programs in the background, possibly under different user identities. The ability to run many programs at once is called *multitasking*.

Each of these programs that your computer keeps in memory runs in a single *process*. A process is an isolated region of memory that contains a program's code and data. All programs run within a process, and code running in one process cannot access the memory within any other process. This prevents one program from interfering with any other program.

The process is started when the program starts and exists for as long as the program is running. When a process is started, Windows sets up an isolated memory area for the program and loads the program's code into that area of memory. It then starts up the main thread for the process, pointing it at the first instruction in the program. From that point, the thread runs the sequence of instructions defined by the program.

Windows supports *multithreading*, so the main thread might execute instructions that create more threads within the same process. These other threads run within the same memory space as the main thread — all sharing the same memory. Threads within a process are not isolated from each other. One thread in a process can tamper with data being used by other threads in that same process. However, a thread in one process cannot tamper with data being used by threads in any other processes on the computer.

At this point you should understand that Windows loads program code into a process and executes that code on one or more threads. The .NET Framework adds another concept to the mix: the *AppDomain*. An AppDomain is very much like a process in concept. Each AppDomain is an isolated region of memory, and code running in one AppDomain cannot access the memory of another AppDomain.

The .NET Framework introduced the AppDomain to make it possible to run multiple, isolated programs within the same Windows process. It turns out to be relatively expensive to create a Windows process in terms of time and memory. It is much cheaper to create a new AppDomain within an existing process.

Remember that Windows has no concept of an AppDomain, it only understands the concept of a process. The only way to get *any* code to run under Windows is to load it into a process. This means that each .NET AppDomain exists within a process. The end result is that all .NET code runs within an AppDomain *and* within a Windows process (see Figure 22-3).

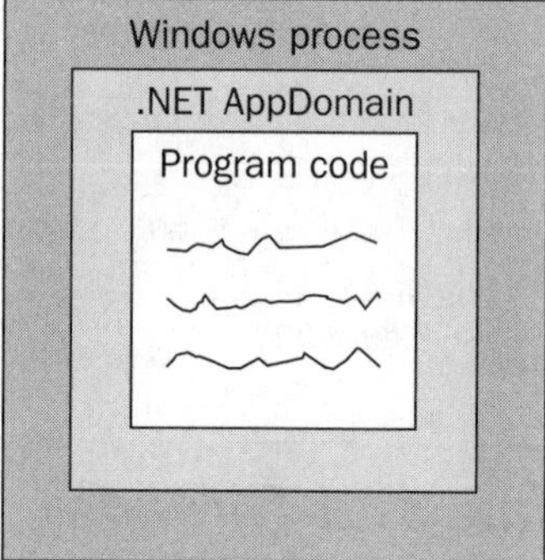

Figure 22-3

In most cases, a Windows process will contain one AppDomain, which will contain our program's code. The main thread of the process will execute our program's instructions. The end result is that the existence of the AppDomain is largely invisible to our program.

In some cases, most notably ASP.NET, a Windows process will contain multiple AppDomains, each with a separate program loaded (see Figure 22-4).

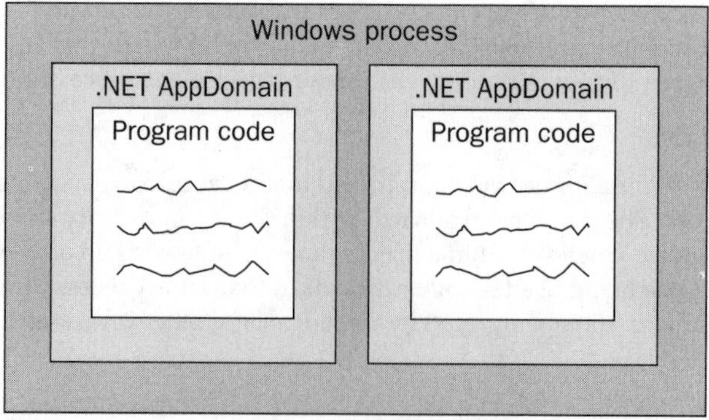

Figure 22-4

ASP.NET uses this technique to isolate Web applications from each other without having to start an expensive new Windows process for each virtual root on the server.

Note that AppDomains do not change the relationship between a process and threads. Each process has a main thread and may have other threads. This means that even in the ASP.NET process, with multiple AppDomains, there is only one main thread. Of course, ASP.NET creates other threads, so multiple Web applications can execute simultaneously, but there's only a single main thread in the entire process.

Thread Scheduling

Earlier in the chapter we noted that visual evidence tells us that multiple programs, and thus multiple threads, execute simultaneously even on a single-CPU computer. This is an illusion created by the operating system through the use of a concept called time slicing or time sharing.

The reality is that only one thread runs on each CPU at a time, again with the exception of hyperthreaded processors, which are essentially multiple CPUs in one. In a single-CPU machine, this means that only one thread is ever executing at any one time. To provide the illusion that many things are happening at the same time, the operating system never lets any one thread run for very long, giving other threads a chance to get a bit of work done as well. The end result is that it *appears* that the computer is executing several threads at the same time.

The length of time each thread gets to run is called a *quantum*. Although a quantum can vary, it is typically around 20 milliseconds. Once a thread has run for its quantum, the operating system stops the thread and allows another thread to run. When that thread reaches its quantum, yet another thread gets to run and so forth. A thread can also give up the CPU before it reaches its quantum. This happens frequently, since most I/O operations and numerous other interactions with the Windows operating system will cause a thread to give up the CPU.

Because the length of time each thread gets to run is so short, we never notice that the threads are getting started and stopped constantly behind the scenes. This is the same concept animators use when creating cartoons or other animated media. As long as the changes happen faster than we can perceive them, we are given the illusion of motion, or in this case, simultaneous execution of code.

The technology used by Windows is called *preemptive multitasking*. It is preemptive because no thread is ever allowed to run beyond its quantum. The operating system always intervenes and allows other threads to run. This helps ensure that no single thread can consume all the processing power on the machine to the detriment of other threads.

It also means that we can never be sure when our thread will be interrupted and another thread allowed to run. This is the primary source of the complexity of multithreading, as it can cause race conditions when two threads access the same memory. If we attempt to solve a race condition with a lock, it can cause deadlock conditions when two threads attempt to access the same lock. We'll discuss these concepts more later. The point you should take away now is that writing multithreaded code can be exceedingly difficult.

The entity that executes code in Windows is the thread. This means that the operating system is primarily focused on scheduling threads to keep the CPU or CPUs busy at all times. The operating system does not schedule processes, nor does it schedule AppDomains. Processes and AppDomains are merely regions of memory that contain our code — threads are what execute the code.

Threads have priorities, and Windows always allows higher priority threads to run before lower priority threads. In fact, if a higher priority thread is ready to run, Windows will cut short a lower priority thread's quantum to allow the higher priority thread to execute sooner. The end result is that Windows has a bias towards threads of higher priority.

Setting thread priorities can be useful in situations where you have a process that requires a lot of processor muscle, but it doesn't matter how long the process takes to do its work. Setting a program's thread to a low priority allows that program to run continuously with little impact on other programs. So if we need to use Word or Outlook or another application, Windows gives more processor time to these applications and less time to the low priority program. This means the computer can work smoothly when the user needs it to, letting the low priority program only use otherwise wasted CPU power.

Threads may also voluntarily suspend themselves before their quantum is complete. This happens frequently, for instance, when a thread attempts to read data from a file. It takes some significant time for the IO subsystem to locate the file and start retrieving the data. We can't have the CPU sitting idle during that time, especially when there are probably other threads that could be running. So what happens is that the thread enters a wait state to indicate that it is waiting for an external event. The Windows scheduler immediately locates and runs the next ready thread, keeping the CPU busy while the first thread waits for its data.

Windows also automatically suspends and resumes our threads depending on its perceived processing needs, the various priority settings, and so on. Say we're running one AppDomain containing two threads. If we can somehow mark the second thread as dormant (in other words, tell Windows that it has nothing to do), there's no need for Windows to allocate time to it. Effectively, the first thread will receive 100 percent of the processor horsepower available to that process. When a thread is marked as dormant we say it's in a *wait state*.

Windows is particularly good at managing processes and threads. It's a core part of Windows' functionality and so its developers have spent a lot of time making sure that it's super-efficient and as bug-free as software can be. This means that creating and spinning up threads is very easy to do and happens very quickly. Threads also only take up a small amount of system resources. However, there is a caveat you should be aware of.

The activity of stopping one thread and starting another is called *context switching*. This switching happens relatively quickly, but only if you're relatively careful with the number of threads you create. Remember that this happens for each active thread at the end of each quantum (or not before) — so after at most 20 milliseconds. If you spin up too many threads, the operating system will spend all of its time switching between different threads, perhaps even getting to a point where the code in the thread doesn't get a chance to run because as soon as you've started the thread it's time for it to stop again.

Creating thousands of threads is not the right solution. What you need to do is find a balance between the amount of threads that your application needs and the amount of threads that Windows can handle. There's no magic number or right answer to the question of "How many threads should I create?" You just need to be aware of context switching and experiment a little.

Take the Microsoft Word spell check example. The thread that performs the spell check is around all the time. Imagine you have a blank document containing no text. At this point, the spell check thread is in a wait state. Imagine you type a single word into the document and then pause. At this point, Word will pass the word over to the thread and signal it to start working. The thread will use its own slice of the processor power to examine the word. If it finds something wrong with the word, it will tell the primary thread that a spelling problem was found and that the user needs to be alerted. At this point, the spell check thread drops back into a wait state until more text is entered into the document. Word doesn't spin up the thread whenever it needs to perform a check—rather the thread runs all the time, but, if it has nothing to do, it drops into this efficient wait state. (You'll learn about how the thread starts again later.)

Again, this is an oversimplification. Word will "wake up" the thread at various times. However, the principle is sound—the thread is given work to do, it reports the results, and then it starts waiting for the next chunk of work to do.

So why is all this important? If you plan to author multithreaded applications, it is important to realize how the operating system will be scheduling our threads as well as the threads of all other processes on the system. Most importantly, you need to recognize that your thread can be interrupted at any time so that another thread can run.

Thread Safety and Thread Affinity

Most of the .NET Framework base class library is not *thread safe*. Thread-safe code is code that can be called by multiple threads at the same time without negative side effects. If code is not thread-safe, then calling that code from multiple threads at the same time will result in unpredictable and undesirable side effects, potentially even blatantly crashing your application. When dealing with objects that are not thread safe, we must ensure that multiple threads never simultaneously interact with the same object.

As an example, if you have a `ListBox` control (or any other control) on a Windows Form and you start updating that control with data from multiple threads, you'll find that your results are undependable. Sometimes you'll see all your data in order, other times it will be out of order, and other times some data will be missing. This is because Windows Forms controls are not thread safe and don't behave properly when used by multiple threads at the same time.

To find out if any specific method in the .NET Base Class Library is thread safe, refer to the online help. If there is no mention of threading in association with the method, then the method is *not* thread safe.

The Windows Forms subset of the .NET Framework is not only not thread safe, but also has *thread affinity*. Thread affinity means that objects created by a thread can only be used by that thread. Other threads should never interact with those objects. In the case of Windows Forms, this means that we must ensure that multiple threads never interact with Windows Forms objects (like forms and controls). This is important, because when we are creating interactive multithreaded applications, we must ensure that only the thread that created a form interacts directly with that form.

As we'll see, Windows Forms includes technology by which a background thread can safely make method calls on forms and controls by transferring the method call to the thread that owns the form.

When to Use Threads

If we regard computer programs as being either application software or service software, we find there are different motivators for each one.

Application software uses threads primarily to deliver a better user experience. Common examples are

- **Microsoft Word** — background spell checker
- **Microsoft Word** — background printing
- **Microsoft Outlook** — background sending and receiving of email
- **Microsoft Excel** — background recalculation

You can see that in all of these cases, threads are used to do "something in the background." This provides a better user experience. For example, I can still edit a Word document while Word is spooling another document to the printer. Or, I can still read emails while Outlook is sending my new e-mail. As an application developer, you should use threads to enhance the user experience. At some point during the application startup, code running in the primary thread would have spun up this other thread to be used for spell checking. As part of the "allow user to edit the document" process, we give the spell checker thread some words to check. This thread separation means that the user can continue to type, even though spell checking is still taking place.

Service software uses threads to deliver scalability and improve the service offered. For example, imagine I had a Web server that receives six incoming connections simultaneously. That server needs to service each of the requests in parallel, otherwise the sixth thread would have to wait for me to finish threads one through five before it even got started. Figure 22-5 shows how IIS might handle incoming requests.

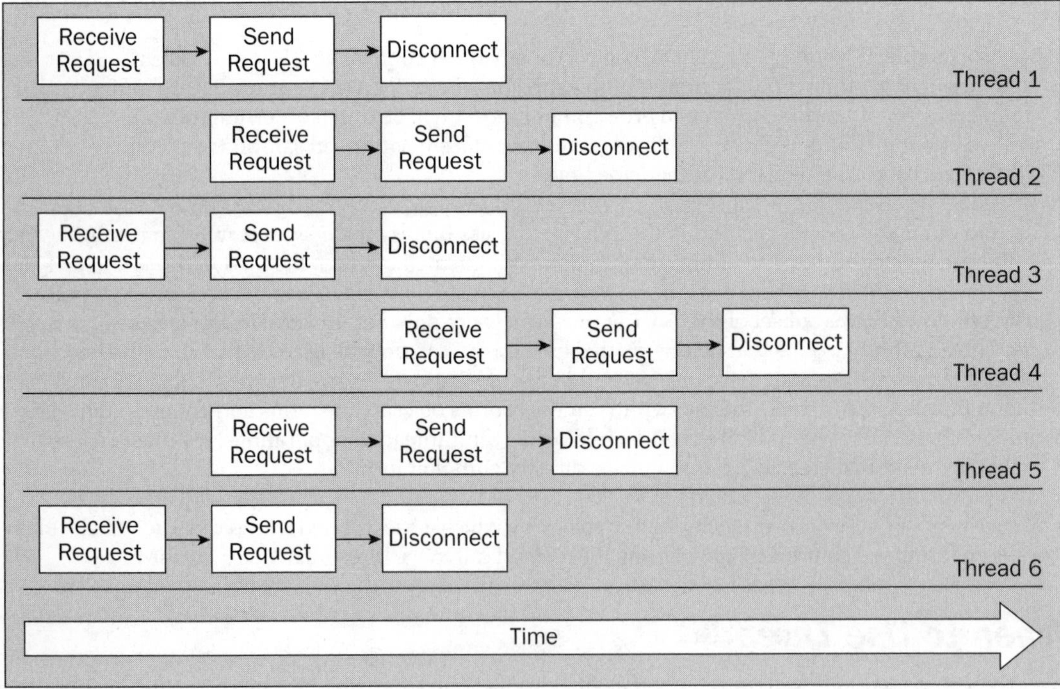

Figure 22-5

The primary motivation for multiple threads in a service like this is to keep the CPU busy servicing user requests even when other user requests are blocked waiting for data or other events. If we have six user requests, odds are high that some, or all of them, will read from files or databases and thus will spend many milliseconds in wait states. While some of the user requests are in wait states, other user requests will need CPU time and can be scheduled to run. The end result is higher scalability because we keep the CPU, IO, and other subsystems of the computer as busy as possible at all times.

Designing a Background Task

The specific goals and requirements for background processing in an interactive application are quite different from a server application. By interactive application, I am talking about Windows Forms or Console applications. While a Web application might be somewhat interactive, the fact is that all our code runs on the server, and so Web applications are server applications when it comes to threading.

Interactive Applications

In the case of interactive applications (typically Windows Forms applications), our design must center around having the background thread do useful work, but also interact appropriately (and safely) with the thread that is managing the UI. After all, we'll typically want to let the user know when the background process starts, stops, and does interesting things over its life. We can summarize these to the following basic requirements for the background thread:

- Indicate that the background task has started
- Provide periodic status or progress information
- Indicate that the background task has completed
- Allow the user to request that the background task cancel

While every application is different, these four requirements are typical for background threads in an interactive application.

As noted earlier, most of the .NET Framework is not thread safe, and Windows Forms is even more restrictive by having thread affinity. We want our background task to be able to notify the user when it starts, stops, and provides progress information. The fact that Windows Forms has thread affinity complicates this, because our background thread can never directly interact with Windows Forms objects. Fortunately, Windows Forms provides a formalized mechanism by which code in a background thread can send messages to the UI thread, so that the UI thread can update the display for the user.

This is done through the use of the `BackgroundWorker` control. This control is found in the Components tab of the toolbox.

The purpose of the `BackgroundWorker` control is to start, monitor, and control the execution of background tasks. The control makes it easy for code on the application's primary thread to start a task on a background thread. It also makes it easy for the code running on the background thread to notify the primary thread of progress and completion. Finally, it provides a mechanism by which the primary thread can request that the background task be cancelled, and for the background thread to notify the primary thread when it has completed the cancellation.

All this is done in a way that safely transfers control between the primary thread (that can update the UI) and the background thread (that cannot update the UI).

Server Applications

In the case of server programs, our design must center around the background thread being as efficient as possible. Server resources are precious, so the quicker the task can complete, the fewer resources we'll consume over time. Interactivity with a UI isn't a concern, since our code is running on a server, detached from any UI. The key to success in server coding is to avoid or minimize locking, thus maximizing throughput because our code never gets stopped by a lock.

For example, Microsoft went to great pains to design and refine ASP.NET to minimize the number of locks required from the time a user request hits the server to the time an ASPX page's code is running. Once the page code is running, no locking occurs, so the page code can just run, top to bottom, as fast and efficiently as possible.

Avoiding locking means avoiding shared resources or data. This is the dominant design goal for server code — to design programs to avoid scenarios where multiple threads need access to the same variables or other resources. Any time that multiple threads may access the same resource, we need to implement locking to prevent the threads from colliding with each other. We'll discuss locking later in the chapter, as sometimes it is simply unavoidable.

Implementing Threading

At this point you should have a basic understanding of threads and how they relate to the process and AppDomain concepts. You should also realize that for interactive applications, multithreading is not a way to improve performance, but rather is a way to improve the end user experience by providing the illusion that the computer is executing more code simultaneously. In the case of server-side code, multithreading enables higher scalability by allowing Windows to better utilize the CPU along with other subsystems such as IO.

A Quick Tour

When a background thread is created, it points to a method or procedure that will be executed by the thread. Remember that a thread is just a pointer to the current instruction in a sequence of instructions to be executed. In all cases, the first instruction in this sequence is the start of a method or procedure.

When using the `BackgroundWorker` control, this method is always the control's `DoWork` event handler. It is important to realize that this method can't be a `Function`. There is no mechanism by which a method running on one thread can return a result directly to code running on another thread. This means that any time you design a background task, you should start by creating a `Sub` in which you write the code to run on the background thread.

Also, because the goals for interactive applications and server programs are different, our designs for implementing threading in these two environments are different. This means that the way we design and code the background task will vary.

By way of explanation, let's work with a simple method that calculates prime numbers. This implementation is naïve, and so can take quite a lot of time when run against larger numbers, so it makes for a useful example of a long-running background task. Do the following:

1. Create a new Windows Forms Application project named `Threading`.
2. Add two `Button` controls, a `ListBox` and a `ProgressBar` control to `Form1`.
3. Add a `BackgroundWorker` control to `Form1`.
4. Set its `WorkerReportsProgress` and `WorkerSupportsCancellation` properties to `True`.
5. Add the following to the form's code:

```
Public Class Form1

#Region " Shared data "

  Private mMin As Integer
  Private mMax As Integer
  Private mResults As New List(Of Integer)

#End Region

#Region " Primary thread methods "

  Private Sub btnStart_Click(ByVal sender As System.Object, _
    ByVal e As System.EventArgs) Handles btnStart.Click

    ProgressBar1.Value = 0
    ListBox1.Items.Clear()
    mMin = 1
    mMax = 10000
    BackgroundWorker1.RunWorkerAsync()

  End Sub


  Private Sub btnCancel_Click(ByVal sender As System.Object, _
    ByVal e As System.EventArgs) Handles btnCancel.Click

    BackgroundWorker1.CancelAsync()

  End Sub


  Private Sub BackgroundWorker1_ProgressChanged( _
    ByVal sender As Object, ByVal e As _
    System.ComponentModel.ProgressChangedEventArgs) _
    Handles BackgroundWorker1.ProgressChanged

    ProgressBar1.Value = e.ProgressPercentage

  End Sub
```

```
  Private Sub BackgroundWorker1_RunWorkerCompleted( _
    ByVal sender As Object, ByVal e As _
    System.ComponentModel.RunWorkerCompletedEventArgs) _
    Handles BackgroundWorker1.RunWorkerCompleted

    For Each item As String In mResults
      ListBox1.Items.Add(item)
    Next

  End Sub

#End Region

#Region " Background thread methods "

  Private Sub BackgroundWorker1_DoWork(ByVal sender As Object, _
    ByVal e As System.ComponentModel.DoWorkEventArgs) _
    Handles BackgroundWorker1.DoWork

    mResults.Clear()

    For count As Integer = mMin To mMax Step 2
      Dim isPrime As Boolean = True

      For x As Integer = 1 To CInt(count / 2)
        For y As Integer = 1 To x
          If x * y = count Then
            ' the number is not prime
            isPrime = False
            Exit For
          End If
        Next
        ' short-circuit the check
        If Not isPrime Then Exit For
      Next

      If isPrime Then
        mResults.Add(count)
      End If

      Me.BackgroundWorker1.ReportProgress( _
        CInt((count - mMin) / (mMax - mMin) * 100))

      If Me.BackgroundWorker1.CancellationPending Then
        Exit Sub
      End If

    Next

  End Sub

#End Region

End Class
```

The `BackgroundWorker1_DoWork` method implements the code to find the prime numbers. This method is automatically run on a background thread by the `BackgroundWorker1` control. Notice that the method is a `Sub`, so it returns no value. Instead, it stores its results into a variable, in this case, a `List(Of Integer)`. The idea is that once the background task is complete, we can do something useful with the results.

When `btnStart` is clicked, the `BackgroundWorker` control is told to start the background task. In order to initialize any data values before launching the background thread, the `mMin` and `mMax` variables are set before the task is started.

Of course, we want to display the results of the background task. Fortunately, the `BackgroundWorker` control raises an event when the task is complete. In this event handler we can safely copy the values from the `List(Of Integer)` into the `ListBox` for display to the user.

Similarly, the `BackgroundWorker` control raises an event to indicate progress as the task runs. Notice that the `DoWork` method periodically calls the `ReportProgress` method. When this method is called, the progress is transferred from the background thread to the primary thread via the `ProgressChanged` event.

Finally we have the need to cancel a long-running task. It is never wise to directly terminate a background task. Instead, we should send a request to the background task asking it to stop running. This allows the task to cleanly stop running so it can close any resources it might be using and shut down properly.

To send the cancel request, call the `BackgroundWorker` control's `CancelAsync` method. This sets the control's `CancellationPending` property to `True`. Notice how this value is periodically checked by the `DoWork` method, and if it is `True`, we exit the `DoWork` method, thus effectively canceling the task.

Running the code now demonstrates that the UI remains entirely responsive while the background task is running, and the results are displayed when available.

Now that we've explored the basics of threading in an interactive application, let's discuss the various threading options that are at our disposal.

Threading Options

The .NET Framework offers two ways to implement multithreading. Regardless of which approach we use, we must specify the method or procedure that the thread will execute when it starts.

First, we can use the thread pool provided by the .NET Framework. The thread pool is a managed pool of threads that can be reused over the life of our application. Threads are created in the pool on an as-needed basis and idle threads in the pool are reused, thus keeping the number of threads created by our application to a minimum. This is important because threads are an expensive operating system resource.

> **The thread pool should be your first choice in most multithreading scenarios.**

Many built-in .NET Framework features already use the thread pool. In fact, we've already used it, because the `BackgroundWorker` control runs its background tasks on thread from the thread pool. Also, any time we do an asynchronous read from a file, URL, or TCP socket, the thread pool is used on our behalf. Any time we implement a remoting listener, a Web site, or a Web service, the thread pool is used. Because the .NET Framework itself relies on the thread pool, there is a high degree of confidence that it is an optimal choice for most multithreading requirements.

Second, we can create our own thread object. This can be a good approach if we have a single, long-running background task in our application. It is also useful if we need fine-grained control over the background thread. Examples of such control include setting the thread priority or suspending and resuming the thread's execution.

Using the Thread Pool

The .NET Framework provides a thread pool in the `System.Threading` namespace. This thread pool is self-managing. It will create threads on demand and, if possible, will reuse idle threads that already exist in the pool.

The thread pool won't create an unlimited number of threads. In fact, it will create at most 25 threads per CPU in the system. If we assign more work requests to the pool than it can handle with these threads, our work requests will be queued until a thread becomes available. This is typically a good feature, as it helps ensure that our application won't overload the operating system with too many threads.

There are five primary ways to use the thread pool: through the `BackgroundWorker` control, by calling `BeginXYZ` methods, via `Delegates`, manually via the `ThreadPool.QueueUserWorkItem` method, or by using a `System.Timers.Timer` control. Of the five, the easiest is to use the `BackgroundWorker` control.

Using the BackgroundWorker Control

The previous quick tour of threading explored the `BackgroundWorker` control, which allows us to easily start a task on a background thread, monitor that task's progress, and be notified when it is complete. It also allows us to request that the background task cancel itself. All this is done in a safe manner, where control is transferred from the primary thread to the background thread and back again without us having to worry about the details.

Using BeginXYZ Methods

Many of the .NET Framework objects support both synchronous and asynchronous invocation. For instance, we can read from a TCP socket by using the `Read` method or the `BeginRead` method. The `Read` method is synchronous, so we are blocked until the data is read.

The `BeginRead` method is asynchronous, so we are not blocked. Instead, the read operation occurs on a background thread in the thread pool. We provide the address of a method that is called automatically when the read operation is complete. This *callback* method is invoked by the background thread, and so the result is that our code also ends up running on the background thread in the thread pool.

Behind the scenes, this behavior is all driven by delegates. Rather than exploring TCP sockets or some other specific subset of the .NET Framework class library, let's move on and discuss the underlying technology itself.

Using Delegates

A delegate is a strongly typed pointer to a function or method. Delegates are the underlying technology used to implement events within Visual Basic, and they can be used directly to invoke a method given just a pointer to that method.

Delegates can be used to launch a background task on a thread in the thread pool. They can also transfer a method call from a background thread to the UI thread. The `BackgroundWorker` control uses this technology behind the scenes on our behalf, but we can use delegates directly as well.

To use delegates, our worker code must be in a method, and we must define a delegate for that method. The delegate is a pointer for the method, so it must have the same method signature as the method itself:

```
Private Delegate Sub TaskDelegate(ByVal min As Integer, ByVal max As Integer)

Private Sub FindPrimesViaDelegate(ByVal min As Integer, ByVal max As Integer)

    mResults.Clear()

    For count As Integer = min To max Step 2
      Dim isPrime As Boolean = True

      For x As Integer = 1 To CInt(count / 2)
        For y As Integer = 1 To x
          If x * y = count Then
            ' the number is not prime
            isPrime = False
            Exit For
          End If
        Next
        ' short-circuit the check
        If Not isPrime Then Exit For
      Next

      If isPrime Then
        mResults.Add(count)
      End If

    Next
End Sub
```

Running background tasks via delegates allows us to pass strongly typed parameters to the background task, thus clarifying and simplifying our code.

Now that we have a worker method and corresponding delegate, we can add a new button and write code in its click event handler to use it to run `FindPrimes` on a background thread:

```
Private Sub btnDelegate_Click(ByVal sender As System.Object)
        ByVal e As System.EventArgs) Handles btnDelegate.Click
  ' run the task
```

```
    Dim worker As New TaskDelegate(AddressOf FindPrimesViaDelegate)
    worker.BeginInvoke(1, 10000, AddressOf TaskComplete, Nothing)
End Sub
```

First we create an instance of the delegate, setting it up to point to the `FindPrimesViaDelegate` method. Then we call `BeginInvoke` on the delegate to invoke the method.

The `BeginInvoke` method is the key here. `BeginInvoke` is an example of the `BeginXYZ` methods we discussed earlier, and as you'll recall, they automatically run the method on a background thread in the thread pool. This is true for `BeginInvoke` as well, meaning that `FindPrimes` will be run in the background and the UI thread is not blocked, so it can continue to interact with the user.

Notice all the parameters we're passing to `BeginInvoke`. The first two correspond to the parameters we defined on our delegate — the `min` and `max` values that should be passed to `FindPrimes`.

The next parameter is the address of a method that will be automatically invoked when the background thread is complete. The final parameter (to which we've passed `Nothing`) is a mechanism by which we can pass a value from our UI thread to the method that is invoked when the background task is complete.

This means that we need to implement the `TaskComplete` method. This method is invoked when the background task is complete. It will run on the background thread, not on the UI thread, so we need to remember that this method can't interact with any Windows Forms objects. Instead it will contain the code to invoke an `UpdateDisplay` method on the UI thread via the form's `BeginInvoke` method:

```
Private Sub TaskComplete(ByVal ar As IAsyncResult)

  Dim update As New UpdateDisplayDelegate(AddressOf UpdateDisplay)
  Me.BeginInvoke(update)

End Sub

Private Delegate Sub UpdateDisplayDelegate()

Private Sub UpdateDisplay()

  For Each item As String In mResults
    ListBox1.Items.Add(item)
  Next

End Sub
```

Notice how a delegate is used to invoke the `UpdateDisplay` method as well, thus illustrating how delegates can be used with a `Form` object's `BeginInvoke` method to transfer control back to the primary thread. The same technique could be used to allow the background task to notify the primary thread of progress as the task runs.

Now when we run the application we'll have a responsive UI, with the `FindPrimesViaDelegate` method running in the background within the thread pool.

Manually Queuing Work

The final option for using the thread pool is to manually queue items for the thread pool to process. This is done by calling `ThreadPool.QueueUserWorkItem`. This is a `Shared` method on the `ThreadPool` class that directly places a method into the thread pool to be executed on a background thread.

This technique doesn't allow us to pass arbitrary parameters to the worker method. Instead it requires that the `worker` method accept a single parameter of type object, through which we can pass an arbitrary value. We can use this to pass multiple values by declaring a class with all our parameter types. Add the following class *inside* the `Form4` class:

```
Private Class params
  Public min As Integer
  Public max As Integer

  Public Sub New(ByVal min As Integer, ByVal max As Integer)
    Me.min = min
    Me.max = max
  End Sub

End Class
```

Then we can make `FindPrimes` accept this value as an Object:

```
  Private Sub FindPrimesInPool(ByVal state As Object)
    Dim params As params = DirectCast(state, params)
    mResults.Clear()

    For count As Integer = params.min To params.max Step 2
      Dim isPrime As Boolean = True

      For x As Integer = 1 To CInt(count / 2)
        For y As Integer = 1 To x
          If x * y = count Then
            ' the number is not prime
            isPrime = False
            Exit For
          End If
        Next
        ' short-circuit the check
        If Not isPrime Then Exit For
      Next

      If isPrime Then
        mResults.Add(count)
      End If

    Next

    Dim update As New UpdateDisplayDelegate(AddressOf UpdateDisplay)
    Me.BeginInvoke(update)

  End Sub
```

This is basically the same method used with delegates, but it accepts an object parameter rather than the strongly typed parameters. Also notice that the method uses a delegate to invoke the `UpdateDisplay` method on the UI thread when the task is complete. When we manually put a task on the thread pool, there is no automatic callback to a method when the task is complete, so we must do the callback in the worker method itself.

Now we can manually queue the worker method to run in the thread pool within our click event handler:

```
Private Sub btnPool_Click(ByVal sender As System.Object, _
      ByVal e As System.EventArgs) Handles btnPool.Click

  ' run the task
  System.Threading.ThreadPool.QueueUserWorkItem( _
    AddressOf FindPrimesInPool, New params(1, 10000))
End Sub
```

The `QueueUserWorkItem` method accepts the address of the worker method — in this case `FindPrimes`. This worker method must accept a single parameter of type `Object` or we'll get a compile error here.

The second parameter to `QueueUserWorkItem` is the object that is to be passed to the worker method when it is invoked on the background thread. In this case, we're passing a new instance of the `params` class we defined earlier. This allows us to pass our parameter values to `FindPrimes`.

When we run this code we'll again find that we have a responsive UI, with `FindPrimes` running on a background thread in the thread pool.

Using System.Timers.Timer

Beyond `BeginXYZ` methods, delegates, and manually queuing work items, there are various other ways to get our code running in the thread pool. One of the most common is through the use of a special `Timer` control. The `Elapsed` event of this control is raised on a background thread in the thread pool.

This is different from the `System.Windows.Forms.Timer` control, where the `Tick` event is raised on the UI thread. The difference is very important to understand, because we can't directly interact with Windows Forms objects from background threads. Code running in the `Elapsed` event of a `System.Timers.Timer` control must be treated like any other code running on a background thread.

The exception to this is if we set the `SynchronizingObject` property on the control to a Windows Forms object such as a Form or Control. In this case, the `Elapsed` event will be raised on the appropriate UI thread rather than on a thread in the thread pool. The end result is basically the same as using `System.Windows.Forms.Timer` instead.

Manually Creating a Thread

Thus far we've been working with the .NET thread pool. It is also possible to manually create and control background threads through code.

To manually create a thread, we need to create and start a `Thread` object. This looks something like the following:

```
  ' run the task
Dim worker As New Thread(AddressOf FindPrimes)
worker.Start()
```

While this seems like the obvious way to do multithreading, the thread pool is typically the preferred approach. This is because there is a cost to creating and destroying threads, and the thread pool helps avoid that cost by reusing threads when possible. When we manually create a thread as shown here, we must pay the cost of creating the thread each time or implement our own scheme to reuse the threads we create.

However, manual creation of threads can be useful. The thread pool is designed to be used for background tasks that run for a while and then complete, thus allowing the background thread to be reused for subsequent background tasks. If we need to run a background task for the entire duration of our application, the thread pool is not ideal, because that thread would never become available for reuse. In such a case, we are better off creating the background thread manually.

An example of this is the aforementioned spell checker in Word, which runs as long as we are editing a document. Running such a task on the thread pool would make little sense, since the task will run as long as the application, so instead it should be run on a manually created thread, leaving the thread pool available for shorter running tasks.

The other primary reason for manual creation of threads is where we want to be able to interact with the `Thread` object as it is running. There are various methods on the `Thread` object we can use to interact with and control the background thread. These are as shown in the following table.

`Abort`	Stops the thread (not recommended, as no cleanup occurs — this is not a graceful shutdown of the thread)
`ApartmentState`	Sets the COM apartment type used by this thread — important if we're using COM `interop` in the background task
`Join`	Blocks our current thread until the background thread is complete
`Priority`	Allows us to raise or lower the priority of the background thread so Windows will schedule it to get more or less CPU time relative to other threads
`Sleep`	Causes the thread to be suspended for a specified period of time
`Suspend`	Suspends a thread — temporarily stopping it without terminating the thread
`Resume`	Restarts a suspended thread

There are many other methods available on the `Thread` object as well; consult the online help for more details.

We can use these methods to control the behavior and lifetime of the background thread, which can be useful in advanced threading scenarios.

Shared Data

In most multithreading scenarios, we have data in our main thread that needs to be used by the background task on the background thread. Likewise, the background task typically generates data that is needed by the main thread. These are examples of *shared data*, or data that is used by multiple threads.

Remember that multithreading means that we have multiple threads within the same process, and in .NET within the same AppDomain. Because memory within an AppDomain is common across all threads in that AppDomain, it is very easy for multiple threads to access the same objects or variables within our application.

For example, in our original prime example, the background task needed the `min` and `max` values from the main thread, and all our implementations have used a `List(Of Integer)` to transfer results back to the main thread when the task was complete. These are examples of shared data. Note that we didn't do anything special to make the data shared — the variables were shared by default.

When we're writing multithreaded code, the hardest issue is that of managing access to shared data within our AppDomain. You don't, for example, want two threads writing to the same piece of memory at the same time. Equally, you don't want a group of threads reading memory that another thread is in the process of changing. This management of memory access is called *synchronization*. It's properly managing synchronization that makes writing multithreaded code difficult.

When multiple threads want to simultaneously access a common bit of shared data, use synchronization to control things. This is typically done by blocking all but one thread, so only one thread can access the shared data. All other threads are put into a wait state by using a blocking operation of some sort. Once the nonblocked thread is done using the shared data, it will release the block, allowing another thread to resume processing and to use the shared data.

The process of releasing the block is often called an event. When we say "event" we are *not* talking about a Visual Basic event. Although the naming convention is unfortunate, the principle is the same — something happens and we react to it. In this case, the nonblocked thread causes an event, which releases some other thread so it can access the shared data.

Although blocking can be used to control the execution of threads, it's primarily used to control access to resources, including memory. This is the basic idea behind synchronization — if we need something, we block until we can access it.

Synchronization is expensive and can be complex. It is expensive because it stops one or more threads from running while another thread uses the shared data. The whole point of having multiple threads is to do more than one thing at a time, and if we're constantly blocking all but one thread then we lose this benefit.

It can be complex because there are many ways to implement synchronization. Each technique is appropriate for a certain class of synchronization problem, and using the wrong one in the wrong place will increase the cost of synchronization.

It is also quite possible to create *deadlocks*, where two or more threads end up *permanently* blocked. You've undoubtedly seen examples of this. Pretty much any time a Windows application totally locks up and must be stopped by the Task Manager, you are seeing an example of poor multithreading implementation. The fact that this happens even in otherwise high-quality commercial applications (such as Microsoft Outlook) is confirmation that synchronization can be very hard to get right.

Avoid Sharing Data

Since synchronization has so many downsides in terms of performance and complexity, the best thing we can do is avoid or minimize its use. If at all possible, we should design our multithreaded applications to avoid reliance on shared data, and to maintain tight control over the usage of any shared data that is required.

Typically, some shared data is unavoidable, so the question becomes how to manage that shared data to avoid or minimize synchronization. There are two primary schemes we can use for this purpose, so let's discuss them now.

Transferring Data Ownership

The first approach is to avoid sharing of data by always passing references to the data between threads. If we also make sure that neither thread uses the same reference, then each thread has its own copy of the data, and no thread needs access to data being used by any other threads.

This is exactly what we did in our prime example where we started the background task via a delegate:

```
Dim worker As New TaskDelegate(AddressOf FindPrimesViaDelegate)
worker.BeginInvoke(1, 10000, AddressOf TaskComplete, Nothing)
```

The `min` and `max` values are passed as `ByVal` parameters, meaning that they are copied and provided to the `indPrimes` method. No synchronization is required here, because the background thread never tries to access the values from the main thread.

We passed copies of the values a different way when we manually started the task in the thread pool:

```
System.Threading.ThreadPool.QueueUserWorkItem( _
  AddressOf FindPrimesInPool, New params(1, 10000))
```

In this case, we created a `params` object into which we put the `min` and `max` values. Again, those values were copied before they were used by the background thread. The `FindPrimesInPool` method never attempted to access any parameter data being used by the main thread.

Transferring Data Ownership

What we've done so far works great for variables that are *value types*, such as `Integer`, and *immutable objects*, such as `String`. It won't work for *reference types*, such as a regular object, because reference types are never passed by value, only by reference.

To use reference types, we need to change our approach. Rather than returning a copy of the data, we'll return a reference to the object containing the data. Then we'll make sure that the background task stops using *that* object, and starts using a new object. As long as different threads aren't simultaneously using the same objects, there's no conflict.

We can enhance our prime application to provide the prime numbers to the UI thread as it finds them, rather than in a batch at the end of the process. To see how this works, we'll alter our original code based on the `BackgroundWorker` control. That is the easiest, and typically the best, way to start a background task, so we'll use it as a base implementation.

The first thing to do is to alter the `DoWork` method so it periodically returns results. Rather than using the shared `mResults` variable, we'll use a local `List(Of Integer)` variable to store the results. Each time we have enough results to report, we'll return that `List(Of Integer)` to the UI thread, and we'll create a new `List(Of Integer)` for the next batch of values. This way we're never sharing the same object between two threads. The required changes are highlighted:

```
Private Sub BackgroundWorker1_DoWork(ByVal sender As Object, _
  ByVal e As System.ComponentModel.DoWorkEventArgs) _
  Handles BackgroundWorker1.DoWork

  'mResults.Clear()
  Dim results As New List(Of Integer)

  For count As Integer = mMin To mMax Step 2
    Dim isPrime As Boolean = True

    For x As Integer = 1 To CInt(count / 2)
      For y As Integer = 1 To x
        If x * y = count Then
          ' the number is not prime
          isPrime = False
          Exit For
        End If
      Next
      ' short-circuit the check
      If Not isPrime Then Exit For
    Next

    If isPrime Then
      'mResults.Add(count)
      results.Add(count)
      If results.Count >= 10 Then
        BackgroundWorker1.ReportProgress( _
          CInt((count - mMin) / (mMax - mMin) * 100), results)
        results = New List(Of Integer)
      End If
    End If

    BackgroundWorker1.ReportProgress( _
      CInt((count - mMin) / (mMax - mMin) * 100))

    If BackgroundWorker1.CancellationPending Then
      Exit Sub
    End If

  Next

  BackgroundWorker1.ReportProgress(100, results)

End Sub
```

Our results are now placed into a local `List(Of Integer)`. Any time the list has 10 values, we return it to the primary thread by calling the `BackgroundWorker` control's `ReportProgress` method, passing the `List(Of Integer)` as a parameter.

The important thing here is that we then immediately create a new `List(Of Integer)` for use in the `DoWorker` method. This ensures that the background thread is never trying to interact with the same `List(Of Integer)` object as the UI thread.

Now that the `DoWork` method is returning results, alter the code on the primary thread to use those results:

```
Private Sub BackgroundWorker1_ProgressChanged( _
  ByVal sender As Object, _
  ByVal e As System.ComponentModel.ProgressChangedEventArgs) _
  Handles BackgroundWorker1.ProgressChanged


  ProgressBar1.Value = e.ProgressPercentage
  If e.UserState IsNot Nothing Then
    For Each item As String In CType(e.UserState, List(Of Integer))
      ListBox1.Items.Add(item)
    Next
  End If

End Sub
```

Any time the `ProgressChanged` event is raised, the code checks to see if the background task provided a state object. If it did provide a state object, we cast it to a `List(Of Integer)` and update the UI to display the values in the object.

At this point we no longer need the `RunWorkerCompleted` method, so it can be removed or commented out.

If we run the code at this point, we'll find that not only is our UI continually responsive, but the results from the background task are displayed as they are discovered rather than in a batch at the end of the process. As you run the application, resize and move the form while the prime numbers are being found. Although the *displaying* of the data may be slowed down as we interact with the form (because the UI thread can only do so much work), the *generation* of the data continues independently in the background and is not blocked by the UI thread's work.

When we rely on transferring data ownership, we are ensuring that only one thread can access the data at any given time by ensuring that the background task never uses an object once it returns it to the primary thread.

Sharing Data with Synchronization

So far, we've seen ways to avoid the sharing of data. However, sometimes we will have a requirement for data sharing, in which case we'll be faced with the complex world of synchronization.

As we discussed earlier, incorrect implementation of synchronization can cause performance issues, deadlocks, and application crashes. Success is dependent on serious attention to detail. Problems may not manifest in testing, but when they happen in production they are often catastrophic. You can't *test* to ensure proper implementation; you must prove it in the same way mathematicians prove mathematical truths — by careful logical analysis of all possibilities.

Built-in Synchronization Support

Some objects in the .NET Framework have built-in support for synchronization, so we don't need to write it ourselves. In particular, most of the collection-oriented classes have optional support for synchronization. These include: `Queue`, `Stack`, `Hashtable`, `ArrayList`, and more.

Rather than transferring ownership of `List(Of Integer)` objects from the background thread to the UI thread as we did in the last example, we can use the synchronization provided by the `ArrayList` object to help mediate between the two threads.

To use a synchronized `ArrayList`, we need to change from the `List(Of Integer)` to an `ArrayList`. Additionally, the `ArrayList` must be created a special way:

```
Private Sub BackgroundWorker1_DoWork(ByVal sender As Object, _
  ByVal e As System.ComponentModel.DoWorkEventArgs) _
  Handles BackgroundWorker1.DoWork

  'mResults.Clear()
  'Dim results As New List(Of Integer)
  Dim results As ArrayList = ArrayList.Synchronized(New ArrayList)
```

What we're doing here is creating a normal `ArrayList`, and then having the `ArrayList` class "wrap" it with a synchronized wrapper. The end result is an `ArrayList` object that is thread safe and automatically prevents multiple threads from interacting with the data in invalid ways.

Now that the `ArrayList` is synchronized, we don't need to create a new one each time we return the values to the primary thread.

Comment out the following line in the `DoWork` method:

```
      If results.Count >= 10 Then
        BackgroundWorker1.ReportProgress( _
          CInt((count - mMin) / (mMax - mMin) * 100), results)
        'results = New List(Of Integer)
      End If
```

Finally, the code on the primary thread needs to be updated to properly display the data from the `ArrayList`:

```
Private Sub BackgroundWorker1_ProgressChanged( _
  ByVal sender As Object, _
  ByVal e As System.ComponentModel.ProgressChangedEventArgs) _
  Handles BackgroundWorker1.ProgressChanged


  ProgressBar1.Value = e.ProgressPercentage
  If e.UserState IsNot Nothing Then
    Dim result As ArrayList = CType(e.UserState, ArrayList)
    For index As Integer = ListBox1.Items.Count To result.Count - 1
      ListBox1.Items.Add(result(index))
```

```
        Next
      End If

    End Sub
```

Since the entire list is accessible at all times, we need to only copy the new values to the `ListBox` rather than looping through the entire list.

This works out well anyway, because the `For..Each` statement isn't threadsafe even with a synchronized collection. To use the `For..Each` statement, we'd need to enclose the entire loop inside a `SyncLock` block like this:

```
Dim result As ArrayList = CType(e.UserState, ArrayList)
SyncLock result.SyncRoot
  For Each item As String in result
    ListBox1.Items.Add(item)
  Next
End SyncLock
```

The `SyncLock` statement in Visual Basic is used to provide an exclusive lock on an object. Here it is being used to get an exclusive lock on the `ArrayList` object's `SyncRoot`. This means that all our code within the `SyncLock` block can be sure that it is the only code that is interacting with the contents of the `ArrayList`. No other threads can access the data while our code is in this block.

Synchronization Objects

While many collection objects optionally provide support for synchronization, most objects in the .NET Framework or in third-party libraries are not thread safe. To safely share these objects and classes in a multithreaded environment, we must manually implement synchronization.

To manually implement synchronization, we must rely on help from the Windows operating system. The .NET Framework includes classes that wrap the underling Windows operating system concepts however, so we don't need to call Windows directly. Instead we use the .NET Framework synchronization objects.

Synchronization objects have their own special terminology. Most of these objects can be acquired and released. In other cases, we wait on an object until it is signaled. Let's explore these terms.

For objects that can be acquired, the idea is that when we have the object we have a lock. Any other threads trying to acquire the object are blocked until we release the object. These types of synchronization objects are like a hot potato—only one thread has it at a time and other threads are waiting for it. No thread should hold onto such an object any longer than necessary, since that slows down the whole system.

The other class of objects are those that wait on the object—which means our thread is blocked. Some other thread will signal our object, which releases us so we become unblocked. Many threads can be waiting on the same object, and when the object is signaled, all the blocked threads are released. This is basically the exact opposite of an acquire/release type object.

The following table lists the primary synchronization objects in the .NET Framework.

Object	Model	Description
`AutoResetEvent`	Wait/Signal	Allows a thread to release other threads that are waiting on the object
`Interlocked`	N/A	Allows multiple threads to safely increment and decrement values that are stored in variables accessible to all the threads
`ManualResetEvent`	Wait/Signal	Allows a thread to release other threads that are waiting on the object
`Monitor`	Acquire/Release	Defines an exclusive application-level lock where only one thread can hold the lock at any given time
`Mutex`	Acquire/Release	Defines an exclusive systemwide lock where only one thread can hold the lock at any given time
`ReaderWriterLock`	Acquire/Release	Defines a lock where many threads can read data, but provides exclusive access to one thread for writing data

Exclusive Locks and the SyncLock Statement

Perhaps the easiest type of synchronization to understand and implement is an *exclusive lock*. When one thread holds an exclusive lock, no other thread can obtain that lock. Any other thread attempting to obtain the lock is blocked until the lock becomes available.

There are two primary technologies for exclusive locking: the `monitor` and `mutex` objects. The `monitor` object allows a thread in a process to block other threads in the same process. The `mutex` object allows a thread in any process to block threads in the same process or in other processes. Because a `mutex` has systemwide scope, it is a more expensive object to use and should only be used when cross-process locking is required.

Visual Basic includes the `SyncLock` statement, which is a shortcut to access a monitor object. While it is possible to directly create and use a `System.Threading.Monitor` object, it is far simpler to just use the `SyncLock` statement (briefly mentioned in the `ArrayList` object discussion), so that is what we'll do here.

Exclusive locks can be used to protect shared data so only one thread at a time can access the data. They can also be used to ensure that only one thread at a time can run a specific bit of code. This exclusive bit of code is called a *critical section*. While critical sections are an important concept in computer science, it is far more common to use exclusive locks to protect shared data, and that's what we'll focus on in this chapter.

You can use an exclusive lock to lock virtually any shared data. As an example, we can change our code to use the `SyncLock` statement instead of using a synchronized `ArrayList`.

Change the declaration of the `ArrayList` in the `DoWork` method so it is global to the form, and it is no longer synchronized:

```
    Private results As New ArrayList
```

This means that we're responsible for managing all synchronization ourselves. First, in the DoWork method, we need to protect all access to the results variable:

```
If isPrime Then
  Dim numberOfResults As Integer
  SyncLock results.SyncRoot
    results.Add(count)
    numberOfResults = results.Count
  End SyncLock
  If numberofresults >= 10 Then
    BackgroundWorker1.ReportProgress( _
      CInt((count - mMin) / (mMax - mMin) * 100), results)
  End If
End If
```

Notice how the code has changed so both the Add and Count method calls are contained within a SyncLock block. This ensures that no other thread can be interacting with the ArrayList while we make these calls.

The SyncLock statement acts against an object. In this case results.SyncRoot.

> *The trick to making this work is to ensure that all code throughout the application wraps any access to* results *within the* SyncLock *statement. If any code doesn't follow this protocol, there will be conflicts between threads!*

Because SyncLock acts against a specific object, we can have many active SyncLock statements, each working against a different object:

```
SyncLock obj1
  ' blocks against obj1
End SyncLock

SyncLock obj2
  ' blocks against obj2
End SyncLock
```

Note that neither obj1 nor obj2 are altered or affected by this at all. The only thing we're saying here is that while we're within a SyncLock obj1 code block, any other thread attempting to execute a SyncLock obj1 statement will be blocked until we've executed the End SyncLock statement.

Next we need to change the UI update code in the ProgressChanged method:

```
ProgressBar1.Value = e.ProgressPercentage
If e.UserState IsNot Nothing Then
  Dim result As ArrayList = CType(e.UserState, ArrayList)
  SyncLock result
    For index As Integer = ListBox1.Items.Count To result.Count - 1
      ListBox1.Items.Add(result(index))
    Next
  End SyncLock
End If
```

Again, notice how our interaction with the ArrayList is contained within a SyncLock block.

While this version of the code will operate just fine, notice how slow it is. In fact, you can pretty much stall out the whole processing by continually moving or resizing the window while it runs. This is because the UI thread is blocking the background thread via the `SyncLock` call, and if the UI thread is totally busy moving or resizing the window, then the background thread can be entirely blocked during that time as well.

Reader–Writer Locks

While exclusive locks are an easy way to protect shared data, they are not always the most efficient. In many cases, our application will contain some code that is updating shared data, and other code that is only reading from shared data. Some applications do a great deal of data reading, and only periodic data changes.

Since reading data doesn't change anything, there's nothing wrong with having multiple threads read data at the same time, as long as we can ensure that no threads are *updating* data while we're trying to read. Also, we typically only want one thread updating at a time.

What we have then is a scenario where we want to allow many concurrent readers, but if the data is to be changed, then one thread must temporarily gain exclusive access to the shared memory. This is the purpose behind the `ReaderWriterLock` object.

Using a `ReaderWriterLock`, we can request either a read lock or a write lock. If we obtain a read lock, we can safely read the data. Other threads can simultaneously also obtain read locks and can safely read the data.

Before we can update data, we must obtain a write lock. When we request a write lock, any other threads requesting either a read or write lock will be blocked. If there are any outstanding read or write locks in progress, we'll be blocked until they are released. Once there are no outstanding locks (read or write), we'll be granted the write lock. No other locks are granted until we release the write lock, so our write lock is an exclusive lock.

Once we release the write lock, any pending requests for other locks are granted, allowing either another single writer to access the data, or allowing multiple readers to simultaneously access the data. We can adapt our sample code to use a `System.Threading.ReaderWriterLock` object. Start by using the code we just created based on the `SyncLock` statement with a `Queue` object as shared data.

First, we need to create an instance of the `ReaderWriterLock` in a form-wide variable:

```
  ' lock object
Private mRWLock As New System.Threading.ReaderWriterLock
```

Since a `ReaderWriterLock` is just an object, we can have many lock objects in an application if needed. We could use each lock object to protect different bits of shared data.

Then we can change the `DoWork` method to make use of this object instead of the `SyncLock` statement:

```
        If isPrime Then
          Dim numberOfResults As Integer
          mRWLock.AcquireWriterLock(100)
          Try
```

```
      results.Add(count)
    Finally
      mRWLock.ReleaseWriterLock()
    End Try
    mRWLock.AcquireReaderLock(100)
    Try
      numberOfResults = results.Count
    Finally
      mRWLock.ReleaseReaderLock()
    End Try
    If numberOfResults >= 10 Then
      BackgroundWorker1.ReportProgress( _
        CInt((count - mMin) / (mMax - mMin) * 100), results)
    End If
  End If
```

Before we write or alter the data in the `ArrayList`, we need to acquire a writer lock. Before we read any data from the `ArrayList`, we need to acquire a reader lock.

If any thread holds a reader lock, attempts to get a writer lock are blocked. When any thread requests a writer lock, any *other* requests for a reader lock are blocked until after that thread gets (and releases) its writer lock. Also, if any thread has a writer lock, other threads requesting a reader (or writer) lock are blocked until that writer lock is released.

The end result is that there can be only one writer, and while the writer is active, there are no readers. But if no writer is active, there can be many concurrent reader threads running at the same time.

Note that all work done while a lock is held is contained within a `Try..Finally` block. This ensures that the lock is released regardless of any exceptions we might encounter.

It is critical that we always release locks we're holding. Failure to do so may cause your application to become unstable and crash or lock up unexpectedly.

Failure to release a lock will almost certainly block other threads, possibly forever—causing a deadlock situation. The alternate fate is that the other threads will request a lock and will time out, throwing an exception and causing the application to fail. Either way, if we don't release our locks, we'll cause application failure.

We also need to update the code in the `ProgressChanged` method:

```
ProgressBar1.Value = e.ProgressPercentage
If e.UserState IsNot Nothing Then
  Dim result As ArrayList = CType(e.UserState, ArrayList)
  mRWLock.AcquireReaderLock(100)
  Try
    For index As Integer = ListBox1.Items.Count To result.Count - 1
      ListBox1.Items.Add(result(index))
    Next
```

```
        Finally
          mRWLock.ReleaseReaderLock()
        End Try
      End If
```

Again, before reading from `results`, we get a reader lock, releasing it in a `Finally` block once we're done.

This code will run a bit smoother than the previous implementation. However, the UI thread can be kept busy with resizing or moving the window, thus causing it to hold the reader lock and thus preventing the background thread from running since it won't be able to acquire a writer lock.

AutoReset Events

Both `Monitor` (`SyncLock`) and `ReaderWriterLock` objects follow the acquire/release model, where threads are blocked until they can acquire control of the appropriate lock.

We can flip the paradigm by using `AutoResetEvent` and `ManualResetEvent` objects. With these objects, threads voluntarily wait on the event object. While waiting, they are blocked and do no work. When another thread signals (raises) the event, any threads waiting on the event object are released and do work.

Signaling an event object is done by calling the object's `Set` method. To wait on an event object, a thread calls that object's `WaitOne` method. This method blocks the thread until the event object is signaled (the event is raised).

Event objects can be in one of two states: signaled or not signaled. When an event object is signaled, threads waiting on the object are released. If a thread calls `WaitOne` on an event object that is signaled, then the thread isn't blocked, and continues running. However, if a thread calls `WaitOne` on an event object that is not signaled, then the thread is blocked until some other thread calls that object's `Set` method, thus signaling the event.

`AutoResetEvent` objects automatically reset themselves to the not signaled state as soon as any thread calls the `WaitOne` method. In other words, if an `AutoResetEvent` is not signaled and a thread calls `WaitOne`, then that thread will be blocked. Another thread can then call the `Set` method, thus signaling the event. This both releases the waiting thread and immediately resets the `AutoResetEvent` object to its not signaled state.

We can use an `AutoResetEvent` object to coordinate the use of shared data between threads. Change the `ReaderWriterLock` declaration to declare an `AutoResetEvent` instead:

```
    Dim mWait As New System.Threading.AutoResetEvent(False)
```

By passing `False` to the constructor, we are telling the event object to start out in its not signaled state. Were we to pass `True`, it would start out in the signaled state, and the first thread to call `WaitOne` would *not* be blocked, but would trigger the event object to automatically reset its state to not signaled.

Next we can update `DoWork` to use the event object. In order to ensure that both the primary and background thread don't simultaneously access the `ArrayList` object, we'll use the `AutoResetEvent` object to block the background thread until the UI thread is done with the `ArrayList`:

```
If isPrime Then
  Dim numberOfResults As Integer
  results.Add(count)
  numberOfResults = results.Count
  If numberOfResults >= 10 Then
    BackgroundWorker1.ReportProgress( _
      CInt((count - mMin) / (mMax - mMin) * 100), results)
    mWait.WaitOne()
  End If
End If
```

This code is much simpler than using the `ReaderWriterLock`. In this case, the background thread assumes it has exclusive access to the `ArrayList` until the `ReportProgress` method is called to invoke the primary thread to update the UI. When that occurs, the background thread calls the `WaitOne` method so it is blocked until released by the primary thread.

In the UI update code, we need to change the code to release the background thread:

```
ProgressBar1.Value = e.ProgressPercentage
If e.UserState IsNot Nothing Then
  Dim result As ArrayList = CType(e.UserState, ArrayList)
  For index As Integer = ListBox1.Items.Count To result.Count - 1
    ListBox1.Items.Add(result(index))
  Next
  mWait.Set()
End If
```

This is done by calling the `Set` method on the `AutoResetEvent` object, thus setting it to its signaled state. This releases the background thread so it can continue to work. Notice that the `Set` method isn't called until after the primary thread is completely done working with the `ArrayList` object.

As with our previous examples, if you continually move or resize the form, the UI thread will become so busy it won't ever release the background thread.

ManualReset Events

A `ManualResetEvent` object is very similar to the `AutoResetEvent` we just used. The difference is that with a `ManualResetEvent` object we are in total control over whether the event object is set to its signaled or not signaled state. The state of the event object is never altered automatically.

This means that we can manually call the `Reset` method rather than relying on it to occur automatically. The end result is that we have more control over the process and can potentially gain some efficiencies.

To see how this works, change the declaration to create a `ManualResetEvent`:

```
  ' wait object
Dim mWait As New System.Threading.ManualResetEvent(True)
```

Notice that we're constructing it with a `True` parameter. This means that the object will be in its signaled state to start with. Until it is reset to a nonsignaled state, `WaitOne` calls won't block on this object.

Then change the `DoWork` method as follows:

```
    If isPrime Then
      mWait.WaitOne()
      Dim numberOfResults As Integer
      results.Add(count)
      numberOfResults = results.Count
      If numberOfResults >= 10 Then
        mWait.Reset()
        BackgroundWorker1.ReportProgress( _
          CInt((count - mMin) / (mMax - mMin) * 100), results)
      End If
    End If
```

This is quite different from the previous code. Before interacting with the `ArrayList` object, the code calls `WaitOne`. This will cause it to block if the primary thread is active. Remember that to start with, the lock object is signaled, so initially the `WaitOne` call will *not* block.

Then, before transferring control to the primary thread to update the UI, we call `mWait.Reset`. The `Reset` event sets the lock object to its nonsignaled state. Until its `Set` method is called, any `WaitOne` methods will block.

No changes are required to the UI update code. It already calls the `Set` method when it is done interacting with the `ArrayList`.

The end result is that the background thread can continue to search for prime numbers while the UI is being updated. The only time the background thread will block is if it finds a prime number before the UI is done with its update process.

Summary

This chapter took a fairly involved look at the subject of threading in .NET and how Visual Basic developers now have access to a rich set of threading functionality.

Proper implementation of multithreaded code is very difficult, and proving that multithreaded code will always run as expected requires careful code walkthroughs, as it can't be proven through testing. Due to this, it is best to avoid the use of multithreading when possible.

However, multithreading can be a useful way to run lengthy tasks in the background, while continuing to provide the user with an interactive experience. If using multithreading, try to avoid using shared data, and instead relay data between the UI and background threads using messaging techniques as shown in this chapter.

If you must share data between multiple threads, make sure to use appropriate synchronization primitives to ensure only one thread interacts with the data at any given time. Beware the performance implications of using synchronization objects, and design carefully to avoid deadlocks.

Threading can be useful in specialized situations, and its use should be limited whenever possible.

23

XML Web Services

This chapter starts with a short history of multitier architecture and network operating systems, a discussion of the early days of the network-as-the-computer, and a discussion of the future. (The reason for this diversion is to understand the rationale behind *Web Services*.)

Next, the chapter looks at a sample Web Service, and walks through making it accessible to the Internet and accessing it from a client application — both with the Visual Studio IDE and using command-line tools. From there, the chapter moves on to a key feature of Web Services, the *Service Repository*, *discovery*, and *Universal Description, Discovery, and Integration* (UDDI), features that allow remote programmers to correctly access Web Services.

Finally, the chapter delves into more in-depth topics during the discussion of the four namespaces found in the .NET Framework class library (`System.Web.Services`, `System.Web.Description`, `System.Web.Services.Discovery`, and `System.Web.Services.Protocols`) that deal with Web Services and how to access them with Visual Basic 2005. Moving on, the chapter discusses serious topics, such as security, transactions, and the downsides of any distributed architecture (including Web Services), followed by a short discussion of where you go from here and how you get there.

Introduction to Web Services

A Web Service is a means of exposing application logic or data via standard protocols such as XML, or more specifically — SOAP (*Simple Object Access Protocol*). A Web Service comprises one or more functions, packaged together for use in a common framework throughout a network. This is shown in Figure 23-1, where Web Services provide access to information through standard Internet Protocols. By using a WSDL (Web Services Description Language) contract, consumers of the Web Service can learn the structure of the data the Web Service provides as well as all the details on how to actually consume it.

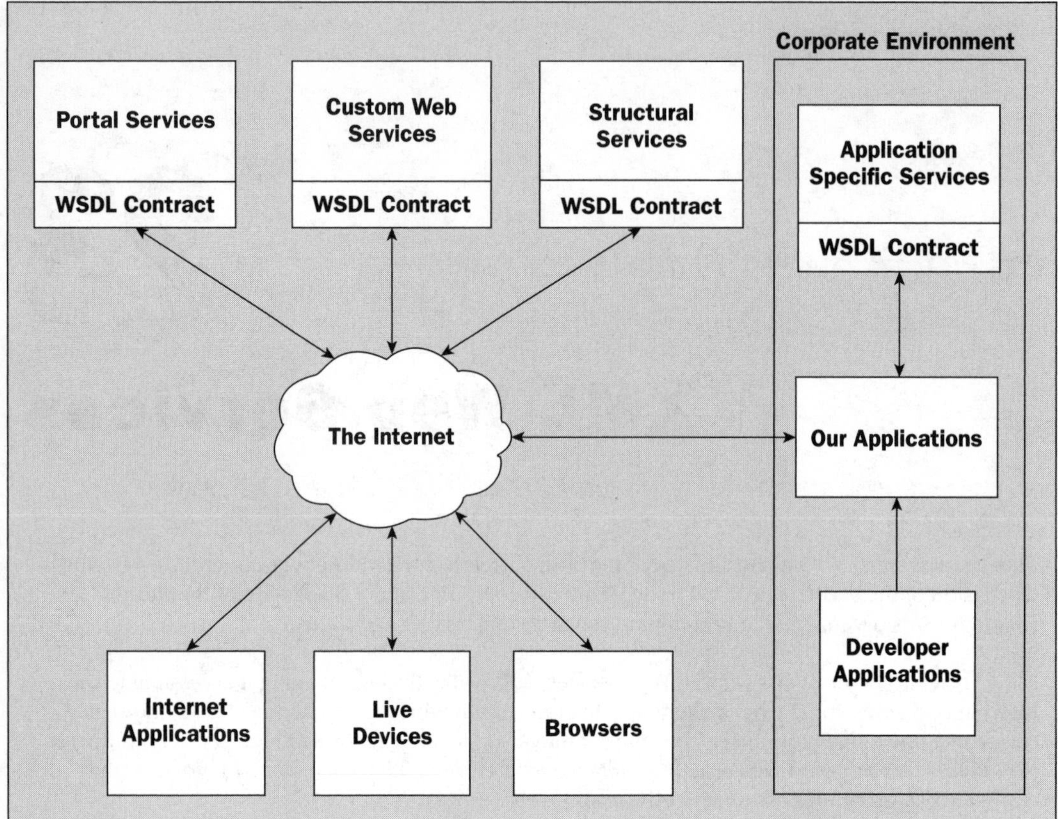

Figure 23-1

This simple concept provides for a very wide variety of potential uses by developers of Internet and enterprise applications alike, as shown in Figure 23-1.

Web Services are going to be the heart of the next generation of systems architecture because they are

- **Architecture neutral** — Web Services don't depend on a proprietary wire format, schema description, or discovery standard.
- **Ubiquitous** — Any service that supports the standards can support the service.
- **Simple** — Creating Web Services is easy, quick, and can be free. The data schema is human readable. Any language can participate.
- **Interoperable** — Since the Web Services all speak the same standards, they can all speak to one another.

In basic terms, a Web Service is an object with an XML document describing all of the methods, properties, and events sitting between the code and the caller. Any body of code written in just about any programming language can be described with this XML document, and then any application that understands

SOAP can access the object. That's because the parameters you'd type after the function name are passed via XML to the Web Service and because SOAP is an open standard.

Microsoft has put a wrapper around all of the XML schemas that support Web Services (including SOAP and WSDL), so they look like .NET or COM objects. Next, we'll talk about how the world views a Web Service, then how Microsoft views Web Services.

Early Architectural Designs

An understanding of the history of the search for a decent *Remote Method Invocation* (RMI) protocol is imperative to your understanding of why Web Services are so important. Each of the RMI systems created before Web Services solved a particular set of problems, and you will see how Web Services represent the next evolution of these ideas and cross-platform boundaries to solve the problems that these other technologies tried to address.

The Network Angle

Throughout the history of computing, the networking operations were largely handled by the operating system. UNIX, the networking host of early computing, featured a body of shell operations that gave remarkable user control over the operations of the network. Personal computing was slower to catch up: Microsoft and Apple software didn't inherently support networking protocols until the mid-1990s. Third-party add-ons by Novell and Banyan were available earlier, but they were only an adjunct to the operating system. The concept of the network being the computer didn't fully infiltrate the development community until the expansion of the World Wide Web.

Application Development

Let's break away from networking for a minute and look at how application development progressed through this time. Early time-sharing operation systems allowed several people to use the same application with its built-in data. These single-tier systems didn't allow for growth in the system size, and data redundancy became the standard, with nightly batch jobs synchronizing the data becoming commonplace through the seventies and early eighties.

Eventually, the opportunity presented by networks became the overriding factor in systems development, and enterprise network developers began offering the loosely termed *Object Request Brokers* (ORBs) on their systems: Microsoft's Transaction Server (MTS), *Common Object Request Broker Architecture* (CORBA), and the like. These ORBs allowed for the separation of the user interface from the business logic using tightly coupled method pooling. This three-tier architecture brings you to the present in development terms, so let's step back for a second and let networking catch up.

Merging the Two with the Web

The HTTP protocol was born in 1990. There had been several other information delivery protocols before, such as Gopher, but what made HTTP different were the extensibility of the related language, HTML, and the flexibility of the transport layer, TCP/IP. Suddenly, movement of many formats of data was possible in a stateless, distributed way. Software-as-a-service was on its way.

Over the next decade, low-level protocols supported by network systems and the Internet became a staple in applications, with SMTP and FTP providing file and information transfer among distributed servers. *Remote procedure calls* (RPC) took things to the next level, but were platform-specific, with UNIX implementations in CORBA and Microsoft's *Distributed COM* (DCOM) leading the pack.

Enterprise development took a clue from the emerging technologies in wide area network (WAN) networking and personal computing, and development for these large-scale business systems began to mature. As usage of networks grew, developers began to solve problems of scalability, reliability, and adaptability, with the traditional flat-format programming model. Multitier development began to spread the data, processing, and user interface of applications over several machines connected by local area networks.

This made applications more scalable and reliable by allowing for growth and providing redundancy. Gradually, vendor compliance and the Java programming language provided adaptability, allowing the applications to run in a variety of circumstances on a variety of platforms.

However, there was a dichotomy between the capabilities of the network and the features of the programming environment. Specifically, after the introduction of XML, there still existed no "killer app" using its power. XML is a subset of Standard Generalized Markup Language (SGML), an international standard that describes the relationship between a document's content and its structure. It enables developers to create their own tags for hierarchical data transport in an HTML-like format. With HTTP as a transport and SOAP as a protocol, there still needed to be an interoperable, ubiquitous, simple, broadly supported system for the execution of business logic throughout the world of Internet application development.

The Foundations of Web Services

The hunt began with a look at the existing protocols. As has been the case for years, the Microsoft versus Sun Alliance debate was heating up among RPC programmers. CORBA versus DCOM was a source of continuing argument for developers using those platforms for distributed object development. After Sun added Remote Method Invocation to Java with Java-RMI, there were three distributed object protocols that fit none of the requirements.

Because DCOM and RMI are manufacturer-specific, it makes sense to start with those. CORBA is centrally managed by the Object Management Group, so it is a special case and should be considered separately.

RMI and DCOM provide distributed object invocation for their respective platforms — extremely important in this era of distributed networks. Both allow for the enterprise-wide reuse of existing functionality, which dramatically reduces cost and time-to-market. Both provide encapsulated object methodology, preventing changes to one set of business logic from affecting another. Finally, similar to ORB-managed objects, maintenance and client weight are reduced by the simple fact that applications using distributed objects are by nature multitier.

DCOM

DCOM's best feature is the fact that it is based on COM, surely one of the most prevalent desktop object models in use today. COM components are shielded from one another, and calls between them are so well defined by the OS-specific languages that there is practically no overhead to the methods. Each

COM object is instantiated in its own space, with the necessary security and protocol providers. If an object in one process needs to call an object in another process, COM handles the exchange by intercepting the call and forwarding it through one of the network protocols.

When you use DCOM, all you are doing is making the wire a bit longer. With Windows NT4, Microsoft added the TCP/IP protocol to the COM network architecture and essentially made DCOM Internet-savvy. Aside from the setup on the client and server, the interobject calls are transparent to the client, and even to the programmer.

Any Microsoft programmer can tell you, though, that DCOM has its problems. First, there is a customer wire transport function, so most firewalls will not allow DCOM calls to get through, even though they are by nature quite benign. There is no way to query DCOM about the methods and properties available, unless you have the opportunity to get the source code or request the remote component locally. In addition, there is no standard data transfer protocol (though that is less of a problem since DCOM is mostly for Microsoft networks).

Remote Method Invocation in Java

RMI is Sun's answer to DCOM. Java relies on a really neat, but very proprietary, protocol called Java Object Serialization, which protects objects marshaled as a stream. The client and server both need to be constructed in Java for this to work, but it simplifies remote method invocation even more, because Java doesn't care if the serialization takes place on one machine or across a continent. Similarly to DCOM, RMI allows the object developer to define an interface for remote access to certain methods.

CORBA

CORBA uses Internet Inter-ORB Protocol to provide remote method invocation. It is remarkably similar to Java Object Serialization in this regard. Since it is only a specification, though, it is supported by a number of languages on diverse operating systems. With CORBA, the ORB does all the work, such as finding the pointer to the parent, instantiating it so that it can receive remote requests, carrying messages back and forth, and disputing arbitration and trash collecting. The CORBA objects use specially designed sub-ORB objects called Basic or Portable Object Adapters to communicate with remote ORBs, allowing developers more leeway in code reuse.

At first sight, it seems CORBA is your ace in the hole. There is only one problem — it doesn't really work that way. CORBA suffers from the same thing the Web browsers do — poor implementations of the standards, causing lack of interoperability between Object Request Brokers. With IE and Netscape, a little differential in the way the pages display is written off as cosmetic. If there is a problem with the CORBA standard though, it is a *real* problem. Not just looks are affected, but network interactions too, as if there were 15 different implementations of HTTP.

The Problems

The principal problem of the DCOM/CORBA/RMI methods is the complexity of the implementation. The transfer protocol of each of these is based on manufacturers' standards, generally preventing interoperability. In essence, the left hand has to know what the right hand is doing. This prevents a company using DCOM from communicating with a company using CORBA, emphasizing platform as a reason for doing business with one another.

First, there's the problem of wire format. Each of these three methods uses an OS-specific wire format that encompasses information only supplied by the operating system in question. The problem with this is that two diverse machines cannot usually share information. The benefit is security; since the client and server can make assumptions about the availability of functionality, data security can be managed with API calls to the operating system.

The second problem is the number of issues associated with describing the format of the protocol. Apart from the actual transport layer, there must be a schema or layout for the data that moves back and forth. Each of the three contemporary protocols makes great assumptions between the client and server. DCOM, for instance, provides ADO/RDS for data transport, whereas RMI has JDBC. While you can endlessly argue the benefits of one over the other, at least agree on the fact that they don't play well together.

The third problem is how to know where to find broadly available services, even within your own network. We've all faced the problem of having to call up the COM+ MMC panel so that we could remember how to spell this component or that method. When the method is resident on a server 10 buildings over and we don't have access to the MMC console, the next step is digging through the text documentation, if there is any.

The Other Players

On a path to providing these services, we stumble across a few other technologies. While *Java Applets* and Microsoft's *client-side ActiveX* aren't technically distributed object invocations, they do provide distributed computing and provide important lessons. Fortunately, we can describe both in the same section since they are largely the same, with different operating systems as their backbone.

Applets and client-side ActiveX are both attempts to use the HTTP protocol to send thick clients to the end user. In a circumstance where a user can provide a platform previously prepared to maintain a thicker-than-HTML client base to a precompiled binary, the ActiveX and Applet protocols pass small applications to the end user, usually running a Web browser. These applications are still managed by their servers, at least loosely, and usually provide custom data transmission, utilizing the power of the client to manage the information distributed, as well as display it.

This concept was taken to the extreme with *Distributed Applet-Based Massively Parallel Processing*, a strategy that used the power of the Internet to complete processor-intense tasks such as 3-D rendering or massive economic models with a small application installed on the user's computer. If you view the Internet as a massive collection of parallel processors, sitting mostly unused, you have the right idea. An example of this type of processing is provided by United Devices (`www.ud.com`).

What you learned here is that HTTP can provide distributed computing. The problem you discovered is that the tightly coupled connection between the client and server had to go, given the nature of today's large enterprises. The HTTP angle did show developers that using an industry recognized transport method did solve problem number one, that is wire format. Using HTTP meant that no matter what the network, the object could communicate. The client still had to know a lot about the service being sent, but the network didn't.

The goal is *Distributed Object Invocation Meets the World Wide Web*. The problems are wire format, protocol, and discovery. The solution is a standards-based, loosely coupled method invocation protocol with a huge catalog. Microsoft, IBM, and Ariba set out in 1999 to create just that, and generated the RFC for Web Services.

What All the Foundations Missed

You may notice that in reviewing the majority of the earlier services there has been little mentioned about language. This is because it was a problem that was overlooked by the foundations. Even RMI didn't see the reality that you can't make everyone use the same language, even if it is a great language.

HTTP — A Language-Independent Protocol

What we really need is a language-independent protocol that allows for a standard wire transfer, protocol language, and catalog service. Java and Remote Scripting and ActiveX taught us that HTTP is the wire transfer of choice.

Why is this? What does HTTP do that is so great? First, it is simple. The header added to a communication by HTTP is straightforward enough that a power user can type it at a command prompt if he or she has to. Second, it doesn't require a special data protocol; it just uses ASCII text. Another reason is that HTTP traffic can easily get through firewalls (port 80 is usually open). Finally, it is extensible. Additional headers can be added to the HTTP header for application-specific needs, and intermediary software just ignores it.

XML — Cross-Language Data Markup

Now that we have the standard wire transfer protocol that we know works, we need a language and a transport mechanism. Existing languages don't really have data description functions, aside from the data management object models like ADO. XML fits the bill because it is self-describing. There's no need for the left hand to know what the right hand is doing. An XML file transported over HTTP doesn't need to know the answering system's network protocol or its data description language. The concepts behind XML are so light and open that everyone can agree to support them. In fact, almost everyone has. XML has become the ASCII of the Web.

XML is important to Web Services because it provides a universal format for information to be passed from system to system. We knew that, but Web Services actually uses XML as the object invocation layer, changing the input and output to tightly formatted XML so as to be platform- and language-independent.

SOAP — The Transfer You Need

Enter Simple Object Access Protocol (SOAP), which uses HTTP to package essentially one-way messages from service to service in such a way that business logic can interpolate a request/response pair. In order for your Web page to get the above listing, for instance, a SOAP request would look something like this:

```
POST /Directory HTTP/1.1
Host: Ldap.companyname.com
Content-Type: text/xml; charset="utf-8"
Content-Length: 33
SOAPAction: "Some-URI"\vs

<SOAP-ENV:Envelope
 xmlns:SOAP-ENV="http://schemas.xmlsoap.org/soap/envelope/"
 SOAP-ENV:encodingStyle="http://schemas.xmlsoap.org/soap/encoding/">
 <SOAP-ENV:Body>
   <m:FindPerson xmlns:m="Some-URI">
     <NAME>Gates</NAME>
   </m: FindPerson>
 </SOAP-ENV:Body>
</SOAP-ENV:Envelope>
```

This is an HTTP page request, just like one you'd see for an HTML page except that the `Content-Type` specifies XML, and there is the addition of the `SOAPAction` header. SOAP has made use of the two most powerful parts of HTTP — content neutrality and extensibility. Here is the response statement from the server:

```
HTTP/1.1 200 OK
Content-Type: text/xml;
charset="utf-8"
Content-Length: 66

<SOAP-ENV:Envelope
 xmlns:SOAP-ENV="http://schemas.xmlsoap.org/soap/envelope/"
 SOAP-ENV:encodingStyle="http://schemas.xmlsoap.org/soap/encoding/"/>
  <SOAP-ENV:Body>
    <m:FindPersonResponse xmlns:m="Some-URI">
      <DIRECTORY>Employees
      <PERSON>
        <NAME>Bill Gates</NAME>
        <FUNCTION>Architect
          <TYPE>Web Services</TYPE>
        </FUNCTION>
        <CONTACT>
          <PHONE TYPE=CELL>123-456-7890</PHONE>
          <PHONE TYPE=HOME>555-111-2222</PHONE>
        </CONTACT>
      </PERSON>
      </DIRECTORY>
    </m: FindPersonResponse >
  </SOAP-ENV:Body>
</SOAP-ENV:Envelope>
```

SOAP allows you to send the XML files back and forth among remote methods. It is tightly similar to XML-RPC, a protocol developed by Dave Winer in parallel with the SOAP protocol. Both protocols provide similar structures, but it is the official SOAP protocol that is used by Visual Basic and the entire .NET platform.

SOAP isn't specific to .NET, either. The SOAP Toolkit is another set of tools that Microsoft's Web Services Team provides free of charge. It contains a wonderful WSDL editor, retrofit objects for Windows 2000 and Windows NT4 servers, and more. You can find it at `http://msdn.microsoft.com/webservices`.

Web Services Description Language

A Web Services Description Language (WSDL) document is a set of definitions. Six elements are defined and used by the SOAP protocol: `types`, `message`, `portType`, `binding`, `port`, and `service`. Essentially adding another layer of abstraction, the purpose of WSDL is to isolate remote method invocations from their wire transport and data definition language. Once again, it is a specification, not a language, so it is much easier to get companies to agree to its use.

Because WSDL is just a set of descriptions in XML, it is not so much a protocol as a grammar. Following is the sample service contract for the `HelloWorld` Web Service you'll be building shortly. You will be able to see this file by visiting `http://localhost/HelloWorldExample/Service.asmx?WSDL` using your Web browser after you install the samples:

```
<?xml version="1.0" encoding="utf-8" ?>
<wsdl:definitions xmlns:soap="http://schemas.xmlsoap.org/wsdl/soap/"
 xmlns:tm="http://microsoft.com/wsdl/mime/textMatching/"
 xmlns:soapenc="http://schemas.xmlsoap.org/soap/encoding/"
 xmlns:mime="http://schemas.xmlsoap.org/wsdl/mime/"
 xmlns:tns="http://localhost/webservice" xmlns:s="http://www.w3.org/2001/XMLSchema"
 xmlns:soap12="http://schemas.xmlsoap.org/wsdl/soap12/"
 xmlns:http="http://schemas.xmlsoap.org/wsdl/http/"
 targetNamespace="http://localhost/webservice"
 xmlns:wsdl="http://schemas.xmlsoap.org/wsdl/">
   <wsdl:types>
      <s:schema elementFormDefault="qualified"
       targetNamespace="http://localhost/webservice">
         <s:element name="HelloWorld">
            <s:complexType />
         </s:element>
         <s:element name="HelloWorldResponse">
            <s:complexType>
               <s:sequence>
                  <s:element minOccurs="0" maxOccurs="1" name="HelloWorldResult"
                   type="s:string" />
               </s:sequence>
            </s:complexType>
         </s:element>
      </s:schema>
   </wsdl:types>
   <wsdl:message name="HelloWorldSoapIn">
      <wsdl:part name="parameters" element="tns:HelloWorld" />
   </wsdl:message>
   <wsdl:message name="HelloWorldSoapOut">
      <wsdl:part name="parameters" element="tns:HelloWorldResponse" />
   </wsdl:message>
   <wsdl:portType name="WebServiceSoap">
      <wsdl:operation name="HelloWorld">
         <wsdl:input message="tns:HelloWorldSoapIn" />
         <wsdl:output message="tns:HelloWorldSoapOut" />
      </wsdl:operation>
   </wsdl:portType>
   <wsdl:binding name="WebServiceSoap" type="tns:WebServiceSoap">
      <wsdl:documentation>
         <wsi:Claim conformsTo="http://ws-i.org/profiles/basic/1.0"
          xmlns:wsi="http://ws-i.org/schemas/conformanceClaim/" />
      </wsdl:documentation>
      <soap:binding transport="http://schemas.xmlsoap.org/soap/http"
       style="document" />
      <wsdl:operation name="HelloWorld">
         <soap:operation soapAction="http://localhost/webservice/HelloWorld"
          style="document" />
         <wsdl:input>
            <soap:body use="literal" />
         </wsdl:input>
         <wsdl:output>
            <soap:body use="literal" />
         </wsdl:output>
```

```
         </wsdl:operation>
      </wsdl:binding>
      <wsdl:binding name="WebServiceSoap12" type="tns:WebServiceSoap">
         <soap12:binding transport="http://schemas.xmlsoap.org/soap/http"
          style="document" />
         <wsdl:operation name="HelloWorld">
            <soap12:operation soapAction="http://localhost/webservice/HelloWorld"
             style="document" />
            <wsdl:input>
               <soap12:body use="literal" />
            </wsdl:input>
            <wsdl:output>
               <soap12:body use="literal" />
            </wsdl:output>
         </wsdl:operation>
      </wsdl:binding>
      <wsdl:service name="WebService">
         <wsdl:port name="WebServiceSoap" binding="tns:WebServiceSoap">
            <soap:address location="http://localhost:40718/Reuters/WebService.asmx" />
         </wsdl:port>
         <wsdl:port name="WebServiceSoap12" binding="tns:WebServiceSoap12">
            <soap12:address
             location="http://localhost:40718/Reuters/WebService.asmx" />
         </wsdl:port>
      </wsdl:service>
   </wsdl:definitions>
```

This is what makes it all work. Notice that each of the inputs and outputs of the `HelloWorldResponse` function is defined as an element in the schema. .NET uses this to build library files that understand how best to format the outgoing requests, so no matter what operating system develops the WSDL, as long as it is well formed, any type of application (it doesn't necessarily need to be a .NET application) can consume it with SOAP and .NET.

In fact, IIS with the .NET Framework is set up to use the WSDL to provide a great auto-generated user interface for developers and consumers to check out and test Web Services. After removing the `?wsdl` from the preceding URL, you'll see a very nicely formatted documentation screen for the service. Click the function name, and you'll get the screen shown in the following figure. This is all dynamically generated from the WSDL document, which is dynamically generated from ASP.NET code. Abstraction makes it all work, as shown in Figure 23-2.

The WSDL can also be expanded in order to define your own descriptions. You can use the `Description` property of both the `WebService()` and `WebMethod()` attributes in order to provide more details for this .NET-generated test page for your XML Web Services.

Building a Web Service

Building Web Services with Visual Studio 2005 is *incredibly* easy. Microsoft has made it a cakewalk to put together a new Web Service application and expose methods off that Web Service.

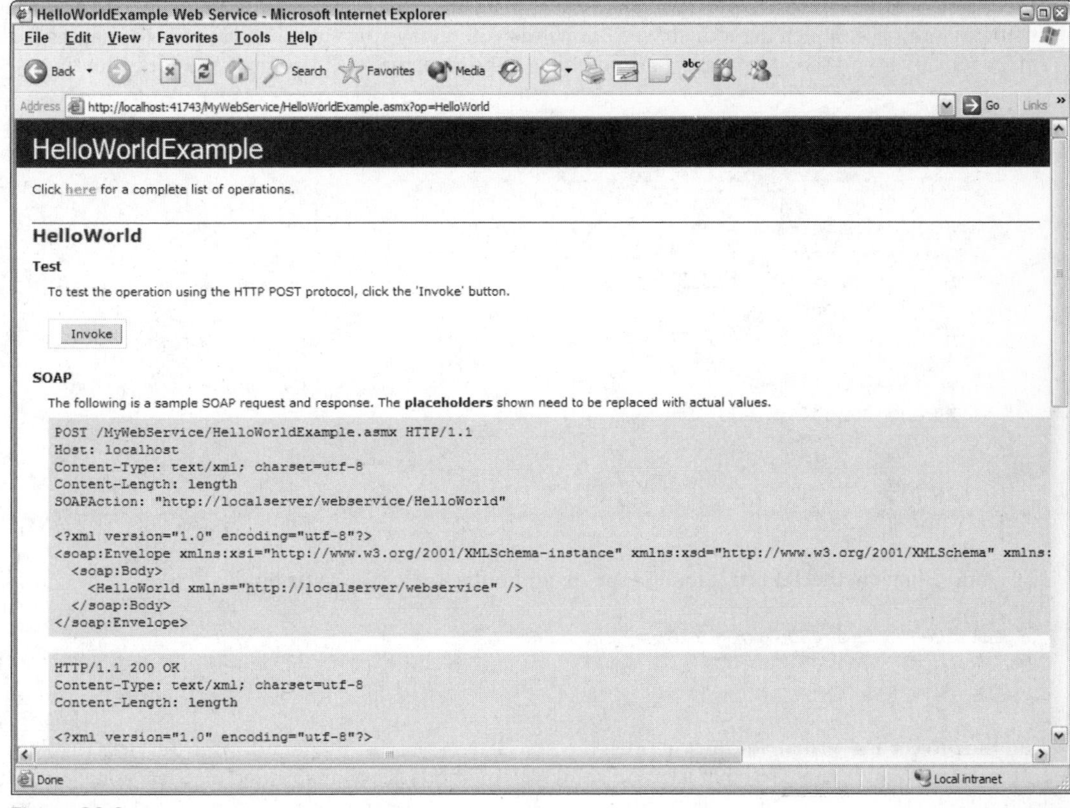

Figure 23-2

To get started, all you need is to create an ASP.NET Web Service application. Find this option by clicking File ⇨ New Web Site in Visual Studio. Then, Visual Studio will ask you for the location of the Web server. Enter this as `C:\WebSites\HelloWordExample`.

Unlike an ASP.NET Web application project, Visual Studio will create an .asmx file rather than an .aspx file. The .asmx file extension is short for Active Server Methods, and its name comes from the fact that it adds methods that will be exposed through the Web Service.

By default, Visual Studio will create the Web Service using the code-behind model for the Web Service page. In addition to the .asmx file, Visual Studio also created a `Service.vb` file and placed this file in the App_Code folder of the project. Instead of focusing on the `Service.asmx` page, the `Service.vb` file opens in the Document window of Visual Studio.

In the Document window, notice that there is a single method on the page and that this method is decorated with the `<WebMethod()>` attribute. This attribute (`System.Web.Services.WebMethodAttribute`) is used to tell ASP.NET to expose this particular method through the Web Service.

Directly before the `WebServiceBinding` attribute, place the `WebService` attribute in code to define a custom namespace, which the industry recommends you always provide. The value of the namespace can be whatever you see fit because it doesn't have to be an actual URL, but just a unique identifier.

```
Imports System.Web
Imports System.Web.Services
Imports System.Web.Services.Protocols

<WebService(Namespace:="http://localhost/helloworldexample")> _
<WebServiceBinding(ConformsTo:=WsiProfiles.BasicProfile1_1)> _
<Global.Microsoft.VisualBasic.CompilerServices.DesignerGenerated()> _
Public Class Service
     Inherits System.Web.Services.WebService

    <WebMethod()> _
    Public Function HelloWorld() As String
        Return "Hello World"
    End Function

End Class
```

Next, add a new method called `GoodbyeWorld`, without a `WebMethod` attribute:

```
Public Function GoodbyeWorld() As String
  Return "Goodbye World"
End Function
```

Run the project and Visual Studio will open the `Service.asmx` file. By default, Web Services display a test interface (see Figure 23-3) that lets you see which methods are available and also lets you execute the methods.

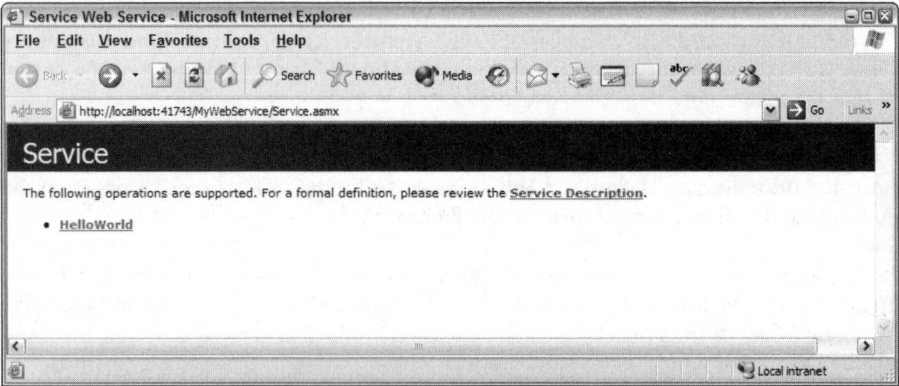

Figure 23-3

Notice that only the `HelloWorld` method is displayed. This is the only method decorated with the `WebMethod` attribute, hence the reason why `GoodbyeWorld` and all of the inherited methods on the `Service` class were not displayed.

Clicking the link gives the option to invoke the method, as shown in Figure 23-4.

Service Web Service - Microsoft Internet Explorer

File Edit View Favorites Tools Help

Back Search Favorites Media

Address http://localhost:41743/MyWebService/Service.asmx?op=HelloWorld Go Links

Service

Click here for a complete list of operations.

HelloWorld

Test

To test the operation using the HTTP POST protocol, click the 'Invoke' button.

Invoke

SOAP

The following is a sample SOAP request and response. The **placeholders** shown need to be replaced with actual values.

```
POST /MyWebService/Service.asmx HTTP/1.1
Host: localhost
Content-Type: text/xml; charset=utf-8
Content-Length: length
SOAPAction: "http://localhost/webservice/HelloWorld"

<?xml version="1.0" encoding="utf-8"?>
<soap:Envelope xmlns:xsi="http://www.w3.org/2001/XMLSchema-instance" xmlns:xsd="http://www.w3.org/2001/XMLSchema" xmlns
  <soap:Body>
    <HelloWorld xmlns="http://localhost/webservice" />
  </soap:Body>
</soap:Envelope>
```

```
HTTP/1.1 200 OK
Content-Type: text/xml; charset=utf-8
Content-Length: length
```

Done Local intranet

Figure 23-4

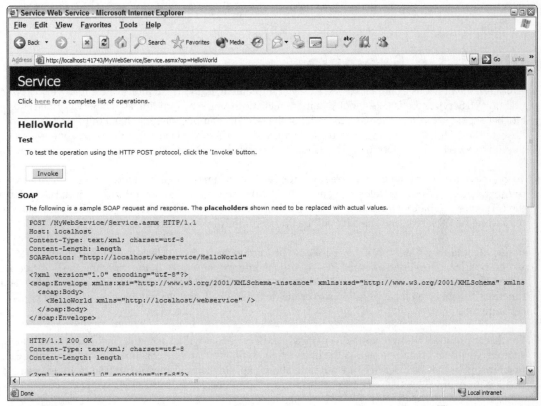

If you do this, the URL `http://localhost:#####/HelloWorldExample/Service.asmx/HelloWorld?` is requested, which happens to be the URL for this specific method (running with the built-in Web server that is provided with Visual Studio). You'll then see the payload of the SOAP document directly in the browser, which contains the results of the call as illustrated in Figure 23-5.

Figure 23-5

That's pretty much all there is to Web Services from an implementation perspective in .NET. .NET deals with all of the plumbing that was discussed in the first part of this chapter (SOAP, WSDL, and so on), which means that all there is to do is add properly decorated methods to the service.

A Realistic Example

Although the previous example was very easy to implement, it doesn't demonstrate a real-world application of Web Services. Let's take a look at a more realistic example by building a Web Service that sends out a richer set of data from a database instead. For the sake of example, imagine that a third-party provider hosts the site. The SQL server is behind a firewall, and the IIS server is in a demilitarized zone — a safe, though exposed, network position. This is illustrated in Figure 23-6.

To get the data from your site to the remote site, call a Web Service on the remote Web server from your intranet. Since the SOAP envelope is sent via HTTP, the firewall will allow it through, and ADO.NET on the IIS server will handle the actual database manipulation. The remote firewall will allow database calls only from the IIS server, and the data will be updated safely because of the security.

In real life, the class file `GetCustomers` would be local to your intranet server, and the database file would be an SQL server on a second PC. Across the Internet, as shown in the diagram, the Web Service would be on an IIS server sitting outside the network firewall. The DLL that actually provides the data functions would be on an application server inside the firewall, and the database would again be on a separate machine.

For this application, though, you will create a Web Service that will expose the Customers table from the sample Northwind database, across the intranet, that will then later be consumed by a Web application. Just remember that Web Services are not only about exposing simple values, but also about exposing a richer dataset of values such as entire tables from a data store (for example, SQL Server).

Start this example by first creating a new Web Service project in Visual Studio called `MyWebService`.

Using Visual Studio 2005 to Build Web Services

The Visual Studio 2005 IDE shows a marked improvement from the add-ins provided for Visual Studio 6 in the SOAP Toolkit. For instance, Web Services are shown as references on a project, rather than in a separate dialog box. The discovery process, discussed later, is used to its fullest, providing much more information to the developer. In short, it is nearly as easy to consume a Web Service with Visual Basic as it is to use DLLs.

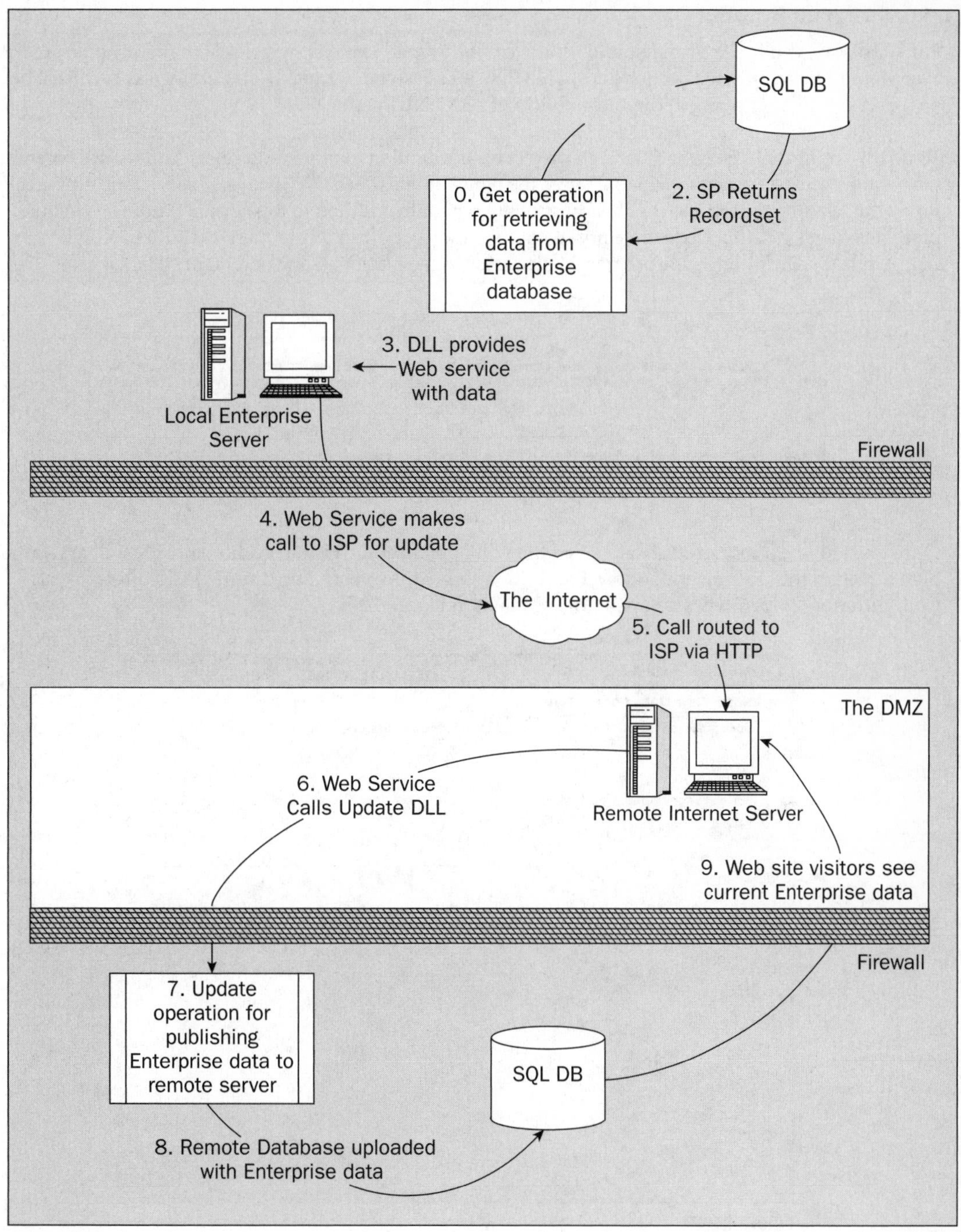
SQL DB
0. Get operation for retrieving data from Enterprise database
2. SP Returns Recordset
3. DLL provides Web service with data
Local Enterprise Server
Firewall
4. Web Service makes call to ISP for update
The Internet
5. Call routed to ISP via HTTP
The DMZ
6. Web Service Calls Update DLL
Remote Internet Server
9. Web site visitors see current Enterprise data
Firewall
7. Update operation for publishing Enterprise data to remote server
SQL DB
8. Remote Database uploaded with Enterprise data

Figure 23-6

Produce a Typed DataSet

For simplicity, you'll use Visual Studio to first create a typed DataSet, which will be returned from the WebMethod that you will later produce. This IDE enables you to quickly and easily create the needed data access without having to dig through lots of ADO.NET code.

To do this, right-click the `MyWebService` project in the Solution Explorer and select Add ➪ Add New Item. One of the options is a new DataSet. Change the name of this file to `MyDataComponent.xsd`. This creates a typed `DataSet` on the fly, and it's already strongly typed. In addition to this, Visual Studio will request to place this file in the App_Code directory of your solution. Confirm this request, because having it in the App_Code directory allows for programmatic access to the DataSet (shown in Figure 23-7).

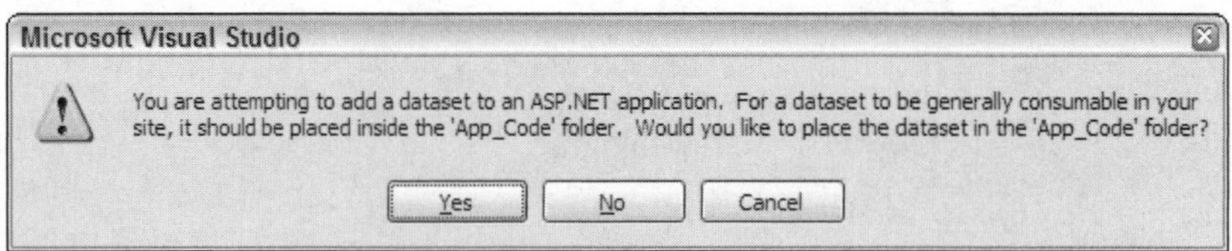

Figure 23-7

Once created, the `MyDataComponent.xsd` file will open itself in Visual Studio. This file will appear as a blue screen in the Document window. In addition to the file opening up, the TableAdapter Configuration Wizard will also open up, as shown in Figure 23-8.

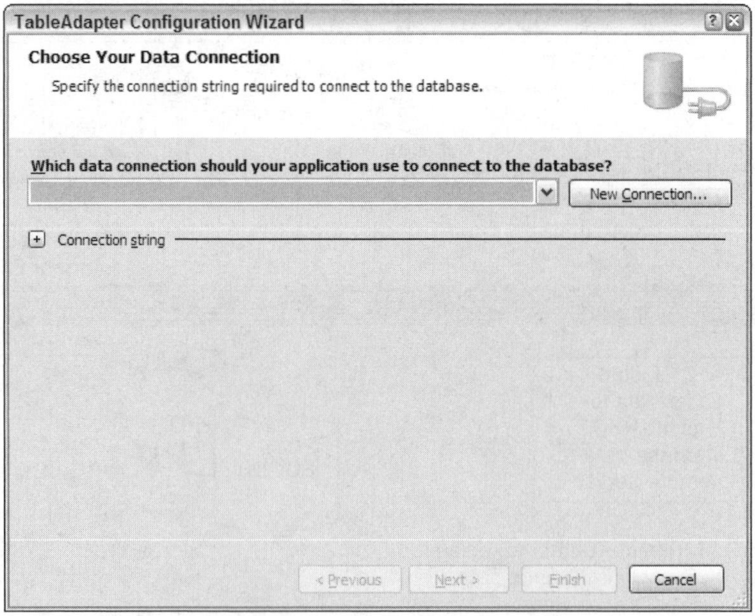

Figure 23-8

The first step in the TableAdapter Configuration Wizard is to establish a data connection. If there is not a connection already in place, create a new connection by clicking on the New Connection button. Using this dialog, make a new connection to the sample Northwind database in Microsoft's SQL Server.

Once the connection is in place, you will be able to see that the wizard will use the `System.Data.SqlClient` provider. Click the Next button, which calls up a dialog that enables you to pick the command type that you are going to want to work with. Typically, the options are working with either direct SQL commands, existing stored procedures, or stored procedures that you can create directly in the wizard. For this example though, choose the first option: Use SQL Statements.

The next page in the wizard asks for the query that you want to use to load the table data. Input the following:

```
SELECT dbo.Customers.* FROM dbo.Customers
```

Clicking the Next button s results in a page that will allow you to pick the methods that the wizard will create. These are the methods used in your Web Service to load data into datasets for transmission. In this case, just accept the default and click the Next button again.

Now you will be at the last page of the wizard. This final page just shows the results of all the actions taken (shown in Figure 23-9).

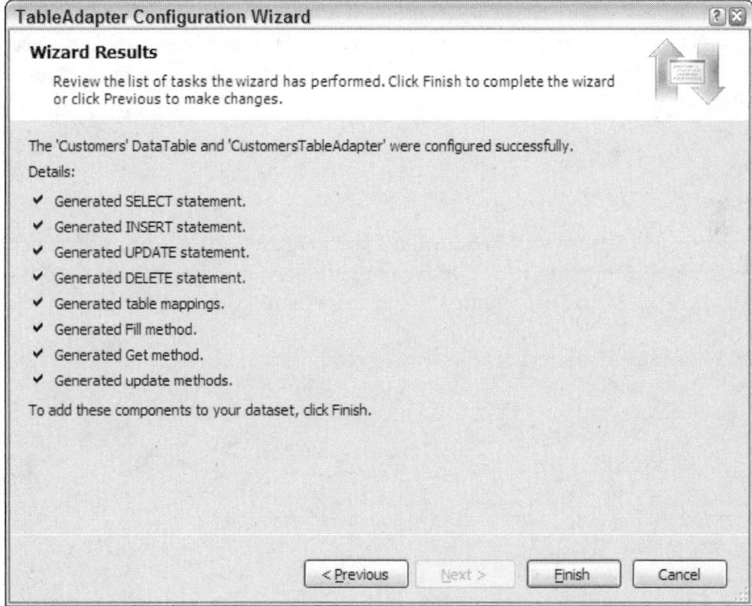

Figure 23-9

Once you click the Finish button, notice that the design surface of the `MyDataComponent.xsd` file changes to reflect the data that comes from the Customers table of the Northwind database. These results are shown in Figure 23-10.

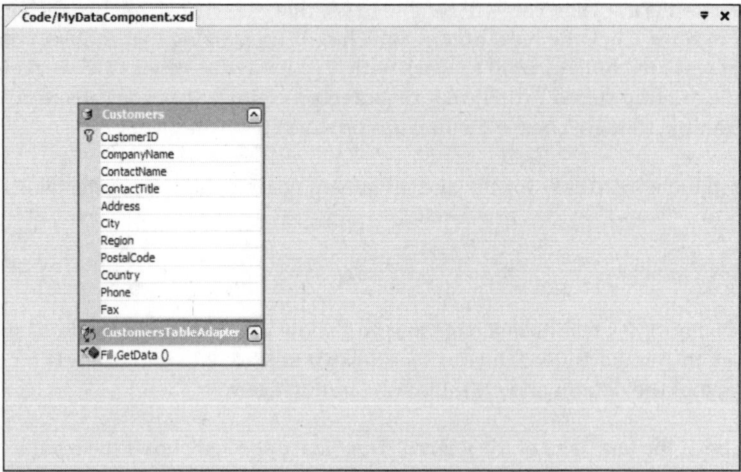

Figure 23-10

The typed dataset is now in place and ready to use by the Web Service. Looking at the results on the design surface of the .xsd file, you can see that indeed the typed `Customers` dataset is in place, but in addition to this there is also a `CustomersTableAdapter` object with `Fill()` and `GetData()` methods in place.

Build the Service

Right-click `Service.asmx` from within Solution Explorer in Visual Studio, and select View Code. Rename the `HelloWorld` function to `GetCustomers`. From here, simply retrieve data from the `CustomersTableAdapter` that was created when you created the .xsd file earlier.

```
<%@ WebService Language="VB" Class="Service" %>

Imports System.Web
Imports System.Web.Services
Imports System.Web.Services.Protocols

<%@ WebService Language="VB" Class="Service" %>
Imports System.Web
Imports System.Web.Services
Imports System.Web.Services.Protocols
<WebService(Namespace:="http://localhost/mywebservice")> _
<WebServiceBinding(ConformsTo:=WsiProfiles.BasicProfile1_1)> _
<Global.Microsoft.VisualBasic.CompilerServices.DesignerGenerated()> _
Public Class Service
Inherits System.Web.Services.WebService
<WebMethod()> _
    Public Function GetCustomers() As MyDataComponent.CustomersDataTable
        Dim da As New MyDataComponentTableAdapters.CustomersTableAdapter()
```

```
            Dim ds As New MyDataComponent.CustomersDataTable()
        da.Fill(ds)
        Return ds
    End Function
End Class
```

Right-click the `Service.asmx` file in Solution Explorer and select View in Browser. If there are no errors, a simple screen listing `GetCustomers` as the sole method of the service appears. Click the Service Description line, and you'll get a screen like that shown earlier in the "Web Services Description Language" section.

Consuming the Service

For this consuming application, provide a Web application called `WSCustomers` by creating a new ASP.NET Web site project with that name. The first step is to create a Web reference to the remote XML Web Service.

Adding a Web Reference

The only bit of magic here is the adding of a Web reference to the project with the Visual Studio IDE. As discussed later, you are really creating a proxy based upon the WSDL file of the service and referencing the proxy in the project, but the IDE makes this all very easy.

To create the proxy that is needed by the consuming application, right-click the `WSCustomers` project in Solution Explorer and select Add Web Reference from the list of options. In this form, enter in the WSDL file of the Web Service that you are wishing to make a reference to. If the Web Service is a .NET Web Service (with an .asmx file extension), simply input the URL of the .asmx file and nothing more because the wizard will know to put `?wsdl` at the end of the input. If you are referencing a Java Web Service, then place the URL for the .wsdl file in this wizard. Enter the URL of your service in the address bar. (This would be at the ISP in your real-life scenario, but if you've been following along it'll be `http://localhost/mywebservice/service.asmx`. If you are using IIS, click on the Web Services in this solution link). The dialog box should appear as displayed in Figure 23-11.

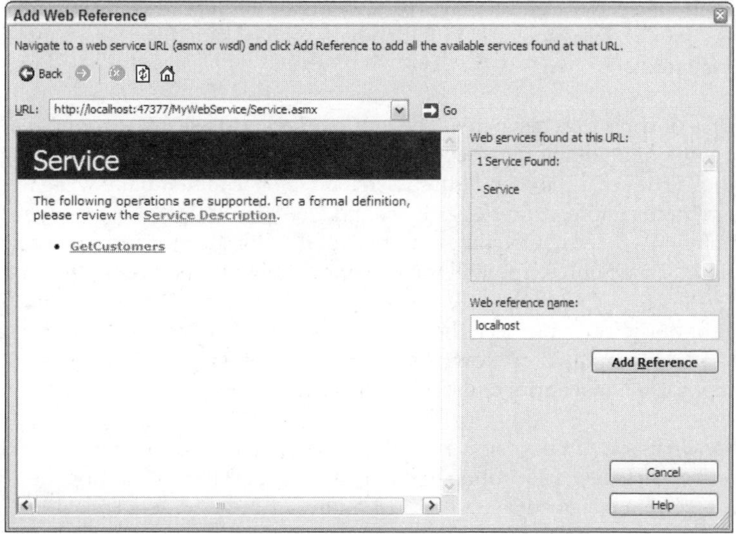

Figure 23-11

The service description page you've just seen when you built your service appears in the left pane of the wizard, with .NET specific information in the right. Click the Add Reference button at the bottom of the window to add this to the project. The service appears in a new folder in Solution Explorer, Web References, as illustrated in Figure 23-12.

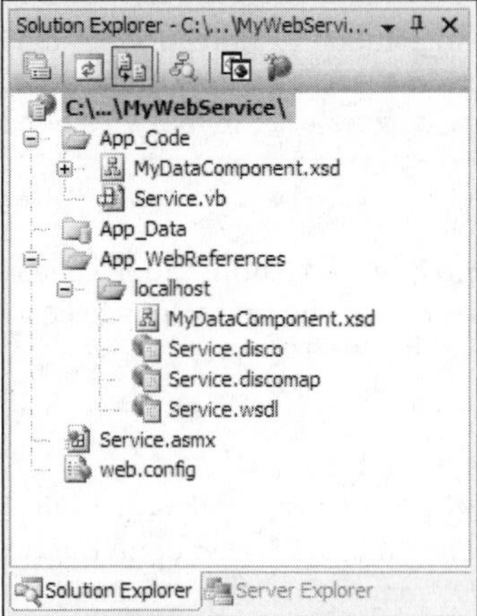

Figure 23-12

Building the Consumer

The COM architecture continually promised "one line of code" to generate great results. Web Services live up to the promise, minus the declarations. Now the only thing left to do is call the referenced Web Service and pass the generated `DataSet`. Compared to the scores of lines of XML needed to pass the `DataSet` in the existing Microsoft technologies, this is a breeze.

The first step of your consuming an .aspx page is simply to make a reference to the proxy that Visual Studio created and then call the `GetCustomers WebMethod` through this instantiated object. The results pulled from the `GetCustomers` method will then be displayed in a `GridView` control, which should be placed on the Web form.

There are a couple of ways to achieve this. The first method is to use an `ObjectDataSource` control, which does the work of invoking the `GetCustomers WebMethod` and then displaying the results in the `GridView` control. (The second method, discussed a bit later, is to manually write the required code.) To work through this example, drop a `GridView` and an `ObjectDataSource` server control onto the design surface of the Web Form. Open the smart tag of the ObjectDataSource control and select the option to Configure Data Source. You will then be presented with the Configure Data Source Wizard.

In the first page of this wizard, uncheck the Show Only Data Components check box and select `localhost.Service` from the drop-down list. Click the Next button to choose the `Select` method that for `ObjectDataSource` control to use (shown in Figure 23-13).

From the drop-down list on this page of the wizard, select `GetData(), returns CustomerDataTable`. Once this is selected, click the Finish button to progress to the next step of binding the `GridView` control to the returned dataset from this `ObjectDataSource` control.

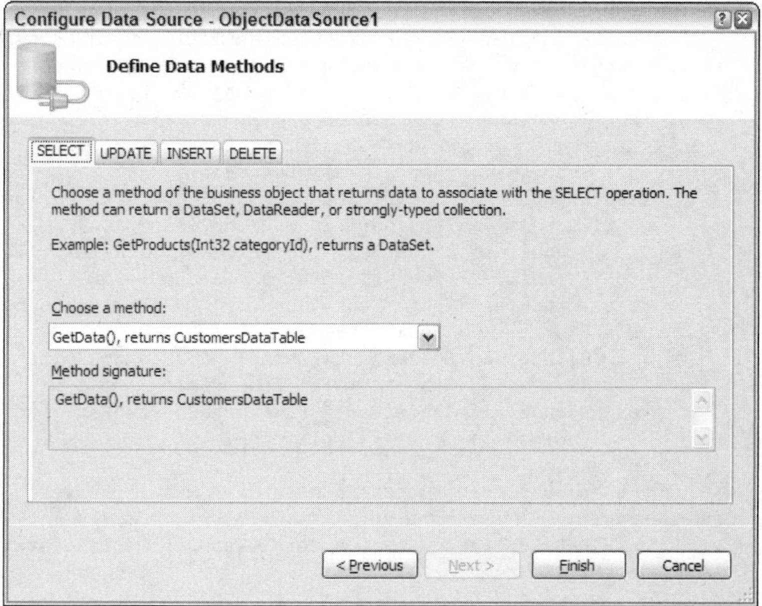

Figure 23-13

Now, focus on the `GridView` control. In configuring this control, open the control's smart tag and select `ObjectDataSource1` as the data source control for this control from the drop-down list. Notice that once you do this, the `GridView` control expands to include all the appropriate columns from the Customers table of the Northwind database.

Then in the same smart tag, enable paging and sorting by selecting the appropriate check boxes. The end code that is generated by Visual Studio is shown here:

```
<%@ Page Language="VB" %>

<html xmlns="http://www.w3.org/1999/xhtml" >
<head runat="server">
    <title>Consuming Application</title>
</head>
<body>
    <form id="form1" runat="server">
    <div>
        <asp:GridView ID="GridView1" Runat="server"
         DataSourceID="ObjectDataSource1" AutoGenerateColumns="False"
         AllowPaging="True" AllowSorting="True">
            <Columns>
                <asp:BoundField HeaderText="CustomerID" DataField="CustomerID"
                 SortExpression="CustomerID"></asp:BoundField>
                <asp:BoundField HeaderText="CompanyName" DataField="CompanyName"
                 SortExpression="CompanyName"></asp:BoundField>
                <asp:BoundField HeaderText="ContactName" DataField="ContactName"
```

```
                    SortExpression="ContactName"></asp:BoundField>
                    <asp:BoundField HeaderText="ContactTitle" DataField="ContactTitle"
                     SortExpression="ContactTitle"></asp:BoundField>
                    <asp:BoundField HeaderText="Address" DataField="Address"
                     SortExpression="Address"></asp:BoundField>
                    <asp:BoundField HeaderText="City" DataField="City"
                     SortExpression="City"></asp:BoundField>
                    <asp:BoundField HeaderText="Region" DataField="Region"
                     SortExpression="Region"></asp:BoundField>
                    <asp:BoundField HeaderText="PostalCode" DataField="PostalCode"
                     SortExpression="PostalCode"></asp:BoundField>
                    <asp:BoundField HeaderText="Country" DataField="Country"
                     SortExpression="Country"></asp:BoundField>
                    <asp:BoundField HeaderText="Phone" DataField="Phone"
                     SortExpression="Phone"></asp:BoundField>
                    <asp:BoundField HeaderText="Fax" DataField="Fax"
                     SortExpression="Fax"></asp:BoundField>
                </Columns>
            <asp:ObjectDataSource ID="ObjectDataSource1" Runat="server"
SelectMethod="GetData"
             TypeName="MyDataComponentTableAdapters.CustomersTableAdapter">
            </asp:ObjectDataSource>
    </div>
    </form>
</body>
</html>
```

Once it is complete, just build and run the page. That's it, there is a table in the Web form with all the data from a remote SQL server that can be paged and sorted — and you didn't have to write *any* code to achieve this functionality! The end page results are shown in Figure 23-14.

Now look at doing the same thing, but instead spend a little time writing some code. This is a good move because it offers more control over the situation (if desired), and it teaches you more about what is going on.

Start by creating a page that only includes a `GridView` control. From here, you get at the data that comes from the Web Service in the `Page_Load` event. This is illustrated in the following example:

```
<%@ Page Language="VB" %>

<script runat="server">
    Sub Page_Load(ByVal sender As Object, ByVal e As System.EventArgs)
        Dim ws As New localhost.Service

        GridView1.DataSource = ws.GetCustomers()
        GridView1.DataBind()
    End Sub
</script>

<html xmlns="http://www.w3.org/1999/xhtml" >
<head runat="server">
```

```
        <title>Consuming Application</title>
    </head>
    <body>
        <form id="form1" runat="server">
        <div>
            <asp:GridView ID="GridView1" Runat="server"
             AllowPaging="True" AllowSorting="True">
            </asp:GridView>
        </div>
        </form>
    </body>
    </html>
```

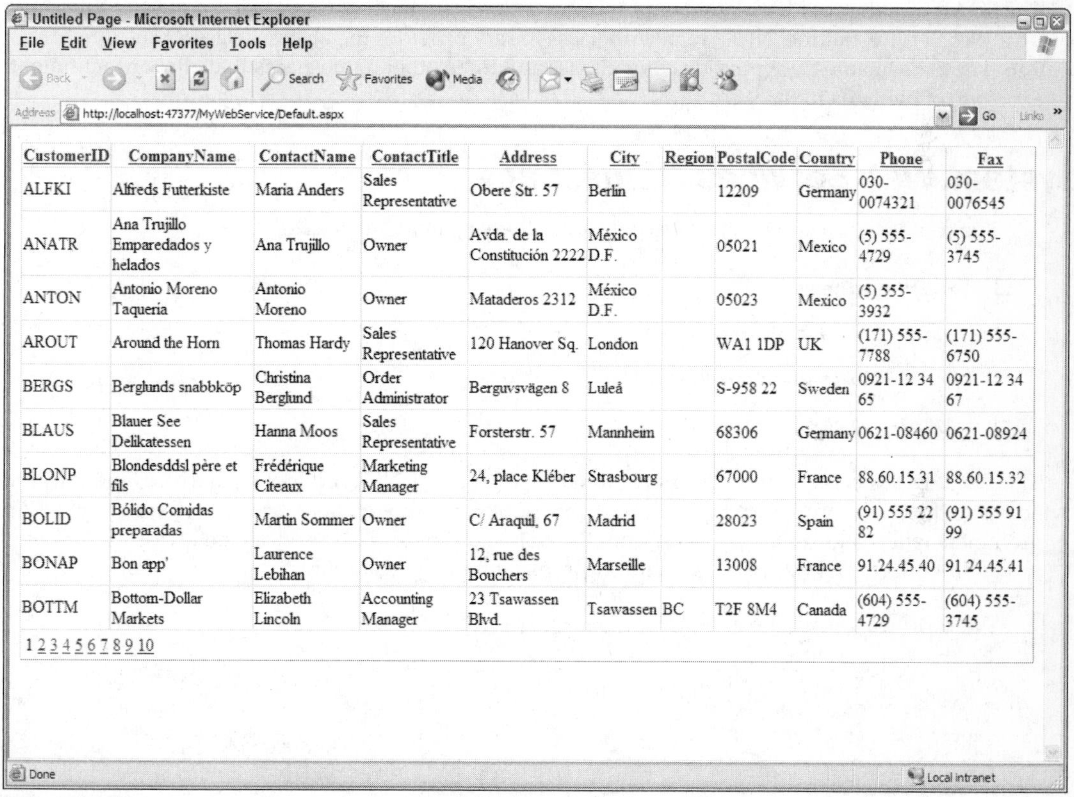

Untitled Page - Microsoft Internet Explorer

File Edit View Favorites Tools Help

Address http://localhost:47377/MyWebService/Default.aspx

CustomerID	CompanyName	ContactName	ContactTitle	Address	City	Region	PostalCode	Country	Phone	Fax
ALFKI	Alfreds Futterkiste	Maria Anders	Sales Representative	Obere Str. 57	Berlin		12209	Germany	030-0074321	030-0076545
ANATR	Ana Trujillo Emparedados y helados	Ana Trujillo	Owner	Avda. de la Constitución 2222	México D.F.		05021	Mexico	(5) 555-4729	(5) 555-3745
ANTON	Antonio Moreno Taquería	Antonio Moreno	Owner	Mataderos 2312	México D.F.		05023	Mexico	(5) 555-3932	
AROUT	Around the Horn	Thomas Hardy	Sales Representative	120 Hanover Sq.	London		WA1 1DP	UK	(171) 555-7788	(171) 555-6750
BERGS	Berglunds snabbköp	Christina Berglund	Order Administrator	Berguvsvägen 8	Luleå		S-958 22	Sweden	0921-12 34 65	0921-12 34 67
BLAUS	Blauer See Delikatessen	Hanna Moos	Sales Representative	Forsterstr. 57	Mannheim		68306	Germany	0621-08460	0621-08924
BLONP	Blondesddsl père et fils	Frédérique Citeaux	Marketing Manager	24, place Kléber	Strasbourg		67000	France	88.60.15.31	88.60.15.32
BOLID	Bólido Comidas preparadas	Martín Sommer	Owner	C/ Araquil, 67	Madrid		28023	Spain	(91) 555 22 82	(91) 555 91 99
BONAP	Bon app'	Laurence Lebihan	Owner	12, rue des Bouchers	Marseille		13008	France	91.24.45.40	91.24.45.41
BOTTM	Bottom-Dollar Markets	Elizabeth Lincoln	Accounting Manager	23 Tsawassen Blvd.	Tsawassen	BC	T2F 8M4	Canada	(604) 555-4729	(604) 555-3745

1 2 3 4 5 6 7 8 9 10

Done | Local intranet

Figure 23-14

The first line of code contained in the `Page_Load` event instantiates the proxy object that was created for you. The next line assigns the `DataSource` property of the `GridView` control to the result set from the `GetCustomers() WebMethod` call. Finally, close everything by calling the `DataBind()` method of the `GridView` control. By compiling and running the XML Web Service, you are able to pull out of the database the entire Customers table from the Northwind database. A returned dataset contains a wealth of information, including:

- An XSD definition of the XML that is contained in the DataSet
- All the customer information from the Customers table of the Northwind database

Then on the consumption side, consumers of this XML Web Service can easily use the XSD definition and the XML that is contained within the DataSet within their own applications. If consumers are then consuming this DataSet into .NET applications, they can easily bind this data to a DataGrid and use it within their applications with minimal lines of code.

Visual Basic and System.Web.Services

The SOAP Toolkit provided a number of wizards to navigate most of the obstacle course required to set up a Web Service, but the .NET Framework class library provides the abstract classes. The System.Web.Services namespace provides four classes and three other namespaces that allow programmatic exposure of methods to the Web.

System.Web.Services Namespace

The System.Web.Services namespace includes these component classes:

- WebService
- WebMethodAttribute
- WebServiceAttribute
- WebServicesBindingAttribute

The WebService class is the base class from which all the ASP.NET services are derived, and it includes access to the public properties for Application, Context, Server, Session, Site, and User. ASP programmers will recognize these objects from the ASP namespace. Web Services can access the IIS object model from the WebService class, including application-level variables:

```
<%@ WebService Language="VB" Class="Util" %>

Imports System.Web
Imports System.Web.Services
Imports System.Web.Services.Protocols

<WebService(Namespace:="http://localhost/util")> _
<WebServiceBinding(ConformsTo:=WsiProfiles.BasicProfile1_1)> _
Public Class Util
    Inherits System.Web.Services.WebService
   <WebMethod(Description = "Application Hit Counter", EnableSession = "False")> _
    Public Function HitCounter() As String

        If (Application("HitCounter") = null) Then
           Application("HitCounter") = 1
        Else
           Application("HitCounter") = Application("HitCounter") + 1
```

```
        End If

        HitCounter = Application("HitCounter")
    End Function

End Class
```

`WebService` is an optional base class, used only if access to ASP.NET objects is desired. The `WebMethodAttribute` class, however, is a necessity if the class needs to be available over the Web.

The `WebServiceAttribute` class is similar to the `WebMethodAttribute` class in that it enables the addition of the description string to an entire class, rather than method by method. We recommend adding it before the previous class declaration:

```
<WebService(Description="Common Server Variables")> _
Public Class ServerVariables
    Inherits System.Web.Services.WebService
```

Instead of using WSDL in the contract to describe these services, the `System.Web.Services` namespace provides programmatic access to these properties. IIS Service Discovery will use these descriptions when queried. This way, we have removed the necessity to struggle with myriad protocols surrounding Service Contract Language and SOAP.

System.Web.Services.Description Namespace

The `System.Web.Services.Description` namespace provides a host of classes that provide total management of the WSDL Descriptions for your Web Service. This object manages every element in the WSDL schema as a class property.

Take this example. In the preceding discussion on the benefits of WSDL description, we mentioned the benefits of being able to query a Web Service about its methods and parameters. The `System.Web.Services.Description` namespace provides methods for the discovery of methods and parameters, gathering the information from the service contract and providing it to the object model in Visual Basic code.

If working on the HTTP GET protocol (as opposed to SOAP, for instance), simply pass in the required `sEmail` parameter through the use of a `querystring`. There are details of this in the Web Service's WSDL description. In the successive `<wsdl:message>` sections, you find all parameter info for all three protocols, including HTTP GET.

```
<wsdl:message name="IsValidEmailHttpGetIn">
   <wsdl:part name="sEmail" type="s:string" />
</wsdl:message>
<wsdl:message name="IsValidEmailHttpGetOut">
   <wsdl:part name="Body" element="tns:boolean" />
</wsdl:message>
```

Invoking this Web Service using HTTP GET, use the following construct:

```
http://localserver/Validate.asmx?sEmail=evjen@yahoo.com
```

It is important to note that HTTP GET is disabled by default because it is deemed a security risk. If you wish to enable HTTP GET for your XML Web Services, then configure it for this in the `web.config` file of your Web Service solution. This is illustrated here:

```
<configuration>
   <system.web>
      <webServices>
         <protocols>
            <add name="HttpGet"/>
         </protocols>
      </webServices>
   </system.web>
</configuration>
```

System.Web.Services.Discovery Namespace

The `System.Web.Services.Discovery` namespace provides access to all of the wonderful features of the .disco files on a dynamic basis. Since Microsoft is currently trying to integrate Web Services as a remoting protocol and is not pushing the public service side as much, you don't see the use of .disco files as often in the Microsoft side of things. Your business partner might be using them, though, so this namespace proves useful. For instance, you can access the `DiscoveryDocument` using the `Discovery` class:

```
Imports System.Web.Services.Discovery

ReadOnly Property DiscoveryDocument(strURL As String) As DiscoveryDocument
   Get
      DiscoveryDocument = DiscoveryClientProtocol.Discover(strURL)
   End Get
End Property
```

Like the `System.Web.Services.Description` namespace, the `System.Web.Services.Discovery` namespace provides many tools to build a .disco document on the fly.

System.Web.Services.Protocols Namespace

All of the wire service problems solved with HTTP and SOAP are handled here in the `System.Web.Services.Protocols` namespace. When handling references to classes also referenced in other Web Services namespaces, the `System.Web.Services.Protocols` namespace proves to be a handy tool. The objects referenced by the `System.Web.Services.Protocols` namespace include (among others):

- Cookies per RFC 2019
- HTML forms
- HTTP request and response
- MIME
- Server
- SOAP, including `SoapException`, the only error-handling mechanism

- URIs and URLs
- XML

The `System.Web.Services.Protocols` namespace is particularly handy for managing the connection type by a client. A consumer of a Web Service can use the HTTP GET or HTTP POST protocol to call a service, as well as the HTTP SOAP protocol. Microsoft's .NET initiative focuses on SOAP as the ultimate means of connecting disparate data sources. The `System.Web.Services.Protocols.SoapDocumentMethodAttribute` class allows the developer to set special attributes of a public method for when a client calls it using SOAP:

```
<%@ WebService Language="VB" Class="Util" %>

Imports System.Web
Imports System.Web.Services
Imports System.Web.Services.Protocols

<WebService(Namespace:="http://localhost/util")> _
<WebServiceBinding(ConformsTo:=WsiProfiles.BasicProfile1_1)> _
<Global.Microsoft.VisualBasic.CompilerServices.DesignerGenerated()> _
 Public Class Util
    Inherits System.Web.Services.WebService

  <SoapDocumentMethod(Action="http://MySoapMethod.org/Sample", _
   RequestNamespace="http://MyNameSpace.org/Request", _
   RequestElementName="GetUserNameRequest", _
   ResponseNamespace="http://MyNameSpace.org/Response", _
   ResponseElementName="GetUserNameResponse") _
   WebMethod(Description="Obtains the User Name")> _
  Public Function GetUserName()
    '...
  End Function
End Class
```

Architecting with Web Services

Web Services impart two remarkable benefits to users—one more obvious, another less so. First, they will replace common binary RPC formats, such as DCOM, CORBA, and RMI. Since these use a proprietary communication protocol, they are significantly less architecturally flexible than Web Services. With appliances utilizing more and more of the Internet, platform-neutrality will be a great advantage. Less obviously but more importantly, Web Services will be used to transfer structured business communications in a secure manner, potentially ending the hold that Sterling has on the Electronic Data Interchange (EDI) market. HTTPS with 128-bit SSL can provide the security necessary for intracompany information transfer. In addition to this, Microsoft has recently (as of this writing) released Web Services Enhancements 2.0 (WSE), which allows you to easily use WS-Security and other advanced protocols to apply credentials, encryption, and digital signing to your SOAP messages in an easy and straightforward manner.

Why Web Services?

So, why Web Services? First, they are remarkably easy to deploy with Visual Basic. The key to remoting with Web Services is the SDL contract—written in the dense WSDL protocol you saw earlier.

IIS 5.0 and 6.0 does that in conjunction with the .NET Framework, analyzing the VB code and dynamically generating the WSDL code for the contract.

Also, Web Services are inherently cross-platform, even if created with Microsoft products. Yes, you've heard this before, but so far this seems to be true. Since the standard XML schemas are centrally managed, and IBM mostly built the WSDL specification, Microsoft seems to have toed the line on this one.

Finally, they best represent where the Internet is going — toward an architecturally neutral collection of appliances, rather than millions of PCs surfing the World Wide Web. Encapsulating code so that you can simply and easily allow cellphones to use your logic is a major boon to developers, even if they don't know it yet.

How This All Fits Together

It is important to note that Web Services are not a feature of the .NET Framework per se. In fact, Web Services run fine on Windows NT4 SP6, with the SOAP Toolkit installed. You can do most anything you are doing here with VB6 and IIS 4.0.

However, the .NET Framework encapsulates the Web Services protocol into objects. It is now an integrated part of the strategy, rather than an add-on. If you are currently working in a VB6 environment, take a look at the SOAP Toolkit (downloadable from MSDN at `http://msdn.microsoft.com/webservices`), and understand that the services you build are available not only to different flavors of Windows, but also to IBM and Sun platforms.

The goal of Web Services is to provide a loosely coupled, ubiquitous, universal information exchange format. Toward that end, SOAP is not the only mechanism for communicating with Web Services — the HTTP GET and HTTP POST protocols are also supported by .NET. Response is via HTTP, just like normal RPCs with SOAP. This allows legacy Web applications to make use of Web Services without the benefit of the .NET Framework.

State Management for XML Web Services

The Internet is *stateless* by nature. Many of the techniques used for managing state in ASP.NET Web applications are the same techniques you can use within the XML Web Services built on the .NET platform. Remember that XML Web Services are part of the ASP.NET model and both application types have the same objects at their disposal.

These sessions can also be run in the same process as the XML Web Service application itself — out of process, using the .NET `StateServer`, or by storing all the sessions within SQL Server.

To use sessions within XML Web Services built on the .NET platform, you actually have to turn on this capability within the `WebMethod` attribute by using the `EnableSession` property. By default, the `EnableSession` property is set to `False`, so to use the `HTTPSessionState` object, you have to set this property to `True`, as shown here:

```
<%@ WebService Language="VB" Class="Service" %>

Imports System.Web
```

```
Imports System.Web.Services
Imports System.Web.Services.Protocols

<WebService(Namespace:="http://localhost/util")> _
<WebServiceBinding(ConformsTo:=WsiProfiles.BasicProfile1_1> _
<Global.Microsoft.VisualBasic.CompilerServices.DesignerGenerated()> _
Public Class Service
    Inherits System.Web.Services.WebService

   <WebMethod(EnableSession:=True)> _
   Public Function SessionCounter() As Integer
      If Session("Counter") Is Nothing Then
         Session("Counter") = 1
      Else
         Session("Counter") = CInt(Session("Counter")) + 1
      End If

      Return CInt(Session("Counter"))
   End Function

End Class
```

The `EnableSession` property goes directly in the parentheses of the `WebMethod` declaration. This property takes a Boolean value and needs to be set to `True` in order to work with the `Session` object.

Using DNS As a Model

How does any computer know where to find a Web page? Every machine doesn't know every location of every page. Rather, there is a big catalog called *DNS* that is replicated by most Internet service providers, which translates domain names (like `yahoo.com`) into IP numbers (like `204.71.200.74`).

The benefit of the DNS system is that it offers a further level of abstraction between the marketing and the wires. It's a lot easier to remember `yahoo.com` than `204.71.200.74`. With Web Services, it becomes even more important, because there is not only a function name but also the parameters to remember.

Three things make up the *Web Service Repository*: a standard format, a language, and a database. You have already seen the language, WSDL. This can be used to lay out the discovery information you need to publicize your Web Service. The format of choice is called *DISCO* (short for DISCOvery of all things). Finally, and most exciting, is the Web Services answer to DNS — *UDDI (Universal Description, Discovery, and Integration)*. Let's talk about DISCO first.

DISCO

One way to enable a repository is to have applications that look for services. To implement this, you drop a DISCO document into the Web Service directory — a file that an application can look for that enables the discovery of the Web Services present in that directory, or on that machine. Alternatively, you can mark each particular service you would like to enable.

Web Service discovery is the process of locating and interrogating Web Service descriptions, which is a preliminary step for accessing a Web Service. It is through the discovery process that Web Service clients learn that a Web Service exists, what its capabilities are, and how to properly interact with it.

Dynamic Discovery with IIS

Admittedly not as fun as it sounds, *dynamic discovery* is Web Services' answer to the `robots.txt` file. Dynamic discovery automatically exposes Web Services beneath a given URL on a Web site. By placing this document at the root of your service's directories, you give a prospective consumer the opportunity to obtain information about all services contained in that directory or subdirectories.

To enable dynamic discovery for your Web Services, create a `<filename>.disco` document at the root of the Web Services directory.

This XML file contains the *excluded* directories within the hierarchy, so that the dynamic discovery process knows where not to go to gather information about Web Services:

```
<?xml version="1.0" ?>
<dynamicDiscovery xmlns="urn:schemas-dynamicdiscovery:disco.2000-03-17">
   <exclude path="_vti_cnf"/>
   <exclude path="_vti_pvt"/>
   <exclude path="_vti_log"/>
   <exclude path="_vti_script"/>
   <exclude path="_vti_txt"/>
</dynamicDiscovery>
```

In order for the dynamic discovery to be noticed by visiting consumers, refer to it in the `<head>` of your default HTML or ASP document:

```
<head>
   <link type='text/xml' rel='alternate' href='Default.disco'/>
   <title></title>
</head>
```

Or, if you have an XML page as your default:

```
<?xml-stylesheet type="text/xml" alternate="yes" href="default.disco" ?>
```

Dynamic discovery is the way to go with IIS; the discovery process is very well tuned. If you work with another Web server, though, or are a hands-on sort, you can roll your own discovery documents for each Web Service.

A *discovery document* is just an XML file with references listed in the `discovery` hierarchy. Within the hierarchy, you can add as many service contracts as you have services and references to other DISCO documents throughout the server:

```
<?xml version="1.0" ?>
<disco:discovery xmlns:disco="http://schemas.xmlsoap.org/disco"
                 xmlns:scl="http://schemas.xmlsoap.org/disco/scl">
  <scl:contractRef ref="http://ServerName/ServiceName.asmx?SDL"/>
  <scl:contractRef ref="http://ServerName/AnotherName.asmx?SDL"/>
  <scl:contractRef ref="http://ServerName/ThirdName.asmx?SDL"/>
  <disco:discoveryRef ref="Folder1/default.disco"/>
  <disco:discoveryRef ref="Folder2/default.disco"/>
  <disco:discoveryRef ref="Folder3/default.disco"/>
</disco:discovery>
```

This is essentially what IIS will do, using dynamic discovery.

The DISCO concept depends on the client knowing where to start. If you don't know that a business offers a particular Web Service, you won't know where to look for a DISCO document. UDDI is all about changing that.

The UDDI Project

The DISCO format allows crawlers to index Web Services just as they index Web sites. The `robots.txt` approach, however, is dependent on the ability of a crawler to locate each Web site and find the location of the service description file on that Web site. The current system relies upon the interlocking nature of Web sites to crawl from site to site — there is no such visible connection between Web Services. This leaves the programmer having to know where to begin looking for a Web Service before he starts.

UDDI (*Universal Description, Discovery, and Integration*) takes an approach that relies upon a distributed registry of businesses and their service descriptions implemented in a common XML format. There is all sorts of helpful information about UDDI at `www.uddi.org`, but we'll give you an introduction to it here and talk about how it relates to Microsoft in general and Visual Basic in particular.

UDDI can be thought of as the Yellow Pages for Web Services. UDDI is a means of defining a standard way to publish and discover information about Web Services, so businesses can provide descriptions of their Web Services in terms of an XML file with white, yellow, and green pages:

- The *white pages* include how and where to find the service.
- The *yellow pages* include ontological classifications and binding information.
- The *green pages* include the technical specification of the service.

In the XML schema for UDDI, this breaks into four elements: `businessEntity`, `businessService`, `bindingElements`, and metadata, or `tModels`. The `tModels` provide additional important technical information that falls outside the `bindingElements` element, but that is necessary for the consumption of the service once it is bound.

You can find the XML schema for this at `www.uddi.org/schema/uddi_1.xsd`, but you don't have to understand it because UDDI provided an API that is built into the .NET Framework, as discussed in the next section. Generally, though, each API function represents a publicly accessible SOAP message used to get or place information about a registry entry. For instance, the `findService` SOAP message lists available services based on the conditions specified in the arguments:

```
<find_service businessKey="uuid_key" generic="1.0" [ maxRows="nn" ]
              xmlns="urn:uddi-org:api" >
  [<findQualifiers/>]
  <name/> | <categoryBag/> | <tModelBag/>
</find_service>
```

The parameters it accepts include `maxRows`, `businessKey`, `findQualifiers`, `name`, `categoryBag`, and `tModelBag`. On success, it returns a `serviceList` as a SOAP response object. On the whole, it's not that much different from the COM world, except that SOAP is entirely an open standard.

Using UDDI

The best thing about UDDI is how easy it is to use. Many of us who started early in the Internet field remember filling out the InterNIC's domain add/change forms, and having our own representative at the NIC to help us when we were stuck. Now, though, the Web handles registration of services—you only need to really have a grasp of the discovery schema if you are going to build a registration site.

In fact, Microsoft has a UDDI mirror if its own at `http://uddi.microsoft.com` where you can register your Web Services, just like adding them to DNS or a search engine. Of course, you'll have to have a Microsoft Passport (another UDDI registered Web Service) to do it, but it is a rather simple task. After registering against your Passport, you enter business and contact information that is stored in your UDDI registry. Then you can add your Web Services.

Where UDDI Is Headed

UDDI is the invisible fourth layer in the stack of protocols that represent Web Services. Like DNS and HTTP, UDDI provides a needed interface between the SOAP messaging and the ubiquity of the service that is so important, but difficult to achieve.

Going forward, UDDI as an organization sees itself being a global provider of discovery services for the business-to-business (B2B) Web Services market, hosted throughout the world. For instance, software companies can build applications that customize themselves based on services information in the UDDI registry on installation. Online marketplaces can back their market sites with UDDI technology to better serve the growing needs of B2B value-added services.

Future services planned by UDDI include the extension of the technology far beyond the specifications in the Open Draft. Eventually, regional and hierarchical searches will be accomplished through simple, effective conventions. The industry's goal is much farther reaching than InterNICs was at the beginning—truly using the lessons learned in the past to shape the future.

Microsoft's commitment to UDDI is apparent from its use within Windows Server 2003. If you have Windows Server 2003 Enterprise Edition, you can enable your server to be a UDDI server, and there is a UDDI database built right in as well.

Security in Web Services

Opening up a procedure call to remoting makes applications vulnerable to accidents, poor end-user implementation, and crackers. Any application design needs to include some level of security. Web Services demand the inclusion of security.

Security problems with Web Services fall into two categories—that of interception and that of unauthorized use. SOAP messages intercepted by crackers potentially expose private information such as account numbers and passwords to the public. Unauthorized use at best costs money and at worst wreaks havoc within a system.

Very few of the concepts discussed here are things we would like to see in the hands of those wearing the black hats. Even the simple validation service handles email addresses—a valuable commodity in this world of "opt in" spamming. If you add Social Security or account numbers to the service, then this becomes even more of a concern. Fortunately, the wire transport of choice—HTTPS—provides a 128-bit solution to these problems.

Also, as mentioned earlier, now by using Microsoft's Web Services Enhancements (WSE) capabilities, you can easily apply security standards such as WS-Security to your SOAP messages.

The Secure Sockets Layer

The Secure Sockets Layer, or SSL, is a protocol consumed by HTTP in the transfer of Internet data from the Web server to browser. On the Web, the process works like this:

1. The user calls a secure Web document, and a unique public key is generated for the client browser, using the server's root certificate.
2. A message, encrypted with the server's public key, is sent from the browser.
3. The server can decrypt the message using its private key.

The protocol in the URI represents how HTTP would appear if it was changed to HTTPS:

```
<address uri="https://aspx.securedomains.com/evjen/Validate.asmx" />
```

Then the service would make an SSL call to the server. Remember that SSL is significantly slower than HTTP, so you will suffer a performance hit. Given the sensitivity of much of the information passing over Web Services, it is probably worth the slowdown.

Directory-Level Security

You also have the option to code security into your applications. This solves different problems from SSL, and, in fact, you may wish to combine the two services for a complete security solution.

Unauthorized access is a potential problem for any remote system, but for Web Services even more so. The open architecture of the system provides crackers with all the information they need to plan an attack. Fortunately, simplicity is often the best defense. Use of the NT security options already on the server is your best bet to defend against unauthorized users.

You can use NTFS permissions for individual directories within an application and require users to provide a valid username and password combination if they wish to access the service.

Web Service security is a large area to cover. For more information, you should refer to the documentation included with the .NET Framework SDK.

The best approach to security is to use SSL and directory-level security together. It is slow, and at times inconvenient, but this is a small price to pay for the heightened level of security. Though this is different from the traditional role-based COM+ security, it is still very effective for running information across the wire.

Other Types of Security

The Windows platform also provides for other forms of security. For instance, the Windows CryptoAPI supplies access to most of the commonly used encryption algorithms—aside from the protocols used in Secure Sockets Layer. Digital certificates (sort of a personal form of SSL `ServerCertificates`) are now rapidly becoming a powerful force in security.

The Downside

There is a downside to any distributed architecture. We've covered most of them in this chapter and suggested workarounds—security, state, speed, and connectivity. Let's go over them once more to help make sure that Web Services are the way to go.

Security

The key to the issue and solution of security problems is the management of client expectations. If Web Services are built securely to begin with, there will be no instances to draw concern or scrutiny. Consider the security of everything you write. It's fairly easy, and the payoff is great.

State

State is less of a problem in a distributed architecture because in Windows DNA, Microsoft has been saying for years that *n*-tier statefulness has to go. Most developers are used to the idea, and if you aren't, then you need to get on the boat with the rest of us. Architect your solutions to be loosely coupled. That's what Web Services are made to do.

Transactions

Web Services are not made for transactional systems. If the Web server at `MyCompany.com` was to access a database at UPS for example, and the connection dropped in the middle, the lock on the database would remain without giving the network system at UPS a chance to solve the problem. Web Services are by nature loosely coupled. They are not designed for tight transactional integration.

A common use of Web Services, communication between differing systems, prompted a number of technology architects to design a number of XML transaction protocols such as 2PC. These packages provide for an understanding between two systems that the network link will remain stable.

Speed and Connectivity

Speed and connectivity are going to be a continuing problem until we have the ubiquitous bandwidth of which George Gilder talks about in his book *Telecosm* (Free Press, 2000). Right now, the majority of Internet devices that could really benefit from Web Services—cellphones, PDAs, and the like—are stuck at the paltry 14,000-bits per second currently supported by most wireless providers.

For application development, this is a concern because when the router goes down, the application goes down. Right now, intranets continue to function when the ISP drops the ISDN. With Web Services running the links to customers and suppliers, that ISDN line becomes the company lifeline. Redundancy of connections and a firm partnership with your service provider are the only solution.

Where We Go from Here

The cellphone is a listening device. It listens for a call to its network address from the cell network. When it receives one, it follows some logic to handle the call. Sound familiar? This works just like the RPC architecture and will be the format for a new host of devices that listen for Web Service calls over the G3 wireless network.

The first lines of the W3C XML group's charter say:

> **"Today, the principal use of the World Wide Web is for interactive access to documents and applications. In almost all cases, such access is by human users, typically working through Web browsers, audio players, or other interactive front-end systems. The Web can grow significantly in power and scope if it is extended to support communication between applications, from one program to another."**

New business communication will be via XML and Web Services, rather than EDI and VANs. Micropayment may actually become a reality. There are scores of promises that the Internet made since its inception that can be fulfilled with Web Services and XML. It won't stop there, though. The power of listening devices will bring Web Services development into user-to-user markets from business-to-business ones.

It sounds far-fetched, but the hope is that you can see how the power of Web Services on .NET could make this possible. SOAP isn't just about replacing the RPC architecture already out there. It is a fundamentally different way to think about the network as the platform.

Summary

This chapter looked at the need for an architecturally neutral, ubiquitous, easy-to-use, and interoperable system to replace DCOM, RMI, and CORBA. It discussed how Web Services fill the gaps successfully because HTTP is used as the language-independent protocol, XML is its language (in WSDL) and transport mechanism, and SOAP allows you to package messages for sending over HTTP.

Then, the chapter moved on to look at how to create and consume Web Services programmatically using Visual Basic. It discussed the abstract classes provided by the .NET Framework class library to set up and work with Web Services. In particular, it looked at the `WebService`, `WebServiceAttribute`, `WebMethodAttribute`, and `WebServiceBindingAttribute` component classes of the `System.Web.Services` namespace, in addition to the `System.Web.Services.Description`, `System.Web.Services.Discovery`, and `System.Web.Services.Protocols` namespaces.

Next, it took a high-level look at some of the technologies supporting Web Services—namely DISCO and UDDI—before briefly covering security in Web Services.

Finally, it talked about some of the downsides to using any distributed architecture (Web Services included), but it finished with an optimistic note on where Web Services might take us in the future.

24

Remoting

Remoting is the .NET technology that allows code in one application domain (`AppDomain`) to call into the methods and properties of objects running in another application domain. A major use of remoting is in the classic n-tier desktop approach, where presentation code on the desktop needs to access objects running on a server somewhere on the network. Another primary use for remoting is when code in ASP.NET Web forms or Web Services needs to call objects running on an application server somewhere on the network. In short, remoting is the technology to use when your *n*-tier code needs to talk to the business or data tier that is running on an application server.

Remoting is conceptually somewhat similar to Web Services. Both remoting and Web Services are TCP/IP-based technologies that allow communication between different machines over an IP network. This means that they both pass through firewalls, and they both provide stateless and connectionless communication between machines. These two technologies share a lot of the same principles.

It is important to recognize that Microsoft intends to merge the functionality of remoting, Web Services, Enterprise Services, and MSMQ (Microsoft Message Queue) into Indigo — the next generation of the technologies.

SOAP's biggest problem is that it is not lightweight. It's designed with maximum platform interoperability in mind, and this puts certain limits on how data can be transferred. For example, imagine that Platform A stores Integer variables as a 4-byte block of memory, with the lowest-value byte appearing first. Now imagine that Platform B also uses a 4-byte block of memory, but this time the highest-value byte appears first. Without some form of conversion, if you copy that block of bytes from Platform A to Platform B, because the encoding of the value is different, the platforms won't be able to agree on what the number actually is. In this scenario, one platform thinks it's got the number 4, whereas the other thinks that the number is actually `536870912`.

SOAP gets around this problem by representing numbers (and everything else) as strings of ASCII characters — as ASCII is a text-encoding standard that most platforms can understand. However, this means that the native binary representations of the numbers have to be converted to text each time the SOAP document has to be constructed. In addition, the values themselves have to be packaged in something that you can read (with a little bit of effort). This leads to two problems: massive bloat (a 4-byte value starts taking hundreds of bytes to store) and wasted CPU cycles used in converting from native encoding to text encoding and back again.

You can live with all these problems if you only want to run your Web Service on, say, Windows 2000, and have it accessed through a client running on a cellphone. SOAP is designed to do this kind of thing.

However, if you have a Windows XP desktop application that wants to use objects hosted on a Windows 2000 server (using the same platform), the bloated network traffic and wastage in terms of conversion is suboptimal at best and ridiculous at worst.

Remoting lets you enjoy the same power of Web Services but without the downside. If you want, you can connect directly to the server over TCP and send binary data without having to do any conversions. If one Windows computer has a 4-byte block of memory holding a 32-bit integer value, you can safely copy the bit pattern to another Windows computer and both will agree on what the number is. In effect, network traffic sanity is restored and processor time isn't wasted doing conversions.

Now that you know what remoting is, you're ready to understand its architecture.

Remoting Overview

It's important to understand several basics about remoting, including the basic terms and related objects, which are covered in the following sections.

Basic Terminology

A normal object is not accessible via remoting. By default, .NET objects are only accessible to other code running within the same .NET `AppDomain`.

A *remote object* is an object that's been made available over remoting by inheriting from `System.MarshalByRefObject`. These objects are often also called `MBROs`. Remote objects are the same kinds of objects that you build normally, with the single condition that they inherit from `MarshalByRefObject` and that you register them with the `Remoting` subsystem to make them available to clients. Remote objects are anchored to the machine and `AppDomain` where they were created, and you communicate with them over the network.

A *serializable object* is an object that's been made available over remoting by marking the class with the `<Serializable()>` attribute. These objects will move from machine to machine or `AppDomain` to `AppDomain`. They are not anchored to any particular location, so they are unanchored objects. A common example of a serializable object is the `DataSet`, which can be returned from a server to a client across the network. The `DataSet` physically moves from server to client via the serialization technology in the .NET Framework.

A *remoting host* is a server application that configures remoting to listen for client requests. Remoting runs within the host process, using the memory and threads of the host process to handle any client requests. The most common remoting host is IIS. You can create custom remoting hosts, which are typically created as a Windows Service, so they can run even when no user is logged in to the server. It is also possible to have any .NET application be a remoting host, which can allow you to emulate ActiveX EXE behaviors to some degree. This last technique is most commonly used when creating peer-to-peer-style applications.

A *channel* is a way of communicating between two machines. Out-of-the-box, .NET comes with two channels: TCP and HTTP. The TCP channel is a lightweight channel designed for transporting binary data between two computers. (You need to think of the TCP channel as being different from the TCP protocol that HTTP also uses.) It works using sockets, something discussed in much more detail in Chapter 26. HTTP, as you already know, is the protocol that Web servers use. The HTTP channel hosted in IIS is recommended by Microsoft.

A *formatter* object is used to serialize or marshal an object's data into a format in which it can be transferred down the channel. Out of the box, you have two formatter objects: `BinaryFormatter` and `SoapFormatter`. The `BinaryFormatter` is more efficient and is recommended. The `SoapFormatter` is not recommended and may be discontinued in future versions of the .NET framework.

A *message* is a communication between the client and server. It holds the information about the remote object and the method or property that's being invoked, as well as any parameters.

A *proxy* is used on the client side to call into the remote object. To use remoting, you don't typically have to worry about creating the proxy — .NET can do it all for you. However, there's a slightly confusing split between something called a *transparent proxy* and a *real proxy*. A transparent proxy is so called because "you can't see it." When you request a remote object, a transparent proxy is what you get. It looks like the remote object (that is, it has the same properties and methods as the original), which means that your client code can use the remote object or a local copy of the would-be-remote object without your having to make any changes and without your knowing that there is any difference. The transparent proxy defers the calls to the real proxy. The real proxy is what actually constructs the message, sends it to the server, and waits for the response. You can think of the transparent proxy as a "fake" object that contains the same methods and properties that the real object contains.

The real proxy is effectively a set of helper functions that manages the communications. You don't use the real proxy directly, instead, the transparent proxy calls into the real proxy on your behalf.

A *message sink* is an "interceptor object." Before messages go into the channel, these are used to do some further processing on them, perhaps to attach more data, reformat data before it is sent, route debugging information, or perform security checking. On the client side, you have an "envoy sink." On the server side, you have a "server context sink" and an "object context sink." In typical use, you can ignore these.

Message sinks are a pretty advanced topic and allow for some powerful extensions to the remoting model. It is not recommended that you create custom sinks, channels, or formatters, so they are not covered in this book. Creating them is not recommended because they will not transfer directly to Indigo, the next generation of the technology from Microsoft. If you do opt to create your own custom sink, formatter, or channel, you must expect to rewrite it from scratch when you upgrade to Indigo.

Figures 24-1 and 24-2 show how these concepts fit together.

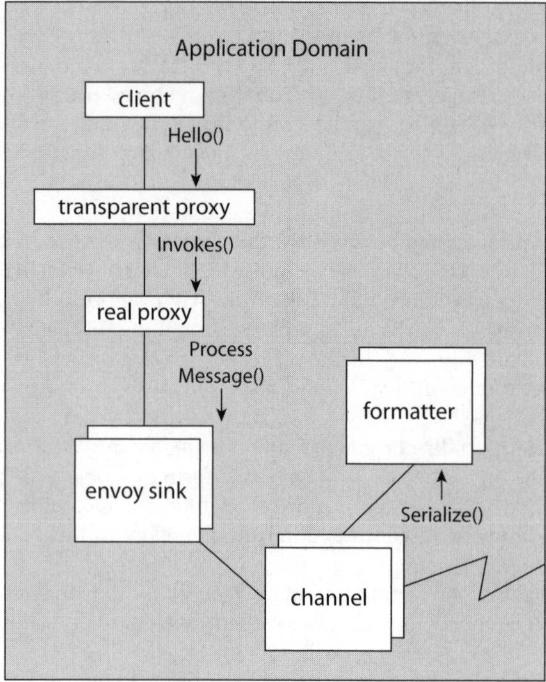

Figure 24-1

Figure 24-1 shows how a client calls the `Hello` method of a transparent proxy object. The transparent proxy looks just like the real object, so the client doesn't even realize that remoting is involved. The transparent proxy then invokes the real proxy, which converts the method call into a generic remoting message.

This message is sent through any messaging sinks configured on the client. These messaging sinks may transform the message in various ways, including adding encryption or compressing the data.

The message is then serialized by the formatter object. The result is a byte stream that is sent to the server by using the channel configured for use on the client.

Figure 24-2 shows how the server handles the message. The message comes into the server via a channel. The message is then deserialized by the formatter object and run through any messaging sinks configured on the server. These messaging sinks typically mirror those on the client, unencrypting or decompressing the data as appropriate.

Finally, the message is decoded by the object context sink, which uses the information in the message to invoke the method on the actual object. The object itself has no idea that it was invoked via remoting, since the method call was merely relayed from the client.

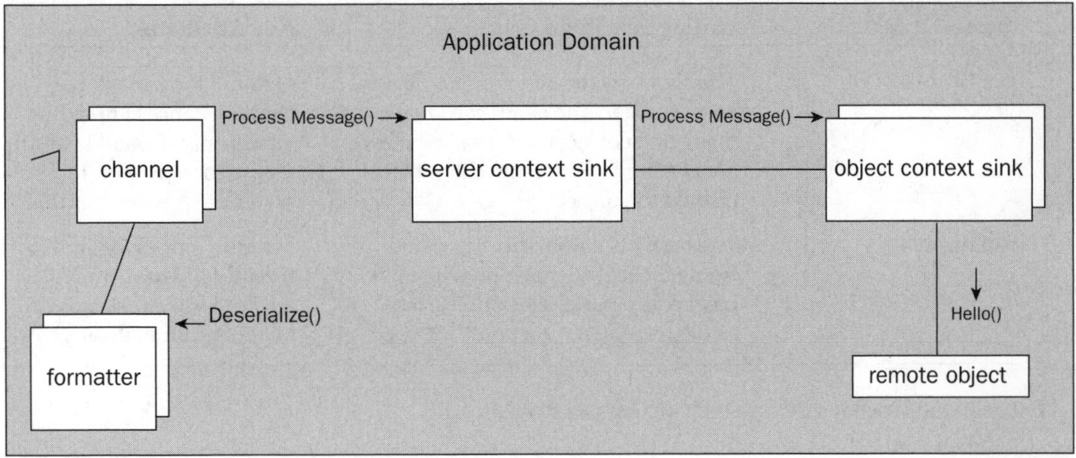

Figure 24-2

SingleCall, Singleton, and Activated Objects

The next step is to look at the way that remoting treats objects. In remoting, objects are divided into three camps: `wellknown` objects, *client-activated* objects, and *serializable* objects.

- `wellknown` objects run on the server and perform a service for the remote application, such as *give me a list of all the customers* or *create an invoice*. They can be configured to act similarly to a Web Service or use what's called a singleton pattern (which is discussed shortly).
- Client-activated (`Activated`) objects are created for each client and maintain state on the server over time. In many ways, these objects act similar to COM objects you accessed via DCOM in the past.
- Serializable objects can move from machine to machine as needed. For instance, a serializable object can be created on the server (by a `wellknown` or `Activated` object), and then returned to a client. When the object is returned to the client, it is physically copied *to the client machine*, where it can be used by client code.

The following table summarizes the types of object.

Type	Calling Semantics	Key Attributes
`SingleCall` (`wellknown`)	An object is created for each client method call made to the server.	Stateless, per-method life time, atomic methods, no-threading issues, anchored to `AppDomain` where created.
`Singleton` (`wellknown`)	One object exists on the server and is used to handle all method calls from all clients.	Stateful, long-lived, shared instance, thread synchronization required, anchored to `AppDomain` where created.

Table continued on following page

Type	Calling Semantics	Key Attributes
`Activated`	The client creates `Activated` objects on the server. The client can create many such objects. `Activated` objects are available only to the client that created the object.	Stateful, long-lived, per-client instances, threading issues only if client is multi-threaded, anchored to `AppDomain` where created.
Serializable	The object is automatically copied from machine to machine when it is passed as a parameter or returned as the result of a function.	Stateful, long-lived, no threading issues, non-anchored (moves across network automatically).

The following sections discuss each in a bit more detail.

SingleCall Objects

`SingleCall` objects act much like typical Web Service objects. Each time a client calls a method on a `SingleCall` object, an object is created specifically to handle that method call. Once the method call is complete, the object is not reused and is garbage collected by the .NET runtime.

`SingleCall` objects also work the way a JIT (just-in-time) `Activated` object does in COM+, and matches the way most people use MTS or COM+ objects. In those environments, good developers typically create a server-side object, make a method call, and then release the object.

These objects must inherit from `System.MarshalByRefObject`, so they are MBROs. This means that they always run in the `AppDomain` and Windows process where they are created. If they are created on a server in a host process, that is where they live and run. Clients interact with them across the network.

The most commonly used type of service object in remoting is the `SingleCall` object. Not only do these objects provide semantics similar to Web Services, MTS, and COM+, but they also provide the simplest programming model.

Since an object is created for each method call, these objects are inherently stateless. Even if an object tried to keep state between calls, it would fail because the object is destroyed after each method is complete. This helps ensure that no method call can be affected by previous method calls or can contaminate subsequent method calls.

Each method call runs on its own thread (from the .NET thread pool, as discussed in Chapter 22). However, since each method call also gets its very own object, there's typically no contention between threads. This means that you don't need to worry about writing synchronization or locking code in your `SingleCall` code.

Technically, it is possible to encounter synchronization issues if there are shared stateful objects on the server. This requires substantial work to create and access such shared objects and is outside the scope of this book. Typically, this type of model is not used, so threading is a nonissue with `SingleCall` *objects.*

Because of their automatic isolation, statelessness, and threading simplicity, `SingleCall` objects are the preferred technology for creation of server code in remoting.

Singleton Objects

Singleton objects are quite different from `SingleCall` objects. Only one `Singleton` object exists at a time, and it may exist for a long time and maintain state. All client method calls from all users are routed to this one `Singleton` object. This means that all clients have equal, shared access to any state maintained by the `Singleton` object.

These objects must inherit from `System.MarshalByRefObject`, so they are MBROs. This means that they always run in the `AppDomain` and Windows process where they are created. If they are created on a server in a host process, that is where they live and run. Clients interact with them across the network.

As with the `SingleCall` scenario, all method calls are run on threads from the .NET thread pool. This means that multiple simultaneous method calls can be running on different threads at the same time. As discussed in Chapter 22, this can be complex since you have to write multithreaded synchronization code to ensure that these threads don't collide as they interact with your `Singleton` object.

`Singleton` objects have a potentially unpredictable lifespan. When the first client makes the first method call to the object, it is created. From that point forward, it remains in memory for an indeterminate period of time. As long as it remains in memory, all method calls from all the clients will be handled by this one object. However, if the object is idle for a long time, remoting may release it to conserve resources. Also, some remoting hosts may recycle their `AppDomain` objects, which will automatically cause the destruction of all your objects.

Because of this, you can never be certain that the data stored in memory in the object will remain available over time. This means that any long-term state data must be written to a persistent store like a database.

Due to the complexity of shared memory, thread synchronization, and dealing with object lifetime issues, `Singleton` objects are more complex to design and code than `SingleCall` objects. While they can be useful in specialized scenarios, they aren't as widely used as `SingleCall` objects.

Activated Objects

Client-activated (or `Activated`) objects are different from both `SingleCall` and `Singleton` objects. `Activated` objects are created by a client application, and they remain in memory on the server over time. They are associated with just that one client, so they are not shared between clients. Also, they are stateful objects, meaning that they can maintain data in memory during their lifetime.

These objects must inherit from `System.MarshalByRefObject`, so they are MBROs. This means that they always run in the `AppDomain` and Windows process where they are created. If they are created on a server in a host process, that is where they live and run. Clients interact with them across the network.

A client can create multiple `Activated` objects on the server. The objects will remain on the server until the client releases the objects or the server `Appdomain` is reset (which can happen with some types of remoting host). Also, if the client doesn't contact the server for several minutes, the server will assume the client abandoned the objects and it will release them.

`Activated` objects typically don't have any threading issues. The only way multiple threads will be running in the same Activated object is if the client is multithreaded and multiple client threads simultaneously make method calls to the same server-side Activated object. If this is the case in your application, then you'll have to deal with shared data and synchronization issues as discussed in Chapter 22.

While long-lived, stateful, per-client objects can be useful in some specialized scenarios, they are not commonly used in most client/server or *n*-tier application environments. By storing per-client state in an object on the server, this type of design reduces the scalability and fault tolerance of a system.

Serializable Objects

While `SingleCall`, `Singleton`, and `Activated` objects are always anchored to the `Appdomain`, Windows process, and machine where they are created, this is not the case with serializable objects.

Serializable objects can move from machine to machine as needed. The classic example of this is the ADO.NET `DataSet`, which can be returned as a result of a function on a server. The `DataSet` physically moves to the client machine, where it can be used by client code. When the client wants to update the `DataSet`, it simply passes the object to the server as a parameter, causing the `DataSet` to physically move to the server machine.

These objects *do not* inherit from `System.MarshalByRefObject`. Instead, they are decorated with the `<Serializable()>` attribute and may optionally implement the `ISerializable` interface. The following is a very basic implementation of a `<Serializable()>` object:

```
<Serializable()> _
Public Class Customer
  Private mName As String = ""

  Public Property Name() As String
    Get
      Return mName
    End Get
    Set(ByVal value As String)
      mName = value
    End Set

    Public Sub Load()
      ' Load data here.
    End Sub
End Class
```

`<Serializable()>` objects are not anchored to the `Appdomain` or Windows process where they were created. The remoting subsystem will automatically serialize these objects' data and transfer it across the network to another machine. On that other machine, a new instance of the objects will be created and loaded with the data, effectively cloning the objects across the network.

When working with serializable objects, it's typically a good idea to use a `SingleCall` object on the server to create the serializable object and call any server-side methods (such as ones to load the object with data from a database). The `SingleCall` object will then return the serializable object to the client as a function result, so the client can then interact with the object. The `SingleCall` object's method might look like the following:

```
Public Function GetCustomer(ByVal ID As Integer) As Customer

  Dim cust As New Customer()
  cust.Load(ID)
  Return cust

End Function
```

The client code might look like this:

```
Dim cust As Customer

cust = myService.GetCustomer(123)
TextBox1.Text = cust.Name()
```

Note that both server and client code have direct, local access to the `Customer` object, because it is automatically copied from the server to the client as a result of the `GetCustomer` method call.

Serializable objects can be very useful in many client/server scenarios, especially if the application is created using object-oriented application design principles.

Implementing Remoting

When you implement an application using remoting, there are three key components to the application.

Client	The application calling the server
Server Library	The DLL containing the objects to be called by the client
Host	The application running on the server that hosts remoting and the Server Library

Basically, you create your server-side objects in a Visual Basic .NET class library project. Then, you expose the classes in that DLL from your server-side remoting host application. With the objects exposed on the server, you can then create client applications that call the objects in the Server Library DLL.

You might also have some other optional components to support various scenarios.

Interface	A DLL containing interfaces that are implemented by the objects in the Server Library
Proxy	A DLL containing generated proxy code based on the objects in the Server Library
Shared Library	A DLL containing serializable objects that must be available to both the Server Library and the client

Each of these is discussed in detail as it is used later in the chapter. For now, it's time to get into some code and see how remoting works.

A Simple Example

To start with, you will create a simple remoting application, consisting of a library DLL that contains the server-side code, a remoting host application, and a client to call the library DLL on the server.

The first thing you need to realize is that both the host and the client need access to the type information that describes the classes in the library DLL. The type information includes the name of the classes in the DLL and the methods exposed by those classes.

The host needs the information because it will be exposing the library DLL to clients via remoting. However, the client needs the information in order to know which objects to create and what methods are available on those objects.

Since you know that the library DLL will be on the server, it is easy enough for the host application to just reference the DLL to get the type information. The client is a bit trickier though, since the library DLL won't necessarily be on the client machine. There are three options for getting the type information to the client.

Reference the library DLL	This is the simplest approach, since the client just references the DLL directly and, thus, has all the type information. The drawback is that the DLL must be installed on the client along with the client application.
Use an interface DLL	This approach is more complex. The classes in the library DLL must implement formal interfaces as defined in this interface DLL. The client can then reference just the interface DLL, so the library DLL doesn't need to be installed on the client machine. The way the client invokes the server is different when using interfaces.
Generate a proxy DLL	This approach is of moderate complexity. The server must expose the objects via HTTP, so you can run the soapsuds.exe command-line utility. The utility creates an assembly containing the type information for the library DLL classes exposed by the server. The client then references this proxy assembly rather than the library DLL.

You'll implement all three options in this chapter, starting with the simplest—referencing the library DLL directly from the client application.

Library DLL

To begin, create the library DLL. This is just a regular `Class Library` project, so open Visual Studio .NET (VS.NET) and create a new class library named `SimpleLibrary. Remove Class1.vb` and add a new class named `Calculator`. Since you're creating a well-known remoting object, it must inherit from `MarshalByRefObject`:

```
Public Class Calculator
  Inherits MarshalByRefObject

End Class
```

That's really all there is to it. At this point, the `Calculator` class is ready to be exposed from a server via remoting. Of course, you need to add some methods that clients can call.

Any and all `Public` methods written in the `Calculator` class will be available to clients. How you design the methods depends entirely on whether you plan to expose this class as `SingleCall`, `Singleton`, or `Activated`. For `SingleCall` you know that an instance of `Calculator` will be created for *each method call*, so there's absolutely no point in using any class-level variables. After all, they'll be destroyed along with the object when each method call is complete.

It also means that you can't have the client call a sequence of methods on your object. Since each method call gets its own object, each method call is entirely isolated from any previous or subsequent method calls. In short, each method must stand alone.

For illustration purposes, you need to prove that the server-side code is running in a different process from the client code. The easiest way to prove this is to return the `thread ID` where the code is running. You can compare this `thread ID` to the `thread ID` of the client process. If they are different, then you are sure that the server-side code really is running on the server (or at least in another process on your machine).

Add the following method:

```
Public Function GetThreadID() As Integer

  Return Threading.Thread.CurrentThread.ManagedThreadId

End Function
```

You can add other `Public` methods as well if you'd like, for instance:

```
Public Function Add(ByVal a As Integer, ByVal b As Integer) As Integer

  Return a + b

End Function
```

Since this is a calculator class, it only seems appropriate that it should do some calculations.

At this point, you have a simple but functional `Calculator` class. Build the solution to create the DLL. Your remoting host application will use this DLL to provide the calculator functionality to clients.

Host Application

With the server-side library complete, you can create a remoting host. It is recommended that you use IIS as a remoting host, but it is quite possible to create a custom host as well. You'll use IIS later in the chapter, but for now let's see how you can create a custom host in a `Console` Application for testing.

Most custom hosts are created as a Windows Service so the host can run on the server even when no user is logged into the machine. However, for testing purposes, a console application is easier to create and run.

The advantage to a custom host is that you can host a remoting server on any machine that supports the .NET Framework. This includes Windows 98 and up. If you use IIS as a host, you can only host on Windows 2000 and up, which is a bit more restrictive.

The drawback to a custom host is that it isn't as robust and capable as IIS, at least, not without a lot of work. For this chapter's example, you're not going to attempt to make your host as powerful as IIS. You'll just stick with the basic process of creating a custom host.

Setting up the Project

Create a new solution in VS.NET, with a console application named `SimpleServer`.

Since the remoting host will be interacting with remoting, you need to reference the appropriate framework DLL. Use the `Add Reference` dialog box to add a reference to `System.Runtime.Remoting`, as shown in Figure 24-3.

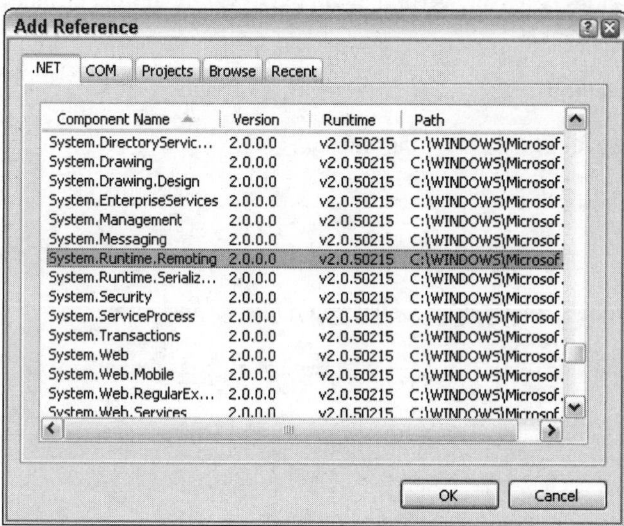

Figure 24-3

Then, in `Module1` you need to import the appropriate namespace:

```
Imports System.Runtime.Remoting
```

At this point, you can configure and use remoting. However, before you do that, you need to have access to the DLL containing the classes you plan to expose via remoting—in this case this is `SimpleLibrary.dll`.

Referencing the Library DLL

There are two ways to configure remoting, via a configuration file or via code. If you opt for the configuration file approach, then the only requirement is that `SimpleLibrary.dll` be in the same directory as your host application. You don't even need to reference `SimpleLibrary.dll` from the host. However, if you opt to configure remoting via code, then your host must reference `SimpleLibrary.dll`.

Even if you go with the configuration file approach, referencing `SimpleLibrary.dll` from the host project allows VS.NET to automatically keep the DLL updated in your project directory, and it means that any setup project you might create will automatically include `SimpleLibrary.dll`. In general, it is a good idea to reference the library DLL from the host and that's what you'll do here.

Add a reference to `SimpleLibrary.dll` by clicking the Browse button in the Add References dialog box and navigating to the `SimpleLibrary\bin\release` directory, as shown in Figure 24-4.

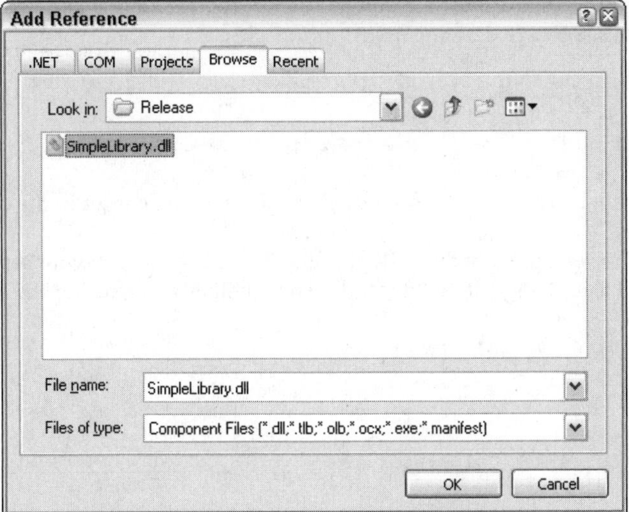

Figure 24-4

All that remains now is to configure remoting.

Configuring Remoting

The typical way to do this is with a configuration file. Open the `app.config` file in the `SimpleServer` project. In this `config` file, you'll add a section to configure remoting. Remember that XML is case-sensitive, so the slightest typo here will prevent remoting from being properly configured:

```
<?xml version="1.0" encoding="utf-8" ?>
<configuration>
  <system.runtime.remoting>
    <application>
      <!- The following section defines the classes you're
            exposing to clients from this host. ->
      <service>
        <wellknown mode="SingleCall"
             objectUri="Calculator.rem"
             type="SimpleLibrary.Calculator, SimpleLibrary" />
      </service>

      <channels>
        <channel ref="tcp" port="49341" />
      </channels>

    </application>
  </system.runtime.remoting>
```

Notice that all configuration is within the `<system.runtime.remoting>` element, and then within an `<application>` element. The real work happens first inside the `<service>` element. The `<service>` element tells remoting that you're configuring server-side components. Within this block is where you define the classes you want to make available to clients. You can define both `wellknown` and `Activated` classes here. In this case you're defining a `wellknown` class:

```
<wellknown mode="SingleCall"
     objectUri="Calculator.rem"
     type="SimpleLibrary.Calculator, SimpleLibrary" />
```

The mode will be either `SingleCall` or `Singleton` as discussed earlier in the chapter.

The `objectUri` is the "end part" of the URL that clients will use to reach your server. You'll revisit this in a moment, but this is basically how it fits (depending on whether you're using the TCP or HTTP protocol):

```
tcp://localhost:49341/Calculator.rem
```

or

```
http://localhost:49341/Calculator.rem
```

The .rem extension on the `objectUri` is important. This extension indicates that remoting should handle the client request, and is used by the networking infrastructure to route the request to the right location. You can optionally use the .soap extension to get the same result. The .rem and .soap extensions are totally equivalent.

Finally, the type defines the full type name and assembly where the actual class can be found. Remoting uses this information to dynamically load the assembly and create the object when requested by a client.

You can have many `<wellknown>` blocks here to expose all the server-side classes you want to make available to clients.

The other key configuration block is where you specify which remoting channel (protocol) you want to use. You can choose between the TCP and HTTP channels.

TCP	Slightly faster than HTTP, but less stable and not recommended
HTTP	Slightly slower than TCP, but more stable and is recommended

Since you'll look at the HTTP channel later, you're using the TCP channel now. Either way, you need to specify the IP port number on which you'll be listening for client requests. When choosing a port for a server, you should keep the following port ranges in mind:

- **0–1023** — Well-known ports reserved for specific applications such as Web servers, mail servers, and so on
- **1024–49151** — Registered ports that are reserved for various widely used protocols such as DirectPlay
- **49152–65535** — Intended for dynamic or private use, such as for applications that might be performing remoting with .NET

You're setting remoting to use a TCP channel, listening on port 49341:

```
<channels>
  <channel ref="tcp" port="49341" />
</channels>
```

With the `config` file created, the only thing remaining is to tell remoting to configure itself based on this information. To do this you need to add code to `Sub Main`:

```
Sub Main()
  RemotingConfiguration.Configure( _
    AppDomain.CurrentDomain.SetupInformation.ConfigurationFile)
  Console.Write("Press <enter> to exit")
  Console.Read()
End Sub
```

The `Console.Write` and `Console.Read` statements are there to ensure that the application stays running until you are ready for it to terminate. The line that actually configures remoting is:

```
RemotingConfiguration.Configure( _
  AppDomain.CurrentDomain.SetupInformation.ConfigurationFile)
```

You are calling the `Configure` method, which tells remoting to read a `config` file and to process the `<system.runtime.remoting>` element in that file. You want it to use your application configuration file, so you pass that path as a parameter. Fortunately, you can get the path from your `AppDomain` object so you don't have to worry about hard-coding the file name.

Configuring Remoting via Code

Your other option is to configure the remoting host via code. To do this you'd write different code in `Sub Main`:

```
Sub Main()

  RemotingConfiguration.RegisterWellKnownServiceType( _
    GetType(SimpleLibrary.Calculator), _
    "Calculator.rem", _
    WellKnownObjectMode.SingleCall)

  System.Runtime.Remoting.Channels.ChannelServices.RegisterChannel( _
    New System.Runtime.Remoting.Channels.Tcp.TcpServerChannel(49341))

  Console.Write("Press <enter> to exit")
  Console.Read()
End Sub
```

You can see that you're providing the exact same information here as you did in the `config` file, only via code. You call `RegisterWellKnownServiceType`, passing the mode, `objectUri`, and type data just as you did in the `config` file. Then, you call `RegisterChannel`, passing a new instance of the `TcpServerChannel` configured to use the port you chose earlier.

The end result is the same as using the config file. Most server applications use a config file to configure remoting because it allows you to change things like the channel and port without having to recompile the host application.

Build the solution. At this point your host is ready to run. Open a Command Prompt window, navigate to the bin directory, and run SimpleServer.exe.

Client Application

The final piece of the puzzle is to create a client application that calls the server.

Setting Up the Project

Here's how to create a new VS.NET solution with a Windows Application named SimpleClient. As discussed earlier, the client needs access to the type information for the classes it wants to call on the server. The easiest way to get this type information is to have it reference SimpleLibrary.dll. Since you'll be configuring remoting, you also need to reference the remoting DLL. Then import the remoting namespace in Form1:

```
Imports System.Runtime.Remoting
```

Now, you can write code to interact with the Calculator class. Add controls to the form as shown in Figure 24-5.

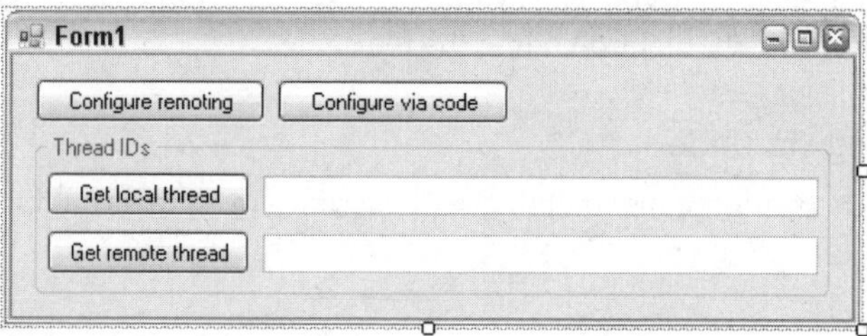

Figure 24-5

Name the controls (in order): ConfigureButton, CodeConfigureButton, LocalThreadButton, LocalThread, RemoteThreadButton, RemoteThread. First, let's write the code to get the thread ID values for each object:

```
Private Sub LocalThreadButton_Click( _
  ByVal sender As System.Object, ByVal e As System.EventArgs) _
  Handles LocalThreadButton.Click

  LocalThread.Text = CStr(Threading.Thread.CurrentThread.ManagedThreadId)

End Sub

Private Sub RemoteThreadButton_Click( _
    ByVal sender As System.Object, ByVal e As System.EventArgs) _
    Handles RemoteThreadButton.Click
```

```
    Dim calc As New SimpleLibrary.Calculator

    RemoteThread.Text = CStr(calc.GetThreadID)

  End Sub
```

Displaying the thread ID of the local process is easily accomplished. More interesting though, is that your code to interact with the `Calculator` class doesn't look special in any way. Where's the remoting code?

It turns out that there's this idea of *location transparency*, where it is possible to write "normal" code that interacts with an object whether it is running locally or remotely. This is an important and desirable trait for distributed technologies, and remoting supports the concept. Looking at the code you've written, you can't tell if the `Calculator` object is local or remoting; its location is transparent.

All that remains is to configure remoting so that it knows that the `Calculator` object should, in fact, be created remotely. As with the server, you can configure clients either via a `config` file or through code.

Before you configure remoting, you need to realize something important. If remoting is not configured before the first usage of `SimpleLibrary.Calculator`, then the `Calculator` object will be created locally. If that happens, configuring remoting won't help, and you'll never create remote `Calculator` objects.

To prevent this from happening, you need to make sure that you can't interact with the class until after remoting is configured. Typically, this is done by configuring remoting as the application starts up, either in `Sub Main` or in the first form's `Load` event. In this case, however, you're going to configure remoting behind some buttons, so a different approach is required.

In `Form_Load`, add the following code:

```
  Private Sub Form1_Load( _
    ByVal sender As System.Object, ByVal e As System.EventArgs) _
    Handles MyBase.Load

    RemoteThreadButton.Enabled = False

  End Sub
```

This prevents you from requesting the remote thread. You won't enable this button until after remoting has been configured either through the `config` file or code.

Configuring Remoting

To configure remoting via a `config` file, you first need to add a `config` file to the project. Use the Project ➪ Add New Item menu to add an Application Configuration File. Make sure to keep the default name of `App.config`. In this file, add the following code:

```
  <?xml version="1.0" encoding="utf-8" ?>
  <configuration>
    <system.runtime.remoting>
      <application>
```

```
        <!- The following section defines the classes you're
              getting from the remote host. ->
        <client>
          <wellknown mode="SingleCall"
               type="SimpleLibrary.Calculator, SimpleLibrary"
              url="tcp://localhost:49341/Calculator.rem" />
          </client>
      </application>
    </system.runtime.remoting>
  </configuration>
```

In this case, you're using the `<client>` element, telling remoting that you're configuring a client. Within the `<client>` block, you define the classes that should be run on a remote server, both `wellknown` and `Activated`. In your case you have a `wellknown` class:

```
<wellknown
      type="SimpleLibrary.Calculator, SimpleLibrary"
     url="tcp://localhost:49341/Calculator.rem" />
```

On the client, you only need to provide two bits of information. You need to tell remoting the class and assembly that should be run remotely. This is done with the type attribute, which specifies the full type name and assembly name for the class, just as you did on the server. You also need to provide the full URL for the class on the server.

You defined this URL when you created the server, though it might not have been clear that you did so. When you defined the class for remoting on the server, you specified an `objectUri` value (`Calculator.rem`). Also, on the server you specified the channel (TCP) and port (49341) on which the server will listen for client requests. Combined with the server name itself, you have a URL:

```
tcp://localhost:49341/Calculator.rem
```

The channel is `tcp://`, the server name is `localhost` (or whatever the server name might be), the port is `49341`, and the object's URI is `Calculator.rem`. This is the unique address of your `SimpleLibrary.Calculator` class on the remote server.

As with the server configuration, you might have multiple elements in the `config` file, one for each server-side object you wish to use. These can be a mix of `<wellknown>` and `<activated>` elements.

With the configuration set up, you just need to tell remoting to read the file. You'll do this behind the `ConfigureButton` control:

```
Private Sub ConfigureButton_Click( _
  ByVal sender As System.Object, ByVal e As System.EventArgs) _
  Handles ConfigureButton.Click

  RemotingConfiguration.Configure( _
    AppDomain.CurrentDomain.SetupInformation.ConfigurationFile)

  ConfigureButton.Enabled = False
  CodeConfigureButton.Enabled = False
  RemoteThreadButton.Enabled = True

End Sub
```

Once remoting is configured in an application, you can't configure it again, so you're disabling the two configuration buttons. Also, you're enabling the button to retrieve the remote thread ID. Now that remoting has been configured, it is safe to interact with `SimpleLibrary.Calculator`.

The line of code that configures remoting is the same as it was in the server:

```
RemotingConfiguration.Configure( _
  AppDomain.CurrentDomain.SetupInformation.ConfigurationFile)
```

Again, you're telling remoting to read your application configuration file to find the `<system.runtime.remoting>` element and process it.

Configuring Remoting via Code

Another option for configuring remoting is to do it via code. You must provide the same information in your code as you did in the `config` file. Put this behind the `CodeConfigureButton` control:

```
Private Sub CodeConfigureButton_Click( _
  ByVal sender As System.Object, ByVal e As System.EventArgs) _
  Handles CodeConfigureButton.Click
  RemotingConfiguration.RegisterWellKnownClientType( _
    GetType(SimpleLibrary.Calculator), "tcp://localhost:49341/Calculator.rem")

  ConfigureButton.Enabled = False
  CodeConfigureButton.Enabled = False
  RemoteThreadButton.Enabled = True

End Sub
```

The `RegisterWellKnownClientType` method requires that you specify the type of the class to be run remotely, in this case `SimpleLibrary.Calculator`. It also requires that you provide the URL for the class on the remote server, just as you did in the `config` file.

Regardless of whether you do the configuration via code or the `config` file, the end result is that the .NET runtime now knows that any attempt to create a `SimpleLibrary.Calculator` object should be routed through remoting, so the object will be created on the server.

Compile and run the application. Try configuring remoting both ways. In either case, you should discover that the local thread ID and the remote thread ID are different, proving that the Calculator code is running on the server, not locally in the Windows application, as shown in Figure 24-6.

Figure 24-6

Note that your specific thread ID values will vary from those shown here. The important part is that they are different from each other, establishing that the local code and remote code are running in different places.

Using IIS As a Remoting Host

You've seen how to create a very basic custom host. In most production environments, however, such a basic host isn't directly useful. You'd need to create a Windows Service, add management and logging facilities, implement security, and so forth.

Or, you could just use IIS as the host and get all those things automatically. Due to this, it is often better to use IIS as a remoting host than to try to create your own.

Creating the Host

Using IIS as a host is a straightforward exercise. The first thing to do is create a Web project. To do this, create a new solution in VS.NET with an Empty Web Site named `SimpleHost`, as shown in Figure 24-7.

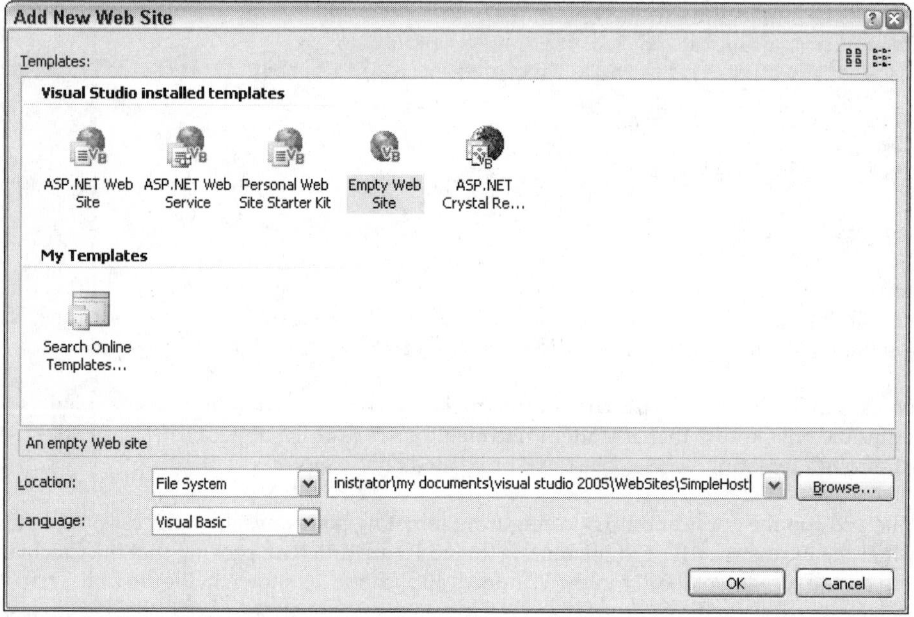

Figure 24-7

When you click OK, VS.NET will properly create and configure the virtual root on your server.

The next task is to ensure that the `SimpleLibrary.dll` is in the `bin` directory under the virtual root. While you could copy the DLL there by hand, it is often easier to simply add a reference to the DLL from the Web site. This allows VS.NET to automatically copy the DLL to the right location, and it has the added side-benefit that if you create a deployment project the DLL will be automatically included as part of the setup.

Add a reference to SimpleLibrary.dll using the Add References dialog box as you did previously in the SimpleServer and SimpleClient projects. This way VS.NET will ensure that the DLL is available as needed.

All that remains now is to configure remoting. The only thing you need to do within an IIS host is add the <system.runtime.remoting> section to the web.config file. Remoting is automatically configured based on web.config by ASP.NET.

Use the Project ➪ Add New Item menu to add a Web Configuration File. Make sure to use the default name of web.config. This adds a web.config file to the project with a series of default settings. You may opt to change some of these settings for your environment. In particular, these settings allow you to control security options and so forth.

More importantly, however, add the remoting configuration to the file:

```
<?xml version="1.0" encoding="utf-8" ?>
<configuration>

  <system.runtime.remoting>
    <application>
      <!- The following section defines the classes you're
            exposing to clients from this host. ->
      <service>
        <wellknown mode="SingleCall"
             objectUri="Calculator.rem"
             type="SimpleLibrary.Calculator, SimpleLibrary" />
      </service>

  </application>
</system.runtime.remoting>
```

An IIS host can only support the HTTP channel. Also, the port on which the host listens is defined by IIS, not by your configuration file. This means that all you really need to do here is define the classes you want to expose to clients. This is done within the <service> element, just like with a custom host. Again, you use a <wellknown> element to define your class:

```
<wellknown mode="SingleCall"
     objectUri="Calculator.rem"
     type="SimpleLibrary.Calculator, SimpleLibrary" />
```

The <wellknown> element shown here is the exact same definition as with the custom host, and you'll get the same end result.

The primary difference between your custom host and the IIS host is that IIS cannot use the TCP channel, but only uses the HTTP channel. This means that the URL for your server-side class is different:

```
http://localhost/SimpleHost/Calculator.rem
```

The channel defines the protocol, which is http://. The server name is localhost (or whatever your server name might be). The virtual root within IIS is SimpleHost, named just like it is with any Web project. And finally, the objectUri value for your class (Calculator.rem) rounds out the URL.

Again note that the .rem extension is important. This extension (or the equivalent .soap extension) tells IIS to route the client request to ASP.NET, and it tells ASP.NET to route the request to remoting so it can be properly handled by invoking your `Calculator` class.

At this point, the remoting host is done and ready to go. Since it is using the HTTP protocol, you can test it with the browser by navigating to the following URL:

```
http://localhost/SimpleHost/Calculator.rem?wsdl
```

This should return an XML description of the host service and all the classes exposed from the host.

Updating the Client Application

With a new host set up, you can change the client application to use this IIS host instead of the custom host. To do this, all you need to do is change the URL for the object when you configure remoting.

If you're using the `config` file to configure remoting, you'd make the following change:

```
<?xml version="1.0" encoding="utf-8" ?>
<configuration>
  <system.runtime.remoting>
    <application>
      <!- the following section defines the classes you're
            getting from the remote host ->
      <client>
        <wellknown
              type="SimpleLibrary.Calculator, SimpleLibrary"
             url="http://localhost/SimpleHost/Calculator.rem" />
       </client>
    </application>
  </system.runtime.remoting>
</configuration>
```

Once making this change to `App.config`, make sure to rebuild the project so VS.NET copies the new `config` file to the `bin` directory and renames it to `SimpleClient.exe.config`.

When configuring remoting via code, change the code to the following:

```
Private Sub CodeConfigureButton_Click( _
  ByVal sender As System.Object, ByVal e As System.EventArgs) _
  Handles CodeConfigureButton.Click

  RemotingConfiguration.RegisterWellKnownClientType( _
    GetType(SimpleLibrary.Calculator), _
    "http://localhost/SimpleHost/Calculator.rem")

  ConfigureButton.Enabled = False
  CodeConfigureButton.Enabled = False
  RemoteThreadButton.Enabled = True

End Sub
```

In either case, you're simply changing the URL, so remoting now routes your calls to the IIS host instead of your custom host.

Using the Binary Formatter in IIS

One thing to note about using IIS as a host is that it always uses the HTTP channel. The HTTP channel defaults to using the `SoapFormatter` instead of the `BinaryFormatter` to encode the data that is sent across the network. While SOAP is a fine format, it is extremely verbose. The `BinaryFormatter` generates about one-third the number of bytes as the `SoapFormatter` to send the same data.

For production code, it's good practice to use the `BinaryFormatter` to reduce the amount of data sent across the network and to improve performance. The formatter is controlled by the client, so you'll need to update the client configuration of remoting.

To change the `config` file, do as follows:

```
<?xml version="1.0" encoding="utf-8" ?>
<configuration>
  <system.runtime.remoting>
    <application>
      <!- the following section defines the classes you're
            getting from the remote host ->
      <client>
        <wellknown
             type="SimpleLibrary.Calculator, SimpleLibrary"
            url="http://localhost/SimpleHost/Calculator.rem" />
      </client>
  <!-- use the binary formatter over the
         http channel ->
  <channels>
     <channel ref="http">
      <clientProviders>
        <formatter ref="binary" />
      </clientProviders>
    </channel>
  </channels>

    </application>
  </system.runtime.remoting>
</configuration>
```

The highlighted XML shown above configures remoting so when it initializes the HTTP channel, it does so with a `BinaryFormatter` instead of the default `SoapFormatter`.

To do the equivalent to the XML configuration in code, you'll want to import a couple namespaces into `Form1`:

```
Imports System.Runtime.Remoting.Channels
Imports System.Runtime.Remoting.Channels.Http
```

This also requires that the `SimpleClient` project reference the `System.Runtime.Remoting.dll` assembly. Do this using the Add References dialog as you did earlier in the `SimpleLibrary` project.

Then add the following when configuring remoting:

```
Private Sub CodeConfigureButton_Click( _
  ByVal sender As System.Object, ByVal e As System.EventArgs) _
  Handles CodeConfigureButton.Click

  RemotingConfiguration.RegisterWellKnownClientType( _
    GetType(SimpleLibrary.Calculator), _
    "http://localhost/SimpleHost/Calculator.rem")

  ' Use the binary formatter with the
  ' HTTP channel.
  Dim clientFormatter As New BinaryClientFormatterSinkProvider
  Dim channel As New HttpChannel(Nothing, clientFormatter, Nothing)
  ChannelServices.RegisterChannel(channel)

  ConfigureButton.Enabled = False
  CodeConfigureButton.Enabled = False
  RemoteThreadButton.Enabled = True

End Sub
```

As with the `config` file approach, you're specifically creating the `HttpChannel` object, specifying that it should use a `BinaryFormatter` rather than the default.

At this point, you've explored the basic use of remoting. You've created a library DLL, a client that uses the library DLL, and two different types of remoting hosts, so the library DLL can run on the server.

There are many other facets of remoting to explore, more than what fits into this single chapter. The remainder of the chapter explores some of the more common features that you might encounter or use in your applications. You'll have to take them pretty fast, but the complete code for each of them is available in the code download for the book, so you can get the complete picture there.

Using Activator.GetObject

In your simple client you configured remoting so that all attempts to use `SimpleLibrary.Calculator` were automatically routed to a specific server via remoting. If you want more control and flexibility, you can take a different approach by using the `System.Activator` class. The full code for this example is in the `ActivatorClient` project.

Instead of configuring remoting to always know where to find the remote class, you can specify it as you create the remote object. Since you won't be configuring remoting, you don't need a reference to `System.Runtime.Remoting.dll`, nor do you need any of the remoting configuration code you had in the client to this point.

All you do is replace the use of the `New` keyword with a call to `Activator.GetObject`. To use the custom host, you'd use the following code to retrieve the remote thread ID:

```
Private Sub RemoteThreadButton_Click( _
  ByVal sender As System.Object, ByVal e As System.EventArgs) _
  Handles RemoteThreadButton.Click
```

```
    Dim calc As SimpleLibrary.Calculator

    calc = CType(Activator.GetObject( _
      GetType(SimpleLibrary.Calculator), _
      "tcp://localhost:49341/Calculator.rem"), _
      SimpleLibrary.Calculator)

    RemoteThread.Text = CStr(calc.GetThreadID)

  End Sub
```

For this to work, the `SimpleServer` application must be running before the `RemoteThread` button is clicked.

The `Activator.GetObject` method accepts the type of object to create (`SimpleLibrary.Calculator`) and the URL where the object can be found. To use the IIS host, you'd change the URL:

```
calc = CType(Activator.GetObject( _
  GetType(SimpleLibrary.Calculator), _

  "http://localhost/SimpleHost/Calculator.rem"), _
  SimpleLibrary.Calculator)
```

Using this approach, you lose location transparency because it is quite obvious looking at your code that you're using a remote object. However, you gain explicit control over where the remote object will be created. This can be useful in some cases, when you want to programmatically control the URL on a per-call basis.

Interface-Based Design

One drawback to the simple implementation you've used thus far is that the library DLL (`SimpleLibrary.dll`) must be installed on the client machine. Sometimes this is not desirable, because you don't want clients to have access to the server-side code. There are a couple of solutions to this problem: using an interface DLL or using a generated proxy. First, take a look at the interface DLL approach.

Interface DLL

To use this approach, you need to create a new DLL that contains interface definitions for your server-side classes and their methods. For instance, in the `SimpleInterface` project, you have the following interface defined:

```
Public Interface  ICalculator
  Function GetThreadID() As Integer
  Function Add(ByVal a As Integer, ByVal b As Integer) As Integer
End Interface
```

This interface defines the methods on your `Calculator` class. You need to update the `Calculator` class to implement this interface. The `SimpleLibrary` project must reference the `SimpleInterface` DLL, then you can do the following in your `Calculator` class:

```
Public Class Calculator
  Inherits MarshalByRefObject

 Implements SimpleInterface.ICalculator
 Public Function GetThreadID() As Integer _
   Implements SimpleInterface.ICalculator.GetThreadID

   Return AppDomain.GetCurrentThreadId

 End Function

 Public Function Add(ByVal a As Integer, ByVal b As Integer) As Integer _
   Implements SimpleInterface.ICalculator.Add

    Return a + b

  End Function

End Class
```

At this point, the `SimpleLibrary.Calculator` class can be invoked either directly or via the `ICalculator` interface.

Make sure to rebuild the custom and IIS host projects so that the new `SimpleLibrary` and the `Simple Interface` DLLs are both copies to the host directories. Note that since (`SimpleLibrary.Calculator`) is still available natively, your existing client applications (`SimpleClient` and `ActivatorClient`) will continue to run just fine.

Updating the Client Application

The `InterfaceClient` project only references `SimpleInterface.dll`, not `SimpleLibrary.dll`. This means that the client machine doesn't need to install `SimpleLibrary.dll` for the client to run, meaning that the client has no access to the actual server-side code.

Since you don't have access to the types in `SimpleLibrary`, you can't use them in your code. The only types you can use come from `SimpleInterface`. This means that your code to retrieve the remote thread ID is a bit different. To use the custom host, you do the following:

```
Private Sub RemoteThreadButton_Click( _
  ByVal sender As System.Object, ByVal e As System.EventArgs) _
  Handles RemoteThreadButton.Click

  Dim calc As SimpleInterface.ICalculator

  calc = CType(Activator.GetObject( _
    GetType(SimpleInterface.ICalculator), _
    "tcp://localhost:49341/Calculator.rem"), _
    SimpleInterface.ICalculator)

  RemoteThread.Text = CStr(calc.GetThreadID)

End Sub
```

Note that the `calc` variable is now declared as type `ICalculator` rather than `Calculator`. Also notice that you're using `Activator.GetType`. This is required when using interfaces, because you can't use the `New` keyword at all. You can't do the following:

```
calc = New SimpleInterface.ICalculator()
```

The result is a compiler error because it isn't possible to create an instance of an interface. Because of this, you can't just configure remoting and use location transparency, you must use `Activator.GetObject` to have remoting create an instance of the object on the server.

Remoting knows how and where to create the object based on the URL you provide. It then converts the object to the right type (`SimpleInterface.ICalculator`) based on the type you provide in the `GetObject` call. If the remote object doesn't implement this interface, then you'll get a runtime exception.

Using Generated Proxies

Another way to create a client that doesn't reference the library DLL is to use the `soapsuds.exe` command-line utility to create a proxy assembly for the service and the classes it exposes. This proxy assembly is then referenced by the client application, giving the client access to the server type information so that it can interact with the server objects.

Proxy DLL

To create the proxy DLL, you just run the `soapsuds.exe` utility with the following command line:

```
> soapsuds -url:http://localhost/SimpleHost/Calculator.rem?wsdl -oa:SimpleProxy.dll
```

Note that you're going against the IIS host here because it uses the HTTP protocol. This won't work against your current custom host, as the `soapsuds.exe` utility doesn't understand the `tcp://` prefix. To use this against a custom host, you'd have to make sure the custom host used the HTTP protocol.

Creating the Client Application

In the code download there's a `ProxyClient` project. This is a Windows application that references only `SimpleProxy.dll`. There is no reference to `SimpleLibrary.dll` or `SimpleInterface.dll` — this client relies entirely on the generated proxy assembly to interact with the server.

The best part of this is that the generated proxy contains the same namespace and class names as the service on the server. In other words, it appears that you are working with `SimpleLibrary.Calculator`, because the proxy is set up with that same namespace and class name. To get the remote thread ID, write the following code:

```
Private Sub RemoteThreadButton_Click( _
  ByVal sender As System.Object, ByVal e As System.EventArgs) _
  Handles RemoteThreadButton.Click

  Dim calc As New SimpleLibrary.Calculator()

  RemoteThread.Text = CStr(calc.GetThreadID)

End Sub
```

Note that this is the same code used in the original simple example. You've come full circle at this point, but now the client application doesn't directly reference your library DLL.

Summary

Remoting is a powerful technology that provides many of the capabilities of Web Services and DCOM, plus some new capabilities of its own. Using remoting, you can create both Windows and Web applications that interact with objects on an application server across the network.

On the server you can create `SingleCall`, `Singleton`, and `Activated` objects. These three object types provide a great deal of flexibility in terms of *n*-tier application design and should be able to meet almost any need. `SingleCall` gives you behavior similar to Web Services or typical COM+ objects. `Activated` gives you objects that act similar to COM objects exposed via DCOM. `Singleton` objects are unique to remoting and allow all your clients to share a single stateful object on the server.

You can also create serializable objects, which can move from machine to machine as needed. Using this type of object allows you to easily move data and business logic from server to client and back again. This technology is particularly exciting for object-oriented development in a distributed environment.

In this chapter, you created a library DLL and exposed it to clients from both a custom and IIS remoting host. You then created client applications to use your server-side code by referencing the library DLL directly, using an interface DLL and using the `soapsuds.exe` utility to create a proxy DLL. These techniques apply not only to `SingleCall` objects but also to `Singleton` and `Activated` objects, so you should have a good grounding in the techniques available for using remoting in your environment.

25

Windows Services

Modern, multitasking operating systems often need to run applications that operate in the background and that are independent of the user who is logged in. In Windows NT, Windows 2000, Windows XP, and Windows Server 2003, such applications are called *Windows Services* (formerly known as NT Services). The tasks carried out by Windows Services are typically long running and have little or no direct interaction with a user (so they don't usually have user interfaces). Such applications may be started when the computer is booted and often continue to run until the computer is shut down.

This chapter looks at:

- The characteristics of a Windows Service
- How to interact with a Windows Service using Visual Studio 2005 and the management applets in the Windows Control Panel
- How to create, install, and communicate with a Windows Service using Visual Basic
- How to debug a Windows Service from within Visual Studio 2005

As VB6 did not offer direct support for the creation of Windows Services, you might be unfamiliar with such applications. So, to help understand the variety of such applications, this chapter examines some scenarios in which a Windows Service application is a good solution.

Example Windows Services

Microsoft SQL Server, Exchange Server, Internet Information Server (IIS), and antivirus software all use Windows Services to perform tasks in response to events that occur on the system overall. Only a background service, or Windows Service, which runs no matter which user is logged in, could perform such operations.

Consider these potential Windows Services:

- **A File Watcher**—Suppose we are running an FTP server that allows users to place files in a particular directory. We could use a Windows Service to monitor and process files within that directory as they arrive. The service runs in the background and detects when files are changed or added within the directory, and then extracts information from these files in order to process orders, or update address and billing information. We'll see an example of such a Windows Service later in this chapter.
- **An Automated Stock Price Reporter**—We could build a system that extracts stock prices from a Web site and then e-mails the information to users. We could set thresholds so that an e-mail is only sent out if the stock price reaches a certain price. This Windows Service can be automated to extract the information every 10 minutes, every 10 seconds, or whatever. Because a Windows Service can contain any logic that does not require a user interface, there is a lot of flexibility in constructing such applications.
- **Microsoft Transaction Server (MTS)**—This (part of COM+ Services in Windows 2000 and later) is an object broker that manages instances of components and is used regularly by professional developers. This service runs constantly in the background and manages components as soon as the computer is booted, just like IIS or Exchange Server.

Characteristics of a Windows Service

To properly design and develop a Windows Service, it's important to understand how a Windows Service differs from a typical Windows program. Here are the most important characteristics of a Windows Service:

- A Windows Service can start before a user logs on. The system maintains a list of Windows Services and they can be set to start at boot time. Services can also be installed so they require a manual startup and will not start at boot.
- A Windows Service can run under a different account from that of the current user. Most Windows Services provide functionality that needs to be running all the time and some load before a user logs on, so they cannot depend on a user being logged on to run.
- A Windows Service has its own process. It does not run in the process of a program communicating with it (Chapter 24 has more information on processes).
- A Windows Service typically has no user interface. This is because the service may be running under a different account from that of the current user, or the service may start at boot time, which would mean that the calls to put up a user interface might fail because they are out of context (it is possible to create a Windows Service with a user interface, but Visual Basic 2005 cannot be used to do it; we'll discuss why later on).
- A Windows Service requires a special installation procedure; just clicking on a compiled EXE won't run it. The program must run in a special context in the operating system, and a specific installation process is required to do the configuration necessary for a Windows Service to be run in this special context.

- A Windows Service works with a *Service Control Manager* (discussed shortly). The Service Control Manager is required to provide an interface to the Windows Service. External programs that want to communicate with a Windows Service (for example, to start or stop the service) must go through the Service Control Manager. The Service Control Manager is an operating-system-level program, but it has a user interface that can be used to start and stop services, and this interface can be accessed through the Computer Management section of the Control Panel.

Interacting with Windows Services

You can view the services that are used on your computer by opening the Services Control Manager user interface. This can be done in Windows 2000 via Administrative Tools ➪ Services in the Control Panel, and in Windows XP Professional via All Programs ➪ Administrative Tools ➪ Services from the Start button. Using the Services Control Manager, a service can be set to automatically start up when the system is booted, or a service can be started manually. Services can also be stopped or paused. The list of services contained in the Services Control Manager includes the current state for each service. Figure 25-1 shows the Services Control Manager in Windows XP.

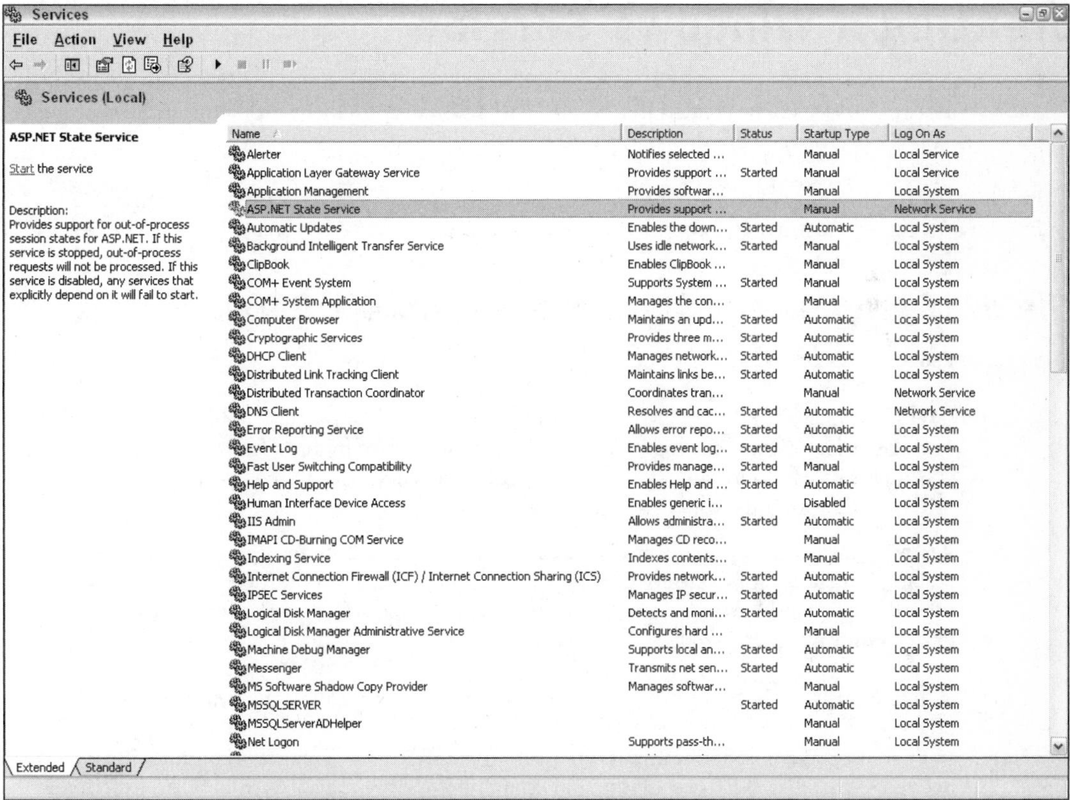

Figure 25-1

The Status column indicates the current state of the service. If this column is blank, the service has not been started since the last time the computer was booted. Other possible values for Status are Started, Stopped, and Paused. You can get access to additional settings and details concerning a service by double-clicking it.

When a service is started, it automatically logs into the system using either a user or system account:

- The user account is a regular NT account that allows the program to interact with the system—in essence, the service will impersonate a user.
- The system account is not associated with a particular user.

The Services Control Manager seen in Figure 25-1 is part of the operating system (which is what supports Windows Services); it is not a part of .NET. Any service run by the operating system is exposed through the Services Control Manager, no matter how the service was created or installed. We can also interact with Windows Services via the Server Explorer in Visual Studio 2005. We'll cover this technique later on.

Creating a Windows Service

Prior to .NET, most Windows Services were created with C++. Third-party toolkits were available to allow Windows Services to be created in VB6 and earlier, but deployment problems and threading issues meant that few developers went down this route.

In .NET, the functionality needed to interface to the operating system is wrapped up in the .NET Framework classes, so any .NET-compliant language can now be used to create a Windows Service.

The .NET Framework Classes for Windows Services

There are several base classes that are needed to create a Windows Service:

- `System.ServiceProcess.ServiceBase`—Provides the base class for the Windows Service. The class that contains the logic that will run in the service inherits from `ServiceBase`. A single executable can contain more than one service, but each service in the executable will be a separate class that inherits from `ServiceBase`.
- `System.Configuration.Install.Installer`—This is a generic class that performs the installation chores for a variety of components. One class in a Windows Service process must inherit and extend `Installer` in order to provide the interface necessary to install the service under Windows Server 2003, XP, 2000, and NT.

Each class that inherits from `Installer` needs to contain an instance of each of these classes:

- `System.ServiceProcess.ServiceProcessInstaller`—This class contains the information needed to install a .NET executable that contains Windows Services (that is, an executable that contains classes that inherit from `ServiceBase`). The .NET installation utility for Windows Services (`InstallUtil.exe`, which we will discuss later) calls this class to get the information it needs to perform the installation.

- `System.ServiceProcess.ServiceInstaller`—This class also interacts with the `InstallUtil.exe` installation program. Whereas `ServiceProcessInstaller` contains information needed to install the executable as a whole, `ServiceInstaller` contains information on a specific service in the executable. If an executable contains more than one service, an instance of `ServiceInstaller` is needed for each one.

For most Windows Services we develop, we can let Visual Studio 2005 take care of `Installer`, `ServiceProcessInstaller`, and `ServiceInstaller`. We'll just need to set a few properties. The class we need to thoroughly understand is `ServiceBase`, as this is the class that contains the functionality of a Windows Service and therefore must inherit from it.

The ServiceBase Class

`ServiceBase` contains several useful properties and methods, but initially it's more important to understand the events of `ServiceBase`. Most of these events are fired by the Service Control Manager when the state of the service is changed. The most important events are as follows.

Event	How and When the Event is Used
`OnStart`	Occurs when the service is started. This is where the initialization logic for a service is usually placed.
`OnStop`	Occurs when the service is stopped. Cleanup and shutdown logic is generally placed here.
`OnPause`	Occurs when the service is paused. Any logic required to suspend operations during a pause goes here.
`OnContinue`	Occurs when a service continues after being paused.
`OnShutdown`	Occurs when the operating system is being shut down.
`OnSessionChange`	Occurs when a change event is received from a Terminal Session service. This method is new in the .NET Framework 2.0.
`OnPowerEvent`	Occurs when the system's power management software causes a change in the power status of the system. Usually used to change the behavior of a service when a system is going in or out of a "suspended" power mode. This is more frequent with end users who are working on a laptop.
`OnCustomCommand`	Occurs when an external program has told the Service Control Manager that it wishes to send a command to the service. The operation of this event is covered in "Communicating with the Service."

The events used most frequently are `OnStart`, `OnStop`, and `OnCustomCommand`. The `OnStart` and `OnStop` events are used in almost every Windows Service written in Visual Basic, and the `OnCustomCommand` is used if any special configuration of the service needs to be done while the service is running.

All of these are `Protected` events, so they are only available to classes that inherit from `ServiceBase`. Because of the restricted context in which it runs, a Windows Service component that inherits from `ServiceBase` often lacks a public interface. While we can add public properties and methods to such a component, they are of limited use because outside programs cannot obtain an object reference to running a Windows Service component.

To be active as a Windows Service, an instance of ServiceBase must be started via the shared Run method of the ServiceBase class. However, normally we don't have to write code to do this because the template code generated by Visual Studio 2005 places the correct code in the Main subroutine of the project for us.

The most commonly used property of ServiceBase is the AutoLog property. This Boolean property is set to True by default. If True, then the Windows Service automatically logs the Start, Stop, Pause, and Continue events to an Event Log. The Event Log used is the Application Event Log and the Source in the log entries is taken from the name of Windows Service. This automatic event logging is stopped by setting the AutoLog property to False.

The following File Watcher example goes into more detail about the automatic logging capabilities in a Windows Service, and about Event Logs in general.

Installation-Oriented Classes

The Installer, ServiceProcessInstaller, and ServiceInstaller classes are quite simple to build and use if you are employing Visual Studio 2005. After you create your Windows Service project, Visual Studio 2005 will create a class file called Service1.vb for you. To add the Installer, ServiceProcessInstaller, and ServiceInstaller classes to your project, simply right-click the design surface of this ServiceBase class, Service1.vb, and select Add Installer. This creates the code framework necessary to use them.

The Installer class (named ProjectInstaller.vb by default in a Windows Service project) generally needs no interaction at all—it is ready to use when created by Visual Studio 2005. However, it may be appropriate to change some properties of the ServiceProcessInstaller and ServiceInstaller classes. You can do this by simply highlighting these objects on the design surface and changing their properties directly in the Properties window of Visual Studio 2005. The properties that are typically modified for ServiceProcessInstaller include:

- Account—This specifies the type of account under which the entire service application will run. Different settings give the services in the application different levels of privilege on the local system. We'll use the highest level of privilege, LocalSystem, for most of the examples in this chapter in order to keep it simple. If this property is set to User (which is the default), then we must supply a username and password, and that user's account is used to determine privileges for the service. If there is any possibility that a service could access system resources that should be "out-of-bounds," then using the User setting to restrict privileges is a good idea. Besides LocalSystem and User, other possible settings for the Account property include NetworkService and LocalService.
- Username—If Account is set to User, then this property determines the user account to use in determining the privileges the system will have and how it interacts with other computers on the network. If this property is left blank, it will be requested when the service is installed.
- Password—This property determines the password to access the user account specified in the Username property. If the password is left blank, it will be requested when the service is installed.
- HelpText—The information about the service that will be displayed in certain installation options.

If the `Account` property is set to `User`, it is good practice to set up a special user account for the service, rather than relying on some existing account that is intended for a live user. The special account can be set up with exactly the appropriate privileges for the service. It also is not as vulnerable to having its password or its privileges inadvertently changed in a way that would cause problems in running the service.

For the `ServiceInstaller` class, the properties we might change include:

- `DisplayName`—The name of the service as displayed in the Service Manager or the Server Explorer can be different from the class name and the executable name if desired, though it's a good convention to make this name the same as the class name for the service.
- `StartType`—This specifies how the service is started. The default is `Manual`, which means we must start the service manually as it won't start by itself after the system boots. If we want the service to always start when the system starts, we can change this property to `Automatic`. The Service Manager can be used to override the `StartType` setting.
- `ServiceName`—The name of the service that this `ServiceInstaller` handles during installation. If we changed the class name of the service after using the Add Installer option, we would need to change this property to correspond to the new name for the service.

`ServiceProcessInstaller` and `ServiceInstaller` are used as necessary during the installation process, so there is no need to understand or manipulate the methods of either.

Multiple Services Within One Executable

It is possible to place more than one class that inherits from `ServiceBase` in a single Windows Service executable. Each such class then allows for a separate service that can be started, stopped, and so on, independently of the other services in the executable.

If a Windows Service executable contains more than one service, it needs to contain one `ServiceInstaller` for each service. Each `ServiceInstaller` is configured with the information used for its associated service, such as the displayed name and the start type (automatic or manual). However, the executable still only needs one `ServiceProcessInstaller`, which works for all the services in the executable. It is configured with the account information that will be used for all the services in the executable.

The ServiceController Class

Another important .NET Framework class for working with Windows Services is the `System.ServiceProcess.ServiceController` class. This class is not used when constructing a service. It is used by external applications to communicate with a running service, allowing operations such as starting and stopping the service. The `ServiceController` class is described in detail in Communicating with the Service.

Other Types of Windows Services

The `ServiceBase` and `ServiceController` classes can be used to create typical Windows Services that work with high-level system resources such as the file system or performance counters. However, some Windows Services need to interact at a deeper level. For example, a service may work at the kernel level, fulfilling functions such as that of a device driver.

Presently, the .NET Framework classes for Windows Services cannot be used to create such lower-level services, which rules out both VB and C# as tools to create them. C++ is typically the tool of choice for these types of services. If the .NET version of C++ is used, the code for such services would typically run in unmanaged mode.

Another type of service that cannot be created with the .NET Framework classes is one that interacts with the Windows desktop. Again, C++ is the preferred tool for such services.

We'll look at the types of services that *are* possible again when we cover the `ServiceType` property of the `ServiceController` class, in "Communicating with the Service."

Creating a Windows Service with Visual Basic

Now it's time to create and use a Windows Service with Visual Basic, using the previously discussed .NET Framework classes. We will demonstrate these tasks later in a detailed example. Here is a high-level description of the necessary tasks:

1. Create a new project of the type Windows Service. By default, the service will be in a module named `Service1.vb`. The service can be renamed as with any other .NET module. (The class that is automatically placed in `Service1.vb` will be named `Service1` by default, and it will inherit from `ServiceBase`.)
2. Place any logic needed to run when the service is started in the `OnStart` event of the service class. You can find the code listing for the `Service1.vb` file by double-clicking this file's design surface.
3. Add any additional logic that the service needs to carry out its operation. Logic can be placed in the class for the service, or in any other class module in the project. Such logic is typically called via some event that is generated by the operating system and passed to the service, such as a file changing in a directory, or a timer tick.
4. Add an installer to the project. This module provides the interface to Windows Server 2003, Windows XP, Windows 2000, or Windows NT to install the module as a Windows Service. The installer will be a class that inherits from `System.Configuration.Install.Installer`, and it will contain instances of the `ServiceProcessInstaller` and `ServiceInstaller` classes.
5. Set the properties of the installer modules as necessary. The most common settings needed are the account under which the service will run and the name the service will display in the Service Control Manager.
6. Build the project. This will result in an EXE file. If the service was named `WindowsService1`, then the executable file would be named `WindowsService1.exe`.
7. Install the Windows Service with a command-line utility named `InstallUtil.exe`. (As previously mentioned, a service cannot be started by just running the EXE file.)
8. Start the Windows Service with the Service Control Manager (available in the Control Panel ➪ Administrative Tools folder in Windows 2000, or the Start ➪ All Programs ➪ Administrative Tools folder in Windows XP) or with the Server Explorer in Visual Studio 2005.

You can also start a service from the command console if the proper paths to .NET are set. The command is "`NET START <servicename>`". Note that the `<servicename>` used in this command is the name of the service, not the name of the executable in which the service resides. Depending on the configuration of your system, a service being started with any of the aforementioned methods will sometimes fail with an error message that says the service did not start in a timely fashion. This may be because the .NET libraries and other initialization tasks did not finish fast enough to suit the Service Control Manager. If this happens, attempt to start the service again, and it will usually succeed the second time.

Note that Steps 2 through 5 can be done in a different order. It doesn't matter if the installer is added and configured before or after the logic that does the processing for the service is added.

At this point, a service is installed and running. The Service Manager or the Server Explorer can stop the service, or it will be automatically stopped when the system is shut down. The command to stop the service in a command console is "`NET STOP <servicename>`".

The service will not automatically start up the next time the system is booted unless the service is configured for that. This can be done by setting the `StartType` property for the service to `Automatic` when developing the service or it can be done in the Service Manager. Right-clicking the service in the Service Manager gives access to this capability.

This process is superficially similar to doing most other Visual Basic projects. There are a few important differences, however:

- We cannot debug the project in the environment as you normally would any other Visual Basic program. The service must be installed and started before it can be debugged. It is also necessary to attach to the process for the service to do debugging. Details about this are included in "Debugging the Service."
- Even though the end result of the development is an EXE, we should not include any message boxes or other visual elements in the code. The Windows Service executable is more like a component library in that sense, and should not have a visual interface. If you include visual elements such as message boxes, the results can vary. In some cases, the UI code will have no effect. In others cases, the service may hang when attempting to write to the user interface.
- Finally, we should be especially careful to handle all errors within the program. Since the program is not running in a user context, a runtime error has no place to report itself visually. We should handle all errors with structured exception handling, and use an Event Log or other offline means to record and communicate runtime errors.

Creating a Counter Monitor Service

To illustrate the outlined steps, we'll create a simple service that will check the value of a performance counter, and when the value of the counter exceeds a certain value, the service will beep every three seconds. This is a good example for stepping through the process of creating, installing, and starting a Windows Service. It contains very little logic, and we can easily tell when it is working.

In the first phase of the example, we create a service that always beeps. Then in the second phase, we add logic to monitor the performance counter and only beep when the counter exceeds a specific value:

1. Start a new Windows Service project using Visual Studio 2005. Name the project `CounterMonitor`.

2. In the Solution Explorer, rename `Service1.vb` to `CounterMonitor.vb`.

3. Click the design surface for `CounterMonitor.vb`. In the Properties window, change the `(Name)` property to `CounterMonitor`, and change the `ServiceName` property from `Service1` to `CounterMonitor` (the `(Name)` property changes the name of the class on which the service is based, while the `ServiceName` property changes the name of the service as known to the Service Control Manager).

4. Right-click the project for the service, and select Properties. You will then be presented with the CounterMonitor Property Pages as one of the paged tabs directly in Visual Studio. From the Application tab, set the Application Type drop-down list to Windows Service and from the drop-down list named Startup Object, select `CounterMonitor`. This is shown in Figure 25-2.

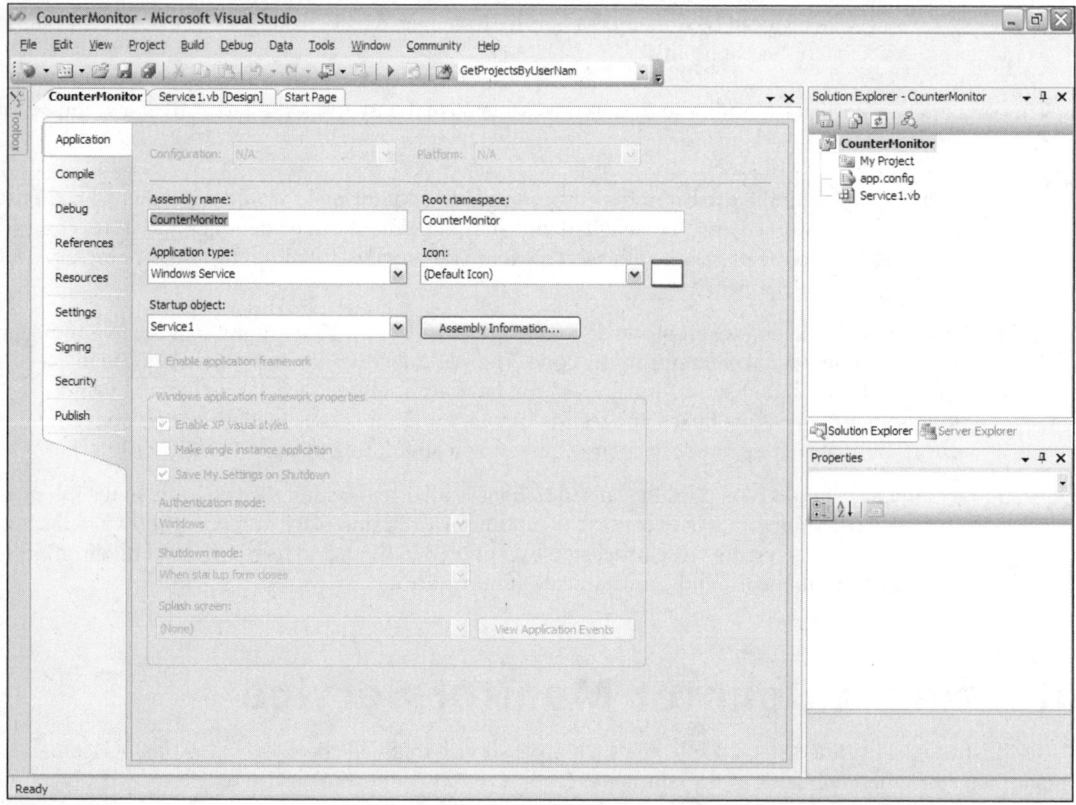

Figure 25-2

5. Go back to the `CounterMonitor.vb` file's design view and open the Visual Studio 2005 Toolbox. Open the Components (not the Windows Forms) tab. Drag a `Timer` control from the Toolbox onto the `CounterMonitor` design surface. It will appear on the design surface with the name `Timer1`.

6. In the Properties window for `Timer1`, change the `Interval` property to a value of `3000` (that's 3,000 milliseconds, which will cause the timer to fire every 3 seconds).

7. Go to the code for `CounterMonitor.vb`. Inside the `OnStart` event handler (which is already created for you in the code), enter the following code:

```
Timer1.Enabled = True
```

8. In the `OnStop` event for the class, enter the following code:

```
Timer1.Enabled = False
```

9. Create an `Elapsed` event for the timer by highlighting `Timer1` in the left-hand drop-down box at the top of the code editor window, and then selecting the `Elapsed` event in the right-hand drop-down box from the code view of the file.

10. In the `Elapsed` event, place the following line of code:

```
Beep()
```

11. Now add an installer to the project. Go back to the design surface for `CounterMonitor` and right-click it. Select Add Installer. A new file called `ProjectInstaller1.vb` is created and added to the project. The `ProjectInstaller1.vb` file will have two components added to its design surface, named `ServiceProcessInstaller1` and `ServiceInstaller1`. This is shown in Figure 25-3.

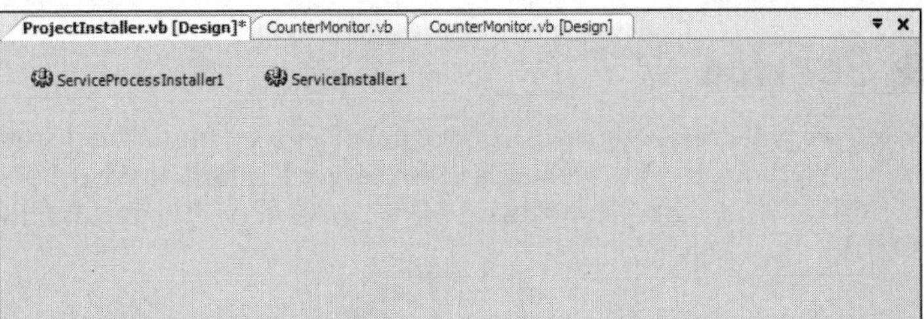

Figure 25-3

12. On the `ProjectInstaller.vb` design surface, highlight the `ServiceProcessInstaller1` control. In its Properties window, change the `Account` property to `LocalSystem`.

13. Highlight the `ServiceInstaller1` control. In its Properties window, type in `CounterMonitor` as the value of the `DisplayName` property.

14. Now build the project by right-clicking on the solution and selecting Build from the menu. An EXE for the service will be created named `CounterMonitor.exe`.

Installing the Service

Now we are ready to install the service. The utility for doing this must be run from a command line. The utility is called `InstallUtil.exe`, and it is located in the .NET utilities directory, which will be found at `C:\WINNT\Microsoft.NET\Framework\v2.0.[xxxx]` on Windows 2000 and NT systems, or `C:\Windows\Microsoft.NET\Framework\v2.0.[xxxx]` on Windows XP and Windows 2003.

You can easily access this utility (and all the other .NET utilities in that directory) using an option off of the Programs menu that is installed with Visual Studio 2005. Choose Microsoft Visual Studio 2005 ➪ Visual Studio Tools ➪ Visual Studio 2005 Command Prompt. This will result in the display of a command window. Change to the directory that contains `CounterMonitor.exe`. By default, when using Visual Studio 2005, you'll find this executable at `C:\Documents and Settings\[ user ]\My Documents\Visual Studio\Projects\CounterMonitor\Projects\CounterMonitor\CounterMonitor\obj\Debug`. Once found, run the following command:

```
InstallUtil CounterMonitor.exe
```

You should look at the messages generated by `InstallUtil.exe` to make sure that the installation of the service was successful. The utility will generate several lines of information, and if it is successful, the last two lines will be

```
The Commit phase completed successfully.

The transacted install has completed.
```

If these two lines do not appear, you will need to read all the information generated by the utility to find out why the install did not work. Reasons might include a bad pathname for the executable, or trying to install the service again when it is already installed (it must be uninstalled before it can be reinstalled).

Starting the Service

Later in this chapter, we will create our own "control panel" screen to start and stop the service. But for now, to test our new Windows Service, we will use the Server Explorer in Visual Studio 2005. Open the Server Explorer in Visual Studio 2005 and expand the Services node. The resulting screen is shown in Figure 25-4.

Figure 25-4

If the `CounterMonitor` service does not appear in the list, the installation was unsuccessful. Try the installation again and check the error messages.

Right-click the `CounterMonitor` service. Select the Start menu option. You will hear the service beep every 3 seconds. You can stop the service by right-clicking it again, and selecting the Stop menu option.

You can also use the Service Control Manager built into Windows to start the `CounterMonitor` service. This is illustrated in Figure 25-5.

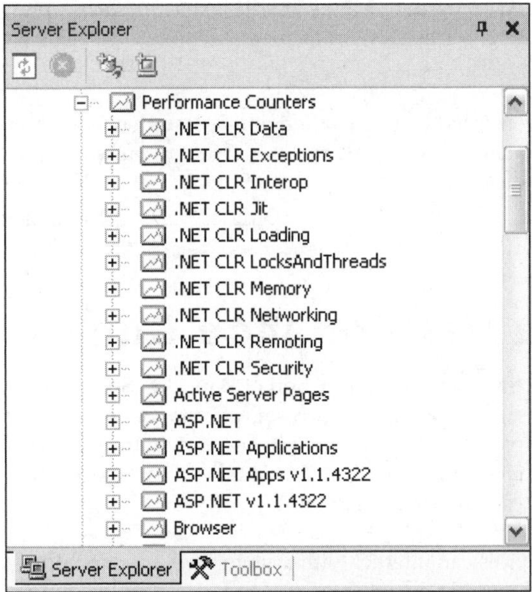

Figure 25-5

Start `CounterMonitor` by right-clicking it and selecting Start or by clicking the Start link. As before, you will hear your computer beep every three seconds. Stop the service by right-clicking `CounterMonitor` and selecting Stop or by clicking the Stop link. Note that if you already started the service via the Server Explorer (as discussed earlier), then it will be in a Started state when you go into the Service Control Manager program.

Uninstalling the Service

Uninstalling the service is very similar to installing it. The service must be in a stopped state before it can be uninstalled, but the uninstall operation will attempt to stop the service if it is running. The uninstall operation is done in the same command window (with the Visual Studio 2005 Command Prompt) as the install operation, and the command used is the same as the one for installation, except that the option `/u` is included just before name of the service. Remember that you will need to navigate to

`C:\Documents and Settings\[ user ]\My Documents\Visual Studio\Projects\CounterMonitor\Projects\CounterMonitor\CounterMonitor\obj\Debug` to run this command.

```
InstallUtil.exe /u CounterMonitor.exe
```

You can tell that the uninstall was successful if the information displayed by the utility contains the following line:

```
Service CounterMonitor was successfully removed from the system.
```

If the uninstall is unsuccessful, read the rest of the information to find out why. Besides typing in the wrong pathname, another common reason for failure is trying to uninstall a service that is in a running state and could not be stopped in a timely fashion.

Once you have uninstalled `CounterMonitor`, it will no longer show up in the list of available services to start and stop (at least after a refresh it won't).

> **A Windows Service must be uninstalled and reinstalled every time you make changes to it. You should uninstall `CounterMonitor` now because we're about to add new capabilities to it.**

Monitoring a Performance Counter

Performance counters are a system-level function of Windows Server 2003, Windows 2000, XP, and NT. They are used to track usage of system resources. Performance counters can be expressed as counts (number of times a Web page was hit), or percentages (how much disk space is left), or other types of information. Many counters are automatically maintained by the operating system, but applications can create and manage their own performance counters.

To demonstrate how services can interact with system-level functionality, we will add the capability to our `CounterMonitor` to monitor a particular performance counter, and only beep when the performance counter exceeds a certain value.

Performance counters can be monitored by a user with the Performance Monitor. There are a variety of performance counters built into the operating system, providing access to information such as the number of threads currently active on the system, or the number of documents in a print queue. Any of these, and any custom performance counters, can be graphed in the Performance Monitor.

Creating a Performance Counter

We will create a performance counter named `ServiceCounter`. Then we will change `CounterMonitor` to check that counter and only beep when its value is over 5. To test it, we will also create a small Windows Forms application that increments and decrements the counter.

Performance counters are typically accessed in Visual Studio 2005 through the Server Explorer tab. To see the available performance counters, open the Server Explorer, which looks much like the screen shown in Figure 25-6.

To see the categories of performance counters, click the plus sign next to the Performance Counters option in the Server Explorer. Several dozen categories will be shown. You can look at the counters in any particular category by clicking the plus sign next to the category.

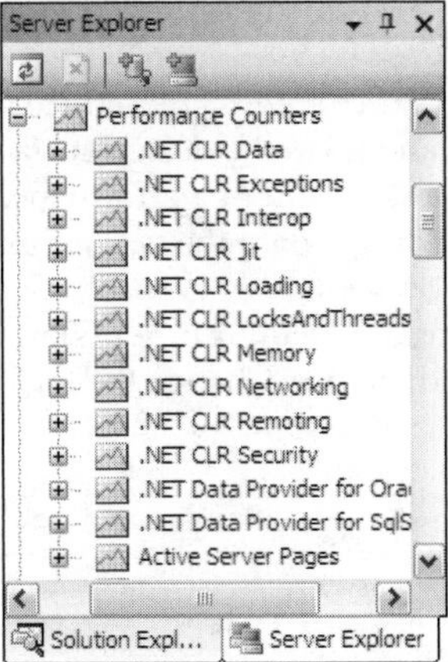

Figure 25-6

You can also create new categories and new counters. For this example, you need to create a new category for our counter called `Service Counters`. To do that, right-click the Performance Counters option in the Server Explorer and select the Create New Category option. In the resulting Performance Counter Builder dialog box (shown in Figure 25-7), enter the name of the category as `Service Counters`, and create a new counter by clicking the New button and entering `TestCounter` for the name. Once that is complete, click the OK button in the dialog box, and Visual Studio 2005 will then create a new category called `Service Counters` that contains a single performance counter called `TestCounter`.

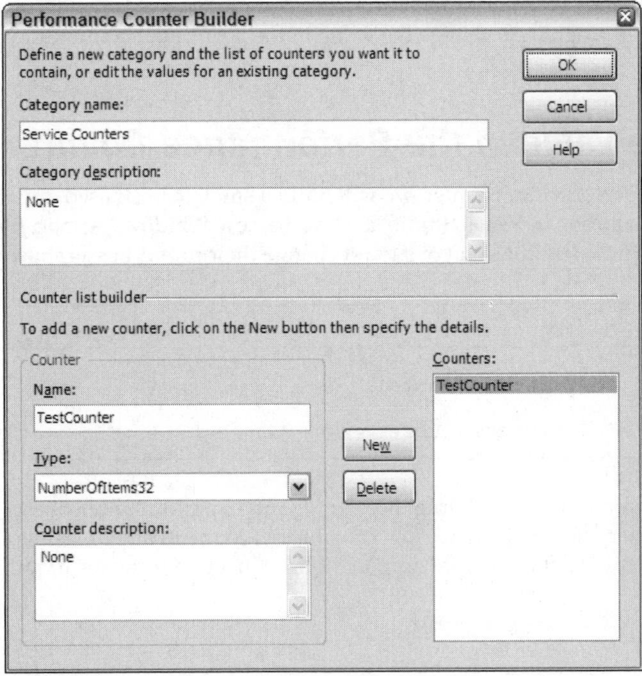

Figure 25-7

Integrating the Counter into the Service

Using a performance counter in the `CounterMonitor` service we created earlier is straightforward. Open the `CounterMonitor` project, and go to the design surface for `CounterMonitor`. Then open the Server Explorer so that it shows the `TestCounter` performance counter we created. Click `TestCounter` from within the Server Explorer and drag it onto the `CounterMonitor.vb` design surface.

A new visual control named `PerformanceCounter1` will now be shown on the page's design surface. The performance counter is now ready to use. Change the logic in the `Elapsed` event for `Timer1` to look like this:

```
If PerformanceCounter1.RawValue > mnMaxValue Then
    Beep()
End If
```

The `RawValue` property being used in this code fetches the unformatted value of the counter. For counters that track whole numbers (such as the number of times a Web page is hit), the `RawValue` property is normally used to get the value of the counter for testing or display. Some other types of counters use a `NextValue` method to get a formatted value. See the `CounterType` property of the `PerformanceCounter` class for more on the types of performance counters available.

Next, put this statement in the code module just under the first line of the `CounterMonitor` class:

```
Dim mnMaxValue As Integer = 5
```

Now build the service again, and install it as we did before. Start the service. It should not beep at this point because the value in the performance counter is zero. You can leave the counter running, because we will now create a program to change the value in the performance counter, and thus make the service begin beeping.

Changing the Value in the Performance Counter

To manipulate the performance counter, we will build a small forms-based application. Close the `CounterMonitor` solution in Visual Studio, and start a new Windows Application Project named `CounterTest`. Place two buttons on `Form1` and change their properties as shown in the following table.

Name	Text
`BtnIncrement`	`Increment Counter`
`BtnDecrement`	`Decrement Counter`

Then, open the Server Explorer and drag the `TestCounter` performance counter onto the form itself, just as you did earlier with the `CounterMonitor` project. As with all nonvisible components from the toolbox, the counter will appear in the component tray (just under the form) rather than on the form design surface.

The `PerformanceCounter1` control for `CounterTest` needs one property change. The `ReadOnly` property of the control needs to be set to `False`. This will allow the application to manipulate the counter. (This change was unnecessary for the `CounterMonitor` Windows Service project because that project only reads the value of the performance counter and does not change it.)

Now double-click `btnIncrement` to get to its click event. Place the following code in the event:

```
PerformanceCounter1.Increment()
```

Double-click the `btnDecrement` to get to its click event. Place the following code in the event:

```
PerformanceCounter1.Decrement()
```

Build and run the program and click the increment button six times. If the `CounterMonitor` service is running, on the sixth click it will begin beeping because the value in the counter has exceeded five. Then click the decrement button a couple of times, and the beeping will stop.

If you want to monitor the current value of the counter, select Control Panel ➪ Administrative Tools ➪ Performance. This program, the Performance Monitor, allows the value of counters to be graphed. You add a counter for display by clicking the New Counter Set button and right-clicking the right-hand portion of the Performance Monitor, and adding a counter in the dialog box that pops up. Change the Performance Object drop-down list to `Service Counters` and add the `TestCounter` performance counter to the list. When completed, press the Close button. The counter that you created will then be monitored by the dialog box. You can use the help for this program for more details on displaying counters in the Performance Monitor.

Communicating with the Service

Up to this point, we've seen how to:

- Create a Windows Service using Visual Basic
- Start and stop a service with the Server Explorer in Visual Studio 2005 or the Service Control Manager in the control panel
- Make a service work with a system level function such as a performance counter

If it is sufficient to start, stop, and check on the service through the Server Explorer or Service Control Manager, and there is no need to do any other communication with the service, then these procedures are all you need. But it is oftentimes helpful to create a specialized application to manipulate your service. This application will typically be able to start and stop a service, and check on its status. The application may also need to communicate with the service to change its configuration. Such an application is often referred to as a *control panel* for the service, even though it does not necessarily reside in the operating system's Control Panel. A commonly-used example of such an application is the SQL Server Service Manager, whose icon appears in the tray on the Taskbar (normally in the lower right section of the screen) if you have SQL Server 2000 installed.

Such an application needs a way to communicate with the service. The .NET Framework base class that is used for such communication is the `ServiceController` class. It is in the `System.ServiceProcess` namespace. You need to add a reference to `System.ServiceProcess.dll` (which contains this namespace) before a project can use the `ServiceController` class.

The `ServiceController` class provides an interface to the Service Control Manager, which coordinates all communication with Windows Services. However, we don't have to know anything about the Service Control Manager to use the `ServiceController` class. We just manipulate the properties and methods of the `ServiceController` class, and any necessary communication with the Service Control Manager is accomplished on our behalf behind the scenes.

It's a good idea to use exactly *one* instance of the `ServiceController` class for each service you are controlling. Multiple instances of `ServiceController` that are communicating with the same service can have timing conflicts. Typically, that means using a module-level object variable to hold the reference to the active `ServiceController`, and instantiating the `ServiceController` during the initialization logic for the application. The following example uses this technique.

The ServiceController Class

The constructor for the `ServiceController` requires the name of the Windows Service with which it will be communicating. This is the same as the name that was placed in the `ServiceName` property of the class that defined the service. We'll see how to instantiate the `ServiceController` class shortly.

The `ServiceController` class has several members that are useful in manipulating services. Here are the most important methods, followed by another table of the most important properties.

Method	Purpose
`Start`	A method to start up the service.
`Stop`	A method to stop the service.
`Refresh`	A method to make sure the `ServiceController` object contains the latest state of the service (needed because the service might be manipulated from another program).
`ExecuteCommand`	A method used to send a custom command to the service. We will cover this method in the section on Custom Commands.

Here are the most important properties.

Property	Purpose
`CanStop`	A property indicating whether the service can be stopped.
`ServiceName`	A property containing the name of the associated service.

Property	Purpose
`Status`	An enumerated property that indicates whether a service is stopped, started, in process of being started, and so on. The `ToString` method on this property is useful for getting the status in a string form for text messages. The possible values of the enumeration are: `ContinuePending` — The service is attempting to continue `Paused` — The service is paused `PausePending` — The service is attempting to go into a paused state `Running` — The service is running `StartPending` — The service is starting `Stopped` — The service is not running `StopPending` — The service is stopping
`ServiceType`	A property that indicates the type of service. The result is an enumerated value. The enumerations are: `Win32OwnProcess` — The service uses its own process (this is the default for a service created in .NET). `Win32ShareProcess` — The service shares a process with another service (this advanced capability is not covered here). `Adapter`, `FileSystemDriver`, `InteractiveProcess`, `KernelDriver`, `RecognizerDriver` — These are low-level service types that cannot be created with Visual Basic because the `ServiceBase` class does not support the types. However, the value of the `ServiceType` property may still have these values for services created with other tools.

Integrating a ServiceController into the Example

To manipulate the service, we'll enhance the `CounterTest` program we created earlier. Here are step-by-step instructions to do that:

1. Add three new buttons to the `CounterTest` form, with the following names and text labels.

Name	Text
`BtnCheckStatus`	"Check Status"
`BtnStartService`	"Start Service"
`BtnStopService`	"Stop Service"

2. Add a reference to the DLL that contains the `ServiceController` class. To do this, select Project ➪ Add Reference. On the .NET tab, highlight the `System.ServiceProcess.dll` option, and press the OK button.

3. Add this line at the top of the code for `Form1`:

```
Imports System.ServiceProcess
```

4. As we discussed, the project needs to use only one instance of the `ServiceController` class. Create a module-level object reference to a `ServiceController` class by adding the following line of code within the `Form1` class:

```
Dim myController As ServiceController
```

5. Create a `Form Load` event in `Form1`, and place the following line of code in it to instantiate the `ServiceController` class:

```
myController = New ServiceController("CounterMonitor")
```

We now have a `ServiceController` class named `myController` that we can use to manipulate the `CounterMonitor` Windows Service. In the click event for `btnCheckStatus`, place the following code:

```
Dim sStatus As String
myController.Refresh()
sStatus = myController.Status.ToString

MsgBox(myController.ServiceName & " is in state: " & sStatus)
```

In the click event for `btnStartService`, place the following code:

```
Try
    myController.Start()
Catch exp As Exception
    MsgBox("Could not start service or the service is already running")
End Try
```

In the `click` event for `btnStopService`, place the following code:

```
If myController.CanStop Then
    myController.Stop()
Else
    MsgBox("Service cannot be stopped or the service is already stopped")
End If
```

Run and test the program. The service may already be running because of one of your previous tests. Make sure the performance counter is high enough to make the service beep, and then test starting and stopping the service.

More About ServiceController

`ServiceController` classes can be created for *any* Windows Service, not just those created in .NET. For example, we could instantiate a `ServiceController` class that was associated with the Windows Service for Internet Information Server (IIS), and use it to start, pause, and stop IIS. The code would look just like the code used earlier for the application that controlled the `CounterMonitor` service. The only difference is that the name of the service would need to be changed in the line that instantiates the `ServiceController` (Step 5).

It's also useful to emphasize that the `ServiceController` is not communicating directly with the service. It is working through the Services Control Manager. That means the requests from the Service Controller to start, stop, or pause a service do not behave synchronously. As soon as the `ServiceController` has passed the request to the `ServicesControlManager`, it continues to execute its own code without waiting for the Service Control Manager to pass on the request, or for the service to act on the request.

Custom Commands

Some services need additional operations besides starting and stopping. For example, for our `CounterMonitor` Windows Service, we might want to set the threshold value of the performance counter that causes the service to begin beeping, or we might want to change the interval between beeps.

With most components, we would implement such functionality through a public interface. That is, we would put public properties and methods on the component. However, we cannot do this with a Windows Service, because it has no public interface that we can get to from outside the service.

To deal with this need, the interface for a Windows Service contains a special event called `OnCustomCommand`. The event arguments include a numeric code that can service as a command sent to the Windows Service. The code can be any number in the range 128 to 255. (Those numbers under 128 are reserved for use by the operating system.)

To fire the event and send a custom command to a service, the `ExecuteCommand` method of the `ServiceController` is used. The `ExecuteCommand` method takes the numeric code that needs to be sent to the service as a parameter. When this method is accessed, the `ServiceController` class tells the Service Control Manager to fire the `OnCustomCommand` event in the service, and to pass it the numeric code.

To see this process in action, let's go through an example. Suppose we want to be able to change the interval between beeps for our `CounterMonitor` service. We cannot directly send the beep interval that we want, but we can pick various values of the interval, and associate a custom command numeric code with each.

Suppose we want to be able to set intervals of 1 second, 3 seconds (the default), or 10 seconds. We could set up the following correspondence.

Custom Command Numeric Code	Beep Interval
201	One second (1,000 milliseconds)
203	Three seconds (3,000 milliseconds)
210	Ten seconds (10,000 milliseconds)

The correspondence between code and times we have chosen is completely arbitrary. We could use any codes between 128 and 255 to associate with our beep intervals. The ones shown in the table were chosen because they are easy to remember.

First, we need to change the CounterMonitor service so that it is able to accept the custom commands for the beep interval. To do that, first make sure the CounterMonitor service is uninstalled from any previous installs. Then open the Visual Studio 2005 project for the CounterMonitor service.

Create an OnCustomCommand event in the service. To do this, first open the code window for CounterMonitor.vb. Then type Protected Overrides OnCustomCommand. By this point, IntelliSense will kick in and you can press the tab key to autocomplete the shell event. Notice how it only accepts a single Integer as a parameter.

```
Protected Overrides Sub OnCustomCommand(ByVal command As Integer)

End Sub
```

In the OnCustomCommand event, place the following code:

```
    Timer1.Enabled = False
    Select Case command
        Case 201
            Timer1.Interval = 1000
        Case 203
            Timer1.Interval = 3000
        Case 210
            Timer1.Interval = 10000
    End Select
    Timer1.Enabled = True
```

Now build the countermonitor service, reinstall it, and start it.

Now we can enhance our CounterTest application that we created earlier to set the interval. To allow the user to pick the interval, we will use radio buttons. On the CounterTest program Form1 (which currently contains five buttons), place three radio buttons. Set their text labels as follows:

```
RadioButton1 - "1 second"
RadioButton2 - "3 seconds"
RadioButton3 - "10 seconds"
```

Then, place a button directly under these option buttons. Name it `btnSetInterval`, and set its text to `Set Interval`. In the `click` event for this button, place the following code:

```
Dim nIntervalCommand As Integer = 203
If RadioButton1.Checked Then
    nIntervalCommand = 201
End If
If RadioButton2.Checked Then
    nIntervalCommand = 203
End If
If RadioButton3.Checked Then
    nIntervalCommand = 210
End If
myController.ExecuteCommand(nIntervalCommand)
```

At this point, `Form1` should look something like the sample screen shown in Figure 25-8.

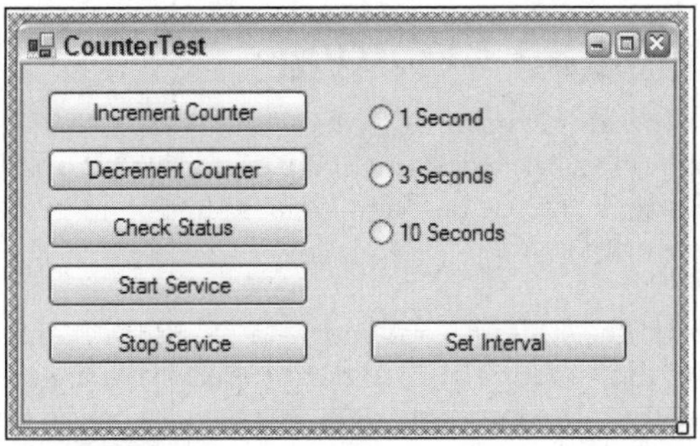

Figure 25-8

Start the `CounterTest` control program, and test the ability to change the beep interval. Remember to make sure the performance counter is high enough so that the `CounterMonitor` service beeps. Also remember that every time you stop and restart the service, it will reset the beep interval to 3 seconds.

Passing Strings to a Service

Since the `OnCustomCommand` event only takes numeric codes as input parameters, we cannot directly pass strings to the service. For example, if we wanted to reconfigure a directory name for a service, we could not just send the directory name over.

Instead it would be necessary to place the information to be passed to the service in a file in some known location on disk. Then a custom command for the service could instruct it to look at the standard file location, and read the information in the file. What the service did with the contents of the file would, of course, be customized for the service.

Creating a File Watcher

Now let's step through another example to illustrate what a Windows Service can do and how to construct one. We will build a service that monitors a particular directory, and reacts when a new or changed file is placed in the directory. The example Windows Service application waits for those files, extracts information from them, and then logs an event to a system log to record the file change.

As before, create a Windows Service from the built-in template named Windows Service in the New Project screen. Start by creating a new project and selecting the Windows Service template. Name this project `FileWatcherService` and click OK. This creates a new service class called `Service1.vb`. Rename this to `FileWatcherService.vb`. Then right-click the design surface, select Properties, and set the `ServiceName` property to `FileWatcherService`.

As in the first example, set the application type to Windows Service and reset the project's start object to `FileWatcherService`. All of this is illustrated earlier in this chapter.

Writing Events Using an Eventlog

The way to ensure the service is doing its job is by having it write events to a system Event Log. Event Logs are available under Windows NT, Windows 2000, Windows XP, and Windows Server 2003. As with many other system-level features, the use of Event Logs is simplified in .NET because a .NET Framework base class does most of the work for you.

There are three Event Logs on the system: `Application`, `Security`, and `System`. Normally, your applications should only write to the `Application` log. A property of a log entry called `Source` identifies the application writing the message. This property does not have to be the same as the executable name of the application, but is often given that name to make it easy to identify the source of the message.

You can look at the events in the Event Log by using the Event Viewer. It is in Control Panel ➪ Administrative Tools ➪ Event Viewer on Windows 2000, and Start ➪ All Programs ➪ Administrative Tools ➪ Event Viewer on Windows XP. We will use the Event Viewer in our example below to make sure our service is generating events.

Early in the chapter, we briefly mentioned that the `AutoLog` property of the `ServiceBase` class determines whether the service automatically writes events to the Application log. The `AutoLog` property instructs the service to use the Application Event Log to report command failures, as well as information for `OnStart`, `OnStop`, `OnPause`, and `OnContinue` events on the service. What is actually logged to the Event Log is an entry saying Service started successfully and Service stopped successfully, and any errors that might have occurred. If you look in the Application Event Log now, you will notice these logged events for the `CounterMonitor` Windows Service that you created and ran earlier in the chapter.

We can turn off the Event Log reporting by setting the `AutoLog` property to `False` in the Properties window for the service. However, we will leave it set to `True` for our example. That means some events will be logged automatically (without us including any code for them). Then, we add some code to our service to log additional events not covered by the `AutoLog` property.

First, though, we need to implement a file monitoring control into the project.

Creating a FileSystemWatcher

For performance reasons, we should do all of our work on a separate thread to our main application thread. We want to leave our main application free to accept any requests from the user or the operating system. We can do this by using some of the different components that create their own threads when they are launched. The `Timer` component and the `FileSystemWatcher` component are two examples. When the `Timer` component fires its `Elapsed` event, a thread is spawned and any code placed within that event will work on that newly created thread. The same thing happens when the events for the `FileSystemWatcher` component fire.

You can learn more about threading in .NET in Chapter 22.

The FileSystemWatcher Component

The `FileSystemWatcher` component is used to monitor a particular directory. The component implements `Created`, `Changed`, `Deleted`, and `Renamed` events, which are fired when files are placed in the directory, changed, deleted, or renamed, respectively.

The operation that takes place when one of these events is fired is up to the application developer. Most often, logic is included to read and process the new or changed files. However, we are just going to write a message to a log file.

To implement the component in the project, drag and drop a `FileSystemWatcher` control from the Components tab of the toolbox onto the designer surface of `FileWatcherService.vb`. This control will automatically be called `FileSystemWatcher1`.

The EnableRaisingEvents Property

The `FileSystemWatcher` control should not generate any events until the service is initialized and ready to handle them. To prevent this, set the `EnableRaisingEvents` property to `False`. This will prevent the control from firing any events. We will enable it during the `OnStart` event in the service.

These events fired by the `FileSystemWatcher` are controlled using the `NotifyFilter` property, discussed later.

The Path Property

Next, the path that we want to monitor is the `TEMP` directory on the `C:` drive, so set the `Path` property to `C:\TEMP` (be sure to check that there is a `TEMP` directory on your `C:` drive). Of course, this path can be changed to monitor any directory depending on your system, including any network or removable drives.

The NotifyFilter Property

We only want to watch for when a file is freshly created, or the last modified value of a file has changed. To do this, set the `NotifyFilter` property to `FileName, LastWrite`. We could also watch for other changes such as attributes, security, size, and directory name changes as well, just by changing the `NotifyFilter` property. Note that we specify multiple changes to watch for by including a list of changes separated by commas.

The Filter Property

The types of files that we will look for are text files. This is done by setting the `Filter` property to `.txt`. Notice that if you were going to watch for all file types, then the value of the `Filter` property needs to be set to `*.*`.

The IncludeSubdirectories Property

If we wanted to watch subdirectories, we would set the `IncludeSubdirectories` property to `True`. In this sample, we're leaving it as `False`, which is the default value.

You should have the following properties set as illustrated in Figure 25-9.

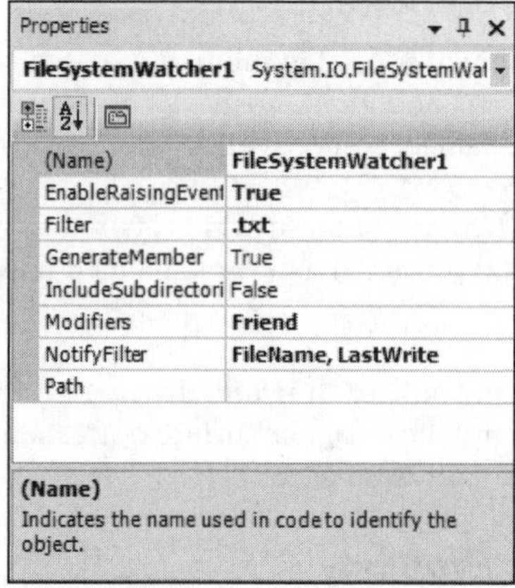

Figure 25-9

Adding FileSystemWatcher Code to OnStart and OnStop

Now that we have some properties set, let's add some code to the `OnStart` event. We need to start the `FileSystemWatcher1` component so it will start triggering events when files are created or copied into the directory we're monitoring, so we set the `EnableRaisingEvents` property to `True`:

```
Protected Overrides Sub OnStart(ByVal args() As String)
    ' Start monitoring for files
    FileSystemWatcher1.EnableRaisingEvents = True

End Sub
```

Once our file monitoring properties are initialized, we are ready to start the monitoring.

When the service stops we need to stop the file monitoring process. Add this code to your `OnStop` event:

```
Protected Overrides Sub OnStop()
    ' Stop monitoring for files
     FileSystemWatcher1.EnableRaisingEvents = False

End Sub
```

The EventLog Component

Now we are ready to place an `EventLog` component in the service to facilitate logging of events. Drag and drop an `EventLog` control from the Components tab of the toolbox onto the designer surface of `FileWatcherService.vb`. This control will automatically be called `EventLog1`.

Set the `Log` property for `Eventlog1` to `Application`, and set the `Source` property to `FileWatcherService`.

The Created Event

Next, we will place some logic in the `Created` event of our `FileSystemWatcher` component to log when a file has been created. This event will fire when a file has been placed or created in the directory that we are monitoring. This event fires because the last modified information on the file has changed.

Select `FileSystemWatcher1` from the Class Name drop-down list and select Created from the Method Name drop-down list, and the `Created` event will be added to your code. Add code to the `Created` event as follows:

```
Public Sub FileSystemWatcher1_Created(ByVal sender As Object, _
        ByVal e As System.IO.FileSystemEventArgs) _
        Handles FileSystemWatcher1.Created

    Dim sMessage As String
    sMessage = "File created in directory - file name is " + e.Name
    EventLog1.WriteEntry(sMessage)

End Sub
```

Notice that the event argument's object (the object named "`e`" in the event parameters) includes a property called `Name`. This property holds the name of the file that generated the event.

At this point, we could add the other events for `FileSystemWatcher` (`Changed`, `Deleted`, `Renamed`) in a similar way and create corresponding log messages for those events. To keep the example simple, we'll just do the `Created` event in this service.

We need to add an `Installer` class to this project to install the application. This is done as it was in the earlier `CounterMonitor` example, by right-clicking the design surface for the service and selecting Add Installer or by clicking on the Add Installer link in the Properties window of Visual Studio 2005. Don't forget to change the `Account` property to `LocalSystem`, or set it to `User` and fill in the `Username` and `Password` properties.

As before, we must install the service using `InstallUtil.exe`. Then, start it with the Server Explorer or the Service Manager.

Upon successful compilation of these steps, we will get a message logged for any file with a `.txt` extension that we copy or create in the monitored directory. So, after dropping some sample text files into our monitored directory, we can use the Event Viewer to check and make sure the events are present.

Figure 25-10 shows the Event Viewer with several example messages created by our service.

If you right-click one of the events for `FileWatcherService`, you'll see a detail screen. Notice that the message corresponds to the Event Log message we constructed in the `Created` event of the `FileSystemWatcher` control in the service as shown in Figure 25-11.

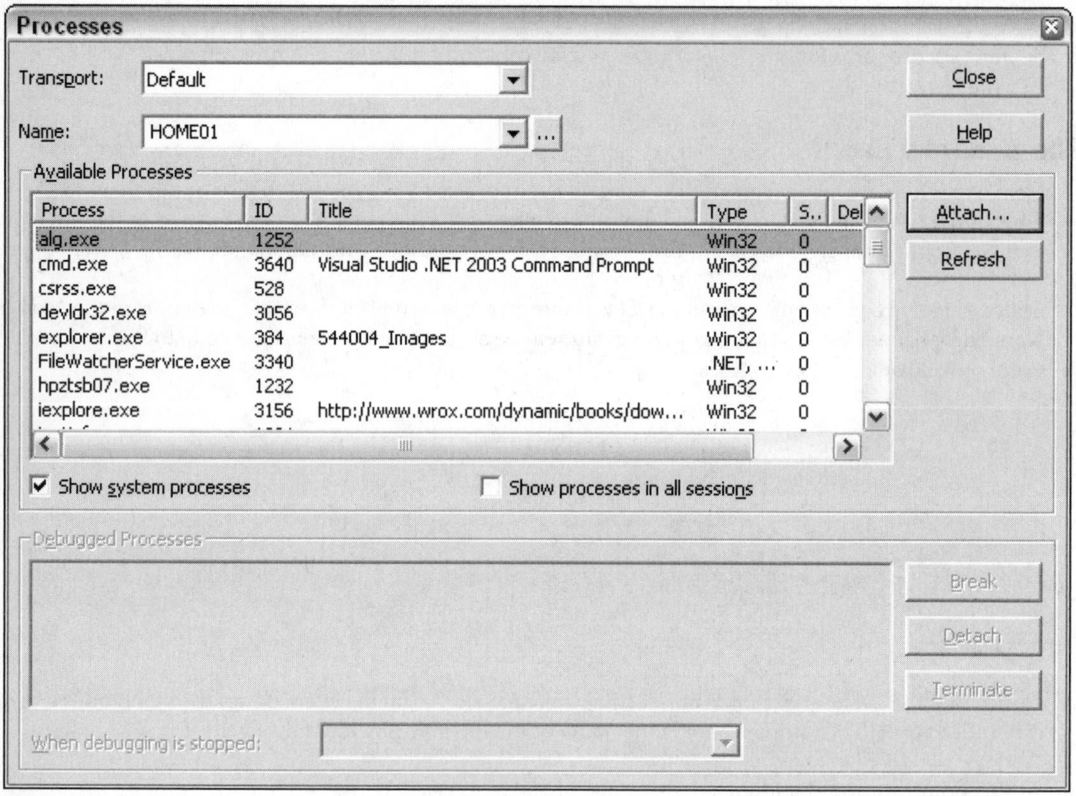

Processes

Transport: Default

Name: HOME01

Available Processes

Process	ID	Title	Type	S..	Del
alg.exe	1252		Win32	0	
cmd.exe	3640	Visual Studio .NET 2003 Command Prompt	Win32	0	
csrss.exe	528		Win32	0	
devldr32.exe	3056		Win32	0	
explorer.exe	384	544004_Images	Win32	0	
FileWatcherService.exe	3340		.NET, ...	0	
hpztsb07.exe	1232		Win32	0	
iexplore.exe	3156	http://www.wrox.com/dynamic/books/dow...	Win32	0	

Close | Help | Attach... | Refresh

Show system processes | Show processes in all sessions

Debugged Processes

Break | Detach | Terminate

When debugging is stopped:

Figure 25-10

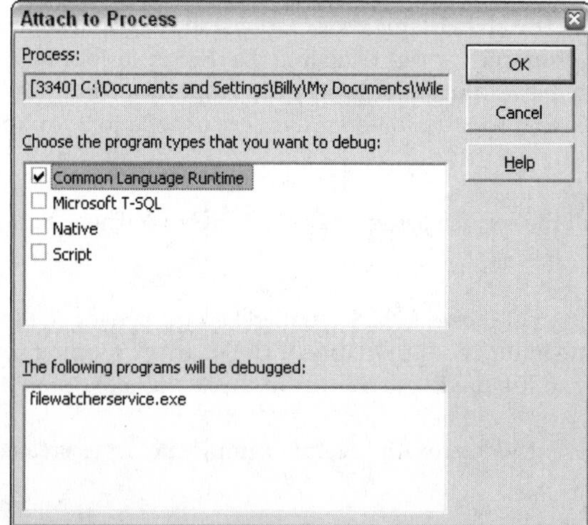

Figure 25-11

Debugging the Service

Because a service must be run from within the context of the Services Control Manager rather than from within Visual Studio 2005, debugging a service is not as straightforward as debugging other Visual Studio 2005 application types. To debug a service, we must start the service and then attach a debugger to the process in which it is running. We can then debug your application using all of the standard debugging functionality of Visual Studio 2005.

> **You should not attach to a process unless you know what the process is and understand the consequences of attaching to and possibly killing that process.**

To avoid going through this extra effort, you may want to test out most of the code in your service in a standard Windows Forms application. This test-bed application can have the same components (`FileSystemWatchers`, `EventLogs`, `Timers`, and so on) as the Windows Service, and thus will be able to run the same logic in events. Once you have checked out the logic in this context, you can just copy and paste it into a Windows Service application.

However, there will be some occasions for which the service itself needs to be debugged directly. So it's important to understand how to attach to the service's process and do direct debugging. The rest of this section explains how to do that.

The only time you can debug a service is when it's running. When you attach the debugger to the service, you are interrupting the service. The service is suspended for a short period while you attach to it. The service will also be interrupted when you place breakpoints and step through your code.

Attaching to the service's process allows you to debug most, but not all, of the service's code. For instance, because the service has already been started, you cannot debug the code in the service's `OnStart` method this way, or the code in the `Main` method that is used to load the service. To debug the `OnStart` event or any of the Visual Studio 2005 designer code, you have to add a dummy service and start that service first. In the dummy service, you would create an instance of the service that you want to debug. You can place some code in a `Timer` object and create the new instance of the object that you want to debug after 30 seconds or so. Allow enough time to attach to the debugger before the new instance is created. Meanwhile, place breakpoints in your startup code to debug those events, if desired.

To Debug a Service

Follow these steps to debug a service:

1. Install the service.
2. Start the service, either from the Services Control Manager, Server Explorer, or from code.
3. In Visual Studio 2005, load the solution for the service. Then select Attach to Process from the Debug menu. The Attach to Process dialog box appears (see Figure 25-12).
4. For a Windows Service, the desired process to attach to is not a foreground process; it's important to make sure to check the check box next to the Show processes from all users option.

5. In the Available Processes section, click the process indicated by the executable name for the service, and then click the Attach button.

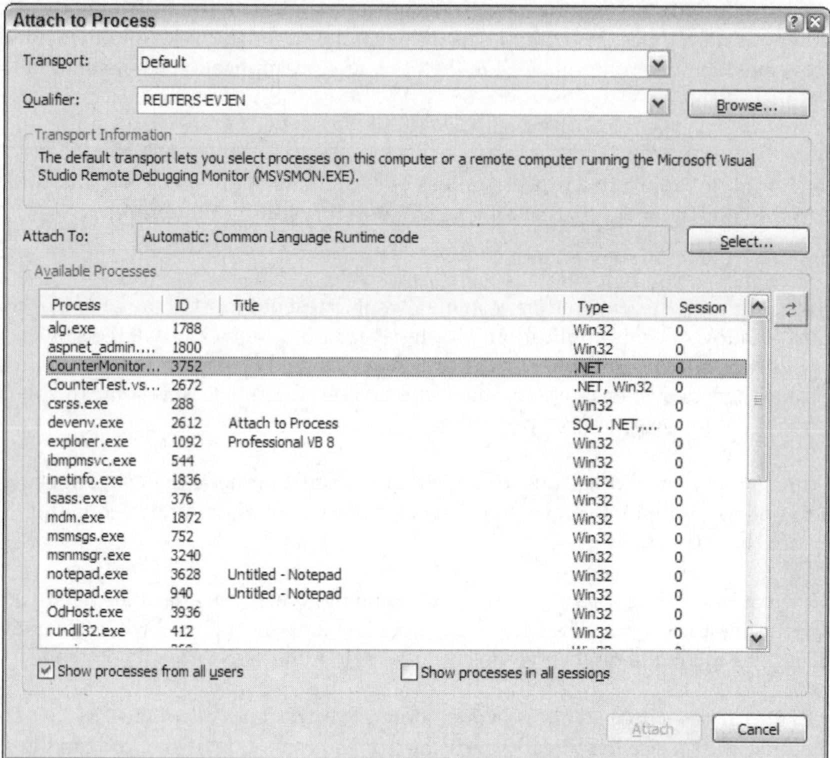

Figure 25-12

6. You can now debug your process. Place a breakpoint in the code for the service at the place you want to debug. Cause the code in the service to execute (by placing a file in a monitored directory, for example).

7. When finished, select Stop Debugging from the Debug menu.

Let's go through an actual scenario, using our earlier `CounterMonitor` example. Bring up both the `CounterMonitor` project and the `CounterTest` project in separate instances of the Visual Studio 2005 IDE. Then make sure that the `CounterMonitor` service has been started. It is best if you hear it beeping—that way you know it is working. If necessary, remember to increment the performance counter to make it beep.

In the `CounterMonitor` project, go to the Debug menu and select Processes, you'll get a dialog box that shows a list of the foreground processes on the system. Check the box next to "Show system processes."

Once you do this, the list of processes will expand, and one of the processes in the list will be `CounterMonitor.exe`. That's the process you want. Highlight it and press the Attach button.

You'll then get a dialog box asking you what program types you are interested in debugging. Since we are working solely within .NET, check the box next to common language runtime and leave the rest unchecked. Then press the OK button on this dialog box, and press the Close button on the Processes dialog box. You are now attached to the process running `CounterMonitor` in the background.

Place a breakpoint on the first line of the `OnCustomCommand` event:

```
Timer1.Enabled = False
```

Now we are ready to check debugging. Bring up the `CounterTest` program, and start it. Press one of the radio buttons to change the beep interval. You will hear the beeping stop, because `CounterMonitor.exe` has entered debugging mode. Switch back to the `CounterMonitor` project, and the cursor will be on the breakpoint line in `OnCustomCommand`. You can use the normal commands at this point to step through the code.

Summary

This chapter presented a general overview of what a Windows Service is and how to create one with Visual Basic. The techniques in this chapter can be used for many different types of background service. A few examples are:

- ❑ Automatically moving statistical files from a database server to a Web server
- ❑ Pushing general files across computers and platforms
- ❑ A watchdog timer to ensure that a connection is always available
- ❑ An application to move and process FTP files, or indeed files received from any source

While Visual Basic cannot be used to create every type of Windows Service, it is effective at creating many of the most useful ones. The .NET Framework classes for Windows Services make this creation relatively straightforward. The designers generate much of the routine code needed, and you as a developer can concentrate on the code that is specific to your particular Windows Service.

26

Network Programming

Just as it is difficult to live your life without talking with people, your applications also need to communicate, perhaps with other programs or perhaps with hardware devices. As we have seen throughout this book, there are a variety of techniques you can use to have your program communicate, including .NET Remoting, Web Services, and Enterprise Services. This chapter looks at yet another way to communicate, using the basic protocols that the Internet and many networks have been built on. You will learn how the classes in `System.Net` can provide a variety of techniques for communicating with existing applications such as Web or FTP servers, or how you can use them to create your own communication applications.

Before getting started on writing applications using these classes, however, it would be good to get some background on how networks are bolted together, and how machines and applications are identified.

Getting Your Message Across: Protocols, Addresses, and Ports

No discussion of a network is complete without a huge number of acronyms, seemingly random numbers, and the idea of a protocol. For example, the World Wide Web runs using a protocol called HTTP or HyperText Transfer Protocol. Similarly, there are File Transfer Protocol (FTP), Network News Transfer Protocol (NNTP), and Gopher protocols. Each application you run on a network communicates with another program using a defined protocol. The protocol is simply the expected messages each program will send the other, in the order that they should be sent. For a real-world example, if you want to go see a movie with a friend, a simplified conversation could look like this:

```
You: Dials phone
Them: Hears phone ringing, answers phone, "Hello"
You: "Hello. Want to go see 'Freddie and Jason Escape from New York part 6?'"
```

```
Them: "No, I saw that one already. What about 'Star Warthogs'?"
You: "OK, 9:30 showing downtown?"
Them: "Yes"
You: "Later"

Them: "See you", hangs up
```

Apart from a bad taste in movies, we can see a basic protocol here. Someone initiates a communication channel. The recipient accepts the channel and signals the start of the communication. The initial caller then sends a series of messages to which the recipient replies, either to signify they have received them, or as either a positive or negative response. Finally, one of the messages indicates the end of the communication channel, and the two disconnect.

Similarly, network applications have their own protocols defined by the application writer. For example, sending an email using SMTP (Simple Mail Transfer Protocol) could look like the following:

```
220 schroedinger Microsoft ESMTP MAIL Service, Version: 6.0.2600.2180 ready at Wed,
6 Oct 2004 15:58:28 -0700
HELO
250 schroedinger Hello [127.0.0.1]
FOO
500 5.3.3 Unrecognized command
MAIL FROM: me
250 2.1.0 me@schroedinger....Sender OK
RCPT TO: him
250 2.1.5 him@schroedinger
DATA
354 Start mail input; end with <CRLF>.<CRLF>
subject: Testing SMTP

Hello World, via mail.
.
250 2.6.0 <SCHROEDINGERKaq65r500000001@schroedinger> Queued mail for delivery
QUIT
221 2.0.0 schroedinger Service closing transmission channel


Connection to host lost.
```

In this case, lines beginning with numbers are coming from the server, while the items in uppercase (and the message itself) were sent from the client. If the client sends an invalid message (as in the "FOO" message in the preceding code example), it receives a gentle rebuff from the server, while correct messages receive either an "OK" or "Go on" reply. Traditionally, for SMTP and many other protocols, the reply is a three-digit number (see the following table) identifying the response (the text after the number, such as, "2.1.0 me@schroedinger .... Sender OK, isn't really needed).

Range	Description
100–199	Message is good, but the server is still working on the request.
200–299	Message is good, and the server has completed acting on the request.

Range	Description
300–399	Message is good, but the server needs more information to work on the request.
400–499	Message is good, but the server could not act on the request. You may try the request again to see if it works in the future.
500–599	The server could not act on the request. Either the message was bad or an error occurred. It likely won't work next time.

Other protocols use this technique as well (leading to the infamous HTTP 404 error for "Page not found"), but they don't have to. Having a good reference is key to your success, and the best reference for existing protocols is the Request for Comments (RFC) for the protocol. These are the definitions that are used by protocol authors to create their implementation of the standard. Many of these RFCs are available at the IETF (`http://www.ietf.org`) and World Wide Web Consortium (`http://www.w3.org`) Web sites.

Addresses and Names

The next important topic necessary to a thorough understanding of network programming is the relationship between the names and addresses of each of the computers involved. Each form of network communication (such as TCP/IP networks, such as the Internet) has its own way of mapping the name of a computer (or host) to an address. The reason for this is simple: Computers deal with numbers better than text, and humans can remember text better than numbers (generally). So, while you may have named your computer something clever like, "l33t_#4x0R," applications and other computers know it by its IP (Internet Protocol) address. This address is a 32-bit value, usually written in four parts (each one a byte that is a number from 0 to 255), like 192.168.1.39. This is the standard the Internet has worked on for many years. However, as there are only about four billion unique addresses using this method, another standard, IPv6, has been proposed. It is called IPv6 as it is the sixth recommendation in the series (the older 32-bit addresses are often called IPv4 to differentiate them). With IPv6, a 128-bit address is used, leading to a maximum number of about $3x10^{28}$ unique addresses. More than enough for every Internet-enabled toaster, I imagine.

This IP (whether IPv4 or IPv6) address must uniquely identify each host on a network (actually subnetwork, but I'm getting ahead of myself). If not, messages will not be routed to their destination properly, and chaos ensues. The matter gets more complicated when another 32-bit number, the Subnet Mask, is brought into the picture. This is a value that is masked (using a Boolean AND operation) over the address to identify the subnetwork of the network that the computer is on.

Because computers and humans use two different means of identifying computers, there must obviously be some way for the two to be related. The term for this process is *name resolution*. In the case of the Internet, a common means of name resolution is done by yet another protocol, Domain Naming System (DNS). Computers, when faced with an unknown text-based name, will send a message to the closest DNS server. It then looks to see if it knows the IP address of that host. If it does, it passes this back to the requestor. If not, it asks another DNS server it knows. This process continues until either the IP address is found, or you run out of DNS servers. Once the IP address is found, all of the servers (and the original computer) store that number for a while in case they are asked again.

Keeping the problems that can ensue during name resolution in mind can often solve many development problems. For example, if you are having difficulty communicating with a computer that should be responding, it may be that your computer simply can't resolve the name of the remote computer. Try using the IP address instead. This removes any name resolution problems from the equation, and may allow you to continue developing while someone else fixes the name resolution problem.

Ports: They're Not Just for Ships

As the previous sections described, each computer or host on a network is uniquely identified by an address. However, how does your computer realize which of possibly many applications running are meant to receive a given message arriving on the network? This is determined by the port the message is targeted at. The port is another number, in this case an integer value from 1 to 32,767. The unique combination of address and port identifies the target application.

For example, assume you currently have a Web server (IIS) running, as well as an SMTP server, and a few browser windows open. If a network message comes in, how does the operating system "know" which of these applications should receive the packet? Each of the applications (either client or server) that may receive a message is assigned a unique port number. In the case of servers, this is typically a fixed number, while client applications, such as your Web browser, are assigned a random available port.

To make communication with servers easier, they typically use a well-known assigned port. In the case of Web servers, this is port 80, while SMTP servers use port 25. You can see a list of common servers and their ports in the file %windows%\system32\drivers\etc\services.

If you are writing a server application, you can either use these common port numbers (and you should if you're attempting to write a common type of server), or choose your own. If you are writing a new type of server, you should likely choose a port that has not been assigned to another server; choosing a port higher than 1024 should prevent any conflicts, as these are not assigned. When writing a client application, there is typically no need to assign a port, as a dynamic port is assigned to the client for communication with a server.

In addition, ports below 1024 should be considered secure ports and applications that use them should have administrative access.

Firewalls: Can't Live with Them, Can't Live without Them

Many people experience a love/hate relationship with firewalls. While they are invaluable in today's network, sometimes it would be nice if they got out of the way. A firewall is a piece of hardware or software that monitors network traffic, either incoming, outgoing, or both. They can be configured to allow only particular ports or applications to transmit information beyond the firewall. They protect against hackers or viruses that may attempt to connect to open ports, leveraging them to their own ends. They protect against spyware applications that may attempt to communicate out from your machine. However, they also "protect" against any network programming you may attempt to do. You must invariably cooperate with your network administrators, working within their guidelines for network access. If they make only certain ports available, then your applications should only use those ports. Alternately, you may be able to get them to configure the firewalls involved to permit the ports needed by your applications.

Thankfully, passing messages is a bit easier with Visual Basic 2005. The following sections demonstrate how.

The System.Net Namespace

Most of the functionality used when writing network applications is contained within the `System.Net` and `System.Net.Sockets` namespaces. The main classes in these namespaces that this chapter covers are

- `WebRequest` and `WebResponse`, and their subclasses, including the new Ftp`WebRequest`.
- `WebClient`, the simplified `WebRequest` for common scenarios.
- `HttpListener`, the new ability to create your own Web server.

Note: There are additional classes, methods, properties, and events that have been added to the `System.Net` *and* `System.Net.Sockets` *namespaces in the .NET Framework 2.0. Please see the updated reference for these namespaces (currently at* `http://msdn2.microsoft.com/library/system.net.aspx` *as of this writing).*

Web Requests (and Responses)

When most people think of network programming these days, they're really thinking of communication via a Web server or client. Therefore, it shouldn't come as a surprise that there should be a set of classes for this communication need. In this case, it is the abstract `WebRequest` class and the associated `WebResponse`. These two classes represent the concept of a request/response communication with a Web server, or similar server. As these are abstract classes, that is, `MustInherit` classes, they cannot be created by themselves. Instead, you create the subclasses of `WebRequest` that are optimized for specific types of communication.

The most important properties and methods of the `WebRequest` class are shown in the following table.

Member	Description
Create	Method used to create specific type of WebRequest. This method uses the URL (either as a string or as an Uri class) passed to identify and create a subclass of WebRequest.
GetRequestStream	Method that allows access to the outgoing request. This allows you to add additional information, such as POST data, to the request before sending.
GetResponse	Method used to perform the request and retrieve the corresponding WebResponse.
Credentials	Property that allows you to set the user id and password for the request if they are needed to perform the request.
Headers	Property that enables you to change or add to the headers for the request.
Method	Property used to identify the action for the request, such as GET or POST. The list of available methods is specific to each type of server.
Proxy	Property allowing you to identify a proxy server for the communication if needed. Note that you generally don't need to set this property as Visual Basic 2005 detects the settings for Internet Explorer and uses them by default.
Timeout	Property that enables you to define the time permitted for the request before you 'give up' on the server.

Each of the subclasses of `WebRequest` supports these methods, giving a very consistent programming model for communication with a variety of server types. The basic model for working with any of the subclasses of `WebRequest` can be written in the following pseudo code:

```
Declare variable as child class
Create the variable based on the URL
Make any changes to the Request object you may need
Use the GetResponse method to retrieve the response from the server
Get the Stream from the WebResponse
Do something with the Stream
```

If you decide to change the protocol (for example, from HTTP to a file-based protocol), the only thing that needs to change is the URL used to retrieve the object.

Working with FileWebRequest and HttpWebRequest

The first two types of `WebRequest` that became available were the `FileWebRequest` and `HttpWebRequest`. `FileWebRequest` is used less frequently; it represents a request to a local file, using the "file://" URL format. You may have seen this type of request if you attempt to open a local file using your Web browser, such as Internet Explorer, Firefox, or Navigator. Generally, however, the subclass most developers will use is `HttpWebRequest`. This class enables you to make HTTP requests to a Web server, without requiring a browser. This could allow you to communicate with a Web server, or, using the time-honored tradition of "screen scraping" to retrieve data available on the Web.

One hurdle many developers encounter when first working with `HttpWebRequest` is that there is no available constructor. Instead, you must use the `WebRequest.Create` (or the `Create` method of your desired subclass) method to create new instances of any of the subclasses. This method uses the URL requested to create the appropriate subtype of `WebRequest`. For example, this would create a new `HttpWebRequest`:

```
Dim req As HttpWebRequest = WebRequest.Create("http://msdn.microsoft.com")
```

Note that if you have `Option Strict` turned on (and you should), the above code will produce an error. Instead, you should explicitly cast the return value of `Create` to the desired type:

```
Dim req As HttpWebRequest = _
  DirectCast(WebRequest.Create("http://msdn.microsoft.com"), _
  System.Net.HttpWebRequest)
```

Putting It Together

In order to demonstrate how to use `WebRequest/WebResponse`, the following example shows how to wrap a Web call into a Visual Basic class. In this case, we'll wrap Google's, `define:` keyword that allows you to retrieve a set of definitions for a word (for example, `http://www.google.com/search?q=define%3A+egregious`), then use that in a sample application. (See Figure 26-1.)

1. Create a new Windows application. I named my project, `DefinePad`.
2. Add a new class to the project. This will hold the actual `WebRequest` code. Call it `GoogleClient`.
3. Add a reference to the `System.Web.DLL`, as we will need access to some of its functionality later.

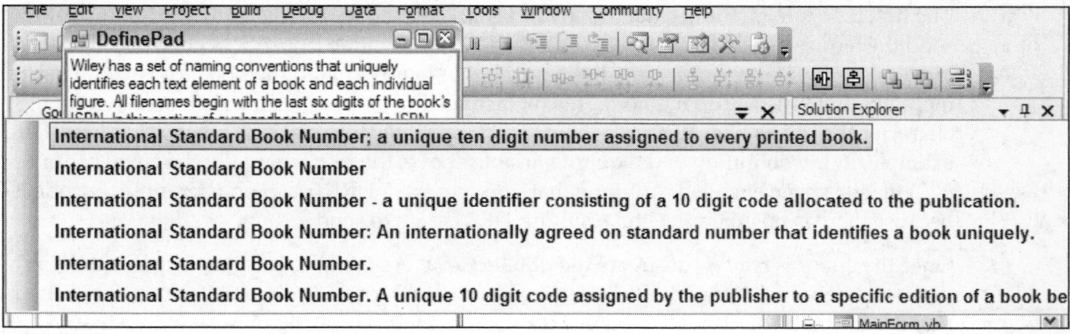
File Edit View Project Build Debug Data Format Tools Window Community Help
DefinePad
Wiley has a set of naming conventions that uniquely identifies each text element of a book and each individual figure. All filenames begin with the last six digits of the book's
Solution Explorer
International Standard Book Number; a unique ten digit number assigned to every printed book.
International Standard Book Number
International Standard Book Number - a unique identifier consisting of a 10 digit code allocated to the publication.
International Standard Book Number: An internationally agreed on standard number that identifies a book uniquely.
International Standard Book Number.
International Standard Book Number. A unique 10 digit code assigned by the publisher to a specific edition of a book be
MainForm.vb

Figure 26-1

4. In the `GoogleClient.vb` file, add import statements to make the coding a little briefer:

```
Imports System.IO
Imports System.Net
Imports System.Web
Imports System.Collections.Generic
```

5. The main function in `GoogleClient` will be a `Define` function that will return an array of strings. Each string will be one definition returned by Google.

```
Public Function Define(ByVal word As String) As String()
    Dim req As HttpWebRequest = Nothing
    Dim resp As HttpWebResponse
    Dim query As String
    Dim result As New List(Of String)

    query = "http://www.google.com/search?q=define%3A" & _
      HttpUtility.UrlEncode(word)

    Try
        req = DirectCast(WebRequest.Create(query), HttpWebRequest)
        With req
            .Method = "GET"
            resp = req.GetResponse
            If resp.StatusCode = HttpStatusCode.OK Then
                ParseResponse(resp.GetResponseStream, result)
            Else
                MessageBox.Show("Error calling definition service")
            End If
        End With
    Catch ex As Exception

    End Try

    Return result.ToArray()

End Function
```

6. The first task is to guarantee that no invalid characters appear in the QueryString when you send the request, such as a space, accented character, or other non-ASCII character. The `System.Web.HttpUtility` class has a number of handy shared methods for encoding strings, including the `UrlEncode` method. This replaces characters with a safe representation of the character that looks like, `%value`, where the value is the Unicode code for the character. For example, in the definition of the query variable above, the `%3A` is actually the colon character (":") that has been encoded. Anytime that you retrieve a URL based on user input, encode it because there is no guarantee the resulting URL is safe to send.

7. Once the query is ready, you create the `WebRequest`. As the URL is for an http resource, an `HttpWebRequest` is created. While the default method for `WebRequest` is a `GET`, it's still good practice to set it. You'll create the `ParseResponse` method shortly to process the stream returned from the server.

8. One other piece of code worthy of mentioning is the return value for this method, and how it is created. In order to return arrays of a specific type (rather than returning actual collections from a method), you either must know the actual size to initialize the array, or you need to use the new `List` generic type or the older `ArrayList`. These classes behave like the Visual Basic 6.0 `Collection` class, which enables you to add items, and it grows as needed. They also have a handy method that allows you to convert the array into an array of any type; you can see this in the return statement. The `ArrayList` requires you to do a bit more work. If you want to use an `ArrayList` for this method, you must identify the type of array you'd like to return. The resulting return statement would look like this using an `ArrayList`:

```
Return result.ToArray(GetType(String))
```

9. The `ProcessRequest` method parses the stream returned from the server, and converts it into an array of items. Note that this is slightly simplified: In a real application, you would likely want to return an array of objects, where each object provides access to the definition and the URL of the site providing it.

```
Private Sub ParseResponse(ByVal input As System.IO.Stream, _
  ByRef output As List(Of String))
        'definitions are in a block beginning with <p>Definitions for...
        'then are marked with <li> tags
        'yes, I should use Regular Expressions for this
        'this format will also likely change in the future.    Dim reader As New
StreamReader(input)
    Dim work As String = reader.ReadToEnd
        Dim blockStart As String = "<p>Definitions of"
        Dim pos As Integer = work.IndexOf(blockStart)    Dim posEnd As Integer
    Dim temp As String

    Do
        pos = work.IndexOf("<p>", pos + 1)
        If pos Then
            posEnd = work.IndexOf("</p>", pos)
            temp = work.Substring(pos + 3, posEnd - pos - 6)
            output.Add(ParseDefinition(temp))
            pos = posEnd + 1
        End If
    Loop While pos

End Sub
```

10. The code is fairly simple, using the time-honored tradition of "screen scraping" — processing the HTML of a page to find the section you need and then removing the HTML to produce the result.

11. The last part of the `GoogleClient` class is the `ParseDefinition` method that cleans up the definition, removing the link and other HTML tags.

```
Private Function ParseDefinition(ByVal input As String) As String
    Dim result As String = ""
        Dim lineBreak As Integer

        lineBreak = input.IndexOf("<br>")
        If lineBreak > 0 Then
            result = input.Substring(0, input.IndexOf("<br>"))
        Else
            result = input
        End If
End Function
```

12. Now, with class in hand, you can create a client to use it. In this case, you'll create a simple text editor that adds the ability to retrieve definitions for words. Go back to the `Form` created for the application, and add controls as shown in Figure 26-2.

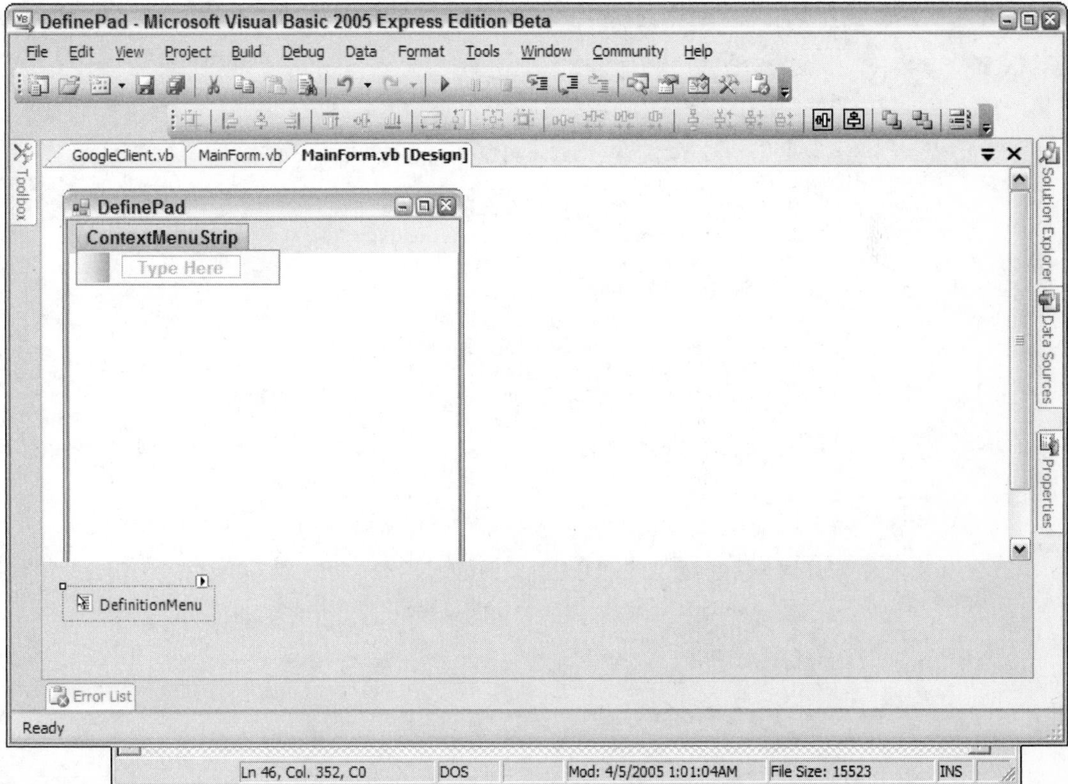

Figure 26-2

13. The user interface for `DefinePad` is simple: a `TextBox` and a `ContextMenuStrip`.

Control	Property	Value
TextBox	Name	TextField
	Multiline	True
	Dock	Client
	ContextMenuStrip	DefinitionMenu
ContextMenuStrip	Name	DefinitionMenu1

14. The only code in the `Form` is for the `Opening` event of the `ContextMenuStrip`. Here, you will add the definitions to the menu. Add the following code to the handler for the `Opening` event.

```
Private Sub DefinitionMenu_Opened(ByVal sender As Object, _
  ByVal e As System.ComponentModel.CancelEventArgs) _
  Handles DefinitionMenu.Opened
    Dim svc As New GoogleClient
    Dim definitions() As String
    Dim definitionCount As Integer

    DefinitionMenu.Items.Clear()

    Try
        'define the currently selected word
        If TextField.SelectionLength > 0 Then
            definitions = svc.Define(TextField.SelectedText)

            'build context menu of returned definitions
            definitionCount = definitions.Length
            If definitionCount > 6 Then
                definitionCount = 6
            ElseIf definitionCount = 0 Then
                'we can't do anymore, so exit
                Dim item As New ToolStripButton
                item.Text = "Sorry, no definitions available"
                DefinitionMenu.Items.Add(item)
                Exit Sub
            End If

            For i As Integer = 1 To definitionCount
                Dim item As New ToolStripButton
                item.Text = definitions(i)
                DefinitionMenu.Items.Add(item)
            Next
        End If

    Catch ex As Exception
        MessageBox.Show(ex.Message, "Error getting definitions", _
            MessageBoxButtons.OK, MessageBoxIcon.Error)

    End Try
End Sub
```

15. The bulk of the code in this event is to limit the number of items displayed in the menu. The actual functional part of the routine is the call to the `Define` method of the `GoogleClient`. If you trace through the code as you run, you'll see the `WebRequest` generated, the call made, and the resulting response stream parsed into the individual items as desired. Finally, you can use the returned list to create a set of menu items (that don't actually do anything), and display the "menu". Clicking on any definition closes the menu.

16. To text the application, run it. Type or copy some text into the `TextBox`, select a word, and right-click on it. After a brief pause, you should see the definitions for the word (see Figure 26-3 for definitions of developer).

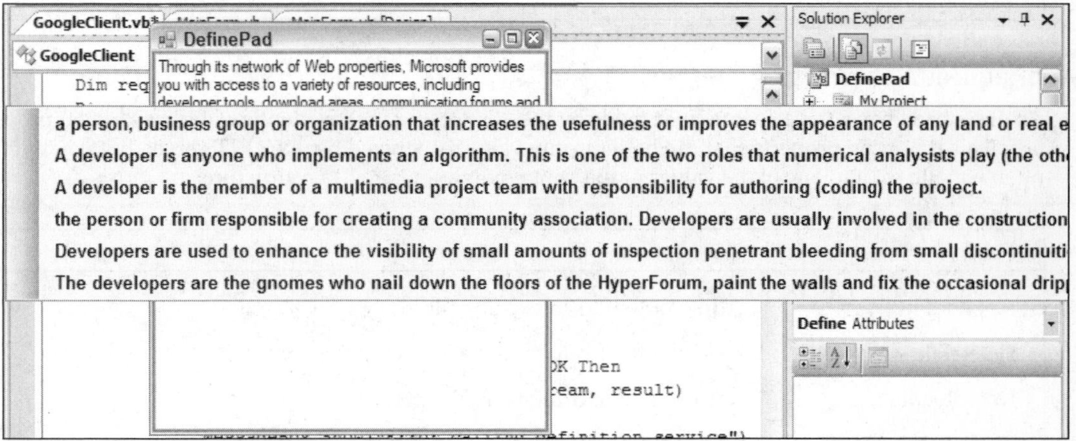

Figure 26-3

While they are not as 'sexy' as Web Services, using this technique (`WebRequest`, screen scraping of the resulting HTML) can provide access to a great deal of the functionality of the Internet for your applications.

Working with FtpWebRequest

One of the new sets of classes added to the `System.Net` namespace in Visual Basic 2005 is another type of Web request — the `FtpWebRequest`. This class, and the related `FtpWebResponse`, is used to communicate with FTP servers. While the `HttpWebRequest/Response` can be used for simple file uploading and retrieving, the `FtpWebRequest` adds the ability to browse or create directories, delete files, and more. The following table describes some of the added functionality in the `FtpWebRequest`.

Member	Description
Abort	Used when performing an asynchronous operation. This command terminates the current operation.
Binary	A Boolean value that determines if the data transfer should be treated as binary or text. Set to true when you are transferring a binary file and text otherwise.

Table continued on following page

Member	Description
Method	While not new, the behavior of this method is quite important with the `FtpWebRequest` as it defines the action to perform. See the section below on `WebRequestMethods.Ftp` that defines the possible values.
Passive	Boolean value that determines how the client and server should communicate. If this is set to true, the server does not initiate communication back to the client. Instead, it waits until the client initiates the communication. This is typically needed when communicating through a firewall that might not allow the server to open a connection to the client machine.

WebRequestMethods.Ftp

As described above, the actual request made by the `FtpWebRequest` is identified by the `Method` property. This is a string property that can be set to any value recognized by your FTP server, but you will often want to set it to one of the values in the `WebRequestMethods.Ftp` structure.

Field	Description
AppendFile	Adds content to an existing file.
DeleteFile	Deletes a file from the server (if you have permission).
DownloadFile	Retrieves a file from the FTP server.
GetDateTimeStamp	Gets the date and time the file was last modified.
GetFileSize	Gets the size of the file on the FTP server.
ListDirectory	Gets the file and directory names for a directory on the FTP server. The data returned is a list of the files, each on a line (that is, separated by CRLF characters). This method doesn't provide an easy way to determine which of the items returned are directories or files.
ListDirectoryDetails	Gets the file and directory information for a directory on the FTP server. This method returns a good deal of information about each item, including attributes, permissions, date of last modification, and size. Just as with the ListDirectory method, each file's (or directory's) information is on a single line.
MakeDirectory	Creates a directory on the server.
PrintWorkingDirectory	Gets the current path on the FTP server.
RemoveDirectory	Removes a directory from the server (if you have permission).
UploadFile	Uploads a file to the FTP server.
UploadFileWith UniqueName	Similar to UploadFile, but this method ensures that the new file has a unique file name. This is great when you allow the user to upload files, but don't want possible name collisions to happen, or if you don't really care what name the file is (for example when the file contents just need processing but not saving).

Creating an FTP Client

In order to demonstrate using the `FtpWebRequest`, the next section covers how to create a simple FTP server browser. The application will allow you to connect to a server, browse the available files, and download files. (See Figure 26-4.)

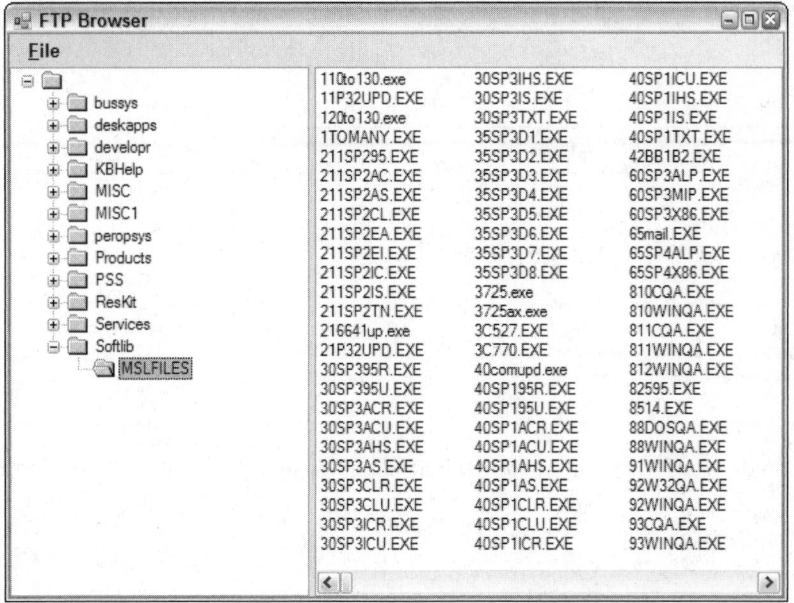

Figure 26-4

Even though this application is a Windows Forms application, we separate the FTP handling to a class for use in other applications.

1. Create a new Windows application called "FTP Browser"
2. Add `MenuStrip` and `SplitContainer` controls to the `Form`. You can leave the names and other properties of these controls at their defaults. Create three items under the File menu: Connect..., Download, and Exit. You may also want to add an `ImageList` control, and populate it with appropriate graphics for open and closed folders.
3. Add a `TreeView` control to the right side of the `SplitContainer`, and a `ListView` to the left side. Set the properties as in the following tables.

TreeView

Property	Value
Name	DirectoryList
Dock	Fill
PathSeparator	/

Table continued on following page

Property	Value
ImageList	The name of your ImageList control
SelectedImageKey	The open image's name
ImageKey	The closed image's name

ListView

Property	Value
Name	FileList
Dock	Fill
MultiSelect	False
View	List

4. Open the Code View for the form. First, add a few private variables to the Form class.

```
Private ftp As New FtpClient
Private baseUrl As String
Private downloadPath As String
```

5. Next, add a handler for the Form Load event; this will initialize the `TreeView` and `FtpClient` objects.

```
Private Sub MainForm_Load(ByVal sender As Object, _
  ByVal e As System.EventArgs) Handles Me.Load
    'initialize form
    With Me.DirectoryTree
        .Nodes.Add("/")
    End With
    'initialize ftp client
    With ftp
        .UserId = My.Settings.user
        .Password = My.Settings.email
    End With
    downloadPath = My.Settings.downloadPath

End Sub
```

6. Notice the calls to `My.Settings` when initializing the `FtpClient`. The Settings collection is available to the My object when you have created settings values in the My Project dialog. Open the Solution Explorer and double-click on the My Project item. Select the Settings tab, and add the three values there (see Figure 26-5).

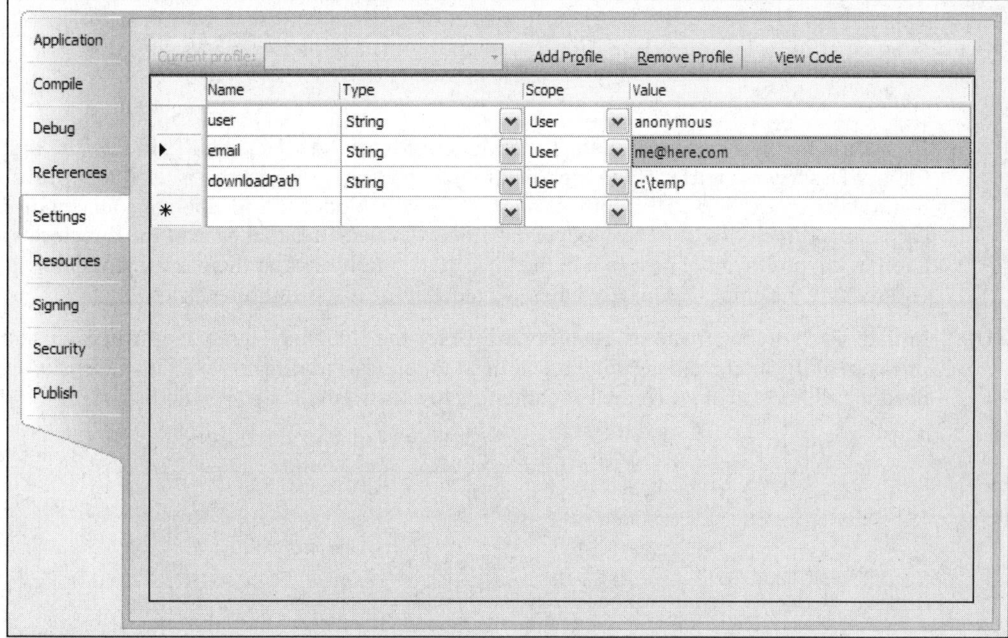

Figure 26-5

7. You can now return to adding the code to the Form. The next step is to enable connecting to the FTP server, and retrieving the initial list of directories to add to the `TreeView`. Add this to the Connect menu item.

```
Private Sub ConnectToolStripMenuItem_Click(ByVal sender As System.Object, _
  ByVal e As System.EventArgs) Handles ConnectToolStripMenuItem.Click
    'makes a new connection to an FTP server

    baseUrl = InputBox("Enter FTP site to open", "FTP Browser", _
      "ftp://ftp.microsoft.com")
    AddNodes(Me.DirectoryTree.Nodes(0), baseUrl)

End Sub
```

8. The event prompts the user for the address of the FTP server to connect with, and then adds it to the `TreeView` via a helper subroutine, `AddNodes`.

```
Private Sub AddNodes(ByVal parent As TreeNode, ByVal url As String)
    Dim dirs() As String

    Me.Cursor = Cursors.WaitCursor

    dirs = ftp.GetDirectories(url)
    For Each dir As String In dirs
        With parent.Nodes.Add(dir)
            .Nodes.Add("NoNodeHere", "empty")
        End With
```

```
        Next

        Me.Cursor = Cursors.Default
    End Sub
```

9. The AddNodes method retrieves the list of directories for the selected URL. In this, the first call for an FTP server, it retrieves the root directory. Later, the same method is used to retrieve subdirectories by requesting a URL containing the full path. Notice the addition of a fake node to each of the directories (the "NoNodeHere" item). This ensures that each of the directories we add has the plus symbol next to it in the TreeView, implying that there is content below it. We will remove the empty node later when we request the actual subdirectories.

10. Initially, each of the directories is empty except for the "NoNodeHere" item. You can use the presence of this node to determine if you need to request subdirectories. If it still exists, you need to call AddNodes when the user attempts to expand the TreeView node.

```
    Private Sub DirectoryTree_BeforeExpand(ByVal sender As Object, _
      ByVal e As System.Windows.Forms.TreeViewCancelEventArgs) _
      Handles DirectoryTree.BeforeExpand
        Dim thisNode As TreeNode

        thisNode = e.Node
        If thisNode.Nodes.ContainsKey("NoNodeHere") Then
            'we haven't retrieved this nodes children yet
            'remove the empty node
            thisNode.Nodes("NoNodeHere").Remove()
            'get the real children now
            AddNodes(thisNode, baseUrl + thisNode.FullPath)
        End If

    End Sub
```

11. If the "NoNodeHere" still exists, you remove it, and then call the AddNodes method again, passing this node, and its path. This calls the FTP server again, retrieving the child directories of the selected directory. You perform this before the node is expanded, so before the user can see the "NoNodeHere" node. If the subdirectories have already been requested, the "NoNodeHere" node won't be in the TreeView anymore, and so the code to call the FTP server won't be called again.

12. After the node has been expanded, it is selected. At this time, retrieve the list of files in that directory to display in the ListView control.

```
    Private Sub DirectoryTree_AfterSelect(ByVal sender As System.Object, _
      ByVal e As System.Windows.Forms.TreeViewEventArgs) _
      Handles DirectoryTree.AfterSelect
        Dim thisNode As TreeNode
        Dim files() As String

        thisNode = e.Node

        'we don't want to do this for the root node
        If thisNode.Text <> "/" Then
```

```
            'get files for this directory
            Me.Cursor = Cursors.WaitCursor
            'clear the current list
            Me.FileList.Items.Clear()
            files = ftp.GetFiles(baseUrl + thisNode.FullPath)
            For Each fil As String In files
                Me.FileList.Items.Add(fil)
            Next

            Me.Cursor = Cursors.Default
        End If
    End Sub
```

13. This code is fairly simple. First, the `ListView` is cleared of existing files. Then, the `FtpClient` is called, retrieving the list of files in the selected directory. These are then added to the `ListView`.

14. That sets up our user interface. Now it's time to begin to add the functionality. Add a new class to the project, called `FtpClient.vb`. This class will be used to create wrapper functionality to make working with `FtpWebRequest` easier. First, add the `Imports` statements for later use.

```
Imports System.IO
Imports System.Net
Imports System.Text
Imports System.Collections.Generic
```

15. Next, add two properties to the class. This is for the user id and password that will be used by the `FtpClient`.

```
    Private _user As String
    Private _pwd As String

    Public Property UserId() As String
        Get
            Return _user
        End Get
        Set(ByVal value As String)
            _user = value
        End Set
    End Property

    Public Property Password() As String
        Get
            Return _pwd
        End Get
        Set(ByVal value As String)
            _pwd = value
        End Set
    End Property
```

16. The code added to the Form above used two methods, `GetDirectories` and `GetFiles`. These two methods are basically identical.

```
Public Function GetDirectories(ByVal url As String) As String()
    'line should look like:
    'dr-xr-xr-x   1 owner    group
    ' 0 Nov 25  2002 bussys"
    ' if the first character is a 'd', it's a directory
    Return GetDirectoryEntries(url, "d")
End Function

Public Function GetFiles(ByVal url As String) As String()
    'line should look like:
    '-r-xr-xr-x   1 owner    group
    ' 1715 May 20  1996 readme.txt
    ' if the first character is a '-', it's a file
    Return GetDirectoryEntries(url, "-")
End Function
```

17. Obviously, both `GetDirectories` and `GetFiles` simply return the result of another helper routing, `GetDirectoryEntries`. The only difference between the information returned for a file and a directory is that directories have the directory attribute set to 'd', while files have a blank ('-') in that position.

```
Private Function GetDirectoryEntries(ByVal url As String, _
    ByVal directoryAttribute As String) As String()

    Dim result As New List(Of String)
    Dim str As Stream = Nothing
    Dim temp As String
    Dim words() As String
    Dim splitChars() As Char = {" "c}

    DoFtpRequest(url, _
        WebRequestMethods.Ftp.ListDirectoryDetails, _
        False, str)
    Try
        Using reader As StreamReader = New StreamReader(str)
            Do
                temp = reader.ReadLine

                If temp <> Nothing Then
                    'split into component parts
                    words = temp.Split(splitChars, _
                      StringSplitOptions.RemoveEmptyEntries)
                    If words(0).StartsWith(directoryAttribute) Then
                        result.Add(words(8))
                    End If
                End If
            Loop While temp <> Nothing
        End Using
    Catch ex As Exception
        MessageBox.Show(ex.Message, "Error getting files from " & url)
    End Try

    Return result.ToArray()

End Function
```

18. The `GetDirectoryEntries` method uses another helper method you'll create shortly to execute the `WebRequestMethods.Ftp.ListDirectoryDetails` method on the FTP server. This method returns the resulting response stream in the str parameter. The code then loops through the returned content. Each of the directory entries appears on a separate line, so `ReadLine` is perfect here. The line is split on spaces, and then added to the return value if it has the desired value for the first character (that represents it if it's a directory or a file).

19. The `GetDirectoryEntries` method calls a helper method that does the actual `FtpWebRequest`. This method returns the resulting stream by way of a `ByRef` parameter.

```
Private Function DoFtpRequest(ByVal url As String, _
  ByVal method As String, ByVal useBinary As Boolean, _
  ByRef data As Stream) As FtpStatusCode
    Dim result As FtpStatusCode


    Dim req As FtpWebRequest
    Dim resp As FtpWebResponse
    Dim creds As New NetworkCredential(UserId, Password)

    req = DirectCast(WebRequest.Create(url), FtpWebRequest)

    With req
        .Credentials = creds
        .UseBinary = useBinary
        .KeepAlive = True

        'make initial connection
        .Method = method
        resp = .GetResponse()

        data = resp.GetResponseStream
        result = resp.StatusCode

    End With

    Return result
End Function
```

20. The appropriate type of `WebRequest` is created, the properties are set, and the final request is sent.

21. You should now be able to run the application and browse an FTP server (see Figure 26-6).

22. Just for a few finishing touches, we'll set the Download menu item to only be usable if a file is selected, and add the code for the Exit menu item. Set the initial value for Enabled to false for the download menu item, and add the following code to the handler for the `ListView`'s `SelectedIndexChanged` event:

```
Private Sub FileList_SelectedIndexChanged(ByVal sender As System.Object, _
  ByVal e As System.EventArgs) Handles FileList.SelectedIndexChanged
    Me.DownloadToolStripMenuItem.Enabled = _
      CBool(Me.FileList.SelectedItems.Count)
End Sub
```

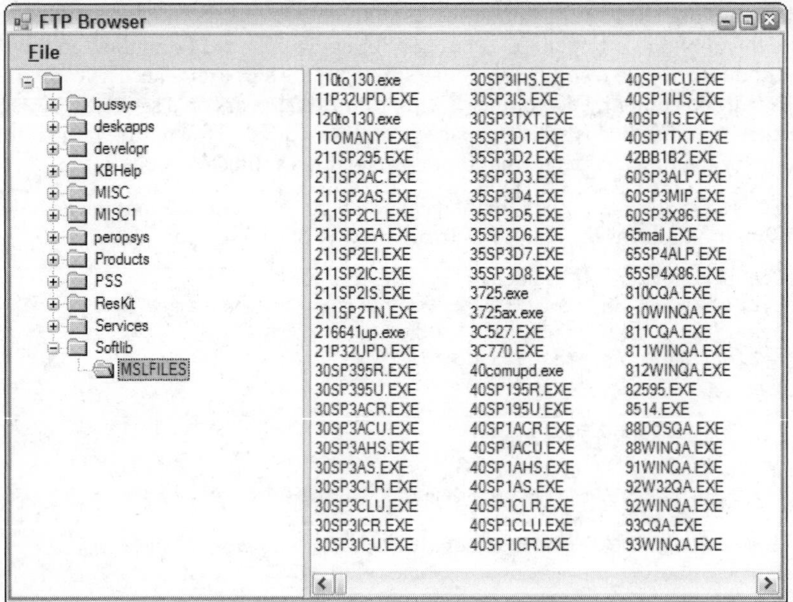

Figure 26-6

23. When there is a selected item, the Count will be > 0, which converts to True. If 0 items are selected, this will be False.

24. The code for the Exit menu item is simple enough:

```
Private Sub ExitToolStripMenuItem_Click(ByVal sender As System.Object, _
  ByVal e As System.EventArgs) Handles ExitToolStripMenuItem.Click
    Me.Close()
End Sub
```

25. Finally, we're ready to add the code for the Download menu item:

```
Private Sub DownloadToolStripMenuItem_Click(ByVal sender As Object, _
  ByVal e As System.EventArgs) Handles DownloadToolStripMenuItem.Click
    'download currently selected file (but only if something is selected)

    ftp.DownloadFile(baseUrl & _
      Me.DirectoryTree.SelectedNode.FullPath & _
      "/" & Me.FileList.SelectedItems(0).Text, _
      downloadPath & Me.FileList.SelectedItems(0).Text)
End Sub
```

26. Obviously, we need to add the `DownloadFile` method to the `FtpClient` class. Here's the code:

```
Public Sub DownloadFile(ByVal url As String, _
  ByVal destination As String)
    Dim str As Stream = Nothing

    DoFtpRequest(url, _
        WebRequestMethods.Ftp.DownloadFile, _
        True, _
        str)

    Using reader As StreamReader = New StreamReader(str)
        Using writer As StreamWriter = _
          New StreamWriter(File.OpenWrite(destination))
            writer.Write(reader.ReadToEnd)
        End Using
    End Using

End Sub
```

Note the repeat use of the `DoFtpRequest` method. However, this time, we pass 'True' for the binary, just in case the file we're transferring is not a text-based file. Using the new 'using' block, we create a new `StreamReader` around the output stream of the response, and a new `StreamWriter` to a local output file. By using the Using block, we guarantee that the associated readers, writers, and streams will all be closed when we're done using them. The `Using` block is functionally identical to the following .NET Framework 1.1 code:

```
Dim reader As StreamReader
Try
    reader = New StreamReader(str)
    ...
Finally
    reader.Flush()
    reader.Close()
    reader = Nothing
End Try
```

Now you can test out the new download code. Run the application again, connect to an FTP server, select a file, and then select Download from the File menu. You should see the newly created file appear in your download directory. (See Figure 26-7.)

While creating a full-blown FTP client would still be a fair bit more work, hopefully you can see that the functionality of the `FtpWebRequest` and `FtpWebResponse` classes makes communicating with an FTP server much easier than before, let alone writing the core functionality yourself using sockets.

Figure 26-7

Simplifying Common Web Requests with WebClient

When I first saw a demo of `WebRequest` back in early 2000, I was delighted. Here was the ability to easily access Internet resources waiting for me to play with. However, one of the other attendees of the demo asked, "Why is that so difficult? You need to do so much to get it to work." The next time I saw the same `WebRequest` demo, the presenter concluded with, "For those of you doing the common scenarios, we have an even easier way." He then went on to show us how to use `System.Net.WebClient`.

For those times when you just want to send a GET or POST request and download a file or the resulting data, you can forget about `WebRequest/WebResponse`. `WebClient` abstracts away all of the little details of making Web requests, and makes it amazingly easy to grab data from the Web. The important methods and properties of the `WebClient` class are described in the following table.

Member	Description
DownloadData	Returns a Byte array of data from the server. This is essentially the same as if you had called the Read method on the stream returned from GetResponseStream. You could then save this to a binary file, or convert to text using an appropriate Encoding. However, see DownloadFile and DownloadString below for two easier ways of performing these tasks.
DownloadFile	Retrieves a file from the server, and saves it locally.
DownloadString	Returns a block of text from the server.
OpenRead	Returns a stream providing data from the server. This is essentially the same stream returned from the call to GetResponseStream.
OpenWrite	Returns a stream you can use to write to the server. This is essentially the same as creating a WebRequest and writing to the GetResponse stream.
UploadData	Sends a Byte array of data to the server. See UploadFile, UploadString, and UploadValues for easier ways of performing this task.
UploadFile	Sends a local file up to the server for processing.
UploadString	POSTs a string to the server. This is very handy when you are simulating HTML form input.
UploadValues	Sends a set of name/value pairs to the server. This is similar to the format used by QueryString values, and this method is quite useful for simulating HTML input.
BaseAddress	The base URL the WebClient will access, for example: http://www.example.com.
Credentials	Credentials that will be used when performing any request. You can either create a new NetworkCredential to use this, or alternately, set the UseDefaultCredentials property to true to use the credentials the user has logged in as.
Headers	Collection of headers that will be used for the request.
Proxy	Overrides the proxy settings from Internet Explorer if set. By default you should never need to set this property as the normal proxy settings are chosen by default.
QueryString	Collection of name/value pairs that will be sent with the request. This represents the values after the '?' on a request.
ResponseHeaders	Collection of headers returned by the server.

All of the `DownloadX` and `UploadX` methods also support an asynchronous version of the method, called `DownloadXAsync`, such as `DownloadFileAsync` or `UploadValuesAsync`. These methods perform the actual request on a background thread, and fire an event when the task is completed. If your application has some form of user interface, such as a Form, you should generally use these methods to keep your application responsive.

As `WebClient` uses the `WebRequest` classes to actually perform its magic, it can greatly simplify network coding. For example, just replace the code used in the `WebRequest` sample created earlier.

Before:

```
Public Function Define(ByVal word As String) As String()
    Dim req As HttpWebRequest = Nothing
    Dim resp As HttpWebResponse
    Dim query As String
    Dim result As New List(Of String)

    query = "http://www.google.com/search?q=define%3A" & _
      HttpUtility.UrlEncode(word)

    Try
        req = DirectCast(WebRequest.Create(query), HttpWebRequest)
        With req
            .Method = "GET"
            resp = req.GetResponse
            If resp.StatusCode = HttpStatusCode.OK Then
                ParseResponse(resp.GetResponseStream, result)
            Else
                MessageBox.Show("Error calling definition service")
            End If
        End With
    Catch ex As Exception

    End Try

    Return result.ToArray()

End Function
```

After:

```
    Public Function Define(ByVal word As String) As String()
        Dim client As New WebClient
        Dim query As String
        Dim result As New List(Of String)

        query = "http://www.google.com/search?q=define%3A" & _
          HttpUtility.UrlEncode(word)

        Try
            result = ParseResponse(client.DownloadString(query))
        Catch ex As Exception

        End Try

        Return result.ToArray()

    End Function
```

`WebClient` avoids all of the stream handling required for `WebRequest`. However, you should still know how `WebRequest` operates, as this knowledge is directly relatable to `WebClient`.

Creating Your Own Web Server with HttpListener

One feature of the .NET Framework 2.0 that got me extremely excited was the new `HttpListener` class (and related classes). This class enables you to very easily create your own Web server. While it likely wouldn't be a replacement for IIS, it can enable you to add Web server functionality to other applications. For example, rather than using Remoting or MSMQ to create a communication channel between two applications, why not use HTTP? Each instance could host its own little Web server, and then you could use `HttpWebRequest` or `WebClient` to communicate between them. Alternately, many applications and hardware devices now provide a built-in Web application enabling you to configure the device or application via a Web browser.

> *The fine print. Unfortunately, the* `HttpListener` *class relies on the new* `Http.sys` *functionality built into IIS 6.0, so you must be using an operating system that includes* `http.sys` *as a systemwide HTTP service. Only Windows Server 2003 and Windows XP SP2 (and future versions of the operating system) include this functionality. So, this is yet another reason to upgrade, and to install Service Packs. Future operating systems should all provide this functionality.*

`HttpListener` works by registering one or more "Prefixes" with `http.sys`. Once this is done, any requests intercepted by the HTTP subsystem will be passed on to the registered listener. An `HttpListenerContext` object is created and passed to your listener. This context contains properties for the Request and Response objects, just as the Context object in ASP.NET does. Again, similar to Web applications, you read the request from the Request property, and write the response to the Response property. Closing the Response sends the resulting page to the user's browser. The following table describes the important members of `HttpListener`.

Member	Description
Abort	Shuts down the server, without finishing any existing requests.
Close	Shuts down the server, after finishing handling any existing requests.
Start	Starts the listener receiving requests.
Stop	Stops the listener from receiving requests.
IsListening	Property that determines if the listener is currently receiving requests.
Prefixes	Collection of the types of requests that this listener will respond to. These are the 'left hand side' of the URL, such as 'http://localhost:8080/' or 'http://serverName:1234/vrootName/'. Note that you must end the prefix in a slash, or you will receive a runtime error. If you have IIS installed on the same server, you can use port 80, as long as a vroot with the same name is not already defined by IIS.

Creating Your Web Server

To demonstrate using `HttpListener`, I'll show you how to create a Windows Service to host its functionality. This could simulate a management or monitoring interface to a Windows Service that would enable authenticated individuals to use the Windows Service remotely or to get other information out of it.

1. Create a new Windows Service application called MiniServer. The server won't do much on its own, but will host an `HttpListener`.
2. From the Components section of the toolbox, add a `BackgroundWorker` component. Call this component BackgroundWork. The other properties can remain at their defaults. This BackgroundWorker will be used to process HTTP requests on a background thread, simplifying the handling of the threads.
3. Switch to code view for the service. Add the Imports statements you need to the top of the file.

```
Imports System.Net
Imports System.IO
Imports System.Web
Imports System.Text
```

4. In the `OnStart` method, set up the list of Prefixes that the server will respond to. This can be as simple as adding a port address to the URL, or include specific vroots. In the sample's case, there are examples of each:

```
Protected Overrides Sub OnStart(ByVal args() As String)
    'args(0) will allow us to override the port
    Dim machineName As String

    machineName = System.Environment.MachineName
    theService = HttpUtility.UrlEncode(Me.ServiceName)

    Me.EventLog.WriteEntry("Service Name: " & Me.ServiceName)

    With listener
        .Prefixes.Add(String.Format("http://{0}:{1}/", _
          "localhost", PORT.ToString))
        .Prefixes.Add(String.Format("http://{0}:{1}/", _
          machineName, PORT.ToString))
        .Prefixes.Add(String.Format("http://{0}/{1}/", _
          "localhost", theService))
        .Prefixes.Add(String.Format("http://{0}/{1}/", _
          machineName, theService))
        .Start()
    End With
    'start up the background thread
    Me.BackgroundWork.RunWorkerAsync()

End Sub
```

In this case, the server will respond to a prefix in any of the formats (the sample computer is called Tantalus):

```
http://localhost:9090/
http://tantalus:9090/
http://localhost/sampleservice/
http://tantalus/sampleservice/
```

> **Note: There is one important point to keep in mind as you add prefixes. They must end in a slash ("/") character. If not, you will get a runtime error when the listener attempts to add that prefix.**

After initializing the Prefixes collection, calling the Start method binds the listener to the appropriate ports and vroots and starts it accepting requests. However, we don't want to actually receive the requests in the OnStart handler. Remember that the service doesn't actually start until after this method has completed. So, having a lot of processing in the OnStart will actually prevent the service from completing. Therefore, we use another of the new features of Visual Basic 2005, the BackgroundWorker component, to handle the requests. Call its RunWorkerAsync to start the background task (in our case, the HttpListener).

5. The OnStop method will serve to shutdown the HttpListener.

```
Protected Overrides Sub OnStop()
    With listener
        .Stop()
        .Close()
    End With
End Sub
```

6. The background task performed by the BackgroundWorker component can be any process that you don't want to interfere with the normal application's processing. If this was a Windows Forms application, having a long running loop or other process running might prevent the application from drawing, or responding to the user's requests. Beyond that, we can do anything we want in the background task, with one exception. Because a Windows Forms application works in a single foreground task, one can't directly access the controls on the Form from the background task. Instead, if the background task must change properties on the controls, it should fire events. The controls can then subscribe to those events, where you can access the properties. In this Windows Service, it has no such user interface, so that problem is avoided.

   The actual work you want the BackgroundWorker to perform is in the DoWork event handler:

```
Private Sub BackgroundWork_DoWork(ByVal sender As System.Object, _
  ByVal e As System.ComponentModel.DoWorkEventArgs) Handles BackgroundWork.DoWork
    Dim context As HttpListenerContext
    Dim path As String

    'this is where we actually process requests
    While listener.IsListening
        context = listener.GetContext
        path = context.Request.Url.AbsolutePath.ToLower

        'strip out the serviceName if you're using the URL format:
        'http://server/servicename/path
        If path.StartsWith("/" & theService.ToLower) Then
            path = path.Substring(theService.Length + 1)
        End If
        Me.EventLog.WriteEntry("Received request for " & path)


        Select Case path
            Case "/time"
                SendPage(context.Response, DateTime.Now.ToLongTimeString)
            Case "/date"
                SendPage(context.Response, DateTime.Now.ToLongDateString)
            Case "/random"
                SendPage(context.Response, New Random().Next.ToString)
            Case Else
                'if we don't understand the request, send a 404
```

```
                context.Response.StatusCode = 404
        End Select

    End While
End Sub
```

Our background task performs its work in a loop as long as the `HttpListener` is actively listening. Every developer knows that performing a set of tasks in a (relatively) tight loop is dangerous, possibly leading to computer or application lockup. However, the `BackgroundWorker` performs this on another thread, leaving our application responsive.

For this application, we first get access to the context for the listener. The context groups together one client's set of communication with our listener. Similar to the `HttpContext` in ASP.NET, the `HttpListenerContext` provides access to the `HttpListenerRequest` and `HttpListenerResponse` objects, so the first step in handling a request should always be to get this context. Next, the code uses a very simple means of determining the request URL. In a more full-featured implementation, this could be more complex, separating any query values from the path requested, etc. For this sample, the listener only responds to three main paths, "/time", "/date", and "/random" to receive the current (server) time or date, or a random Integer value. If the user requests anything else, we return a 404.

7. The `SendPage` subroutine simply writes out a basic HTML page, and the value determined.

```
Private Sub SendPage(ByVal response As HttpListenerResponse, _
  ByVal message As String)
    Dim sb As New StringBuilder

    'build string
    With sb
        .Append("<html><body>")
        .AppendFormat("<h3>{0}</h3>", message)
        .Append("</body></html>")
    End With

    Me.EventLog.WriteEntry(sb.ToString)

    'set up content headers
    With response
        .ContentType = "text/html"
        .ContentEncoding = Encoding.UTF8
        .ContentLength64 = sb.ToString.Length
        Me.EventLog.WriteEntry(sb.ToString.Length.ToString)

        Try
            Using writer As New StreamWriter(.OutputStream)
                With writer
                    .Write(sb.ToString)
                    .Flush()
                End With
            End Using

        Catch ex As Exception
            Me.EventLog.WriteEntry(ex.Message, EventLogEntryType.Error)
```

```
        Finally
            'close the response to end
            .Close()
        End Try
    End With
End Sub
```

Hopefully there isn't much surprising in this code. Using a `StringBuilder`, a response is built. Then the content is written back to the browser (see Figure 26-8) using a `StreamWriter` that is created on top of the `Response.OutputStream`. Remember to Close the `Response`, or the request will never close until it times out.

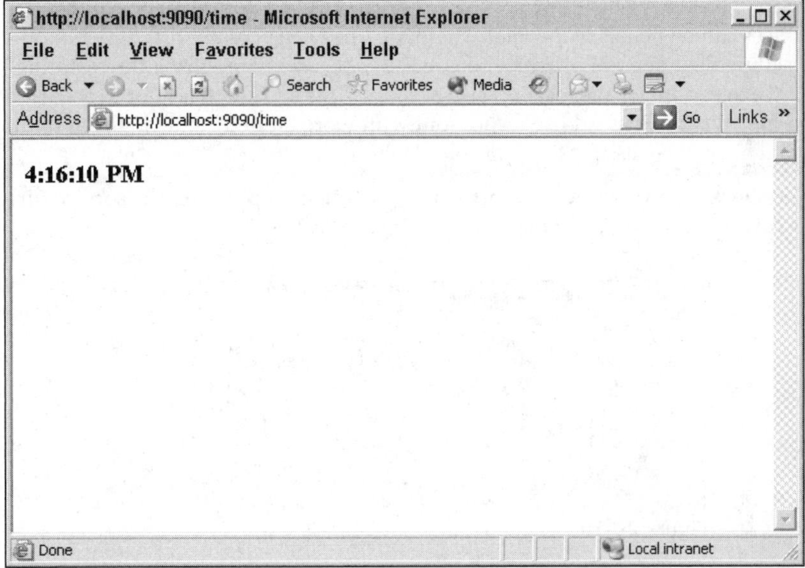

Figure 26-8

8. Before you can install and test your Windows Service, however, it must be installed. On the Properties window for the actual service, click Add Installer (see Figure 26-9). This adds a new file to the project called `ProjectInstaller.vb`, and adds two components to the file, `ServiceInstaller1` and `ServiceProcessInstaller1`. You can either keep these names or change them as you desire. In addition, set the properties as in the following table.

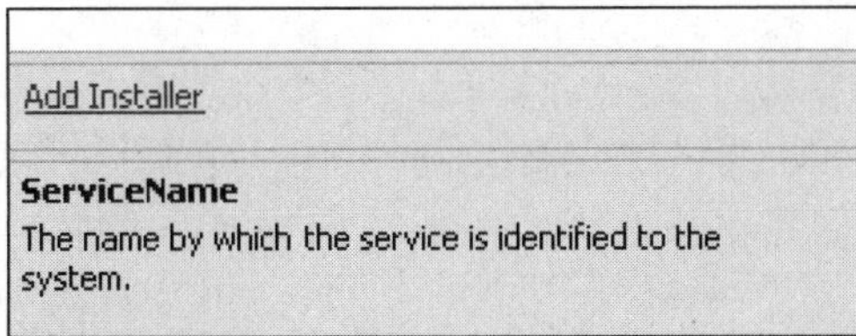

Figure 26-9

Component	Property	Value
ServiceInstaller1	Description	Sample Service from Wrox Professional Visual Basic 2005
	DisplayName	Sample Service
	ServiceName	SampleService
ServiceProcessInstaller1	Account	LocalSystem

Most of these properties only affect the display values for the Windows Service. However, the `Account` property of the `ServiceProcessInstaller` deserves special mention. Windows Services run on behalf of the user. Therefore, they can actually run under another user account. By setting the `Account` property to `LocalSystem`, you are setting the resulting Windows Service to run under the local system account. This account has a lot of access to the system, so you may want to instead use an account with more limited rights to the system; however you would have to create this account separately.

9. Build the Windows service. Unfortunately, if you attempt to run the service directly from Visual Basic, you will get an error message (see Figure 26-10).

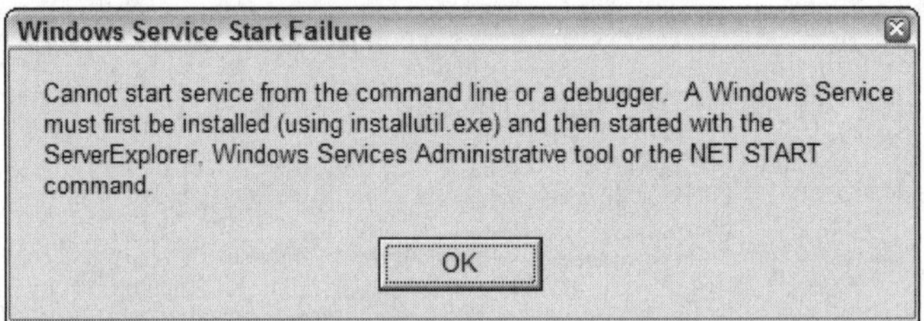

Figure 26-10

A Windows Service can only run if it has been installed into the system, and this task is performed using a command-line utility `InstallUtil.exe`. Open the Visual Studio Command Prompt and navigate to the directory where you have built `MiniServer.exe`. Run `installutil miniserver.exe`, and hopefully you'll be greeted with a success message (see Figure 26-11).

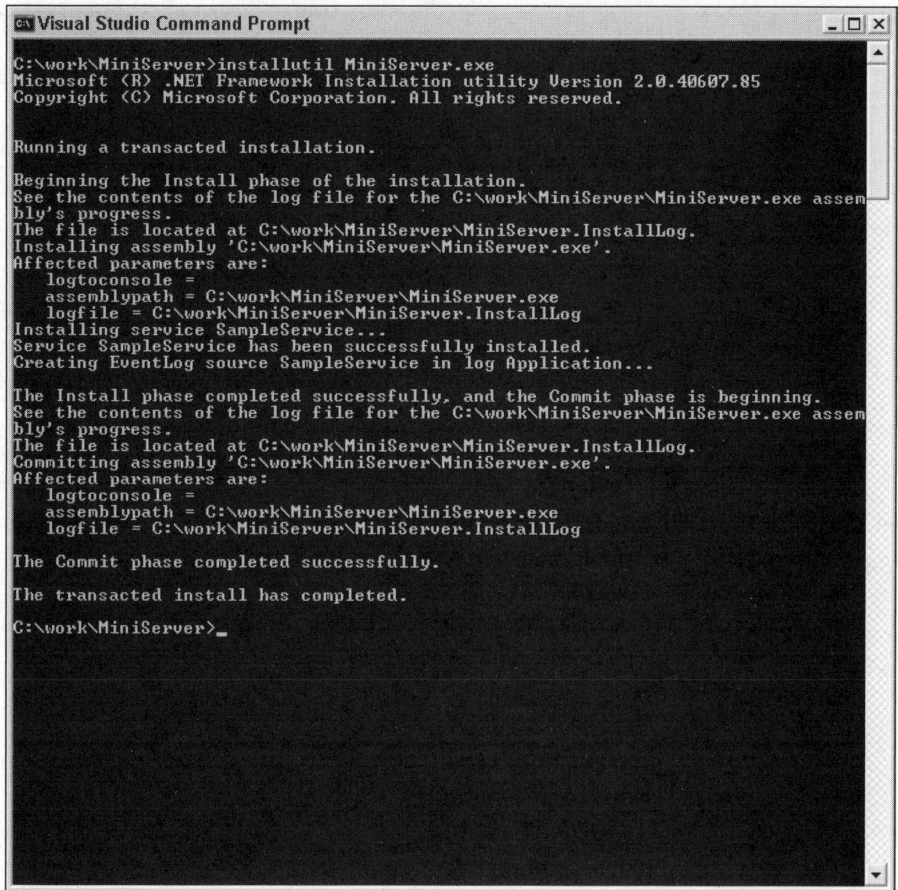

Visual Studio Command Prompt
C:\work\MiniServer>installutil MiniServer.exe
Microsoft (R) .NET Framework Installation utility Version 2.0.40607.85
Copyright (C) Microsoft Corporation. All rights reserved.
Running a transacted installation.
Beginning the Install phase of the installation.
See the contents of the log file for the C:\work\MiniServer\MiniServer.exe assem
bly's progress.
The file is located at C:\work\MiniServer\MiniServer.InstallLog.
Installing assembly 'C:\work\MiniServer\MiniServer.exe'.
Affected parameters are:
logtoconsole =
assemblypath = C:\work\MiniServer\MiniServer.exe
logfile = C:\work\MiniServer\MiniServer.InstallLog
Installing service SampleService...
Service SampleService has been successfully installed.
Creating EventLog source SampleService in log Application...
The Install phase completed successfully, and the Commit phase is beginning.
See the contents of the log file for the C:\work\MiniServer\MiniServer.exe assem
bly's progress.
The file is located at C:\work\MiniServer\MiniServer.InstallLog.
Committing assembly 'C:\work\MiniServer\MiniServer.exe'.
Affected parameters are:
logtoconsole =
assemblypath = C:\work\MiniServer\MiniServer.exe
logfile = C:\work\MiniServer\MiniServer.InstallLog
The Commit phase completed successfully.
The transacted install has completed.
C:\work\MiniServer>_

Figure 26-11

10. Finally, you can start your new service. Open the Services application from Start ➪ All Programs ➪ Administrative Tools. Find the Sample Service in the list (see Figure 26-12), and click Start. You should now be able to request one of the items the service is listening to, such as `http://localhost:9090/time` (see Figure 26-13).

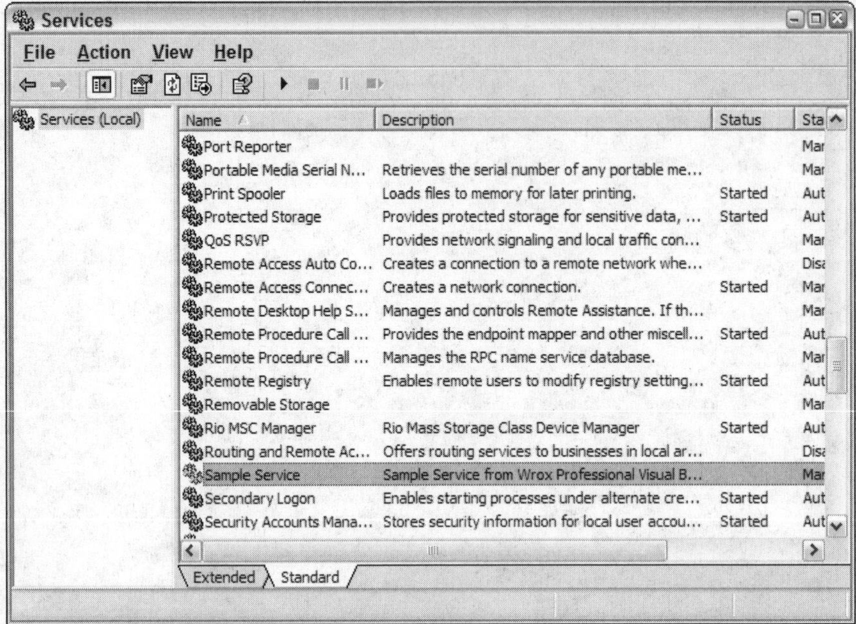

Figure 26-12

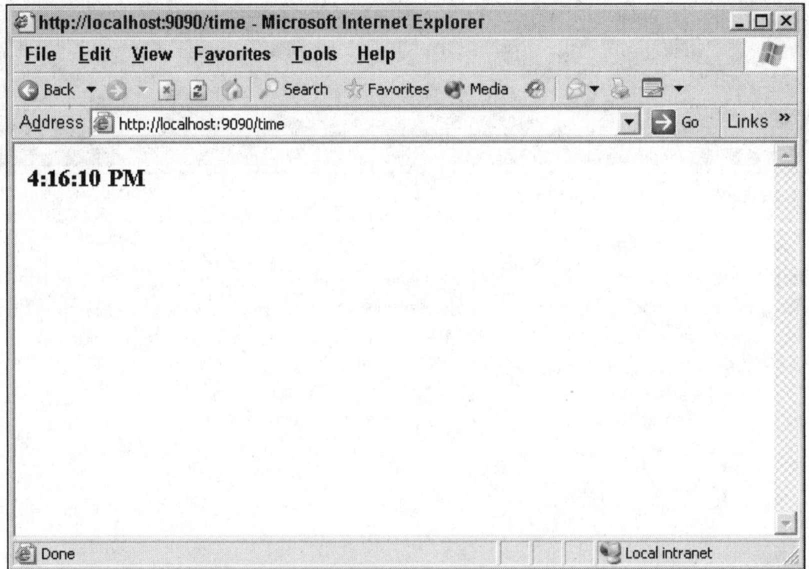

Figure 26-13

Just to confirm that all of the Prefixes work, you can also request one of the values using the vroot rather than using the port (see Figure 26-14).

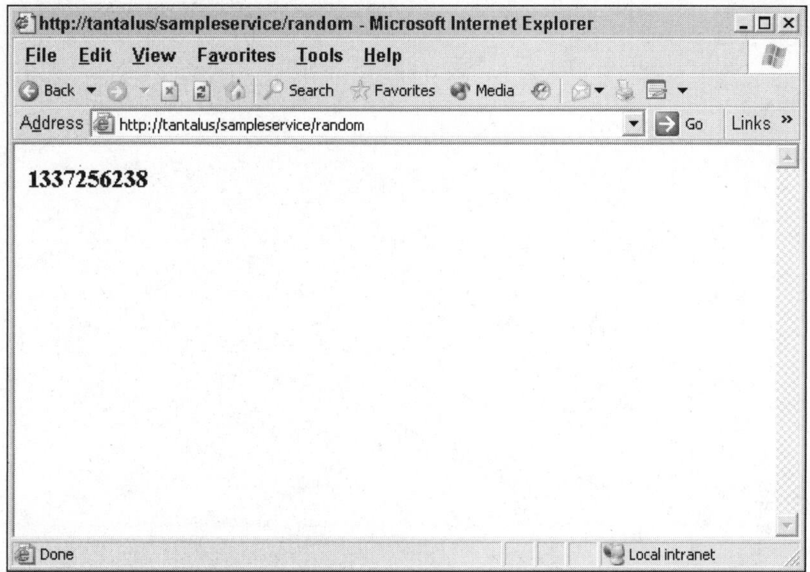

Figure 26-14

The `HttpListener` adds yet another powerful way for your applications to communicate. It gives you the ability to extend the reach of your applications out to Web browser clients, without requiring the additional administrative and management overhead of IIS to your deployment.

Summary

Programming directly to the network provides a great deal of power and flexibility. Of course, all of that power and flexibility comes at a cost. Many of the services provided by higher-level technologies, such as Web Services or Remoting, aren't available, and must often be re-created. However, in those situations where you must communicate with an existing application, or when you need the ultimate in control and speed, using the classes in `System.Net` make life easier than it would be otherwise.

This chapter looked at many of the classes that expose network programming. You've seen how to make Web requests without a browser, so you could use the data on the Internet in your applications; you've seen how you can leverage the bare sockets layer to write your own communication protocols, and finally, you've seen some of the new classes in Visual Basic 2005 for creating FTP clients and Web servers.

27

Visual Basic and the Internet

In today's network-centric world, it's very likely that applications will need to work with other computers over a private network, the Internet, or both.

This chapter details how to:

- Download resources from the Web
- Design your own communication protocols
- Reuse Internet Explorer in your applications

A good place to start working with network resources is with a look at how to download content from the Web.

Downloading Internet Resources

Downloading content from the Web is very easy, so you'll throw together a basic application before getting onto some more meaty topics. This application will download HTML from a Web page and display it in a text box. Later on, you'll look at how you can display HTML properly by hosting Internet Explorer (IE) directly using the new `WebBrowser` control in Windows Forms applications, but for now you'll just use plain text.

In order to download a Web page, you need to be able to identity the remote page that you wish to download, make a request of the Web server that can provide that page, listen for the response, and download the data for the resource.

The relevant classes for this example are `System.Uri`, `System.Net.WebRequest`, `System.Net.HttpWebRequest`, and `System.Net.HttpWebResponse`:

- `System.Uri` is a useful general-purpose class for expressing a *Uniform Resource Identifier* (URI). A *Uniform Resource Locator* (URL) is a type of URI (although in reality the terms are so confused that they are often used interchangeably). A URI, however is "more than" a URL, which is why this .NET class is `Uri` and not `Url`. `System.Uri` has many properties for decoding a URI. For example, if you had a string like `www.pretendcompany.com:8080/ myservices/myservice.asmx?WSDL`, you could use the `Port` property to extract the port number, the `Query` property to extract the query string, and so on.
- A `WebRequest` expresses some kind of Internet resource whether it is located on the LAN or WAN (so in my opinion a better name for this class would be `NetRequest`, as the classes aren't specifically related to the Web protocol).
- Protocol-specific descendants of `WebRequest` carry out the actual request: `HttpWebRequest` expresses an HTTP download and `FileWebRequest` expresses a file download, for example `file://c:/MyFile.txt`.
- An `HttpWebResponse` is returned once a connection to the Web server has been made and the resource is available to download.

There are another two major classes related to working with the Internet in the .NET Framework. One is `System.Net.WebClient` and the other is `System.Net.WebProxy`. `WebClient` is basically a helper class that wraps the request and response classes previously mentioned.

As this is a professional-level book, I'm going to show you what to do behind the scenes, in effect, reengineer what `WebClient` can do. I'll talk about `WebProxy` later, which allows you to explicitly define a proxy server to use for Internet communications.

Let's use these classes to build an application. Create a new Windows application, create a new form, and add controls to it as shown in Figure 27-1.

Figure 27-1

The control names are: `textUrl`, `buttonGo`, and `textData`. The `Anchor` properties of the controls are set so that the form resizes properly. The control `textUrl` should be set to `Top, Left, Right`; `buttonGo` to `Top, Right`; and `textData` to `Top, Left, Bottom, Right`.

Add these namespace import declarations to the form's code:

```
Imports System.IO
Imports System.Net
Imports System.Text
```

To keep the code simple, you'll include all the functionality into the `Click` handler of `buttonGo`. In an ideal world, you want to break the code in the handler out to a separate method. This enriches the interface of the object and promotes good reuse.

The first thing you do here is create a new `System.Uri` based on the URL that the user enters into the text box:

```
Private Sub buttonGo_Click(ByVal sender As System.Object, _
 ByVal e As System.EventArgs) Handles buttonGo.Click

   Dim uri As New Uri(textUrl.Text)
```

Then, you'll illustrate some of the useful properties of `System.Uri`:

```
Dim builder As New StringBuilder
builder.Append("AbsolutePath: " & uri.AbsolutePath & VbCrLf)
builder.Append("AbsoluteUri: " & uri.AbsoluteUri & VbCrLf)
builder.Append("Host: " & uri.Host & VbCrLf)
builder.Append("HostNameType: " & uri.HostNameType.ToString() & _
               VbCrLf)
builder.Append("LocalPath: " & uri.LocalPath & VbCrLf)
builder.Append("PathAndQuery: " & uri.PathAndQuery & VbCrLf)
builder.Append("Port: " & uri.Port & VbCrLf)
builder.Append("Query: " & uri.Query & VbCrLf)
builder.Append("Scheme: " & uri.Scheme)
MsgBox(builder.ToString())
```

The shared `Create` method of `System.Net.WebRequest` is used to create the actual object that you can use to download the Web resource. Notice how you don't create an instance of `HttpWebRequest`; you're working with a return object of type `WebRequest`. However, you'll actually be given an `HttpWebRequest` object, and `WebRequest` chooses the most appropriate class to return based on the URI. This allows you to build your own handlers for different network resources that can be used by consumers who simply supply an appropriate URL.

To make the request and get the response back from the server (so ultimately you can access the data), you call the `GetResponse` method of `WebRequest`. In your case, you'll get an `HttpWebResponse` object—once more it's up to the implementation of the `WebRequest`-derived object, in this case `HttpWebRequest`, to return an object of the most suitable type.

If the request is not okay, you'll get an exception (which for the sake of simplicity you won't bother processing). If the request is okay, you can get the length and the type of the response using properties of the `WebResponse` object:

```
Dim request As WebRequest = WebRequest.Create(uri)
Dim response As WebResponse = request.GetResponse()
builder = New StringBuilder
```

```
    builder.Append("Request type: " & request.GetType().ToString() & VbCrLf)
    builder.Append("Response type: " & response.GetType().ToString() & VbCrLf)
    builder.Append("Content length: " & response.ContentLength & _
          " bytes" & VbCrLf)
    builder.Append("Content type: " & response.ContentType & VbCrLf)
    MsgBox(builder.ToString())
```

It just remains for you to download the information. You can do this through a stream (`WebResponse` objects return a stream by overriding `GetResponseStream`), and what's more, you can use a `System.IO.StreamReader` to download the whole lot in a single call by calling the `ReadToEnd` method. This method will only download text, so if you want to download binary data you'll have to use the methods on the `Stream` object directly, or use a `System.IO.BinaryReader`.

```
    Dim stream As Stream = response.GetResponseStream()
    Dim reader As New StreamReader(stream)
    Dim data As String = reader.ReadToEnd()
    reader.Close()
    stream.Close()
    textData.Text = data
  End Sub
```

If you run the application, enter a URL of `www.reuters.com`, and click the Go button, you'll see debugging information about the URL, as shown in Figure 27-2.

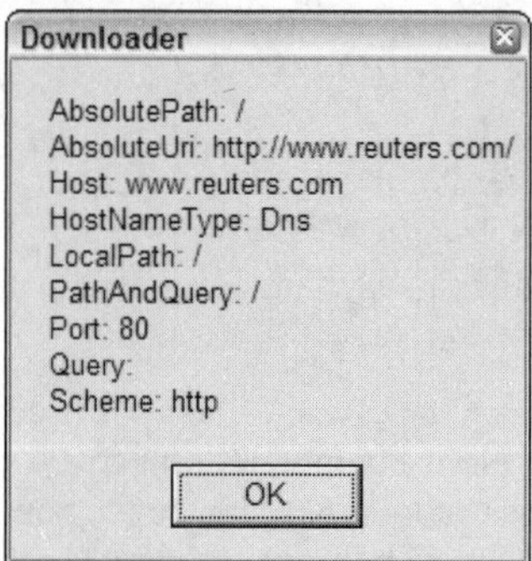

Figure 27-2

This is a simple URL. The application tells you that the scheme is `http`, and the host name type is `Dns`. If, for example, you enter an IP into the URL to be requested rather than a host name, this type will come back as `IPv4`. This tells you where the host name came from; in this case, it's a general Internet host name.

Next, the application as shown in Figure 27-3 provides information about the response.

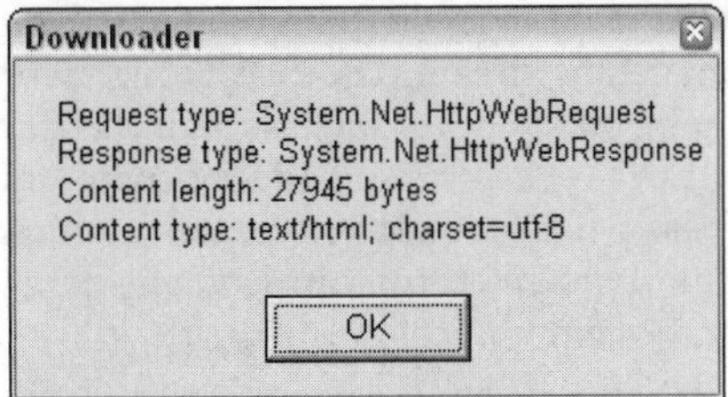

Figure 27-3

Finally, you get to see the response data itself as illustrated in Figure 27-4.

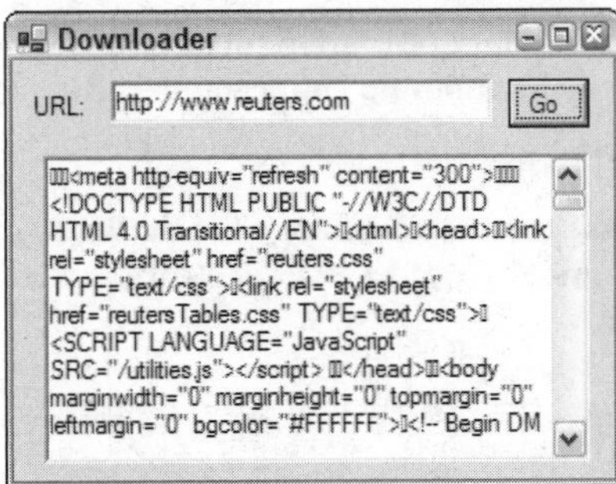

Figure 27-4

Perhaps the most important exception to be aware of when using these classes is the `System.Net.WebException` exception. If anything goes wrong on the `WebRequest.GetResponse` call, this exception will be thrown. Among other things, this exception provides access to the `WebResponse` object through the `Response` property. The `StatusCode` property of `WebResponse` tells you what actually happened through the `HttpStatusCode` enumeration. For example, `HttpStatusCode.NotFound` is the equivalent of the HTTP 404 status code.

Sockets

There may be times when you need to transfer data across a network (either a private network or the Internet) when the existing techniques and protocols don't exactly suit your needs. For example, you wouldn't be able to download resources using the techniques discussed at the start of this chapter, and you can't use Web Services (as described in Chapter 23) or remoting (as described in Chapter 24). When this happens, the best course of action is to roll your own protocol using *sockets*.

TCP/IP, and therefore, the Internet itself, is based on sockets. The principle is simple, establish a port at one end and allow clients to "plug in" to that port from the other end. Once the connection is made, applications can send and receive data through a stream. For example, HTTP nearly always operates on port 80. So, a Web server opens a socket on port 80 and waits for incoming connections (Web browsers, unless told otherwise, attempt to connect to port 80 in order to make a request of that Web server).

In .NET, sockets are implemented in the `System.Net.Sockets` namespace and use classes from `System.Net` and `System.IO` to get the stream classes. Although working with sockets can be a little tricky outside of .NET, the Framework includes some superb classes that enable you to open a socket for inbound connections (`System.Net.TcpListener`) and for communication between two open sockets (`System.Net.TcpClient`). These two classes, in combination with some threading shenanigans, allow you build your own protocol, through which you can send any data you like. With your own protocol, you have ultimate control over the communication.

To demonstrate these techniques, you're going to build Wrox Messenger, a very basic instant messenger application similar to MSN Messenger.

Building the Application

You'll wrap all the functionality of your application into a single Windows application. This application will act as both a server that waits for inbound connections and a client that has established outbound connections.

Create a new project called `WroxMessenger`. Change the title of `Form1` to `Wrox Messenger` and add a `TextBox` control called `textConnectTo` and a `Button` control called `buttonConnect`. The form should appear as shown in Figure 27-5.

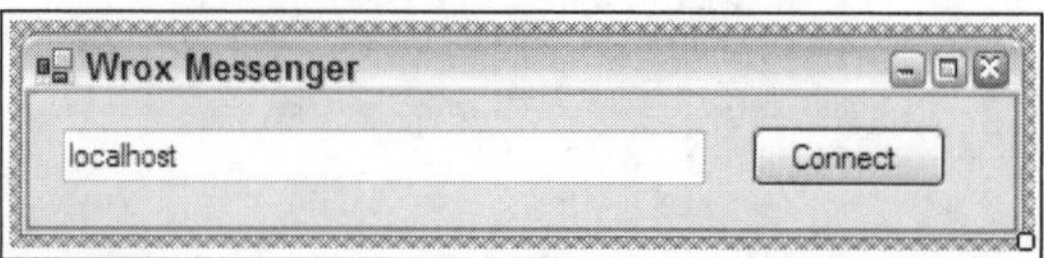

Figure 27-5

We'll talk about this in more detail in a little while, but for now it's very important that all of your UI code runs in the same thread, and that the thread is actually the main application that creates and runs `Form1`.

To keep track of what's happening, you'll add a field to `Form1` that allows you to store the ID of the startup thread and also report that ID on the caption. This will help you gain an understanding of the thread/UI issues that are discussed later. You'll also need some namespace imports and a constant specifying the ID of the default port. Add this code to `Form1`:

```
Imports System.Net
Imports System.Net.Sockets

Public Class Form1
   Inherits System.Windows.Forms.Form

   Private Shared _mainThreadId As Integer
   Public Const ServicePort As Integer = 10101
```

Next, open the designer file for Form1 (`Form1.Designer.vb`) and add this code to the constructor that populates the field and changes the caption:

```
<System.Diagnostics.DebuggerNonUserCode()> _
Public Sub New()
   MyBase.New()

   'This call is required by the Windows Form Designer.
   InitializeComponent()

   mainThreadId = System.Threading.Thread.CurrentThread.GetHashCode()

   Text &= "-" & _mainThreadId.ToString()

End Sub
```

Note that you can get to the `Form1.Designer.vb` file by starting from the `Form1.vb` file and using Visual Studio by selecting `Form1` and `New` in the uppermost drop-downs in the document window. This will cause the `Form1.Designer.vb` file to open for you.

To listen for incoming connections, you'll create a separate class called `Listener`. This class will use an instance of `System.Net.Sockets.TcpListener` to wait for incoming connections. Specifically, this will open a TCP port that *any* client can connect to — sockets are absolutely not platform-specific. Although connections are always made on a specific, known port, the actual communication takes place on a port of the TCP/IP subsystem's choosing, which means you can support many inbound connections at once, despite the fact that each of them connects to the same port. Sockets are an open standard available on pretty much any platform you care to mention. For example, if you publish the specification for your protocol, developers working on Linux would be able to connect to your Wrox Messenger service.

When you detect an inbound connection, you'll be given a `System.Net.Sockets.TcpClient` object. This is your gateway to the remote client. To send and receive data, you need to get hold of a `System.Net.NetworkStream` object (returned through a call to `GetStream` on `TcpClient`), which returns a stream that you can use.

Create a new class called `Listener`. This thread needs members to hold an instance of a `System.Threading.Thread` object and also a reference back to the `Form1` class that is the main form in the application. We won't go into a discussion of how to spin up and spin down threads, nor are we going to talk about synchronization. (You should refer back to Chapter 22 if you need more information on this.)

Here's the basic code for the `Listener` class:

```
Imports System.Net.Sockets
Imports System.Threading

Public Class Listener

 Private _main As Form1
 Private _listener As TcpListener
 Private _thread As Thread

 Public Sub New(ByVal main As Form1)
  _main = main
 End Sub
```

```
    Public Sub SpinUp()

      ' create and start the new thread...
      _thread = New Thread(AddressOf ThreadEntryPoint)
      _thread.Start()
    End Sub
  End Class
```

The obvious missing method here is `ThreadEntryPoint`. This is where you need to create the socket and wait for inbound connections. When you get them, you'll be given a `TcpClient` object, which you need to pass back to `Form1`, where the conversation window can be created.

To create the socket, create an instance of `TcpListener` and give it a port. In your application, the port you're going to use is `10101`. This port should be free on your computer, but if the debugger breaks on an exception when you instantiate `TcpListener` or call `Start`, try another port. Once you've done that and called `Start` to configure the object to listen for connections, you drop into an infinite loop and call `AcceptTcpClient`. This method will block until the socket is closed, or a connection becomes available. If you get `Nothing` back, either the socket is closed or there's a problem, so you drop out of the thread. If you get something back, then you pass the `TcpClient` over to `Form1` through a call to the (not yet built) `ReceiveInboundConnection` method:

```
  ' ThreadEntryPoint...
  Protected Sub ThreadEntryPoint()

    ' Create a socket...
    _listener = New TcpListener(Form1.ServicePort)
    _listener.Start()

    ' Loop infinitely, waiting for connections.
    Do While True

      ' Get a connection...
      Dim client As TcpClient = _listener.AcceptTcpClient()
      If client Is Nothing Then
       Exit Do
      End If
      ' Process it...
      _main.ReceiveInboundConnection(client)
      Loop
  End Sub
```

It's in the `ReceiveInboundConnection` method that you'll create the Conversation form that the user can use to send messages.

Creating Conversation Windows

When building Windows Forms applications that support threading, there's always the possibility of running into a problem with the Windows messaging subsystem. This is a very old part of Windows (the idea has been around since version 1.0 of the platform, although the implementation on modern Windows versions is far removed from the original) that powers the Windows user interface.

Even those who are not familiar with old-school Windows programming, such as MFC, Win32, or even Win16 development, should be familiar with events. When you move a mouse over a form, you get `MouseMove` events. When you close a form, you get a `Closed` event. There's a mapping between these events and the messages that Windows passes around to support the actual display of the windows. For example, whenever you receive a `MouseMove` event, a message called `WM_MOUSEMOVE` is sent to the window, by Windows, in response to the mouse driver. In .NET, and in other Rapid Application Development (RAD) environments like VB and Delphi, this message is converted into an event that you can write code against.

Although this is getting way off the topic — you know how to build Windows Forms applications by now and don't need the details of messages like `WM_NCHITTEST` or `WM_PAINT` — it has an important implication. In effect, Windows creates a message queue for each thread into which it posts the messages that the thread's windows have to work with. This queue is looped on a virtually constant basis, and the messages are distributed to the appropriate window (remember, small controls like buttons and text boxes are also windows). In .NET, these messages are turned into events, but unless the message queue still gets looped the messages don't get through.

Imagine that Windows needs to paint a window. It will post a `WM_PAINT` message to the queue. A message loop implemented on the main thread of the process containing the window detects the message and dispatches it on to the appropriate window where it is processed. Now, imagine that the queue isn't looped. The message never gets picked up, and the window will never get painted.

In a Windows application, a single thread is usually responsible for message dispatch. This thread is usually (although it doesn't have to be) the main application thread, the one that's created when the process is first created. If you create windows in a different thread, then that new thread has to support the message dispatch loop so that messages destined for the windows get through. However, with `Listener`, you have no code for processing the message loop and there's little point in writing any, because the next time you call `AcceptTcpClient` you're going to block and everything will stop working.

The trick then is to create the windows only in the main application thread, which is the thread that created `Form1` and that is processing the messages for all the windows created in this thread. You can pass calls from one thread to the other by calling the `Invoke` method of `Form1`.

This is where things start to get complicated. There is an awful lot of code to write to get to a point where you can see that the socket connection has been established and get conversation windows to appear. Here's what you need to do:

- ❑ Create a new Conversation form. This form will need controls for displaying the total content of the conversation, plus a `TextBox` control for adding new messages.
- ❑ The Conversation window will need to be able to send and receive messages through its own thread.
- ❑ `Form1` needs to be able to initiate new connections. This will be done in a separate thread that is managed by the thread pool. When the connection has been established, a new Conversation window needs to be created and configured.
- ❑ `Form1` also needs to receive inbound connections. When it gets one of these, a new Conversation needs to be created and configured.

Let's look at these problems one at a time.

Creating the Conversation Form

The simplest place to start is to build the new Conversation form. This needs three `TextBox` controls (`textUsername`, `textMessages`, and `textMessage`) and a `Button` control (`buttonSend`). The form is shown in Figure 27-6.

Figure 27-6

This class requires a number of fields and an enumeration. It needs fields to hold the username of the user (which you'll default to `Evjen`), the underlying `TcpClient`, and the `NetworkStream` returned by that client. The enumeration indicates the direction of the connection (which will help you when debugging):

```
Imports System.Net
Imports System.Net.Sockets
Imports System.Text
Imports System.Threading
Imports System.Runtime.Serialization.Formatters.Binary

Public Class Conversation
 Inherits System.Windows.Forms.Form

 Private _username As String = "Evjen"
 Private _client As TcpClient
 Private _stream As NetworkStream
 Private _direction As ConversationDirection

 Public Enum ConversationDirection As Integer
  Inbound = 0
  Outbound = 1
 End Enum
```

We won't look into the issues of establishing a thread for exchanging messages at this stage, but we will look at implementing the `ConfigureClient` method. This method will eventually do more work than this, but, for now, it sets a couple of fields and calls `UpdateCaption`:

```
Public Sub ConfigureClient(ByVal client As TcpClient, _
              ByVal direction As ConversationDirection)
  ' Set it up...
```

```
  _client = client
  _direction = direction

  ' Update the window...
  UpdateCaption()
 End Sub

 Protected Sub UpdateCaption()

  ' Set the text.
  Dim builder As New StringBuilder(_username)
  builder.Append(" - ")
  builder.Append(_direction.ToString())
  builder.Append(" - ")
  builder.Append(Thread.CurrentThread.GetHashCode())
  builder.Append(" - ")
  If Not _client Is Nothing Then
   builder.Append("Connected")
  Else
   builder.Append("Not connected")
  End If
  Text = builder.ToString()
 End Sub
```

One debugging issue that you have is that if you're connecting to a conversation on the same machine, you need a way of changing the name of the user sending each message; otherwise, things will get confusing.

That's what the topmost `TextBox` control is for. In the constructor, set the text for the `textUsername.Text` property:

```
 Public Sub New()
  MyBase.New()
   'This call is required by the Windows Form Designer.
  InitializeComponent()

  'Add any initialization after the InitializeComponent() call
  textUsername.Text = _username
 End Sub
```

On the `TextChanged` event for this control, update the caption and the internal `_username` field:

```
 Private Sub textUsername_TextChanged(ByVal sender As System.Object, _
                    ByVal e As System.EventArgs) _
                    Handles textUsername.TextChanged
  _username = textUsername.Text
  UpdateCaption()
 End Sub
```

Initiating Connections

`Form1` needs to be able to both initiate connections and receive inbound connections—the application is both a client and a server. You've already created some of the server portion by creating `Listener`, and now you'll look at the client side.

The general rule when working with sockets is that any time you send anything over the wire, you must perform the actual communication in a separate thread. Virtually all calls to send and receive do so in a blocking manner; that is, they block until data is received, block until all data is sent, and so on.

If threads are used well, the UI will keep running as normal, irrespective of the problems that may occur during transmitting and receiving. This is why in the `InitiateConnection` method on `Form1` you defer processing to another method called `InitiateConnectionThreadEntryPoint`, which is called from a new thread:

```
Public Sub InitiateConnection()
 InitiateConnection(textConnectTo.Text)
End Sub

Public Sub InitiateConnection(ByVal hostName As String)

 ' Give it to the threadpool to do...
 ThreadPool.QueueUserWorkItem(AddressOf _
 Me.InitiateConnectionThreadEntryPoint, hostName)
End Sub

Private Sub buttonConnect_Click(ByVal sender As System.Object, _
                ByVal e As System.EventArgs) _
                Handles buttonConnect.Click

 InitiateConnection()
End Sub
```

Inside the thread, you try to convert the host name that you're given into an IP address (`localhost` is used as the host name in the demonstration, but it could be the name of a machine on the local network or a host name on the Internet). This is done through the shared `Resolve` method on `System.Net.Dns` and returns a `System.Net.IPHostEntry` object. As a host name can point to multiple IP addresses, you'll just use the first one that you're given. You take this address expressed as an IP (for example, `192.168.0.4`) and combine it with the port number to get a new `System.Net.IPEndPoint`. You create a new `TcpClient` from this `IPEndPoint` and try to connect.

If at any time an exception is thrown (which can happen because the name couldn't be resolved or the connection could not be established), you'll pass the exception over to `HandleInitiateConnectionException`. If it succeeds, you'll pass it to `ProcessOutboundConnection`. Both of these methods will be implemented shortly:

```
Private Sub InitiateConnectionThreadEntryPoint(ByVal state As Object)

 Try
    ' Get the host name...
  Dim hostName As String = CStr(state)

   ' Resolve...
  Dim hostEntry As IPHostEntry = Dns.Resolve(hostName)
  If Not hostEntry Is Nothing Then

    ' Create an end point for the first address.
```

```
      Dim endPoint As New IPEndPoint(hostEntry.AddressList(0), ServicePort)

      ' Create a TCP client...
      Dim client As New TcpClient
      client.Connect(endPoint)

      ' Create the connection window...
      ProcessOutboundConnection(client)
     Else
      Throw New ApplicationException("Host '" & hostName & _
       "' could not be resolved.")
      End If
    Catch ex As Exception
     HandleInitiateConnectionException(ex)
    End Try
   End Sub
```

When it comes to `HandleInitiateConnectionException`, you start to see the inter-thread UI problems that were mentioned earlier. When there is a problem with the exception, you need to tell the user, which means that you need to move the exception from the thread-pool-managed thread into the main application thread. The principle for this is the same, you need to create a delegate and call that delegate through the `Invoke` method of the form. This method does all the hard work in marshaling the call across to the other thread.

Here's what the delegates look like. They have the same parameters of the calls themselves. As a naming convention, it's a good idea to use the same name as the method and tack the word `Delegate` on the end:

```
Public Class Form1
 Inherits System.Windows.Forms.Form
 Private Shared _mainThreadId As Integer
```

```
 ' delegates...
 Protected Delegate Sub HandleInitiateConnectionExceptionDelegate( _
                                             ByVal ex As Exception)
```

In the constructor for `Form1`, you capture the thread caller's thread ID and store it in `_mainThreadId`. Here's a method that compares the captured ID with the ID of the current thread:

```
Public Shared Function IsMainThread() As Boolean
 If Thread.CurrentThread.GetHashCode() = _mainThreadId Then
  Return True
 Else
  Return False
 End If
End Function
```

The first thing you do at the top of `HandleInitiateConnectionException` is to check the thread ID. If it doesn't match, you create the delegate and call it. Notice how you set the delegate to call back into the same method, because the second time it's called you would have moved to the main thread; therefore, `IsMainThread` will return `True`, and you can process the exception properly:

```
Protected Sub HandleInitiateConnectionException(ByVal ex As Exception)

  ' main thread?
  If IsMainThread() = False Then

    ' Create and call...
    Dim args(0) As Object
    args(0) = ex
    Invoke(New HandleInitiateConnectionExceptionDelegate(AddressOf _
     HandleInitiateConnectionException), args)    ' return
    Return
  End If

  ' Show it.
  MsgBox(ex.GetType().ToString() & ":" & ex.Message)
End Sub
```

The result is that when the call comes in from the thread-pool-managed thread, `IsMainThread` returns `False`, and the delegate is created and called. When the method is entered again as a result of the delegate call, `IsMainThread` returns `True` and you see the message box.

When it comes to `ProcessOutboundConnection`, you have to again jump into the main UI thread. However, the magic behind this method is implemented in a separate method called `ProcessConnection`, which can handle either inbound or outbound connections. Here's the delegate:

```
Public Class Form1
    Inherits System.Windows.Forms.Form

  Private Shared _mainThreadId As Integer

  Private _listener As Listener

  Protected Delegate Sub ProcessConnectionDelegate(ByVal client As _
      TcpClient, ByVal direction As Conversation.ConversationDirection)

  Protected Delegate Sub HandleInitiateConnectionExceptionDelegate(ByVal _
        ex As Exception)
```

Here's the method itself, which creates the new Conversation form and calls the `ConfigureClient` method:

```
Protected Sub ProcessConnection(ByVal client As TcpClient, _
  ByVal direction As Conversation.ConversationDirection)

  ' Do you have to move to another thread?
  If IsMainThread() = False Then

    ' Create and call...
    Dim args(1) As Object
    args(0) = client
    args(1) = direction
    Invoke(New ProcessConnectionDelegate(AddressOf ProcessConnection), _
        args)
```

```
    Return
  End If
   ' Create the conversation window...
  Dim conversation As New Conversation
  conversation.Show()
  conversation.ConfigureClient(client, direction)
End Sub
```

Of course, `ProcessOutboundConnection` needs to defer to `ProcessConnection`:

```
Public Sub ProcessOutboundConnection(ByVal client As TcpClient)
 ProcessConnection(client, Conversation.ConversationDirection.Outbound)
End Sub
```

Now that you can connect to something on the client side, let's look at how to receive connections (on the server side).

Receiving Inbound Connections

You've already built `Listener`, but you haven't created an instance of it, nor have you spun up its thread to wait for incoming connections. To do this, you need a field in `Form1` to hold an instance of the object, and you also need to tweak the constructor. Here's the field:

```
Public Class Form1
  Inherits System.Windows.Forms.Form

 Private _mainThreadId As Integer

 Private _listener As Listener
```

Here is the new code that needs to be added to the constructor:

```
Public Sub New()
 MyBase.New()

 'This call is required by the Windows Form Designer.
 InitializeComponent()

_ mainThreadId = Thread.CurrentThread.GetHashCode()
  Text &= " - " & _mainThreadId.ToString()

  ' listener...
 _listener = New Listener(Me)
 _listener.SpinUp()
End Sub
```

When inbound connections are received, you'll get a new `TcpClient` object. This is passed back to `Form1` through the `ReceiveInboundConnection` method. This method, like `ProcessOutboundConnection`, defers to `ProcessConnection`. Because `ProcessConnection` already handles the issue of moving the call to the main application thread, `ReceiveInboundConnection` looks like this:

```
Public Sub ReceiveInboundConnection(ByVal client As TcpClient)
 ProcessConnection(client, Conversation.ConversationDirection.Inbound)
End Sub
```

If you run the project now, you should be able to click the Connect button and see two windows—one inbound and one outbound, as shown in Figure 27-7.

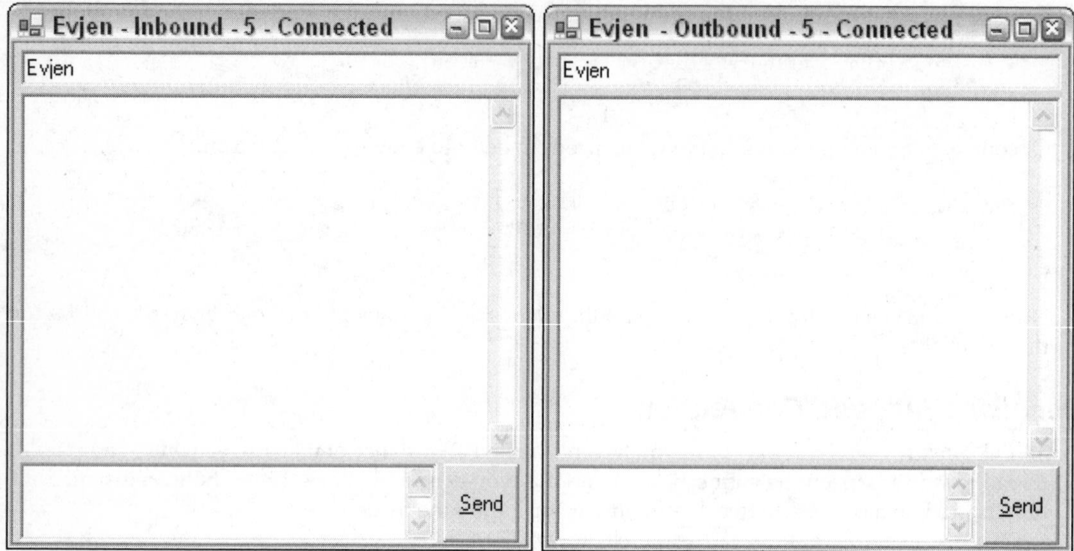

Figure 27-7

If you close all three windows, the application will keep running because you haven't written code to close down the listener thread, and having an open thread like this will keep the application open. Use the Debug ➪ Stop Debugging menu option in Visual Studio to close the application down by killing all running threads.

By clicking the Connect button, you're calling `InitiateConnection`. This spins up a new thread in the pool that resolves the given host name (`localhost`) into an IP address. This IP address, in combination with a port number, is then used in the creation of a `TcpClient` object. If the connection can be made, `ProcessOutboundConnection` is called, which results in the first of the conversation windows being created and marked as "outbound."

Your example is somewhat artificial, as the two instances of Wrox Messenger should be running on separate computers. On the remote computer (if you're connecting to `localhost`, this will be the same computer), a connection is received through the `AcceptTcpClient` method of `TcpListener`. This results in a call to `ReceiveInboundConnection`, which, in turn, results in the creation of the second conversation window, this time marked as "inbound."

Sending Messages

The next step is to work out how to exchange messages between the two Conversation windows. You already have a `TcpClient` in each case so all you have to do is squirt binary data down the wire on one side and pick it up at the other end. As the two Conversation windows act as both client and server, both need to be able to send and receive.

There are three problems to solve:

- You need to establish one thread to send and another thread to receive data.
- Data sent and received needs to be reported back to the user so that he or she can follow the conversation.
- The data that you want to send has to be converted into a wire-ready format, which in .NET terms usually means serialization.

The power of sockets means that you can define whatever protocol you like for data transmission. If you wanted to build your own SMTP server, you could implement the (publicly available) specifications, set up a listener to wait for connections on port 25 (the standard port for SMTP), wait for data to come in, process it, and return responses as appropriate.

It's best to work in this way when building protocols. Unless there are very strong reasons for not doing so, make your server as open as possible: Do not tie it to a specific platform. This is the way that things are done on the Internet. To an extent, things like Web Services should negate the need to build your own protocols; as you go forward, you will rely instead on the "remote object available to local client" paradigm.

Now it's time to think ahead to the idea of using the serialization features of .NET to transmit data across the network. After all, you've already seen this in action with Web Services and remoting. You can take an object in .NET, use serialization to convert it to a string of bytes, and expose that string down to a Web Service consumer, or remoting client, or even to a file.

Chapter 24 discussed the `BinaryFormatter` and `SoapFormatter` classes. You could use either of those classes, or create your own custom formatter, to convert data for transmission and reception. In this case, you're going to create a new class called `Message` and use `BinaryFormatter` to crunch it down into a wire-ready format and convert it back again for processing.

This approach isn't ideal from the perspective of interoperability, because the actual protocol used is lost in the implementation of the .NET Framework, rather than being under your absolute control.

If you want to build an open protocol, this is *not* the best way to do it. Unfortunately, the best way to do it is beyond the scope of this book, but a good place to start is to look at existing protocols and standards and model any protocol on their approach. `BinaryFormatter` is quick and dirty, which is why you're going to use it.

The Message Class

The `Message` class contains two fields, `_username` and `_message`, which form the entirety of the data that you want to transmit. The code for this class follows; notice how the `Serializable` attribute is applied to it so that `BinaryFormatter` can change it into a wire-ready form. Also notice how you're providing a new implementation of `ToString`:

```
Imports System.Text

<Serializable()> Public Class Message

 Private _username As String
 Private _message As String
```

```
    Public Sub New(ByVal name As String)
     _username = name
    End Sub

    Public Sub New(ByVal name As String, ByVal message As String)
     _username = name
     _message = message
    End Sub

    Public Overrides Function ToString() As String
     Dim builder As New StringBuilder(_username)
     builder.Append(" says:")
     builder.Append(ControlChars.CrLf)
     builder.Append(_message)
     builder.Append(ControlChars.CrLf)
     Return builder.ToString()
    End Function

   End Class
```

Now, all you have to do is spin up two threads, one for transmission and one for reception, updating the display. You need two threads per *conversation*, so if you have 10 conversations open, you'll need 20 threads plus the main UI thread, plus the thread running `TcpListener`.

Receiving messages is pretty easy. When calling `Deserialize` on `BinaryFormatter`, you give it the stream returned to you from `TcpClient`. If there's no data, this blocks. If there is data, it's decoded into a `Message` object that you can display. If you have multiple messages coming down the pipe, `BinaryFormatter` will keep processing them until the pipe is empty. Here's the method for doing this, and this should be added to `Conversation`. Remember, you haven't implemented `ShowMessage` yet:

```
   Protected Sub ReceiveThreadEntryPoint()

    ' Create a formatter...
    Dim formatter As New BinaryFormatter
    ' Loop
    Do While True

     ' Receive...
     Dim message1 As Message = formatter.Deserialize(_stream)
     If message1 Is Nothing Then
      Exit Do
     End If

     ' Show it...
     ShowMessage(message1)
    Loop
   End Sub
```

Transmitting messages is a touch more complex. What you want is a queue (managed by a `System.Collections.Queue`) of outgoing messages. Every second, you'll examine the state of the queue. If you find any messages, you'll use `BinaryFormatter` to transmit them. Because you'll be accessing this queue from multiple threads, you'll use a `System.Threading.ReaderWriterLock` to control access. To minimize the amount of time you spend inside locked code, you'll quickly transfer the contents of the shared queue into a private queue that you can process at your leisure. This allows the client to continue to add messages to the queue through the UI, even though existing messages are being sent by the transmit thread.

First, add these members to `Conversation`:

```
Public Class Conversation
    Inherits System.Windows.Forms.Form

  Private _username As String = "Evjen"
  Private _client As TcpClient
  Private _stream As NetworkStream
  Private _direction As ConversationDirection

  Private _receiveThread As Thread
  Private _transmitThread As Thread
  Private _transmitQueue As New Queue()
  Private _transmitLock As New ReaderWriterLock()
```

Now, add this method again to `Conversation`:

```
Protected Sub TransmitThreadEntryPoint()

 ' Create a formatter...
 Dim formatter As New BinaryFormatter
 Dim workQueue As New Queue
 ' Loop
 Do While True

  ' Wait for the signal...
  Thread.Sleep(1000)

  ' Go through the queue...

  _transmitLock.AcquireWriterLock(-1)
  Dim message As Message
  workQueue.Clear()
  For Each message In _transmitQueue
   workQueue.Enqueue(message)
  Next
  _transmitQueue.Clear()
  _transmitLock.ReleaseWriterLock()

  ' Loop the outbound messages...
  For Each message In workQueue

   ' Send it...
   formatter.Serialize(_stream, message)

  Next

 Loop

End Sub
```

When you want to send a message, you call one version of the SendMessage method. Here are all of the implementations, and the Click handler for buttonSend:

```
Private Sub buttonSend_Click(ByVal sender As System.Object, _
 ByVal e As System.EventArgs) Handles buttonSend.Click

 SendMessage(textMessage.Text)
End Sub

Public Sub SendMessage(ByVal message As String)
 SendMessage(_username, message)
End Sub

Public Sub SendMessage(ByVal username As String, ByVal message As String)
 SendMessage(New Message(username, message))
End Sub

Public Sub SendMessage(ByVal message As Message)

 ' Queue it
 _transmitLock.AcquireWriterLock(-1)
 _transmitQueue.Enqueue(message)
 _transmitLock.ReleaseWriterLock()

 ' Show it...
 ShowMessage(message)
End Sub
```

ShowMessage is responsible for updating textMessages so that the conversation remains up to date (notice how you add the message both when you send it and when you receive it so that both parties have an up-to-date thread). This is a UI feature, so it is good practice to pass it over to the main application thread for processing. Although, the call in response to the button click comes off the main application thread, the one from inside ReceiveThreadEntryPoint does not. Here's what the delegate looks like:

```
Public Class Conversation
  Inherits System.Windows.Forms.Form

 ' members...
 Private _username As String = "Evjen"
 Private _client As TcpClient
 Private _stream As NetworkStream
 Private _direction As ConversationDirection
 Private _receiveThread As Thread
 Private _transmitThread As Thread
 Private _transmitQueue As New Queue()
 Private _transmitLock As New ReaderWriterLock()

 Public Delegate Sub ShowMessageDelegate(ByVal message As Message)
```

Here's the method implementation:

```
Public Sub ShowMessage(ByVal message As Message)

    ' Thread?
    If Form1.IsMainThread() = False Then

        ' Run...
        Dim args(0) As Object
        args(0) = message
        Invoke(New ShowMessageDelegate(AddressOf ShowMessage), args)

        ' Return...
        Return
    End If

    ' Show it...
    textMessages.Text &= message.ToString()
End Sub
```

All that remains now is to spin up the threads. This should be done from within `ConfigureClient`. Before the threads are spun up, you need to get hold of the stream and store it in the private `_stream` field. After that, you create new `Thread` objects as normal:

```
Public Sub ConfigureClient(ByVal client As TcpClient, _
        ByVal direction As ConversationDirection)

    ' Set it up...
    _client = client
    _direction = direction

    ' Update the window...
    UpdateCaption()

    ' Get the stream...
    _stream = _client.GetStream()
    ' Spin up the threads...
    _transmitThread = New Thread(AddressOf TransmitThreadEntryPoint)
    _transmitThread.Start()
    _receiveThread = New Thread(AddressOf ReceiveThreadEntryPoint)
    _receiveThread.Start()
End Sub
```

At this point, you should be able to connect and exchange messages, as shown in Figure 27-8.

Note that the screen shots show the username of the inbound connection as `Tuija`. This was done with the `textUsername` text box so that you can follow which half of the conversation comes from where.

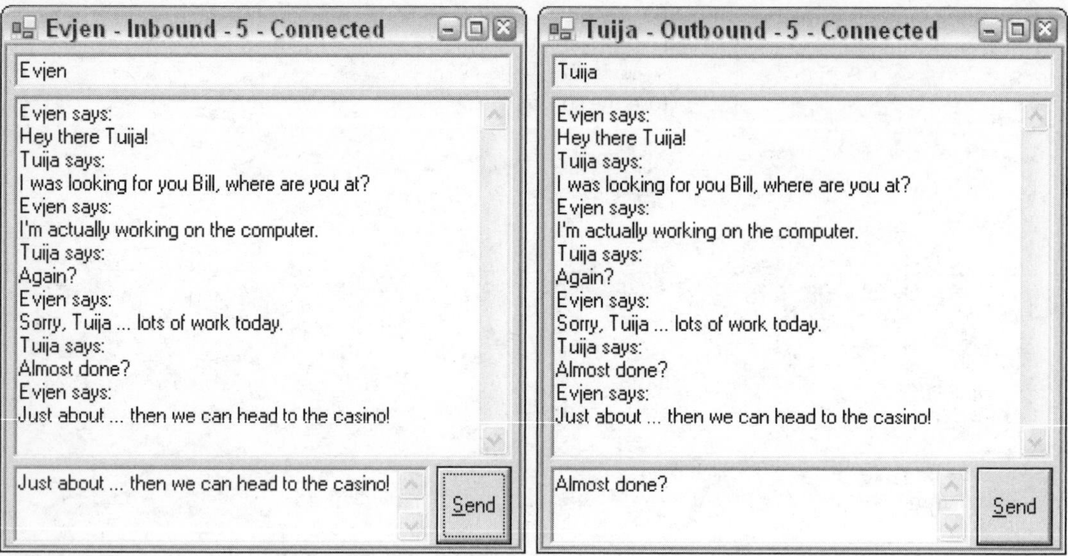

Figure 27-8

Shutting Down the Application

You've yet to solve the problem of neatly closing the application, or, in fact, dealing with one person in the conversation closing down his or her window, indicating a wish to end the conversation. When the process ends (whether "neatly" or forcefully), Windows automatically mops up any open connections and frees up the port for other processes.

Imagine, if you will, that you have two computers, one window per computer as you would in a production environment. If you close your window, you're indicating that you want to end the conversation. You need to close the socket and spin down the transmission and reception threads. At the other end, you should be able to detect that the socket has been closed, spin down the threads, and tell the user that the other user has terminated the conversation.

This all hinges on being able to detect when the socket has been closed. For some reason, Microsoft has actually made this very hard, thanks to the design of the `TcpClient` class. `TcpClient` effectively encapsulates a `System.Net.Sockets.Socket` class, providing methods for helping to manage the connection lifetime and communication streams. However, `TcpClient` does not have a method or property that answers the question, "Am I still connected?" What you need to do is get hold of the `Socket` object that `TcpClient` is wrapping and then you can use its `Connected` property to find out if the connection has been closed.

`TcpClient` does support a property called `Client` that returns a `Socket`. However, this property is protected, meaning that you can only access it by inheriting a new class from `TcpClient`. But, there is another way — you could use reflection to get at the property and call it without having to inherit a new class.

Microsoft claims that this is a legitimate technique, even though it appears to violate every rule in the book about encapsulation. Reflection is designed not only for finding out which types are available, and learning which methods and properties each type supports, but also for invoking those methods and properties whether they're protected or public.

So, in `Conversation`, you need to store the socket:

```
Public Class Conversation
 Inherits System.Windows.Forms.Form

 Private _username As String = "Evjen"
 Private _client As TcpClient
 Private _socket As Socket
```

In `ConfigureClient`, you need to use `Reflection` to peek in to the `Type` object for `TcpClient` and dig out the `Client` property. Once you have a `System.Reflection.PropertyInfo` for this property, you can retrieve its value by using the `GetValue` method. Here's the code. Don't forget to import the `System.Reflection` namespace:

```
Public Sub ConfigureClient(ByVal client As TcpClient, _
             ByVal direction As ConversationDirection)

 ' Set it up...
 _client = client
 _direction = direction

 ' Update the window...
 UpdateCaption()

 ' Get the stream...
 _stream = _client.GetStream()

 ' Get the socket through reflection...
 Dim propertyInfo As PropertyInfo = _
   _client.GetType().GetProperty("Client", _
    BindingFlags.Instance Or BindingFlags.NonPublic)
 If Not propertyInfo Is Nothing Then
  _socket = propertyInfo.GetValue(_client, Nothing)
 Else
  Throw New Exception("Couldn't retrieve Client property from TcpClient")
 End If

 ' Spin up the threads...
 _transmitThread = New Thread(AddressOf TransmitThreadEntryPoint)
 _transmitThread.Start()
 _receiveThread = New Thread(AddressOf ReceiveThreadEntryPoint)
 _receiveThread.Start()
End Sub
```

Applications are able to check the state of the socket either by detecting when an error occurs because you've tried to send data over a closed socket or by actually asking if the socket is connected. If you either don't have a `Socket` available in _socket (that is, it is `Nothing`), or if you have one and it tells you you're disconnected, you give the user some feedback and exit the loop. By exiting the loop, you effectively exit the thread, which is a neat way of quitting the thread. Notice as well that you might not have a window at this point (you might be the one that closed the conversation by closing the window), so you wrap the UI call in a `Try Catch` (the other side will see a `<disconnect>` message):

```
Protected Sub TransmitThreadEntryPoint()

 ' Create a formatter...
 Dim formatter As New BinaryFormatter
 Dim workQueue As New Queuevs

 ' name...
 Thread.CurrentThread.Name = "Tx-" & _direction.ToString()

 ' Loop...
 Do While True
 ' Wait for the signal...
 Thread.Sleep(1000)

 ' Disconnected?
 If _socket Is Nothing OrElse _socket.Connected = False Then
  Try
   ShowMessage(New Message("Debug", "<disconnect>"))
  Catch
  End Try
  Exit Do
 End If

 ' Go through the queue...
```

`ReceiveThreadEntryPoint` also needs some massaging. When the socket is closed, the stream will no longer be valid and so `BinaryFormatter.Deserialize` will throw an exception. Likewise, you quit the loop and, therefore, neatly quit the thread:

```
Protected Sub ReceiveThreadEntryPoint()

 ' Create a formatter...
 Dim formatter As New BinaryFormatter

 ' Loop...
 Do While True

  ' Receive...
  Dim message As Message = Nothing
  Try
   message = formatter.Deserialize(_stream)
  Catch
  End Try
  If message Is Nothing Then
   Exit Do
  End If

  ' Show it...
  ShowMessage(message)
 Loop
End Sub
```

So, how do you deal with actually closing the socket? Well, you tweak the `Dispose` method of the form itself (you will find this method in the Windows-generated code section of the file), and if you have a `_socket` object you close it:

```
Protected Overloads Overrides Sub Dispose(ByVal disposing As Boolean)
 If disposing Then
  If Not (components Is Nothing) Then
   components.Dispose()
  End If
 End If

 ' Close the socket...
 If Not _socket Is Nothing Then
  _socket.Close()
  _socket = Nothing
 End If

 MyBase.Dispose(disposing)
End Sub
```

Now, you'll be able to start a conversation, and if one of the windows is closed, `<disconnect>` will appear in the other. This is illustrated in Figure 27-9. In the background, the four threads (one transmit, one receive per window) will spin down properly.

Figure 27-9

However, the application itself will still not close properly, even if you close all the windows. That's because you need to stop the `Listener` when `Form1` closes. To do this, you'll make `Listener` implement `Idisposable`:

```
Public Class Listener
  Implements IDisposable
 Public Sub Dispose() Implements System.IDisposable.Dispose

  ' Stop it...
  Finalize()
  GC.SuppressFinalize(Me)

 End Sub
```

```
    Protected Overrides Sub Finalize()

     ' Stop the listener...
     If Not _listener Is Nothing Then
      _listener.Stop()
      _listener = Nothing
     End If

     ' Stop the thread...
     If Not _thread Is Nothing Then
      _thread.Join()
      _thread = Nothing
     End If

     ' Call up...
     MyBase.Finalize()

    End Sub
```

Now all that remains is to call `Dispose` from within `Form1`. A good place to do this is in the `Closed` event handler:

```
   Protected Overrides Sub OnClosed(ByVal e As System.EventArgs)
    If Not _listener Is Nothing Then
     _listener.Dispose()
     _listener = Nothing
    End If
   End Sub
```

After the code is compiled again, the application can be closed.

Using Internet Explorer in Your Applications

A common requirement of modern applications is to display HTML files and other files commonly used with Internet applications. Although the .NET Framework has considerable support for common image formats (such as GIF, JPEG, and PNG), working with HTML used to be a touch trickier in versions 1.0 and 1.1 of the .NET Framework. Today, life has been made considerably easier with the inclusion of the new `WebBrowser` control in the .NET Framework 2.0.

> **For information on how to accomplish this task using the .NET Framework 1.0 or 1.1, please review the second and third editions of this book.**

You don't want to have to write your own HTML parser, so using this new control to display HTML pages is, in most cases, one of your only options. Microsoft's Internet Explorer was implemented as a stand-alone component comprising a parser and a renderer, all packaged up in a neat COM object. The new `WebBrowser` control that you all use "simply" utilizes this COM object. There's nothing to stop you from using this COM object directly in your own applications, but you will find it considerably easier to use this new control for hosting Web pages in your applications.

Yes, a COM object. There is no managed version of Internet Explorer for use with .NET. Considering that writing an HTML parser is extremely hard, and writing a renderer is extremely hard, the natural conclusion is that it's much easier to use interop to get to Internet Explorer in the .NET applications than have Microsoft try and rewrite a managed version of it just for .NET. Maybe you will see "Internet Explorer .NET" within the next year or two, but for now you do have to use interop.

Windows Forms and HTML — No Problem!

These sections demonstrate how to build a mini-browser application. In some cases, you might want to display HTML pages without giving the user the UI widgets like a toolbar or the ability to enter his or her own URLs. You might also want to use the control in a nonvisual manner. For example, using the `WebBrowser` control, you can retrieve Web pages and then print the results that are retrieved without ever needing to display the contents. Let's start though by first creating a simple form that contains only a `TextBox` and a `WebBrowser` control.

Allowing Simple Web Browsing in Your Windows Application

The first step is to create a new Windows Forms application called `MiniBrowser`. On the default form, place a single `TextBox` control and the new `WebBrowser` control so that your form looks as shown in Figure 27-10.

Figure 27-10

The idea is that when the end user presses the Enter key (Return key), the URL that is entered into the text box will be the HTML page that is retrieved and displayed in the `WebBrowser` control. To accomplish this task, use the following code for your form:

```
Public Class Form1

    Private Sub TextBox1_KeyPress(ByVal sender As Object, _
       ByVal e As System.Windows.Forms.KeyPressEventArgs) Handles TextBox1.KeyPress

        If e.KeyChar = Chr(13) Then
            WebBrowser1.Navigate(TextBox1.Text)
        End If

    End Sub

End Class
```

For this simple example, you check the key presses that are made in the `TextBox1` control, and if the key press is a specific one — the Enter key — then you use the `WebBrowser` control's `Navigate` method to navigate to the requested page. The `Navigate` method can take a single `String` value, which represents the location of the Web page to retrieve. The example shown in Figure 27-11 shows the Wrox Web site.

Figure 27-11

Launching Internet Explorer from Your Windows Application

Sometimes, the goal is not to host a browser inside of the application but instead to allow the user to find the Web site in a typical Web browser. For an example of this task, create a Windows Form that has a `LinkLabel` control on it. For instance, you can have a form that has a `LinkLabel` control on it that simply states, "Visit your company Web site!"

Once this control is in place, use the following code to launch the company's Web site in an independent browser as opposed to directly in the form of your application:

```
Public Class Form1

    Private Sub LinkLabel1_LinkClicked(ByVal sender As System.Object, _
       ByVal e As System.Windows.Forms.LinkLabelLinkClickedEventArgs) Handles _
       LinkLabel1.LinkClicked

        Dim wb As New WebBrowser
        wb.Navigate("http://www.wrox.com", True)

    End Sub

End Class
```

In this example, when the `LinkLabel` control is clicked by the user, a new instance of the `WebBrowser` class is created. Then, using the `WebBrowser`'s `Navigate` method, the code specifies the location of the Web page as well as a `Boolean` value that specifics whether this end point should be opened within the Windows Form application (a `False` value) or from within an independent browser (a `True` value). By default, this is set to `False`. With the preceding construct, when the end user clicks on the link found in the Windows application, a browser instance will be instantiated and the Wrox Web site will be immediately launched.

Updating URLs and Page Titles

Notice that when working with the `MiniBrowser` example in which the WebBrowser control is directly in the form, when you click the links, the text in the `TextBox1` control is not updated. You can fix this by listening for events coming off the `WebBrowser` control and adding handlers to the control.

Updating the form's title with the HTML page's title is easy. You just have to create a `DocumentTitle Changed` event and update the `Text` property of the form:

```
Private Sub WebBrowser1_DocumentTitleChanged(ByVal sender As Object, _
   ByVal e As System.EventArgs) Handles WebBrowser1.DocumentTitleChanged

    Me.Text = WebBrowser1.DocumentTitle.ToString()

End Sub
```

In this case, when the `WebBrowser` control notices that the page title has changed (due to changing the page viewed), the `DocumentTitleChanged` event will fire. In this case, you change the Form's `Text` property (its title) to the title of the page being viewed using the `DocumentTitle` property of the `WebBrowser` control.

The next thing you want to do is to update the text string that appears in the Form's text box, based on the complete URL of the page being viewed. To do this, you can use the `WebBrowser` control's `Navigated` event.

```
Private Sub WebBrowser1_Navigated(ByVal sender As Object, _
   ByVal e As System.Windows.Forms.WebBrowserNavigatedEventArgs) Handles _
   WebBrowser1.Navigated

    TextBox1.Text = WebBrowser1.Url.ToString()

End Sub
```

In this case, when the requested page is finished being downloaded in the `WebBrowser` control, the `Navigated` event is fired. You simply update the `Text` value of the `TextBox1` control to be the URL of the page. This means that once a page is loaded in the `WebBrowser` control's HTML container and if the URL changes in this process, then the new URL will be shown in the text box. For instance, if you employ these steps and navigate to the Wrox Web site (`www.wrox.com`), you will notice that the page's URL will immediately change to `http://www.wrox.com/WileyCDA/`. This process also means that if the end user clicks on one of the links contained within the HTML view, then the URL of the newly requested page will also be shown in the text box.

Now, if you run the application with the preceding changes put into place, the form title and address bar will work as they do in Microsoft's Internet Explorer, as demonstrated in Figure 27-12.

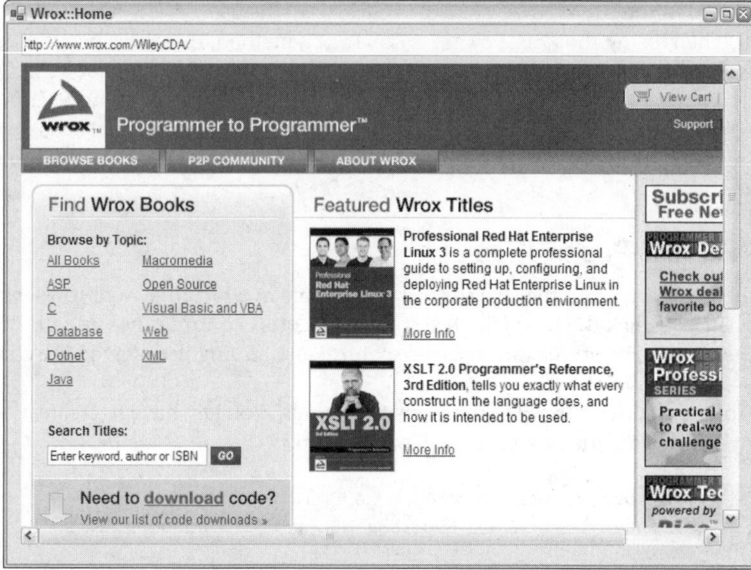

Figure 27-12

Creating a Toolbar

Next, you'll add a simple toolbar to the top of the control that gives you the usual features you'd expect from a Web browser, that is Back, Forward, Stop, Refresh, and Home.

Rather than using the `ToolBar` control, you'll add a set of button controls at the top of the control where you currently have the address bar. Add five buttons to the top of the control, as illustrated in Figure 27-13.

I've just changed the text on the buttons to indicate their function. Of course, you can use a screen capture utility to "borrow" button images from IE and use those. The buttons should be named `buttonBack`, `buttonForward`, `buttonStop`, `buttonRefresh`, and `buttonHome`. To get the resizing to work properly, make sure that you set the `Anchor` property of the three buttons on the right to `Top, Right`.

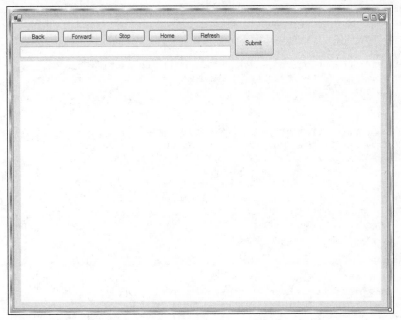

Figure 27-13

On startup, `buttonBack`, `buttonForward`, and `buttonStop` should be disabled because there is no point to the buttons if there is no initial page loaded. You will later tell the `WebBrowser` control when to enable and disable the Back and Forward buttons, depending on where the user is in the page stack. Also, when a page is being loaded, you will need to enable the Stop button—but you will also need to disable the Stop button once the page has finished being loaded.

First off though, you'll add the functionality behind the buttons. The `WebBrowser` class itself has all of the methods that you need, so this is all very straightforward:

```
Public Class Form1
    Private Sub Form1_Load(ByVal sender As System.Object, _
     ByVal e As System.EventArgs) Handles MyBase.Load
        buttonBack.Enabled = False
        buttonForward.Enabled = False
        buttonStop.Enabled = False
    End Sub

    Private Sub buttonBack_Click(ByVal sender As System.Object, _
     ByVal e As System.EventArgs) Handles buttonBack.Click
        WebBrowser1.GoBack()
        TextBox1.Text = WebBrowser1.Url.ToString()
    End Sub

    Private Sub buttonForward_Click(ByVal sender As System.Object, _
     ByVal e As System.EventArgs) Handles buttonForward.Click
```

```
        WebBrowser1.GoForward()
        TextBox1.Text = WebBrowser1.Url.ToString()
    End Sub

    Private Sub buttonStop_Click(ByVal sender As System.Object, _
     ByVal e As System.EventArgs) Handles buttonStop.Click
        WebBrowser1.Stop()
    End Sub

    Private Sub buttonRefresh_Click(ByVal sender As System.Object, _
     ByVal e As System.EventArgs) Handles buttonRefresh.Click
        WebBrowser1.Refresh()
    End Sub

    Private Sub buttonHome_Click(ByVal sender As System.Object, _
     ByVal e As System.EventArgs) Handles buttonHome.Click
        WebBrowser1.GoHome()
        TextBox1.Text = WebBrowser1.Url.ToString()
    End Sub

    Private Sub buttonSubmit_Click(ByVal sender As System.Object, _
     ByVal e As System.EventArgs) Handles buttonSubmit.Click
        WebBrowser1.Navigate(TextBox1.Text)
    End Sub

    Private Sub WebBrowser1_CanGoBackChanged(ByVal sender As Object, _
     ByVal e As System.EventArgs) Handles WebBrowser1.CanGoBackChanged
        If WebBrowser1.CanGoBack = True Then
            buttonBack.Enabled = True
        Else
            buttonBack.Enabled = False
        End If
    End Sub

    Private Sub WebBrowser1_CanGoForwardChanged(ByVal sender As Object, _
     ByVal e As System.EventArgs) Handles WebBrowser1.CanGoForwardChanged
        If WebBrowser1.CanGoForward = True Then
            buttonForward.Enabled = True
        Else
            buttonForward.Enabled = False
        End If
    End Sub

    Private Sub WebBrowser1_Navigated(ByVal sender As Object, _
     ByVal e As System.Windows.Forms.WebBrowserNavigatedEventArgs) Handles _
     WebBrowser1.Navigated
        TextBox1.Text = WebBrowser1.Url.ToString()
        Me.Text = WebBrowser1.DocumentTitle.ToString()
    End Sub

    Private Sub WebBrowser1_Navigating(ByVal sender As Object, _
     ByVal e As System.Windows.Forms.WebBrowserNavigatingEventArgs) Handles _
     WebBrowser1.Navigating
        buttonStop.Enabled = True
    End Sub
```

```
    Private Sub WebBrowser1_DocumentCompleted(ByVal sender As Object, _
     ByVal e As System.Windows.Forms.WebBrowserDocumentCompletedEventArgs) _
     Handles WebBrowser1.DocumentCompleted
        buttonStop.Enabled = False
    End Sub

End Class
```

There are a lot of different activities going on in this example, since there are so many options for the end user when using this `MiniBrowser` application. First, for each of the button `Click` events, there is a specific `WebBrowser` class method assigned as the action to initiate. For instance, for the Back button on the form, you simply use the Web Browser control's `GoBack()` method. And for the other buttons, it is the same — for the Forward button you have the `GoForward()` method, and for the other buttons you have methods such as `Stop()`, `Refresh()`, and `GoHome()`. This makes it fairly simple and straightforward to create a toolbar that will give you actions similar to those of Microsoft's Internet Explorer.

When the form is first loaded, the `Form1_Load` event disables the appropriate buttons. From there, the end user can enter a URL into the text box and click the Submit button to have the application retrieve the desired page.

To manage the enabling and disabling of the buttons, you have to key in a couple of events. As mentioned before, whenever downloading begins you need to enable Stop. For this, you simply add an event handler for the `Navigating` event to enable the Stop button:

```
Private Sub WebBrowser1_Navigating(ByVal sender As Object, _
 ByVal e As System.Windows.Forms.WebBrowserNavigatingEventArgs) Handles _
 WebBrowser1.Navigating
    buttonStop.Enabled = True
End Sub
```

Then the Stop button is again disabled when the document has finished loading:

```
Private Sub WebBrowser1_DocumentCompleted(ByVal sender As Object, _
 ByVal e As System.Windows.Forms.WebBrowserDocumentCompletedEventArgs) _
 Handles WebBrowser1.DocumentCompleted
    buttonStop.Enabled = False
End Sub
```

Enabling and disabling the appropriate Back and Forward buttons really depend on the ability to go backward or forward in the page stack. This is achieved by using both the `CanGoForwardChanged` and the `CanGoBackChanged` events.

```
Private Sub WebBrowser1_CanGoBackChanged(ByVal sender As Object, _
 ByVal e As System.EventArgs) Handles WebBrowser1.CanGoBackChanged
    If WebBrowser1.CanGoBack = True Then
        buttonBack.Enabled = True
    Else
        buttonBack.Enabled = False
    End If
End Sub
```

```
Private Sub WebBrowser1_CanGoForwardChanged(ByVal sender As Object, _
 ByVal e As System.EventArgs) Handles WebBrowser1.CanGoForwardChanged
    If WebBrowser1.CanGoForward = True Then
        buttonForward.Enabled = True
    Else
        buttonForward.Enabled = False
    End If
End Sub
```

Run the project now, and visit a Web page and click through a few links. You should also be able to use the toolbar to enhance your browsing experience. The end product is shown in Figure 27-14.

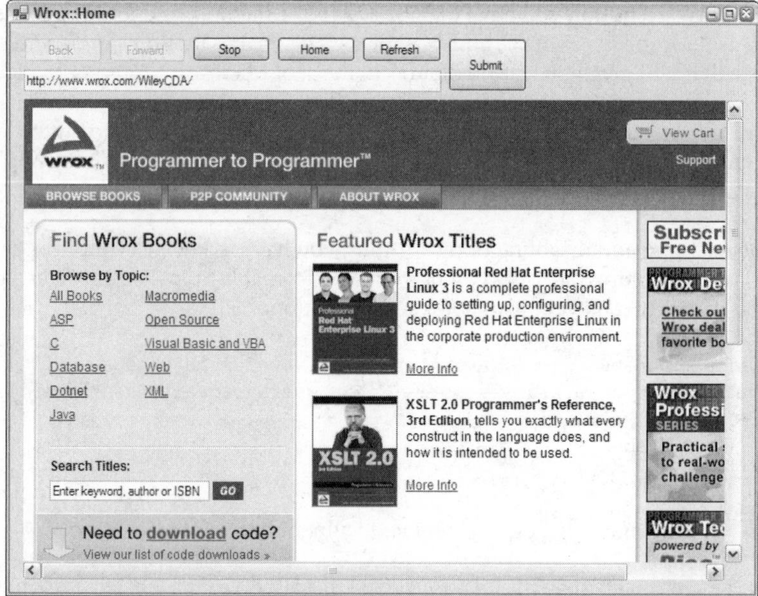

Figure 27-14

Showing Documents Using the WebBrowser Control

You are not limited to using just Web pages within the `WebBrowser` control. In fact, you can allow the end user to view many different types of documents. So far, you have seen how to use the `WebBrowser` control to access documents that have been purely accessible by defining a URL. Though, the `WebBrowser` control also allows you to use an absolute path and define end points to files such as Word documents, Excel documents, PDFs, and more.

For instance, let's suppose that you are using the following code snippet:

```
WebBrowser1.Navigate("C:\Financial Report.doc")
```

This would open the Word document in your application. Not only would the document appear in the `WebBrowser` control, but the Word toolbar would also be present. This is illustrated in Figure 27-15.

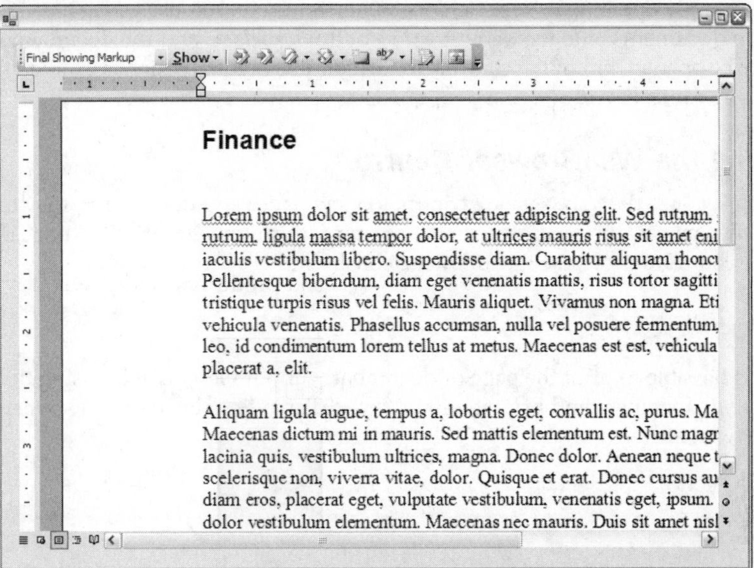

Figure 27-15

In Figure 27-16, the `WebBrowser` control shows an Adobe PDF file.

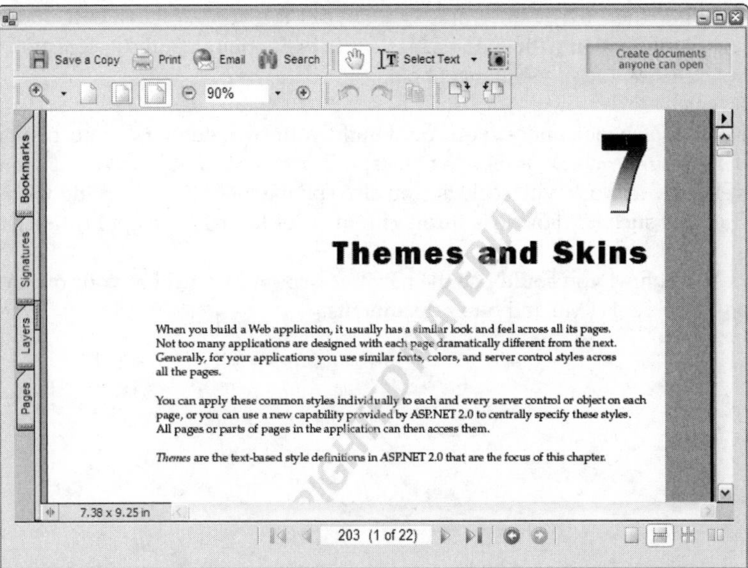

Figure 27-16

In addition to simply opening up specific documents in the control, users also have the ability to drag and drop documents onto the WebBrowser control's surface, and the document dropped will automatically be opened within the control. To turn off this ability (which is enabled by default), set the WebBrowser control's AllowWebBrowserDrop property to False.

Printing Using the WebBrowser Control

Not only can users use the WebBrowser control to view pages and documents, they can also use the control to send these pages and documents to the printer for printing. To print the page or document being viewed in the control, simply use the following construct:

```
WebBrowser1.Print()
```

As before, it is possible to print the page or document without viewing it by using the WebBrowser class to load an HTML document and print it without even displaying the loaded document. This is accomplished as shown here:

```
Dim wb As new WebBrowser
wb.Navigate("http://www.wrox.com")
wb.Print()
```

Summary

This chapter kicked off by looking at just how easy it is to download resources from a Web server using classes built into the .NET Framework. System.Uri lets you express a URI, and System.Net.WebRequest, in combination with System.Net.HttpWebRequest and System.Net.HttpWebResponse, lets you physically get hold of the data.

The second section took a look at how you could build your own network protocol by using sockets, implemented in the System.Net.Sockets namespace. You looked at how TcpListener and TcpClient make it relatively easy to work with sockets. You also spent a lot of time working with threads and the various UI issues that such kind of work throws up in order to make the application as usable as possible.

Finally, you looked at how you could use the new WebBrowser control in your own Windows Form application to work with HTML and other documents.

The Visual Basic Compiler

When the .NET Framework was first introduced, one nice addition for the Visual Basic developer was the inclusion of a stand-alone language compiler. This meant that you weren't required to have the Visual Studio .NET 2002 IDE in order to build Visual Basic applications. In fact, you could take the .NET Framework from the Microsoft Web site (for free), and build Web applications, classes, modules and more simply using a text editor such as Notepad. You could then take the completed files and compile them using the Visual Basic compiler.

The Visual Basic compiler is included along with the default .NET Framework install. The name of the compiler is `vbc.exe` and can be found at:

```
C:\WINDOWS\Microsoft.NET\Framework\v2.0.[version]\vbc.exe
```

The vbc.exe.config File

In addition to the `vbc.exe` file, you will also notice that there is a `vbc.exe.config` file in the directory as well. This XML file is used to specify the versions of the .NET Framework the compiler should build applications for. Now that there are three versions of the .NET Framework available for our applications to work with, it is important to understand how this configuration file actually works.

With the .NET Framework 2.0 installed, you will find the `vbc.exe.config` file with the following construction:

```
<?xml version ="1.0"?>
<configuration>
    <startup>
        <supportedRuntime version="v2.0.40607" safemode="true"/>
        <requiredRuntime version="v2.0.40607" safemode="true"/>
    </startup>
</configuration>
```

Note that the actual build number of your version might be different than what is shown in the above example.

This .config file is basically a typical .NET Framework configuration file with the default <configuration> root element included. Nested within the <configuration> element, you will need to place a <startup> element. This is the only child element that is possible in the vbc.exe's configuration file.

Nested within the <startup> element, you can use two possible elements: <supportedRuntime> and <requiredRuntime>.

The <requiredRuntime> element really is only needed if your application is going to run on the .NET Framework 1.0 (the very first iteration of the .NET Framework). If your application is going to run from the .NET Framework 1.0, then you would build the vbc.exe.config file as such:

```
<?xml version ="1.0"?>
<configuration>
    <startup>
        <requiredRuntime version="v1.0.3705" safemode="true"/>
    </startup>
</configuration>
```

Though today, working with three different versions of the .NET Framework, you may wish to compile your applications using the Visual Basic compiler so that they work with multiple versions of the framework. To do this, you could use the <supportedRuntime> element as shown here:

```
<?xml version ="1.0"?>
<configuration>
    <startup>
        <supportedRuntime version="v2.0.40607" safemode="true"/>
        <supportedRuntime version="v1.1.4322" safemode="true"/>
    </startup>
</configuration>
```

This construction states that the application should first try to run on version 2.0.40607 of the .NET Framework, and if this version of the .NET Framework is not found, then the next preferred version of the framework in which the compiled object should work with is version 1.1.4322 of the .NET Framework. When working in this kind of construction, you need to order the framework versions in the XML file so that the most preferred version of the framework in which you want to utilize should be the uppermost element, and the least preferred version of the framework should be last in the node list.

It is important to note that the <supportedRuntime> element is meant for .NET Framework versions 1.1 and above. If you are going to utilize the .NET Framework version 1.0, then you should use the <requiredRuntime> element.

The <supportedRuntime> element contains two possible attributes — version and safemode. Both attributes are optional. The attribute version allows you to specify the specific version you want your application to run against, while safemode specifies whether the registry should be searched for the particular framework version. The safemode attribute takes a Boolean value and the default value is false, meaning that the framework version will not be checked.

Simple Steps to Compilation

To show how the Visual Basic compiler works in the simplest manner, let's start by taking a look at how to compile a single class file.

1. To accomplish this task, create a module called `MyModule.vb`. Let's keep the module simple as this example is meant to show you just how to compile the items using the `vbc.exe` compiler.

```
Module Module1

    Sub Main()
        Console.WriteLine("Howdy there")
        Console.ReadLine()
    End Sub

End Module
```

2. Once your file is in place, it is then time to use the Visual Basic compiler. There are really a couple of ways around this. First off, if you do have Visual Studio 2005 on the computer, you can open the Visual Studio Command Prompt (found at Start ➪ All Programs ➪ Microsoft Visual Studio 2005 ➪ Visual Studio Tools ➪ Visual Studio Command Prompt). Once open, you then just navigate to the location of the file and then run the compiler against the file (shown shortly).

3. In most cases, you are probably going to be using the Visual Basic compiler on computers that do not have Visual Studio on them. In those cases, copy and paste the `vbc.exe`, `vbc.exe.config`, and the `vbc.rsp` files to the folder where the class file you wish to compile is located. Then you can open up a command prompt by selecting Run from the Start menu and typing `cmd` in the text box.

   Another option is to add the compiler to the path itself. This is done by typing the following at the command prompt:

```
path %path%;C:\WINDOWS\Microsoft.NET\Framework\v2.0.50215
```

   Now you can work with the compilation normally and the `vbc.exe` compiler will be found upon compilation.

4. Once the command prompt is open, navigate to the folder that contains both the Visual Basic compiler and the class file that needs compiling. From this location, type the following command at the command prompt:

```
vbc.exe MyModule.vb
```

There are many options in how items can be compiled using the Visual Basic compiler — but this is the absolute simplest way to compile this module. This command simply compiles the .vb file so that it can then be utilized by your applications. Running this command produces the following results:

```
C:\CoolStuff>vbc.exe MyModule.vb
Microsoft (R) Visual Basic .NET Compiler version 8.0.40607.16
for Microsoft (R) .NET Framework version 2.0.40607.16
Copyright (C) Microsoft Corporation 1987-2003. All rights reserved.
```

So what does this operation actually do? Well, in this case, it has created an .exe file for you in the same directory as the `MyModule.vb` file. Looking there, you will find `MyModule.exe` all ready to run.

The Visual Basic compiler has a number of options that are available for use which allow you to dictate what sorts of actions the compiler will take with the compilation process. These flags will be defined soon, but you can specify additional settings by using a forward-slash followed by the name of the option and the setting assigned to the option. For instance, if you were going to add a reference to `Microsoft.VisualBasic.dll` along with the compilation, you would construct your compiler command as follows:

```
vbc.exe MyModule.vb /reference:Microsoft.VisualBasic.dll
```

Compiler Output

Now, take a comprehensive look at all the available options for the Visual Basic compiler. Note that you can get a full list of options by typing the following command:

```
vbc.exe /?
```

/nologo

This option causes the compiler to perform its compilation without producing the compiler information set that was previously shown in our examples. This is really only useful if you are invoking the compiler in your application, showing the results coming from the compiler to the end user of your application, and if you have no desire to show this information to them in the result set.

/utf8output

By default, when you use the Visual Basic command-line compiler, it will not do the compilation using UTF-8 encoding. In fact, the Visual Studio 2005 IDE will not even allow this to occur, but by using `/utf8output` in the command-line compiler, you will use this encoding type.

/verbose

Adding this command will cause the compiler to output a complete list of what it is doing, including the assemblies that are being loaded and the errors that it receives in the compilation process. You would use it in the following fashion:

```
vbc.exe MyModule.vb /reference:Microsoft.VisualBasic.dll /verbose
```

This would produce results such as (note that there is only room to show small examples of the result output as it is rather lengthy):

```
Adding assembly reference 'C:\WINDOWS\Microsoft.NET\Framework\v2.0.40607\System.
Data.dll'
```

As well as:

```
Adding import 'System'
Adding import 'Microsoft.VisualBasic'
Adding file 'C:\MyModule.vb'
Adding assembly reference 'C:\WINDOWS\Microsoft.NET\Framework\v2.0.40607\Microso
ft.VisualBasic.dll'
Compiling...
```

And then the compiler starts loading assemblies:

```
Loading C:\WINDOWS\Microsoft.NET\Framework\v2.0.40607\mscorlib.dll.

Loading C:\WINDOWS\Microsoft.NET\Framework\v2.0.40607\Microsoft.VisualBasic.dll.
```

Until it finishes:

```
Building C:\MyModule.vb.

Building 17d14f5c-a337-4978-8281-53493378c1071.vb.

Compilation successful
```

Optimization

The following sections discuss the optimization features available.

/filealign

Though, most likely not used by most developers, the `/filealign` setting allows you to specify the alignment of sections, or blocks of contiguous memory, in your output file. You would use the following construction when using this option:

```
vbc.exe MyModule.vb /filealign:2048
```

The number assigned is the byte size of the file produced, and valid values include `512`, `1024`, `2048`, `4096`, `8192`, and `16384`.

/optimize

If you go to your project's property page (found by right-clicking on the project in the Visual Studio Solution Explorer), then you will see that there is a page for compilation settings. From this page, you can make all sorts of optimizations on how the application should be compiled. To have your command-line compiler not ignore these instructions, you should set the `/optimize` flag in your compilation instructions.

```
vbc.exe MyModule.vb /optimize
```

By default, optimizations are turned off.

Output files

The following sections explain the output files.

/doc

By default, the compiler does not produce the XML documentation file upon compilation. This new feature of Visual Basic 2005 allows developers to put structured comments in their code which can then be turned into an XML document for easy viewing (along with a style sheet). Including the `/doc` option causes the compiler to create this documentation. You would structure your command as follows if you wanted to produce this XML documentation file.

```
vbc.exe MyModule.vb /doc
```

You can also specify the name of the XML file in the following manner:

```
vbc.exe MyModule.vb /doc:MyModuleXmlFile.xml
```

/netcf

This option is not possible to execute from Visual Studio 2005 itself, but you can use this flag from the Visual Basic command-line compiler. Using `/netcf` causes the compiler to build your application so that the result is targeted for the .NET Compact Framework and not to the full .NET Framework itself. To accomplish this, you should use the following construct:

```
vbc.exe MyModule.vb /netcf
```

/out

Using the `/out` option allows you to change the name and extension of the file that was produced from the compilation. By default, it will be the name of the file that contains the `Main()` procedure or the first source code file in a DLL. To modify this yourself instead of using the defaults, you could use something similar to the following:

```
vbc.exe MyModule.vb /out:MyReallyCoolModule.exe
```

/target

This setting allows you to specify what exactly is output from the compilation process. For this, there are four options. You can have the compiler output an EXE, a DLL, a module, or a Windows program.

`/target:exe` — Produces an executable console application. This is the default if no `/target` option is specified.

`/target:library` — Produces a dynamic link library (also known as a DLL).

`/target:module` — Produces a module.

`/target:winexe` — Produces a Windows program.

You can also use a short form of this by just using `/t:exe`, `/t:library`, `/t:module`, or `/t:winexe`.

.NET Assemblies

The following sections detail the .NET assemblies for use.

/addmodule

This option is also not available to Visual Studio 2005, but is possible when using the Visual Basic compiler. Using `/addmodule` allows you to add a `.netmodule` file to the resulting output of the compiler. For this, you would use something similar to the following construction:

```
vbc.exe MyModule.vb /addmodule:MyOtherModule.netmodule
```

/delaysign

This is a compiler option that needs to be used in conjunction with the `/key` or `/keycontainer` option, which deals with the signing of your assembly. When used with the `/delaysign` option, the compiler will create a space for the digital signature that will later be used to sign the assembly instead of actually signing the assembly at that point. You would use this option in the following manner:

```
vbc.exe MyModule.vb /key:myKey1.sn /delaysign
```

/imports

A commonly used compiler option, the `/imports` option allows you to import namespaces into the compilation process. For instance:

```
vbc.exe MyModule.vb /imports:System
```

You can also add multiple namespaces by separating the namespaces with a comma:

```
vbc.exe MyModule.vb /imports:System, System.Data
```

/keycontainer

This command causes the compiler to create a sharable component and places a public key into the component's assembly manifest while signing the assembly with a private key. You would use this option in the following manner:

```
vbc.exe MyModule.vb /keycontainer:myKey1
```

If your key container that contains the key has a name that includes a space, then you will have to place quotes around the value as shown here:

```
vbc.exe MyModule.vb /keycontainer:"my Key1"
```

/keyfile

Similar to the `/keycontainer` option, the `/key` option causes the compiler to place a public key into the component's assembly manifest while signing the assembly with a private key. To use this option, you would use the following construction:

```
vbc.exe MyModule.vb /key:myKey1.sn
```

If your key has a name that includes a space, then you will have to place quotes around the value as shown here:

```
vbc.exe MyModule.vb /key:"my Key1.sn"
```

/libpath

When making references to other assemblies when using the /reference compiler option (mentioned next), you will not always have these referenced assemblies in the same location as the object getting compiled. For this reason, you can use the /libpath option to specify the location of the referenced assemblies. This is illustrated here:

```
vbc.exe MyModule.vb /reference:MyAssembly.dll /libpath:c:\Reuters\bin
```

If you want the compiler to search for the referenced DLLs in more than one location, you can specify the multiple locations using the /libpath option by separating the locations with a comma. This is shown here:

```
vbc.exe MyModule.vb /reference:MyAssembly.dll /libpath:c:\Reuters\bin, c:\
```

This command means that the compiler will look for the MyAssembly.dll in both the C:\Reuters\bin directory as well as the root directory found at C:\.

/reference

The /reference option allows you to make references to other assemblies in the compilation process. This is done in the following manner:

```
vbc.exe MyModule.vb /reference:MyAssembly.dll
```

You can also shorten the command option by using just /r:

```
vbc.exe MyModule.vb /r:MyAssembly.dll
```

You would make a reference to multiple assemblies by using a comma to separate the referenced assemblies:

```
vbc.exe MyModule.vb /reference:MyAssembly.dll, MyOtherAssembly.dll
```

Debugging and Error-Checking

The following sections address the many features available for error-checking and debugging.

/bugreport

This option creates a file that is a full report of the compilation process. The /bugreport option will create this file which will contain your code, as well as version information on the computer's operating system as well as the compiler itself. You would use this option in the following manner:

```
vbc.exe MyModule.vb /bugreport:bugsy.txt
```

/debug

By default, the Visual Basic compiler will not build objects with attached debugging information included in the generated object. Using the `/debug` option will cause the compiler to place this information in the created output file. The use of this option is shown here:

```
vbc.exe MyModule.vb /debug
```

/nowarn

The `/nowarn` option actually suppresses the compiler from throwing any warnings. There are a couple of ways in which you can use this option. The first is by simply using the `/nowarn` option without any associated values as shown here:

```
vbc.exe MyModule.vb /nowarn
```

Instead of suppressing all the warnings that can come from the compiler, the other option at your disposal is in specifying the exact warnings you wish the compiler to suppress. This is shown here:

```
vbc.exe MyModule.vb /nowarn:42016
```

In this case, you are telling the compiler not to throw any warnings when it encounters a 42016 error (an implicit conversion warning error). To interject more than one warning code, you would separate the warning codes with a comma as illustrated here:

```
vbc.exe MyModule.vb /nowarn:42016, 42024
```

You can find a list of available warnings by searching for 'Configuring Warnings in Visual Basic' in the MSDN documentation.

/quiet

Like some of the other compiler options, the `/quiet` option is only available to the command-line compiler and is not available when compiling your applications using Visual Studio. The `/quiet` option removes some of the error notifications from the error text output that is typically generated. What normally occurs when the compiler encounters an error that disallows further compilation, is that the error notification will be shown with a line of code in the file where the error occurred. The line of code that is presented will have a squiggly line underneath the bit of code which is the exact point of error occurrence. Using the `/quiet` option causes the compiler to only show the notification line and to leave the code line out of the output. This might be desirable in some situations.

/removeintchecks

By default, the Visual Basic compiler checks all your integer calculations for any possible errors. Possible errors include division by zero or overflow situations. Using the `/removeintchecks` causes the compiler to not look for these kinds of errors in the code of the files being compiled. You would use this option in the following manner:

```
vbc.exe MyModule.vb /removeintchecks
```

/warnaserror

The compiler can not only find and report errors, but the compiler can also encounter situations that are only considered warnings. Even though warnings are encountered, the compilation process will still continue to proceed. Using the `/warnaserror` option in the compilation process causes the compiler to treat all warnings as errors. This option would be used as illustrated here:

```
vbc.exe MyModule.vb /warnaserror
```

You might not want each warning to cause an error to be thrown, but instead only specific warnings. For these occasions, you can state the warning ID number that you want to look out for. This is shown here:

```
vbc.exe MyModule.vb /warnaserror:42016
```

You can also check for multiple warnings by separating the warning ID numbers with commas:

```
vbc.exe MyModule.vb /warnaserror:42016, 42024
```

Help

The following sections address the help features.

/?

When you're without this book for reference, you can use the Visual Basic compiler to give you a list of options for the compiler by using the `/?` option. This is shown here:

```
vbc.exe /?
```

This will cause the entire list of options and their definitions to be displayed in the command window.

/help

The `/help` option is the same as the `/?` option. Both of these options will produce the same results. The `/help` option produces a list of options that can be used with the compiler.

Language

The following sections detail the language options.

/optionexplicit

Always a good idea, using the `/optionexplicit` causes the compiler to check to see if any variables in the code are used before they are even declared (yes, this is possible and very bad practice). If it is found that there are variables that are used before they are even declared, the compiler will throw an error stating such if this option is in use. By default, the compiler will not check the code using the `option explicit` option. Using this option is shown here in the following example:

```
vbc.exe MyModule.vb /optionexplicit
```

/optionstrict

Another good idea is the use of the `/optionstrict` option in the compilation process. Using this option causes the compiler to check if you are making any improper type conversions in your code. Widening type conversions are allowed, but when you start performing narrowing type conversions, then with the use of the option — an error will be thrown by the compiler. By default, the compiler is not looking for these types of possible errors with your type conversions. Using this option is illustrated here:

```
vbc.exe MyModule.vb /optionstrict
```

/optioncompare

By default, the Visual Basic compiler compares strings using a binary comparison. If you wish the string comparisons using a text comparison, then you would use the following construction:

```
vbc.exe MyModule.vb /optioncompare:text
```

Preprocessor: /define

The `/define` option allows you to define conditional compiler constants for the compilation process. This is quite similar to using the `#Const` directive in your code. This can be used in something similar to the following:

```
vbc.exe MyModule.vb /define:Version="4.11"
```

You can also place definitions for multiple constants as shown here:

```
vbc.exe MyModule.vb /define:Version="4.11", DebugMode=False
```

To place multiple constants, you just need to separate the constants with commas.

Resources

The following sections elaborate on the resources in the compiler.

/linkresource

Instead of imbedding resources directly in the generated output file (such as the case with the `/resource` option), the `/linkresource` allows you to just create the connection between your resulted objects and the resources that they require. You would use this option in the following manner:

```
vbc.exe MyModule.vb /linkresource=MyResourceFile.res
```

You can then specify if the resource file is supposed to be public or private in the assembly manifest. By default, the resource file is referenced as public.

```
vbc.exe MyModule.vb /linkresource=MyResourceFile.res, private
```

You can shorten the `/linkresource` option to just `/linkres` if you desire.

/resource

The `/resource` option allows you to reference managed resource objects. The referenced resource is then embedded in the assembly. You would do this in the following manner:

```
vbc.exe MyModule.vb /resource=MyResourceFile.res
```

Like the `/linkresource` option, you can specify whether the reference to the resource should be done using either public or private. This is done in the following way (again the default is public):

```
vbc.exe MyModule.vb /resource=MyResourceFile.res, private
```

You can shorten the `/resource` option to just `/res` if you desire.

/win32icon

This option allows you to embed an .ico file (an image that is actually the application's icon) in the produced file. This is done as illustrated here in the following example:

```
vbc.exe MyModule.vb /win32icon:MyIcon.ico
```

/win32resource

This option allows you to embed a Win32 resource file into the produced file. This is done as shown here in the following example:

```
vbc.exe MyModule.vb /win32resource=MyResourceFile.res
```

Miscellaneous

Finally, the following sections address some of the more random but very useful features in the compiler.

One great feature of the Visual Basic compiler is in the use of response files. If you have a compilation that you frequently perform or one that is rather lengthy, you can instead create an .rsp file (the response file), which is a simple text file that contains all of the compilation instructions that you need for the compilation process. Here is an example .rsp file:

```
# This is a comment
/target:exe
/out:MyCoolModule.exe
/linkresource=MyResourceFile.res
MyModule.vb
SomeOtherClassFile.vb
```

Save this as `MyResponseFile.res` and then you can use this as shown here in the following example:

```
vbc.exe @MyResponseFile.rsp
```

You can also specify multiple response files as illustrated here:

```
vbc.exe @MyResponseFile.rsp @MyOtherResponseFile.rsp
```

/baseaddress

When creating a DLL using the `/target:library` option, you can assign the base address of the DLL if you wish. This, by default, is done for you by the compiler, but if you wish to make this assignment yourself, you can. To accomplish this, you would use something similar to the following:

```
vbc.exe MyClass.vb /target:library /baseaddress:0x11110000
```

All base addresses are specified as hexadecimal numbers.

/codepage

By default, the compiler compiles your files expecting all the files to be using an ANSI, Unicode, or UTF-8 code page. Using the `/codepage` option of the compiler, you can specify the code page that the compiler should actually be using. Setting it to one of the defaults is shown here:

```
vbc.exe MyClass.vb /codepage:1252
```

`1252` is used for American English and most European languages. Though setting it to Japanese Kanji would be done in the following manner:

```
vbc.exe MyClass.vb /codepage:932
```

/main

Using the `/main` option, you can point the compiler to the class or module that contains the `SubMain` procedure. This is done in the following manner:

```
vbc.exe MyClass.vb /main:MyClass.vb
```

/noconfig

By default, the Visual Basic compiler uses the `vbc.rsp` resource file in the compilation process. Using the `/noconfig` option, you are telling the compiler to avoid the use of this file in the compilation process. An example of this is shown here:

```
vbc.exe MyClass.vb /noconfig
```

/recurse

The `/recurse` option tells the compiler to compile all the specified files within a specified directory. Also included will be all of the child directories of the directory specified. One example of the use of the `/recurse` option is shown here:

```
vbc.exe /target:library /out:MyComponent.dll /recurse:MyApplication\Classes\*.vb
```

This command takes all of the .vb files from the `MyApplication/Classes` directory and creates a DLL called `MyComponent.dll`.

/rootnamespace

This option allows you to specify the namespace to use for the compilation process. This is illustrated here in the following example:

```
vbc.exe MyClass.vb /rootnamespace:Reuters
```

/sdkpath

This option allows you to specify the location of `mscorlib.dll` and `Microsoft.VisualBasic.dll` if it is located someplace other than the default location. This setting was really meant to be used with the `/netcf` option, which was described earlier, and should be used in some way similar to the following:

```
vbc.exe /sdkpath:"C:\Program Files\Microsoft Visual Studio 8
   \CompactFrameworkSDK\v1.0.5000\Windows CE" MyModule.vb
```

Looking at the vbc.rsp File

As stated earlier, the `vbc.rsp` file is there for the compiler's sake. When a compilation is being done, the Visual Basic compiler uses the `vbc.rsp` file for each compilation (unless you specify the `/noconfig` option). Inside this .rsp file, you will find a list of compiler commands:

```
# This file contains command-line options that the VB
# command-line compiler (VBC) will process as part
# of every compilation, unless the "/noconfig" option
# is specified.

# Reference the common Framework libraries
/r:Accessibility.dll
/r:Microsoft.Vsa.dll
/r:System.Configuration.Install.dll
/r:System.Data.dll
/r:System.Design.dll
/r:System.DirectoryServices.dll
/r:System.dll
/r:System.Drawing.Design.dll
/r:System.Drawing.dll
/r:System.EnterpriseServices.dll
/r:System.Management.dll
/r:System.Messaging.dll
/r:System.Runtime.Remoting.dll
/r:System.Runtime.Serialization.Formatters.Soap.dll
/r:System.Security.dll
/r:System.ServiceProcess.dll
/r:System.Web.dll
/r:System.Web.Mobile.dll
/r:System.Web.RegularExpressions.dll
/r:System.Web.Services.dll
/r:System.Windows.Forms.Dll
/r:System.XML.dll

# Import System and Microsoft.VisualBasic
/imports:System
/imports:Microsoft.VisualBasic
```

These commands are the references and imports which are done for each item that you compile using this command-line compiler. The nice thing is that you can also feel free to play with this file as you choose. If you wish to add your own references, then add them to the list and save the file, and from then on, every compilation that you make will then include this reference. As you get into using the Visual Basic command-line compiler, you will see a lot of power in using .rsp files—even the default Visual Basic one.

Visual Basic Resources

On the Web

The MSDN Visual Basic Developer Center	`msdn.microsoft.com/vbasic`
Blogs of the Microsoft VB team	`blogs.msdn.com/vteam`
VB DotNet Heaven	`www.vbdotnetheaven.com`
The Microsoft Windows Forms site	`www.windowsforms.net`
The Microsoft ASP.NET site	`www.asp.net`
VB City	`www.vbcity.com`
GotDotNet	`www.gotdotnet.com`
VB.NET Forums	`www.vbdotnetforums.com`
vbAccelerator.com	`www.vbaccelerator.com`
DotNetJunkies	`www.dotnetjunkies.com`
4 Guys from Rolla	`www.4guysfromrolla.com`
123ASPX	`www.123aspx.com`
International .NET Association	`www.ineta.org`
Microsoft Newsgroups	`msdn.microsoft.com/newsgroups`
Microsoft Developer Centers	`msdn.microsoft.com/developercenters`
VBRun: Microsoft's Visual Basic 6.0 site	`msdn.microsoft.com/VBRun`

Books

Professional ASP.NET 2.0 (ISBN: 0764576100)

Wrox's Visual Basic 2005 Express Edition Starter Kit (ISBN: 0764595733)

ASP.NET 2.0 Website Programming: Problem Design Solution (ISBN: 0764584642)

Beginning VB.NET Databases (ISBN: 0764568000)

Beginning Visual Basic 2005 Databases (ISBN: 076458994X)

Beginning ASP.NET 2.0 (ISBN: 0764588508)

Index

Index

B

C

D

E

F

G

H

I

J

K

L

N

O

P

Q

R

S

V

W

X

Z